Introduction to Comparative Politics

CONTRIBUTORS

Ervand Abrahamian
BARUCH COLLEGE

Christopher S. Allen
UNIVERSITY OF GEORGIA

Amrita Basu
AMHERST COLLEGE

Joan DeBardeleben
CARLETON UNIVERSITY

Louis DeSipio
UNIVERSITY OF CALIFORNIA, IRVINE

Shigeko N. Fukai
OKAYAMA UNIVERSITY

Haruhiro Fukui
UNIVERSITY OF CALIFORNIA, SANTA
BARBARA

Merilee S. Grindle
HARVARD UNIVERSITY

William A. Joseph
WELLESLEY COLLEGE

Mark Kesselman
COLUMBIA UNIVERSITY

Darren Kew
UNIVERSITY OF MASSACHUSETTS,
BOSTON

Atul Kohli
PRINCETON UNIVERSITY

Joel Krieger
WELLESLEY COLLEGE

Peter Lewis
AMERICAN UNIVERSITY

Alfred P. Montero
CARLETON COLLEGE

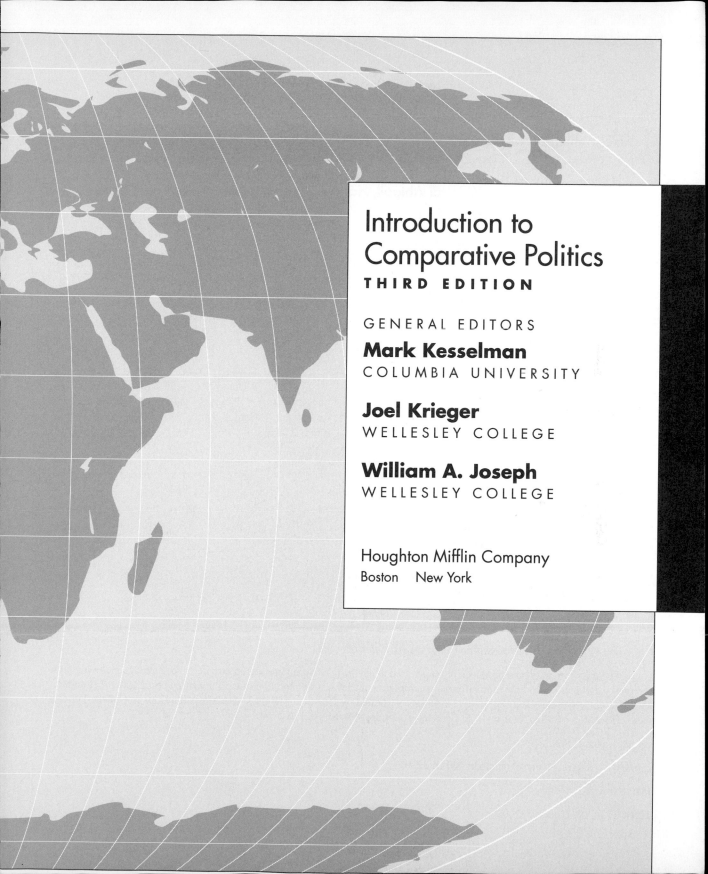

Introduction to Comparative Politics

THIRD EDITION

GENERAL EDITORS

Mark Kesselman
COLUMBIA UNIVERSITY

Joel Krieger
WELLESLEY COLLEGE

William A. Joseph
WELLESLEY COLLEGE

Houghton Mifflin Company
Boston   New York

To our children, who are growing up in a complex and ever more challenging world:
MK—for Ishan and Javed
JK—for Nathan and Megan
WAJ—for Abigail, Hannah, and Rebecca

Sponsoring Editor: Katherine Meisenheimer
Senior Development Editor: Frances Gay
Senior Project Editor: Ylang Nguyen
Editorial Assistant: Wendy Thayer
Senior Manufacturing Coordinator: Marie Barnes
Production / Design Coordinator: Jennifer Meyer Dare
Marketing Manager: Nicola Poser

Cover Image: Three globes showing different parts of the world © Stuart Hunter / Getty Images / Taxi.

Printed in the U.S.A.

Library of Congress Control Number: 2001133289

ISBN: 0-618-21446-1

123456789-MV-07 06 05 04 03

BRIEF CONTENTS

CONTENTS

5 Japan   193

Shigeko N. Fukai and Haruhiro Fukui

PART ❸ Developing Democracies   344

8 Russia   345

Joan DeBardeleben

11 Nigeria   513

Darren Kew and Peter Lewis

PREFACE

We began the preface to the second edition of *Introduction to Comparative Politics: Political Challenges and Changing Agendas:* "These are exciting yet daunting times to teach comparative politics. After years in which the contours of the subject matter were quite familiar, the democratic revolutions of recent years have challenged scholars and teachers to think anew about the field's geographical, national, and intellectual boundaries. Even as countries ruled for decades by communist and authoritarian regimes adopted democratic institutions, other countries that held out against the democratic tide found themselves on the defensive internationally and at home, while long-established democracies have been buffeted by new economic, cultural, and political challenges. For the countries included in *Introduction to Comparative Politics*, there seems to be no end to history."

No end indeed. We do not claim to be prophets. Who could have predicted the protests at the ministerial meeting of the World Trade Organization (WTO) in Seattle in 1999 (as well as at numerous meetings of the WTO, the International Monetary Fund, and the World Bank since then); the attacks on the World Trade Center and Pentagon on September 11, 2001; and, in 2003, U.S.-led military action against Iraq, the worldwide protests that followed, and the diplomatic rift between the United States and some of its key European allies such as Germany and France? It appears that a reshuffling of the geopolitical order is in progress—the results of which cannot be predicted. We are all struggling to make sense of the awesome challenges of globalization, ethnonationalism, and state-sponsored and non-state-based violence in the brave new world of the twenty-first century. These developments fundamentally affect the internal politics and policies of countries throughout the world in complex and highly variable ways. We hope that this thoroughly revamped edition of *Introduction to Comparative Politics* will help students analyze new (and old) political challenges and changing (and persistent) agendas.

Structure of the Book

The core elements of *Introduction to Comparative Politics* have not changed. We are pleased that instructors and students have generously praised the analytical framework, lively writing, and high level of scholarship in *Introduction to Comparative Politics*. In the third edition, we have retained the basic framework and approach of the second edition. We aim to make the book accessible to students with little or no background in political science. We have used readable, direct prose as free of jargon as possible, and have maximized symmetry among chapters in order to facilitate comparison.

Introduction to Comparative Politics emphasizes patterns of state formation, political economy, domestic politics, and the politics of collective identities within the context of globalization. A distinctive feature of the book is the use of four comparative themes to frame the presentation of each country's politics. We explain the themes in Chapter 1 and present an intriguing "puzzle" for each to stimulate student thinking. These themes—treated in each country study—focus attention on the continuities and contrasts among the twelve countries:

- **A World of States** highlights the importance of state formation and the interstate system for political development.
- **Governing the Economy** analyzes state strategies for promoting economic development and stresses the effects of economic globalization on domestic politics.
- **The Democratic Idea** explores the challenges posed by citizens' demands for greater control and participation in both democracies and non-democracies.
- **The Politics of Collective Identities** considers the political consequences of race, ethnicity, gender, religion, and nationality and their complex interplay with class based politics.

Through our four themes, the methods of comparative analysis come alive as students examine similarities and differences among countries and within and between political systems. This thematic approach facilitates timely and comprehensive analysis of political challenges and changing agendas within countries.

Introduction to Comparative Politics uses a country-by-country approach and strikes a balance between the richness of each country's national political development and more general comparative analysis. Chapter 1 explains the comparative method, analyzes the four key themes of the book, and describes core features of political institutions and processes. Each country chapter that follows consists of five sections. **Section 1** treats the historic formation of the modern state, its geographic setting, and critical junctures in its political development. **Section 2** describes the political economy of past and current national development. **Section 3** outlines the major institutions of governance and policy-making. **Section 4** explains the widely varying processes of representation, participation, and contestation. Finally, **Section 5** reflects on the major issues that confront the country and are likely to shape its future.

Several special features assist in the teaching and learning process.

At the beginning of each chapter, students will find a page of basic demographic, social, economic, and political information to aid in comparing countries. Throughout the chapters a wide array of maps, tables, charts, photographs, and political cartoons enliven the text and present key information in clear and graphic ways. Each country study includes four to six boxes that highlight interesting and provocative aspects of politics—for example, **Leaders,** biographies of important political leaders; **Institutional Intricacies,** important features of a political system that need clarification; **Citizen Action,** unconventional forms of participation; **Global Connection,** examples of connections between domestic and international politics; and **Current Challenges,** issues of today and the future. Key terms are set in boldface when first introduced and are defined in the Glossary at the end of the book. Students will find that the Glossary defines many key concepts that are used broadly in comparative politics.

New to This Edition

We have updated the material on each of the countries to take account of major events and regime changes. We pay particular attention in this edition of *Introduction*

to Comparative Politics to the challenges posed by globalization and issues involving security in a world reshaped by the events of September 11.

We retain the classification of countries used in the last edition, with one relatively minor change: we group countries as established democracies, developing democracies (in previous editions we called this middle group transitional democracies), and non-democracies. With the change in terminology we try to recognize that democratization is often a protracted process with ambiguous results, rather than a clearly delineated path toward completion. Some may question assigning a particular country to a particular category. Fine! We do not claim that the boundaries dividing the three groups are airtight. For one thing, politics is a moving target—a coup or other upheaval may bump a developing democracy into the category of non-democracy. Or the start of a democratic transition may suggest moving a non-democracy into the category of developing democracy. For another, scholars disagree about the appropriate criteria for classifying regime types as well as how to apply the criteria to particular cases. Indeed, instructors may well find that conducting discussion about how to best characterize a given country (or the conceptual scheme that we suggest for classifying countries) can be stimulating and fruitful.

The present edition of *Introduction to Comparative Politics* also provides instructors with much greater flexibility and choice regarding the countries that they may include in their course. For those who prefer the convenience of a preselected set of countries, the regular third edition contains the same countries covered in the second edition. However, instructors who would prefer to cover fewer countries or a different selection of countries can now easily and inexpensively arrange for a **customized edition** of *Introduction to Comparative Politics* to be produced for their course. All the chapters of the regular edition are posted in an **online database**. Also in the database will be six additional country choices, which will only be available in a customized edition. We are delighted that David Ost has written a chapter on East-Central Europe and Tom Lodge has written a chapter on South Africa, which will be online in 2003. In 2004, we will add chapters on the Republic of Korea and on Indonesia. In 2005, Cuba and Turkey will be included in the database of countries that instructors can select for their course. To learn more about the database, or to create a custom edition, visit the Houghton Mifflin online catalog at http://www.college.hmco.com or contact your Houghton Mifflin representative.

Acknowledgments

We want to thank the following for their assistance in preparing some of the country chapters for this edition: Nagraj Adve (India); Bertha Angulo (Mexico); Stuart Chandler, Natalia Joukovskaia, and Yevgen Shevchenko (Russia); Alicia Gourdine, Andrei Ogrezeanu, and John Paetsch (Germany); Jamie Hodari, Mehmet Tabak, and Nicholas Toloudis (France); and Jason Richardson (Brazil). We are also very grateful to those colleagues who have reviewed and critiqued the previous editions of this book:

Michael Bratton, Michigan State University; **William Crowther,** University of North Carolina, Greensboro; **Louise K. Davidson-Schmich,** University of Miami; **Chris Hamilton,** Washburn University; **Kenji Hayao,** Boston College; **Maria Perez Laubhan,** College of Lake County; **Richard Leich,** Gustavus Adolphus College; **Mahmood Monshipouri,** Quinnipiac University.

Finally, our thanks to the talented and professional staff at Houghton Mifflin, especially Katherine Meisenheimer, sponsoring editor; Fran Gay, senior development editor; Ylang Nguyen, senior project editor; and Nicola Poser, marketing manager.

M. K.
J. K.
W. A. J.

Introduction to Comparative Politics

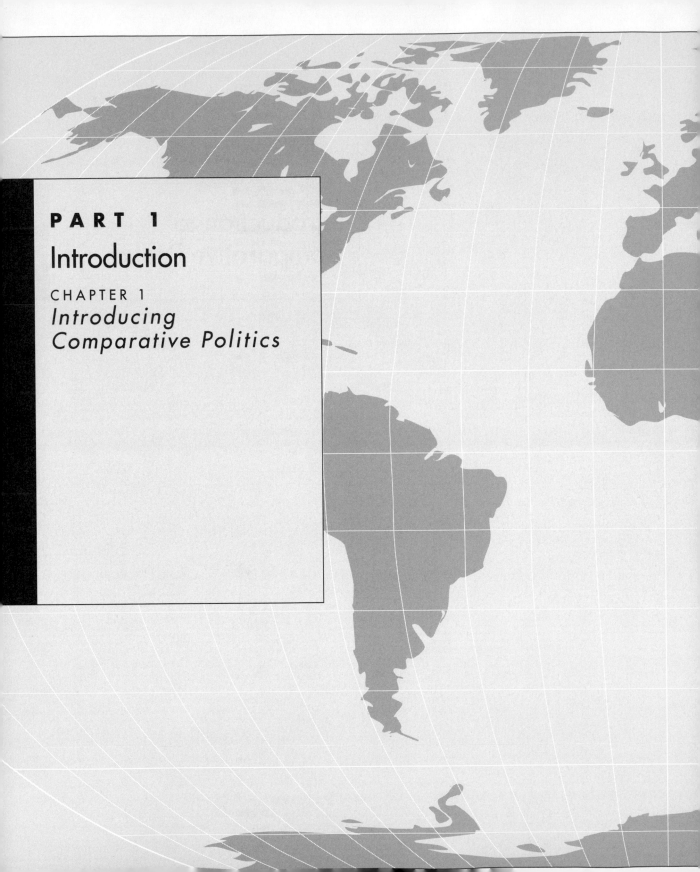

PART 1

Introduction

CHAPTER 1
Introducing Comparative Politics

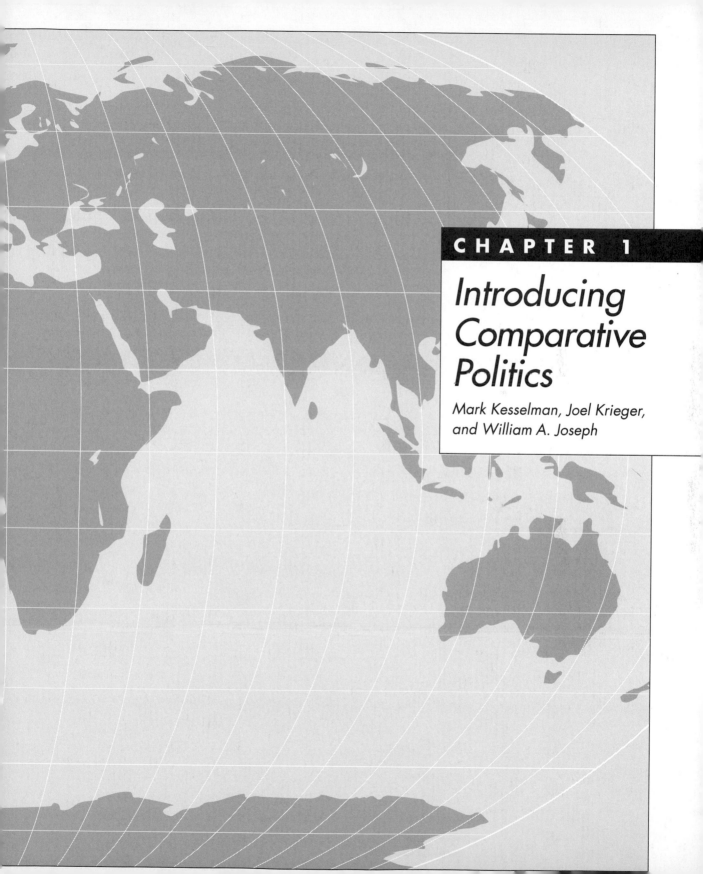

CHAPTER 1

Introducing Comparative Politics

Mark Kesselman, Joel Krieger, and William A. Joseph

Section ❶ The Global Challenge of Comparative Politics

Politics throughout the world seems more troubled today than even a few years ago, when celebrations around the globe ushered in the new millennium. Of course, no one expected that the start of a new century would spell an end to ethnic cleansing, brushfire wars, horrifying epidemics, famine, currency crises that wiped out years of economic development, and the growing marginalization of whole regions of the globe.

Yet there were positive developments on the horizon. The new century began with vivid accounts of the widening circle of opportunities associated with democratization and economic development. (In the United States, especially, the stock market boom of the 1990s was historically unprecedented.) Memories were still fresh of the grim and potentially deadly **cold war,** which ended when the communist regimes in the Soviet Union and East Central Europe imploded beginning in 1989. It looked as if international politics would be driven much more by global economic competition than by hard-edged national enmities.

In 2000, although a world order had not fully crystallized, a new lens for analyzing politics within and among—and behind the backs of—countries seemed to focus everyone's attention: **globalization.** The key new question that promised to dominate the political agenda of the early twenty-first century was whether the processes of globalization—the global diffusion of investment, trade, production, and extraordinary communication technologies—would promote a worldwide diffusion of opportunity and enhancement of human development, or would reinforce the comparative advantages of the more prosperous and powerful regions and peoples, undermine local cultures, and intensify regional conflicts.

These issues are very much with us today and they continue to frame the country studies in this book. Yet the terrorist attacks of September 11, 2001, on the United States and their aftermath have partially reframed our thinking about globalization. Until September 11, the economic aspects of globalization claimed major attention. Since September 11, political and military concerns have been at the forefront, involving how American power will recast global alliances and affect both national politics and people's lives throughout the world. But these issues do not replace concerns about economic globalization. Instead, we are challenged to develop a more complex understanding of globalization and how it frames both politics and the study of comparative politics.

Globalization and Comparative Politics

The terms *globalization* and *global era* are everywhere applied as a general catch phrase to identify the growing depth, extent, and diversity of cross-border connections that are a key characteristic of the contemporary world. Discussion of globalization begins with accounts of economic activities, including the reorganization of production and the global redistribution of the work force (the "global factory") and in the increased extent and intensity of international trade, finance, and foreign direct investment. Globalization involves the movement of peoples due to migration, employment, business, and educational opportunities.

Globalization includes other profound changes that are less visible but equally significant. For example, new applications of information technology (such as the Internet and CNN) blur the traditional distinction between what is around the world and what is around the block, thereby instantly transforming cultures and eroding the boundaries between the local and global. These technologies make instantaneous communication possible and link producers and contractors, headquarters, branch plants, and suppliers in real time anywhere in the world. Employees may be rooted in time and place, but employers can take advantage of the ebb and flow of a global labor market. A secure job today is gone tomorrow. Globalization fosters insecurity in everyday life and presents extraordinary challenges to government.

It forges new forms of international governance, from the **European Union** to the World Trade Organization. And as we all know, international terror networks can strike anywhere—from New York to Bali to Mobassa. In an attempt to regulate and stabilize

5

the myriad international flows, an alphabet soup of international organizations—NATO, the UN, IMF, WTO, OECD, NAFTA, to name but a few—has been enlisted.

All of these processes complicate politics as they erode the ability of even the strongest countries to control their destinies. No state can secure economic and life cycle security for its citizens. None can preserve pristine national models of economic governance or distinctly national cultures, values, understandings of the world, or narratives that define a people and forge their unity.

It is clear that countries face a host of challenges simultaneously from above and below. The capacities of states to control domestic outcomes and assert sovereignty are compromised by regional and global technological and market forces, as well as growing security concerns. The very stability and viability of countries are simultaneously assaulted by ethnic, nationalist, and religious divisions that often involve both internal and external components. The bright line separating domestic and international politics has been rubbed out by the complex set of cross-border economic, cultural, technological, governance, and security processes, institutions, and relations that constitute the contemporary global order.

Making Sense of Turbulent Times

It is not surprising that in the flash of newspaper headlines and television sound bites, the upheavals, rush of events, and sheer range and complexity of the cross-border phenomena of globalization tend to make politics look chaotic beyond comprehension. Although the study of comparative politics can help us understand current events in a rapidly changing world, it involves much more than snapshot analysis or Monday-morning quarterbacking. *Introduction to Comparative Politics* describes and analyzes in detail the government and politics of a range of countries and identifies common themes in their development that explain longer-term causes of both changes and continuities. The book provides cross-national comparisons and explanations based on four themes that we believe are central for understanding politics in today's world:

- The interaction of states within the international order
- The role of the state in economic management
- The pressures for more democracy and the challenges of democratization
- The political impact of diverse attachments and sources of group identity, including class, gender, ethnicity, and religion

We also expect that these four themes will be useful for analyzing where countries may be heading politically in the first decades of the twenty-first century. Moreover, the themes illustrate how comparative politics can serve as a valuable tool for making political sense of even the most tumultuous times. The contemporary period presents an extraordinary challenge to those who study comparative politics, but the study of comparative politics also provides a unique opportunity for understanding this uncertain era.

In order to appreciate the complexity of politics and political transitions in countries around the world, we must look beyond our own national perspectives. Today, business and trade, information technology, mass communications and culture, immigration and travel, as well as politics, forge deep connections among people worldwide. It is particularly urgent that we adopt a truly global perspective as we explore both the politics of different countries and their growing interdependence.

There is an added benefit: by comparing political institutions, values, and processes in countries around the world, the student of comparative politics acquires analytical skills that can be used at home. After you study comparative politics, you begin to think like a comparativist. As comparison becomes almost automatic, you look at the politics of your own country differently, with a wider focus and new insights.

The contemporary world provides a fascinating laboratory for the study of comparative politics and gives unusual significance to the subject. We hope that you share our sense of excitement and join us in the challenging effort to understand the complex and ever-shifting terrain of contemporary politics throughout the world. We begin by exploring what comparative politics actually compares and how comparative study enhances our understanding of politics generally.

Section ❷ What—and How—Comparative Politics Compares

To "compare and contrast" is one of the most common human exercises, whether in the classroom study of literature or politics or animal behavior—or in selecting dorm rooms or listing your favorite movies. In the observation of politics, the use of comparisons is very old, dating at least from Aristotle, the ancient Greek philosopher. Aristotle categorized Athenian city-states in the fifth century B.C. according to their form of political rule: rule by a single individual, rule by a few, or rule by all citizens. He added a normative dimension (a claim about how societies should be ruled), by distinguishing ("contrasting") good and corrupt versions of each type. The modern study of comparative politics refines and systematizes the age-old practice of evaluating some feature of X by comparing it to the same feature of Y in order to learn more about it than isolated study would permit.

The term **comparative politics** refers to a field within the academic study of politics (that is, political science), as well as to a method or approach to the study of politics.[1] The subject matter of comparative politics is the domestic politics of countries or peoples. Within the discipline of political science, comparative politics is one of four areas of specialization. In addition to comparative politics, most political science (or government) departments in U.S. colleges and universities include courses and academic specialists in three other fields: political theory, international relations, and American politics.

Because it is widely believed that students living in the United States should study American politics intensively and with special focus, the two fields remain separate. The pattern of distinguishing the study of politics at home from politics abroad is also common elsewhere, so students in Canada may be expected to study Canadian politics as a distinctive specialty, and Japanese students would be expected to master Japanese politics.

However, there is no logical reason that study of the United States should not be included within the field of comparative politics—and good reason to do so. In fact, many important studies in comparative politics (and an increasing number of courses) have integrated the study of American politics with the study of politics in other countries. Comparative study can place U.S. politics into a much richer perspective and at the same time make it easier to recognize what is distinctive and most interesting about other countries.

The comparative approach principally analyzes similarities and differences among countries by focusing on selected institutions and processes. As students of comparative politics (we call ourselves **comparativists**), we believe that we cannot make reliable statements about most political observations by looking at only one case. We often hear statements such as: "The United States has the best health care system in the world." Comparativists immediately wonder what kinds of health care systems exist in other countries, what they cost and how they are financed, who is covered by health insurance, and so on. Besides, what does "best" mean when it comes to health care systems? Is it the one that provides the widest access? The one that is the most technologically advanced? The one that is the most cost-effective? The one that produces the healthiest population? We would not announce the "best movie" or the "best car" without considering other alternatives or deciding what specific factors enter into our judgment.

Comparativists often analyze political institutions or processes by looking at two or more cases deliberately selected to isolate their common and contrasting features. The analysis involves comparing similar aspects of politics in more than one country—for example, the executive branches of government in the United States, Britain, and Canada.[2] Some comparative political studies take a thematic approach and analyze broad issues, such as the causes and consequences of revolutions in different countries.[3]

Level of Analysis

Comparisons can be very useful for political analysis at several different levels. Political scientists often compare developments in different cities, regions, provinces, or states. Comparative analysis can also focus on specific institutions and processes in different countries, such as the legislature, executive, political parties, social movements, or court systems. The organization of

Introduction to Comparative Politics reflects our belief that the best way to begin the study of comparative politics is with **countries.** Countries, which are also sometimes referred to as **nation-states,** comprise distinct, politically defined territories that encompass political institutions, cultures, economies, and ethnic and other social identities.

Although often highly divided internally, countries have historically been the most important source of a people's collective political identity and are the major arena for organized political action in the modern world. Therefore, countries are the natural unit of analysis for most domestic political variables and processes. These include:

- **political institutions:** the formal and informal rules and structured relationships that organize power and resources in society
- **political culture:** attitudes, beliefs, and symbols that influence political behavior
- **political development:** the stages of change in the structures of government.

Within a given country, the state is almost always the most powerful cluster of institutions. But just what is the state? The way the term is used in comparative politics is probably unfamiliar to many students. In the United States, it usually refers to the states in the federal system—Texas, California, and so on. But in comparative politics, the **state** refers to the key political institutions responsible for making, implementing, enforcing, and adjudicating important policies in a country. The most important state institutions are the national **executive,** notably, the president and/or prime minister and **cabinet,** along with the military, police, and administrative **bureaucracy,** the legislature, and courts. In many ways, the state is synonymous with what is often called the "government."

States claim, usually with considerable success, the right to issue rules—notably, laws, administrative regulations, and court decisions—that are binding for people within the country. Even democratic states, in which top officials are chosen by procedures that permit all citizens to participate, can survive only if they can preserve enforcement (or coercive) powers both internally and with regard to other states that may pose challenges. A number of countries have highly repressive states whose political survival depends largely on military and police powers. But even in such states, long-term stability requires that the ruling regime have some measure of political **legitimacy;** that is, a significant segment of the citizenry must believe that the state is entitled to command. Political legitimacy is greatly affected by the state's ability to "deliver the goods" through satisfactory economic performance and an acceptable distribution of economic resources. Moreover, in the contemporary period, legitimacy seems to require that states represent themselves as democratic in some fashion, whether or not they are in fact. Thus, *Introduction to Comparative Politics* looks closely at, first, the state's role in governing the economy and, second, the pressures exerted on states to develop and extend democratic participation.

The fact that states are the fundamental objects of analysis in comparative politics does not mean that all states are the same. Indeed, the organization of state institutions varies widely, and these differences have a powerful impact on political and social life. Hence, each country study in this book devotes considerable attention to variations in institutions of governance, participation, and representation and their political implications. Each country study begins with an analysis of how the institutional organization and political procedures of the state have evolved historically. This process of **state formation** fundamentally influences how and why states differ politically.

Causal Theories

Because countries are the basic building blocks in politics and because states are the most significant political organizations and actors, these two are the critical units for comparative analysis. The comparativist looks at similarities and differences among countries or states. One influential approach in comparative politics involves developing causal theories—hypotheses that can be expressed formally in a causal mode: "If X happens, then Y will be the result." Such theories include factors (the independent variables, symbolized by X) that are believed to influence some outcome and the outcome (the dependent variable, symbolized by Y) to be explained. For example, it is commonly argued that if a country's economic pie shrinks, conflict among groups for resources will intensify. This hypothesis suggests what is called an inverse correlation between variables: as X varies in one direction, Y varies in the opposite direction. As the total national economic product (X) decreases, then political and social conflict over economic shares (Y) increases. Even when the explanation does not involve the explicit testing of hypotheses (and often it does not), comparativists try to identify similarities and differences among countries and significant patterns.

It is important to recognize the limits on just how "scientific" political science—and thus comparative politics—can be. Two important differences exist between the "hard" (or natural) sciences like physics and chemistry and the social sciences. First, social scientists study people who exercise free will. Because people have a margin for free choice, their choices, attitudes, and behavior cannot be fully explained by causal analysis. This does not mean that people choose in an arbitrary fashion. We choose within the context of material constraint, institutional dictates, and cultural prescriptions. Indeed, comparative politics analyzes how these and other factors orient political choices in systematic ways. But there will probably always be a wide gulf between the natural and social sciences because of their different objects of study.

A second difference between the natural and social sciences is that in the natural sciences, experimental techniques can be applied to isolate the contribution of distinct factors to a particular outcome. It is possible to change the value or magnitude of a factor—for example, the force applied to an object—and measure how the outcome has consequently changed. However, like other social scientists, political scientists and comparativists rarely have the opportunity to apply such experimental techniques.

In the real world of politics, unlike in a laboratory, variables cannot easily be isolated or manipulated. Statistical techniques can be used in an attempt to identify the specific causal weight of different variables in explaining variations in political outcomes. But it is difficult to measure precisely how, for example, a person's ethnicity, gender, or income influences her or his choice when casting a ballot. Nor can we ever know for sure what exact mix of factors—conflicts among elites, popular ideological appeals, the weakness of the state, the organizational capacity of rebel leaders, or the discontent of the masses—precipitates a successful revolution. Indeed, different

revolutions may result from different configurations of factors, such that one cannot develop a theory of revolution.

There is a lively debate about whether the social sciences should seek comparable scientific explanation to what prevails in the natural sciences, such as physics. Some claim that political scientists should seek to develop what has been called covering laws to explain political outcomes, that is, political phenomena should be explained by universal laws in a similar way to how physicists develop universally applicable laws to explain specific features of the physical world. On the other side of the debate, critics of this view claim that the social world is essentially different from the natural world. Some contend that the social sciences should seek to identify particular mechanisms that operate in different settings—but that discerning recurrent mechanisms do not fully explain outcomes. Another group claims that the social scientist should focus on identifying unique configurations that coexist in a particular case but that, once again, the result will not be full explanation or the development of what has been called universal or covering laws.[4] And yet a fourth group advocates what one practitioner described as "thick description," which seeks to convey the rich and subtle texture of any given historical situation, including the subjective and symbolic meaning of that situation for its participants. For the last group, and possibly the second and third group as well, the aim is thus not to provide causal explanations of particular events.

Leaving aside the knotty issue of causality, most comparativists probably agree on the value of steering a middle course that avoids focusing exclusively on one country as well as combining all countries indiscriminately. If we study only individual countries without any comparative framework, then comparative politics would become merely the study of a series of isolated cases. It would be impossible to recognize what is most significant in the collage of political characteristics that we find in the world's many countries. As a result, the understanding of patterns of similarity and difference among countries would be lost, along with an important tool for evaluating what is and what is not unique about a country's political life.

If we go to the other extreme and try to make universal claims that something is always true in all countries, we would either have to stretch the truth or ignore the interesting differences and patterns of variation. The political world is incredibly complex, shaped by an extraordinary array of factors and an almost endless interplay of variables. Indeed, after a brief period in the 1950s and 1960s when many comparativists tried—and failed—to develop a "grand theory" that would apply to all countries, most comparativists now agree on the value of **middle-level theory,** that is, theories focusing on specific features of the political world, such as institutions, policies, or classes of similar events, such as revolutions or elections.

For example, comparativists have analyzed the process in which many countries with authoritarian forms of government, such as military **dictatorships** and one-party states, have developed more participatory and democratic regimes. In studying this process, termed *democratic transitions,* comparativists do not treat each national case as unique or try to construct a universal pattern that ignores all differences. Applying middle-level theory, we identify the influence on the new regime's political stability of specific variables

such as institutional legacies, political culture, levels of economic development, the nature of the regime before the transition, and the degree of ethnic conflict or homogeneity. Comparativists have been able to identify patterns in the emergence and consolidation of democratic regimes in southern Europe in the 1970s (Greece, Portugal, and Spain) and have compared them to developments in Latin America, Asia, and Africa since the 1980s and in Eastern and Central Europe since the revolutions of 1989.[5]

The study of comparative politics has many challenges, including the complexity of the subject matter, the fast pace of change in the contemporary world, and the impossibility of manipulating variables or replicating conditions. What can we expect when the whole political world is our laboratory? When we put the method of comparative politics to the test and develop a set of themes derived from middle-level theory, we discover that it is possible to find explanations and discern patterns that make sense of a vast range of political developments and link the experiences of states and citizens throughout the world.

Section ❸ Themes for Comparative Analysis

We began this introduction by emphasizing the extraordinary importance and fluid pace of the global changes currently taking place. Next, we explained the subject matter of comparative politics and described some of the tools of comparative analysis. This section describes the four themes we use to organize the information on institutions and processes in the country chapters in *Introduction to Comparative Politics.*

These themes help explain continuities and contrasts among countries and demonstrate what patterns apply to a group of countries and why, and what patterns are specific to a particular country. We also suggest a way that each theme highlights some puzzle in comparative politics.

Before we introduce the themes, a couple of warnings are necessary. First, our four themes cannot possibly capture the infinitely varied experience of politics throughout the world. Our framework in *Introduction*

to Comparative Politics, built on four core themes, provides a guide to understanding many features of contemporary comparative politics. But we urge students (and rely on instructors!) to challenge and expand on our interpretations. Second, we want to note that a textbook builds from existing theory but does not construct or test new hypotheses. That task is the goal of original scholarly studies. The themes are intended to distill some of the most significant findings in the field of contemporary comparative politics.

Theme 1: A World of States

The theme that we call a world of states reflects the fact that since the beginning of the modern era about 500 years ago, states have been the primary actors on the world stage. Although international organizations and private actors like transnational corporations play a crucial role, for the most part it is the rulers of states who send armies to conquer other states and territories. It is the legal codes of states that make it possible for businesses to operate within their borders and beyond. States provide for the social protection of citizens through the provision—in one way or another—of health care, old age pensions, aid to dependent children, and assistance to the unemployed. It is states that regulate the movement of people across borders through immigration law. And even the most influential contemporary international organizations in large part reflect the balance of power among member states. That said, the trend is toward courses in international relations integrating a concern with how internal political processes affect states' behavior, and courses in comparative politics highlighting the importance of transnational forces for understanding what goes on within a country's borders. Therefore, in *Introduction to Comparative Politics,* we emphasize the interactive effects of domestic politics and international forces.

No state, even the most powerful, such as the United States, is unaffected by influences originating outside its borders. Today, a host of processes associated with globalization underscore the heightened importance of various cross-national influences. A wide array of international organizations and treaties, including the United Nations, the European Union, the World Trade Organization, and the North American Free Trade Agreement, challenge the sovereign control of national governments. Transnational corporations, international banks, and currency traders in New York, London, Frankfurt, and Tokyo affect countries and people throughout the world. A country's political borders do not protect its citizens from global warming, environmental pollution, or infectious diseases that come from abroad. More broadly, developments linked to technology transfer, the growth of an international information society, immigration, and cultural diffusion have a varying but undeniable impact on the domestic politics of all countries. For example, thanks to the global diffusion of radio, television, and the Internet, people in every part of the world are remarkably informed about international developments. This knowledge may fuel popular local demands that governments intervene in faraway Kosovo, Rwanda, or elsewhere. And heightened global awareness may make citizens more ready to hold their own government to internationally recognized standards of human rights.

In the first decade of this new century, all nation-states are experiencing intense pressures from an expanding and increasingly complex mix of external influences. But international political and economic influences do not have the same impact in all countries, nor do all states equally shape the institutional form and policy of international organizations in which they participate. It is likely that the more advantaged a state is, as measured by its level of economic development, military power, and resource base, the more it will shape global influences. Conversely, the policies of less advantaged countries are more extensively molded by other states, international organizations, and broader international constraints. With the world of states theme, we emphasize one key feature of the international arena: the impact on a state's domestic political institutions and processes of its relative success or failure in competing economically and politically with other states. What sphere of maneuver is left to states by imperious global economic and geopolitical forces? How do CNN, the Internet, McDonald's, television, and films (whether produced in Hollywood or in "Bollywood," that is, Bombay, by India's thriving film industry) shape local cultures and values, influence citizen perceptions of and demands of government, and affect political outcomes?

The theme we identify as a world of states includes a second important focus: similarities and contrasts among countries in state formation. Here we consider the effects of the global order long before the contemporary era of globalization. We study the ways that states have developed historically, diverse patterns in the organization of political institutions, the processes and limits of democratization, the ability of the state to control social groups and sustain power, and the state's economic management strategies and capacities. We draw special attention to the linkage between state formation and the position of states in the international order. Certain countries, such as Britain, India, and Nigeria, are connected by colonial histories; others, like China and Russia, share developmental patterns that for decades were shaped by communist ideologies, political structures, and approaches to economic organization. Today, global security concerns shape a host of developments. The issue decisively affected the U.S. and British attack in 2003 on the regime of Saddam Hussein of Iraq, which the United States and British governments considered a global threat. The action provoked intense controversy and widespread opposition throughout the world. The post–September 11 events have also exerted a ripple effect on conflicts long predating September 11, such as the Kashmir dispute that bitterly divides predominantly Hindu India and mostly Muslim Pakistan.

A puzzle: To what extent do states still remain the basic building blocks of political life? Increasingly, the politics and policies of states are shaped by diverse external factors often lumped together under the category of globalization. At the same time, many states face increasingly restive constituencies who challenge the power and legitimacy of central governments. In reading our country case studies, try to assess what impact pressures from both above and below—outside and inside—have had on the role of the state in carrying out its basic functions and in sustaining the political attachment of its citizens. Can the most powerful states (above all, the United States) preserve a great degree of decision-making autonomy and simply impose their will on others? Or are all states losing their ability to control policy and secure political outcomes? Is a significant degree of local and national autonomy and political innovation for the many states in the developing world compatible with globalization?

Theme 2: Governing the Economy

The success of states in maintaining their authority and sovereign control is greatly affected by their ability to ensure that an adequate volume of goods and services is produced to satisfy the needs of their populations. Certainly, the inadequate performance of the Soviet economic system was an important reason for the rejection of communism and the disintegration of the Soviet Union. It is important to analyze, for example, how countries differ in the balance between agricultural and industrial production in their economies, how successful they are in competing with other countries that offer similar products in international markets, and the relative importance of market forces

versus government control of the economy. How a country "governs the economy"[6]—how it organizes production and intervenes to manage the economy—is one of the key elements in its overall pattern of political as well as economic development.

An important goal of all countries in the contemporary world is to achieve durable economic development. In fact, effective economic performance is near the top of every state's political agenda. The term **political economy** refers to how governments affect economic performance and how economic performance in turn affects a country's political processes. We accord great importance to political economy in *Introduction to Comparative Politics* because we believe that politics in all countries is deeply influenced by the relationship between government and the economy in both domestic and international dimensions. However, the term "economic performance" conveys the impression that there is a single standard by which to measure performance. In fact, the matter is far more complex. Should economic performance be measured solely by how rapidly a country's economy grows? By how equitably it distributes the fruits of economic growth? By the quality of life of its citizenry, as measured by such criteria as life expectancy, level of education, and unemployment rates? (For additional analysis of this point, see "Global Connection: How is Development Measured?" in Section 4.) We invite you to consider these questions as you study the political economies of the countries analyzed in this book.

A puzzle: What political factors promote successful national economic performance? This is a question that students of political economy have long pondered, and to which there are no easy answers. Consider, for example, the apparently straightforward question: Are democratic states more or less able to pursue effective developmental strategies? Although all economies, even the most powerful, experience ups and downs, the United States, Canada, and the countries of the European Union—all democracies—have been notable economic success stories. Yet until the East Asian economic crisis that began in 1997, several countries with **authoritarian** regimes also achieved remarkable records of development. The Republic of Korea (South Korea), Taiwan, and Singapore surged economically in the 1960s and 1970s, and Malaysia and Thailand followed suit in the 1980s and 1990s. China has enjoyed the highest growth rate in the world since the early 1990s. Today, Europe faces high unemployment and worries about a loss of competitiveness that critics allege is due to the high costs of wages and social welfare protections, the result of decades of democratic pressures from center-left parties and working-class interests. Much of East Asia remains in the throes of an economic downturn and loss of international confidence by investors and international financial organizations such as the IMF, which question whether the nondemocratic elements of political regimes will allow them to effectively reform institutions and stabilize their economies. The Nobel Prize–winning economist and comparative public policy analyst Amartya Sen has argued recently, "There is no clear relation between economic growth and democracy in *either* direction."[7] At another level, all countries are facing trade-offs between more market-driven and more state-regulated economic strategies. As you read the country studies, try to reach your own conclusions about what factors—such as the responsiveness of political institutions to participation and popular pressure and approaches to economic management—lead to economic success and whether any consistent patterns apply across countries.

Theme 3: The Democratic Idea

Our comparative case studies reveal a surprising level of complexity in the seemingly simple fact of the rapid spread of democracy throughout much of the world in recent years. First, they show the strong appeal of the democratic idea, by which we mean the claim by citizens that they should, in some way, exercise substantial control over the decisions made by their states and governments. As authoritarian rulers have recently learned in the former Soviet Union, Brazil, Mexico, Iran, South Africa, Nigeria, and China, once persistent and widespread pressures for democratic participation develop, they are hard (although not impossible) to resist. A good indication of the near-universal appeal of the democratic idea is that even authoritarian regimes proclaim their attachment to democracy, usually asserting that they embody a superior form to that prevailing elsewhere. For example, leaders of the People's

Republic of China claim that their brand of "socialist democracy" represents the interests of the vast majority of citizens more effectively than do the "bourgeois democracies" of capitalist societies. As Sen puts it, "While democracy is not yet uniformly practiced, nor indeed uniformly accepted, in the general climate of world opinion, democratic governance has now achieved the status of being taken to be generally right."[8]

Second, the case studies draw attention to diverse sources of support for democracy. Democracy has proved appealing for many reasons. In some historical settings, it may represent a standoff or equilibrium among political contenders for power, in which no one group can gain sufficient strength to control outcomes alone.[9] Democracy may appeal to citizens in authoritarian settings because democratic regimes often rank among the world's most stable, affluent, and cohesive countries. Another important pressure for democracy is born of the human desire for dignity and equality. Even when dictatorial regimes appear to benefit their countries—for example, by promoting economic development or nationalist goals—citizens are still likely to demand democracy. Although authoritarian governments can suppress demands for democratic participation, the domestic and (in recent years) international costs of doing so are high.

Third, the country studies show that democracies vary widely in concrete historical, institutional, and cultural dimensions. We pay close attention to different electoral and party systems, to the distinction between parliamentary and presidential systems, and to differences in the values and expectations that shape citizens' demands in different countries.

Fourth, many of the country studies illustrate the potential fragility of democratic transitions. The fact that popular movements or leaders of moderate factions often displace authoritarian regimes and then hold elections does not mean that democratic institutions will prevail or endure: a wide gulf exists between a transition to democracy and the consolidation of democracy. Historically, powerful groups have often opposed democratic institutions because they fear that democracy will threaten their privilege. On the other hand, disadvantaged groups may oppose the democratic process because they see it as unresponsive to their deeply felt grievances. As a result, reversals of democratic regimes have occurred in the past and will doubtless occur in the future. The country studies do not support a philosophy of history or theory of political development that identifies a single (democratic) end point toward which all countries will eventually converge. One important work, published in the early phase of the most recent democratic wave, captured the tenuous process of democratization in its title: *Transitions from Authoritarian Rule: Tentative Conclusions About Uncertain Democracies.*[10] Some suggest that it is far easier for a country to hold its first democratic election than its second or third. Hence, the fact that the democratic idea is so powerful does not mean that all countries will adopt or preserve democratic institutions.

Finally, our democratic idea theme requires us to examine the incompleteness of democratic agendas in countries with the longest and most developed experiences of representative democracy. In recent years, many citizens in virtually every democracy have turned against the state when their living standards were threatened by high unemployment and economic stagnation. At the same time, **social movements** have targeted the state because of its actions or inactions in such varied spheres as environmental regulation, reproductive rights, and race or ethnic relations. Comparative studies confirm that the democratic idea fuels political conflicts no matter how long established the democracies are because a large gap usually separates democratic ideals and the actual functioning of democratic political institutions. Moreover, social movements are often organized because citizens perceive political parties, presumably an important established vehicle for representing new demands in representative democracies, as ossified and distant. Thus, even in countries with impressive histories of democratic institutions, citizens may invoke the democratic idea to demand that their government be more responsive and accountable.

A puzzle: democracy and stability. Comparativists have intensely debated whether democratic institutions contribute to political stability or, on the contrary, to political disorder. On the one hand, democracy by its very nature permits political opposition: one of its defining characteristics is competition among those who aspire to gain high political office. Political life in democracies is turbulent and unpredictable. On the other hand, the fact that political opposition and competition are legitimate in democracies appears to deepen support for the state even among opponents of a particular government. History reveals far more cases of durable democratic regimes than durable authoritarian regimes in the modern world. In your country-by-country studies, look for the stabilizing and destabilizing consequences of democratic transitions, as well as the challenges that long-standing democracies face.

Theme 4: The Politics of Collective Identity

How do individuals understand who they are in political terms, and on what basis do groups of people come together to advance common political aims? In other words, what are the sources of collective political identity? At one point, social scientists thought they knew the answer. Observers argued that the age-old loyalties of ethnicity, religious affiliation, race, gender, and locality were being dissolved and displaced by economic, political, and cultural modernization. Comparativists thought that **social class**—solidarities based on the shared experience of work or, more broadly, economic position—had become the most important source of collective identity. They believed that most of the time, groups would pragmatically pursue their interests in ways that were not politically destabilizing.[11] We now know that the formation of group attachments and the interplay of politically relevant collective identities are far more complex and uncertain.

In many long-established democracies, the importance of identities based on class membership has declined, although class and material sources of collective political identity remain significant in political competition and economic organization. By contrast, contrary to earlier predictions, in many countries (both long-established and developing democracies) non-class identities have assumed growing, not diminishing, significance. These affiliations develop from a sense of belonging to particular groups based on language, region, religion, ethnicity, race, nationality, or gender.

The politics of collective political identity involves struggles to define which groups are full participants in the political community and which are marginalized or even ostracized. It also involves a constant tug of war over relative power and influence, both symbolic and substantive, among groups. Issues of inclusion, political recognition, and priority remain pivotal in many countries, and they may never be fully resolved.

In addition, questions of representation are hard to resolve: Who is included in an ethnic minority community, for example, or who speaks for the community or negotiates with a governmental authority on its behalf? One reason that conflict around these questions can be so intense is that political leaders in the state and in opposition movements often seek to mobilize support by exploiting ethnic, religious, racial, or regional rivalries and manipulating the issue of representation.

Identity-based conflicts can be found in every multiethnic society. And given the pace of migration and the tangled web of postcolonial histories that link colonizer to colonized, what country is not multiethnic? In Britain, France, and Germany, issues of nationality, citizenship, and immigration, often with ethnic or racial overtones, have been hot-button issues and have often spilled over into electoral politics. Often these conflicts are particularly intense in postcolonial countries, such as Nigeria, where colonial powers forced ethnic groups together in order to carve out a country and borders were drawn with little regard to preexisting collective identities. This process of state formation sowed seeds for future conflict in Nigeria and elsewhere and threatens the continued survival of many postcolonial countries.

A puzzle: collective identity and distributional politics. Once identity demands are placed on the political agenda, can governments resolve them by distributing political, economic, and other resources in ways that redress the grievances of the minority or politically weaker identity groups? Collective identities operate at the level of symbols, attitudes, values, and beliefs and at the level of material resources. However, the contrast between material- and nonmaterial-based identities and demands should not be exaggerated. In practice, most groups are animated by both feelings of attach-

ment and solidarity and by the desire to obtain material benefits and political influence for their members. But the analytical distinction between material and nonmaterial demands remains useful, and it is worth considering whether the nonmaterial aspects of the politics of collective identities make political disputes over ethnicity or religion or language or nationality especially divisive and difficult to resolve.

In a situation of extreme scarcity, it may prove nearly impossible to reach any compromise among groups with conflicting material demands. But if an adequate level of material resources is available, such conflicts may be easier to resolve because groups can negotiate at least a minimally satisfying share of resources. This process of determining who gets what or how resources are distributed is called **distributional politics.** However, the demands of ethnic, religious, and nationalist movements may be difficult to satisfy by a distributional style of politics. The distributional style may be quite ineffective when, for example, a religious group demands that the government require all citizens to conform to its social practices, or a dominant linguistic group insists that a single language be used in education and government throughout the country. In such cases, political conflict tends to move from the distributive realm to the cultural realm, where compromises cannot be achieved by simply dividing the pie of material resources. The country studies examine a wide range of conflicts involving collective identities. It will be interesting (and possibly troubling) to ponder whether and under what conditions they are subject to the normal give-and-take of political bargaining.

These four themes provide our analytic scaffold. With an understanding of the method of comparative politics and the four themes in mind, we can now discuss how we have grouped the country studies that comprise *Introduction to Comparative Politics* and how the text is organized for comparative analysis.

Section ④ Classifying Political Systems

There are nearly 200 states, each with a political regime, in the world today. How can we classify them in a manageable way? One possibility would be not to classify them at all, but simply to treat each state as different and unique. However, comparativists are rarely content with this solution—or nonsolution. It makes sense to highlight clusters of states that share important similarities, just as it is useful to identify what distinguishes one cluster of relatively similar states from other clusters. When comparativists classify a large number of cases into a smaller number of types or clusters, they call the result a **typology.** Typologies facilitate comparison both within the same type as well as between types of states. For example, what difference does it make that Britain has a parliamentary form of government and France a semipresidential one? Both are long-established democracies and highly developed countries, but their different mix of institutions provides an interesting laboratory case to study the impact of institutional variation.

We can also compare across clusters or types. In this type of comparison—comparativists call this **most different case analysis**—we analyze what produces the substantial differences we observe. What difference does it make that the world's two most populous countries, China and India, have two such different political systems? How do their different political regimes affect such important issues as economic development, human rights, and the role of women?

How do we go about constructing typologies of states? Typologies exist as much in the eye of their beholder as in the nature of the beast. Typologies are artificial constructs, made rather than born. What counts in evaluating a typology is not whether it is "true" or "false," but whether it is useful, and for what purpose. Typologies are helpful to the extent that they permit us to engage in useful comparisons.

What is the most useful typology for classifying states? For almost half a century, from the end of World War II until the 1980s, there was a general consensus on the utility of one typology. Political scientists classified states as industrial (and primarily Western) democracies, the "First World"; communist states as the "Second World"; and poor countries in Asia, Africa, and Latin America that had recently gained independence as the "Third World." It was an imperfect attempt. For example, where should one assign Japan, a country not in the West that rapidly developed in the 1960s and 1970s and became the world's second leading economic power? Nevertheless, the typology was a generally adequate, if imperfect, way to distinguish broad groups of countries because it corresponded to what appeared to be durable and important geopolitical and theoretical divisions in the world.

Today, the typology of First, Second, and Third Worlds is less common because historical change has meant that a large number of countries no longer fit comfortably within this framework. For one thing, in the past two decades, scores of countries have become democratic that are neither highly industrialized nor located in the North Atlantic region, the geographic base of the "First World." From Argentina to Zambia, countries that were formerly colonies or undemocratic states adopted democratic institutions in the past several decades, one of the most important and promising changes in the modern world.

Linked to the swelling of the ranks of democratic countries has been the near-disappearance of communist regimes, that is, the "Second World." Beginning in 1989, the implosion of communism in the former Soviet Union and Eastern and Central Europe set off a revolutionary change in world politics. Only a handful of countries in the world—China, Cuba, Vietnam, Laos, and the Democratic People's Republic of (North) Korea—are now ruled by communist parties and declare an allegiance to communist ideology. It follows that the "Second World" is no longer a useful category to classify countries.

Finally, the "Third World" has also become less useful as a way to understand the many countries formerly classified in this cluster. Countries that are often called "Third World" share few features, other than being less economically developed than industrialized nations (see "Global Connection: How Is Development Measured?"). Their colonial legacies have receded further and further into the past. In addition, some of them have become more industrialized and

Global Connection: *How Is Development Measured?*

One frequently used measure of a country's level of economic development is its gross domestic product (GDP) per capita. This figure is an estimate of a country's total economic output (including income earned from abroad) divided by its total population. Such estimates are made in a country's own currency, such as pesos in Mexico or rubles in Russia.

In order to make comparisons of GDP per capita across countries, it is necessary to convert the estimates to a common currency, usually the U.S. dollar. This is done using official international currency exchange rates, which, for example, would tell you how many pesos or rubles it takes to buy U.S.$1. But many economists believe that an estimate of GDP per capita in dollars based on official exchange rates does not give a very accurate sense of the real standards of living in different countries because it does not tell what goods and services (such as housing, food, and transportation) people can actually buy with their local currencies.

An alternative and increasingly popular means of comparing levels of economic development across countries is to use exchange rates based on purchasing power parity (PPP). PPP-based exchange rates take into account the actual cost of living in a particular country by figuring what it costs to buy the same bundle of goods in different countries. For example, how many pesos does it take to buy a certain amount of food in Mexico or rubles to pay for housing in Russia? Many analysts think that PPP provides a more reliable (and revealing) tool for comparing standards of living among countries.

The data boxes at the start of each country chapter in this text give both GDP per capita at official exchange rates and using PPP. As you will see, the differences between the two calculations can be quite dramatic, especially for developing countries. However, income comparisons based on either GDP per capita or PPP do not provide a complete picture of a country's level of development, since these measurements do not necessarily capture what might be considered ways of measuring the quality of life. As a result, the United Nations has introduced another concept that is useful in making socioeconomic comparisons among nations: the Human Development Index (HDI). Based on a formula that takes into account the three factors of longevity (life expectancy at birth), knowledge (literacy and average years of schooling), and income (according to PPP), the United Nations assigns each country of the world, for which there are enough data, an HDI decimal number between 0 and 1; the closer a country is to 1, the better is its level of human development.

Out of 173 countries ranked according to HDI by the United Nations Development Programme in 2002, Norway (.942) was at the top and Sierra Leone (.275) was ranked last. Countries such as the United States (6), Japan (9), France (12), Britain (13), Germany (17), Israel (22), Singapore (25), the Republic of Korea or South Korea (27) and Poland (37) scored as having "high human development"; Mexico (54), Russia (60), Brazil (73), China (96), Iran (98), India (124), and Kenya (134) had "medium human development"; and Pakistan (138) and Nigeria (148) were ranked as having "low human development."

---

economically powerful, including Brazil and Mexico. Nevertheless, even in the post–cold war era, the term "Third World" retains some significance as a shorthand way to refer to the roughly 130 countries that the United Nations classifies as "developing" and are still separated from the 50 or so industrialized nations by a vast economic gulf. Within the "Third World" there are about four dozen countries—for example, Afghanistan, Ethiopia, and Haiti—that are classified by the UN as "least developed" and are so poor that the term "Fourth World" is sometimes used to describe them.

If the "three worlds" method of classification is no longer as useful as it once was, what is a preferred alternative? At present, there is no agreement among comparativists on this question. We suggest a typology based on the concept of democracy that identifies one of the most important dimensions for understanding differences among regimes in the contemporary world. However, we preface the discussion by emphasizing that the categories we use are not airtight. Further, one might imagine an altogether different typology for classifying regimes. We invite students to think critically about how to make sense of the great variety of regimes in the world today.

Our typology distinguishes among regimes that are *established democracies, developing democracies,* and *nondemocracies.*[12] Our selection of a typology reflects the bedrock distinction between democratic and nondemocratic regimes. For a regime to qualify as democratic, it must include the following characteristics:

- **Political accountability.** There must be formal procedures by which those who hold political power are chosen and held accountable to the people of the country. The key mechanism for such accountability is regular, free, and fair elections in which all citizens are eligible to cast ballots to elect candidates for office.
- **Political competition.** Political parties must be free to organize, present candidates for office, express their ideas, and compete in fair elections. The winning party must be allowed to take office, and the losing party must relinquish power through legal and peaceful means.
- **Political freedom.** All citizens must possess political rights and civil liberties. These include the right to participate in the political process, free of government reprisals; freedom of assembly, organization, and political expression (including the right to criticize the government); equality before the law; and protection against arbitrary state intrusion into citizens' private lives. A judiciary not subject to direct political control is a common institutional means for safeguarding these freedoms.
- **Political equality.** All citizens must be legally entitled to participate in politics (by voting, running for office, and joining an interest group), and their votes must have equal weight in the political process. Men and women of political, ethnic, religious, or other minority groups must have equal rights as citizens.

We believe that in understanding similarities and differences among regimes, it is fundamentally important to focus on whether a regime is democratic. We make a further distinction in this book between established and developing democracies. We do so on the basis of whether democratic institutions and practices are solidly and stably established. Thus, we claim there is a difference of kind, and not just of degree, between what comparativists call *consolidated democracies* and more fragile democracies, which we term here *developing democracies.*

Established democracies are regimes in which there is a quite durable tradition of respecting the democratic procedures that we specified above. We do not mean to claim that established democracies do not violate democratic procedures—and sometimes in very important respects. For example, one can point to numerous instances in countries high in the democratic rankings, like Britain and the United States, of police abuse and of unequal treatment of citizens who are poor or from a racial or ethnic minority. Indeed, political conflicts in established democracies often involve demands for more and better-quality democracy. Examples of established democracies around the world are Britain, France, Germany, Japan, India, and the United States.

The reason we identify two varieties of democracy becomes clearer when we turn to the second category of democracy. In developing democracies, as compared to established democracies, it is much less certain that political parties will be free to compete, that votes will be counted honestly, and that political officials will be held accountable through elections and independent judiciary. Moreover, respecting these important democratic practices at one point in time is sufficient to warrant classifying a regime as a developing democracy. But a relatively lengthy period of democratic practice is required for us to consider a regime as an established democracy. We classify Russia, Brazil, Mexico, and Nigeria as developing democracies for two reasons. First, they respect the checklist of democratic procedures specified above to a lesser extent than is the case for the group of established democracies. Extensive political corruption, troubling state-sanctioned violence against opponents, or executive interference in judicial processes is often found in developing democracies, despite their official adherence to democratic guarantees. Second, developing democracies are characterized as practicing democracy for a relatively brief period. There is no hard and fast line to determine how long democracy must be practiced (as well as simply preached) for us to classify it as established. Again, then, our typology is not meant to suggest that the classification is rigid or unchangeable. When a new edition of this book appears, several countries classified in this edition as developing democracies may be classified as established democracies—or as non-democratic.

We want to emphasize that there is no inevitable escalator that carries a country from one category to the next higher one. History has demonstrated that one should beware of subscribing to a theory of inevitable progress—whether political, economic, or social. Through time, countries may become more democratic—or less so. Thus, democratic institutions may be subverted so that a democratic regime becomes nondemocratic. How should we define nondemocratic

regimes? The answer is mostly by reversing the sign in the checklist of democratic requisites specified above. Thus, we classify nondemocratic regimes as those in which there are poorly developed or respected procedures for selecting and holding accountable political leaders, political competition is severely restricted, citizens have little freedom to participate in and dissent from official policies, and citizens of different genders, racial groups, religions, ethnicities, and so on do not enjoy equal rights. Examples of nondemocratic regimes are Iran and China. We conclude our discussion of the typology for classifying regimes by repeating that the categories we use do not divide regimes in a hard and fast fashion or once and for all. For example, we consider India an established democracy: since it gained independence in 1947, political competition and elections have generally been free and fair, and the other checklist items of democratic procedures have been respected. However, to cite only one important violation of democratic rights, India has all too often been the scene of horrific communal violence, in which religious minorities have been targeted, sometimes with the active complicity of state officials. Closer to home, credible evidence exists that racial inequalities in voter registration and vote counting are not a thing of the past in some states of the United States.

Section ❺ Organization of the Text

The core of this book consists of case studies selected for their significance in terms of our comparative themes and ability to provide a reasonable cross-section of types of political regimes and geographic regions. Although each of the country studies makes important comparative references, the studies are primarily intended to provide detailed descriptions and analyses of the politics of individual countries. At the same time, the country studies have common section and subsection headings to help you make comparisons and explore similar themes across the various cases. The following are brief summaries of the main issues and questions covered in the country studies.

1: The Making of the Modern State

Section 1 in each chapter provides an overview of the forces that have shaped the particular character of the state. We believe that an understanding of the contemporary politics of any country requires some familiarity with the historical process by which its current political system was formed. "Politics in Action" uses a specific event to illustrate an important political moment in the country's recent history and to highlight some of the critical political issues it faces. "Geographic Setting" locates the country in its regional context and discusses the political implications of its geographic setting. "Critical Junctures" looks at some of the major stages and decisive turning points in state development. This discussion should give you an idea of how the country assumed its current political order and a sense of how relations between state and society have developed over time. "Themes and Implications" shows how the past pattern of state development continues to shape the country's current political agenda. "Historical Junctures and Political Themes" applies the text's core themes to the making of the modern state: How was the country's political development affected by its place in the world of states? What are the political implications of the state's approach to economic management? What has been the country's experience with the democratic idea? What are the important bases of collective identity in the country, and how do these relate to the people's image of themselves as citizens of the state? "Implications for Comparative Politics" discusses the broader significance of the country for the study of comparative politics.

2: Political Economy and Development

Section 2 in each chapter traces the country's recent and contemporary economic development. It explores the issues raised by the core theme of governing the economy and analyzes how economic development has affected political change. The placement of this section near the beginning of the country study reflects our belief that an understanding of an economic situation is essential for analyzing its politics. "State and Economy" discusses the basic organization of the country's economy, with an emphasis on the role of the state in managing economic life and on the relationship between the government and other economic actors. How do the dynamics and historical timing of the country's insertion into the world economy—and its current position and competitiveness within the globalized economy—affect domestic political arrangements and shape contemporary challenges? This section also analyzes the state's social welfare policies, such as health care, housing, and pension programs. "Society and Economy" examines the social and political implications of the country's economic situation. It asks who benefits from economic change and looks at how economic development creates or reinforces class, ethnic, gender, regional, or ideological

cleavages in society. "The International Political Economy" considers the country's global role: How have patterns of trade and foreign investment changed over time? What is the country's relationship to regional and international organizations? To what degree has the country been able to influence multilateral policies? How have international economic issues affected the domestic political agenda?

3: Governance and Policy-Making

In Section 3, we describe the state's major policy-making institutions and procedures. "Organization of the State" lays out the fundamental principles—as reflected in the country's constitution, its official ideology, and its historical experience—on which the political system and the distribution of political power are based. It also sketches the basic structure of the state, including the relationship among different levels and branches of government. "The Executive" encompasses whatever key offices (for example, presidents, prime ministers, communist party leaders) are at the top of the political system, focusing on those who have the most power, how they are selected, and how they use their power to make policy. It looks at the national bureaucracy and its relationship to the chief executive and the governing party and its role in the policy-making. "Other State Institutions" generally looks at the military, the judiciary and the legal system, state-run corporations, and subnational government. "The Policy-Making Process" summarizes how public policy gets made and implemented. It describes the roles of formal institutions and procedures, as well as informal aspects of policy-making, such as patron-client relations and interest group activity.

4: Representation and Participation

The relationship between the state and the society it governs is the topic of Section 4. How do different groups in society organize to further their political interests, how do they participate and get represented in the political system, and how do they influence policy-making? Given the importance of the U.S. Congress in policy-making, American readers might expect to find the principal discussion of "The Legislature" in Section 3 ("Governance and Policy-Making") rather than

Section 4. But the United States is rather exceptional in having a legislature that is very nearly a coequal branch of government with the executive in the policy process. In most other political systems, the executive dominates the policy process, even when it is ultimately responsible to the legislature, as in a parliamentary system. In most countries other than the United States, the legislature functions primarily to represent and provide a forum for the political expression of various interests in government; it is only secondarily (and in some cases, such as China, only marginally) a policy-making body. Therefore, although this section does describe and assess the legislature's role in policy-making, its primary focus is on how the legislature represents or fails to represent different interests in society. "Political Parties and the Party System" describes the overall organization of the party system and reviews the major parties. "Elections" discusses the election process and recent trends in electoral behavior. It also considers the significance of elections (or lack thereof) as a vehicle for citizen participation in politics and in bringing about changes in the government. "Political Culture, Citizenship, and Identity" examines how people perceive themselves as members of the political community: the nature and source of political values and attitudes, who is considered a citizen of the state, and how different groups in society understand their relationship to the state. The topics covered may include political aspects of the educational system, the media, religion, and ethnicity. How has globalization shaped collective identities and collective action? "Interests, Social Movements, and Protests" discusses how various groups pursue their political interests outside the party system. When do they use formal organizations (such as unions) or launch movements (such as Green environmental or "antiglobalization" movements)? What is the relationship between the state and such organizations and movements? When and how do citizens engage in acts of protest? And how does the state respond to such protests?

5: Politics in Transition

In Section 5, each country study returns to the book's focus on the major challenges that are reshaping our world and the study of comparative politics. "Political Challenges and Changing Agendas" lays out the major unresolved issues facing the country and assesses which are most likely to dominate in the near future. "Politics in Comparative Perspective" returns to the four themes and highlights what this case study tells us about politics in other countries that have similar political systems or that face similar kinds of political challenges.

It is quite a challenge to understand the contemporary world of politics. We hope that the timely information and thematic focus of *Introduction to Comparative Politics* will both prepare and inspire you to explore further the endlessly fascinating terrain of comparative politics.

Key Terms

cold war	bureaucracy
globalization	legitimacy
European Union	state formation
comparative politics	middle-level theory
comparativists	dictatorship
country	political economy
nation-state	authoritarian
political institutions	social movements
political culture	social class
political development	distributional politics
state	typology
executive	most different case
cabinet	analysis

Suggested Readings

Anderson, Benedict. *Imagined Communities: Reflections on the Origins and Spread of Nationalism*. Rev. ed. London: Verso, 1991.

Anderson, Lisa, ed. *Transitions to Democracy*. New York: Columbia University Press, 1999.

Berger, Suzanne, and Dore, Ronald, eds. *National Diversity and Global Capitalism*. Ithaca, N.Y.: Cornell University Press, 1996.

Brady, Henry E., and Collier, David, eds. *Rethinking Social Inquiry: Diverse Tools, Shared Standards*. Boulder, Colo.: Rowman and Littlefield, forthcoming.

Cammack, Paul. *Capitalism and Democracy in the Third World: The Doctrine for Political Development*. London: Leicester University Press, 1997.

Diamond, Larry, and Plattner, Marc F., eds. *The Global Resurgence of Democracy*. 2d ed. Baltimore: Johns Hopkins University Press, 1996.

Diamond, Larry, Plattner, Marc F., Chu, Yun-han, and Tien, Hung-mao, eds. *Consolidating the Third Wave of Democracy.* 2 vols. Baltimore: Johns Hopkins University Press, 1997.

Evans, Peter. *Embedded Autonomy: States and Industrial Transformation.* Princeton, N.J.: Princeton University Press, 1995.

Evans, Peter B., Rueschemeyer, Dietrich, and Skocpol, Theda, eds. *Bringing the State Back In.* Cambridge: Cambridge University Press, 1985.

Hall, Peter A., and Soskice, David, eds. *Varieties of Capitalism: The Institutional Foundations of Comparative Advantage.* New York: Oxford University Press, 2001.

Katznelson, Ira, and Milner, Helen V., eds. *Political Science: The State of the Discipline.* New York: Norton, 2002.

King, Gary, Keohane, Robert O., and Verba, Sidney. *Designing Social Inquiry: Scientific Inference in Qualitative Research.* Princeton, N.J.: Princeton University Press, 1994.

Lichbach, Mark Irving, and Zuckerman, Alan S., eds. *Comparative Politics: Rationality, Culture, and Structure.* Cambridge: Cambridge University Press, 1997.

Linz, Juan J., and Stepan, Alfred. *Problems of Democratic Transition and Consolidation: Southern Europe, South America, and Post-Communist Europe.* Baltimore: Johns Hopkins University Press, 1996.

Mahoney, James, and Rueschemeyer, Dietrich, eds. *Comparative Historical Analysis in the Social Sciences.* Cambridge: Cambridge University Press, 2003.

Marx, Anthony. *Making Race and Nation: A Comparison of the United States, South Africa, and Brazil.* Cambridge: Cambridge University Press, 1998.

O'Donnell, Guillermo A., Schmitter, Philippe C., and Whitehead, Laurence, eds. *Transitions from Authoritarian Rule.* 4 vols. Baltimore: Johns Hopkins University Press, 1986.

Przeworski, Adam. *Democracy and the Market: Political and Economic Reforms in Eastern Europe and Latin America.* Cambridge: Cambridge University Press, 1991.

————, et al. *Democracy and Development: Political Institutions and Well-Being in the World, 1950–1990.* Cambridge: Cambridge University Press, 2000.

Putnam, Robert, with Leonardi, Robert, and Nanetti, Raffaella Y. *Making Democracy Work: Civic Traditions in Modern Italy.* Princeton, N.J.: Princeton University Press, 1992.

Scott, James C. *Seeing Like a State: How Certain Schemes to Improve the Human Condition Have Failed.* New Haven, Conn.: Yale University Press, 1998.

Stark, David, and Bruszt, Laszlo. *Postsocialist Pathways: Transforming Politics and Property in East Central Europe.* Cambridge: Cambridge University Press, 1998.

Stiglitz, Joseph E. *Globalization and Its Discontents.* New York: Norton, 2002.

Tarrow, Sidney. *Power in Movement: Social Movements and Contentious Politics.* 2d ed. Cambridge: Cambridge University Press, 1998.

Tilly, Charles. *Coercion, Capital and European States,* A.D. *990–1992.* Cambridge: Blackwell, 1990.

Woo-Cummings, Meredith, ed. *The Developmental State.* Ithaca, N.Y.: Cornell University Press, 1999.

Suggested Websites

CIA World Factbook
www.odci.gov/cia/publications/factbook/index.html
Elections Around the World
www.electionworld.org/
Foreign Government Resources on the Web
www.lib.umich.edu/govdocs/foreignnew.html
Freedom House
www.freedomhouse.org/
Political Resources on the Net
www.politicalresources.net/
World Audit
www.worldaudit.org/

Notes

[1] See Philippe Schmitter, "Comparative Politics," in Joel Krieger, ed., *The Oxford Companion to Politics of the World,* 2nd ed. (New York: Oxford University Press, 2001), 160–165. For a more extended discussion and different approach, see David D. Laitin, "Comparative Politics: The State of the Subdiscipline," in Ira Katznelson and Helen V. Milner, eds., *Political Science: The State of the Discipline* (New York: Norton, 2002), 630–659.

[2] See, for example, Colin Campbell, *Governments Under Stress: Political Executives and Key Bureaucrats in Washington, London, and Ottawa* (Toronto: University of Toronto Press, 1983).

[3] See, for example, Theda Skocpol, *Social Revolutions in the Modern World* (Cambridge: Cambridge University Press, 1994).

[4] For diverse views, see Gary King, Robert O. Keohane, and Sidney Verba, *Designing Social Inquiry: Scientific Inference in Qualitative Research* (Princeton, N.J.: Princeton University Press, 1994); Mark Irving Lichbach and Alan S. Zuckerman, eds., *Comparative Politics: Rationality, Culture, and Structure* (Cambridge: Cambridge University Press, 1997); and Katznelson and Milner, eds., *Political Science;* Henry E. Brady and David Collier, eds., *Rethinking Social Inquiry: Diverse Tools, Shared Standards* (Boulder, Colo.: Rowman and Littlefield, forthcoming).

[5] For a fine example, see Juan J. Linz and Alfred Stepan, *Problems of Democratic Transition and Consolidation: Southern Europe, South America, and Post-Communist Europe* (Baltimore: Johns Hopkins University Press, 1996).

[6] This term is borrowed from Peter A. Hall, *Governing the Economy: The Politics of State Intervention in Britain and France* (New York: Oxford University Press, 1986).

[7] Amartya Sen, "Democracy as a Universal Value," *Journal of Democracy* 10, no. 3 (July 1999): 3–17. (http://muse.jhu.edu/demo/jod/10.3sen.html). Another influential study of this question reaches a similar conclusion: Adam Przeworski et al., *Democracy and Development: Political Institutions and Well-Being in the World, 1950–1990* (Cambridge: Cambridge University Press, 2000).

[8]Sen, p. 3 (Internet text version).

[9]This view has been developed well by Adam Przeworski, *Democracy and the Market: Political and Economic Reforms in Eastern Europe and Latin America* (Cambridge: Cambridge University Press, 1991).

[10]Guillermo O'Donnell and Philippe Schmitter, *Transitions from Authoritarian Rule: Tentative Conclusions About Uncertain Democracies* (Baltimore: Johns Hopkins University Press, 1986).

[11]For a survey of political science literature on this question, see Mark Kesselman, "The Conflictual Evolution of American Political Science: From Apologetic Pluralism to Trilateralism and Marxism," in J. David Greenstone, ed., *Public Values and Private Power in American Democracy* (Chicago: University of Chicago Press, 1982), 34–67.

[12]The term *developing democracies* is borrowed and adapted from Larry Diamond, *Developing Democracy: Toward Consolidation* (Baltimore: Johns Hopkins University Press, 1999).

PART 2

Established Democracies

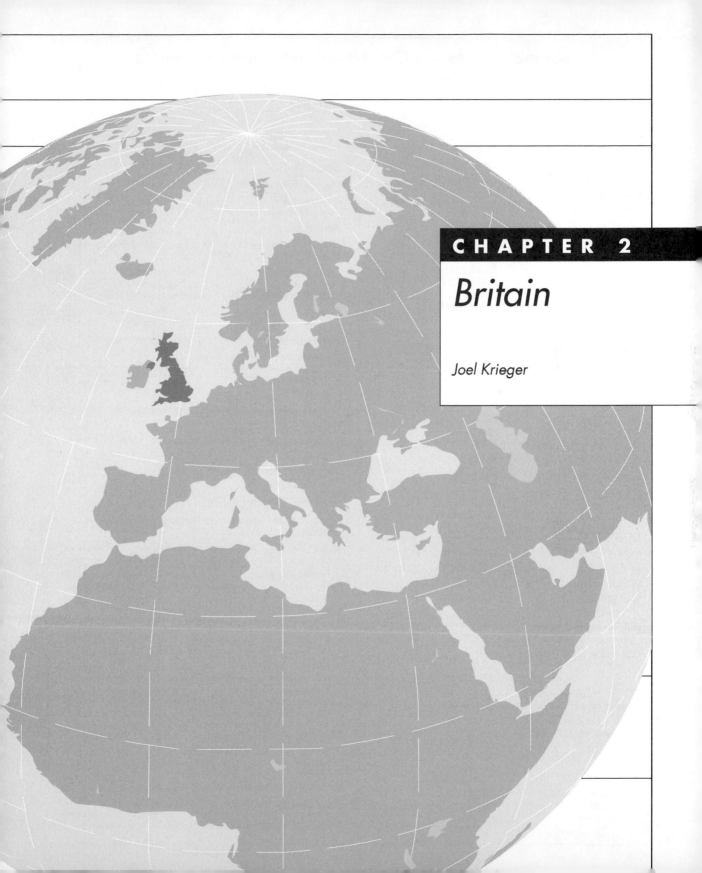

CHAPTER 2

Britain

Joel Krieger

United Kingdom of Great Britain and Northern Ireland

Land and People

Capital	London	
Total area (square miles)	94,251 (Slightly smaller than Oregon)	
Population	59.4 million	
Annual population growth rate (%)	1975–2000	0.2
	2000–2015 (projected)	0.1
Urban population (%)	89.5	
Ethnic composition (%)	White	92.2
	Indian	1.7
	Pakistani	1.3
	Bangladeshi	0.5
	Other Asian	0.4
	Black Caribbean	1.0
	Black African	0.9
	Chinese	0.3
	Hybrid Identity	0.8
	Other	0.6
	Not Stated	0.2
Major language(s)	English	
Religious affiliation (%)	Church of England/ Anglican	29.8
	Roman Catholic	9.2
	Presbyterian	3.5
	Baptist or Methodist	3.4
	Other Christian	9.3
	Islam/Muslim	2.0
	Hindu	1.0
	Jewish	0.8
	Sikh	0.4
	Other non-Christian	0.5
	Refusal/Not Answered/ Didn't Know	0.6
	None	39.5

Economy

Domestic Currency	Pound Sterling	
Total GDP (US$)	1.41 trillion	
GDP per capita (US$)	24,058	
Total GDP at purchasing power parity (US$)	1.40 trillion	
GDP per capita at purchasing power parity (US$)	23,509	
GDP annual growth rate (%)	1997	3.5
	2000	3.1
	2001	2.2
GDP per capita average annual growth rate (%)	1975–2000	2.0
	1990–2000	2.2
Inequality in income or consumption (1999) (%)	Poorest 20%	8
	Next 20%	12
	Middle 20%	16
	Next 20%	22
	Richest 20%	42
	Gini Index (1991)	36.1
Structure of production (% of GDP)	Agriculture	1.0
	Industry	28.8
	Services	70.2

Labor force distribution (% of total)	Agriculture	1
	Industry	25
	Services	74
Exports as % of GDP	27	
Imports as % of GDP	29	

Society

Life expectancy at birth	77.7	
Infant mortality per 1000 live births	6	
Adult literacy (%)	99*	

*The OECD estimates that Britain has a functional illiteracy rate of about 22%

Access to information and communications (per 1000 population)	Telephone lines	589
	Mobile phones	727
	Radios	1432
	Televisions	653
	Personal Computers	338

Women in Government and Economy

Women in the national legislature	Lower house (%)	17.9
	Upper house (%)	16.4
Women at ministerial level (%)	33.3	
Female economic activity rate (age 15 and above) (%)	52.8	
Female labor force (% of total)	44	
Estimated earned income (PPP US$)	Female	17,931
	Male	29,264
2002 Human Development Index Ranking *(out of 173 countries)*		13

Political Organization

Political System   Parliamentary Democracy, Constitutional monarchy.

Regime History   Long constitutional history, origins subject to interpretation, usually dated from the seventeenth century or earlier.

Administrative Structure   Unitary state with fusion of powers. UK parliament has supreme legislative, executive, and judicial authority. Reform in process to transfer limited powers to representative bodies for Scotland, Wales, and Northern Ireland.

Executive   Prime Minister, answerable to House of Commons, subject to collective responsibility of the cabinet; member of Parliament who is leader of party that can control a majority in Commons.

Legislature   Bicameral. House of Commons elected by single-member plurality system with no fixed term but a five-year limit. Main legislative powers: to pass laws, provide for finance, scrutinize public administration and government policy. House of Lords, unelected upper house: limited powers to delay enactment of legislation and to recommend revisions; specified appeals court functions. Reform introduced to eliminate voting rights of hereditary peers and create new second chamber.

Judiciary   Independent but with no power to judge the constitutionality of legislation or governmental conduct. Judges appointed by Crown on recommendation of PM or lord chancellor.

Party System   Two-party dominant, with regional variation. Principal parties: Labour, and Conservative; a center party (Liberal Democrats); and national parties in Scotland, Wales, and Northern Ireland.

Section ❶ The Making of the Modern British State

The Statue of Liberty declares, "Give me your tired, your poor / Your huddled masses, yearning to breathe free." The *Economist* recently pondered the question of what a similar European Union (EU) monument in Brussels might proclaim and proposed the following: "We have vacancies for a limited number of computer programmers and will reluctantly accept torture victims with convincing scars. Migrants looking for a better life can clear off."[1] What might a British Statue of Liberty announce to potential immigrants, refugees, and asylum seekers?

There is a sense of urgency about the "huddled masses" in Europe. A great many European voters are preoccupied with high unemployment and a host of insecurities about national identities and material security that are endemic to this era of European integration and globalization. Right-wing populist anti-immigrant parties have gained electoral strength by manipulating these fears and blaming society's ills on immigrants. The center-left has lost its dominance in Europe and is scrambling to regain the initiative.

In one sense, Britain is an exception, with Tony Blair's New Labour riding high and no significant challenge in sight from either the mainstream Conservative right or the extreme right. Yet, in another sense, Britain is swept up in the frenzy of a fortress Europe mentality. Evidence suggests that the increase in applications for asylum in the U.K.—from roughly 1,500 in the first quarter of 2001 to nearly 20,000 in the first quarter of 2002—has fueled anger among many Britons that the U.K. is a "soft touch." Polling data in May 2002 also suggests that Britons vastly exaggerate the number of refugees and asylum seekers. Although the U.K. hosts just under 2 percent of the world's refugees and asylum seekers, the public estimates the number at more than ten times higher, believing on average that the country hosts almost 23 percent of the world total.[2]

Tony Blair is leading the get-tough policy, determined to show everyone that Britain is as harsh on asylum seekers and illegal immigrants as its neighbors are and making sure that no one doubts the resolve of the center-left on this highly charged issue. The government introduced a bill in Parliament in June 2002, that would allow Britain to deport failed asylum seekers within days; make a knowledge of English, Gaelic, or Welsh mandatory for those seeking British nationality; and keep the children of asylum seekers segregated from children in British schools for six months by placing them in special classes in asylum centers. The Nationality, Immigration and Asylum Act was approved by both houses of Parliament in November 2002 and came into force in January 2003.

At the EU summit in Seville in June 2002, the British prime minister and his Spanish counterpart led a campaign to harden trade policy and suspend foreign aid to developing countries that refuse to take back refugees whose applications for asylum have been rejected. The plan was turned down by the summit, which went no further than to require a migration clause and commitment to re-admission in all new trade agreements with non-EU countries and to review existing agreements in cases of non-cooperation. Blair's rebuff occasioned tabloid headlines about his humiliation at Seville, even as his attempts to put a good face on things inspired familiar attacks on his proclivity to favor spin over substance. Blair suffered recriminations from immigrant and human rights groups, European allies (the Swedish prime minister blasted the proposal as "stupid, unworkable and an historic mistake"), and even from his own minister for development (who called the proposal "morally repugnant"). The French president, Jacques Chirac, who knows something about outmaneuvering the far right on immigration issues, opposed any conditionality on aid, insisting, "You are not going to solve problems by brandishing a sword, especially a wooden one." Meanwhile, the British and the French worked on resolving a dispute over a Red Cross camp for refugees at Sangatte, near Calais, and close to the entrance to the Channel Tunnel joining England and France. Endless coverage of the camp's residents flocking onto trains bound for Britain have made Sangatte a potent symbol of the "invasion" of Britain and intensified the diplomatic efforts to secure French agreement to close the camp altogether. (The Sangatte camp closed in December 2002.)

The Seville impasse suggests the contortions involved in Britain's effort to maximize its influence in the world of states. Britain is a stalwart champion of

America's war on terror and a voice for moderation in U.S. foreign policy. It is thus a global power beyond the scope of European affairs and yet something of an outlier in the EU unable to shape European policy. One of only three members of the EU who has not yet joined the euro zone, the U.K. is reluctant to throw in its lot completely with Europe as the pace of economic integration quickens. Perhaps even more telling, British sensibilities remain out of step with Europe, and its hopes to counter-balance reduced economic policy influence with greater foreign policy clout suffered a set back in Seville. In particular, asylum policy has strained relations with France and a handful of other EU partners.

The Seville summit as well as widespread discussion of the Nationality, Immigration and Asylum Act also raised important issues about collective identities in the U.K. Both press reports and statements by ministers muddied discussion about immigration policy in a way that seemed to invite anti-immigrant feeling and raise concerns in the ethnic minority communities. Perfectly lawful requests for asylum and refugee status were routinely labeled "illegal immigration," and immigration was unfairly associated with crime. On recent evidence, if there were a Statue of Liberty built in Dover, it might proclaim something like: "Don't give us your poor, your huddled masses / We have more than enough. And please shut down Sangatte. We are tired of the invasion of asylum seekers and refugees and don't know what to do with them."

Geographic Setting

Britain is the largest of the British Isles, a group of islands off the northwest coast of Europe, and encompasses England, Scotland, and Wales. The second largest island comprises Northern Ireland and the independent Republic of Ireland. The term *Great* Britain encompasses England, Wales, and Scotland but not Northern Ireland. We use the term *Britain* as shorthand for the United Kingdom of Great Britain and Northern Ireland.

Covering an area of approximately 94,000 square miles, Britain is roughly two-thirds the size of Japan or approximately half the size of France. In 1995, the population of the United Kingdom was 58.6 million people; the population is projected to peak at 61.2 million people in 2023.[3] To put the size of this once immensely powerful country in perspective, it is slightly smaller than Oregon.

Although forever altered by the Channel Tunnel, Britain's location as an offshore island adjacent to Europe is significant. Historically, Britain's island destiny made it less subject to invasion and conquest than its continental counterparts, affording the country a sense of security. The geographic separation from mainland Europe has also created for many Britons a feeling that they are both apart from and a part of Europe, a factor that has complicated relations with Britain's EU partners to this day.

Critical Junctures

Our study begins with a look at the historic development of the modern British state. History shapes contemporary politics in very important ways. Once in place, institutions leave powerful legacies, and issues placed on the agenda in one period and left unresolved may present challenges for the future.

In many ways, Britain is the model of a united and stable country with an enviable record of continuity and resiliency. Nevertheless, the history of state formation reveals how complex and open-ended the process can be. Some issues that plague other countries, such as religious divisions, were settled long ago in Great Britain proper (although not in Northern Ireland). Yet others, such as multiple national identities, remain on the agenda.

British state formation involved the unification of kingdoms or crowns (hence the term United *Kingdom*). After Duke William of Normandy defeated the English in the Battle of Hastings in 1066, the Norman monarchy extended its authority throughout the British Isles. Although Welsh national sentiments remained strong, the prospects for unity with England were improved in 1485 by the accession to the English throne of Henry VII of the Welsh House of Tudor. With the Acts of Union of 1536 and 1542, England and Wales were legally, politically, and administratively united. The unification of the Scottish and English crowns occurred when James VI of Scotland ascended to the English throne as James I. Thereafter, England, Scotland, and Wales were known as Great Britain. Scotland and England remained divided politically, however, until the Act of Union of 1707. Henceforth, a common Parliament of Great Britain replaced the two separate parliaments of Scotland and of England and Wales.

Britain

0   100 Miles

0   100 Kilometers

Shetland Islands

Orkney Islands

Outer Hebrides

Inner Hebrides

SCOTLAND

North Sea

★Edinburgh

•Glasgow

NORTHERN IRELAND

★Belfast

Isle of Man

Irish Sea

REPUBLIC OF IRELAND

Dublin★

Isle of Anglesey

•Manchester

•Liverpool

ENGLAND

•Birmingham

WALES

Cardiff★

•Bristol

Thames

London✪

Chunnel

Southampton•

Isle of Wight

★•Plymouth

English Channel

ATLANTIC OCEAN

FRANCE

At the same time, the making of the British state included a historic expression of constraints on monarchical rule. At first, the period of Norman rule after 1066 strengthened royal control, but the conduct of King John (1199–1216) fueled opposition from feudal barons. In 1215, they forced the king to consent to a series of concessions that protected feudal landowners from abuses of royal power. These restrictions on royal prerogatives were embodied in the Magna Carta, a historic statement of the rights of a political community against the monarchical state. Soon after, in 1236, the term *Parliament* was first used officially to refer to the gathering of feudal barons summoned by the king whenever he required their consent to special taxes. By the fifteenth century, Parliament had gained the right to make laws.

The Seventeenth-Century Settlement

The making of the British state in the sixteenth and seventeenth centuries involved a complex interplay of religious conflicts, national rivalries, and struggles between rulers and the fledgling Parliament. These conflicts erupted in the Civil War of the 1640s and the forced abdication of James II in 1688. The bloodless political revolution of 1688, subsequently known as the Glorious Revolution, marked the "last successful political coup d'état or revolution in British history."[4] It also confirmed the power of Parliament over the monarchy. Parliament required the new monarchs, William and Mary, to meet with it annually and to agree to regular parliamentary elections. This contrasted dramatically with the arrangement enjoyed in France by Louis XIV (1643–1715), who gained power at the expense of the French nobility and operated without any constraint from commoners.

By the end of the seventeenth century, the framework of a constitutional (or limited) monarchy, which would still exercise flashes of power into the nineteenth century, was established in Britain. For more than 300 years, Britain's monarchs have been answerable to Parliament, which has held the sole authority for taxation and the maintenance of a standing army.

The Glorious Revolution also resolved long-standing religious conflict. The replacement of the Roman Catholic James II by the Protestant William and Mary ensured the dominance of the Church of England (or Anglican church). To this day, the Church of England remains the established (official) religion, and approximately two dozen of its bishops and archbishops sit as members of the House of Lords, the upper house of Parliament.

Thus, by the end of the seventeenth century, a basic form of parliamentary democracy had emerged, and the problem of religious divisions, which continue to plague many countries throughout the world, was settled. Equally important, these seventeenth-century developments became a defining moment for how the British perceive their history to this day. However divisive and disruptive the process of state building may have been originally, its telling and retelling have contributed significantly to a British political culture that celebrates democracy's continuity, gradualism, and tolerance.

As a result of settling its religious differences early, Britain has taken a more secular turn than most other countries in western Europe. The majority of Britons do not consider religion a significant source of identity, and active church membership in Britain, at 15 percent, is very low in comparison with other west European countries. In Britain, religious identification has less political significance in voting behavior or party loyalty than in many other countries. By contrast to France, where devout Catholics tend to vote right of center, there is relatively little association between religion and voting behavior in Britain (although Anglicans are a little more likely to vote Conservative). Unlike Iran or India, for example, politics in Britain is secular. No parties have religious affiliation, a factor that contributed to the success of the Conservative Party, one of the most successful right-of-center parties in Europe in the twentieth century.

As a consequence, except in Northern Ireland where religious divisions continue, the party system in the United Kingdom has traditionally reflected class distinctions and remains free of the pattern of multiple parties (particularly right-of-center parties) that occur in countries where party loyalties are divided by both class and religion.

The Industrial Revolution and the British Empire

Although the British state was consolidated by the seventeenth century, its form was radically shaped by the

---

Critical Junctures in Britain's Political Development

1688	Glorious Revolution establishes power of Parliament
c. 1750	Industrial Revolution begins in Britain
1832	Reform Act expands voting rights
1837–1901	Reign of Queen Victoria; height of British Empire
1914–1918	World War I
1929–1939	Great Depression
1939–1945	World War II
1945–1979	Establishment of British welfare state; dismantling of British Empire
1973	Britain joins the European Community
1979–1990	Prime Minister Margaret Thatcher promotes "enterprise culture"
1997	Tony Blair elected prime minister

timing of its industrial development and the way that process transformed Britain's role in the world. The Industrial Revolution in the mid-eighteenth century involved rapid expansion of manufacturing production and technological innovation. It also led to monumental social and economic transformations and resulted in pressures for democratization. Externally, Britain used its competitive edge to transform and dominate the international order. Internally, the Industrial Revolution helped shape the development of the British state and changed forever the British people's way of life.

The Industrial Revolution.   The consequences of the Industrial Revolution for the generations of people who experienced its upheavals can scarcely be exaggerated. The typical worker was turned "by degrees . . . from small peasant or craftsman into wage-labourer," as historian Eric Hobsbawm observes. Cash and market-based transactions replaced older traditions of barter and production for local need.[5]

Despite a gradual improvement in the standard of living in the English population at large, the effects of industrialization were often profound for agricultural laborers and particular types of artisans. With the commercialization of agriculture, many field laborers lost their security of employment, and cottagers (small landholders) were squeezed off the land in large numbers. The mechanization of manufacturing, which spread furthest in the cotton industry, upset the traditional status of the preindustrial skilled craft workers and permanently marginalized them.

The British Empire.   Britain had assumed a significant role as a world power during the seventeenth century, building an overseas empire and engaging actively in international commerce. But it was the Industrial Revolution of the eighteenth century that established global production and exchange on a new and expanded scale, with particular consequences for the making of the British state. Cotton manufacture, the driving force behind Britain's growing industrial dominance, not only pioneered the new techniques and changed labor organization of the Industrial Revolution but also represented the perfect imperial industry. It relied on imported raw materials and, by the turn of the nineteenth century, already depended on overseas markets for the vast majority of its sales of finished goods. Growth depended on foreign markets rather than domestic consumption. This export orientation fueled an expansion

far more rapid than an exclusively domestic orientation would have allowed.

With its leading industrial sector dependent on overseas trade, Britain's leaders worked aggressively to secure markets and expand the empire. Toward these ends, Britain defeated European rivals in a series of military engagements, culminating in the Napoleonic Wars (1803–1815), which confirmed Britain's commercial, military, and geopolitical preeminence. The Napoleonic Wars also secured a balance of power on the European continent favorable for largely unrestricted international commerce (**free trade**). Propelled by the formidable and active presence of the British navy, international trade helped England take full advantage of its position as the first industrial power. Many scholars suggest that in the middle of the nineteenth century, Britain had the highest per capita income in the world (it was certainly among the two or three highest), and in 1870, at the height of its glory, its trade represented nearly one-quarter of the world total, and its industrial mastery ensured highly competitive productivity in comparison to trading partners (see Table 1).

During the reign of Queen Victoria (1837–1901), the British Empire was immensely powerful and encompassed fully 25 percent of the world's population. Britain presided over a vast formal and informal empire, with extensive direct colonial rule over some four dozen countries, including India and Nigeria. At the same time, Britain enjoyed the advantages of an extensive informal empire—a worldwide network of independent states, including China, Iran, and Brazil—whose

Table 1

World Trade and Relative Labor Productivity

	Proportion of World Trade (%)	Relative Labour Productivity[a] (%)
1870	24.0	1.63
1890	18.5	1.45
1913	14.1	1.15
1938	14.0	0.92

[a]As compared with the average rate of productivity in other members of the world economy.

Source: Robert O. Keohane, After Hegemony: Cooperation and Discord in the World Economy, p. 36. Copyright © 1984 by Princeton University Press. Reprinted by permission of Princeton University Press.

economic fates were linked to it. Britain ruled as a **hegemonic power,** the state that could control the pattern of alliances and terms of the international economic order, and often could shape domestic political developments in countries throughout the world. Overall, the making of the British state observed a neat symmetry. Its global power helped underwrite industrial growth at home. At the same time, the reliance of domestic industry on world markets, beginning with cotton manufacture in the eighteenth century, prompted the government to project British interests overseas as forcefully as possible.

Industrial Change and the Struggle for Voting Rights. The Industrial Revolution shifted economic power from landowners to men of commerce and industry. As a result, the first critical juncture in the long process of democratization began in the late 1820s, when the "respectable opinion" of the propertied classes and increasing popular agitation pressed Parliament to expand the right to vote (**franchise**) beyond a thin band of men with substantial property, mainly landowners. With Parliament under considerable pressure, the Reform Act of 1832 extended the franchise to a section of the (male) middle class.

In a very limited way, the Reform Act confirmed the social and political transformations of the Industrial Revolution by granting new urban manufacturing centers, such as Manchester and Birmingham, more substantial representation. However, the massive urban working class created by the Industrial Revolution and populating the cities of Charles Dickens's England remained on the outside looking in. In fact, the reform was very narrow and defensive. Before 1832, less than 5 percent of the adult population was entitled to vote—and afterward, only about 7 percent.

In extending the franchise so narrowly, the reform underscored the strict property basis for political participation and inflamed class-based tensions in Britain. Following the Reform Act, a massive popular movement erupted in the late 1830s to secure the program of the People's Charter, which included demands for universal male suffrage and other radical reforms intended to make Britain a much more participatory democracy. The Chartist movement, as it was called, held huge and often tumultuous rallies, and organized a vast campaign to petition Parliament, but it failed to achieve any of its aims.

Expansion of the franchise proceeded very slowly. The Representation of the People Act of 1867 increased the electorate to just over 16 percent but left cities significantly underrepresented. The Franchise Act of 1884 nearly doubled the size of the electorate, but it was not until the Representation of the People Act of 1918 that suffrage included nearly all adult men and women over age thirty. How slow a process was it? The franchise for men with substantial incomes dated from the fifteenth century, but women between the ages of twenty-one and thirty were not enfranchised until 1928. The voting age for both women and men was lowered to eighteen in 1969. Except for some episodes during the days of the Chartist movement, the struggle for extension of the franchise took place without violence, but its time horizon must be measured in centuries. This is British gradualism—at its best and its worst (see Figure 1).

World Wars, Industrial Strife, and the Depression (1914–1945)

With the matter of the franchise finally resolved, in one sense the making of the British state as a democracy was settled. In another important sense, however, the development of the state was just beginning in the twentieth century with the expansion of the state's direct responsibility for management of the economy and the provision of social welfare for citizens. The making of what is sometimes called the *interventionist state* was spurred by the experiences of two world wars.

The state's involvement in the economy increased significantly during World War I (1914–1918). The state took control of a number of industries, including railways, mining, and shipping. It set prices and restricted the flow of capital abroad and channeled the country's resources into production geared to the war effort. After World War I, it remained active in the management of industry in a rather different way. Amid a set of tremendous industrial disputes, the state wielded its power to fragment the trade union movement and resist demands for workers' control over production and to promote more extensive state ownership of industries. This considerable government manipulation of the economy openly contradicted the policy of **laissez-faire** (minimal government interference in the operation of economic markets). The tensions between free-market principles and interventionist practices

Figure 1

Expansion of Voting Rights

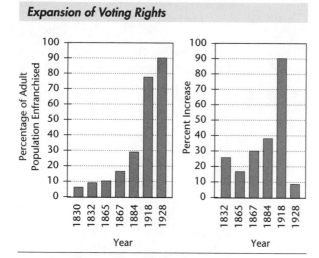

Expansion of the franchise in Britain was a gradual process. Despite reforms dating from the early nineteenth century, nearly universal adult suffrage was not achieved until 1928. *Source:* Jorgen S. Rasmussen. *The British Political Process,* p. 151. Copyright © 1993 Wadsworth Publishing Company. Reprinted with permission of the publisher.

deepened with the Great Depression beginning in 1929 and continuing through much of the 1930s and the experiences of World War II (1939–1945). The fear of depression and the burst of pent-up yearnings for a better life after the war helped transform the role of the state and ushered in a period of unusual political harmony.

Collectivist Consensus (1945–1979)

In the postwar context of shared victory and common misery (almost everyone suffered terrible hardships immediately after the war), reconstruction and dreams of new prosperity and security took priority over ideological conflict. In Britain today, a debate rages among political scientists over whether there was a postwar consensus. Critics of the concept contend that disagreements over specific policies concerning the economy, education, employment, and health, along with an electorate divided on partisan lines largely according to social class, indicated politics as usual.[6] It seems fair to say, however, that a broad culture of reconciliation and a determination to rebuild and improve the conditions of life for all Britons helped forge a postwar

settlement based broadly on a collectivist consensus that endured until the mid-1970s.

Collectivism is the term coined to describe the consensus that drove politics in the harmonious postwar period when a significant majority of Britons and all major political parties agreed that the state should take expanded responsibility for economic governance and provide for the social welfare in the broadest terms. They accepted as a matter of faith that governments should work to narrow the gap between rich and poor through public education, national health care, and other policies of the **welfare state,** and they accepted state responsibility for economic growth and full employment. Collectivism brought class-based actors (representatives of labor and management) inside politics and forged a broad consensus about the expanded role of government.

Throughout this period, there was a remarkable unity among electoral combatants, as the Labour and Conservative mainstream endorsed the principle of state responsibility for the collective good in both economic and social terms. Although modest in comparative European terms, the commitment to state management of the economy and provision of social services marked a new era in British politics. In time, however, economic downturn and political stagnation caused the consensus to unravel.

Margaret Thatcher and the Enterprise Culture (1979–1990)

In the 1970s, economic stagnation and the declining competitiveness of key British industries in international markets fueled industrial strife and kept class-based tensions near the surface of politics. No government appeared equal to the tasks of economic management. Each party failed in turn. The Conservative government of Edward Heath (1970–1974) could not resolve the economic problems or the political tensions that resulted from the previously unheard-of combination of increased inflation and reduced growth (stagflation). The Labour government of Harold Wilson and James Callaghan (1974–1979) fared no better. As unions became increasingly disgruntled, the country was beset by a rash of strikes throughout the winter of 1978–1979, the "winter of discontent." Labour's inability to discipline its trade union allies hurt the party in the election just a few months later in May 1979. The traditional centrist Conservative and Labour alternatives within the collectivist mold seemed exhausted, and many Britons were ready for a new policy agenda.

Margaret Thatcher more than met the challenge. Winning the leadership of the Conservative Party in 1975, she wasted little time in launching a set of bold policy initiatives, which, with characteristic forthrightness, she began to implement after the Conservatives were returned to power in 1979. Reelected in 1983 and 1987, Thatcher served longer without interruption than any other British prime minister in the twentieth century and never lost a general election.

Thatcher transformed British political life by advancing an alternative vision of politics. She was convinced that collectivism had contributed to Britain's decline by sapping British industry and permitting powerful and self-serving unions to hold the country for ransom. To reverse Britain's relative economic slide, Thatcher sought to jump-start the economy by cutting taxes, reducing social services where possible, and using government policy to stimulate competitiveness and efficiency in the private sector.

The term *Thatcherism* embraces her distinctive leadership style, her economic and political strategies, as well as her traditional cultural values: individual responsibility, commitment to family, frugality, and an affirmation of the entrepreneurial spirit. These values combined nostalgia for the past and a rejection of permissiveness and disorder. Taken together and referred to as the *enterprise culture,* they stood as a reproach and an alternative to collectivism.

In many ways, the period of Margaret Thatcher's leadership as prime minister (1979–1990) marks a critical dividing line in postwar British politics. She set the tone and redefined the goals of British politics like few others before her. In November 1990, a leadership challenge within Thatcher's own Conservative Party, largely over her anti-EU stance and high-handed leadership style, caused her sudden resignation and replacement by John Major. Major served as prime minister from 1990 to 1997, leading the Conservative Party to a victory in the 1992 general election before succumbing to Tony Blair's New Labour in 1997.

New Labour's Third Way

Some twenty electoral records were toppled, as New Labour under the leadership of Tony Blair (see "Lead-

With characteristic aplomb, Prime Minister Margaret Thatcher greeted the annual Conservative Party Conference at the seaside resort Bournemouth in October 1986. *Source:* Stuart Franklin/Magnum Photos, Inc.

ers: Tony Blair") won 419 of the 659 seats in Parliament, the largest majority it has ever held. Blair was propelled into office as prime minister with a 10 percent swing from Conservative to Labour, a postwar record. More women (120) and members of ethnic minorities (9) were elected than ever before. In addition, the political undertow of this electoral tsunami was fierce. The Conservative Party, which had been in power since Margaret Thatcher's 1979 victory and was one of Europe's most successful parties in the twentieth century, was decimated. More cabinet ministers lost their seats than ever before. The Conservatives were nearly wiped off the map in London and other major cities and were shut out altogether in Scotland and Wales.

Blair's Agenda for Britain.   After Tony Blair's election in 1997, there was an unmistakable sense in Britain that something extremely interesting and potentially significant was happening. New Labour aspired to recast British politics, offering what it referred to as a "third-way" alternative to the collectivism of traditional Labour and Thatcherism. Everything was at issue, from the way politics is organized to the country's underlying values, institutions, and policies. In electoral terms, New Labour rejected the notion of interest-based politics, in which unions and working people naturally look to Labour and businesspeople and the more prosperous look to the Conservatives. Labour

won in 1997 by drawing support from across the socio-economic spectrum. It rejected the historic ties between Labour governments and the trade union movement, choosing instead to emphasize the virtues of a partnership with business.

In institutional and policy terms, New Labour's innovations were intended to reverse the tendency of previous Labour governments in Britain to provide centralized statist solutions to all economic and social problems. Blair promised new approaches to economic, welfare, and social policy; British leadership in Europe; and far-reaching constitutional changes to revitalize democratic participation and devolve (transfer) specified powers from the central government to Scotland, Wales, and Northern Ireland.

In the early months of his premiership, Blair

Leaders: *Tony Blair*

Born in 1953 to a mother from Donegal, Ireland (who moved to Glasgow after her father's death), and a father from the Clyde-side shipyards, Tony Blair lacks the typical pedigree of Labour Party leaders. It is very common in the highest ranks of the Labour Party to find someone whose father or grandfather was a union official or a Labour MP. The politics in the Blair family, by contrast, were closely linked to Conservatism (as chairman of his local Conservative party club, his father Leo had a good chance to become a Conservative MP). Often, like Tony Blair's two predecessors—Neil Kinnock from Wales and John Smith from the West of Scotland—leaders of the Labour Party also have distinctive regional ties. In contrast, Blair moved to Durham in the north of England when he was five, but spent much of his youth in boarding schools, moved south when he was old enough to set out on his own, studied law at Oxford, and specialized in employment and industrial law in London—and returned to the north only to enter the House of Commons from Sedgefield in 1983. Thus, Blair has neither the traditional political or regional ties of a Labour Party leader.*

Coming of political age in opposition, Blair joined the Shadow Cabinet in 1988, serving in

turn as shadow minister of energy, then employment, and finally as shadow home secretary. An MP with no government experience, he easily won the contest for party leadership after his close friend and fellow modernizer, John Smith, died of a sudden heart attack in the summer of 1994. From the start, he boosted Labour Party morale and raised expectations that the party would soon regain power. As one observer put it, "The new Leader rapidly made a favorable impression upon the electorate: his looks and affability of manner appealed to voters whilst his self-confidence, lucidity and clarity of mind rendered him a highly effective communicator and lent him an air of authority."† Blair has gone from strength to strength, combining winning style with firm leadership, eclectic beliefs, and bold political initiatives. A figure to reckon with—some have predicted he will become the dominant figure in British politics for the next quarter-century—his lack of familiar roots and ideological convictions make Blair, for many, an enigmatic figure.

---

*See Andy McSmith, *Faces of Labour: The Inside Story* (London: Verso, 1997), 7–96.

†Eric Shaw, *The Labour Party Since 1945* (Oxford: Blackwell, 1996), 195.

displayed effective leadership in his stewardship of the nation during the period after Lady Diana's death and his aggressive efforts to achieve a potentially historic peace agreement for Northern Ireland, with far-reaching constitutional implications. By the summer of 2000, however, a rash of embarrassing leaks from Blair's inner sanctum, including a document written by the prime minister that revealed him stewing over "a sense that the government—and this even applies to me—are somehow out of touch with gut British instincts," contributed to a growing sense that New Labour was spinning its wheels. Many observers, Labour supporters among them, suggested that Blair and his team were better at coming up with innovative-sounding ideas than at delivering the goods. Factionalism in the party and among the leadership was reemerging and skepticism growing that key promises, for example, in health care and education (respectively, to reduce waiting lists for hospital services and class sizes) might not be met. In addition, a set of crises—from a set of fatal train crashes since 1997 to protests over the cost of petrol (gasoline) in September 2000 to an outbreak of mad cow disease in spring 2001—have made Blair more politically vulnerable and his grand promises seem a little shopworn. Nevertheless, Blair remained a formidable leader, and New Labour won what it most sought: an electoral mandate in June 2001 for a second successive term.

After September 11. In the aftermath of the September 11, 2001, attacks on the World Trade Center and the Pentagon in the United States, Blair showed decisive leadership in assuming the role of a key ally to the United States in the war on terrorism. With Britain willing and able to lend moral, diplomatic, and military support, September 11 lent new credence to the "special relationship"—a bond of language and culture that creates an unusually close alliance—that has governed U.S.-U.K. relations and catapulted Blair to high visibility in world affairs. For a time, the war on terrorism seemed to bridge the gap between American and European foreign policy objectives. Before long, however, parliamentary opponents and editorial writers were mocking Blair's high-profile visits to trouble spots around the world (dubbed "designer diplomacy" by the Conservatives) and accusing him of neglecting pressing problems at home, from transportation to education and health care. From the British perspective,

it was clear that Blair's willingness to run interference with allies and add intellectual ballast and nuance to President George W. Bush's post-9/11 plans was a big help to the United States, but what was in it for Britain? Would the partnership yield results measured in changes in American policy or just pull Britain into deeper waters? We will return to the implications of the Blair-Bush special relationship in Section 5.

Themes and Implications

The processes that came together in these historical junctures continue to influence developments today in powerful and complex ways. Our four core themes in this book, introduced in Part I, highlight some of the most important features of British politics.

Historical Junctures and Political Themes

The first theme suggests that a country's relative position in the world of states influences its ability to manage domestic and international challenges. A weaker international standing makes it difficult for a country to control international events, shape the policy of powerful international organizations, or insulate itself from external pressures. Britain's ability to control the terms of trade and master political alliances during the height of its imperial power in the nineteenth century confirms this maxim. In a quite different way, the theme of the world of states is also confirmed by Britain's reduced standing and influence today.

As the gradual process of decolonization defined Britain's changing relationship to the world of states, Britain fell to a second-tier status during the twentieth century. Its formal empire began to shrink in the interwar period (1919–1939) as the "white dominions" of Canada, Australia, and New Zealand gained independence. In Britain's Asian, Middle Eastern, and African colonies, the pressure for political reforms leading to independence deepened during World War II and in the immediate postwar period. Beginning with the formal independence of India and Pakistan in 1947, an enormous empire of dependent colonies more or less dissolved in less than twenty years (although the problem of white-dominated Rhodesia lingered until it achieved independence as Zimbabwe in 1980). Finally, in 1997, Britain returned the commercially vibrant

Playing Robin to President Bush's Batman may have turned Tony Blair into a foreign policy superhero in the aftermath of September 11, but within a few months many Britons were wondering where future adventures might lead him. *Source:* © Dave Simonds.

crown colony of Hong Kong to China. The process of decolonization ended any realistic claim Britain could make to be a dominant player in world politics.

Is Britain a world power or just a middle-of-the-pack country in western Europe? It appears to be both. On the one hand, as a legacy of its role in World War II, Britain sits as a permanent member of the United Nations Security Council, a position denied more powerful and populous countries such as Germany and Japan. On the other hand, Britain has remained an outsider in the EU, more often than not playing second fiddle in its special relationship to the United States and declining in influence in the Commonwealth (an association of some fifty states that were once part of the British empire). In particular, British governments face persistent challenges in their dealings with the EU. As Margaret Thatcher learned too late to save her premiership, Europe is a highly divisive issue. Can Britain afford to remain aloof from the fast-paced changes of economic integration symbolized by the headlong rush toward a common currency, the euro, already embraced, despite growing qualms, by every leading member state except the United Kingdom? It is clear that Britain does not have the power to control EU policy outcomes. Can it offset the weakness expressed by its status outside the euro zone by emphasizing its role as an honest broker between the United States and Europe on a host of important issues, from European defense to global warming protocols to the

Bush administration's commitment to regime change in Iraq? Will British governments, beginning with Tony Blair's, find the right formula for limiting the political fallout of EU politics and at the same time find the best approach to economic competitiveness?

A second theme examines the strategies employed in governing the economy and the political implications of economic performance and the choices government makes in the distribution of economic goods and public services. Since the dawn of Britain's Industrial Revolution, prosperity at home relied on superior competitiveness abroad, and this is even truer in today's environment of intensified international competition and global production.

When Tony Blair took office in 1997, he inherited a streak of prosperity in Britain dating from 1992—an enviable circumstance. The Blair government could thus work to modernize the economy and determine its budgetary priorities from economic strength. Will Britain's "less-is-more" laissez-faire approach to economic governance, invigorated by New Labour's business partnership, continue to compete effectively in a global context? Can Britain achieve a durable economic model with—or without—fuller integration into Europe? How can we assess the spending priorities and distributive implications of the third-way politics of the Blair government? Britain will never again assume the privileged position of hegemonic power, so a lot depends on how well it plays the cards it does have.

A third theme is the potent political influence of the democratic idea, the universal appeal of core values associated with parliamentary democracy as practiced first in the United Kingdom. Even in Britain, issues about democratic governance, citizen participation, and constitutional reform have been renewed with considerable force.

As the traditionally sacrosanct royal family has been rocked by scandal and improprieties, questions about the undemocratic underpinning of the British state are asked with greater urgency. Few reject the monarchy outright, but, especially after the perceived insensitivity of the royal family in the aftermath of Diana's death, the pressure to modernize the monarchy, scale it down, and reduce its drain on the budget ($50 million a year) gained new intensity. Nevertheless, the outpouring of affection during a four-day national holiday in June 2002 celebrating fifty years on the throne for Queen Elizabeth II could leave no doubt about the emotional and patriotic hold of the queen on the nation. Perhaps most significant, questions about the role of the monarchy helped place on the agenda broader issues about citizen control over government and constitutional reform. As a result, in November 1999, a bill was enacted to remove hereditary peers from Britain's upper unelected chamber of Parliament, the House of Lords, although to facilitate passage, the government agreed to keep ninety-two hereditary peers as an interim measure in the modified second chamber.

Long-settled issues about the constitutional form and unity of the state have also reemerged with unexpected force. How can the interests of England, Wales, Scotland, and Northern Ireland be balanced within a single nation-state? Can the perpetual crisis in Northern Ireland be finally resolved? Tony Blair has placed squarely on the agenda a set of policies designed to reshape the institutions of government and reconfigure fundamental constitutional principles to address the "troubles" in Northern Ireland and modernize the architecture of the United Kingdom to recognize the realities of a multi-nation-state. Key policy initiatives include the formation of a Scottish Parliament and a Welsh Senedd (or Assembly), and the negotiation of a peace agreement for Northern Ireland that contains a comprehensive set of new political institutions and power-sharing arrangements—some involving the Republic of Ireland—with far-reaching constitutional ramifications. Clearly, democracy is not a fixed result even

in the United Kingdom, but a highly politicized and potentially disruptive process, as constitutional reform has taken a place front and center as perhaps the boldest item on Tony Blair's agenda.

Finally, we come to the fourth theme, collective identities, which considers how individuals define who they are politically in terms of group attachments, come together to pursue political goals, and face their status as political insiders or outsiders by virtue of these group attachments. In Britain, an important aspect of the politics of collective identities is connected to Britain's legacy of empire and its aftermath. Through the immigration of its former colonial subjects to the United Kingdom, decolonization helped create a multiracial society, to which Britain has adjusted poorly. As we shall see, issues of race, ethnicity, and cultural identity have challenged the long-standing British values of tolerance and consensus and now present important challenges for policy and the prospects of cohesion in Britain today. Indeed, the concept of "Britishness"— what the country stands for and who comprises the political community—has come under intense scrutiny. For many, the controversial asylum policy is as much a statement about immigrants and a backlash against multi-ethnic Britain as it is a practical policy for policing borders and controlling the flow of refugees. At the same time, **gender** politics remains a significant theme, from voting patterns (where in recent years a **gender gap** first favored the Conservatives, then Labour, and now has dissolved) to questions of equality in the workplace and positions of political leadership. Moreover, the specific needs of women for equal employment opportunities and to balance the demands of work and family have assumed an important place in debates about social and employment policies.

Implications for Comparative Politics

Britain's privileged position in comparative politics textbooks (it almost always comes first among country studies in these books) seems to follow naturally from the important historical firsts it has enjoyed. Britain was the first nation to industrialize, and for much of the nineteenth century, the British Empire was the world's dominant economic, political, and military power, with a vast network of colonies throughout the world. Britain was also the first nation to develop an effective parliamentary democracy (a form of representative government in which the executive is drawn from and answerable to an elected national legislature). As a result of its vast empire, Britain had tremendous influence on the form of government introduced in countries around the globe, including India and Nigeria in this book. For these reasons, British politics is often studied as a model of representative government. Named after the building that houses the British legislature in London, the **Westminster model** emphasizes that democracy rests on the supreme authority of a legislature—in Britain's case, the Parliament. Finally, Britain has served as a model of gradual and peaceful evolution of democratic government in a world where transitions to democracy are often turbulent, interrupted, and uncertain.

Today, more than a century after the height of its international power, Britain's significance in comparative terms must be measured in somewhat different ways. *Modernization* is the watchword of the Blair government, and the level of public support given Blair ever since his 1997 victory, the advantages bestowed on prime ministers by the formidable levers of power they control, and the relative strength of the British economy provide a platform for success. Particularly in the aftermath of September 11, with signs of intolerance rampant, all economies facing new challenges, and European center-left politics in disarray, the stakes are high. Blair's ability to succeed (or not) in sustaining economic competitiveness, resolving the euro dilemma, and revitalizing the center-left will send important signals to governments throughout the world. Is significant innovation possible in established democracies? Can a politics beyond left and right develop coherent policies and sustain public support? Can constitutional reforms help bind together a multiethnic, multinational state? In fact, contemporary Britain may help define an innovative new model for middle-rank established democracies in a global age.

Section ❷ Political Economy and Development

The timing of industrialization and of a country's insertion into the world economy are important variables in explaining both how and how successfully the state intervenes in economic governance. Both the specific policies chosen and the relative success of the economic strategy have significant political repercussions. Economic developments often determine political winners and losers, influence broad changes in the distribution of resources and opportunities among groups in society, and affect a country's international standing.

In analyzing our *governing the economy* theme, some scholars have suggested that states that have institutionalized effective relationships with organized economic interests (such as France and Germany in Europe and also Japan) have enjoyed more consistent growth and stronger economic competitiveness. It is true that Britain's annual growth rates were lower than those of Japan, Germany, and France from the end of World War II through the 1970s. Rather than institutionalizing a dense network of relationships among government agencies, business, and labor, Britain preserves arm's-length state relationships with key economic actors. With British political culture trumpeting the benefits of free-market individualism and with New Labour reinforcing Thatcherism's appeal to entrepreneurship, competition, and industriousness in the private sector, the British experience becomes a critical test case for analyzing the relative merits of alternative strategies for governing the economy.

In the early years of the new century, it appears that the trend toward greater government management of the economy has reversed, breathing new life into the old economic doctrine of laissez-faire. In large part because of the relative success of the British and U.S. economies, laissez-faire economics—or **neoliberalism,** as it is called today—seems to have the upper hand. Neoliberalism is a touchstone premise of Tony Blair's New Labour. Government policies aim to promote free competition among firms, interfere with the prerogatives of entrepreneurs and managers as little as possible, and create a business-friendly environment to help attract foreign investment and spur innovation. At the same time, Britain's Labour government insists that its third way, as distinct from conventional center-left projects, can blend the dynamism of market forces with the traditional center-left concern for social justice and commitment to the reduction of inequalities. How "new" is New Labour's approach to economic management? Are Britons across the spectrum enjoying the fruits of relative prosperity? How has the growing importance of the EU and the economic processes of globalization changed the political equation? In this section, we analyze the politics of economic management in Britain and consider the implications of Britain's less-is-more, laissez-faire approach.

State and Economy

Whereas late industrializers, like Germany and Japan, relied on powerful government support during their industrial take-off period, England's Industrial Revolution was based more on laissez-faire, or free-market, principles. When the state intervened in powerful ways, it did so primarily to secure free markets at home and open markets for British goods (free trade) in the international sphere.

With control of crucial industries during World War I and the active management of industry by the state in the interwar years, the state assumed a more interventionist role. After World War II, the sense of unity inspired by the shared suffering of war and the need to rebuild a war-ravaged country helped crystallize the collectivist consensus. In common with other western European states, the British state both broadened and deepened its responsibilities for the overall performance of the economy and the well-being of its citizens. The leading political parties and policy-making elites agreed that the state should take an active role in governing the economy.

The state nationalized some key industries, assuming direct ownership of them. It also accepted the responsibility to secure low levels of unemployment (referred to as a policy of full employment), expand social services, maintain a steady rate of growth (increase the output or gross domestic product, GDP), keep prices stable, and achieve desirable balance-of-payments and exchange rates. The approach is called *Keynesian demand management,* or **Keynesianism** (after the British economist John Maynard Keynes, 1883–1946). State budget deficits were used to expand demand in an effort to boost both consumption and investment when the economy was slowing. Cuts in government spending and a tightening of credit and finance were used to cool demand when high rates of growth brought fears of inflation or a deficit in balance

of payments. Taken together, this new agenda of expanded economic management and welfare provision, sometimes referred to as the Keynesian welfare state, directed government policy throughout the era of the collectivist consensus.

Two central dimensions, economic management and welfare policy, capture the new role of the state. Analysis of these policy areas also reveals how limited this new state role was in comparative terms.

Economic Management

Like all other states, whatever their commitment to free markets, the British state intervenes in economic life, sometimes with considerable force. However, the British have not developed the institutions for state-sponsored economic planning or industrial policy that have been created by some countries with which they compete for global market share in key economic sectors. Instead, apart from its management of nationalized industries, the British state has limited its role mainly to broad policy instruments designed to influence the economy generally (**macroeconomic policy**) by adjusting state revenues and expenditures. The Treasury and the Bank of England dominate economic policy, which has often seemed reactive and sometimes skittish. As senior officials in these key finance institutions respond to fluctuations in the business cycle, the government reacts with short-term political calculations that abruptly shift policy agendas. As a result, state involvement in economic management has traditionally been relatively ineffectual.

Despite other differences, this generally reactive and minimalist orientation of economic management strategies in Britain bridges the first two eras of postwar politics in Britain: the consensus era (1945–1979) and the period of Thatcherite policy orientation (1979–1997). How has the orientation of economic policy developed and changed during the postwar period? How new is New Labour when it comes to economic policy?

The Consensus Era. Before Thatcher became leader of the Conservative Party in 1975, Conservative leaders in Britain generally accepted the terms of the collectivist consensus. These Conservatives were also modernizers, prepared to manage the economy in a way consistent with the Keynesian approach and to maintain the welfare state and guarantee full employment.

Declining economic competitiveness made the situation for mainstream Conservatives and, indeed, for any other government, more complex and difficult. By the 1970s, public officials no longer saw the world as one they understood and could master; it had become a world without economic growth and with growing political discontent. Edward Heath, the Conservative centrist who governed from 1970 to 1974, was the first prime minister to suffer the full burden of recession and the force of political opposition from both traditional business allies and resurgent trade union adversaries. Operating in an era marked by increased inflation and reduced growth (stagflation), Heath could never break out of the political constraints imposed on him by economic decline.

From 1974 to 1979, the Labour government of Harold Wilson and James Callaghan reinforced the impression that governments could no longer control the swirl of events. The beginning of the end came when trade unions became increasingly restive under the pinch of voluntary wage restraints pressed on them by the Labour government. Frustrated by wage increases well below inflation rates, the unions broke with the government in 1978. The number of unofficial work stoppages increased and official strikes followed, all fueled by a seemingly endless series of leapfrogging pay demands that erupted throughout the winter of 1978–1979 (the "winter of discontent"). There is little doubt that the industrial unrest that dramatized Labour's inability to manage its own allies, the trade unions, contributed mightily to Thatcher's election just a few months later in May 1979. If a Labour government could not manage its trade union allies, whom could it govern? More significant, the winter of discontent helped write the conclusion to Britain's collectivist consensus and discredit the Keynesian welfare state.

Thatcherite Policy Orientation. In policy terms, the economic orientations that Thatcher pioneered and that Major substantially maintained reflected a growing disillusionment with Keynesianism. In its place, **monetarism** emerged as the new economic doctrine. Keynesian demand management assumed that the level of unemployment could be set and the economy stabilized through decisions of government (monetary and fiscal or budgetary policy). By contrast, monetarism assumed that there is a "natural rate of unemployment" determined by the labor market itself. Monetary and fiscal policy should be passive and intervention limited (so far as this was possible) to a few steps that would help foster appropriate rates of growth in the money supply and keep inflation low.

By implication, the government ruled out spending to run up budgetary deficits as a useful instrument for stimulating the economy. On the contrary, governments could contribute to overall economic efficiency and growth by reducing social expenditure and downsizing the public sector, by reducing its work force or privatizing nationalized industries. Monetarism reflected a radical change from the postwar consensus regarding economic management. Not only was active government intervention considered unnecessary; it was seen as undesirable and destabilizing.

New Labour's Economic Policy Approach. Can New Labour thinking on macroeconomic policy end the "short-termism" of economic policy and provide the cohesion previously lacking? In British commentaries on New Labour, much has been made of the influence of revitalized Keynesian ideas and reform proposals.[7] In some ways, government policy seems to pursue conventional market-reinforcing and pro-business policies (neoliberalism). In other ways, the New Labour program stands as an alternative to Thatcherite monetarism and traditional Keynesianism. Whether New Labour's approach to economic management constitutes a distinctive third way or a less coherent blend of disparate elements is a matter of political debate.

The first shot fired in the Blair revolution was the announcement within a week of the 1997 election by the chancellor of the exchequer (finance minister), Gordon Brown, that the Bank of England would be given "operational independence" in the setting of monetary policy. The decision transferred from the cabinet a critical, and highly political, prerogative of government. With Brown attuned to the pressures of international financial markets, and the control of inflation and stability the key goals of macroeconomic policy, the transfer of authority over monetary policy confirmed the neoliberal market orientation of economic policy.

In other ways, however, New Labour's approach may signal a third way. Above all, it emphasizes pragmatism in the face of global economic competition. Since capital is international, mobile, and not subject to control, industrial policy and planning that focus on the domestic economy alone are futile. Rather, government can improve the quality of labor through education and training, maintain the labor market flexibility inherited from the Thatcher regime, and help attract investment to Britain. Strict control of inflation, low taxes, and tough limits on public expenditure help promote both employment and investment opportunities. At the same time, economic policy is directed at enhancing the competitive strength of key sectors and developing a partnership with business through research and development, training, technology, and modernization policies. New Labour is very focused on designing and implementing policies to create new jobs and get people, particularly young people, into the work force; amid skepticism, there are some indications of success. Blair, his economic policy team, and his supporters hope that this approach will help build a stable and competitive economy, one in which all Britons have a stake (New Labour refers to its vision as "the stakeholder economy").[8]

Political Implications of Economic Policy. Differences in economic doctrine are not what matter most in policy terms. In fact, British governments in the past have never consistently followed any economic theory, whether Keynesianism or monetarism. Today, the economic policy of New Labour is pragmatic and eclectic. The political consequences of economic orientations are more significant: each economic doctrine helps to justify a broad moral and cultural vision of society, provide motives for state policy, and advance alternative sets of values. Should the government intervene, work to reduce inequalities through the mildly redistributive provisions of the welfare state, and sustain the ethos of a caring society (collectivism)? Should it back off and allow the market to function competitively and thereby promote entrepreneurship, competitiveness, and individual autonomy (Thatcherism)? Or should it help secure an inclusive stakeholder economy in which business has the flexibility, security, and mobility to compete and workers have the skills and training to participate effectively in the global labor market (New Labour)? As these questions make clear, economic management strategies are closely linked to social or welfare policy.

Social Policy

Observers have noted that the social and political role of the welfare state depends as much on policy goals and instruments as on spending levels. Does the state provide services itself or offer cash benefits that can be used to purchase services from private providers? Are benefits limited to those who fall below an income threshold (means-tested) or universal? Are they designed to meet the temporary needs of individuals or to help reduce the gap between rich and poor?

The expanded role of government during World War II and the increased role of the Labour Party during the wartime coalition government led by Winston Churchill prepared the way for the development of the welfare state in Britain. The 1943 Beveridge Report provided a blueprint for an extensive but, in comparative European terms, fairly shallow set of provisions. The principal means-tested program is **social security,** a system of contributory and noncontributory benefits to provide financial assistance (not services directly) for the elderly, sick, disabled, unemployed, and others similarly in need of assistance.

In general, welfare state provisions interfere relatively little in the workings of the market, and policymakers do not see the reduction of group inequalities as the proper goal of the welfare state. The National Health Service (NHS) provides comprehensive and universal medical care and has long been championed as the jewel in the crown of the welfare state in Britain, but it remains an exception to the rule. Compared to other western European countries, the welfare state in Britain offers relatively few comprehensive services, and the policies are not very generous. For the most part, Britons must rely on means-tested safety net programs that leave few of the recipients satisfied.

The Welfare State Under Thatcher and Major. The record on social expenditure by Conservative governments from 1979 to 1997 was mixed. Given Britons' strong support for public education, pensions, and health care, Conservative governments attempted more limited reform than many at first anticipated. The

Thatcher and Major governments encouraged private alongside public provision in education, health care (insurance), and pensions. They worked to increase efficiency in social services, reduced the value of some benefits by changing the formulas or reducing cost-of-living adjustments, and contracted out some services (purchased them from private contractors rather than providing them directly). In addition, in policy reforms reminiscent of U.S. "workfare" requirements, they tried to reduce dependency by denying benefits to youths who refused to participate in training programs. Despite these efforts, the commitment to reduced spending could not be sustained, partly because a recession triggered rises in income support and unemployment benefits.

To a degree, however, this general pattern masks specific and, in some cases, highly charged policy changes in both expenditures and the institutionalized pattern of provision. In housing, the changes in state policy and provision were the most extensive, with repercussions in electoral terms and in changing the way Britons think about the welfare state. By 1990, more than 1.25 million council houses (public housing maintained by local government) were sold, particularly the attractive single-family homes with gardens (quite unlike public housing in the United States). Two-thirds of the sales were to rental tenants. Thatcher's housing policy was extremely popular. By one calculation, between 1979 and 1983 there was a swing (change in the percentage of vote received by the two major parties) to the Conservative Party of 17 percent among those who had bought their council houses.[9]

Despite great Conservative success in the campaign to privatize housing, a strong majority of Britons remain stalwart supporters of the principle of collective provision for their basic needs. Thus, there were limits on the government's ability to reduce social spending or change institutional behavior. For example, in 1989, the Conservative government tried to introduce market practices into the NHS, with general practitioners managing funds and purchasing hospital care for their patients. Many voiced fears that the reforms would create a two-tier system of medical care for rich and poor.

More generally, a lack of confidence in the Conservatives on social protection hurt Major substantially in 1992, and it has continued to plague the party.

Nothing propelled the Labour landslide in 1997 more than the concern for the "caring" issues. The traditional advantage Labour enjoys on these issues also helped secure victory for Blair in June 2001.

New Labour Social Policy. As with economic policy, social policy for New Labour presents an opportunity for government to balance pragmatism and innovation, while borrowing from traditional Labour as well as from Thatcherite options. Thus, the Blair government rejects both the attempted retrenchment of Conservative governments that seemed mean-spirited as well as the egalitarian traditions of Britain's collectivist era that emphasized entitlements. Instead, New Labour focuses its policy on training and broader social investment as a more positive third-way alternative. At the same time, New Labour draws political strength from the "Old Labour" legacy of commitment on the "caring" social policy issues.

For example, following Bill Clinton, his New Democratic counterpart in the United States, the prime minister promised a modernized, leaner welfare state, in which people are actively encouraged to seek work. The reform of the welfare state emphasizes efficiencies and attempts to break welfare dependency. Efforts to spur entry into the labor market combine carrots and sticks. Positive inducements include training programs, especially targeted at youth, combined with incentives to private industry to hire new entrants to the labor market. The threats include eligibility restrictions and reductions in coverage. Referred to as the "New Deal" for the young unemployed, welfare reform in the United Kingdom has emphasized concerted efforts to create viable pathways out of dependence. Although beginning with a focus on moving youth from welfare to work, New Deal reform efforts expanded in several directions. The New Deal was quickly extended to single parents and the long-term unemployed. In 1999, the government launched a "Bridging the Gap" initiative to provide a more comprehensive approach for assisting sixteen- to eighteen-year-olds not in education, employment, or training to achieve clear goals by age nineteen through a variety of "pathways" (academic, vocational, or occupational). "Better Government for Older People" was launched in 1998 and followed quickly by *All Our Futures,* a government report issued in the summer of 2000 with twenty-eight recommendations to improve the quality of life and the delivery of public services for senior citizens. A new initiative, "The IT New Deal," was launched in 2001 as a government-business partnership to address skill shortages in information technologies.

Although the jury is still out on the follow-through and effectiveness of New Labour social and welfare policy initiatives, the intent to create innovative policies and approach social policy in new and more comprehensive ways is clearly there. Late in 1997, the government inaugurated the Social Exclusion Unit, staffed by civil servants and external policy specialists, located within the cabinet office, and reporting directly to the prime minister. It was charged broadly with addressing "what can happen when people or areas suffer from such problems as unemployment, poor skills, low incomes, poor housing, high crime environments, bad health, and family breakdown." The Social Exclusion Unit has been actively involved in developing the New Deal initiative as well as in writing reports and recommending policies to take on problems such as truancy and school exclusion, homelessness, neighborhood renewal, and teenage pregnancy. This effort to identify comprehensive solutions to society's ills and reduce the tendency for government to let marginalized individuals fall by the wayside captures the third-way orientation of the Blair project.

Nevertheless, New Labour, like all other governments in Britain and many other countries, will be accountable above all for the failure or success of more traditional social policies, especially health care and education. The Department of Health acknowledged in a report issued in 2000 that the NHS suffered from chronic underfunding, overcentralization, and insufficient incentives to improve performance. In its annual *Survey* of the U.K. in the same year, the Organization for Economic Cooperation and Development (OECD) gave the Blair government low marks on health care, noting that the ratio of doctors to population and level of spending are low for a developed country. It cautioned that health care results in the United Kingdom are in some ways mediocre, with cancer survival rates, for example, more typical of eastern than western European norms, and raised doubts about the effectiveness of NHS reforms. The 2001–2002 OECD *Survey* noted that some of the endemic problems in the NHS were being addressed with new budgetary allocations

to add hospital beds, equip hospitals and doctors' offices with up-to-date information technology, and hire significant numbers of doctors and nurses, as well as specific targets to guarantee quicker appointments with primary care doctors and specialists. Until class sizes and waiting lists for treatment are reduced, the electorate will not let New Labour off the hook on education and health care. For a great many Britons, these core policies, much more than the battle against social exclusion, will determine the measure of success of New Labour's social policy.

Society and Economy

What were the *distributional effects*—the consequences for group patterns of wealth and poverty—of the economic and social policies of Thatcher and Major? To what extent are the policies of Tony Blair's Labour government designed to continue, or to reverse, these trends? How has government policy influenced the condition of minorities and women? It is impossible to ascertain when government policy creates a given distribution of resources and when poverty increases or decreases because of a general downturn or upswing in the economy. The evidence is clear, however, that economic inequality grew in Britain during the 1980s before it stabilized or narrowed slightly in the mid-1990s, and that ethnic minorities and women continue to experience significant disadvantages.

In general, policy initiated by the Conservative Party particularly during the Thatcher years tended to deepen inequalities. The economic upturn that began in 1992, combined with Major's moderating effects on the Thatcherite social policy agenda, served to narrow inequality by the mid-1990s. Since 1997, as one observer noted, Labour has "pursued redistribution by stealth, raising various indirect levies on the better-off to finance tax breaks for poorer workers."[10] As a result, Britain has witnessed a modest downward redistribution of income since 1997. Attention to social exclusion in its many forms, a 1999 pledge by the prime minister to eradicate child poverty, and projected growth for 2003 above all the G7 economies but the U.S.'s and Canada's (the G7 is a group of seven high-level advanced economies including the United States, Japan, Germany, Britain, France, Italy, and Canada), augur well for a further modest narrowing of the gap between rich and poor in Britain. But, as a 2000 report, *Poverty and Social Exclusion in Britain,* indicates, there is much more work to be done to improve the standards of living of many Britons. The report found almost a quarter of households in Britain living in poverty in 1999, compared to 14 percent in 1983. Comparative analysis of poverty rates indicates that the U.K. has greater problems regarding income inequality than do most of its EU counterparts (see Figure 2).

Inequality and Ethnic Minorities

Poverty and diminished opportunity disproportionately characterize the situation of ethnic minorities (a term applied to peoples of non-European origin from the former British colonies in the Indian subcontinent, the Caribbean, and Africa). Official estimates place the ethnic minority population in Britain at 4.5 million in 2001/2002, or 7.6 percent of the total population of the U.K. Indians comprise the largest ethnic minority, at 21.7 percent; Pakistanis represent 16.7

percent; Bangladeshis represent 6.1 percent; and Afro-Caribbeans and other blacks, 27.1 percent.[11] Due to past immigration and fertility patterns, the ethnic minority population in the United Kingdom is considerably younger than the white population. More than one-third of the ethnic minority population is younger than age sixteen, nearly half is under age twenty-five, and more than four-fifths is under age forty-five. Thus, despite the often disparaging reference to ethnic minority individuals as "immigrants," the experience of members of ethnic minority groups is increasingly that of a native-born population.[12]

Britain has adjusted slowly to the realities of a multicultural society. The postwar period has witnessed the gradual erosion of racial, religious, and ethnic tolerance in Britain and a chipping away at the right of settlement of postcolonial subjects in the United Kingdom. During the Thatcher era, discussion of immigration and citizenship rights was used for partisan political purposes and assumed a distinctly racial tone. Ethnic minority individuals, particularly young men, are subject to unequal treatment by the police

Figure 2

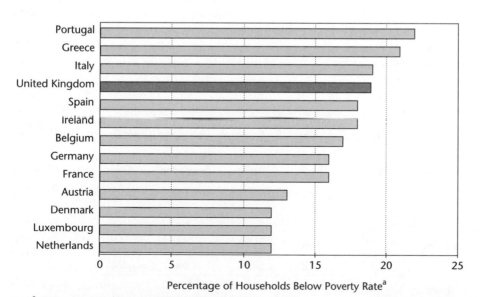

U.K. Poverty Rates in Comparative European Perspective

Percentage of Households Below Poverty Rate[a]

[a]Poverty rate is defined as income below 60 percent of the national median.

Britain has experienced more persistent problems with poverty and income inequality than most of EU Europe. New Labour's attention to social exclusion and a relatively strong economy suggest that poverty may decrease in the years ahead, but there is surprisingly little evidence of improvement to date. Source. "Poverty," from *OECD Economic Surveys 2001–2002.* Copyright © OECD, 2001–2002.

and considerable physical harassment by citizens. They have experienced cultural isolation as well as marginalization in the educational system, job training, housing, and labor markets. There is considerable concern about the apparent rise in racially motivated crime in major metropolitan areas with significant ethnic diversity. Recognizing these problems, in 2000 the government brought to Parliament a bill to amend the Race Relations Act 1976 by outlawing direct and indirect discrimination in all public bodies and placing a "positive duty" on all public officials and authorities to promote racial equality. The Race Relations (Amendment) Act 2000 received final parliamentary approval in November 2000.

In general, poor rates of economic success reinforce the sense of isolation and distinct collective identities. Variations among ethnic minority communities are quite considerable, however, and there are some noteworthy success stories. For example, among men of African, Asian, Chinese, and Indian descent, the proportional representation in the managerial and professional ranks is actually higher than that for white men (although they are much less likely to be senior managers in large firms). Also, Britons of South Asian, and, especially, Indian descent enjoy a high rate of entrepreneurship. Nevertheless, despite some variations, employment opportunities for women from all minority ethnic groups are limited.[13] In addition, a distinct gap remains between the job opportunities available to whites and those open to ethnic minorities in Britain (see Table 2). It is clear that people from ethnic minority communities are overrepresented among low-income households in the United Kingdom. Nearly two-thirds of Pakistani or Bangladeshi households are in low-income households (defined by income below 60 percent of the median), while only 17 percent of white people may be found in such households. More than one-quarter of black (of African or Caribbean descent), Indian, and people from other ethnic minority groups are in low-income households.

Inequality and Women

Women's participation in the labor market when compared to that of men also indicates marked patterns of inequality. In fact, most women in Britain work part-time, often in jobs with fewer than sixteen hours of work per week and often with fewer than eight hours (in contrast, fewer than one in every fifteen men is employed part-time). More than three-quarters of women working part-time report that they did not want a full-time job, yet more women than men (in raw numbers, not simply as a percentage) take on second jobs. Although employment conditions for women in Britain trail those of many of their EU counterparts, the gap in the differential between weekly earnings of men and women in the U.K. has narrowed in recent decades. Between 1970 and 1999, women's weekly earnings rose to 74 percent of the earnings of men compared to 54 percent in 1970. Because even women who work full-time tend to work fewer hours per week than their male counterparts, the gender gap in hourly earnings is somewhat narrower. In 1999, women earned 82 percent of the hourly earnings of men.[14]

Table 2

People in Households Below 60 Percent Median Income: By Economic Status and Ethnic Group, 1996–1998[a]

	White	Black	Indian	Pakistani/ Bangladeshi	Other	All
All above pensionable age	24%	—	—	—	—	24%
Other households						
No members in work	47	52	55	75	40	49
At least one member in work	9	—	20	56	23	10
All households	17	28	27	64	29	18

[a]Combined financial years: 1996–97 and 1997–98.

Source: Jill Matheson and Carol Summerfield, eds., Office for National Statistics *Social Trends 30* (London: Stationery Office, 2000), 94. Reprinted by permission of Her Majesty's Stationery Office.

The Blair government remains committed to gender equality in the workplace and affirmed its resolve to address women's concerns to balance work and family responsibilities. It has taken a number of steps to aid women at work and help reconcile the demands of family and employment. The government has implemented (or proposed) a set of "family-friendly" work-related policies, including unpaid parental leave of up to three months (the EU standard accepted by the United Kingdom under Blair as part of the Social Charter, an EU commitment to enhanced wage earner rights that was included in the 1991 Maastricht Treaty on European Union, to which previous U.K. governments had opted out). The unpaid leave supplements the statutory leave package (six weeks at 90 percent pay plus twelve weeks at half-pay plus roughly $90 per week) and the right to refuse to work more than forty-eight hours per week. Other measures include a commitment in principle to filling half of all public appointments with women, a review of the pension system to ensure better coverage for women, draft legislation to provide for the sharing of pensions after divorce, tax credits for working families as well as for child care, and a National Childcare Strategy. Nevertheless, the United Kingdom is likely to remain an EU outlier in the provision of day care, with responsibilities remaining primarily in private hands and the gap between childcare supply and demand far greater than elsewhere in western Europe. Moreover, the government has continued the Conservative policy of promoting management flexibility, so it seems likely that the general pattern of female labor market participation and inequality in earnings will change relatively little in the years ahead. A spring 1999 report commissioned by the cabinet office's Women's Unit confirms a significant pattern of inequality in lifetime earnings of men and women with an equal complement of skills, defined by both a gender gap and a "mother gap."

Britain and the International Political Economy

The term *globalization* is often applied as a general catch phrase to identify the growing depth, extent, and diversity of cross-border connections that are a signal characteristic of the contemporary world. Some have argued that the radical mobility of factors of production, especially the capital of the "electronic herd" of investors and financiers who can shift vast sums of money around the globe at the speed of a mouse-click, has fatally weakened the capacities of nation-states. Students of comparative politics by and large argue, however, that claims of the demise of national policy controls and national economic models have been exaggerated. Each country study in this book will illuminate the particular features of national economic models as they are shaped by the international political economy, all set against the critical backdrop of domestic policy legacies and political constituencies and programs.

In the case of Britain, the dilemmas of European integration most vividly illustrate the interplay between economics and politics in an era of global interdependence. Many Britons remain skeptical about the advantages of Britain's political and economic integration with Europe and are uneasy about the loss of sovereignty that result from EU membership.

Economic Integration and Political Disintegration

During the Thatcher and Major years, the issue of economic integration bedeviled the prime minister's office and divided the Conservative Party. The introduction of the European Monetary System (EMS) by the European Economic Community (predecessor to the European Community and, in turn, to the EU) in 1979 set the stage for the political dramas that followed. The EMS fixed the exchange rates among member currencies (referred to as the exchange rate mechanism, or ERM), and permitted only limited fluctuation above or below. Thatcher opposed British participation in the ERM throughout the 1980s, insisting on British control of its economic policy. However, when her domestic economic policy failed to stem Britain's rampant inflation, Thatcher's anti-European Community (EC) stance pitted her against senior ministers and leaders of Britain's EC partners, as well as against the bulk of the British business community. In the end, Thatcher succumbed to the pressure and permitted Britain to join the ERM in October 1990. Ironically, just one month later, she was toppled from office by a coup led by those in her own party who most deeply resented her grudging attitude toward European integration.

For the new government of Prime Minister Major, participation in the ERM held enormous symbolic and political significance. As chancellor of the exchequer, he had quietly pressed Thatcher to join, and as prime minister, he staked his reputation on its success.

He hoped that participation would stabilize European trade, reduce inflation, and pull Britain out of a stubborn recession. In September 1992, the EMS collapsed under the impact of downward pressures in the British economy and the strains of German unification. Major never recovered, and it took several years before plans for economic integration in the EU were put back on track. Remarkably, a single European policy (the ERM) led to Thatcher's downfall and politically haunted John Major throughout his premiership.

Developments in European integration present a formidable hurdle for Tony Blair or any successor government (this is discussed further in Section 5). Since Tony Blair's Britain wants to assume leadership in Europe and position itself on the cutting edge of globalization, Britain faces a significant dilemma over the euro. The U.K. cannot maximize its influence in Europe while remaining nothing more than a sympathetic outsider when it comes to monetary union. The political repercussions of economic and monetary considerations will help shape the challenges that New Labour, future governments, and the country face in the years ahead.

Making the Most of Globalization?

Britain plays a particular role within the European and international economy, one that has been reinforced by international competitive pressures in this global age. For a start, **foreign direct investment** (FDI) favors national systems, like those of Britain (and the United States), that rely more on private contractual and market-driven arrangements and less on state capacity and political or institutional arrangements. Due to such factors as low costs, political climate, government-sponsored financial incentives, reduced trade union power, and a large pool of potential non-unionized recruits, the United Kingdom is a highly regarded location in Europe for FDI.

From the mid-1980s onward, the single-market initiative of the EU has attracted foreign investment by according insider status to non-EU-based companies, so long as minimum local content requirements are met. Throughout this period, all British governments have, for both pragmatic and ideological reasons, promoted the United Kingdom as a magnet for foreign investment. For the Thatcher and Major governments, FDI was a congenial market-driven alternative to state intervention as a means to improve sectoral competitiveness, especially in the automobile industry. It had the added benefit of exposing U.K. producers to lean production techniques and management cultures and strategies that reinforced government designs to weaken unions and enforce flexibility. New Labour has continued this approach, which helps advance its key third-way strategy orientation to accept globalization as a given and seek ways to improve competitiveness through business-friendly partnerships.

FDI is only one part of a bigger picture. In very important ways, New Labour accepted the legacy of eighteen years of Conservative assaults on trade union powers and privileges. It has chosen to modernize, but not reshape, the system of production in which nonstandard and insecure jobs without traditional social protections proliferate, a growing sector in which women and ethnic minorities are significantly overrepresented. As a result, within EU Europe, Britain has assumed a specialized profile as a producer of low-technology, low-value-added products through the use of a comparatively low-paid, segmented, weakly organized, and easily dismissible work force. Tony Blair's Britain preaches this model of "flexible labour markets" throughout EU Europe, and its success in boosting Britain's economic performance in comparison to the rest of Europe has won some reluctant admirers, even converts. Thus, Britain has been shaped by the international political economy in important ways and hopes to take full advantage of the economic prospects of globalization, even as it tries to reshape other European national models in its own image.

As our world-of-states theme suggests, a country's participation in today's global economic order diminishes national sovereign control, raising unsettling questions in even the most established democracies. Amid complicated pressures, both internal and external, can state institutions retain the capacity to administer policy effectively within distinctive national models? How much do the growth of powerful bureaucracies at home and complex dependencies on international organizations such as the EU limit the ability of citizens to control policy ends? We turn to these questions in Section 3.

Section ③ Governance and Policy-Making

An understanding of British governance begins with consideration of Britain's constitution, which is notable for two significant features: its form and its antiquity. Britain lacks a formal written constitution in the usual sense; that is, there is no single unified and authoritative text that has special status above ordinary law and can be amended only by special procedures. Rather, the British constitution is a combination of statutory law (mainly acts of Parliament), common law, convention, and authoritative interpretations. Although it is often said that Britain has an unwritten constitution, this is not accurate. Authoritative legal treatises are written, of course, as are the much more significant acts of Parliament that define crucial elements of the British political system. These acts define the powers of Parliament and its relationship with the Crown, the rights governing the relationship between state and citizen, the relationship of constituent nations to the United Kingdom, the relationship of the United Kingdom to the EU, and many other rights and legal arrangements. Thus, it is probably best to say that "what distinguishes the British constitution from others is not that it is unwritten, but rather that it is part written and uncodified."[15]

More than its form, however, the British constitution's antiquity raises questions. It is hard to know where conventions and acts of Parliament with constitutional implications began, but they can certainly be found dating back to the seventeenth century, notably with the Bill of Rights of 1689, which helped define the relationship between the monarchy and Parliament. "Britain's constitution presents a paradox," a British scholar of constitutional history has observed. "We live in a modern world but inhabit a pre-modern, indeed, ancient, constitution."[16] For example, several industrial democracies, including Spain, Belgium, and the Netherlands, are constitutional monarchies, in which policy-making is left to the elected government and the monarch fulfills largely ceremonial duties. In fact, western Europe contains the largest concentration of constitutional monarchies in the world. However, Britain alone among Western democracies has permitted two unelected hereditary institutions, the Crown

and the House of Lords, to participate in governing the country (in the case of the Lords, a process of reform was begun in 1999).

More generally, the structure and principles of many areas of government have been accepted by constitutional authorities for so long that appeal to convention has enormous cultural force. Thus, widely agreed-on rules of conduct, rather than law or U.S.-style checks and balances, set the limits of governmental power.

This reality underscores an important aspect of British government: absolute principles of government are few. At the same time, those that exist are fundamental to the organization of the state and central to governance, policy-making, and patterns of representation.

Organization of the State

The core constitutional principle of the British political system and cornerstone of the Westminster model is **parliamentary sovereignty:** Parliament can make or overturn any law; the executive, the judiciary, and the throne do not have any authority to restrict or rescind parliamentary action. Only Parliament can nullify or overturn its own legislation. In a classic **parliamentary democracy,** the prime minister is answerable to the House of Commons (the elected element of Parliament) and may be dismissed by it. That said, by passing the European Communities Act in 1972 (Britain joined the European Economic Community in 1973), Parliament accepted significant limitations on its ability to act with power. It acknowledged that European law has force in the United Kingdom without requiring parliamentary assent and acquiesced to the authority of the European Court of Justice (ECJ) to resolve jurisdictional disputes. To complete the circle, the ECJ has confirmed its prerogative to suspend acts of Parliament.[17]

Second, Britain has long been a **unitary state.** By contrast to the United States, where powers not delegated to the national government are reserved for the states, no powers are reserved constitutionally for subcentral units of government in the United Kingdom. However, the Labour government of Tony Blair introduced a far-reaching program of constitutional reform that created, for the first time, a quasi-federal system in Britain. Specified powers have been delegated (the British prefer to say *devolved*) to legislative bodies in Scotland and Wales, and in Northern Ireland (although conflict there leaves the ultimate shape of the constitutional settlement still in doubt). In addition, some powers have been redistributed from the Westminster Parliament to an authority governing London with a directly elected mayor, and additional powers may be devolved to regional assemblies as well.

Third, Britain operates within a system of **fusion of powers** at the national level: Parliament is the supreme legislative, executive, and judicial authority and includes the monarch as well as the House of Commons and the House of Lords. The fusion of legislature and executive is also expressed in the function and personnel of the **cabinet.** Whereas U.S. presidents can direct or ignore their cabinets, which have no constitutionally mandated function, the British cabinet bears enormous constitutional responsibility. Through its collective decision making, the cabinet, and not an independent prime minister, shapes, directs, and takes responsibility for government. Cabinet government stands in stark contrast to presidential government and is perhaps the most important feature, certainly the center, of Britain's system of government.

Finally, sovereignty rests with the Queen-in-Parliament (the formal term for Parliament). Britain is a **constitutional monarchy.** The position of head of state passes by hereditary succession, but nearly all powers of the Crown must be exercised by the government or state officials. Taken together, parliamentary sovereignty, parliamentary democracy, and cabinet government form the core elements of the British or Westminster model of government, which many consider a model democracy and the first effective parliamentary democracy.

It may seem curious that such a venerable constitutional framework is also vulnerable to uncertainty and criticism. Can a willful prime minister overstep the generally agreed limits of the collective responsibility of the cabinet and achieve an undue concentration of power? How well has the British model of government stood the test of time and radically changed circumstances? What are the constitutional implications of Blair's reform agenda? These questions underscore the problems that even the most stable democracies face. They also help identify important comparative themes, because the principles of the Westminster model were, with some modifications, adopted widely by former colonies ranging from Canada, Australia, and New Zealand to India, Jamaica, and Zimbabwe. British success (or failure) in preserving citizens' control of their government has implications reaching well beyond the British Isles.

The Executive

The term cabinet government is useful in emphasizing the key functions that the cabinet exercises: responsibility for policy-making, supreme control of government, and coordination of all government departments. However, the term does not capture the full range of executive institutions or the scale and complexity of operations. The executive reaches well beyond the cabinet. It extends from ministries (departments) and ministers to the civil service in one direction, and to Parliament (as we shall see in Section 4) in the other direction.

Cabinet Government

After a general election, the Crown invites the leader of the party that emerges from the election with control of a majority of seats in the House of Commons to form a government and serve as prime minister. The prime minister usually selects approximately two dozen ministers to constitute the cabinet. Among the most significant assignments are the Foreign Office (equivalent to the U.S. secretary of state), the Home Office (ministry of justice or attorney general), and the chancellor of the exchequer (a finance minister or a more powerful version of the U.S. treasury secretary).

The responsibilities of a cabinet minister are immense. "The Cabinet, as a collective body, is responsible for formulating the policy to be placed before Parliament and is also the supreme controlling and directing body of the entire executive branch," notes S. E. Finer. "Its decisions bind all Ministers and other officers in the conduct of their departmental business."[18] In contrast to the French Constitution, which prohibits a cabinet minister from serving in the legislature, British constitutional tradition *requires* overlapping membership between Parliament and cabinet. Unlike the informal status of the U.S. cabinet, its British counterpart enjoys considerable constitutional privilege and is a powerful institution with enormous responsibility for the political and administrative success of the government.

The cabinet system is a complex patchwork of conflicting obligations and potential divisions. Each cabinet member who is a departmental minister has responsibilities to the ministry that he or she must run, and unless the cabinet member is a member of the House of Lords, he or she is also linked to a constituency, or electoral district (as an elected member of Parliament, or MP), to the party (as a leader and, often, a member of its executive board), to the prime minister (as an appointee who shares in the duties of a plural executive), and to a political tendency within the party (as a leading proponent of a particular vision of government).

The cabinet room at 10 Downing Street (the prime minister's official residence) is a place of intrigue as well as deliberation. From the perspective of the prime minister, the cabinet may appear as loyal followers or as ideological combatants, potential challengers for party leadership, and parochial advocates for pet programs that run counter to the overall objectives of the government. Against this potential for division, the convention of collective responsibility normally ensures the continuity of government by unifying the cabinet. In principle, the prime minister must gain the support of a majority of the cabinet for a range of significant decisions, notably the budget and the legislative program.

The only other constitutionally mandated mechanism for checking the prime minister is a defeat on a vote of no confidence in the House of Commons (discussed in Section 4). Since this action is rare and politically dangerous, the cabinet's role in constraining the chief executive remains the only routine check on his or her power. Collective responsibility is therefore a crucial aspect of the Westminster model of democracy. Prime ministers, however, reserve the option to develop policies in cabinet committees, whose membership can be manipulated to ensure support, and then to present policy to the full cabinet with little

chance for other ministers to challenge the results. In addition, the principle of collective responsibility requires that all ministers support any action taken in the name of the government, whether or not it was brought to cabinet. Does collective responsibility effectively constrain the power of prime ministers, or does it enable the prime minister to paint "presidential" decisions with the veneer of collectivity?

A politician with strong ideological convictions and a leadership style to match, Margaret Thatcher often attempted to galvanize loyalists in the cabinet and either marginalize or expel detractors. In the end, Thatcher's treatment of the cabinet helped inspire the movement to unseat her as party leader and stretched British constitutional conventions. John Major returned to a more consultative approach, in keeping with the classic model of cabinet government. "When John Major became Prime Minister it was as though he had read textbooks on British constitutional theory, had observed very closely the circumstances of Margaret Thatcher's downfall, and had come to the conclusion that he was going to do things differently—very differently."[19] After Thatcher's tight control, ministers were delighted with their new freedom, but in time the collegiality of Major's cabinet broke down.

Tony Blair, like Thatcher, has narrowed the scope of collective responsibility. Cabinet meetings are dull and perfunctory, and debate is rare. Decisions are taken in smaller gatherings by the prime minister, a few key cabinet members, and a handful of advisers. In a striking example of this process early in the Blair premiership, right after the election when the full cabinet had not yet met, the government announced the decision to free the Bank of England to set interest rates. Blair has accentuated the tendency for shorter cabinet meetings (they are usually less than an hour) that cannot seriously take up (much less resolve) policy differences.

Both Blair and his close aides seem skeptical about the effectiveness of the cabinet as well as cabinet committees. The prime minister prefers to coordinate strategically important policy areas through highly politicized special units in the Cabinet Office such as the Social Exclusion Unit, the Women's Unit, and the U.K. Anti-Drugs Co-ordination Unit. Finally, Blair has vastly expanded the role of one-on-one meetings with ministers. In a lecture at the London School of

Economics that caused quite a stir, a highly regarded historian and former writer for the *Economist,* Peter Hennessy, quoted a variety of Whitehall insiders (*Whitehall* is a street name referring to the London nerve center of the civil service) who lamented that Blair had killed off cabinet government. One of the luminaries was quoted as saying that "Blair makes Margaret Thatcher look like a natural consulter; to be a minister outside the inner loop is hell."[20]

On balance, cabinet government represents a durable and effective formula for governance. It is important to remember that the cabinet operates within a broader cabinet system or core executive as it is sometimes called (see Figure 3). Because the prime minister is the head of the cabinet, his or her office helps develop policy, coordinates operations, and functions as a liaison with the media, the party, interest groups, and Parliament. Both cabinet committees (comprising ministers) and official committees (made up of civil servants) supplement the work of the cabinet. In addition, the treasury plays an important coordinating role through its budgetary control, while the cabinet office supports day-to-day operations. Leaders in both the Commons and the Lords, the *whips,* help smooth the passage of legislation sponsored by the government, which is more or less guaranteed by a working majority.

The cabinet system ensures that there is no Washington-style gridlock (the inability of legislature and executive to agree on policy) in London. On the contrary, if there is a problem at the pinnacle of power in the United Kingdom, it is the potential for excessive concentration of power by a prime minister who is prepared to manipulate cabinet and flout the conventions of collective responsibility.

Bureaucracy and Civil Service

Policy-making at 10 Downing Street may appear to be increasingly concentrated in the prime minister's hands. At the same time, when viewed from Whitehall, the executive may appear to be dominated by its vast administrative agencies. The range and complexity of state policy-making mean that in practice, the cabinet's authority must be shared with a vast set of unelected officials.

How is the interaction between the civil service and the cabinet ministers (and their political assistants) coordinated? A very senior career civil servant, called a permanent secretary, has chief administrative responsibility for running a department. The permanent secretaries are assisted, in turn, by other senior civil servants, including deputy secretaries and undersecretaries. There are approximately 75,000 senior executives a few rungs down from the level of interaction with ministers and junior ministers. In addition, the minister reaches into his or her department to appoint a principal private secretary, an up-and-coming civil servant who assists the minister as gatekeeper and liaison with senior civil servants. In April 2001, there were 482,690 permanent civil servants (measured in full-time equivalents, FTEs) or almost 2 percent of the work force, down from a height of 751,000 FTEs in 1976, a decline of one-third.

Successful policy requires the effective translation of policy goals into policy instruments. Since nearly all legislation is introduced on behalf of the government and presented as the policy directive of a ministry, much of the work of conceptualizing and refining legislation that is done by committee staffers in the U.S. Congress is done by civil servants in Britain. Civil servants, more than ministers, assume operational duties and, despite a certain natural level of mutual mistrust and incomprehension, the two must work closely together. To the impartial, permanent, and anonymous civil servants, ministers are too political, unpredictable, and temporary—whereas *they* are tireless self-promoters who may neglect or misunderstand the needs of the ministry. To a conscientious minister, the permanent secretary may be protecting *his* or *her* department too strenuously from constitutionally proper oversight and direction. Whatever they may think, no sharp line separates the responsibilities of ministers and civil servants, and they have no choice but to execute policy in tandem. Many of the activities traditionally undertaken by civil servants are now carried out in executive agencies established since a 1988 report on more effective government management. In addition, quite a range of administrative functions previously performed in-house are now provided through contracting out services to the private sector.

Figure 3

The Cabinet System

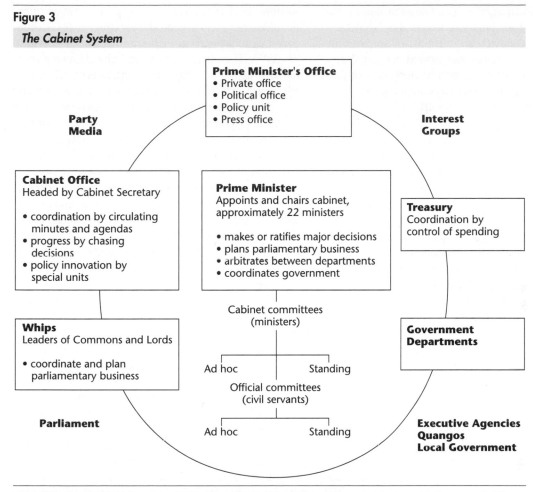

The cabinet is supported by a set of institutions that help formulate policy, coordinate operations, and facilitate the support for government policy. Acting within a context set by the fusion of legislature and executive, the prime minister enjoys a great opportunity for decisive leadership that is lacking in a system of checks and balances and separation of powers among the branches of government. *Source: British Politics: Continuities and Change,* Third Edition, by Dennis Kavanagh, p. 251. Copyright © 1996 by Oxford University Press. Reprinted by permission.

Like ministers, civil servants are servants of the Crown, but they are not part of the government (taken in the more political sense, like the term *the administration* in common American usage). The ministers, not the civil servants, have constitutional responsibility for policy and are answerable to Parliament and the electorate for the conduct of their departments. The significant influence of civil servants (and the size of

even a streamlined bureaucracy) raises important questions about the proper role of unelected officials in a democratic polity. Indeed, the civil service has been assaulted from many directions. Since the early 1980s, the pace of change at Whitehall has been very fast, with governments looking to cut the size of the civil service, streamline its operations, replace permanent with casual (temporary) staff, and enhance its accountability to citizens. Beyond these pressures, the frustration of civil servants was deepened by Thatcher's evident impatience with the customs of impartiality and drawn-out procedures that slowed her aggressive policy agenda. In addition, the reinvigoration of parliamentary select committees has complicated the role of the civil service. Although tradition requires senior civil servants to testify on behalf of their ministers, the more aggressive stance of select committees in recent years has for the first time pressed them to testify, in effect, *against* their ministers if necessary to satisfy parliamentary concerns about misconduct or poor judgment. Some describe a situation of uncertainty and loss of morale.

As a result of the ongoing modernization of Whitehall (known as new public management, NPM), the civil service inherited by New Labour is very different from the civil service of thirty years ago. It has been downsized and given a new corporate structure (divided into over 120 separate executive agencies). Few at the top of these agencies (agency chief executives) are traditional career civil servants. More generally, a tradition of a career service, in which nearly all the most powerful posts were filled by those who entered the bureaucratic ranks in their twenties, is fading. Many top appointments are advertised widely and filled by "outsiders." The Blair government seems unlikely to reverse the NPM trends toward accountability, efficiency, and greater transparency in the operations of the executive bureaucracy. Some have expressed concern, however, that New Labour has done—and will continue to do—whatever it can to subject the Whitehall machine to effective political and ministerial direction and control.[21]

Public and Semipublic Institutions

Like other countries, Britain has institutionalized a set of administrative functions that expand the role of the state well beyond the traditional core executive functions and agencies. The ebb and flow of alternative visions of government in the postwar period, from collectivist consensus to Thatcherism to New Labour, have resulted in substantial changes in emphasis. We turn now to a brief discussion of "semipublic" agencies—entities sanctioned by the state but without direct democratic oversight.

Nationalized Industries. The nationalization of basic industries was a central objective of the Labour government's program in the immediate period after World War II. Nationalization symbolized Labour's core socialist aspiration affirmed in the famous Clause IV of its party constitution ("to secure for the workers by hand or brain the full fruits of their industry . . . upon the basis of common ownership of the means of production, distribution and exchange"). Between 1946 and 1949, the Bank of England was nationalized, and coal, iron and steel, gas and electricity supply, and the bulk of the transport sector became public corporations. By 1960, nationalized industries accounted for about 18 percent of total fixed investment, produced about one-tenth of the national income, and employed some 8 percent of the U.K. work force.[22]

During the eighteen years of Conservative government beginning in 1979, nearly 1 million workers transferred from public to private sector employment, and by 1995, the output of the nationalized sector was less than half the percentage of GDP it had been in 1975. In his first speech as leader to the Labour Party conference in October 1994, Blair argued that a revision of Clause IV was necessary to make it clear that the Labour Party had broken with its past. Within months, a new Clause IV was in place that speaks to middle-class aspirations and rejects the notion that the capitalist market economy is immoral or inherently exploitative. For New Labour, a return to the program of public ownership of industry is unthinkable. Instead, when thinking of expanding state functions, we can look to a growing set of semipublic administrative organizations.

Nondepartmental Public Bodies. Since the 1970s, an increasing number of administrative functions have been transferred to quasi-nongovernmental organizations, better known as **quangos.** Quangos have increasing policy influence and enjoy considerable administrative and political advantages. They take responsibility for specific functions and can combine governmental and private sector expertise. At the same time, ministers can distance themselves from controversial areas of policy, such as arms sales or race relations.

Despite Thatcher's attempts to reduce their number and scale back their operations, by the early 1990s a new generation of powerful, broadly defined, and well-funded quangos had replaced the smaller-scale quangos of the past. In 1990–1991, quangos were spending three times as much as they had in 1978–1979. The growth was particularly significant in locally appointed agencies, including bodies with responsibility for education, job training, health, and housing. By the late 1990s, there were some 6,000 quangos, 90 percent operating at the local level. They were responsible for one-third of all public spending and staffed by approximately 50,000 people. Key areas of public policy previously under the authority of local governments are now controlled by quangos, which are nonelected bodies.

Some observers have expressed concern that the principle of democratic control is being compromised by the power of quangos, which are not accountable to the electorate. Some argue that the growth of local quangos has contributed to the centralization of power, as agencies appointed by ministers take over many functions of local government. Although critical of the "quango state" while in opposition, New Labour took a more measured approach once in government, emphasizing reforms and more democratic scrutiny. The elected authority in London, as well as the Welsh Assembly and Scottish Parliament, acquired extensive powers to review and reform many of the quangos under their responsibility. We will return later to consider local government in Britain, but we move now to a discussion of a set of formal institutions within and outside the executive.

Other State Institutions

Although British public administration extends well beyond its traditional focus on finance or foreign affairs or law and order, these policy areas remain critical. In this section, we examine the military and the police, the judiciary, and subnational government.

The Military and the Police

From the local bobby (a term for a local police officer derived from Sir Robert Peel, who set up London's metropolitan police force in 1829) to the most senior military officer, those involved in security and law enforcement have enjoyed a rare measure of popular support in Britain. Constitutional tradition and profes-

sionalism distance the British police and military officers from politics. Nevertheless, both institutions have been placed in more politically controversial and exposed positions in recent decades.

In the case of the military, British policy in the post–cold war period remains focused on a gradually redefined set of North Atlantic Treaty Organization (NATO) commitments. Still ranked among the top five military powers in the world, Britain retains a global presence, and the Thatcher and Major governments deployed forces in ways that strengthened their political positions and maximized Britain's global influence. In 1982, Britain soundly defeated Argentina in a war over the disputed Falkland/Malvinas Islands in the South Atlantic. In the Gulf War of 1991, Britain deployed a full armored division in the UN-sanctioned force arrayed against Iraq's Saddam Hussein. Under Blair's leadership, Britain was the sole participant alongside the United States in the aerial bombardment of Iraq in December 1998. In 1999, the United Kingdom strongly backed NATO's Kosovo campaign and pressed for ground troops. Blair's stalwart role alongside George W. Bush in the war against terrorism continued and deepened the U.K. role as stalwart U.S. ally and muscular presence in global military initiatives.

Until Britain's special relationship to the United States put the prospect of active U.K. participation in a second war against Iraq very much in play, the use of the military in international conflicts generated little opposition. The role of the military in the dispute in Northern Ireland, however, has been controversial for more than three decades. After a civil rights movement calling for Catholic political and economic equality helped provoke Protestant riots in the autumn of 1969, the British government sent troops to Northern Ireland. In a context set by paramilitary violence on all sides, the reputation of the army was tarnished by its use of techniques that were found to violate the European Convention on Human Rights (ECHR) as well as by accusations that it was used as a partisan political instrument to repress Irish nationalism.

As for the police, which traditionally operate as independent local forces throughout the country, the period since the 1980s has witnessed growth in government control, centralization, and level of political use. During the coal miners' strike of 1984–1985, the police operated to an unprecedented, and perhaps unlawful, degree as a national force coordinated through Scotland Yard (London police headquarters). Police menaced strikers and hindered miners from participating in strike support activities. This partisan use of the police in an industrial dispute flew in the face of constitutional traditions and offended some police officers and officials. During the 1990s, concerns about police conduct focused on police-community relations, including race relations, corruption, and the interrogation and treatment of people held in custody. In particular, widespread criticism of the police for mishandling their investigation into the brutal 1993 racist killing of Stephen Lawrence in South London resulted in a scathing report by a commission of inquiry in 1999. The case raised basic questions about police attitudes toward ethnic minorities, as well as their conduct in racially sensitive cases, and focused renewed attention on necessary reforms. New Labour has advocated expanding police-community partnerships and improving relations with ethnic minority groups. At the same time, it considers tough action on crime as part of its broader approach to community that places considerable emphasis on the responsibilities of individuals and citizens (communitarianism).

The Judiciary

In Britain, the principle of parliamentary sovereignty has limited the role of the judiciary. Courts have no power to judge the constitutionality of legislative acts (judicial review). They can only determine whether policy directives or administrative acts violate common law or an act of Parliament. Hence, the British judiciary is generally less politicized and influential than its U.S. counterpart. In recent decades, however, governments have pulled the courts into political battles over the rights of local councils (municipal government), the activities of police in urban riots, and the role of police and trade unions in industrial disputes. For example, in the 1984–1985 coal miners' strike, the courts interpreted the new Employment Act of 1982 very broadly and froze the entire assets of the miners' union.

Jurists have also participated in the wider political debate outside court, as when they have headed royal commissions on the conduct of industrial relations, the struggle in Northern Ireland, and riots in Britain's inner cities. Some observers of British politics are concerned that governments have used judges in these ways to secure partisan ends, deflect criticism, and weaken the tradition of parliamentary scrutiny of government policy. Nevertheless, Sir Richard Scott's harsh report on his investigation into Britain's sales of military equipment to Iraq in the 1980s, for example, indicates that inquiries led by judges with a streak of independence can prove highly embarrassing to the government and raise important issues for public debate.

Thus, it seems that the courts, newly activist and politicized (by British, if not U.S., standards), are increasingly called into the breach when the normal interplay of party, interest organization, and institutional politics cannot resolve contemporary disputes. Constitutional reform may increase the set of highly politicized demands on the judiciary in the United Kingdom to resolve jurisdictional disputes.

The European dimension has also significantly influenced law and the administration of justice. As a member of the EU, Britain is bound to abide by the European Court of Justice (ECJ), as it applies and develops law as an independent institution within the EU. For example, two decisions by the ECJ led to the enactment of the Sex Discrimination Act of 1986, since previous legislation did not provide the full guarantees of women's rights in employment mandated to all members by the EU's Equal Treatment Directive. Moreover, as a signatory to the ECHR with the passage of the Human Rights Act in 1998, Britain is required to comply with the rulings of the European Court of Justice on Human Rights (ECJHR). This has far-reaching potential for advancing a "pluralistic human rights culture" in Britain and providing new ground rules in law for protecting privacy, freedom of religion, and a wider respect for human rights.[23] Perhaps an indication of its broad influence to come, the adoption of the ECHR forced Britain to curtail discrimination against gays in the military.

Subnational Government

Since the United Kingdom is a state comprising distinct nations (England, Scotland, Wales, and Northern Ireland), the distribution of powers involves two levels below the central government: national government and local (municipal) government. Because the British political framework has traditionally been unitary, not federal, no formal powers devolved to either the nation within the United Kingdom or subnational units (states or regions) as in the United States or Germany. Initiatives undertaken by Blair's government involve far-reaching constitutional changes in the distribution of power between the U.K. government and subcentral national units.

Although no powers have been constitutionally reserved to local governments, they historically had considerable autonomy in financial terms and discretion in implementing a host of social service and related policies. Before 1975, elected local governments set their own spending and taxation levels through the setting of rates (local property taxes). In the context of increased fiscal pressures that followed the 1973 oil crisis, the Labour government introduced the first check on the fiscal autonomy of local councils (elected local authorities) by introducing cash limits (ceilings on spending) beginning in fiscal year 1976–1977. In 1980, the newly elected Thatcher government introduced the Local Government, Planning and Land Act, further tightening the fiscal constraints on local government. Finally, in 1982, the central government set a ceiling on local rates (a rate cap). The outright abolition of London's progressive and multiculturally oriented city government (the Greater London Council, GLC) under the leadership of Ken Livingstone, and several other metropolitan councils in March 1986, completed the political onslaught on local autonomy.

In 1989, the Thatcher government introduced a poll tax, an equal per capita levy for local finance, to replace the age-old system of rates. This radical break with tradition, which shifted the burden of local taxes from property owners and businesses to individuals, and taxed rich and poor alike, was monumentally unpopular. The poll tax proved a tremendous political liability, maintained the local edge to national politics, and helped lead to Thatcher's departure.

Although much of New Labour's agenda concerning subcentral government is focused on the political role of nations within Britain, devolution within England is also part of the reform process. Regional Development Agencies (RDAs) were introduced throughout England in April 1999 as part of a decentralizing agenda, but perhaps even more to facilitate economic development at the regional level. Despite the fairly low-key profile of RDAs and their limited scope (they are unelected bodies with no statutory authority), they open the door to popular mobilization in the long term for elected regional assemblies. In addition, the Blair government placed changes in the governance of London on the fast track. The introduction of a directly elected mayor of London in May 2000 proved embarrassing to Blair, as the government's efforts to keep Livingstone out of the contest backfired and he won handily. With characteristic panache, Livingstone began his victory speech with an obvious allusion to the abolition of the GLC: "As I was saying before I was so rudely interrupted 14 years ago . . . I want an all-embracing administration that will speak with one voice on behalf of London." Even before the debacle of the mayor's race in London, Blair and New Labour appeared genuinely ambivalent about decentralization with the loss of direction and control it entails. In the aftermath, it was even clearer that constitutional reform, once begun, can take on a life of its own.

The Policy-Making Process

Parliamentary sovereignty is the core constitutional principle of the British political system. However, when it comes to policy-making and policy implementation, the focus is not on Westminster but rather on Whitehall. In many countries, such as Japan, India, and Nigeria, personal connections and informal networks play a large role in policy-making and implementation. How different is the British system?

Unlike the U.S. system, in which policy-making is concentrated in congressional committees and subcommittees, Parliament has little direct participation in policy-making. Policy-making emerges primarily from within the executive. There, decision making is strongly influenced by policy communities—informal networks with extensive knowledge, access, and personal connections to those responsible for policy. In this private hot-house environment, civil servants, ministers, and members of the policy communities work through informal ties. A cooperative style develops as the ministry becomes an advocate for key players in its policy community and as civil servants come perhaps to overidentify the public good with the advancement of policy within their area of responsibility.

This cozy insider-only policy process has been challenged by the delegation of more and more authority to the EU. As one observer neatly summarized this development, "The result is a new kind of multi-level political system in which political power is shared between the EU, national and subnational levels, and decisions taken at one level shape outcomes at others."[24] Both ministers and senior civil servants spend a great deal of time in EU policy deliberations and are constrained both directly and indirectly by the EU agenda and directives. More than 80 percent of the rules governing economic life in Britain are determined by the EU. Even where Britain has opted out, as in the case of the common currency, decisions by the Council of Finance Ministers and the European Central Bank shape British macroeconomic, monetary, and fiscal policies. Even foreign and security policy, the classic exercises of national sovereignty, are no longer immune from EU influences, since multilevel governance has been extended to these spheres by the EU's Common Foreign and Security Policy.[25]

As we will see in Section 4, not only the broad principles and practices of governance, but also the organization of interests and the broad dynamics of representation and political participation have been fundamentally reshaped in recent decades.

Section ④ Representation and Participation

As discussed in Section 3, parliamentary sovereignty is the core constitutional principle defining the role of the legislature and, in a sense, the whole system of British government. No act of Parliament can be set aside by the executive or judiciary, nor is any Parliament bound by the actions of any previous Parliament. Nevertheless, in practice, the control exerted by the House of Commons (or Commons) is not unlimited. In this section, we investigate the powers and role of Parliament, both Commons and Lords, as well as the party system, elections, and contemporary currents in British political culture and citizenship. We also assess the political significance of collective identities in Britain (social class, nationality, ethnicity, and gender) and discuss patterns of political participation and social protest.

The Legislature

Is Parliament still as sovereign in practice as it remains in constitutional tradition? Clearly, it is not as powerful as it once was. From roughly the 1830s to the 1880s, it collaborated in the formulation of policy, and members amended or rejected legislation on the floor of the House. Today, the Commons does not so much legislate as assent to government legislation, since (with rare exceptions) the governing party has a majority of the seats and requires no cross-party voting to pass bills. In addition, the balance of effective oversight of policy has shifted from the legislature to executive agencies. In this section, we discuss, in turn, the legislative process, the House of Commons, the House of Lords, and reforms and pressures for change.

Legislative proceedings are conducted according to time-honored customs and procedures. A law begins in draft form as a parliamentary bill. Although there are private bills that concern matters of individual or local interest, most bills are public bills sponsored by the government. The most important of these have generally passed through an extensive process before they reach the floor of the House, where they undergo additional extensive scrutiny before proceeding to the Lords. The elaborate path followed by prospective legislation is described in "Institutional Intricacies: The Legislative Process."

House of Commons

In constitutional terms, the House of Commons, the lower house of Parliament (currently with 659 members), exercises the main legislative power in Britain. Along with the two unelected elements of Parliament, the Crown and the House of Lords, the Commons has three main functions: (1) to pass laws, (2) to provide finance for the state by authorizing taxation, and (3) to review and scrutinize public administration and government policy.

Institutional Intricacies: *The Legislative Process*

To become law, bills must be introduced in the House of Commons and the House of Lords, although approval by the latter is not required. The procedure for developing and adopting a public bill is quite complex. The ideas for prospective legislation may come from political parties, pressure groups, think tanks, the prime minister's policy unit, or government departments. Prospective legislation is then normally drafted by civil servants, circulated within Whitehall, approved by the cabinet, and then refined by one of some thirty lawyers in the office of Parliamentary Counsel.*

According to tradition, in the House of Commons the bill usually comes to floor three times (referred to as *readings*). The bill is formerly read upon introduction (the *first reading*), printed, distributed, debated in general terms, and after an interval (from a single day to several weeks), given a *second reading*, followed by a vote. The bill is then usually sent for detailed review to a standing committee of between sixteen and fifty members chosen to reflect the overall party balance in the House. It is then subject to a report stage during which new amendments may be introduced. The *third reading* follows; normally, the bill is considered in final form (and voted on) without debate.

After the third reading, a bill passed in the House of Commons follows a parallel path in the House of Lords. There the bill is either accepted without change, amended, or rejected. According to custom, the House of Lords passes bills concerning taxation or budgetary matters without alteration, and can add technical and editorial amendments to other bills (which must be approved by the House of Commons) to add clarity in wording and precision in administration. After a bill has passed through all these stages, it is sent to the Crown for royal assent (approval by the queen or king, which is only a formality), after which it becomes law and is referred to as an Act of Parliament.

*See Dennis Kavanagh, *British Politics: Continuities and Change*, 3d ed. (Oxford: Oxford University Press, 1996), 282–288.

In practical terms, the Commons has a limited legislative function; nevertheless, it serves a very important democratic function. It provides a highly visible arena for policy debate and the partisan collision of political world views. The Commons comes alive when opposition members challenge the government, spark debates over legislation, and question the actions of cabinet members. During question time, a regular weekly feature of Commons debate, ministers give oral replies to questions submitted in advance by members of Parliament (MPs) and offer off-the-cuff responses to follow-up questions and sarcastic asides (often to the merriment of all in attendance). The exchanges create extraordinary theater and can make and unmake careers. The ability to handle parliamentary debate with style and panache is considered a prerequisite for party leadership.

The high stakes and the flash of rhetorical skills bring drama to the historic chambers, but one crucial element of drama is nearly always missing: the outcome is seldom in doubt. The likelihood that the Commons will invoke its ultimate authority, to defeat a government, is very small. MPs from the governing party who consider rebelling against their leader (the prime minister) are understandably reluctant in a close and critical vote to force a general election, which would place their jobs in grave jeopardy. Only once since the defeat of Ramsay MacDonald's government in 1924 has a government been brought down by a defeat in the Commons (in 1979). Contemporary constitutional conventions provide a good deal of wiggle room for the government. It was once taken for granted that defeat of any significant motion or bill would automatically result in cabinet resignation or a dissolution of Parliament. However, it is now likely that only defeat on a motion that explicitly refers to "confidence in Her Majesty's government" still mandates dissolution. Today, the balance of institutional power has shifted from Parliament to the governing party and the executive.

House of Lords

The upper chamber of Parliament, the House of Lords (or Lords), is an unelected body that comprises hereditary peers (nobility of the rank of duke, marquis, earl, viscount, or baron), life peers (appointed by the Crown on the recommendation of the prime minister), and law lords (appointed to assist the Lords in its judicial duties and who become life peers). The Lords also includes the archbishops of Canterbury and York and two dozen senior bishops of the Church of England. There are roughly 1,200 members of the House of Lords, but there is no fixed number, and membership changes with the appointment of peers. Not surprisingly, the Conservatives have a considerable edge in the upper house, with just over one-half of peers; Labour runs a distant second at roughly one-sixth. About one-third are crossbenchers, or independents.

The House of Lords is also the final court of appeal for civil cases throughout Britain and for criminal cases in England, Wales, and Northern Ireland. This judicial role, performed by the law lords, drew international attention in 1998 and 1999 when a Spanish court attempted to extradite General Augusto Pinochet of Chile on charges of genocide, torture, and terrorism. In modern times, however, the Lords, which has the power to amend and delay legislation, has served mainly as a chamber of revision, providing expertise in redrafting legislation. Recently, for example, the House of Lords, which considered the Nationality, Immigration and Asylum Bill too harsh, battled the government for weeks and forced revisions before approving the legislation.

In 1999, the Blair government appointed a Royal Commission on the Reform of the House of Lords (the Wakeham commission) and in the same year introduced legislation to remove the right of hereditary lords to speak and vote. In January 2000, the commission recommended a partly elected second chamber, enumerating alternative models. In February 2003, the Commons rejected seven options ranging from a fully appointed chamber (Blair's preference) to an entirely elected one. The failure of a joint committee of MPs and peers to achieve consensus left reform plans in tatters.

Reforms in Behavior and Structure

How significant are contemporary changes in the House? How far will they go to stem the tide in Parliament's much-heralded decline?

Behavioral Changes: Backbench Dissent. Since the 1970s, backbenchers (MPs of the governing party who have no governmental office and rank-and-file opposition members) have been markedly less deferential than in the past. A backbench rebellion against the Major government's EU policy took a toll on the prestige of the prime minister and weakened him considerably. Until the war in Iraq, Blair seemed less likely to face significant rebellion from Labour MPs, although divisions did occur, for example, over social welfare policy and the treatment of trade unions. The defection of some one-third of Labour MPs on key votes in February and March 2003 authorizing force to disarm Iraq represents a far more historic rebellion. It is likely that any decision to join the euro would inspire significant backbench dissent once more. After Major's problems with backbenchers over the EU, many argued that weaker party discipline had become a permanent condition, and the rupture in the Labour party over Iraq will fuel speculation that party discipline may no longer quell opposition on matters of great moment that inspire deep convictions.

Structural Changes: Parliamentary Committees. In addition to the standing committees that routinely review bills during legislative proceedings, in 1979 the Commons revived and extended the number and "remit" (i.e., responsibilities) of select committees. Select committees help Parliament exert control over the executive by examining specific policies or aspects of administration.

The most controversial select committees are watchdog committees that monitor the conduct of major departments and ministries. Select committees hold hearings, take written and oral testimony, and question senior civil servants and ministers. They then issue reports that often include strong policy recommendations at odds with government policy. As one side effect of the reform, the role of the civil service has been complicated. For the first time, they have been required to testify in a manner that might damage their ministers, revealing culpability or flawed judgments. As discussed in Section 3, the powerful norms of civil service secrecy have been compromised and the relationship with ministers disturbed. On balance, the committees have been extremely energetic, but not very powerful.

In 1997, the Modernisation Committee was established, providing an avenue for the Commons to assess procedures and conventions critically. The committee's reforms have been generally regarded as productive but limited. Perhaps the most significant modernizing reform was the 1998 change in the system of scrutinizing EU affairs. These included the introduction of new committees and the strengthening of informal links with EU institutions. The prospects of parliamentary reform are limited by its very character and function within the broader political system. The dominance of party and executive constrains Parliament, not to mention "the fundamental fact that Parliament is a legislature in which the ambition of most of its members is to join the executive."[26] As a consequence, demands for significantly greater scrutiny over government are not likely to be made and are even less likely to be accepted.

Political Parties and the Party System

Like the term *parliamentary sovereignty,* which conceals the reduced role of Parliament in legislation and the unmaking of governments, the term *two-party system,* which is commonly used to describe the British party system, is somewhat deceiving. It is true that since 1945, only leaders of the Labour or Conservative parties have served as prime ministers. Also, from 1945 through 2001, the Conservative and Labour parties each won eight general elections. It is also true that throughout the postwar period, these two parties have routinely divided some 90 percent of the seats in the House of Commons. But a variety of other parties—centrist, environmental, nationalist, and even neofascist—have complicated the picture of party competition. (In addition, Britain has several national parties, which are described below in "Trends in Electoral Behavior.")

Labour Party

As one of the few European parties with origins outside electoral politics, the Labour Party was launched by trade union representatives and socialist societies in the last decade of the nineteenth century and formally took its name in 1906. From its inception in a Labour Representation Committee, supporters sought to advance working-class political representation and to further specific trade unionist demands. In the years preceding World War I, the party expanded its trade union affiliation but made only weak progress at the polls. Labour secured only 7.1 percent of the vote in 1910, but the radicalizing effects of the war and the expansion of the franchise in 1918 nearly tripled its base of support. In 1918, it received 22.2 percent, even with a shift of emphasis from the defense of trade union rights to explicitly socialist appeals. Its landslide 1945 victory promoted the party to major player status. At the same time, Labour began moderating its ideological appeal and broadening its electoral base.

Early in the postwar period, it was clear that Labour Party fundamentalism, which stressed state ownership of industry and workers' control of production, would take a back seat to a more moderate perspective that advocates the projects of the collectivist consensus (called *revisionism* or *Labourism* by contemporaries). In the 1950s and early 1960s, those not engaged in manual labor voted Conservative three times more commonly than they did Labour; more than two out of three manual workers, by contrast, voted Labour. During this period, Britain conformed to one classic pattern of a western European party system: a two-class/two-party system.

The period since the mid-1970s has been marked by significant changes in the party system and a growing disaffection with even the moderate social democracy associated with the Keynesian welfare state and Labourism. The party suffered from divisions between its trade unionist and parliamentary elements, constitutional wrangling over the power of trade unions to determine party policy at annual conferences, and disputes over how the leader would be selected. In 1981, a centrist breakaway of leading Labour MPs further destabilized the party.

Divisions spilled over into foreign policy issues as well. Although Labour has been generally internationalist, persistent voices within the party challenged participation in the European Community (EC) on the grounds that EC policy would advance the interests of business over labor. However, the EC's adoption of the

Social Charter to extend workers' rights and protections in 1989 helped turn Labour into a pro-EC party. On defense issues, there was a strong pacifist and an even stronger antinuclear sentiment within the party. Support for unilateral nuclear disarmament (the reduction and elimination of nuclear weapons systems with or without comparable developments on the Soviet side) was a decisive break with the national consensus on security policy and contributed to the party's losses in 1983 and 1987. Unilateralism was then scrapped.

The 1980s and 1990s witnessed a period of relative harmony within the party, with moderate trade union and parliamentary leadership agreeing on major policy issues. Tony Blair's immediate predecessors as party leaders—Neil Kinnock (who served from 1983 until Labour's defeat in the March 1992 election) and John Smith (who replaced Kinnock and served as leader until his death in May 1994)—helped pave the way for New Labour by abandoning socialism and taking the party in a new pragmatic direction. Labour has become a moderate left-of-center party in which ideology takes a back seat to performance and electoral mobilization, although divisions over the war in Iraq have inspired some soul searching about what the party stands for.

Conservative Party

The pragmatism, flexibility, and organizational capabilities of the Conservative Party, a party that dates back to the eighteenth century, have made it one of the most successful and, at times, innovative center-right parties in Europe. In contrast to some leading conservative parties in Italy and Germany, it has been a secular party wholly committed to democratic principles, free of the association with fascism during World War II that tainted the others. Although it has fallen on hard times in recent years, it would be unwise to underestimate its potential as both an opposition and a governing party.

Although the association of the Conservative Party with the economic and social elite is unmistakable, it is also true that it was the Conservative government of Prime Minister Benjamin Disraeli (1874–1880) that served as midwife to the birth of the modern welfare state in Britain. The creation of a "long-lasting alliance between an upper-class leadership and a lower-class following" made the Conservative Party a formidable player in British politics.[27] Throughout the postwar period, it has also routinely (with some exceptions) provided the Tories, as Conservatives are colloquially called, with electoral support from about one-third or more of the manual working class. Even in Labour's recent landslide victories, the Tories continued to attract significant working-class support. In 1997, 28 percent of skilled manual workers and 24 percent of unskilled manual workers voted for the Conservatives, and in 2001 the corresponding figures were 31 percent and 25 percent.[28]

Contemporary analysis of the Conservative Party must emphasize the cost to the party of its internal divisions over Britain's role in the EU. The Tories have seldom, if ever, experienced divisions over an area of policy as serious as those over Europe in the 1990s. Wrangling among the Conservatives over Europe lead to Thatcher's demise as leader and weakened Major throughout his years as prime minister. The bitter leadership contest that followed Major's resignation after the 1997 defeat only reinforced the impression of a party in turmoil. The new party leader, a centrist, William Hague, had his work cut out for him. The Conservatives were divided between the "Euroskeptics," who reject further European integration, and those who support integration balanced by a firm regard for British sovereignty. In addition, despite party support for a unitary, not a federal, arrangement, the Conservatives under Hague had no choice but to find credible positions on the constitutional reforms that were already in the pipeline and some, like devolution, that have very considerable support, especially in Scotland. Finally, although economic and social policy divisions were eclipsed by the clash over Europe, Conservatives faced inner disagreements on social policy, industrial policy, and the running of the economy.

The pro-business and pro-market orientation of Blair's Labour Party and its perceived centrism limit the options for Conservatives in advancing economic and social policy that would mark out a distinctive alternative to Blair. In a clear effort to differentiate the Conservatives from Blair's third way, Hague launched a "British Way" initiative, appealing to "Middle England" and traditional values of entrepreneurship, individualism, and loyalty to local and national institutions.[29] In a related development, the party adopted hard-line positions on asylum seekers, gays, and ethnic minority rights that raised questions about tolerance and its much trumpeted compassion.

Whatever the divisions and policy challenges, the Conservatives faced the 2001 election with a confidence they had not experienced for several years, hoping for a good showing, although not expecting victory. But the election proved a stunning repudiation. A bid to lower taxes backfired with an electorate demanding better public services. Nor did the anti-euro stance gain support. Within hours of the result, Hague announced his resignation. His successor as Conservative leader, Iain Duncan Smith, elected in September 2001, was viewed by many as a poor, even a suicidal, choice to revitalize the party. Since Hague was defeated fighting a "save the pound" campaign, what advantage would be gained by choosing a leader who was even more anti-euro and more right-wing on social issues? Starting from such low expectations, Smith has done tolerably well. The party has not split over Europe and has tried with some success to reposition itself, emphasizing the salient issue of improved public services and using the "war on terrorism" to raise questions about civil liberties. It has yet, however, to become a credible electoral threat to New Labour.

Liberal Democrats and Other Parties

Since the 1980s, a changing roster of centrist parties has posed a potentially significant threat to the two-party dominance of Conservative and Labour. Through the 1970s, the Liberal Party, a governing party in the pre–World War I period and thereafter the traditional centrist third party in Britain, was the only centrist challenger to the Labour and Conservative parties. In 1981, the Social Democratic Party (SDP) formed out of a split within the Labour Party. In the 1983 election, the Alliance (an electoral arrangement of the Liberals and the SDP) gained a quarter of the vote. The strength of centrist parties in the mid-1980s led to expectations of a possible Alliance-led government (which did not occur), and observers of British politics began to talk about a party system with "four major national parties" (Conservative, Labour, Liberal, and SDP). After the Conservative victory in 1987, the Liberal Party and

most of the SDP merged to form the Social and Liberal Democratic Party (now called the Liberal Democrats, or the LD).

Under the leadership of Paddy Ashdown, the Liberal Democrats fought the 1992 election from the awkward stance of "equidistance" from the two major parties. After a disappointing result—17.8 percent of the vote and only twenty seats in the Commons—the party changed its position in 1994 and began working more closely with Labour. Most important, the two parties created the Joint Constitutional Committee, which developed a degree of unity on proposals for constitutional reform. Many credit the Liberal Democrats with inspiring Blair's constitutional agenda. Nevertheless, under Ashdown's effective leadership, the Liberal Democrats preserved their independence in the 1997 election. They targeted the seats where they had the greatest chance of victory, with impressive results. Although their share of the vote slipped slightly between 1992 and 1997 (from 17.8 to 16.8 percent), they won more than twice as many seats (forty-six).

Amid a growing debate about the relationship between Labour and the Liberal Democrats, early in 1999 Ashdown unexpectedly resigned as leader and was succeeded by Charles Kennedy, an MP from the Scottish Highlands. The success of the Liberal Democrats in the 2001 general election (discussed in "Trends in Electoral Behavior" below) positioned the party as a potentially powerful center-left critic of New Labour. The local government elections in May 2002 resulted in some significant gains (as well as some reversals), but did little to sustain the party's momentum. As the Blair government fought to emphasize its willingness to save public services (especially the NHS) at almost any cost, Kennedy's luster as leader and the optimism of the Liberal Democrats experienced at least a temporary decline.

The appeal of smaller parties in Britain is constantly shifting. One party, the Greens (formed in 1973 by environmentalists and the oldest Green Party in Europe), surprised everyone (themselves included) by achieving a 15 percent third-place showing in the June 1989 elections to the European Parliament (but winning no seats). With public opinion surveys ranking "pollution and the environment" as the third-most common concern, the major parties hustled to acquire a greenish hue. But the Green Party failed to capitalize on its 1989 showing. By the mid-1990s, party membership declined, and environmental activists focused on a wide range of grass-roots initiatives. In 1997, it ran only 95 candidates (down from 253 in 1992), with very little impact (it averaged only 1.4 percent in the constituencies it contested). A likely sign of the alienation of voters from the mainstream parties, in 2001 the Greens doubled their share of the vote in the constituencies they contested.[30]

The National Front (formed in 1967), a far-right, neofascist, anti-immigrant party, won seats on local councils and entered candidates (unsuccessfully) for Parliament. After the National Front faded in the late 1970s, the British National Party (BNP), formed in 1983, emerged as the most visible far right party. Concentrating its electoral strategy on impoverished inner-city constituencies, in 1997 it ran fifty-seven candidates who registered a meager 1.3 percent average share of the votes cast. The most dramatic and troubling result of the 2001 election was the performance of the far-right white racist BNP. Electioneering on the violent riots and racial tensions that enflamed Oldham, a town near Manchester, some ten days before the election, the BNP leader registered 16 percent of the vote in Oldham West and Royton and party candidates won 11 percent in each of two neighboring constituencies. Although hardly rivaling Le Pen's National Front in France, the BNP results were a shock in the U.K., representing the strongest showing of the far right in a general election in more than fifty years.

In addition to these center, environmental, far right, and single-issue parties, Britain has several national parties, which are described below as part of the discussion of trends in electoral behavior.

Elections

British elections are exclusively for legislative posts. The prime minister is not elected as prime minister but as an MP from a single constituency (electoral district) averaging about 65,000 registered voters. Parliament has a maximum life of five years, with no fixed term. General elections are held after Parliament has been dissolved by the Crown at the request of the prime minister. However, for strategic political reasons, the prime minister may ask the Crown to dissolve Parliament at any time. The ability to control the timing of

elections is a tremendous political asset for the prime minister. This contrasts sharply with a presidential system, characteristic of the United States, with direct election of the chief executive and a fixed term of office.

Electoral System

Election for representatives in the Commons (who are called members of Parliament, or MPs) is by a "first-past-the-post" (or winner-take-all) principle in each constituency. In this single-member plurality system, the candidate who receives the most votes is elected. There is no requirement of a majority and no element of proportional representation (a system in which each party is given a percentage of seats in a representative assembly roughly comparable to its percentage of the popular vote). Table 3 shows the results of the general elections from 1945 to 2001.

This winner-take-all electoral system tends to exaggerate the size of the victory of the largest party and reduce the influence of regionally dispersed lesser parties. Thus, in 2001, with 40.7 percent of the popular vote, Labour won 413 seats. With 18.3 percent of the vote, the Liberal Democrats, despite targeting their most winnable constituencies, won only 52 seats. Thus, the Liberal Democrats achieved a share of the vote that was approximately 45 percent of that achieved by Labour, while winning fewer than 13 percent of the seats won by Labour. Such are the benefits to the victor of the system.

With a fairly stable two-and-a-half party system (Conservative, Labour, and Center), the British electoral system tends toward stable single-party government. However, the electoral system raises questions about representation and fairness. The system reduces the competitiveness of smaller parties with diffuse pockets of support. In addition, the party and electoral systems have contributed to the creation of a Parliament that has been a bastion of white men. In 1992, 60 women were elected as MPs out of 650 seats (9.2 percent), an increase from 42 members in 1987 (6.3 percent). The 1997 election represented a breakthrough for women: the number of women MPs nearly doubled to a record 120 (18.2 percent). The 2001 election saw the number of women MPs decline to 118 (17.9 percent). In an effort to improve the prospects for female

Table 3

British General Elections, 1945–2001

		Percentage of Popular Vote						Seats in House of Commons					
	Turnout	Conserv-ative	Labour	Liberal[a]	National Parties[b]	Other	Swing[c]	Conserv-ative	Labour	Liberal[a]	National Parties[b]	Other	Government Majority
1945	72.7	39.8	48.3	9.1	0.2	2.5	−12.2	213	393	12	0	22	146
1950	84.0	43.5	46.1	9.1	0.1	1.2	+3.0	299	315	9	0	2	.5
1951	82.5	48.0	48.8	2.5	0.1	0.6	+0.9	321	295	6	0	3	17
1955	76.7	49.7	46.4	2.7	0.2	0.9	+2.1	345	277	6	0	2	60
1959	78.8	49.4	43.8	5.9	0.4	0.6	+1.2	365	258	6	0	1	100
1964	77.1	43.4	44.1	11.2	0.5	0.8	−3.2	304	317	9	0	0	4
1966	75.8	41.9	47.9	8.5	0.7	0.9	−2.7	253	363	12	0	2	95
1970	72.0	46.4	43.0	7.5	1.3	1.8	+4.7	330	288	6	1	5	30
Feb. 1974	78.7	37.8	37.1	19.3	2.6	3.2	−1.4	297	301	14	9	14	−34[d]
Oct. 1974	72.8	35.8	39.2	18.3	3.5	3.2	−2.1	277	319	13	14	12	3
1979	76.0	43.9	37.0	13.8	2.0	3.3	+5.2	339	269	11	4	12	43
1983	72.7	42.4	27.6	25.4	1.5	3.1	+4.0	397	209	23	4	17	144
1987	75.3	42.3	30.8	22.6	1.7	2.6	−1.7	376	229	22	6	17	102
1992	77.7	41.9	34.4	17.8	2.3	3.5	−2.0	336	271	20	7	17	21
1997	71.4	30.7	43.2	16.8	2.6	6.7	−10.0	165	419	46	10	19	179
2001	59.4	31.7	40.7	18.3	2.5	6.8	+1.8	166	413	52	9	19	167

[a]Liberal Party, 1945–1979; Liberal/Social Democrat Alliance, 1983–1987; Liberal Democratic Party, 1992–2001.

[b]Combined vote of Scottish National Party (SNP) and Welsh National Party (Plaid Cymru).

[c]"Swing" compares the results of each election with the results of the previous election. It is calculated as the average of the winning major party's percentage point increase in its share of the vote and the losing major party's decrease in its percentage point share of the vote. In the table, a positive sign denotes a swing to the Conservatives, a negative sign a swing to Labour.

[d]Following the February 1974 election, the Labour Party was thirty-four seats short of having an overall majority. It formed a minority government until it obtained a majority in the October 1974 election.

Source: Anthony King, ed., *New Labour Triumphs: Britain at the Polls* (Chatham, N.J.: Chatham House, 1998), p. 249. Copyright © 1998 by Chatham House. Reprinted by permission. For 2001 results, http://news.bbc.co.uk/hi/english/static/vote2001/results_constituencies/uk_breakdown/uk_full.stm.

parliamentary representation, the Sex Discrimination (Election Candidates) Act, which received Royal Assent (the formal approval given by the queen after both parliamentary houses have approved an act) in February 2002, removes legal barriers to parties taking positive action to increase the number of women candidates, for example, through the use of women-only shortlists in the selection of candidates to run for Parliament (as Labour used from 1993 to 1996).

Also in 1992, 6 ethnic minority candidates were elected, up from 4 in 1987, the first time since before World War II that Parliament included minority members. The number of ethnic minority MPs rose in 1997 to 9 (1.4 percent) and to 12 in 2001 (1.8 percent). Although the numbers of successful candidates remain very low, recruitment has improved substantially: there were 57 ethnic minority candidates in 2001 compared to 5 in 1979. Another positive sign is that two of the ethnic minority MPs represent constituencies that do not have sizeable ethnic minority populations. Despite the general trend of increased representation of women and minorities, they remain substantially underrepresented in Parliament.

Trends in Electoral Behavior

Recent general elections have deepened geographic and regional fragmentation on the political map. British political scientist Ivor Crewe has referred to the emergence of *two* two-party systems: (1) competition between the Conservative and Labour parties dominates contests in English urban and northern seats, and (2) Conservative-Center party competition dominates England's rural and southern seats.[31] In addition, a third two-party competition may be observed in Scotland, where Labour–National Party competition dominates.

The national parties have challenged two-party dominance since the 1970s. The Scottish National Party (SNP) was founded in 1934 and its Welsh counterpart, the Plaid Cymru, in 1925. Coming in a distant second to Labour in Scotland in 1997, the SNP won 21.6 percent of the vote and six seats. In 2001, support for the SNP declined by 2 percent, and the party lost one of its seats. Both electoral and polling data indicate that Scottish voters are more inclined to support the SNP for elections to the Scottish parliament than to Westminster and that devolution may have stemmed the rising tide of nationalism.[32] In both 1997 and 2001, the Plaid Cymru won four seats where Welsh is still spoken widely. In both Scotland and Wales, Labour is the dominant party, with the overwhelming majority of seats. Its experience is another illustration of the effects of the first-past-the-post system. With the Tories shut out in both Wales and Scotland in 1997 and with only one Scottish seat for the Conservatives in 2001, the prospects of a common two-party pattern of electoral competition throughout Britain are more remote than ever before.

For now, the winner-take-all electoral system has preserved two-party dominance in parliamentary representation. But the popular vote tells a different story. Except for 1979, the center and national parties combined have received more than one-fifth of the vote in every general election between February 1974 and 1992. They slipped slightly to 19.4 percent in 1997

and then, with the strong showing of the Liberal Democrats, rebounded to 20.8 percent in 2001. But the winner-take-all system preserves two-party dominance in parliamentary representation at roughly 90 percent. The British electoral system is more complicated than it seems at first glance.

In fact, one of the most significant features of the 2001 election was the further weakening of two-party dominance. With Charles Kennedy, the leader of the Liberal Democrats, running an effective, plainspoken campaign—arguing, for example, that improvement in public services would require tax increases—the party increased its vote tally by nearly one-fifth overall. It won fifty-two seats, the most since 1929, and knocked the Tories into fourth place in the popular vote in Scotland. As the Conservatives entered a period of introspection, the Liberal Democrats could credibly claim that they were, in effect, the leading opposition party, although translating that boast into an effective critique of New Labour is easier said than done.

Political Culture, Citizenship, and Identity

In their classic study of the ideals and values that shape political behavior, political scientists Gabriel Almond and Sidney Verba wrote that the civic (or political) culture in Britain was characterized by trust, deference to authority and competence, pragmatism, and the balance between acceptance of the rules of the game and disagreement over specific issues.[33] Many have considered these characteristics the model for active, informed, and stable democratic citizenship. Viewed retrospectively, the 1970s appear as a crucial turning point in British political culture and group identities. It is too early to be certain, but the electoral earthquake of 1997 may represent another critical shift in British politics and culture.

During the 1970s, the long years of economic decline culminated in economic reversals in the standard of living for many Britons. Also for many, the historic bonds of occupational and social class grew weaker. Union membership declined with the continued transfer of jobs away from the traditional manufacturing sectors. More damaging, unions lost popular support as they appeared to bully society, act undemocratically, and neglect the needs of an increasingly female and minority work force. At the same time, a growing number of conservative think tanks and the powerful voice of mass-circulation newspapers, which are overwhelmingly conservative, worked hard to erode the fundamental beliefs of the Keynesian welfare state. **New social movements (NSMs),** such as feminism, antinuclear activism, and environmentalism, challenged basic tenets of British political culture. Identities based on race and ethnicity, gender, and sexual orientation gained significance. Thus, a combination of economic strains, ideological assaults, and social dislocations helped foster political fragmentation and, at the same time, a shift to the right in values and policy agendas.

Thatcher's ascent reflected these changes in political culture, identities, and values. It also put the full resources of the state and a bold and determined prime minister behind a sweeping agenda for change. As a leading British scholar put it, "Thatcher's objective was nothing less than a cultural revolution."[34] Although most observers agree that she fell considerably short of that aim, Thatcherism cut deep. It touched the cultural recesses of British society, recast political values, and redefined national identity.

To the extent that the Thatcherite worldview took hold (and the record is mixed), its new language and ethos helped transform the common sense of politics and redefined the political community. Monetarism (however modified) and the appeal to an enterprise culture of competitive market logic and entrepreneurial values fostered individualism and competition—winners and losers. It rejected collectivism, the redistribution of resources from rich to poor, and state responsibility for full employment. Thatcherism considered individual property rights more important than the social rights claimed by all citizens in the welfare state.

In addition to her positive appeals to the enterprise culture, Thatcher's reform agenda included negative appeals. A review of Thatcher's first general election reveals the repoliticization of race. She promised tougher nationality legislation to restrict immigration, expressed sympathy for those who harbored "fear that [Britain] might be swamped" by nonwhite Commonwealth immigrants, and associated minorities with lawlessness. In a similar vein, during the 1984–1985 miners' strike, she denounced the coal miners as the "enemy within," comparing them to the external Argentine enemy during the Falklands/Malvinas war of 1982. Thatcher symbolically expelled some groups—ethnic minority communities and the unrepentant miners—from the national community. In this way, Thatcherism involved an attempt to redefine national identity by implicit appeals to a more secure, provincial, and unified Britain. In addition, pressure for devolution and growing nationalist sentiment in Scotland and Wales fueled a center versus periphery division. Finally, working-class identity and politics were stigmatized as government sharply criticized the behavior of unions. The traditional values of "an honest day's work for an honest day's pay" and solidarity among coworkers in industrial disputes were characterized as "rigidities" that reduced productivity and competitiveness.

Under the Conservative leadership of Thatcher and Major, governments held class-based interests at arm's length and worked to curb their political and industrial power. A formidable combination of legislated constraints, trade union defeats in industrial disputes, and massive unemployment (particularly in the traditionally unionized manufacturing sectors) helped crystallize a pattern of decline in union membership, militancy, and power. Although Blair's reasons are different—he emphasizes the realities of the new global economic competition—he has done little to create a more cooperative or productive relationship with the unions. As many have noted, "tough on the unions" is a core premise of New Labour, and this has contributed to a fundamental erosion of the ability of working people in the United Kingdom to improve their lot through collective bargaining or to exert influence over public policy through the political muscle of the trade union movement. Class still matters in the U.K., but not in the dominating way that it did in the nineteenth century or in the collectivist era.

The sources and relative strength of diverse group attachments have shifted in Britain in recent decades under the combined pressures of decolonization, which created a multiethnic Britain, and a fragmentation of the experiences of work, which challenge a simple unitary model of class interest. National identity has become especially complicated in the United Kingdom.

At the same time, gender politics has emerged as a hot-button issue.

Citizenship and National Identity

As political scientist Benedict Anderson has observed, national identity involves the belief in an "imagined community" of belonging, shared fates, and affinities among millions of diverse and actually unconnected citizens.[35] Since the 1970s, the question of what constitutes "Britishness"—who is included and who is excluded from the national political community—has become increasingly vexing. What constitutes "Britishness"? Of what may citizens be justifiably proud? How has the imagined nation stood the test of time? These questions are increasingly difficult to answer.

Questions about fragmented sovereignty within the context of the EU, the commingled histories of four nations (England, Scotland, Wales, and Ireland/Northern Ireland), and the interplay of race and nationality in postcolonial Britain have created doubts about British identity that run deep. As ethnicity, intra-U.K. territorial attachments, and the processes of Europeanization and globalization complicate national identity, it becomes increasingly difficult for U.K. residents automatically to imagine themselves Britons, constituting a resonant national community.

Thus, the imagined community of Britain fragmented into smaller communities of class, nation, region, and ethnicity that existed side by side but not necessarily in amiable proximity. Can New Labour recreate a more cohesive political culture and foster a more inclusive sense of British identity? Unlike Thatcher, Blair is a conciliator, and he has worked hard to revitalize a sense of community in Britain and extend his agenda to the socially excluded. The efforts of the Blair government to forge unity and build community and the obstacles it faces are discussed in Section 5.

Ethnicity

Britain is a country of tremendous ethnic diversity. As noted in Section 2, 4.5 million Britons (7.6 percent of the total population) are of African, African-Caribbean, or Asian descent. In Greater London, a little more than one-third of the population have community backgrounds outside Britain, and slightly more than one-fifth have backgrounds in Africa, Asia, or the Caribbean. The authors of a recent commission report on multi-ethnic Britain explained:

> Many communities overlap; all affect and are affected by others. More and more people have multiple identities—they are Welsh Europeans, Pakistani Yorkshirewomen, Glaswegian Muslims, English Jews and black British. Many enjoy this complexity but also experience conflicting loyalties.[36]

In political terms, the past two decades have seen increased attention, both negative and positive, to the role of ethnic minorities in the United Kingdom. The politicization of immigration in the 1979 election marked an intensification of this process. It also underscored the resentment white Britons felt toward minority communities that maintained their own religious beliefs and cultures. Ethnic minority communities have experienced police insensitivity, problems in access to the best public housing, hate crimes, and accusations that they are not truly British if they do not root for Britain's cricket team. In a similar vein, the current controversy over immigration and asylum, coming as it does in the wake of intense scrutiny of the Muslim community post–September 11, contributes to the alienation of the ethic minority community, particularly sections of the Muslim citizenry. The home secretary's talk about asylum seekers "swamping" public services, an almost eerie echo of Thatcher's remark a quarter-century ago, makes it look as if little has changed. And yet, in the aftermath of the attack on the World Trade Center and the Pentagon, public debate included a range of articulate, young, and confident Muslims from a variety of perspectives, and Faz Hakim, chief race relations adviser to the prime minister, had played a visible public insider role. It is true that the experience of Islamic Britain has been framed by September 11 and by the riots in northern towns in the summer of 2001 (British Pakistanis in Bradford were responsible for the worst of the violent episodes). But it is equally true that Muslim university graduates are assuming leading roles in the professions, there are more than 160 Muslim elected city councillors, and British society has become increasingly sensitive to Muslim concerns.[37] (The challenges of multiethnic Britain are discussed further in Section 5.)

Gender

Historically, the issues women care about most—child care, the treatment of part-time workers, domestic violence, equal pay, and support for family caregivers—have not topped the list of policy agendas of any political party in Britain. Has New Labour significantly changed the equation?

In 1997, Labour made a concerted effort to attract female voters and was handsomely rewarded. In addition to specific policy statements, the appointment of a series of shadow ministers for women, who worked hard to mobilize support through women's networks and organizations, contributed to Labour's success in closing the gender gap in 1997.[38] (See "Current Challenges: The Gender-Generation Gap.") It is probably fair to say, on balance, that Labour does well among women voters less because of any specific policies and more because it has made the effort to listen to concerns that women voice. Labour stalwarts would insist that they have addressed key concerns that women (and men) share concerning health care, crime, and education. They would point with pride to the policy directions spurred by the social exclusion and women's units.

In the absence of concrete policy achievements linked to women's experiences of work and family life, it is hard to place women decisively in Labour's column. Many women in Britain are quick to suggest that tax credits for working families and efforts to encourage businesses to adopt more family-friendly policies, however laudable, have not changed the basic equation. This puts in context the gender voting patterns in June 2001. Before the election, some New Labour enthusiasts called Labour "the natural party of women," but the votes did not turn out that way. Both men and women gave Labour about 46 percent of the vote, and both swung about 3 percent in the direction of the Conservatives, compared to 1997. New Labour has obliterated the old gender gap in which women favored the Conservatives but has not established a new pro-Labour women's vote.[39]

Interests, Social Movements, and Protests

Since the 1970s, movements based on ethnic and gender attachments (NSMs) have grown in significance. By contrast to the traditional interest-group-oriented social movements, the NSMs tend to be more fluidly organized and democratic, less oriented to immediate payoffs for their group, and more focused on fundamental questions about the values of society. For example, in the 1970s and 1980s, the women's peace movement protested Britain's participation in NATO's nuclear defense and organized a string of mass demonstrations. In general, following the NSM approach, the women's movement in Britain has remained decentralized and activist. It has emphasized consciousness raising, self-help, and lifestyle transformations and spawned dozens of action groups, ranging from health clinics to battered women's and rape crisis shelters, to feminist collectives and black women's groups, to networks of women in media, law, and other professions. More recently, women have confronted government over inadequate child care and the difficulties posed by women's daily struggle to juggle the demands of work and family.

Simultaneously, the subcultures and countercultures of black Britain have been a vital source of NSM activity, often expressed in antiracist initiatives. "Rock Against Racism" concerts in the 1970s brought reggae and skinhead bands together in public resistance to the National Front; today, lower-profile efforts are made to sensitize local councils to the cultural and material needs of ethnic minorities and to publicize their potential political clout. Efforts to secure improved housing have been a persistent focus of ethnic minority political mobilization. Like the women's movement, such movements are decentralized and culturally engaged.

In recent years, partly in response to globalization, political protest has been on the rise in Britain. A radical strain of anticapitalist anarchism has gained strength. As protesters demand more accountability and transparency in the operations of powerful international trade and development agencies, a "reclaim the Streets" march in London in June 1999 resulted in over eighty arrests and the equivalent of over $3 million damage to the City of London (the equivalent of Wall Street). In addition, London became the site of

Current Challenges: The Gender-Generation Gap

The issue of a gender gap in voting behavior has long been a mainstay of British electoral studies. From 1945 to 1992, women were more likely than men to vote Conservative. In addition, since 1964 a "gender-generation" gap has become well established. The phenomenon was very clear in the 1992 election. Among younger voters (under 30 years old), women preferred Labour while men voted strongly for the Conservatives; producing a 14-point gender gap favoring Labour; among older voters (over 65 years old), women were far more inclined to vote Conservative than were their male counterparts, creating a gender gap of 18 points favoring the Conservatives.

What happened to the gender gap in the 1997 election? The modest all-generation gender gap that favored the Tories in 1992 (6 percent) was closed in 1997, as a greater percentage of women shifted away from the Conservatives (11 percent) than did men (8 percent). As a result, women and men recorded an identical 44 percent tally for Labour. The gender-generation gap continued, however, with younger women more pro-Labour than younger men, and the pattern reversing in the older generation. Moreover, one of the most striking features of the 1997 election was the generational dimension: the largest swing to Labour was among those in the 18–29 age group (+18 percent), and among first-time voters; there was no swing to Labour among those over 65.

What are the implications of this overlay of gender and generational voting patterns? For one thing, it seems that a party's ability to recognize and satisfy the political agendas of women in Britain may offer big political dividends. Studies suggest, first, that issues at the top of the list of women's concerns (e.g., child care, the rights and pay of part-time workers, equal pay, support for family caregivers, domestic violence) do not feature strongly in the existing policy agendas of the political parties. Second, to the extent that women and men care about the same broadly defined issues, women often understand the issues differently than men do and express different priorities. For example, while men (and the three major parties) consider unemployment the central employment issue, women emphasize equal pay and pensions, access to child care, and the rights of part-time workers. Third, research indicates that distinct sets of issues concern different groups of women. For example, older women are most concerned about pensions and transportation. Due to the overrepresentation of women in lower-paid part-time jobs, working women express particular concern about the minimum wage and the treatment of part-time workers. Mothers find the level of child benefit more important than issues of tax cuts. Finally, younger women strongly support policies that would help them balance the responsibilities of work, family, and child care.

Sources: Pippa Norris, Electoral Change in Britain since 1945 (Oxford: Blackwell Publishers, 1997), 133–135; Joni Lovenkuski, "Gender Politics: A Breakthrough for Women?" Parliamentary Affairs 50, no. 4 (October 1997): 708–719.

protests timed to correspond with the Seattle meeting of the World Trade Organization (WTO), which generated some 100,000 protesters in November 1999.

Above all, since the mid-1990s, the level and intensity of environmental activism have been unprecedented. The combined membership of Greenpeace and Friends of the Earth swelled substantially above 600,000 by 1993, but the level of environmental activism really took off with the growing attention to genetically modified (GM) crops in the late 1990s. A newly radicalized movement, worried that long-term consumption of GM food might be harmful and that once let loose, GM crops—referred to derisively as "Frankenstein food"—might cross-pollinate with "normal" plants, captured the popular imagination. A host of direct-action protests erupted in the summer of 1999, some including the destruction of crops. Opinion polls indicated that nearly 75 percent of the population did not want GM crops in the United Kingdom, and in November 1999, the government announced a ban on commercially grown GM crops in Britain.

In a movement that galvanized the country and

raised critical questions about Blair's leadership, massive demonstrations that cut across constituencies and enjoyed huge popular support erupted in September 2000 to protest high fuel prices. (See "Citizen Action: The Fuel Crisis.")

A quite different kind of activism spread to the countryside among a population not usually known for political protest. Farmers who had been badly hurt by the BSE (bovine spongiform encephalopathy, more popularly known as "mad cow disease") crisis and other rural populations concerned about the perceived urban bias of the Labour government launched massive protests.[40] As the banning and licensing of fox hunting roiled Parliament, the Countryside Alliance, which represents country dwellers who see restrictions on fox hunting as emblematic of domineering urban interests, held mass demonstrations at party conferences and in London in an effort (thus far successful) to block restrictive legislation. Competing for attention with antihunt protestors, nearly a quarter of a million people gathered on the day after Christmas 2002, for traditional Boxing Day hunts, possibly the last such meeting in the present form if the government bans or restricts hunts in 2003 as promised.

On the far more significant matter of war in Iraq, a series of antiwar rallies were held in London. In September, 2002, a huge protest rally was organized in London, led by the Stop the War Coalition and the Muslim Association of Britain. Organizers reported that 400,000 people joined in the Saturday march from the Embankment to a rally in Hyde Park, while police said that they counted more than 150,000 marchers. Whatever the exact number of protestors, it was one of Europe's biggest antiwar rallies. The mayor of London, Ken Livingstone, no stranger to social movement mobilizations, called it the largest march for peace that he had seen in thirty years. Another antiwar rally in mid-February 2003 challenged Blair's stand on Iraq with at least 750,000 demonstrators.

Both within the U.K. and among observers of British politics and society, many still endorse the Almond and Verba view of the political culture. Although pragmatism, trust, and deference may still be found in good measure, the persistence and mobilizing potential of a wide range of social movements suggest that quite powerful political subcurrents persist in Britain, posing significant challenges for British government.

Section ⑤ British Politics in Transition

In the fall of 1994, cease-fire declarations made by the Irish Republican Army (IRA) and the Protestant paramilitary organizations renewed hope for a peace settlement in Northern Ireland. Then, in a dramatic new development in early spring 1995, British prime minister John Major and Irish prime minister John Bruton jointly issued a framework agreement, inspiring mounting optimism about a political settlement. Although Major did what he could to secure public and parliamentary support, he lacked the necessary political capital to bring the historic initiative to fruition.

With his 1997 landslide victory, Tony Blair had political capital to spend, and he chose to invest a chunk of it on peace in Northern Ireland. Blair arranged to meet Gerry Adams, president of Sinn Fein, the party in Northern Ireland with close ties to the IRA—and shook his hand. He was the first prime minister to meet a head of Sinn Fein since 1921. Blair later spoke of the "hand of history" on his shoulder.

Under deadline pressure imposed by Blair and the new Irish prime minister, Bertie Ahern, and thirty-three hours of around-the-clock talks, an agreement was reached on Good Friday 1998. It specified elections for a Northern Ireland assembly, in which Protestants and Catholics would share power, and the creation of a North-South Council to facilitate "all-Ireland" cooperation on matters such as economic development, agriculture, transportation, and the environment. Much was left unclear—for example, the details of how and when the IRA would give up its weapons (called "decommissioning" in Northern Irish parlance) and questions about the release of prisoners affiliated with the paramilitary groups. It did not address the reform of the police force in Northern Ireland, which was overwhelmingly Protestant and partisan and does not enjoy the confidence of the Catholic community. Nevertheless, despite doubts about the fine print, both parts of Ireland voted yes in May 1998

Citizen Action: *The Fuel Crisis*

The familiar maxim, "A week can be a long time in politics," took on new meaning in Britain during September 2000 as a fuel crisis quickly erupted into a serious political challenge to Prime Minister Tony Blair. On September 7, 2000, the story broke that angry farmers and truck drivers were mounting protests outside an oil refinery in northwest England. French truckers are famously contentious and had won concessions from their government in the form of a 15 percent reduction on fuel taxes the previous week, but few expected a similarly aggressive turn to direct action in Britain. But by the weekend, protests were threatening delivery at every refinery in Britain as discontent over high fuel prices spread across Europe.

The rising cost of gasoline in Europe has presented a huge headache to motorists. In Britain, as elsewhere, the high cost of petrol (gasoline) has become a serious threat to those whose livelihood puts them behind the wheel or requires that their products be transported by vehicle. As the ninth ranking oil producer in the world, the United Kingdom is in far better shape about oil than other European countries. Nevertheless, the prices in Britain are the highest of all, with premium unleaded gas at the time of the protest costing about US $4.37 a gallon. Although the Blair government tried to turn the mounting anger against oil companies and the Organization of Petroleum Exporting Countries, it was clear as the week wore on that Blair was on the hot seat. For a start, taxes account for a higher percentage of the cost—a whopping 76.2 percent—than anywhere else in the EU countries (gasoline taxes in the United States count for 22.8 percent of the pump price, less than one-third the levy paid by Britons). Moreover, it is clear that the ferocity and effectiveness of the protests took the government by surprise and that Blair, who is often accused of aloofness and arrogance, misplayed his initial response.

On September 11, as panic buying mounted and fears grew that hospitals might soon be forced to cancel nonemergency procedures and schools might have to shut down, Blair refused to compromise on fuel taxes and seemed tone deaf to the protesters' laments. "We cannot and will not alter government policy on petrol through blockades and pickets," intoned a defiant prime minister. "That's not the way to make policy in Britain." By the following evening, 90 percent of the petrol stations in Britain had run out of unleaded gas. Overnight, Queen Elizabeth, on the advice of the prime minister and cabinet, declared a state of emergency. By September 13, hospitals, schools, and social services were being hard hit, small businesses were crippled by the protests, and food stocks were dwindling. Blair's promise to get things back to normal by evening only inflamed the situation, but by the end of the workweek, the protest's informal leaders called off their action. They had proved their point, nearly bringing Britain to a halt, and focused the country's attention on their concerns. The protesters quit while they were ahead without promises of concessions, but amid strong hints that the next budget would include cuts in fuel taxes—and before they could be blamed for loss of life or the failure of critical services. As the blockades came down, opinion polls showed 80 percent of the country behind the protests and, for the first time in eight years, the Conservatives surging past Labour.

"Fuel Tax Protestors Tie up Chancellor." This cartoon shows Chancellor Gordon Brown trapped by protesters in September 2000 demanding reduced taxes on fuel. The government refused to give in to demands during the heat of the direct action campaign, but Brown's prebudget statement in November was calculated to relieve pressure on the government before the anticipated general election. *Source: Spectator,* September 16, 2000, p. 12. Drawing by Jonathan Wateridge, courtesy of the *Spectator.*

in a referendum to approve the peace agreement. It appeared that a new era was dawning in Northern Ireland.

Like the spiral of political violence that can imperil peace efforts in the Middle East at any time, handshake or not, devastating bombs have exploded in Northern Ireland since the agreement, and violent turf battles within and between each camp have created fear and repeated crises in the peace process. The Northern Ireland secretary felt compelled to suspend the devolved power-sharing government in February 2000, less than three months after it began, under Protestant Unionist pressure concerning the timetable for decommissioning of IRA weapons amid allegations of bad faith on both sides. Through the winter of 2001, recurring crises over weapons—deadlines, procedures governing inspections by an international commission, what sort of interim meetings could take place—strained relations between the parties to the dispute and threatened to disrupt the Good Friday Agreement. Insisting that Sinn Fein cabinet ministers be barred from discussion until the IRA disarmed, hard-liners in the Protestant camp created a rash of challenges to David Trimble, the Ulster Unionist leader who remained committed to the success of the process. Sinn Fein, in turn, accused Trimble of sabotage and warned that the IRA would not be able to control its own dissidents if the power-sharing arrangements were unilaterally dismantled.

In October 2001, the IRA began disarming under the sponsorship of third-party diplomats, and yet violence rose despite cease-fires by paramilitary groups: police reported 18 killed in 2001 (mostly by the Protestant paramilitary groups) and more than 300 "punishment beatings" inflicted equally by Protestant and Catholic gangs. The spring and summer of 2002 were rife with accusations and denials of the IRA training Colombian guerrillas in bomb-making techniques, fomenting street violence in Belfast, and stealing police antiterrorist intelligence in the U.K. Was it a time of hope or a time of despair? In May 2002, a group of Palestinian and Israeli political leaders met in the English Midlands with figures who had negotiated the Good Friday Agreement. They hoped to return to the Middle East with lessons about how a dangerous stalemate born of mistrust and violence could be resolved through negotiations. Yet, in October 2002,

home rule government was suspended and British direct rule was reimposed. Tony Blair and his Irish Republic counterpart Bertie Ahern pledged to redouble efforts to get Northern Ireland's faltering peace process back on track, but little progress was achieved by early 2003.

The never-ending crises in Northern Ireland confirm the important proposition that unresolved tensions in state formation shape political agendas for generations. Northern Ireland, however, is but one of a host of challenges facing Britain on Tony Blair's watch.

Political Challenges and Changing Agendas

As our democratic idea theme suggests, no democracy, however secure it may be, is a finished project. Even in Britain, with its centuries-old constitutional settlement and secure institutional framework, issues about democratic governance and citizens' participation remain unresolved.

Constitutional Reform

Questions about the role of the monarchy and the House of Lords have long been simmering on Britain's political agenda. Since the traditionally admired royal family was battered by scandal and misconduct in the 1990s, these concerns about the undemocratic foundations of the British state have gained credibility. "Why is the House of Commons not sovereign?" wondered one observer somewhat caustically. "Why does it have to share sovereignty with other, unelected institutions?"[41] The balance of power among constitutionally critical institutions remains a major issue of contemporary political debate. Parliament is hamstrung by strong, centrally controlled parties and is easily overpowered by an executive whose strength in relation to that of the legislature may be greater than in any other Western democracy. Add to these concerns the role of the unelected House of Lords and the absence of an "entrenched" bill of rights (one that Parliament cannot override), and it seems appropriate to raise questions about the accountability of the British government to its citizens.

In fact, constitutional reform may become New Labour's most enduring legacy. The Blair government has begun to implement far-reaching reforms of Parliament, including the removal of the right of hereditary peers to speak and vote in the House of Lords and the redesign of the historic upper chamber. In addition, the European Convention on Human Rights has been incorporated into U.K. law. Moreover, new systems of proportional representation have been introduced for Welsh and Scottish elections, as well as for the European Parliament, and the possible use of proportional representation in U.K. general elections has been placed on the reform agenda (although reform in this area seems unlikely for now). New Labour's inability to control the outcome of London's historic mayoral contest in May 2000 illustrates the difficulties that may accompany far-reaching measures to devolve and decentralize power.

Finally, the initiatives in Northern Ireland and power-sharing arrangements between Westminster and national assemblies in Scotland and Wales raise the prospect of further basic modifications of U.K. constitutional principles. Devolution implies both an element of federalism and some compromise in the historic parliamentary sovereignty at the heart of the Westminster model, with uncertain and potentially unsettling consequences. It is too early to be sure about the success of these reform initiatives, but it is certain that the constitutional reform agenda is highly significant. The range and depth of New Labour's constitutional reform agenda represent a breathtaking illustration of a core premise of our democratic idea theme: that even long-standing democracies face pressures to narrow the gap between government and citizens. If the British feel themselves removed from day-to-day control over the affairs of government, they are hardly alone. And despite the questions Britons raise about the rigidities of their ancient institutional architecture, others throughout the world see the Westminster model as an enduring exemplar of representative democracy, stability, tolerance, and the virtues of a constitutional tradition that balances a competitive party system with effective central government.

Identities in Flux

Although the relatively small scale of the ethnic minority community limits the political impact of the most divisive issues concerning collective identities, it is probably in this area that rigidities in the British political system challenge tenets of democracy and tolerance most severely. Given Britain's single-member, simple-plurality electoral system and no proportional representation, minority representation in Parliament is very low, and there are deep-seated social attitudes that no government can easily transform. The issues of immigration, refugees, and asylum still inspire fear among white Britons of multiculturalism and conjure very negative and probably prejudiced reactions. In fall 2000, the report of the Commission on the Future of Multi-Ethnic Britain raised profound questions about tolerance, justice, and inclusion in contemporary U.K. society. In a powerful and controversial analysis, the report concluded that "the word 'British' will never do on its own. . . . Britishness as much as Englishness, has systematic, largely unspoken, racial connotations."[42]

How about other dimensions of collective identity? The situation is fluid. The electoral force of class identity has declined in Britain for the time being, and the Labour government's first term in office was free of pay disputes and strikes. New Labour's efforts to develop a partnership with business and to keep trade unions at arm's length appeared to weaken the labor movement, positioning it as an "internal opposition" with little ability to challenge the government on industrial relations and economic policy. By Labour's second term, however, the country faced an upsurge in industrial action. Public sector workers such as local government staff and firefighters have led the unrest. A new generation of militant leaders in two railway unions, the postal workers union, and the government and health workers union have created new challenges for the government. Against this backdrop, a dramatic series of work stoppages by firefighters in the autumn and winter of 2002 to 2003 were particularly noteworthy. The stoppages dramatized the return of industrial militancy in unforgettable images and raised difficult questions about Blair's ability to reform and improve public services, a pledge he takes very seriously and one the electorate will not soon forget. Early in 2003, many were asking whether the New Labour government could effectively resolve the upswing in industrial action and, at the same time, meet its commitment to modernize and upgrade public services.

In political terms, the gender gap has closed for the

time being, but concerns about women's employment, the disparate impact of social policy, the problems of balancing family and work responsibilities, and parliamentary representation remain. The prospects for a political settlement in Northern Ireland, such as they are, offer the hope that discord over national identity may be reduced in a profound way. More unsettling, the agreement in Northern Ireland, the constitutional reforms in Scotland and Wales, and the processes of Europeanization all involve some weakening of the central authority of Westminster and Whitehall. Thus, British identity, which is already weakly felt, will lose some of its institutional security at the same time that European identity is pulling from above and regional, ethnic, and national identities are pulling from below.

European Integration

From 1989 to 1997, the seemingly endless backbiting over policy toward Europe in the Conservative Party sidetracked Thatcher and Major and cost them dearly in political terms. Britain's traumatic withdrawal from the Exchange Rate Mechanism in 1992 stands as a warning that deeper European integration can be economically disruptive and politically dangerous. In the years ahead, Britain's decision whether, when, and under what conditions to join the single currency will almost certainly prove a serious challenge to New Labour's managerial skills and unity.

Thus far, the government has opted to play down the political significance of the euro. At first, Blair and his followers began to make the case for the "yes" campaign, despite government assurances that the promised referendum on the euro would not be held until after the subsequent general election. Despite some strong hints early in 1999 that the government would ultimately support entry, the Foreign Secretary at the time, Robin Cook claimed that "the high-water mark of European integration has already been reached." Chancellor of the Exchequer Gordon Brown has repeatedly assured listeners that the decision on entry into the single currency will be based on how high the euro scores on a series of five key economic tests, and Blair has conceded the point.

Most observers note, however, that the issues swirling around British participation in the single currency are profoundly political and that the tide of European integration is rising. In fact, the matter of Britain's participation in the euro seems likely to create significant political pressures for New Labour. Unofficially, the prime minister and quite a few other key members of the government have for years supported British participation in the single currency, and the decision to free the Bank of England from direct government control was a powerful indication that Blair and Brown intended to create the proper conditions for British entry. However, the prospect of all but irreversible and comprehensive European integration has inspired significant resistance within New Labour and among the public. By spring 2002, public opinion seemed to be tipping toward the euro. Perhaps the introduction of euro coins and bills since the start of the new year lent an everyday reality and familiarity to the common currency, even to the British. The growing buoyancy of the euro against the dollar with the rash of American business scandals through the summer and fall of 2002 added momentum to the "yes" campaign, and Blair made it increasingly clear that he would like to decide in 2003 on a firm date for having a referendum on entry. Still, the guessing game continued amidst reports of public bickering between Blair and Brown. Sparks fly between the two rivals at the head of government, with Brown wary, and Blair unwilling thus far to force the issue without the Chancellor's support.

For countries that have joined the euro club (or want to curry favor and influence with those who have joined), the European Central Bank has acquired critical economic policy powers that have reduced national sovereign control. Participation holds significant consequences for price stability and for the capacity of national governments to manipulate interest rates and exchange rates to cushion declines in demand and limit unemployment. In addition, the euro will create pressure for coordination of tax policies. Economic and monetary integration therefore has potentially quite significant repercussions for standards of living and distributional politics at home.

Inevitably New Labour will have to face head-on these issues and the political divisions that will almost certainly follow. The euro will cast a long shadow over New Labour's strategies for governing the economy, and perceptions about Blair's handling of the U.K.

position on the euro are likely to have tremendous political repercussions for years to come.

Post–9/11: Britain's Special Relationship with the United States

In the immediate aftermath of the terror attacks on the United States, Blair's decisive support for President Bush struck a resonant cord in both countries, and (despite some grumbling) boosted Britain's influence in Europe. By spring and summer 2002, Blair's dalliance with Bush was looking more and more like a liability. The "axis of evil" motif of President Bush's State of the Union address in January 2002 worried many Britons (including foreign secretary Jack Straw), who considered it simplistic and potentially destabilizing. Would the special relationship—at the national level and between the two leaders—mean that Blair could moderate Bush's foreign policy and stall the plans for pre-emptive war against Iraq? Would it influence U.S. policy or at least calm the rhetoric about North Korea and Iran? As Britons' instinctive post–September 11 support for America faded, many wondered whether Tony Blair had boxed himself into a corner by aligning himself too closely with George W. Bush, not knowing where the president's foreign policy initiatives might lead in the Middle East and Asia, and in a host of policy areas from trade policy to the conduct of the continuing campaign in Afghanistan to global warming to the International Criminal Court. Through the start of the war in Iraq, Blair persevered in his staunch support for Bush's stance despite widespread opposition from Labour MPs, opinion polls indicating that only a quarter of the public supported war without a UN mandate, and the cabinet resignation of Robin Cook, leader of the House and former foreign minister. Speculation mounted that Blair's support for Bush might in time imperil his political future.

British Politics in Comparative Perspective

For many reasons, both historical and contemporary, the British case represents a critical one in comparative terms, even though Britain is no longer a leading power. How well have three centuries of constitutional government and a culture of laissez-faire capitalism prepared Britain for a political and economic world that it has fewer resources to control? Does Britain still

Since the terror attacks of September 11, Tony Blair has risked a lot on his relationship with George Bush. As critical policy disagreements emerge, will the prime minister be able to influence American policy? *Source/ Credit:* Rex Features.

offer a distinctive and appealing model of democracy? What are the lessons that may be drawn from Blair's New Labour, a modernizing politics that aspires to go beyond Left and Right?

Until the Asian financial crisis that began in 1997, it was an axiom of comparative politics that economic success required a style of economic governance that Britain lacks. Many argued that innovation and competitiveness in the new global economy required the strategic coordination of the economy by an interventionist state. Interestingly, however, the United Kingdom escaped the recession that plagued the rest of Europe for much of the 1990s, with six solid years of uninterrupted growth between 1992 and 1998, and it outperformed Germany throughout much of the 1980s and 1990s. Although growth has slowed since summer 2000, the U.K. is outperforming most major world economies and exhibits a good overall performance, declining unemployment, and relatively low inflation. The government recognizes that investment in both physical and human capital has been weak and that the biggest economic challenge facing the U.K. is to improve productivity (see Figure 4).[43] Britain is not an economic paradise, but there is cause for optimism, notwithstanding the uncertainties of the post–September 11 environment and the drag of U.S.

financial markets following the revelations about corporate scandals.

The reasons for Britain's success and its economic prospects for the future continue to fuel debate inside the United Kingdom and attract considerable attention elsewhere. Perhaps Britain has already reaped the competitive benefits of ending restrictive labor practices and attracting massive foreign investment looking for a European base with few restrictions, and it is time to introduce a German-style high-skill, high-wage work force and give it similar opportunities to participate in management. Or perhaps Britain's "less is more" approach to economic management, augmented by Tony Blair's business partnership and welfare reforms that encourage active participation in the labor force, provides an important and timely alternative to the more state-centered and interventionist strategies of Germany, France, and Japan. Time will tell, and partisan debate will probably never end, but the British approach has gained favor in recent years. In many countries throughout the world, politicians are looking for an economic model that can sustain economic competitiveness while preserving individual liberties and improving the plight of the socially excluded. Tony Blair's third way—a political orientation that hopes to transcend left and right in favor of practical

Figure 4

Comparative Investment in Human and Physical Capital

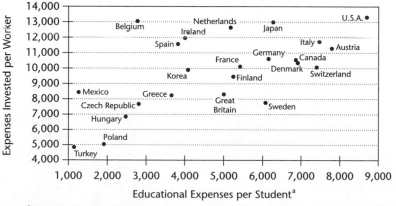

Despite improvements in recent years, Britain trails many countries in terms of investment per worker and educational spending per student. After the June 2001 election, the government stressed its determination to boost innovation and productivity through greater investment in human and physical capital." *Source:* "Investment in Human and Physical Capital," from *OECD Economic Surveys 2001–2002.* Copyright © OECD, 2001–2002.

[a]Expenditure per student on public and private institutions for all levels of education (based on full-time equivalents).

and effective policies—will be carefully watched and, if it is successful, widely emulated.

Beyond the impressive size of Blair's victory, nothing about the May 1997 election was clearer than the unprecedented volatility of the electorate. In previous elections, commitment to party (partisan identification) and interests linked to occupation (class location) had largely determined the results. In 1997, attachments to party and class had far less influence.

Beginning with the historically low turnout, the 2001 election underscored, as one journalist put it, that "instinctive party support" based on class and partisan traditions has been replaced by "pick and choose" politics. The tendency of voters to behave as electoral shoppers lends a perpetual air of uncertainty to elections. It seems that Blair's success in transforming Labour into New Labour blunted the social basis of party identification. At the same time, the modernization agenda of New Labour resolutely emphasized fiscal responsibility over distributive politics. As a result, it seems that specific issues and the needs of voters mattered more than deep-seated attachments. People voted as consumers of policies: they asked themselves who would make it easier for them to pay their mortgage, get the health care their family needs, best educate their children—and what role the government would play in underwriting or providing these goods.

As the fuel crisis illustrates, without the traditional constraints of partisan and class identities, citizens (whether as voters or as political activists) can shift allegiances with lightning speed. "What have you done for me lately?" becomes the litmus test for leaders and politicians. In Blair's case, it appeared by November that September's crisis was old news. The prebudget statement by Chancellor Gordon Brown promised a package of freezes and cuts in fuel taxes plus large reductions in vehicle excise duties amounting to the equivalent of $3.2 billion, or some 24 cents a gallon for ordinary motorists and twice that for truck drivers. Perhaps not coincidentally, the government was back on top, with snapshot polls giving Labour 45 percent and the Conservatives 34 percent.

The election in June 2001 was, paradoxically, a landslide and a powerful reminder that much of the electorate was waiting to be convinced that New Labour could deliver on its core promises of improved schools, hospitals, transport, and protection against crime. In winning 40.7 percent of the popular vote and a very commanding majority of 167 in the Commons, Labour achieved a historic result. For the first time, the party won two emphatic electoral victories in a row and was poised to lead the country for two full successive terms. Nevertheless, despite the overwhelming mandate, at 59.4 percent, the lowest turnout for a general election in Britain since 1918 indicated widespread apathy and skepticism (although, of course, a low turnout also reflected a sense that the outcome was never in doubt). Many wondered aloud whether in its second term, New Labour could dispel the notion that it was "more spin than substance." Even an exuberant Tony Blair noted that the mood in 2001 was more sober and less euphoric than it had been on election night four years earlier. Everyone seemed painfully aware of unfulfilled promises and the challenges that lay ahead.

In this era of uncertain democratic transitions, divided leadership, and intense global pressures on economic competitiveness, Britain's response to contemporary challenges will be closely watched. These are tough times for national governments to maintain popular support and achieve desirable goals. Can a popular and resolute leader who is riding a wave of solid economic achievement in one of the most secure democracies govern effectively? If not, many will conclude that these tough times just got tougher.

Key Terms

free trade	social security
hegemonic power	globalization
franchise	foreign direct investment
laissez-faire	parliamentary
welfare state	sovereignty
gender	parliamentary democracy
gender gap	unitary state
Westminster model	fusion of powers
neoliberalism	cabinet
Keynesianism	constitutional monarchy
macroeconomic policy	quangos
monetarism	new social movements

Suggested Reading

Beer, Samuel H. *Britain Against Itself: The Political Contradictions of Collectivism*. New York: Norton, 1982.

Driver, Stephen, and Martel, Luke. *New Labour: Politics After Thatcherism*. Cambridge: Polity Press, 1998.

Dunleavy, Patrick, et al. *Developments in British Politics, 6*. New York: St. Martin's Press, 2000.

Giddens, Anthony. *The Third Way: The Renewal of Social Democracy*. Cambridge: Polity Press, 1998.

Gilroy, Paul. *"There Ain't No Black in the Union Jack": The Cultural Politics of Race and Nation*. Chicago: University of Chicago Press, 1991.

Hall, Peter A. *Governing the Economy: The Politics of State Intervention in Britain and France*. New York: Oxford University Press, 1986.

Hall, Stuart, and Jacques, Martin, eds. *The Politics of Thatcherism*. London: Lawrence and Wishart, 1983.

Hobsbawm, E. J. *Industry and Empire*. Harmondsworth: Penguin/Pelican, 1983.

Kavenagh, Dennis, and Seldon, Anthony. *The Powers Behind the Prime Minister: The Hidden Influence of Number Ten*. London: HarperCollins, 1999.

King, Anthony, ed. *Britain at the Polls, 2001*. New York: Chatham House, 2002.

King, Anthony, et al. *New Labour Triumphs: Britain at the Polls*. Chatham, N.J.: Chatham House, 1998.

Krieger, Joel. *British Politics in the Global Age: Can Social Democracy Survive?* New York: Oxford University Press, 1999.

Landes, David S. *The Unbound Prometheus: Technological Change and Industrial Development in Western Europe from 1750 to the Present*. Cambridge: Cambridge University Press, 1969.

Lewis, Philip. *Islamic Britain: Religion, Politics and Identity Among British Muslims*. London: I. B. Taurus, 2002

Marsh, David, et al. *Postwar British Politics in Perspective*. Cambridge: Polity Press, 1999.

Marshall, Geoffrey. *Ministerial Responsibility*. Oxford: Oxford University Press, 1989.

Middlemas, Keith. *Politics in Industrial Society: The Experience of the British System Since 1911*. London: André Deutsch, 1979.

Norris, Pippa. *Electoral Change in Britain Since 1945*. Oxford: Blackwell Publishers, 1997.

Parekh, Bhiku, et al., *The Future of Multi-Ethnic Britain: The Parekh Report*. London: Profile Books, 2000.

Pierson, Paul. *Dismantling the Welfare State? Reagan, Thatcher, and the Politics of Retrenchment*. New York: Cambridge University Press, 1994.

Riddell, Peter. *The Thatcher Decade*. Oxford: Basil Blackwell, 1989.

Särlvik, Bo, and Crewe, Ivor. *Decade of Dealignment: The Conservative Victory of 1979 and Electoral Trends in the 1970s*. Cambridge: Cambridge University Press, 1983.

Shaw, Eric. *The Labour Party Since 1945*. Oxford: Blackwell Publishers, 1996.

Thompson, E. P. *The Making of the English Working Class*. New York: Vintage, 1966.

Wright, Tony, ed. *The British Political Process*. London: Routledge, 2000.

Suggested Websites

British Broadcasting Corporation
www.bbc.co.uk
Cabinet office
www.cabinet-office.gov.uk
Market and Opinion Research International (MORI), Britain's leading political polling organization.
www.mori.com
Scottish Parliament
www.scottish.parliament.uk
The U.K. government official website
www.ukonline.gov.uk
The U.K. Parliament
www.parliament.uk

Notes

[1]"Huddled Masses, Please Stay Away," *The Economist,* June 15, 2002, p. 49.

[2]Market and Opinion Research International (MORI), http://www.mori.com/polls/2002/refugee.shtml

[3]Jenny Church, ed., *Social Trends* 27 (London: The Stationery Office, 1997), p. 28.

[4]Jeremy Black, *The Politics of Britain, 1688–1800* (Manchester: Manchester University Press, 1993), p. 6.

[5]E. J. Hobsbawm, *Industry and Empire* (Harmmondsworth: Penguin/Pelican, 1983), pp. 29–31.

[6]See Duncan Fraser, "The Postwar Consensus: A Debate Not Long Enough?" *Parliamentary Affairs* 53, no. 2 (April 2000): 347–362.

[7]Will Hutton, *The State We're In* (London: Jonathan Cape, 1995).

[8]See Stephen Driver and Luke Martell, *New Labour Politics After Thatcherism* (Cambridge: Polity Press, 1998), pp. 32–73.

[9]Ivor Crewe, "Labor Force Changes, Working Class Decline, and the Labour Vote: Social and Electoral Trends in Postwar Britain," in Frances Fox Piven, ed., *Labor Parties in Postindustrial Societies* (New York: Oxford University Press, 1992), p. 34. See also David Marsh and R. A. W. Rhodes, "Implementing Thatcherism: Policy Change in the 1980s," *Parliamentary Affairs* 45, no. 1 (January 1992): 34–37.

[10]Steven Fielding, "A New Politics?" in Patrick Dunleavy et al., eds., *Developments in British Politics 6* (New York: St. Martin's Press, 2000), p. 2.

[11]National Statistics Online, Ethnicity, http://www.statistics.gov.uk/cci/nugget.asp?id=273

[12]Office of National Statistics Social Survey, *Living in Britain: Results from the 1995 General Household Survey* (London: The Stationery Office, 1997).

[13]Gail Lewis, "Black Women's Employment and the British Economy," in Winston James and Clive Harris, eds., *Inside Babylon: The Caribbean Diaspora in Britain* (London: Verso, 1993), pp. 73–96.

[14]Jill Matheson and Carol Summerfield, eds., *Social Trends 30* (London: The Stationery Office, 2000), p.88.

[15]See Philip Norton, *The British Polity,* 3rd ed. (New York: Longman, 1994), p. 59, for a useful discussion of the sources of the British constitution.

[16]Stephen Haseler, "Britain's Ancien régime," *Parliamentary Affairs* 40, no. 4 (October 1990): 415.

[17]See Philip Norton, "Parliament in Transition," in Robert Pyper and Lynton Robins, eds., *United Kingdom Governance* (New York: St. Martin's Press, 2000), pp. 82–106.

[18]S. E. Finer, *Five Constitutions* (Atlantic Highlands, N.J.: Humanities Press, 1979), p. 52.

[19]Anthony King, "Cabinet Co-ordination or Prime Ministerial Dominance? A Conflict of Three Principles of Cabinet Government," in Ian Budge and David McKay, eds., *The Developing British Political System: The 1990s,* 3rd ed. (London: Longman, 1993), p. 63.

[20]Chris Brady, "Collective Responsibility of the Cabinet: An Ethical, Constitutional or Managerial Tool?" *Parliamentary Affairs* 52, no.2 (April 1999): 214–229.

[21]Kevin Theakston, "Ministers and Civil Servants," in Pyper and Robins, eds., *United Kingdom Governance,* pp. 39–60.

[22]Simon Mohun, "Continuity and Change in State Economic Intervention," in Allan Cochrane and James Anderson, eds., *Politics in Transition* (London: Sage, 1989), p. 73.

[23]See Bhiku Parekh et al., *The Future of Multi-Ethnic Britain: The Parekh Report* (London: Profile Books, 2000), pp. 90–102.

[24]Simon Hix, "Britain, the EU and the Euro," in Dunleavy et al., *Developments in British Politics 6,* p. 48.

[25]For a useful discussion of the repercussions of the EU on British governance, see Simon Hix, "Britain, the EU and the Euro," in Dunleavy et al., *Developments in British Politics 6,* pp. 47–68.

[26]Tony Wright et al., *The British Political Process* (London: Routledge, 2000), p. 232.

[27]Samuel H. Beer, *The British Political System* (New York: Random House, 1973), p. 157.

[28]John Bartle, "Why Labour Won—Again," in Anthony King, ed., *Britain at the Polls, 2001* (New York: Chatham House, 2002), p. 168.

[29]For an excellent treatment of Hague's strategy, see Steven Felding, "A New Politics?" in Patrick Dunleavy et al., eds., *Developments in British Politics 6* (New York: St. Martin's Press, 2000), pp. 10–28. 13, no. 6 (July 1990): 4.

[30]Ivor Crewe, "A New Political hegemony?," in Anthony King, ed., *Britain at the Polls, 2001,* (New York: Chatham House, 2002), p.228.

[31]Ivor Crewe, "Great Britain," in I. Crewe and D. Denver, eds., *Electoral Change in Western Democracies* (London: Croom Helm, 1985), p. 107.

[32]John Bartle, "Why Labour Won—Again," in Anthony King, ed., *Britain at the Polls, 2001* (New York: Chatham House, 2002), p. 171.

[33]See Gabriel A. Almond and Sidney Verba, *The Civic Culture: Political Attitudes and Democracy in Five Nations* (Princeton, N.J.: Princeton University Press, 1963); Almond and Verba, eds., *The Civic Culture Revisited* (Boston: Little, Brown, 1980); and Samuel H. Beer, *Britain Against Itself: The Political Contradictions of Collectivism* (New York: Norton, 1982), Beer, *Britain Against Itself,* pp. 110–114.

[34]Ivor Crewe, "The Thatcher Legacy," in Anthony King et al., eds., *Britain at the Polls 1992,* ed. Anthony King, et al. (Chatham, N.J.: Chatham House, 1993), 18.

[35]Benedict Anderson, *Imagined Communities,* rev. ed. (London and New York: Verso, 1991).

[36]Bhiku Parekh et al., *The Future of Multi-Ethnic Britain: The Parekh Report* (London: Profile Books, 2000), p.10.

[37]For an excellent treatment of the complex experiences of British Muslims, see: Philip Lewis, *Islamic Britain* (London and New York: I.B. Tauris Publishers, 2002).

[38]For a detailed account of the efforts by Labour, as well as the Conservatives and Liberal Democrats, to attract women voters, see Joni Lovenduski, "Gender Politics: A Breakthrough for Women?" *Parliamentary Affairs* 50, no. 4 (1997): 708-719.

[39]See John Bartle, "Why Labour Won—Again," in Anthony King, ed., *Britain at the Polls, 2001* (New York: Chatham House, 2002), pp. 168–169.

[40]For an excellent discussion of social movements and protest from which this account of anticapitalist and environmental mobilization was drawn, see Helen Margetts, "Political Participation and Protest," in Dunleavy et al., *Developments in British Politics 6,* pp. 185–202.

[41]Stephen Haseler, "Britain's Ancien Régime," *Parliamentary Affairs* 40, no. 4 (October 1990): 418.

[42]Bhiku Parekh et al., *The Future of Multi-Ethnic Britain: The Parekh Report* (London: Profile Books, 2000), p. 38.

[43]Organisation for Economic Co-Operation and Development, *OECD Economic Surveys 2001–2002: United Kingdom,* (Paris: OECD: 2002).

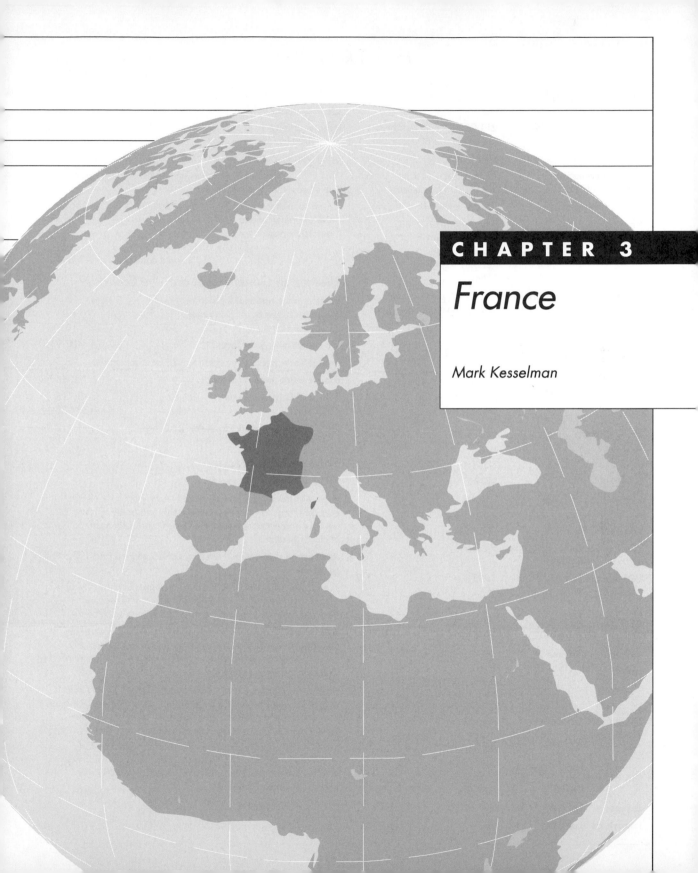

CHAPTER 3

France

Mark Kesselman

French Republic

Land and People

Capital	Paris
Total area (square miles)	211,208 (Slightly less than twice the size of Colorado)
Population	60.7 million

Annual population growth rate (%)	1975–2000	0.5
	2000–2015 (projected)	0.3

Urban population (%)	75.4

Ethnic composition* (%)	French-born	91
	Other European	3
	North African (mostly Algerian)	4
	Other	2

*French law prohibits gathering statistics in public opinion polls and census surveys on ethnic or racial identity, so the figures provided are rough estimates.

Major language(s)	French

Religious affiliation (%)	Roman Catholic	83–88
	Protestant	2
	Jewish	1
	Muslim	5–10
	Unaffiliated	4

Economy

Domestic currency	Euro US$1: (US $1.15)	
Total GDP (US$)	1.29 trillion	
GDP per capita (US$)	21,848	
Total GDP at purchasing power parity (US$)	1.43 trillion	
GDP per capita at purchasing power parity (US$)	24,223	

GDP annual growth rate (%)	1997	1.9
	2000	3.1
	2001	2.0

GDP per capita average annual growth rate (%)	1975–2000	1.7
	1990–2000	1.3

Inequality in income or consumption (1995) (%)	Share of poorest 10%	2.8
	Share of poorest 20%	7.2
	Share of richest 20%	40.2
	Share of richest 10%	25.1
	Gini Index (1995)	32.5

Structure of production (% of GDP)	Agriculture	2.9
	Industry	26.1
	Services	70.9

Labor force distribution (% of total)	Agriculture	4
	Industry	25
	Services	71

Exports as % of GDP	29
Imports as % of GDP	27

Society

Life expectancy at birth	78.6
Infant mortality per 1000 live births	4
Adult literacy (%)	99*

*The OECD estimates that France has a functional illiteracy rate of about 17 percent.

Access to information and communications (per 1000 population)	Telephone lines	579
	Mobile phones	493
	Radios	950
	Televisions	628
	Personal computers	304

Women in Government and the Economy

Women in the national legislature		
Lower house or single house (%)		12.1
Upper house (%)		10.9
Women at ministerial level (%)		37.9
Female economic activity rate (age 15 and above) (%)		48.5
Female labor force (% of total)		45
Estimated Earned Income (PPP US$)	Female	18,715
	Male	30,022
2002 Human Development Index Ranking (out of 173 countries)		12

Political Organization

Political System Unitary republic.

Regime History Semipresidential system; popularly elected president, popularly elected parliament, and prime minister and government appointed by president and responsible to National Assembly.

Administrative Structure Unitary, with 22 regions and 100 departments.

Executive Dual executive: president (seven-year term); PM appointed by president, generally leader of majority coalition in National Assembly, and responsible to National Assembly.

Legislature Bicameral. Senate (upper house) has power to delay legislation passed by lower house. National Assembly (lower house) can pass legislation and force government to resign by passing a censure motion.

Judiciary A nine-member independent Constitutional Council named for nonrenewable nine-year terms; president of republic names three members, president of each house of parliament names three. They exercise right of judicial review.

Party System Multiparty. Principal parties: Socialist Party (PS); Rally for the Republic (RPR), Union for French Democracy (UDF); minor parties: National Front (FN), Communist Party (PCF), and Green Party.

Section ① The Making of the Modern French State

Politics in Action

As France's Christmas season began to move into high gear in late November 2002, a looming crisis cast a pall over the approaching festivities. French truckers, who haul the bulk of freight vital to sustaining the French economy, called a strike to press for higher wages. Truckers who own their own rigs complained that their business was being undermined by foreign competition and lower-paid truckers from eastern Europe. To press their claims, they set up roadblocks throughout France, despite threats from the government that truckers mounting such blockades would be arrested and fined and would have their licenses revoked.

The government hoped that forcible action would prevent a repetition of similar trucker strikes in the 1990s, when freight movements throughout France were halted, gas stations closed, and road traffic throughout Europe was disrupted when freight piled up at France's borders. There were two additional reasons that the government sought to restore normal trucking operations. First, officials from the European Union (EU), the political and economic union of European countries of which France is a leading member, warned that the French government would be subject to stiff penalties if the strikes impeded European commerce. Second, the government feared that if the truckers' strike succeeded, it would spread to other areas of the economy. In particular, unions of public sector workers in transportation, including the Paris subway, bus lines, and air traffic controllers, as well as unions of hospital, postal, electricity, and telecommunications workers, issued notices for a one-day walkout scheduled at the start of the truckers' strike. Public sector workers had different grievances from the truckers: they struck to protest government plans for benefit cuts and further privatization of public services. If the truckers' strike succeeded and public sector workers stayed home, it could signify the beginning of a more sustained period of strikes that could paralyze the country. If that happened, it would not be the first time. Strikes of this magnitude—whose impact is far greater than when a single firm or industry is shut down—are fairly frequent in France. Such far-flung strikes occurred in 1968, 1987, 1993, and, as described in Section 5, 1995.

It turned out that the actual strikes were only partially successful. Road traffic was only partially disrupted. Similarly, although most of the 4,300 flights in France were canceled for a day, normal traffic was quickly restored. Consequently, the 2002 strikes will not be included in the list of historic strike waves. But another one might well occur when you are reading this book!

Why is it useful to begin our study of French politics with a description of the 2002 strikes? What do they teach us about French politics? As for the first question, the 2002 strikes illustrate an important pattern in French politics: that politics in France consists of more than political parties competing for votes and government seeking to persuade parliament to pass legislation. Alongside institutionalized politics, there is an important tradition of protest politics in France whose origins may be dated from the French Revolution of 1789, when the French monarchy was overthrown and the First French Republic was created. Ever since then, political regimes have periodically been threatened by direct challenges.

The reasons that the 2002 strikes were only partially successful is also instructive. Four of France's six truckers' unions reached a settlement with management just before the strike deadline. Only the remaining two unions called on their members to strike. This situation of union fragmentation highlights the existence of fractures and divisions within the French body politic. It has historically been more difficult in France than many neighboring countries to negotiate national-level deals between government and private actors because private actors are weak and divided. Finally, it is doubtful that the EU's threatened sanctions played much of a direct role in ending the strikes. But they may have been indirectly important, because the French government did not want to bear the cost of sanctions and did not want to be singled out for criticism within the tightly integrated EU. The 2002 strikes thus highlight that France is no longer—if it ever was—an island isolated from its neighbors. Globalization—

and, in this case, regionalization—are an important part of the story of the 2002 strikes, and of French politics more generally in the twenty-first century.

Geographic Setting

France is among the world's favored countries, thanks to its temperate climate, large and fertile land area, relatively low population density, and high standard of living. The natural beauty of the country and its superb architecture, culture, and cuisine have made France by far the world's most popular tourist destination. How-

ever, the country is poorly endowed in natural resources. For example, France imports most of its petroleum, which prompted the government to sponsor an intensive nuclear power program since the 1950s. France must also import most minerals. In order to compete internationally, it must therefore produce high-value-added products.

With a population of 60.7 million, France is among the most populous countries in Western Europe, but its large size—210,000 square miles—means that its population density is low. An unusual feature of French national territorial boundaries is that some overseas

France

territories, such as the Caribbean islands of Guadeloupe and Martinique and the Pacific island of Réunion, are considered an integral part of the country, comparable to Alaska and Hawaii for the United States. Their inhabitants are French citizens who enjoy full civil rights and liberties; for example, like other French citizens, they elect representatives to the French legislature to represent their locality. France's gross national product (GNP) of over $1 trillion and per capita income of $24,200 are among the highest in the world. France ranked twelfth among the 174 countries of the world in the 2002 UNDP Human Development Index, a leading measure of the overall quality of life compiled by the United Nations.

France occupies a key position in Europe, bordering the Mediterranean Sea in the south and sharing borders with Belgium, Switzerland, and Germany on the north and east, Spain in the southwest, and Italy in the southeast. France is Britain's closest continental neighbor; the two are separated by a mere twenty-five-mile stretch of the English Channel, a distance that has shrunk since the opening in 1994 of the "Chunnel," the railroad tunnel under the English Channel that links the two countries. France has quite secure natural borders of mountains and seas on all sides, save for the open plains of the northeast. The flat, open terrain separating France from Germany enabled German forces to invade France three times in the nineteenth and twentieth centuries.

France has a modern economy, and most people work in the industrial and service sectors. Nevertheless, agriculture continues to occupy a significant place in the economy and, because the country was predominantly rural until quite recently, an even stronger place in the country's collective memory. Moreover, the proportion of French who live in rural areas and small towns remains high. No other French city rivals Paris, the capital, in size and influence, and Paris, Lyons, and Marseilles are the only large cities in France.

Critical Junctures

A central feature of French history from premodern times to the present has been the centrality of the state. France was created by monarchs who for centuries laboriously knit together the diverse regions and provinces of what is present-day France—actions that

provoked periodic protest. The French have often displayed toward the state both enormous respect for its achievements and intense resentment because of its frequently high-handed intrusion into local life. Moreover, the state played the key role in structuring French political life. The pattern of vigorous state activity and popular backlash persisted until recent times. However, the increasing political and economic importance of globalization, especially the impact of French membership in the EU, the adoption of economic policies since the 1980s that have reduced state regulation, and decentralization reforms initiated in the 1980s have jostled the French state's preeminence. Until the 1990s, for better or worse, political attention and energies were exclusively focused on Paris, the national capital and seat of the admired and feared ministries that governed French life. Now, Paris must vie for preeminence with regional and local governments throughout the country, as well as Brussels, headquarters of the EU, Frankfurt, where the European Central Bank is located, London and New York, the world's financial capitals, and Strasbourg, home of the European Parliament.

Creating Modern France

For five centuries at the beginning of the modern era, the area that is now France was part of the Roman Empire. It was called Gaul by the Romans (the source of the term *Gallic,* sometimes used to describe the French). It took its current name from the Franks, a Germanic tribe that conquered the area in the fifth century A.D., with the breakup of the Roman Empire. The Merovingian dynasty ruled France for several centuries, during which time most of the population became Christian. It was succeeded by the Carolingian dynasty, whose most noteworthy ruler, Charlemagne, briefly brought much of West Europe under his control during the Holy Roman Empire in the ninth century. Following Charlemagne's death in 814, the empire disintegrated.

During the next two centuries, a succession of powerful French monarchs sought to overcome the fierce resistance of powerful provincial rulers and groups in Burgundy, Brittany, and other regions. France was nearly overrun by the English during the Hundred Years' War (1337–1453). Joan of Arc, a peasant, eventually led French forces to victory over the invading English army. Along with Charlemagne and a handful of other historic figures, she remains a symbol of intense national pride.

France flourished during the next several centuries, especially after Henri IV (who ruled from 1589 to 1610) ended religious wars between Catholics and Huguenots (Protestants) in 1598 by issuing the Edict of Nantes. The edict granted Protestants limited religious toleration. In the sixteenth century, France and England competed in acquiring colonial domination over North America. The rivalry between the two eventually ended with France's defeat. By signing the Treaty of Paris in 1763, France accepted British domination in North America and India. (At a later period, France engaged in further colonial conquests in Africa, Asia, and the Caribbean.)

The seventeenth and early eighteenth centuries were the high point of French economic, military, and cultural influence. France was the most affluent and powerful country in Europe. It was also the artistic and scientific capital of Europe and home of the Enlightenment in the eighteenth century, the philosophical movement that emphasized the importance of using scientific reason to understand and change the world.

The Ancien Régime

French political life was shaped for centuries by the attempt of French monarchs to undermine local loyalties and foster uniform rules throughout the country. A turning point came when King Louis XIV (1643–1715) sponsored the creation of a relatively efficient state bureaucracy, separate from the Crown's personal domain and the feudal aristocracy. France was a pioneer in developing the absolutist state, which has shaped French development ever since.

But the modernizing, absolutist state created by Louis XIV and his successors coexisted with an intricate and burdensome system of feudal privileges that peasants and other common people increasingly resented. Another target of popular discontent was the Catholic Church, a large landowner, tax collector, and ally of the feudal authorities. This complex patchwork of institutions was later called the *ancien régime,* or old regime.

For most of the period from the mid-seventeenth to the mid-eighteenth century, France was at war with its

Critical Junctures in Modern French Political Development
Until 1789   *Ancien régime* (Bourbon monarchy)
1789–1799   Revolutionary regimes
Constituent Assembly, 1789–1791 (Declaration of Rights of Man, Aug. 26, 1789)
Legislative, 1791
Convention, 1792–1795: Monarchy abolished and First Republic established, 1792
Directory, 1795–1799
1800–1814   Consultat and First Empire (Napoleon Bonaparte)
1814–1830   Restoration
1830–1848   July Monarchy
1848–1851   Second Republic
1852–1870   Second Empire (Louis Napoleon)
1871   Paris Commune
1871–1940   Third Republic
1940–1944   Vichy regime
1946–1958   Fourth Republic
1958–Present   Fifth Republic

neighbors. As historian Simon Schama notes, "No other European power attempted to support both a major continental army and a transcontinental navy at the same time."[1] France was the most powerful nation in Europe in the seventeenth century. But in the eighteenth century, Britain began to challenge France's preeminence, thanks to the economic advantages that Britain reaped from the Agricultural and Industrial Revolutions. France could not generate the resources to compete with an increasingly productive England. When Louis XVI tried to raise taxes, the bulk of which fell on the common people, the reaction this provoked sealed the fate of the French monarchy.

The Two Faces of the French Revolution, 1789–1815

An angry crowd burst through the gates of Paris's Bastille prison on July 14, 1789, and freed the prisoners, launching the French Revolution. A succession of revolutionary regimes followed in rapid succession, including the Constituent Assembly (which issued the famous Declaration of the Rights of Man and the Citizen), the Legislative Assembly, the Convention, and the Directory. The most important changes included the abolition of the French monarchy, the abolition of the entire *ancien régime* of nobility and feudal privileges, and the proclamation of the First Republic in 1792. These momentous events marked the beginning of a new era in French and world history.

France was the first European nation in which a **revolution** abolished the monarchy and established a **republic** based on the belief that all citizens, regardless of social background, were equal before the law. The French Revolution also involved a revolution in people's thinking. Historian Lynn Hunt observes, "The chief accomplishment of the French Revolution was the institution of a dramatically new political culture. . . . The French Revolution may be said to represent the transition to political and social modernity, the first occasion when the people entered upon the historical stage to remake the political community."[2]

The revolution was at the same time a *national* revolution, which affirmed the people's right to choose their own political regime; an *international* revolution, which inspired national uprisings elsewhere in Europe and sought to expand French revolutionary values internationally (often through military means); a *liberal* revolution, which championed the value of individual liberty in the political and economic spheres; and a *democratic* revolution, which proclaimed that a nation's identity and the legitimacy of its government depend on all citizens having the right to participate in making key political decisions. These provocative ideas have since been diffused on a global level.

The revolution was not without flaws. At the same time that the revolutionary regime was proclaiming the values of liberty, equality, and fraternity, it was brutal toward opponents. (At the extreme, during the Reign of Terror, the Revolution guillotined those found guilty by revolutionary tribunals.) Historian Joan Landes has analyzed how, despite some reforms responsive to women's demands (for example, short-lived divorce legislation), the revolutionary ferment was quite hostile to women: "The [First] Republic was constructed against women, not just without them, and nineteenth-century Republicans did not actively counteract this masculinist heritage of republicanism."[3]

In other ways, too, the revolution left a complex legacy. Alexis de Tocqueville, a French aristocrat and writer in the nineteenth century, brilliantly analyzed how the French Revolution both produced a rupture with the *ancien régime* and shared the goal pursued by French monarchs of strengthening state institutions. In particular, many of the centralizing institutions created by Napoleon Bonaparte, the popular general who seized power and proclaimed himself emperor in 1802, remain to this day. Napoleon established the system by which state-appointed officials called **prefects** administer localities. And he promulgated the Napoleonic Code of Law, an elaborate legal framework.

Ever since the Revolution, French politics has often revolved around the question of how to reconcile state autonomy—the state's independence from pressure coming from groups within society—with democratic participation and decision making. The French state has traditionally intervened extensively to regulate important as well as quite trivial areas of social life. While citizens have often sought state help, they also resent its heavy hand and periodically take to the streets in opposition. The result has been extensive political instability.

Many Regimes, Slow Industrialization: 1815–1940

France spent much of the nineteenth and twentieth centuries digesting and debating the legacy of the Revolution. The succession of regimes and revolutions for more than a century after 1814 can be interpreted as varied attempts to combine state autonomy and direction with democratic participation and decision making. After Napoleon's removal from power in 1815, there were frequent uprisings, revolutions, and regime changes. The monarchy was restored to power in 1814–1815 (hence the name, the Restoration, to refer to this change), but it was overthrown in a popular uprising in 1830, and a distant royal cousin, Louis Philippe, was installed as king. (His regime is known as the July Monarchy.) In 1848, another revolution produced yet another regime: the short-lived Second Republic. Louis Napoleon, the nephew of Napoleon Bonaparte, overthrew the republic and proclaimed himself emperor of the Second Empire in 1852. When France lost the Franco-Prussian War of 1870–1871, the Second Empire was swept away by a revolutionary upheaval that produced the Paris Commune in 1871, a brief experiment in worker-governed democracy. The Commune was violently crushed after a few months, to be succeeded by the Third Republic, created in 1871 under the shadow of military defeat and civil war.

Although the Third Republic was born from France's military defeat, and it never commanded widespread support, it turned out to be France's most durable modern regime, lasting until 1940. (The current regime, the Fifth Republic, created in 1958, is next in longevity.) The Third Republic survived the terrible ordeal of World War I and held firm against extremist forces on the right during the 1920s and 1930s, when republics were crumbling in Germany, Italy, and Spain. However, when France was defeated by Germany in World War II, in part a result of the Third Republic's inability to mount an effective military challenge to the Nazi forces, the republic was abolished.

The succession of regime changes in the nineteenth and twentieth centuries highlights the existence of sharp cleavages and the absence of political institutions capable of regulating conflict. In sharp contrast with the dizzying pace at which regimes came and went, the rate of economic change in France during this period was quite gradual. Compared to Germany, its dynamic neighbor to the northeast, France chose economic stability over modernization.

There have been endless attempts to explain why France did not become an industrial leader in the nineteenth century. Although it began the century as the world's second most important economic power, fairly close to Britain in terms of economic output, by 1900 France trailed the United States, Great Britain, and Germany in industrial development. A large peasantry acted as a brake on industrialization, as did the fact that France is poorly endowed with key natural resources. Historians also point to the relatively underdeveloped entrepreneurial spirit in France. Within the ranks of the middle class, professionals, administrators, and shopkeepers outnumbered industrial entrepreneurs.

Another factor inhibiting industrial development was the slow growth of the French population. In the middle of the nineteenth century, France was the second most populous nation in Europe (after Russia).

However, whereas the British population more than tripled in the nineteenth century and the number of Germans more than doubled, France's population increased by less than one-half. France had 15 percent of Europe's population in 1800 but only 8 percent in 1950.[4] Slow population growth reduced the demand for goods, and business firms had less incentive to invest and increase productivity.

More important than technical or demographic factors was the role of the state. In Britain, the government removed restrictions on the free operation of market forces, and in Prussia (later Germany), the powerful Chancellor Otto von Bismarck imposed industrialization from above. By contrast, the French state aimed to "maintain an equilibrium among industry, commerce, and agriculture and attempted to insulate France from the distress and upheaval that had struck other nations bent upon rapid economic advance."[5] France retained some of the highest tariff barriers in Western Europe in the nineteenth and early twentieth centuries. These **protectionist policies** were designed to shield small producers—farmers, manufacturers, and artisans—from foreign competition.

Yet the state did not simply oppose economic modernization. In a tradition dating back to Colbert, the finance minister of Louis XIV who directed the creation of the French merchant marine, the state sponsored a number of large-scale economic projects. For example, in the 1860s under Louis Napoleon, the state organized an integrated national rail network, encouraged the formation of the Crédit Mobilier, an investment bank to finance railroad development, and guaranteed interest rates on the bonds sold to underwrite railroad construction.

On balance, however, through much of the nineteenth century and well into the twentieth, the state chose to favor social stability over economic modernization. What eventually reversed this orientation was France's humiliating defeat by Germany in 1940.

Vichy France (1940–1944) and the Fourth Republic (1946–1958)

World War II was one of the bleakest periods in French history. When France was overrun by Germany in 1940, Marshal Pétain, an aged military hero, took the lead in destroying the Third Republic. He signed an armistice with the Nazi regime that divided France in two. The north was under direct German occupation; the south was controlled by Pétain's puppet regime, whose capital was at Vichy. The Vichy government collaborated with the Nazi occupation by providing workers and supplies for the German war machine. It had the dubious distinction of being the only government in Western Europe not directly under German occupation that delivered Jews to the Nazis. About 76,000 Jews, including 12,000 children, were sent to Nazi death camps.

Although the vast majority of French quietly accepted France's defeat, a small resistance movement developed. Charles de Gaulle, a prominent general in the Third Republic, defiantly proclaimed the need for armed opposition. He assumed leadership over communist, socialist, and progressive Catholic opposition forces and consolidated them into what became known as the Resistance. Although France actually contributed quite little to the Allied victory, de Gaulle enabled France to gain acceptance as a member of the victorious coalition.

In 1945, following the Nazi defeat, de Gaulle sought to sponsor a regime that would avoid the errors that in his view had weakened France and contributed to its moral decline and defeat. He believed that the institutional design of the Third Republic, in which the executive was completely dependent on parliament, blurred the responsibility for governing and prevented forceful leadership. He proposed creating a regime in which the government was independent and powerful.

De Gaulle failed at first. Having just overthrown the **authoritarian** Vichy regime, French citizens opposed designing a new republic that included a strong executive. When De Gaulle could not persuade political leaders to support a strong executive, he abruptly resigned as leader and opposed the newly created Fourth Republic, on the grounds that it resembled the Third Republic too closely.

The Fourth Republic lasted for merely a dozen years (1946–1958). It embodied an extreme form of parliamentary rule and weak executive. The constitution made parliament all-powerful, and parliaments used (or misused) their power to vote governments out of office on average every six months. One reason for the lack of a stable parliamentary majority was that the system of **proportional representation** used to elect members

of the National Assembly, the powerful lower house, enabled many parties to gain parliamentary representation. As in the Third Republic, parliamentary fragmentation, rapid shifts in party alliances, and a lack of discipline within parties meant that governments lacked the cohesion and authority to make tough decisions and develop long-range policies.

Despite some important achievements, notably setting France on the road to economic expansion and modernization, the Fourth Republic was often unable to act decisively. De Gaulle seized the opportunity to regain power when the Algerian independence movement challenged French domination of its key North African colony. By threatening to lead a military rebellion against the republic, de Gaulle blackmailed parliament into supporting his return to power and authorizing him to propose a new constitutional framework. The constitution of the Fifth Republic, drafted under his direction, provided for a vastly strengthened executive and weakened parliament.

The Fifth Republic (1958 to the Present)

The contrast between the Fourth and Fifth republics provides a textbook example of how institutions matter. The Fourth Republic could be described, unkindly but accurately, as an example of all talk and no action: while parliament endlessly debated and voted to make and unmake governments, political leaders failed to address the nation's pressing problems. In sharp contrast, the Fifth Republic enabled leaders to act decisively but did not provide mechanisms to hold them accountable to parliament or public opinion.

Although de Gaulle became the first president of the Fifth Republic in the unsavory circumstances of a possible military intervention, he commanded wide popular support because of his historic position as Resistance hero and was able to persuade the French to support a regime in which democratic participation was strictly limited. De Gaulle's high-handed governing style and the centralized institutions of the Fifth Republic eventually provoked widespread opposition. The most dramatic example was in May 1968, when students and workers engaged in the largest general strike in West European history. For weeks, workers and students occupied factories, offices, and universities, and the regime's survival hung in the balance.

Although de Gaulle temporarily regained control of the situation, he was discredited and resigned from office the following year.

The Fifth Republic was again severely tested in 1981. Until then, the same **conservative** forces that had gained power in 1958 won election after election. In 1981, Socialist Party candidate François Mitterrand was elected president, and in the parliamentary elections that followed, his allies swamped the conservative coalition. Despite fears that the Fifth Republic would not be able to survive a **socialist** government, the institutions of the Fifth Republic proved highly successful at accommodating political alternation.

President Mitterrand's government sponsored one of the most ambitious reform agendas in modern French history, including changes that strengthened the autonomy of the judiciary, the media, and local governments. The centerpiece was the **nationalization** of many of France's largest industrial firms and banks. However, by seeking to extend the sphere of public control of the economy, France was swimming against the international economic and political tide. During the 1980s, the predominant tendency elsewhere in the industrialized world was to strengthen private market forces

rather than extend public control. When France experienced an economic and financial crisis in 1983–1984, the government reversed course. Since then, although frequent changes in the governing coalition have occurred, governments of left and right alike have pursued market-friendly policies.

Does the convergence between the major political parties of center-left and center-right mean the end of major political conflict and the growth of a broad consensus in France? Far from it, as the 2002 presidential elections demonstrated.

The Le Pen Bombshell

Two rounds of elections are usually required to select a French president. If no candidate at the first round gains an absolute majority (the typical case), a runoff election is held between the two front-runners.

When the presidential election campaign began in 2002, it was universally assumed that the two candidates who would face off in the decisive runoff election would be the workhorses of mainstream French politics: Lionel Jospin, Socialist prime minister, and Jacques Chirac, incumbent president and candidate of the center-right. These perennial opponents had competed in the runoff in the previous presidential election, held in 1995, that resulted in Chirac's election as president. Virtually everyone assumed that the first ballot in 2002, when a record sixteen candidates competed, was a mere formality whose purpose was to narrow the field to Chirac and Jospin. A best-selling book published in early 2002, *The Duel,* whose cover featured a photo of Jospin and Chirac in classic dueling position, said it all.

Given that the real action would not occur until the second ballot, it was understandable why the first-ballot campaign was lackluster. A day before the first ballot, a *New York Times* reporter explained why voters were so bored: "Part of the problem, experts say, is that there is little suspense."[6]

However, soon after the polls closed on April 21, apathy turned to stupefaction as the outcome produced the greatest surprise in the nearly fifty-year history of the French Fifth Republic. Although Chirac came in first, according to script, Jospin was nudged out for second place by Jean-Marie Le Pen, a far-right demagogue whose targets include Muslim immigrants, Jews, and mainstream politicians (see "Leaders: Jean-Marie Le

"What!?? The president's a Socialist and the Eiffel Tower is still standing!??" "Incredible!" *Source:* Courtesy Plantu, from *Le Monde,* May 1981.

Leaders: Jean-Marie Le Pen

Born in Brittany in 1928, the son of a fishing boat owner-fisherman, Jean-Marie Le Pen became politically active in a far-right organization as early as 1947. He quickly displayed a knack for arousing crowds by his charismatic presence and fiery oratory. He became a paratrooper in 1953 and fought briefly in France's last-ditch (and unsuccessful) effort to retain its empire in Indochina. When he returned to France, Le Pen joined a right-wing populist political movement led by Pierre Poujade and in 1956, at the age of twenty-seven, was elected to the National Assembly, the youngest deputy in France. He volunteered to fight in the French army during the Suez expedition in 1956 and also served in Algeria, when the French army was engaged in a brutal war with the Algerian independence movement. In 2002, several Algerians publicly testified that Le Pen had tortured them at this time (he had admitted this earlier, in a published interview).

In 1960, Le Pen helped found a small right-wing political movement whose aim was to prevent Algeria from gaining independence. When this effort failed, he engaged in a variety of unsuccessful political ventures. For example, in the early 1970s, he created a neofascist movement called New Order (Ordre nouveau) and later helped create the National Front (FN). Assisted by former members of the French branch of the Nazi SS, he tried to consolidate the many small groups on the far right. For years, the movement was stalled.

The FN scored its first big victory in the 1983 municipal elections at Dreux, a small city in Normandy, where a member of the party was elected mayor on an anti-immigrant platform. Le Pen, head of the FN, began to appear on television talk shows, his blunt, crude humor contrasting dramatically with the approach of most other politicians.

The FN scored a major breakthrough in the 1984 European elections, where the party received 11 percent of the vote. The system of proportional elections used in the election facilitated voters choosing smaller parties like the FN. Commentators attributed the FN's performance to citizens on the far right who blamed center-right parties for allowing the Socialist-Communist coalition to gain election in 1981.

Following 1984, Le Pen was much more successful in building a personal following than in creating an effective party organization. In what later proved to be a preview of the 2002 elections, he received an amazingly high 14.5 percent of vote in the 1988 presidential elections, coming in third behind incumbent president François Mitterrand and challenger Jacques Chirac. Le Pen's electorate, which had at first been based on the far right and among lower-middle-class shopkeepers, began to expand to working-class and popular elements who felt betrayed by the Socialist government's right turn in the mid-1980s.

Le Pen also captured wide media attention by his flamboyant use of inflammatory phrases—at the same time that he was convicted in French courts for defending war crimes, as well as for provoking racial discrimination and violence. In the 1980s, Le Pen also began to oppose the EU, economic liberalism, and globalization because, he claimed, they damaged France's economic well-being and national identity. He coupled these themes with a denunciation of policies that permitted the arrival of large numbers of Muslim (often Arab) immigrants. The result, he charged, was to jeopardize the Catholic heritage of white France. Thus, Le Pen proved masterful in constructing a single response—expel immigrants—to multiple insecurities, consisting of unemployment, crime, restructuring of commerce that eliminated many small retail stores, and industrial restructuring that resulted in the layoffs of many manual workers.

Le Pen slightly improved his performance in the 1995 presidential elections and appeared headed for further success. However, he suffered a severe setback in 1999 when he was indicted on a charge of assaulting a politician and prohibited from running for political office for several years. One of his closest associates bolted the FN to form a rival organization, taking with him many of the FN's top leaders. The FN's support declined significantly to about 9 percent in the 1999 European elections. The aging Le Pen—seventy-three years old during the 2002 presidential elections—appeared headed for forced retirement. However, his dramatic breakthrough in 2002 resulted from skillfully capitalizing on citizens' apathy and disgust with the prevailing political class, as well as the media's nonstop coverage of France's rising crime rate in early 2002. It was a heaven-sent opportunity for Le Pen to claim that he was the only candidate who advocated tough measures to restore law and order.

Le Pen has shifted from an exclusive appeal to anti-immigrant and antisemitic sentiment toward right-wing libertarian economic and social populism. Among his specific proposals were eliminating the income tax, France's withdrawal from the EU, protectionism, outlawing abortion, and restricting immigrants' access to social benefits, jobs, and citizenship. In a statement following his first-round victory in 2002, he declared, "I'm a man of the people, I'll always be on the side of those who suffer, because I myself have known cold, hunger, and poverty." Le Pen asked for support of "miners, metalworkers, and workers from industries ruined by EU-style globalization, as well as of farmers doomed to a miserable retirement and victims of insecurity [that is, crime]." The fact that so many voters answered his call invites analysis of weaknesses in French democracy.

Pen"). The fact that Le Pen outpolled Jospin by under 1 percent (17.0 percent to Jospin's 16.1 percent) was less important than that the runoff would pit Le Pen against Chirac. Commentators used terms like *bombshell* and *earthquake* to describe the first-ballot results in France. It was literally unthinkable that a politician regarded by a large majority of the French (and citizens from around the world) as a barely disguised racist would be one of only two candidates competing in the runoff election.

Le Monde, France's influential newspaper, spoke for the vast majority of French when it began its front-page editorial the day after the election: "France is wounded."[7] A cartoon in *Le Monde* graphically depicted Le Pen's success as France's equivalent of the September 11, 2001, attack against the United States.

Immediately after the first ballot results were announced, massive anti–Le Pen marches and demonstrations were organized throughout France in preparation for the runoff election. The high point occurred on May 1, a holiday traditionally commemorating workers' struggles, when about 1.5 million people participated in demonstrations in Paris and other cities. *Le Monde* observed that "May 1, 2002 will go down in history as one of the largest popular demonstrations that the capital has ever experienced."[8] A poll reported that one young French person in two participated in a demonstration between the two ballots.[9]

At the runoff ballot on May 5, Chirac outpolled Le Pen by 82 to 18 percent, the most lopsided vote in the history of the Fifth Republic.[10] *Le Monde*'s editor announced in the newspaper on May 7 that "the insult to France from Jean-Marie Le Pen's first round result . . . has been washed clean by the massive vote in favor of Jacques Chirac." Nevertheless, many questioned whether Chirac's overwhelming second-round victory offset the damage from Le Pen's first-ballot performance.

France in the Euro Era

France's close involvement in the EU, highlighted by the adoption of the euro, represents an important shift in the country's relationship to the world beyond French borders. The euro symbolizes the powerful way that France's fate is now intensely intertwined with that of the EU. Few national symbols are as important as a country's currency. In 2002, euro notes replaced national currencies in most member states of the EU.

Along with Germany and several smaller European countries, France helped form the EU to promote economic growth and political stability. Has French membership achieved that aim? The answer is mixed. France is among the world's economic success stories, but its economic performance can hardly be qualified as a complete success. Our major focus in this book is on political developments. On that score, the news may

Le Monde's cartoonist compares Le Pen's attack on Chirac and Jospin to the bombing of the twin towers of the World Trade Center. *Source:* Plantu, *Le Monde,* April 23, 2001, p 1.

be even less promising. A cluster of recent developments suggests intense strains within French politics.

Consider the rapid-fire series of electoral shifts that have occurred. From 1981 to 2002, there were six parliamentary elections in France. In every single one, control shifted from the incumbent ruling coalition to the opposition. Voters thus seized the opportunity to demonstrate displeasure with the "ins"—although it does not take them long to register displeasure with the new ruling coalition. A second ingredient is that countless political scandals have tarnished the reputation of many leading politicians, including party leaders, cabinet ministers, and the two most recent presidents (Mitterrand, president from 1981 to 1995, and Chirac, president since 1995). Third, many French citizens reject the major governing parties of both left and right, preferring to abstain or support fringe parties. Particularly troubling in the 2002 presidential elections was that many citizens chose to express their discontent by supporting Le Pen's thinly veiled racist appeal. Fourth, underlying these changes is an increasingly severe cleavage in France between those who lack the resources to participate fully in French political, social, and economic life and those who have benefited from France's participation in the globalized political economy.

Following the terrorist attacks on the United States of September 11, 2001, France has been even more closely connected to the complex conflicts of global politics. Zacarias Moussaoui, a French citizen, was tried in the United States in 2002 on charges that he helped plan the September 11 attack. In late 2001, Richard Reid, a British citizen, was subdued by passengers and crew members during a flight from Paris to Miami when he attempted to ignite explosives in his shoe. In 2003, he was convicted and sentenced to life imprisonment. In 2003, French antiterrorist police detained eighteen Algerians and Pakistanis in the Paris area on charges that they were accomplices of Reid as well as members of a network of Islamic militants linked to al Qaeda. In 2002, fourteen French technicians working in Pakistan were murdered. In a separate incident that year, a French oil tanker near Yemen was damaged by an explosive charge. France is therefore deeply involved in the post–September 11 realignments occurring in the world.

Themes and Implications

We have identified some key moments in French history. We can gain greater clarity on French politics by highlighting the distinctive ways that France has addressed the four key themes that frame our country analyses of comparative politics.

Historical Junctures and Political Themes

France in a Globalized World.   France's relationship to the rest of Europe and other regions of the world, particularly Asia and Africa, has heavily shaped state formation. For over a century following Napoleon's defeat in 1815, the country displayed an inward, isolationist orientation. Nevertheless, France participated aggressively in the new imperialism of the late nineteenth century, creating an empire in Southeast Asia, North and sub-Saharan Africa, the Caribbean, and the Pacific. For close to a century, France exploited the resources of its colonies. The arrangement shielded France from competing in the global economy, although it contributed to France's relatively slow pace of technological and industrial development.

France's tortured relationship with Germany—the two countries fought each other in three devastating wars in less than a century—has weighed heavily on state development. The fact that the two countries developed cordial relations after World War II, in part thanks to the EU and the expansion of the European and world economy, has provided France with a vastly increased measure of security.

No longer in the first rank militarily, France nevertheless remains an important player on the world stage. For example, it is a major nuclear power and among the world's leading arms exporters. It has been an important participant in the Western alliance led by the United States. But in contrast to Britain and Germany, for example, France has often been a gadfly to the United States. For example, it publicly opposed U.S. plans to launch military action in Afghanistan and Iraq in the aftermath of the September 11 attacks. France's wary attitude toward the United States has been evident periodically throughout the postwar period, such as when President de Gaulle publicly criticized U.S. military action in Vietnam in the 1960s.

The French state has been a powerful, capable instrument helping the country adapt to the challenges posed by global economic competition. In recent decades, the state has skillfully promoted internationally acclaimed high-tech industrial projects, including high-speed rail travel (the TGV), leadership in the European consortium that developed an efficient wide-bodied airplane (the Airbus), an electronic telephone directory and data bank (the Minitel), and relatively safe and cheap nuclear power plants. Yet France's **statist** tradition is under siege as a result of increased international economic integration and competition, highlighted by French participation in the EU, as well as ideological shifts and citizens' demands for more autonomy.

Governing the Economy.   Following World War II, the French pioneered in developing methods to steer and strengthen the economy. As a result of planning, state loans and subsidies to private business, and crash programs to develop key economic sectors (e.g., the steel industry), the French economy soared. However, state direction has created problems in the current era, when rapidly changing technology and economic globalization have put a premium on flexibility.

The Democratic Idea.   France has had a complex relationship to the democratic idea: its deeply rooted statist tradition is quite hostile to democratic participation and decision making, yet it has been deeply attached to two divergent democratic currents. The first dates back to eighteenth-century philosopher Jean-Jacques Rousseau. The theory of direct democracy that Rousseau inspired claims that citizens should participate directly in political decisions rather than merely choose leaders who monopolize political power.

A second powerful democratic current in French political culture, fearful that direct democracy can culminate in demagogic leadership, stresses the value of representative democracy. Many opponents of de Gaulle criticized him for violating the representative democratic tradition and furthering *le pouvoir personnel* (personal power). The parliamentary tradition opposes anything that smacks of direct democracy.

France's democratic theory and institutions face important challenges. One stems from French participation in the EU, which exhibits what has been dubbed a "democratic deficit," that is, too much administrative direction and too little democratic participation and representation. Another challenge involves reconciling state autonomy and democratic participation within France. The democratic deficit that underlies the EU may also be said to characterize France's own political system.

Politics of Collective Identity.   French national identity has always been closely linked to state formation. The Revolution championed the idea that anyone who accepted republican values could become French. The French approach to citizenship and national identity encourages immigrants to become French—as long as they accept France's dominant cultural and political values. Such an approach stresses that what binds people are shared political values rather than common racial or ethnic (i.e., inherited) characteristics.

The traditional French model of assimilation that helped produce a coherent pattern of French national identity has been challenged recently by conflicts fueled by ethnic differences and globalization. After World War II, a large wave of immigrants from North Africa contributed to French economic reconstruction and industrialization. Although immigration was restricted following the economic slowdown in the 1970s, the issue of immigrants and their status in French society erupted into the political arena beginning in the 1980s. Le Pen's political party, the National Front, gained support by blaming many of France's problems, especially unemployment, urban decay, and crime, on immigrants and their children.

French national identity is also jostled by French participation in the EU and, more broadly, the broadening of France's geographic and cultural horizons as a result of globalization. Decisions affecting French citizens are increasingly made outside France. The French are especially fearful that the United States is seeking to dominate the world and impose its political, economic, and cultural preferences on others. Following the terrorist attacks of September 11, 2001, the French expressed sympathy and solidarity with the United States. But this quickly changed when many French came to believe that the United States sought to use the attacks to strengthen its international dominance by pressuring allies like France to support U.S. military action in Afghanistan and Iraq. In 2003, France threatened to veto a possible UN Security Council resolution authorizing a U.S.-British invasion of Iraq.

At the same time, France seeks to participate in decisions made outside its borders. Along with Britain and Germany, France is one of the "big three" of the EU and a world-class economic competitor. A key issue is how effectively France confronts the challenge of closer integration in the European and world political economy.

Implications for Comparative Politics

The study of French politics offers rich lessons for students of comparative politics. France has continually tried to reshape its destiny by conscious political direction, and it provides a natural laboratory in which to test the importance of variations in institutional design. To illustrate, comparativists debate the impact of electoral procedures. Because French electoral laws (along with many other features of political institutions) have often changed in a brief period, comparativists can assess the impact of institutional variation.

At a more general level, the French have often looked to the state to achieve important economic and political goals. In countries without a statist tradition (for example, the United States and Britain), private groups rely to a greater extent on their own efforts. What can we learn from comparing the two approaches? What are the strengths and weaknesses of statism?

France also provides a fascinating case of a country seeking to combine a strong state and strong democracy. The French do not believe that a state that acts vigorously need be undemocratic. In practice, however, combining state vigor and democratic practice is no easy matter. How successful is the French attempt? What can it teach us about this issue?

As a leading participant in the EU and the global political economy, France is an excellent case of a country seeking to forge close economic and political ties with its neighbors while retaining an important measure of autonomy. What kinds of strains have been produced within France as a result of its participation in the EU and the international political economy?

A place to begin our analysis of current French politics is France's political economy, for the way that a country engages in economic management deeply influences the functioning of its political system.

Section ❷ Political Economy and Development

France is among the world's leading economic powers, and it ranks fourth highest among all countries in the size of its national production (GNP), fourth highest in world trade, and second in the volume of import and export of capital. The state has long played a key role in promoting French economic development. However, since the 1980s, when states throughout the world have taken a back seat to private market forces, France's style of vigorous state economic management has come under severe stress.

State and Economy

During the early period of industrialization in Western Europe in the eighteenth and nineteenth centuries, the French state pursued an unusual goal. In Britain, the world's first industrialized power, the state acted vigorously to create a framework of free markets. The United States copied this model. In Prussia (which merged with neighboring states to become Germany in 1871), the state sponsored a crash program of industrialization to catch up in the competition with its European neighbors. Although the French state did play a key role in promoting economic modernization—for example, it helped organize an extensive system of railroad transportation in the nineteenth century—its major goal was not economic modernization but social stability. Following the upheaval of the French Revolution, the French state generally sought to preserve the dominance of artisans, shopkeepers, and small-scale manufacturers against the aristocratic remnants of the *ancien régime* and crafts and industrial workers.

This situation could last only so long as the state was able to protect France's economy and the nation from external threat. That task became increasingly difficult in the late nineteenth and early twentieth centuries once Germany, France's eastern neighbor, achieved economic parity and developed aggressive political goals. France was severely weakened by the wars that it fought with Germany; the low point was reached when the Third Republic collapsed in 1940.

The New French Revolution

Following World War II, an important shift occurred in the French state's economic orientation. Many believed that France's poor economic performance was a key reason for its defeat and proposed making economic modernization a high priority. "After the war," economic historian Richard Kuisel observes, "what was distinctive about France was the compelling sense of relative economic backwardness. This impulse was the principal stimulus for economic renovation and set France apart from other countries."[11] Two scholars have described the postwar shift as "a new French Revolution. Although peaceful, this has been just as profound as that of 1789 because it has totally overhauled the moral foundations and social equilibrium of French society."[12]

Given its strong statist tradition, France was potentially well equipped to develop the institutional capacity to steer the economy. From guardian of the status quo, the state became sponsor of social and economic progress.

Planning. Soon after World War II, the French developed what was termed **indicative planning.** A government agency, the Planning Commission (the Commissariat général du plan), established overall national economic and social priorities for the next several years. The commission was assisted by modernization commissions composed of public and private officials that established targets for specific economic and social sectors. Perhaps more important than particular goals was that planning promoted new patterns of cooperation and fostered the belief that change was to be welcomed, a sharp contrast to the past conservative pattern.

Planning did not represent interests equally. Small businesses, trade unions, and consumers were largely ignored. The process was dominated by a close alliance between the state and dynamic producer interests, especially large, technologically advanced firms seeking to compete in world markets. Critics charged that planning was undemocratic because important decisions affecting France's future were made behind closed doors by a small group unrepresentative of France's diverse interests.

Dirigisme **Under de Gaulle.**   Although planning began in the Fourth Republic, the first steps were halting and uncertain. Vigorous leadership to overcome opposition to the attempt to modernize French capitalism was provided after 1958, when Charles de Gaulle, the most influential politician in twentieth-century French history, regained power and created the Fifth Republic. De Gaulle was a complex and controversial figure. On the one hand, he was a faithful representative of traditional France, deeply attached to the values of order and hierarchy, which earned him the enmity of the left. On the other hand, he believed that if France was to play a leading role on the world stage, shock therapy was needed to strengthen the French political economy.

De Gaulle presided over a period of state-led industrialization and growth based on indicative planning. The state developed a variety of instruments to promote economic modernization. The new relationship between the state and economy was termed *dirigiste* (directorial), highlighting the state's importance in steering the economy.

The *dirigiste* approach had the following key elements:

- Intensive efforts to coordinate economic policymaking through the planning process, legislation, and governmental direction.
- State subsidies, loans, and tax write-offs to achieve industrial concentration, specialization in new fields, and technological innovation. Until the 1970s, the state provided the bulk of capital for new investment, limited the outflow of French capital, created a host of parapublic banking institutions, and controlled private bank loans. The state provided favored sectors with cheap credit—and starved low-priority sectors and inefficient firms.
- Restructuring key sectors, including steel, machine tools, and paper products, by steering credit and pressuring medium-sized industrial firms to merge in order to create "national champions" able to compete in world markets.
- Creating and managing entire industries. Some state-created and -managed firms were in the vanguard of

technological progress throughout the world. A prime example was nuclear power. Given France's dependence on imported petroleum, the government gave high priority to developing safe and reliable nuclear energy. France became a world leader in designing, building, and operating nuclear power installations.

In sum, in the French economic model, the state was a (indeed, *the*) chief economic player.

France's Economic Miracle

During the period that one French economist dubbed "the thirty glorious years" (1945–1975), French growth rates were among the highest of any European nation and second only to that of Japan, a striking contrast with the 1930s, when the French economy declined at the rate of over 1 percent annually (see Table 1).

Economic growth produced higher living standards. The average French citizen's income nearly tripled between 1946 and 1962, resulting in a wholesale transformation of consumer patterns. For example, the proportion of homes with running water more than doubled in this period. The number of automobiles registered in France tripled between 1959 and 1973. The number of housing units built annually nearly doubled during the same period. In sum, after a century of economic stagnation, France leapfrogged into the twentieth century.

May 1968 and Beyond: Economic Crisis and Political Conflict

Political scientist Peter A. Hall identified a central dilemma in the planning process: "The reorganization of production to attain great[er] efficiency tends to intensify the social conflict that planning is also supposed to prevent."[13] Furthermore, Gaullist-sponsored economic modernization was planned in a high-handed manner that provided few cushions to reduce social dislocations and inequalities.

The most dramatic evidence of the regime's fragility occurred in a massive wave of strikes and demonstrations in May 1968 by diverse groups united in their opposition to the way that a distant state was deciding their fate with little grass-roots consultation or participation. Although the opposition movement was overcome after a few weeks, it was followed by a period of intense labor mobilization. A rapid increase in female employment beginning in the early 1970s also provoked strikes by women, who protested unequal treatment.

As a result of their militance, workers gained increased rights and benefits. Building on this success, the two largest left-wing opposition parties, the Communist Party (*Parti communiste français,* PCF) and the Socialist Party (reformed and renamed the *Parti socialiste,* PS, in 1969), forged a coalition in 1972 that advocated radical reforms, including nationalizing privately owned banks and industrial firms, increasing workers' rights in the firm, and expanding social programs.

Economic Instability

The left's fortunes were further improved because economic strains in the 1970s tarnished the reputation of the governing conservative coalition. France was badly damaged by international economic shocks in the 1970s. Despite its many nuclear power plants, the French economy remained dependent on imported oil and was squeezed when petroleum prices increased sharply in the 1970s. At the same time, developing nations such as Taiwan, South Korea, and Brazil mounted efficient new firms in basic industrial sectors like textiles, steel,

Table 1

Average Growth Rates in Gross National Product, 1958–1973	
Japan	10.4%
France	5.5
Italy	5.3
West Germany	5.0
Belgium	4.9
Netherlands	4.2
Norway	4.2
Sweden	4.1
United States	4.1
United Kingdom	3.2

Source: Reprinted by permission of the State University of New York Press, from *The Fifth Republic at Twenty* by William G. Andrews and Stanley Hoffmann (Eds). © 1981 State University of New York. All rights reserved.

Students and workers unite in a mass demonstration on the Left Bank of Paris, May 27, 1968. *Source:* AP/Wide World Photos.

and shipbuilding. Hundreds of thousands of jobs in France were eliminated in these three industries alone. The French economy was also battered when the U.S. and Japanese producers captured markets in microelectronics, bioengineering, and robotics, sectors in which French firms were hoping to gain favored positions.

French Socialism in Practice—and Conservative Aftermath

After conservative governments failed to meet the economic challenges of the 1970s, the left finally gained the chance to try. A new era began in 1981 when, after twenty-three years of conservative government, Socialist Party candidate François Mitterrand was elected president and his Socialist Party won the parliamentary elections that followed his election. Mitterrand

appointed a government composed of Socialist and Communist ministers with a mandate to revive and democratize the ailing economy, create jobs, and recapture domestic markets. The government's audacious reform agenda included:

- A hefty boost in social benefits, including increases in the minimum wage, family allowances, old-age pensions, rent subsidies, and state-mandated paid vacations (from four to five weeks each year)
- The creation of public sector employment
- An increased emphasis on industrial policy, including state assistance to develop cutting-edge industrial technologies (including biotech, telecommunications, and aerospace)
- Nationalizing a large number of private companies in the industrial and banking sectors
- Increased attention to environmental concerns

Figure 1

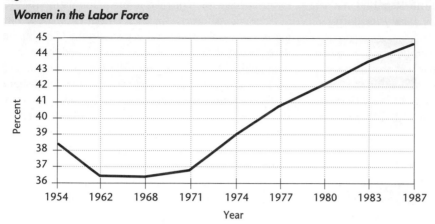

Women in the Labor Force

The expansion of women working outside the home. *Source:* INSEE, in Louis Dirn, *La Société française en tendances* (Paris: PUF, 1990), 108.

The Socialist government created a cabinet-level ministry of the environment and promised to reconsider France's heavy emphasis on nuclear energy. After declaring a moratorium on building new nuclear plants, it scaled back France's nuclear energy program but did not end the construction of new plants.

The Socialist approach was a radicalized version of the postwar *dirigiste* approach, in which the state was used to promote programs to compensate for what were regarded as market failures. Many French citizens reaped significant benefits from the Socialist program. Moreover, many of the newly nationalized firms, which were in financial difficulty when they were nationalized, were put on a firmer footing with the infusion of government subsidies. But the program failed to revive economic growth, which was sorely needed to create new jobs and generate tax revenues to finance additional government spending. There were two reasons. First, French business executives and international investors were hostile to the government's policy orientation. Rather than investing in French industry, they exported capital to safe havens abroad. Second, an international economic recession in the early 1980s came at the worst time. International economic growth would have given French industry a needed boost and might have unleashed an upward spiral of job creation and economic growth within France.

Although many of the Socialist reforms were socially progressive and eventually helped to modernize

the French economy, society, and state, the short-run result was to provoke a severe economic crisis that drove France to the brink of bankruptcy. Budget deficits soared, international investors avoided France like the plague, and French international currency reserves were rapidly exhausted. Something had to give—and fast.

The crisis cruelly demonstrated how limited was the margin of maneuver for a medium-rank power like France. Mitterrand's government was soon forced to choose between abandoning its reformist course or adopting protectionist measures to discourage foreign imports. The latter strategy involved high risks, because it would require France to pull out of EU monetary arrangements. Further, France risked international isolation because conservative governments in office at the time in Britain, Germany, Japan, and the United States—the world's other major industrialized countries—were introducing quite opposite reforms. Rather than expanding state management, these governments were sponsoring **deregulation,** tax cuts, and leaner states.

After intense soul searching in 1983, Mitterrand ordered an about-face in economic policy. France trimmed social benefits and other spending, raised taxes, deregulated financial and other markets, and reversed the policy of nationalization by embarking on a program to privatize some state-owned firms. The decision to reject radical statism—and question the state model of economic management more generally—was a turning point within the Fifth Republic and set France on a course from which it has not departed since.

France's failure to achieve autonomous, state-led development in the early 1980s has had profound ideological and policy consequences both within the country and elsewhere. First, it served to discredit France's traditional statist pattern and the possibility of nationally based radical or democratic socialism. Observing France's difficulties, socialist movements elsewhere decided to scale back their own radical goals.

Second, the indirect effect of the French failure was to propel European integration forward. French policymakers, from Mitterrand down, concluded that if France was to play an important role in the world, it could not go it alone. They turned to the EU as second best. As one scholar observes, "It was only in 1983, with the turn-around in the economic policy of the French government, that the French started . . . to become more pro-European, and started to see European integration as a way of compensating for the loss of policy autonomy."[14] Scaling back statism aligned French economic management with the process of European unification based on EU-wide (privately controlled) markets in goods, capital, and population movements.

France's Neoliberal Modernization Strategy

Whereas in the past, state administrators played a key role in organizing and running the economy, the new orientation, which Peter Hall describes as France's neoliberal modernization strategy, involved state officials' deferring to private decision makers on key economic matters. Among the elements comprising the strategy were privatization, deregulation and liberalization, and fiscal policies in conformity with EU directives.[15]

Privatization.   A key element of the "right turn" in 1983 involved reversing the process of nationalization that the Socialists had initiated in 1981. Since 1983, socialist and conservative governments alike have sold scores of public sector industrial firms, banks, and insurance companies to private investors. The state retains ownership of many public transportation, power, and communications systems, but even some of these key sectors have been privatized, and many public sector firms have been opened to private investment.

Opponents of privatization, primarily on the left of the political spectrum, and especially the Communist Party, charged that the process represented the sale of vital public assets at bargain-basement prices and that the most affluent citizens were reaping the lion's share of the benefits. In some cases, employees of firms slated for privatization have waged highly disruptive strikes, on the grounds that their hard-won gains—good wages and fringe benefits, job security, and rights to be consulted—would be endangered. Their fears were often justified. Indeed, a principal reason to privatize is often to facilitate cutting employee benefits and laying off workers.

Privatization has occurred in many countries around the world. However, the move is especially noteworthy in France because it marks such a departure from the traditionally preeminent role of the state.

Deregulation and Liberalization.   Before the shift from *dirigisme* in 1983, the state exercised close supervision over the economy. State regulations mandated technical standards; specified market share; set prices, interest rates, and terms of credit; and even decided where investments would be located. Policymakers erected tariffs to shield producers from foreign competition. The state limited employers' freedom to schedule work time and promote and fire workers. For example, employers required administrative authorization for layoffs, and workers could not be fired unless the firm provided substantial severance benefits.

Much state regulation was beneficial. Consumers benefited when the administration set high standards and rigorously enforced them. For example, the French transportation network had an enviable safety record. Workers benefited when state labor inspectors prevented arbitrary employer actions. But there was general agreement that France was drowning in a sea of red tape. What was needless regulation for one group was regarded as welcome protection by others.

Since 1983, one economic area after another has been deregulated. Deregulation has been especially sweeping in the financial sector, where the dense framework of state supervision, subsidized loans, differential interest rates, and credit rationing has been substantially eliminated. Today, market forces, not

Global Connection: *France and the European Union*

France has been a charter member and one of the most powerful states in the European Union since it was founded in 1958. (The EU was originally known as the European Economic Community.) Before World War II, France had preferred isolation to international cooperation. But three devastating wars in less than a century between France and Germany taught both countries that there was no alternative but to cooperate. The EU has proved to be the most effective mechanism for fostering closer ties between the two countries and the other member states of the organization. (The number of members has steadily increased, from the original seven to twenty-five by 2004.) Indeed, French and German support for the EU has been essential to the EU's success. The EU has gained great credit from having contributed to the vast increase in prosperity and political stability in Western Europe in the past decades. As a result of the EU's sponsorship of lower tariffs among member states, as well as other measures to liberalize trade and investment, France has developed extremely close economic relations with its West European neighbors. The EU has emerged as one of the three major economic regions in the world, along with North America and East Asia.

France has played a leading role within the EU from the beginning, although when Charles de Gaulle was president between 1958 and 1969, he did not hesitate to provoke some notable crises to prevent the organization from limiting France's freedom of action. The two most powerful leaders of the EU have both been French: Jean Monnet, the first director of the organization (he came to be known as the Father of Europe), and Jacques Delors, president of the European Commission, the administrative directorate of the EU, from 1984 to 1994.

French participation in the EU has not been costless. Many French citizens fear that France's distinctive culture and identity are somehow diluted by membership in the EU. Some EU decisions have produced painful results for France, including economic austerity and the need to alter some government policies and decisions to conform with EU regulations.

The introduction of the euro in 1999 ushered in a new and even closer phase of economic integration. It resulted from a historically unprecedented decision by France and other members of the European Monetary Union (linked to the EU) to delegate key decisions over monetary policy to the newly created, independent European Central Bank. In its first years, the euro's value declined substantially against the dollar, and an international economic recession produced slow growth throughout the EU member nations (as well as most countries of the world). However, the euro reversed its downward course in 2002, and the future outlook for the EU and its member states has improved. Will the future produce solid gains—or more economic hardship and a political backlash? Stay tuned.

---

administrative officials, determine who qualifies for loans, at what amount, and at what interest rates. In brief, the new policy stance relies heavily on market competition to achieve economic and technological modernization.

The increased freedom enjoyed by managers has enabled them to streamline the French economy and keep France internationally competitive. But French employees have paid a steep price for the rapid pace of change. Many citizens blame the major political parties, which have alternated in government, for the trend toward greater economic instability. This helps explain the increased support for fringe parties of left and right in France, a topic that we analyze in Section 4.

The End of *Dirigisme* or *Dirigiste* Disengagement?
If the French have adopted a trend of reduced state economic management, they have done so in a distinctively French manner that retains an important role for state direction. In recent years, the state has supervised the retrenchment of industries like steel and shipbuilding rather than their expansion, as occurred in the earlier period. It has steered the French economy toward integration within the EU and has shifted its efforts toward

exerting influence on EU institutions. This is *dirigisme* of a different—and less overbearing—sort, but for better or worse, statism is still alive and well in France.[16] Moreover, reduced state control does not necessarily signify increased freedom for French consumers, citizens, or workers, because it has been accompanied by increased control by the EU and transnational corporations headquartered in France or elsewhere.

Society and Economy

Welfare State

In part because of working-class pressure, exercised in the streets and through political parties, the French have enacted among the most extensive array of welfare state programs in the world. State-provided and -financed social services (the social security system, as it is called in France) go beyond even cradle to the grave: they begin before birth with free prenatal care provided to pregnant women, and extend through old age, with pensions, subsidies for home care, and low-cost health care. Mothers are entitled to six months' paid maternity leave, and, in a reform beginning in 2002, fathers receive two weeks of paid paternity leave. French families have access to excellent low-cost public day care facilities, staffed by highly qualified teachers. Families with more than one child receive a state subsidy, and the government headed by Jean-Pierre Raffarin sponsored legislation in 2003 to provide all mothers of young children with subsidies.

Public education is excellent in France, and students who pass a stiff high school graduation exam are entitled to virtually free university education. The state provides extensive public housing and rent subsidies. Workers receive a fairly ample minimum wage, five weeks of paid vacation annually, and the right to job training throughout their working lives. If they are laid off, they are entitled to job retraining and relatively ample unemployment insurance payments. The long-term unemployed receive a minimum income.

The extensive system of social provision promotes solidarity and enables most French citizens to live in dignity. However, the price tag for the welfare state (and other government services) is steep. Public expenditures by the state, local governments, and welfare state agencies constitute about 55 percent of France's annual production (GDP). President Chirac's 2002 electoral platform proposed hefty cuts in taxes and state spending. Yet there are limits to how much state spending can be trimmed because the French are fiercely attached to their system of extensive social protection.

Although the French system provides relatively generous benefits to most citizens, economic inequalities are extensive. One unusually sharp cleavage in France pits those with jobs against the unemployed. During the 1980s and 1990s, France's unemployment rate was among the highest in Western Europe, exceeding 12 percent in the mid-1990s. For years, voters consistently ranked unemployment the most important problem in France, and governments' inability to reduce unemployment contributed to the frequent electoral gyrations of the recent period. International economic expansion in the late 1990s helped reduce unemployment, although the downturn from 2001 reversed this trend. More than 8 percent of French were unemployed in 2003, with youth, immigrants, and women considerably more likely to be out of work.

The French have coined the term *the social fracture* (*la fracture sociale*) to describe the existence of a permanently excluded group of citizens—those without stable jobs, the long-term unemployed, the poor, and the homeless. The government estimates the number of homeless in France at between 200,000 and 500,000, and soup kitchens organized by nonprofit organizations serve 500,000 meals daily to the poor. Nearly 2 million citizens receive grants under the minimum income program for the impoverished and long-term unemployed.

A related dilemma in recent years involves the rising costs of the welfare state. On one hand, the *Sécu* (shorthand for the social security system of health and retirement benefits) is among the most popular public programs in France. Prior to 1995, not even conservative governments dared attack it frontally. However, social programs are increasingly costly due to rising medical costs, high levels of unemployment, a slowdown in birthrates (which means fewer active workers are available to contribute to finance welfare benefits), and a growing ratio of retired to younger workers. The proportion of elderly will double by 2050. Currently, three French adults work for every retired worker; in 2050, the ratio will drop to 1.5 workers for every retired worker.

The conservative government of Jean-Pierre Raffarin, elected in 2002 following Chirac's reelection, proposed a hefty cut in income taxes on the grounds that this would provide employers and consumers with more money, thus increasing demand and giving the economy a shot in the arm. Whether this approach will be effective in reducing unemployment is not yet known.

Inequality and Ethnic Minorities

France long prided itself on its ability to integrate ethnic minorities. Yet its vaunted openness was partially misleading, for there was also a strong current of suspicion (or worse) toward the foreign born. Immigrants face significantly greater hardships in the labor market. In 2002, a study issued by the Economic and Social Council (a political institution described in Section 3) reported extensive racial discrimination and the existence of a glass ceiling that limits social mobility among immigrants and first-generation French citizens. The report documented that first-generation French have twice the unemployment rate of native-born French.[17]

Inequality and Women

The place of women in French society is double-edged. Because of social services like excellent public and nonprofit day care facilities, one scholar observes that France's female-friendly and family-friendly policies are "at the forefront of developments in employment policy designed to make child-bearing compatible with employment."[18] As a result, the proportion of women aged twenty-five to forty-nine years old in the paid labor force soared from 49 percent in 1970 to 79 percent in 1998. Nevertheless, French women are far from achieving economic and social equality. They are paid 20 percent less than men for comparable work. Within the sphere of political representation, although a landmark reform (described in Section 4) mandates gender political equality, women remain distinctly subordinate.

The Generation Gap

An ironic result of France's extensive welfare state arrangements is to create a sharp generation gap. While welfare state programs provide generous treatment for the elderly, young people are treated much less well. Moreover, the legal protections and economic benefits enjoyed by stably employed workers limit job creation. Thus, young people disproportionately absorb the costs of a generous welfare state, creating an unusually deep generation gap in France. For example, whereas in the United States the unemployment rate for young workers is double that for older workers, in France it is five times higher.[19]

France and the International Political Economy

France's relatively large size, abundant skilled workers, and large internal market enabled it to achieve an enviable economic position for centuries. France gained additional benefits after carving out a colonial empire in Africa, Asia, and the Caribbean, from which it extracted raw materials on favorable terms and to which it exported French industrial products. As global economic integration and competition increased from the 1970s, France chose to pool its resources with other European countries within the framework of the EU in order to remain a major economic power. Although France is inserted in the global economy in ways other than EU membership, we focus on the EU because of its importance for the French economy.

Impact of the European Union

Along with Germany, France has been the key country shaping EU institutions. Membership in the EU has tied France tightly to its European neighbors. When the EU was created in 1958, French trade with other EU countries accounted for about one-quarter of its international trade. A decade later, nearly half of French trade took place within the EU, and it has since increased to about 60 percent.

France's membership in the EU has been accompanied by less statist and more free-market-oriented economic policies. For example, the Maastricht Treaty negotiated in 1991 required member states to adopt austerity measures, called *convergence criteria,* in order to participate in the common European currency, the euro. States had to cut annual budget deficits to under 3 percent of the GDP, limit total public debt to under 60 percent of GDP, and grant their central banks independence with the mandate of pursuing anti-inflationary economic policies. The European Central Bank, created by EU treaty agreements, was authorized to regulate interest rates throughout the EU and sponsor the euro, a new currency that in 2002 replaced the national currency of most member states of the EU. The euro has made it easier for firms in the EU to invest and trade across borders of the member states. The resultant gains in efficiency should be of mutual benefit.

But the adoption of the euro, as well as other measures promoting greater economic integration, also involve costs for states and citizens. When states like France authorize EU officials the power to regulate the currency, interest rates, and the exchange rate, state officials and citizens lose control over core elements of sovereignty. For example, following his reelection as president in 2002, Jacques Chirac announced plans to cut income taxes by 5 percent. The EU Commission promptly warned the French government that doing so might violate the government's agreement to reduce budget deficits and balance the budget by 2004. After first blustering at the EU's warning, the government announced that it would respect its treaty obligations, although budget deficits in 2002 exceeded the convergence criteria, caused tense negotiations between French and EU officials, and provoked an EU reprimand in 2003 for France's projected budgetary deficit. Recall, too, that when French truckers mounted a strike in late 2002, the EU threatened to impose stiff fines if the government failed to ensure that EU commerce would move freely through France.

The EU prohibits states from engaging in the kind of *dirigisme* that was the hallmark of the French state in the postwar period—for example, credit rationing, subsidies, and monopoly state ownership. It thus poses a particular challenge for France. EU membership has contributed to French economic growth and has provided important financial assistance to particular sectors of the French economy. France is the largest beneficiary of EU's generous farm subsidies, and the government has fiercely resisted eliminating this protectionist program. But the EU's emphasis on deregulation has harmed vulnerable economic groups and challenged the state-led pattern by which France achieved economic success and cultural distinctiveness. Most of the smaller party candidates in the 2002 presidential election opposed what they claimed was EU infringement on French sovereignty. The strong support for anti-EU candidates, who received a hefty majority of the votes, suggests that this theme strikes a responsive chord with the French electorate.

France in the Global Economy

France is highly integrated in the global economy. Imports and exports account for fully half of its GDP. Foreign investors, especially American pension funds, own nearly half of all stock traded on the French stock exchange. France ranks third in the world as a source of investment capital throughout the world and second only to the United States as a location for foreign investment. Some of the world's largest banks and transnational corporations are based in France. An example close to home is that Houghton Mifflin, publisher of *Introduction to Comparative Politics,* was owned for several years by the French media giant Vivendi Universal. (Vivendi sold Houghton Mifflin in 2002.)

France is also a major player on the world's geopolitical stage. It is one of the five permanent members of the United Nations Security Council and an important member of the World Trade Organization and the G-8 group of industrialized nations. France is notorious for pursuing an independent course internationally and, in particular, for being a gadfly toward the United States. For example, when the United States sought international support for military action in Iraq in 2002–2003, France was among the most outspoken critics of the U.S. action. Politics and economics may have been closely intertwined in this dispute as in so many others. One reason for French opposition to the U.S. action was rumored to be France's concern that if Saddam Hussein were toppled, U.S. oil companies would replace French companies as potential partners in exploiting Iraq's immense petroleum reserves. Another frequently cited reason was France's concern that the United States was exercising global dominance. President Chirac's highly public defiance of the United States was widely popular in France and throughout the world, although it fuelled strong anti-French sentiment in the United States.

Section ③ Governance and Policy-Making

Despite frequent changes of regimes in France in the past two centuries, three important features of the French state remained constant. That all three have changed recently suggests a bedrock transformation in the character of the French state. First, for centuries, there was a strong consensus on the value of a unitary state. Even before the French Revolution, subnational governments were regarded as an administrative arm of the state based in Paris. Beginning in the 1980s, when the Socialist government transferred substantial powers to local governments, a new spirit of local autonomy became evident.

Second, the long-established tradition that claims the state should play an active role in directing the society and economy has been challenged within recent years. The third change involves limits on state action from within the state itself. Until recently, a nation that emphasized the importance of formalized legal codes and, along with the United States, boasts the modern world's first written constitution, did not consider that the constitution should be scrupulously respected. The French tradition of parliamentary sovereignty held that the legislature, as the people's representatives, should have a free hand to govern free of constitutional or judicial restraint. This too has changed in the recent past. The Constitution of the Fifth Republic has generally come to be regarded as the authoritative source for allocating power among political institutions, and the judiciary has gained a vital new power to interpret the Constitution.

Organization of the State

The Fifth Republic is usually described as a semipresidential system, one that combines elements of presidential and parliamentary systems, because of the design of the executive and legislature. In a wholly presidential system, such as in the United States, the executive and the legislature are chosen separately and are not accountable to each other. The legislature and executive possess independent powers; neither controls the agenda of the other. Moreover, both institutions have fixed terms in office. Neither the government nor the legislature can force the other to resign and face new elections. The one exception to this generalization in a presidential system is that the legislature can impeach

and force the president to resign when it deems that the president has committed treason or other grave misdeeds. There is a similar impeachment procedure in the French Fifth Republic, although it has never been used: for a French president to be impeached, a text must be voted in identical terms by an absolute majority of both houses of parliament. The president's case is then judged by a High Court of Justice comprising twelve deputies and twelve senators elected from and by the two houses.

In a parliamentary system, as in Britain, the executive and legislature are fused. The government is accountable to Parliament and must resign if Parliament passes a motion of no confidence. At the same time, the government has substantial control over the parliamentary agenda and can dissolve Parliament, thereby provoking new elections.

In the Fifth Republic, both the president and parliament are directly elected, as in a presidential system. However, the French system differs from both presidential and parliamentary systems in that the president appoints a prime minister and government who are answerable to parliament.

Why is the Fifth Republic a *semi*presidential system? The "semi" refers to the fact that in several respects—notably, the existence of a government responsible to parliament—the legislature and executive are not wholly separate, as they are in a pure presidential system. The system is called semi*presidential,* not semi*parliamentary,* because the executive dominates parliament, not the other way around. In every respect in which the political system of the Fifth Republic deviates from the purely parliamentary or the purely presidential model, the result is to strengthen the executive (which, in periods other than **cohabitation,** described below, mainly means the president). As in a pure parliamentary system, the executive mostly controls the parliamentary agenda and can dissolve parliament. The fusion of executive and legislative powers characteristic of parliamentary regimes strengthens the executive. It is further strengthened by the fact that in contrast to parliamentary regimes, the French parliament cannot vote a motion of no confidence in the president. Although the French National Assembly can vote a censure motion of the government, thus forcing it to resign, the president, is not answerable to parliament. In this key respect, there is a separation of powers found in presidential systems. The coexistence within the Fifth Republic of presidential and parliamentary features provides the executive with decisive advantages over the legislature exceeding those occurring in both the classic parliamentary and presidential regimes.

The Executive

Besides Russia, France is the only major country with a semipresidential system. In parliamentary regimes, the head of state—the monarch in Britain, for example, and the president, as in Germany—exercises purely ceremonial duties, while the bulk of executive power is wielded by the prime minister, who is the head of government and is responsible to parliament. In France, the president is the head of state but also enjoys substantial political, policy-making, and executive power.

The president shares executive and policy-making powers with the prime minister and the cabinet. This situation of a dual executive—president and prime minister—poses few problems when the two officials are allies and lead the same political coalition; it poses a major problem during periods when opposing political coalitions win presidential and parliamentary elections, what the French term *cohabitation,* or power sharing, whose result is that the president and prime minister are political opponents. Dissatisfaction with this situation, which occurred repeatedly from the 1980s, led to a constitutional reform in 2000 that reduced the president's term from seven to five years. By making the president's term the same length as that of the members of the National Assembly and holding elections for the two institutions in the same period, the reform was designed to minimize the chance of cohabitation. In 2002, in the first elections held under the new system, Jacques Chirac was resoundingly reelected president, and his political supporters won a large majority in the National Assembly. For the foreseeable future, then, there will be unified control of key political institutions.

The President

When both the executive and the legislature are controlled by the same party coalition, the powers of the French president are immense. At these times, the president combines the independent powers of the U.S. president—notably, command of the executive establishment and independence from legislative control—with the powers that accrue to the government in a parliamentary regime—namely, control over parliament's agenda and the ability to dissolve parliament. The result is a greater degree of executive dominance than in virtually any other democratic nation.

The president has become so powerful for three reasons: the towering personalities of the republic's most powerful presidents, the ample powers conferred on the office by the Constitution, and the political practices of the Fifth Republic.

Presidential Personalities. Charles de Gaulle (1890–1970) was unquestionably the most influential politician in modern French history. He first achieved prominence in leading the Resistance forces in France during World War II. Later, in 1958, he toppled the Fourth Republic and designed the Fifth Republic to facilitate strong leadership. As first president in the Fifth Republic, from 1958 to 1969, de Gaulle exercised towering leadership.

The next president who used presidential powers to the full was François Mitterrand, president from 1981 to 1995. A youthful leader in the Resistance during World War II and at first an ally of de Gaulle, Mitterrand broke with de Gaulle after the war. In the 1960s and 1970s, Mitterrand assembled a leftist coalition to oppose de Gaulle. During this period, Mitterrand twice ran for president, losing both times. However, he was elected on his third try, in 1981, when he defeated incumbent president Valéry Giscard d'Estaing. Thus began Mitterrand's fourteen-year reign (1981–1995), the longest presidential term in the history of the Fifth Republic.

Ironically, President Mitterrand's governing style was strikingly similar to that of his archrival, de Gaulle. As he humorously remarked soon after taking office in 1981, "The institutions of the Fifth Republic weren't created with me in mind, but they suit me fine!" The result was that, under Mitterrand, the left, which had opposed the Fifth Republic at first, became fully integrated within the institutions of the regime and supported the kind of strong presidential leadership that it had opposed when de Gaulle occupied the Elysée (the presidential palace).

It is unclear what legacy incumbent president Jacques Chirac, who succeeded Mitterrand as president, will leave. During much of his first term in office, he was forced to share power with Socialist prime minister Lionel Jospin, who led the Socialist coalition that dominated the National Assembly. The situation changed dramatically following Chirac's landside reelection in 2002 when Chirac's major opponent, Jospin, was eliminated from the runoff ballot by Le Pen. Immediately following his reelection, Chirac began to assert presidential dominance in a manner strikingly reminiscent of de Gaulle and Mitterrand. Nothing better demonstrates the importance of the contrast between cohabitation and unified control of the executive. Time will tell whether Chirac will continue to exercise unbridled presidential power or will sponsor constitutional reforms creating a more balanced regime.

The Constitutional Presidency.   The Constitution of the Fifth Republic endows the president with the ceremonial powers of head of state, the role occupied by the president in previous regimes. He resides in the resplendent Elysée Palace in a fashionable section of Paris, he is the symbolic embodiment of the majestic French state, and he represents France at international diplomatic gatherings.

The Constitution grants the president important political powers that belonged to the prime minister in the past republics, as well as entirely new powers. Thus, the president both symbolizes the unity and majesty of the state and actively participates in political decision making.

The president is the only political official directly chosen by the entire French electorate, a source of powerful personal support and legitimacy for the entire regime. Presidents are eligible for reelection without

Table 2

Presidents of the Fifth Republic	
President	**Term**
Charles de Gaulle	1958–1969
Georges Pompidou	1969–1974
Valéry Giscard d'Estaing	1975–1981
François Mitterrand	1981–1995
Jacques Chirac	1995–Present

limit. Unlike the U.S. Constitution, there is no minimum age requirement or requirement to be a French citizen. In order to be nominated, five hundred local elected officials must sign a nominating petition. Because France has several hundred thousand local elected officials, many candidates compete in each presidential election. The record was 2002, when the field contained fifteen candidates, including several proposing quite bizarre platforms. One example was the candidate from the Hunters, Fishing Enthusiasts, Nature, and Tradition Party (*Parti chasse, pêche, nature et traditions,* CNPT), who managed to garner 4.3 percent of the popular vote.

Although only candidates nominated by major political parties stand a realistic chance of winning, minor party candidates can have an important influence on the outcome, notably by influencing which candidates make it to the runoff ballot. The most dramatic example occurred in 2002, when Lionel Jospin, the major center-left candidate, failed to make the runoff because he came in third, behind Chirac and far-right candidate Jean-Marie Le Pen. One reason for Jospin's poor showing was that the large number of leftist candidates fragmented the left electorate. Among minor-party candidates were Jean-Pierre Chevènement, a former associate of Jospin who broke with him; three ultraleft candidates; Green Party and PCF candidates; and Christiane Taubira, the first ever black candidate, nominee of a small party allied with the Socialist Party.

The Constitution grants the president vital powers, including the right to:

- Name the prime minister and approve the prime minister's choice of other cabinet officials, as well as name other high-ranking civil, military, and judicial officials.
- Preside over meetings of the Council of Ministers (the government). Note that the president, not the prime minister, is charged with this responsibility.
- Conduct foreign affairs, through the power to negotiate and ratify treaties, as well as to name French ambassadors and accredit foreign ambassadors to France.
- Direct the armed forces, bolstered by a 1964 decree that grants the president exclusive control over France's nuclear forces.
- Dissolve the National Assembly and call for new

elections. The Constitution specifies that if the president has dissolved the National Assembly, he or she cannot do so again for a year.

- Appoint three of the nine members of the Constitutional Council, including its president, and refer bills passed by parliament to the council to determine if they conform to the Constitution. (The president shares this last power with the prime minister and the presidents of the two houses of parliament.)

Several other constitutional grants of power strengthen the president's position. Article 16, for example, authorizes the president to assume emergency powers when, in his judgment, the institutions of the republic, the independence of the nation, the integrity of its territory, or the execution of France's international (treaty) commitments are threatened. (The masculine form is used because there has never been a female president or even a female candidate with a serious chance of winning.)

Article 89 authorizes the president, with the approval of the prime minister, to propose constitutional amendments. An amendment must be approved by a majority of both houses of parliament and ratified by either a national **referendum** or a three-fifths vote of a congress comprising both houses of parliament. The amendment procedure has been used with increasing frequency in recent years. Eleven of the Constitution's fifteen amendments have been added since 1992; most were ratified by vote of parliament meeting as a congress.

The president's ability to call a referendum represents a potentially powerful weapon. The referendum was used several times in the early years of the Fifth Republic to consolidate support for de Gaulle. But calling a referendum carries risks. When voters rejected a referendum that de Gaulle sponsored in 1969 to restructure the Senate and create regional governments, he resigned from office, on the grounds that he had lost popular confidence.

Because of the example that de Gaulle set, his successors have been reluctant to sponsor referenda. President Pompidou sponsored one; President Giscard d'Estaing, none; President Mitterrand, two; and President Chirac, two. Although all five referenda were approved, turnout was so low that the "victories" probably caused the president as much harm as good.

Article 5 directs the president "to ensure, by his arbitration, the regular functioning of the governmental authorities, as well as the continuance of the State. He shall be the guarantor of national independence, of the integrity of the territory, and of respect for . . . agreements and treaties." Because the president is the sole official charged with arbitrating and guaranteeing national independence, the Constitution confers on the office enormous legitimacy and power over the state machinery.

The Political President. The Constitution creates a powerful office on paper. But to be effective, a president must translate formal powers into the actual exercise of influence. One important resource is that the president is the only official to be elected by the entire nation. The democratic legitimacy conferred by electoral victory provides a powerful weapon against the opposition and can also be useful in keeping the president's own political allies in line.

Presidential leadership is given a powerful boost when the president commands the majority party coalition in the National Assembly. At these times, the president appoints loyal political supporters to lead the government, and parliament generally supports the president's policy proposals.

This situation of unified control prevailed for nearly three decades after the founding of the Fifth Republic. During this long period, De Gaulle and his successors used their formal and informal powers to the hilt. Two developments further strengthened the president at this time. First, in addition to the constitutional power to designate prime ministers, presidents successfully claimed the right (not specified in the Constitution) to dismiss them as well. Thus, the tradition developed that the government was responsible not only to the National Assembly, as formally specified in the Constitution, but informally to the president as well. Second, although the Constitution delegates the prime minister and government the power to develop policy, presidents successfully asserted the right to shape policy in virtually any domain that they choose.

The situation of presidential preeminence prevailed for nearly thirty years in the Fifth Republic. However, a fundamental break occurred in political practice during the first period of cohabitation, when a conservative parliamentary majority opposed to President Mitterrand was elected in the 1986 legislative elections. Mitterrand accepted the inevitable and appointed a conservative prime minister, Jacques Chirac, who eventually was elected president himself in 1995.

During this unprecedented situation, opposing forces quickly developed informal rules of the game to ensure political stability. Although Mitterrand retained the ceremonial trappings of the presidency, his control over policy-making was vastly reduced. He retained great power over foreign and defense policy, as specified in the Constitution. But whereas in his first years as president, he played the decisive role in shaping policy, after 1986 he was often little more than a spectator.

Mitterrand nevertheless played his cards shrewdly. When his first term expired in 1988, he won reelection by outmaneuvering Chirac, who ran against Mitterrand in the presidential elections that year. After Mitterrand was reelected, he dissolved the National Assembly and the Socialists won a narrow victory, thus reestablishing unified control. Since then, periods of cohabitation (1993–1995 and 1997–2002) have alternated with periods of unified control.

The contrast in policy-making between periods of unified control and cohabitation is so great they can be considered two different political systems: one dominated by the president and the other by the prime minister. Moreover, after 1997, cohabitation proved highly unpopular because of the sniping that occurred between President Chirac and Prime Minister Jospin, a major reason for reducing the president's term to five years. In 2002, the first elections held with the shortened presidential term, Chirac was reelected, and his conservative allies won the legislative elections held a month later. There is thus a high probability of unified control until at least 2007, when the terms of the president and National Assembly expire.

The Prime Minister and Government

Reading the Constitution would be poor preparation for understanding who makes the key policy decisions in the Fifth Republic. The Constitution designates the government, not the president, as the preeminent policy-making institution. Article 20 states that the government "shall determine and direct the policy of the nation. It shall have at its disposal the administration and the armed forces." And Article 21 authorizes the prime minister to "direct the action of the government.

He [the prime minister] is responsible for national defense. He assures the execution of the laws." During periods of unified control, governments follow the president's lead because of political dynamics rather than constitutional directive.

The prime minister is the second most powerful official in the Fifth Republic. The president usually appoints as prime minister a leader of the party coalition that wins a majority of parliamentary seats. The president has greater discretion in choosing a prime minister in periods of unified control. Thus, President Chirac named Jean-Pierre Raffarin as prime minister in 2002 from among a handful of leaders of the president's coalition later named the Union for a Popular Movement (UMP). The Constitution specifies that the prime minister directs the bureaucracy (Article 20) and the government (Article 21) and has exclusive responsibility for issuing regulations, which have the force of law (Articles 21 and 37). Thus far in the Fifth Republic, there has been one female prime minister, Édith Cresson, who directed a Socialist government in 1992–1993.

The prime minister nominates and the president appoints other cabinet ministers. The government (also known as the cabinet) is a collective body under the prime minister's leadership. Given France's multiparty system, described in the next section, one party rarely gains an absolute parliamentary majority, although this occurred in 2002 when the umbrella party, the UMP, was formed to support Chirac. The typical situation is that ideologically allied parties form coalitions to contest parliamentary elections. Cabinet ministers are usually powerful members of the majority coalition that controls parliament. They are typically (but not always) members of the National Assembly or Senate, the two houses of parliament. The Constitution specifies that members of parliament who are named to the cabinet must resign their parliamentary seat. The distribution of positions allotted parties in the cabinet is roughly proportional to their strength in the majority parliamentary coalition. Cabinet ministers direct government departments and propose policy initiatives in their domain. If supported by the government and president, these proposals are added to the legislative and administrative agenda.

The prime minister and other government ministers have extensive staff assistance to help them develop

Institutional Intricacies: *Of Presidents and Prime Ministers*

The relationship between the president and prime minister is a key element in the Fifth Republic. There are two possible situations: (1) when the president and prime minister are political allies and (2) the periods of cohabitation, when the two are political opponents. The first situation occurred from the beginning of the Fifth Republic in 1958 until 1986. During this long period, when the president enjoyed the support of a parliamentary majority, he was able to name a close political ally as prime minister. The result was undisputed presidential supremacy. Most of the time, presidents selected the prime minister from the ranks of leaders of the majority party coalition. Loyal prime ministers can provide the president with important political assets: parliamentary support for the government's policies, skill in gaining sympathetic media treatment, and experience in directing the state bureaucracy.

Nevertheless, even when the same political coalition controls the presidency and parliament, tensions between the prime minister and president are inevitable. Prime ministers are constantly tempted to stake out a position independent of the president in the hope that, one day, they will move from the Matignon (the prime minister's official residence) to the Elysée. In order to do so, a prime minister must be more than a presidential lapdog.

During cohabitation, the balance shifts from open displays of cooperation to open displays of rivalry. The president cannot expect the prime minister and parliament to support presidential initiatives. The president is now forced to assume the mantle of dignified and ceremonial head of state, while the prime minister assumes the responsibility—and risks—of policy leadership. The situation somewhat resembles that in parliamentary regimes—save that the French prime minister must also contend with the ever-present danger that the president may publicly criticize the prime minister's decisions (the parallel situation in Britain—that the queen would openly oppose the government—is unthinkable). When cohabitation in France occurred in 1986, following the election of a Conservative parliamentary majority, it lasted only briefly because the electoral calendar provided for a presidential election to be held within two years. Mitterrand won reelection that year, dissolved the National Assembly, and persuaded the electorate to produce a Socialist victory (thus ending divided control).

In 1997, the Socialists' victory in legislative elections occurred only two years into President Chirac's seven-year term. This meant that cohabitation lasted for five long years, an experience that prompted extensive criticism. A constitutional reform was enacted in 2000 reducing the president's term to five years, in part with the aim of minimizing the chances of cohabitation.

When President Chirac was reelected in 2002 and a center-right coalition swept the legislative elections that followed, cohabitation ended, and the chances were that it would not recur for many years. Few lamented its passing.

---

policy proposals and direct the immense and far-flung bureaucracy. For example, the prime minister's office includes the general directorate of the public service, the general secretariat of the government, and the general secretariat of defense. These agencies coordinate policy and supervise its implementation by the departments that comprise the executive. During periods of unified control, there is an informal division of labor between the president and prime minister: the president is responsible for formulating overall policy orientations and the prime minister for translating these into specific programs, directing parliament, and supervising the cabinet and bureaucracy. At these times, there is no uncertainty about who is preeminent within the executive.

The prime minister's most unpleasant function during periods of unified control is to serve as a lightning rod to deflect criticism from the president. Typically, therefore, prime ministers become increasingly unpopular and are replaced by the president after two or three years in office.

As with cabinets in most other political systems, cabinet meetings in France are not the occasion for searching policy debate or collective decision making.

They are where the president or prime minister announces decisions made earlier and elsewhere, and they fulfill formalities required by the Constitution, such as approving nominations to high administrative positions. The most important policy decisions are made at the Elysée Palace or Matignon (the prime minister's official residence), or by interministerial committees composed of ministers from several departments meeting under the direction of the president and prime minister to focus on a specific policy question.

Bureaucracy and Civil Service

The most prominent officials in the French state are found in the Elysée, the Matignon, and ornate government ministries scattered throughout Paris. The day-to-day work of the state, however, is performed by a veritable army of administrators numbering 2.5 million—one for every twenty-four French citizens. Given France's long-standing *dirigiste* tradition, the bureaucracy has enormous influence over the country's social and economic life. The Fifth Republic further bolstered the influence of the bureaucracy by limiting parliament's legislative power and authorizing the bureaucracy, under the prime minister's direction, to issue regulations with the force of laws.

Key positions at the top of the bureaucracy, the sector on which we focus here, command great power. Top posts are reserved for graduates of highly selective educational institutions, called **grandes écoles.** Competition for admission to these schools is intense; of the over 1 million students enrolled in higher education at any given time, only 3,000 attend a *grande école* at the very top of the educational pyramid.[20]

Students who graduate at the top of their class, especially those at the two most prestigious institutions, the École Nationale d'Administration and the École Polytechnique, are admitted into an even more select fraternity: one of the **grands corps,** small, specialized, cohesive networks of civil servants. Membership in a *grand corps* is for life and guarantees a fine salary, an excellent position, and considerable power and prestige. Members of a *grand corps* leapfrog to the top of the bureaucracy at a young age. Recently, its members have also gained top executive positions in large public and private industrial firms and banks. Many have launched political careers by running for parliament

after compiling some administrative experience. Countless members of the *grands corps* have become cabinet ministers, several became prime minister, and two—Valéry Giscard d'Estaing and Jacques Chirac—were elected president.

Among the many influential bureaucratic positions, particular mention should be made of what the French term a ministerial *cabinet,* that is, the personal staff advising a government minister. (In order to distinguish the *cabinet,* or personal staff, from the cabinet composed of government ministers, we italicize *cabinet* when referring to the former agency.) Members of a *cabinet* advise the minister on policy and partisan matters and informally supervise the bureaucracy in the minister's name. French ministers gain considerable power over the line bureaucracy thanks to the help provided by their *cabinets.*

Despite its reputation for competence, honesty, and influence, all is not well in the French administration. The retreat of the state has affected the morale and social position of civil servants. The increased power of the private sector, as well as the EU's increased role, signifies that the once preeminent civil service is no longer larger than life. When there is unified control of government, as followed the 2002 elections, there are charges that the government favors its political allies in appointments to top administrative positions.

Semipublic Agencies

Since World War II, France has had an important array of public sector enterprises in basic industry, transportation, energy, telecommunications, banking, and services. Although broadly speaking under political control, they enjoyed enormous power and autonomy. For example, Electricity of France possessed a monopoly on the distribution of electricity throughout France and has often been described as a state within the state. However, the public industrial and financial sector has been sharply reduced by the sale of state-owned enterprises beginning in the mid-1980s. There are still large and powerful semipublic agencies that remain. But even state-owned bastions like Electricity of France, France Télécom, Air France, and the Renault automobile company have been fully or partially privatized.

Other State Institutions

Among many other state institutions, we focus on those that are exceptionally important or are created by the Constitution.

The Military and the Police

In all countries, the military and the police are key executive agencies that provide the coercive force to maintain law and order. But an important distinction between democratic and undemocratic regimes is whether the armed forces and police are servants, not masters, of civilian authorities. In France, the army has rarely been an active participant in politics. However, there are important exceptions, most recently in 1958, when the army helped topple the Fourth Republic and enabled de Gaulle to return to power.

The French armed forces traditionally recruited by universal conscription, with young Frenchmen from diverse social backgrounds subject to the draft. The army was regarded as an important agency, along with public schools, for socializing French youth to republican values. However, the French pattern began to appear costly, old-fashioned, and ineffective in an age of high-tech warfare. In 1996, President Chirac cut back the size of the army and replaced conscription by professional recruitment.

For many years, France repeatedly deployed its armed forces to protect brutal, pro-French dictators in its former colonies in Africa and the Pacific. In the process, France made a mockery of its proclaimed commitments to democracy and universal human rights. A particularly horrific instance was when France supported a Hutu-dominated regime in Rwanda in the 1990s that engaged in extensive genocide against the country's Tutsi population. Prime Minister Jospin partially reversed France's repressive policy when he announced that French troops would no longer intervene militarily in France's former colonies.

The police forces in France enjoy considerable freedom—far too much, according to many. The "forces of order," as they are called in France, have a reputation for abusing power, and the judiciary and high executive officials have often turned a blind eye. Immigrants and French citizens from Algeria and other predominantly Arab countries in North Africa, black Africa,

and the Caribbean are often subject to identity checks, strip searches, and other indignities.

The police have gained additional powers in recent years in response to both rising crime and widespread public concern. The Jospin government made it easier for the police to conduct searches and engage in electronic surveillance. Nonetheless, in the 2002 presidential campaign, Chirac and Le Pen repeatedly denounced the Jospin government for its alleged laxity in controlling crime. Indeed, the issue of law and order dominated the campaign and heavily contributed to Jospin's first-round defeat. Immediately following Chirac's re-election, he announced the creation of regional security committees, and the Raffarin government sponsored legislation giving the police added powers to engage in surveillance (including wiretapping) and retain suspects longer without formal charges.

The Judiciary and the Constitutional Council

Traditionally, French courts have had little autonomy and were considered an arm of the executive. In the past two decades, however, this condition has changed dramatically, as the Constitutional Council increased its reach and independent administrative authorities gained the power to regulate such varied sectors as the audiovisual industry, stock exchange, and commercial competition.

No other political institution in the Fifth Republic has gained more power since the founding of the Fifth Republic than the Constitutional Council. One study observes, "Originally an obscure institution conceived to play a marginal role in the Fifth Republic, the Constitutional Council has gradually moved toward the center stage of French politics and acquired the status of a major actor in the policy-making system."[21]

The nine members of the council are named for staggered nine-year nonrenewable terms. The president of the republic and the presidents of the National Assembly and Senate each appoints three members of the council. The president of the republic names the council's president. Members of the Constitutional Council are generally distinguished jurists or elder statesmen. The first woman was appointed to the council in 1992.

Three changes have been key in strengthening the Constitutional Council and the judiciary more generally.

First was broadening access to the Constitutional Council. At first, only the president of the republic and the presidents of the two houses of the legislature could bring cases to the council. A constitutional amendment passed in 1974 authorized sixty deputies or sixty senators to bring suit. As a result, the council is now asked to rule on most important legislation.

Second, the council has successfully assumed the power of **judicial review,** that is, the right to strike down legislation that it judges to be in violation of the Constitution. This development is unprecedented in French history. Although important council judgments have provoked intense controversy, no one questions the council's right of judicial review.

Third is transferring the power to appoint judges from the executive to magistrates elected from among the rank of judges. This change required a constitutional amendment in 1993. The same amendment created a new Court of Justice of the Republic to try cases against government ministers accused of criminal acts committed while in office.

The French judicial system of Roman law is based on a host of legal codes, most notably, the Napoleonic Code, which regulates legal relations in such areas as criminal justice, industrial relations, and local government activity. This pattern differs from the system prevailing in Britain, the United States, and other nations inspired by the common law system. French courts accord little importance to judicial precedent; their judgments are based on legislation that is codified in specific subfields, such as labor law and local governmental regulation.

In criminal cases, a judicial authority, the *juge d'instruction,* is responsible for preparing the prosecution's case. French judges play an active role in questioning witnesses and recommending verdicts to juries. Criminal defendants enjoy fewer rights against the prosecution than in the U.S. or British system of criminal justice, although the Jospin government sponsored reforms that increased defendants' rights.

State Council.   Administrative courts in France play an important role in regulating the bureaucracy and the scope of administrative regulations (recall that many areas regulated by legislation in other democratic systems are the subject of administrative regulation in France). There are about thirty administrative courts

in France. At the apex is the *Conseil d'État* (State Council), which hears cases brought by individuals alleging that their rights have been violated by administrative regulations or bureaucratic actions. The State Council's other responsibility is to advise the government when new legislation is drafted concerning the constitutionality, legality, and coherence of proposed laws. The council is charged with being a watchdog on the executive, especially important in the French political system, where the executive possesses such great autonomy.

The Economic and Social Council

The Economic and Social Council is a consultative body composed of representatives from business, agriculture, labor unions, social welfare organizations, and consumer groups, as well as leading citizens from cultural and scientific fields. Created by the Constitution, the council has issued influential reports on important public issues, including job discrimination toward immigrants and reorganization of the minimum wage system. The council has no legislative power, is relatively unknown, and exercises relatively little political influence.

Subnational Government

Until the 1980s, locally elected municipal governments were weak, and the local governmental structure was extremely fragmented. There are over 36,000 village and city governments in France, more than the total number of local governments in all other major Western European countries combined. Responsibility for regulating local affairs was mainly in the hands of nationally appointed field officers, who reported to national cabinet ministers.

The Socialist government fundamentally overhauled local government in the 1980s. State supervision of local governments was reduced, regional administrative units were transformed into governmental authorities, and localities were given substantially greater power to levy taxes and sponsor programs. The Socialist government also cut back on the system known as the *cumul des mandats* (accumulation of mandates), which permitted a politician simultaneously to be elected mayor, president of the departmental council, deputy or senator, and member of the European Parliament. The Raffarin government announced plans to further restrict the *cumul*.

The European Dimension

Although we review political institutions of the French state in this section, political institutions in France, like those in other member states of the EU, no longer function in isolation from EU institutions. There is such tight integration between the two levels that domestic French public officials spend much of their time helping to shape and implement EU decisions. The process begins at the top, since the president, prime minister, and cabinet ministers are constantly involved in meetings with their counterparts to help make EU decisions. The process continues right down the bureaucratic hierarchy. Jacques Delors, a French political leader who for years served as president of the Commission of the EU, claimed that about 80 percent of the legislation regulating French affairs originates in Brussels (the seat of the EU). Whether the topic is the quantity of fish that French commercial trawlers are permitted to harvest or standards for French pharmaceuticals, French administrative regulations usually must incorporate EU directives. When analyzing the way that French political institutions function, it is sometimes difficult to unravel where the "EU" begins and "France" leaves off.

The Policy-Making Process

Until the first period of cohabitation in 1986, there was great unity of purpose and a nearly hierarchical chain of command linking the French president, government, bureaucracy, and parliament. The president, often in consultation with the prime minister, formulated major policy initiatives. The government, assisted by the formidable bureaucracy, developed detailed legislative proposals and administrative regulations for implementing policy. The parliament generally approved the government's proposals. And the powerful bureaucracy thereupon took over to implement policy.

During periods of cohabitation, as we have seen, the policy-making process was significantly different. The prime minister gained the dominant voice in policy-making, and the president retreated to the political wings. The fact that the UMP has firmly controlled all major political institutions since 2002 means that presidential dominance is all but assured.

In France there are few opportunities for private groups to influence executive decisions. The Constitution enshrines executive dominance at the expense of the legislature and popular participation. Nonetheless, the executive is not all-powerful. Strikes and demonstrations have periodically erupted and altered policy. The Constitutional Council can influence the policy process. Finally, the executive and French state more generally have been severely limited by France's participation in the global economy, especially French membership in the EU.

As France has become more integrated within the EU and the wider global arena, the gulf has widened between political decision makers and ordinary citizens. Many fear that decisions made behind closed doors in Brussels and elsewhere benefit privileged interests at the expense of vulnerable groups. One result has been periodic strikes and protests, as we describe below. In order to address this democratic deficit, there have been many proposals for institutional reforms. One response was the reduction of the French president's term to five years. But the change has not ended criticism of the imbalanced nature of the semipresidential system. Recently proposed constitutional reforms to strengthen representative elements include authorizing parliament to participate in setting budgetary priorities, limiting the president's power to dissolve parliament, and the most audacious—but by far the least likely—eliminating direct election of the president.

Section **4** Representation and Participation

A principal feature guiding the construction of the Fifth Republic was Charles de Gaulle's belief that political parties and parliament had overstepped their proper role in the Third and Fourth Republics, thereby preventing vigorous executive leadership. To correct what he regarded as this dangerous imbalance, the Constitution of the Fifth Republic grants the executive an astonishing array of powers and severely limits popular participation, representation, and legislative autonomy.

Although de Gaulle did succeed in limiting parliament's role, he failed completely to curb the importance of political parties. Ironically, however, the development of strong, well-organized, centralized parties early in the Fifth Republic—squarely contrary to de Gaulle's intentions—is a principal buttress of decisive leadership and political stability, de Gaulle's highest priorities.

What explains this curious turn of events? De Gaulle's decision to provide for popular election of the presidency powerfully contributed to the development of strong parties. In an attempt to win the all-important presidential contest, the formerly decentralized parties of the Fourth Republic reorganized to become centralized, unified organizations. The result was to facilitate strong executive leadership, although parties have not been especially useful in fostering popular participation and representation. As a result, France's centuries-old tradition of popular protest against state authority persists.

The Legislature

In the Third and Fourth Republics, parliament was regarded as the sole voice of the sovereign people. By granting the executive exceptionally powerful weapons to limit parliament, the Constitution of the Fifth Republic rejects the tradition of parliamentary sovereignty. The French parliament does not provide an important forum for national debates, fails to represent conflicting interests adequately, and is a weak check on executive abuses of power.

The French parliament is bicameral, consisting of the more powerful National Assembly and the Senate.

Article 34 of the Constitution, which defines the scope of parliament's legislative jurisdiction, represented a minor revolution in French constitutional law. Rather than authorizing parliament to legislate in all areas except those it designates as off-limits, the Constitution enumerates areas in which parliament *is* competent and prohibits it from legislating in other domains. The Constitution authorizes the executive to issue regulations and decrees in domains outside parliament's jurisdiction.

Within the limited area of lawmaking, the Constitution grants the government extensive powers to control legislative activity. The government is mostly responsible for establishing the parliamentary agenda. As in other parliamentary regimes, the government, not backbenchers or the opposition, initiates most bills passed into law. (In a typical year, over 90 percent of the laws voted by the legislature are government sponsored.)

The government possesses a raft of other devices to control parliament. The executive can choose to dissolve the National Assembly before its normal five-year term ends, thus forcing new legislative elections. When the executive dissolves the National Assembly, it cannot do so again for a year. The executive cannot dissolve the Senate, but this matters little, since the Senate lacks two vital powers enjoyed by the National Assembly: the right to refuse to approve legislation and thus prevent it from passing, and the power to force the government to resign by voting censure.

Under Article 44, the government can call for a single vote, known as the *vote bloquée* ("blocked vote," or package vote), on all or a portion of a bill. When it invokes this procedure, the government can select which amendments will be included with the text. Governments have used—abused, according to the opposition—the package vote procedure to restrict debate and limit parliament's ability to amend proposed legislation.

The government can further curb the National Assembly by calling for a confidence vote on its overall policies or on a specific bill (Article 49). When the government declares a confidence vote, the motion is considered approved, even without a vote supporting the government, unless the National Assembly votes censure within twenty-four hours. To be approved, an absolute majority of deputies must vote in favor of the censure motion. Deputies who are absent or abstain are in effect counted as opposing censure. (Members of the National Assembly are known as deputies; members of the Senate are known as senators. Together the two groups are known as members of parliament.)

Deputies can also submit motions to censure the government on their own initiative. Such a motion must be signed by one-tenth of all deputies in the National Assembly. The procedure for passing this kind of censure motion is the same as that called by the government. Deputies who sign a censure motion cannot do so again during the life of legislature. The result is to limit the number of parliament-initiated censure motions.

Given the fact that the government typically commands majority support in the National Assembly, it rarely need worry about being forced to resign by a vote of censure. Although several censure motions are proposed every legislative session, only one has ever passed in the history of the Fifth Republic.

Parliament has quite limited control over the budgetary process. The government prepares the budget, and members of parliament are prohibited from introducing amendments that will raise expenditures or lower revenues. Furthermore, unless parliament approves the budget within seventy days after it has been submitted, the government can enact it by decree (although this has never occurred in the Fifth Republic).

In some parliamentary systems, parliamentary committees—the French term them commissions—play a vital role. But not in the Fifth Republic. There are six permanent commissions: foreign policy; finances and economy; defense; constitutional changes, legislation, and general administration; cultural, family, and social affairs; and production and exchange. Special commissions may also be appointed to examine especially important bills, such as occurred when the Socialist government introduced nationalization reforms in 1981.

Commissions are responsible for reviewing proposed legislation and can amend bills. However, the government can reject unwanted changes. The Constitution also authorizes parliament to create commissions of inquiry to control the executive, but the few that have been created—for example, one that studied

the shortening of the work week (1998), another that evaluated the activities of the police forces in Corsica (1999)—have proved quite ineffective.

In recent years, parliament has modestly increased its standing. A constitutional amendment in 1995 increased the opportunities for members of parliament to pose questions to the government. Members of parliament have skillfully exploited the right to amend government-sponsored bills, or at least to delay passage by proposing endless amendments. But these changes have not fundamentally reduced the imbalance between the executive and legislature in the Fifth Republic.

The National Assembly is by far the more powerful chamber of parliament. It possesses two key powers that the Senate lacks: only the National Assembly can vote censure of the government and pass a law despite the Senate's opposition. The Senate is fully equal to the National Assembly in one important area: a constitutional amendment cannot be proposed for ratification without the support of both houses.

Most bills that receive serious parliamentary consideration are introduced by the government, typically in the National Assembly, sometimes in the Senate. After review and possible amendment by one of the six standing commissions in the relevant chamber, the bill is submitted to the full house for debate, further amendment, and vote. If it is approved, the text is sent for consideration to the second chamber.

If passed in identical form by both houses, a bill becomes law (unless struck down by the Constitutional Council). If the two houses vote different versions or the Senate rejects a text approved by the National Assembly, a joint commission of members from the two chambers seeks to negotiate a compromise. The new text is again considered by both houses. Failing agreement, the process is repeated. However, the government can request that both houses reconsider and approve an identical text. If all else fails, the government can ask the National Assembly to override the Senate. If the National Assembly approves the text, it becomes law despite the Senate's opposition.

After a bill is passed, the Constitution authorizes the president of the republic, president of either chamber of the legislature, or sixty deputies or senators to request review by the Constitutional Council. The council can strike down those portions of a bill or an entire text that it judges to be in violation of the

Constitution. The council must be asked to rule within one month after a bill is passed. If a suit is not brought, the law can never be reviewed by the council.

Why might the National Assembly and Senate have different positions on a policy issue? One reason is that members of the two houses are elected by different procedures and represent different interests. Deputies are chosen from single-member districts for five years (unless the government dissolves the chamber before the end of its normal term). There are currently 577 deputies elected to the National Assembly—555 elected from mainland France and 22 from France's overseas departments and territories. Thus, there are 577 districts. A two-ballot procedure is used, similar to the one for presidential elections. To be elected at the first ballot, a candidate must receive an absolute majority of the votes cast in the district. If no candidate gains a majority—the usual situation (although highly popular deputies are reelected at the first ballot)—a runoff election is held. Unlike the presidential election, in which only the two front-running candidates may compete in the runoff, any candidate receiving at least 12.5 percent of the votes at the first ballot can compete in the runoff.

Typically, however, parties on the left and those on the right negotiate alliances in which they agree to support the best-placed candidate from the alliance in each district. The result is that parties agree to withdraw those less well-placed candidates in the coalition who obtain over 12.5 percent of the vote. Parties entering into these agreements stand a much better chance of seeing their candidates elected. However, fringe parties can exercise an important influence as spoilers if many of their candidates clear the 12.5 percent threshold and remain in the runoff. Parties that elect at least 20 deputies are entitled to form a parliamentary group, which provides the party with the right to representation on parliamentary commissions and other privileges.

Since alliances in runoff elections typically reflect the left-right divide, the system used to elect the National Assembly contributes to polarization within French politics. The major effect of the system is to maximize the chances that a stable majority will emerge in parliament. This is why political scientist Jean Charlot claims that the two-ballot single-district system "has proved . . . one of the most solid underpinnings of the Fifth Republic. The electoral law . . . weakens or even

neutralizes the natural tendency of the French and their parties toward division."[22]

The 322 senators are chosen by indirect election for nine-year terms, and the way they are chosen makes the Senate responsive to different interests. Most senators are elected by mayors and town councilors from France's 100 *départements* (the administrative districts into which mainland and overseas France is divided). Twelve senators are elected by nonresident French citizens. The Senate is a quite conservative body because rural interests are substantially overrepresented. After many years of intense criticisms about the Senate's unrepresentative character, a Senate commission proposed shortening the length of senatorial terms to six years and increasing urban representation; the reform will likely be enacted in coming years.

Political Parties and the Party System

We have described the irony that the emergence of powerful political parties—a factor that de Gaulle feared would nurture division, instability, and paralysis—has promoted political stability in the Fifth Republic. Parties have facilitated stable leadership and political alternation in office. In recent years, however, the ideological distance between the major parties has shrunk, and many French citizens feel unrepresented by the major alternatives. The result has been falling turnout, declining support for the large, established parties, and increased support for smaller or fringe parties. The most dramatic example was Le Pen's breakthrough in the 2002 presidential elections.

The 1962 reform providing for popular election of the president transformed the French party system. Until adoption of the reform, political parties were highly decentralized. Since their main goal was to elect deputies to the National Assembly, they were mostly based in districts throughout France. Once the president became popularly elected, parties adapted their programs, internal organization, and alliance strategy to winning the next presidential election. Parties chose leaders who projected an appealing image and performed well on television. They shaped their program to capture the widest possible audience, which promoted ideological moderation. As French parties have moved in this direction, some observers have described French politics as becoming "Americanized," for the emphasis on winning presidential elections, on candidates' personalities, and ideological centrism are major features of American politics.

Counterpressures, however, constantly challenge these trends. In particular, when the major parties drift toward the ideological center, the number of voters who feel abandoned grows, along with support for fringe parties. The point was dramatically illustrated by the performance of Le Pen and other "minor-party" candidates in the 2002 presidential elections.

The Major Parties

In the past several decades, three major parties vied for dominance, and each held top offices within the Fifth Republic. Yet the French party system is in rapid flux. In particular, the bombshell of the 2002 presidential elections has reshaped the party system.

Union pour un mouvement populaire. Parties on the right of the French political spectrum have traditionally been numerous and fragmented. However, this changed when de Gaulle returned to power in 1958. A new party, formed to support de Gaulle's attempt to safeguard France's national independence, provide strong political leadership within France, and modernize French society and economy while retaining France's distinctive cultural heritage, dominated the Fifth Republic in the early years.

From the mid-1970s until 2002, the Gaullist party (called most recently the *Rassemblement pour la République,* RPR) slipped. Jacques Chirac, who became party leader in 1974, lost presidential bids in 1981 and 1988. The RPR regained its premier role in the Fifth Republic when Chirac won the 1995 presidential elections, and it became even more powerful when Chirac was reelected in 2002.

Le Pen's success at the first ballot in 2002 proved a surprise for Chirac. He capitalized on the widespread revulsion toward Le Pen to form what became known as the *Union pour un mouvement populaire* (UMP, Union for a Popular Movement), an umbrella grouping designed to consolidate the diverse parties of the center-right. In late 2002, the new party formally replaced the RPR (although RPR cadres dominated the UMP). More important, the UMP absorbed most members and leaders of the other major center-right party, the *Union des démocrates pour la France* (UDF, Union of

Democrats for France). The UMP now virtually monopolizes the center-right of the political spectrum, an unprecedented situation in contemporary French history.

The social base of the UMP reflects its conservative orientation. Business executives, professionals, the highly educated, the wealthy, and the elderly are especially likely to support the party.

Parti socialiste. From a party of aging local politicians and schoolteachers in the Fourth and early Fifth Republics, the *Parti socialiste* (PS) became the vanguard of a new France in 1981 when it swept presidential and parliamentary elections under the leadership of François Mitterrand. The PS helped shape present-day France by integrating oppositionist left forces within the institutions of the Fifth Republic, reorienting the left in a more moderate direction, and sponsoring important policy reforms within the Fifth Republic.

The PS reached power in 1981 by advocating substantial, even radical, changes, and it sponsored a flurry of reforms in its first years in office. However, when President Mitterrand sponsored a dramatic about-face in 1983–1984 after the government encountered severe economic difficulties, French socialism lost its ideological bite. Although Mitterrand and his successor, Lionel Jospin, did not reorient the Socialist Party in as thoroughly centrist fashion as did Tony Blair, leader of the British Labour Party, they cast the PS as a responsible, reformist governing party.

The PS experienced a stunning setback when Jospin failed to make the runoff in the 2002 presidential elections. Without a leader—Jospin immediately retired from political life after his defeat—the party groped for a new direction. It will probably remain in the opposition for at least five years following the 2002 elections (although it remains the largest opposition party in the National Assembly).

Small Parties

The two major political parties that dominate the French political system command dwindling political support. Especially as their programs have converged, many voters judged that the major parties were unresponsive to their concerns. As a result, support for small parties has grown. Hence, along with the consolidation of the center-left under the PS and the center-right under the UMP, there has been a tendency toward increased fragmentation within the French party system. In the 2002 presidential elections, candidates from parties other than the UMP and PS garnered well over half the popular vote. We describe here several quite important small parties. But as the 2002 presidential elections illustrated, there are many other splinter parties in France, and their support reveals important political currents. For example, candidates of the Communist and three ultraleft parties in the 2002 elections received a quite hefty 14 percent of the votes.

Parti communiste français (PCF).   From 1945 until 1981, the PCF was one of the largest political parties in France. It saw itself as heir to the French revolutionary tradition and was proud of its close links to both the French working class, whose electoral support was key to the party's strong position, and the Soviet Union. For much of this period, the PCF's stated goal was to replace France's capitalist system, which, it argued, was undemocratically organized and exploitative, with public ownership and control of the economy.

PCF support began to dwindle because it adapted too little and too late to the political, social, and economic modernization that transformed France beginning in the 1960s. Its support slipped from over 20 percent of the vote in the postwar period to under 10 percent by the 1980s. Although the PCF joined Socialist-led governments as a junior partner between 1981–1984 and 1997–2002, it failed to gain credit for the government's achievements. At the same time, it was deserted by many voters, who gravitated to small ultraleft opposition parties as well as to the National Front.

The PCF's low point was the 2002 presidential elections, where its candidate won a mere 3.4 percent of the vote. It continues to enjoy representation in the National Assembly but is a pale shadow of its former self.

Front national (FN).   The FN has existed for decades, but its rapid rise in the 1980s was fueled by high unemployment, fears about increased crime, and the choice of a handy scapegoat: immigrant workers and their families.

In 1981, FN leader Jean-Marie Le Pen failed to gain the required number of signatures from local politicians to run for president. Twenty years later, Le Pen came in second in the presidential elections. The party's slogan, "France for the French," does not answer the question, "Who (and what) is French?" However, the phrase implies that immigrants, especially those who are not white, are not truly French. Unfortunately, the FN's simplistic and racist approach has had wide resonance.

Although party leaders have engaged in anti-Semitic and anti-immigrant rhetoric across the board, their favorite target has been Arabs from Algeria, France's former North African colony. The FN advocates depriving immigrants of employment, social benefits, and education and, if possible, deporting them.

Le Pen powerfully contributed to the FN's success. In both the 1988 and 1995 presidential elections, he gained 15 percent of the first ballot vote, and came in third, behind the major candidates. Although the party split in 1998, Le Pen retained a popular following. By outpolling Jospin in the 2002 presidential elections, he made front-page headlines around the world.

Les Verts **(Greens).**   The state's relative indifference to environmental concerns provided the potential for a Green movement in France. For example, France has the largest nuclear power program in Western Europe, and the Greens first reached public notice by sponsoring antinuclear protests.

The Greens achieved a major breakthrough in the 1989 European elections by gaining 10.6 percent of the vote, in part because of proportional representation. The Greens have been intensely divided by the question of whether the movement should maintain a distance from both left and right parties or whether it should ally with the left in order to build support among left parties for environmental concerns. The larger grouping of the Greens allied with the PS in the 1997 parliamentary elections, and their leader served as minister of environment in the Jospin government.

Union des démocrates pour la France.   The Union of Democrats for France (UDF) was created in 1978 by a variety of small conservative parties opposed to de Gaulle and the RPR. The party was a major force in French politics, and its leader, Valéry Giscard d'Estaing, was president from 1974 until 1981.

For years, the RPR and the UDF dominated the center-right, allying in legislative elections against the Socialist Party but conflicting on many issues. The UDF opposed de Gaulle, the RPR passionately supported him; the RPR supported European integration, the RPR was divided on the issue; the UDF championed free enterprise, the RPR favored state direction of the economy. However, the two parties increasingly converged in their positions, and by the 1980s, they were divided mainly by the personal rivalries of Giscard d'Estaing and Chirac. The RPR's superior organization and Giscard's age eventually tipped the balance in the RPR's favor. The turning point occurred in 1995, when Giscard decided not to challenge Chirac in the presidential elections. Following Chirac's victory, Giscard began withdrawing from active political life. In 2001, by now an elder statesman, he was designated by the EU Commission to preside over a convention to propose changes in EU governance.

The UDF presented a candidate in the presidential elections, François Bayrou, but he gained a mere 7 percent of the vote. Most UDF leaders and members bolted the UDF after the election to join the newly formed UMP, although the UDF managed to win enough seats in the 2002 legislative elections to form a separate parliamentary group.

Elections

French voters go to the polls nearly every year to vote in a referendum or in elections for municipal, departmental, or regional councilor, deputy to the European Parliament or National Assembly, and president. The most important elections are the legislative and presidential elections, whose results are provided in Tables 3 and 4. Many scholars believe that France is experiencing a crisis of political representation and the party system and point to the following evidence:

- Support for fringe parties opposed to the select "cartel" of governmental parties has soared. In the 1995 presidential election, peripheral candidates, that is, those not nominated by the major governing parties, garnered 38 percent among citizens who voted. In 2002, it soared to over half of those voting. Even more dramatically, under one-quarter of the electorate in 2002 voted for the major established candidates, Chirac or Jospin. More than one-quarter of citizens abstained, and well over half of those who voted supported candidates from small parties.
- Voting turnout has steadily dwindled. In the 2002 elections, abstentions reached record levels: 28 percent in the first ballot of the presidential elections (along with an additional 3 percent who cast a spoiled or blank ballot), 36 percent in the first ballot of the legislative elections.
- Voting patterns have been increasingly unstable. Political scientist Pascal Perrineau notes, "A new type

Table 3

Electoral Results, Elections to National Assembly, 1958–2002 (percentage of those voting)

	1958	1962	1967	1968	1973	1978	1981	1986	1988	1993	1997	2002
Far Left	2%	2%	2%	4%	3%	3%	1%	2%	0%	2%	2%	3%
PCF	19	22	23	20	21	21	16	10	11	9	10	5
Socialist Party/Left Radicals	23	21	19	17	22	25	38	32	38	21	26	25
Ecology	—	—	—	—	—	2	1	1	1	12	8	4
Center	15	15	18	10	16	21*	19*		19*	19*	15*	
Center-Right	14	14	0	4	7			42*				5*
UNR-RPR-UMP	18	32	38	44	24	23	21	—	19	20	17	34
Far Right	3	1	1	0	3	0	3	10	10	13	15	12
Abstentions	23	31	19	20	19	17	30	22	34	31	32	36

*Number represents the percentage of combined votes for Center and Center-Right parties.

Sources: Françoise Dreyfus and François D'Arcy, *Les Institutions politiques et administratives de la France* (Paris: Economica, 1985), 54; *Le Monde,* March 18, 1986; *Le Monde, Les élections législatives* (Paris: *Le Monde,* 1988). Ministry of the Interior, 1993, 1997. *Le Monde,* June 11, 2002.

Table 4

Presidential Elections in the Fifth Republic (percentage of those voting)

	December 1965		June 1969		May 1974		April–May 1981		April–May 1988		April–May 1995		April–May 2002	
	Candidate	Ballot Percentage	Candidate	Ballot Percentage	Candidate	Ballot Percentage	Candidate	Ballot Percentage	Candidate	Ballot Percentage	Candidate	Ballot Percentage	Candidate	Ballot Percentage
Extreme Right									Le Pen (FN)	14.4	Le Pen (FN)	15.0	Le Pen (FN)	17.0 (17.9)
Center Right	de Gaulle (Center-Right)	43.7 (54.5)	Pompidou (UNR)	44.0 (57.6)			Chirac (RPR)	18.0	Chirac (RPR)	19.9 (46.0)	Chirac (RPR)	20.8 (52.6)	Chirac (RPR)	19.9 (82.1)
Center	Lecanuet (Opposition-Center)	15.8	Poher (Center)	23.4 (42.4)	Giscard	32.9 (50.7)	Giscard	28.3 (48.2)	Barre	16.5	Balladur (UDF)	18.9	Bayou (UDF)	6.8
													Saint-Josse (CNPT)	4.3
													Madelin (PR)	3.9
Center Left	Mitterrand (Socialist-Communist)	32.2 (45.5)	Defferre (PS)	5.1	Mitterrand (PS)	43.4 (49.3)	Mitterrand (PS)	25.8 (51.8)	Mitterrand (PS)	34.1 (54.0)	Jospin (PS)	23.3 (47.4)	Jospin (PS)	16.1
													Chevènement	5.3
													Mamère (Greens)	5.3
Left			Duclos (PCF)	21.5			Marchais (PCF)	15.3	Lajoinie (PCF)	6.8	Hue (PCF)	8.6	Hue (PCF)	3.4
													3 candidates (Extreme Left)	10.6
Abstentions		15.0 (15.5)		21.8 (30.9)		15.1 (12.1)		18.9 (14.1)				20.6		27.9 (19.9)

Note: Numbers in parentheses indicate percentage of vote received in second ballot. Percentages of votes for candidates do not add to 100 because of minor party candidates and rounding errors.

Sources: John R. Frears and Jean-Luc Parodi, *War Will Not Take Place: The French Parliamentary Elections of March 1978* (London: Hurst, 1976), p. 6; *Le Monde, L'Élection présidentielle: 26 avril–10 mai 1981* (Paris: Le Monde, 1981), pp. 98, 138; *Le Monde*, April 28 and May 12, 1998; *Journal officiel*, May 14, 1995; *Le Monde*, May 5–6, 2002; *Le Monde*, May 7, 2002.

of voter is emerging, less docile to social and territorial allegiances, less faithful to a party or political camp, and less involved in the act of voting. . . . Voters are likely to change their minds from one election to another, or even from one ballot to another in the same election."[23] The 2002 presidential elections furnish an extreme example of voters' volatility. A poll found that fully one-sixth of voters did not decide which candidate to support until just before the election. But the trend originated earlier. In every one of the six legislative elections held between 1981 and 2002, the governing majority has alternated between the center-left and center-right parties. Such shifts were unthinkable in the first decades of the Fifth Republic. Laurent Fabius, a former prime minister, probably identified the most important reason for this electoral instability when he observed after the 2002 elections, "For the past 20 years, the principal feature of our political life is the rejection of incumbents."[24]

- Political leaders and parties have been implicated in countless financial scandals. In recent years, former cabinet ministers, the president of the Constitutional Council, and large-city mayors have been hauled into court. In response to the public outcry, four party finance laws were passed between 1988 and 1995. The legislation authorizes public funds for parties and candidates, limits private political gifts for parties and candidates, and establishes ceilings for campaign expenditures in elections at all levels. An independent election commission can disqualify candidates who violate campaign finance laws.

   These reforms have not ended the revelations of corruption in high places, however. President Chirac himself has been implicated in several major scandals. Convincing evidence has surfaced that while he was mayor of Paris in the 1970s and 1980s, he received lavish kickbacks from housing contractors for luxurious vacations and illicit political contributions. If courts had not held that a sitting president cannot be prosecuted while in office, President Chirac would doubtless have been indicted on corruption charges.

- Public disgust with political leaders is at record highs. A public opinion poll in the May 10, 2002, issue of *Le Monde* reported that 84 percent of young people believe that politicians habitually lie. The

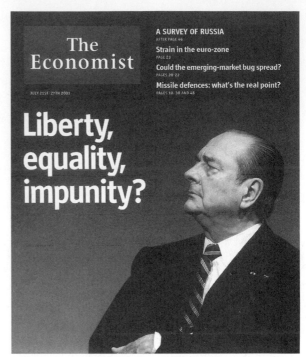

Allegations of corruption by President Chirac. *Source:* Reuters.

low turnover within the political class may contribute to popular distrust toward politicians. For example, President Chirac first served in high national political office in 1967. Most other major politicians have been fixtures of political life for decades. When Prime Minister Jospin retired from political life after his defeat in the 2002 presidential elections, his example was nearly unprecedented. (An earlier important example was when President de Gaulle resigned as president in 1969, after voters rejected a referendum he sponsored.) Le Pen's barbs that target the political class proved so effective in the light of this situation.

Political Culture, Citizenship, and Identity

Economic restructuring, changing state-society relations, and France's changing relations with the rest of the world have posed important challenges to traditional French political culture, ideologies, and collective identities.

Citizenship and National Identity

France has traditionally granted citizenship rights in a quite inclusive fashion. Sociologist Rogers Brubaker's classic comparison of the two major continental states of West Europe, Germany and France, describes how the French conception of citizenship has traditionally been based on the principle of territory and political values, whereas the German conception was based on blood or ethnicity.[25] Anyone born on French soil, including the offspring of parents who are not citizens, automatically possesses citizenship rights. Furthermore, France has traditionally imposed few restrictions on immigrants becoming French citizens.

France's approach to citizenship and national identity is double-edged. On the one hand, its inclusive conception of citizenship and national identity, dating from the Revolution of 1789, specifies that anyone who accepts French political ideals and culture deserves to be granted legal rights of citizenship. On the other hand, this approach also mandates that ethnic, religious, and cultural affiliations have no place in public life and should be considered private preferences. An illustration: polling organizations and the census are prohibited from asking citizens about their religious or ethnic identity. (It should also be noted that this republican ideal of citizenship, dominant since 1789, has been contested by an older tradition based in a Catholic and conservative social milieu.) In the republican French self-conception, the political community should be secular and culturally homogeneous. The republican ideal of citizenship strongly opposes what is termed multiculturalism in the United States.

However, there have been cracks in the consensus around this assimilationist approach, as a result of globalization and the migration of Muslims with very different cultural values from those of native-born French. Since the 1980s, there have been important conflicts and intense debates about what it means and should mean to be French.

Ethnicity and Immigration

France has traditionally attracted large numbers of immigrants. According to political sociologist Charles Tilly, France has "served as Europe's greatest melting pot."[26] Currently, one French citizen out of four has at least one foreign-born grandparent.

So what? Historian Gérard Noiriel's path-breaking studies provide an answer. Noiriel suggests that successive waves of immigration enabled France to compensate for a low birthrate and "preserve its rank on the international scene, whereas many observers in the late nineteenth century had predicted its irremediable decline."[27] After World War II, immigrants helped fuel French economic growth by laboring for low wages under harsh working conditions in the construction and manufacturing sectors. Moreover, immigrants have contributed to French scientific and cultural renown. Examples include scientist Marie Curie, philosopher Henri Bergson, writers Paul Verlaine and Guillaume Apollinaire, painters Pablo Picasso and Marc Chagall, and composer Igor Stravinsky.

There were often conflicts between immigrants and native-born French, for example, early in the twentieth century, between immigrants arriving from Poland, Italy, and Portugal and native-born French. But conflicts around the issue of immigration have been particularly acute in recent decades, a result of economic instability, cultural conflict, and native-born citizens' anxiety about France's identity in an era of globalization.

The majority of immigrants in recent decades have been Muslims from North Africa, especially Algeria, France's former colony with which the French fought a long and bitter war. Many native-born French resent their presence, and tensions run especially high in the high-rise housing developments and poor urban neighborhoods where there are fewer public facilities and resources. There are over 4 million Muslims in France, of whom about 2 million are French citizens. During France's economic boom in the 1960s, the government actively recruited workers from North Africa to fill jobs that native-born French rejected. Since the mid-1970s, with the onset of economic stagnation, successive governments have reversed course, often by brutal means. Since 1993, new immigration has been prohibited, save for families of already established immigrants and applicants for political asylum. As a result, the number of new immigrants arriving yearly has fallen from between 250,000 and 300,000 to between 100,000 and 120,000. At the same time, issues involving immigration have been important sources of conflict within French politics and society.

Social Class

For centuries, France was among the countries in which class cleavages periodically fueled intense political conflicts, and even revolutions. A watershed change in collective identities occurred during the 1970s and 1980s. Under the impact of economic change and ideological reorientation, large numbers of French citizens (especially manual workers) shed their self-identification as members of a social class. The political impact of declining identification has been especially great among workers. Until the 1980s, workers often looked to the PCF for support. Now, many see the FN as an ally in the face of a hostile world.

The millions of French who are unemployed, low paid, or in marginal economic sectors and various categories of workers periodically mount strikes and demonstrations. However, social class no longer constitutes a major dimension of partisan cleavage.

Gender

France can be considered the home of modernist feminist thought. Philosopher and novelist Simone de Beauvoir's *The Second Sex,* published after World War II, is a landmark in this regard. In the 1960s and 1970s French feminist theorists contributed to reshaping literary studies throughout the world. However, there is considerable gender inequality in France.

State policy often has been unresponsive to women's concerns. Contraception, for example, was illegal in France until 1967 and abortion until 1974. A weak law outlawing sexual harassment was passed in 1992; it was considerably stiffened in 2001. On the other hand, legislation prohibits publishing sexist material, and extensive welfare state programs enable women to work outside the home, including paid parental leave, subsidized child care and preschool facilities, and public health care.

For many years, women were highly underrepresented in politics. Although over half the electorate, women constituted no more than 10 percent of the National Assembly. After years of mobilization by women, a constitutional amendment passed in 1999 and legislation adopted in 2000 addressed the issue and put France at the forefront of countries seeking to increase women's political representation. The parity law, as it is called, reduces public funds for political parties that fail to nominate an equal number of men and women.

The results to date have been mixed. The 2001 municipal elections, the first held since the reform was adopted, produced a dramatic increase in women's representation. From one election to the next, the number of women among the 83,000 municipal councilors on the governing councils in towns above 3,500 population to which the law applies skyrocketed from about 7,000 to 39,000.

Yet the parity law does not mandate gender equality; it merely reduces public funding if parties do not nominate an equal number of women. A party may observe the letter of the law but violate its spirit by reserving safe or close seats for men. Moreover, a party may ignore the law altogether. In the 2002 legislative elections, only one-fifth of the candidates nominated by the UMP, the major winner in the election, were women. As a result, although the proportion of female candidates in 2002 nearly doubled from the 1997 legislative elections (20 percent in 1997 to 39 percent in 2002), the proportion of women elected to the National Assembly rose only slightly.

Interests, Social Movements, and Protests

Organized Interests

The overbearing French state has typically tended to view autonomous interest groups and social movements with distrust. This tendency was reinforced when the Fifth Republic strengthened the executive, enabling it to make and implement policy with little regard for popular opinion. Yet favored sectors may enjoy privileged access to the state. For example, the National Federation of Farmers' Unions (FNSEA) has traditionally been well represented on the administrative commissions that regulate agricultural prices and farm subsidies. Indeed, it is difficult to distinguish where the bureaucracy ends and the FNSEA begins. The extraordinary success of the French farm lobby is reflected in the fact that the EU provides enormous subsidies to agricultural products, with French farmers receiving the largest share. Another powerful organization is the major business association, the Movement of French Business Firms (Medef). Trade associations and labor unions play an important part in administering the far-flung public health system, as well as state-financed vocational training programs. Representatives of interest groups also serve on the Economic and Social Council, the peak-level advisory body described in Section 3 (see "Citizen Action: French Trade Unions").

Social Movements and Protest

France has a long tradition of direct protest. During the nineteenth century, regimes were periodically toppled by mass opposition in the streets. Although Fifth Republic institutions were designed to discourage citizens

---

Citizen Action: **French Trade Unions**

The character of the French trade union movement and its relationship to politics explain much about protest in France. In many industrialized democracies, such as Britain, Germany, and Japan, trade unions in specific sectors—for example, steel, transportation, teaching, the civil service—are allied in a central trade union confederation. As a consequence, organized labor speaks with relatively one voice. In addition, the central union confederation is usually allied with the country's major left-of-center political party: the Labour Party in Britain, Social Democratic Party in Germany, and Socialist Party in Japan.

The situation is very different in France. Rather than one umbrella trade union confederation, there are four, as well as a number of other independent unions. Each confederation pursues its own economic and political agenda. The confederations compete with each other in recruiting members and in elections to representative bodies (called works councils) based in shopfloors and offices. Traditionally, divisions have been heightened because each confederation was loosely allied with a competing political party. The largest confederation was closely allied with the Communist Party, while other confederations had links to the Socialist and centrist parties. The confederations' ties to political parties have weakened in recent years, but their rivalry with each other continues.

Since French labor often speaks with discordant voices, and relatively few workers belong to unions, trade unions have little direct influence in shaping public policy. Although the French trade union movement is among the oldest in the world, the rate of union membership has traditionally been among the lowest of the industrialized democracies. In the 1990s, with the downsizing of manufacturing, which produced high levels of unemployment, the union movement suffered a further loss of members and power. Membership has sagged to under 10 percent of the labor force, a historic low in the postwar period.

This description suggests that because of their small numbers, organizational and political divisions, and meager clout, unions are a weak force in French politics and society. And in "normal" times, French unions do indeed play a marginal role. But the strength of unions needs to be measured in other ways than the members holding a union card. First, unions play a key role in some public and private institutions. For example, union nominees often dominate elected works councils of French business firms. Unions have participated in managing the social security health, pension, and unemployment insurance funds. Second, unions can mobilize large numbers of members and nonmembers alike when they call strikes and demonstrations. And, third, at these crisis points, French unions gain strength because they are the only organized actor with which employers and the state can negotiate in order to restore order.

During normal periods, French employers and the state are tempted to ignore unions and workers' interests on the assumption that unions are not a significant force. But when strikes and demonstrations shut down plants, firms, economic sectors, and even large regions or the entire country, employers and the state must court union leaders. Feverish all-night negotiations are held among management, government officials, and union leaders, which often produce settlements providing wage gains and institutional reforms, whereupon the cycle of "normalcy" resumes, and unions retreat to a more marginal position—until the next explosion.

from acting autonomously, they have not always succeeded. For example, the May 1968 uprising was "the nearest thing to a full-blown revolution ever experienced in an advanced industrial society" and a vivid reminder of how fragile political stability can be in France.[28] A repeat performance occurred in 1995, when transportation workers brought Paris and other large cities to a halt. The strikes in late 2002, which opened this chapter, demonstrate that strikes continue to produce widespread disruption. Although overall strike levels have been low in recent years due to high unemployment, a host of groups have mounted strikes and demonstrations, including farmers, fishing interests, postal workers, teachers, high school students, truckers, railway workers, air traffic controllers, and health care workers—to provide a partial list. As should be clear, strikes are not confined to manual workers. For example, French doctors waged a five-month slowdown in the winter of 2001 and spring of 2002 to demand that the government raise medical fees and limit on-call obligations. A strike on Christmas 2001 overloaded emergency rooms and resulted in prefects ordering doctors to work to ensure minimum medical services. In March 2002, 30,000 doctors and other health workers marched through Paris to press their demands. The minister of health angrily declared that doctors "have eyes larger than their stomachs."

In the past decade, new issues have generated widespread mobilization, including AIDS, the homeless, human rights, and the mistreatment of immigrants. As described in Section 5, France has been at the forefront of protests over globalization.

Although, as we have seen, the tradition of popular contention remains strong, there has been a sharp rise in the number of civic associations whose aims are to promote sports, leisure, and culture. Whereas in the 1970s, about 20,000 new civic associations were created each year, the number has increased to 60,000. Nonetheless, France lags behind neighboring countries in this respect: whereas 39 percent of the French report belonging to one or more associations, the comparable figures for France's neighbors are 53 percent of citizens in Britain, 58 percent in Belgium, 67 percent in Germany, and 84 percent in the Netherlands.[29]

The Fifth Republic strengthened the state's capacity to make and implement policy but failed to sponsor comparable reforms to broaden opportunities for participation and representation. (Two exceptions might be cited: popular election of the president and decentralization reforms.) As we review in the next section, the French political system confronts the explosive challenge in the twenty-first century of dealing with daunting new and old problems when state capacity has declined while representative political institutions and civil society remain weak.

Section ⑤ French Politics in Transition

The pace of change throughout the world has rapidly accelerated as space and time are compressed by the incredible technological advances of recent decades, and national borders become more porous as a result of increased transnational economic, political, social, and cultural flows. While the extent and character of the changes wrought by globalization are complex, controversial, and often obscure, the fact that the world is changing cannot be disputed. These observations apply to France no less than to other countries in the world. What kinds of changes—and continuities—in French politics emerge from our analysis?

Political Challenges and Changing Agendas

What a distance separates French political patterns in the new century from those that prevailed for the half-century following World War II. Political parties and conflicts in the earlier period could be arrayed quite neatly along a left-right ideological continuum linked to social class divisions. For example, in the 1970s, attention was riveted on the opposition between a Communist and Socialist alliance advocating a radical reformist program, and the conservative alliances of center-right parties. In the early 1980s, the reform initiatives of the Socialist government dominated the news. When the center-right coalition gained a parliamentary majority in 1986, its first priority was to roll back many of the reforms.

By the mid-1990s, however, the center-left and center-right were considerably closer to agreeing on the major political priorities. The large governing parties accepted France's mixed economy, consisting of the coexistence of a strong role for the state combined with heavy reliance on private market forces. They agreed that for the sake of further European integration (notably, the launching of the euro), it was worth making unpopular economic policy choices, in order to reduce government deficits and the public debt. By the mid-1990s, then, it appeared that significant ideological controversy, at least among the major political parties, had ended.

Yet in retrospect, the calm was but a prelude to the storm. We review here four dramatic political challenges in the brief period since the mid-1990s that highlight continuities and changes in France's political agenda. All four raise disturbing questions about the adequacy of the existing political system to confront that agenda.

The Strikes of December 1995: May 1968 Redux?

In late 1995, France was rocked by a series of strikes and demonstrations whose extent and intensity recalled those of May 1968. The origins of the massive strikes in 1995 may be found in the conjunction of France's severe economic difficulties, the expectations raised by Jacques Chirac's 1995 presidential election campaign advocating change, and the disillusionment created when Chirac renounced his electoral pledges.

Section 2 reviewed how France has undergone extensive economic restructuring, involving both modernization for many industries and extensive dislocations for entire regions and sectors of the population. Since the Socialists' "right turn" in 1983, governments of left and right alike have promoted the intensive modernization of French industry by a program involving deregulation, privatization, high interest rates, social retrenchment, and European integration.

In the 1995 presidential election, Chirac attempted to differentiate himself from another conservative candidate, as well as from Socialist Party candidate Lionel Jospin, by holding out the hope that things could

be different. A journalist commented that Chirac "was forced to adopt the strategy of an outsider, gambling that victory would go not to a candidate proposing continuity, but to the candidate who advocated change."[30] Chirac's strategy was electorally successful but soon proved politically costly. Only months after he had promised that things could be different, he abruptly announced an about-face in a television interview in late 1995. The need to comply with the strict fiscal requirements of the Treaty of Maastricht collided with electoral promises, and the promises lost.

Immediately after Chirac's interview, Prime Minister Alain Juppé announced a series of major reforms that represented virtually a declaration of war on labor unions, especially those in the public sector. He proposed reducing civil servants' pensions and ending preferential retirement benefits for workers in key public sectors, including railroads, electrical and gas distribution, and the post office. Among slated changes in the social security system were raising social contributions, reducing benefits, and limiting future spending, as well as increasing government control (and weakening the unions' role) regarding social spending. At the same time, Juppé projected reduced spending on universities, including cutbacks in hiring and new construction.

Reaction to the proposed reforms was swift and massive. Transportation workers soon struck, with France brought to a halt when service shut down on Air France flights, railroads, buses, and the Paris Métro. The transportation strikes soon spread to other public services, and in a short time the postal system ground to a halt, garbage accumulated on city streets, schools closed, and power slowdowns occurred. Demonstrations in support of the strikes attracted wide support from French consumers and private sector workers. The high point was in early December, when two million turned out in Paris and throughout France in solidarity with the strikers. The strikes wound down when the government abandoned many of the proposed changes.

The 1995 strikes reveal the continuing vitality of the French tradition of popular protest, as does the 2002 strike described at the beginning of this chapter. It also highlights the importance of France's participation in the global and European economy, both for shaping French policy and provoking popular opposition. This was not the last occasion when such a lesson would be driven home.

Oui *to Roquefort Cheese,* Non *to Genetically Engineered Products*

Several years after the 1995 strikes challenged social cutbacks, another movement developed to protest constraints imposed by the process of globalization and Europeanization. The movement is quite diverse and includes environmentalists, reenergized ultraleftists, intellectuals, and farmers. One of the movement's leaders is José Bové, a sheep farmer from southwestern France, where famed Roquefort cheese is produced. Bové helped found an organization of small farmers in 1987 that opposed the agribusiness orientation of the National Federation of Farmers' Unions. Small farmers like Bové oppose the standardized methods of farming that agribusiness corporations seek to impose (including the use of genetically modified seed), as well as low-priced farm imports from the EU, and farmers' loss of autonomy resulting from centralization of food distribution and processing by large corporations. Bové achieved worldwide prominence in early 1999 when he led a march of several hundred people that ransacked a McDonald's construction site in southwest France. For Bové and his supporters, who soon numbered in the millions, McDonald's symbolizes what is wrong about the EU and globalization: a U.S. multinational promoting standardized fast food that might include genetically engineered products (genetically modified organisms, GMOs) and purveying meals that are an insult to traditional French cuisine.

Bové was arrested and sentenced to a stiff fine and prison sentence, an unusually harsh penalty for property damage. He served six weeks in prison for the McDonald's attack and was sentenced to an additional prison term for an attack on genetically engineered crops in 1998. Bové received support from across the political spectrum. President Chirac announced that he too dislikes McDonald's food and that he supports Bové's project of seeking to protect traditional French farming, cuisine, and lifestyles from the homogenizing forces of globalization.

When the World Trade Organization met in Seattle in 1999 to strengthen regulations requiring governments to guarantee free trade and investment, the French agriculture minister, who was a delegate, invited Bové to attend the conference and praised his efforts. (Bové managed to smuggle 100 pounds of Roquefort with him to Seattle and distributed it to the protestors.) After the EU banned American hormone-injected beef from European markets, the United States imposed punitive tariffs on EU food imports to the United States. Is it merely a coincidence that Roquefort cheese was included on the list?

Bové became a leading participant in the worldwide struggle against globalization. He participated in the World Social Forums held at Porto Alegre, Brazil, in 2001 and 2002, where popular movements from around the world considered how to promote social justice. At the 2001 Forum, Bové participated in an assault on a nearby agricultural research facility run by Monsanto, a U.S. biotech firm, and helped destroy genetically modified corn and soybean plants. In short order, Bové became an international celebrity because of his opposition to what he described as U.S. economic and cultural imperialism.

France is a center of the worldwide protests against globalization and the EU. In 1998, an organization named ATTAC was created, with over 25,000 members and nearly 200 local committees in France and other

Globalization. This appeared when José Bové traveled to the Seattle meeting of the World Trade Organization in 1999. *Source:* Plantu, Cartoonists & Writers Syndicate, from *Cassettes, mensonges et vidéo* (Paris: Le Seuil, 2000), p. 36.

countries. ATTAC has sponsored forums and demonstrations to oppose free trade and capital movements and to support a plan, originally proposed by Nobel economics prize laureate James Tobin, to impose a tax on international financial speculation. ATTAC helped organize the World Social Forums mentioned above.

The Challenge of Le Pen

The 1995 strike wave and current antiglobalization movement are responses to France's changing position in a changing world. The Le Pen phenomenon and ethnic conflicts are others. The FN rose to political prominence in the mid-1980s by attacking what it alleged was the Socialist government's laxity toward Muslim immigrants. The FN's simplistic and racist response to rising unemployment, extensive layoffs in key industries, growing European integration, and budgetary austerity was to blame immigrants. Le Pen advocated reserving jobs and social benefits such as public housing for French citizens—"national preference" were his code words for the proposal. He also proposed expelling immigrants from France. Muslims were his major but not only target. He appealed to antisemitic sentiment by crude jokes about Jewish politicians and by characterizing the Holocaust as "a historical detail." Other targets of his ire were the United States—he opposed the U.S.-led military operation against Iraq during the 1991 Gulf War—and mainstream French politicians, whom he denounced as corrupt and soft on crime. A leading specialist observes, "What the National Front proposes to the French people . . . is a magical solution to their distress, to their loss of confidence in grand political visions of the nation and in the legacy of the Enlightenment, now in disarray."[31] Le Pen's base of support was at first primarily on the far right of the political spectrum. However, the FN eventually gained the support of a significant segment of the working class. In the 2002 presidential elections, one-third of Le Pen's electorate was unemployed.[32] More workers voted for Le Pen than for any other candidate.

There is a strong link between the decline of the PCF—the party that for decades successfully presented itself as the representative of the working class—and the rise of FN. And as was true for the PCF in its heyday, the FN's success may be due less to the substance of its ideas than to its position as fierce critic of the established system. Polls show that a large majority of FN supporters do not share the party's ideas but instead regard a vote for Le Pen as the most effective way to protest against the established system of parties and politicians. Yet at the same time, the ideas championed by the FN have gained increased support. The proportion of French reporting that they agree with the party's program rose from 11 percent in 1999 to 17 percent in 2000 and 28 percent in 2002.[33] Because the FN has helped to reshape the entire French political agenda, political scientist James Shields claims that its rise "is arguably the most important political development of the past fourteen years."[34]

Muslim-Jewish Tensions

The FN has reaped a political harvest from the presence of Muslims in French society. At the same time that Muslims have been targeted, a small number have resorted to violence in face of frustration and anger at their difficulties in France, although Israel's military action in the West Bank in early 2002 was the catalyst for the most recent violence. Beginning in February 2002, Muslim youths launched numerous attacks against French Jews and Jewish institutions, including synagogues, cemeteries, schools, kosher restaurants, and sports clubs. If the Middle East ignited passions, the form they took often failed to distinguish between Israel's actions, French Jews, and Judaism. For example, a star of David and the words "Dirty Jew" were painted on a statue in Paris of Alfred Dreyfus, the French Jewish army officer falsely convicted of treason in the late nineteenth century. After synagogues were torched in Marseille, Strasbourg, and Lyon over the 2002 Passover-Easter weekend, the government stationed police with submachine weapons outside synagogues throughout France. Although the attacks ended, the damage was done.

According to one specialist, these "incidents are linked to some very real social problems in France, where many Arabs who are having a hard time or are frustrated with what is going on in Palestine are taking it out on Jews."[35] One reason for unusually high Muslim-Jewish tensions is that France is home to the largest number of both Muslims and Jews of any country in Europe. Moreover, the character of French political institutions, notably, the dominance of the executive, weakness of representative mechanisms, and the ethnic and color-blind conception of citizenship, makes it difficult for the political system to process religious and ethnic conflicts.

Institutional Strains and New Issues and Sources of Partisan Conflict: Economy and Identity

French politics has entered a new era. Traditional ideological conflicts have waned, and established political parties have moved closer together. The center-left Socialist Party has drained much of the support that in the past made the *Parti communiste français* (PCF) one of France's largest parties. The UMP has consolidated the bulk of support on the center-right. Furthermore, debates involving how best to organize the economy have been replaced by a centrist, pragmatic managerialism. There is thus widespread acceptance of a mixed economy blending state regulation and market competition.

Significant institutional reforms in the past two decades, including decentralization, shortening the presidential term, and mandating gender parity in political representation, have produced a more balanced and equitable regime. Political institutions permitted orderly alternation and cohabitation. Yet the challenges described in this section have generated lively debate about additional institutional reforms. Some proposals call for fundamental restructuring of the regime—for example, creating a wholly presidential system by abolishing the office of prime minister and prohibiting the president from dissolving parliament. Other proposals involve less fundamental changes—for example, increasing parliament's role in preparing the budget, reforming the quite unrepresentative Senate, and further restricting politicians' right to hold multiple elected mandates (the *cumul des mandats*). Debates about institutional reform will doubtless persist because France has not yet devised a way to combine vigorous political leadership and vibrant democratic participation.

Underlying the issue of institutional reform is a more general problem of political participation and representation. As we saw in Section 4, established parties command ever smaller levels of support. Citizens are voting with their feet by supporting dissident political parties or not voting at all. In brief, established French political parties have been relatively unable to resolve two major issues: the economic challenge of ensuring adequate living standards for all French citizens and the cultural issue of French national identity. Each is a difficult issue; in tandem, the two pose a daunting challenge confronting the French political system.

"It's the Economy, Stupid."   Bill Clinton became president of the United States in 1992 when, with the nation in recession, he promised to "focus like a laser" on the economy. This is a useful reminder that governments generally flourish when the economy flourishes and are punished when the economy stagnates. The uneven performance of the French economy in the past several decades helps explain the political gyrations that have occurred. Although the French economy has been considerably modernized and strengthened in the recent period, many French have paid a heavy price, notably by high rates of unemployment and a large number of marginalized, excluded citizens.

French economic difficulties are compounded by the French style of economic governance. In the postwar period, the French excelled at state-directed promotion of large firms producing projects for captive markets at home and abroad (the latter negotiated with foreign states), as well as at crash programs of industrial development (such as rail and road transport, aerospace, and telecommunications). In the current economic race, victory goes not to the large but to the flexible, and state direction may prove a handicap, not an advantage. Moreover, the cost of innovation in many new spheres now exceeds the capacity of a medium-sized power such as France.

A related issue is the dilemma of how to preserve France's extensive welfare state. The French oppose the American model in which access to medical care and other social services depends on the size of one's pocketbook. The French claim that all citizens should be entitled to access to the goods and services essential for a dignified existence. But can this conception survive when unemployment is high, the proportion of the working population (which finances such programs) is declining, and EU treaty obligations impose severe fiscal constraints?

The Challenge of European and Global Integration

Can the French meet the challenge posed by the EU and globalization to French national distinctiveness, identity, and political, economic, and cultural autonomy? It is no coincidence that rising support for fringe parties coincides with the deepening of European integration in the past two decades. Similarly, there has been a resurgence of demands for regional autonomy and, in the case of the island of Corsica, for independence from France. Corsica has engendered especially bitter and often violent conflict. Reforms proposed by the Jospin government to grant Corsica extensive regional autonomy were shelved by the Raffarin government, which proposed reforms to grant increased authority to all regions, not just to Corsica.

At a general level, French values of liberty, equality, and fraternity have become more widely shared and less distinctive, yet France's assimilationist model has failed to integrate the large Muslim minority. Although France outlaws racial discrimination, it "has not gone beyond the color-blind frame and the model of individual discrimination to embrace a more collective approach that attempts to compensate for inequalities between groups."[36]

A commission charged by the government to analyze France's capacity to confront the future asserted that the country's traditional patterns pose severe handicaps. It asked, "Will the road toward democratic maturity, within the context of the globalization of values and a reduced role for national states, be more arduous in France than in other nations?"[37] In the light of the previous discussion, the answer seems quite obvious.

French Politics in Comparative Perspective

France provides a fascinating case for comparative analysis. The rapid succession of regimes enables us to analyze the impact of institutions on political practice. Consider the Fourth and Fifth Republics, when the same country was governed in two dramatically different ways within a short time. The experiment teaches what to avoid as much as what to emulate. The Fourth Republic demonstrated the pitfalls of a fragmented multiparty system with undisciplined parties and a parliamentary regime with a weak executive. The Fifth Republic's semipresidential system provides an instructive case for analysis in its own right and for comparison with parliamentary and presidential systems. Although there have been halting steps toward developing more balanced institutions, including a larger role for the Constitutional Council, stronger local governments, and a shorter term for the president, the Fifth Republic demonstrates the danger of an isolated and overly powerful executive. At the same time, given the Fifth Republic's generally strong economic and political performance, its semipresidential system may prove attractive to countries seeking lessons in political-institutional design.

France also provides an exciting opportunity to analyze the efficacy of institutional changes to address inequalities in political representation. By adopting the gender parity reform in 2000, France is among the first countries in the world to promote equal political representation for men and women. As this bold experiment unfolds, its results will be widely scrutinized for the lessons it provides to comparativists and concerned citizens.

France pioneered another institutional reform involving intergroup relations when legislation was passed in 1999 creating a civil union between couples of the same or opposite sex, the civil solidarity pact (*pacte civil de solidarité,* or *Pacs*). The *Pacs* provides couples who register their association some of the legal rights hitherto enjoyed only by married couples. The innovation signifies a liberalization of French cultural attitudes, although it has been sharply contested by conservative groups.

On the level of political culture more generally, France has prided itself on its universalist yet distinctive role in history, deriving from its revolutionary heritage of liberty, equality, and fraternity. But we have analyzed how these values have become less effective in demarcating what is distinctive about France and in promoting cohesion among French citizens. Another challenge to French political culture and national pride is that the French language, revered by the French for its beauty and precision, and for centuries the favored medium for international diplomatic communication, has largely been eclipsed by English. The French have devoted considerable efforts to preserving the place of

French in the world—as well as in France (where English has made important inroads through advertising, television, and popular music). But here again, it is not certain whether the struggle will succeed in preserving France's distinctive heritage.

Yet another question that invites us to analyze French political culture in a comparative context is the troubling question of Le Pen's electoral success in 2002. One should not overestimate Le Pen's success; particular features of the presidential election, such as the record number of candidates, help explain why Le Pen nosed out Jospin for second place. But the importance of the election should not be underestimated, either. More generally, how can democratic institutions be preserved, even in face of those who mount racist attacks on minorities within a country?

In terms of France's position on the world stage, students can analyze how France seeks to maintain a favored position while no longer being able to occupy a preeminent rank. France is not alone in seeking to maintain national cohesion in the face of internal diversity and close integration in the international economic and political order. Nor is it the only country seeking to balance political cohesion with the right of diverse groups to maintain their distinct identity. Confronting these challenges will help shape the French political agenda in coming years. In brief, more than thirty years after youthful French protesters chanted in May 1968, "The struggle continues," the words have lost none of their relevance.

Key Terms

ancien régime	statist
revolution	indicative planning
republic	dirigisme
prefects	dirigiste
protectionist	deregulation
authoritarian	cohabitation
proportional representation	referendum
conservative	grandes écoles
socialist	grands corps
nationalization	judicial review

Suggested Readings

Birnbaum, Pierre. *Jewish Destinies: Citizenship, State, and Community in Modern France.* New York: Hill & Wang, 2000.

———. *The Idea of France.* New York: Hill & Wang, 2001.

Brubaker, Rogers. *Citizenship and Nationhood in France and Germany.* Cambridge, Mass.: Harvard University Press, 1992.

Chapman, Herrick, Kesselman, Mark, and Schain, Martin A., eds. *A Century of Organized Labor in France: A Union Movement for the Twenty-First Century?* New York: St. Martin's Press, 1998.

Daley, Anthony. *Steel, State, and Labor: Mobilization and Adjustment in France.* Pittsburgh: University of Pittsburgh Press, 1996.

———, ed. *The Mitterrand Era: Policy Alternatives and Political Mobilization in France.* New York: New York University Press, 1996.

Duyvendak, Jan Willem. *The Power of Politics: New Social Movements in France.* Boulder, Colo.: Westview, 1995.

Favell, Adrian. *Philosophies of Integration: Immigration and the Idea of Citizenship in France and Britain.* New York: St. Martin's Press, 1998.

Gaffney, John, and Milne, Lorna, eds. *French Presidentialism and the Election of 1995.* Brookfield, Vt.: Ashgate, 1997.

Gopnik, Adam. *Paris to the Moon.* New York: Random House, 2000.

Gordon, Philip A., and Meunier, Sophie. *The French Challenge: Adapting to Globalization.* Washington, D.C.: Brookings, 2001.

Hall, Peter A. *Governing the Economy: The Politics of State Intervention in Britain and France.* New York: Oxford University Press, 1986.

Hall, Peter, Hayward, Jack, and Machin, Howard, eds. *Developments in French Politics 2.* New York: Macmillan, 1998.

Haus, Leah. *Unions, Immigration, and Internationalization: New Challenges and Changing Coalitions in the United States and France.* New York: Palgrave Macmillan, 2002.

Howell, Chris. *Regulating Labor: The State and Industrial Relations Reform in Postwar France.* Princeton, N.J.: Princeton University Press, 1992.

Huber, John D. *Rationalizing Parliament: Legislative Institutions and Party Politics in France.* Cambridge: Cambridge University Press, 1996.

Ireland, Patrick. *The Policy Challenge of Ethnic Diversity: Immigrant Politics in France and Switzerland.* Cambridge, Mass.: Harvard University Press, 1994.

Keeler, John T. S., and Schain, Martin A., eds. *Chirac's Challenge: Liberalization, Europeanization, and Malaise in France.* New York: St. Martin's Press, 1996.

Levy, Jonah. *Tocqueville's Revenge: Dilemmas of Institutional Reform in Post-Dirigiste France.* Cambridge, Mass.: Harvard University Press, 1999.

Lewis-Beck, Michael S., ed. *How France Votes.* New York: Chatham House, 2000.

Mazur, Amy G. *Gender Bias and the State: Symbolic Reform at Work in Fifth Republic France.* Pittsburgh: University of Pittsburgh Press, 1996.

Noiriel, Gérard. *The French Melting Pot: Immigration, Citizenship, and National Identity.* Minneapolis: University of Minnesota Press, 1996.

Pierce, Roy. *Choosing the Chief: Presidential Elections in France and the United States.* Ann Arbor: University of Michigan Press, 1995.

Sa'adah, Anne. *Contemporary France: A Democratic Education.* Lanham, Md.: Rowman and Littlefield, 2003.

Schmidt, Vivien A. *From State to Market? The Transformation of French Business and Government.* Cambridge: Cambridge University Press, 1996.

Simmons, Harvey G. *The French National Front: The Extremist Challenge to Democracy.* Boulder, Colo.: Westview, 1996.

Smith, W. Rand. *The Left's Dirty Job: The Politics of Industrial Restructuring in France and Spain.* Pittsburgh: University of Pittsburgh Press, 1998.

Stone, Alec. *The Birth of Judicial Politics in France.* New York: Oxford University Press, 1992.

Tiersky, Ronald. *François Mitterrand: The Last French President.* New York: St. Martin's Press, 2000.

Tilly, Charles. *The Contentious French: Four Centuries of Popular Struggle.* Cambridge, Mass.: The Belknap Press of Harvard University Press, 1986.

Suggested Websites

French Embassy site in Washington, D.C.
www.ambafrance-us.org/fnews.htm
French foreign ministry
www.diplomatie.gouv.fr/actualite/actu.asp
National Assembly site
www.assemblee-nationale.fr
Prime minister's site
www.premier-ministre.gouv.fr/en
The Tocqueville Connection
www.ttc.org

Notes

[1] Simon Schama, *Citizens: A Chronicle of the French Revolution* (New York: Knopf, 1989), 62.

[2] Lynn Hunt, *Politics, Culture, and Class in the French Revolution* (Berkeley: University of California Press, 1984), 15, 56.

[3] Joan B. Landes, *Women and the Public Sphere in the Age of the French Revolution* (Ithaca, N.Y.: Cornell University Press, 1988), 171–172.

[4] William H. Sewell, Jr., *Work and Revolution in France: The Language of Labor from the Old Regime to 1848* (Cambridge: Cambridge University Press, 1980), 199. Georges Dupeux, *La société française, 1789–1970* (Paris: Armand Colin, 1974), 10.

[5] Richard F. Kuisel, *Capitalism and the State in Modern France* (Cambridge: Cambridge University Press, 1981), 15.

[6] Suzanne Daley, "As French Campaign Ends, Many Focus on Next Round," *New York Times,* April 20, 2002.

[7] *Le Monde,* April 23, 2002.

[8] *Le Monde,* May 3, 2002.

[9] *Le Monde,* May 10, 2002.

[10] *Le Monde,* May 7, 2002.

[11] Kuisel, *Capitalism and the State,* p. 277.

[12] Henri Mendras with Alistair Cole, *Social Change in Modern France: Towards a Cultural Anthropology of the Fifth Republic* (Cambridge: Cambridge University Press, 1991), 1.

[13] Peter A. Hall, *Governing the Economy: The Politics of State Intervention in Britain and France* (New York: Oxford University Press, 1986), 163.

[14] Amy Verdun, *European Responses to Globalization and Financial Market Integration: Perceptions of Economic and Monetary Union in Britain, France and Germany* (New York: St. Martin's Press, 2000), 177.

[15] Peter A. Hall, "From One Modernization Strategy to Another: The Character and Consequences of Recent Economic Policy in France" (paper presented to the Tenth International Conference of Europeanists, Chicago, March 15, 1996).

[16] The best study of the process in English is Vivien A. Schmidt, *From State to Market? The Transformation of French Business and Government* (Cambridge: Cambridge University Press, 1996), chaps. 5–6.

[17] *Le Monde,* June 4, 2002.

[18] J. Fagnani, "Family Policies and Working Mothers: A Comparison of France and West Germany," in M. D. Garcia-Ramon and J. Monk, eds., *Women of the European Union: The Politics of Work and Daily Life* (London: Routledge, 1996), 133.

[19] Fondation Saint-Simon, *Pour une nouvelle république sociale* (Paris: Calmann-Lévy, 1997), 44.

[20] Ezra Suleiman, "Les élites de l'administration et de la politique dans la France de la Ve République: Homogénéité, puissance, permanence," in Ezra Suleiman and Henri Mendras, eds., *Le recrutement des élites en Europe* (Paris: La Découverte, 1995), 33.

[21] John T. S. Keeler and Alec Stone, "Judicial-Political Confrontation in Mitterrand's France: The Emergence of the Constitutional Council as a Major Actor in the Policy-making Process," in Stanley Hoffmann, George Ross, and Sylvia Malzacher, eds., *The Mitterrand Experiment: Continuity and Change in Mitterrand's France* (New York: Oxford University Press, 1987), 176.

[22] Jean Charlot, *La Politique en France* (Paris: Livre de Poche, 1994), 21.

[23] Pascal Perrineau, "Election Cycles and Changing Patterns of Political Behavior in France," *French Politics and Society* 13, no. 1 (Winter 1995): 53.

[24] *Libération,* July 4, 2002.

[25] Rogers Brubaker, *Citizenship and Nationhood in France and Germany* (Cambridge, Mass.: Harvard University Press, 1992).

[26]Charles Tilly, Foreword to Gérard Noiriel, *The French Melting Pot: Immigration, Citizenship, and National Identity* (Minneapolis: University of Minnesota Press, 1996), vii.

[27]Noiriel, *The French Melting Pot,* 240.

[28]Stephen Bornstein, "States and Unions: From Postwar Settlement to Contemporary Stalemate," in Stephen Bornstein, David Held, and Joel Krieger, eds., *The State in Capitalist Europe: A Casebook* (Winchester, Mass.: George Allen & Unwin, 1984), 64.

[29]Commissariat général du plan, *Rapport sur les perspectives de la France* (Paris: La Documentation Française, 2000), 86.

[30]Patrick Jarreau, *La France de Chirac* (Paris: Flammarion, 1995), 9.

[31]Pierre Birnbaum, *The Idea of France* (New York: Hill & Wang, 2001), 278–279.

[32]*Le Monde,* April 30, 2002.

[33]*Le Monde,* May 29, 2002.

[34]James G. Shields, "Le Pen and the Progression of the Far-Right Vote in France," *French Politics and Society* 13, no. 2 (Spring 1995): 37.

[35]*New York Times,* February 26, 2002.

[36]Robert C. Lieberman, "Weak State, Strong Policy: Paradoxes of Race Policy in the United States, Great Britain, and France?" *Studies in American Political Development* 16 (Fall 2002): 139.

[37]Bernard Cazes, Fabrice Hatem, and Paul Thibaud, "L'État et la société française en l'an 2000," *Esprit,* no. 165 (October 1990): 95.

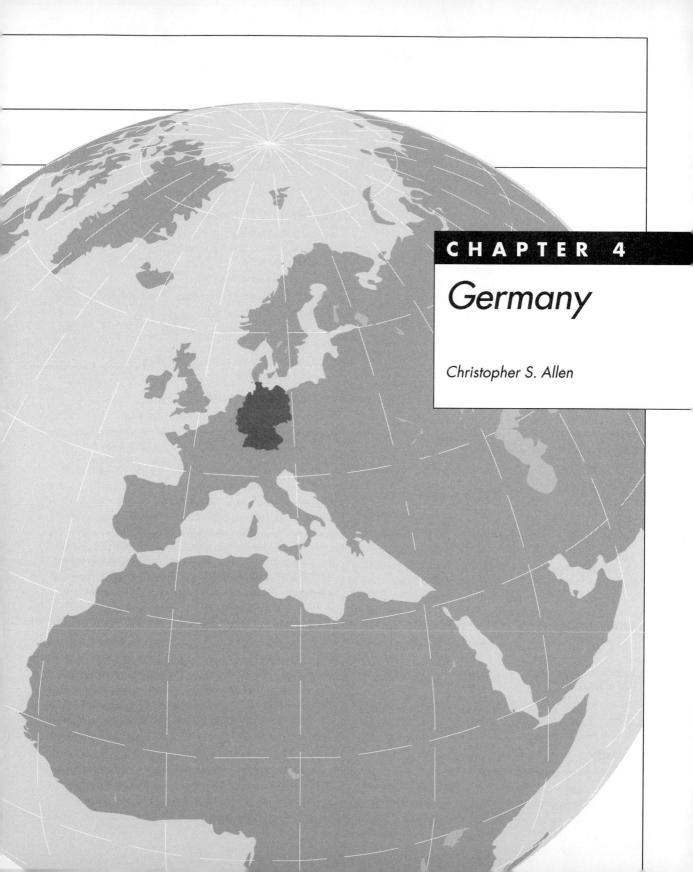

CHAPTER 4

Germany

Christopher S. Allen

Federal Republic of Germany

Land and People

Capital	Berlin
Total area (square miles)	137,830 (Slightly smaller than Montana)
Population	82.0

Annual population growth rate (%)	1975–2000	0.2
	2000–2015 (projected)	–.1

Urban population (%)	87.5

Ethnic composition (%)	German	91.5
	Turkish	2.4
	Other	6.1

Major language(s)	German

Religious affiliation (%)	Protestant	34
	Roman Catholic	34
	Muslim	3.7
	Unaffiliated or other	28.3

Economy

Domestic currency	Euro
Total GDP (US$)	1.87 trillion
GDP per capita (US$)	22,753
Total GDP at purchasing power parity (US$)	2.06 trillion
GDP per capita at purchasing power parity (US$)	25,103

GDP annual growth rate (%)	1997	1.4
	2000	3.0
	2001	0.6

GDP per capita average annual growth rate (%)	1975–2000	1.9
	1990–2000	1.2

Inequality in income or consumption (1994) (%)	Share of poorest 10%	3.3
	Share of poorest 20%	8.2
	Share of richest 20%	38.5
	Share of richest 10%	23.7
	Gini Index (1994)	30.0

Structure of production (% of GDP)	Agriculture	1.2
	Industry	31.2
	Services	67.6

Labor force distribution (% of total)	Agriculture	2.8
	Industry	33.4
	Services	63.8

Exports as % of GDP	33
Imports as % of GDP	33

Society

Life expectancy at birth	77.7
Infant mortality per 1000 live births	5

Adult literacy (%)	99*

The OECD estimates that Germany has a functional illiteracy rate of about 14%.

Access to information and communications (per 1,000 population)	Telephone lines	611
	Mobile phones	586
	Radios	948
	Televisions	586
	Personal computers	336

Women in Government and the Economy

Women in the National Legislature		
Lower house or single house (%)		32.2
Upper house (%)		24.6
Women at ministerial level (%)		35.7
Female economic activity rate (age 15 and above) (%)		47.9
Female labor force (% of total)		42
Estimated earned income (PPP US$)	Female	16,904
	Male	33,653
2002 Human Development Index Ranking (out of 173 countries)		17

Political Organization

Political System   Parliamentary democracy.

Regime History   After Third Reich's defeat, Germany was partitioned and occupied by Allies in 1945. In 1949 the Federal Republic of Germany (FGR) was established in the west and the German Democratic Republic (GDR) was established in the east. The two German states unified in 1990.

Administrative Structure   Federal, with 16 states. Germany does not have sharp separation between levels of government.

Executive   Ceremonial president is the head of state, elected for a five-year term (with a two-term limit) by the Federal Convention. Chancellor is head of government and is a member of the *Bundestag* and a leader of the majority party or coalition.

Legislature   Bicameral. *Bundestag* Senate (603 members at 2002 federal election) elected via dual ballot system combining single-member districts and proportional representation. Upper house (*Bundesrat*) comprises 69 members who are elected and appointed officials from the 16 states.

Judiciary   Autonomous and independent. The legal system has 3 levels: Federal High Court, which is the criminal-civil system; Special Constitutional Court, dealing with matters affecting Basic Law; and Administrative Court, consisting of Labor, Social Security, and Finance courts.

Party System   Multiparty. Major parties are Social Democratic Party (SDP), the Greens, Christian Democratic Union (CDU), Christian Social Union (CSU), Free Democratic Party (FDP), and Party of Democratic Socialism (PDS).

Section ❶ The Making of the Modern German State

Politics in Action

Any journey to Berlin today produces a powerful first impression. Construction equipment is virtually everywhere, and the noise and bustle accompanying this frenetic activity seem almost overwhelming to both first-time visitors as well as those who have not been there for several years.

Two things are driving this structural overhaul of Germany's largest city. First, as a result of unification of the formerly divided Germany in 1990, the capital has moved from Bonn, its former site. The erection of new ministry offices is responsible for much of this construction boom as older buildings are rehabilitated and newer ones spring up seemingly overnight. Second, Berlin's location deep within the former East Germany has presented German governments during the past decade with both an opportunity and an obligation to rebuild that region after forty years of Communist underdevelopment. The structural rebuilding of the city has had a powerful effect in raising the values of both commercial and residential properties. It also has reinvigorated cultural and political life, as the former divided city once again becomes a world capital.

The merging of the two states in 1990 was the second unification in modern Germany's brief history. The principalities that joined in 1871 to form the first modern German state, called the Second Reich, produced a remarkable—and often catastrophic—variety of political outcomes: an authoritarian pseudo-democracy, World War I, the ill-fated Weimar Republic, the fascist Nazi regime (the Third Reich), World War II and the Holocaust, the postwar partition into two Germanies, and finally, a modern reunification. Unlike Britain, whose democracy developed gradually over many centuries, Germany established a stable democracy only after great fluctuations in regimes, two military defeats, and a foreign occupation, and then only in part of its former territory. A highly repressive Communist government until unification in 1990 ruled East Germany, which remained within the Soviet Union's sphere of influence.

The return of the capital to Berlin not surprisingly has generated some fears as well as enthusiasm among both Germans and other Europeans. In many ways, the change in Berlin's physical and political status is a metaphor for both the challenges and the opportunities that Germany faces in the twenty-first century. Some of its neighbors fear that Germany will once again become a menace to the European continent as it did twice during the early to mid-twentieth century. The rebuilding of the *Reichstag,* the parliament building constructed by Otto von Bismarck, who founded modern Germany in 1871 and used by Hitler, drives some of the foreign anxiety about Germany's role in the new century. Realistically, an aggressive Germany is highly unlikely, but the country's unique history still worries skeptics. Second, the frenetic, expensive, and often ostentatious building boom in the new capital contrasts sharply with the dilapidated condition of much of eastern Germany that surrounds Berlin. Eastern Germans complain that western Germans use their disproportionately high wealth to behave as carpetbaggers in the former German Democratic Republic (GDR). The faster that Berlin grows, the more obviously eastern Germans believe they lag behind. Third, Berlin's rapid growth and Europe's open borders have served as an economic magnet for eastern Germans but also for migrants from both Eastern Europe and the rest of the world. The rapid immigration of foreigners into a part of Germany that was both ethnically and culturally homogeneous during the Communist years has proved combustible. Now, eastern Germans perceive the influx of immigrants as both an economic and a cultural threat. Finally, the growth of Berlin as Germany's new capital raises once again in some minds the question of whether we are witnessing the evolution of a German Europe or a European Germany.

The new Berlin—and Germany as a whole—stand at a turning point that could lead in one of two directions. The first might see a consolidation of postwar successes in which the former East Germans achieve the material prosperity and democratic political culture of their western counterparts. This could help Germany to become the anchor in the expanding European Union (EU) as a partner with, not a conqueror of, its neighbors. The second path would be much more dangerous. It could see rising social conflict, unstable domestic institutions, uncertain international relations including a weakened EU, and difficulties in responding to global economic competition. Success or failure will most likely depend on how well Germany and the rest of Europe combine economic growth with social equity and inclusionary and politically accountable forms of democratic representation.

Geographic Setting

Germany is located in central Europe and has been as much a Western European nation as an Eastern European one. It has a total area of 137,803 square miles (slightly smaller than the state of Montana). Its population of 82 million, comprising about 90 percent Germans, all of whom speak German as the primary language, is roughly evenly divided between Roman

Catholics and Protestants. Germany has been relatively homogeneous ethnically; however, the presence of several million Turks in Germany, first drawn to the Federal Republic as *Gastarbeiter* (guest workers) in the 1960s, suggests that ethnic diversity will continue to grow. Furthermore, increased migration across borders by EU citizens will also decrease cultural homogeneity.

For a densely populated country, Germany has a surprisingly high 54 percent of its land in agricultural production. It is composed of large plains in northern Germany, a series of smaller mountain ranges in the center of the country, and the towering Alps to the south at the Austrian and Swiss borders. It has a temperate climate with considerable cloud cover and precipitation throughout the year. For Germany, the absence of natural borders in the west and east has been an important geographic fact. For example, on the north, it borders both the North and Baltic seas and the country of Denmark, but to the west, south, and east, it has many neighbors: the Netherlands, Belgium, Luxembourg, France, Switzerland, Austria, the Czech Republic, and Poland. Conflicts and wars with its neighbors were a constant feature in Germany until the end of World War II.

Germany's lack of resources—aside from iron ore and coal deposits in the Ruhr and the Saarland—has shaped much of the country's history. Since the Industrial Revolution in the nineteenth century, many of Germany's external relationships, both commercial and military, have revolved around gaining access to resources it lacks within its national borders. Germany is divided into sixteen **federal states** (*Bundesländer*), many of which correspond to historic German kingdoms and principalities (e.g., Bavaria, Saxony, Hesse) or medieval trading cities (e.g., Hamburg, Bremen).

Critical Junctures

Nationalism and German Unification (1806–1871)

The first German state was the Holy Roman Empire, founded by Charlemagne in 800 A.D. (sometimes referred to as the First Reich). But this loose and fragmented "*Reich*" (empire) bore little resemblance to a modern nation-state. The empire was composed of as

Critical Junctures in Germany's Political Development	
1806–1871	Nationalism and German Unification
1871–1918	Second Reich
1919–1933	Weimar Republic
1933–1945	Third Reich
1939–1945	World War II
1945–1990	A Divided Germany
1990–1998	The Challenge of German Unification
1990–Present	Germany in the Euro Era

many as three hundred sovereign entities and included the territories of present-day Germany, Austria, and the Czech Republic.

Two main factors hindered German state formation: uncertain geographic boundaries and religious division.[1] The geographic and religious divisions caused the German language and German physical and cultural traits to define German national identity to a much greater extent than in other European states. For many nineteenth-century Germans, the lack of political unity stood in sharp contrast to the strong influence of German culture in such literary and religious figures as Goethe, Schiller, and Luther.

The victories of the French emperor Napoleon against Prussia and Austria brought an end to the Holy Roman Empire. But defeat and occupation aroused strong German nationalist sentiment, and in 1813–1814 the Prussians led an alliance of German states in a "War of Liberation" culminating in a new German confederation.

In 1819, authoritarian Prussian leaders confidently launched a tariff union with neighboring German states that by 1834 encompassed almost all of the German Confederation except Austria, greatly expanding Prussian influence at Austria's expense. But free-market capitalism and democracy did not take root in the Prussian-dominated Germanic principalities. Instead, there surfaced qualities such as a strong state, the dominance of a reactionary group of noble landlords in eastern Prussia called *Junkers,* a patriotic military, and a political culture dominated by honor, duty, and service to the state.

The European revolutions of 1848 sparked many pro-democracy uprisings, including Berlin and Vienna, respectively the Prussian and Austrian capitals. But these revolutionary democratic movements in Germany and Austria were violently and quickly suppressed. Germany would be united instead by a "revolution from above" led by Count Otto von Bismarck who became minister-president of Prussia in 1862.[2] A *Junker* who reflected the values and authoritarian vision of his class, Bismarck realized that Prussia needed to industrialize and modernize its economy to compete with Britain, France, and the United States. He created an unlikely and nondemocratic coalition of northeastern rural *Junkers* and northwestern Ruhr Valley iron industrialists. The coalition relied on a support of elites rather than on the democratic working class and peasant/farmers, as had the French and American revolutions. Very simply, Bismarck was contemptuous of democracy, preferring "blood and iron" as his primary political tools. He was also as good as his word, launching three short wars—against Denmark (1864), Austria (1866), and France (1870)—that culminated in the unification of Germany.[3] The so-called Second Reich, excluding Austria and with the king of Prussia as *Kaiser* (emperor), was proclaimed in 1871.

The Second Reich (1871–1918)

The Second Reich (a term not used at the time but only retrospectively in the twentieth century) was an authoritarian regime that was democratic in appearance only. Undemocratic forces (industrial and landed elites) controlled political and economic power. Bismarck's regime was symbolically democratic in that the "Iron Chancellor" allowed for universal male suffrage for the lower house (*Reichstag*) of the bicameral legislature, but real decision-making authority lay in the hands of the upper house (*Landtag*), which Bismarck controlled.

The primary goal of the Second Reich was rapid industrialization, supported by state power and a powerful banking system geared to foster large-scale industrial investment rather than by the trial-and-error methods of free markets.[4] This path was so successful that Germany had become a leading industrial power by 1900, emphasizing such industries as coal, steel, railroads, dyes, chemicals, industrial electronics, and machine tools. The state pushed the development of such heavy industries at the expense of those producing consumer goods. Lacking a strong domestic consumer goods economy, Germany had to sell a substantial portion of what it produced on world markets.

Rapid transformation of a largely agrarian society in the 1850s to an industrial one by the turn of the twentieth century created widespread social dislocation and growing opposition to the conservative regime. A small middle class of professionals and small-business owners with rising expectations pressured the government to democratize and provide basic **liberal** (i.e., free-market) rights. Industrialization also promoted the growth of a manually skilled working class and the corresponding rise of a militant Social Democratic Party (*Sozialdemokratische Partei Deutschlands,* SPD). The Social Democrats' primary goals were economic rights in the workplace and democratization of the political system. The party was greatly influenced by the founders of socialism, Germans Karl Marx and Friedrich Engels. Socialist philosophy argues that workers, as producers of society's goods and services, should receive a greater share of economic and political power. The SPD grew as fast as the pace of German industrialization.

As German chancellor from 1871 to 1890, Bismarck alternately persecuted and grudgingly tolerated the democratic and socialist opposition. He banned the Social Democratic Party yet created the first welfare state as a way to blunt the effects of rapid economic growth. Social welfare benefits included health insurance and the first forms of state-sponsored old-age pensions. This combination of welfare with political repression is sometimes referred to as Bismarck's iron fist in a velvet glove.

Bismarck also significantly influenced German political culture by creating a strong and centralized German state. The ***Kulturkampf*** (cultural struggle) he initiated was a prime example of Prussian and Protestant dominance. Essentially a movement against the Catholic Church, it sought to remove educational and cultural institutions from the church and place them under the state. This action, which polarized the church and many Catholic Germans, left a powerful political legacy.

By 1900, Germany's primary economic problem consisted of obtaining necessary raw materials and accessing world markets to sell their finished goods, thus sustaining rapid economic growth. Germany then embarked on an imperial adventure sometimes called "the scramble for Africa."[5] However, as a latecomer on this continent, Germany could colonize only resource-poor southwestern Africa. From 1871 until World War I, Germany tried and failed to extend its colonial and economic influence. This failure inflamed German nationalists and pushed German leaders to rapidly develop the shipbuilding industry and a navy to secure German economic and geopolitical interests.

An undemocratic domestic political system, the lack of profitable colonies, an exposed geopolitical position in central Europe, and increasingly inflamed nationalism heightened Germany's aggression toward other nations and ultimately prompted it to launch World War I in 1914.

German leaders expected the war to be brief and victorious. It turned into a protracted conflict, however, and cost Germany both its few colonial possessions and its imperial social order. The Second Reich collapsed in November 1918, leaving a weak foundation for the country's first attempt to establish a parliamentary democracy. The costs of defeat were substantial and fatally compromised Germany's first democratic regime, the Weimar Republic.

The Weimar Republic (1918–1933)

Kaiser Wilhelm II abdicated at the end of World War I, and the Weimar Republic (the constitution was drafted in that eastern German city) replaced the Second Reich. The SPD, the only remaining party not discredited by the failed war, found itself in charge of Germany's first democracy. Its first unwelcome task was to surrender to the Allies.

The new government was a procedural democracy; holding regular elections and comprising multiple parties from the far left to the far right. Yet it had a fatal flaw: the many right-wing political parties and social forces, as well as the Communists on the left, refused to accept the legitimacy of democratic government.

From the beginning, the SPD leadership was on shaky ground: it foolishly asked the undemocratic military to "guarantee" order and stability; the SPD's signing the Treaty of Versailles and its onerous reparations payments allowed the right to accuse the government of having "stabbed Germany in the back"; and it failed to address the ruinous inflation of 1923, when the government was forced to print worthless Reichmarks to pay the huge war reparations.

Into this turmoil stepped Adolf Hitler, a little-known, Austrian-born former corporal in the German army, who became the leader of the Nazi Party in 1920 (**Nazi** is a German acronym for National Socialist German Workers' Party). Taking advantage of a deepening economic crisis, the Nazis mobilized large segments of the population by preaching hatred of the left and of "inferior, non-Aryan races."

After the Great Depression spread to central Europe in 1931, Germany became more unstable, with none of the major parties able to win a majority or even form durable government coalitions. Frequent elections produced ever shakier minority governments.

The Nazis relentlessly pressed for political power from a population that continued to underestimate Hitler's real intentions and viewed his hate-filled speeches as merely political rhetoric. The Nazis were rewarded in early 1933 when Hitler outmaneuvered President Paul von Hindenburg, a former World War I general, to become chancellor in a Nazi-Nationalist coalition government sworn in on January 30. Under the Weimar Constitution, as in many other parliamentary systems, the head of state chose the next head of government when no one party or coalition received a majority of the seats. Once in power, the Nazis arranged for a fire at the *Reichstag* that they falsely blamed on the Communists. After Hindenburg issued emergency decrees that suspended free speech, free press, and other liberties in March 1933, Hitler rammed through the *Reichstag* the infamous Enabling Act. This legislation gave sweeping powers to the Nazi-dominated cabinet, rendering the *Reichstag* irrelevant as a representative political body.

The Third Reich (1933–1945)

After the Nazis had obtained the chancellorship, establishing social control was their next major priority, and the initial step was banning political parties and then all civic and religious institutions. Ultimately, the Nazis employed propaganda and demagoguery in the absence of democratic opposition to mobilize large segments of the German population. Using mesmerizing speeches and a relentless propaganda ministry led by Joseph Goebbels, Hitler exercised total control of

Hitler strides triumphantly through a phalanx of Nazi storm troopers (SA) in 1934.   *Source:* © Ullstein Bilderdienst.

political power and the media to reshape German politics to his party's vision. This vision allowed no opposition, even within the party.

Initial Nazi domestic policy was focused on two major areas: centralization of political power and the rebuilding of an economy devastated by the depression of the early 1930s. The Nazis concentrated all political authority in Berlin, removing any regional political autonomy. The main purpose of this top-down system was to ensure that Nazi policy regarding the repression of political opposition and Jews and other minorities was carried out to the minutest detail.

The Nazis' economic program was also autocratic in design and implementation. Because free trade unions had been banned, both private and state-run industries

forced workers, including slave laborers during World War II, to work long hours for little or no pay. The program emphasized heavier industries that required massive investment from the large manufacturing cartels, the banking system, and the state itself. Although some segments of big business had initially feared Hitler before he took power, most of German industry eventually endorsed Nazi economic policies. The Nazis also emphasized massive public works projects, such as building the *Autobahn* highway system, upgrading the railroad system, and constructing grandiose public buildings. Almost all favored Nazi industries had direct military application. Even the *Autobahn* was built more for easing military transport than for encouraging pleasure driving.

Hitler incited German nationalism by glorifying the warrior tradition in German folklore and exulting in imperial Germany's conquests in the nineteenth century. Touting a mythically glorious and racially pure German past, he made scapegoats out of homosexuals, ethnic minorities such as gypsies, and especially the Jews. Antisemitism proved a powerful political force that allowed Hitler to blame Germany's problems on an "external" international minority and to target them as enemies to be relentlessly persecuted, suppressed, and exterminated.

The Nazis refused to abide by the provisions of the 1919 Treaty of Versailles and began producing armaments in large quantities and remilitarized the Rhineland. Hitler rejected the territorial divisions of World War I, claiming that a growing Germany needed increased space to live (*Lebensraum*) in eastern Europe. He ordered a forced union with Austria in March 1938 and the occupation of the German-speaking Sudetenland areas of Czechoslovakia in September 1938. The Third Reich's attack on Poland on September 1, 1939, finally precipitated World War II.

Hitler's visions of German world domination were dramatically heightened by Germany's conquest of much of Europe in 1939 and 1940. In 1941, he turned his attention to the Soviet Union, the only continental power that stood in his way. Assuming that the USSR would fall as easily as did his other conquests, he attacked it in the summer of 1941, violating the Nazi-Soviet Nonaggression Pact of 1939. Ultimately, the failed attack not only ended German military successes but also began the defeat of the Third Reich, a process that would grind on for almost four more years. Yet even as defeat loomed for Germany in May 1945, Hitler wanted the country totally destroyed rather than have it surrender "national honor."

The most heinous aspect of the Nazi regime was the systematic extermination of 6 million Jews and millions of other civilians in concentration camps. Hitler explicitly stated in his book *Mein Kampf* (*My Struggle*) that the Germans were the master race and all those of non-Aryan ethnicity, especially Jews, were inferior. The Nazis placed most of the extermination camps in occupied countries like Poland; the most infamous one in Germany was Dachau, just outside Munich.

A Divided Germany (1945–1990)

Germany was occupied by the victorious Allied powers from 1945 to 1949. However, cold war tensions soon led to the formal division of Germany: the Federal Republic of Germany (FRG) in the west and the communist German Democratic Republic (GDR) in the east.

During the years of occupation, FRG and Allied officials reduced the powers of the central state in domestic politics, which were partly assumed by regional governments. Western German reformers also rebuilt the party system, helping to create parties with more broad-based interests and ideological considerations. The most significant political development was the merger in 1946 of Roman Catholic and Protestant interests into the Christian Democratic Party, as was not the case during the Weimar period, when the Catholics had their own separate party.

Nation-statehood was restored to the two Germanys in 1949, but neither of the two parts of divided Germany was fully sovereign. The FRG deferred to the United States in matters of international relations, as did the GDR to the Soviet Union. Neither of the two Germanys joined the cold war's international alliances—NATO (North Atlantic Treaty Organization) and the Warsaw Pact, respectively—until 1955. The United

"Enemies of the Third Reich"   *Source:* Courtesy of The Trustees of the Boston Public Library, Rare Books and Manuscripts. Reproduced with the permission of Alexandra Szyk Bracie, daughter of Arthur Szyk, in cooperation with The Arthur Szyk Society, www.syzk.org

States and the USSR felt it was necessary to restrict their respective German client states, a condition that continued for decades.

In 1949, the Federal Republic became a democracy, characterized by constitutional provisions for free elections, civil liberties and individual rights, and an independent judiciary. Its main political institutions were a bicameral parliamentary system, a **chancellor** (head of government), a president (head of state), a multiparty system, and an independent judiciary.

The Federal Republic's democratic system produced rapid economic growth and remarkable political stability for the first forty years of its existence. Alternation from a moderate center-right government to a moderate center-left one, and back again, produced high standards of living and a genuine democratic regime. Under Christian Democratic chancellors Konrad Adenauer (1949–1963) and Ludwig Erhard (1963–1966) the FRG saw the establishment of a new parliamentary regime, an extensive system of social welfare benefits, a politically regulated market economy, and the re-establishment of strong regional governments, which assumed responsibilities formerly handled by the central government. Under Social Democratic chancellors Willy Brandt (1969–1974) and Helmut Schmidt (1974–1982) the FRG first enjoyed robust full employment and a large increase in social services. The SPD also advocated a more equal distribution of income. The government passed legislation requiring in-plant works councils and company-wide **co-determination,** that is, trade union participation on company boards. For most of the post–World War II period, this rank-and-file democratic participation, often called **democratic corporatism,** helped alleviate much of the social tension that had plagued Germany before 1945.[6] But later in the 1970s, two economic recessions produced increased unemployment and forced Chancellor Schmidt to introduce moderate cutbacks in social services. Yet unlike many Western capitalist countries in the 1980s, West Germany's postwar welfare state retained many of its services and most of its public support.

The Christian Democrats returned to power in 1982 under the leadership of Chancellor Helmut Kohl, who formed a center-right coalition with the Free Democratic Party (FDP), a moderate centrist party that had coalesced with both of the two major parties in

most governments since 1949. The coalition enthusiastically embraced the concept of the single European market and pragmatically moved to reunite East and West Germany. The 1949–1990 period established the viability of constitutional democracy in the Federal Republic, as the country maintained a firm commitment to parliamentary government and political stability.

In the meantime, the German Democratic Republic (a "people's democracy," in communist parlance) was established in Soviet-occupied East Germany in 1949. The GDR was a one-party state under the control of the communist party, which was known as the Socialist Unity Party (SED, *Sozialistische Einheits Partei*). Although the state provided full employment, housing, and various social benefits to its citizens, it was a rigid, bureaucratic, Stalinist regime that tightly controlled economic and political life under the leadership of party chairmen Walter Ulbricht, Willi Stoph, and finally Eric Honnecker. East Germany assumed a universal consensus about the correctness of communism and suppressed public dissent as deviationist and undermining the "true path of socialism." East Germans caught trying to flee to the West were subject to execution on the spot. In August 1961, East Germany erected the Berlin Wall to keep its citizens from fleeing to West Germany.

For more than forty years, the international role of the two Germanys was limited. Because of NATO's geopolitical restrictions, West German energies were focused on rebuilding the economy and pursuing European economic integration. East Germany was similarly restricted. Although it became the strongest of the Warsaw Pact's economies, it also loyally toed the Soviet line in international affairs.

The Challenge of German Unification (1990–1998)

Germany's unification in 1990 took place rapidly, surprising West and East Germans alike. When the Berlin Wall was opened in November 1989, the two German states envisioned a slow process of increased contacts and cooperation while maintaining separate sovereign states for the short term. When a currency reform provided East Germans with valuable West German deutsche marks, this move fueled the migration westward in the summer of 1990. After a referendum on unification and intense negotiations in the late summer, the former East Germany was incorporated into the FRG as five new West German states (*Länder*).

Formal unification took place in the fall of 1990 as Helmut Kohl, the "unification chancellor," won a strong reelection victory for his center-right Christian Democratic–Free Democratic coalition. But unification euphoria did not last, as its costs strained Germany's budget and democratic institutions. The process proved much more difficult than expected. Before unification, East Germany was considered the strongest of the Eastern European Communist economies. But the border opening and eventual unification soon showed that the East German economy was far more backward than most economists had thought. The Communist planned economy (sometimes called a *command economy*) was not sensitive to market signals since production of goods was determined more by rigid government dictates than by real consumer needs. The East German level of technology was decades behind, and the unified German government spent billions just to rebuild communication networks. Politically, East Germany was a state in which open political discourse and expression had been discouraged, if not prohibited. Of course, people would meet and speak candidly among family or close friends, but a liberal democratic political culture did not exist.

Incorporating the disadvantaged Eastern Germany into the FRG had an adverse impact on a wide range of public policies, including unemployment expenses, structural-rebuilding funds, and the large tax increases necessary to pay for it all. The large number of unemployed in eastern Germany—approximately 20 percent, which was more than twice the figure in the prosperous west—helped fuel scattered ultra-right-wing political movements. They sought out foreigners (often Turks) as scapegoats, and there were several vicious attacks on minority groups in the 1990s.

The difficulties of unification were complicated by raised expectations by the Kohl government throughout the 1990s. In order to win the support of eastern Germans, he sugarcoated the enormity of the unification process as well as its duration. In order to win the support of western Germans, he had to convince them that the 7.5 percent "unification tax" imposed on them

in the early 1990s would be money well spent. Unfortunately for Kohl, the longer the unification process remained incomplete, the less willing the German electorate was to give him continued support. He was able to convince voters to continue to support the Christian Democratic–Free Democratic government in the 1994 election, in which the coalition was returned to power, albeit with a significantly reduced majority.

By 1998, however, Kohl's center-right coalition had run out of both gas and ideas. Successfully convincing Germans that a change was necessary, newly elected SPD Chancellor Gerhard Schröder, a generation younger than Kohl, entered into a coalition government with the environmentalist Green Party for the first time in the nation's history. Significant too was the continued high support for the former communist party (PDS, Party of Democratic Socialism) in eastern Germany (over 20 percent), which enabled it to gain more than 5 percent of the total German vote. With almost 54 percent of the electorate voting for parties of the left, clearly a new era had arrived in Germany.

The speed with which East Germany came apart after the fall of the Berlin Wall surprised everyone, not the least Helmut Kohl. The former chancellor can certainly be faulted for misjudging the economic and political costs of German unification. In fact, his overpromising of the pace of East German transformation in the early 1990s was a critical factor in his electoral loss in 1998. However, in acting quickly to integrate East Germany as five new *Länder,* when an independent, noncommunist East Germany proved unworkable in the spring and summer of 1990, Kohl helped alleviate what could have been a politically disastrous situation for both Germany and the rest of Europe.

Germany in the Euro Era (1998–)

Germany's leaders from Adenauer through Schröder have all been strongly enthusiastic toward European integration. Why? In its relations with other states after World War II, Germany has faced two different kinds of criticism. First was the fear of a too-powerful Germany, a country that had run roughshod over its European neighbors for most of the first half of the twentieth century. Second is the opposite problem, the so-called economic giant–political dwarf syndrome in which Germany was accused of benefiting from a strong world economy for much of the past fifty years, while taking on none of the political responsibility. The fact that these are mutually contradictory points of view did not spare Germany from criticism.

An integrated Europe promised the possibility of solving both problems simultaneously. Germany will likely remain the economic anchor of the EU, and its membership in the EU will enable it to do things and take on needed political responsibilities that it would be unable to do on its own. Germany, like all of the other European nations that supported integration, has tended to see the glass as half-full. From Germany's viewpoint, meeting both criticisms in the context of the EU was a positive-sum outcome.

However, the comprehensive integration process that began with the Maastricht Treaty of 1992, which radically restructured the European Community (EC), formally established the European Union, and committed the EC to the Economic and Monetary Union by 1999 at the latest, had an unusual mechanism of dealing with issues. European leaders, faced with both easy and difficult tasks, made the choice to begin with the former and then address the latter. This meant that they took relatively straightforward steps of easing intra-European trade and travel and allowing for workers to cross borders for employment as long as they already had the requisite linguistic and job skills. The more complicated and difficult decisions, such as a single currency, monetary and fiscal policy, and democratic governance, were delayed. Optimistic European leaders, including the Germans, believed that a positive momentum, if not a "europhoria," would develop and thereby ease the transition toward continued integration.

In retrospect, the accelerating pace of European integration placed additional pressures on the Federal Republic. The movement toward a common monetary policy, a European central bank, and a single currency in 1999 for all bank and credit card transactions, followed by the physical elimination of all national currencies in favor of the euro in 2002, proved daunting. Many Germans wondered whether the anchor of stability represented by the redoubtable deutsche mark (DM) and the inflation-fighting *Deutsche Bundesbank* would begin to drift in the uncertain sea of the EU. By the early twenty-first century, many Germans began to

realize the costs associated with European integration that might threaten the economic and political stability that they had so long prized during the first fifty years of the Federal Republic. The fall in value of the euro by some 25 percent in relation to the dollar from 1999 to 2001 was worrisome to Germans, long accustomed to a stable and rock-hard DM. While the lower value of the euro meant it was easier for German industry to export goods, the higher prices for imported goods threatened to rekindle the age-old fear of German inflation. These fears eased somewhat when the euro moved close to parity with the dollar in 2003, but uncertainty remained.

With open borders and seemingly free-flowing immigration, Germans also wondered whether Europeanization threatened to erode what it meant to be German. At the same time that immigration and political asylum increased in Germany during the 1990s, the birthrate, particularly in the former GDR, dropped precipitously. Far-right and even some moderate right-wing politicians used these demographic changes to whip up nationalist support for decreasing the flow of migrants to the FRG. The terrorist attacks of September 11, 2001, and the discovery that some of the terrorists lived in Germany prior to the attacks only added to the tension. For a country that had prided itself in generously granting political asylum in the wake of the Nazi period, increased antiterrorist security requirements threatened to uproot decades of FRG postwar policy. Ironically, these demographic changes also coincided with the increased inability of the highly regarded secondary educational system to produce enough skilled workers for the information age. Germany's vocational educational system and integrated apprenticeship system have worked exceptionally well for traditionally strong German industries, but they have been less effective in producing highly qualified information sector workers. This "tech shortage" reached such a critical mass in the early 2000s that the Schröder government began to recruit scientists and engineers from other countries, particularly India, who eventually would be granted citizenship status. In other words, a new wave of *Gastarbeiter* was arriving precisely when some Germans were increasingly agitated about the immigration boom in the face of almost 10 percent unemployment. In fact, some conservative politicians reacted to the arrival of the Indian computer specialists with the phrase *Kinder statt Inder* (children instead of Indians), meaning that they would prefer that the government train German adolescents instead of inviting another wave of immigrants. The problem, however, was that the German economy needed to embrace technically skilled workers immediately and could not wait for other solutions. The country needed both to increase Germany's presence in this sector and enable its traditionally strong industries to adapt to new forms of international competition. The economic pressures did not allow the luxury of waiting the several years for the German secondary educational system to get up to speed. In late 2002, however, the German Supreme Court struck down a law on procedural ground that would have allowed up to 50,000 foreign technical workers to move to Germany. The Schröder government had to go back to the drawing board.

Finally, the issue of democratic governance was an additional European challenge. Like most other forms of increased integration among nation-states throughout history, economic integration generally precedes political integration. The EU has been no exception. However, in the rush toward integration, questions of political accountability have been less well emphasized. With fiscal and monetary policy essentially determined by either Brussels or the European Central Bank, where does democratic governance really lie?

Themes and Implications

Historical Junctures and Political Themes

Germany's role in the world of states is contentious. For all states, military strength is a basic tool used to shape and consolidate. But in Germany, the rise of militarism and a corresponding authoritarian political culture was exaggerated for several reasons. Germany's exposed position in the central plains of Europe encouraged military preparedness because any of its many neighbors could mount an attack with few constraints. Since various German-speaking lands lacked a solid democratic or liberal political culture before unification in 1871, Prussian militarism exerted a dominant influence over political and civic life. In other words, late unifi-

cation accompanied by war created a state that caused tremendous fear among Germany's neighbors. The conduct of World War I and especially the Third Reich of the Nazis and World War II intensified this fear. Although more than fifty years have passed since the end of World War II and although Germany's independent political actions are constrained by the EU, many Europeans remain wary of Germany's international role.

The second theme, governing the economy, has been colored profoundly by Germany's late unification and the issue of state building. Clearly, nation-states can promote economic growth more easily than can politically fragmented entities. Delayed unification and industrialization in Germany prevented it from embarking on the race for empire and raw materials until the late nineteenth century. By the time Germany joined the global economy, it lagged behind Britain and France in industrializing and securing access to the natural resources of developing countries. Thus, pursuit of fast economic growth and an awakened sense of German nationalism in the late nineteenth century produced an aggressive, acquisitive state in which economic and political needs overlapped. The fusion of state and economic power is what enabled Hitler to build the Third Reich. Consequently, post–World War II policymakers and political leaders desired to remove the state from actively governing the economy.

Thus, the postwar period saw the development of *Modell Deutschland* (the German Model), a term often used to describe the Federal Republic of Germany's distinctive political and socioeconomic features: coordinated banking and industrial relations, democratic participation by workers on the job, and extensive public sector benefits.[7] This model was unlike either the free-market traditions of countries like the United States and Great Britain or the more state-centered policies of democracies like France and Japan. Rather, postwar Germany developed an organized capitalist model that placed primacy on coordination among private sector actors to promote efficiency and competitiveness. As a counterweight to concentrated economic power, the Federal Republic also developed a strong labor movement that used democratic corporatism to participate in fundamental decisions often left to management in other countries. This model served Germany exceptionally well until the late 1990s, but its future is uncertain in the new era of the EU. It remains an open question whether previously successful German economic institutions will continue to function well in a unified Europe.

The democratic idea, our third theme, is one that developed much later in Germany than in most other advanced industrialized countries. It was not until 1918 and the shaky Weimar Republic that Germany attained democracy at all. Despite a formal democratic constitution, Weimar was a prisoner of forces bent on its destruction. Unlike stable multiparty political systems in other countries, the Weimar Republic was plagued by a sharp and increasing polarization of political parties. The constitution of the Federal Republic in 1949 was designed to overcome Weimar's shortcomings. A system of federalism, constitutional provisions to encourage the formation and maintenance of coalitions, and a streamlined political party system proved solid foundations for the new democracy. Electoral turnout of between 80 and 90 percent for almost all elections since 1949 suggests that Germans have embraced democracy, although skeptics once argued that Germans voted more out of duty than anything else.[8] However, four peaceful electoral regime changes in the past fifty years, in which both the government and the opposition functioned more smoothly than in most other democratic regimes, may finally put doubts about German democracy to rest. The remaining uncertainty is how well and how quickly the democratic culture will penetrate former communist eastern Germany.

The fourth theme, the politics of collective identity, offers a unique look at the intersection of democracy and collectivity. More than in other democratic countries, German political institutions, social forces, and patterns of life emphasize collective action rather than the individualism characteristic of the United States. This should not imply that German citizens have less freedom compared to those in other developed democracies or that there is no conflict in Germany. It means that political expression, in both the state and civil society, revolves around group representation and cooperative spirit in public action. Certainly Germany's history from Prussian militarism through Nazism has led many observers to believe that collectivist impulses should be eradicated. However, to expect Germany to embrace an individualistic democ-

racy like that of the United States with no deep history of this is misguided. Germany's development of a collective identity since 1945 has relied on a redefinition of Germany in a European context. For example, one of the first provisions of the SDP-Green coalition agreement was to alter Germany's restrictive immigration law to legitimize those who have lived in Germany for decades without citizenship. German collective identity is changing.

Implications for Comparative Politics

Germany differs from other developed countries in substantial ways. First, Britain and France are unitary states, whereas Germany is a federal one. Second, Germany's later industrialization, like that of Japan, produced a strong though unbalanced economic growth until after World War II. Combining nationalism and militarism in the late nineteenth and early twentieth centuries, Germany, like Japan, was feared by its neighbors with good reason. Third, Germany experienced delayed development of democratic forms of representation until the Weimar Republic, again sharing a similarity with Japan. Destroyed by the Third Reich, parliamentary democracy did not return until the founding of the Federal Republic in 1949. The most significant difference between Germany and other Western European states is, of course, the Nazi period and the destruction that the Third Reich wrought. Such concerns are somewhat tempered however, by the general stability of Germany's and the rest of Europe's postwar development, the successful development of its democratic institutions, and a political economy characterized by a highly organized business community and active worker participation within a strong labor movement. The parallels with Japan continue here as well.

Unification continues to present Germany with unique challenges. The economic, political, cultural, and physical strains of uniting two disparate societies have placed great stress on the Federal Republic's politics and institutions. Last, Germany's role in the EU presents both opportunities and challenges to Germany and its neighbors. As the strongest European power, Germany has many economic and political advantages in integrating Europe. However, it must deal with the suspicions that its history has aroused among its neighbors and confront the question of whether its post–World War II political institutions, so well suited to Germany, will also fit its partners in the EU.

Germany's significance for the study of comparative politics lies in several areas: the contrast between its nationalistic history and democratization in an integrating Europe; its unique form of organized capitalism that is neither state led nor laissez-faire; its successful form of representative democracy that combines widespread participation and representation of the entire electorate in a stable parliamentary regime; and a politics of identity that builds on existing collectivities in an increasingly multifaceted political culture.

Some suggest that to enjoy sustained economic growth, a state should have a balanced relationship among its various social and economic interests and between the means of production and exchange. The state should promote an independent economic strategy but work closely with influential economic sectors within society, including financial institutions, trade unions, and business elites, in order to make more informed decisions. According to this theory, neither state nor market interests should overpower the other. The Federal Republic of Germany comes close to approximating this model. Germany has taken a development path that emphasizes cooperative interaction between the state and a dense interest group network made up of key social and economic participants. In this way, post–World War II Germany has avoided the imbalances that plague many nation-states, such as when powerful private interests—typically leaders from one sector of the economy—capture or dominate state policy or when the state dominates or captures private interests. As we suggest later, the Federal Republic's unique form of organized capitalism combined with a social market economy have spared Germany an economic policy of unpredictable changes and boom-or-bust cycles.

Section ❷ Political Economy and Development

State and Economy

Germany is an organized capitalist country—the world's third largest and with one of the highest standards of living—in which the state plays a leading but not a directing role. Numerous powerful business organizations, some of which represent industry generally and others employers specifically, play significant coordinating roles. Rather than emphasizing individual entrepreneurship and small business as its defining characteristics, the German economy has relied on an organized network of small and large businesses working together. In addition, much of the banking system and financial community are directly involved in private investment and engage in little of the financial speculation characteristic of Wall Street brokers. Excepting the largest internationally oriented financial institutions, the banks' primary role is to provide long-term investments to support the internationally competitive manufacturing industries that are the foundation of the economy. For example, unlike their U.S. counterparts, German banks are legally allowed to develop close financial ties with firms in other industries, including owning the stock of such firms, granting them long-term loans, having representatives on their boards of directors, and voting as stockholders or on behalf of third-party investors. The end result is that much private investment is based on long-term relationships among familiar partners rather than the short-term deals common among banks, investors, and firms in the United States. Although the universal applicability of these practices has eroded somewhat in the face of globalization, deregulation, and Europeanization, the core principles of this arrangement remain particularly among small and medium-sized firms and financial institutions.

The Role of the State Before 1945

In the years before unification in 1871, many of Germany's regional governments played a strong role in promoting economic growth and development. They worked directly and indirectly with private economic interests, thus blurring distinctions between the state and the market.

The economic powers assumed by the modern states (*Länder*) of the Federal Republic after 1945 were also derived from their century-long involvement in promoting industrialization. The most common way to analyze industrial growth in Germany during the nineteenth century has been economic historian Alexander Gerschenkron's late industrialization thesis. He maintained that Germany's transformation from a quasi-feudal society to a highly industrialized one during the latter two-thirds of the nineteenth century was characterized by explicit coordination among big business, a powerful universal banking system (universal in the sense that banks, then as now, handle all financial transactions and were not segmented into savings and commercial branches, for example), and government. This progress has often been called rapid German industrialization, although a more accurate term might be rapid Prussian industrialization because it was Bismarck's vision and mobilization of Prussian interest groups that proved the dominant force.

Unlike Britain and the United States, Germany did not experience the kind of trial-and-error capitalism that characterized much of the early nineteenth century. By 1871, a unified Germany was forced to compete with a number of other countries that had already developed industrialized capitalist economies. German business and political elites realized that a gradual, small-firm-oriented economy would face ruinous competition from countries such as Britain, France, and the United States. To be competitive, the German state became a significant and powerful force in the German economy. This meant building on the foundations established by the formerly independent and autonomous states such as Prussia and Bavaria, which became part of a united Germany in 1871.

The foundations for economic growth were established, and the most spectacular early leaps of industrial modernization happened, before Germany's unification in 1871. The creation of the customs union (*Zollverein*) in 1834 from eighteen independent states with a population of 23 million people propelled industrial modernization by greatly facilitating trade among these states after centuries of economic stagnation. Prussian leaders initiated this process long before Bismarck was on the scene. Yet it was Bismarck who became the dominant symbol for Prussia's hegemonic position in brokering the interests of grain-growing *Junkers* in the east with those of the coal and steel barons in the Ruhr. Bismarck used the development of the railroad as a catalyst for this "marriage of iron and rye."[9] He astutely realized that although railroads were a primary consumer of coal and steel, they also provided an effective way to transport the *Junkers'* grain from the relatively isolated eastern part of Germany to market. The image of Prussian-led, rapid, state-enhanced industrial growth is important, but the opening of trade among these independent principalities did not dislodge the distinct patterns of modernization that the less powerful states had developed on their own. Small-scale agricultural production remained in many parts of the southern states, particularly in Bavaria, and small-scale craft production continued in Württemberg as well as in many other regions where feudal craft skills were adapted to the patterns of industrial modernization.

Because each state had different material needs and social circumstances, their regional governments may have done a more effective job of fulfilling needs than a central state could have done. Certainly, Bismarck's welfare state measures brought economies of scale to those programs that needed to be implemented on a national basis. However, the strong role of the regional governments in meeting certain needs continued, especially during the Second Reich (1871–1918). Later, when the Weimar regime was succumbing to the Third Reich, regional governments tried to resist the Nazi state's goal of massive centralization of policy but were unsuccessful.

During the Third Reich, between 1933 and 1945, the state worked hand-in-glove with German industry to suppress workers, employ slave labor, and produce military armaments. As a result, a number of leading industrialists, notably those of the Krupp steel works and the IG Farben chemical complex, were tried and convicted of war crimes after the Allied victory.

The Social Market Economy

German economic policy is indirect and supportive rather than heavy-handed and overly regulatory. Although the government sets broad guidelines, it encourages the formation of voluntary associations to coordinate negotiations among employers, banks, trade unions, and regional governments in order to reach the government's policy objectives. Its economic policy-making is flexible in two ways.

First, German regulation establishes a general framework for economic activity rather than detailed standards. The government sets rigorous but broad licensing and performance standards for most professions and industries. For example, German banks must possess greater capital reserves than internationally accepted minimums, and their officers must demonstrate competence to hold their positions to a semipublic institution, the Federal Bank Supervisory Office. Government policymakers believe that once their core requirements are met and their general objectives known, private actors can be trusted to achieve government goals without detailed regulation. Failure to uphold government standards can result in fines or, in some criminal cases, imprisonment. In contrast, the United States has no such core requirements but often produces many layers of detailed—and sometimes contradictory—regulations in the wake of banking failures and financial abuses.

Second, among the major European economies, Germany has the smallest share of industry in national government hands, but it allows state governments to have considerable power. This is called cooperative federalism, which delegates to the states (*Länder*) the administrative powers of laws and regulations passed at the federal level.

Postwar policymakers avoided a dominating role for the state in the Federal Republic's economic life. Unlike the French and the Japanese states, which have intervened much more in the economy, the German state has evolved a careful balance between the public and private sectors. Rather than creating a state-versus-market standoff, the German public and private sectors have evolved a densely interpenetrated association. Germany has avoided the opposite pattern as well: the frequently antigovernment, free-market policies of Britain and the United States since the 1980s.

In other words, the relationship between state and market in Germany is neither free market nor state dominant. Rather, the state sets clear general ground rules, acknowledged by the private sector, but then allows market forces to work relatively unimpeded within the general framework of government supervision. Since the time of the first postwar chancellor, Christian Democrat Konrad Adenauer, the Germans have referred to this approach as the **social market economy** (*Sozialmarktwirtschaft*). Basically, the term refers to a system of capitalism in which fundamental social benefits are essential, not antagonistic, to the workings of the market. Among the many social components of the German economy are such diverse public benefits as health care, workers' rights, public transportation, and support for the arts. In some respects, these benefits are similar to those provided by other European governments. However, the provision of some public benefits through organized private interests (the quasi-public "sickness funds" that provides for health insurance is one example) makes the German social market economy a blend of public and private actions that support and implement public policies. The social market economy blurs state market distinctions in the hope of producing a socially responsible capitalism.

The social component of the social market economy is unique to Germany. Several programs, such as savings subsidies and vocational education, contribute to the production of income. The former contributes to a stable pool of investment capital, while the latter helps create a deep pool of human capital that has enabled Germany to produce high-quality goods throughout the postwar period.

The German system of framework regulation is best explained in the words of economist Wilhelm Röpke, one of the shapers of post–World War II economic policy:

> [Our program] consists of measures and institutions which impart to competition the framework, rules, and machinery of impartial supervision, which a competitive system needs as much as any game or match if it is not to degenerate into a vulgar brawl. A genuine, equitable, and smoothly functioning competitive system cannot in fact survive without a judicious moral and legal framework and without regular supervision of the conditions under which competition can take place pursuant to real efficiency principles. This presupposes mature economic discernment on the part of all responsible bodies and individuals and a strong impartial state.[10]

This system has enabled German economic policy to avoid the sharp lurches between laissez-faire and state-led economic policy that have characterized Britain during the post–World War II period.

Germany, for most of its postwar history, has been a high-wage, high-welfare nation that has maintained its competitive world position far better than most other advanced industrialized states since the oil crisis of 1973. Its success in combining strong competitiveness with high wages and social spending surpassed a faltering Japan before the start of the new century. An emphasis on high skills in key export-oriented manufacturing industries was the specific path that German economic policy took to maintain its competitive position. An elaborate vocational education system combined with apprenticeship training underlay this policy, which was implemented through the **works councils,** firm level institutions elected by every worker in all German companies with five or more employees. This system of advanced skills training enabled Germany for many years to resist the siren song of the postindustrial service sector–oriented world that countries such as the United States and Britain have embraced.

Relying extensively on this elaborate apprenticeship training program, Germany maintained a competitive position in such traditional manufacturing industries as automobiles, chemicals, machine tools, and industrial electronics. By stressing the value that its highly skilled work force adds to raw materials, Germany resisted for many years the claim that it must lower its wage costs to match those of newly industrializing countries. Germany's record suggested that a developed country in a globalized world economy could still compete in manufacturing by raising product quality rather than by lowering wage costs. Despite a lack of natural resources, Germany has maintained a trade surplus and still has a large working-class population that historically has spurned protectionism. With one in every three jobs devoted to exports (one in two in the four manufacturing industries just mentioned), protectionism would be self-defeating for German unions. The skills of its workers have helped German industry overcome the costs of acquiring resources and paying high wages; in fact, German industry has emphasized that high quality and high productivity offset these costs. This has enabled Germany's highly skilled blue-collar workers to drive expensive German automobiles and enjoy six weeks of paid vacation each year.

Germany's research and development strategy has enhanced these economic policies. Rather than push for specific new breakthroughs in exotic technologies or invent new products that might take years to commercialize, the strategy is to adapt existing technologies to traditional sectors and refine already competitive sectors. This was the exact opposite of U.S. research and development strategy. During the postwar years, this policy has enabled Germany to maintain a favorable balance of trade and a high degree of competitiveness. However, German unification and European integration have forced German industry and policy-makers to reexamine and perhaps modify this model. Taking others' core discoveries and quickly applying them to production is a delicate task that requires coordinated policies among all producer groups. The primary challenge since the 1990s has been trying to institute West German policies among former GDR workers raised in a different industrial culture. One of the major tasks for 1998 SPD-Green coalition has been to improve Germany's vocational education system, particularly in the five eastern states.

Other than the government, the German institution that, until recently, was most responsible for shaping economic policy was the very independent *Bundesbank.* This institution was both a bankers' bank, in that it set interest rates, and the agency that determined the amount of money in circulation. This second role proved especially contentious during the 1980s and early 1990s. The *Bundesbank* preferred low inflation, both because this is a traditional demand of all central bankers and because of Germany's history of ruinous inflation during the Weimar Republic. The relevance for economic policy is that when the government wished to expand the economy by increasing spending or reducing taxes, the *Bundesbank* always preferred policies that favored monetary restrictions before fast economic growth. As a result, the government and the *Bundesbank* disagreed on economic policy repeatedly in the years since unification. Since the introduction of the euro, however, the European Central Bank (ECB) has usurped the *Bundesbank*'s role. Although the ECB is modeled on the *Bundesbank* (and is also located in Frankfurt), it signifies a change in German economic policy from the national to the European level.

Despite the long success of the German model, the last years of the Kohl era ushered in period of deep introspection questioning these previously effective yet high-cost practices. Upon its election in 1998, the Gerhard Schröder–led SPD-Green government pledged to maintain the core features of the *Sozialmark-twirtschaft*. But it too found each of these traditionally successful policies facing mounting challenges from Europeanization, globalization, and a powerful deregulatory free enterprise ideology.

Domestically, not all Germans consider this organized capitalist model a complete success either. The Greens, the environmental political party that first won *Bundestag* seats in 1983 and became the junior coalition partner of the SPD in 1998, and the free-market-oriented business sector questioned the dominant economic policy model. Both felt that this pattern favors those inside the system (such as industry organizations, employer groups, and the banking community) and excludes those who are outside. Moreover, the Greens criticize many business policies as not being sufficiently protective of the environment. They were able to use their position in the cabinet to only partial success, however. The primary complaint of the small-business sector is that the organized nature of large-firm-dominant capitalism is not sufficiently flexible in the creation of new products and industries. However, neither group has been able to dislodge the dominant position of German organized capitalism in the shaping of economic policy. Of course, with the Greens as junior members of the Schröder government, previously unassailable nonecologically friendly government policies have been modified. One of the first ecological changes that the Greens won in coalition with the SPD was the commitment to phase out nuclear power in Germany eventually, although the completion date is at least two decades in the future. In addition, the Greens were able to push for several important environmental goals, one of which was an increase in the gasoline tax. The party also used its position in the cabinet to force the German government to challenge the United States on such policies as genetically modified foods, the American failure to maintain its commitment to the Kyoto protocols, which committed world governments to reduce greenhouse gas emissions on a strict schedule, and military action against Iraq.

Welfare Provision

Welfare policies can be described as the social part of the social market economy. The Federal Republic's social welfare expenditures are consistent with historically generous West European standards. Although they are not as extensive as ones in Scandinavia, public services in the Federal Republic dwarf those in the United States. From housing subsidies to savings subsidies, health care, public transit, and the rebuilding of the destroyed cities and public infrastructure of the former GDR, the Federal Republic is still remarkably generous in its public spending. Even under the moderately conservative rule of the CDU-led Adenauer coalition during the 1950s and early 1960s, there was a strong commitment to provide adequate public services. This strategy recalls Bismarck's efforts to use public services to forestall radical demands in the late nineteenth century. For nondemocratic conservatives like Bismarck and for democratic conservatives like Adenauer, comprehensive welfare benefits were not philanthropic but a blunting and softening of the demands of the Social Democratic Party and the trade unions. Thus, welfare in Germany has never been a gift but a negotiated settlement, often after periods of conflict between major social forces that have agreed to compromise.

The development of welfare services has been tremendously enhanced as well by the European Christian social tradition, a major force in the CDU/CSU coalition. Roman Catholic and Protestant churches both advocate public spending for services as a responsibility of the strong for the welfare of the weak. Similarly, the unions' and the SPD's demands for increased public spending ensured that both the left and the right shared a commitment to public provision of social services throughout the Federal Republic's history.

During the mid-1970s, when unemployment grew from 1 or 2 percent to roughly 4 percent and when some social welfare measures were capped (but not reduced), citizens of the Federal Republic spoke of the crisis of the welfare state. Yet non-German observers were hard-pressed to find indications of crisis. Clearly, contraction of substantial welfare state benefits in no way approximated the cutbacks of the United States and Britain in the 1980s and 1990s.

Since the 1980s, continued high unemployment (by German standards) and the costs of support for workers who had depleted their benefits presented difficult dilemmas for the welfare state. German jobs tend to be highly paid, so employers have tried to avoid creating part-time jobs, preferring to wait to hire until the need for employees is sustainable. During times of recession, the number of new jobs created can be minuscule.

Current Strains on the Social Market Economy

Uncertain economic conditions in the early 1980s cost Social Democratic Chancellor Helmut Schmidt his position. Yet even during his successor Helmut Kohl's sixteen-year tenure, the heady days of less than 1 percent unemployment never returned. Unemployment has not dropped below 6 percent since then. One persistent problem facing successive German governments has been shouldering the cost of sustaining the long-term unemployed through general welfare funds. More seriously, how could the Federal Republic's elaborate vocational education and apprenticeship system absorb all the new entrants into the labor market? This problem could have undermined one of the strengths of the German economy: the continued supply of skilled workers. Despite these threats in the mid-1980s, both the unemployment compensation system and the vocational education and apprenticeship system survived under the Kohl government. However, this issue resurfaced with the large increase in the unemployment rate following unification in 1990, particularly in the eastern German states.

"Find the Money" German policy-makers worrying about the costs of the welfare state. *Source:* Atelier Rabenau/ *Frankfurter Allgemeine Zeitung.*

In the early 1990s, the idea of a smoothly functioning German economic juggernaut faltered. First, the Kohl government badly misjudged the costs of unification. In 1992, Kohl finally acknowledged that the successful integration of the eastern economy into the western one would cost much more and require longer than originally predicted. Second, the structural challenges that the German political economy faced in the mid-1990s proved far more extensive than the Federal Republic had encountered since the 1950s. The amount budgeted in the early 1990s for reconstruction of eastern Germany's infrastructure was approximately 20 percent of the entire national budget. In addition, funds from private firms, regional governments, and other subsidies amounted to another DM50 billion, yet even these huge sums were not enough to help smooth the assimilation process, and today a large gap in productivity levels exists between the two regions. Third, the western German democratic corporatist institutions, composed of employers and trade unions with a long history of cooperation, became difficult to transfer as a model to eastern Germany since they had to be created from scratch. If present, they could have been effective mediating institutions to soften the costs of transition for eastern Germans. In their absence, the *Treuhandanstalt* (the government reconstruction agency— *Treuhand,* for short) took the path of least resistance and simply privatized some 7,000 of the total of 11,000 firms that it had inherited from East Germany. One of the most significant costs of this transition from state to private ownership was high unemployment in the eastern sector. Some 1.2 million workers were officially unemployed, and in the early 1990s, another 2 million enrolled in a government-subsidized short-term program combined with job training (this program's funds were later slashed as part of an austerity budget).

The costs of the social market economy, particularly during unification, stressed the upper limits of Germany's capacity to pay for them. Massive budget cuts became imperative by the early and mid-1990s. The completion of the EU's single market, the grand culmination of a post–cold war spirit of German and European unity, has placed additional strains on the German government. Its alleged immediate benefit will likely strengthen the trends toward decentralization and deregulation already begun in Western Europe.

More significant for the German regime, the EU has begun to disturb the organized capitalism of its small and large businesses, which features an intricate, mutually reinforcing pattern of government and business self-regulation. In addition, the growing push for deregulation in European finance could threaten Germany's distinctive finance-manufacturing links, which depend on long-term relationships between the two parties, not on short-term deals.[11] Thus, the trend toward Europeanization, on a path that challenges Germany's preeminent position, may be incompatible with the consensus-oriented and coordinated nature of Germany's political and social institutions.

Tensions have also flared up between former East and West Germans. The East German economy was strong by Communist standards and provided jobs for virtually all adults who wanted one. But East German industry, as in most other former Communist countries, was inefficient by Western standards, and most firms were not able to survive the transition to capitalism. Among the most serious problems were overstaffing and inadequate quality controls. Consequently, many easterners lost their jobs when newly privatized firms then had to compete in a capitalist economy. For a time, eastern Germans were generously supported by western subsidies, but recovery in the five new eastern states lagged much more than the Kohl government had anticipated. Easterners resented the slow pace of change and high unemployment, and western Germans were bitter about losing jobs to easterners and paying, through increased taxes, for the cleanup of the ecological and infrastructural disaster inherited from the former East German regime.

In short, the magnitude of the problems in eastern Germany threatened to overwhelm the institutional capacity to handle them. It certainly helped contribute to the defeat of Helmut Kohl's CDU/CSU-FDP center-right coalition government in 1998. Some pessimistic observers began to suggest that these stresses placed the German political economy in a precarious position. Germany's economic prowess has depended on certain manufacturing industries that produce eminently exportable goods but whose technologies must constantly be upgraded and whose labor costs continue to rise. Complicating the demands on Germany's economic institutions is the obligation to align Germany's economic policies with those of its European neighbors.

Thus, early in the twenty-first century, the German political economy seemed less rosy than in previous decades. European integration, German unification, and globalization have forced German industry and policy-makers to examine whether this model remains appropriate or needs fundamental reexamination. Depending on others to make core discoveries and then quickly applying the technology to production is a delicate task that requires coordinated policies among all producer groups. Trying to institute the western German policy among former GDR workers who come from a different industrial culture has begun to prove difficult.

In fact, the speed of the information age and the penetration of the Internet into all facets of economic and public life have caught the German model somewhat unprepared. Are Germany's prevailing economic practices and policy styles still relevant for the new information industries, as well as existing industries transformed by the process? Can the primary, secondary, and vocational-apprenticeship systems produce the kind of workers needed in the new century? The answer is uncertain, because despite unemployment at between 7 and 8 percent, German industry had to recruit programmers, web designers, and network specialists from Asia to meet gaping shortages in these fields in Germany. However, the deregulation of Deutsche Telekom, the former state-run telephone service, has begun to spur a belated development in Internet and information infrastructure technology. The question for observers of German political economy is whether the traditional German industrial pattern of integrating and applying innovations first developed elsewhere will apply to the information age economy as well.

Society and Economy

During the boom years of the mid-twentieth century, German economic growth provided a sound foundation for social development. The social market economy of the Christian Democrats was augmented by governments led by Social Democrats from 1969 to 1982, when the supportive social programs of the 1950s and 1960s were extended and enhanced. This growth, with its corresponding social policies, helped Germany to avoid the kind of occupational and regional conflict common to many other countries. Germany is a prosperous country with a high standard of living, high savings rates, and a well-paid work force. The strong role of trade unions and the consequent unwillingness of employers to confront workers on wage and workplace issues have minimized stratification of the society and the workplace. There is some stratification, however, within the labor force. The primary workplace fault line lies between the core of mostly male, high-skilled blue-collar workers in the largest competitive industries and less-skilled workers, often employed in smaller firms with lower wages and not always full-time work. A significant number of women and immigrants are among the less-skilled workers.

The most controversial social issues for German society since the 1990s have been race and ethnicity, with profound implications for Germany's ideology and political culture. Racist attacks against Turkish immigrants and other ethnic minorities have forced Germans to confront the possibility that almost fifty years of democracy have not tamed the xenophobic aspects of their political culture. The issue of ethnic minorities affected the economy and society during the 1980s and was exacerbated in the 1990s by unification and European integration. Nationalism apparently has not disappeared. East Germans were raised in a society that did not celebrate, or even value, toleration or dissent and in which official unemployment did not exist. East Germany was a closed society, as were most other Communist regimes, and many of its citizens had little contact with foreign nationals before 1989. In contrast, since the 1960s, West Germany has encouraged the migration of millions of guest workers (*Gastarbeiter*) from southern Europe. The Federal Republic has also provided generous provisions for those seeking political asylum, in an effort to overcome—to some degree at least—the legacy of Nazi persecution of non-Germans from 1933 to 1945.

The *Gastarbeiter* program originated after 1961 when the construction of the Berlin Wall caused a labor shortage because East Germans could no longer emigrate to the West. Thus, temporary workers were recruited from southern Europe with the stipulation that they would return to their native countries if unemployment increased. However, the economic boom lasted so long that by the time the economy did turn down in the mid-1970s, it was difficult for these so-called guests to return to homes in which they had not lived for a decade or more. And as semipermanent residents, they were eligible for welfare benefits. These foreign workers produced heightened social strain in the 1970s and 1980s, a time of increasing unemployment. Because German citizenship was not granted to the guest workers or their children, the problem remained unresolved. Although not as severe as in the Second Reich, the clash between German and *Gastarbeiter* cultures increased in intensity into the 1980s, particularly in areas where Turkish workers were highly concentrated. However, in a significant departure from past practice, the Schröder-led SPD-Green government made the changing of the immigration law one of its first items of business. The new government in 1999 adopted a much easier immigration policy, allowing second- and third-generation *Gastarbeiter* to attain German citizenship or maintain dual citizenship.

Upon unification, when different ethnic minorities flooded into the former East and West Germanies, few former GDR citizens were able to respond positively. Instead of guaranteed lifetime employment, they faced a labor market that did not always supply enough jobs, one where structural unemployment idled up to 25 percent of the work force. And they were expected to embrace completely and immediately a much more open and ethnically diverse society than they had ever known. Thus, immigrants and asylum seekers became the scapegoats for the lack of employment, and Germans who were falling through the cracks of the welfare state were susceptible to racist propaganda blaming ethnic minorities for the rapid upheaval that had occurred.

Another important issue has been the role of women in German society. Until the late 1970s, men traditionally dominated all positions of authority in management and the union movement. The union movement has made greater strides than management in expanding leadership opportunities for women, but men still hold the dominant positions in most unions. More than half of all German women entered the work force by the late 1970s, but their participation plateaued at about 62 percent in the 1990s, while the male participation rate remained steady at 80 percent (see Table 1).

Beyond the workplace, the differences between the laws of the former East and West Germanies have created a firestorm of controversy. In the East, women had

Table 1

Labor Force Participation Rates (Ages 15–65)			
	1996	*1999*	*2001*
Male	80.3%	80.3%	80.1%
Female	62.8	63.8	64.9

Source: Federal Statistical Office, Germany, 2002.

made far greater social and economic progress than in the West, and both women and men had received generous government support for child care and family leave. During the last Kohl government, one of the most heated debates concerned the cancellation of the more liberal East German policies toward women (including abortion) in favor of the more conservative and restrictive ones of the Federal Republic. Even with the election in 1998 of Gerhard Schröder's left-wing government, supposedly more sympathetic to issues of primary concern to females, German policy toward women and women's issues did not develop as much as its supporters had first hoped.

Perhaps the most significant obstacle that German women have to overcome is not so much the substance of the benefits that they receive but the premise on which women's role in German society is defined.[12] By any measure, Germany's universal welfare state benefits are generous to all citizens, including women, but it is helpful to understand the context within which rights are granted.

German welfare is a creation of conservatives and Christian Democrats and not of the left. It was Bismarck who created the first modern welfare state in the late nineteenth century—not out of the goodness of his heart but to stave off socialist revolution and preserve traditional German cultural values. Similarly, the postwar Christian Democratic creation of the social part of the social market economy was based on Christian values and envisioned a world of male breadwinners and women at home caring for—and having more—children. To be sure, the years of Social Democratic governance (1969–1982 and since 1998) have expanded benefits for women, but at its foundation, women's benefits in German society have been tied more to their roles within the family than as individuals. This

means that within the context of the labor market, individual German women face discriminatory aspects and assumptions about their career patterns that American women have greatly overcome. As increasing numbers of women enter the German work force, it is harder for them to achieve positions of power and responsibility as individuals than it is for their American counterparts. Perhaps this is one more manifestation of the differences between collectivist and individualist societies.

A final social cleavage is the generation gap, which has two dimensions. The younger part of this gap is the so-called postmaterialist social movement, which focuses on lifestyle concerns rather than bread-and-butter economic issues. It has not relied on class as a primary category to define itself, as many within this group tend to be university-educated children of the middle class. This group has not, however, been able to create an identity strong enough to challenge the highly skilled working class's dominance in the structure of the Federal Republic. The still-dominant working-class culture of the Federal Republic has acted as a barrier to the postmaterialist social movement's attaining further influence. However, this group has attained an important vehicle for systematic political representation in the Green Party.

The next aspect of the generation gap comes at the other end of the demographic scale: pensioners and older workers. The German birthrate fell markedly in the last decade of the twentieth century, particularly in the former GDR. Demographically, this has placed great pressure on the German welfare state because the combination of the low birthrate and the increasing age of the baby boom generation means that fewer younger workers will be contributing to the welfare and retirement benefits of an increasing elderly population. This time bomb has not yet fully hit German politics, largely because the Kohl government during the 1980s and 1990s essentially ignored it. Only in 2000 did the Schröder government begin to address it in the context of the tax reform package. The Red (i.e., Social Democratic)-Green government augmented the beleaguered public pension system with additional tax funds that will help Germans diversify their retirement options by developing tax-supported private pensions to accompany the public ones.

Germany and the International Political Economy

Germany's relationship to the regional and international political economy is shaped by two factors: the EU and globalization.

The European Union

The EU was embraced by most Germans and by the political and industrial establishment, especially in the first few years after unification. As Europe's leading economic power, Germany has benefited greatly from European integration because its position of strength has been enhanced by wider market opportunities for successful global competition. Many actions and policies that might once have been viewed by its neighbors as German domination have become more acceptable when seen as Germany's active participation as a member of the larger EU.

As for how quickly European integration proceeds, countries that might consider emulating German institutions require not just strategies but also the means of implementing them. The lack of a cohesive European-wide institutional framework would severely hinder efforts to develop strategies appropriate to meeting the domestic and international challenges of European unification. Most other European nations can identify their goals: a highly skilled work force able to compete in international markets on some basis other than a combination of low labor costs and high-tech production strategies. But whether they can or want to follow Germany's example remains to be seen, especially in the light of recent German economic difficulty. Is Germany a model for other countries? The preoccupation of Germany with its immediate domestic issues and the German-specific nature of the institutions of its political economy have partially diminished the luster of German-style policies for a Europe increasingly defined by the EU.

Several difficult issues confront Germany's international position in the early twenty-first century. One concern is whether successful German-specific institutional arrangements, such as its institutionalized system of worker (and union) participation in management, its tightly organized capitalism, and its elaborate system of apprenticeship training, will prove adaptable or durable in wider European and global contexts. What works well for Germany may be derived from indigenous institutional, political, or cultural patterns that will not successfully transfer beyond the Federal Republic.

Another concern involves Germany's political role on the global stage. After German unification and European integration, many observers in Europe, Japan, and North America assumed that Germany would take on greater political responsibility. However, indecision and inaction in world affairs by the Kohl regime in the 1990s suggested Germany's unwillingness or inability to assume the responsibilities of a world power. Examples of this inaction are visible in the failure of leadership in areas such as forging a common European policy toward Iraq and especially the crisis in the former Yugoslavia. Kohl's initial inaction paralyzed German (and European) foreign policy and contributed to Serbian aggression against its neighbors.

The arrival of Gerhard Schröder as chancellor in 1998 seemed to have moved Germany's foreign policy in a more decisive direction. As the first chancellor with no direct memory of World War II (he was born in 1944), he is less willing to defer to the United States and NATO on all international issues. His successful 2002 reelection campaign in which he openly challenged President Bush's position on a possible invasion of Iraq is the most obvious example. In fact, the combination of moving the capital to Berlin and Schröder's more independent foreign policy stance suggests that Germany's international political role might increase. German participation in the UN peacekeeping mission in Bosnia was one example, and agreeing to participate in opposition to Serbian aggression in Kosovo in 1998 was another. This was the first time that Germany had exercised military force abroad since World War II, and there were considerable debates about the constitutionality of doing so. In opposition, the SPD and Greens had argued that because of the Third Reich's aggressive military expeditions to the east in World War II, it was impossible for the German military, under either UN or NATO auspices, to play a constructive role in eastern Europe. Yet once in government, the SPD and Greens faced increased international pressure that Germany play a leading role in European foreign policy and not shirk the responsibility; witness its developing an alternative position to that of President Bush concerning Iraq. While some European neighbors might express anxiety about increased German political power in Europe, the alternative was a political vacuum by an indecisive EU, hardly a stronger option.

Germany in a Globalizing World

Germany clearly has enjoyed a greater degree of institutional stability since World War II in its political economy than at any other time in its history. Yet the momentous European and German changes since the late 1980s may have begun to undermine the political structure. Until the turn of the century, dominant economic and political leaders have maintained stability by retaining a balance between the private and public sectors in order to maintain international competitiveness. Nineteenth-century history showed Germans the important role that the state played in the unification of the country and the development of an industrial economy that could compete on a world stage. Yet twentieth-century German history—both the Nazi years and the GDR experience—showed Germans the dangers in placing too heavy a reliance on centralized state authority. Even the left realized that it must maintain a strong presence in both public and private sectors. The major actors in the Federal Republic's postwar political economy learned that a balance must be struck between the public and private sectors to be a major

force in the world political economy. For much of this period, they thought they had found that balance.

However, issues such as trade, economic competition with East Asia and North America, the introduction of the euro, the general pace of economic integration, and patterns of financial regulation have challenged these postwar policies. Germany, as a goods-exporting nation, has always favored an open trading system. Management and unions realize that exports represent both profits and jobs and that seeking refuge in protectionism would be self-defeating. Yet international competition has caused unemployment to remain persistently high (near 10 percent). With respect to banking regulation, the Schröder government sponsored a law that enabled banks to sell their prodigious shares in companies. This altered the prevailing postwar policy of encouraging banks to maintain equity holdings in other firms as a form of long-term-oriented investment. This took the German model perilously close to the Anglo-American world of highly mobile capital investment. Very simply, many of the large German banks saw themselves more as international players than German ones. Some have suggested that the pressures of competing in a globalized world economy have made the German-specific patterns of the country's political economy more of a liability than an asset. Similar criticisms have been raised since the mid-1970s, but the challenges to the German model in the early twenty-first century seem the most fundamental yet.

Section ❸ Governance and Policy-Making

The primary goals at the Federal Republic's founding in 1949 were to work toward eventual unification of the two Germanies and, more important, to avoid repeating the failure of the Weimar Republic. When unification was blocked indefinitely, the founders instituted the **Basic Law** (*Grundgesetz*) as a compromise. They preferred to wait until Germany could be reunited before using the term *constitution* (*Verfassung*). After unification in 1990, however, the term *Basic Law* was retained because of the FRG's unqualified post-WWII success.

Their other goal, ensuring a lasting democratic order, presented a more complicated problem. Two

fundamental institutional weaknesses had undermined the Weimar government: (1) provisions for emergency powers had enabled leaders to arbitrarily centralize authority and suspend democratic rights, and (2) the fragmentation of the political party system had prevented stable majorities from forming in the *Reichstag*. This second weakness, instability, encouraged the first: the use of emergency powers to break legislative deadlocks. It was, of course, Weimar's weakness that made possible the Nazi takeover, and thus the primary motivation of state rebuilding after World War II was to minimize the risk of extremism.

Organization of the State

The Basic Law and Promoting Stability

Under Allied occupation guidance, the builders of the postwar government sought to inhibit centralized power by establishing a federal system with significant powers for the states (*Länder*). It is paradoxical that a document that owes so much to the influence of foreign powers has proved so durable. Under the Basic Law of the Federal Republic, many functions that had formerly been centralized during the imperial, Weimar, and Nazi periods, such as the educational system, the police, and the radio networks, now became the responsibility of the states. Although the federal *Bundestag* (lower house) became the chief lawmaking body, the implementation of many laws fell to the state governments. Moreover, the state governments sent representatives to the *Bundesrat* (upper house), which was required to approve bills passed in the *Bundestag*.

There was little opposition from major actors within the Federal Republic to this shift from a centralized to a federal system. The Third Reich's arbitrary abuse of power had created strong sentiment for curbing the state's repressive capacities. In addition, political leaders, influenced by advisers from the United States, were inclined to support a federal system. Further, the development of a federal system was not a departure but a return to form. Prior to the unification of Germany in 1871, the various regions of Germany had formed a decentralized political system with such autonomous institutions as banks, universities, vocational schools, and state administrative systems.

Several methods were used to surmount party fragmentation and the inability to form working majorities. The multiplicity of parties, a characteristic of the Weimar Republic, was partly controlled in the FRG by the **5 percent rule:** a political party had to receive at least 5 percent of the vote to obtain seats in the *Bundestag* or in state or municipal governments. Under the 5 percent rule, smaller parties tended to fade, with most of their members absorbed by the three major parties. However, the Green Party in the early 1980s and the former communist party of East Germany, reformed as the Party of Democratic Socialism, in the 1990s surpassed the threshold and appear likely to remain in the *Bundestag*. No extreme right-wing parties,

however, have ever achieved 5 percent of the national vote to attain seats in the *Bundestag*.

The *Bundestag* is more likely to achieve working majorities than the Weimar government did for several other reasons. Because the interval between elections is set at four years (except under unusual circumstances), governments have a fair opportunity to implement their programs and take responsibility for success or failure. The electoral system was also changed from a pure proportional representation system under the Weimar government to a combination of proportional representation and single-member electoral districts. New constitutional provisions limited the possibility for the *Bundestag* to vote a government from office. Under the Weimar constitution, majorities of disparate forces could be mustered to unseat the chancellor but were unable to agree on the choice of a replacement. In the Federal Republic, a **constructive vote of no confidence** is required, an institutional mechanism designed to force majorities to propose a constructive alternative. In other words, to vote out one chancellor, the *Bundestag* must simultaneously vote in another. In addition, the chancellor's powers are now more clearly defined. As the leader of the dominant party or coalition of parties, the chancellor now has control over the composition of the cabinet, so that the federal president is merely the ceremonial head of state. Under the Weimar Constitution the president could wield emergency powers, but FRG presidents have been stripped of such broad power.

The principles of the Federal Republic's government contained in the Basic Law give the nation a solid foundation, one that appeared capable of assimilating the five *Länder* of the former GDR when unification occurred in 1990. After surviving for over a half-century, the Federal Republic has clearly attained its most important goals. However, in the 1990s, threats of neo-Nazi movements and racist violence surprised many observers, who thought these sentiments had long since been purged from German politics. Some observers have suggested that until the arrival of the Federal Republic, Germany had been a premodern country.[13] From 1949 until unification, it appeared much like other Western industrialized countries. After unification in 1990, with the difficulties in integrating the two regimes and the uncertainties regarding European integration, some of the more pessimistic assumptions about a reformed, democratic Germany have resurfaced. Yet other observers might cite such factors as another successful democratic alternation of power, this time to the Red-Green coalition in 1998; the continued support for the democratized former communist party (PDS) in the east; and the minuscule support for undemocratic right-wing parties. These examples would point to the durability and maturity of democracy in Germany.

Government Institutions

Germany is organized as a federal system, with sixteen *Länder* (states), each with considerable powers (see Figure 1). The states have the right to raise revenue independently as well as to own and operate firms, usually in partnership with private industry. As a parliamentary democracy, the German government resembles the parliamentary systems of Britain and Japan: there is a fusion of powers in that the chancellor, the executive or head of government, is also the leader of the leading party (or coalition) in the *Bundestag*. This contrasts with the separation-of-powers system used in the United States, in which the president and cabinet offi-

cials cannot simultaneously serve in the Congress. Generally, the executive dominates the legislative in the Federal Republic, but this authority derives from the chancellor's role as party leader and a high level of party discipline. Most members of the governing parties support the chancellor at all times, as their own positions depend on a successful government. This loyalty diffuses the lone-ranger syndrome, so common in the U.S. House of Representatives and Senate, where individual members of Congress often act as independent political entrepreneurs.

The Federal Republic's legislature is bicameral, with the 603-member *Bundestag* as the lower house and the 69-member *Bundesrat* as the upper house. Unlike the U.S. Senate and the British House of Lords, the *Bundesrat* is composed of elected and appointed officials of the sixteen states. In this way, Germany's constitutional system allows more governmental overlap than countries that are unitary (Britain) or have a sharp separation of powers within the federal government and between federal and state governments (United States). The *Bundestag* members are elected in a "personalized" proportional representation system (see Section 4), and the leader of the major party, who

---

Figure 1

Constitutional Structure of the German Federal Government

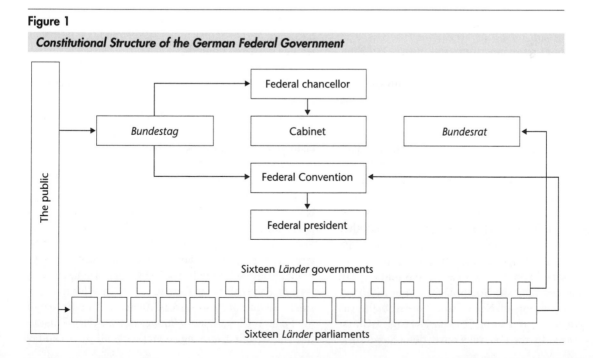

is usually the leader of the largest party in a two- or three-party coalition, becomes chancellor. As in most other parliamentary systems, the chancellor must maintain a majority for the government to survive, with the added provision (i.e., the constructive vote of no confidence) that the opposition must have a replacement ready to assume office.

The Executive

The division between the head of government (the chancellor) and the head of state (the president) is firmly established in the Federal Republic, with major political powers delegated to the chancellor. Responsibilities and obligations are clearly distinguished between the two offices. For example, the chancellor can be criticized for the government's policies without the criticism being perceived as an attack against the state itself. This division of power in the executive branch was essential to establish respect for the new West German state after Hitler assumed both offices as the *Führer*.

The German president is the head of state, a much weaker position than that of the chancellor. Like constitutional monarchs in Britain, for example, German presidents stand above the political fray, which means that their role is more ceremonial than political. Among the most common functions are signing treaties, presiding at formal state functions, and overseeing *Bundestag* protocols. German presidents are almost always semiretired politicians who are moderates within their respective parties and thus broadly acceptable to the electorate. However, if there were a political crisis affecting the chancellor, the president would remain as a caretaker of the political process, thus providing continuity in a time of national calamity. For example, should a parliamentary crisis arise and no candidate can command the support of an absolute majority of *Bundestag* members, the president can exercise a specific form of influence. He or she can decide whether the country is to be governed by a minority administration under a chancellor elected by a plurality of deputies or whether new elections are to be called.[14] In 1999, Johannes Rau, the Social Democratic *Minister-Präsident* (governor) of North Rhine–Westphalia was elected president, replacing Roman Herzog, a Christian Democrat, by the Federal Convention (*Bundesver-*

sammlung), an assembly of all *Bundestag* members and an equal number of delegates elected by the state legislatures according to the principle of proportional representation (the equivalent of an electoral college). The presidential term is five years, with a limit of two terms. All federal presidents to date have been men—and all from the Rhineland—so when Herzog announced he would serve only one term, many Germans hoped that a woman might get a chance to serve in this post. But in 1999, the *Bundestag* and *Bundesrat* nominated only men, and Rau was elected.

The chancellor is elected by a majority of the members of the *Bundestag*. In practice, this means that the chancellor's ability to be a strong party leader (or leader of a coalition of parties) is essential to the government's success. A government is formed after a national election or, if the chancellor leaves office between elections, after a majority of the *Bundestag* has nominated a chancellor in a constructive vote of no confidence. The new leader consults with other party (and coalition) officials to make up the cabinet. These party leaders have considerable influence in determining which individuals receive ministries. In the event of a coalition government, party leaders often designate during the election campaign who will receive certain ministries. Negotiations on which policies a coalition will pursue can often become heated, so the choice of ministers for particular ministries is made on policy as well as personal grounds.

From their party or coalition, chancellors select members of the cabinet who can best carry out the duties of the executive branch. The most significant cabinet ministries are those of finance, economics, justice, interior, and foreign policy (the Foreign Ministry). Decision making within the cabinet meetings is often pro forma, since many of the important deliberations are conducted beforehand. In many cases, chancellors rely on strong ministers in key posts, but some chancellors have taken ministerial responsibility themselves in key areas such as economics and foreign policy. Helmut Schmidt and Willy Brandt, respectively, fit this pattern. The economics and finance ministries always work closely with the European Central Bank (ECB).

Once the cabinet is formed, the chancellor has considerable authority to govern, thanks to the power of the Federal Chancellery (*Bundeskanzleramt*). This office is the first among equals of all the cabinet ministries, enabling the chancellor to oversee the entire government as well as mediate conflicts among the other ministries. It is a kind of superministry with wide-ranging powers in many areas.

The office of the chancellor has played a pivotal role in the Federal Republic. Its clearly defined role within the federal framework has resulted in a series of far more effective heads of government than was the case in the Weimar period. On the other hand, the chancellor's more limited role within the context of a federal system has constrained the ability of the central government to take sweeping action. To many Germans, the limitation of centralized executive power has been a welcome improvement.

Perhaps the most significant source of the chancellor's powers is the constructive vote of no confidence. To avoid the weakness of the Weimar cabinet governments, the drafters of the Basic Law added a twist to common parliamentary practice in which a prime minister is brought down on a vote of no confidence. In most parliamentary democracies, prime ministers who lose such a vote must step down or call for new elections. In the Federal Republic, however, such a vote must be "constructive," meaning that a chancellor cannot be removed unless the *Bundestag* simultaneously elects a new chancellor (usually from one of the opposition parties). This constitutional provision strengthens the chancellor's power in at least two ways: (1) chancellors can more easily reconcile disputes among cabinet officials without threatening their own position, and (2) the opposition must come up with concrete and specific alternatives to the existing government, thus preventing confrontation for its own sake.

Chancellors also face significant limits on their power. As discussed in Section 4, the *Bundesrat* (upper house) must ratify all legislation passed in the *Bundestag* (lower house) unless overridden by a two-thirds vote. In addition, since the *Bundesrat* generally implements most legislation, chancellors have to consider the position of the upper house on most issues.

The Bureaucracy

An essential component of the executive is the national bureaucracy. In Germany, it is very powerful and protected by long-standing civil service provisions. Firing or otherwise removing a bureaucrat is very difficult. **Civil servants** maintain the conviction that their work is a profession, not just a job.

Surprisingly, the federal government employs only about 10 percent of civil servants, with the remainder employed by state and local governments. Today, most civil servants either are graduates from major German universities or come from positions within the political parties. The federal bureaucrats are primarily policy-makers who work closely with their ministries and the legislature. The bureaucrats at the state and local levels are the predominant agents of policy implementation because the states must administer most policies determined at the national level. This overlapping and coordinating of national, regional, and local bureaucracies is supported by the importance that Germans give to the provision of public services. The ongoing institutionalized relationship among the various levels of the bureaucracy has produced a more consistent and effective public policy than is found in other countries, where federal and state governments are often at odds with one another.

Overlapping responsibilities on policy issues make it difficult to demarcate specifically the responsibility of federal institutions from the national to the regional level and from the regional to the local level. City-states such as Berlin, Bremen, and Hamburg can be so affected.

During the Second and Third Reichs, German civil servants had a reputation for inflexibility and rigidity. The modern German bureaucracy, still renowned for being officious, rigid, and unfriendly, has nevertheless won high, if grudging, respect from the population. It is generally seen as efficient, although sometimes arcane. Some bureaucrats, mostly top federal officials, are appointed on the basis of party affiliation; following the traditional German pattern of proportionality, all major political groupings are represented in the bureaucracy. However, in the 1970s, the Social Democratic Brandt government attempted to purge the bureaucracy of suspected left-wing radicals by issuing the so-called Radicals Decree, a move that tarnished its reputation for impartiality and fairness. But the majority of civil servants are chosen on the basis of merit, with elaborate licensing and testing for those in the highest positions. German bureaucrats enjoy a well-deserved reputation for competence, especially when compared to the bureaucracies of most developed states.

Semipublic Institutions

In the late 1940s, the idea of a strong central state in Germany was discredited for two reasons: the excesses of Nazism and the American occupation authorities' strong affinity for the private sector. West German authorities faced a dilemma. How would they rebuild society if a strong public sector role were prohibited? The answer was to create modern, democratic versions of those nineteenth-century institutions that blurred the differences between the public and private sectors. These semipublic institutions have played a crucial role in the German political economy, one that has long been unrecognized.

Semipublic institutions are powerful, efficient, and responsible for much national policy-making. The most influential include the *Bundesbank,* the health insurance funds that administer the national health care system, and the vocational education system (which encompasses the apprenticeship training system). These are part of the integrated system of democratic corporatism in which national (and state) governments delegate certain policy-making authority to these institutions, which engage in continuous dialogue with all relevant participants in the policy community until appropriate policies are found.

In countries that had a guild system in the Middle Ages, such as Germany, an inclusionary, democratic corporatist form of representation is common. Here, various professions or organized groups form to represent the interests of their members. In return for access to deliberation and power, these groups are expected to aggregate the interests of their members and act responsibly. Semipublic institutions with their democratic corporatist membership combine aspects of both representation and implementation. German semipublic institutions differ greatly from pluralist representation in countries such as the United States, where interest groups petition public authority for redress of grievances while keeping at arm's length from the implementation process. The democratic corporatist interest groups are also very much intertwined with the Federal Republic's semipublic agencies, which are institutions crucial for the functioning of the German political economy. For example, implementation of the health care system requires an intricate set of negotiations among many semipublic institutions. Gray areas encompassing both public and private responsibilities, these institutions are an apparent seamless web that shapes, directs, implements, and diffuses German public policy.

The political scientist Peter Katzenstein has written extensively about the semipublic agencies, calling them *detached institutions.*[15] He sees them as primarily mediating entities that reduce the influence of the central state. Katzenstein finds that they have tended to work best in areas of social and economic policy. Among the most important semipublic agencies are the Chambers of Industry, the Council of Economic Advisors (known colloquially as the Six Wise Men), and the institutions of worker participation (co-determination and the works councils). Even areas of the welfare system are semipublic because the distribution system for welfare benefits is often administered by organizations not officially part of the state bureaucracy. The most significant example of this are the **health insurance funds** (*Krankenkassen*), which bring all major health interests together to allocate costs and benefits through an elaborate system of consultation and group participation.

Another important set of semipublic institutions is the unions, which participate in industrial relations through the system known as co-determination (*Mitbestimmung*) (see "Citizen Action: Co-Determination"). This group of institutions is discussed here because co-determination legally gives workers opportunities to shape public policy.

Co-determination provides that workers, including union members, participate on the boards of directors of all medium and large firms, thus giving unions an inside look at the workings of the most powerful firms in the Federal Republic. Unions can thus understand, if not control, major corporate decisions on such issues as investment and application of technology. Based on laws passed in the early 1950s and expanded in the 1970s, co-determination gives workers (and unions) up to one-half of the seats on company boards. The unions' problem in challenging management positions on contentious issues is that (with the exception of the coal and steel industries) the laws also give management one additional, usually tie-breaking, vote.

Another uniquely German institution, the works

Citizen Action: **Co-Determination**

Co-determination is an institutional relationship between organized labor and business that gives labor movements the right to participate in major decisions that affect their firms and industries. Found in northern Europe, including the Netherlands and Scandinavia, but best known in the Federal Republic of Germany, co-determination (*Mitbestimmung*) allows representatives of workers and trade unions to obtain voting seats on the supervisory boards of directors of firms with 2,000 or more employees.

German co-determination has two official forms: one for the coal and steel industries and one for all other industries. The former provides full parity for worker representatives in all decisions on the supervisory board, whereas the latter provides nearly full parity between worker and employer representatives because a representative of management always has the tie-breaking vote. Post–World War II roots of co-determination sprang from the anger of German workers toward the complicity of German industrialists with the Nazi war machine. This was especially true of the coal and steel barons; hence, the full parity in those industries. The idea of placing workers and union representatives on the boards of directors of these firms was seen by many as a way to ensure accountability from German capitalism.

The laws governing co-determination, first passed in the early 1950s and expanded in the 1970s, reflect the powerful role of the trade unions in the politics of the Federal Republic. They give the workers—and indirectly their unions for those firms so organized—a form of institutionalized participation through membership on the supervisory boards of German firms. This participation, rather than making German firms uncompetitive, actually had the opposite effect. Workers and unions can comprehend, if not unilaterally determine, corporate decisions regarding investment and the introduction of new technologies. Co-determination has allowed German workers a broader and deeper knowledge of the goals and strategies of the firms for which they work.

But co-determination has not been conflict free. In 1976, at the time of the broadening of some of the unions' powers, the Constitutional Court ruled that worker representatives could never attain majority representation on the supervisory board, since such a provision could compromise private property. Despite this residual tension, however, co-determination has provided substantial benefits to German business, workers, and the entire society. The most pressing challenge for co-determination in the future will be whether these German-specific institutional patterns will infiltrate other European countries or whether they will be overtaken by European-wide labor relations policies that take other forms.

councils (*Betriebsräte*), gives German workers access to the policy implementation process. In contrast to co-determination, which gives trade unions input outside the plant (i.e., on the board), the works councils represent workers inside the workplace and address shop-floor and plant-level affairs. The trade unions have historically addressed collective bargaining issues, whereas the works councils have concentrated on social and personnel matters. With the trend to more flexible workplaces since the late 1980s, these lines of demarcation have blurred.

The unions have clout on the boards because they are a countrywide, multi-industry organization representing a large number of diverse workers. The works councils, on the other hand, owe their primary allegiance to their local plants and firms. The distribution of power between these two bodies causes rivalries, periodic rifts, and competing spheres of interest. Despite an 85 percent overlap in personnel between unions and works councils and despite a structural entanglement between these two major pillars of labor representation in the Federal Republic, these divisions can produce tensions among organized labor. A period of general flux and plant-related, management-imposed flexibility beginning in the mid- and late 1980s and sporadically continuing since, particularly in eastern

Germany, has exacerbated these tensions. However, the unions have usually avoided the proliferation of any serious plant-level divisions among workers that might have eroded their stature in the German economy in the 1990s and early 2000s.

Other State Institutions

In addition to the institutions discussed so far, the military, the judiciary, and subnational governments are essential institutions for governance and policy-making.

The Military and Police

From the eighteenth century (when it was the Prussian military) through World War II, the German military was powerful and aggressive. After World War II, the military was placed completely under civilian control and tightly circumscribed by law and treaty. The end of the cold war produced two other important changes in German military policy: the reduction in U.S. armed forces stationed in Germany and payments made to Russia for removal of soldiers and materiel from the former East Germany.

Germany has a universal service arrangement requiring all citizens over the age of eighteen to perform one year of military or civilian service. In 1990, Germany had about 600,000 men and women in the military, but in 1994 the Federal Government fixed the figure at approximately 340,000. Germany spends approximately 1.5 percent of its GDP on the military. Germany's armed forces have been legally proscribed from extranational activity, first by the Allied occupation and later by the German Basic Law. Under the provisions of the Basic Law, the German military is to be used only for defensive purposes within Europe, and then in coordination with NATO authorities. Only very limited military activity under tightly circumscribed approval (via NATO) has altered the general prohibition. German participation in the UN peacekeeping mission in Bosnia was one example, and agreeing to participate in opposition to Serbian aggression in Kosovo in 1999, a decision made by the Red-Green government, was another.

Since World War II, two generations of Germans have been educated to deemphasize the military and militarism as a solution to political problems. The irony is that it is now politically—and until recently, constitutionally—difficult for Germany to commit troops to regional conflicts, even under UN auspices. The dilemmas intensify when the issues of Bosnia, Serbia, and the catastrophe of the former Yugoslavia are considered. In opposition, the SPD and the Greens had argued that because of the Third Reich's aggressive military expeditions to the east in World War II, it was impossible for the German military, under either UN or NATO auspices, to play a constructive role in Eastern Europe. Yet after coming to power, the Red-Green government broke precedent and allowed Germany to take on more geopolitical responsibility in the context of NATO and the EU. This has not been an easy issue, and it is made all the more difficult by the need for the Greens and left-leaning elements in the SPD to accommodate themselves to their power and responsibility. Perhaps it is this latter dimension that enabled Gerhard Schröder to challenge President Bush's position on Iraq in 2002 and 2003.

Discussion of the German police needs to focus on three areas. The first is that of the postwar experience in the FRG, where police powers have been organized on a *Land* basis and, given the excesses of the Third Reich, have been constitutionally circumscribed to ensure that human and civil rights remain inviolate. To be sure, there have been episodes of exceptions, as the German police will never be as well regarded as the British "bobby." For example, during the dragnets for the Red Army *Faktion* terrorists in the late 1970s, many forces in the SPD and among the *Bürgerinititiven* (citizen action groups), the precursors to the Greens, argued that German police forces compromised civil liberties in their desire to capture the terrorists.

The second is that of the GDR's notorious secret police, the *Stasi*. The Ministry for State Security (*Stasi*'s formal name) comprised some 91,000 official employees; moreover, in 1989, more than 180,000 East Germans and perhaps 4,000 West Germans worked as informants for the *Stasi*.[16] In proportion to the 16 million GDR citizens, the *Stasi* was more encompassing in the GDR than was the Gestapo during Nazi rule. It spied on virtually the entire society and arbitrarily arrested and persecuted thousands of citizens. Since unification, *Stasi* archives have been open to all, as the East Germans and later the FRG believed that full and open disclosure of *Stasi* excesses was essential in a democratic state. In so doing, however, names of informants were made public, which created bitter confrontations among former friends and neighbors.

The third is the heightened concern for security in Germany in the wake of 9/11. Germany is particularly concerned about terrorism, since numerous members of the al Qaeda terrorist organization, including several of the 9/11 bombers, lived for years in apartments in Hamburg and other German cities, easily escaping detection. Germany will need to balance the pressing demand for terrorist surveillance with the understandable concerns for maintaining civil liberties in a democratic society only a little more than fifty years old.

The Judiciary

The German judiciary is an independent institution whose rulings are almost always consistent with accepted constitutional principles. Judges are appointed by federal or state governments, depending on the court, and are drawn from practitioners of the law, similar to the pattern in other countries. In 2001, there were over 21,000 judges in Germany, with approximately 25 percent of them female. The German judiciary remains outside the political fray on most issues, although a ruling in 1993 limiting access to abortion for many women, in direct opposition to a more liberal law in East Germany, was a clear exception to the general pattern. The judiciary was also criticized in the 1990s for showing too much leniency toward perpetrators of racist violence.

The court system in the Federal Republic is three-pronged. One branch consists of the criminal-civil system, which has as its apex the Federal High Court. It is a unified rather than a federal system and tries to apply a consistent set of criteria to cases in the sixteen states. The Federal High Court reviews cases that have been appealed from the lower courts, including criminal and civil cases, disputes among the states, and matters that would be viewed in some countries as political, such as the abortion ruling.

The Special Constitutional Court deals with matters directly affecting the Basic Law. A postwar creation, it was founded to safeguard the new democratic order. Precisely because of the Nazis' abuses of the judiciary, the founders of West Germany added a layer to the judiciary, basically a judicial review, to ensure that

the democratic order was maintained. The most notable decisions of the Constitutional Court in the 1950s were the banning of both the ultraright Socialist Reich Party and the leftist Communist Party as forces hostile to the Basic Law. During the early 1970s, when the so-called Radicals Decree was promulgated, the Constitutional Court ruled that several individuals who had lost their jobs were "enemies of the constitution." During the brief terrorist wave of the late 1970s, when several prominent individuals were kidnapped or killed by the ultraradical Red Army *Faktion,* this court was asked to pass judgment on the government's action in response to the terrorists' attacks. At that time, it sanctioned a wide, indiscriminate sweep for all those who might be supporters of the Red Army *Faktion,* questioning and arresting several thousand innocent citizens. In a state that claimed to be an adherent of Western-style liberalism, and in one ruled by the SPD-led government, such far-reaching action alarmed many who were concerned about individual freedoms and due process.

The **Administrative Court** system is the third branch of the judiciary. Consisting of the Labor Court, the Social Security Court, and the Finance Court, the Administrative Court system has a much narrower jurisdiction than the other two branches. Because the state and its bureaucracy have such a prominent place in the lives of German citizens, this level of the court system acts as a check on the arbitrary power of the bureaucracy. Compared to Britain, where much public policy is determined by legislation, German public policy is more often determined by the administrative actions of the bureaucracy. Citizens can use these three courts to challenge bureaucratic decisions—for example, if authorities improperly take action with respect to labor, welfare, or tax policies.

The judiciary has always played a major role in German government because of the state's deep involvement in political and economic matters. But the worst abuses of the judiciary for political purposes came during the Nazi regime, when it was induced to make a wide range of antidemocratic, repressive, and even criminal decisions. Among these were banning non-Nazi parties, allowing the seizure of Jewish property, and sanctioning the deaths of millions.

The Federal Republic's founders were determined that the new judicial system would avoid these abuses.

One of the first requirements was that the judiciary explicitly safeguard the democratic rights of individuals, groups, and political parties, stressing some of the individual freedoms that had long been associated with the American and British legal systems. In fact, the Basic Law contains a more elaborate and explicit statement of individual rights than exists in either the U.S. Constitution or in British common law.

However, the Federal Republic's legal system differs from the common law tradition of Britain, its former colonies, and the United States. The common law precedent-based system is characterized by adversarial relationships between contending parties, in which the judge (or the court itself) merely provides the arena for the struggle. In continental Europe, including France and Germany, the legal system is based on a codified legal system with roots in Roman law and the Napoleonic code.

In the Federal Republic, the judiciary is thus an active administrator of the law rather than solely an arbiter. Specifically, judges have a different relationship with the state and with the adjudication of cases. This judicial system relies on the concept of the capacity of the state to identify and implement certain important societal goals. And if the task of the state is to create the laws to attain these goals, then the judiciary should safeguard their implementation. In both defining the meaning of very complex laws and in implementing their administration, German courts go considerably beyond those in the United States and Britain, which supposedly have avoided political decisions. The German courts' role in shaping policy has been most evident in the ruling on whether to allow the unions to obtain increased co-determination rights in 1976. The court allowed the unions to obtain near parity on the boards of directors but stated that full union parity with employers would compromise the right of private property.

In the 1990s, the courts came under great pressure to resolve the intractable policy issues that unification and European integration brought about. As they were drawn deeper into the political thicket, their decisions came under increased scrutiny. Clandestine searches for terrorists in the late 1970s left many observers believing that the rights of citizens who were unaffiliated with any terrorist organizations had been compromised. Many critics wish that today's courts would show the same diligence and zeal in addressing the crimes of neo-Nazism, not to mention potential al Qaeda terrorists, as the courts did in the 1970s, when Germany was confronted with violence from small ultraleftist groups. The judicial system as a whole now must walk a very fine line between maintaining civil rights in a democratic society and providing security from various sources of extremist violence.

Subnational Government

There are sixteen states in the Federal Republic; eleven composed the old West Germany and five the former East Germany. Among the best-known regions are Bavaria, the Rhineland including the industrial Ruhr River valley, the Black Forest area in the southwest, and the city-states of Berlin, Hamburg, and Bremen. Unlike the weakly developed regional governments of Britain and France, German state governments enjoy considerable autonomy and independent powers. Each state has a regional assembly (*Landtag*), which functions much like the *Bundestag* does at the federal level. The governor (*Minister-Präsident*) of each *Land* is the leader of the largest party (or coalition of parties) in the *Landtag* and forms a government in the *Landtag* in much the same way as does the chancellor in the *Bundestag*. Elections for each of the sixteen states are held on independent, staggered four-year cycles, which generally do not coincide with federal elections and only occasionally coincide with elections in other *Länder*. Like the semipublic institutions, subnational governments in Germany are powerful, important, and responsible for much national policy implementation.

Particularly significant is Germany's "marble-cake" federalism—the interaction among state and federal government that sees the former implement many of the laws passed by the latter. A good way to show how it works is to cite the example of **industrial policy** (*Ordnungspolitik*). Regional governments are much more active than the national government in planning and targeting economic policy and therefore have greater autonomy in administering industrial policy. Since the *Länder* are constituent states, they are able to develop their own regional versions of industrial policy. Because the different regions have different economic needs and industrial foundations, most voters see these powers as legitimate and appropriate.

The state governments encourage banks to make direct investment and loans to stimulate industrial development. They also encourage cooperation among regional firms, many in the same industry, to spur international competition. This coordination avoids violation of the Cartel Law of 1957, Germany's principal antitrust law, because it does not impede domestic competition. State governments also invest heavily in vocational education to provide the skills needed for manufacturing high-quality goods, the core of the German economy. Organized business and organized labor have a direct role in shaping curricula to improve worker skills through the vocational education system. These *Land* governments have improved industrial adaptation by shaping the state's competitive framework rather than adopting a heavy-handed regulatory posture.

The states do not pursue identical economic policies, and there are various models of government involvement in economic policy. The specific patterns identified have included the organized yet flexible specialization of Baden-Württemberg, the late industrialization of Bavaria, and the managed decline and adjustment of North Rhine–Westphalia.

In the Federal Republic, state politics is organized on the same political party basis as the national parties. This does not mean that national politics dominates local politics. However, the common party names and platforms at all levels let voters see the connection among local, regional, and national issues. Because parties adopt platforms for state and city elections, voters can see the ideological differences among parties and not be swayed solely by personalities. This does not mean that personalities do not play a role in German regional politics. Rather, the German party system encourages national political figures to begin their careers at the local and state levels. Regional and local party members' careers are tied closely to the national, regional, and local levels of the party. Thus, ideological and policy continuity across levels is rewarded. Some observers suggest that this connection in the Federal Republic among national, regional, and local politics may be one reason that voter turnout in German state elections far exceeds that of equivalent U.S. elections.

Local governments in the Federal Republic can raise revenues by owning enterprises, and many do. This has partly resulted from the historical patterns of public sector involvement in the economy but also from the assumption that these levels of government are the stewards of a collective public good. By operating art museums, theater companies, television and radio networks, recreational facilities, and housing complexes and by providing various direct and indirect subsidies to citizens, local governments attempt to maintain the quality of life in modern society. Even during the various recessions since the early 1980s, there have been remarkably few cutbacks in ownership of public enterprises or in these various types of social spending.

The Policy-Making Process

The chancellor and the cabinet have the principal responsibility for policy-making, but their power cannot be wielded in an arbitrary fashion. The policy-making process in Germany is largely consensus based, with contentious issues usually extensively debated within various public, semipublic, and private institutions. Although the legislature has a general role in policy-making, the primary driving forces are the respective cabinet departments and the experts on whom they call.

Policy implementation is similarly diffuse. Along with corporatist interest groups and various semipublic organizations, the *Bundesrat* (upper house) also plays a significant role. Among the areas of policy most likely to be shaped by multiple actors are vocational education, welfare, health care, and worker participation. Germany's status as a federal state and one populated by a broad range of democratic corporatist groups and parapublic institutions means that policy implementation has many participants. Even in such areas as foreign and security policy, the federal cabinet departments sometimes rely on business interests in policy implementation. EU policy is shaped by both national and regional governments, as well as by private sector interests that use corporatist institutions to participate in the process.

Many observers do not understand exactly why and how institutions support the Federal Republic's economic policy-making process. The role that the various institutions have played in the process of flexible adaptation to competitive pressures has been substantial. It has enabled the German economy to outperform the economies of most other industrialized countries for most of the post–World War II period. At first glance, it seems that such institutions are merely regulatory agencies that inhibit economic freedoms. A closer examination, however, reveals that German institutions regulate not the minute details but the general framework. Because all economic actors are clear on the general parameters, German regulatory policy is remarkably free of the microregulations common in many other countries. Moreover, many policies, especially in the banking and manufacturing industries, are reinforced by industry self-regulation that makes heavy-handed government intervention unnecessary.

What components of this policy-making process actually create economic policy? First, corporatism is a system and not just a collection of firms or discrete policies. In this system, business, labor, and the government bargain hard from the outset of the process, finally developing consensual policy solutions to national, regional, state, and local issues. The Germans have spoken of their "social" (not "free") market economy because of the deeply entrenched belief that business must share in the responsibility to provide a stable order for the economy and indirectly for society.

German business, labor, and government support for the **framework regulations** has produced a system that often appears externally rigid but internally flexible (in the sense that large institutions and firms are often surprisingly flexible in adapting applied technologies to produce specialized goods). In short, this system regulates not the details, but the general rules of the game under which all actors must play.

Some would criticize such a system as being too cumbersome and inflexible. However, the Germans praise their system for generally producing agreement on major policy direction without major social dislocation. Once agreement has been informally worked out among all the major parties, it is easier to move forward with specific legislation. This process is generally less conflict oriented than in Britain because the German parliamentary system takes steps to secure support from major interest groups.

The extraordinary nature of unification issues and the increasing significance of the EU as a policy-making entity have greatly challenged this consensual system. Both changes have put this informal style of policy-making under tremendous pressure. Among the issues that proved most intractable at the domestic level are those of political asylum, racist violence, and scandals that tarnished the reputations of major public figures in the political system and in major interest groups. At the European level, issues such as the euro and counter-terrorism remain difficult. Moreover, for all of its system-maintaining advantages, the German consensual system contains a certain intolerance of dissent. Among examples are the structure of the party system that forces politicians to work slowly through the organization, the 5 percent threshold for party representation, and judicial banning of political parties. This helps to explain the protest from outside the parties that started in the 1960s and has continued on and off ever since.

Section ❹ Representation and Participation

In the aftermath of unification and European integration, Germany continues to strive for democratic participation that is both inclusive and representative. The nation still struggles with issues surrounding collective identities. Incorporating disparate political cultures (east and west, for example) when respect for dissent and dialogue is not deeply ingrained is a dilemma for any society. The key issue for Germany is how to develop a system of democratic participation that encompasses both extrainstitutional groups and organized political institutions.

The Legislature

The legislature occupies a prominent place in the political system, with both the lower house (*Bundestag*) and the upper house (*Bundesrat*) holding significant and wide-ranging powers. The Federal Republic is similar to other parliamentary regimes that have a fusion of power in which the executive branch derives directly from the legislative branch. In other words, there is not a sharply defined separation of powers between cabinet and legislature.

The process for choosing members of the two houses differs substantially. The *Bundestag* elects its members directly; voters choose both individual district representatives and the political parties that represent their interests. The *Bundesrat's* members, on the other hand, are officials who are elected or appointed to the regional (*Länder*) governments. Both branches of the legislature are broadly representative of the major interests in German society, although some interests such as business and labor are somewhat overrepresented, whereas ecological and noneconomic interests are somewhat underrepresented.

The executive branch introduces legislation in accordance with the Basic Law, which requires that the executive initiate the federal budget and tax legislation. Although most bills are initiated in the cabinet, this does not diminish the influence of *Bundestag* or *Bundesrat* members. In fact, because the chancellor is the leader of the major party or coalition of parties, no sharp division exists between the executive and legislative branches. There is generally strong consensus within parties and within coalitions about what legislation should be introduced. Parties and coalitions, which depend on party discipline to sustain majorities, place a high value on agreement regarding major legislation.

When the chancellor and the cabinet propose a bill, it is sent to a relevant *Bundestag* committee. Most of the committee deliberations take place privately so that the individual committee members can have considerable latitude to shape details of the legislation. The committees will call on their own expertise as well as that of relevant government ministries and testimony from pertinent interest groups. This may appear to be a kind of insiders' club, and to some degree it is. However, the committees generally call on a wide range of groups, both pro and con, that are affected by the proposed legislation. By consulting the corporatist interest groups, a more consensus-oriented outcome is achieved. In contrast, legislative sessions in countries with a more pluralist (less inclusive) form of lobbying, such as Britain and the United States, tend to be contentious and less likely to produce agreement. Under pluralism, it is relatively easy for groups to articulate issues; however, without a coordinated institutional structure, policy-making is more haphazard.

After emerging from committee, the bill has three readings in the *Bundestag*. The debate in the *Bun-*

destag often produces considerable criticism from the opposition and sharp defense by the governing parties. The primary purpose of the debate is to educate the public about the major issues of the bill. Following passage in the *Bundestag,* the *Bundesrat,* whose assent includes determining how a particular law will be implemented at the regional level, must approve the bill. Finally, the federal president must sign it.

Most of the members of the national legislature are male, middle-class professionals, even in the supposedly working-class Social Democratic Party, which had a much greater proportion of blue-collar deputies in the 1950s. There were few women lawmakers until the 1980s and 1990s, when the Greens elected an increasing number of female *Bundestag* members, and women began to gain slots on the Social Democrats' electoral lists.[17] Fewer than 10 percent of *Bundestag* members were women through the 1983 election, but since 1987, the number of women has increased substantially, reaching 32.2 percent with the 2002 election (see Table 2). The addition of newer parties such as the worker-oriented ex-communist Party of Democratic Socialism (PDS) and the continued presence of the Greens with their counterculture lifestyles have increased the variety of backgrounds among *Bundestag* members. In fact, the proportional representation system used in Germany increases the number of women and minorities elected to the *Bundestag*. Many parties, particularly the Social Democrats, the Greens, and the PDS, select candidates for their electoral lists based on gender and diversity.

Table 2

Percentage of Women Members of the Bundestag

Year	Percentage	Year	Percentage
1949	6.8	1976	7.3
1953	8.8	1980	8.5
1957	9.2	1983	9.8
1961	8.3	1987	15.4
1965	6.9	1990	20.5
1969	6.6	1994	26.3
1972	5.8	1998	30.2
		2002	32.2

Source: Bundeszentrale für Politische Bildung, 2002.

The Bundestag

The lower house of the legislature, the *Bundestag,* consists of 603 seats. This large number (and unification caused it to increase by over 100 members) caused a strain on the facilities in Bonn. When the capital moved to Berlin in 1999 to the rebuilt *Reichstag,* all *Bundestag* members could finally be accommodated.

Bundestag members almost always vote with their parties. This party unity contributes to consistency in the parties' positions over the course of a four-year legislative period and enables the electorate to identify each party's stance on a range of issues. Consequently, all representatives in the *Bundestag* can be held accountable based on their support for their parties' positions. Party discipline, in turn, helps produce more stable governments.

The tradition of strong, unified parties in the *Bundestag* has some drawbacks. The hierarchy within parties relegates newer members to a comparatively long stint as backbenchers. Since party elders and the Federal Chancellery control the legislative agenda and key policy decisions, individual legislators have few opportunities to make an impact. Some of the most prominent national politicians preferred to serve their political apprenticeship in state or local government, where they would have more visibility. Chancellors Gerhard Schröder and Helmut Kohl took this route as governors of Lower Saxony and Rhineland Palatinate, respectively.

The Bundesrat

The *Bundesrat* has a different role from the U.S. Senate or the British House of Lords. The *Bundesrat* is the mechanism that makes the federal system work. It is responsible for the distribution of powers between national and state governments and grants to the states the rights to implement federal laws. It is the point of intersection for the national and the state governments and is made up of sixty-nine members from the sixteen state governments. Each state sends at least three representatives to the *Bundesrat,* depending on its population. States with more than 2 million residents have four votes, and states with more than 6 million people have five votes.

The political composition of the *Bundesrat* at any given time is determined by which parties are in power in the states. Each state delegation casts its votes on legislation in a bloc, reflecting the views of the majority party or coalition. Consequently, the party controlling the majority of state governments can have a significant effect on legislation passed in the *Bundestag*. And because state elections usually take place between *Bundestag* electoral periods, the *Bundesrat* majority can shift during the course of a *Bundestag* legislative period.

The *Bundesrat* must approve all amendments to the constitution as well as all laws that address the fundamental interests of the states, such as taxes, territorial integrity, and basic administrative functions. It exercises a **suspensive veto;** that is, if the *Bundesrat* votes against a bill, the *Bundestag* can override the *Bundesrat* by passing the measure again by a simple majority. If, however, a two-thirds majority of the *Bundesrat* votes against a bill, the *Bundestag* must pass it again by a two-thirds margin. In usual practice, the *Bundesrat* has not acted to obstruct. When the legislation is concurrent—that is, when the state and national governments share administrative responsibilities for implementing the particular policy—there is almost always easy agreement between the two houses. Also, a party or coalition that has achieved a stable majority in the *Bundestag* can overcome any possible obstruction by the *Bundesrat*.

The *Bundesrat* introduces comparatively little legislation, but its administrative responsibilities are considerable. Most of the members of the *Bundesrat* are also state government officials, well experienced in the implementation of particular laws. Their expertise is frequently called on in the committee hearings of the *Bundestag,* which are open to all *Bundesrat* members. This overlapping is a unique feature of the Federal Republic. Many U.S. observers make the mistake of equating German and U.S. federalism; however, Germany has a qualitatively different relationship between national and state governments. The Federal Republic avoids the jurisdictional problems that sometimes plague other decentralized federal countries because many of the laws passed in the *Bundestag* are implemented at the *Land* level.

The *Bundesrat*'s strong administrative role is a key component of the government. In different ways, this system avoids the shortcomings of both the fragmented legislative practices of the United States and the overly centralized policies of previous German governments. Because the *Bundesrat* is concerned with implementation, its role is more purposeful than that of the U.S. Congress, where laws that overlap or contradict previous legislation are frequently passed. For example, the *Bundesrat* administers a major television network (ARD) and coordinates the link between regional and national economic policies and vocational education systems. The *Bundesrat*'s structure positions it close to the concerns and needs of the entire country and provides a forum for understanding how national legislation will affect each of the states.

Although the *Bundesrat* was originally envisioned to be more technocratic and less politically contentious than the popularly elected *Bundestag,* debates in the *Bundesrat* became strongly politicized beginning in the 1970s. The most common occurrence was the conflict that emerged when regional elections caused a change in control of the *Bundesrat,* especially when this change gave more influence to the party, or group of parties, that was in opposition to the *Bundestag*. For example, part of Helmut Kohl's difficulty in his last term (1994–1998) resulted from the Social Democrats' controlling a majority of state governments, where they occasionally blocked national legislation. After Schröder's narrow victory in the 2002 Federal elections and the CDU victory in two *Land* elections in early 2003, many observers expected similar conflict for the remainder of the SPD-Green second term.

Political Parties and the Party System

Germany has often been called a **party democracy** because its parties are so important in shaping state policy. Its multiparty system has proved quite stable for most of the post–World War II period. Until the early 1980s, Germany had a "two-and-a-half" party system, composed of a moderate-left Social Democratic Party (SPD), a moderate-right Christian Democratic grouping (CDU in all of West Germany except Bavaria, where it is called the CSU), and a small centrist Free Democratic Party (FDP). The ideological distance between these parties was not great. The SPD broadened its base from its core working-class constituency to include more middle-class supporters beginning in the late 1950s. The CDU/CSU includes both Catholics (mostly from the Bavarian-based CSU) and Protestants. The FDP is liberal in the European sense and favors free-market solutions to economic problems and extensive personal freedoms for individuals. With only 5 to 10 percent of the vote, it is a pragmatic party and until 1998 usually chose to ally itself with one of the two larger parties to form a government. During their time as the only parties on the political landscape (1949–1983), these groups presided over a stable, growing economy and a broad public consensus on economic and social policies.

During the 1980s and 1990s, two new parties emerged to challenge the "two-and-a-half" major parties (see Table 3) and to complicate Germany's comparatively tidy political landscape.[18] These were the Greens/Bündnis '90, generally of the left and favoring ecological, environmental, and peace issues; and the Party of Democratic Socialism (PDS), the former Communist Party of East Germany. Two other small right-wing parties, the Republicans (*Republikaner*) and the German Peoples Union (*Deutsche Volksunion,* DVU), also emerged. Much more conservative than the CDU/CSU, they emphasized nationalism and aggression toward immigrants and ethnic minorities. Neither of these two right-wing parties has yet won seats in the *Bundestag* because of the 5 percent rule. Both have exceeded 5 percent in regional elections, however, and have won seats in those bodies.

The Greens entered the political scene in 1979 and have won seats at national and regional levels ever since. The PDS is concentrated in the five states of the former East Germany, and although it has received as much as 25 percent of the vote in some regional and local elections, it draws well under the 5 percent mark in the states of the former West Germany.

The Social Democratic Party

As the leading party of the left in Germany, the *Sozialdemokratische Partei Deutschlands* (SPD) has had a long and durable history. The SPD was founded in 1875 in response to rapid industrialization. After surviving Bismarck's attempts in the 1880s to outlaw it, it grew to be the largest party in the *Reichstag* by 1912.[19] Following World War I, it became the leading party—but without a majority—of the Weimar Republic during its early years.

Despite strong influence in postwar Germany from

Table 3

FRG Election Results, 1949–2002

Year	Party	Percentage of Vote	Government	Year	Party	Percentage of Vote	Government
1949	Voter turnout	78.5	CDU/CSU-FDP	1983	Voter Turnout	89.1	CDU/CSU-FDP
	CDU/CSU	31.0			CDU/CSU	48.8	
	SPD	29.2			SPD	38.2	
	FDP	11.9			FDP	7.0	
	Others	27.8			Greens	5.6	
1953	Voter turnout	86.0	CDU/CSU-FDP		Others	0.5	
	CDU/CSU	45.2		1987	Voter turnout	84.3	CDU/CSU-FDP
	SPD	28.8			CDU/CSU	44.3	
	FDP	9.5			SPD	37.0	
	Others	16.7			FDP	9.1	
1957	Voter turnout	87.8	CDU/CSU		Greens	8.3	
	CDU/CSU	50.2			Others	1.3	
	SPD	31.8		1990	Voter turnout	78.0	CDU/CSU-FDP
	FDP	7.7			CDU/CSU	43.8	
	Others	10.3			SPD	33.5	
1961	Voter turnout	87.8	CDU/CSU-FDP		FDP	11.0	
	CDU/CSU	45.3			Greens	3.8	
	SPD	36.2			PDS	2.4	
	FDP	12.8			Bündnis '90	1.2	
	Others	5.7			Others	3.5	
1965	Voter turnout	86.8	CDU/CSU-SPD	1994	Voter turnout	79.0	CDU/CSU-FDP
	CDU/CSU	47.6	Grand		CDU/CSU	41.5	
	SPD	39.3	Coalition		SPD	36.4	
	FDP	9.5			FDP	6.9	
	Others	3.6			Greens	7.3	
1969	Voter turnout	86.7	SPD-FDP		PDS	4.4	
	CDU/CSU	46.1			Others	3.5	
	SPD	42.7		1998	Voter turnout	82.3	SPD-Greens
	FDP	5.8			CDU/CSU	35.1	
	Others	5.4			SPD	40.9	
1972	Voter turnout	86.0	SPD-FDP		FDP	6.2	
	CDU/CSU	44.9			Greens	6.7	
	SPD	45.8			PDS	5.1	
	FDP	9.5			Others	6.0	
	Others	16.7		2002	Voter turnout	79.1	SPD-Greens
1976	Voter turnout	90.7	SDP-FDP		SPD	38.5	
	CDU/CSU	48.2			CDU/CSU	38.5	
	SPD	42.6			Greens	8.6	
	FDP	7.9			FDP	7.4	
	Others	0.9			PDS	4.0	
1980	Voter Turnout	88.6	SPD-FDP		Others	3.0	
	CDU/CSU	44.5					
	SPD	42.9					
	FDP	10.6					
	Others	0.5					

Source: German Information Center, 2002.

1945 to 1948, the SPD was able to obtain only about 30 percent of the popular vote from 1949 until the early 1960s. In an attempt to broaden its constituency, it altered its party program at a 1959 party conference in Bad Godesberg. Deemphasizing its primary reliance on Marxism, its new goal was to broaden its base and become what the political scientist Otto Kirchheimer has called a "catchall party."[20] The SPD did not relinquish Marxism completely and continued to represent the working class, but it also began to seek and attract support from groups outside the traditional blue-collar working class. The Bad Godesberg conference transformed the SPD into a party similar to other western European social democratic parties.

The SPD finally took office as the leading member of a majority coalition, with the FDP, in 1969 and remained in power for thirteen years under chancellors Willy Brandt and Helmut Schmidt. The SPD brought to the coalition a concern for increased welfare and social spending.[21] This as due partly to pressure by left-wing extraparliamentary opposition groups and student demonstrations in 1968. The FDP brought its support for increased individual freedom of expression at a time when youths in all industrialized societies were seeking a greater voice. The principal factor cementing these two dissimilar parties for such a long time was the strong performance of the economy. The coalition finally broke up in the early 1980s, when an economic recession prevented the increased social spending demanded by the SPD left wing.

During the 1980s and 1990s when it was out of power, the SPD failed to formulate clear alternative policies to make itself attractive to its members, supporters, and voters. In 1998, the Kohl regime was exhausted and had overpromised the speed of transformation in eastern Germany. An effective campaign by Gerhard Schröder enabled the SPD to increase its share of the vote by 5 percent over its 1994 percentage and emerge as Germany's leading party (see Figure 2 and "Leaders: Gerhard Schröder"). It retained this position, albeit with a reduced majority in the 2002 *Bundestag* election.

The Greens

The Green Party is a heterogeneous party that first drew support from several different constituencies in the early 1980s: urban-based **Citizens Action Groups,**

Figure 2

Distribution of Seats

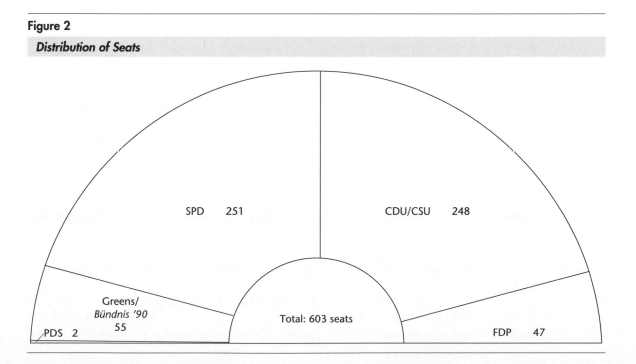

SPD   251

CDU/CSU   248

Greens/
Bündnis '90
55

Total: 603 seats

PDS   2

FDP   47

Leaders: *Gerhard Schröder*

Gerhard Schröder, the chancellor of Germany elected in 1998, is the first German political leader truly of the postwar generation. Schröder was born at the war's cusp, in 1944, in the small Lower Saxony town of Rosenburg. He was profoundly affected by the war in one sense; his father, a German soldier, was killed on the eastern front in Romania. As a young man, Gerhard Schröder had to work while he completed his education, serving a stint in a hardware store before completing the first phase of his university studies.

In his twenties, Schröder became active in Social Democratic party politics, belonging to the Jungsozialisten (Young Socialists), or Jusos, as they are known colloquially. He embraced Marxism, as did most other Jusos at the time; this fact is not surprising given the Marxist roots of virtually all Social Democratic, Socialist, and Labor parties. By the time Schröder received his law degree from Göttingen University in 1976, he had already become an influential young politician in the SPD. He became a member of the Bundestag in 1980 and in 1990 was elected Minister-Präsident (governor) of Lower Saxony. Even in his early years in public life, Schröder had high ambitions. One evening in Bonn in the 1980s, Schröder, who had taken perhaps an extra glass of wine or two, was walking past the gate to the chancellor's office then occupied by Helmut Kohl; he put his hands on the gate and exclaimed: "I want to be in there!" Schröder's personal life is not without controversy; he has been married and divorced three times and is now married to his fourth wife. During the 1998 campaign, the youth wing of Helmut Kohl's CDU used a critical slogan urging voters to reject Schröder and the SPD, stating, "Three women can't be wrong."

During the 1998 election campaign, Schröder was compared with British Prime Minister Tony Blair and former U.S. President Bill Clinton. Observers stressed one apparent thread that tied the three young (all were in their forties or fifties) political leaders together. As heads of nominally left parties in their respective countries, they seemed to share an affinity for moving their parties toward more centrist positions. In fact, the SPD slogan for the 1998 campaign was "die neue Mitte" (the New Middle), suggesting just such a moderating tendency.

Yet a funny thing happened on Schröder's way toward the center: German politics. Unlike Bill Clinton, who often operated without regard to his own Democratic Party's concerns, or Tony Blair, who controls and shapes the policy of his majority Labour Party, Gerhard Schröder has been much more institutionally constrained. For one thing, the SPD is in coalition with another party, the Greens, and does not have a majority by itself. Just as important, though, is the institutional structure of the SPD, with its various factions and constituencies. One other influence inhibited Schröder's move toward the center: he was brought up by his widowed mother, and he retains a powerful commitment to maintaining a strong welfare state and a social benefits package that will sustain widows like his mother in their old age.

Following his narrow 2002 reelection, these constraints placed Schröder in a tight squeeze. The left-wing members of the SPD, as well his Greens' coalition partners, resisted massive cutbacks, yet the rising unemployment, globalization, and the strictures of EU membership prevented him from bold expansionary economic policies. By the start of his second term, his honeymoon with the German people appeared to be over as some forces in the SPD even wanted to replace him as chancellor.

environmental activists, farmers, anti-nuclear power activists, the remnants of the peace movement, and small bands of Marxist-Leninists. After overcoming the 5 percent hurdle in the 1983 *Bundestag* elections, the Green Party went on to win seats in most subsequent state elections by stressing noneconomic quality-of-life issues. The electoral successes of this "antiparty party" generated a serious division within the party between the *realos* (realists) and the *fundis* (fundamentalists). The *realos* believed it was important to enter political institutions to gain access to power; the *fundis* opposed any collaboration with existing parties, even if this meant sacrificing some of their goals.

The realists gained the upper hand, but there was no guarantee of long-term success for the Greens because all the other parties began to include environmental and qualitative issues in their party programs. Until the merger with the eastern German Bündnis '90 in 1993, the Greens' position looked bleak. The squabbling between *fundis* and *realos* undercut the party's credibility among potential new voters. Its inability to develop positions to address the problems of unification made the party appear unwilling to deal with reality. The Greens' failure to motivate its own core constituency during the early 1990s greatly hampered the party. The unexpected death (by suicide) of a former party leader—the American-born Petra Kelly, a *fundi*—and the moderation of a current party leader (and foreign minister), Joschka Fischer, signaled the transformation of the Greens into a dependable, innovative coalition partner.

The persistent ecological problems of the former East German states have presented the Greens a tremendous opportunity. After gaining over 6 percent of the vote in the 1994 and 1998 elections and becoming the junior coalition partner in the SPD-Green coalition, the party's firm base seemed to waver as the 2002 election approached. This was caused by its defending coalition policy on which its own members did not always agree. However, the Greens rebounded and increased their share of the vote to 8.6 percent and now appear to be a permanent fixture in the German *Bundestag*.

The Christian Democrats

The Christian Democrats combine the Christian Democratic Union (CDU, in all Länder except Bavaria) and the Christian Social Union (CSU, the affiliated Bavarian grouping). Unlike the older parties (SPD and FDP) of the Federal Republic, the CDU/CSU was founded immediately after World War II, when most nonleftist parties worked to avoid the bickering and divisiveness of the Weimar period and establish a counterweight to the SPD. The CDU/CSU united Catholics and Protestants in one confessional (Christian) party and served as a catchall party of the center-right.

Programmatically, the CDU/CSU stressed the social market economy, which blended elements of European Catholic social concerns about the poor and workers with market economy concerns to create a program that was capitalist but with a paternalistic sense of social responsibility.[22] Under Chancellors Adenauer and Erhard, the Christian Democrats held political power for almost twenty years. Its social policies during this period were paternalistic and moderately conservative. As mentioned above, social policy assumed a male breadwinner and a wife who stayed at home. The CDU/CSU even explicitly codified this approach with their phrase *Kinder, Kirche, Kuche* (children, church, and kitchen) which defined the Christian Democrats' view of women's primary roles.

After the SPD and FDP established their center-left coalition in 1969, the CDU/CSU spent thirteen years as the opposition party. Returning to power in 1983 under the leadership of Helmut Kohl, the CDU/CSU with their FDP coalition partners continued their traditions of a moderate center-right regime and retained power through four elections until 1998. During his first three terms (1982–1990) Kohl and the Christian Democrats successfully maintained a successful mixed economy and a still-generous social welfare state. However, the most significant and historic accomplishments—truly twin legacies—of the long Kohl regime are German unification and Germany's integration into the EU.

The Free Democratic Party

The philosophy of the FDP comes closest to the individualistic ideals of British liberal and American libertarian parties. (It must be emphasized again that *liberal* is used in the European sense of an emphasis on the individual as opposed to an activist state tradition.) The FDP's major influence is its role as a swing party because it has allied with each of the two major parties (SPD and CDU/CSU) at different periods since 1949. Regularly holding the foreign and economics ministries in coalition with the Christian Democrats, the FDP's most notable leaders were Walter Scheel, Otto Graf Lambsdorff, and Hans-Dietrich Genscher.

The FDP's perspective encompasses two ideologies, broadly characterized here as economic liberalism and social liberalism. During the postwar period, the FDP relied on two philosophies to align itself with the two major political groupings, the CDU/CSU and the SPD. It remained in power until 1998, when the

FDP was shut out of the cabinet for only the third time since 1949: the two previous occurrences were the CDU/CSU majority from 1957 to 1961 and the Grand Coalition from 1966 to 1969. For its strategy of co-governing with first one major party and then the other, the FDP has occasionally been accused of lacking strong political convictions.

The Party of Democratic Socialism

The Party of Democratic Socialism (PDS), a new party concentrated in the former East Germany, has had a long and volatile history. It sprang from the Communist Party of Germany, which was founded after World War I. In the late 1940s, the Communist Party flourished in the Soviet zone and under USSR acquiescence forced a merger with the Social Democrats in the east. The merged Communist/Socialist party was renamed the Socialist Unity Party (*Sozialistische Einheits Partei,* SED). It dominated all aspects of life in East Germany under the leadership of Walter Ulbricht, Willi Stoph, and Erik Honnecker and was considered the most Stalinist and repressive regime in Eastern Europe.

With unification in 1990, reality confronted the SED. Its reformist leader, Gregor Gysi, quickly changed its name, and it showed considerable strength in the five states of the former East Germany. Throughout the 1990s, the difficulties of unification helped to renew the strength of the PDS. It gained over 20 percent of the vote in the five new German states in the 1994, 1998, and 2002 elections and won seats in the *Bundestag* in four consecutive elections. In the mid-1990s, it formed regional coalitions with the SPD in eastern Germany and even was a junior member of the Berlin city and state governments in 2001.

Whether the PDS could ever be considered a potential coalition partner at the national level is uncertain. To some observers, the most interesting development is that the PDS is not a "communist" party anymore. Rather, it has become a regionally based party beseeching the national government for greater resources. In this sense, it seems to be a left-wing eastern German version of the right-wing Bavaria-based CSU.

Elections

Germany's two-ballot electoral system has produced two significant outcomes. First, the proportional representation electoral system produces multiple parties that help reinforce the constitution's specific support for the parties as essential institutions in a democratic polity. Second, the 5 percent hurdle ensures that only parties with sufficient support attain seats in the Bundestag. This has helped Germany avoid the wild proliferation of parties that plagues some democracies, such as Italy and Israel, where coalition formation is extremely difficult.

The German parliamentary system represents a synthesis between the British and U.S. traditions of a single legislator representing one district and the European tradition of proportional representation in which the percentage of the vote is equal to the percentage of the parliamentary seats. (see "Institutional Intricacies: Proportional Representation and the Story of the German 'Double Ballot.'") Single-member district voting systems tend to produce a two-party system, and the Germans wanted to ensure that all major parties were represented, not just two. The German hybrid system, known as **personalized proportional representation,** requires citizens to cast two votes on each ballot: the first for an individual candidate in the local district and the second for a list of national/regional candidates grouped by party affiliation (see Figure 3). This system has the effect of personalizing list voting because voters have their own local representative, but they also can choose among several parties representing various ideologies. To ensure that only major parties are represented, only those that get 5 percent of the vote or that have three candidates who directly win individual seats can gain representation in the Bundestag.

Allocation of seats by party in the *Bundestag,* however, works more like proportional representation. Specifically, the percentage of total seats won per party corresponds strongly with the party's percentage of the popular vote. For example, if a party's candidate wins a seat as an individual member, his or her party loses one seat from those won via list voting. In practice, the two large parties, the Social Democrats and the Christian Democrats, win most of the district seats because the district vote is winner-take-all. The smaller parties' representatives are almost always elected through the party lists. Thus, the list system creates stronger, more coherent parties.

One direct result of the party discipline is that the Federal Republic has high electoral participation (80

Institutional Intricacies: *Proportional Representation and the Story of the German "Double Ballot"*

Proportional representation is a method of electing representatives in parliamentary democracies. In the more commonly used list form, proportional representation attempts to provide for political parties the same ratio of seats in a parliamentary body that these parties received in an election. For example, if a political party received 20 percent of the vote in an election, under proportional representation this party would receive 20 percent of the seats in the legislative body. The much less widely used Hare system (named for the nineteenth-century British political reformer Thomas Hare) is a complicated mechanism where individual candidates can be ranked by the voters in an order of preference.

Proportional representation is most common in continental Europe and it is most unlike the nonproportional single-member district, "first-past-the-post" electoral system characteristic of the United Kingdom, the United States, and many other English-speaking countries. Proportional representation's origins date from the late nineteenth and early twentieth centuries when the proliferation of political parties representing specific groups in continental European societies (nobility, peasants, industrialists, workers, religions) made the Anglo-American system impractical and unfair. For example, if a district had individual candidates from five different parties and the leading candidate received 25 percent of the vote, that candidate would win 100 percent of the seat with only 25 percent of the vote under the Anglo-American "first-past-the-post" rule.

The Anglo-American preference for single-member district, first-past-the-post electoral systems derives from the earlier introduction of democracy, the greater role given to individual representation, and a smaller number of parties in those countries. In the United States, a generally weaker party system also reinforced the preference for choice based on individual candidates. In fact, the relationship between the number of parties and the choice between proportional representation and an Anglo-American system is somewhat of a chicken-and-egg issue. With fewer parties, there is less likelihood of a perceived need for proportional representation. Yet a well-entrenched single-member, first-past-the-post system is biased in favor of only two parties and thus makes the effective formation of a third—or more—parties inherently more difficult.

Most countries using proportional representation today have the political parties provide a list of candidates so that voters may choose to give their vote to the party that most closely represents their ideological preference. In other words, the party as a collective entity is the primary vehicle for organizing political expression. This system encourages the parties to place the candidates whom they would most like to see elected near the top of the list, as the candidates are chosen for the legislature on the basis of the proportion of their votes that the party receives. In multiparty systems, voters often have a wider range of political choices, which often correlates with higher voter participation than in Anglo-American systems. Some countries (Sweden and Germany) provide a minimum threshold (4 percent and 5 percent, respectively) to prevent the proliferation of a large number of tiny parties. Other countries, such as Israel, have minimal (1.5 percent) thresholds, producing large numbers of political parties. There are also variations in how candidates are chosen.

For example, Germany uses a combination of single-member districts and proportional representation (see the sample ballot in Figure 3), but the allocation of seats in the Bundestag still depends on the proportion of the vote that the parties obtain in the votes by party list. In other words, for each candidate who is elected directly on the "first" ballot, there is one fewer member of that party's list elected from the "second" ballot. The advantage of this system is that every voter has his or her "own" local representative, yet the entire *Bundestag* comprises members who reflect the respective share of each party's total vote. The Germans came up with this unique system somewhat accidentally. At the foundation of the Federal Republic, the German party leaders preferred the proportional representation system that they knew from Weimar (and other continental countries). The American postwar advisers, not surprisingly, preferred the Anglo-American first-past-the-post, single-member district system. An impasse resulted, followed by a compromise that produced the German "double ballot." The irony, of course, is that measure whereby each district seat won on the "first ballot" is subtracted from the total of that party's seats on the "second (proportional) ballot" means that the system is proportional, a fact that the Americans may not have understood at the time. Not surprisingly, the two largest parties get most of the first ballot seats, while virtually all of the smaller parties' seats come from the second (list) ballot.

The primary criticisms of proportional representation by advocates of Anglo-American systems are that there is too great a proliferation of parties and that the formation of working majorities is made more difficult. As the examples of the threshold provision indicate above, a large number of parties—and the chances of a failure to attain an effective majority—can be alleviated by modifying proportional representation systems in ways similar to the Swedish and German experiences.

From *The Oxford Companion to Politics of the World,* edited by Joel Krieger. Copyright © 1993 by Oxford University Press, Inc. Used by permission of Oxford Press, Inc.

Figure 3

Bundestag Election Ballot

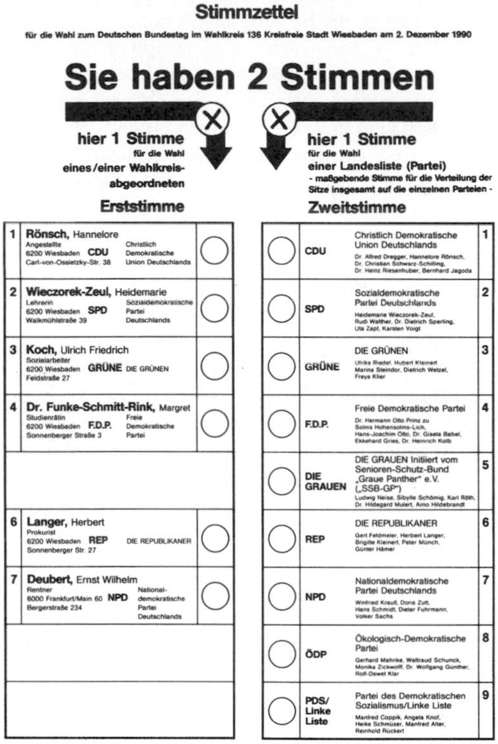

Stimmzettel

für die Wahl zum Deutschen Bundestag im Wahlkreis 136 Kreisfreie Stadt Wiesbaden am 2. Dezember 1990

Sie haben 2 Stimmen

hier 1 Stimme für die Wahl eines/einer Wahlkreis-abgeordneten — **Erststimme**	hier 1 Stimme für die Wahl einer Landesliste (Partei) - maßgebende Stimme für die Verteilung der Sitze insgesamt auf die einzelnen Parteien - — **Zweitstimme**
1 **Rönsch,** Hannelore, Angestellte, 6200 Wiesbaden, Carl-von-Ossietzky-Str. 38 — **CDU** Christlich Demokratische Union Deutschlands	**CDU** Christlich Demokratische Union Deutschlands — Dr. Alfred Dregger, Hannelore Rönsch, Dr. Christian Schwarz-Schilling, Dr. Heinz Riesenhuber, Bernhard Jagoda 1
2 **Wieczorek-Zeul,** Heidemarie, Lehrerin, 6200 Wiesbaden, Walkmühlstraße 39 — **SPD** Sozialdemokratische Partei Deutschlands	**SPD** Sozialdemokratische Partei Deutschlands — Heidemarie Wieczorek-Zeul, Rudi Walther, Dr. Dietrich Sperling, Uta Zapf, Karsten Voigt 2
3 **Koch,** Ulrich Friedrich, Sozialarbeiter, 6200 Wiesbaden, Feldstraße 27 — **GRÜNE** DIE GRÜNEN	**GRÜNE** DIE GRÜNEN — Ulrike Riedel, Hubert Kleinert, Marina Steindor, Dietrich Wetzel, Freya Klier 3
4 **Dr. Funke-Schmitt-Rink,** Margret, Studienrätin, 6200 Wiesbaden, Sonnenberger Straße 3 — **F.D.P.** Freie Demokratische Partei	**F.D.P.** Freie Demokratische Partei — Dr. Hermann Otto Prinz zu Solms Hohensolms-Lich, Hans-Joachim Otto, Dr. Gisela Babel, Ekkehard Gries, Dr. Heinrich Kolb 4
	DIE GRAUEN DIE GRAUEN Initiiert vom Senioren-Schutz-Bund „Graue Panther" e.V. („SSB-GP") — Ludwig Neise, Sibylle Schömig, Karl Röth, Dr. Hildegard Mulert, Arno Hildebrandt 5
6 **Langer,** Herbert, Prokurist, 6200 Wiesbaden, Sonnenberger Str. 27 — **REP** DIE REPUBLIKANER	**REP** DIE REPUBLIKANER — Gert Feldmeier, Herbert Langer, Brigitte Kleinert, Peter Münch, Günter Hämer 6
7 **Deubert,** Ernst Wilhelm, Rentner, 6000 Frankfurt/Main 60, Bergerstraße 234 — **NPD** National-demokratische Partei Deutschlands	**NPD** Nationaldemokratische Partei Deutschlands — Winfried Krauß, Doris Zutt, Hans Schmidt, Dieter Fuhrmann, Volker Sachs 7
	ÖDP Ökologisch-Demokratische Partei — Gerhard Mahnke, Waltraud Schunck, Monika Zickwolff, Dr. Wolfgang Günther, Rolf-Dewet Klar 8
	PDS/Linke Liste Partei des Demokratischen Sozialismus/Linke Liste — Manfred Coppik, Angela Knof, Heike Schmüser, Manfred Alter, Reinhold Rückert 9

With their "first vote," voters from the Bonn electoral district can choose a candidate by name from the lefthand column. The "second vote" in the right hand column is cast for a party list at the federal level.

to 90 percent at the federal level), which is strongly enhanced by clear party ideology. The newer parties, Greens and PDS with similar kinds of ideological coherence, appear to confirm this. For nearly fifty years in the Federal Republic, voting participation rates matched or exceeded those in all other West European countries.

As Table 3 suggests, Germany has been a country without volatile electoral swings. There have been five major periods of party dominance (plus the Grand Coalition) between 1949 and 2002:

1. CDU/CSU-FDP coalition (1949–1966)
2. Grand Coalition (CDU/CSU-SPD) interregnum (1966–1969)
3. SPD-FDP coalition (1969–1982)
4. CDU/CSU-FDP coalition (1982–1998)
5. SPD-Green coalition (1998–)

Germany has enjoyed relatively stable electoral allegiance, despite unification, European integration, and the introduction of two new parties in the *Bundestag* during the decade of the 1990s.

Political Culture, Citizenship, and Identity

With political parties representing such a broad ideological spectrum, there is wide-ranging political debate in Germany. This diversity is reflected in the media, where newspapers appeal to a broad range of political opinion. The major print media range from the mass-market tabloid *Bild Zeitung* (literally, picture newspaper) on the right, to conservative and liberal broadsheet newspapers such as *Die Welt* of Hamburg, the *Süddeutscher Zeitung* of Munich, and the *Frankfurter Allgemeine Zeitung*. The *Frankfurter Rundschau* is close to the SPD in its editorial positions, while the *TAZ* of Berlin is closest to the Greens. There is a wide variety of private TV cable channels, but the three main networks are public channels, and they are careful to provide a balance of major party positions. Until the late 1990s, most public channels prohibited paid TV campaign commercials during the two-month electoral campaigns. Instead, the networks present roundtable discussions in which all parties participate. This approach has prevented the bigger and richer parties from buying a larger share of the popular vote, although some parties have begun advertising on private channels.

The wide range of public opinion has helped dispel the view that Germany's high voting turnout is due to a sense of duty and not to any real commitment to democracy. There is a strong participatory ethic among the democratic left, fostered by the many opportunities for participation at the workplace through co-determination and the works councils. Moreover, one of the primary appeals of the Greens has been their emphasis on **grass-roots democracy**—that is, rank-and-file participation. The strength of the Greens, and now the PDS, has forced the traditional parties to focus on mobilizing their supporters and potential supporters. The arrival of the Greens and the PDS has also helped remove from German political culture some of the old stereotypes about the country's legendary preference for consensus, order, and stability.

Germany's educational system has also changed since the Federal Republic was created, particularly in terms of the socialization of German citizens. The catalyst was the student movement of the 1960s. At that time, the university system was elitist and restrictive and did not offer sufficient critical analysis of Germany's bloody twentieth-century history. Not only did the student mobilizations of the 1960s open up the educational system to a wider socioeconomic spectrum, they also caused many of the so-called '68 Generation (1968 was the year of the most significant demonstrations) to challenge their parents about attitudes shaped by the Nazi period and before. Even in the 1990s, many critics of the German educational system argued that some of the older attitudes toward non-Germans remain and that the educational system should increase its efforts to build a tolerant citizenry.

Germany's social market economy enjoys broad acceptance among Germans, with the possible exception of some Greens, the PDS, and the extreme right. The social market economy provides benefits to almost all segments of the population, including public transit, subsidies for the arts, virtually free higher and vocational education, and a generous welfare state. Thus, there is a general tolerance for a wide variety of political and artistic opinion and very little of the squabbling and acrimony over public funding of the arts that is common in some other countries.

However, antiethnic and anti-immigrant violence in the late 1980s, mid-1990s, and early 2000s challenged the optimistic view that Germany has become a typical parliamentary democracy. The attacks on foreign immigrants, including families who had lived in Germany for more than thirty years, raised questions among some observers regarding the genuineness of German toleration. Given Germany's persecution of Jews, homosexuals, political opponents, and all non-Germans during the first half of the twentieth century and the unimaginable horrors of the Holocaust, such concerns must be taken extremely seriously. Although Germany is not alone among industrialized nations in racist violence, its history brings German citizens the burden to confront and overcome any display of intolerance if it is to gain the world's respect as a decent nation.

The Schröder Red-Green government began to change the rules on citizenship, democracy, and participation in Germany. Until 1998, German citizenship was based on blood, that is, German ethnicity. Unlike many other European nations, Germany made it difficult for residents without native ethnicity to be naturalized, no matter how long they had lived in the country, and it denied citizenship even to the children of noncitizens born on native soil. Ethnic Germans whose ancestors had not lived in Germany for centuries were allowed to enter Germany legally and to become citizens immediately. One of the first acts of the Schröder government was to allow expedited citizenship for long-time foreign residents.

Perhaps the most contentious citizenship/identity problem has surrounded the political asylum question. Following World War II, Germany passed one of the world's most liberal political asylum laws, in part to help atone for the Nazis' political repression of millions. With the end of the cold war and the opening up of East European borders, the trickle of asylum seekers turned into a flood. This influx drove the Kohl government to curtail drastically the right of political asylum, a step that put into question whether German democracy was as mature and well developed as it had claimed it was during the stable postwar period. Germany's commitment to democratic rights appeared to contain some new conditions, and many of them involved a definition of identity that looked remarkably insular in a Europe that was becoming more international and global.

Interests, Social Movements, and Protest

Germany remains a country of organized collectivities: major economic producer groups such as the BDI (Federal Association of German Industry), BDA (Federal Association of German Employers), and DGB (German Trade Union Confederation); political parties (in which authentic participatory membership remains higher than in most other countries); and social groups. Germany has never been a country with a strong individualistic ethos. Occasionally, individuals stand out in German politics amid the powerful organized collectivities, but they are in the minority. In fact, the ascension of most individuals to political prominence in Germany owes as much to their skills in working the organizations as it does to individual initiative. Leaders

Current Challenges: *The Complicated Politics of Immigration*

Germany, like virtually all other Western Europe nations, has discovered that it has become an immigrant country. To be sure, a nation-state that did not achieve unity until 1871 faced calamitous questions of immigration and nationality. In fact, the nationalism unleashed in the late nineteenth century in the wake of economic and political upheaval caused catastrophe for nonethnic Germans. Because of that late-nineteenth- and early- to mid-twentieth-century oppression of racial and ethnic minorities, the Federal Republic realized in the postwar period that it had a special obligation to both Jews and other ethnic minorities whom the Nazis had persecuted and killed. It was this history that caused the new FRG government to pass generous asylum laws allowing those who faced political persecution to come to a democratic West Germany and obtain residency, if not citizenship.

Citizenship was a more difficult proposition for immigrants to Germany. The 1913 Immigration Law (until liberalized by the SPD/Green Schröder government in 1999) stipulated that citizenship was based on blood (*jus sanguis*) and not naturalization (*jus solis*). This meant that German citizenship was easy to obtain for "ethnic" Germans who had lived in Russia or Eastern Europe for generations and did not speak German, but difficult for the *Gastarbeiter* (guest workers) who had lived in Germany since the 1960s.

In fact, the tension between cultural conceptions of citizenship and the economic demands of both Germany and the EU lie at the heart of the complicated politics of immigration. On the one hand, some Germans and Europeans are fearful of what immigration will do to traditional conceptions of what being a "German" actually is. Racist violence is an extreme manifestation of this sentiment. On the other hand, globalization and Europeanization have opened up the Continent to increasing migration, which, to some, is the very point of the process. Adding to the economic pressures on European countries to increase immigration is the demographic bomb that affects almost all Western European countries: a population decrease of the "native" or "ethnic" portions of their population, fueling the fears of some among this population. Yet this aging population is also relying on a welfare and pension system that demands that there be a young work force to pay for it. Western European policy-makers now realize that a partial solution to the fiscal obligations that an aging population represents is new, young, immigrant workers who will both revitalize economic growth and help fund the pension and welfare obligations. To do so, however, requires that Germany—and many of its neighbors—fundamentally reconsider what it means to be a citizen.

such as Helmut Kohl, Gerhard Schröder, Joschka Fischer, and the late Petra Kelly obtained prominence by knowing how organizations and institutions work and taking advantage of the system.

From the descriptions of organized business and organized labor in Section 3, it is clear that interest groups in Germany operate differently than they do in the United States and Britain. In the Federal Republic, interest groups are seen as having a societal role and responsibility that transcend the immediate interests of their members. Germany's codified legal system specifically allows private interests to perform public functions, albeit within a clearly specified general

framework. Thus, interest groups are seen as part of the fabric of society and are virtually permanent institutions. This view places a social premium on their adaptation and response to new issues. To speak of winners and losers in such an arrangement is to misunderstand the ability of existing interest groups to make incremental changes over time.

Strikes and demonstrations on a wide range of economic and noneconomic issues do occur, but they should be counted as evidence of success. Political institutions sometimes are mistakenly seen as fixed structures that are supposed to prevent or repress dissent.[23] A more positive way to analyze such conflicts is to interpret them as mechanisms pressuring institutions and policies to be responsive. In the absence of protest, the tendency would be for the corporatist system in Germany to become overly rigid and out of step with citizens' concerns. Rather than being detrimental to democratic participation, such "bottom-up" protests embody its essence.

Such a system does not encourage fractious competition; instead, it creates a framework within which interest groups can battle yet eventually come to an agreement on policy. Moreover, because they aggregate the interests of all members of their group, they often take a broader, less parochial view of problems and policy solutions. As part of the fabric of German society, interest groups have an institutional longevity that surpasses the duration of interest groups in most other industrialized countries. How does the German state mediate the relationship among interest groups? Peter Katzenstein observes that in the Federal Republic, "the state is not an actor but a series of relationships," and these relationships are solidified in what he has called "parapublic institutions."[24] The parapublics encompass a wide variety of organizations, among which the most important are the *Bundesbank,* the institutions of co-determination, the labor courts, the social insurance funds, and the employment office. Under prevailing German public law, which is rooted in pre-1871 feudal traditions, the parapublics have been assigned the role of "independent governance by the representatives of social sectors at the behest of or under the general supervision of the state." In other words, German organizations, seen as mere interest groups in other countries, are combined with certain quasi-government agencies to fill a parapublic role in the Federal Republic.

Other important groups include the Protestant and Catholic churches, the Jewish synagogues, the Farmers Association, the Association of Artisans, and the Federal Chamber of Physicians. Each of these groups has been tightly integrated into various parapublic institutions to perform a range of essential social functions that in other countries might be performed by state agencies. These groups also act as the nation's conscience. One example is the vocal Jewish community's demand for reparations to be paid to Israel and to survivors of slave labor factories during World War II. A second is the demand by Turkish residents for Muslim education to accompany Christian teachings in the schools. These organizations assume a degree of social responsibility, through their roles in policy implementation, which goes beyond what political scientist Arnold Heidenheimer has called the "freewheeling competition of 'selfish' interest groups."[25] For example, through the state, the churches collect a church tax on all citizens born into either the Protestant or Roman Catholic churches. This provides the churches with a steady stream of income, ensuring them institutional permanence while compelling them to play a major role in the provision of social welfare and aid to the families of foreign workers. The Farmers Association has been a pillar of support for both the FDP and the CDU/CSU and for decades has strongly influenced the agricultural ministry. It has also resisted the attempts by the EU to lower direct subsidies paid to European farmers as part of the EU's common agricultural policy. The Association of Artisans is a major component of the German Chamber of Commerce, to which all firms in Germany must belong, and the Chamber of Physicians has been intimately involved with the legislation and implementation of social and medical insurance.

These interest groups and the parapublic agencies limit social conflict by regular meetings and close coordination as part of a small-scale democratic corporatism. However, this system is subject to the same problems that have plagued corporatism in more centralized industrial societies such as Sweden and France; that is, it must express the concerns of member organizations, channel the conflicts, and recommend (and sometimes implement) public policy. If the system fails and conflicts are allowed to go unresolved, the effectiveness of the institutions is questioned, and some elements of society may go unrepresented. A partial failure of certain interest groups and institutions led to a series of social movements during the 1960s and 1970s, particularly around university reform, wage negotiations, and foreign policy. The very existence of the Green Party in the 1980s and 1990s is a prime example of a movement that responded to the inability of existing institutions to address, mediate, and solve certain contentious issues.

Until recently, most conflicts and policy responses were encompassed within this system. Yet not all individuals found organizations to represent their interests. Germany's openness, new parties, and European integration place strains on German institutions. Those who are outside the organized groups fall into several categories. Political groups that fail to meet the 5 percent electoral threshold, such as the *Republikaner* and the German Peoples Union (DVU), belong in this category, along with smaller right-wing groups. The substantial Turkish population, comprising 2.3 percent of Germany's inhabitants, might be included here until it obtains citizenship. Many Turks have resided in Germany for decades, but unlike workers from EU countries like Italy and Spain, Turkish residents have had few rights in Germany. Finally, the once-active leftist community of revolutionary Marxists still retains a small presence, mostly in large cities and university towns. Some of these left-wing parties contest elections, but they never get more than 1 percent of the vote.

Since the student mobilizations of the late 1960s, Germany has witnessed considerable protest and mobilization of social forces outside established channels. Among the most significant social forces in the postwar Federal Republic have been feminists, the peace movement, the antinuclear movement, and the peaceful church-linked protests in East Germany in 1989 that were a catalyst for the breakdown of the communist regime. All four groups, in different ways, challenged fundamental assumptions about German politics and highlighted the inability of the institutional structure to respond to their needs and issues. The spirit of direct action has animated German politics in ways that were not possible earlier. Such examples as opposition to a restrictive abortion law in the 1970s, demonstrations against the stationing of nuclear missiles on German soil in the 1980s, regular protests against nuclear power plants since the 1970s, and courageous challenges to communism have shown the vibrancy of German protest.

The 1990s witnessed less protest from the left than from the right. Illegal neo-Nazi groups were responsible for racist attacks. Significantly, all of these attacks by the right-wing fringe were met with spontaneous, peaceful marches of 200,000 to 500,000 people in various cities. This reaction suggests that social protest, as a part of an active democratic political discourse, has matured in the face of this new threat from the right. As stated at the beginning of this section, the challenge for German politics is to maintain a system of democratic participation that encompasses both extrainstitutional groups and specific organized political institutions in a way that enhances democracy rather than destroys it.

Section ⑤ German Politics in Transition

Political Challenges and Changing Agendas

German politics is truly in transition. The unprecedented election of a Red-Green coalition in 1998 and its reelection in 2002 has taken German politics in a new direction after sixteen years of center-right government. These elections also represented another stage of Germany's journey toward becoming a more "normal" country. After fifty years of democratic rule with high electoral participation and the alternation of power between right and left for the fourth time, perhaps German politics has finally matured.

Yet the legacy of two major events in the 1990s—celebration of unification and residual racial hatred in parts of Germany—causes a tempering of unalloyed enthusiasm for Germany's prospects for the new century. Is contemporary Germany best represented as a revitalized democracy exemplified by the celebration and joy for increased freedoms unleashed by the destruction of the Berlin Wall? Or is Germany again becoming a place hostile to foreigners and those who do not appear German, as suggested by the firebombs thrown at a hostel housing immigrants? An accurate picture of contemporary German politics lies between these two extremes. Nevertheless, both represent aspects of modern Germany, and it remains a political challenge for the SPD-Green government—and for all German citizens—to cultivate the spirit of freedom while discouraging the outrages of xenophobia.

The path taken by German politics will be determined by the resolution of the four core themes identified in Section 1. The more optimistic direction would be continued integration of eastern Germany into the fabric of the Federal Republic as a whole; however, mutual suspicions between eastern and western Germans remain high. The former resent the so-called elbow society of the West, in which material goods appear high in the order of societal goals, while the latter resent the huge costs and increased taxation required to rebuild the eastern states. Yet successful economic, political, and social integration demands patience and a sound institutional foundation on the part of the government. Only with a sound and effective foundation of domestic polity will Germany be able to address successfully the larger issue of European integration.

The more pessimistic direction may mean a less-than-robust economy with consequent social tensions and conflict, possibly exacerbated by tensions within the Red-Green coalition. There are now five significant political parties in Germany's political landscape rather than the customary three. Can Germany's organized society and institutional political structure sustain the increased cooperation necessary to maintain a vibrant democracy? And what of Germany's economic giant–political dwarf syndrome? Can Germany assume the political responsibility that accompanied its economic stature? Do its European neighbors really want it to do so? And what of Germany's high-wage and welfare structure in the face of increased economic competition from lower-wage countries in East Asia and elsewhere? Will using the euro instead of the deutsche mark enable Germany to thrive, or will it undermine the previous strengths of the German economy? And what is the state of the German economy in the face of domestic structural challenges as well as globalization of the international economy and the evolution of "Euroland," as those countries that have adopted the euro as their currency are called? Following the 2002 elections, the Schröder government faces daunting pressures to make significant economic policy reforms to overcome a sluggish economy. Failure to address these questions effectively could compromise satisfactory outcomes for Germany and its neighbors.

For many years, Germany was held up as a model for other industrialized societies to emulate. But there have been significant changes in Germany since unification, and the *Modell Deutschland* of the 1970s and 1980s is less appropriate. Can Germany evolve peacefully and democratically in a region where increased integration will become more likely? The expansion of the EU since the 1990s has enabled more European citizens to live and work outside their home countries. What will happen to German collective identity given this fluidity and the change in German citizenship laws by the SPD-Green government? Can the elaborate and long-effective institutional structure that balances private and public interests be maintained? Will the EU augment or challenge Germany's position in Europe? Will these challenges threaten Germany's enviable position in the face of increased globalization of the world economy?

The future of German politics depends on how the country addresses the four primary themes identified in this analysis of the Federal Republic: a state's position in the world of states, governing the economy, the democratic idea, and collective identities. For much of the post–World War II period, Germany enjoyed a spiral of success that enabled it to confront these issues with confidence and resolve. For example, problems of collective identities were handled in a much less exclusionary way as women, nonnative ethnic groups, and newer political parties and movements began to contribute to a stable and healthy diversity in German politics that had been lacking for most of the country's history. Democratic institutions effectively balanced participation and dissent, offsetting the country's turbulent and often racist past by almost fifty years of a stable multiparty democracy. Even while a moderate-conservative Christian Democratic Party governed Germany, the country still contained one of the most powerful and respected Social Democratic parties in the world. Germany's economic success has been significant and unique. The country is a stronghold of advanced capitalism yet supports an extensive state welfare program and mandates worker/trade union/works councils' participation in managerial decision-making. These successes have helped Germany participate more effectively on the international scene. Since the late 1980s, Germany has confidently, and with the support of its neighbors and allies, taken a leading role in European integration. It is firmly anchored in Western

Europe but is uniquely positioned to assist in the transition of the former communist central and eastern European states toward economic and political modernization and EU membership.

However, close examination of these four major themes reveals that Germany's path is not yet certain. Can the country continue to succeed in all four areas, or will tensions and difficulties undermine its success and produce a period of economic, political, and social instability? In the area of collective identities, Germany faces many unresolved challenges. Turkish and other non-German guest workers remain essential to Germany's economy, and now some will be able to obtain German citizenship. The long-term acceptance of the opposition CDU/CSU, not to mention the smaller ultraright parties, will likely be key to a fundamental change in the concept of who is a German. The influx of refugees and asylum seekers has placed great strains on German taxpayers and increased ethnic tensions. German nationalism, suppressed since the end of World War II, has shown some signs of resurgence. Two generations after the end of World War II, some younger Germans are asking what being German actually means. The change in citizenship laws will complicate this issue, for although this search for identity can be healthy, its dark side is manifested by various extremist groups, which still preach exaggerated nationalism and hatred of foreigners and minorities. Such tendencies are fundamentally incompatible with Germany's playing a leading role in a unifying Europe.

Democracy in Germany appears well established after nearly fifty years of the Federal Republic. It features high voter turnout, a stable and responsible multiparty political system, and a healthy civic culture.[26]

Many observers believe that broad-based participation is part of the fabric of German political life. The overriding challenge for Germany's political institutions is the assimilation of the five eastern states. Can eastern Germans who have lost jobs and benefits in the transition to capitalism understand that ethnic minorities are not the cause of their plight? Can tolerance and understanding develop while a right-wing fringe is preaching hatred and searching for scapegoats to blame for the costs of unification? Also, what is the legacy of a bureaucratic state that as recently as the 1970s, under a Social Democratic–led government, purged individuals who appeared to have radical tendencies? In other words, if social tensions continue to grow, how will the German state respond?

There is some reason for optimism. Eastern Germans have shown that they understand and practice democracy amazingly well. After years of authoritarian communist rule, many East Germans saw dissent not as political participation but as treason. However, the evolution of the PDS into an effective political party that articulates the interests of its voters offers considerable promise. In the 1998 elections, the PDS was considered not suitable as a potential coalition partner because of its origins as a communist party. However, when the Greens first obtained seats in the *Bundestag* in 1983, observers, many of whom were SPD officials, refused to consider the Greens as a coalition partner. Yet fifteen years later, the Greens have joined the SPD in the first left-wing majority government in German history. The lesson to be learned from the Greens' transformation from a motley crew of *alternativen* (counter culture) to a governing coalition partner is that continued participation in democratic institutions can have positive results for both the party and the institutions. Although if the party fails to maintain at least 5 percent of the vote, critics will say that the party has sold out and lost its distinctive edge in the process of becoming integrated into governing coalitions. In general, rather than marginalizing dissent, the German practice of including parties that attain 5 percent of the vote enables these parties to represent their distinct constituencies. And by participating in the *Bundestag* in opposition, such parties convince others that they play by the same democratic rules as do other parties. In time, such a path may produce new "suitable" coalition partners.

Germany's approach to governing the economy was also challenged in the late 1990s. For many years, the German economy was characterized as "high everything" in that it combined high-quality manufacturing with high wages, high fringe benefits, high worker participation, and high levels of vacation time (six weeks per year).[27] Since the first oil crisis in 1973, critical observers have insisted that such a system could not last in a competitive world economy. Nevertheless, the German economy has remained among the world's leaders. But the huge costs of unification, the globalization of the world economy, and the exaggerated emphasis on laissez-faire principles in many of its neighboring countries challenge the German model anew. Together they have caused many of the old criticisms about an extended, inflexible, and overburdened economy to surface again.

Pessimists began to suggest that the stresses of the late 1990s and early 2000s placed the German political economy in a precarious position. This "anti–German Model" consisted of several related arguments.[28] First, Germany's economic prowess resided in manufacturing industries (such as automobiles and machine tools) whose goods were exportable but whose technologies were decidedly "low." As wage costs in these sectors continued to rise, German exports would inevitably be less competitive. Second, the costs of the social market economy, particularly with unification, pressed on the upper limits of Germany's capacity to pay for them. In addition, economic tensions remained at the heart of conflict between former East and West Germans. While easterners resented the slow pace of change and high unemployment, western Germans were bitter about losing jobs to easterners and paying for the cleanup of the ecological and infrastructural disasters inherited from the former East German regime. The larger issue in this argument was that German economic strength has been predicated on specific "organized capitalist" institutions that worked well with traditional manufacturing industries. In a globalizing economy of service sector industries, software, telecommunications, and financial mobility, what happens to German organized capitalism? And in its relationship with the EU, far from being a model of fiscal probity, Germany risked being called to account by the EU for exceeding the 3 percent ceiling on budget deficits.

The primary economic task of the Schröder government has been to address the competitiveness issue and manage the transition to an economy that can confront the technological and globalizing pressures that German firms continue to face. The trend toward Europeanization may be incompatible with the consensus-oriented and coordinated nature of Germany's adjustment patterns. In fact, economic tensions within the SPD regarding stimulating economic policy caused the forced resignation of the left-leaning SPD finance minister, Oskar Lafontaine, in early 1999, five months after taking office. And as Europe becomes more open to the world economy, how well will Germany's "high everything" system be able to withstand

increased global economic competition? The completion of the single market of the EU has also complicated Germany's relationship with other states. Although the EU was supposedly the grand culmination of a post–cold war spirit of European unity, it has proved more difficult to establish than first anticipated. Its manifestations in the early twenty-first century have only strengthened the trends toward decentralization and deregulation already under way in western Europe rather than enhancing integration. More significant for the German economy, such deregulatory tendencies, if spread throughout Europe, could potentially disturb the organized capitalism of Germany's small and large businesses. In addition, the apparent deregulation in European finance threatens Germany's distinctive finance-manufacturing links.

The effects of introducing the euro have also caused uncertainty (see "Global Connection: The EU and the Euro"). Administration of the currency has required a European central bank, a common monetary policy of all twelve "Euroland" nations, and a common set of fiscal policies. In short, fundamental tools that in the past had defined sovereignty for nation-states now are subject to European, not national, control. Germany has tried to model the European Central Bank after the *Bundesbank* (it is located in Frankfurt, not Paris or London). However, the coordination of monetary and fiscal policies by the European Central Bank since the introduction of the euro has not always been what German governments and German firms have come to expect.

Politically, can Germany continue to emerge from its reticent status and play a leadership role in integrating central and eastern European states into a wider EU? As long as the cold war prevailed, Germany had the luxury of deferring to the United States and NATO in foreign policy initiatives, yet the cold war has been over for more than a decade, and Europe desperately needs clear and purposeful political leadership. Given their electoral strength and the positions of their countries, the two most likely candidates are Tony Blair and Gerhard Schröder. However, with the former supporting the United States on Iraq and the latter opposing it, Europe's foreign policy may see much more vibrant debates than it once did.

At the time of Schröder's election in 1998, the first majority left-wing victory in FRG history, all other

Global Connection: The EU and the Euro

One of the Federal Republic's most lasting legacies—in addition to German unification—at the end of the twentieth century was its commitment to European integration. As early enthusiasts of European unity, Germany's postwar political leaders realized the positive opportunity that a more formally united continent would present. In its relations with other states after World War II, Germany faced two different kinds of criticism. First was the fear of a too-powerful Germany, a country that had run roughshod over its European neighbors for most of the first half of the twentieth century. Second was the opposite problem: the so-called economic giant–political dwarf syndrome in which Germany was accused of benefiting from a strong world economy for fifty years while taking on none of the political responsibility. The fact that these are mutually contradictory positions did not spare Germany from criticism. Yet both Chancellors Kohl and Schröder during the 1990s realized that an integrated Europe promised the possibility of solving both problems simultaneously. Germany remains the economic anchor of the EU, while Germany's membership in the EU has enabled it to take on political responsibilities that it would be unable to assume on its own, such as UN peacekeeping operations in Eastern Europe. Both men realized this and were firm advocates of measures that would assist in a smooth, stable, and comprehensive EU.

The euro was a crucial part of this broader European goal. Beginning in the mid-1980s, most European countries realized that they were in global economic competition with two other regions in the world economy: North America and East Asia. Yet the problem of multiple currencies in major European governments were also led by left-of-center parties. However, electoral changes in Italy and France since then (and Tony Blair's continuing moderation after reelection in 2001) have ended that ephemeral configuration. These changes have likely eroded the possibility of a European-wide political movement that could aggressively defend a "social" Europe and act as a brake on some of the ruthless and

Europe, the largest of the three regions, was inhibiting European financial influence. This challenge represented a problem for Germany. Although the deutsche mark was the very foundation of postwar German economic performance and contributed mightily to German self-confidence, it remained as one currency among many in Europe, thereby disadvantaging Europe economically in relation to both North America and East Asia. Kohl and Schröder realized that economic success for both Germany and Europe depended on creating a stronger economic foundation, which is where the euro came in.

Formally introduced among eleven (now twelve) countries as a virtual currency in 1999 (for credit cards and intracountry bank transfers, for example) it "went live" on January 1, 2002. Gone was the redoubtable DM in favor of a currency that had no human beings on the notes, only nonspecific buildings, bridges, and arches. In the first few months of the "physical" euro, the currency continued to trade below the value of the dollar, as it had since its virtual inception three years earlier. Considerable uncertainty among Germans mounted as to whether adopting the new currency was a good idea. In addition, some Germans accused businesses of "rounding up" the value of the euro when making the pricing conversion of goods and services from DM to euro, once again raising inflation worries. Yet by the middle of 2002, the financial scandals in the United States caused the euro to rise in value and achieve parity with the dollar in July. This gave the usually financially angst-ridden Germans some tangible assurance that the new currency might show some promise after all.

destabilizing free-market tendencies of a globalizing economy.

German Politics in Comparative Perspective

Germany offers important insights for comparative politics. First, can Germany remake its political culture and institutions in the wake of a fascist past? Countries such as Japan, Italy, and Spain among developed states also bear watching on this point. Many have hoped that Germany's impressive democratic experience during the first fifty years of the Federal Republic has completely exorcised the ghosts of the Third Reich. But not all observers are certain. To what extent have the educational system, civil service, and the media addressed the Nazi past? To what extent do they bear some responsibility for the recent rise of right-wing violence? Have the reforms in the educational system since the 1960s provided a spirit of critical discourse in the broad mainstream of society that can withstand right-wing rhetoric? Can judges effectively sentence those who abuse the civil rights of ethnic minorities? Will the news media continue to express a wide range of opinion and contribute to a healthy civic discourse? Or will strident, tabloid-style journalism stifle the more reasoned debate that any democracy must have to survive and flourish?

Second, Germany's historical importance on the world political stage during the past 150 years means that understanding its transition is essential for comparative purposes. It was late to achieve political unity and late to industrialize. These two factors eventually helped produce a catastrophic first half of the twentieth century for Germany and the whole world. Yet the country's transition to a successful developed economy with an apparently solid democratic political system would seem to suggest lessons for other countries. Those that might derive the most benefit might be industrializing nations that could learn from the successes and failures of countries such as Germany as they also attempt to achieve economic growth and develop stable democracies.

Third is the role of organized capitalism. Germany offers a model for combining state and market in a way that is unique among advanced industrialized nations. Many models of political analysis choose to emphasize the distinctions between state and market. Debates about whether nationalized industries should be privatized and whether welfare should be reduced in favor of private charity, for example, are symptomatic of the conflict between state and market that animates the politics of most developed countries. Germany's organized capitalism, together with its social market economy, has blurred the distinction between the public and private sectors. It has refused to see public policy as a stark choice between these two alternatives, preferring to emphasize policies in which the state and

market work together. The German state pursues development plans that benefit from its cooperative interaction with a dense network of key social and economic participants. Despite Germany's prominence as a powerful, advanced, industrialized economy, this model remains surprisingly understudied. Regardless of Germany's current economic challenges brought about by unification and the uncertain terrain of Europeanization, it remains a model worthy of comparative analysis.

The fourth insight concerns Germany's development as a collectivist democracy. In many developed states, democracy is approached from the perspective of individual rights. Some scholars, following a formalized interpretation called rational choice, suggest that the base of politics is a series of individual choices, much as a consumer would choose to buy one product or another in a supermarket. Germany, however, has evolved a different model, which, while sometimes underplaying a more individualistic democracy, does offer insights for participation and representation in a complex society. German democracy has emphasized participation among groups. In other words, it has stressed the role of the individual not as a sole actor in isolation from the rest of society, but as a citizen in a wider set of communities, organizations, and parties that must find ways of cooperating if the nation-state is to maintain its democracy. It is clearly within this complex of policies that Germany is wrestling with its treatment of different groups within the Federal Republic.

Germany offers a fifth insight on the issues of tolerance and respect for civil rights for ethnic minorities. The Schröder government has modified Germany's immigration policies to allow long-time foreign workers to participate and make a meaningful contribution to German democracy. Can residual ethnic tensions, perhaps in response to this major change in immigration policy, be resolved in a way that enhances democracy rather than undermines it? Clearly, the issue of collective identities offers both powerful obstacles and rich opportunities to address one of the most crucial noneconomic issues that Germany faces at the dawn of a new century.

Finally, what is the role of a middle-rank power as the potential leader of a regional world bloc of some 400 million people? To some extent this issue also confronts Japan, as it struggles to take on political responsibilities commensurate with its economic successes.

Germany is facing intense pressures from within its borders, such as conflict among ethnic groups, and from a complex mix of external influences. Its role as both a western and an eastern European power pulls at it in different ways. Should the country emphasize the Western-oriented EU and build a solid foundation with its NATO allies? Or should it turn eastward to step into the vacuum created by the demise and fragmentation of the former USSR? Can Germany's twentieth-century history allow either its western or eastern neighbors to let it play the geopolitical role that its low-profile postwar political status has only postponed? To some extent, the political cover of the EU will allow Germany to do more as the leading country in a powerful international organization than it ever could do as a sovereign nation-state with its unique political baggage.

Key Terms

Gastarbeiter (guest workers)
federal state
Junkers
liberal
Kulturkampf
Nazi
chancellor
co-determination
democratic corporatism
Zollverein
social market economy
works councils
Basic Law
5 percent rule
constructive vote of no confidence
civil servants
overlapping responsibilities
health insurance funds
Administrative Court
industrial policy
framework regulations
suspensive veto
party democracy
Citizens Action Groups
personalized proportional representation
grass-roots democracy

Suggested Readings

Braunthal, Gerard. *The Federation of German Industry in Politics.* Ithaca, N.Y.: Cornell University Press, 1965.
———. *Parties and Politics in Modern Germany.* Boulder, Colo.: Westview Press, 1996.
Craig, Gordon. *The Politics of the Prussian Army.* Oxford: Oxford University Press, 1955.
Dahrendorf, Ralf. *Society and Democracy in Germany.* Garden City, N.Y.: Anchor, 1969.
Deeg, Richard. *Finance Capital Unveiled: Banks and Economic Adjustment in Germany.* Ann Arbor: University of Michigan Press, 1998.
Eley, Geoff. *Reshaping the German Right: Radical Nationalism and Political Change After Bismarck.* New Haven, Conn.: Yale University Press, 1980.

Esping-Anderson, Gøsta. *Three Worlds of Welfare Capitalism.* Princeton, N.J.: Princeton University Press, 1990.
Evans, Peter B., Rueschemeyer, Dietrich, and Skocpol, Theda, eds. *Bringing the State Back In.* Cambridge: Cambridge University Press, 1985.
Gerschenkron, Alexander. *Bread and Democracy in Germany.* 2d ed. Ithaca, N.Y.: Cornell University Press, 1989.
Hirschman, Albert O. *Exit, Voice, and Loyalty.* New Haven, Conn.: Yale University Press, 1970.
Inglehart, Ronald. *Culture Shift in Advanced Industrial Society.* Princeton, N.J.: Princeton University Press, 1990.
Katzenstein, Peter. *Policy and Politics in West Germany: The Growth of a Semi-Sovereign State.* Philadelphia: Temple University Press, 1987.
———. *Tamed Power: Germany in Europe.* Ithaca, N.Y.: Cornell University Press, 1997.
Kemp, Tom. *Industrialization in Nineteenth Century Europe.* 2d ed. London: Longman, 1985.
Markovits, Andrei S., and Reich, Simon. *The German Predicament: Memory and Power of the New Europe.* Ithaca, N.Y.: Cornell University Press, 1997.
Moore, Barrington. *Social Origins of Dictatorship and Democracy.* Boston: Beacon Press, 1965.
Piore, Michael, and Sabel, Charles. *The Second Industrial Divide.* New York: Basic Books, 1984.
Rein, Taagepera, and Shugart, Matthew Soberg. *Seats and Votes: The Effects and Determinants of Electoral Systems.* New Haven, Conn.: Yale University Press, 1989.
Röpke, Wilhelm. "The Guiding Principle of the Liberal Programme." In H. F. Wünche, ed., *Standard Texts on the Social Market Economy.* New York: Gustav Fischer Verlag, 1982.
Rueschemeyer, Dietrich, Stephens, Evelyne Huber, and Stephens, John D. *Capitalist Development and Democracy.* Chicago: University of Chicago Press, 1992.
Schmitter, Philippe C., and Lembruch, Gerhard, eds. *Trends Toward Corporatist Intermediation.* Beverly Hills, Calif.: Sage, 1979.
Shirer, William. *The Rise and Fall of the Third Reich.* New York: Simon & Schuster, 1960.
Steinmo, Sven, Thelen, Kathleen, and Longstreth, Frank, eds. *Structuring Politics: Historical Institutionalism in Historical Perspective.* New York: Cambridge University Press, 1992.
Tilly, Charles, ed. *The Formation of National States in Western Europe.* Princeton, N.J.: Princeton University Press, 1975.
Turner, Lowell, ed. *Negotiating the New Germany: Can Social Partnership Survive?* Ithaca, N.Y.: Cornell University Press, 1997.

Suggested Websites

American Institute for Contemporary German Studies, Johns Hopkins University
www.aicgs.org
German Embassy, German Information Center
www.germany-info.org/sf_index.html
German Studies Web, Western European Studies Section
www.dartmouth.edu/~wess/

German News (in English) 1995–Present
www.mathematik.uni-ulm.de/de-news/
Max Planck Institute for the Study of Societies, Cologne
www.mpi-fg-koeln.mpg.de/index_en.html
WZB, Social Science Research Center, Berlin
www.wz-berlin.de/default.en.asp

Notes

[1]Charles Tilly, ed., *The Formation of National States in Western Europe* (Princeton, N.J.: Princeton University Press, 1975).

[2]Barrington Moore, *Social Origins of Dictatorship and Democracy* (Boston: Beacon Press, 1965).

[3]Gordon Craig, *The Politics of the Prussian Army* (Oxford: Oxford University Press, 1955).

[4]Tom Kemp, *Industrialization in Nineteenth Century Europe,* 2d ed. (London: Longman, 1985).

[5]Geoffrey Barraclough, *An Introduction to Contemporary History* (Baltimore: Penguin, 1967).

[6]Philippe Schmitter and Gerhard Lembruch, eds., *Trends Toward Corporatist Intermediation* (Beverly Hills, Calif.: Sage, 1979).

[7]William E. Paterson and Gordon Smith, *The West German Model: Perspectives on a Stable State* (London: Cass, 1981).

[8]Ralf Dahrendorf, *Society and Democracy in Germany* (Garden City, N.Y.: Anchor, 1969).

[9]Alexander Gerschenkron, *Bread and Democracy in Germany,* 2d ed. (Ithaca, N.Y.: Cornell University Press, 1989.

[10]Wilhelm Röpke, "The Guiding Principle of the Liberal Program," in H. F. Wünche, ed., *Standard Texts on the Social Market Economy* (New York: Gustav Fischer Verlag, 1982), 188.

[11]Richard Deeg, F*inance Capital Unveiled: Banks and Economic Adjustment in Germany* (Ann Arbor: University of Michigan Press, 1998).

[12]Joyce Mushaben, "Challenging the Maternalist Presumption: Gender and Welfare Reform in Germany and the United States," in Ulrike Liebert and Nancy Hirschman, eds*., Women and Welfare: Theory and Practice in the U.S. and Europe* (Rutgers, N.J.: Rutgers University Press, 2001).

[13]Dahrendorf, *Society and Democracy in Germany.*

[14]http://eng.bundespraesident.de.

[15]Peter Katzenstein, *Policy and Politics in West Germany: The Growth of a Semi-Sovereign State* (Philadelphia: Temple University Press, 1987).

[16]John O. Koehler, *Stasi: The Untold Story of the East German Secret Police* (Boulder, Colo.: Westview Press, 1999).

[17]Frank Louis Rusciano, "Rethinking the Gender Gap: The Case of West German Elections," *Comparative Politics* 24, no. 3 (April 1992): 335–358.

[18]Christopher S. Allen, ed., *Transformation of the German Political Party System: Institutional Crisis or Democratic Renewal?* (New York: Berghahn, 2001).

[19]Carl E. Schorske, *German Social Democracy, 1905–1917: The Development of the Great Schism* (Cambridge, Mass.: Harvard University Press, 1983).

[20]Otto Kirchheimer, "The Transformation of the Western European Party System," in Roy C. Macridis, ed., *Comparative Politics: Notes and Readings,* 6th ed. (Chicago: Dorsey Press, 1986).

[21]Gerard Braunthal, *The German Social Democrats Since 1969: A Party in Power and Opposition,* 2d ed. (Boulder, Colo.: Westview Press, 1994).

[22]Aline Kuntz, "The Bavarian CSU: A Case Study in Conservative Modernization" (Ph.D. diss., Cornell University, 1987).

[23]Sven Steinmo, Kathleen Thelen, and Frank Longstreth, eds., *Structuring Politics: The New Institutionalism in Comparative Perspectiv*e (Cambridge: Cambridge University Press, 1992).

[24]Katzenstein, *Policy and Politics in West Germany.*

[25]Arnold J. Heidenheimer, *Comparative Public Policy: The Politics of Social Choice in America, Europe and Japan,* 3d ed. (New York: St. Martin's Press, 1990).

[26]Gabriel A. Almond and Sidney Verba, eds., *The Civic Culture Revisited* (Newbury Park, Calif.: Sage, 1989).

[27]Lowell Turner, ed., *Negotiating the New Germany: Can Social Partnership Survive?* (Ithaca, N.Y.: Cornell University Press, 1997).

[28]Gary Herrigel, "The Crisis in German Decentralized Production," *European Urban and Regional Studies* 3, no. 1 (1996): 33–52.

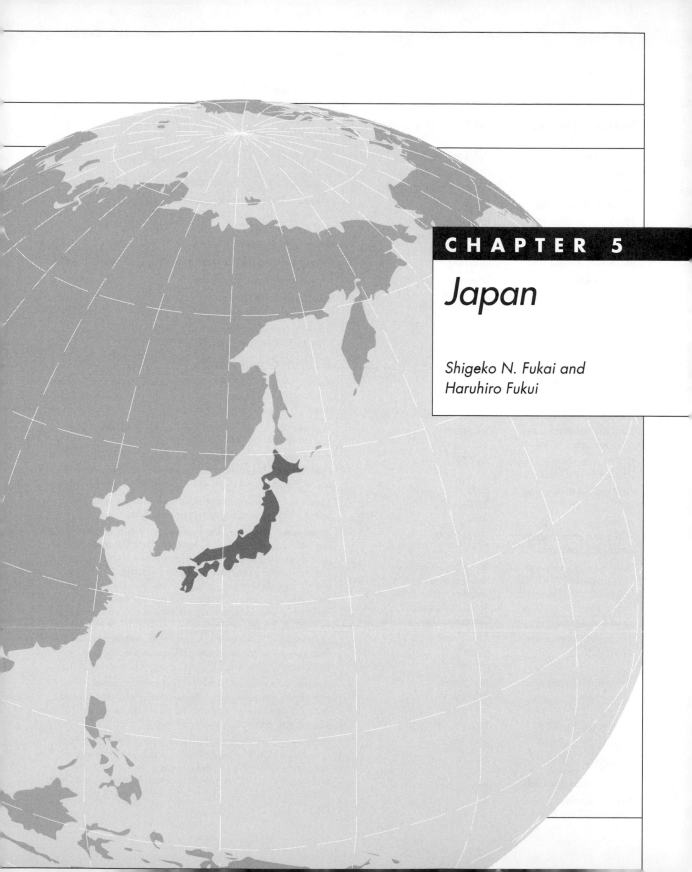

CHAPTER 5

Japan

Shigeko N. Fukai and
Haruhiro Fukui

Japan

Land and People

Capital	Tokyo
Total area (square miles)	145,845 (Slightly smaller than California)
Population	127.1 million

Annual population growth rate (%)

1975–2000	0.5
2000–2015 (projected)	0

Urban population (%)	78.8

Ethnic composition (%)

Japanese	99
Others (including Korean, Chinese, Brazilian, Filipino)	1

Major language(s)	Japanese

Religious affiliation (%)

Observe both Shinto and Buddhism	84
Other (including Christian 0.7)	16

Economy

Domestic Currency	Yen (JPY)	
	US$1: 125.2 JPY (2002 av.)	
Total GDP (US$)	4.8 trillion	
GDP per capita (US$)	37,494	
Total GDP at purchasing power parity (US$)	3.4 trillion	
GDP per capita at purchasing power parity (US$)	26,775	

GDP annual growth rate (%)

1997	1.8
2000	2.4
2001	–0.4

GDP per capita average annual growth rate (%)

1975–2000	2.7
1990–2000	1.1

Inequality in income or consumption (1993) (%)

Share of poorest 10%	4.8
Share of poorest 20%	10.6
Share of richest 20%	35.7
Share of richest 10%	21.7
Gini Index (1993)	24.9

Structure of production (% ofGDP)

Agriculture	1.6
Industry	33.7
Services	64.7

Labor force distribution (% of total)

Agriculture	5
Industry	30
Services	65

Exports as % of GDP	10
Imports as % of GDP	8

Society

Life expectancy at birth	81
Infant mortality per 1,000 live births	4
Adult literacy (%)	99

Access to information and communications (per 1,000 population)

Telephone lines	586
Mobile phones	528
Radios	956
Televisions	725
Personal computers	315

Women in Government and the Economy

Women in the national legislature

Lower house or single house (%)	7.3
Upper house (%)	15.4

Women at ministerial level (%)	5.7
Female economic activity rate (age 15 and above) (%)	50.8
Female labor force (% of total)	41

Estimated earned income (PPP US$)

Female	16,601
Male	37,345

2002 Human Development Index Ranking (out of 173 countries)	9

Political Organization

Political System   Parliamentary democracy and constitutional monarchy, in which the Emperor is merely a symbol of national unity.

Regime History   Current constitution promulgated in 1946 and in effect since 1947.

Administrative Structure   Unitary state, 47 units of intermediate-level subnational government called prefectures and 3232 lower-level units called city, town, or village.

Executive   Prime minister selected by legislature; a cabinet of about 20 ministers appointed by prime minister.

Legislature   Bicameral. The upper house (House of Councillors) has 247 members (to be reduced to 242 in 2004) elected for six-year terms. Half of the members are elected every three years. One hundred and fifty-one members (146 after 2004) are elected from multiple-seat prefecture-wide districts; 96 are elected nationally by a party list proportional representation method. The lower house (House of Representatives) has 480 members elected for four-year terms, which may be shortened by the dissolution of the house. Three hundred lower house members are elected from single-seat constituencies; 180 are elected by party list proportional representation from 11 regional electoral districts.

Judiciary   Supreme Court has 15 judges appointed by the cabinet, except chief judge who is nominated by the cabinet and appointed by the emperor; all eligible to serve until 70 years if age, subject to popular review.

Party System   One-party dominant (Liberal Democratic Party) since mid-1950s; has become considerably more competitive since early 1990s. Major parties: Liberal Democratic Party, Liberal Party, Conservative Party, Democratic Party of Japan, Clean Government Party, Social Democratic Party, Japan Communist Party.

Politics in Action

Japanese politics took several dramatic turns in the first year and a half of the new millennium. At the beginning of 2001, a three-party coalition government led by contemporary Japan's most successful party, the Liberal Democratic Party (LDP), was on the verge of a collapse with a record-low public approval rating: below 20 percent. The government did fall a few months later and was replaced by a new coalition government headed by another LDP leader, Junichiro Koizumi, a change that raised the public approval rate of the government overnight to nearly 80 percent. This surge of popularity was largely due to the new prime minister's widely publicized call for a thorough reform of the nation's outdated, inefficient, and corruption-prone political and economic systems. But the Koizumi government's popularity lasted less than a year before it plummeted in early 2002 to below 50 percent and continued to slide until it was under 40 percent by early May. The sudden dissipation of Koizumi's appeal among the Japanese people was due largely to the slow progress of the reform effort. The prime minister's troubles reflected widespread public dissatisfaction with the existing state of Japanese politics and, especially, the economy, which had been badly depressed since the early 1990s and was not showing any sign of significant improvement in the near future.

These dramatic developments in Japanese politics had been preceded by a period of considerable political instability ushered in by the historic defeat of the LDP in the 1993 House of Representatives (lower house) general election and the formation of a government without LDP participation for the first time since the mid-1950s. The LDP had governed Japan without interruption for nearly forty years, presiding over what seemed to be a uniquely stable and prosperous democracy. By contrast, the multiparty non-LDP government formed in the summer of 1993 lasted for less than a year, and a new LDP-led coalition returned to power in 1994. Since that time, the Liberal Democrats have stayed in power through a succession of coalition governments, but in sharp contrast with the three and half decades of LDP rule, volatility and the potential for

難航！ 難航！   小島 功

Danger! Danger! The Koizumi-maru ship with a banner marked "Reform" sails right into a monstrous wave of negative 0.8 percent GDP growth rate. *Source:* Isao Kojimo, *Asahi shinbun*, September 8, 2001.

unexpected twists and turns appear to have become basic features of Japanese politics.

Geographic Setting

A group of islands lying off the eastern coast of Asia, Japan is physically a relatively small country prone to a host of recurrent natural disasters, such as earthquakes, typhoons, and tidal waves. The group comprises 6,852 islands, all but four of which—Honshu, Hokkaido, Kyushu, and Shikoku—are less than 500 square miles in size each. The country is divided into forty-seven provinces, known as prefectures. With a territory of about 145,900 square miles, Japan is slightly smaller than California, slightly larger than Germany, and only about one-twenty-fifth the size of China.

Japan is the eighth most populous country in the world, with about 127 million people. With about 850 people per square mile, it is the ninth most densely

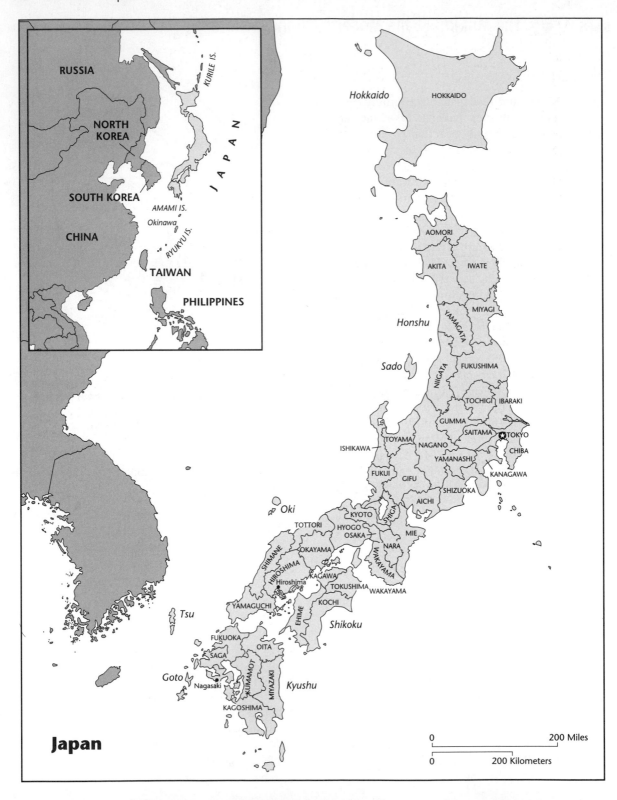

RUSSIA

NORTH
KOREA

SOUTH KOREA

CHINA

TAIWAN

PHILIPPINES

KURILE IS.

J A P A N

AMAMI IS.

Okinawa

RYUKYU IS.

Hokkaido HOKKAIDO

AOMORI

AKITA IWATE

MIYAGI

Honshu YAMAGATA

Sado NIIGATA FUKUSHIMA

TOCHIGI IBARAKI

GUMMA

SAITAMA TOKYO

TOYAMA NAGANO CHIBA

ISHIKAWA YAMANASHI KANAGAWA

FUKUI GIFU

SHIZUOKA

AICHI

Oki KYOTO SHIGA

TOTTORI HYOGO MIE

OSAKA

SHIMANE OKAYAMA NARA

WAKAYAMA

HIROSHIMA KAGAWA

Hiroshima TOKUSHIMA WAKAYAMA

YAMAGUCHI KOCHI

Tsu EHIME *Shikoku*

FUKUOKA

SAGA OITA

Goto KUMAMOTO

Nagasaki MIYAZAKI *Kyushu*

KAGOSHIMA

Japan

0   200 Miles

0   200 Kilometers

populated among countries with a population of 1 million or more. It is about twelve times as crowded as the United States, three times as crowded as France, and one and a half times as crowded as Great Britain or Germany. Slightly less than 80 percent of the Japanese today live in the urban areas within the boundaries of about 670 cities, most with a population of 50,000 or more.

Japan is poorly endowed with natural resources, particularly coal, petroleum, metal ores, and timber. The only exception is water from normally plentiful rainfall that feeds the ubiquitous paddy fields and supplies the nation more rice than is needed for immediate domestic consumption, at least for the present. Consequently, Japan is unusually reliant on hydroelectric and nuclear energy as well as on imports of oil from the Middle East. Indeed, Japan must import from abroad large quantities of most of the resources essential for modern industry.

Only about 15 percent of land in Japan is arable, compared to more than 20 percent in the United States and Great Britain and well over 30 percent in Germany and France. Other than rice, Japanese farms cannot supply enough food for the nation, and Japan ranks lowest, at about 60 percent in the early 2000s, among the advanced industrial states in the degree of self-sufficiency in overall food supply. As a result of its need to import natural resources and food, modern Japan has been a natural trading state.

Japan's closest and most accessible neighbors are Korea, 30 miles west across the Sea of Japan, and China, some 500 miles west across the East China Sea. Ancient and medieval Japan imported enormous amounts of not only goods but also science, technology, and culture—such as religions, customs, laws, literature, architecture, and fine arts—from both Korea and China. Medieval Japan also developed extensive trading and diplomatic relationships with many Southeast Asian peoples across the South China Sea, such as those in contemporary Indochina, Thailand, Malaysia, and Indonesia. Since the mid-nineteenth century, Japan has had extensive contacts—and sometimes conflict— with Russia to the north and, most important, the United States to the east across the wide Pacific Ocean.

Critical Junctures

Ancient and Medieval Japan

Archeological evidence shows that the Japanese archipelago was inhabited by tribes of hunters and gatherers as early as about 30,000 B.C. By about 7000 B.C. some of the early inhabitants of the island domain apparently began to build and live in small settlements and even raise some livestock. By the middle of the third century A.D., a modest state had emerged in the southwestern region of what is now Japan.

Broader control over this ancient state was established by a tribal chief who probably had ancestral roots in Korea and claimed to be a "heavenly king" descended from a mythical sun goddess. The early rulers of this small, insular state frequently sent diplomatic missions to Korea and China, which brought back products of an advanced culture, including the teachings of the Chinese philosopher Confucius (551 479 B.C.). Confucian ideas, particularly about the moral foundations of the political and social order based on reverence for one's ancestors and submission to authority, had a profound and enduring effect on Japanese society. Buddhism, with its origins in India reached Japan via China and Korea in the middle of the sixth century, and there it thrived among the rulers and people alike, despite dividing into a number of competing sects. Together with a native cult of nature and ancestor worship known as Shinto ("ways of the spirits"), Confucianism and Buddhism continue to shape everyday life in Japan.

For more than fifteen centuries, Japan has remained a unified and independent state, except for several years immediately following World War II, when the country was militarily occupied by the United States and other Allied powers. Up to the late twelfth century, Japan was ruled first by shifting coalitions of tribal groups, then by those claiming the title of heavenly emperor and their regents. The latter founded the world's longest—and still surviving—monarchy. During Japan's medieval era, which began in the late twelfth century, the monarchy remained intact but yielded effective power to a succession of military leaders, or shoguns.[1] The most successful of these military leaders founded a durable dynasty known as the Tokugawa Shogunate.

The Tokugawa Shogunate (1603–1867)

The shogunate was a feudal autocracy founded by Ieyasu Tokugawa, the ultimate winner of the series of civil wars fought in the last decades of the sixteenth century. Under the iron hand of a succession of fifteen hereditary rulers, the Tokugawa dynasty ruled the nation for 265 years through an effectively centralized and complex system of administration and military power headquartered in the city of Edo, the site of today's Tokyo.

Beyond Edo, Japan was divided into lands owned and administered by the central government, which accounted for about 15 percent of the productive lands and included all the major cities and mining towns, and 270 or so fiefs owned and governed, subject to the central government's approval, by local lords. Roughly half of these fiefs belonged to lords closely tied to the Tokugawa family by kinship or historical association and regarded as totally loyal to central government. The remainder belonged to lords who were not so unquestionably trustworthy. The lands owned by the central government and its close and dependable allies were deliberately scattered among the lands owned by the others, so that the potentially disaffected and rebellious lords could be watched by the loyal ones. All local lords were required to visit Edo and pay homage to the shogun every few years and frequently contribute both funds and labor to a variety of public works undertaken by the central government. For two and a half centuries, these mandatory requisitions kept all the feudal lords of the era relatively poor and subservient to the shogunate.

Social classes in Tokugawa Japan were strictly segregated, living and working separately, each within officially demarcated neighborhoods. Under the official classification system, there were six classes—warriors (the ruling class), farmers, artisans, merchants, "filthy hordes," and "nonhumans"—although the last two categories were often lumped together as the "outcaste" class. "Filthy hordes" and "nonhumans" referred, respectively, to those who, barred from "normal" occupations for whatever reasons, made their living by collecting and working on hides of dead and discarded cows and horses and to those who did so by begging.[2] Both, but especially the former, were forbidden, either by law or by custom, to share dwellings, baths, furniture, and so on, with "normal" people. The majority of

those who belonged to the ruling warrior class, known as *bushi* or, more popularly, samurai, accounted for about 8 percent of the population, or about ten times the proportion of knights in medieval England or France. Women in Tokugawa Japan were treated as inherently inferior and subordinate to men and were denied participation in public affairs even at the village level.[3]

There was also a minuscule class of nobles at the imperial court in Kyoto, where the figurehead emperor resided, but it had long since lost all of its political power to the samurai. The monarchy survived as a traditional source of political legitimacy in a nation founded on the myth of the divine origin of its imperial family.

As a rule, boys from samurai families—and increasingly the sons of well-to-do merchant and farm families and even some girls—had access to primary school education. In addition to reading, writing, and simple arithmetic, children were taught the idea of Japan as a nation separate from but equal to other nations. They were taught, above all, the Confucian principles of correct social order and proper personal behavior.[4]

Japan in the Meiji-Taisho Era (1868–1925)

The revolt that eventually toppled the autocratic Tokugawa regime in 1868 known as the Meiji Restoration, resulted partly from growing political tension within Japan caused by gradual but nevertheless profound socioeconomic changes. It also resulted from rising pressure exerted by a number of Western powers to integrate Japan, which the Tokugawa rulers had gone to extreme measure to keep isolated from the outside world, into a rapidly expanding global political-economic system. Most immediately, the revolution was brought about by the forced entry of a small flotilla of American warships into the Bay of Shimoda, less than 100 miles west of Edo, in 1853 and 1854 in defiance of the centuries-old ban on the entry of unauthorized foreigners into Japanese territory.[5] The arrival of U.S. Navy Commodore Matthew C. Perry's squadron and the shogun's capitulation to the demand that Japan open its ports to American naval and merchant ships gave its enemies an excuse to revolt against the shogunate.

The young samurai revolutionaries who overthrew the Tokugawa regime and founded modern Japan quickly consolidated their position as a new ruling oligarchy. They derived their legitimacy to govern the

Critical Junctures in Modern Japan's Political Development

1867   Meiji Restoration inaugurates rapid Japanese industrialization and modernization.

1889   Constitution of the Great Empire of Japan establishes a bicameral legislature, the Imperial Diet.

1900–1901   Constitutional Party of Political Friends (Seiyukai) formed.

1912–1926   Taisho Democracy period.

1925   Universal Manhood Suffrage Law promulgated. Japan Trade Union Council founded.

1931–1932   Japanese army takes control of Chinese Manchuria without orders from the government in Tokyo.

1932   Military officers attempt but fail to take over government.

1937   Japan invades China.

1941   Japan attacks U.S. naval base in Pearl Harbor. United States declares war on Japan.

1945   Atomic bombs dropped on Hiroshima and Nagasaki. Soviet Union declares war on Japan. Japan surrenders. Allied occupation and reform of Japan begin.

1947   New Constitution of Japan promulgated featuring a democratic government and a peace clause (Article 9) renouncing the right to make war.

1951   Japanese Peace Treaty and United States–Japan Mutual Security Treaty signed in San Francisco.

1955   Socialist parties unite to form Japan Socialist Party (JSP); conservative parties merge into Liberal Democratic Party (LDP).

1976   Lockheed scandal and arrest of former Prime Minister Kakuei Tanaka: the first of the major scandals that will rock the Japanese government.

1985   Telecommunications and tobacco industries privatized. Equal Employment Law enacted.

1989   Showa emperor, Hirohito, dies. LDP loses in House of Councilors election.

1990   Prince Akihito ascends throne as Heisei emperor.

1992   Japan New Party (JNP) founded by LDP dissidents.

1993   LDP loses in House of Representatives general election; first non-LDP government since 1955 formed by coalition centered on the JNP.

1994   New House of Representatives election law passed. LDP returns to power in coalition with the JSP.

1996   LDP forms first single-party cabinet since 1993.

1997   Asian financial crisis shakes Japanese stock market and economy.

1998   LDP cabinets implement a series of measures to resuscitate stagnant economy, but to no significant effect. Japan's economy remains depressed into the first years of the twenty-first century.

2001   National government ministries and agencies reorganized. Self-Defense Force ships dispatched to Indian Ocean to assist U.S. Navy in its antiterrorism operations.

nation from their self-proclaimed role as the official representatives of the emperor, whom they had "restored" as Japan's true and divine ruler after centuries of usurpation by the Tokugawa shoguns. Over the next fifty years, this oligarchy, ruling in the name of the Meiji (so-called according to the specific reign title given each Japanese monarch) emperor, would spearhead a "revolution from above" that would transform the feudal nation into one of the world's major industrial and military powers.

A prime goal of the Meiji state from the beginning was to renegotiate the "unequal treaties" that had been concluded between Japan and a dozen Western powers in the last years of the Tokugawa era. These treaties contained two types of "unequal" clauses. One provided for extraterritoriality, or the right of foreign diplomats to try citizens of their countries for offenses committed in Japanese territory. The other granted foreign governments the right to veto changes in Japanese tariff rates. After protracted and frustrating negotiations, the extraterritoriality provisions were eliminated by the last decade of the nineteenth century, and Japan regained full control of its tariff policy by the first decade of the twentieth century.

Meiji Japan was no longer a nation isolated from the rapidly expanding world of modern capitalism. In fact, the opening of Japan was not only sudden but also complete. The new government let foreigners visit the country for diplomatic, commercial, and other purposes and sent Japanese nationals abroad, especially to the United States and Western Europe, to acquire the knowledge and technology deemed necessary for modernizing the nation as quickly as possible. To catch up with the most economically advanced and powerful states of the late nineteenth and early twentieth centuries, Japan imported a wide array of Western institutions, ideas, and practices. For example, in 1871, a 110-member mission was sent to the United States and Europe, where they spent twenty months in a dozen different countries, visiting government offices and military academies, as well as shipyards, factories, banks, and chambers of commerce.[6] After their return to Japan in the fall of 1873, leading members of the group, such as Hirobumi Ito, who later became Japan's first prime minister, spearheaded Japan's drive to build a "rich nation with a strong army," following in the footsteps of the Western powers.

Japanese society in this era was characterized by sharp economic, social, and political inequalities among its people. The countryside was in the grip of a small group of landlords who presided over a vast class of tenant farmers, while urban Japan was dominated by a handful of giant industrial and financial conglomerates, known as *zaibatsu*. The government bureaucracy, which acted as the primary agent of the ruling oligarchy, was dominated by graduates of a single government-funded and -controlled university created as the incubator of able and obedient servants of the autocratic state. Despite the Westernization of some of its political, social, and economic institutions, Meiji Japan was not fundamentally different from Tokugawa Japan as far as the vast majority of Japanese people were concerned. But one significant difference was that they now had access to free and compulsory primary school education, which helped some of them climb out of the lower classes into the middle classes, though almost never into the upper classes.

In its effort to unite and mobilize the nation in the drive for military and economic parity with the West, the Meiji government replaced the six-class system of the Tokugawa period with a three-class system. The samurai class was retained, but farmers, artisans, and merchants were consolidated into a single "commoner" class and the outcastes were combined into a "new commoner" class. This change of names did not lead to a significant change in either the social status or the economic conditions of members of each class, however. Members of the new commoner class, in particular, continued to face open, systematic, and officially condoned discrimination and harassment until the early 1920s, when their leaders founded a national organization that launched a vigorous campaign to attain equality for its members.

Conflicts arising from social divisions were kept under control before World War II by an ideology of national unity and cooperation, which was propagated through the centrally controlled education system and conformist mass media. This ideology focused the attention and energies of the Japanese people on a drive to catch up with the Western powers.[7]

Meiji Japan imported not only economic models and cultural forms from abroad, but political ideas as well. By the 1880s, Japanese translations of John Stuart Mill's *On Liberty* and Jean Jacques Rousseau's *The Social Contract* were published and widely read by Japanese intellectuals, as were a dozen political treatises by Japanese authors that were either based on or inspired by the works of Western writers. The spread of the democratic idea in Japan gave rise to a "freedom and people's rights" movement led by two proto-political parties: the Liberal Party, which espoused radical democracy in the spirit of the French Revolution, and the Reform Party, which advocated moderate change associated with British political tradition. Led by former members of the early Meiji oligarchy who had left the government in a disagreement over policy issues, both parties called for the adoption of parliamentary and other democratic institutions as the best means to mobilize the entire country in pursuit of national goals. The oligarchic government responded to their call in 1889 by promulgating a constitution modeled after the conservative Prussian prototype and instituting a bicameral legislature, the Imperial Diet, modeled after the British Parliament (though named after its Prussian counterpart).

The 1889 constitution, or the Constitution of the

Great Empire of Japan, merely formalized the leading role of the Meiji oligarchy. The charter guaranteed civil rights and freedoms to the emperor's subjects "subject to the limitations imposed by law" and required every law to be enacted with the consent of the Imperial Diet. But the emperor retained the prerogative to sanction and promulgate all laws; open, close, and adjourn the Diet; and, in his capacity as the supreme commander of the armed forces, declare war, make peace, and conclude treaties.

In practice, however, the emperor's powers were exercised by the ruling oligarchs. They dominated the powerful nonelective institutions of government, such as the Privy Council, the House of Peers (the upper chamber of the Imperial Diet), and, above all, the civil and military services. The elected representatives of the emperor's subjects spoke ineffectually through the less powerful lower chamber of the Diet, the House of Representatives, and a few legally recognized political parties. The House of Representatives could block legislation of which its members did not approve, but the oligarchy could easily bully them into changing their minds or, if that did not work, they could simply have the emperor legislate by decree.

There was some progress toward political liberalization in Japan during the era known as **Taisho Democracy** (1912–1926), Taisho being the reign title of the Meiji emperor's son who succeeded to the throne in 1912.[8] Two conservative parties (descendants of the Liberal and Reform parties), the Constitutional Party of Political Friends (Seiyukai) and the Constitutional Government Party (Kenseito), alternately formed a government through electoral competition.[9]

The most important political development of the Taisho Democracy period was the 1925 revision of the House of Representatives Election Law, better known as the Universal Manhood Suffrage Law. This event represented the culmination of a tortuous campaign that had been launched in the last years of the nineteenth century but had gathered momentum only in the "democratic '20s." The revision removed the restrictions on the grant of the vote to Japanese male adults based on the amounts of national taxes paid, although it did not extend the suffrage to adult women.

Taisho Democracy was short-lived. As Japan's economy became mired in a protracted recession after World War I and then devastated by the Great Depression in the early 1930s, the advocates of democracy at home and peace abroad came under increasingly savage attack. Military and right-wing groups within and outside the civilian bureaucracy blamed the parties and liberal politicians for all of Japan's woes.

Japan Under Military Rule and in War

The political power and influence of the military grew steadily throughout the Meiji-Taisho era, importantly as a result of the establishment of the Army General Staff Office in 1878 and the Naval General Staff Office in 1886. These offices were invested with control over the armed forces, subject only to the will of the throne, thereby placing the military beyond the control of the civilian government. The extraconstitutional status thus acquired eventually led the military to practice what amounted to its own diplomacy, often at cross-purposes with that of the civilian authorities, and to dominate decision making on critical domestic and foreign policy issues.

An even more significant factor in the rise of militarism in Japan was the Japanese victories in the 1894–1895 Sino-Japanese War and the 1904–1905 Russo-Japanese War. Accompanied by rapid growth of heavy industry, these wars marked the successful achievement of Meiji Japan's major goals of turning an economically underdeveloped and militarily vulnerable semifeudal nation into a burgeoning imperial power poised to expand into neighboring territories. It was not until the late 1920s, however, that the Japanese military began seriously to seek full control of the country's government.

Another crucial step on the road to war was taken when the government led by Giichi Tanaka, an army general elected president of the Constitutional Party of Political Friends in 1925 and appointed prime minister in 1927, decided to bring northeastern China, known as Manchuria, under Japanese control in order to secure a market that absorbed 70 percent of Japan's exports at the time. Tanaka's policy encouraged Japanese army units in Manchuria to take matters into their own hands and expand their operations against local Chinese forces without prior authorization from the government in Tokyo.[10]

The events in Manchuria provoked such intense international protest against and criticism of Japanese policy that Tanaka was forced to resign. He was succeeded by a liberal civilian, Osachi Hamaguchi, who directed Japan's participation in the 1930 London Naval Disarmament Conference. Japan not only reaffirmed an earlier agreement to limit the tonnage of its large warships to 60 percent of those of the United States and Great Britain, but also agreed to additional restrictions on the growth of its naval power. The acceptance of these limitations by the Japanese delegation to the conference caused an uproar among the military and right-wing groups at home and led to the assassination of Hamaguchi a few months later. Thereafter, the military steadily consolidated its control of the Japanese government with the emperor's acquiescence, if not explicit support. The military silenced its critics by propaganda, blackmail, and the use or threat of force.

Hamaguchi's immediate successors, either civilians or moderate military leaders, failed to control radical younger officers bent on conquering northeastern China and eventually the rest of China and Southeast Asia as a vast resource base for Japanese industry and armed forces. In an unsuccessful coup attempt in May 1932, a band of young naval officers attacked several government offices and fatally shot the prime minister. In a similar attempt in February 1936, army troops led by radical officers invaded a number of government offices, murdered the finance minister and several other government leaders, and occupied the central part of Tokyo for four days.[11] Neither action succeeded in immediately installing a military government, but both helped to intimidate opponents of the military not only in the government but also in business circles, academia, and the mass media. Political parties were not only silenced but disbanded by 1941.

When the League of Nations condemned the Japanese invasion of northern China in 1933, the Japanese government, already under strong military and right-wing pressure, chose to withdraw from the League, an action followed by Nazi Germany later in the same year. As the international criticism of Japanese action in China intensified, Japan entered into an ostensibly defensive anticommunist military alliance with Nazi Germany in 1936, which was joined by fascist Italy the following year. In the summer of 1937, Japanese army units in China used a skirmish between Japanese and Chinese troops at Lugouqiao (Marco Polo) Bridge near Beijing to embark on a full-scale invasion of China and, in December of the same year, unleashed a rampage against Chinese civilians in the then Chinese capital,

Nanjing, an incident known as the "Rape of Nanking." When the United States terminated its trade agreement with Japan in 1939, thus blocking Japan's access to a major source of petroleum and raw materials, the government in Tokyo decided to seek an alternative source of supplies in Southeast Asia. In July 1941, Japan moved its troops into French Indochina. In response, Washington froze Japanese-owned assets in the United States and banned the sale of petroleum to Japan.

Faced with the prospect of exhausting its limited fuel supplies, the Japanese government, now led by General Hideki Tojo, made the fateful decision to start a war against the United States and its allies.[12] On December 7, 1941, Japanese naval air units executed a carefully planned surprise attack on the major U.S. naval base at Pearl Harbor in Hawaii. The United States immediately declared war on Japan.

Japan enjoyed some notable military successes at the outset of the war, but in less than a year it began to lose one major battle after another. By late 1944, its effort was reduced to a desperate defense of its homeland from increasingly frequent and destructive air raids by American bombers. In August 1945, Japan's resistance was broken by the nearly total destruction of two major cities, Hiroshima and Nagasaki, by the first and only atomic bombs so far used in war. By then, virtually all major Japanese cities, including Tokyo, had been reduced to rubble by American bombing raids.

Department-store display of destruction resulting from dropping of atomic bomb on two Japanese cities. *Source:* © Kitamura/Gamma Press Image.

The Allied Occupation (1945–1952)

The Allied Occupation of Japan following World War II transformed a fundamentally autocratic state into a fundamentally democratic one.[13] The occupation, which lasted from 1945 to 1952, was formally a joint operation by the major Allies, including the United States, the British Commonwealth, the Soviet Union, and China. In practice, it was nearly exclusively an American operation, led by General Douglas MacArthur, who held the title of **Supreme Commander for the Allied Powers (SCAP).**

During the first year and a half of the occupation, SCAP made a determined effort to achieve its two major goals: the complete demilitarization and democratization of Japan. The Japanese armed forces were swiftly dismantled, troops were demobilized, military production was halted, and wartime leaders were either purged or arrested. Seven of those leaders, including General Tojo, were executed for war crimes. Almost as swiftly, Japanese workers' right to organize was recognized, women were given the vote for the first time, and many family-controlled conglomerates (*zaibatsu*) were dissolved. Virtually all other important political, legal, economic, and social institutions and practices were subjected to close scrutiny, and many were abolished for their allegedly militaristic or antidemocratic character.

By far the most important step taken for the democratization of Japan was the promulgation of a new constitution. Based on a draft prepared by a handful of American lawyers at General MacArthur's behest in 1946, and thereafter known as the 1947 Constitution or the "MacArthur Constitution," the document was intended to legitimize and perpetuate the extensive occupation-sponsored reforms. It was a radically democratic and uniquely pacifist constitution, which also bore the unmistakable marks of its American authorship in its overall tone and language.

The 1947 Constitution relegated the emperor to a purely symbolic role while making the Japanese people the sovereign of the nation. It made all members of both chambers of the Diet directly elected by the people and elevated the Diet to the position of nation's highest and sole lawmaking organ. In a provision unprecedented in the history of constitutions, the document forbade Japan to maintain any form of military power or engage in war as a means to settle international disputes. The constitution's preamble proclaims: "We, the Japanese people, desire peace for all time and are deeply conscious of the high ideals controlling human relationship, and we have determined to preserve our security and existence, trusting in the justice and faith of the peace-loving peoples of the world." In the main body of the document that follows, Article 9, known as the peace clause, reads:

> Aspiring sincerely to an international peace based on justice and order, the Japanese people forever renounce war as a sovereign right of the nation and the threat or use of force as means of settling international disputes.
>
> In order to accomplish the aim of the preceding paragraph, land, sea, and air forces, as well as other war potential, will never be maintained. The right of belligerency of the state will not be recognized.

The spirit, if not the letter, of this provision has long since been violated by the creation in the early 1950s of the so-called **Self-Defense Forces (SDF),** one of the largest and best-equipped military forces in the world today. But the pacifist spirit that the provision represents lives on in the minds of the majority of Japanese more than a half-century later.

Contemporary Japan (1952 to the Present)

Party politics was also revived after the war, with SCAP's blessing and encouragement. The offspring of the prewar Constitutional Party of Political Friends was renamed the Japan Liberal Party, despite its conservative ideology; it dominated Japanese politics for much of the occupation period. The Liberals' major rival was the Japan Socialist Party (JSP). The Socialists won a slim plurality in the Diet elections in 1947 and formed a coalition government with the descendant of the other prewar party, the Constitutional Government Party, which had been renamed the Japan Progressive Party and was later to be called the Democratic Party. The JSP-led coalition government lasted for a little over a year and a half before the Liberals returned to power and began to consolidate their hold on the Diet. The conservative domination of Japanese government became unassailable after the Liberals merged with the Democrats in 1955 to form the Liberal Democratic Party (LDP).

From 1955 to 1993, the LDP managed to win either a majority or large plurality of seats in every Diet election and thus had nearly monopolistic control of the Japanese government for nearly four decades. This prevented any alternation of governing parties and led to the emergence of a stable **predominant-party regime.** But the long era of LDP rule was not uneventful.

One major political crisis occurred in 1960 over the revision of the U.S.-Japan Mutual Security Treaty that had been signed in 1951 at the end of the occupation. The LDP government's proposal to revise the treaty but keep it in force provoked fierce opposition not only in the Diet but also in the streets of Tokyo and other major cities. Hundreds of thousands of protesters, led by JSP Diet members and leaders of the left-wing General Council of Trade Unions of Japan (*Sohyo*) and the National Federation of Students' Self-Government Associations (*Zengakuren*), marched against the treaty and Prime Minister Nobusuke Kishi's LDP government. The protesters argued that the treaty would make Japan a semipermanent military ally of the United States and an enemy of Japan's powerful neighbors, the People's Republic of China and the Soviet Union. Nonetheless, the government eventually railroaded the revised treaty through the Diet in defiance of the widespread public outcry. The revised treaty was to remain in force for the next ten years (until 1970) and thereafter be indefinitely renewable unless renounced by either side.

The government's action caused such a violent public reaction with an anti-American tinge that President Eisenhower's scheduled official visit to Japan was canceled and Prime Minister Kishi and his cabinet were forced to resign soon after. The JSP, which led the protest movement, split amid the turmoil, as a group of its less radical Diet members formed a separate party, the Democratic Socialist Party (DSP), in January 1960. The split caused considerable long-term damage to the JSP and its major trade union ally, *Sohyo,* while helping their conservative rivals: the newly formed DSP, the LDP, and the Japanese Confederation of Labor (*Domei*).

The experience of the 1960 political crisis led Kishi's successors to avoid tackling controversial foreign and security policy issues and concentrate on eco-

Demonstrators against renewal of U.S.-Japan Mutual Security Treaty in front of Diet Building in Tokyo, May 1960. *Source:* AP/Wide World Photos.

nomic matters. This change in the LDP's strategy ushered in an era of political stability and phenomenal economic growth for Japan. The tendency of Japanese public and media attention to focus increasingly on economic issues became considerably more evident after the oil shocks of the 1970s.

The first of these shocks came in 1973 when the Organization of Petroleum Exporting Countries (OPEC) announced its decision to drastically raise the price of crude oil exported by its members and, in some cases, suspend the export altogether. The decision, intended to force all major industrial nations dependent on Middle Eastern oil for their industries to support the Arab states in their protracted conflict with Israel, caused an immediate and widespread panic in Japan, as well as in many other oil-importing nations, followed by a sharp economic downturn.

The second oil shock, in 1979, caused by the Islamic revolution in Iran, did not have as dramatic and devastating an impact on the Japanese economy, thanks mainly to the effective energy-saving and storage measures that had been implemented after the first shock. The Japanese economy, however, has never regained the remarkable growth rates that it experienced during the preceding two decades. Paradoxically, the economic difficulties did more damage to the opposition than to the ruling party; the LDP maintained its majority position in the Diet through the 1980s, while the opposition, especially the JSP, failed to make any political headway.

The lackluster electoral performance of the socialist parties was due mainly to the weakening position of organized labor in Japan, particularly left-wing unions affiliated with *Sohyo*. The proportion of union members among Japanese workers steadily declined, from about 35 percent in 1970 to 30 percent in 1980, 25 percent in 1990, and 19 percent in 2000. *Sohyo* was the largest national federation of Japanese labor in 1960, but second to the more conservative *Domei* by 1967. In 1987, a new national labor organization, the Japanese Trade Union Confederation (***Rengo***), was formed under Domei's leadership. *Sohyo* joined *Rengo* two years later. This development marked the end of the militant labor movement in postwar Japan and inevitably weakened the power of workers relative to management and that of the JSP relative to the LDP. It also reflected the growing global influence of the free-market ideology and the faith in labor market flexibility that were hallmarks of the governments of President Ronald Reagan in the United States and Prime Minister Margaret Thatcher in the United Kingdom.

Japanese politics in the last decades of the twentieth century was rocked by a series of political scandals, many of which implicated top LDP leaders. In the Lockheed scandal of 1976, for example, a former prime minister, Kakuei Tanaka, was charged with, and later found guilty of, accepting bribery from the Lockheed Corporation for his intervention in the purchase of Lockheed's planes by a Japanese airline. In the Recruit scandal of 1988, more than a dozen LDP leaders and senior bureaucrats were charged with receiving expensive gifts and contributions from a job-placement company.

Such scandals hurt the LDP's electoral performance, but not to the extent of threatening its control of government, until the country was hit by another sudden economic downturn in the early 1990s. Unlike the oil shocks of the 1970s, the new economic trouble

was blamed directly on a series of wrong or unwise policies implemented by the LDP government. The first of these missteps dated back to the mid-1980s when the government drastically reduced interest rates on loans in order to stimulate the economy. The enormous amount of money borrowed as a result of this policy went mostly into highly speculative investments in the stock and real estate markets, sending the prices in both skyrocketing. This brought about a wild but short-lived boom, soon to be remembered as the "bubble economy."

The specter of runaway inflation scared the government into putting on the brakes by raising the interest rate as drastically and abruptly as it had cut it in 1986. These actions popped the bubble, but they also killed the engine of economic growth, throwing Japan into a sudden recession. The government then reversed gears again, cutting interest rates sharply during the first half of the 1990s, but without any success in restarting the country's economic engine.

From 1955 to 1990, Japan had been viewed as an "uncommon democracy" under the seemingly permanent rule by a powerful conservative party in a stable and cozy alliance with an even more powerful administrative bureaucracy. This image of the country was shattered in the last decade of the twentieth century: Japan was no longer economically superdynamic or politically superstable, and the once-dominant LDP and the once-prestigious national bureaucracy were now widely perceived both at home and abroad as bungling, and often corrupt, amateurs.

The first straw in the wind that the political times were changing in Japan was the LDP's failure, for the first time since its founding in 1955, to maintain its majority position in the House of Councilors (the upper house) of the National Diet in 1989. This was followed by the LDP's even more dramatic defeat in the 1993 general election of the much more powerful House of Representatives and the subsequent formation of two multiparty coalition governments without the LDP's participation and, in short order, another made up of the LDP and its long-time principal socialist rivals, by then renamed the Social Democratic Party.[14]

The LDP also suffered another embarrassing defeat in the 1998 elections for the House of Councilors, when it lost more than 25 percent of the seats it was contesting. Since 1993, the LDP has remained a partner, and the senior partner after 1996, in a series of coalition governments, but it has never regained the predominant position it had held from the mid-1950s.

The continuing political instability and uncertainty in Japan have so far not directly threatened the basic strength and health of its democratic system. But combined with a protracted and worsening economic recession, the political stalemate could drive the disillusioned electorate to reject the current constitutional form of Japanese democracy and move toward support for truly radical change. Thus, at the dawn of the new millennium, Japan appeared to stand at another potentially hazardous political crossroads as it has done several times since it entered the modern world one and a half centuries ago.

Themes and Implications

Historical Junctures and Political Themes

The fact that Japan joined the modern world of states in the late nineteenth century after two and a half centuries in a weak economic and military position compared with the more developed and powerful Western nations has strongly colored the Japanese perception of, and attitude toward, the rest of the world. To pre–World War II Japanese leaders, the world was divided between powerful, imperious, and self-aggrandizing states, on the one hand, and powerless, often conquered, and humiliated states, on the other.

To survive in such a world, a state had to build strong armed forces and develop a highly productive industrial economy—Japan's policy during most of the prewar period—or secure the protection of a powerful ally—Japan's policy since World War II. The experiences during World War II, particularly the atomic bombs, led most Japanese to abandon their faith in an independent military force as a way to ensure their national security. The only alternative now was alliance, or at least cooperation, with other nations, particularly the most powerful ones. Contemporary Japan is thus an avowed internationalist state, but with a degree of realist, even fatalistic, cynicism in its view of international relations. This element of cynicism often makes the Japanese appear to the rest of the world, including their allies and trading partners, to be unreliable and at times even treacherous.

Japan's entry into the modern world also exposed the country to the democratic idea. By the 1890s, Japan had become a nominally constitutional monarchy with a partially elected parliament and vocal political parties. Its government was faced with persistent popular demands for more democracy and greater participation in government. But pre–World War II Japan remained far more committed to rapid industrialization and military buildup than to democratization. Nor was it committed to social justice and economic equality among its people. Prejudice and discrimination against descendants of the medieval outcaste classes, for example, continued until after World War II, as did the prejudice and discrimination against women.

Democracy became fully accepted both ideologically and institutionally in Japan only after 1945. Nonetheless, the experiment with democratic government in prewar Japan, however half-hearted and ultimately unsuccessful it may have been, helped the Japanese accept the idea of democracy and practice it with considerable skill and success in the postwar period. This history and experience contribute to the durability and stability of democracy in contemporary Japan. Candidates and their supporters in Japanese elections may make liberal use of money as a means to influence voters' decisions, as do their counterparts in the United States. But tampering with ballot boxes or refusing to accept the verdict of an election are virtually unheard of in Japan.

Meiji Japan developed an advanced industrial economy in a country that lacked both the natural resources and the modern technologies long thought to be essential for industrialization. The method involved extensive and systematic intervention by the state in the management of the national economy, later known as **industrial policy.** As discussed in Section 2, this approach was spectacularly successful in both prewar and postwar Japan, and it was studied and copied by many other nations, especially those in East Asia. The approach, however, ceased to work as effectively in the global economy of the late twentieth century, as economic national boundaries virtually disappeared and the role of the state in the economy significantly declined. As the Asian markets for Japanese goods collapsed one by one in the latter half of the 1990s, Japan found itself mired in a protracted recession that seemed to defy any industrial policy–based remedy.

The Japanese began to develop a strong sense of national identity early in their history, and among its elite as early as the late seventh century. This was due partly to their nation's high degree of ethnic homogeneity and partly to the deliberate construction and propagation of a nationalist ideology by its early rulers. Japan's insular position also helped by enabling its rulers in the Tokugawa period to pursue an effective isolationist policy for two and a half centuries. The early development of a national identity tended to suppress the growth of strong regional, communal, and class-based collective identities.

Implications for Comparative Politics

Japan occupies an intermediate or borderline position among the states in the contemporary world in several senses. It is geographically and ethnically an Asian nation, but the patterns of its political and economic development have more in common with those of some North American and Western European nations than those of its Asian neighbors. It was a late developer in modernization and economic development relative to some Western nations, notably Britain and the United States, but an early developer compared to most others. Once one of the most aggressive militarist nations, it is now one of the most pacifistic. Its intermediate position in these and other aspects makes Japan an exceptionally interesting and versatile case to be compared with either advanced Western industrial nations or newly industrialized or developing non-Western nations.

Nonetheless, Japan's geographical, historical, and cultural attributes make it particularly sensible and interesting to compare Japanese politics—its past, present, and future—with those of other Asian nations, especially those in the Confucian cultural zone of Northeast Asia: China, Taiwan, and North and South Korea. Japan also shares the "rice paddy culture" and has had close historical ties with most nations in Southeast Asia as well. This culture has encouraged, on the one hand, early development of sophisticated water- and watershed-management, irrigation, and hydraulic engineering technologies necessary for the successful cultivation of rice and, on the other, certain humility and deference to the forces and whims of nature, often verging on fatalism. The culture lies behind many traditional and contemporary religious rites, festivals, and art forms throughout the region.

The evident physical and cultural similarities and affinities between Japan and other East Asian nations encourage us to try to understand and explain differences between them through comparative analysis.[15] Why, for example, did Japan begin to modernize its political system and social institutions and industrialize its economy so much earlier and apparently more successfully than the others, despite their physical and cultural similarities? Why has Japan experienced a stable one-party rule in a democratic system, while most others have experienced either stable but authoritarian government or unstable multiparty politics? And does the Japanese experience with modernization, industrialization, and democratization lend itself to meaningful reference, if not emulation, by other East Asian nations?

On the other hand, Japan's geographical, historical, and cultural attributes are markedly different from those of nations in Western Europe and North America. Yet politics and economy in medieval and especially modern Japan also share a number of similar characteristics with some nations in those two regions. Why, for example, did the Japanese develop a national identity and unite the nation as early and as fast as, or even earlier and faster than, most Western European nations? Why did Japan succeed in modernizing its politics and society and industrializing its economy as quickly and as effectively as, if not more quickly and more effectively than, most nations in Western Europe and North America?

This line of inquiry might lead to an attempt to explain in particular the similarities between modern Japan and modern Germany. Both entered the modern world about the same time in the nineteenth century, pursued rapid economic development, became major military powers by the early twentieth century, fought and lost World War II, were occupied and democratized by their wartime enemies, and returned to the postwar world as two of the most economically powerful and politically stable democracies. How can we explain these remarkable similarities? What lessons may we learn from the two nations' experiences?

Japan lends itself, as few other nations do, to important comparisons with nations in very different geographic regions and cultural zones of the world. The sections that follow suggest a number of specific aspects of Japanese politics that invite comparisons with those of one or more nations in Asia, Europe, and North America.

Section ❷ Political Economy and Development

Politics and economics often seem to move in tandem as if they were two sides of the same coin. That is certainly the impression one gets from a glance at the history of modern Japan. For example, economic development was one of Meiji Japan's two central objectives and commitments at its birth in the mid-nineteenth century, as suggested by its official slogan, "rich nation with a strong army." Moreover, the Japanese state thrived in the subsequent decades as long as its economy grew at a rapid and steady pace. But after World War I, as its economy fell into a serious and protracted slump, the Japanese state began to face domestic political turmoil. The devastation of its economy by the worldwide depression a decade later set Japan on a course of increasingly harsh authoritarian rule at home and militarist expansionism abroad. The course led eventually to a fatal war with the United States and its allies.

Politics and economics in post–World War II Japan repeat the same story. Lessons learned the hard way led postwar Japan to abandon the "strong army" part of the earlier national agenda and concentrate on the "rich nation" part. This policy generated a long period of economic growth and political stability. The good times came to an end, however: the economic bubble burst in the 1990s, and at the beginning of the new century, Japan also found itself beset with deep political uncertainties.

It is thus hard to escape the conclusion that politics and economics in Japan are closely and presumably causally related to each other. This section looks in some detail at how they interact, in what institutional and cultural contexts, and with what significant effects on citizens' lives.

State and Economy

Wars and Japanese Economic Development

The rapid growth of the Japanese economy in the late 1950s through the early 1970s is rightly called an economic miracle. The impressive performance of the Japanese economy, however, did not begin after World War II. The economy had grown steadily by an average of 3 percent per year from the Meiji Restoration in 1868 through the early twentieth century and the growth rate accelerated to more than 5 percent in the 1930s. On the eve of World War II, Japan was already one of the prewar world's fastest-growing and most competitive economies.[16]

The rapid growth of the Japanese economy was due to a combination of domestic factors, such as government policy, the entrepreneurial talent and initiative of business leaders, and a hard-working, literate, and increasingly skilled work force. International factors and circumstances, including wars, were also significant. The Sino-Japanese War (1894–1895) and the Russo-Japanese War (1904–1905) contributed to the growth of Japanese heavy industry, especially the munitions industry. World War I was a windfall for Japanese business. Taking advantage of the disruption of the existing European-dominated trade networks caused by the war, especially in Asia, Japanese textile, steel, machine tool, chemical, and shipping industries quickly expanded. The wartime boom brought Japan's trade balance into the black for the first time in the nation's history.[17]

Even World War II, which devastated Japan physically and psychologically, was in a sense a blessing in disguise for its economy. The prewar Japanese economy had been hobbled with a structural problem that impeded growth and development: the grossly uneven distribution of income and wealth. Extensive poverty not only generated considerable social tension, but also prevented the formation of a sufficiently large domestic market for Japan's own manufactures, not to mention imports from abroad.

The Allied Occupation–sponsored reforms significantly reduced the concentration of wealth and economic power in Japan. The assets and control of the largest *zaibatsu* corporations were divided up into several new and independent firms. Well over half of Japan's urban workers were unionized by the end of the 1940s. Most of the landlord-owned farmland was redistributed among poor farmers, which reduced the tenant population from nearly 30 percent to about 5 percent of Japanese famers.[18] This latter measure transformed rural farmers from an important source of prewar political radicalism into one of the most reliable blocs of conservative (i.e., LDP) voting in postwar Japan.

Altogether, these changes vastly expanded Japan's middle class and its domestic consumer markets.

Furthermore, the Allied Occupation's demilitarization program forced Japan not only to disarm but also to get out of the arms trade. This freed Japan from the heavy burden of military spending, which had swallowed up about one-third of the total budget in the early 1930s and three-quarters at the beginning of the war in the Pacific. Henceforth, Japan was able to devote its capital, labor, and technology almost exclusively to the production of goods and services for civilian consumption. This shift soon helped facilitate Japan's emergence as one of the most productive, competitive, and wealthiest nations in the postwar world.

The Korean War of the 1950s and the Vietnam War of the 1960s were also highly beneficial for the Japanese economy. Japanese factories were the main suppliers of the goods and services required by the U.S. military during both wars, which triggered a series of long economic booms. By the time these war-induced booms ended in the early 1970s, Japan had become the second largest market economy in the world.

The cold war contributed to the Japanese economic miracle too. U.S.-Soviet rivalry led to a dramatic shift in American policy toward both Germany and Japan. By 1948, Washington's primary objectives were no longer the total demilitarization and democratization of both occupied nations, but their swift economic recovery and incorporation into the U.S.-led anticommunist bloc. After China came under communist rule in 1949 and the Korean War broke out in 1950, Japan's new role as a key ally of the United States in Asia became even more evident. Japan was granted privileged access to the export markets and advanced industrial technologies of the United States and its allies. This helped Japan turn itself into a formidable export machine that was producing large trade surpluses by the mid-1960s.

From 1947 to 1951, the United States helped Japan rebuild its war-devastated economy by providing goods, including food, worth about $1.8 billion. The occupation authorities also helped the Japanese government overcome postwar economic chaos, especially rampant inflation, by balancing the government budget, raising taxes, imposing price and wage freezes, and resuming limited foreign trade. After Japan regained its independence in 1952, the United States continued to help by opening its markets to Japanese exports and granting Japanese firms access to advanced industrial technology developed by U.S. firms. The United States supported Japan's admission to the United Nations, the International Monetary Fund (IMF), the World Bank, and the General Agreement on Tariffs and Trade (GATT). Membership in such international organizations helped Japan gain access to raw materials, merchandise and capital markets, and advanced industrial technology and scientific information.

In the late 1970s and the early 1980s, surging Japanese exports began to be viewed by some countries, especially the United States, as a serious threat to their own industries. This led to a series of policies aimed at slowing the growth of Japanese imports. Deprived of their former privileged position in the American market, Japanese manufacturers faced increasingly intense competition not only abroad but also at home, where Japan's heavily protected markets were gradually forced open to foreign imports by rising international pressure. Under these changing circumstances, the annual growth rate of the Japanese economy fell from over 10 percent in the 1960s to about 4.5 percent in the 1970s and 1980s. Although the economy appeared to rebound in the late 1980s, this was largely a reflection of the bubble economy created by hyperactive stock and real estate markets. When the bubble burst at the end of the decade, coinciding with the end of the cold war, the Japanese economy slipped into a protracted recession, with the growth rate dipping below zero by 1997 amid the Asia-wide financial crisis. This spelled the end of the "economic miracle."

The State's Role in the Economy

The actions of the government have played a key role in the development of the modern Japanese economy from the very beginning. In the mid-nineteenth century, the Meiji state founded and operated munitions factories, mines, railroads, telegraph and telephone companies, and textile mills. Within a decade and a half, most of these businesses were sold at token prices to private entrepreneurs, some of whom subsequently emerged as heads of huge and powerful *zaibatsu* conglomerates.[19] During the rest of the nineteenth century and especially the first forty years of the twentieth century, these formidable and increasingly transnational corporate empires dominated Japanese industry. The *zaibatsu* spearheaded the rapid expansion of the economy in cooperation with an ambitious, disciplined, and highly nationalistic state bureaucracy.[20] The bureaucracy provided a variety of incentives for rapid expansion to *zaibatsu*-affiliated firms: direct subsidies, tax breaks, tariff protection, and the construction of roads, railroads, port facilities, and communications networks.

The state's role as the patron and protector of domestic industry continued after the post–World War II Allied Occupation. In fact, no sooner had the occupation ended in 1952 than the Japanese government began to devise and implement policies and programs to jump-start the war-ravaged economy. Under what became known as industrial policy, the government provided investment funds, tax breaks, foreign exchange, and foreign technologies to specifically targeted strategic industries, including electric power, steel, transportation, and coal mining. Subsequently added to this package of special favors for the chosen industries was a system of informal government counsel known as **administrative guidance.** Such counsel often led to mergers and the formation of cartels, which gained significant advantages in competing with domestic rivals and foreign competitors.

Over the years, the benefits of industrial policy shifted to the semiconductor, computer, aerospace, and other high-tech industries. The forms of government favors also changed. The new strategies included nontariff barriers against foreign imports, public funds for corporate research and development projects, and joint public-private projects for development of cutting-edge technologies.[21] As Japan's gross national product (GNP) grew and its trade balance sheet began to show chronic surpluses after the mid-1960s, Japanese industrial policy in general and trade policy in particular began to draw increasingly vocal foreign criticism. By then, many Japanese manufacturers and traders had grown strong enough to compete successfully in international markets without as much government help as before. These circumstances led to a gradual withdrawal of the Japanese state from the private sector of the economy. Nevertheless, the Japanese economy, especially its agricultural sector, remains heavily protected from foreign competition.

The hardest agricultural market for foreigners to enter is the huge rice market (about 10 million tons per year). Until the early 1990s, LDP-dominated Japanese governments had maintained a nearly total ban on the import of foreign rice in response to the politically powerful farmers. A sudden shortage caused by an exceptionally poor crop in 1993 led the first non-LDP government since 1955 to permit the import of about 2 million tons of foreign rice. At the end of that same year, as part of a series of multilateral trade negotiations held under GATT auspices, Japan agreed to expand import quotas gradually, from 3 percent of domestic consumption in 1995 to 8 percent by 2000. This deal was made acceptable to angry Japanese farmers by giving them a little over 6 trillion yen (then about $60 billion) compensation. At the end of 1998, however, the Japanese government decided, with the farmers' acquiescence, to replace the quotas on imported rice with tariffs at prohibitive rates (about 1,000 percent ad valorem) beginning in the spring of 1999.

Japan's financial sector has been under as strong or even stronger state control and protection. Administrative guidance has led the nation's major banks and securities firms to form among themselves networks of mutual cooperation and assistance. These have been backed by an implicit government commitment to bail out those in such serious trouble that the networks alone cannot rescue them. In other words, the state has assumed an implicit lender of last resort role that has helped weak and internationally uncompetitive banks and securities firms survive and burden the Japanese economy in the long recession of the 1990s. Government policy failures have come under increasing criticism as an important cause of the prolonged recession. The government has been accused especially of putting off the badly needed structural reform of the banking system, which is sinking under the weight of bad loans that keep growing as stock and real estate prices keep falling.

The Financial Services Agency, set up in January 2001 to help devise such reforms, has since mediated a series of bank mergers that has created some of the largest financial institutions in the world. This, however, has not helped to move the huge amount of money that still sits in their safes to businesses starved of funds. As a result, more than 19,000 firms—most of them small businesses, which have long driven the Japanese economy as the major source of innovation and competitive power—went bankrupt in 2001 alone, and others continue to follow. The creation of the giant banks has therefore not helped to create new jobs, spark new demand, and lift Japan out of the decade-long recession. The banking system remains one of the most vulnerable sectors of the Japanese economy.

Underlying this type of policy failure is an entrenched political system that endows central ministry bureaucrats with immense discretionary power to guide the nation's industries in murky ways effectively removed from public view because of highly inadequate rules concerning the disclosure of information about the activities of government officials. A thorough revamping of this system was at the core of the structural reform that Prime Minister Koizumi pledged to take on when he assumed office in early 2001, but so far there have been few tangible results.

Society and Economy

The Private Sector

The private industrial sector of the Japanese economy is characterized by the interdependence and networking among a small number of giant firms, on the one hand, and a vast number of small firms, on the other. In 2002, nearly 98 percent of some 772,000 companies in the manufacturing sector were small businesses with fewer than one hundred employees per firm. Most big businesses are affiliated with one or another of several huge business groups, commonly known as *keiretsu.* Each *keiretsu* is composed of a major bank and several large manufacturing, trading, shipping, construction, and insurance companies. It is a group of firms of comparable size and capability horizontally linked with one another. There are also more than a dozen similar but smaller groups, including those built around the major automobile manufacturers, notably Toyota and Nissan. These too are often called *keiretsu,* but they are characterized more by vertical ties that link several large firms to numerous smaller ones. The latter serve as subcontractors to the former.

The Mitsubishi Group is a good example of a horizontally organized *keiretsu.* Although it is a descendant of a pre–World War II *zaibatsu* group with the same name, today's Mitsubishi Group is no longer controlled by a single family. It is composed of about thirty formally independent, coequal corporations whose presidents form an informal executive committee called the Friday Club, which, as its name suggests, meets once a week. Each of the member corporations is a leading firm in its own line of business, including Mitsubishi automobiles, Nikon cameras, and Kirin beer.

In contrast, the Toyota Group, led by Toyota Motor Corporation, represents a vertically organized *keiretsu.* Under the automobile maker's direct control are a dozen large corporations that maintain subcontracting relationships with about 250 small firms. In turn, many of these subcontractors hand down some of their work to even smaller firms. In other words, the Toyota Group is a huge pyramid made up of several hundred legally independent but operationally interdependent firms.

The subcontracting system provides small businesses with jobs and access to both markets and some of the advanced technologies in the possession of the big businesses within their group. The big businesses benefit even more, since they can avoid keeping certain kinds of workers on their regular payroll by using subcontractors' employees on an as-needed basis. During an economic downturn, the big firms protect themselves by reducing orders placed with their subcontractors or delaying payment for orders already filled.

Both types of *keiretsu* are now faced with the threat posed by the rapidly increasing acquisition of large ownership shares of Japanese firms by foreign investors. As Japanese businesses struggled to survive the hard times in the last decade of the twentieth century by restructuring themselves, many came under foreign firms' control through mergers and acquisitions. *Keiretsu* have not perished in the process, but ties among many of their members have been substantially loosened.

Small businesses in Japan hire large numbers of temporary and part-time workers, most of them women. Part-timers are paid, on average, far less than half as much per hour as regular employees. The wage differentials between regular employees (mostly male) and temporary and part-time employees (mostly female) help keep production costs down and profits up. This **dual-structure system,** or double-deck system, has also contributed to the international competitiveness of Japan's major export companies. Big firms pass on part of the savings to some of their regular employees in the form of job security and wages that rise with the length of service almost independently of employees' performance.

Women account for about 50 percent of Japan's labor force. Their ranks have grown in recent decades for several reasons, including women's rising educational level. In a little over one decade, between 1990 and 2001, the rate of women high school graduates who go to junior college or university increased more than 10 percent, from about 37.4 percent to 48.5 percent.[22] Women with college diplomas tend to work outside the home before, and increasingly after, they marry. Another reason is the diffusion of home appliances such as refrigerators and washing machines, which free housewives from many of the traditional housekeeping chores and permit them to seek part-time jobs. The downturn in the overall economic conditions since the 1970s, especially the significant deterioration in the 1990s, is still another reason. Many families find it increasingly hard to make ends meet with one income. The growing number of women seeking jobs for additional income has been matched by the increasing need of service industries for low-paid temporary and part-time employees. The average female worker's pay in the manufacturing and service sectors was 65.5 percent of the average male worker's in Japan in 2002, compared to 81.3 percent in the United Kingdom and 87.8 percent in Sweden.[23]

Another well-known characteristic of the Japanese economy is the close, and normally cooperative, relationships between labor unions and management. As discussed in Section 1, several labor federations merged in the late 1980s into a larger national organization, the General Confederation of Japanese Labor (*Rengo*). This merger was the result of the growing weakness of the labor movement, which had seen a decline in the proportion of unionized labor in Japan's industrial work force fall from well over 50 percent in the late 1940s to less than half that by the end of the 1980s. In addition, many union leaders, especially those in the private sector, had lost much of their political control over their rank-and-file members and had become increasingly willing to cooperate with management. While the larger unions continue to participate in the nationally coordinated annual wage negotiations with employers, known as the **spring labor offensive,** the radicalism and militancy that once characterized labor's position in such negotiations have steadily diminished.

By the time Japan's economic miracle ended around 1990, it had become a nation virtually free of violent labor disputes and, more generally, free of a sharp popular awareness of class divisions among its people. Thanks to a generally egalitarian pattern of income distribution (see Table 1), most Japanese came to identify themselves as members of the middle class, that is, as economically well off as most other Japanese. This popular perception, however, began to change in the late 1990s as the Japanese economy not only ceased to grow, but actually shrank.

Employment, Social Security, and Taxation

Japanese workers earn wages comparable to those earned by most North American and Western European workers, though they are paid in a somewhat different way. The typical Japanese wage or salary consists of relatively low basic monthly pay, several allowances of variable amounts, and substantial semiannual bonuses. Allowances are paid, for example, for dependents, housing costs, and commuting costs, and the two bonuses, paid in midsummer and at year-end, often amount to nearly one-third of the basic annual wage. Retirement benefits for most employees consist of lump-sum severance pay equal to about thirty-five months' pay and, for those who satisfy the age and length-of-service requirements, a contribution-based pension. Many employees of large firms are provided with company-subsidized housing and the privilege of using company-owned recreational, sporting, and vacationing facilities.

Table 1

Income Distribution in Major Industrial Nations

		Percentage Share of National Income		
Nation	Data Year	Bottom 20%	Middle 60%	Top 20%
Japan	1993	10.6	53.8	35.7
United States	1997	5.2	48.5	46.4
Britain	1991	6.6	50.5	43.0
Germany	1994	8.2	53.4	38.5
France	1995	7.2	52.6	40.2

Source: World Development Report 2000/2001: Attacking Poverty by World Bank. Copyright © 2000 by the International Bank for Reconstruction and Development/The World Bank. Used by permission of Oxford University Press, Inc.

As Japan's economy continued to grow through the 1970s, the demand for young and cheap labor continued to grow. But the birth and population growth rates began to level off in the mid-1950s and to decline in the mid-1970s. The result was a perennially tight labor market and low unemployment rate, conditions welcome to most Japanese citizens. In order to attract and keep skilled workers under these circumstances, many employers would guarantee such workers, explicitly or implicitly, security of employment until retirement at a certain age–usually the mid-fifties. This practice was known as the **lifetime employment** system.

Conditions, however, changed radically in the early 1990s as the Japanese economy fell into a protracted recession. The hard times forced many firms to abandon the traditional practices of lifetime employment and virtually automatic annual pay raises. Many firms began to pay their employees on the basis of performance

("merit") and retire or transfer them to lower-paying positions, often in subsidiary firms, at much younger ages than previously. As in the United States, increasing numbers of people of all ages started to work on a part-time, consulting, work-on-call, or work-at-home basis.

These changes caused considerable hardships to many families, particularly because the Japanese social security system is relatively undeveloped compared to its counterparts in most Western European nations. It was not until after World War II that the Japanese government made a systematic effort to provide a minimum level of social security for all citizens. The development of a comprehensive national social security system was mandated by the 1947 constitution: "In all spheres of life, the State shall use its endeavors for the promotion and extension of social welfare and security, and of public health." During the four decades following the Allied Occupation, a number of state-sponsored and

Current Challenges: *The Protracted Recession*

Known as a country with prohibitively high consumer prices in the 1970s and 1980s, Japan remains in the early twenty-first century one of the most expensive countries not only for foreign visitors but also for its own citizens. According to a 1999 study by Japan's Economic Planning Agency, compared with New York City, dry cleaning in Tokyo cost about 20 percent more, a man's shirt 40 percent, one liter of milk 50 percent, one kilo of oranges and granulated sugar 60 percent, movie tickets 70 percent, one can of beer 80 percent, one kilo of rice 170 percent, and golfing fee per golfer 200 percent!

Nonetheless, the consumer price gaps between Japan and other advanced industrial nations have slowly but steadily shrunk, mainly due to a gradual but continuing decline in the Japanese prices. Alone among the major industrial nations, Japan has experienced a steady and uninterrupted streak of negative monthly changes in consumer prices since mid-1999. Even housing prices, which had risen sixfold in the quarter-century between 1960 and 1985, have followed the same downward trend of other prices since the mid-1900s.

The lower prices should be a boon to Japanese citizens and foreign visitors alike. They are not necessarily so, however, when they result from a protracted recession with its unpleasant, often devastating, causes and consequences. The current Japanese recession, which began with the burst of the "bubble economy" of the 1980s, has depressed not only consumer prices but also investment and employment. The decline in private investments reflects in large measure a decline in funds available from banks and other lending institutions saddled with huge piles of nonperforming loans, many dating back to the bubble economy days. The decline in private funds available for investment was made up for largely by public funds generated not by tax revenue, which has also declined, but by government bonds regularly floated by both the national and local governments.

As a result, the outstanding balance of long-term public bonds, to be eventually repaid by the taxpayers of either this or future generations, has come to amount to about 700 trillion yen, or 140 percent of Japan's GDP. How to deal with this mounting public debt is one of the biggest challenges that the Japanese government and people face.

wholly or partially state-financed social security programs were established. But in the wake of the 1973 oil crisis, the government began to attempt to shift the major burden of financing the rapidly expanding social security system to the private sector.

This so-called Japanese-style welfare society approach failed to contain the growth of public or private welfare expenditures in subsequent years. Today, social security claims over 20 percent of the annual government budget and is the largest public expenditure item in Japan. The tax-financed pension, medical insurance, unemployment insurance, and workers' compensation programs provide virtually all Japanese citizens some social security benefits. However, given the extremely high cost of living in contemporary Japan, the amounts of the benefits are far from adequate to meet the needs of most citizens.

Like citizens in most other countries, Japanese pay both direct and indirect taxes. The former include income, corporate, inheritance, and land-value taxes; the latter include consumption (sales), alcohol, tobacco, petroleum, and stock exchange taxes. A capital gains tax was introduced in 1989. The maximum rates of national and local income taxes are, as of 2003, 37 percent and 13 percent, respectively. The average Japanese taxpayer pays about 23 percent of his or her annual income in national and local taxes. This is only a little lower than the rate paid by the average U.S. taxpayer but considerably lower than that paid by the average Western European taxpayer. The average Japanese, however, does not enjoy as many tax-supported social welfare benefits and public amenities as the average Western European does. This makes the average Japanese consumer chary of nonessential purchases, an attitude that collectively helps to suppress overall demand and prolong the recession. The Japanese government has begun to address the issue but has not yet solved it.

Japan and the International Political Economy

The Trading State

Since the Meiji Restoration of 1868, Japan's government and business leaders have pursued rapid industrialization initially by exporting relatively cheap products of labor-intensive industries, such as textiles, and then by exporting higher-value-added products of more capital-intensive industries, including iron and steel, shipbuilding, and machinery. If implemented successfully, as it was in Japan, such an export-led strategy of development makes it possible for a nation with few natural, financial, and technological resources and a small home market to industrialize by importing resources from abroad and paying for them with foreign exchange earned by exports. Since the 1960s a number of developing nations have followed this strategy. The best-known examples are the newly industrializing countries in East Asia: South Korea, Taiwan, and Singapore. By the early 1990s they had been joined by other Asian nations, such as Thailand, Malaysia, Indonesia, and China.

By the mid-1970s, Japan's export-led development strategy had paved the way for the country to become an economic superpower, with the second largest GNP after the United States.[24] By the early 1990s, Japan was the leading source of official development assistance (ODA) to the Third World (a position it held until 2001), the third largest source of foreign direct investments after the United States and Britain, and the third largest trading nation after the United States and Germany.

Nearly 90 percent of Japan's $479 billion exports in 2000 consisted of industrial goods, especially machinery and automobiles, and 40 percent of its $379 billion imports in the same year consisted of fuels, industrial raw materials, and food. Japan continues to import raw materials, turn them into industrial products, and sell them back to the rest of the world, often at large profits. However, Japanese imports of such industrial goods as machinery, equipment, and textiles from neighboring Asian nations have vastly increased as industrialization has progressed in the region.

Japan continues to have chronic deficits (imports exceeding exports) in its trade balances with nations that export fuels, raw materials, and food, including most Middle Eastern nations, some South American nations such as Brazil and Chile, and Canada, Australia, and New Zealand. These deficits are more than made up for by chronic and larger surpluses (exports exceeding imports) in Japan's trade with the United States, some major European nations such as Germany and Britain, and, above all, most nations in Asia with the exception of China and Vietnam. In 2000, Japan's overall trade surplus (exports minus imports) amounted

Table 2

Japanese Trade with the World and the United States (US$ millions)

	1970	1975	1980	1985	1990	1995	2000
Exports to World	19,316	54,734	121,413	174,015	280,374	443,265	479,175
Imports from World	18,880	49,706	132,210	118,029	216,846	335,991	379,450
Balance with World	436	5,028	−10,797	55,986	63,528	107,274	99,725
Exports to U.S.	6,015	11,149	31,649	65,278	90,322	127,193	142,487
Imports from U.S.	5,565	11,608	24,448	25,793	52,369	64,039	72,180
Balance with U.S.	450	−459	7,201	39,485	37,953	63,154	70,307

Sources: Keizai kikakucho chosakyoku [Research Bureau, Economic Planning Agency], ed., *Keizai yoran* (Heisei 6-nen ban) [Economic handbook, 1994 edition] (Tokyo: Ministry of Finance Printing Office, 1994), 188–189, 192–193; Somucho tokeikyoku [Management and Coordination Agency Bureau of Statistics], ed., *Sekai no tokei* [Statistics of the World] (Tokyo: Ministry of Finance Printing Office, 1998), 202, 220–221; Somusho tokeikyoku and Tokei kenshujo [Ministry of Public Management, Home Affairs, and Posts and Telecommunications Bureau of Statistics, and Statistics Institute], eds., *Sekai no tokei 2002* [Statistics of the World] (Tokyo: Ministry of Finance Printing Office, 2002), 226, 243–244.

to about $116 billion.[25] By far the largest of Japan's trading partners and also the largest contributor to Japan's overall trade surplus has been the United States (see Table 2). The U.S. contribution to Japan's trade surplus in 2000 was about $70 billion, or more than 60 percent of the total.

Washington has repeatedly charged Tokyo with unfair trade practices of one kind or another, and the two governments have been engaged in trade disputes and negotiations for the last four decades, although they have become noticeably less acrimonious during the past decade. In the 1950s, Japan was accused of adopting a protectionist policy of high tariffs on foreign manufactured goods. After tariffs were substantially lowered in the 1960s, the U.S. criticism shifted to a variety of **nontariff barriers,** such as import quotas, discriminatory application of safety and technical standards against imports, and a government procurement policy favoring domestic products.[26] In the 1980s, Japan was accused of creating and maintaining structural impediments to foreign imports and investments, including a complex domestic distribution system, collusive business practices among *keiretsu* companies, and exorbitant rents in metropolitan areas. According to U.S. critics, these practices made it virtually impossible for U.S. and other foreign companies to enter Japan's domestic markets and successfully compete with Japanese producers. Japanese companies were also charged with engaging in predatory trade practices abroad, such

as dumping (selling goods at prices lower than those charged at home).

Over the years, Japan has become more sensitive and responsive to such criticisms, and it has removed or significantly reduced the tariff and nontariff import barriers and abandoned many of the alleged predatory trade practices. By the mid-1980s, there was growing realization among Japanese both within and outside the government that Japan, as a trade-dependent nation, not only had greatly benefited from the global system of free trade that had been constructed largely on U.S. initiative and under Washington's leadership but could not continue to prosper without it. This realization has made them increasingly willing to abandon most of the protectionist policies and practices that had once served them well but had begun to hurt their long-term national interests.

Meanwhile, China has replaced Japan as the trading partner of the United States with the largest surplus in their bilateral trade account. Fueled by surging foreign investments that flow into the country, lured by its huge market, low production costs, highly skilled labor, and ample and cheap land, China has become the "world factory" and a formidable competition for Japanese industry. As Japanese manufacturers shift their plants to China, the resulting negative impact on domestic industry, including rising unemployment, has become an intractable and highly divisive issue in Japanese politics.

Japan in International Organizations

Japan is a leading member of the United Nations and most of its specialized agencies, including the IMF and the International Bank for Reconstruction and Development (the World Bank). It joined these latter two organizations only a few months after the end of the Allied Occupation in 1952 and is today the second largest subscriber to each organization's equity and operating funds after the United States. Since each of the five largest subscribers has the right to appoint its own representative on the board of executive directors, Japan effectively has a permanent seat on the boards of the IMF and the World Bank.

Japan joined the UN only in 1956, mainly because of the initial opposition of the Soviet Union to the admission of a major U.S. ally at the height of the cold war. Japan is now the second largest contributor to the UN budget. Since the mid-1990s, it has been seeking, so far unsuccessfully, to join the United States, Britain, France, Russia, and China as a permanent member of the Security Council. Japan has been very active and visible in Asian and Pacific economic organizations. It is not only the largest contributor to the **Asian Development Bank (ADB)** but has also provided all its past governors. It is a founding member and a major promoter of the **Asia-Pacific Economic Cooperation (APEC)** forum and actively supports the **Association of Southeast Asian Nations (ASEAN).**

The Asia-Pacific region has been of special economic and strategic interest to Japan since the nineteenth century. The rising tide of regionalism around the world in recent years, highlighted by the consolidation and expansion of the European Union (EU), the conclusion of the North American Free Trade Agreement (NAFTA), and, above all, China's increasingly active involvement in the East Asian regional economy and politics, has reinforced Japan's interest in enhancing regional cooperation in its own backyard. So far, however, it has not significantly influenced, much less guided, the slow and erratic progress of East Asian or Asia-Pacific regionalism in the face of the growing Chinese power and the continuing stagnation of the Japanese economy.

Section ❸ Governance and Policy-Making

Often cited as a typical strong state, contemporary Japan is governed by coalitions of ruling party members of the national legislature and national civil servants. The latter develop the majority of new policies and draft the majority of new bills to be debated and voted into law by the former. The policies approved and laws enacted by legislators are then implemented by civil servants. In this process of governance and policy-making, civil servants, or bureaucrats, tend to lead, and legislators, or politicians, to follow, rather than the other way around. Policies and laws elicit diverse reactions from citizens and especially from organized special interests. Their reactions in turn lead bureaucrats and politicians to develop new policies and enact new laws. This section discusses various aspects of this cyclical process: its major participants, its institutional and cultural environment, and its significant consequences.

Organization of the State

Japan is a unitary state with forty-seven prefectures (provinces) that range from the entire island of Hokkaido, a little larger than the state of Maine, to Kagawa, about two-thirds the size of Rhode Island. Major cities, including Tokyo, Osaka, and Kyoto, are parts of prefectures bearing the same name. The prefectures are subdivided into 3,229 municipalities (as of 2000), ranging from large cities like Yokohama, with about 3.4 million people, to half a dozen villages with no more than a few hundred inhabitants. The prefectures and municipalities are subordinate, both economically and politically, to the central government and enjoy a much narrower range of decision-making power than their counterparts in federal states, such as the United States and Germany.

Under the 1947 Constitution, which remains in

force, Japan is a constitutional monarchy and a parliamentary democracy, much like Britain and Sweden. In theory, the people are sovereign. The emperor is no longer considered to be divine; he is merely the symbol of the nation and the unity of its people.

The Japanese people exercise their sovereign power through their elected representatives, who work at the national level through the highest organ of the state and its sole lawmaking body, the National Diet. The Diet designates the prime minister, who then forms a government by appointing other members of the cabinet. By law, at least half of the cabinet positions must be filled by members of the Diet; in practice, all but a very few have been filled by ruling party members of the Diet. Laws enacted by the Diet are implemented by the executive branch of government, which is led by the cabinet and operates through a national civil service. The cabinet is constitutionally subordinate and collectively answerable to the Diet. The national civil service operates under the direction of the cabinet and is therefore indirectly answerable to the Diet.

The constitution invests the Diet with the power to enact laws, approve the government budget, ratify international treaties, and audit the financial transactions of the state. The Diet is bicameral, consisting of an upper chamber, the House of Councilors, and a lower chamber, the House of Representatives. Both houses consist exclusively of popularly elected members. The lower house is the larger and more powerful of the two, with the power to override the opposition of the upper house in votes on the budget and ratification of treaties. The Diet also has the power to investigate any matter of national concern, whereas the prime minister and the cabinet have the obligation to report to the Diet on the state of the nation and its foreign relations. In fulfilling this obligation, cabinet ministers regularly attend meetings of Diet committees and answer members' questions.

In theory, the prime minister and the cabinet ("the government") serve only as long as they have the confidence of the Diet. If the House of Representatives passes a motion of no confidence against a cabinet or refuses to pass a motion of confidence in a cabinet, the government must either dissolve the lower house within ten days or resign. This leads either to the formation of a new cabinet or to a new lower house general election. For example, in 1993, a motion of no confidence against an LDP cabinet passed with the support of a dissident LDP faction. This led to splits in the ruling party and the birth of two splinter parties, which in turn led to the LDP's historic defeat in the general election that followed and the formation of the first non-LDP coalition government since the powerful conservative party was founded in 1955.

Constitutional theory notwithstanding, however, it is the cabinet rather than the Diet that has initiated most legislation and in effect made laws in the past. This has been mostly because members of the Diet have virtually no legislative staffs of their own, whereas cabinet ministers enjoy easy access to the substantial staff and resources of the civil service. During the LDP's long one-party rule, civil servants drafted the majority of bills. Most of these bills then passed the Diet with the unanimous support of ruling party members. By comparison, bills introduced by individual Diet members, especially those sponsored by opposition members alone, were few in number and far less successful; only those receiving nonpartisan support, and usually sponsored by a whole standing or ad hoc committee, enjoyed a good chance of passage.

The Japanese Monarchy and the Royal Family

Japan has the oldest surviving monarchy in the world. The present occupant of its Chrysanthemum Throne—so called after the flower chosen as the crest of the imperial family in 1868—Akihito, is the one hundred and twenty-fifth in an unbroken line of emperors and empresses, according to legend. His ancestors were Japan's actual rulers from the mid-sixth through the early tenth centuries and thereafter remained the nation's titular rulers until shortly after the end of World War II. Under the Meiji Constitution (1889–1947), the emperor was not only Japan's sovereign ruler but a demigod whose person was considered sacred and inviolable. The 1947 Constitution relegated the emperor to the status of a symbol of the Japanese state whose new sovereign was its people. Akihito's father, Hirohito (1901–1989), was thus the sovereign ruler of the Empire of Japan during the first half of his long reign (1926–1989) but a mere figurehead of the democratized Japan during the second half of his life.[27] The Japanese monarchy has survived both the devastating war and the far-reaching postwar reforms and continues to thrive.

Compared to his aloof and enigmatic father, who

led Japan into and out of the disastrous world war and whose role in that war remains controversial, Emperor Akihito is a far more modern and cosmopolitan monarch. An eleven-year-old boy at war's end, he lived through the austere early postwar years as an impressionable young man, mingled freely with classmates from ordinary families, learned English from a female American Quaker, and married a businessman's daughter (née Michiko Shoda). Nonetheless, the Japanese royal family remains sheltered and hidden from public view to a much greater extent than any of the Western European royal families. In this sense, the Japanese monarchy is an extraordinarily tradition-bound institution in the contemporary world.

Rigid adherence to the tradition of strict privacy and secrecy about all matters related to the imperial household has shielded the Japanese royal family from the constant and uncontrolled exposure in the mass media that has dogged British royalty in recent years.

But it has also severely restricted the personal life of members of the royal family and their contact with people outside the small circle of family members and their close friends. The resulting isolation from the public is likely to erode genuine public interest in, if not curiosity about, the royal family and its role, especially among young people.

The Executive

The Cabinet

As suggested above, the executive branch, led by the cabinet, is the source of most legislative and administrative initiatives in Japan. Moreover, the long dominance of the Diet by a single party, the LDP, has made the executive branch much stronger than one might infer from the constitutional definition of its position and status relative to the Diet.

Leaders: *Japan's Royal Family*

Emperor Akihito and Empress Michiko have two sons and one daughter. Both sons, Crown Prince Naruhito and Prince Fumihito, studied at Oxford University after graduating from a Japanese university, and both married commoners' daughters. The youngest child, Princess Sayako, also graduated from a Japanese university and has visited both Britain and the United States. Prince Fumihito's marriage to his college sweetheart, Kiko Kawashima, in 1990 was the year's biggest media event in a country where the royal family remains an object of intense popular interest, though no longer of awe and reverence. Crown Prince Naruhito's wedding in 1993 caused an even greater sensation, partly because the prince's apparent difficulty in finding a suitable and willing bride had been a hot topic in the tabloid press for several years. But it was also partly because his bride and the future empress, Masako Owada, was a young diplomat who had graduated from Harvard with a degree in economics and had also studied at Oxford and the University of Tokyo.

The nation's tabloid press, and many others, waited as long and as eagerly for the arrival of a child in the crown prince's family, an event that occurred on December 1, 2002. Had the newborn baby been a boy, he would have been automatically eligible to succeed his father, Crown Prince Naruhito, to the Chrysanthemum Throne. It was, however, a baby girl, a fact that rekindled an old controversy over the provision in the Imperial Household Law that limits eligibility to ascend the throne to male members of the imperial family. Since no boy has been born to any married couple in the imperial family in the past thirty-eight years or so and, after the Crown Prince and Prince Fumihito, the four most eligible to inherit the throne are Emperor Akihito's brother, uncle, and two cousins, all in their mid-fifties or older, the controversy takes on both seriousness and urgency. With an overwhelming majority of the nation's political leaders and people apparently in favor of "democratizing" the succession rule, the controversial section of the Imperial Household Law is likely to be amended in the near future to allow a female to succeed to the world's oldest throne.

The cabinet is headed by a prime minister who is elected by the Diet. Each house separately elects a candidate for prime minister by a simple majority during a plenary session. If different candidates are elected by the two houses, the one elected by the lower house becomes prime minister. If no candidate wins an absolute majority, a runoff election is held between the top two candidates. Until the LDP's defeat in the 1993 general election, the Diet had consistently elected the leader (i.e., president) of the LDP as prime minister. The LDP's party rules provide for the selection of the party's president by ballot. In practice, however, LDP presidents have been chosen as often by backroom negotiation among leaders of the several factions of LDP Diet members from among themselves. When an election was held, large amounts of money were often spent by the factions to buy votes, directly or indirectly, for their own candidates.

Once elected, the Japanese prime minister has nearly absolute authority to appoint or dismiss any member of his cabinet. (Although there is no legal restriction on the gender of the Japanese prime minister, no woman has ever held the office. One woman has served as the leader of a major party, the Social Democratic Party, and another of a minor one, the Conservative Party.) The appointment of members of an LDP cabinet has been dictated mainly by the prime minister's desire to maintain a balance of power among the several intraparty factions in order to preserve the unity of the party and prolong his own tenure as prime minister. The coalition cabinets that have governed the nation since August 1993, the first two of which did not include the LDP, have been composed of representatives of the coalition parties chosen on the basis of the same principle of balance among the several parties. In order to be appointed to a cabinet-level office in the Japanese government, one must have good standing (which simply means seniority, as a rule) in his or her faction or party but not necessarily special knowledge or experience in any particular policy area or areas.

The prime minister has the constitutional right to submit bills to the Diet in the name of the cabinet; report to the Diet on the state of the nation and its foreign relations; exercise control and supervision of the national civil service; and in rare cases, suspend a cabinet member's constitutionally guaranteed immunity from a legal action during his or her tenure in office.

The prime minister is also the nation's commander in chief and may order, subject to the Diet's consent, the Self-Defense Forces to take appropriate action in a national emergency. If a prime minister resigns or otherwise ceases to hold his office, the cabinet as a whole must also resign.

The executive powers and responsibilities of the Japanese cabinet are wide ranging. In addition to those common to the executive branch of government in most other industrial democracies, they include the following:

- Advising and taking responsibility for any of the emperor's actions that are of concern to the state (such as the promulgation of laws and international treaties, convocation of the Diet, dissolution of the House of Representatives, and receiving foreign ambassadors and ministers)
- Designating the chief justice of the Supreme Court, who is formally appointed by the emperor
- Appointing all other judges of the Supreme Court and those of the lower courts
- Calling the Diet into extraordinary session and the upper house into emergency session
- Approving expenditure of the state's reserve funds

In a sweeping reorganization of the national public service implemented in January 2001, many ministries and agencies were either consolidated or abolished, and, as a result, the membership of the cabinet underwent a significant change. As of mid-2002, it consisted of nineteen members, ten of whom each headed a ministry, one directed the Defense Agency, one chaired the National Public Safety Commission, and five had their offices within the Cabinet Office. The prime minister and the chief cabinet secretary completed the roster of the cabinet. Cabinet positions as of mid-2002 are listed in Table 3.

Although a minister in theory supervises the work of an entire ministry, his or her supervisory power and responsibility are often more nominal than real. (Recent cabinets have included one or two women.) This is largely because ministers are chosen, as a rule, not for their ability in a given policy area but on the basis of seniority in the ruling party or parties. Seniority is determined mainly by the number of times one has been reelected to the Diet. As a result, many cabinet members are inexperienced in the policy areas to which they are assigned and are at the mercy, rather

Table 3

Cabinet Positions (July 2002)

Prime Minister

Minister of Public Management, Home Affairs, Posts and Telecommunications

Minister of Justice

Minister of Foreign Affairs

Minister of Finance

Minister of Education, Culture, Sports, Science and Technology

Minister of Health, Labor and Welfare

Minister of Agriculture, Forestry, and Fisheries

Minister of Economy, Trade and Industry

Minister of Land, Infrastructure and Transport

Minister of the Environment

Chief Cabinet Secretary

Minister of State: Disaster Management

Minister of State: Defense

Minister of State: Okinawa and Northern Territories Affairs, Science and Technology Policy

Minister of State: Financial Services

Minister of State: Economic and Fiscal Policy

Minister of State: Administrative Reform, Regulatory Reform

Chairman of the National Public Safety Commission

than in command, of the career civil servants who are their subordinates.

Since every LDP faction and every coalition party has a long waiting list of candidates for appointment to cabinet posts, the prime minister is under constant pressure to replace incumbents with new people at short intervals. The result has been an average ministerial tenure of no more than a year or so. The short tenure denies cabinet members the time needed to learn the ropes of their ministry, reinforcing their dependence on career bureaucrats for even routine ministerial duties, including answering legislators' questions in the Diet.

The National Bureaucracy

At the core of the contemporary Japanese state are fifteen or so central government ministries, each with more or less exclusive jurisdiction over a specific area or areas of public administration, such as the ministries of

Finance; Public Management, Home Affairs, Postal Services, and Telecommunications; Economy, Trade, and Industry; Land, Infrastructure, and Transport; and Agriculture, Forestry, and Fisheries. Each ministry's mandate as defined by law and by practice includes both regulatory and custodial powers over individuals, corporations, and other organizations. The regulatory power is exercised mainly through the enforcement of legal and quasi-legal requirements for licenses, permits, or certificates for virtually any kind of activity with actual or potential effects on the public interest. The custodial power is used to provide various types of public assistance to private citizens and groups, such as subsidies and tax exemptions for particular industries. Abuse of these powers was at the root of the pervasive political corruption that has erupted in periodic and sensational scandals in postwar as well as prewar Japan.

Japan's central government ministries are all very much alike in organization and behavior. Each is headed by a minister and one or two senior vice ministers, one to three parliamentary secretaries, one vice minister, and one or two deputy ministers. The first three offices are held by members of the Diet, as a rule, while the last two are held by career officials of the ministry concerned. The core organization of a ministry consists of a minister's secretariat, several staff bureaus, and several line bureaus, each subdivided into divisions and departments. The staff bureaus are concerned mainly with broad policy issues, while the line bureaus are responsible for implementation of specific policies and programs. These core components are supplemented by, as a rule, several auxiliary organizations named variously as agencies, commissions, committees, institutes, and so forth.

For example, staff bureaus of the Ministry of Economy, Trade, and Industry (METI) initiate and develop policies and programs in the areas of industrial policy, international trade, economic cooperation, industrial technology and the environment, and information collection and processing. METI's line bureaus are responsible for the development and implementation of policies for all major manufacturing industries (for example, iron and steel, nonferrous metals, chemicals, industrial machinery, automobile, aircraft, weapons, and textiles). The ministry's work is supplemented by the work of its auxiliary organizations: the Natural

Resources and Energy Agency, Small and Medium Enterprise Agency, Japan Patent Office, and eight regional bureaus and their local offices. METI's predecessor, MITI (Ministry of International Trade and Industry), played a central role in the rehabilitation and development of the post–World War II Japanese economy by providing wide-ranging and nationally coordinated policy guidance and assistance to the nation's war-ravaged industries.[28]

As a result of the rapid turnover of political appointees among their senior officials, including the minister, senior vice ministers, and parliamentary secretaries, ministries are run in practice by career officials, namely, the vice minister and deputy ministers. These officials are civil servants with many years of service in the same ministry. A ministry is thus a bureaucracy with considerable autonomy and discretionary power of its own, particularly with regard to its internal organization and personnel decisions.

Ministerial autonomy has often verged on ministerial chauvinism and seriously interfered with cooperation among ministries. **Vertically divided administration** has thus been a common characterization of the way the Japanese civil service operated. For example, in the aftermath of the devastating earthquake that hit Kobe City in January 1995, ministerial egoism and parochialism were widely blamed for long delays, often with tragic consequences, in the Tokyo government's response.

As an editorial writer of a national daily newspaper observed at that time, whenever disaster struck, each government ministry held its own meetings, dispatched its own fact-finding teams, and implemented its own relief measures, with little regard for what other

---

Institutional Intricacies: *Vicissitudes of Bureaucratic Power and Pride*

In the 1970s and 1980s, Japan's government bureaucracy, epitomized by the Ministry of Finance (MOF) and the Ministry of International Trade and Industry (MITI), was greatly admired, both within the nation and abroad, as the uniquely intelligent, energetic, and dedicated architect of the nation's post–World War II economic success. Its policy-making prowess was acclaimed in books such as Ezra Vogel's *Japan As Number One!* (1979) and Chalmers Johnson's *MITI and the Japanese Miracle* (1982).

By the end of the 1990s, however, the enviable reputation of these institutions had completely dissipated. For example, a March 1998 *Asahi Shimbun* poll found that only 1 percent of respondents trusted ministry bureaucrats very much and 25 percent did so to some extent, while 50 percent did not trust them much and 21 percent not at all. What caused this dramatic turnaround in the image of Japan's public officials?

A combination of factors and circumstances seems to have been responsible. First and foremost, the depressed state of the Japanese economy, with all its attendant problems, was blamed, fairly or unfairly, on the bureaucrats. Second, a series of headline-grabbing corruption and malpractice scandals involving ministry bureaucrats that hit from the late 1980s through the early 2000s tainted the public image of not only the individual ministries directly involved—such as the Ministry of Finance, the Ministry of Health and Welfare, and the Ministry of Foreign Affairs—but the entire national bureaucracy.

Third, politicians began to claim and, to some extent, succeed in winning a greater share of policy-making power at the expense of bureaucrats, though with dubious consequences. Fourth, diminishing tax revenue and tighter spending discipline spelled a shrinking war chest for the bureaucrats to tap into for greasing their iron triangle relationships with politicians and special interest groups, thus seriously eroding their influence. Finally, largely as a result of these developments, the bureaucrats themselves began to lose much of their original sense of mission and purpose, which had guided their bold, and often innovative, decisions and actions in the better times and to succumb to a sense of powerlessness and drift.

The morale of the Japanese national government bureaucracy in the first years of the twenty-first century is thus nearly as depressed as the nation's economy. Moreover, neither shows significant signs of early recovery.

ministries and agencies were doing. The first priority was always coordination within each ministry rather than cooperation with other ministries and organizations. The January 2001 reorganization of the ministries was an attempt to correct this situation, but how much difference it will make to the officials' deeply ingrained mindsets and behavior pattern remains to be seen.

The cabinet usually meets twice a week, on Tuesdays and Fridays, although the prime minister may call additional meetings on his own initiative or at the request of other members of his cabinet. The director-general of the Cabinet Legislation Bureau and two deputy chief cabinet secretaries are also regular participants. However, most outstanding issues are settled in advance, at a meeting of vice ministers, which is normally held the day before the cabinet meeting. There has been a movement to abolish or pare down the decision-making power of the vice ministers with a view to reducing the bureaucrats' power and influence and increase that of the Diet. No specific action has been taken so far, however.

The power and prestige of the national civil service derive to an important extent from the unique position it occupies among the political institutions of contemporary Japan. Alone among prewar Japan's public institutions, the central government bureaucracy survived the occupation-sponsored postwar reforms virtually intact. The only notable casualty was the Home Ministry, which was divided into several smaller ministries and agencies. The national civil service actually became stronger after the reforms, which destroyed outright or drastically weakened other institutions, and played the leading role in Japan's postwar recovery.

During most of the postwar period, institutional autonomy and discretionary power, combined with adequate though not exceptionally high pay and guaranteed job security, gave Japan's national civil service enormous prestige. The prestige attracted a large number of university graduates to the annual civil service entrance examinations and ensured that only the best performers were appointed to fast-track positions in the central ministries and auxiliary organizations, especially the most prestigious among them, such as the Ministry of Finance (MOF), Ministry of International Trade and Industry (MITI; later reorganized and renamed METI), and Ministry of Foreign Affairs (MOFA). As Japan grew richer, the attractiveness of

careers in the private sector, especially in one of the conglomerate-affiliated giant corporations, rose rapidly, while the relative popularity of civil service careers declined. During the late 1980s, the number of applicants taking the civil service entrance examination in the most competitive fast-track category, officially called Class I, declined by nearly one-third. Still, the competition in this category remains stiff, and only about one out of thirty applicants survives it to win a civil service appointment.

By custom, though not by law, Japan's national civil servants retire at a relatively young age, usually about fifty-five, with fairly modest retirement benefits. This forces most retired civil servants to seek new jobs. Many find high-paying jobs in public or semipublic corporations or in the major private firms. This way of gaining postretirement employment is known as *amakudari,* or "descent from heaven." The "descent" is usually arranged in advance between the ministry ("heaven") from which the official is retiring and one of the public, semipublic, or private enterprises with which the ministry has a close relationship. The Japanese civil service law forbids employment of a retired civil servant within two years of his or her retirement by a private enterprise that has had a close relationship with the government office where the retired official was employed in the last five years. This restriction may be lifted at the National Personnel Authority's discretion, however, and has routinely been lifted for several dozen retiring senior bureaucrats each year. Moreover, there are no legal restrictions on the "descent" of a retired official to a public or semipublic organization.

In 2001, Japan's national government, including its auxiliary organizations, employed about 1.12 million people, or a little less than 2 percent of the employed work force of about 64.5 million people. The Japanese central government budget claimed a somewhat larger share of the nation's gross domestic product (GDP) than Germany's but less than that of the United States or France and less than half of that of Italy or Great Britain (see Figure 1). It is difficult to compare the efficiency of different nations' public bureaucracies, but it is probably reasonable to call Japan's relatively lean and thrifty. However, its traditional image as a group of unselfish, public-minded, and incorruptible mandarins— their antecedents in Imperial China—was seriously compromised in the 1990s and early 2000s by a series of scandals involving senior and middle-level officials in some of the traditionally most powerful and prestigious ministries and agencies, such as the ministries of Finance, Foreign Affairs, and Agriculture, Forestry, and Fisheries, and the Defense Agency.

Public and Semipublic Agencies

In 2002, Japan had seventy-eight national public and semipublic enterprises. They may be divided into three broad groups:

1. Nonprofit public financial institutions, including two government-owned banks (Japan Bank for International Cooperation and the Development Bank of Japan) and half a dozen public funds. All receive their capital from the central government and make loans to organizations or individuals engaged in activities of public interest, such as small businesses, farm and fishing families, and home buyers. Their budgets and expenditures are subject to approval and audit by the Diet.

2. Public corporations funded by either the central government or jointly by the central and local governments. These are involved in large public works projects, such as development and conservation of natural resources, and construction and management of highways, railroads, and airports.

3. Businesses that are wholly or partially supported by public funds. The activities of these businesses range from the development of advanced industrial technologies and the conservation of the environment to the construction and maintenance of transport and medical facilities and assistance to small businesses, livestock farmers, social and welfare services, and private schools.

The number of Japanese public and semipublic enterprises has been gradually declining for the past quarter-century, a trend substantially accelerated in the 1980s by the global deregulation and privatization movement led by President Ronald Reagan in the United States and Prime Minister Margaret Thatcher in Britain. The movement gained considerable public support in Japan partly because many of Japan's public and semipublic enterprises were chronically losing money and required constant infusions of taxpayer funds in order to keep operating. The Japanese National Railways (JNR) is a good example. Saddled with huge debts, JNR was on the verge of bankruptcy when it was privatized and divided into six private railroad companies in 1987. Nevertheless, many of the survivors, notably the Japan Highway Public Corporation, continue to pile up debts, which must be picked up by taxpayers.

Another important reason that many Japanese citizens are skeptical about public and semipublic enterprises is that they are believed to serve mainly as providers of lucrative "descent from heaven" postretirement employment for senior ministry bureaucrats. The practice gives senior civil servants an unfair advantage over others in the postretirement job market, such as most employees of private companies who retire at comparable ages. But since privatization means the elimination or downsizing of the targeted public and semipublic companies, it is opposed by many civil servants and has not gone very far. Japan is likely to remain home to dozens, if not hundreds, of public and semipublic enterprises for a long time to come.

Figure 1

National Government Expenditures as Percentage of Gross Domestic Product, 1995

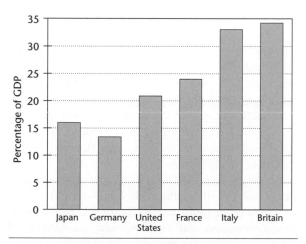

Source: International Department, Bank of Japan, *Comparative Economic and Financial Statistics: Japan and Other Major Countries 1997* (Tokyo: Bank of Japan, 1997), 109–110. Table 32.

Other State Institutions

The Military

Japan's military establishment was totally dismantled by the Allied Occupation authorities after World War II. Article IX of the 1947 Constitution renounces "war as a sovereign right of the nation" and declares that "land, sea and air forces, as well as other war potential, will never be maintained." In 1950, the outbreak of the Korean War led the Japanese government to launch a rearmament program at the urging of the U.S. government. Initially, a "police reserve force" was created, to avoid provoking controversy over its constitutionality. By 1954 this force had evolved into the Self-Defense Forces (SDF). In 1959, the Supreme Court ruled that Article IX allowed Japan to take necessary measures to defend itself as an independent nation. The SDF have since grown into substantial armed forces.

More important in the long run is the gradual erosion, due in large measure to Washington's persistent pressure, of the Japanese antipathy to war and arms born of their harrowing experiences in World War II. By the late 1990s, the majority of Japanese people had come to accept the SDF as constitutional, and a plurality of them favored a revision of the constitution and its war-renouncing article. According to the results of public opinion polls taken by one of Japan's major newspapers, the *Asahi Shimbun*, the ratios of those who favored a revision and those who opposed were reversed between 1983, when it was 26 percent in favor to 47 percent opposed, and 2001, when it had changed to 47 percent in favor and 36 percent opposed. In 1994, the newly elected prime minister and leader of the Socialist Party, which had long and relentlessly denounced the SDF and the U.S.-Japan Mutual Security Treaty as unconstitutional, suddenly declared both to be constitutional. By the end of the decade, the Japan Communist Party (JCP), which had been an even more vociferous opponent of the Japanese military and the military alliance with the United States, had de facto withdrawn objections. Following the September 11, 2001, terrorist attacks on the United States, the Japanese government dispatched, with little overt public or media opposition, half a dozen warships to the Indian Ocean to assist the U.S. forces in their military operations in and around Afghanistan.

The government failed, however, in a subsequent attempt to pass a set of bills to deal with future military emergencies by expanding the SDF's powers and requiring local governments and individual citizens to cooperate in the SDF's war efforts. The bills were introduced and debated in the 2002 Diet session, but were withdrawn before they were voted on in the face of strong and widespread opposition. They may be reintroduced in future Diet sessions, but their fate in the 2002 session testified to the continuing wariness among Japanese citizens of their nation's growing military power and increasing involvement in military and paramilitary actions abroad.

With the use of its own military power constitutionally circumscribed and possessing no advanced strategic weapons, such as long-range bombers and aircraft carriers, not to mention nuclear weapons, Japan relies on U.S. forces for protection against potential armed attack by a foreign power. This arrangement is based on the 1960 Treaty of Mutual Cooperation and Security between Japan and the United States. By virtue of the treaty and the Agreement on the Status of U.S. Armed Forces, which stipulates detailed rules for the implementation of the provisions of the treaty, the United States maintains an extended network of military bases and facilities and has about 40,000 U.S. troops regularly stationed in Japan

For historical as well as logistical reasons, three-quarters of the U.S. military bases and facilities in Japan are concentrated in the nation's southernmost prefecture, Okinawa. They take up about 10 percent of the total land area, and 18 percent of that of the largest of the islands that make up the nation's fourth smallest prefecture. The presence of so many foreign military bases has been a perennial source of disaffection and resentment among the local population since Okinawa was returned to Japan in 1972 after twenty-seven years of military occupation by the United States following the end of World War II.

Local sentiment in Okinawa has not only been critical of the U.S. bases but highly equivocal about the treatment of the prefecture and its people by the Japanese government and its relationship to the rest of Japan. This sentiment derives partly from the memory of the incorporation by force of what was then a semi-independent kingdom known as the Ryukyus into the expanding Japanese state in the late nineteenth century.

Institutional Intricacies: *Japan's Self-Defense Forces*

In the opening years of the twenty-first century, the Japanese military, euphemistically called the Self-Defense Forces (SDF), is equal, in operational capability, if not in physical size, to the armed forces of any major Western European nation. Japan's defense spending—about $45 billion in 2002—is larger than that of any other nation, except the United States and Russia (estimated) and perhaps France. It is, according to a Japanese source, more than twice as large as China's, more than two and a half times South Korea's, and nearly eight times North Korea's. Even though Japan spends only about 1 percent of its GNP on defense, it can afford to, and does, buy very large amounts of advanced weapons and military technologies.

From Washington's point of view, however, Japan's defense spending is too small relative to its overall economic power. In 2002, the United States spent about $379 billion, or nearly nine times as much as Japan. Not surprisingly, U.S. leaders have persistently demanded a larger defense effort by Tokyo, and Japan has responded by, among other things, expanding the scope of its participation in UN-sponsored peacekeeping operations (PKO) in various regions of the world. Beginning with the dispatch of three civilian election watchers to Angola in 1992, Japanese, including SDF troops in an increasing number of cases, have participated during the past decade in PKO activities in Cambodia, Mozambique, El Salvador, Rwanda, Syria/Golan Heights, Bosnia/ Herzegovina, and East Timor.

During the 1991 Persian Gulf War, Japan contributed a substantial amount of funds ($13 billion) to the efforts of the Coalition Forces, although no Japanese troops participated in the war itself. Following the September 11, 2001, terrorist attacks on the United States, the Japanese government promptly enacted the Anti-Terrorism Special Measures Law and dispatched several Maritime SDF ships to the Indian Ocean to assist the U.S. forces in their war against al Qaeda. One of these ships,

a destroyer, was replaced in December 2002 by another equipped with a cutting-edge air defense system known as Aegis, a system boasting highly advanced radar-tracking, information-processing, and missile-firing capabilities. Under the Koizumi government's direction, Japan thus appeared poised to play a much more active role in UN- or U.S.-led military actions not only in its immediate vicinity but even in remoter parts of the world.

Such government actions, however, have not necessarily met with approval from the Japanese public. A December 2002 *Asahi Shimbun* poll found 40 percent of respondents approving and 48 percent disapproving the dispatch of the Aegis destroyer to the Indian Ocean and 29 percent approving and 57 percent disapproving Japanese cooperation in a U.S.-led war against Iraq. Koizumi and his cabinet were thus attempting to please Washington at the risk of antagonizing the Japanese public, a dangerous game to play in a democracy.

Comparative Defense Expenditures

	US$ billions	Percentage of GDP
East Asia		
Japan	$44.4	1.0%
China	41.2	5.3
South Korea	14.5	2.7
North Korea	2.0	13.9
Taiwan	17.2	5.6
NATO and Russia		
United States	294.7	3
France	33.8	2.55
Germany	28.2	1.6
Great Britain	33.9	2.4
Italy	20.6	1.9
Russia	58.8	5

Source: The Statesman's Yearbook 2003. London: Palgrave Macmillan, 2003.

More important, it comes from the fresher memory of the Battle of Okinawa, which cost the lives of over 100,000 Japanese and 12,000 American troops and 140,000 local civilians in an extremely brutal three-month engagement in the last phase of World War II. The prefecture was then "given away" to the U.S. military by the Japanese government after World War II and remained under American control for twenty years after the rest of Japan had been freed from the Allied Occupation. Worse still, the return to Japanese jurisdiction did not lead to any significant reduction in the absolute or relative scale of U.S. military presence. The bases, especially those in the crowded urban areas of the main island, continued to cause not only noise and other nuisances but also serious safety hazards and crimes by American military personnel in the adjacent neighborhoods. In 1995, a local elementary school girl was gang-raped by three U.S. marines.

The rape incident sharply escalated the local opposition to the bases and threatened to lead to a prefecture-wide demand for the closing or relocation of many, if not all, of the major American bases and facilities. Concerned about the potentially deleterious impact of such a development on overall bilateral U.S.-Japan security and economic relations, the governments of both nations have attempted to defuse local tensions by proposing relocation of the most contentious bases and facilities. No tangible results have been achieved so far, however, and local discontent remains strong. Despite the substantially increased financial aid provided to Okinawa by the central government, it still remains the poorest of Japan's forty-seven prefectures.

The Judiciary

The judicial branch of the Japanese government operates according to the rules and decisions of the Supreme Court and is theoretically free from interference by the other two branches of government or any private interest group. The Supreme Court consists of the chief judge and fourteen other judges. All judges are appointed by the cabinet, except the chief judge of the Supreme Court, who is nominated by the cabinet and appointed by the emperor. Supreme Court judges are subject to popular review and potential recall in the first House of Representatives election following their appointment and every ten years thereafter. Otherwise, judges of all courts may serve until the mandatory

retirement ages: seventy for Supreme Court and small claims court judges and sixty-five for all others. In the eighteen popular reviews of Supreme Court judges held through 2002, no judge received a negative vote from much more than 10 percent of the voters. The recall provision is thus no more than a ritual of no practical import.

The Supreme Court, eight higher (regional) courts, and fifty district (prefectural) courts are invested with and occasionally use the constitutional power of judicial review. But the Supreme Court has been extremely reluctant to do so and especially to declare an existing law unconstitutional. For example, lower courts have twice found the SDF in violation of the war-renouncing Article IX of the 1947 Constitution: once in the late 1950s and again in the late 1970s. On each occasion, the Supreme Court reversed the lower court's verdict on the grounds that the issue was too political to be amenable to judicial review; this amounted to indirectly declaring the SDF constitutional. During the half-century of its existence up to 2002, the Supreme Court upheld lower court verdicts on the unconstitutionality of existing laws in only five cases, none of which involved a controversial political issue.

The passive posture of the Supreme Court helped sustain LDP domination of the Diet and the cabinet until the early 1990s. The court refused to order major changes in the distribution of Diet seats among the nation's election districts to reflect the massive postwar population movement from the country to the cities. As a result, in 1993 voters in the most overrepresented rural districts elected 2.8 times as many lower house members and 6.7 times as many upper house members per voter as their counterparts in the most underrepresented urban districts. In that year, the Supreme Court acknowledged, as it had done in 1976, the unconstitutionality of such gross malapportionment, but it refused, as it had done on the previous occasion, to invalidate the results of the elections already held.

The reluctance of the Japanese Supreme Court to use its power of judicial review may be attributed to several factors. First, there is an influential legal opinion that holds that the judiciary should not intervene in highly political acts of the legislative or executive branches of government, which represent the people's will more directly than the judiciary. Second, Japan has a much weaker case law tradition than either the United States or Britain. This makes judges less inclined to challenge the constitutionality of new legislation on the basis of precedents. Third, most of the Supreme Court judges appointed by the LDP governments were conservative in their outlook and inclined to approve decisions made by the conservative party in power. Fourth, judicial passivity may reflect the traditional reluctance of the Japanese people to resort to litigation to settle disputes. Finally, Japan lacks a tradition of judicial review. Under the Meiji Constitution, the emperor was above the law, and the courts did not have the power to deny the legality of any executive act taken in his name.

Subnational Government

The Japanese prefecture and its subdivisions are under the extensive administrative and financial control of the central government and enjoy only limited decision-making authority. In this respect, Japan differs from most other industrial democracies except France.

The lopsided distribution of decision-making power is sustained by an equally lopsided division of taxing power. The central government collects nearly two-thirds of the taxes collected by all governments and provides the funds for nearly one-third of local governments' expenditures through extensive grants-in-aid and subsidies programs. Some scholars believe that the relationship between the national and local governments in postwar Japan has been far less lopsided than widely believed.[29] However, the findings and recommendations of an expert committee appointed by the central government in accordance with a 1995 law leave little room for doubt about the extremely limited scope of local autonomy under the existing system. The grossly skewed central-local relations are a major factor impeding the development of greater democracy in Japan because they discourage citizens from participating in local government and politics.

The Policy-Making Process

The majority of bills passed by the Diet originate in the national civil service. When the LDP is in power, the draft bills are reviewed and approved by the party's Policy Research Council—and, if power is shared with a coalition partner or partners, also by its counterparts in the allied parties—before being sent to the Diet. The LDP's council operates through a dozen standing committees, each corresponding to a government ministry, and as of 2002, about one hundred ad hoc committees. Some of these ad hoc committees are concerned with broad, long-term policy issues, such as revision of the constitution, fiscal policy, and the educational system. Others deal with more specific issues, such as government assistance to depressed industries, treatment of foreign workers, and response to problems related to U.S. military bases in the country. Their recommendations are presented to the executive committee of the Policy Research Council and then to the party's Executive Council. If approved by both, these usually become LDP policies to be implemented through legislative actions of the Diet or administrative actions of the bureaucracy.

Most LDP policy committees are led by veteran Diet members who are experienced and knowledgeable in specific policy areas. Over the years, they have formed close personal relationships with senior civil servants and leaders of special interest groups. These LDP legislative bosses, who form among themselves what are popularly known as *zoku* (tribes), work through informal policy-making networks with their bureaucratic and business allies. Such groups dominate policy-making in all major policy areas, but especially in such areas as agriculture, construction, education, telecomunications, and transportation. Many of the bills drafted by bureaucrats and introduced in the Diet by an LDP cabinet originate in a tribe, as do many administrative measures implemented by a government ministry.

Through such policy-making partnerships, or **iron triangles,** special interests are promoted by friendly politicians and bureaucrats, bureaucrats have their turfs protected and often extended by sympathetic politicians, and politicians have their campaign war chests filled with contributions from the interest groups. The LDP tribes are thus the principal actors in pork-barrel politics and the major sources of political corruption and scandals. As a result, LDP government policies tend to be conservative, their main purpose being to protect the well-organized, well-connected, and well-to-do special interests. Big businesses, small shop owners, farmers, builders, insurers, and doctors are all represented by their own tribes and protected against those who threaten their interests, whether they are Japanese consumers, insurance policy holders, patients, foreign producers, exporters, or providers of various services.

Prime Minister Koizumi has the Postal Reform Service Bill introduced in the Diet against much opposition in his own party. Koizumi is running hard and fast with the bill. Veteran Postal Service Tribe politicians look on; one says, "Don't worry, he is not getting anywhere," and another says, "He is just exhausting himself!" *Source:* Mitsuru Yaku, *Asahi shinbun,* April 25, 2002.

郵政改革法案　強行提出
やく　みつる

This iron triangle process and its consequences were dramatically illustrated by the evolution of the administrative reform campaign launched with great fanfare by Prime Minister Ryutaro Hashimoto and his LDP government in 1997. An interim report by a blue-ribbon panel chaired by the prime minister himself proposed to eliminate or consolidate all nonessential or redundant government offices. The proposal provoked ferocious opposition not only from the targeted ministries and agencies but also from their allied interest groups and "tribesmen" in the LDP and other parties' executive offices and policy board committees. The consolidation of the central government ministries and agencies, mostly through mergers and renaming of existing organizational units, was accomplished by January 2001. It led, however, to few substantive changes in the organizations' functions and performance.

Hashimoto's was by no means the first government to call for reforming the bureaucracy. All three coalition governments that preceded it from 1993 to 1997 had promised thoroughgoing reform, but none had been able to deliver on their promises in the face of determined opposition by an assortment of iron triangles. Nor was Hashimoto the last reformist prime minister. All of his successors, especially Junichiro Koizumi

who took over as prime minister in the spring of 2001, arrived with a bold reformist agenda. Koizumi promised, above all, a prompt disposition of the bad public and private loans, the total amount of which in 2002 was estimated to exceed two-thirds of the nation's GDP, and the privatization of the postal services, including the highly lucrative postal savings and postal insurance services. As will be discussed in Section 5, his reform agenda provoked as fierce and determined resistance among the threatened iron triangles as his predecessors' had done, and it was substantially whittled down within a year of its inauguration.

As the term suggests, an iron triangle is characterized by strong solidarity among its members on the one hand, and rivalry and competition with outsiders on the other. The policy-making process that revolves around dozens of such triangles is inevitably disjointed and incoherent. Decisions made by one triangle in one policy area are seldom coordinated with decisions made in another. The medley of policies that often run at cross-purposes are then passed by the Diet or announced as new government policies. As a result, there are myriad laws and regulations in contemporary Japan but few comprehensive, coherent, long-term policies.

Section ④ Representation and Participation

The principal official forums in which the interests of Japanese citizens are expressed and considered in the conduct of government are the national and local legislatures. The principal official actors who represent them are the legislators, most of whom are affiliated with political parties. Citizens exercise a degree of control over the legislators' conduct and performance as their representatives through periodic elections. There are also other organizations and activities that express and represent citizens' interests and opinions outside the legislatures, such as interest groups and social movements. This section discusses the main features and problems of these organizations and activities in contemporary Japan.

The Legislature

Even during the period of LDP domination from the mid-1950s through the early 1990s, the Japanese national legislature played a central and indispensable role in the operation of democratic government as the most authoritative arena for public debates on important issues. The postwar constitution declares the Diet the highest and sole lawmaking organ of state. How the Diet is constituted and how it operates are therefore critical questions in assessing the current state and future prospects of democracy in Japan.

The House of Councilors, or the upper house of the bicameral Diet, currently has 247 seats (to be reduced to 242 in 2004). Upper house members have a fixed term of six years. As is the case with U.S. senators, their terms are staggered so that half of them are elected every three years. Ninety-six of the members (forty-eight in each triennial upper house election) are elected by a party (or closed) list proportional representation (PR) method. Each qualified party—one that has at least five current Diet seats or won at least 2 percent of the vote in the most recent Diet election or has at least ten candidates in the current election—submits a ranked list of its candidates to the election management committee in advance of the election. Each voter marks a ballot for her or his preferred candidate in just one party. Seats in the House of Councilors are then allocated to the parties in numbers proportionate to their shares of the total vote, and those seats are given, in turn, to the party's candidates according to their rank on the party list. The remaining 151 (146 after 2004) members of the House of Councilors are elected from multiple-seat prefecture-wide districts by a method known as single nontransferable vote (SNTV). Upper house members were originally expected to bring a broad national perspective to parliamentary deliberations and be less influenced by parochial local interests than lower house members. In practice, however, this distinction has long been lost, and the two houses are virtually indistinguishable.

The House of Representatives, or the lower house, currently has 480 seats. The full term of office for its members is four years, but the actual term served by a member averages about two and a half years. This is because, unlike the upper house, the lower house may be dissolved by the cabinet when the house passes a motion of no confidence against the cabinet or refuses to pass a motion of confidence in the cabinet. In either case, the cabinet must choose either to resign or to dissolve the lower house and call a new election. The cabinet may voluntarily choose to dissolve the lower house at other times as well. The constitution gives the emperor the right to dissolve the lower house with the advice and consent of the cabinet; in fact, he cannot refuse such a request from the cabinet. The cabinet chooses to dissolve the lower house when it lacks an effective control of the house but believes that the ruling party will win a new general election.

A speaker and a vice speaker preside in the lower house; a president and a vice president preside in the upper house. Unlike their counterparts in the U.S. Congress, the presiding officers of the Japanese Diet are expected to be nonpartisan in discharging their duties. When a member of the Diet is elected to any of these four positions, the member nominally gives up his or her party affiliation and becomes an independent.

An ordinary session of the Diet sits for 150 days each year, beginning in late January. If necessary, it may be extended once. An extraordinary session may be called at any time by the cabinet or by a quarter of the members of either house. As in the U.S. Congress, a good deal of business is conducted in the standing and ad hoc committees of each house. In 2002, there were seventeen standing committees in each house and eight and ten ad hoc committees, respectively, in the lower and upper houses. The quorum for the plenary session and the meeting of a committee of either house is uniformly a simple majority. So is the number of votes required for the passage of a bill or a resolution by either house or its committee.

A bill may be introduced in either house but must be considered and approved by both houses in order to become a law. In practice, an overwhelming majority of bills have been introduced first in the lower house and later referred to the upper house. A bill may be introduced by the cabinet, the house, a committee of the house, or a member or members of the house. In all cases, it is first presented to the presiding officer of the house, then referred by him or her to an appropriate committee of the house for initial consideration, unless the introducer requests for special reasons that it be immediately sent to and considered by the entire house. A member's bill that does not require a budget appropriation must be cosigned by twenty or more lower house members or ten or more upper house members; one that requires a budget appropriation must be cosigned by fifty or more lower house or twenty or more upper house members.

A bill approved by a committee of either house is referred to and debated by the whole house and, if approved, transmitted to the other house, where the same process is repeated. A bill that has been approved by both houses, with or without amendments, is signed by the speaker of the lower house or the president of the upper house, whichever has approved it last, and presented to the emperor for promulgation. Promulgation is purely a formality that does not entail the approval or endorsement of the bill by the emperor.

The lower house is the more powerful of the two houses of the Diet. If a bill has been approved by the lower house but disapproved by the upper house, it may still become a law by being passed again with a two-thirds majority in the lower house. The annual government budget must be introduced to the lower house and may be passed by that house alone, regardless of the upper house's action or opinion. The lower house enjoys the same privilege with regard to the ratification of international treaties.

Japanese Diet members normally vote strictly along party lines, unlike members of the U.S. Congress but like those in the parliaments of most parliamentary democracies. In the 1950s and early 1960s, the rigid enforcement of party discipline in Diet voting contributed to frequent confrontations between the LDP and the opposition, which sometimes led to fistfights on the floor of the Diet. By the mid-1960s, however, the opposition had given up violent tactics in favor of delaying maneuvers such as repeated submissions of no-confidence motions against a cabinet. Since the early 1970s, parliamentary battles between the ruling party and the opposition have become increasingly ritualized. The opposition first uses a boycott or other means to stall Diet proceedings and kill a government proposal, but eventually accepts a settlement mediated by the presiding officer of either house. The ruling party repays the opposition for its cooperation by making limited concessions.

Most Japanese legislators are men. While female voters' turnout has been consistently higher than male voters' in local elections since the late 1950s and in Diet elections since the early 1970s, there are few female legislators at either the national or local level.[30] As of late 2002, 35 of the 480 (7.3 percent) lower house members and 38 of the 247 (15.4 percent) upper house members were women. On a list compiled at that same time by the Inter-Parliamentary Union, Japan was tied with the Central African Republic for ninety-sixth place out of 123 ranked nations in the percentage of women among those elected to either a unicameral parliament or the more powerful lower house of a bicameral parliament in the country's most recent election. Sweden was first, with 45 percent.

Japanese women also play a limited role in the executive and judicial branches of Japan's national government and in prefectural and local governments. This is partly due to the traditional Japanese political culture that discourages women's participation in public affairs. More important, however, it is a consequence of the standard rules used in the selection of candidates in national and local elections by all major Japanese political parties. These rules give priority to incumbents, candidates chosen by the party's local branches, and candidates who are likely to win, roughly in this order. Nearly all are under the control of male politicians.

When an incumbent retires or dies, he or she is likely to be succeeded by a relative, typically a son, or a close aide. Thanks to the campaign organization and personal networks bequeathed by the predecessor, such a successor has significant advantage over rival candidates in securing the support of the local party branch by convincing its leaders that he or she can win. In the 2000 lower house general election, such "hereditary" candidates accounted for 25 percent of all winners and 36 percent of the LDP affiliates, and with their counterparts in the upper house, they accounted for 30 percent of all Diet members in 2002.

In the Japanese Diet, as in the U.S. Congress, committee deliberations, where special interest groups can exert their influence most effectively, play the central part in the legislative process. By comparison, sessions of the whole chamber seldom lead to substantial changes in a bill that has already been approved by a committee. While in most Western democracies, bills are read three or more times by the entire membership of a house, there is only one reading in the plenary session of the Japanese Diet. As a result, entrenched special interests represented by their own tribes and iron triangles in committee deliberations are likely to have

their cases heard far more sympathetically than newer and less organized interests that are not so represented, such as women and youth.

The interests of the national civil service are also effectively represented in the work of Diet committees. Civil servants are in a position to interpret laws almost as they please by issuing administrative orders, which are supposed to help implement a law but often have the effect of modifying or even replacing it. Japanese laws tend to lack specific and detailed provisions, which gives bureaucrats wide discretion in interpreting them. As a result, bureaucratic interests, as well as entrenched private interests, tend to prevail over those of the broader public.

Political Parties and the Party System

For nearly forty years, from the mid-1950s, when the Liberal and Democratic parties merged, to the early 1990s, the LDP dominated the Diet. The party owed its success mainly to a booming economy, a generally satisfied electorate, and a divided and bickering opposition. By the late 1980s, however, a series of scandals began to take their toll on the party. In the 1993 lower house election, the party lost enough seats to the opposition to give up government for the first time in its

Table 4

Percentage Shares of Seats and Proportional Representation Votes by Party

| | Lower House | | | | Upper House | | | |
| | Seats | | Votes | | Seats | | Votes | |
	1996	2000	1996	2000	1998	2001	1998	2001
Liberal Democratic Party	47.8%	48.5%	32.0%	20.3%	34.9%	53.7%	25.2%	38.6%
Japan Renewal Party	31.2	–	28.0	–	–	–	–	–
Democratic Party of Japan	10.4	26.5	16.1	25.2	21.4	21.5	21.7	16.4
Japan Communist Party	5.2	4.2	13.1	11.2	11.9	4.1	14.6	7.9
Social Democratic Party	3.0	4.0	6.4	9.4	3.9	2.5	7.8	6.6
New Party Harbinger	0.4	–	1.0	–	0.0	–	1.4	–
Liberal Party	–	4.6	–	11.0	4.8	5.0	9.3	7.7
Clean Government Party	–	6.5	–	13.0	7.1	10.7	13.8	15.0
Other parties & independents	2.0	5.8	2.6	1.9	15.9	2.5	6.1	7.7

Sources: Asahi shinbun, October 21, 1996, 1, 3; October 21, 1996, evening ed., 3; July 13, 1998, 1, 4; July 13, 1998, evening ed., 1; July 14, 1998, 7; June 26, 2000, 1; June 27, 2000, 5, 9; July 31, 2001, 3, 10.

history. This event ushered in a period of uncertainty and instability in Japanese politics characterized by the rapid rise and fall of parties new and old, as well as of cabinets, at short intervals (see Table 4).

At the end of the 1980s, there were five parties regularly contesting Diet elections: the LDP, the Japan Socialist Party (JSP), the Clean Government Party (CGP), the Democratic Socialist Party (DSP), and the Japan Communist Party (JCP). The LDP, the JSP, and the JCP were descendants of prewar parties that had been disbanded (banned in the JCP's case) before and revived after World War II. The DSP was formed in 1960 by defectors from the JSP. The CGP was founded in 1964 as the political arm of the national organization of lay members of the Buddhist sect called *Sokagakkai* (Value Creation Academy).

The LDP's defeat in the 1993 lower house election was triggered by a series of scandals, the LDP government's unpopular tax and trade policies, and, above all, Japan's economic downturn. The voter revolt against the LDP was exploited by three new parties: the Japan New Party (JNP), the New Party Harbinger (NPH or Sakigake), and the Japan Renewal Party (JRP). The JNP had been founded in 1992 by a disgruntled former LDP

upper house member, while the NPH and the JRP were both formed by LDP defectors less than a month before the election. In the following years, the LDP regained power (in coalition governments) while most of the other parties reorganized and renamed themselves

As of late 2002, there were seven political parties in Japan (see Table 5). The LDP draws its electoral and financial support mainly from the big- and small-business communities and farmer groups. The Social Democratic Party (formerly the Japan Socialist Party) has been supported by public sector labor unions, and the Communist Party relies on urban workers and intellectuals. The Clean Government Party, originally sponsored by the lay group of a large Buddhist sect, formally declared independence from the religious organization in 1970 but still gets a lot of support from sect members. The three newer parties—the Democratic Party of Japan (DPJ), the Liberal Party (LP), and the Conservative Party (CP)—all draw the bulk of their support from disaffected former supporters of the LDP or SDP. None of the three has yet built a well-defined and reliable base of electoral and financial support.

The Liberal Democrats and the Conservatives stand at the right end and the Communists at the left end of

Table 5

Japanese Political Parties, February 2002

Ideological Tendency	Party Name	Year Founded	Diet Seats HR	Diet Seats HC
Right	Liberal Democratic Party (LDP)	1955	242	111
	Conservative Party (CP)	2000	7	5
Center	Democratic Party of Japan (DPJ)	1996	124	58
	Clean Government Party (CGP)	1998 (1964)*	31	23
	Liberal Party (LP)	1997	22	8
Left	Social Democratic Party (SDP)	1955	19	7
	Japan Communist Party (JCP)	1945	20	20
Others			7	6
Independents			7	8
Vacancies			1	1
Totals			480	247

Note: HR = House of Representatives; HC = House of Councillors.

*Year originally founded in parentheses

Source: Kokkai binran (Diet handbook), 108th edition (Tokyo: Nihon keizai shinbunsha, February 2002), 406–11.

an ideological spectrum, while the Liberal Party, Clean Government Party, Democratic Party of Japan, and Social Democratic Party range from right to left between them, roughly in that order. Japanese politics in general and party politics in particular have not been intensely ideological since the end of the Vietnam War in the mid-1970s and have become even less so since the end of the cold war. The JCP's official platform, revised most recently in 1985, continues to refer to Japanese monopoly capitalism and American imperialism. Nonetheless, the party now calls for the formation of a democratic coalition government in cooperation with conservative opposition parties and with the support of conservative but independent voters. The party has also abandoned its opposition to both the Japanese Self-Defense Forces and the United States–Japan Mutual Security Treaty as unconstitutional. In both its domestic and foreign policy, the JCP today is thus as pragmatic and politically astute as any other Japanese party.

Although the LDP remains the largest party in the Diet, it still suffers from perennial factional divisions that militate against strong and stable party leadership. Since its birth in 1955, the party has been divided into several well-defined and deeply entrenched rival factions, each led by a veteran Diet member. Until recently, the boss of each faction and his followers were bound by patron-client relationships of mutual help and dependence. The boss helped his followers with campaign funds at election time and advocated their appointment to Diet, cabinet, and party offices. His followers reciprocated by pledging their support for the boss's actual or expected bid for the highest party office, the LDP presidency, which was, given the LDP's control of the Diet, virtually synonymous with Japan's premiership. A large factional following was therefore an essential asset for a boss with prime ministerial ambitions.

The LDP factions thus functioned primarily as intraparty campaign machines intent on promoting themselves at each other's expense. They influenced the policy-making process inasmuch as all important Diet, cabinet, and party offices were allocated on the basis of the standing of the factions in the party and members' standing in their own faction. In the early days of the LDP, the personal role of the faction boss was particularly great, and his death or retirement often resulted in splits or disintegration of the faction. After the late 1970s, however, the extant factions became

increasingly institutionalized, so that the departure of their bosses no longer threatened the groups' survival. Amid the complex party realignment process set off by the LDP's fall from power in 1993, all the factions declared themselves disbanded by the end of 1994. The declaration was, however, no more than a public relations gimmick, and the factions remained alive and active when the LDP returned to power in less than a year. However, the ties between a faction's leader and his or her followers and among faction members in general had substantially loosened and the factions' influence on LDP Diet members' legislative and other actions had declined. On the other hand, groups of Diet members formed around specific policy issues, often crossing party lines, have increased in number and gained in influence.

The SDP (formerly JSP) and the DPJ, too, have been host to entrenched intraparty factions. In fact, theirs have been as contentious as, and, in some ways, more destructive than, their counterparts in the LDP. While the LDP factions are concerned primarily with fundraising and the distribution of government and party offices among its Diet members, the SDP's and, to a lesser extent, the DPJ's have been primarily ideological and/or policy groups. For example, some are more willing than others to have SDF units participate in UN-sanctioned collective self-defense actions abroad or to revise the 1947 Constitution or to join the LDP in a coalition government. The failure of the SDP and the DPJ to make much headway in Diet and local elections may be attributed mainly to their members' inability to rally behind a leader or a leadership group in pursuit of well-defined and consistent party lines on controversial policy issues. This inability has been a direct result of internal factional conflicts.

Elections

The House of Representatives election system was drastically changed in 1994. Under the old system, all lower house members, as well as some of the House of Councilors, were elected by the single nontransferable vote (SNTV) method that had been in effect in Japan since the mid-1920s but was very rare in national-level elections elsewhere. According to this method, two or more members are elected in each district but each voter casts a single ballot for a particular candidate, which may not be transferred to another candidate even of the same party. The candidates with the largest numbers of votes in each district win. At the time of the 1993 lower house election, Japan was divided into 129 lower house election districts, each of which elected between two and six members. This system permitted a candidate to win a seat with as little as 10 to 15 percent of the votes cast in the district and enabled smaller parties to win at least some seats.

The SNTV system, however, forced candidates of the same party to compete by highlighting their qualifications and strengths in matters other than their views on policy issues. This tendency was particularly pronounced because all Japanese parties required their Diet members to support the party line on all major policy issues. Under such circumstances, the most common way to win voters' support was to offer them a variety of constituency services, ranging from finding jobs for constituents or their children to lobbying for government subsidies for local firms. Constituency service activities were carried out primarily by the candidate's personal campaign organization, known as *koenkai* (support association).

The *koenkai* mobilized local community groups, such as agricultural cooperatives and shopkeepers' associations, into solid blocs of voters for their candidates. It took enormous amounts of money and hard work to set up and maintain a viable *koenkai* organization, not so much to buy votes outright but to rent office space, pay salaries, and finance constituency services. The funds were provided mainly by local businesses and business associations. The LDP's long rule depended on the extensive and sturdy networks of patron-client relationships (**clientelism**) between LDP politicians, local businessmen and business associations, and *koenkai* organizations.

The LDP also owed its success to gross malapportionment that gave significant advantage to rural voters over urban voters. This malapportionment had its roots in a census taken right after World War II when Japan's major cities had been evacuated in the face of Allied air raids and the majority of Japanese were living in the countryside. Thus, the rural areas were given a larger share of representatives in the Diet, a situation that has since been perpetuated to the present time, despite the enormous population shifts from rural to urban areas that occurred in the next several decades. The LDP

consistently championed farmers' interests (e.g., by strict limitations on imported rice) and succeeded in turning rural Japan into a solid bloc of staunchly pro-LDP voters. The LDP's interest in farmers' votes has not significantly diminished even as farmers and their families have become a minority of only about 10 percent of the total population in today's Japan. Nearly 30 percent of LDP Diet members are former local politicians who have been elected with farmers' votes and who would risk losing in a future election without those votes.

This type of systematic bias in the election system and the "money politics" that led to recurrent scandals involving top LDP leaders and business executives raised serious doubts about the quality of democracy in Japan. Many Japanese critics, including some LDP leaders, were calling for reform for nearly a quarter-century. But the determined opposition of those who benefited from the status quo had effectively blocked any meaningful change. The dramatic reversal in the electoral fortunes of the LDP in the early 1990s at long last led to some serious attacks on these decades-old problems.

In 1994, the lower house election system was "reformed": the SNTV system was replaced by a combination of a single-member district (SMD) and proportional representation (PR) system, in the belief that the change would help rid lower house elections of money politics. The existing 129 multimember districts that elected 511 lower house members were replaced with 300 single-member districts and 11 regional districts that would elect an additional 200 members by a party list–based PR method. Candidates were allowed to run simultaneously in both an SMD and a PR district and could get elected by winning in one district while losing in the other. The "reform," however, did not significantly affect the basic pattern of Japanese parliamentary and party politics. In the 1993 lower house election, the LDP had won 223 of the 511 seats, or 43.6 percent. In the first lower house election held under the new mixed system in 1996, the LDP won 239 of the 500 seats, or 47.8 percent of the total, or 4.2 percent more than in the 1993 election. In another "reform" implemented in 2000 on the eve of the most recent lower house election, the number of the house's seats was reduced to 480. In the election that followed, the LDP won 233 seats, or 48.5 percent of the total, 0.7 percent more than in 1996.

Voter turnout in postwar Diet elections fluctuated between about 68 and 77 percent in lower house elections and 57 and 75 percent in upper house elections until the late 1980s. Both hit the low points in the mid-1990s, at about 60 percent and 45 percent, respectively, but have since recovered somewhat, respectively, to a little over 62 percent in the 2000 lower house election and a little over 56 percent in the 2001 upper house election.

Political Culture, Citizenship, and Identity

Japan is an ethnically and culturally homogeneous country whose citizens have a well-developed sense of national identity. This sense was molded into a strong and aggressive nationalist ideology in prewar Japan, leading it to attempt to build a colonial empire in East Asia on the model of those erected by European powers around the world. Japan's defeat in World War II put an end to the aggressive nationalist ideology and the dreams of empire. The strong sense of national identity, however, survived the war.

At the heart of prewar Japanese national identity and nationalism was the quasi-Shinto cult of emperor worship. The cult inspired the drive to build a "rich nation with a strong army" in the nineteenth century and an East Asian empire in the 1920s and 1930s. Whether a secular religion or a substitute for a religion, the emperor cult had been fused with and nourished by another philosophy, Confucianism, which was imported from Korea by the fifth century. Confucianism, even more than Shinto or the quasi-Shinto emperor cult, has influenced and shaped the Japanese way of life, particularly attitudes toward the state, family, work, and education.

Religion has not been an important factor in modern Japanese politics or society. The postwar Japanese constitution, like its U.S. model, provides for the separation of state and religion. Most Japanese are nominally Buddhist and/or Shintoist, but their religious observance usually consists of visiting a shrine or temple on a festival day, hearing a Shinto priest intone at wedding ceremonies, or listening to a Buddhist monk's chant at a funeral service. The generally casual, often cavalier, attitude toward religion is reflected in the fact that many Japanese are not sure whether they are Buddhist or Shintoist and are in fact counted as both. For example,

in 2000, when the total Japanese population was about 125 million, there were about 106 million Japanese Shintoists, nearly 96 million Japanese Buddhists, 1.7 million Christians, and a little over 10 million followers of other faiths. In other words, the average Japanese belong to two religious communities or groups.

The Japanese have built a society concerned nearly exclusively with matters of this world, such as economic success and material comfort. They enjoy the longest life expectancy at birth and one of the lowest infant mortality rates in the world. The enrollment rates of Japanese children in elementary and secondary schools are among the highest in the world. Virtually all Japanese families own a wide assortment of home appliances and electronic gadgets, such as color televisions, washing machines, vacuum cleaners, refrigerators, and automobiles.

At the same time, Japan remains a society with a Confucian distaste for social conflict and a longing for order and harmony among and within all classes. In prewar Japan, a combination of Confucian and Shinto precepts nurtured the idea of the unique nation ruled and protected by descendants of its original divine creator, which was to be revered by all its subjects as the source of their collective identity and the object of their boundless loyalty and devotion. In postwar Japan, the nation as the object of personal loyalty has been largely replaced by a smaller organization or group, such as a firm; but the group-centered rather than individualistic view of life and society continues to prevail, with important political implications and consequences. For example, a company's management and labor union often jointly sponsor a particular candidate in a Diet election.

The Japanese are among the best-educated people in the world. The six-year elementary and three-year lower secondary school education is compulsory, and virtually all children finish it. Moreover, over 95 percent of lower secondary school graduates go to three-year upper secondary schools, and nearly half of upper secondary school graduates go to two-year junior colleges or four-year universities. Schools are predominantly public, and private schools differ little from public schools in either organization or curriculum. All schools use similar textbooks in all subject areas, thanks to the textbook certification system. All drafts of textbooks must be submitted to the Ministry of

Education, Science, Sports, and Culture—known as the Ministry of Education prior to the January 2001 reorganization and hereafter cited by its old name—for inspection, often extensive revisions, and certification before they can be used in schools. This censorship system ensures that textbooks are generally consistent with the opinions, preferences, and prejudices of Ministry of Education inspectors. As a result, the history and social studies textbooks used in Japanese schools tend to avoid detailed discussion of any controversial political issues. For example, they say little about the role of the emperor in the series of wars fought by Japan in the nineteenth and twentieth centuries, the controversy over the constitutionality of the Self-Defense Forces, or the causes and consequences of corruption in Japanese government and society. They have also been relatively silent on Japanese wartime atrocities, such as the Rape of Nanking.

The most important function of the school in contemporary Japan is to prepare students for entrance into either the job market or higher-level schools. Which school and, in particular, which university one attends largely determines what kind of job one will hold after graduation. Some universities are believed to prepare students better than others for the most prestigious companies or government agencies and therefore attract more and better-performing applicants to their entrance examinations. The preparatory mission common to all Japanese schools absorbs the bulk of their teachers' and students' time and energy, leaving little of either for acquiring knowledge for its own sake, learning to enjoy art, or developing critical faculties. On the other hand, the centralized and rigidly controlled educational system produced a literate, hard-working, and dedicated labor force during the period when the modern Japanese economy grew rapidly in the late nineteenth century through the late twentieth century.[31]

With a 99 percent literacy rate, contemporary Japan is also one of the most media-saturated societies. It has less than one-tenth as many daily newspapers as the United States and one-third as many as Germany, but many have far larger circulations than their U.S. or European counterparts. As a result, Japan boasts the highest total and per person newspaper circulation among the major industrial nations. This is also true for books and magazines: some 56,000 new books per year and nearly 3,000 monthly magazines are published. More-

over, the average Japanese family owns two color televisions. The Japanese are thus exposed to a huge amount of media-purveyed information, although the bulk of it is about cultural, social, and economic, rather than political, topics.

Japan's mainstream mass media are politically and socially conservative by American standards, due to the indirect but pervasive influence of the government and corporate management. Such influence is a function mainly of two characteristic features of the news business in contemporary Japan: the influence of the press club and the importance of revenue from advertising. A press club consists of one or more reporters from each accredited member newspaper, television station, radio station, or news service agency. Each club is provided with office space by the organization it covers, and its members gather information mainly from the organization's official spokespersons. A reporter who seeks unofficial information risks losing good standing with the host organization and even club membership. The system thus works to suppress publication of news critical of the organizations concerned, such as a government ministry or a major firm. Moreover, all major Japanese newspapers and privately owned television and radio stations depend on advertisements for substantial portions of their income and tend to avoid publishing information that could embarrass or offend their advertisers.

The ethnic and cultural homogeneity of the Japanese society has been gradually eroded by its increasing contact with the outside world, especially in the last few decades of the twentieth century when the process of globalization significantly intensified. Compared with the industrial nations of North America and Western Europe, however, Japan remains far less exposed to and penetrated by foreign ethnic and cultural influences. The number of foreign residents in Japan at the turn of the twenty-first century, for example, was about 1.5 million, or only about 1.2 percent of Japan's total population. Moreover, about 40 percent of these foreigners were Koreans, nearly 20 percent were Chinese, and 15 percent were Japanese Brazilians. In other words, about three-quarters of them were those with ethnic and cultural backgrounds very similar to, if not identical with, those of the Japanese.

This was even truer of foreign students studying at Japanese universities: there were only about 56,000 of them altogether, and more than 45 percent were Chinese, 20 percent were Koreans, and another 25 percent were other Asians. More significant for the cultural, if not ethnic, diversification of Japan were probably the effects of tourism: no more than about 5 million foreigners visited Japan in 2000, but nearly 18 million Japanese visited foreign countries in the same year. These Japanese tourists' experiences abroad and those of the Japanese who met foreign tourists in Japan may have a far-reaching long-term impact on the Japanese collective identities and behavior.

Interests, Social Movements, and Protests

Although Japan may appear politically conservative and quiescent (except at election time), it is not entirely free of political controversies. For example, the development and use of nuclear power by electric companies remains controversial in the only nation that has ever experienced the effects of an atomic bomb used as a weapon in wartime.

Energy and Environmental Issues

The electric power industry and the LDP leadership have vigorously pushed the construction of nuclear reactors as an alternative to imported fuels, especially oil from the Middle East. Japan is today one of the world's major users of nuclear energy, with fifty-two reactors supplying about 13 percent of Japan's energy consumption as of 2002. Still, a number of local communities and governments have vigorously opposed the construction of reactors in their own backyards. The opposition stiffened following the 1979 Three Mile Island accident in the United States and the 1986 Chernobyl disaster in the Soviet Union. It gained considerably greater momentum following accidents at one of Japan's major nuclear power plant sites, **Tokai Village.**

In the first of these accidents in 1997, a fire at a plutonium reprocessing plant exposed about three dozen workers to low-level radiation, although none suffered serious physical damage. Two and a half years later, another accident at a uranium processing facility in the same village exposed three employees to much heavier doses of irradiation and led to the deaths of two. The succession of these accidents has deepened the public concern about the safety of nuclear power plants

and led to the suspension of construction plans and even the operation of some existing reactors at a number of sites around the country.

Rapid industrialization and urbanization have also given rise to intense conflicts over a number of other environmental issues. In fact, a series of extremely severe cases of industrial pollution in the 1950s and 1960s made Japan one of the world's best-known and most frequently cited victims of environmental hazards resulting from reckless industrialization. These cases included fatal mercury poisoning known as **Minamata disease,** which first occurred in Minamata City in central Kyushu and later in northern Honshu, cadmium poisoning in central Honshu, and asthma in southwestern Honshu.

A set of stiff antipollution laws passed by the Diet in the early 1970s has helped prevent a recurrence of such devastating disasters. But citizens' concern about the continuing deterioration of the environment still spurs battles in courtrooms and protests in the streets. Local citizens' opposition to noise, for example, often blocks or delays construction of new highways, railroads, and airports.

Ethnic Minorities: Ainu, Outcastes, Koreans, and Immigrants

Belying its stereotype as a homogeneous society, contemporary Japan does have some serious identity problems to contend with, although they are neither as widespread nor as intense as those found in a number of other nations. Such issues are of concern particularly to the numerically minuscule but increasingly vocal ethnic minority known as the Ainu, the much larger and far more vocal minority of former outcaste people, and Koreans and other resident foreigners

The Ainu are descendants of the hunter-gatherers believed to have once inhabited the greater part of the northern half of Japan. The traditional Ainu society had no concept of private property, and most of its communally owned land was taken by and distributed among new settlers from other regions of the country in a land "reform" undertaken by the Meiji government. The Ainu were left with only the land on which they lived in Japan's northernmost prefecture, Hokkaido. They were also forced to abandon hunting by government decree. Most Ainu quickly fell into extreme poverty.

As the number of non-Ainu immigrants to Hokkaido grew, intermarriage increased. Today, about 24,000 Japanese are known to have some Ainu blood, but the number of full-blooded Ainu is estimated to be no more than a few hundred.

Until the late 1990s, the Ainu were ostensibly protected by a nineteenth-century Law to Protect Former Native Inhabitants of Hokkaido, but in practice little was done to protect or help them. The Ainu community had long been afflicted with a high incidence of alcoholism, tuberculosis, and venereal disease. These problems, and the plight of the Ainu in general, were almost completely ignored by the Japanese government and public until the mid-1980s. In 1986, a prime minister's reference to Japan as a homogeneous nation led leaders of the Ainu community to protest publicly and the prefectural government of Hokkaido to propose a new law to protect Ainu human rights, improve their social and economic conditions, and preserve and promote their traditional culture. The long-ignored problems of an important ethnic minority in the nation were thus addressed at last. An Ainu scholar-author, Shigeru Kayano, ran as a candidate on the JSP proportional representation list in the 1992 upper house election and became the runner-up; two years later, he filled a vacancy left by a deceased JSP member and became the first Ainu ever to serve in the Diet. He was instrumental in the enactment of the 1997 Law to Promote Ainu Culture, which replaced the archaic Meiji law.

One type of class-based segregation that began in the Tokugawa period and survived until after World War II is that imposed on Japan's outcaste class. For centuries, its members were condemned to pariah status associated with particular residential areas, known in recent times as "discriminated hamlets" or "unliberated hamlets" and types of work once regarded as unclean, such as disposing of carcasses and working with hides and leather. The Japanese caste system was not as complex as the Hindu caste system in India, but was similar to systems found in early medieval Europe and especially in premodern and early modern China and Korea. As in China and Korea, the system has been legally abolished, but the prejudice it nurtured for centuries has not completely disappeared.

The movement for the liberation of the descendants of outcaste people picked up steam after World War II.

In the 1970s, a series of laws were passed to help abolish the approximately 4,600 "discriminated hamlets" that still existed, mostly in the southwestern half of the country, and integrate the more than 1 million people who lived there into the broader national community. Since then, considerable improvement has been made in the economic conditions of former outcaste communities, but complete equality and full integration into the national community, especially in areas such as employment and marriage, remain unfulfilled goals.

After the Meiji Restoration and especially after Japan annexed Korea in 1910, many Koreans migrated to Japan. Initially, they came to Japan voluntarily. By the 1930s, however, they were increasingly brought by force to work in some of the nation's most poorly equipped and accident-prone factories and mines. At the end of World War II, more than 2 million Koreans were living in Japan. Most of them returned to South or North Korea, while a small minority acquired Japanese citizenship. About 660,000 Koreans currently live in Japan as resident aliens, some by choice but many because they are denied citizenship under the rules of Japanese immigration and naturalization policy.

There is substantial public support for allowing resident foreigners in general and Koreans in particular to vote and run as candidates in local elections, though not in Diet elections. More than 1,200 local legislatures, or well over one-third of the total, have adopted resolutions in favor of recognizing Korean residents' right to participate in local politics. The Supreme Court decided in 1995 that such a move would be constitutional. But the LDP and the Ministry of Public Management, Home Affairs, and Posts and Telecommunications (known as the Ministry of Home Affairs prior to the January 2001 reorganization) continue to oppose the move and have blocked it so far.

The most important and difficult issue raised by ethnic minorities is not the physical hardships or material deprivations inflicted on them by deliberate government policy. In fact, many former outcaste communities have received generous financial assistance from both the national and local governments during the last three decades and today enjoy greatly improved community facilities, such as paved roads, well-equipped schools, public libraries, and community centers. Many Korean residents own successful businesses, mostly small enterprises such as restaurants and game parlors. The core problem facing the minorities in Japan is the social and cultural discrimination that they continue to face, especially in employment and marriage.

Like many other advanced industrial societies, contemporary Japan has attracted foreign workers who legally enter the country but often stay illegally after their visas have expired. About 660,000 foreign workers, mainly from Asia and the Middle East, were employed in Japan in the late 1990s. They are a potential source of social tension over the issue of collective identities. Most have come to Japan in search of jobs, mostly menial and sometimes exploitative (including the sex industry), that pay them much higher wages than jobs available in their own countries. Some of these laborers are indispensable to many Japanese businesses suffering from chronic shortages of young and cheap workers. As in most high-wage industrial nations of North America and Western Europe, foreign workers are feared and resented by some Japanese, who see them as a threat to their own wages, pensions, free medical care, and even jobs in a period of recession. Unlike the situation in some European countries with much larger numbers of foreign workers and much higher unemployment rates, no organized violence against foreign workers by Japanese citizens has been reported so far.

Women's Movement

The movement to improve the social and political status of women in Japan has a long history, dating back to the early part of the Meiji period. The movement had its origins in the democratic idea imported from the West at the time and was an important part of the "freedom and people's rights" movement in the 1880s. Japan's first major women's organization was the Tokyo Women's Temperance Union, founded in 1886, which campaigned mainly for the abolition of prostitution. The Bluestocking Society, formed in 1911 by a group of younger women writers, attacked the traditional patriarchal family system and called for the expansion of educational and professional opportunities for women.

The Taisho Democracy era after World War I saw the birth of women's organizations more explicitly committed to achieving gender equality in politics. The Society of New Women founded in 1920 successfully lobbied the Imperial Diet to amend the Peace and Police Law, which prohibited women's participation in political parties and other political organizations. This was followed by the formation of Japan's first suffragist organization in 1924 and first openly socialist women's organization in 1929. In the militarist climate of the 1930s, however, all of these liberal women's organizations were disbanded and replaced by organizations promoting the traditional status and role of women as good homemakers, wives, and mothers.

The emancipation of women was one of the most important goals of the postwar reforms undertaken during the Allied Occupation. Japanese women were enfranchised for the first time and began to participate actively in politics as voters. Numerous women's organizations were founded, including the League of Japanese Women Voters, the Women's Democratic Club, and the Federation of Women's Organizations. Their presence and activities have helped to improve Japanese women's social status and political role. However, the actual participation of Japanese women in the nation's government and policy-making remains very limited.

Japan: A Classless Society?

Japanese society, which has been strongly influenced by the Confucian view of the state as one big family where order and harmony prevail and everybody accepts his or her proper station, has never been hospitable to class-based identities. As Japan became increasingly affluent after World War II, what little class consciousness that had developed among Japanese workers during harder times steadily eroded. A high degree of social mobility also contributed to the decline of class consciousness by blurring the boundaries between the classes. By the early 1970s, about 90 percent of Japanese identified themselves as members of the middle class, somewhere between the very rich and the very poor. Japan is often depicted as a classless society in which class distinctions have virtually disappeared in terms of income, wealth, consumption habits, lifestyles, levels of education, and basic values.

The emergence of the "classless" society has had an important political impact. In the mid-1950s, slightly more than half of white-collar and blue-collar workers supported the Japan Socialist Party, while one-third supported the LDP; by the mid-1980s, the ranks of JSP supporters had diminished to about one-fifth of the total, while the ranks of LDP supporters had increased to well over half. Businesspeople and farmers have supported the LDP far more consistently. It is doubtful, however, that their partisanship results from class consciousness alone. It is more likely based on

their personal and organizational involvement with the LDP and its Diet members. Class has been a weak basis for collective political action in contemporary Japan.

Apart from the sound trucks of various extreme right-wing groups, bedecked with the national flag and driven noisily around the streets of Tokyo and other major cities to promote their causes, today's Japan is basically a politically quiet society whose citizens grumble privately rather than protest publicly.

Section ❺ Japanese Politics in Transition

Japan entered the twenty-first century a disappointed, frustrated, and confused nation. The economy, which had been hailed as a fast-growing miracle just a few decades before, was wallowing in a decade-long recession with no end in sight. In fact, the nation's GDP had not only stopped growing, but had shrunk in the last years of the twentieth century, unemployment was at a record high level, the total amount of public debt was larger than the nation's GDP and averaged more than 4 million yen (about $40,000) per capita, and a number of major firms in the key industries, such as automobile, machine tool, and home appliances, had moved their plants and jobs abroad.

The situation in Japanese politics was no better. Despite the LDP's historic defeat in the 1993 lower house general election and the subsequent changes of governments, nothing much had changed in the way politicians and bureaucrats went ineffectually about the business of governing the nation. Corruption and scandals continued to hit the headlines just as often as, or even more often than, before. The only notable difference was the increasing involvement of central government bureaucrats, who had once been regarded as incorruptible and highly competent, in the scandals. Between 1992 and 2002, senior and middle-level officials in the ministries of Health and Welfare, Labor, Agriculture, Forestry and Fisheries, Finance, and Foreign Affairs, the Defense Agency, and the Bank of Japan were charged with, and often found guilty of, corrupt acts, usually in collusion with politicians and businessmen. Combined with the perception of their incompetence and inability to solve Japan's very serious economic problems, these recurrent scandals further

eroded the already low public trust in government leaders as guardians of the public interest. They also added to the public pressure for a radical reform of the nation's political, economic, and social institutions and practices.

Junichiro Koizumi was elected LDP leader and Japanese prime minister in April 2001 as the champion of a radical reform program, with special emphasis on the deregulation and privatization of the numerous publicly owned or publicly regulated services and industries. All of his immediate predecessors had come to power with similar promises of sweeping reform, but none had actually delivered on their promises.

Koizumi entered the April 2001 LDP presidential election, a necessary step to becoming the prime minister of Japan, as an underdog against his main rival, former prime minister Ryutaro Hashimoto. However, public opinion favored Koizumi by a margin of four to one. On the eve of the election, this apparently caused a decisive shift among LDP Diet members, who would select the next head of their party, leading to Koizumi's surprising and decisive victory. Public expectations for real reform were so high that nearly 80 percent of the respondents to a poll taken after the election approved of Prime Minister Koizumi and his proclaimed agenda.

But no sooner had Koizumi begun to try to implement his reform program than it ran into strong and widespread opposition from the iron triangles that guarded the interests of the targeted industries and professions. These included, among others, the state-owned mail service, the state-regulated health service, and the state-subsidized highway and railroad construction and maintenance industries. Even the LDP's official decision-making body, the Executive Council, charged Koizumi with claiming and exercising "dictatorial powers." Koizumi nonetheless continued to push his reform agenda, but increasingly in words only rather than in action, with few tangible results.

The "Koizumi boom" ended in early 2002 as suddenly as it had begun less than a year before. The immediate cause of this turnabout was the sacking of an immensely popular member of the Koizumi cabinet and Japan's first woman foreign minister, Makiko Tanaka. Tanaka's performance during her brief tenure in office had been lackluster, but she had earned a reputation as an even more committed reformer than the prime minister. She had been embroiled in bitter battles with a number of senior officials in her own ministry and fellow LDP politicians over both policy and personnel issues. Koizumi dismissed her because he apparently wanted to put an end to these battles, which distracted attention from his main policy agenda. But by firing the most popular member of his cabinet, he lost the trust of many of those who had supported him because of his apparent commitment to reform.

Political Challenges and Changing Agendas

Despite the sorry state of the economy and an exasperating political stalemate, Japan remains an affluent and socially stable nation. Even after a decade of recession, its standard of living is among the highest in the world. Although rocked by heinous crimes from time to time, the frequency of such incidents in Japan is far lower than in any other advanced industrial nation: in 1995, less than half that of Britain, about one-fifth Germany's, and less than one-eighth that in the United States. And while the number of dropouts from elementary and lower secondary school significantly increased in the 1990s—threefold at the elementary and twofold at the secondary school level—they accounted in 1998 for no more than about a third of 1 percent and 2.5 percent, respectively, of the total number of students.

A problem of much greater concern is the aging, or graying, of Japan's population. Japan has the world's longest average life expectancy: eighty-one years. At the same time, the country's current birthrate of about 10 per 1,000 is among the lowest in the world. As a result of these two trends, Japan is expected to have the highest percentage (22.5 per 1,000) of citizens over sixty-five years of age in the world by the year 2010. This will inevitably lead to a sharp rise in the cost of health care for elderly people and a significant shortfall in the number of younger, productive workers. Alarmed by these trends, some municipalities in Japan now offer monetary rewards to parents with new babies. But this has made little difference to the overall picture of steadily and irreversibly declining birthrates in the country as a whole.

Koizumi speaking in the upper house after naming another female member of his cabinet, Environment Minister Yoriko Kawguchi, as Tanaka's replacement. *Source:* AP/Wide World Photos.

In the area of foreign policy and relations, the top priority remains the formation and maintenance of the closest and friendliest possible relationship with the United States, a goal set in the early post–World War II period and, by and large, successfully achieved by a long succession of Japanese governments. The United States has consistently been chosen as the most likable foreign country by a large plurality of respondents in every major public opinion poll taken in Japan during the past decade. It is small wonder, then, that over 5 million Japanese visit the United States each year for business or pleasure. This is more than twice as many as those who visit South Korea, three times as many as those who visit China, and six times as many as those who visit any of the other popular destinations, such as Hong Kong, Taiwan, and Thailand.

From the 1970s through the early 1990s, bilateral trade was a chronic, and often highly contentious, issue in Japanese-U.S. relations. A succession of U.S. administrations, both Republican and Democratic, kept complaining about the aggressive Japanese export drive targeted at U.S. markets and protectionism at home. As the Japanese economy lost its competitive vigor both at home and abroad in the 1990s, U.S. complaints about and criticisms of Japanese trade policy were considerably toned down, except on the issue of Japan's tightly protected agricultural, especially rice, markets. This change occurred even as the chronic Japanese surplus and U.S. deficit in the annual bilateral trade account continued.

Until about a decade ago, the United States–Japan Mutual Security Treaty was routinely condemned as warmongering and in violation of the peace clause of the 1947 Japanese Constitution not only by the Communist and Socialist parties but also by many others, especially in academia and the labor movement. According to the results of recent public opinion polls, however, an overwhelming majority of Japanese now considers the treaty beneficial to Japanese national interests. Moreover, Japanese were increasingly receptive to the long-standing U.S. demand that Japan participate more willingly and extensively in both bilateral and multilateral peacekeeping operations, especially those undertaken under UN auspices. Ever since a few Japanese civilians were sent to Angola in 1992 to watch a post–civil war election, Japan has participated, though rather peripherally in most cases, in a series of UN-sponsored operations in such diverse places as Cambodia, Mozambique, Rwanda, Bosnia-Herzegovina, and East Timor.

Next to its relationship with the United States, Japan has consistently given high priority to the cultivation of friendly relationships with its immediate neighbors in East Asia. Its effort on that score has been generally successful, with its relationships with China, South Korea, and all the Southeast Asian nations steadily improving during the last quarter of the twentieth century. The progress, however, has been disrupted, and often even reversed, by disputes over two highly charged and closely related issues.

First, every summer, usually on August 15 (the day of Japan's surrender in World War II), since the mid-1980s, Japanese prime ministers and most cabinet members have visited the controversial Yasukuni ("Nation at Peace") Shinto Shrine to pay their respects to the souls of the nearly 2.5 million "heroes" killed in the wars fought by Japan since the Meiji Restoration of the mid-nineteenth century. The Japanese leaders' visits are objectionable to many in the neighboring nations mainly for two reasons. First, the overwhelming majority (86 percent) of the "war heroes" commemorated are those killed in World War II, including the seven top wartime government and military leaders who were found guilty of crimes against peace by the International Military Tribunal for the Far East and executed. Second, the shrine's exhibitions and inscriptions cling steadfastly to the position that the war, which it calls the "Greater East Asia War," was fought by Japan for its self-defense and that the postwar trials of the Japanese leaders and soldiers were totally arbitrary, biased, and unjustified. Despite the outcries of the governments and citizens of the neighboring nations, especially China and South Korea, however, Japanese leaders, including Koizumi, have continued to make annual visits to the shrine, albeit ostensibly in their capacity as private citizens.

The second controversy involves the official authorization of secondary school history and social studies textbooks that subscribe to the same Japanocentric ideology that the Yasukuni Shrine espouses. In the latest round of this decades-old controversy, a textbook compiled by a group of right-wing historians was approved by Ministry of Education reviewers for use in schools. The news provoked instant and angry outcries among government leaders and intellectuals in China, South and North Korea, and several Southeast Asian nations. They charged that the textbook either completely ignored or papered over the Japanese aggression and brutalities committed in their countries before and during World War II.

The Yasukuni Shrine and textbook episodes point to the presence and, in some quarters, expansion of a nationalistic, and potentially chauvinistic, ideology and movement in contemporary Japanese society. Prime Minister Koizumi's insistence on his right to make a ritual visit to the controversial Shinto shrine, no matter how much it may shock and anger many foreign governments and citizens, is emblematic of this aspect of Japanese political culture at the turn of the new millennium. So is the immense popularity of Tokyo's governor and a well-known nationalist ideologue, Shintaro Ishihara, who is a potential future prime minister. His recent remark—no doubt made with his tongue in his cheek, but highly inflammable all the same—that if China keeps bullying Japan, then Japan should threaten to arm itself with nuclear weapons, provoked little public and media attention or criticism. These are very disconcerting episodes to those who treasure the reputation of post–World War II Japan as a genuinely democratic and pacifist nation.

It would, however, be rash to jump to the conclusion that the nationalists, especially the more chauvinistic among them, have taken over Japan. Koizumi's visits to Yasukuni Shrine in August 2001, April 2002, and January 2003 were, in large measure, an obligatory gesture dictated by a promise he had made to war-bereaved families at the time of his election as LDP president. The controversial secondary school textbook has been adopted by very few schools and fewer than 1,300 copies—a minuscule number for courses enrolling nearly 1.3 million students—have been sold.

Japan's role in the world is undergoing notable, but often confusing, changes in other ways too, including its defense policy. The events of September 11, 2001, had a powerful impact on Japanese public opinion: in an October 2001 poll by Japan's largest newspaper, the *Yomiuri Shinbun*, "antiterrorism measures" ranked at the top of the list of the most urgent policies for the government to act on. Nonetheless, and although Japan did send several SDF ships to the Indian Ocean to assist the U.S. effort in Afghanistan, public opinion

remained wary of the use of military means in antiterrorist, or any other, operations abroad. Polls taken by another major newspaper at the same time found those opposed to the deployment of SDF troops abroad outnumbering, 46 percent to 42 percent, those approving such actions. Those opposed to relaxing restrictions on the use of arms by SDF troops, too, outnumbered 51 percent to 39 percent those who approved it.

Another factor affecting Japan's role in the world is the sharp decline of the country's global economic power during the past decade. Once touted as the world's most dynamic industrial economy, Japan was ranked thirtieth on a forty-nine-nation relative economic competitiveness list compiled by the International Institute for Management Development of Lausanne, Switzerland. The largest donor of official development assistance (ODA) funds throughout the 1990s, Japan yielded pride of place to the United States in 2001. Moreover, the continuing weakness of its economy is likely to lead to further cuts in Japan's ODA budgets in the coming years, which will likely lead to a decline in Japan's political and diplomatic influence in the region.

Japanese Politics in Comparative Perspective

Postwar Japan's economic success inspired many other Asian nations, including South Korea, Taiwan, Thailand, Malaysia, and Indonesia, to adopt the Japanese model of development. Like Japan, these countries used an assortment of government policies and institutions to facilitate human capital formation (especially education), high savings and investment rates, efficient resource allocation, and export expansion to encourage the rapid growth of their national economies. But today's Japan is no longer an economic miracle or model.

Japan thus presents a model of state-led development that worked successfully for more than a century but faltered badly in the 1990s. This experience raises some interesting questions about the relationship between the state and the economy:

• Why did the Japanese model of economic development work for so long, but then prove unable to adapt to changing domestic and international circumstances? Particularly, what role did the state play in both the successes and limitations of Japan's development model?

- Will state-led development ever work again in Japan in the future and, if so, under what conditions? How would the role of the government have to change in order to help revive the Japanese economy?
- Could the Japanese model work successfully in other nations and, if so, under what domestic or international conditions and at what stages of national development?

Japan has also often been cited as a model of so-called Asian-style democracy. The Western model of democratic government emphasizes active citizen participation in the affairs of the state, the role of independent political parties and interest groups, and the periodic alternation of power among competing political parties. The Japanese model is said to rely on a passive and compliant citizenry and monopoly of power by one party or the government bureaucracy. Japan and most of its Asian neighbors have placed far greater emphasis on economic growth and political stability than on citizen participation in politics or the protection of political and human rights. This emphasis is particularly agreeable to those who believe in the Confucian ideal of an orderly, hierarchical, harmonious society governed by a wise and benevolent ruler or ruling elite with the support of a loyal and obedient citizenry. This model has often been used to justify repressive governments in post–World War II Asia, but has weakened to some extent as democratization has spread to formerly authoritarian states, including South Korea and Taiwan.

The instability of Japanese politics since the LDP's electoral defeats in the 1990s also calls into question the long-term viability of such a model of governance in contemporary Asia. Where there are deep economic, social, or ideological divisions in society, democracy inevitably gives rise to political contention. Japan experienced just such intense political conflict during the formative period (1947–1960) of its postwar democracy. In fact, it took a major political crisis caused by a massive popular protest against the undemocratic and high-handed manner in which the government pursued the 1960 revision of the U.S.-Japanese Mutual Security Treaty to usher in a period of compromise and consensus that lasted for the next three decades and helped produce both stability and prosperity.

In other words, it took Japan a decade and a half of intense political conflict—and several more decades if one considers the struggle for democracy in prewar Japan—to learn to practice democracy in peace. After the traumatic experience of 1960, the ruling LDP began to take the opposition's opinion and policies seriously and often to co-opt them. Long before its dominance of Japanese politics ended in the early 1990s, the LDP had begun to co-opt and incorporate into its own programs many of the interests of organized labor, though not necessarily of unorganized workers or consumers, through informal consultations and deals made with the opposition, if only to avert another political crisis.

Democracy thus did not get established in Japan in the absence of political conflict but rather in and through conflict, just as in Western Europe and the United States. The rupture of consensus and return of open conflict that led to the change of government in 1993 did not mean a breakdown of democracy in Japan. On the contrary, it reflected the strength and maturity of Japanese democracy by proving the ability of Japanese citizens to "throw the rascals out" through the ballot box. Moreover, this changing of the guard gave the opposition an opportunity to learn how to govern and the LDP an opportunity to learn how to oppose within the framework of democratic government.

While this first change of government in Japan in nearly forty years did not last long, it has helped to reduce oligarchic influences and increase democratic elements in contemporary Japanese politics. The succession of coalition governments that have been formed and have governed the nation since 1993 have proved, by and large, more sensitive to public opinion and less beholden to special interests than earlier LDP-dominated governments. Nevertheless, a few years into the twenty-first century, the first order of business for Japan remains the real and effective reform of its many moribund political, economic, and social institutions, for the sake not only of its own people but also for many others in the Asia-Pacific region and, indeed, in the increasingly interdependent world.

Key Terms

bushi (samurai)	nontariff barriers
zaibatsu	Asian Development Bank
Taisho Democracy	Asia-Pacific Economic Cooperation
Supreme Commander for the Allied Powers	Association of Southeast Asian Nations
Self-Defense Forces	vertically divided administration
predominant-party regime	amakudari
Sohyo	Aegis
Domei	zoku
Rengo	iron triangles
industrial policy	koenkai
administrative guidance	clientelism
keiretsu	Tokai Village
dual-structure system	Minamata disease
spring labor offensive	
lifetime employment	

Suggested Readings

Abe, Hitoshi, Shindo, Muneyuki, and Kawato, Sadafumi. *The Government and Politics of Japan*. Trans. James White. Tokyo: University of Tokyo Press, 1994.

Barnhard, Michael A. *Japan Prepares for Total War: The Search for Economic Security, 1919–1941*. Ithaca, N.Y.: Cornell University Press, 1987.

Calder, Kent E. *Crisis and Compensation: Public Policy and Political Stability in Japan, 1949–1986*. Princeton, N.J.: Princeton University Press, 1988.

Dower, John W. *Embracing Defeat: Japan in the Wake of World War II*. New York: Norton, 2000.

Francks, Penelope. *Japanese Economic Development: Theory and Practice*. London: Routledge, 1992.

Fruin, W. Mark. *The Japanese Enterprise System: Competitive Strategies and Cooperative Structures*. Oxford: Clarendon Press, 1992.

Gluck, Carol. *Japan's Modern Myths: Ideology in the Late Meiji Period*. Princeton, N.J.: Princeton University Press, 1985.

Hall, John Whitney, et al., eds., *The Cambridge History of Japan*, 6 vols. Cambridge: Cambridge University Press, 1988–1993.

Hook, Glenn D., et al. *Japan's International Relations: Politics, Economics and Security*. London: Routledge, 2001.

Johnson, Chalmers A. *MITI and the Japanese Miracle: The Growth of Industrial Policy, 1925-1975*. Stanford: Stanford University Press, 1982.

Katz, Richard. *Japanese Phoenix: The Long Road to Economic Revival*. Armonk, N.Y.: M. E. Sharpe, 2002.

Kohno, Masaru. *Japan's Postwar Party Politics*. Princeton, N.J.: Princeton University Press, 1997.

Lincoln, Edward J. *Japan's New Global Role*. Washington, D.C.: Brookings Institution, 1993.

Lockwood, William W. *The Economic Development of Japan: Growth and Structural Change, 1868–1938*. Princeton, N.J.: Princeton University Press, 1954.

Miyashita, Kenichi, and Russell, David. *Keiretsu: Inside the Hidden Japanese Conglomerates*. New York: McGraw-Hill, 1994.

Mulgan, Aurelia George. *Japan's Failed Revolution: Koizumi and the Politics of Economic Reform*. Canberra: Asia Pacific Press, 2002.

Nakamura, Takafusa. *The Postwar Japanese Economy: Its Development and Structure, 1937–1994*. 2nd ed. Trans. Jacqueline Kaminski. Tokyo: University of Tokyo Press, 1995.

Pempel, T. J. *Regime Shift: Comparative Dynamics of the Japanese Political Economy*. Ithaca, N.Y.: Cornell University Press, 1998.

Ramseyer, J. Mark, and Rosenbluth, Frances M. *The Politics of Oligarchy: Institutional Choice in Imperial Japan*. Cambridge: Cambridge University Press, 1995.

Samuels, Richard J. *"Rich Nation, Strong Army": National Security and the Technological Transformation of Japan*. Ithaca, N.Y.: Cornell University Press, 1994.

Stockwin, J. A. A. *Governing Japan: Divided Politics in a Major Economy*. 3rd ed. Oxford: Blackwell. 1999.

Vogel, Ezra A. *Japan As Number One: Lessons for America*. Cambridge, Mass.: Harvard University Press, 1979.

Suggested Websites

Asahi Newspaper (English)
www.asahi.com/english/english.html
Embassy of Japan in the United States
www.embjapan.org/
Japan Guide
jguide.stanford.edu/
Japan Politics Central
www.people.virginia.edu/~ljs2k/webtext.html
Japan Politics
ist-socrates.berkeley.edu/~jaytate/japanpolitics.html
Resources on the WWW for the Study of the Japanese Polity
www.lib.duke.edu/ias/eac/polsciww.html

Notes

[1]George Sansom, *A History of Japan, 1334–1615* (Stanford, Calif.: Stanford University Press, 1961); A. L. Sadler, *A Short History of Japan* (Sydney: Angus and Robertson, 1963), Ch. 4–6.

[2]George De Vos and Hiroshi Wagatsuma, eds., *Japan's Invisible Race: Caste in Culture and Personality* (Berkeley: University of California Press, 1966); Frank K. Upham, *Law and Social Change in Postwar Japan* (Cambridge, Mass.: Harvard University Press, 1987), Ch. 3.

[3]Mikiso Hane, *Modern Japan: A Historical Survey* (Boulder, Colo.: Westview Press, 1986), 35–37.

[4]Ronald P. Dore, *Education in Tokugawa Japan* (London: Athlone, 1965).

[5]Alfred Tamarin, *Japan and the United States: Early Encounters 1791–1860* (London: Macmillan, 1970); Peter Booth Wiley, with Korogi Ichiro, *Yankees in the Land of the Gods: Commodore Perry and the Opening of Japan* (New York: Viking, 1990).

[6]W. G. Beasley, *Japan Encounters the Barbarian: Japanese Travellers in America and Europe* (New Haven, Conn.: Yale University Press, 1995), Ch. 9.

[7]Richard J. Samuels, *"Rich Nation, Strong Army": National Security and the Technological Transformation of Japan* (Ithaca, N.Y.: Cornell University Press, 1994), Ch. 2.

[8]Robert A. Scalapino, *Democracy and the Party Movement in Prewar Japan* (Berkeley: University of California Press, 1962), Ch. 2–4.

[9]Peter Duus, *Party Rivalry and Political Change in Taisho Japan* (Cambridge, Mass.: Harvard University Press, 1968).

[10]Sadako N. Ogata, *Defiance in Manchuria: The Making of Japanese Foreign Policy, 1931–1932* (Berkeley: University of California Press, 1964), Pt. II.

[11]Ben-Ami Shillony, *Revolt in Japan: The Young Officers and the February 26, 1936 Incident* (Princeton, N.J.: Princeton University Press, 1973).

[12]Herbert Feis, *The Road to Pearl Harbor: The Coming of the War Between the United States and Japan* (Princeton, N.J.: Princeton University Press, 1950).

[13]Robert E. Ward and Sakamoto Yoshikazu, eds., *Democratizing Japan: The Allied Occupation* (Honolulu: University of Hawaii Press, 1987).

[14]Haruhiro Fukui and Shigeko N. Fukai, "The End of the Miracle: Japanese Politics in the Post–Cold War Era," in *The Rise of East Asia: Critical Visions of the Pacific Century*, ed. Mark T. Berger and Douglas A. Borer (New York: Routledge, 1997), 37–60.

[15]Charles C. Ragin, *The Comparative Method: Moving Beyond Qualitative and Quantitative Strategies* (Berkeley: University of California Press, 1987), Ch. 3; Adam Preworski and Henry Teune, *The Logic of Comparative Social Inquiry* (New York: Wiley-Interscience, 1970).

[16]Hugh Patrick and Henry Rosovsky, "Japan's Economic Performance: An Overview," in *Asia's New Giant: How the Japanese Economy Works,* ed. Hugh Patrick and Henry Rosovsky (Washington, D.C.: Brookings Institution, 1976), 7–9; Kazuo Yamaguchi, "Early Modern Economy (1868–1945)," in *Kodansha Encyclopedia of Japan*, vol. 2 (Tokyo: Kodansha Ltd., 1983), 151–154.

[17]William W. Lockwood, *The Economic Development of Japan: Growth and Structural Change, 1868–1938* (Princeton, N.J.: Princeton University Press, 1954), 38–39.

[18]Ronald P. Dore, *Land Reform in Japan* (London: Oxford University Press, 1959), 176, Table 9.

[19]Lockwood, *The Economic Development of Japan*, 14–15.

[20]Hidemasa Morikawa, *Zaibatsu: The Rise and Fall of Family Enterprise Groups in Japan* (Tokyo: University of Tokyo Press, 1992).

[21]Daniel I. Okimoto, *Between MITI and the Market: Japanese Industrial Policy for High Technology* (Stanford, Calif.: Stanford University Press, 1989), Ch. 2.

[22]Somusho tokeikyoku, and Tokei kenshujo [Bureau of Statistics and Statistics Center, Ministry of Public Management, Home Affairs, Postal Services and Telecommunications], eds. *Nihon no tokei 2002* [Japanese statistics, 2002] (Tokyo: Zaimusho insatsukyoku, 2002), 307, Table 20-17.

[23]Somusho tokeikyoku, and Tokei kenshujo [Bureau of Statistics and Statistics Center, Ministry of Public Management, Home Affairs, Postal Services and Telecommunications], eds. *Sekai no tokei 2002* [World statistics, 2002] (Tokyo: Zaimusho insatsukyoku, 2002), 80-81, Table 3-10.

[24]Richard Rosecrance, *The Rise of the Trading State* (New York: Basic Books, 1986).

[25]Naikakufu keizaishakai-sogokenkyujo (Cabinet office institute for integrated economic and social research), ed. *Keizai yoran 2002* (Economic handbook)(Tokyo: Zaimusho insatsukyoku, 2002), 174–75.

[26]Stephen D. Cohen, *Cowboys and Samurai: Why the United States Is Losing the Industrial Battle and Why It Matters* (New York: HarperBusiness, 1991).

[27]Herbert P. Bix, *Hirohito and the Making of Modern Japan* (New York: HarperCollins, 2000); Stephen S. Large, *Emperor Hirohito and Showa Japan: A Political Biography* (London: Routledge, 1992).

[28]Chalmers Johnson, *MITI and the Japanese Miracle: The Growth of Industrial Policy, 1925–1975* (Stanford, CA: Stanford University Press, 1982).

[29]Michio Muramatsu, *Local Power in the Japanese State*, trans. Betsey Sheiner and James White (Berkeley: University of California Press, 1997).

[30]Haruhiro Fukui, "Japan," in *Passages to Power: Legislative Recruitment in Advanced Democracies,* ed. Pippa Norris (Cambridge, U.K.: Cambridge University Press, 1997), 106–108.

[31]Thomas P. Rohlen, *Japan's High Schools* (Berkeley: University of California Press, 1983). For an overview of contemporary Japanese school education, see Thomas P. Rohlen and Chris Björk, eds., *Education and Training in Japan,* 3 vols. (London: Routledge, 1998).

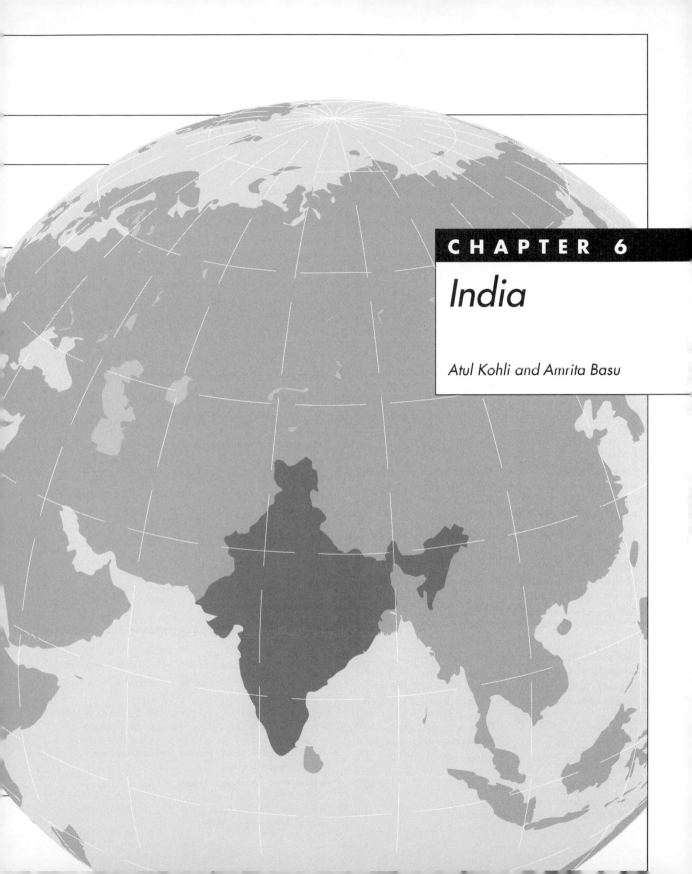

CHAPTER 6

India

Atul Kohli and Amrita Basu

Republic of India

Land and People

Capital	New Delhi	
Total area (square miles)	1,269,338 (slightly more than one-third the size of the U.S.)	
Population (2001)	1.09 billion	
Annual population growth rate (%)	1975–2000	1.9
	2000–2015 (projected)	1.3
Urban population (%)	27.7	
Major languages* (%)	Hindi	40
	Telugu	8
	Bengali	8
	Marathi	7.3
	Tamil	6.6
	Gujarati	4
	Urdu	5
	Other	22

*Hindi is the main language, but English is the most important language for political, commercial, and other national-level communication.

Religious affiliation (%)	Hindu	81.3
	Muslim	12
	Christian	2.3
	Sikh	1.9
	Buddhist and other	2.5

Economy

Domestic currency	Rupee (INR) US$1: 47.9 INR (2002 average)	
Total GDP (US$)	457 billion	
GDP per capita (US$)	476	
Total GDP at purchasing power parity (US$$)	2.4 trillion	
GDP per capita at purchasing power parity (US$)	2,358	
GDP annual growth rate (%)	1997	4.4
	2000	3.9
	2001	4.5
GDP per capita average annual growth rate (%)	1975–2000	3.2
	1990–2000	4.1
Inequality in income consumption (1997) (%)	Share of poorest 10%	3.5
	Share of poorest 20%	8.1
	Share of richest 20%	46.1
	Share of richest 10%	33.5
	Gini index (1997)	37.8
Structure of production (% of GDP)	Agriculture	24.9
	Industry	26.9
	Services	48.2
Labor force distribution (% of total)	Agriculture	60
	Industry	23
	Services	17

Exports as % of GDP	14
Imports as % of GDP	17
Electricity consumption per capita (kwh)	448
Carbon dioxide emissions per capita (metric tons)	1

Society

Life expectancy	Female	63
	Male	62.8
Doctors per 100,000 people		48
Infant mortality (per 1,000 live births)		69
Adult literacy (%)	Female	45.4
	Male	68.4
Access to information and communications (per 1,000 people)	Telephone lines	32
	Mobile phones	4
	Radios	121
	Televisions	78
	Personal computers	4.5

Women in Government and Economy

Women in the national legislature		
Lower house or single house (%)		8.8
Upper house (%)		9.1
Women at ministerial level (%)		10.1
Female economic activity rate (age 15 and above) (%)		50
Female labor force (% of total)		32
Estimated earned income (PPP US$)	Female	1,267
	Male	3,383

2002 Human Development Index ranking (out of 173 countries)	124

Political Organization

Political System   Parliamentary democracy and a federal republic.

Regime History   Current government formed by the Bharatiya Janata Party (BJP), under the leadership of Atal Behari Vajpayee.

Administrative Structure   Federal, with 28 state governments.

Executive   Prime minister, leader of the party with the most seats in the parliament.

Legislature   Bicameral, upper house elected indirectly and without much substantial power; lower house, the main house, with members elected from single-member districts, winner-take-all. Judiciary Independent constitutional court with appointed judges.

Party System   Multiparty system. The Bharatiya Janata Party (BJP) is the dominant party; major opposition parties include the Congress Party, Janata Dal, and the Communist Party of India, Marxist (CPM).

Politics in Action

On December 6, 1992, thousands of Hindus, encouraged by the Bharatiya Janata Party (BJP, Indian People's Party), stormed and destroyed a Muslim mosque in Ayodhya, India. In the accompanying riots, 1,700 people were killed.

In May 1998, the BJP-led coalition government proclaimed that India was a nuclear power, since it had successfully detonated five underground nuclear explosions.

*In late February and early March 2002, groups instigated by the **Hindu** nationalists attacked and killed well over 1,000 **Muslims** in the state of Gujarat, in apparent retaliation for an attack on a train bringing Hindu activists back from Ayodhya.*

The tense, tumultuous, bloody trek from Ayodhya to the nuclear bomb, back to Ayodhya, highlights the turbulent nature of Indian democracy in the early twenty-first century. It challenges images of an earlier era in which India exemplified principles of secularism, stability, and nonviolence. And yet, with it all, Indian democracy has endured and succeeded for well over half a century.

The Ayodhya incident was triggered by the electoral mobilization strategies of the BJP, a religious, nationalist party that had been courting the electoral and political support of Hindus, India's largest religious group at over 80 percent of the country's population. BJP leaders argued that the mosque at Ayodhya, a place of worship for India's Muslims, who constitute nearly 11 percent of India's population, had been built on the birthplace of the Hindu god Rama. They wanted to replace the mosque with a Hindu temple. The BJP mobilized Hindus, including unemployed youth and small traders, throughout India, in political protest. The political use of religious symbols touched a raw nerve in a multiethnic society in which religious conflict has a long history and memories of communal hostility and suspicion are ever present. After all, Indian independence in 1947 was achieved at the same time that the "jewel in the crown" of Britain's colonial empire was dismembered into mostly Hindu India and mostly Muslim Pakistan. The partition was achieved by vast migration between the two countries and widespread religious violence.

The BJP's successful use of religious divisions enabled it to emerge as India's ruling party in the 1998 parliamentary elections and again in general elections a year later. Shortly afterward, in fulfillment of one of

A crowd of Hindu nationalists listens to speeches by leaders around a disputed mosque in Ayodhya, a town in northern India, on December 6, 1992. The mosque was later torn down by belligerent volunteers, precipitating a major political crisis. *Source:* Bettmann/Corbis.

the BJP's electoral promises, the BJP-led coalition government gate-crashed the nuclear club, triggering a nuclear arms race in South Asia. Although the Indian government cited regional threats from China and Pakistan as the key reason, the decision to become a nuclear state can also be traced directly to the evolution of Indian democracy since the late 1980s. Electoral mobilization along ethnic lines (religious, language, or caste) in an atmosphere of economic turmoil and poverty prompted political parties to mobilize Indians' national pride, thereby deflecting attention from domestic economic and political problems. Within a few weeks, India's archenemy and neighbor, Pakistan, responded by testing its own bomb. Swift worldwide condemnation followed as many countries, including the United States, punished both countries with the imposition of economic and technology sanctions.

The riots in Gujarat in the spring of 2002 were among the worst that India has experienced in the postindependence period, compared even to the violence that accompanied the destruction of the mosque in Ayodhya. The catalyst for the violence was an attack on a trainload of pilgrims returning from Ayodhya, in which fifty-nine Hindus were killed. In the weeks that followed, Hindu groups engaged in a campaign of terror against the Muslim population of Gujarat. The rampage was a particularly grave challenge to democratic prin-

ciples because it was sanctioned by leading political officials of the BJP state government in Gujarat. Unlike riots of the past, which were an urban phenomenon, this one spread to the villages and gained the support of untouchables, the lowest caste in the Hindu caste hierarchy, and tribals, or indigenous peoples The violence often included sexual assaults on women. However, the tragedy far surpassed the immediate destruction of lives and property. With tacit support from the national government, the BJP government in Gujarat called for early elections in 2002 and won a landslide victory by capitalizing on the electoral support of the Hindus that it had mobilized during the riots.

These incidents capture three important themes in contemporary Indian politics. First, political struggles in a relatively poor, multicultural democracy are especially likely to be contentious. Many of these struggles readily become ethnic conflicts, broadly concerned with questions of religion, language, and caste. The most violent conflicts in India in the recent past have been religious and have often involved Hindus and Muslims. Protracted ethnic conflicts over territory have also acquired religious overtones, especially in Kashmir, a state in northern India in which Hindu-Muslim divisions are especially strong.

Second, although ethnic conflicts appear to be the products of primordial animosities, they are often

Indian nuclear test, May 1998.
Source: Baldev/Sygma.

instigated by political parties and the state. In recent years, the growing strength of the BJP, both in opposition and in office, has heavily contributed to religious polarization. As the development of the nuclear bomb and the riots suggest, the BJP's anti-Muslim stance has influenced both its domestic and foreign policy.

Although growing conflicts often push Indian democracy to the brink, the democratic system has managed to absorb the crises and muddle through for over half a century, albeit with strains. An important question for students of Indian politics, and comparative politics more generally, is how and why the second most populous country in the world, and one of the poorest, has maintained democratic institutions since it gained independence after World War II.

Geographic Setting

India is a big, populous, and geographically and culturally diverse country. Its large size, approximately 2,000 miles in both length and width, is rivaled in Asia only by China. Its rich geographic setting includes three diverse topographic zones (the mountainous northern zone, the basin formed by the Ganges River, and the peninsula of southern India) and a variety of climates (mountain climate in the northern mountain range; dry, hot weather in the arid, northern plateau; and subtropical climate in the south). Along with its neighbors Pakistan and Bangladesh, the region is physically isolated from the rest of Asia by the Himalayas to the north and the Indian Ocean to the east, south, and west. The northwest frontier is the only permeable frontier, and it is the route that successive invaders and migrants have used to enter this region.

India's population of over 1 billion people makes it the second largest country in the world, after its neighbor China. It is the world's largest democracy and the oldest democracy among the developing countries of Asia, Africa, and Latin America. India has functioned as a democracy with full adult suffrage since 1947, when it emerged as a sovereign nation-state following the end of British colonial rule. The durability of Indian democracy is especially intriguing considering the diversity of Indian society. Some fourteen major languages and numerous dialects are spoken. India contains many different ethnic groups, a host of regionally concentrated tribal groups, as well as adherents of vir-

tually all the world's major religions. In addition to the majority Hindu population, India includes Muslims, **Sikhs,** Jains, Buddhists, Christians, and even several tiny Jewish communities. Furthermore, Indian society, especially Hindu society, is divided into myriad caste groupings. Although these are mainly based on occupation, they also tend to be closed social groups in the sense that people are born into, marry, and die within their caste. India is still largely an agrarian society; 73 percent of the population lives in far-flung villages in the rural areas. The major cities, Bombay, Calcutta, and New Delhi, the national capital, are densely populated.

Critical Junctures

India is among the most ancient civilizations of the world, dating back to the third millennium B.C. The Indian subcontinent, comprising Pakistan, India, and Bangladesh, has witnessed the rise and fall of many civilizations and empires. Only five of the most recent legacies that have shaped present-day politics are reviewed here.

The Colonial Legacy (1757–1947)

Motivated by a combination of economic and political interests, the British started making inroads into the Indian subcontinent in the late seventeenth and early eighteenth centuries. Since 1526, large sections of the subcontinent had been ruled by the Mughal dynasty, which hailed from Central Asia and was Muslim by religion. As the power of the Mughal emperors declined in the eighteenth century, lesser princely contenders vied with one another for supremacy. In this environment, the British East India Company, a large English trading organization with commercial interests in India and strong backing from the British Crown, was able to play off one Indian prince against another, forming alliances with some, subduing others, and thus strengthening its control through a policy of divide and rule.

This informal empire was replaced in the mid-nineteenth century with a more formal one. After a major revolt by an alliance of Indian princes against growing British power, known as the Sepoy Rebellion or the Mutiny of 1857, the British Crown assumed direct control of India. British rule over India from 1857 to

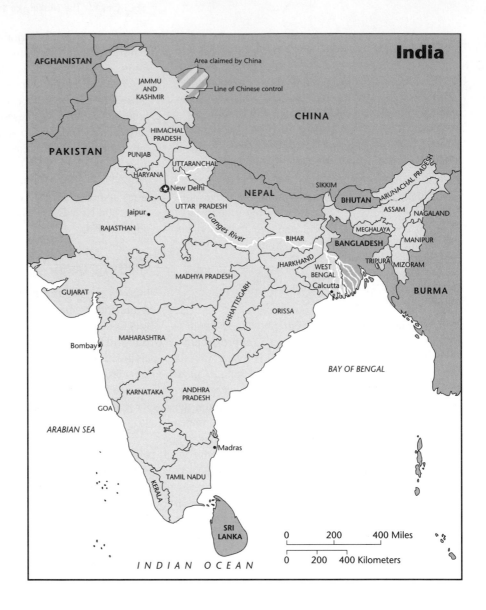

1947 left important legacies. Like other colonies, India contributed to Britain's Industrial Revolution because it was a source of cheap raw materials and provided an outlet for both British manufactured goods and investment. Colonial rule in India also provided a model for subsequent British colonial ventures.

In order to consolidate its political and economic hold over India, the British created three main varieties of ruling arrangements. First, numerous small- to medium-sized states, as many as five hundred covering an area equal to two-fifths of the subcontinent,

continued to be ruled throughout the colonial period by traditional Indian princes, the **Maharajas.** In exchange for accepting British rule, these Indian princes were allowed a relatively free hand within their realms. Second, in other parts of India, British indirect rule penetrated more deeply than in the princely states, for example, in the Bengal area (currently Bihar, West Bengal, and Bangladesh). In these regions, the British transformed traditional Indian elites, who controlled much agricultural land, into legal landlords, the *zamindars,* in exchange for periodic payments to the

---

Critical Junctures in Modern India's Development

1526	Mughal dynasty founded.
1612–1690	British East India Company establishes trading stations at Surat, Bombay, and Calcutta.
1757	Britain establishes informal colonial rule.
1857	Britain establishes formal colonial rule in response to Sepoy Rebellion.
1885	Indian National Congress is created.
1947	India achieves independence from Britain; India and Pakistan are partitioned; modern Indian state is founded.
1947–1964	Jawaharlal Nehru is prime minister.
1966–1984	Indira Gandhi is prime minister (except for a brief period from 1977 to 1980).
1990–Present	Rise of the Bharatiya Janata Party and India's emergence as a nuclear power.

---

colonial administration. Third, the British established direct rule in the remaining regions of India, for example, in Bombay and the Madras presidencies (large areas around the cities of the same name), where British civil servants were directly responsible for collecting land taxes and adjudicating law and order.

Whatever its particular forms, British rule seldom reached very deep into Indian society, especially in rural areas, which were organized into countless relatively self-sufficient villages. Social life within villages was further divided by religiously sanctioned caste groups. Typically, a few landowning castes dominated many other castes lower in the ritual, occupational, and income hierarchies.

The British sought to create a semblance of coherence in India through the creation of a central government that controlled and led these various territories and indigenous authority structures. Important instruments included the creation of an all-India civil service, police force, and army. Although at first only British nationals could serve in these institutions, with the introduction of modern educational institutions, some educated Indians were incorporated into government services. Unlike many other colonies, particularly in Africa, the British helped create a relatively effective state structure in India. When India emerged from

British rule in 1947, it inherited, maintained, and expanded colonial institutions. The civil administration, police, and armed services in contemporary India continue to be organized along the principles established by the British colonialists in the last century. Thus, there is close continuity between the modern Indian state and the British colonial tradition.

The Nationalist Movement (1885–1947)

With the growth of commerce, education, and urbanization, groups of urban, educated upper caste Indian elites emerged as the new Indian leaders. They both observed and closely interacted with their colonial rulers and often felt slighted by their treatment as second-class citizens. Even at this stage, a secular-religious divide was apparent. Some of them were Hindu nationalists who believed that a reformed Hinduism could provide a basis for a new, modern India. Others were attracted to British liberal ideas and invoked these to seek greater equality with the British.

Two centuries of British colonial rule witnessed growing intellectual and cultural ferment in India. The British colonial rulers and traditional Indian elites had become allies of sorts, squeezing from the poor Indian peasantry resources that were simultaneously used to maintain the colonial bureaucratic state and support the conspicuous lifestyles of a parasitic landlord class. It was not long before Indian nationalists opposed these arrangements through the Indian National Congress (INC), which was actually formed by an Englishman in 1885. Its aim was to right the racial, cultural, and political wrongs of colonial rule. In its early years, the INC was mainly a collection of Indian urban elites who periodically met and petitioned India's British rulers, invoking liberal principles of political equality and requesting greater Indian involvement in higher political offices. The British largely ignored these requests, and over time, the requests turned into demands, pushing some nationalists into militancy and others into nonviolent mass mobilization.

World War I was an important turning point for Indian nationalists. After the war, as great European empires disintegrated, creating new sovereign states in Europe and the Middle East, the principle of self-determination for people who considered themselves a nation gained international respectability. Indian nationalists were also inspired by the Russian revolution of 1917, which they viewed as a successful uprising against imperialism.

The man most responsible for helping to transform the INC from a narrow, elitist club to a mass nationalist movement was Mohandas Karamchand Gandhi, called Mahatma ("great soul") by his followers, one of the most influential and admirable leaders of the twentieth century. After becoming the leader of the INC in the 1920s, Gandhi successfully mobilized the middle classes, as well as a segment of the peasantry, into an anti-British movement that came to demand full sovereignty for India.

Three characteristics of the nationalist movement greatly influenced state building and democracy in India. First, the INC came to embody the principle of

Leaders: *Mahatma Gandhi*

Born in 1869 in western India, Mohandas Gandhi studied law in London for two years and worked in Durban, South Africa, as a lawyer and an activist for twenty-one years before returning home to join the Indian nationalist movement. His work among the different communities in South Africa helped him to develop the political strategies of nonviolence, or *satyagraha* (grasp of truth). On his arrival in India in 1915, he set about transforming the Indian National Congress into a mass party by reaching out to the urban and rural poor, non-Hindu religious groups, and the scheduled castes, whom he called *Harijans,* or Children of God. Following the British massacre of unarmed civilians gathered in protest in the Punjab (at the Jallianwala Bagh, a location well-known in Indian history) in April 1919, Gandhi and Jawaharlal Nehru proposed a noncooperation movement. This required a boycott of British legal and educational institutions as well as British merchandise, for which were substituted indigenous, or *swadeshi,* varieties. (The image of Gandhi weaving his own cloth is familiar to many.) Gandhi believed that mass civil disobedience could succeed only if people were truly committed. The involvement of some Congress workers in a violent incident in 1922 greatly disturbed him, causing him to call off the noncooperation movement. Gandhi was strongly opposed to the partition of India along religious lines in 1947, but because he had resigned from the Congress in 1934, his protests went unheard. Nevertheless, he dominated India's nationalist movement for more than two decades until he was assassinated in January 1948, five months after India achieved its goal of self-rule, or *swaraj.* He is often referred to as the Mahatma, or "great soul."

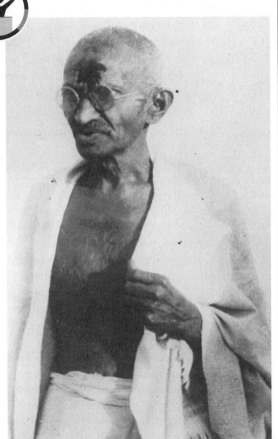

Mahatma Gandhi, the leader of India's independence movement as he appeared at the head of a 200-mile march, staged in defiance of the statute establishing a government salt monopoly by the British colonial government in 1930. *Source:* UPI/Bettmann.

unity within diversity, which served India well in creating and maintaining a relatively stable political system. Because the INC became a powerful political organization committed to establishing an Indian nation, many conflicts could play themselves out within the INC without undermining its unity. Second, although a variety of Indians in their encounter with the British discovered what they had in common with each other, they also recognized their differences. The most serious conflict was between Hindus and Muslims. A segment of the Indian Muslim elite refused to accept the leadership of Gandhi and the INC, demanded separate political rights for Muslims, and called for an independent Muslim state when the INC refused.

The resulting division of the subcontinent into two sovereign states in 1947—the Muslim state of Pakistan and the secular state of India—was turbulent and bloody. Millions of Muslims fled from India to Pakistan, and millions of Hindus fled the other way; nearly 20 million people migrated, and up to 3 million may have died in communal violence. The euphoria of independence in India was thus tempered by the human tragedy that accompanied the subcontinent's partition.

Third, the nationalist movement laid the foundations for democracy in India. Although Gandhi pioneered the use of civil disobedience to challenge British laws that he regarded as unjust, he did so on the basis of profound ethical commitments and nonviolent means. Many of the INC's prominent leaders, like Jawaharlal Nehru, were educated in England and were committed democrats. Moreover, the INC participated in limited elections allowed by the British, ran democratic governments with limited powers in various British-controlled Indian provinces, and chose its own leaders through internal elections. These preindependence democratic tendencies were valuable assets to Indian democracy.

During the 1920s and 1930s, Gandhi, Nehru, and other leaders of the INC were increasingly successful in mobilizing Indians in an anti-British nationalist movement for India's independence. The more successful the movement became, the more the British either had to repress the INC or make concessions, and they tried both. However, World War II consumed Britain's energies, and the economic and symbolic costs of colonization became extremely onerous. In order to gain Indian support for its war efforts, the British promised Indians independence following the war. India became a sovereign state in August 1947, when the British, weakened from World War II, decided to withdraw from the subcontinent.

The Nehru Era (1947–1964)

Within India, Jawaharlal Nehru, who Gandhi favored, emerged as the leader of the new nation. Soon after, a militant member of the extremist anti-Muslim Hindu cultural organization, the *Rashtriya Swayam Sevak Sangh* (RSS), assassinated Gandhi, who had opposed partition and later ardently defended Muslims within India. Nehru became the uncontested leader of a new India, a position he maintained until his death in 1964. The years of Nehru's rule shaped the dominant patterns of India's future development.

Nehru's India inherited an ambiguous legacy from British rule: a relatively strong central government and a weak economy. Nehru, a committed nationalist and social democrat, sought to strengthen India's independence and national power and to improve its economy and the lives of the Indian poor. He used the governmental machinery that India had inherited to accomplish these tasks.

At independence, India was confronted with major political problems, including a massive inflow of refugees, war with Pakistan over the disputed state of Kashmir, situated between the two countries, and the need to consolidate numerous Indian princely states into a coherent national state. Concerned about India's capacity to deal with such problems, Nehru and other leaders depended on and further strengthened the civil, police, and armed services that were legacies of colonial rule.

After independence, India adopted a democratic constitution and established a British-style democracy with full adult suffrage. Because political power now required winning elections, the INC had to transform itself from an opposition movement into a political party, the Congress Party. It was highly successful in doing so, in part by establishing a nationwide patronage system. Another important change in the decade following independence was the linguistic reorganization of states. As in the United States, the Indian constitution defines India as a federal system. The contentious political issue in the 1950s was the criterion by which Indian political groups could demand a state within the federal union. With Indians divided by the languages they speak, an

Leaders: *The Nehru-Gandhi Dynasty*

Jawaharlal Nehru

Jawaharlal Nehru was a staunch believer in liberal democratic principles. Along with Gandhi and others, he was at the forefront of India's nationalist movement against the British. When India became independent in 1947, Nehru became prime minister as head of the Congress Party and retained that position until his death in 1964. During this period, he established India as a socialist, democratic, and secular state in theory, if not always in practice. On the international front, he helped found the nonaligned movement, a forum for expressing the interests and aspirations of developing countries that did not want to ally with the United States or the Soviet Union during the cold war. Nehru attempted to set India on a rapid road to industrialization by establishing heavy industry. His efforts to effect redistribution of wealth through land reform were combined with an equally strong commitment to democratic and individual rights, such as the right to private property. Upon his death, India inherited a stable polity, a functioning democracy, and an economy characterized by a large public sector and an intricate pattern of state control over the private sector.

Indira Gandhi

Indira Gandhi became prime minister shortly after the death of her father, Jawaharlal Nehru, and dominated the Indian political scene until her assassination in 1984. Her years in power strengthened India's international position, but her domestic policies weakened the organizational structure of the Congress Party. Her tendencies toward centralization and the personalization of authority within the Congress and the concomitant use of populist rhetoric in electoral campaigns contributed to the erosion of the Congress Party. By presenting the regional conflict in the Punjab and problems with Pakistan as Hindu-Sikh and Hindu-Muslim problems, respectively, she contributed to further erosion of the party's secular base and to rising religious factionalism. Her decision to send troops into the holiest of the holy Sikh temples in Amritsar deeply alienated Sikhs, a small but important religious group in India. The ensuing bloodshed culminated in her assassination by one of her Sikh bodyguards in 1984. Her assassination ushered in a new generation of the Nehru-Gandhi dynasty, as her son Rajiv Gandhi served as prime minister until 1989.

obvious basis for the federal system was to organize constituent units based on language groups. Hindi is the most widely spoken Indian language; however, most Hindi speakers are concentrated in the north-central part of the country. Indians living in the south, east, and parts of the west speak a variety of other languages. Concerned about domination by Hindi speakers, many of these non-Hindi groups demanded a reorganization of the Indian union into linguistically defined states. Initially, Nehru resisted this demand, worried that linguistic states within a federation might become secessionist and demand sovereignty. As demands for linguistic states mounted, especially from south Indian groups, Nehru compromised in 1956: the new Indian union was organized around fourteen linguistically defined states. Following subsequent changes, there are now twenty-eight major states within India.

Another legacy of the Nehru era is noteworthy. Jawaharlal Nehru was an internationalist who wanted India to play a global role. However, as he was consolidating power in India, the cold war was unfolding between the Soviet Union and the United States. Together with postcolonial leaders of Asia and Africa, Nehru initiated what became known as the nonaligned movement, which united those countries wishing to maintain a distance from the two superpowers. India and many other developing countries viewed both Western capitalism and Soviet communism with suspicion. Under Nehru, India played a leadership role among other nonaligned developing countries while pursuing mixed economic policies at home that were neither fully capitalist nor fully socialist (see Section 2).

Nehru's initiatives put India firmly on a stable, democratic road. However the strong, centralized state that

Nehru created also had some negative long-term consequences. The new Indian state came to resemble the old British Indian state that Nehru and others had so vociferously opposed. The colonial state's tendency to favor traditional Indian elites carried over into the Nehru era. Powerful groups in the society, including elite bureaucrats, wealthy landowners, entrepreneurs, and leaders of well-organized ethnic movements, enjoyed a favored position. While Nehru and the Congress Party continued to maintain a pro-poor, socialist rhetoric, they generally failed to deliver on their promises.

The Indira Gandhi Era (1966–1984)

When Nehru died in 1964, the Congress Party was divided over the choice of a successor and hurriedly selected mild-mannered Lal Bahadur Shastri to be prime minister. When he died of a heart attack in 1966 and rivalry again broke out over his successor, party elites found a compromise candidate in Nehru's daughter, Indira Gandhi. They chose her to capitalize on the fact that as Nehru's daughter, she would help the Congress Party garner the electoral support it needed to remain in power. They also calculated that she would be a weak woman who could be manipulated by competing factions within the party. They were right about the first point, but decisively wrong about the second.

As prime minister from 1966 to 1984, except for the brief period of 1977 to 1980, Indira Gandhi's rule had several long-term legacies for contemporary Indian democracy. First, Indian politics became more personalized, populist, and nationalist. To bolster her popularity, Indira Gandhi deliberately whipped up Indian nationalism. During the late 1960s, the Bengali-speaking eastern half of Pakistan, which was separated from its western half by nearly 1,000 miles of Indian territory, demanded sovereignty. As violence escalated within Pakistan and refugees from East Pakistan began pouring into India, Gandhi ordered Indian forces to intervene. This led to the creation of the sovereign state of Bangladesh. Because the United States sided with Pakistan in that conflict (and the Soviet Union backed India), Indira Gandhi was able to mobilize Indian nationalist sentiment against both Pakistan and the United States. This war-related victory added to her popularity. She soon consolidated her leadership over the Congress Party, forcing out leaders who opposed her and

replacing them with loyal allies. The result was to create a new Congress Party in her own image. Subsequently, she portrayed the old Congress elite as defending the status quo and preventing her from helping the poor. Gandhi's populist rhetoric won her immense popularity among India's poor. From 1971 to 1984, she dominated Indian politics as much as Mahatma Gandhi or her father ever had.

A second legacy of Indira Gandhi's rule was to further centralize the Indian political system. During the Nehru era, local elites had helped select higher political officeholders, but in the 1970s, Indira Gandhi directly appointed officeholders at both the national and regional levels. Although this strategy enabled her to gain a firm grip over the party, it isolated her from broader political forces and eroded the legitimacy of local leaders.

A third important legacy of Indira Gandhi's rule was her failure to translate populist rhetoric into real gains for India's poor. She was unable to redistribute agricultural land from large landowners to those who worked the land or generate employment, provide welfare, or improve access by the poor to education and medical services. The reasons are complex and controversial. Some analysts argue that she was never sincere in her commitment to the poor and that her populism was mainly a strategy for gaining votes. Given the magnitude of India's poverty, however, even sincere efforts faced a monumental task.

Indian politics became more and more turbulent under Indira Gandhi, a fourth legacy of her rule. As her popularity soared, so did the opposition to her. The old Congress elite denounced her populist political style, arguing that her government was corrupt and that India needed to oust her from power and clean up the government. Led by a credible follower of Mahatma Gandhi, Jai Prakash Narain, they began organizing mass demonstrations and strikes to press their case. During 1974, the political situation in India became unstable, with the opposition organizing general strikes and Indira Gandhi threatening massive state repression. When Narain called on the Indian armed forces to mutiny, Gandhi declared a national **Emergency,** suspended many democratic rights, and arrested most opposition leaders. The Emergency lasted nearly two years, the only period since 1947 when India was not a democracy.

In 1977, Indira Gandhi rescinded the Emergency

and called for national elections, confidently expecting that she would win. To her surprise, she was soundly defeated, and for the first time since independence, a non-Congress government came to power. Various groups that had opposed Gandhi hastily joined together in a loosely organized party (the Janata Party) and won power. Indira Gandhi's authoritarian measures during the Emergency were so unpopular that the newly formed party was able to unite India's fragmented opposition groups and achieve electoral success. However, soon after the elections, Janata leaders became factionalized and the Janata government collapsed, providing a new opportunity for Indira Gandhi to regain power in the 1980 parliamentary elections.

Indira Gandhi's tenure in power between 1980 and 1984 resembled the preceding period, in that it was marked by a personal and populist political style, an increasingly centralized political system, failure to implement antipoverty policies, and growing political turbulence. However, she departed from her previous approach in two ways. The first was in the realm of the economy. During the 1970s, India's industrial establishment grew relatively slowly because the government spent too much on buying political support and too little on investment; incomes of the poor were not improving and therefore demand for new products was limited; and excessive rules and regulations were counterproductive, both for domestic entrepreneurs and for integrating India into the world economy. With few means to rechannel government spending or improve the spending capacity of the poor, Gandhi started liberalizing the rules that governed India's economy.

The second important change concerns the strategy Indira Gandhi employed to achieve electoral support. It was clear that continuing appeals to poverty alleviation would not provide a successful electoral strategy, because poverty had not diminished and would not without greater government intervention. Meanwhile government policy was tending toward liberalization. With the loss of populist promises as a strategy to win support, the prime minister needed to devise alternative appeals to socialism and secularism, which both she and her father had championed since the 1950s. In the early 1980s, Indira Gandhi began to use religious appeals to mobilize India's Hindu majority. By introducing religion into politics, the Congress Party sowed

the seeds for the growth of the Hindu nationalist BJP and thereby accelerated its own demise.

Religious conflicts began to reenter Indian politics in the early 1980s, as illustrated by the growing conflict between the Sikh religious minority, based in the Punjab, and the national government. During the course of the conflict, Indian security forces invaded and extensively damaged the holiest Sikh shrine, the Golden Temple in the city of Amritsar, to attack Sikh militants besieged there. The resulting alienation of Sikhs from Gandhi peaked when she was assassinated in 1984 by one of her Sikh bodyguards.

Immediately after her assassination, rampaging mobs of Hindus brutally murdered Sikhs in New Delhi, Kanpur, and other north Indian cities. Most of the 3,700 Sikh victims were poor. Anti-Sikh violence was not spontaneous but orchestrated by some leading figures within the Congress Party. In this respect, it resembled the anti-Muslim violence organized by BJP party and state leaders in the following decade.

Indira's son, Rajiv Gandhi, won a landslide victory in the subsequent national elections as a result of the sympathy wave that his mother's assassination generated. He came to office promising clean government, a high-tech economy that would carry India into the next century, and reduced ethnic conflict. He was somewhat successful in ameliorating tensions in the state of Punjab, helped by the fact that the Sikh independence movement lost popular support and was repressed by the state. But Rajiv Gandhi inflamed tensions between Hindus and Muslims by sponsoring a law that placed Muslim women under the purview of the family. He left office in 1989 under a cloud after a scandal involving an arms deal with the Swedish Bofors company.

With Indira Gandhi's death, the tradition of powerful and populist prime ministers came to an end. India has since been facing a crisis of governance that began during the Indira Gandhi era. This was evident in increasing factionalism within the Congress Party, India's dominant party since independence. Moreover, other secular political parties proved unable to fill the vacuum in government caused by the Congress Party's disintegration. Since 1984, only two governments, both Congress led, have lasted their full terms: under Rajiv Gandhi (1984–1989) and under Narasimha Rao (1991–1996). Rao rode to victory on a sympathy vote for

Congress when Rajiv Gandhi was assassinated in 1991 while campaigning for election. However, the Congress Party split in 1995, further contributing to the fragmentation of the entire party system.

Coalition Governments and the Growth of the BJP (1989 to the Present)

In the five general elections since 1989, no single party has won a majority of seats in parliamentary elections. A succession of unstable coalition and minority governments ruled from 1989 to 1998. Since then, India has been led by BJP coalition governments, with Atal Behari Vajpayee as prime minister.

The tendency for Indian elections to produce unstable and short-lived coalitions at the national level has grown because no party has been able to fill the vacuum created by the Congress Party's decline. Coalition governments at the national level and in most states have generally been hurriedly arranged and poorly conceived. The cement that binds coalitions together has more often been negative than positive. For example, opposition to Congress brought governments to power in 1977 and 1989. By the early 1990s, when the Congress had crumbled and hence was not an attractive target to oppose, opposition to the BJP provided the major incentive for coalitional arrangements among regional and lower caste parties (see Table 1).

Politics in India today is characterized by governments of precarious coalitions, weakened political institutions, and considerable political activism along ethnic lines. These developments have generated policies that range from limited action on the economic front to nationalist outbursts on the military front. Whether any party or charismatic leader capable of unifying the country across the salient cleavages will emerge remains to be seen.

Themes and Implications

Historical Junctures and Political Themes

India in a World of States. India's domestic difficulties both reflect and influence its changing status in the world of states. In an increasingly interdependent global political and economic system, India's attainment of nuclear power signaled the dawn of a new era. As a

Table 1

Prime Ministers of India, 1947–Present

	Years in Office	Party
Jawaharlal Nehru	1947–1964	Congress
Lal Bahadur Shastri	1964–1966	Congress
Indira Gandhi	1966–1977	Congress
Morarji Desai	1977–1979	Janata
Charan Singh	1979–1980	Janata
Indira Gandhi	1980–1984	Congress
Rajiv Gandhi	1984–1989	Congress
V. P. Singh	1989–1990	Janata
Chandra Shekhar	1990–1991	Janata (Socialist)
Narasimha Rao	1991–1996	Congress
Atal Bihari Vajpayee	1996 (13 days)	BJP & allies
H. D. Deve Gowda	1996–1997	United Front
I. K. Gujral	1997–1998	United Front
Atal Bihari Vajpayee	1998–1999, 1999–	BJP & allies

result, simmering historical tensions over territories such as Kashmir will need to be managed very carefully. India now shares borders with two nuclear powers, China and Pakistan, and has engaged in wars and periodic border skirmishes with both. With the end of the cold war, managing regional tensions poses problems. India and Pakistan have fought three wars, and their politicians have exploited the tensions between them during domestic political crises. The challenge facing the Indian state is how to prevent domestic pressures from escalating into international belligerence.

Governing the Economy. Successful economic performance is necessary for India to fulfill its national and domestic ambitions. Indian policy-makers initially sought economic self-sufficiency through a policy of state-led industrialization focused on meeting the needs of its large internal market. This protectionist economic strategy had mixed results. Although it resulted in the development of some important basic industries, it also generated extensive inefficiencies and did little to alleviate the country's severe poverty. Like many other developing nations, India must adjust its economic strategy to meet the demands of increasingly competitive and interdependent global markets.

But in a global environment that requires making quick decisions and grasping ephemeral opportunities, the halting steps taken by Indian economic liberalizers have fallen short of expectations. How can India prevent its liberalization policy from being held hostage by entrenched elites? How can policy-makers simultaneously pursue economic reforms and provide for social benefits through well-aimed schemes that avoid clientalism and patronage? Will liberalization of India's state-controlled economy provide a basis for increased wealth in an extremely poor country? These are among the daunting challenges that face Indian leaders and observers concerned about the future of this continent-sized, poor democracy.

The Democratic Idea.   The democratic idea has been sustained in India for over half a century, barring a short period of authoritarianism between 1977 and 1979. India can boast of a vibrant and vigilant civil society, periodic elections, unfettered media, and relatively autonomous courts and bureaucracy. However, these institutions have been corroded over the years. For example, Indira Gandhi's radical posturing brought turbulence to Indian democracy, damaged the economy, and never provided real benefits to the poor. Since the late 1980s, political parties have deployed electoral strategies that have exacerbated ethnic tensions. The challenge that India faces is how to balance an increasingly divided society with the demands of social, economic, and political citizenship for all. Given the fact that the vast majority of India's citizens are Hindu, the danger is that political parties will be tempted to mobilize on the basis of Hindu religious identity and thereby marginalize India's religious minority communities. Indeed, this is precisely the scenario that brought the BJP to power in 1998.

Paradoxically, Indian democracy has become more democratic in some ways and less so in others. More groups with more diverse identities are participating in politics than ever before. They are joining a larger range of political parties from more diverse regions of the country. The Indian political class can no longer be identified with a single region, caste, and class. However, a key ingredient of democracy is the protection of minority rights, and on this count, India is less democratic than in the past. Sikhs, Christians, and above all Muslims have suffered brutal attacks since the mid-1980s. Muslims have been rendered especially vulnerable. Democracy and identity politics have become intricately linked, often in destructive fashion, in contemporary Indian politics.

The Politics of Collective Identity.   That there are intense conflicts around the issue of collective identity is not surprising in multicultural India. What is alarming is how mobilization of the electorate on ethnic grounds could corrode democratic values. Democracy is supposed to provide a level playing field for a tussle between different interests and identities. But the victory of the BJP, a Hindu nationalist party, has deepened regional and religious divisions and changed the nature of Indian democracy. India faces the challenge of reconciling domestic electoral strategies of ethnic mobilization to capture power with the demands of moderation demanded in the exercise of such power and the challenge of coping with demands of multiethnic and multiclass groups and sustaining economic growth.

Implications for Comparative Politics

There are exceptional political features of the Indian state that have great significance for the study of comparative politics. First, India is a poor yet vibrant democracy. Most Indians value their citizenship rights and exercise them vigorously, despite widespread poverty and illiteracy. Theories of modernization have usually posited that democracy and economic growth are conjoined, but India stands out as an exception. At independence, the country was struggling with problems of nation building, poverty, poor human development indicators, and managing a transition to democracy. Against all odds, India became and remains a thriving democracy, an achievement especially striking when compared to the authoritarian fate of other newly independent British colonies in Asia and Africa.

Second, unlike other multiethnic states such as Yugoslavia and the former Soviet Union, which disintegrated with the advent of democracy, the Indian state has managed to remain cohesive and stable—although this must be qualified by the severe turmoil at various times in the states of Assam, Punjab, Gujarat, and especially Kashmir. Indian politics thus offers a case study of the tempering influence of democracy on ethnic cleavages. Contrast the exclusionary rhetoric of

Hindu nationalism during the BJP's tenure as an opposition party with its rhetorical shift toward moderation as India's ruling party. In an attempt to stabilize a fractious multiparty coalition government, the BJP was forced to put contentious religious issues such as the temple in Ayodhya on a back burner.

Third, as home to 1 billion people with diverse cultural, religious, and linguistic ties, Indian democracy offers an arena for testing and studying various theories and dilemmas of comparative politics. For instance, one dilemma in comparative politics is how multiethnic democracies can develop a coherent institutional system that gives representation to diverse interests without degenerating into authoritarianism or total collapse. The history of the Congress Party until the Indira Gandhi era demonstrates how one party successfully managed to unite diverse and multiple ethnic identities under one umbrella.

Fourth, theorists dealing with recent transitions to democracy in Latin America and Eastern Europe have puzzled over the question of what constitutes a consolidated democracy and how one achieves such consolidation. Here, a comparison of India with Pakistan would help us evaluate the role of historical junctures, leaders, and their interaction with institutions. At independence, Pakistan adopted a centralized, authoritarian, system, while India created a federal, parliamentary state. These decisions had critical implications. India has functioned as a democracy for all but two years since 1947, whereas Pakistan has functioned as an authoritarian state for most of the same period. Moreover, the Indian experience with authoritarianism during the Emergency era in the late 1970s, and the resurgence of democratic norms when Indira Gandhi was voted out by an angry populace, shows the importance of elections. It also shows that the existence of democratic institutions and procedures leads to the diffusion of democratic norms throughout the society.

Fifth, comparativists have focused on the dilemma of whether democracy and social equity can be achieved simultaneously in poor countries. The case of Kerala, a state in southern India, suggests an affirmative answer. Although it is one of the poorer states in India, Kerala has achieved near total literacy, long life expectancy, low infant mortality, and high access to medical care. Kerala's development indicators compare favorably with the rest of India, other low-income countries, and even wealthy countries like the United States.

This discussion of critical junctures in Indian history highlights the central challenge of contemporary Indian politics: how to establish a coherent, legitimate government and use its power to facilitate economic growth and equitable distribution. The former requires forming durable electoral coalitions without exacerbating political passions and ethnic conflicts. The latter requires careful implementation of policies that simultaneously help entrepreneurs produce goods and ensure a fair distribution of the growth in production. The remainder of this chapter describes how India is coping with these challenges.

Section ❷ Political Economy and Development

At the time of independence, India was largely a poor, agricultural economy. Although it still has a very large agricultural sector and considerable poverty, India today also has a quite substantial industrial base and a vibrant middle class. Since the introduction of economic liberalization policies under Narasimha Rao's Congress government in 1991, all Indian governments have supported economic reform. Before discussing what liberalization entails, why it has become a priority, and what its implications are for Indian politics, we review the development of the Indian political economy historically.

State and Economy
The Economy Under British Rule

During the colonial period, the Indian economy was largely agricultural, with hundreds of millions of poor peasants living in thousands of small villages, tilling the land with primitive technology, and producing at a low level of efficiency. The British, along with Indian landlords, extracted extensive land revenues, land taxes, and tributes from Indian princes. However, they reinvested only a small portion of this surplus into improving agricultural production. Most resources were squandered through conspicuous consumption by Indian princes and landlords or used to finance the expensive colonial government. The result of this mismanagement of resources was that Indian agricultural productivity, that is, the amount of wheat, rice, and other products produced from one unit of land, mostly stagnated in the first half of the twentieth century. Agricultural productivity in India was considerably lower in 1950 than in Japan or even China.

Some industry developed under colonial rule, but its scope was limited. The British sold their own manufactured goods to India in exchange for Indian raw materials. Because the British economy was more advanced, it was difficult for Indians to compete successfully. Indigenous manufacturing, especially of textiles, and artisanal production were ruined by the forced opening of the Indian market to British goods. Thus, the Indian economy at independence in 1947 was relatively stagnant, especially in agriculture and industrial development.

The Economy After Independence

One of the central tasks facing Indian leaders after 1947 was to modernize the sluggish economy. During Nehru's rule, India adopted a model of development based largely on private property, although there was extensive government ownership of firms and government guidance to private economic activity. Nehru created a powerful planning commission that, following the Soviet model, made five-year plans for the Indian economy, outlining the activities in which government investment would be concentrated. Unlike the plans in communist party states, however, the Indian plans also indicated priority areas for private entrepreneurs, who remained a powerful force in the Indian economy.

The Indian government levied high tariffs on imports, arguing that new Indian industries, so long disadvantaged under colonial rule, required protection from foreign competitors. The government tightly regulated the start-up and expansion of private industries under the presumption that the government was a better safeguard of the public interest than private entrepreneurs. This government-planned private economy achieved mixed results. It helped India create an impressive industrial base but did little to help the poor, and its protected industries were quite inefficient by global standards.

Nationalist in temperament, Nehru and other Congress Party leaders were suspicious of involving foreign investors in India's economic development. The government thus undertook a series of coordinated economic activities on its own. It made significant public sector investments to create such heavy industries as steel and cement; protected Indian entrepreneurs from foreign competition; where possible, further subsidized these producers; and finally, created elaborate rules and regulations controlling the activities of private producers. As a result, India developed a substantial industrial base over the next few decades.

Congress leaders promised to redistribute land from landowners to tenants in order to weaken the former supporters of the colonial government and motivate the tillers of the land to increase production. Although some of the largest landowners were indeed eliminated in the early 1950s, poor tenants and agricultural laborers received very little land. Unlike the communist government in China, India's nationalist government had neither the will nor the capacity to undertake radical property redistribution. Instead, most of the land remained in the hands of medium- to large-sized landowners. Many became part of the Congress political machine in the countryside. This development further weakened the Congress Party's capacity to assist the rural poor and undermined its socialist commitments.

The failure of land reforms led to a new agricultural strategy in the late 1960s known as the **green revolution.** Instead of addressing land redistribution, the state sought to provide landowners with improved seeds and access to subsidized fertilizer. Because irrigation was essential for this strategy to succeed and because irrigation was assured only to larger farmers in some regions of India, the success of the green revolution was uneven. Production increased sharply in some areas, such as the Punjab, but other regions (and especially the poorer farmers in these regions) got left behind. Nevertheless, as a result of this strategy, India became self-sufficient in food (and even became a food exporter), thus avoiding the mass starvation and famines that had occurred in the past.

Between 1950 and 1980, the Indian government facilitated what has been described as **state-led economic development.** This development policy consisted of an expansion of the public sector, protection of the domestic sector from foreign competition, and rules and regulations to control private sector activity. Political leaders hoped to strengthen India's international position by promoting self-sufficient industrialization. To a great extent, the Indian government succeeded in achieving this goal. By 1980, India was a major industrial power able to produce its own steel, airplanes, automobiles, chemicals, military hardware, and many consumer goods. On the agricultural side, although land reforms failed, the revised agricultural strategy improved food production.

State-led development insulated the Indian economy from global influences while aligning the Indian state with business and landowning classes. The strategy resulted in modest economic growth—not as impressive as that of Brazil, Mexico, or the Republic of Korea but better than that of Nigeria. The main beneficiaries were business classes, medium and large landowning farmers, and political and bureaucratic elites. A substantial urban middle class also developed during this phase. However, state-led development was associated with a number of problems. First, given the lack of competition, much industry was inefficient by global standards. Second, the elaborate rules and regulations controlling private economic activity encouraged corruption, as entrepreneurs bribed bureaucrats to get around the rules. And third, the focus on heavy industry directed a substantial portion of new investment into buying machinery rather than creating jobs. As a result, 40 percent of India's population, primarily poor tenant farmers and landless laborers, did not share in the fruits of this growth. And because population growth continued, the number of desperately poor people increased substantially during these decades.

Economic Liberalization

A number of global and national changes moved India toward **economic liberalization** beginning in the 1980s and accelerating after 1991. Throughout the 1980s, socialist models of development came under attack. Within India, political and economic elites were increasingly dissatisfied with India's relatively sluggish economic performance, especially compared with dynamic East Asian economies. For example, during the 1970s, whereas India's economy grew at the rate of 3.4 percent per year, South Korea's grew at 9.6 percent. New elites coming to power in India, less nationalist

and socialist than their predecessors, interpreted the country's slow economic growth as a product of excessive governmental controls and of India's relative insulation from the global economy. India's business and industrial classes increasingly found government intervention in the economy more of a hindrance than a help. Realizing that the poverty of most Indians limited the possibility for expanding domestic markets, they increasingly sought to export their products.

India's economy did relatively well during the 1980s and 1990s, growing at nearly 5 percent per year, a record especially noteworthy when compared to the dismal performance of many debt-ridden Latin American and African economies, such as Brazil and Nigeria. Some of this improved performance resulted from economic liberalization that further integrated India into the global economy. Some resulted from public loans to small factory owners and farmers and public investments in their enterprises. However, a large part of economic growth in the 1980s was based on increased borrowing from abroad, which represented a shift from a fairly conservative fiscal policy. This expansionary fiscal policy, largely funded by foreign loans, was risky because India's exports to other countries did not grow very rapidly. For example, its exports during the 1980s grew at approximately 6 percent per year in comparison to 12 percent per year for both South Korea and China. As a result, the need to repay foreign loans put enormous pressure on the government toward the end of the decade. India was forced in the early 1990s to borrow even more from such international agencies as the International Monetary Fund (IMF) and World Bank. In return for fresh loans, these international organizations required the Indian government to reduce its deficit through such controversial measures as reducing subsidies to the poor and selling government shares in public enterprises to the private sector. Critics allege that the government sold many public enterprises at prices well below their market value.

Liberalization has both a domestic and an international component. The government has sought to dismantle controls over private sector economic activities, especially in industry. More recently, new industries have been created, including oil and natural gas, transportation infrastructure, telecommunications, and power generation. The government has provided a variety of incentives to industry, including tax breaks, eliminating customs duties on the import of equipment, and underwriting losses.

Over the years, the government has progressively increased the scope of stockholding by foreign enterprises and of foreign direct investment in key industries, including pharmaceuticals, and coal mining. For the first time, it allowed multinational investment in natural resources. The government invited bids from private and foreign companies to invest in twenty-five oil and gas exploration blocks in the country. The agreement provides for a seven-year tax holiday from the date of commencement of commercial production; no customs duty on imports required for petroleum operations; a 100 percent cost recovery on exploration, production, and development; and full recovery of all royalties paid to the Indian government for the oil or gas extracted.[1] Such arrangements would have been unthinkable until a few years ago.

Foreign investment has increased significantly, from $100 million a year between 1970 and 1991 to nearly $4 billion annually between 1992 and 1998. In 2000, the government authorized increased foreign direct investment in eight areas: pharmaceuticals, coal and lignite for power plants, tourism, mining, prospecting for gold and diamonds, advertising, pollution control machinery, and the film industry. However, the level of foreign direct investment in India—2 to 3 percent of the annual gross domestic product (GDP)—is relatively modest; China and Brazil receive several times that volume each year.[2] Furthermore, because foreign investment focuses on the domestic market, it has not always facilitated export promotion, which is potentially one of its major benefits in poor countries.

One high-tech sector in which India has excelled is computer software. Indian firms and multinational corporations with operations in India take ample advantage of India's highly skilled and poorly paid scientific and engineering talent to make India a world leader in the production of software. India can boast the equivalent of Silicon Valley in the boom area around Bangalore in southern India, home to a large number of software firms.

Considerable pressure is being brought to bear on the Indian government to liberalize banking, insurance, and other services as part of the World Trade Organization's (WTO) agreement on trade in services. Over forty foreign banks operate independently in India,

and the government is now allowing foreign holdings in Indian banks. It has also opened up the insurance sector to private and foreign investment. Small borrowers in agriculture and small-scale industrialists have found their access to bank lending curtailed. Loans to rural areas and poorer regions have fallen. Foreign banks have focused on retail banking in profitable urban areas, ignoring less lucrative areas of lending.

Under the WTO regime, the Indian government has removed restrictions on the volume of imports. Three-fourths of India's tariffs now have a ceiling beyond which they cannot be raised. Import duties have also been reduced. From 35 percent in 1997–1998, they fell marginally to 32 percent in 2001–2002 and are scheduled to come down to 29 percent in 2002–2003. The government has announced that it will create a two-tier duty structure of 10 and 20 percent by 2004–2005.[3]

Alongside government reforms aimed at opening up and privatizing the economy have been policy moves to cut the work force in public enterprises in order to reduce public spending and deficits. The government has announced measures to reduce the size of the work force by not filling vacancies when employees retire. The goal is to reduce the labor force in public enterprises by 2 percent a year, or 10 percent over five years. In 2002, the government sponsored a voluntary retirement scheme for government employees, under which they could take early retirement.

The government has also been considering reducing workers' legal protections. Industrialists have demanded that the government revise a law requiring government authorization before firms can lay off workers or close factories that employ a minimum of a hundred workers; industry has demanded that the threshold be raised to a thousand. Industry has also sought easing restrictions on hiring temporary workers. In the face of this pressure, the government in 1999 appointed the Second Labor Commission to recommend reforming existing labor laws. The commission proposed replacing the forty-hour week with a sixty-four-hour week, abolishing employment security, enlarging possibilities for employing temporary workers, making government authorization of retrenchment and plant closures easier, and restricting workers' rights to form unions. Recent court decisions have also contributed to the hostility toward workers' organizing, striking, and defending traditional benefits.

Unions and workers have resisted these measures. In 2001, unions prevented the privatization of the Uttar Pradesh State Electricity Board. The privatization of some government enterprises has generated spirited resistance from workers who feared that their jobs were threatened. In 2002, in the largest action ever against the economic reforms, 10 million workers across the country went on strike opposing proposed changes to the labor laws and moves toward privatization.

There has also been opposition to economic liberalization from segments of Indian business. The BJP government that came to power in 1998 based much of its campaign on nationalist rhetoric. It gained support from powerful Indian businesses whose monopolies were threatened by imports and foreign investors. This reaction has slowed the liberalization process, especially when compared to countries in Latin America or Eastern Europe.

To summarize, India's economy during the 1990s grew at a relatively impressive annual growth rate, averaging between five and six percent (see Figure 1). While liberalizing economic policies might have contributed to this robust economic performance, their impact needs to be kept in perspective. Economic liberalization in India, especially external opening and privatization, has been relatively limited. Furthermore, liberalization policies have failed in their intentions of accelerating industrial growth. The significant growth of the Indian economy is most likely propelled by a number of other factors: the share of the slower growing agricultural economy in the overall economy continues to decline steadily, both the knowledge and the stock of modern technology continues to grow, and the closer relationship between government and business has increased the share of private investment in overall investment, thereby increasing production.

Reforms in Agriculture

India's agricultural production made steady and modest progress during the 1990s, helped by good rains during the decade. Weather patterns, especially the timeliness of seasonal rains (the monsoons), continue to have significant bearing on Indian agriculture. Drought hit large parts of the countryside and affected agricultural production and employment opportunities in 2002. Unable to find work or buy food, starvation, suicide, and

mass migration occurred in Rajasthan, Madhya Pradesh, and other states. The victims were invariably from the poorest, lowest-caste segments of the rural population.

The impact of economic liberalization on agriculture has been growing. With the goal of reducing subsidies, the central government excluded millions of impoverished families just above the poverty line from receiving publicly subsidized food supplies. Furthermore, the government linked the price of food sold under the public distribution system to costs incurred, resulting in a sharp increase in prices. Sixty million tons of food grain have been rotting in the storage centers of the Food Corporation of India because it is too costly for the poor to afford.[4]

The removal of restrictions on imports under the WTO has important implications for the agrarian sector. Agricultural producers, such as coffee farmers in south India, are being harmed by increased imports. At a time when prices of primary commodities are falling worldwide, and the United States and other industrialized countries are putting up trade barriers and subsidizing agriculture, India's agriculture economy is being opened up to global forces without safety nets in place.

There has been no unified response to the economic reforms from rural groups. Medium and small peasant farmers, who cultivate between five and thirty acres of land, are scattered across different regions of the country and are divided by language, culture, and caste. They do not constitute a unified political entity. The largest landowning peasant farmers in more affluent states like Punjab and Haryana are more of a political force. They have organized mass demonstration when the national government has removed fertilizer subsidies and implemented other policies that adversely affect their interests.

Economic reforms have had mixed results thus far. India's foreign exchange reserves are much higher than they were in the past. Some industries, such as information technology, have taken off. The service sector is expanding and contributing significantly to India's economic growth. However, as noted earlier, economic liberalization is only partly responsible for robust economic growth. A variety of other long-term factors such as closer relations between a right-wing nationalist government and Indian business also help explain larger and more efficient private investments and economic growth.

Source: World Bank, WDI Data Query, http://devdata.
worldbank.org/data-query/

Figure 1

Recent GDP Growth, 1997–2001

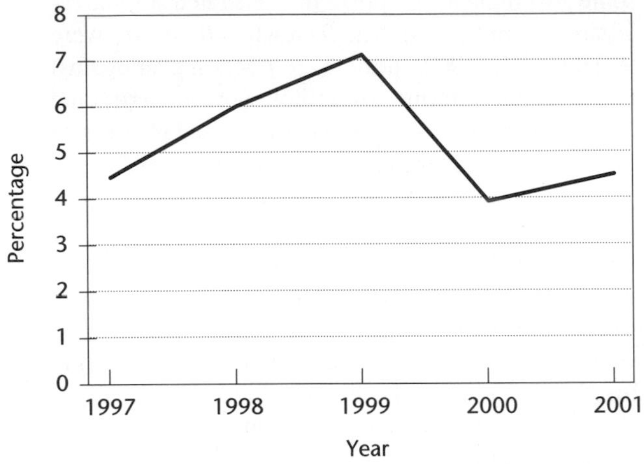

If Indian economic growth has been moderately impressive, numerous other problems remain. Most significantly, the state's capacity to facilitate development directly remains rather limited because of its organizational limitations and the interests it represents. For example, the state has been unable to increase public revenues through improved tax collection but has provided tax relief to business groups. As a result, the state has not spent on such critical areas of development as infrastructure, education, and health. The focus on economic liberalization also detracts its attention away from the question of poverty. Whether economic growth is helping India's poor or not is a controversial question. What is clear is that India has an enormous number of poor people and their numbers grow each year.

Social Welfare Policy

India's poor are a diverse, heterogeneous, and enormous group constituting more than one-third of the population. Since independence, the percentage of the poor has been cut in half. However, because of India's rapid population growth, this advance has not been sufficient to reduce the absolute number of poor, which increased from around 200 million in the 1950s to about

350 million by the late 1990s. India has the sad distinction of having the largest concentration of poor people in the world. Nearly two-thirds of the Indian population and three-fourths of the poor live in rural areas. Although urban poverty accounts for only one-fourth of the poor population, the number of poor urban people, over 70 million, is staggering.

India's poorest people are illiterate women and children and untouchables and tribals. They are peasant farmers who own little land, agricultural tenants, landless laborers in villages, and those without regular jobs in cities who eke out a living on society's margins, often huddled into shantytowns that lack sanitary facilities and electricity or living on the streets of cities like Calcutta or Bombay.

Although most poor people are politically unorganized, their political weight is felt in several ways. First, their sizable numbers impel many Indian politicians to adopt populist or socialist electoral platforms. Second, because many of the poor share a lower-caste status (especially within specific states), their group identity and united electoral behavior can have a considerable impact on electoral outcomes. In some states, notably West Bengal and Kerala, there is a long history of radical politics; the poor in these states are well organized by communist or socialist parties and periodically help elect left-leaning governments. Third, the anger and frustration of the poor provide the raw material for many contemporary movements of rage within India.

Over the years, Indian governments have tried different programs aimed at poverty alleviation. Some have been partly successful, but most have not. Redistribution of agricultural land to the poor was mostly a failure compared to results in countries like China, where radical land redistribution was a key component of a successful assault on poverty. As a communist dictatorship, however, China used government coercion to implement property redistribution. In some Indian states, such as West Bengal and Kerala, elected communist governments have been somewhat successful in land redistribution. Overall, however, land reforms have proved to be nearly impossible in India's democracy.

India has very few Western-style welfare programs such as unemployment insurance, comprehensive public health programs, or guaranteed primary education. The size of the welfare problem is considerable and would tax the resources of any government. No Indian government has ever attempted to provide universal primary education, although there has been considerable pressure from both Western and Indian sources to do so.

The one set of welfare-enhancing programs that has had modest success in India are public employment programs. These programs enable the national and state governments to allocate a portion of the public budget to such projects as the construction of roads and bridges and the cleaning of agricultural waterways. Because the rural poor are unemployed for nearly half the year when agricultural jobs are not available, public employment programs become their off-season source of employment and income. Many surveys have demonstrated that such programs help the poor, though the impact merely improves living conditions in the short run and usually fail to reach the poorest. In the 1990s, however, under the impact of liberalization policies, government budgets came under considerable pressure, creating a squeeze on public investments, especially in such areas as public employment.

Many respected observers have repeatedly stated that development spending, public investment, and bank credit to the rural sector were crucial to economic growth in the 1980s and remain critical today. Food-for-work programs, however inefficient, leaky, and corrupt, not only deal with surplus stock but also help generate nonfarm employment, and consequently generate demand for local manufactures, stimulate industry, and hence help savings and investment.[5] Food-for-work spending was only US$170 million in 2001, and budgeted at $259 million for 2002–2003, whereas its food stocks are valued at $10.6 billion.

Society and Economy

Wealth and income present intense contrasts in Indian society. At the top are a small number of incredibly affluent people who have made their fortunes in basic business and industry. The personal fortunes of the wealthiest industrial families, for example, the Ambanis, Tatas, and Birlas, rival the wealth of the richest corporate tycoons in the world. Below them, a much larger group, nearly 100 million Indians (approximately 10 percent) are relatively well off and enjoy a standard of living comparable to that of the middle classes in many developed countries. India has a sophisticated, technologically developed industrial sector that produces a variety of consumer products, military technologies, nuclear energy, and computers. For instance, India's nuclear explosions were the product of indigenous scientific and technological research.

India's lower middle classes, about half of all Indians, are mainly small farmers or urban workers. Relatively poor by global standards, they barely eke out a living. Finally, at the bottom of the class structure, about a third of the population is extremely poor and is concentrated mostly in India's thousands of villages as landless laborers or as the urban unemployed in city slums. Low levels of literacy, poverty, and primitive technology characterize a good part of India's rural society.

India's large population continues to grow at a relatively rapid pace. India will surpass China as the world's largest country in a few years. Since India already has more labor than it can use productively, rapid population growth hinders economic growth. Simply put, the more people there are, the more mouths there are to feed, and the more food and economic products must be produced simply to maintain people's standard of living.

Why should India's population continue to grow at such a rapid pace? The comparison with China provides part of the explanation. The communist-led Chinese government has pursued strict birth control policies of one child per family since the late 1970s. In part, coercion was used to implement these policies. The result was to reduce birthrates dramatically. India's democratic government, by contrast, has found it difficult to implement population control policies.

Coercion is not the only means of reducing population growth rates. By 1995, the national rate of population growth was around 2 percent per year, while the rate in Kerala was 1.4 percent, close to that of China in the early 1990s. An important reason was that Kerala has one of the highest literacy rates, especially female literacy rates, in India. Whereas the average literacy rate in India is around 37 percent for females (and 65 percent for males), Kerala's female literacy rate is 87 percent. Literate women are more likely to marry later, have more options in the work force, have greater power in personal relationships, and practice birth control.

India is one of the few countries in the world that has a lower percentage of females than men: 52 percent of the population is male and 48 percent female. Indian society favors boys over girls, as evidenced by all social indicators, from lower female literacy and nutrition rates to lower survival of female versus male infants. The favoring of males over females is reinforced through such traditions as the dowry system (the Hindu custom of giving the groom and his family some assets, a dowry, at the time of a daughter's wedding). These traditions, deeply rooted and slow to change, confine the majority of Indian women, particularly poor women, to a life of fewer opportunities than those available to men.

India also has the world's largest population of child labor. Children are employed widely, not only in agricultural labor but also in such urban enterprises as match making and rug weaving and selling tea or sweets at train stations. Children usually work long hours at low wages and are unable to receive an education and consequently lose the chance for upward social mobility. The issue of child labor is closely related to India's failure to provide universal primary education (see Figure 2). If school-age children were required to be in school, they could not be readily employed as full-time laborers. Many Indian elites argue that in their poor country, compulsory primary education is an unaffordable luxury. However, this argument is not very persuasive; many poor African countries have higher rates of primary school enrollments than does India (and recall the example of Kerala, among India's poorer states). The more likely obstacle to universal primary education is poverty and caste inequality. Many upper-caste elites do not see lower-caste children as their equals and do not consider the issue of educating lower-caste children a priority. Child labor is directly linked to poverty and survival, since many poor families see larger numbers of children as a form of insurance. Yet for most poor families, a larger family also means not being able to invest in each child's education and depending on their children's labor for survival.

Caste issues pervade many other aspects of India's political and economic life (See "Institutional Intricacies: The Caste System"). First, by assigning people to specific occupations, it impedes the free movement of labor and talent. Although the link between caste and occupation has been weakening in India, especially in urban areas, it remains an important organizing principle

Figure 2

Educational Levels by Gender

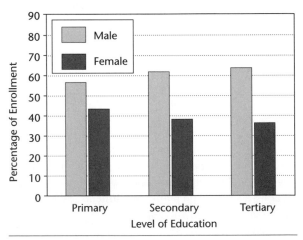

Source: UNESCO Institute for Statistics, http://www.uis.unesco.org/en/stats/stats

for employment Second, in the political arena, caste is a powerful force around which political groups and voting blocs coalesce. Because caste is usually organized at the local level, Indian politics often takes on a local and segmented quality. Related to this, caste cuts across class, making it difficult for labor, business, and other economic classes in India to act in a politically cohesive manner. Third, the Indian government often uses caste as a basis for **reservations,** the Indian version of affirmative action. The government reserves some jobs, admissions into universities, and similar privileges for members of specific underprivileged castes. This has become a highly contentious issue in Indian politics. And last, those who suffer the most in India's caste system are those at the bottom of the caste hierarchy: the untouchables. Nearly 10 percent of India's population, or some 90 million people, is categorized by the Indian census as belonging to the untouchables or scheduled castes, as they are officially known. Notwithstanding considerable government efforts, the social stigma that members of this group suffer runs deep in India.

India and the International Political Economy

After a prolonged colonial experience, nationalist India in the 1950s shunned economic links with the outside world. Although India pursued an active foreign policy as a leader of the **nonaligned bloc,** it was defensive in its economic contacts. A prolonged and successful nationalist movement help explain both India's urge to play a global political role and its desire to protect its economy from foreign influence. India's political and economic elites favored protectionism in trade and sought to limit foreign investment. Although three decades of this policy helped generate an industrial base and domestic capitalism, it gave rise to problems that led to economic liberalization, from which new problems arose.

During the decades of relatively autarkic development, powerful groups emerged that now have vested interests in maintaining the old order. Many bureaucrats abused the system of government controls over private economic activities by accepting bribes to issue government licenses to start private businesses. Indian industry

---

Institutional Intricacies: *The Caste System*

Originally derived from the Portuguese word *castas,* today the word *caste* inevitably evokes images of a rigid hierarchy that characterizes Indian society. In reality, however, castes are less immutable and timeless categories than suggested by the popular image.

Historically, the **caste system** compartmentalized and ranked the Hindu population of the Indian subcontinent through rules governing various aspects of daily life, such as eating, marriage, and prayer. Sanctioned by religion, the hierarchy of caste is based on a conception of the world as divided into realms of purity and impurity. Each hereditary and endogamous group (that is, a group into which one is born and within which one marries) constitutes a *jati,* which is itself organized by *varna,* or shades of color. The four main *varna* are the **Brahmin,** or priestly, caste; the Kshatriya, or warrior and royal, caste; the Vaishyas, or trading, caste; and the Shudra, or artisan, caste. Each of these *varna* is divided into many *jatis* that often approximate occupational groups (such as potters, barbers, and carpenters). Those who were not considered members of organized Hindu society because they lived in forests and on hills rather than in towns and villages, or were involved in "unclean" occupations such as sweepers and leather workers were labeled **untouchables,** outcastes, or **scheduled castes.** Because each *jati* is often concentrated in a particular region, it is sometimes possible to change one's *varna* when one moves to a different part of the country by changing one's name and adopting the social customs of higher castes, for example, giving up eating meat. Some flexibility within the rigidity of the system has contributed to its survival across the centuries.

was often relatively inefficient because neither cheaper foreign goods nor foreign investors were readily allowed into India. Moreover, organized labor, especially in government-controlled factories, had a stake in maintaining inefficient factories because they offered a greater number of jobs. These well-entrenched groups resisted liberalization and threatened to throw their political weight behind opposition parties, making the ruling government hesitant to undertake any decisive policy shift.

The other significant component of India's performance in the international political economy concerns its regional context. India is a giant among the South Asian countries of Pakistan, Bangladesh, Sri Lanka, Nepal, and Bhutan, though its northern neighbor, China, is an even bigger and more powerful giant. Since 1947, India has periodically experienced regional conflict: a war with China in 1962; three wars with Pakistan, the last of which was fought in 1971 and precipitated the breakup of Pakistan into the two states of Pakistan and Bangladesh; a military intervention into strife-torn Sri Lanka in the 1980s; and on-and-off troubled relations with Nepal.

The net effect is that India has not developed extensive economic interactions with its neighbors. Figure 3 compares exports as a percentage of gross national product (GNP) for India and its major trading partners; India's export quantity and rate of growth are relatively low. As nations increasingly look to their neighbors

Figure 3

Exports of India and Its Trading Partners, 1980 and 2000

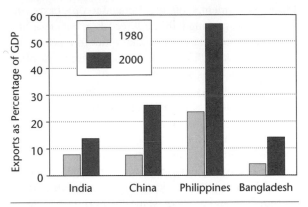

Source: World Bank Country at a Glance, www.worldbank.org/data/countrydata/countrydata.html

for trade and investment, the pressure on India and its neighbors to put aside their mutual conflicts for increased economic contact is likely to grow. Some movement in this direction was already evident in the first half of the 1990s, especially toward China, but there is still a long way to go before South Asia develops an integrated zone of economic activity.

Section ❸ Governance and Policy-Making

Organization of the State

India is a democratic republic with a parliamentary and federal system of government. The constitution adopted in 1950 created this system, and although there have been many profound changes since then in the distribution and use of power, the basic character of India's political system has remained unchanged. For much of this period, India has been a stable, democratic country with universal suffrage and periodic elections at local, state, and national levels. This continuity and democratic stability are remarkable among developing countries. To simplify a complex reality, Indian democracy has proved so resilient because its political

institutions, while always under pressure, have been able to accommodate many new power challenges and to repress the most difficult ones.

India's constitution is lengthy. In contrast to the British constitution on which it is modeled, it is a written document that has been periodically amended by legislation. Among its special features, three are worth noting. First, unlike many other constitutions, the Indian constitution directs the government to promote social and economic equality and justice. The constitution thus goes beyond stipulating formal procedures of decision making and allocating powers among political institutions, and outlines policy goals. Although the impact of these constitutional provisions on government policies is limited, the provisions ensure that issues of welfare and social justice are not ignored. Second, the Indian constitution, similar to the U.S. Constitution, provides for freedom of religion and defines India as a secular state. This was an especially controversial issue in Indian politics during the late 1990s because the ruling BJP was committed to establishing Hinduism as a state-sanctioned religion. And third, the constitution allows for the temporary suspension of many democratic rights under conditions of emergency. These provisions were used, somewhat understandably, during wars with Pakistan or China. But they have also been invoked, more disturbingly, to deal with internal political threats, most dramatically during the national Emergency from 1975 to 1977, when a politically vulnerable Indira Gandhi suspended many democratic rights and imprisoned her leading political opponents.

India's federal system of twenty-eight states and several other special political units is relatively centralized. The central government controls the most essential government functions such as defense, foreign policy, taxation, public expenditures, and economic planning, especially industrial planning. State governments formally control such policy areas as agriculture, education, and law and order within the states. Because they are heavily dependent on the central government for funds in these policy areas, however, the power of the states is limited.

India is a parliamentary democracy designed on the British model. The Indian parliament, known as the *Lok Sabha,* or House of the People, is the most significant political institution. The leader of the political party with the most seats in the *Lok Sabha* becomes the prime minister, who nominates a cabinet, mostly from the ranks of other members of parliament belonging to the ruling coalition. The prime minister and the cabinet, along with permanent civil servants, control much of the government's daily functioning. The prime minister is the linchpin of the system because effective power is concentrated in that office, where most of the country's important policies originate. By contrast, the office of the president is largely ceremonial. In periodic national elections, 544 members of the *Lok Sabha,* the lower house of the bicameral parliament, are elected. The *Lok Sabha* is much more politically significant than the **Rajya Sabha,** the upper

house. The prime minister governs with the help of the cabinet, which periodically meets to discuss important issues, including any new legislation that is likely to be initiated. Individually, cabinet members are the heads of various ministries, for example, Foreign Affairs or Industry, that direct the daily work of the government and make up the permanent bureaucracy.

The Executive

The President and the Prime Minister

The president is the official head of the state and is elected indirectly every five years by an electoral college composed of elected representatives from the national and state governments. In most circumstances, the president acts on the advice of the prime minister and is thus not a very powerful political figure. The presidency is a ceremonial office, symbolizing the unity of the country, and it is supposedly above partisan politics. Under exceptional circumstances, however, especially when the selection of a prime minister becomes a complex issue, the president can play an important political role. For example, in the 1998 election, there was a hung parliament, with no party gaining a clear majority. The president then requested the party with the largest percentage of votes, the BJP, to show that it could muster enough allies to form a government.

The prime minister and other cabinet ministers are the most powerful political figures in India. Because they represent the majority party coalition in parliament, the passage of a bill is not as complicated a process as it can be in a presidential system, especially one with a divided government. The prime minister and the cabinet also head various ministries, so that after legislation is passed, they oversee its implementation. In practice, the permanent bureaucracy, especially the senior and middle-level bureaucrats, are responsible for policy implementation. Nevertheless, as in most other parliamentary systems, such as those in Britain, Germany, and Japan, there is considerable overlap in India between the executive and the legislative branches of the government, creating a greater degree of centralization of power than is initially evident. The duration of the prime minister's tenure in office has become steadily truncated over time. Between 1947 and 1984, except for a few brief interludes, India had only two prime ministers: Nehru and Indira Gandhi (see Table 1). This is nearly unique among democracies; it underlines the powerful hold that the Nehru-Gandhi family had on India's political imagination. Since then, there has been a more rapid turnover. Rajiv Gandhi, Indira Gandhi's son, succeeded his mother after her assassination in 1984. When he lost power four years later, there were short-lived governments under the leadership of V. P. Singh and Chandra Shekhar. Narasimha Rao lasted his full term in office. Atal Behari Vajpayee is serving an entire term since his election in 1999, unlike his previous truncated terms.

The method of selecting a prime minister in India is fairly complex. The original choice of Nehru was a natural one, given his prominent position in the nationalist movement and his relationship to founding father Mahatma Gandhi. The choice of Indira Gandhi was less obvious. She was chosen to head the Congress Party by a group of prominent second-tier party leaders, because of her national name, which they calculated would reap handsome electoral rewards. A similar logic prevailed when Rajiv Gandhi was chosen by party elites to succeed his mother. Rajiv Gandhi benefited from the wave of sympathy generated by his mother's assassination, and he led the Congress Party back to power in 1984 with a handsome electoral majority.

Following Rajiv Gandhi's assassination, the Nehru-Gandhi family line appeared to have reached an end, since Rajiv Gandhi's wife, Sonia Gandhi, was an Italian national and their children were too young to enter politics. In 1991, Narasimha Rao was brought back as an elder statesman, nonthreatening and acceptable to competing factions within the Congress Party. He was the first prime minister from south India; all the previous heads of state had been from the north. Both subsequent United Front prime ministers were compromise candidates who lacked the personality and power to manage their disparate coalitions. In 1998, the Congress Party attempted to resurrect its fortunes by choosing Sonia Gandhi to head their party, creating the possibility that the political rule of the Nehru-Gandhi family would continue. Despite criticisms that Sonia was not born in India, she has proved an able and popular politician.

The Cabinet

The prime minister chooses the cabinet, mostly from among the party's members elected to parliament. Seniority, competence, and personal loyalty are the main criteria that a prime minister takes into account when choosing cabinet ministers. Regional and caste representation at the highest level of government must also be considered. During Indira Gandhi's rule, personal loyalty was critical in the choice of senior ministers. Rajiv Gandhi, by contrast, put a high premium on competence, which unfortunately he equated with youth and technical skills, at the expense of political experience. Since Vajpayee was able to form a government only with the help of many smaller parties, the heads of these parties had to be accommodated, producing a vast, eclectic, and disparate cabinet.

The Bureaucracy

The prime minister and cabinet ministers run the government in close collaboration with senior civil servants. Each senior minister oversees what is often a sprawling bureaucracy, staffed by some very competent, overworked, senior civil servants and by many not-so-competent, underworked, lowly bureaucrats, well known for taking long tea breaks while they stare at stacks of unopened files.

The **Indian Administrative Service** (IAS), an elite corps of top bureaucrats, constitutes a critical but relatively thin layer at the top of India's bureaucracy. The competence of the IAS is a central reason that India is moderately well governed. Because political leaders come and go, whereas senior civil servants stay, many civil servants possess a storehouse of knowledge and expertise that makes them very powerful. Higher-level civil servants in India reach their positions after considerable experience within the government. They are named to the IAS at a relatively young age, usually in their early twenties, by passing a highly competitive entrance exam. Some of India's most talented young men and women were attracted to the IAS during the 1950s and 1960s, reflecting the prestige that service in national government used to enjoy in Indian society. The attraction of the IAS has declined, however, and many talented young people now go into engineering or business administration or leave the country for better opportunities abroad. Government service has become tainted as areas of corruption have developed and the level of professionalism within the IAS has eroded, mainly because politicians prefer loyalty over merit and seniority when making promotions. Nevertheless, the IAS continues to recruit very talented young people, many of whom become dedicated senior civil servants who still constitute the backbone of the Indian government.

Below the IAS, the level of talent and professionalism drops rather sharply. Within each ministry at the national level and in many parallel substructures at the state level, the bureaucracy in India is infamous for corruption and inefficiency. These problems contribute to the gap between good policies made at the top and their poor implementation at the local level.

Other State Institutions

The Military and the Police

Unlike the militaries in many other developing countries, say, Brazil and Nigeria, the Indian military has never intervened directly in politics. The Indian military, with more than 1 million well-trained and well-equipped members, is a highly professional organization. Over the years, the continuity of constitutional, electoral politics and a relatively apolitical military have come to reinforce and strengthen each other. Civilian politicians provide ample resources to the armed forces and, for the most part, let them function as a professional organization. The armed forces, in turn, obey the orders of democratically elected leaders, and although they lobby to preserve their own interests, they mostly stay out of the normal tumble of democratic politics.

Since the 1970s, two factors have weakened this well-institutionalized separation of politics and military. First, during Indira Gandhi's rule, loyalty to political leaders became the key criterion for securing top military jobs. This policy tended to politicize the military and narrow the separation between politics and military.

Second, there were growing regional and ethnic demands for secession (see Section 4). As these demands became more intense in some states, notably in Kashmir, and as militants began to resort to armed conflict,

occasionally with the help of India's often hostile neighbor Pakistan, the Indian government called in the armed forces. However, soldiers are not trained to resolve political problems; rather, they are trained to use force to secure compliance from reluctant political actors. As a result, not only have democratic norms and human rights been violated in India, but the distance between politics and the military has narrowed.

A similar trend toward politicization and de-professionalization has occurred in India's sprawling police services, but with a difference. The Indian police organization was never as professionalized as the armed forces, and the police services come under the jurisdiction of state governments, not the central government. Because state governments are generally less well run than the national government, the cumulative impact is that the Indian police are not apolitical civil servants. State-level politicians regularly interfere in police personnel issues, and police officers in turn regularly oblige the politicians who help them. The problem is especially serious at lower levels. The police are widely regarded as easily bribed and often allied with criminals or politicians. In some states, such as Bihar and Uttar Pradesh, police often take sides in local conflicts instead of acting as neutral arbiters or enforcers of laws. When they do, they tilt the power balance in favor of dominant social groups such as landowners or upper castes or the majority Hindu religious community.

In addition to the regular armed forces and the state-level police forces, paramilitary forces, controlled by the national government, number nearly half a million men. As Indian politics became more turbulent in the 1980s, paramilitary forces steadily expanded. Because the national government calls on the regular armed forces only as a last resort in the management of internal conflicts and because state-level police forces are not very reliable, paramilitary forces are viewed as a way to maintain order. A large, sprawling, and relatively ineffective police service remains a problematic presence in Indian society.

The Judiciary

An independent judiciary is another component of India's state system. But unlike Britain, where the judiciary's role is limited by parliamentary sovereignty, a fundamental contradiction is embedded in the Indian constitution between the principles of parliamentary sovereignty and judicial review. Over the years, the judiciary and the parliament have often clashed, with the former trying to preserve the constitution's basic structure and the latter asserting its right to amend the constitution (See "Institutional Intricacies: The Executive Versus the Judiciary"). The judiciary comprises an apex court, atop a series of national courts, high courts in states, and lower courts in districts.

The supreme judicial authority is the Supreme Court, comprising a chief justice and seventeen other judges, appointed by the president, but as in most other matters of political significance in India, only on the advice of the prime minister. Once appointed, judges cannot be removed from the bench until retirement at age sixty-five. The caseload on the Supreme Court, as on much of the rest of the Indian legal system, is extremely heavy, with a significant backlog.

The main political role of the Supreme Court is to ensure that legislation conforms with the intent of the constitution. Because the Indian constitution is very detailed, however, the need for interpretation is not as great as in many other countries. Nevertheless, there are real conflicts, both within the constitution and in India's political landscape, that often need to be adjudicated by the Supreme Court. For example, the constitution simultaneously protects private property and urges the government to pursue social justice. Indian leaders have often promulgated socialist legislation, for example, requiring the redistribution of agricultural land. Legislation of this nature is considered by the Supreme Court because it potentially violates the right to private property. Many Supreme Court cases have involved the conflict between socialistically inclined legislation and constitutional rights. Cases involving other politically significant issues, for instance, rights of religious minorities such as Muslims and the rights of women, also periodically reach the Supreme Court.

Like many other Indian political institutions, the Supreme Court lost much of its autonomy in the 1980s. The process began during Indira Gandhi's rule, when she argued that the court was too conservative and an obstacle to her socialist program. To remedy this shortcoming, she appointed many pliant judges, including the chief justice. The Supreme Court itself more or less complied with her wishes during the two years of Emergency (1975–1977), when the political and civil rights of many Indians were violated. No such dramatic instance of a politicized Supreme Court has recurred since the late 1970s.

The Supreme Court often functions as a bulwark for citizens against state invasiveness, as is evident from many landmark civil rights judgments. The Court introduced a system of public interest litigation that enabled bonded laborers, disenfranchised tribal people, the homeless, and indigent women to redress their claims. In recent years, the Supreme Court has defended environmental causes. To protect the Taj Mahal, India's most treasured national monument, from damage by air pollution, it ordered 212 nearby businesses that had chronically violated environmental regulations to close. It similarly shut down almost 200 polluters along the Ganges River. The Court enforced clean water and air laws in New Delhi in 1996–1997 by ordering that polluting cars and buses be removed from the roads and shutting down polluting enterprises. It required central and state governments to prevent starvation by releasing food stocks and to promote education by providing school lunches and day care facilities.

Subnational Government

Under India's federal system, the balance of power between the central and state governments varies by time and place. In general, the more powerful and popular the central government and prime minister are, the less likely states are to pursue an independent course. During the rule of Nehru and especially under Indira Gandhi, the states were often quite constrained. By contrast, a weaker central government, like the BJP-led alliance that took office in 1998, enlarges the room for state governments to maneuver. When state governments are run by political parties other than the national ruling party—and this is often true in contemporary India—there is considerable scope for center-state conflict. For example, a popular communist government in West Bengal has often disagreed with the national government in New Delhi, charging it with discriminatory treatment in the allocation of finances and other centrally controlled resources.

Institutional Intricacies: *The Executive Versus the Judiciary*

Over the years, the Supreme Court has clashed head-to-head with the parliament as a result of the contradiction between principles of parliamentary sovereignty and judicial review that is embedded in India's constitution. For instance, during the early years of independence, the courts overturned state government laws to redistribute land from landlords (*zamindars*), saying that the laws violated the *zamindars'* fundamental rights. In retaliation, the parliament passed the first of a series of amendments to the constitution to protect the executive's authority to promote land redistribution. But matters did not end there. The Supreme Court responded by passing a judgment stating that the parliament did not have the power to abrogate fundamental rights. In 1970, the court also invalidated the bank nationalization bill and a presidential order abolishing privy purses (including titles and privileges of former rulers of India's princely states). In retaliation, the parliament passed a series of amendments that undercut the Supreme Court's rulings, thus moving the power balance toward parliamentary sovereignty. The Supreme Court responded that the court still reserved for itself the discretion to reject any constitutional amendments passed by parliament on the grounds that the amendments could not change the constitution's basic structure. During the Emergency period, the parliament passed yet another amendment that limited the Supreme Court's judicial review to procedural issues. The Janata government in the post-Emergency era, however, reversed these changes, thus reintroducing the tension between the executive and judiciary.

Since the 1980s, the courts have increasingly functioned as a bulwark for citizens by protecting their civil liberties from state coercion. For instance, since 1993, it has enforced a policy of compensating victims of violence while in police custody. In 1985, the Supreme Court upheld a verdict finding two people guilty of murdering their wives on the grounds that the dowry was insufficient and sentenced them to life imprisonment. In the mid-1980s, the Supreme Court clashed with parliament on its interpretation of personal law over the Shah Bano case. In India, in keeping with a secular ethos, personal law falls under the purview of religion, although an individual can choose secular alternatives. However, this recourse is circumscribed: a woman married under religious law cannot seek divorce or alimony under secular law. Neither Muslim nor Hindu personal law entitles women to alimony. The British colonial government had passed a law entitling destitute divorced women to maintenance by their husbands. Shah Bano, a destitute seventy-five-year-old woman abandoned and later divorced by her husband, filed for maintenance under this law. The Supreme Court upheld Shah Bano's right to maintenance on the grounds that secular laws transcended personal law (religious law). The parliament, succumbing to pressures from religious leaders, passed a bill excluding Muslim women from the purview of secular laws.

The battle between the executive and the judiciary has taken a toll on the autonomy of the courts. The judiciary has been affected by the general malaise of institutional decay that has affected Indian politics over the years. The backlog of cases has grown phenomenally, while expeditious judgment of cases has declined dramatically.

While the political parties at the national and the state levels may differ, the formal structure of the twenty-eight state governments parallels that of the national government. The chief minister of each state heads the state government. The chief minister is the leader of the majority party (or the party with most seats) in the lower house of the state legislature. The chief minister appoints cabinet ministers who head various ministries staffed by a state-level, permanent bureaucracy. The quality of government below the national level is often poor, contributing to regional and ethnic conflicts.

In lieu of a president, each state has a governor, appointed by the national president. The governors, like the president, are supposed to serve on the advice of the chief minister, but in practice, they often become politically powerful, especially in states where the national government is at odds with the state government or where state governments are unstable. Governors can dismiss elected state governments and proclaim temporary presidential rule if they determine state governments to be ineffective. When this happens, the elected government is dissolved and the state is governed from New Delhi until fresh elections are called and a new government is elected. Although this provision is intended to be a sensible constitutional option, an intrusive national government has often used it for partisan purposes.

The power struggle between the central government and the states is ongoing. With many Indian states inhabited by people with distinctive traditions and cultures, including language, and with conflicting political parties in power at the national and state levels, central-state relations can be fueled by substantial political and ethnic conflicts.

In recent years, Indian politics has become increasingly regionalized. Three new states were formed in 2000 out of existing states. Furthermore states have become increasingly autonomous economically and politically. As a result of economic liberalization, states have acquired rights and opportunities to seek out investors independent of the national government. One consequence is that regional inequalities are widening as some states, for example, Haryana, Punjab, Maharashtra, Gujarat, Andhra Pradesh, Karnataka, and Tamil Nadu, have aggressively sought investments while some of the largest and poorest states in the north and east have fallen behind.

The twenty-eight states of India's federal system have also come to play an increasingly important role in national governance. In each of the national elections since 1989, parties based in a single state have been key to the success of coalition governments. According to the Election Commission's classification of parties, in the four national elections between 1991 and 1998, the vote share of national parties (those with a base in many states) dropped from 77 to 67 percent, and the proportion of seats they controlled slipped from 78 to 68 percent. By contrast, parties based in single

states increased their percentage share of the votes from 17 to 27 percent and their seats from 16 to 29 percent. Since 1989, every coalition government has depended on regional parties for its survival. This development has double-edged implications for democracy. On the one hand, governing coalitions that are established by disparate parties with little ideological or programmatic cohesion are likely to be unstable. On the other hand, national governments are less likely than they were in the past to seek the dismissal of state governments because national governments are likely to be composed of regional political parties.

The *panchayats,* which function at the local, district, and state levels, represent the most important attempts at the devolution of power. The *panchayats* are a precolonial institution that was responsible historically for administering justice by abjudicating conflicts and presiding over community affairs in the rural areas. In 1959, the Indian government introduced a three-tier model of *panchayats,* linked together by indirect elections. However, it gave the *panchayats* meager resources, for members of Parliament and the Legislative Assembly saw them as potential rivals to their authority. By the mid-1960s, the *panchayats* were stagnating and declining.

Some states revived the *panchayats* on their own initiative. In 1978, the communist government of West Bengal overhauled the *panchayat* system by providing for direct elections and giving them additional resources and responsibilities. Other states followed suit. In 1992, the government amended the constitution to enable all states to strengthen the *panchayats*, although states were free to create their own models. It envisaged the *panchayats'* primary role as implementing development programs and encouraging greater local involvement in government. The amendment stipulated that *panchayat* elections would be held every five years and made provisions for reserving 33 percent of the seats for women and seats proportional to the population for scheduled castes and tribes. In the first elections held under the new framework (in 1993), 700,000 women were elected to office. Most states met and several exceeded the 33 percent women's reservations at all three levels.

The abilities of women who were elected to the *panchayats* varied widely. Women who had a prior history of political activism were most likely to use the *panchayats* to benefit women. Some were responsible for the *panchayats'* sponsoring important local development projects. Others sought *panchayat* action on behalf of women over issues like marriage, divorce, and alcoholism. However, most women elected to the *panchayats* had no prior history of activism and became tokens who were silenced, marginalized, and, in extreme situations, even harassed and attacked. Many women ran for election in order to represent the interests of powerful men. In some cases, when women threatened male candidates, they were often accused of sexual immorality. Women were often ignorant about the functions of the *panchayats* and relied on their husbands for advice. Female *panchayat* members were often inhibited from participating actively.

More generally, the resources and planning capabilities of the *panchayats* are relatively limited. State legislatures determine how much power and authority the *panchayats* can wield. Very few states have engaged in a serious devolution of the *panchayats'* development functions. Most *panchayats* are responsible for implementing rural development schemes but not devising them. Policy is made at the national and state levels. Although considerable resources pass through them, local governments seldom enjoy formal discretion over how these resources are allocated. Local political elites, bureaucrats, and others with influence often collude as they determine where projects will be located, who gets a contract, and who is hired on public projects. They often siphon off a healthy share of the public money. Thus, many local governments in India tend to be corrupt, ineffective, and wasteful. City streets are not kept clean, potholes are not repaired, irrigation canals are not properly maintained, and rural schools are so poorly built that they leak as soon as the monsoons start.

The Policy-Making Process

Major policies in India are made by the national government, in New Delhi. The prime minister and senior cabinet ministers are generally responsible for initiating policies. Behind the scenes, senior civil servants in each ministry, as well as in cross-ministry offices like the prime minister's secretariat and the planning commission, play a critical role in identifying problems, synthesizing data, and presenting to political leaders alternative solutions and their implications. After decisions have been made at the highest level, many require new legislation. Because the prime minister usually has a clear majority in parliament, passage of most legislation is ensured except in extremely controversial areas.

The real policy drama in India occurs early on, when major bills are under consideration, and during the process of implementation. Consider economic liberalization policies, which represented a major policy change. The new course was formulated at the highest level of government, involving only a handful of senior ministers and bureaucrats. To reach the decision, however, a fairly complex set of political activities took place. Decision makers consulted some of the most important interest groups, such as associations of Indian businessmen and representatives of international organizations like the World Bank and the IMF. Others, including those who might be adversely affected, were heard; organized labor, for example, might call a one-day general strike (it actually did) to warn the government that any attempt to privatize the public sector would meet considerable resistance. Newspapers, magazines, and intellectuals also expressed support or opposition. Political parties got into the act. Members of the ruling party, the Congress in this case, did not necessarily support the political thinking of their own leaders at the early stage; rather, they worried about the political implications of policies for intraparty power struggles and future elections. Opposition parties, in turn, worried about the interests of their constituents. These pressures modified the policy that the government eventually adopted.

After policies have been adopted, their implementation is far from assured. Continuing with the liberalization example, some aspects of the new policy package proved easier to implement than others. Changing the exchange rate (the value of the Indian rupee in relation to the U.S. dollar) was relatively easy to implement because both the policy decision and its implementation require the actions of only a handful of politicians and bureaucrats. By contrast, the attempts to simplify the procedures for Indian or foreign business executives to create new business enterprises proved far more complicated. Implementation of such policies involves layers of bureaucrats, most of whom benefit from the control they already exercise. When forced to relinquish power, many dragged their feet and, where possible, sabotaged the newly simplified procedures.

Another example is the policies aimed at improving

the standard of living for the Indian poor. Since the 1960s, the national government has attempted to redistribute agricultural land and create public works programs to help India's rural poor. The national government set the broad outlines for land reforms and allocated funds for public works programs but left refinement of these policies, as well as their implementation, to state governments. State governments vary in terms of social classes in the state, ruling party coalitions, and the quality of their bureaucracies. The result is that the implementation of antipoverty policies within India has been quite uneven.

Land redistribution involves taking land from well-off, powerful landlords and redistributing it to poor tenants or agricultural laborers. This is a highly controversial process, requiring some combination of forceful actions by state governments and the organization of the poor beneficiaries. Generally, attempts at land redistribution have been relatively unsuccessful in most Indian states because the interests of landowning classes are well represented, and state-level bureaucrats often have close links to these landowning groups. Partial exceptions to these trends are found in the states of Kerala and West Bengal, where communist state governments and the well-organized poor have made some progress in land reform.

Attempts to generate extra employment for the rural poor through public works projects (such as road construction and canal cleaning) have been somewhat more successful than land redistribution policies because they do not involve any direct confiscation of property. The main issues in the implementation of these policies are the quality of projects chosen, whether they target the poor, and how honestly they are completed. Because the quality of local governments in implementing national policies varies (although it is rarely very high), many of the funds spent on poverty alleviation programs have been wasted. Public works policies have been most effectively implemented in the states of Maharashtra and West Bengal, where there is considerable political pressure from caste or class politics, and in some southern states, where the local bureaucracy is more efficient.

To review, the policy-making process in India, though relatively centralized, takes into account various interests and frequently produces well-developed policies. By contrast, the process of implementation is quite decentralized and relatively ineffective. What often start out as sound policy ideas and positive intentions do not reach fruition because policies are diluted as they get redefined at the state level and because of lackluster implementation.

Section ❹ Representation and Participation

Over the years, India has become a participatory democracy, as previously excluded social groups such as the poor, the landless, and backward castes entered the political arena and used their influence to shape the political process. In the early years of independence, the Congress Party mobilized most groups. However, in recent years, there has been a proliferation of political parties that have appealed to the Indian masses on ethnic grounds (particularly caste and religion), a trend initiated by Indira Gandhi. Simultaneously, the adoption of the democratic idea in the institutional sphere led to an explosion of social movements in civil society. Poor women have marched on the streets of Andhra Pradesh demanding prohibition of the sale of liquor (because of the economic toll it inflicts and its role in domestic violence), while poor tribals in Maharashtra have protested their displacement by the construction of large dams. The democratic idea is so deeply rooted that today thousands of nongovernmental organizations function in the country, representing causes ranging from welfare issues to the environment to human rights. Some social movements have transformed themselves into political parties, while others militantly oppose the established political system. Thus, ironically, while Indian democracy has become more truncated in some respects, as it has experienced institutional decline and decay, political participation through social movements and political parties has grown and flourished.

The Legislature

A good place to begin the discussion of representation and participation in a democracy is with the legislature. The Indian parliament is bicameral, consisting of the

Rajya Sabha and the *Lok Sabha.* Although the government dominates the parliament, election to the *Lok Sabha* is much sought after in India. First, the outcome of parliamentary elections determines which party coalition will control the government. Second, although members of parliament are unable to influence policies directly, they enjoy considerable status, personal access to resources, and influence over allocations of government monies and contracts within their constituencies.

Elections to the *Lok Sabha* must be held at least every five years, but, as in other parliamentary systems, the prime minister may choose to call elections earlier. India is divided into 544 electoral districts of roughly equal population, each of which elects and sends one representative to the national parliament. The major political parties nominate most candidates. Elections in India are won or lost mainly by parties, especially by party leaders, so most legislators are beholden to party leaders for securing a party ticket. Success in elections therefore does not depend on having an independent power base but on belonging to a party whose leader or whose programs are popular. Given the importance of the party label for nominations, members of parliament maintain strong voting discipline in the *Lok Sabha.* The main business of the *Lok Sabha* is to pass new legislation as well as to debate the pros and cons of government actions. Although members sometimes introduce bills, the government introduces most new legislation. After bills are introduced, they are assigned to parliamentary committees for detailed study and discussion. The committees report the bills back to the *Lok Sabha* for debate, possible amendment, and preliminary votes. They then go to the *Rajya Sabha,* the upper house, which is not a powerful chamber; it generally approves bills passed by the *Lok Sabha.* Most members of the *Rajya Sabha* are elected indirectly by state legislatures. After any final modifications by the *Rajya Sabha,* bills return to the *Lok Sabha* for a third reading, after which they are finally voted on in both houses and forwarded to the president for approval.

To understand why the *Lok Sabha* does not play a significant independent role in policy-making, keep in mind that (1) the government generally introduces new legislation; (2) most legislators, especially those belonging to the Congress Party, are politically beholden to party leaders; and (3) all parties use party whips to ensure voting along party lines. One implication of

parliament's relative ineffectiveness is that routine changes in its social composition do not have significant policy consequences. Whether members of parliament are business executives or workers, men or women, members of upper or lower castes, is not likely to lead to dramatic policy shifts. Nevertheless, groups in society derive satisfaction from having one of their own in the parliament, and dramatic shifts in social composition are bound to influence policy.

The typical member of parliament is a male university graduate between forty and sixty years old. Over the years, there have been changes in the social composition along some criteria but not others. For example, legislators in the 1950s were likely to be urban men and were often lawyers and members of higher castes. Today, nearly half the members of parliament come from rural areas, and many have agricultural backgrounds. Members of the middle castes (the so-called backward castes) are also well represented today. These changes reflect some of the broad shifts in the distribution of power in Indian society. By contrast, the proportion of women and of poor, lower-caste individuals in the parliament remains low. The representation of women in parliament has not increased much from the 4.4 percent (or 22 women) in the first parliament (1952–1957) to 8.8 percent (48 women) who were elected in the 1998 elections, the largest number ever (see Figure 4).

Three successive governments since 1996 have supported a constitutional amendment guaranteeing at least 33 percent reserved seats for women in Parliament and the Legislative Assemblies. However although most political parties have endorsed the bill in their election manifestos, they have not supported its passage in Parliament. It was defeated most recently in December 2000, when a range of parties expressed either ambivalence or opposition to it. As a compromise measure, Home Minister L. K. Advani supported the chief election commissioner's proposal to require all political parties to reserve 33 percent of their nominations for women contestants. Critics fear that political parties will nominate women in unwinnable constituencies. Thus far, parties' records in nominating women candidates have been poor. In the 1996 parliamentary elections, for example, political parties allotted less than 15 percent of the total number of tickets to women. Women constitute only 10 to 12 percent of the membership of political parties.[6]

Figure 4

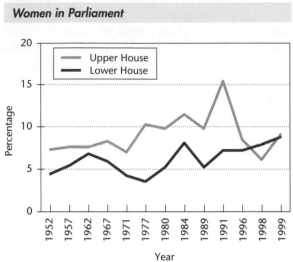

Women in Parliament

Source: India Together, http://indiatogether.org/manushi/issue116/Table-1.htm

There has been far more resistance to state and national reservations for women by political parties than by the broad public. A survey by *India Today* indicates that 75 percent of women and 79 percent of men favor the active participation of women in politics, and 75 percent of men and women favor reservations in legislative bodies. Opposition from parties has been both gendered and caste based. Parties that represent the lower middle castes have opposed the reform because it makes no provision for reservations on a caste basis.

Political Parties and the Party System

Political parties and elections are where much of the real drama of Indian politics occurs. Parties in control of a majority of seats in the national or state parliaments form the national or state governments and control government resources. Parties thus devote substantial political energy to contesting and winning elections. Since independence, the party system has evolved from being dominated by the Congress Party to one in which Congress is among the major parties but far from dominant (see Table 2). Thus, what began as virtually a one-party system has evolved into a real multiparty system, with three main political tendencies: centrist, center-left,

and center-right. Within this framework, there are at least four potentially significant national parties and many regional parties competing for power. The four parties with significant national presence are the Congress, the Janata Party, the BJP, and the Communist Party of India (Marxist; CPM). Whereas the CPM is a left-leaning party and the BJP is a religious, right-leaning one, both Congress and the Janata are more or less centrist parties. Furthermore, coalitions among these parties have occurred in the past. For example, the Janata Party joined forces with the CPM and other smaller parties in the 1996 elections to form the United Front and has been able to form two short-lived left-leaning governments.

The Congress Party

Congress was India's premier political party until the 1990s. Many aspects of this party have already been discussed because it is impossible to analyze Indian politics without referring to its role. To summarize briefly, the Congress Party built its electoral network by creating patrons who would mobilize electoral support for the party during elections. Once in power, the Congress Party would channel government resources to these people, further enhancing their local position and ensuring their support.

This patronage system (some call it machine politics) worked quite well for the Congress Party for nearly two decades. Nevertheless, even when the party was electorally successful, this strategy generated internal contradictions. The pro-poor Congress Party of India, with a socialist shell, came to be internally dominated by high-caste, wealthy Indians.

By the early 1950s, with Nehru at its helm, Congress was the unquestioned ruling party of India. Over the years, especially since the mid-1960s, this hegemony came to be challenged. By the time Indira Gandhi assumed power in 1966, the old Congress Party had begun to lose its political sway, and anticolonial nationalism was fading. The spread of democratic politics mobilized many poor, lower-caste citizens who depended less and less on village big men for political guidance. As a result, numerous regional parties started challenging Congress's monopoly on power. Weather-related food shortages in the mid-1960s also hurt the Congress Party in the 1967 elections.

Table 2

Major Party Election Results

	1991		1996		1998		1999	
	%	Seats	%	Seats	%	Seats	%	Seats
Congress (I)	37.3	225	29	143	25.4	140	28.4	112
BJP & Allies	19.9	119	24	193	36.2	250	41.3	296
Janata	10.8	55	Joined with UF		Joined with UF		1	1
United Front	—	—	31	180	20.9	98	—	—
Communistsª	—	48	Joined with UF		Joined with UF		5.4	32
Others							23.9	107

ªIncludes both the CPM and the CPI.

Source: India Today, July 15, 1991, March 16, 1998; *Economic Times* website http://economictimes.indiatimes.com.

Indira Gandhi sought to reverse the decline in the Congress's electoral popularity through mobilizing India's vast majority, the poor, by promising poverty alleviation as the core of her political program. This promise struck a popular chord, propelling Indira Gandhi to the top of India's political pyramid. Her personal success, however, came at a cost to the party. The old Congress split into two parties, with one branch, the Congress (O), becoming moribund and leaving the other, Congress (I) (the "I" stands for Indira) to inherit the position of the old undivided Congress. Nevertheless, the Congress Party formed all governments from independence to 1989, with just one interlude, when the Janata Party formed the government, (1977–1980). Since 1989, however, Congress headed the government only from 1991 to 1996.

Prior to Indira Gandhi's prime ministership, rank-and-file party members elected the lowest-level Congress Party officers, who in turn elected officers at higher levels of the party organization, up to the position of the party leader, who was the prime minister during the long period when the Congress formed the government. Indira Gandhi reversed this bottom-up party structure by creating a top-down party in which leaders appointed party officers. With some modifications, including some limited internal party elections, this is basically how the contemporary Congress Party is organized. The top-down structure enables the leaders to control the party, but it is a major liability when grassroots support is necessary. As the nation's oldest party, the Congress continues to attract substantial

electoral support. If this support ever declined sharply, most likely the party rank-and-file would demand its reorganization.

Whereas Congress during the 1970s had a left-of-center, pro-poor political platform, beginning in 1984 it moved toward the ideological center under Rajiv Gandhi (see Section 2 for the reasons behind this shift). Today, the Congress Party tilts right-of-center, championing issues of economic efficiency, business interests, and limited government spending over the rights of the poor and the working people and over social questions of health, education, and welfare.

As a nationalist party, the Congress Party is intimately associated with the stability of the Indian nation and the state in Indian political culture. Regardless of its economic program, therefore, the Congress has always attracted support from diverse social groups: rich and poor, upper and lower castes, Hindus and Muslims, northerners and southerners. Nevertheless, elections in the 1990s indicate that Congress has lost some of its traditional constituencies among the poor, lower castes, and Muslims.

The Janata Party

The Janata Party, India's other centrist party, formed short-lived national governments in 1977, 1989, and together with other parties through the United Front in 1996 and 1997. The Janata Party, however, is not so much a political party as an umbrella for various parties and factions that change with the political circumstances. The Janata Party was created in 1977 when several small parties that opposed Indira Gandhi's Emergency hurriedly united to contest her and, much to their own surprise, won the national elections. This loose coalition lasted only a little over two years, when conflicting leadership ambitions tore it apart.

During the late 1980s, the Janata Party enjoyed another brief term as a national government under the leadership of a breakaway Congress leader, V. P. Singh. With these appeals, the party won enough seats in the national parliament to form a minority government in 1989. Once again, factionalism overwhelmed any attempt at a stable government, and this second attempt with a non-Congress-led government collapsed after a little over two years. Since then, the Janata Party has been able to survive only under the umbrella of the United Front, which is a collection of smaller parties, including the CPM.

The Janata Party has a very weak organizational structure and lacks a distinctive, coherent political platform. To distinguish itself from Congress, it claims that it is more Gandhian, a reference to Mahatma Gandhi's vision that modern India should be more decentralized and village oriented, and less pro-Brahmin. Although most of its efforts at political self-definition have not been very successful, V. P. Singh undertook one major policy initiative while in power that identified the Janata Party with a progressive cause. This was the acceptance of the Mandal Commission's recommendation that India's **"Other Backward Classes,"** generally, the middle, rural castes that constitute a near majority in the Indian countryside, be provided substantial reservations (or reserved access) to government jobs and educational institutions. The government's acceptance of this recommendation produced a nationwide outburst of riots and violence, led by upper castes, who felt threatened. The uproar eventually contributed to the downfall of V. P. Singh's government. Nevertheless, Singh's acceptance of what has been called "Mandal" associated the Janata Party with the interests of the backward castes. How strongly backward castes will continue to identify with this party in the future is unknown. For now, the Janata Party is viewed, especially in north-central India, as a party of small, rural agriculturalists who generally fall somewhere in the middle of the rigid caste hierarchy between Brahmins and untouchables.

The Bharatiya Janata Party (BJP)

The BJP, the major political party in contemporary India, is a direct descendant of the Jana Sangh Party, which entered the Indian political scene in 1951. The Jana Sangh joined the Janata Party government in 1977 but then split off and formed the BJP in 1980. The BJP is a right-leaning, Hindu-nationalist party, the first major party to mobilize explicitly on the basis of religious identity and to often adopt an anti-Muslim stance. In comparison to both the Congress and the Janata, the BJP is better organized; it has disciplined party members, who after a prolonged apprenticeship become party cadres, and the authority lines within the party are relatively clear and well respected.

The party is closely affiliated with many related organizations, the most significant of which is the RSS. Most BJP leaders were at one-time members of the RSS, which recruits young people (especially educated youth in urban areas) and involves them in a fairly disciplined set of cultural activities, including the study of a chauvinistic reinterpretation of India's "great Hindu past." These young people, uniformed in khaki shorts and shirts, can often be seen in Indian cities doing group exercises in the mornings and evenings and singing songs glorifying India's Sanskritic civilization (Sanskrit is the classical language in which some of the ancient Hindu scriptures are written). Recalling the pursuits of right-wing fascist groups of interwar Europe, the activities of these youth groups, seemingly no more than an appeal to cultural pride, dismay many non-Hindu minorities and Indian liberals, who fear the havoc that cultural pride can produce, as it did in Nazi Germany.

Those traditionally attracted to the Jana Sangh and the BJP were mainly urban, lower-middle-class groups, especially small traders and commercial groups. As long as this was its main source of support, the BJP remained a minor actor on the Indian political scene. Since the mid-1980s, however, the BJP has widened its base of support appreciably by appealing to Hindu nationalism, especially in north-central India. The decline in the Congress Party's popularity created a vacuum that the BJP was well positioned to fill. Moreover, the BJP found in Indian Muslims a convenient scapegoat for the frustrations of various social groups and successfully mobilized Hindus in an attempt to create a religiously oriented political force where none had existed before. The electoral success of the BJP in 1989 and 1991 and its formation of the government in 1999 underscore the party's rapid rise to power. The BJP's early efforts resulted in its ruling four states from 1991 to 1993, though it lost power in three of the four in 1993. During the 1999 parliamentary elections, the BJP scored a major success and formed the national government.

The growth of the BJP in recent years represents a break with past traditions. In the aftermath of independence, the RSS and its affiliated organizations were widely regarded as divisive, anti-Muslim organizations. The BJP's predecessor, the *Bharatiya Jana Sangh,* responded to its stigmatization by adopting a relatively moderate, centrist position through the 1984 elections, when it won only two seats in parliament. Its fortunes began to rise after the 1989 elections, when it emerged as the third largest party after the Congress and Janata parties. In 1991, the BJP held the second largest number of seats in parliament. To capitalize on the Hindu support it had been mobilizing, the BJP acquiesced in the demolition of the Babri Masjid (a Muslim mosque) in Ayodhya in 1992.

Six years later, as a result of the failures of other parties to lead effective governments, the BJP formed a governing coalition, the National Democratic Alliance, led by Prime Minister Atal Behari Vajpayee. However, its mismanagement of the economy soon generated a popular backlash against the BJP. The BJP performed very badly in four state government assembly elections in 1998, losing to the Congress Party in three states and to a regional party in the fourth state. The BJP government collapsed in 1999, just thirteen months after taking power.

The BJP formed a new electoral coalition, the National Democratic Alliance government, headed by Atal Behari Vajpayee, which was elected in 1999. It was more broadly based than previous BJP-led coalition governments because it attracted the support of regionally based political parties in various states. The result not only strengthened the BJP's hold on power but also strengthened trends toward the regionalization of Indian politics.

Another reason for the greater strength of the BJP-led government in 1999 was its cultivation of a more moderate, centrist stance. In 1996, most political parties shunned an alliance with the BJP, for it was tainted by its militant identity. Even in 1998, the BJP put together a governing coalition with great difficulty. In 1999, the BJP went to great lengths to project Atal Behari Vajpayee as a moderate, centrist leader. Moreover, the National Democratic Alliance platform shelved contentious issues that identified it with the interests of Hindus over and against those of religious minorities.

The BJP has not fully swung to the political center or abdicated its militance. It continues to retain strong ties to the RSS and periodically demonstrates its commitment to constructing a temple in Ayodhya. Its handling of the Gujarat riots in 2002 revealed its reluctance to act decisively to bring the guilty to trial either during the riots or in their aftermath for fear of alienating hard-line supporters.

A number of factors have prevented the BJP from moving in a wholly centrist direction. The first and most important concerns its close ties to the RSS and the Hindu religious organization, the *Visva Hindu Parishad* (VHP). Since its formation in 1964, the VHP has sought to strengthen Hindu identity in a chauvinist and exclusionary fashion. In the 1960s, its activities centered on converting Muslims, who, it claimed, had been forcibly converted to Hinduism. Since the 1980s, it has been active around the construction of the temple in Ayodhya.

There are clearly some important differences in the orientation of these organizations. The RSS is committed to economic nationalism, the BJP to liberalization. The VHP has been implicated in violence, whereas the BJP has promised stability. Despite these differences, the BJP has maintained a close relationship to the RSS and the VHP. The RSS has intervened to mend rifts within the party in various states. It has helped ensure that the BJP, unlike most Indian political parties, has never split. Moreover, it is hard to imagine a complete severance between the two organizations when the highest-ranking BJP members are of RSS backgrounds, and many of them have continuing ties to the RSS. The BJP's relationship to the VHP, though conflictual at times when the BJP is in office, has also been salutary. RSS and VHP activists have regularly participated in the electoral campaigns of the BJP in state and general elections. Moreover, the riots that the VHP has engineered have polarized the electorate along Hindu-Muslim lines and expanded the BJP's electoral fortunes.

The BJP's continuing commitment to privileging the interests of the Hindu majority, evident in response to the Gujarat riots, the temple construction in Ayodhya, and policies in Kashmir, has increased the vulnerability of the Muslim community. Although the BJP has consistently proclaimed its attachment to secular principles, it has taken steps to undermine the conditions under which secularism flourishes. Its promises of providing clean, honest governance have been marred in recent years by disclosures of corruption by high-ranking officials, for example, in the discriminatory distribution of relief after a massive earthquake in Gujarat in 2001, in charges that the army had engaged in corruption after a border clash with Pakistan in 1999, and in patterns of bribery in defense procurement in 2001.

The Communist Party of India (CPM)

The CPM is an offshoot of the Communist Party of India, which was formed during the colonial period and has existed nearly as long as the Congress Party. Although the contemporary CPM has a national presence in that it nearly always elects representatives to the *Lok Sabha,* its political base is concentrated in two of India's states, West Bengal and Kerala. These states have often been ruled by the CPM, and they often elect *Lok Sabha* members who run on a CPM ticket.

The CPM is a disciplined party, with party cadres and a hierarchical authority structure. Other than its name and internal organization, however, there is nothing communist about the CPM; rather, it is a social democratic party like the British Labour Party or the German Social Democratic Party. The CPM accepts the framework of democracy, regularly participates in elections, and often wins them in West Bengal and Kerala. In these two states, the CPM enjoys the support of the lower-middle and lower classes, both factory workers and poorer peasants. Within the national parliament, CPM members often strongly criticize government policies that are likely to hurt the poor. On occasion, the CPM joins with other parties against the BJP, as it did in the 1996 elections by joining the United Front. Where the CPM runs state governments, for example, in West Bengal and Kerala, it has provided a relatively honest and stable administration. It has also pursued a moderate but effective reform program,

ensuring the rights of agricultural tenants (such as preventing their evictions), providing services to those living in shanty towns, and encouraging public investments in rural areas.

Elections

Elections in India are a colossal event. Nearly 500 million people are eligible to vote, and close to 300 million do so. The turnout rate in the 1990s was over 60 percent, considerably higher than in the United States. The level of technology used in both campaigning and the conduct of elections is fairly low. Television plays an increasingly important role, but much campaigning still involves face-to-face contact between politicians and the electorate. Senior leaders fly around the country, making speeches to millions of potential supporters at political rallies held in tiny villages and district towns. Lesser politicians and thousands of their party supporters travel the dusty streets, blaring music and political messages from loudspeakers mounted on their vehicles.

Given the high rate of illiteracy, pictures of party symbols are critical: a hand for the Congress (I); a lotus for the BJP; a hammer and sickle for the CPM. Illiterate voters signify their vote for a candidate in the polling booth by putting thumb marks on one of these symbols. During the campaign, therefore, party representatives work very hard to associate certain individuals and election platforms with specific symbols. A typical election slogan is, "Vote for the hammer and sickle because they stand for the rights of the working people."

India's electoral system, like the British system, is a first-past-the-post system. A number of candidates compete in an electoral district; the candidate who has the most votes wins. For example, if the Congress candidate wins the most votes, say 35 percent of the vote from a district, and the candidates of other parties split the remaining votes, the Congress candidate is victorious. This system privileges the major political parties. It also generates considerable pressure for opposition parties to collaborate as a single voice against the government. In practice, however, given the differences between opposition parties and the considerable clash of leadership ambitions, many parties compete, enabling the candidates of the larger party to squeeze by as winners.

Village women wait in line to get voting slips at a polling station in a village in India's Orissa state, March 7, 1995.
Source: Bettmann/Corbis.

One of the pillars of Indian democracy is its system of free and fair elections. Credit for this goes in part to the Election Commission, a constitutionally mandated central body that functions independently of the executive. Particularly since 1991, with the appointment of an honest and respected chief, the Election Commission has defended free and fair elections.

Political Culture, Citizenship, and Identity

The only generalization that can be made about Indian political culture is that in such a large and culturally diverse country, no single set of cultural traits is shared by the entire population. Nevertheless, three important tendencies or habits of mind are worth noting. These political cultural traits reflect India's hybrid political style, as a rigid, hierarchical, and village-oriented old civilization adapts itself to modern socioeconomic changes, especially to democratic politics.

One important tendency is that India's political and public spheres are not sharply divided from personal and private spheres of activity. The idea that public

office is not a legitimate means for personal enrichment or for furthering the interests of family members or of personal associates is not yet fully accepted in India. As a result, there is fairly widespread misuse of public resources for personal gain, that is, widespread corruption in political life.

Second, the Indian elite is highly factionalized. The roots of such behavior are complex, reflecting India's fragmented social structure. Although some important exceptions exist, generally the personal political ambitions of Indian leaders prevent them from pursuing such collective goals as forming cohesive political parties, running a stable government, or focusing on problems of national development. In contrast to many East Asian countries, where the norms of consensus are powerful and political negotiation is often conducted behind closed doors, politics in India veers toward the other extreme, and open disagreements and conflicts are the norm.

The third, and possibly most important, political cultural tendency that deserves mention concerns the fragmentation of political life in India. Indian society is highly segmented. Different regions have different languages and cultures; within regions, villages are poorly connected with each other; and within villages, different castes often live in isolation from one another. Politics is often fragmented along caste lines, but even caste grievances tend to remain local rather than accumulate nationally or even regionally. Some observers of India find this segmented quality of Indian politics a blessing because it localizes problems, facilitating political stability, but others find it a curse because it stymies the possibility of national reforms to improve the lot of the poorest members of society.

Democracy is relatively well established in India. Most Indians value their citizenship rights and, in spite of poverty and illiteracy, exercise them with vigor. However, the spread of democratic politics can simultaneously fuel political conflicts. The spread of democracy is undermining many of India's political givens, including some of the most rigid hierarchies, and has begun to produce new political patterns.

The most significant of these recent developments concerns identity politics, whereby the dynamics of democratic politics mobilizes social identities in the service of political conflicts. Region, language, religion, and caste all help Indians define who they are. Such differences have generated political cleavages in India, underlining the importance and yet the malleability of collective identities, for example, the Hindu-Muslim conflict at the time of independence. Some of these identity conflicts remained dormant when Nehru's secular nationalism and Indira Gandhi's poor-versus-rich cleavage defined the core political issues. In the 1980s and 1990s, however, with the relative decline of the Congress Party and with developments in telecommunications and transportation that have made people more aware of each other's differences, identity-based political conflicts have mushroomed in India.

Two of the more significant conflicts deserve mention. First, caste conflicts, though usually confined to local and regional politics, have taken on a national dimension in recent years, for example, former prime minister V. P. Singh's acceptance of the Mandal Commission recommendations. These recommendations were meant to benefit India's backward castes, who are numerically significant and tend to be rural agriculturalists by occupation and somewhere in the middle of the caste hierarchy. Groups of backward castes had made a political mark in many states, but prior to Mandal, they were seldom a cohesive factor in national politics. In all probability, V. P. Singh hoped to create a powerful support base out of these disparate groups. However, the move backfired. The threatened upper castes reacted sharply with demonstrations, riots, and political violence. Not only did this disruption contribute to the downfall of Singh's government, but it also converted the conflict between castes from a local and regional issue to a divisive national issue.

The second identity-based political conflict that has reemerged has pitched Hindus and Muslims against each other. Tensions between these religious communities go back several centuries, when Muslim rulers from Central Asia established the Moghul dynasty in India. Stories and memories of the relative greatness of one community over the other, or of atrocities and injustices unleashed on one community by the other, abound in India's popular culture. For the most part, these legends fan low-level hostilities that do not prevent peaceful coexistence. However, political circumstances, especially political machinations by ambitious leaders, can inflame these tendencies and instigate overt conflict. This is what has happened since the mid-1980s, as the BJP has whipped up anti-Muslim

sentiments in an effort to unite disparate Hindu groups into a political force. The resulting victimization of Muslims in acts of political violence, including destruction of life, property, and places of worship, illustrates the dangers of identity-based political passions.

There are many poor or otherwise frustrated social groups in India whose anger is available for political mobilization. Whether the BJP will succeed in tapping this anger in the longer term cannot be predicted. What can be said is that democracy and large pockets of social frustration provide a combustible mix that will continue to generate unexpected outcomes in Indian politics.

Interests, Social Movements, and Protest

India has a vibrant tradition of political activism that has both enriched and complicated the workings of democracy. Social movements, nongovernmental organizations (NGOs), and trade unions have put pressure on the state to be attentive to the interests and needs of underprivileged groups and have checked its authoritarian tendencies.

Among the groups that are politically active, labor has played a significant but not leading role. Labor unions are politically fragmented, particularly at the national level. Instead of the familiar model of one factory/one union, several political parties often organize within a single factory. Above the factory level, several labor organizations compete for labor's support. The government generally stays out of labor-management conflicts. India's industrial relations are thus closer to the pluralist model practiced in Anglo-American countries than to the corporatist model of, say, Mexico. The political energies of unions are channeled into frequent local battles involving strikes, demonstrations, and a peculiarly Indian protest technique called *gherao,* which entails workers' encircling and holding executives of the firm hostage until their demands are met.

Social movements, the most important form of civil society activism, date back to the mid-1970s. During the period of the national Emergency (1975–1977) when the government imprisoned members of the opposition, activists began to come together to form political parties and social movements, often with close ties to one another. In 1977, the Gandhian Socialist leader Jai Prakash Narain organized the movement for total democracy that ultimately brought about the downfall of Congress and the election of the Janata Party. A decade later, V. P. Singh resigned from Congress and formed the *Jan Morcha* (Peoples' Front), an avowedly nonpolitical movement that brought new groups into politics and helped bring the National Front to power in 1989.

Social movements continued to grow and assume new organizational forms in the 1980s. Some engaged in grassroots activism, and others worked more closely with the state. The number of NGOs also expanded. Until the early 1980s, when Indira Gandhi was prime minister, the state was distrustful of what is commonly known in India as the voluntary sector and sought to restrict its activities. When Rajiv Gandhi came to power, he attempted to cultivate a closer relationship with NGOs, for he recognized their potential for taking over some of the development work that the state had traditionally performed. Over the years, financial support for NGOs from the national government has steadily increased. During the seventh five-year plan (1985–1990), the federal government spent about US$11 million each year through NGOs; by 2002 this had increased to over $44 million annually. Today there are 20,000 voluntary organizations listed with the Ministry of Home Affairs, and the actual number is much higher. The most significant social movements organized around either distinctive themes or identities include the women's movement, the environmental movement, and the *dalit* (a term of pride used by untouchables) movement. In recent years, there has also been the growth of antinuclear, civil liberties activism. The extraordinarily large number and extensive activities of social movements make India quite distinctive among developing countries.

The environment movement is organized by educated urban activists and some of India's poorest and most marginal groups. Their activism has been spurred by the magnitude of the country's environmental crisis and the ineffectiveness of its environmental laws. India suffers from severe air pollution in large cities and contaminated lakes and rivers. The shortage of drinking water is worsened by salinization, water overuse, and groundwater depletion. The emission of carbon dioxide has contributed to the greenhouse effect, leading to an increase in temperature, a rise in the sea level, and the destruction of coastal crop lands and fisheries.

Commercial logging, fuel wood depletion, and urbanization have caused serious problems of deforestation, which is associated with droughts, floods, and cyclones.

Successive governments have chosen to promote increased production at the expense of environmental protection. Effective enforcement of environmental laws and policies would put many firms out of business and slow economic growth. Moreover, it would be very time-consuming and difficult for the government to monitor and control all small-scale industries. Although the Congress Party sponsored most of India's environmental laws, it also catered to the interest of big business at the expense of environmental protection. The United Front parties have been strong supporters of environmental issues but have tended to target only big business rather than small businesses. The Bharatiya Janata Party has explicitly placed business interests over environmental concerns. Thus, the major sources of support for environmental protection have been social movements and NGOs.

The Chipko movement against deforestation in the Himalayas, which emerged in the early 1970s, has been one of the longest-lasting movements against deforestation and has influenced similar forms of activism in other regions of the country. Large-scale protest at the 1984 Union Carbide disaster in Bhopal demanded greater compensation for victims of the gas leak, as well as more environmental regulations to prevent similar disasters in the future. This resulted in the creation of the Central Pollution Control Board in 1986 and a series of environmental statutes, regulations, and protocols.

The largest and most significant environmental movement in India has protested the construction of the Sardar Sarvodaya Dam in western India. The Narmada Bachao Andolan (NBA), led by a woman named Medha Pathkar, has organized opposition to the construction of the dam on grounds that it will benefit already prosperous regions to the detriment of poor regions, lead to the large-scale displacement of people, and put in place vastly inadequate resettlement schemes. A large proportion of those who would be displaced are tribals who do not possess land titles. The movement has galvanized tens of thousands of people to engage in nonviolent protest to oppose the construction of the dam. The protest caused the World Bank to rescind promised loans, but the Indian government is still pursuing the project.

Women and questions of gender inequality have been at the forefront of environmental struggles like the Chipko and Narmada movements. The 1980s also witnessed the formation of a number of autonomous urban women's organizations. They campaigned around rape in police custody, dowry murders, *sati* (the immolation of widows on their husbands' funeral pyres), female feticide (through the use of amniocentesis), misrepresentation of women in the media, protest against harmful contraception dissemination, coercive population policies, and, most recently, the adverse impact of the economic reforms.

The *dalit* movement looks back to Dr. Ambedkar, the *dalit* author of the Indian constitution, as the founding father of the movement. He was responsible for the creation of the Republican Party in the late 1960s The disintegration of the party gave rise to the emergence of a radical youth movement that called itself the Dalit Panthers. The movement organized *dalits* to demand to be treated with dignity, to be provided better educational opportunities, and to become more politically active. Today, the *dalit* movement reflects dalits' growing aspirations for electoral power and public office.

Kanshi Ram formed the Bahujan Samaj Party (BSP) in 1989 with the goal of achieving political power for the *dalits*. The BSP experienced significant growth in the 1990s. With a share of 4.7 percent of the national vote in 1998 and 4.2 percent in 1999, it is almost as strong as the CPM (5.4 percent). However, its strength is mainly confined to Uttar Pradesh. Other small lower-caste parties have been active in Maharashtra and Tamil Nadu. However, none of these parties is able to play a national role other than participating in and influencing electoral alliances. Moreover, these parties have confined themselves to seeking political power for *dalits* and lack a broader vision of social transformation. Tensions have emerged within the *dalit* community. Some of the poorer and lower-status *dalits* feel that the better-off, higher-status *dalits* have benefited from reservations at their expense. Radical sections within the *dalit* movement argue that *dalits* ought not to depend entirely on reservations or the state, but should initiate a mass movement of their own that highlights issues of employment, education, and landlessness.

Three important developments have influenced the character and trajectory of social movements in recent years. First, many social movements have been drawn into a closer relationship to the state and to electoral politics. In the past, social movements tended to be community based and issue specific. Once they had achieved some success, around, say, the felling of forest trees, the construction of a dam, or higher prices for agricultural subsidies, the movement would subside. Although many social movements continue to be confined by their focus, duration, and geographic reach, some of them have sought to overcome these difficulties by engaging in electoral politics. The *dalit* movement and Hindu nationalism are two of the most important examples. Participation in electoral politics has in turn shaped and influenced these movements' goals. Other movements have sought to work with particular branches of the state. The women's movement, for example, has worked closely with the bureaucracy and the courts. In part because of the closer relationship between social movements and the state, an enduring broad left-wing formation consisting of left-wing parties and social movements has not emerged. By contrast, Hindu nationalists, particularly under the auspice of the VHP, have sustained their strong connections to the BJP.

Second, the growth of the religious right has confronted left-wing social movements with a serious challenge and dilemma. Unlike some other regions of the world where the religious right and the secular left disagree on most issues, the situation in India is more complex. Segments of the religious right, like parts of the left, oppose economic liberalization and globalization. For example, both feminists and Hindu nationalists oppose the commodification of women's bodies that occurs in international beauty pageants. Similarly, the women's movement has put on the back burner its demand for a uniform civil code that would provide equal treatment of men and women of all religious communities under the law because the BJP has made this very demand, albeit for very different reasons.

A third important development has been that many NGOs and social movements have developed extensive transnational connections. The consequences for social movements have been double-edged. On the positive side, funding from foreign sources has been vital to the survival of NGOs and social movements. India lacks a tradition of donating to secular-philanthropic causes, and corporate funding is limited and tightly controlled. However, organizations receiving foreign funding are often viewed with suspicion and have difficulty establishing their legitimacy. Moreover, foreign funding has created a sharp division between activists with and without access to foreign donors.

If these developments have complicated the agendas of social movements, there is also a strong potential for NGOs and social movements to grow stronger. There are greater opportunities than ever before for social movement and NGO activists to take advantage of the resources that the state is making available to the local level. Some groups have already done this by putting candidates up for elections at the local level, as we have seen in the case of the *panchayats*.

To review, political participation over the years in India has broadened in scope and deepened in intensity. A single-party system dominated by the Congress Party has slowly been supplanted by a multiparty system of parties on the left and the right. Similarly, old hierarchies of caste have eroded in Indian society, and upper castes cannot readily control the political behavior of those below them. The result is that many groups in society increasingly feel empowered and hope to translate this new consciousness and sense of efficacy into material gains by influencing government policies.

Section ⑤ Indian Politics in Transition

Political Challenges and Changing Agendas

As a large country with a legitimate government and sizable armed forces, India has not readily been influenced by external forces. For example, India tested nuclear bombs in 1998 and successfully withstood international condemnation and sanctions. However, in an increasingly interdependent global economic context, India has become far more vulnerable to global pressures. The changing geopolitical environment in the aftermath of the September 11 terrorist attacks has drawn India into closer relations with the United States. India today must confront major challenges at home and abroad if it is to preserve and strengthen its democratic institutions and improve its economic performance.

Kashmir Within a World of States

Of all the challenges that India has faced since independence, among the most enduring and intractable is its relationship to Kashmir, the state located in northern India on the border with Pakistan. The roots of conflict within Kashmir have often been attributed to the ethnic and religious diversity of the state, which is roughly 65 percent Muslim and 35 percent Hindus and other minorities. The non-Muslim minorities—Hindus, Sikhs, and Buddhists, who are concentrated in the areas of the state called Jammu and Ladakh—largely wish to live under Indian sovereignty. The Kashmir Valley, which is predominantly Sunni Muslim, is mostly in favor of Kashmir's becoming an independent country or part of Pakistan. However, separatist sentiments cannot be explained primarily by ethnic differences. Rather, one must ask what led many Kashmiri Muslims to become progressively radicalized against India.

Heightened separatist, fundamentalist, and terrorist activities have resulted from the frustrations many Kashmiris have experienced as a result of the central government's actions. At independence, Nehru promised that a referendum would be held in Kashmir to decide the status of the region. However, the Indian government never honored this pledge, mainly because it has feared a pro-independence vote. With the partial exceptions of 1947–1953 and 1977–1984, Kashmir has been directly ruled from New Delhi. This has retarded democratic participation and institutional development in the state. As demands for independence grew, so too did the repressive actions of the Indian state, leading to spiraling cycles of insurgent militance and state-sanctioned violence. Pakistan also contributed significantly to the insurgency by training and supporting the militants. Whether the fate of Kashmiris can be resolved today through democratic means is an open question.

More than any other conflict, the Kashmir dispute is triggered and sustained by the international context. The timing of Indian independence and simultaneous partition of the subcontinent into India and Partition fueled tensions in Kashmir and created uncertainty over its status within the Indian union. Superpower rivalry in the cold war deterred India and Pakistan from reaching an agreement on the status of Kashmir that would be acceptable to India, Pakistan, and the population of Kashmir itself.

Kashmir represents an important case study of the pitfalls and possibilities of democratic governance in India. It reveals the limits of democracy, for the national government has ruled Kashmir more undemocratically than any other state in India, through a combination of repression, direct control, and intervention to uphold unrepresentative governments. The constant rigging of elections has prevented the development of free and autonomous competition among political parties. While elections were held in most parts of the country from 1952 onward, in Kashmir elections to the Legislative Assembly were held in only 1962 and to the Parliament only in 1967. Most elections in Jammu and Kashmir were fraudulent. The most recent elections in 2002 are a partial exception to this. Although these elections witnessed the police and army forcing people to vote, in part in response to the separatists' support for an electoral boycott, they were more open and inclusive than previous elections. The National Conference, which had been in power for over two decades and had become an ally of the BJP government at the national level, lost heavily. The BJP, which had previously had a strong presence in the Hindu-dominated Jammu region, faced an even bigger setback. After strenuous negotiations, the People's Democratic Party (PDP) and the Congress Party formed a coalition government with PDP's Mufti Mohammad Sayeed as chief minister. The new government proclaimed that it would not implement the undemocratic Prevention of Terrorism Act. It also released several prominent political prisoners. Both policies have already led to friction with the national BJP government.

In addition to ethnic conflict within Kashmir, the other serious impediment to resolving the Kashmiri dispute is continuing tensions between India and Pakistan. These tensions are one of the important reasons for the two countries' high military expenditures (see Figure 5). As recently as the summer of 1999, Pakistani units infiltrated the Indian border and launched a massive air and land campaign. After six weeks of fighting in May and June 1999, Pakistan's prime minister, Musharaf, agreed to withdraw Pakistani troops. Frosty relations between India and Pakistan began to thaw

only a year later. In November 2000, Prime Minister Vajpayee proclaimed a cease-fire, and firing along the Line of Control, the border between India and Pakistan, almost came to a halt. However, the gains of the cease-fire were partial. Within Kashmir, violence by the Indian army and militants continued. Vajpayee and Musharaf held a summit in Agra in July 2001, where the two sides made some progress on numerous secondary issues dividing the two countries, including peace and security, terrorism, drug trafficking, and economic and commercial cooperation. But they failed to make progress on resolving the status of Kashmir, which remains the fundamental cause of tensions between the two countries. Indeed, following the attacks in the United States of September 11, 2001, relations became even more fraught. Understanding why requires putting the aftermath of September 11 in a wider context.

The Effects of September 11

The terrorist attacks of September 11 had important implications for India's relations with its neighbors and with the United States. Prior to September 11, the

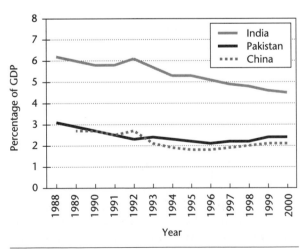

Figure 5

Military Expenditure

Source: Information from the Stockholm International Peace Research Institute (SIPRI), Military Expenditure Database, http://first.sipri.org/non_first/result/milex.php

Pakistani regime had been a major supporter of the Taliban government. With the overthrow of the Taliban and the establishment of the Hamid Karzai government, the new Afghan government established close diplomatic, civil, and commercial ties to India.

In the aftermath of September 11, India began to depict opposition forces in Kashmir as part of international Islamic militancy and demanded that one front in the global U.S. war against terror was militant groups operating from Pakistan to destabilize Kashmir. As a result, tensions increased between India and Pakistan. Soon after September 11, there was an exchange of fire on the border between the two countries. Relations plummeted further with an attack on the Jammu and Kashmir Legislative Assembly in early 2001 and, far more serious, following an attack on the Indian parliament later that year. India charged that the attacks on a key political institution were orchestrated by Pakistan. Following the attack on parliament, India prepared for war with Pakistan by recalling its high commissioner from Islamabad, the Pakistani capital, terminating train and bus service between the two countries, and, most alarming, massing most of its 1.2 million troops near the Pakistani border. Pakistan responded in kind, and for several weeks, nuclear conflagration seemed a distinct possibility. Intense intervention by the United States helped to defuse the situation, and Pakistan and India withdrew most of their troops from the border. However, relations between the two countries remain tense.

Relations between India and the United States became much closer after September 11. Abandoning its previous policy of nonalignment, India allowed the United States to establish a military presence in the country. The United States has been more involved than ever before in negotiating Indo-Pakistan tensions over Kashmir, in the conflict in Sri Lanka over a separate Tamil state, and in Nepal, which has experienced bitter conflict between the monarchy and Maoist militants for over six years.

Nuclear Power Status

One major political challenge for India is how to negotiate with the rest of the world, particularly the United States, on its emergence as a nuclear weapons state. Following India's nuclear tests of May 1998, the focus of international, and particularly U.S., diplomacy sought to enforce a universal nonproliferation agreement. The Vajpayee and the Clinton administrations engaged in several rounds of delicate arms control talks in which Clinton tried to persuade India to sign the Comprehensive Test Ban Treaty (CTBT) and the Nuclear Non-Proliferation Treaty (NPT) in exchange for completely lifting U.S. sanctions. India opposed the NPT on the grounds that it was unfair to nonnuclear countries because it did not establish a procedure for eventual phase-out of nuclear weapons by the nuclear powers. The United States urged India to exercise restraint on its nuclear weapons and missiles programs, while New Delhi insisted on its right to minimum nuclear deterrence. In late 1998, India announced its intention to sign the CTBT if talks with the United States ended successfully and also signaled its willingness to join other nuclear control groups. In February 1999, during a historic visit to Pakistan by the Indian prime minister, both countries agreed to continue their declared nuclear moratoriums on further nuclear tests.

Can India combine its new nuclear power status with responsible use of such weapons? Can it negotiate with its nuclear neighbors, Pakistan and China, to ensure that South Asia does not set off a nuclear disaster? How India confronts challenges on the nuclear front is closely tied to its success in several other areas, including resolution of the Kashmir dispute, the management of increasing ethnic tensions, and its economic performance.

Civil Liberties

Compared to other comparably large, multiethnic democracies, India has generally shown great respect for the pillars of civil rights: a free and lively press, legal protections for citizens' rights, and an independent judiciary. India's media, especially its newspapers and magazines, are as free as any in the world. They represent a wide variety of viewpoints, engage in vigorous investigative reporting and analysis, and maintain pressure for public action. The combination of a vocal intellectual stratum and a free press is a cherished element in India's democracy.

Nevertheless, India's tradition of a strong, interventionist state has enabled the state to violate civil liberties, and the trend since the mid-1980s has been troubling. Global events conjoined with national ones resulted in a restriction of civil liberties in the aftermath of the September 11. The BJP-led government used the war against terrorism as justification for depicting pro-independence groups in Kashmir and Muslim groups throughout India as terrorist.

Soon after September 11, the Indian government banned the Students Islamic Movement of India (SIMI), the students' wing of the radical Islamic political party, the Jamaat-e-Islami, in Pakistan. However, the government did not ban the Bajrang Dal, the militant organization with ties to the VHP that has repeatedly organized anti Muslim violence, most recently in Gujarat in 2002.

After September 11, the Indian government issued the Prevention of Terrorism Ordinance (POTO), later enacted into law by parliament. Its definition of terrorism is extremely vague, and a citizen need not have committed a specific act to be charged under POTO: conspiring, attempting to commit, advocating, abetting, advising, or inciting such acts are punishable, with penalties ranging from stiff prison sentences to death. Membership in a terrorist organization is punishable with life imprisonment. Confessions made to police officers are admissible as evidence in courts, contrary to ordinary law, and confessions are brutally extracted in Indian police stations. The right to bail is severely restricted. An accused person can be kept in police custody for one month and in jail for six months without even being charged.[7] In certain regions, merely possessing arms is punishable with life imprisonment.

Predictably, POTO has been used mostly against Muslims and political dissidents. The largest number of arrests took place in India's newest state, Jharkhand, where members and supporters of Marxist-Leninist groups have been taken into custody under POTO. Marxist-Leninist parties such as CPI (ML)–People's War Group, and the Maoist Communist Center have been banned. By 2002, twenty-three organizations had been banned under POTO.

The Challenge of Ethnic Diversity

The future of Indian democracy is closely bound up with how the country confronts the growing political impact of ethnic identities. Mobilized ethnic groups seeking access to state power and state-controlled economic resources are a basic component of the contemporary Indian political scene. Caste, language, and religion all provide identities around which political mobilization can be galvanized. Identification with a group is heightened by the democratic context, in which parties and leaders freely choose to manipulate such symbols. When studying Indian politics, it is difficult to separate interest- and identity-based politics. For example, caste struggles in India are simultaneously struggles for identity, power, and wealth. Identity politics in India is likely to be characterized by two trends: considerable political ferment, with a variety of dissatisfied groups making demands on parties and governments, and pressure on political parties to broaden their electoral appeal to disadvantaged groups, especially those belonging to the middle and lower strata, many of whom are very poor. India's political leaders will thus continue to experience pressures to expand their support base by promising economic improvements or manipulating nationalist symbols. Under what conditions will such political forces engage in constructive rather than destructive actions? Will democracy succeed in merely tempering the effect of such forces, or will it in the long run promote a positive channeling of identity politics? A factor that will affect an answer to these questions is India's economic performance.

Economic Performance

Comparativists debate how well an economy is governed. India's economic experience is neither a clear success nor a clear failure. If many African countries have done poorly economically and many East Asian countries (prior to 1997) have had dramatic successes, India falls somewhere in the middle. Three conditions may explain this outcome. The first is the nature and the quality of the government for promoting economic growth. In this, India has been fortunate to have enjoyed relatively good government since independence: its democratic system is mostly open and stable, its most powerful political leaders are public spirited, and its upper bureaucracy is well trained and competent. These positive attributes stand out in comparison with many African countries, such as Nigeria.

The second condition concerns India's strategy for economic development. India in the 1950s chose to insulate its economy from global forces, limiting the role of trade and foreign investment and emphasizing the role of government in promoting self-sufficiency in heavy industry and agriculture. The positive impact of this strategy was that India now produces enough food to feed its large and growing population while it simultaneously produces a vast range of industrial goods. This strategy, however, was not without costs. Most of India's manufactured goods are produced rather inefficiently by global standards. India sacrificed the additional economic growth that might have come from competing effectively in the global markets and by selling its products abroad. It also gave up another area of potential economic growth by discouraging foreign investment. And last, during the phase of protective industrialization, India did little to alleviate its staggering poverty: land redistribution failed, job creation by heavy industries was minimal, and investment in the education and health of the poor was minuscule in relation to the magnitude of the problem. The poor also became a drag on economic growth because they were unable to buy goods and stimulate demand for increased production and because an uneducated and unhealthy labor force is not a productive labor force.

A stable government and an emphasis on self-sufficiency have promoted modest economic growth in India; higher growth rates, however, have been difficult to achieve without greater links to the outside world and the alleviation of poverty. This leads to the third condition regarding India's middling political economy. India's continuing economic weakness has made it more vulnerable to global forces. The country's economic crisis in the early 1990s during the Gulf War exposed its vulnerability and prompted a shift toward a more open economy. This shift was associated with improved economic growth in the 1990s. However, the continuation of staggering levels of poverty in India is disturbing. If India is to sustain high levels of growth, the Indian government must address the issues of literacy, health, and welfare for the poor, enabling them to join the economy as truly productive participants. The challenge that Indian politicians face is to reconcile the demands of promoting an efficient economy with those of winning elections. The latter involves encouraging an expansion of government programs and subsidies to discontented groups, while the former calls for austerity. Restricting government's role conflicts with

implementing distributive or populist programs; opening the national economy to foreign economic actors and products is likely to aggravate nationalist sentiments.

Indian Politics in Comparative Perspective

Given its large size, diversity, and vibrant social and political system, India is an exceptionally good case study for analyzing themes of general significance in comparative politics. In this concluding section, we first examine the implications of the study of India for comparative politics and then assess how Indian politics and its economy will influence developments in a regional and global context.

Some comparative scholars suggest that citizens' widespread desire to exercise some control over their government is a potent force encouraging democracy. This assumption is clearly illustrated in India. Although democracy was introduced to India by its elites, it has established firm roots within society. A clear example is when Indira Gandhi declared Emergency rule (1975–1977) and curtailed democratic freedoms. In the next election, in 1977, Indian citizens decisively voted Indira Gandhi out of power, registering their preference for democratic rule. Most Indians value democracy and use its institutions to advance their claims.

Comparativists debate whether democracy or authoritarianism is better for economic growth. In the past, India did not compare well with the success stories of East Asian and Chinese authoritarian-led countries. The collapse in the late 1990s of several East Asian economies and the subsequent rise of instability within those societies makes a study of Indian democracy more relevant to understanding the institutional and cultural factors underpinning economic stability in the long run.

Another theme has been to assess the implications of establishing democracy in multiethnic societies. The rising tide of nationalism and the breakup of the Soviet Union and Yugoslavia, among others, have prompted closer examination of how and why India continues to exist as a cohesive entity. By studying India's history, particularly the post-1947 period, comparativists could explore questions of how cleavages of caste, religion, and language in India balance one another and cancel the most destructive elements in each. Comparativists have also puzzled about the conditions under which multiple and contradictory interests could be harnessed within a democratic setup to generate positive economic and distributional outcomes. Here, the variable performance of different regions in India can serve as a laboratory. For instance, two communist-ruled states, Kerala and West Bengal, have (to a certain extent) engaged in land redistribution policies. An examination of factors such as the role of the mobilizing parties and the interaction between the landless poor and the entrenched landed elite could provide answers. The main elements of the Kerala model are a land reform initiative that abolished tenancy and landlord exploitation, effective public food distribution that provides subsidized rice to low-income households, protective laws for agricultural workers, pensions for retired agricultural laborers, and a high rate of government employment for members of low-caste communities.

Another question engaging comparativists is whether success in providing education and welfare inevitably leads to success in the economic sphere. Again, the case of Kerala provides pointers for further research. Kerala scores high on human development indicators such as literacy and health, but paradoxically has not performed well in terms of achieving economic growth.

What are the international and domestic challenges that India faces at the dawn of the twenty-first century? How will it cope with its new-found status as a nuclear power? How can it prevent further escalation of conflict in the region that could end in a nuclear conflagration? A worst-case scenario would be a conventional war with Pakistan that could escalate into a nuclear war. Domestically, both countries are wracked with ethnic tensions, one with a military dictatorship and the other with an elected coalition government. In an attempt to hold on to power, the leaders of each country could try to divert attention toward a national security threat from its neighbor, a ploy that has been used effectively in the past by politicians in both countries. The history of three wars between India and Pakistan, the simmering tensions over Kashmir, and both countries' possession of nuclear arms could prompt a nuclear war. The challenge for India is to establish a stable relationship with its nuclear neighbors, Pakistan and China, that would eschew proliferation of their nuclear and ballistic missiles arsenals and engage in constructive diplomatic and economic cooperation. India's history of wars with both countries is not an encouraging starting point, but the engagement of Western powers in generating a dialogue between these countries is a portent for the future. The visit to Pakistan by the Indian prime minister in 1999, the first visit in ten years and only the third ever, provides grounds for optimism. Whether such overtures will result in fruitful negotiations on Kashmir and on economic cooperation in the region remains to be seen. Answers to these questions depend at least in part on developments in the sphere of domestic politics.

Fifty years of democracy in India have been a double-edged sword. Winning elections involves attracting votes. While avoiding authoritarianism, the practice of democracy, particularly electoral politics, has worsened ethnic relations between Hindus and Muslims, upper and lower castes, and north and south. With the spread of democracy, many dissatisfied groups are finding their voices and becoming politically mobilized. The challenge for Indian politics is how to repair the divide within a democratic framework. Current voter emphasis on good governance and sound economic management rather than on religious or nationalistic issues might transform electoral platforms in the twenty-first century. In any case, on this score Indian politics will continue to tread a shaky path, as witnessed by the intensification of communal tensions marked by the macabre killing of a Christian missionary and his two young sons in Orissa in January 1999 by Hindu nationalists, as well as other attacks on Christians in scattered regions. Will India be able to manage its domestic tensions and enlarge social, political, and economic rights for its citizens?

Another challenge for India is how to combine its global ambitions of becoming a strong power with its program for economic liberalization. The increasing interdependence of global economies as manifested in global effects of the 1997 East Asian crisis and the dependence of developing countries on investor confidence and external aid should not be underestimated. While India was protected from the East Asian debacle because of the partially closed nature of its economy, the country nevertheless suffered economic blows in the aftermath of becoming nuclear in the form of frozen aid programs worth billions. In addition, a decrease in foreign direct investment followed from the loss of investor confidence as a result of the downgrading of India's credit rating. The economic woes engendered by the sanctions were accentuated by the BJP government's lack of progress on the economic liberalization front. The Indian case embodies the tensions inherent in combining democracy with economic liberalization. Political parties in India face pressures to expand their support base by promoting contradictory economic improvements or by manipulating nationalist symbols. But simultaneously, these promises clash with the task of economic liberalization. The challenge faced by Indian governments is how to combine the task of economic liberalization with the conflicting demands of electoral politics. If the economic problems are not addressed swiftly and effectively, the world will be confronted by an India that is poor, ethnically mobilized, and controlling a formidable nuclear arsenal. This would compromise both regional and global security.

How India reconciles its national political ambitions, domestic political demands for greater economic redistribution, and global pressures for an efficient economy will affect its influence on regional and global trends. Will India be able to capitalize on some of its positive achievements, such as the long-standing democratic ethos framed by functioning institutions, a vibrant civil society and media, and a growing middle class imbued with the desire to succeed economically? Or will it be crippled by ethnic hostility resulting in inaction at best and total disintegration of the country at worst? If the Congress Party is able to remobilize its old umbrella party constituency (such as Muslims and backward castes) under Sonia Gandhi, we might see a return to the era of one-party rule in India. However, if current trends are any indication, the stage seems set for a scenario of two-party rule, with either a BJP-led or a Congress-led coalition ruling at the center. There also seems to be some room for optimism with regard to voter needs and interests on the international and domestic fronts. For instance, during Vajpayee's February 1999 visit to Pakistan, public opinion polls showed that an overwhelming number of people in India and Pakistan wanted improved relations between the two countries. On the domestic side, the preoccupation of voters with economic management, law and order, and other governance issues was evident from the results of the 1998 assembly elections. Of course, balancing the demands of simultaneously achieving equity and efficiency generates its own problems. The understanding of evolving political trends in India will remain matters of continuing significance.

Key Terms

Hindu

Muslims

Sikhs

Maharajas

zamindars

Emergency

green revolution

state-led economic development

economic liberalization

reservations

nonaligned bloc

caste system

Brahmin

untouchables

scheduled castes

Lok Sabha

Rajya Sabha

Indian Administrative Service

panchayats

"Other Backward Classes"

Suggested Readings

Bardhan, Pranab. *The Political Economy of Development in India.* New Delhi: Oxford University Press, 1984.

Basu, Amrita. *Two Faces of Protest: Contrasting Modes of Women's Activism in India.* Berkeley: University of California Press, 1992.

————, and Kohli, Atul, eds. *Community Conflicts and the State in India.* New Delhi: Oxford University Press, 1998.

Bayly, C. A. *The New Cambridge History of India: Indian Society and the Making of the British Empire.* Vol. 2, no. 1. Cambridge: Cambridge University Press, 1988.

Brass, Paul R. *The New Cambridge History of India: The Politics of India Since Independence.* Vol. 4, no. 1. Cambridge: Cambridge University Press, 1990.

————. *The Theft of an Idol.* Princeton, N.J.: Princeton University Press, 1997

Carras, Mary C. *Indira Gandhi: In the Crucible of Leadership.* Boston: Beacon Press, 1979.

Chatterjee, Partha, ed. *State Politics in India.* New Delhi: Oxford University Press, 1997.

Cohen, Stephen P. *The Indian Army: Its Contribution to the Development of a Nation.* Berkeley: University of California Press, 1971.

Dreze, Jean, and Amartya, Sen, eds. *Economic Development and Social Opportunity.* New Delhi: Oxford University Press, 1995.

Frankel, Francine. *India's Political Economy, 1947–1977.* Princeton, N.J.: Princeton University Press, 1978.

Gopal, Sarvepalli. *Jawaharlal Nehru: A Biography.* Vols. 2 and 3. New Delhi: Oxford University Press, 1984.

Graham, Bruce. *Hindu Nationalism and Indian Politics.* Cambridge: Cambridge University Press, 1990.

Hardgrave, Robert L., Jr., and Kochanek, Stanley A. *India: Government and Politics in a Developing Nation.* 4th ed. New York: Harcourt Brace Jovanovich, 1986.

Hasan, Zoya. *Quest for Power: Oppositional Movements and Post-Congress Politics in Uttar Pradesh.* Delhi: Oxford University Press, 1998.

Jaffrelot, Christophe. *The Hindu Nationalist Movement and Indian Politics, 1925 to the 1990s: Strategies on Identity Building, Implantation and Mobilization.* New York: Columbia University Press, 1996.

Jalal, Ayesha. *Democracy and Authoritarianism in South Asia.* Cambridge: Cambridge University Press, 1995.

Jalan, Bimal. *India's Economic Crisis: The Way Ahead.* New Delhi: Oxford University Press, 1991.

Kohli, Atul. *Democracy and Discontent: India's Growing Crisis of Governability.* Cambridge: Cambridge University Press, 1991.

———, ed. *The State and Poverty in India: The Politics of Reform.* Cambridge: Cambridge University Press, 1987.

———. *The Success of India's Democracy.* Cambridge: Cambridge University Press, 2001.

Misra, B. B. *Government and Bureaucracy in India: 1947–1976.* New Delhi: Oxford University Press, 1986.

Nayar, Baldev Raj. *India's Mixed Economy.* Bombay: Popular Prakashan, 1989.

Rothermund, Dietmar. *An Economic History of India: From Pre-Colonial Times to 1986.* London: Croom Helm, 1988.

Rudolph, Lloyd, and Rudolph, Susanne. *In Pursuit of Lakshmi: The Political Economy of the Indian State.* Chicago: University of Chicago Press, 1987.

Sarkar, Sumit. *Modern India: 1885 to 1947.* Madras: Macmillan, 1983.

Varshney, Ashutosh. *Ethnic Conflict and Civic Life: Hindus and Muslims in India.* New Haven, Conn.: Yale University Press, 2002.

Weiner, Myron. *The Child and the State in India.* Princeton, N.J.: Princeton University Press, 1992.

———. *The Indian Paradox: Essays in Indian Politics.* New Delhi: Sage, 1989.

Suggested Websites

BJP Party
www.bjp.org
Economic and Political Weekly, a good source of information on Indian politics
www.epw.org
Frontline, a magazine with coverage of Indian politics
www.flonnet.com
Hindu, an English daily paper in India
www.hinduonnet.com
Hindustan Times
www.hindustantimes.com
Indian government
www.nic.in
Sabrang Communications, providing coverage of human rights issues in India
www.sabrang.com

Notes

[1] Sudha Mahalingam, "Petroleum Sector: An Ambitious Roadshow," *Frontline,* March 3–16, 2001, pp. 99–100.

[2] *Times of India,* September 7, 2002.

[3] C. P. Chandrashekhar, "FDI and the Balance of Payments in the 1990s," www.macroscan.com, June 2000.

[4] Madhura Swaminathan, "Food Security: No Panacea?" *Frontline,* October 14–27, 2000; Jayati Ghosh, "Wasted Food, Wasted Opportunities?" *Frontline,* September 30–October 13, 2000.

[5] Prabhat Patnaik, "Budget 2002: The Poverty of Economic Policy?" *Frontline,* March 16–29, 2002.

[6] Shirin M. Rai, "Gender and Representation: Women MPs in the Indian Parliament," in Anne Marie Goetz, ed., *Getting Institutions Right for Women and Development* (London: Zed Books, 1997), p. 105.

[7] People's Union for Democratic Rights, Resisting POTO, People's Union for Democratic Rights, "No Vakeel, No Daleel, No Appeal," *Delhi,* November 2001. pp. 5–9; also see V. Venkatesan, "Terror Through Ordinance," *Frontline,* November 23, 2001, pp. 26–29, and Gautam Navlakha, "POTO: Taking the Lawless Road," *Economic and Political Weekly,* December 8, 2001, pp. 4520–4522.

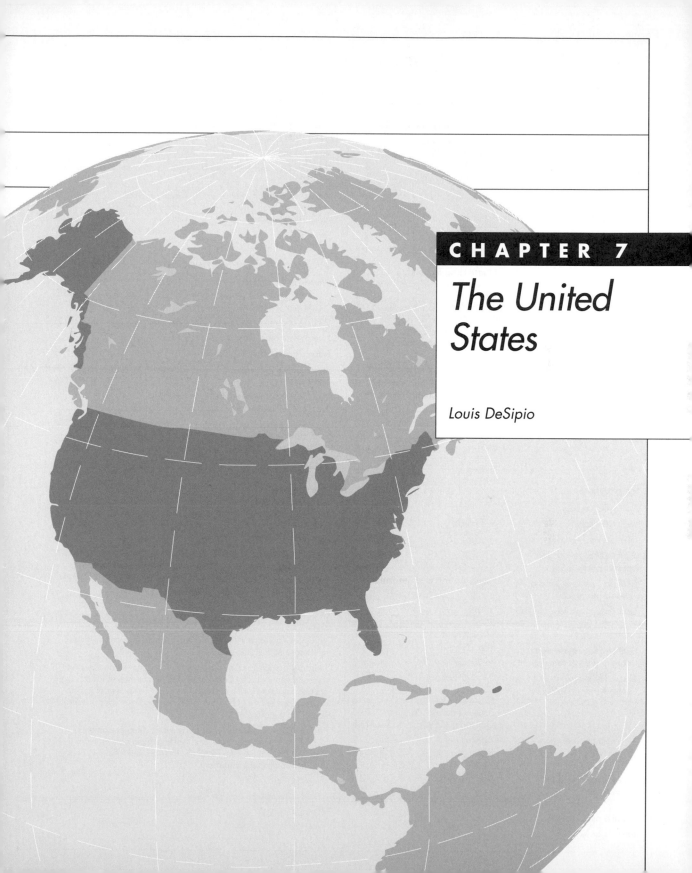

CHAPTER 7

The United States

Louis DeSipio

United States of America

Land and People

Capital	Washington, D.C.
Total area (square miles)	3,794,083 (About one half the size of Russia)
Population	283.2 million

Annual population growth rate (%)

1975–2000	1.0
2000–2015 (projected)	0.8

Urban population (%)	77.2

Ethnic composition (%)

White	77.1
Black	12.9
Asian	4.2
Amerindian and Alaska native	1.5
Native Hawaiian and other Pacific islander	0.3
Other	4

Note: Hispanics make up about 12% of the U.S. population. The 2000 Census did not have a separate listing for Hispanic because the Census Bureau considers Hispanic to mean a person of Latin American descent living in the U.S. who may be of any race or ethnic group (white, black, Asian, etc.).

Major language(s)	English; Spanish (about 28 million U.S. residents over the age of 5 speak Spanish at home)

Religious affiliation (%)

Protestant	56
Roman Catholic	28
Jewish	2
Other	4
None	10

Economy

Domestic currency	U.S. Dollar USD
Total GDP (US$)	9.8 trillion
GDP per capita (US$)	34,637
Total GDP at purchasing power parity (US$)	9.6 trillion
GDP per capita at purchasing power parity (US$)	34,142

GDP annual growth rate (%)

1997	4.5
2000	4.2
2001	1.2

GDP per capita average annual growth rate (%)

1975–2000	2.0
1990–2000	2.2

Inequality in income or consumption (1997) (%)

Share of poorest 10%	1.8
Share of poorest 20%	5.2
Share of richest 20%	46.4
Share of richest 10%	30.5
Gini Index (1997)	40.8

Structure of production (% of GDP)

Agriculture	2
Industry	26
Services	72

Labor force distribution (% of total)

Agriculture	2.4
Industry	24.1
Services	73.5

Exports as % of GDP	11
Imports as % of GDP	13

Society

Life expectancy at birth	77.0
Infant mortality per 1000 live births	7
Adult literacy (%)	99

*The OECD estimates that the US has a functional illiteracy rate of about 21%.

Access to information and communications (per 1000 population)

Telephone lines	700
Mobile phones	398
Radios	2118
Televisions	854
Personal Computers	582

Women in Government and the Economy

Women in the national legislature (2002)

Lower House or Single House (%)	13.8
Upper House (%)	13.0

Women at ministerial level (2000) (%)	31.8
Female economic activity rate (age 15 and above) (%)	58.8
Female labor force (% of total)	46

Estimated earned income (PPP US$)

Female	26,259
Male	42,246

2002 Human Development Index Ranking (out of 173 countries)	6

Political Organization

Political System   Presidential system.

Regime History   Representative democracy, usually dated from the signing of the Declaration of Independence (1776) or the Constitution (1787).

Administrative Structure   Federalism, with powers shared between the national government and the fifty state governments; separation of powers at the level of the national government among legislative, executive, and judicial branches.

Executive   President, "directly" elected (with Electoral College that officially elects president and vice president) for four-year term; cabinet is advisory group selected by president to aid in decision-making but with no formal authority.

Legislature   Bicameral. Congress composed of a lower house (House of Representatives) of 435 members serving two-year terms and an upper house (Senate) of 100 members (two from each state) serving six-year terms; elected in single-member districts (or, in the case of the Senate, states) by simple plurality.

Judiciary   Supreme Court with nine justices nominated by president and confirmed by Senate, with life tenure; has specified original and appellate jurisdiction and exercises the power of judicial review (can declare acts of the legislature and executive unconstitutional and therefore null and void).

Party System   Essentially two-party system (Republican and Democrat), with relatively weak and fractionalized parties; more than in most representative democracies, the personal following of candidates remains very important.

Section ❶ The Making of the Modern American State

Politics in Action

On the morning of September 11, 2001, President George W. Bush was in an elementary school class in Florida. He had both policy and political objectives for spending time in Florida, like many other activities of sitting presidents. His visit to the school reflected a continuing desire to position himself as an education reformer, a theme that he had raised in his campaign the year before. The choice of Florida as the site of a visit to a class reflected political objectives. Bush had won the presidency only because he won the **Electoral College** votes of Florida. The state's popular vote was nearly evenly divided (Bush won by 537 votes), and Bush's advisers realized that Florida would again be critical to a Bush victory in the 2004 presidential election. In the shorter term, the success of President Bush's brother, Jeb, in his 2002 campaign for reelection as governor of Florida would be taken by many as a sign of the president's likely success in 2004.

The president's September 11 visit was one of many in the first nine months of the Bush presidency. President Bush demonstrated his connection to the state not just with visits, but also with a series of policy decisions designed to appeal to Florida voters, such as the allocation of approximately $3.9 billion in federal funds to protect the Everglades. As a result of the terrorist attacks in New York and at the Pentagon, many of the policy goals of his administration changed. Nevertheless, the underlying political need for popular support, as well as the longer-term objective of successful reelection remained. This balance between policy and politics has shaped the U.S. response to the events of September 11.

In the hours and days after the terrorist attacks on the World Trade Center and the Pentagon, the U.S. government (as well as that of many states and localities) refocused its energies on security issues. In a way that the framers of the **Constitution** could not have envisioned, the president and his senior advisers became the focal point of this policy-making. For a brief period, Congress deferred to the president on almost all matters of the U.S. response. In part, the power of the president came from his being one official and not a multi-member legislative body. When immediate decisions needed to be made on September 11, the president and his senior advisers were best positioned to respond.

These new expectations for the president were not just a matter of convenience: they reflected the ultimate power of the presidency, one of just two nationally elected offices (along with the vice presidency). Popular outrage at what had happened on September 11 and the national will that there be a decisive response drove presidential popularity to record highs that remained for many months after the attacks. This popular support for the way President Bush was conducting the presidency, which exceeded 80 percent for several months, gave the presidency a national power that was not envisioned in the Constitution. Recognizing the power inherent in these levels of popularity, Congress initially deferred to the White House in many key areas of policy creation.

Two initial victories for the president demonstrate how a very popular president is able to use power (See "Leaders: George Walker Bush"). In the days after the September 11 attacks, Congress appropriated up to $50 billion in emergency **appropriations** that included large shares for disaster recovery activities in New York, Virginia, and Pennsylvania; for direct grants, subsidies, and insurance to U.S. airlines as compensation for losses incurred in the days after September 11; and for direct payments to the families of victims of the attacks (which protected the airlines and the Port Authority of New York and New Jersey from lawsuits that could have proved ruinous to them). The following month, Congress passed a bill that came to be known by its acronym, the "USA Patriot Act." This bill granted the executive branch broad investigative powers when it suspected that individuals might be planning terrorist activities. The level of surveillance against both U.S. citizens and foreign nationals in the USA Patriot Act was unprecedented in American history. Neither of these bills was extensively debated in Congress prior to their passage.

Despite high popularity ratings, Congress quickly reasserted its constitutionally designed role of challenging presidents who seek to add powers to the executive branch. For nearly a year, Congress blocked

A jet crashes into the World Trade Center on September 11, 2001. *Source: © Moshe Bursurker/AP/Wide World Photos.*

the establishment of the **Department of Homeland Security.** Congress also demanded a voice in authorizing war against Iraq, a policy objective spearheaded by President Bush in the wake of the September 11 attacks. President Bush, however, also had tools at his disposal. He used the bully pulpit of the presidency to speak directly to the citizenry and gained support for his policies. In the 2002 election, he took the risk of campaigning for a large number of Republican candidates. Had these candidates lost, he would have come to be perceived as without political capital and would be less likely to be able to accomplish his policy objectives. This did not happen. Instead, Republican candidates supported by the president won several key senatorial races and added to the Republican majority in the U.S. House of Representatives. The Senate victories switched control of the Senate from the Democrats to the Republicans.

While this outcome will initially ensure that President Bush is able to pursue his policy objectives both at home and abroad, the natural tension between the president and Congress will likely reappear relatively quickly. U.S. politics in action often, and by constitutional design, includes a great deal of inaction. September 11 obscured this recurring feature of American government but is unlikely to eliminate it.

Leaders: *George Walker Bush*

George Bush is the forty-third president of the United States. He was elected in a disputed election in 2000, but saw his popularly increase considerably in the period since the September 11 terrorist attacks on the World Trade Center and the Pentagon. Bush was elected on a platform of educational reform, tax cuts, the introduction of private sector managerial approaches to government, and ethics in government. His administration saw an early success in cutting taxes, but since September 11, its focus has shifted to national security.

President Bush was born in 1946 and grew up in Texas, where his father had moved after World War II to make his fortune in the oil industry. President Bush grew up in a political family. His father served as the forty-first president of the United States (1989–1993) and his grandfather served as senator from Connecticut (1952–1963). His brother Jeb was elected governor of Florida in 1998 and reelected in 2002.

Previous U.S. presidents have seen similar multigenerational success in election to the nation's highest offices. John Adams, for example, served as the second president of the United States, and his son John Quincy Adams was the sixth. The large number of Bushes in politics has begun a conversation about whether they are a dynasty. In the past, political success has dwindled after the second or third generation in most political families.

President Bush surprised many by his quick rise in politics, including perhaps many in his own family, who expected Jeb to follow his father in the White House. Prior to President Bush's election to the Texas governorship in 1994, he had a rather undistinguished academic and professional career. He had followed his father into the oil business and had seen his investments fail. Nevertheless, he was able to turn a small investment in the Texas Rangers baseball club into a sizable profit. He used his innate political skills, as well as perhaps some of his father's political connections, to negotiate a very favorable plan for building a new stadium for the team at public expense. He moved from this position to the Texas governorship. Although the Texas governorship is relatively weak, he used what political capital he had to promote educational reform and business development. He was reelected by an overwhelming margin in 1998, and most Texans expected that he would run for president in 2000.

In that election, he easily defeated his Republican opponents and was able to unify the moral conservative and economic conservative wings of the Republican Party (which had not been able to cooperate in the 1990s) to win a come-from-behind victory. Bush benefited, in an odd way, from the low expectations that many held for him. In the presidential debates in particular, he did much better than people expected. He also benefited from his ability to identify skilled staff people to direct his campaign. Most notable among these is Karl Rove, who had guided President Bush's political career from its start. Rove now serves as senior adviser to the president in the White House.

President Bush's future looks bright for reelection. His popularity ratings, which had been dropping below 50 percent prior to September 11, have stayed higher since (although they have declined from their post-September 11 highs). His campaigning in the 2002 off-year elections is credited with giving the Republicans a majority in the Senate and an increased majority in the House of Representatives. He will be able to raise a record amount of money for his reelection and will probably forgo federal matching funds so that he can spend an unlimited amount on his own campaign. Bush is further advantaged by the absence of a strong field of Democratic opponents.

All presidents, however, face risks. In Bush's case, the continued weakness in the economy and his support for tax cuts rather than more direct economic stimuli causes some in the electorate to question his leadership. A failure in national defense or homeland security could end a very successful streak of seizing political opportunities.

Geographic Setting

The 3.79 million square miles of the United States occupy approximately half of the North American continent and represent an area about half of the size of the Russian Federation and slightly larger than China. Its population, approximately 290 million people, is dwarfed by the populations of China and India.

The United States has only two neighbors, Mexico and Canada, which do not present a military threat and are linked in a comprehensive trade agreement: the **North American Free Trade Agreement (NAFTA).** U.S. territory is rich in natural resources (such as coal, oil, and metals), arable land, navigable rivers, and protected ports. The abundance of land and natural resources has engendered a national ethos that there will always be enough resources to meet national needs. This abundance explains in part the low support for environmental protection laws in the United States. Finally, the nature of the land leads to a final characteristic of U.S. society: the territory has always had low population densities and has served as a magnet for international migration. In 2001, for example, there were approximately 79 people per square mile. This compares to 897 people per square mile in India and 17,849 in Singapore.[1]

Although the time period is regularly debated, the settlement of the territory that is now the United States appears to have begun at least 12,000 years ago, with the arrival of migrants from Asia in what is now Alaska. European settlers and involuntary African migrants came much later, but in the end, they came in

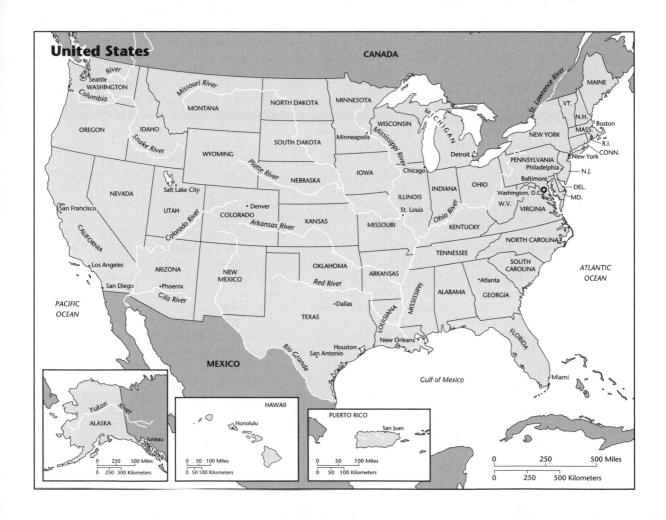

larger numbers. By the 1800s, migration, particularly from Europe, had caused the nation's population to double, and then double again.

European colonization led to the eventual unification of the territory that became the United States under one government and the expansion of that territory from the Atlantic Ocean to the Pacific Ocean. This process began in the early 1500s and reached its peak in the nineteenth century, when rapid population expansion was reinforced by an imperialist national ideology (**manifest destiny**) to push the westward boundary of the nation from the Appalachians to the Pacific. The indigenous residents of the western territories were pushed aside in the process of expansion. The United States experimented with colonialism at the turn of the twentieth century, leading to the annexation of Hawaii, Guam, the Northern Marianas Islands, and Puerto Rico. Hawaii became a state in 1959.

The United States faces little challenge to its territorial boundaries today. Although some in Puerto Rico seek independence, most want either a continuation of commonwealth or statehood. Commonwealth status for Puerto Rico reflects something of a semantic compromise. Puerto Rico is a colony of the United States that has been granted broad autonomy by the U.S. Congress in terms of governance within Puerto Rico, but has limited autonomy in areas such as trade and foreign policy. Puerto Ricans are U.S. citizens by birth and can travel freely to the United States. Guam is officially an "unincorporated territory" of the United States (a U.S. territory that is not on the road to statehood and does not have all of the protections of the U.S. Constitution). The Northern Marianas petitioned for and received commonwealth status in 1975. Neither Guam nor the Northern Marianas has active independence movements.

Critical Junctures

The critical junctures in U.S. political history appear at points when mass discontent becomes sufficiently organized to alter governing institutions or relationships. Each of these junctures challenged dominant paradigms of who should have a voice in democratic government and what the relationship between government and citizen should be. Although these demands for democratic voice and changed citizen-state relations are ongoing in U.S. political history, four periods of focused popular

demand making are explored here: the period from the beginning of the American Revolution through the ratification of the U.S. Constitution, the Civil War and Reconstruction, the New Deal, and a contemporary period of routinely divided national government that began with the 1968 national elections. This final period, which is ongoing, is somewhat less focused than the other three because we cannot know its ultimate outcome.

The outcomes of these eras of mass discontent are not necessarily those envisioned by the initial proponents of the changes. Each of these periods, however,

---

Critical Junctures in U.S. Political Development

1776	Independence from Great Britain declared.
1788	U.S. Constitution replaces Articles of Confederation.
1803	Supreme Court establishes judicial review in *Marbury* v. *Madison*.
1803	Louisiana Purchase.
1830s	Mass political parties emerge, and electorate expands to include a majority of white men.
1861–1865	U.S. Civil War.
1865–1876	Reconstruction era. The United States establishes but fails to guarantee voting rights for freed slaves.
1896	Voter turnout in elections begins century-long decline.
1933–1940	The New Deal responds to the economic distress of the Great Depression.
1941–1945	U.S. participates in World War II.
1964	Tonkin Gulf Resolution authorizes military actions in Vietnam.
1974	Richard Nixon resigns the presidency in the face of certain impeachment.
1978	California passes Proposition 13.
1996	Federal government ends the guarantee of social welfare programs to the poor established during the New Deal.
1998–1999	U.S. House of Representatives impeaches and the U.S. Senate acquits President Clinton.

proved central to development of the modern American nation.

The Revolutionary Era (1773–1789)

The American Revolution was sparked by mass and elite discontent with British colonial rule that resulted in the signing of the **Declaration of Independence** on July 4, 1776. The Revolution itself was only the beginning of a process of creating a new form of government. Mass interests sought to keep government close to home, in each colony, and wanted each colony to have substantial autonomy from the others. Elite interests advocated a national government with control over foreign policy, national assumption of state Revolutionary War debts, and the ability to establish national rules for commerce.

Mass interests won this battle initially. From 1777 to 1788, the **Articles of Confederation** governed the nation. The Articles' weaknesses, specifically the inability of the national government to implement foreign or domestic policy, to tax, or to regulate trade between the states without the acquiescence of the individual governments of each of the states, allowed elite interests to gain support for their replacement with the Constitution. The limited powers of the national government under the Articles rested in a legislature, but the states had to ratify most key decisions. In this period, states established their own foreign policies, which were often divergent with each other. They also established their own fiscal policies and financed state budgets through extensive borrowing.

The Constitution maintained most power with the states but granted the federal (or national) government authority over commerce and foreign and military policy. It also provided the federal government with a source of financing independent of the states. And, most important, it created an executive officer, the president, who had powers independent of the legislature. Initially, the U.S. presidency was quite weak, but its power grew in the twentieth century. The Constitution delegated specific, but limited, powers to the national government. These included establishing post offices and roads, coining money, promoting the progress of science, raising and supporting an army and a navy, and establishing a uniform rule of naturalization. These powers can be found in Article I, Section 8 of the Constitution and tend to vest the federal government with the power to create a national economy. Finally, the Constitution sought to limit the citizenry's voice in government. Presidents were elected indirectly, through the Electoral College. Members of the Senate were elected by state legislatures. Only the House of Representatives was elected by the people, but regulation of who could vote for members of the House were left to the states. (See "Institutional Intricacies: The Electoral College.")

As popular support for ratification of the Constitution began to rise, many who had supported the Articles of Confederation made a new demand: that the newly drafted U.S. Constitution include enumerated protections for individuals from governmental power. Meeting this demand for a **Bill of Rights,** a specific set of prohibitions on the new national government, was necessary to ensure the ratification of the Constitution. Although the specific rights guaranteed in the Bill of Rights had little substantive meaning for Americans in the 1790s, over time they came to offer fundamental guarantees against the excesses of national and state government. Interpretation of the meaning of these rights ensured that the federal courts would play an increasingly significant role in U.S. national government, particularly in the twentieth century.

The Civil War and Reconstruction (1861–1876)

The second critical juncture in U.S. political history was the Civil War. While the morality of slavery convulsed the nation prior to the war, the war itself began over the question of whether the states or the national government should be dominant. Despite the seeming resolution of this question during the Revolutionary era, many states still believed they could nullify actions of the federal government. The Civil War resolved this issue in favor of the indivisibility of the union. A second long-term consequence was to establish an enforceable national citizenship to supplement the state citizenship that had predated the ratification of the Constitution.[2] This establishment of a national citizenship began a slow process that culminated in the New Deal, as the nation's citizens looked to the federal government to meet their basic needs in times of national crisis.

As part of the process of establishing full citizenship

Institutional Intricacies: *The Electoral College*

Until votes started to be counted in the 2000 election, most Americans did not realize that voters do not directly elect the president or the vice president. Instead, they learned, the president and vice president are elected by the Electoral College, which in turn is elected by the voters on Election Day.

The framers of the Constitution designed the Electoral College to act as a check on the passions of the citizenry. Like the indirect election of senators by state legislatures that survived until 1913, the Electoral College was a device to place community leaders between voters and the selection of leaders. Senators are now elected directly, but the Electoral College remains. On Election Day, voters actually vote for a slate of electors who are pledged to vote for a particular candidate. The number of electors in a state is equal to the state's number of representatives plus its two senators. The District of Columbia also has three electors, although it has no voting representation in Congress. To win, a candidate must earn half the total number plus one, or 270, of the Electoral College votes.

The electors, who are not named on the ballot, are selected by the state parties and, in some cases, by the candidates. They are usually state party leaders who are named as an honor for past service. As a result, they are very likely to support the candidate to whom they are pledged when the electors meet in each state capital early in December. Most states also require (by law) that an elector vote for the candidate to whom he or she is pledged. But there are examples, as recently as the 2000 election, where electors did not vote for their pledged candidate.

Such "faithless" electors have not affected the outcome of any election so far. What would happen in a close election if a handful of electors did not vote for the candidate to whom they were pledged? Congress, under the Constitution, would have to count their votes as reported. Thus, in this hypothetical close election, a few stray electors could deny the winner a majority by voting for a third candidate. This would throw the election into the House of Representatives. More unlikely, the electors could vote for the losing candidate and give him or her the ultimate victory in the Electoral College.

As the 2000 election demonstrated, the Electoral College system can make a winner out of the person who places second in the popular vote. Al Gore won the popular vote by more than 500,000 votes, but he lost the Electoral College by a vote of 271 to 266 (one faithless elector from the District of Columbia did not vote for Al Gore who had won a majority of the District's popular vote). All but two states award electoral votes on a winner-take-all basis. This practice maximizes the influence of their voters and increases the likelihood that candidates will campaign in that state; no large state is likely to sacrifice this practice unless all do. Thus, the candidate who receives the most votes in these winner-take-all states wins all of the state's Electoral College votes. In races with three or more serious candidates, these votes can be awarded to candidates who received far less than a majority of the state's votes.

In the 2000 election, President Bush won small victories in key states, including the disputed victory by 537 votes in Florida. These victories, even by small margins, ensured him all of these states' electoral votes. Gore won some of the largest states by large margins. Thus, he won the popular vote but not the Electoral College vote. This scenario almost occurred in 1976 when Jimmy Carter defeated Gerald Ford. When the electorate is evenly divided, the Electoral College winner may not be the popular vote winner.

---

for the freed slaves after the war, Congress revisited the question of individual liberties and citizenship for the first time since the debate over the Bill of Rights at the end of the Revolutionary era. These post–Civil War debates on the relationship of citizens to the national government established several important principles in the Fourteenth Amendment to the Constitution (1868) that shape citizenship today. First, it extended the protections of the Bill of Rights to cover actions by states as well as the federal government (the courts slowed the implementation of this provision). Second, it extended citizenship to all persons born in the United States. This made U.S. citizens of freed slaves (a legal necessity because an 1857 Supreme Court ruling, *Dred Scott* v. *Sanford,* had held that all blacks, slave or free, were not and could never be U.S. citizens) but also guaranteed that children of the tens of millions of immigrants who migrated after 1868 would become U.S. citizens at birth. Without this constitutional protection, the children of immigrants could have formed a legal underclass—denied citizenship but with no real tie to a foreign land. (This kind of excluded status characterized the children of many immigrants to Germany until 2000.) Third, Congress sought to establish some federal regulation of voting and to grant the vote to African Americans (these provisions were strengthened in the Fifteenth Amendment, ratified in 1870). Failure of the federal government to continue to enforce black voting rights meant that African Americans could not routinely exercise the vote until the passage of the Voting Rights Act in 1965. These fundamental guarantees that ensure electoral opportunities today limit prerogatives recognized as the states' responsibilities in the Constitution. The Voting Rights Act and subsequent nationalization of voting rights and voting procedures would have likely been found to be unconstitutional without these Civil War–era amendments.

The New Deal Era (1933–1940)

The third critical juncture in U.S. political development was the New Deal, which came in response to the economic crisis of the Great Depression. The federal government tapped its constitutional powers to regulate interstate commerce to vastly expand federal regulation of business (which had begun tentatively around the turn of the century with antitrust legislation). It also established assistance programs for targeted groups, such as social security to provide benefits to the elderly who had worked, housing programs to provide housing for the working poor, and food subsidies for children in poor households. Finally, the federal government began to directly subsidize the agricultural sector and to offer farmers protections against the cyclical nature of demand. These programs, which had traditionally been understood as being within the purview of the states to the extent that they existed at all,

expanded dramatically in the fifty years after the New Deal. The legislative and judicial battles to establish such policies are direct outcomes of the New Deal and represent a fundamental expansion of the role of the federal government in the lives of individual Americans.

This juncture also saw the federal government assert dominance over the states in delivering services to the people that gave substantive meaning to the national citizenship that was established in the Civil War and Reconstruction critical juncture. Equally important, the New Deal critical juncture saw the presidency assert dominance over the Congress in terms of policy-making. The U.S. president during the New Deal era, Franklin D. Roosevelt, found powers that no previous president had exercised and permanently changed the office of the presidency. Despite many changes in U.S. politics since 1933 and a significant reduction in the scope of federal assistance programs to the poor, all post–New Deal presidents remain much more powerful than any of their predecessors, except perhaps for Abraham Lincoln, who served during the Civil War.

The expanded role of the federal government in this era should be seen in the context in demands for even more dramatic changes. Unemployment rates as high as 40 percent, a worldwide decline in demand for U.S. manufactures, and climatological changes that made much agricultural land unproductive spurred widespread demand for wealth redistribution and centralization of power in the federal government that had not been seen either before or after in American politics. Thus, while the New Deal programs represented a significant change from the policies that preceded the Great Depression, they also reflected underlying American political values (see Section 4) relative to other visions for the U.S. government that were discussed in the era. Even in the New Deal era, class-based politics was kept to a minimum.

This New Deal era expansion in the federal regulation, establishment of a federal role in providing support for the elderly, and federal assistance programs for the poor were not the only changes in federal responsibilities in this era. As the depression came to a close, the United States geared up for its involvement in World War II. Although the United States had previously been involved in an international conflict beyond its borders (World War I), the experience of World War II was different at the inception of U.S. involvement and at the conclusion. The United States entered the war after U.S. territory was attacked (the Japanese bombing of Pearl Harbor). Throughout the war, U.S. leaders made a commitment not to follow the U.S. pattern of isolation after World War I. Although the lessons of World War I and its aftermath may have driven this response, the expansive multilateral approach to the post–World War II era must also be seen as a response to popular support for the newly interventionist U.S. government that emerged during the New Deal. In both domestic and foreign policy, the New Deal critical juncture expanded the scope and breadth of federal government policies and popular expectations for it. In this period of national consensus, in the early years of the New Deal and in the U.S. prosecution of the war against Germany and Japan, the constitutional constraints on the federal government were less evident. Once that consensus disappeared, however, the limits quickly reappeared.

Divided Government and Political Contestation of the Scope of Government (1968 to the Present)

The fourth critical juncture, which began with the 1968 presidential election, is ongoing today. This critical juncture has two dimensions. First, the national government is routinely divided between the two political parties. This division exacerbates the inefficiency that was designed into the American constitutional order and increases popular distrust of government (see Section 3). The second dimension of the contemporary critical juncture began a few years later but emerges from the apparent inefficiency caused by divided government.

Many in the United States began to question the steady increase in the scope of governmental services that was ongoing throughout the twentieth century, and particularly since the New Deal. The electoral roots of this popular discontent can be found in the passage of Proposition 13 by California voters in 1978. Proposition 13 limited governments' abilities to increase **property taxes.** The dissatisfaction expressed by Californians with the cost and scope of government, and efforts to limit them, soon spread to other states. The passage of Proposition 13 began an era that continues today, in which many citizens reject the expansion of government and its role in citizens' lives that began with the New Deal.

The 1968 election saw the election of Richard Nixon (a California Republican) to the presidency. Nixon replaced Democrat Lyndon Johnson, who did not run for reelection, and defeated Johnson's vice president, Hubert Humphrey. Through Nixon's term and that of his Republican successor, Gerald Ford, the Democrats maintained control of both houses of Congress. Although the parties in control of the presidency and of the House of Representatives and the Senate shifted over the next forty-five years, the 1968 election initiated a new norm in American politics: divided government in which one party controlled the presidency and the other party controlled at least one, and frequently both, of the houses of the U.S. Congress. In the period since 1968, one of the parties has controlled the presidency, the U.S. Senate, *and* the U.S. House of Representatives only four times. The Democrats controlled all three from 1977 to 1981 and from 1993 to 1995. The Republicans controlled all three from late January to early June 2001 and again beginning in January 2003.

This division of the federal government between the parties and the emergence by the end of the 1990s of a near equal division between the parties in Congress (and of the electorate in the 2000 election) make it more difficult for government to respond to national needs. The division also reflected a growing division in the populace about the size and scope of government. Although the roots of this debate can be traced to the nation's earliest days, the origin of its current manifestation can be traced to California's passage of Proposition 13 in 1978. California, like a handful of other states, allows citizens to propose ballot initiatives—legislation that appears on the state ballot. If passed by the voters, it cannot be reversed by the legislature. This is one of the few forms of direct democracy in the U.S. system.

Popular discontent in the contemporary era is not limited to taxes; it also focuses on the scope of government. This same period saw popular mobilization to reshape government's involvement in "values" issues. This era saw the emergence of pro- and antiabortion movements, advocates of "traditional" values and movements of people (such as feminists, gay men, and lesbians) who oppose their exclusion from such agendas, and fundamentalist religious movements. Each group seeks to use the government to protect its interests, while condemning government for allegedly promoting the interests of groups with alternative positions on the same issues. As will be evident in the discussion of the constitutional structure of American government and its policy-making institutions, the U.S. government offers individuals and groups with differing positions the opportunity to influence policy in different (governmental) arenas. As a result, U.S. governing institutions cannot directly resolve conflicts over values issues.

Popular concerns about the scope of government reached their apogee with the passage by Congress in 1996 of the Personal Responsibility and Work Opportunity Reconciliation Act, better known as the welfare reform bill. This legislation was quickly signed into law by President Clinton. The consequences of this bill were twofold. First, it ended a commitment that the federal government had made to poor people during the Great Depression and established time limits for eligibility for needs-based federal social welfare programs, such as food stamps and Aid to Families with Dependent Children (renamed Temporary Aid to Needy Families). The entitlement, based largely on low incomes and having minor children in the household, was replaced with a lifetime period of eligibility and the requirement that the parent receiving the benefit train for employment during this period of limited eligibility. Second, the legislation eliminated permanent residents (immigrants who have entered the country legally but have not been naturalized as U.S. citizens) from eligibility for most social welfare benefits, at least during their initial years of U.S. residence. That this bill received support in Congress from many Democrats and was signed with moderate enthusiasm by a Democratic president indicates how far the national debate about the size and scope of government had come since California passed Proposition 13 in 1978.

While divided government had become the norm in 1968, the division became even more razor thin in the late 1990s. Until 1994, the Democrats routinely won sixty-seat majorities in the House of Representatives. This Democratic advantage disappeared in the 1994 elections, when the Republicans took control of the House. Their majority was never as large, numbering no more than twenty seats and routinely fifteen or fewer. Thus, each election raises the possibility of a switch in partisan control of the House and the intense focus of both parties and **interest groups** on winning the handful of seats that could switch from one party to the other. These are very narrow margins by historical standards. The Senate has seen an even narrower gap between the parties. The 107th Congress was initially divided evenly. Democrats retained the "majority" during Vice President Gore's last weeks in office since he could break ties in favor of the Democrats. This advantage shifted to the Republicans with the inauguration of Vice President Dick Cheney, who could break ties in favor of the Republicans. This Republican advantage lasted slightly more than five months, until Senator James Jeffords of Vermont shifted from the Republican Party to an independent status and began to vote with the Democrats on leadership questions, returning the "majority" to them. The 2002 elections returned the majority to the Republicans, but by a razor-thin two-vote margin, which could again shift before the 2004 election.

It is in this environment—one of routinely divided government and national and local debates of the size and scope of government—that the United States responded to the September 11, 2001, terrorist attacks. Although Congress initially rallied behind the president to support financial assistance for New York City, the families of the victims of the attack, and the airlines, partisan divisions and concerns about the powers the president was seeking for the federal government (a concern related to the size and scope of government) quickly began to appear. With Congress so closely divided and neither side actively seeking compromise, the nation soon saw the consequences of the structure and scope of government in the period of the fourth critical juncture. Although the 2002 elections established Republican control over both houses of Congress, the end of divided government is likely only temporary.

Themes and Implications

Historical Junctures and Political Themes

The conflict between the president and Congress, the centralization of federal power in the twentieth century, and the growing opposition to the cost and scope of government represent ongoing themes in U.S. politics. These are not quickly or easily resolved in the United States because the Constitution slowed resolution of such conflicts by creating a system of federalism and separation of powers (see Section 3). When the

Constitution was drafted in 1787, its framers were wary of allowing the federal government to intervene too readily in matters of individual liberties or states' prerogatives, so they created a governing system with multiple powers. These limits remain today even as the United States has achieved sole superpower status in the world, and other nations, as well as U.S. citizens, expect the nation to lead.

In the modern world, the United States may be at a disadvantage with such a system relative to other governing systems that can react more quickly and decisively to societal needs and shifts in public opinion. Leadership in parliamentary systems changes when leaders lose support from the legislature. In parliamentary systems, even when they are burdened by the compromises necessary to maintain coalition governments, a prime minister can exercise power in a way that a U.S. president or Congress can never expect to do. When a prime minister loses the support of his or her party on key issues, elections are called. In the United States, elections are held on a regular cycle, and the presidency and Congress have come to be routinely controlled (since 1968) by the two major opposing parties. In addition to the differences between the parliamentary and the presidential systems, U.S. **federalism** (a division of governing responsibilities between the national government and the states) further slows government action.

The tensions inherent in a system designed to impede governmental action are seen in each of the cross-national themes explored in this book: the world of states, governing the economy, the democratic idea, and the politics of collective identities.

Until the New Deal era and World War II, the United States pursued a contradictory policy toward the rest of the world of states: it sought isolation from international politics but unfettered access to international markets. World War II changed the first of these stances, at least at elite levels (see Section 2): the United States sought to shape international relations through multilateral organizations and military force. It designed the multilateral organizations so that it could have a disproportionate voice (for example, in the United Nations Security Council). The United States used military force to contain communism around the world. The nation's experience in Vietnam in the 1960s and early 1970s dampened its interest in military

involvement abroad (the citizenry would not support such activities for long), but it did maintain its new internationalism. With the decline of communism and the end of the cold war, this postwar internationalism has declined somewhat, and some now call for a reduced role of the U.S. government in the world of states or, at a minimum, a greater willingness to use a unilateral response to international military crises. This decline in interest in the U.S. role in the world among some in U.S. society reflects the fact that foreign policy has never been central to the evolution of U.S. politics and governance. Because the founders designed the Constitution to impede government, both proponents and opponents of an active U.S. role in the world can find a forum to represent their views.

The U.S. government and the states have sought to manage the economy by building domestic manufacturing and exploiting the nation's natural resources while interfering little in the conduct of business (see Section 2). Thus, the United States has governed the economy only selectively. To build industry and exploit resources, the government built roads and other infrastructure, educated citizens, and opened its borders to guarantee a work force. It also sought access to international markets. Only in exceptional circumstances has it limited the operations of business through antitrust regulation. Yet its ability to continue to promote the nation's commerce is today limited by the challenge to the size and scope of government.

The democratic idea inspired the American Revolution and all subsequent efforts to secure and increase freedom and liberty. The democratic idea in the U.S. context was one of an indirect, representative democracy with checks on democratically elected leaders. The emergence of a strong national government after the New Deal era meant that national coalitions could often focus their demands on a single government. The decline in mediating institutions that can channel these demands reduces the ability of individual citizens to influence the national government (see Section 4).

A continuing challenge in U.S. governance is the politics of collective identities. As a nation of immigrants, the United States must unite immigrants and descendants of immigrants from Europe, Africa, Latin America, and Asia with the established U.S. population. Previous waves of immigrants experienced only one to two generations of political and societal exclusion based on their differences from the larger society. Whether today's immigrants experience the same relatively rapid acculturation remains an open question. Preliminary evidence indicates that the process may be even quicker for immigrants with skills and education but slower for those without these. National economic decline or the rise of a virulent anti-immigrant sentiment could slow or even stop the acculturation process. Despite the acculturation of previous waves of immigrants and their children, the United States has never fully remedied its longest-lasting difference in collective identities with full economic and political incorporation of African Americans.

Implications for Comparative Politics

Scholars of U.S. politics have always had to come to terms with the idea of American exceptionalism—the idea that the United States is unique and cannot easily be compared to other nations. In several respects, the United States *could* be considered exceptional. As indicated, its geography and natural resources offer it an advantage that few other nations can match. Its experi-ence with mass representative democracy is longer than that of other nations. It has been able to expand the citizenry beyond the descendants of the original members. And, finally, U.S. society has been much less divided by class than have the societies of other states.[3]

The United States has influenced other nations both because of its success and because it sometimes imposes its experiences on others. The U.S. Constitution, for all of its limitations, has served as the model for the constitutions of many newly independent nations. Some form of **separation of powers** (see Section 3) has become the norm in democratic states. Similarly, district-based and single-member-plurality electoral systems (see Section 4) have been widely adapted to reduce conflict in multiethnic states, of which the United States was the first large-scale example. Through its active role in multilateral institutions such as the United Nations (UN) and international financial institutions such as the International Monetary Fund (IMF), the United States also attempts to impose its will on other nations. Thus, for all of its strengths and weaknesses, it is necessary to know about the U.S. experience to understand more fully the shape of modern democracies throughout the world.

Section ❷ Political Economy and Development

State and Economy

When national leaders present the accomplishments of the United States, they often hold its economy up as an example of what the nation offers to the world and what it offers to its citizens. By governing the economy less, the United States allows the private economy to thrive. In this simplified version of this story, the private sector is the engine of national growth, and this private sector is most successful when left alone by government. Economic success, then, is tied to the **free market**—the absence of government regulation and the opportunity for entrepreneurs to build the nation's economy.

Relative to other advanced democracies, the U.S. economy is much less regulated. The U.S. government has traditionally taken a **laissez-faire** attitude toward economic actors. This absence of regulation allowed for the creation and expansion of many new types of production that subsequently spread throughout the world, such as the assembly line early in the twentieth century, industrialized agriculture at midcentury, and Internet commerce at its end.

The Constitution reserves for the federal government authority to regulate interstate commerce and commerce with foreign nations. As a result, state and local governments—those most knowledgeable about business or consumer interests in their areas—are limited in their ability to shape the economy. When states have tried to regulate commerce, their efforts have been ruled unconstitutional by the Supreme Court. Over time, states have established the ability to regulate workplace conditions as part of their **police powers** or of jurisdiction over public health and safety.

With the exception of agriculture, higher education, and some defense-related industries, the size of various sectors of the economy is almost entirely the result of the free market. The federal government does try to incubate some new industrial sectors, but it primarily uses grants to private agencies—often universities—to accomplish this end. This stimulation of new economic activity makes up a very small share of the nation's gross national product (GNP). The United States also occasionally supports ailing industries, as it did with grants and subsidies to the airline industry in the days after the September 11 attacks, for example. While these account for more in terms of federal expenditures than does stimulation for new industries, political support for propping up ailing industries usually dies quickly. With limited government intervention, the shape of the economy is determined almost entirely by market forces.

Agriculture is something of an exception to this pattern. Since the New Deal, the federal government has guaranteed minimum prices for most agricultural commodities and has sought to protect agriculture by paying farmers to leave some land fallow. It has also considerably reduced the costs of production and risks associated with agriculture by providing subsidized crop insurance, subsidies for canals and aqueducts to transport water, and flood control projects. It has subsidized the sale of U.S. agricultural products abroad. In the 1990s, the federal government began to move away from the guarantees of minimum prices for crops, although it continued to provide funds to sell U.S. crops abroad. Although a less explicit, and perhaps less intentional, form of subsidy, weak regulation of U.S. immigration laws has ensured that agriculture has always had a reliable and inexpensive labor source.

The federal government has also limited its own ability to regulate the economy. With the formation of the **Federal Reserve Board** in 1913, for example, it removed control of the money supply from democratically elected officeholders. Today, unelected leaders on the Federal Reserve Board, many with ties to the banking industry, control the volume of money in the economy and the key interest rates that determine rates at which private lenders lend. Furthermore, the United States has not regulated the flow of capital, which has allowed many large U.S.-based firms to evolve over time into multinational corporations and hence remove themselves from much U.S. government regulation and taxation.

While the United States has taken a more laissez-faire approach to its economy than have other advanced democracies, it is important to recognize that from the nation's earliest days, the federal government has promoted agriculture and industry, spurred exports, and (more recently) sought to stabilize the domestic and international economy. These promotional efforts included tariffs, which sought to disadvantage products that competed with U.S. manufactures; roads and canals, so that U.S.-produced goods could be brought to market cheaply and quickly; the distribution of federally owned lands in the West to individuals and to railroads, so that the land could contribute to national economic activity; and large-scale immigration, so that capital would have people to produce and consume goods (see Section 3).

These efforts to promote U.S. industry often came at the expense of individual citizens, who are less able to organize and make demands of government. Tariffs, for example, kept prices high for domestic consumers, and the enhanced road system and consequent cheap transportation forced native producers to compete in a world economy where their locally produced goods might be more expensive than the same goods produced elsewhere in the United States or abroad.

Through much of the nation's history, the United States used its diplomatic and military resources to establish and maintain markets for U.S.-produced commodities and manufactures abroad. During the nineteenth century, as industry and agriculture geared up to produce for mass markets domestically and abroad, the United States entered into bilateral trading agreements to sell its natural resources, agricultural produce, and manufactured products abroad. The U.S. military protected this commerce. Today, the United States uses its position in the world economy and on multilateral lending institutions to open markets, provide loans for nations facing economic distress, and protect some U.S.-produced goods from foreign competition. In sum, despite national rhetoric to the contrary, the United States has consistently promoted economic development, though not by regulating production or spurring specific industries.

The U.S. economy has increasingly come to rely on two unintentional forms of international subsidy. First, it has built up a steadily increasing international trade deficit. In other words, the United States has bought much more abroad than it has sold. In 2001, for example, the United States imported $347.5 billion more in goods and services than it exported. This represented a substantial decline from the record $375.7 billion trade deficit in 2000. Although some aspects of these trade deficits could well reflect a strength in the U.S. economy (for example, being able to purchase goods produced inexpensively abroad), continuing deficits of this level will act as a downward pressure on the U.S. dollar in the long run (see Figure 1). Slowing this downward pressure for the time being is the second form of international subsidy: the U.S. dollar has become the international reserve currency. This means that many nations and individual investors keep their reserves (their savings) in dollars, or more specifically in dollar-denominated bonds issued by the U.S. government. By doing this, they keep demand for the dollar up, and this reduces the downward pressure that comes from repeated annual trade deficits. To the extent that they are buying U.S. government bonds, they are lending the United States money.

As the European common currency, the euro, increasingly comes to be used as a reserve currency, the United States may see less demand for dollar-denominated investments. This could lead to a decline in the value of the dollar relative to the euro (and other currencies) and an increasing cost for goods produced abroad. Purchases of some of these goods might decline, or they could be produced domestically as their costs increase, but some goods, such as oil, cannot be produced domestically, at least in the quantity used by the U.S. economy. Over time, such a scenario will damage the U.S. economy.

The government, both federal and state, regulates aspects of the economy and employer-labor relations. Beginning in 1890, the United States enacted antitrust legislation that gave it the ability to break up large businesses that could, by the nature of their size, control an entire market. These antitrust powers have been used sparingly—in the oil industry early in the century and in the long-distance telephone and computer industries more recently. Antitrust legislation gives the government a power that is very much at odds with a laissez-faire ideology, but its unwillingness to use this authority except in the most egregious cases (and the courts' occasional rejection of government antitrust initiatives) reflects the underlying hands-off ideology.

In the twentieth century, the U.S. government took on new responsibilities to protect citizens and to tax businesses, in part, to provide government-mandated services for workers. The government also expanded regulation of workplace safety, pension systems, and other worker-management relations issues that limit the ability of industry to operate in a free market relative to its workforce (see Section 3). Despite this expansion of the government role in providing protections to workers, the United States offers fewer guarantees to its workers than do other advanced democracies.

The public sector has traditionally been smaller in the United States than in other advanced democracies. Nevertheless, the U.S. government and the states conduct activities that many believe could be better

Source: U.S. Bureau of the Census, Foreign Trade Statistics, various tables. http://www.census.gov/foreign-trade/Press-Release/current_press_release/press.html#prior (accessed November 29, 2002).

Figure 1

U.S. Trade Deficit, 1994–2001

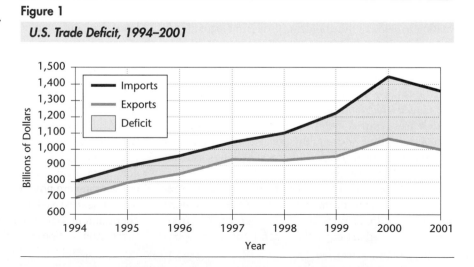

conducted by the private sector. The federal government operates hospitals for veterans (through the Veterans Administration), provides water and electrical power to Appalachian states (through the Tennessee Valley Authority), manages lands in the West and Alaska (through the Department of Interior), runs the civilian air traffic control system (through the Federal Aviation Administration), and, after September 11, manages luggage screening at commercial airports. Some localities own local electric and gas utilities and provide trash service (though in most places these services are privately owned). There has never been a U.S. national airline in the United States, but roads have traditionally been built and maintained by the state and federal governments, and waterways have been kept navigable (and opened to recreational use) by the federal government.

After victories in the 2002 congressional races giving the Republicans majorities in both the House and the Senate, President Bush has proposed the most massive privatization of the federal civil service in history. As many as 875,000 federal jobs (or about half of the federal work force) could be filled with contracted private sector labor. It is not possible at this writing to anticipate whether Congress would accept such a wholesale change in the structure of the federal bureaucracy. One significant fear is that that the newly contracted labor, which would not have job protections, could be used by sitting presidents to reward electoral supporters. It was to avoid such a situation that the federal civil service was established in the 1880s.

The federal government has privatized some activities in recent years. The postal service, for example, became a semi-independent corporation in 1970. The federal government is now trying to end subsidies for the semi-independent passenger rail corporation (Amtrak) that it inherited when the company's private sector owners went bankrupt.

Often left out of the story of the development of the U.S. economy is the role of its natural resources and the environment. The nation's territory is unique. Although it is not the largest country in the world, it is the most diverse in terms of natural resources and environments, stretching from tropical to arctic. The territory includes arable land that can produce more than enough year round for the domestic market as well as for extensive exports. These lands have not been subject to invasion for much of the nation's history. Land has become increasingly concentrated in a few hands,

but in the past, it was held in small plots tilled at least in part by the owners. This tradition of equitable land distribution (encouraged by government policies in the nineteenth century that distributed small plots to resident landholders) dampened the class tensions that appeared in societies with entrenched landholding elites. Not all Americans were eligible for this land-giveaway, however. The recently freed slaves could not obtain free lands in the West, and some share of the gap in wealth between whites and blacks today can be attributed to the access that whites had to western lands in the last century.[4] In today's economy, public benefits and public employment are increasingly limited to U.S. citizens. Over time, these policies could enhance differences between the non-Hispanic white and black populations, on the one hand, and ethnic groups with large shares of immigrants, such as Latinos and Asian Americans, on the other.

The United States has also been advantaged in terms of trade. It has protected ports and navigable rivers and few enemies that can challenge U.S. control over these transportation resources. For over a century, it was able to expand trade while not investing in a large standing military to defend its trade routes. This long history of safety in U.S. territory made the events of September 11 (and Pearl Harbor before it) all the more unnerving for Americans. The symbolic importance of the name of one of the September 11 targets, New York's World Trade Center, raised for many Americans questions about whether the buildings were targeted in part because they represented the increasing presence of American commerce abroad.

One area in which the United States has taken a limited role in regulating the activities of private actors in the American economy is environmental regulation. When the environment first became an issue in international politics, the United States took aggressive action to clean the air and the nation's oceans and navigable waterways. In each of these regulatory areas, federal legislation had dramatic impacts. Emissions standards, in particular, have made the air, even in the nation's most car-focused cities such as Los Angeles, much healthier. Waterways that were dangerous to the touch are now open to swimming.

These 1970s era environmental **regulations** have not been followed by a continuing national commitment to environmentalism. President Ronald Reagan sought to open federal lands to further commercial exploitation and was partially successful in his objectives. President George W. Bush has sought to open the Arctic National Wildlife Refuge (ANWR) to oil exploration and, with Republican control of Congress beginning in 2003, will likely succeed at opening areas within ANWR to oil and gas development. Presidents of both parties have reduced fuel efficiency standards, which would both benefit the environment and reduce demand for imported oil. In some sense, the successes of the early environmental regulations, which had a tangible and visible impact in areas where most Americans live, has reduced the salience of environmental issues, particularly those that would have impact in areas where few people live. As the environment has diminished as a popular concern, traditional laissez-faire attitudes toward governmental regulation have allowed presidents and Congress to trade economic gains for environmental losses.

Society and Economy

The United States adheres more strictly to its laissez-faire ideology in terms of the outcomes of the economic system. The distribution of income and wealth is much more unequal in the United States than in other advanced democracies. In 2001, for example, the richest fifth of families earned approximately 51 percent of the nation's income. The poorest fifth, on the other hand, earned just 4 percent of the nation's income. The top 5 percent alone earned more than 22 percent of the total amount earned in the United States in 2001 (see Figure 2). The nation has always tolerated these conditions and sees them as an incentive for people at the lower end of the economic spectrum. Wealth and income have become more skewed since 1980 (when the top 20 percent of households earned approximately 44 percent of what was earned), a phenomenon that has not been an issue of national political concern. In fact, the mere mention of the class implications of a policy, particularly tax policy, in an election will usually lead to the charge of fomenting class warfare.

Federal income taxation of individuals is progressive, with higher income people paying a higher share of their income in taxes, and could have the effect of reducing gaps in wealth. Rates range from 0 percent for individuals with incomes less than $7,700 to 38.6 percent for individuals with incomes exceeding approximately $315,000. These rates are scheduled to decline

Figure 2

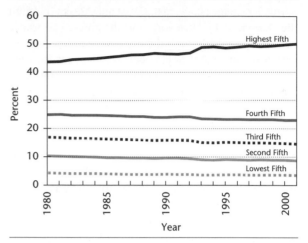

Share of Aggregate Income Received by Households, Quintiles, 1980–2001

Source: U.S. Bureau of the Census, Historical Income Data, Table H-2A "Historical Income Tables – Households." http://www.census.gov/hhes/income/histinc/h02.html (accessed November 29, 2002).

between now and 2010. The highest rate will drop to 33 percent. The progressive nature of federal taxes is reduced considerably by two factors. Upper-income taxpayers receive a much higher share of their income from investments, which are taxed at lower rates. Second, all taxpayers with salary income are subject to a flat or, arguably, regressive tax for social security and disability benefits. A flat tax is a tax at the same percentage for all taxpayers, regardless of income. The tax for social security and Medicare is currently 7.65 percent paid by the worker and 7.65 percent paid by the employer. The social security share of this tax is imposed only on the first $84,900 of income and not at all on higher incomes. This is a regressive tax, in that higher income taxpayers pay a lower share of their income for social security than do lower income taxpayers.

State and local taxes tend to be much less progressive. Most states levy a sales tax. This is a flat tax, ranging between 3 and 9.5 percent depending on the state, on most consumption; some states exempt food and other items from sales taxation. For lower-income people, sales taxes act as a flat tax on most or all of their income. Upper-income people pay a smaller share of their income because they do not have to dedicate all of their income to consumption. Not all states have income taxes. Among those that do, many levy a flat tax, and no states have an income tax that is as progressive as the federal income tax. The final major form of individual taxation is property taxes. All people pay these in one way or another. Property owners pay them directly and can deduct the tax payment from their federal and, in some cases, state income taxes. Renters pay them as part of their rent payment but do not directly get any tax benefits.

Thus, the vast gap between rich and poor in the United States is not remedied by progressive taxation. This gap might well have led to the emergence of class-based political movements, but immigration policy, which also promoted economic development, focused workers' attention away from class and toward cultural differences that reduced the salience of class divisions in U.S. society. Unions, which could also have promoted a class-based politics and focused workers' attentions on income inequalities, have traditionally been weak in the United States. This weakness reflects individual-level antipathy toward unions, but also state and federal laws that limit the abilities of unions to organize and collectively bargain. Today, approximately 14 percent of American workers are unionized; this rate steadily declined in the twentieth century.

Agriculture and industry could not have grown in the United States without the importation of this immigrant labor. With only a few exceptions, the nation has sought to remedy labor shortages with policies that encouraged migration. Today, the United States is one of just four countries that allow large-scale migration of those who do not already have a cultural tie to the receiving nation. (The others—Canada, Australia, and New Zealand—share a colonial history with the United States.) Contemporary immigration to the United States numbers approximately 800,000 people annually, who immigrate under the provisions of the law to a permanent status that allows for eventual eligibility for U.S. citizenship.[5] Another 400,000 migrate without legal status each year and stay (many more migrants to undocumented immigrants come and go during any year). Migration at this level adds about 4 percent to the U.S. population each decade. (See Figure 3.)

Although the United States tolerates the unequal

Figure 3

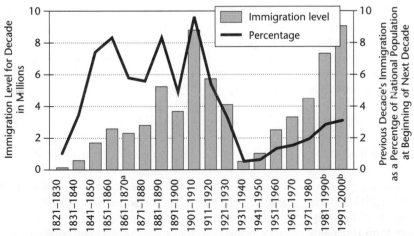

Immigration to the United States, 1821–2000

Legend: Immigration level; Percentage

Y-axis (left): Immigration Level for Decade in Millions
Y-axis (right): Previous Decace's Immigration as a Percentge of National Population at Beginning of Next Decade
X-axis: 1821–1830, 1831–1840, 1841–1850, 1851–1860, 1861–1870[a], 1871–1880, 1881–1890, 1891–1900, 1901–1910, 1911–1920, 1921–1930, 1931–1940, 1941–1950, 1951–1960, 1961–1970, 1971–1980, 1981–1990[b], 1991–2000[b]

Source: Adapted from DeSipio, Louis and Rodolfo O. de la Garza, 1998. *Making Americans/Remaking America: Immigration and Immigrant Policy* (Boulder, Colo.: Westview Press), Table 2.1.

a Until 1867, the federal government recorded as immigrants only people who arrived at seaports.

b These figures include recipients of legalization under the Immigration Reform and Control Act of 1986 who immigrated to the United States prior to 1982 but were recorded as having entered in the year in which they received permanent residence.

distribution of income and wealth, in the twentieth century it intervened directly in the free market to establish protections for workers and, to a lesser degree, to guarantee the welfare of the most disadvantaged in the society. The programs for workers, which are primarily distributive policies, receive much more public support than do programs to assist the poor, which are primarily redistributive policies. **Distributive policies** allocate resources into an area that policy-makers perceive needs to be promoted without a significant impact on income or wealth distribution. **Redistributive policies** take resources from one person or group in society and allocate them to a more disadvantaged group in the society. It should be noted that most worker benefits, such as health insurance, child care, and pensions, are provided by private employers, if they are provided at all, but are regulated by the government.

In 2002, approximately 41 million people, or about one in seven Americans, did not have health insurance. Although this number declined in the late 1990s as the national economy improved, the number of the uninsured is again on the increase. The vast majority of the uninsured are workers who do not receive insurance through their employers. More than 32 million of the uninsured are full-time workers. Many poor families are eligible for a needs-based health insurance program, Medicaid, provided by the federal government. In the early 1990s, Congress and President Bill Clinton sought to craft a policy solution to insure the uninsured, but their efforts collapsed around questions of cost and control. With health care costs again on the rise, employers and the health care industry will again look to government for assistance in providing insurance, and the uninsured (and the potentially uninsured) will demand government action, but it seems even less likely today than it did in the early 1990s that the federal government will assume a responsibility for providing health insurance to the American populace. The cost, which some estimate to be at least $123 billion annually, is too high, and there is no consensus in Congress as to who should manage such a program: the public or private sectors. Finally, President Bush (and future presidents) learned a lesson from the Clinton administration's experience with trying to reform health care: that there is little to be gained because the financial cost of successful health care reform is very high and any reform would require new taxes that would generate much opposition in the electorate and there is much to be lost because Congress, not the president, would ultimately control the design of the new health insurance program. The president will be unlikely to lead such an effort despite the extensive public need.

Best known among the federal programs aimed toward workers is social security, which taxes workers and their employers to pay for benefits for retired and disabled workers (and nonworker spouses). In the past, retirees almost always received more than they had paid into the system (a form of intergenerational redistribution), but it will take some reform to guarantee that this outcome continues when today's workers reach retirement age. The government also established a minimum wage and a bureaucratic mechanism to enforce this wage. Some states and localities established higher minimum wages than the federal minimum wage. Citizen groups in several cities nationwide over the past decade have promoted a further expansion of the idea of a minimum wage to a "living wage," a wage sufficient to live in high-cost cities and is often double the federal minimum wage. These living wage campaigns seek to force cities and municipal contractors to pay such wages.

In addition to social security retirement benefits and the minimum wage, the federal government has established a health insurance program for elderly retirees and their nonworking spouses (Medicare), paid for by workers and their employers; programs to provide financial and health care assistance for disabled workers (through social security); and insurance for private pension plans (paid for by employers). With health care costs on the rise and the number of elderly Americans increasing, the federal government faces a shortage in taxes to pay for Medicare from employers and workers. Sometime early in the 2010s, the government will face the dilemma of having to lower benefits or of paying for health care for the elderly out of general revenues. Changing the tax basis of Medicare now (or lowering benefits now) would delay this point of reckoning, but there is little incentive for Congress to act in this area and suffer the political consequences.

The states also regulate worker-employer relations through unemployment insurance and insurance against workplace injuries. These programs, unlike the federal programs, are paid for entirely by the employer. Benefits and eligibility requirements vary dramatically by state, though the federal governmental mandates that all workers be eligible for twenty-six weeks of benefits (assuming the worker has been employed for at least six months). In times of high unemployment, the federal government often adds an extra thirteen weeks of benefit eligibility paid for with federal taxes.

Beginning in the 1930s, the United States also established social welfare programs to assist the economically disadvantaged. As one would expect in a system organized around the free market, these programs have never been as broad based or as socially accepted as in other economies. These programs, which expanded in the 1960s and 1970s and were restructured in 1996, provided food, health care, housing assistance, some job training, and some cash assistance to the poor. The states administered these programs with a combination of federal and state funds, established benefit levels, and were responsible for moving recipients off the programs. Eligibility and benefit levels varied dramatically from state to state. Prior to 1996, there was a federal guarantee of some food and cash assistance for everyone who met eligibility thresholds.

This guarantee disappeared in 1996 with the passage of comprehensive welfare reform. After 1996, recipients were limited in the duration of their eligibility, and states were entrusted with developing programs to train recipients for work and to get them jobs. Some states have taken these responsibilities seriously, and others have not. It is too early to judge the success of these reforms, though all observers acknowledge that they were helped considerably by the strength of the U.S. economy in the late 1990s. The states are now facing the point where they must end welfare eligibility for large numbers of recipients. Although enacted separately from the 1996 welfare reform, the federal government also reduced the availability of federally managed housing for the poor and expanded subsidies for the poor to secure housing in the private market.

The federal and state governments have one final recurring impact on the national economy that is more indirect but will likely be of increasing importance in the coming years: both the federal and state governments are entering a period of high deficit spending. Spurred by declines in the economy (reducing the amount of income tax being paid by individuals and increasing the number of people collecting needs-based social welfare programs) and the stock market

(reducing capital gains taxes paid), the federal government and the states are not raising as much money as they are spending. Current estimates suggest that the federal government spent $159 billion more than it raised in 2002. The states face a deficit of at least $40 billion. Most states will be required to close this deficit very quickly by raising taxes or cutting services. The federal government, on the other hand, can continue to run a large annual deficit (as it did from the early 1980s until 1997).

Current projections show that the federal government will continue to have deficits in the $200 to $300 billion range throughout the rest of the decade. These deficits will add to the approximately $6.4 trillion national debt (which reflects the cumulative deficits of the past 215 years of national history). Deficits can have a salutary effect on the national economy during weak economic times because the federal government can more easily borrow and then spend this money to stimulate the economy and support individuals who are out of work. In the long run, however, this federal debt absorbs money that could be invested in private sector activities and will slow national economic growth. In 2002, the federal government paid approximately $333 billion in interest on its debt.

The United States and the International Political Economy

Since colonial times, the United States has been linked to world trade. By the late twentieth century, the United States had vastly expanded its role to international finance and was an importer of goods produced abroad (often in low-wage countries that could produce goods less expensively than U.S. factories) as well as an exporter of agricultural products.

After World War II, the United States reversed its traditional isolationism in international politics to take a leading role in the regulation of the international economy. The increasing interdependence of global economies was the result, in part, of conscious efforts by world leaders at the end of World War II, through the Bretton Woods Agreement, to establish and fund multinational lending institutions. These were to provide loans and grants to developing economies in exchange for their agreement to reduce government regulation of their economies and open their domestic markets to internationally produced goods. Chief among these institutions were the World Bank and the International Monetary Fund. Since their establishment in the 1940s, they have been supplemented by a network of international lending and regulatory agencies and regional trading agreements. The Group of Eight (G-8), for example, conducts annual meetings of the leaders of the eight largest industrial democracies (the United States, Japan, Germany, Britain, France, Italy, Canada, and Russia).

The United States is also part of regional trading networks, such as NAFTA with Canada and Mexico. NAFTA did not initially have extensive support in Congress, but President Clinton used all the powers of the presidency to win the support of members of his own party, and the treaty narrowly passed. Despite the initial opposition of many in Congress to NAFTA, it has come to be seen as a boon to the American economy. After its passage, the United States entered into an agreement with neighboring countries in the Carib-

bean to reduce tariffs on many goods. This Caribbean Basin Initiative was not as wide-ranging as NAFTA, but expanded export opportunities for manufactures made in the Caribbean (and also satisfied lawmakers from Florida who initially opposed NAFTA out of fears that it would disadvantage Caribbean nations relative to Mexico in their efforts to penetrate the U.S. market).

NAFTA and the Caribbean Basin Initiative are likely the precursors of other regional trading agreements in the Americas. In 2002, Congress passed, and the president signed into law, authority for the president to negotiate an expansion of regional trading alliances along the lines of NAFTA. This legislation, in a fundamental sense, allows the president to circumvent constitutional limits on the powers of the office. By passing this legislation, Congress agreed that it would review any trade agreement negotiated by the president with a simple yes or no vote. In other words, Congress will not have power to amend trade legislation in any way. Advocates

In order to ensure the passage of the North American Free Trade Agreement, President Clinton had to negotiate with wavering members of Congress. Although he didn't wax any cars, he made government programs and resources available to win votes.
Source: Doonesbury © 1993, G.B. Trudeau. Reprinted with permission of Universal Press Syndicate. All rights reserved.

of expanded trade agreements argue that this presidential authority is necessary so that other nations entering into the agreement with the United States can be assured that what they negotiate will become the law. Critics note that such trade authority circumvents constitutional mandates that the Congress have a role in shaping policy and limits the ability of labor and environmental interests (or other groups who might oppose freer trade) to shape trade relations. Now that the president holds this trade authority, it raises the likelihood that the United States will enter into a free trade area of the Americas that could potentially include as many as thirty-four nations in the Americas and would serve as a counterweight to the European Community (and currency zone).

The U.S. government plays a central role in the international political economy. It achieves this through its domination of international lending agencies and regional defense and trade organizations. Although these international organizations reflect a desire by policymakers to address some international financial issues multilaterally (at least with the other advanced democracies), these efforts are ultimately limited by domestic politics. Some in Congress and a significant minority of the citizenry oppose U.S. involvement in multilateral organizations. Thus, while presidents may promote an international agenda, Congress often limits the funding for international organizations. The United States then appears to many outside the country as a hesitant and sometimes resentful economic leader.

In recent years, another multilateral institution has emerged that can potentially challenge U.S. economic dominance. The European Union (EU) is much more than a trading alliance. It is an organization of fifteen European nations (and thirteen nations, largely East European, waiting for membership) with growing international influence. On January 1, 1999, most EU members entered into a currency union (not included were Britain, Denmark, Greece, and Sweden). Greece joined the euro states in 2001. As the euro comes into widespread use, the dollar will face its first challenge in many years as the world's dominant trading currency. Increasingly, the euro has joined the dollar as a reserve currency for nations and wealthy individuals and is also being used a pricing currency for international trade. Each of these trends has the potential to reduce the dominance of the dollar in the world financial markets.

In addition to contributing to multilateral institutions, the United States funds binational international lending through such agencies as the Export-Import Bank and the Overseas Private Investment Corporation. These agencies make loans to countries and private businesses to purchase goods and services from U.S.-owned businesses. The United States also provides grants and loans to allies to further U.S. strategic and foreign policy objectives or for humanitarian reasons.

The new role of the United States in multilateral economic and defense organizations and the growth in bilateral aid reflect a change in the nation's approach to its role in the world economy. The United States has slowly, and grudgingly, adapted to a world where it can no longer rest on its exceptionalism or simply assert its central role. Its economy and the larger society feel the effects of economic changes abroad. Thus, the U.S. government and, more slowly, the American people have seen their problems and needs from a global perspective. This incorporation into the larger world is certainly not complete. The separation of powers between the executive and legislative branches, and the local constituencies of members of Congress, ensures continuing resistance to this new international role.

The role of the United States in the international economy may be tested in coming years in a way that it has not been since the formation of the multilateral organizations after World War II. The strength of these international organizations is inherently limited by the increasing presence of multinational corporations that are able to transfer capital and production across national boundaries with little control by governments. While this change in the political economy is a political problem that all countries will face in the twenty-first century, the United States is and will be central to this problem. As the domestic U.S. economy is increasingly shaped by these international forces, U.S. citizens will demand economic stability from their government. The U.S. government was designed to be weak (see Section 3), so it will not easily be able to respond. The seeming lack of response will lead to strengthened calls by some in U.S. society to isolate the United States from the regulation of the international economy that it has helped shape. If these voices become dominant, the United States may find itself at odds with the international organizations that it helped create and that promote U.S. trade internationally.

Section ❸ Governance and Policy-Making

Organization of the State

The governing document of the United States is the Constitution. It was drafted in 1787 and ratified by the necessary nine states the following year (all thirteen colonies had ratified it by 1790). The Constitution was not the first governing document of the United States. It was preceded by the Articles of Confederation, which concentrated most power in the states. The revision of the Articles established a central government that was independent of the states but left the states most of their preexisting powers (particularly police powers and public safety, the most common area of interaction between citizens and government). Although it had limited powers, the new U.S. government exercised powers over commerce and foreign policy that were denied to the states.

The Constitution has been amended twenty-seven times since 1787. The first ten of these amendments make up the Bill of Rights, the set of protections of individual rights that were a necessary compromise to ensure that that the Constitution was ratified. These first ten amendments were ratified in 1791. The remaining seventeen amendments have extended democratic election practices and changed procedural deficiencies in the original Constitution that came to be perceived as inconsistent with democratic practice. Examples of amendments to extend democratic election practices would be the extension of the vote to women and to eighteen to twenty year olds (the Nineteenth and Twenty-Sixth Amendments, respectively) or the prohibition of poll taxes, the imposition of a tax that had to be paid before an individual could vote (the Twenty-Fourth Amendment). Changes to procedural deficiencies in the Constitution included the linking of presidential and vice-presidential candidates on a single ticket, replacing a system where the candidate with the most votes in the Electoral College won the presidency and the second-place candidate, often the president's primary opponent, won the vice presidency (the Twelfth Amendment) or establishing procedures to replace a president who becomes incapacitated (the Twenty-Fifth Amendment).

Each amendment requires three-quarters of the states to agree to the change. Although the Constitution allows states to initiate amendments, all twenty-seven have resulted from amendments passed by Congress. When Congress initiates an amendment to the Constitution, two-thirds of senators must vote in favor of the amendment before it is sent to the states. States set their own procedures for ratifying constitutional amendments. In some, a simple majority in the legislature is sufficient while others require support from a higher share of the legislature (such as two-thirds of those voting). Some require that a special convention be called to review the amendment.

Understanding two principles is necessary to understand American constitutional government: federalism and separation of powers. Federalism is the division of authority between multiple levels of government. In the case of the United States, the division is between the federal and state governments. Separation of powers is an effort to set government against itself by vesting separate branches with independent powers so that any one branch cannot permanently dominate the others.

These two characteristics of American government—federalism and separation of powers—were necessary compromises to guarantee the ratification of the Constitution. They should not, however, be viewed simply as compromises. On the contrary, they reflect a conscious desire by the constitutional framers to limit the federal government's ability to control citizens' lives. To limit what they perceived of as an inevitable tyranny of majorities over numerical minorities, the framers designed a system that set each part of government against all the other parts. Each branch of the federal government could limit the independent action of the other two branches, and the federal government and the states could limit each other. Although the potential for tyranny remained, the framers hoped that the individual ambitions of the members of each branch of government would cause each branch to fight efforts by other branches to undermine individual liberties.[6]

Federalism and separation of powers have a consequence that could not be fully anticipated by the framers of the Constitution: U.S. government is designed to be inefficient. Because each part of government is set against all others, policy-making is difficult. Inefficiencies can be partly overcome through extragovernmental mediating institutions such as political parties, but no single leader or branch of government can unequivocally dominate policy-making as the prime minister can in a parliamentary system, for example. Although a consensus across branches of government can sometimes appear in times of national challenge, such as in the period immediately after the September 11 attacks, this commonness of purpose quickly dissolves as each branch of government seeks to protect its prerogatives and position in the policy-making process.

Federalism is the existence of multiple sovereigns. A citizen of the United States is simultaneously a citizen of the nation and of one of the states. Each citizen has responsibilities to each of these sovereigns and can be held accountable to the laws of each. Over the nation's 200-year history, the balance of power between the two principal sovereigns has shifted, with the federal government gaining power relative to the states, but to this day, states remain responsible for many parts of citizens' lives and act in these areas independently of the federal government.

Over time, many powers traditionally reserved to the states have shifted to the federal government. The period of the most rapid of these shifts was the New Deal, when the federal government tapped its commerce regulation powers to create a wide range of programs to address the economic and social needs of the people.

The second organizing principle of American government is separation of powers. While each of the states has adopted some form of separation of powers, its purest form exists at the federal level. Each of the three branches of the federal government—the executive, the legislature (see Section 4), and the judiciary—shares in the responsibilities of governing and has some oversight over the other two branches. In order to enact a law, for example, Congress (the legislative branch) must pass the law, and the president (the executive branch) must sign it. The president can block the action of Congress by vetoing the law. Congress can override the president's veto through a two-thirds vote in both houses of Congress. The courts (the judiciary) can review the constitutionality of laws passed by Congress and signed by the president. Congress and the states acting in unison, however, can reverse a Supreme Court ruling on the constitutionality of a law by passing a constitutional amendment by a two-thirds vote

that is subsequently ratified by three-quarters of the states. The Senate (the legislative branch) must ratify senior appointments to the executive branch, including members of the cabinet, as well as federal judges. The president nominates these judges, and Congress sets their salaries and much of their jurisdiction (except in constitutional matters). In sum, the separation of powers allows each branch to limit the others and prevents any one branch from carrying out its responsibilities without the others' cooperation. It also allows a phenomenon unanticipated by the framers of the Constitution: the divided government in which different political parties control the executive and legislative branches of government, which has been the norm for the federal government since 1968 (but that was not the case when Congress reconvened in 2003).

Federalism and separation of powers create a complexity in U.S. government that cannot be found in other advanced democracies. This complexity encourages an ongoing competition for political power that is reflected in the battle between the president and Congress over impeachment, but more regularly in battles over policy. The states traditionally played a greater role in these battles but are relatively less important now than they were before the 1930s.

The Executive

The Presidency

The American presidency has grown dramatically in power since the nation's first days. The president, who is indirectly elected, serves a fixed four-year term and is limited to two terms by a constitutional amendment ratified in 1951. The president is both head of state and head of government. The roots of presidential power are found in these roles more than in the powers delegated to the presidency in the Constitution.

Through much of the political history of the United States, the president was not at the center of the federal government. Quite the contrary. The Constitution established Congress as the central branch of government and relegated the president to a much more poorly defined role whose primary responsibilities are administering programs designed and funded by Congress. Although twentieth-century presidents found new powers and exercised powers unimaginable to earlier presidents, the structural weaknesses of the presidency remain. The president must receive ongoing support from Congress to ensure the implementation of his agenda. But the president cannot control Congress except to the degree that public opinion (and, to a much lesser degree, party loyalty) encourages members of Congress to support the president.

The president is the commander in chief of the military and may grant pardons, make treaties (which are ratified with the approval of two-thirds of the Senate), and make senior appointments to the executive branch and to judicial posts (again with congressional concurrence). The president is required to provide an annual state of the union report to Congress and may call Congress into session. Finally, the president manages the bureaucracy, which at the time of the Constitution's ratification was small but has subsequently grown in size and responsibility. Thus, in terms of formal powers, the president is far weaker than Congress is.

With one exception, presidents until the turn of the twentieth century did not add considerably to the delegated powers. Instead, nineteenth-century presidents largely served as clerks to the will of Congress. During the War of 1812, for example, Congress directed battle strategy. In the 1880s, Congress directed the president to negotiate for the best deal with shipbuilders to outfit the newly growing navy. The exception among nineteenth-century presidents was Abraham Lincoln, who dominated Congress during the Civil War. His example was one that twentieth-century presidents followed. He became a national leader and was able to establish his own power base directly in the citizenry. Lincoln realized that each member of Congress depended on a local constituency (a district or state) and was able to label their activities as being local or sectional. Lincoln created a national power base for the presidency by presenting himself as the only national political leader, an important position during the Civil War. He had an advantage in being commander in chief during wartime; however, the foundation of his power was not the military but his connection to the people.

In the twentieth century, presidents discovered that they had a previously untapped resource. Beginning with Theodore Roosevelt, twentieth-century presidents used the office of the president as a bully pulpit to speak to the nation and propose public policies that met national needs. No member of Congress or the Senate could claim a similar national constituency (though several have tried in the last fifty years). Roosevelt began a trend that has been tapped by each of his successors. He used the mass media (in his case, newspapers) to present a national agenda to the American people. The most successful of his successors used newly available media to reach over the heads of Congress to the people. Most successful among these twentieth-century presidents using new media technologies was Franklin Roosevelt, whose radio broadcast Fireside Chats unified much of the nation in support of elements of the New Deal.

Later in the twentieth century, presidents found a new power. As the role of the federal government expanded, they managed a much larger federal bureaucracy that provided goods and services used by nearly all citizens. Thus, a program like social security connects almost all citizens to the executive branch. Although Congress appropriates the funds for social security and played a significant role in its design, it is the executive branch that sends the checks each month. Beginning with the New Deal, presidents proposed programs that expanded the federal bureaucracy and, consequently, the connection between the people and the president.

Finally, twentieth-century presidents learned an important lesson from the experience of Abraham Lincoln. The president has an authority over the military that places the office at the center of policy-making in military and international affairs. This centrality is particularly evident in times of war or conditions perceived as warlike and when immediate decisions may have to be made, such as in an era with nuclear weapons. Thus, in the period from World War II to the collapse of the Soviet Union, the presidency was empowered by the widely perceived need for a single decision maker. In the period after September 11, the president, and the executive branch, assumed direction of the U.S. response. Initially, Congress ceded this responsibility.

Even as Congress balked at some presidential initiatives in the post-9/11 period, the public looked to the executive branch, and more specifically President Bush, to lead. President Bush used these popular expectations very strategically in the 2002 elections to support Republican candidates in close races. This investment of his political capital resulted in the victories of several Republican candidates. Overall, the Republicans won control of the Senate and gained several seats in the House of Representatives. The gains by the incumbent party in an off-year election are unusual in politics today and ensure that President Bush will be more able to pursue his agenda during the third and fourth years of his term than he was in the first and second.

Although the presidency gained powers in the twentieth century, the office remains structurally weak relative to Congress. Despite popular expectations for presidential leadership in the period after 9/11, presidential dominance in policy-making has declined relative to the period between World War II and the end of the cold war. Presidential power is particularly undercut by the norm of divided government. The bureaucracy is a weak link on which to build institutional power. Congress has significant powers to shape it. Congress has become increasingly restive about ceding power in international affairs to the president. Since Congress retains the power to appropriate funds, the president must ultimately yield to its will on the design and implementation of policy.

To date, all presidents have been men, all have been white, and all but one (John F. Kennedy) have been Protestant. While being a former general was once a stepping-stone to the presidency, in today's politics having served as a governor works to a candidate's advantage. Presidents from 1976 to 2003 included four former governors (Georgia's Jimmy Carter, California's Ronald Reagan, Arkansas's Bill Clinton, and Texas's George W. Bush). Only President George Herbert Walker Bush had extensive service in the federal government (including serving as President Reagan's vice president) prior to winning the presidency. Despite a common assumption, only four vice presidents have been elected to the presidency immediately at the end of their terms. It is more common for vice presidents to move to the presidency on the death (or, in one case, the resignation) of the president. As the media have become more central to the electoral process, presidents (as well as presidential candidates) have on average been getting younger. Bill Clinton was forty-six when he was elected president in 1992. George W. Bush was fifty-four in 2000.

The Cabinet and the Bureaucracy

To manage the U.S. government, the president appoints (and the Senate confirms) senior administrators to key executive branch departments. The chief offi-cers at each of the core departments make up the president's cabinet. These senior officers include heads of prominent departments such as the secretary of state, the attorney general, and the secretary of defense, as well as lesser-known officials such as the secretary of veterans affairs. Contrary to the case in parliamentary systems, the U.S. cabinet has no legal standing, and presidents frequently use it only at a symbolic level. The president is also free to extend membership to other senior appointed officials (such as the U.S. ambassador to the United Nations), so the number of cabinet members fluctuates from administration to administration.

The senior officers of the executive branch agencies manage a work force of approximately 1.8 million civilian civil servants (the bureaucracy). Although formally part of the executive branch, the bureaucracy must also be responsive to Congress. Under certain circumstances, it operates independent of both elective branches and, rarely, under the direction of the courts. The presidential appointees establish broad policy objectives and propose budgets that can expand or contract the responsibilities of executive branch offices. Congress must approve these budgets, and it uses this financial oversight to encourage bureaucrats to behave as their congressional monitors wish. Although the size of the federal bureaucracy had been in steady decline since the early 1980s, the new federal military and security responsibilities established after the September 11 attacks have reversed this trend. The federalization of airport baggage screening alone will add approximately 54,000 workers to the federal bureaucracy.

September 11 also spurred a challenge to the protections traditionally guaranteed to the federal bureaucracy that would not have been politically possible prior to the attacks. When President Bush proposed that a department of homeland security be formed to bring together under one agency (and one member of the cabinet) federal agencies responsible for domestic security, he sought an exemption from civil service rules for the approximately 170,000 federal workers in the twenty-two agencies that would be moved to this department. Democrats in Congress balked at exempting these workers from the job protections shared by other civil servants. But with the Republican victories in the 2002 elections, Democrats conceded, and President Bush won, the ability to hire and fire workers in the new agency. Bush argued that this change would ensure the agency would be more responsive to public security threats. Opponents express concern that the Bush administration, or a subsequent administration, will use the new Department of Homeland Security to reward political supporters with patronage appointments and impede its mission of homeland security. Perhaps coincidentally, soon after his victory with eliminating civil service protections at the Department of Homeland Security, President Bush proposed contracting out many current federal civil service jobs, arguing that the services could be provided more cheaply by the private sector.

Arguably, the inability of either Congress or the president to control the bureaucracy fully should give it an independence. Although this may be true in the case of policy areas that are of little interest to the elected branches, the bureaucracy as a rule does not have the resources to collect information and shape the laws that guide their operations. Interest groups have steadily filled this informational role, but the information comes at a cost. Bureaucracies often develop symbiotic relations with the interests that they should be regulating. The interest groups have more access to Congress and can shape the operations of the regulatory agencies. These iron triangle relationships (between a private interest group, a congressional committee or subcommittee overseeing the policy in questions, and a federal agency implementing the policy) often exclude new players who represent alternative views on how policies should be implemented. Thus, without an independent source of authority, the bureaucracy is dependent not just on the elected branches but also on interest groups.

Other State Institutions

Besides the presidency and the Congress (see Section 4), three other institutions are central to the operation of U.S. government: the military, the judiciary, and state and local governments.

The Military

The U.S. Army, Navy, and Air Force are made up of approximately 1.4 million individuals. The president is commander in chief of the U.S. military, but on a day-to-day basis, U.S. forces serve under the command of a nonpolitical officers corps made up primarily of graduates of the nation's military academies.

Because of the unique geographic advantages of the United States, the military has had to dedicate few of its resources to defending U.S. territory. In the nineteenth century, its primary responsibilities were to defend U.S. shipping on the high seas and to colonize the West. In the twentieth century, U.S. troops have seen more service abroad. Beginning with the new U.S. geopolitical role after World War II, the military was given new responsibilities to support U.S. multilateral and regional defense agreements. In the 1990s, the U.S. military was committed to multilateral military operations and United Nations peacekeeping efforts. In Kosovo, for example, the North Atlantic Treaty Organization (NATO) sought to remove President Milosevic from power in response to his government's attacks on ethnic Albanians. The United States committed 31,600 troops to the NATO force of approximately 114,000. These troops were supported by a U.S. aircraft carrier battle group. U.S. involvement in multilateral military operations and UN peacekeeping efforts is highly controversial among the American public and some members of Congress, but it is happening with sufficient frequency to suggest that it will be an ongoing responsibility.

The United States increasingly looks to its allies to support U.S. military objectives abroad. In preparation for war with Iraq in 2003, U.S. military leaders designed an invasion force numbering approximately 130,000, with 100,000 ground troops and the remainder in support positions abroad. These 100,000 U.S. military ground troops were supported by at least 15,000 British ground troops. This military force was much smaller than the 500,000 troops marshaled in the 1991 Gulf War. New technologies such as advanced cruise missiles and precision bombs launched from U.S. military aircraft reduced the need for ground troops.

As was the pattern in the civilian bureaucracy in the 1990s, the military saw its size reduced. Military personnel in the armed forces numbered approximately 2 million in 1990. By 2000, this number had declined to approximately 1.4 million. Many of the traditional responsibilities of the military, such as support of troops and specialized technical activities, have been transferred to reserve units. Reserve troops are now called to active duty more frequently and for longer periods. This pattern, exacerbated since September 11, has made it more difficult to recruit and retain reserve troops.

With the increased expectations for the military came increased reliance on defense technologies. U.S. nuclear weapons, intelligence technologies, and space-based defense technologies, as well as the maintenance of conventional weaponry and troop support, have significantly raised the cost of maintaining the military. This has led to ongoing national debates about the cost of the military and whether defense resources should be expended for technology or for troops. Industries have emerged to provide goods and services to the military. Proposals to cut defense spending often face opposition from these industries.

In response to the September 11 attacks, the president quickly proposed and Congress appropriated a record increase in defense spending of more than 10 percent, from approximately $330 billion to $380 billion. These new funds include pay raises for the U.S. troops, resources to expand the size of the military, and the creation of a reserve fund for a possible sustained military engagement abroad. A considerable share, however—as much as a third of the increase— is dedicated to grants to state and local governments for homeland security. These funds will provide operating funds to local police and fire and rescue departments. While U.S. policy-makers have long used the military budget to support the domestic economy (military base placement, for example), this $15 billion in new commitments represents an unprecedented new use of the defense budget to support state and local activities.

The Judiciary

Of the three branches of federal government, the courts are the most poorly defined in the Constitution. Initially, it was unclear what check the courts had on other branches of government. Equally important, the courts were quite dependent on the president, who appointed judges, and on Congress, which approved the nomination of judges and set the jurisdictional authority for the courts. The early days of the federal courts confirmed this weakness. In the Judiciary Act of 1789, Congress created a Supreme Court and a network of lower federal courts—thirteen district courts and three circuit courts. Judges, who often had to travel from city to city

to hear cases, saw a higher turnover in its early years than in any subsequent period of American history.

In 1803, the Supreme Court established the foundation for a more substantial role in federal policy-making. It ruled in *Marbury* **v.** *Madison* that the courts inherently had the right to review the constitutionality of the laws. This ruling, though used rarely in the nineteenth century, gave the judiciary a central place in the system of **checks and balances.** The Court that ruled in *Marbury* v. *Madison* recognized the weakness of the federal courts in this era. While asserting their power to review the constitutionality of a piece of federal legislation, the substantive effect of the ruling was to give a political victory to the sitting president, Thomas Jefferson, against the partisan and ideological interests of a majority of the members of the Court. The majority of the Court at the time had been nominated to the federal bench by political opponents of Jefferson. Had the same justices ruled against President Jefferson, he would likely have disregarded this ruling and demonstrated the fundamental weakness of the federal courts.

Even with the power of judicial review, the judicial branch remained weaker than the other branches. In addition to Congress's ability to establish court jurisdiction in nonconstitutional cases and the president's ability to fill the courts with people of his choosing, the courts have other weaknesses. They must rely on the executive branch to enforce their decisions. Enforcement proves particularly difficult when a court's rulings are not in line with public opinion, such as when the courts ruled that organized prayer did not belong in the public schools or that busing should be used as a tool to accomplish racial integration in the schools. The courts' own rules have also limited their powers. Traditionally, the courts limit standing—the ability to bring suits—to those who are individually affected by some action of government.

Beginning in the second half of the twentieth century, the federal courts gained power relative to the other branches of government. In part, this was accomplished by expanding the rules of standing and by maintaining longer jurisdiction over cases as a tool to establish limited enforcement abilities. The courts also gained relative power because of the expansion of federal regulatory policy. Unclear laws and regulations, often requiring technical expertise to implement, placed the courts at the center of many policy debates. The courts have also gained power because they became a venue for individuals and groups in society whose interests were neglected by the democratically elected institutions but who could make claims based on constitutional guarantees of civil rights or civil liberties. African Americans, for example, received favorable rulings from federal courts before Congress and the president responded to their demands. Similarly, courts expanded protections to federal prisoners in the 1960s and 1970s (before reversing themselves). The courts have become the primary venue for seeking remedies to the denial of civil liberties. Since the September 11 attacks, when the executive branch and majorities in Congress have manifested a willingness to limit individual rights in a search for collective security, several courts have challenged the detention procedures used by the Bush administration to detain Arab immigrants and combatants detained in Afghanistan. Each of these rulings has been overturned on appeal, but the courts remain the most likely venue to challenge post–September 11 challenges to civil liberties and due process.

The steady increase in judicial power in the twentieth century should not obscure the fundamental weaknesses of the courts relative to the elected branches. Although courts in some cases have been able to establish connections with the citizenry around specific issues, the courts are more dependent on the elected branches than the elected branches are on them.

Subnational Government

State governments serve as an important part of government in the United States. Their responsibilities include providing services to people more directly than does the federal government. Most important among these is education, which has always been a state and local responsibility in the United States. Until the New Deal era, state and local governments served as the primary point of interaction between the citizenry and the government.

States and localities continue to serve a critical function in contemporary U.S. governance. They are able to experiment with new policies. If a policy fails in a single state, the cost is much lower than if the entire nation had undertaken a new policy that eventually failed. Successes in one state can be copied in others

or nationally. For example, Wisconsin experimented with welfare reform in the early 1990s before the federal government changed national welfare laws in 1996. In the Wisconsin experiment, the state limited the amount of time that a household could receive welfare benefits, particularly Aid to Families with Dependent Children (AFDC), which provided food subsidies to households with incomes below designated levels. In exchange, Wisconsin dedicated additional resources to training welfare recipients for work and to finding them jobs (though none were guaranteed). Wisconsin also lowered AFDC benefits for welfare recipients who moved to Wisconsin from states with lower benefits. Policy-makers outside Wisconsin saw these reforms as a success and implemented similar (though more draconian) reforms nationally. Had these reforms not been perceived to be successful in Wisconsin, they would not have become the model for federal welfare reform, and the cost of experimentation would have been confined to Wisconsin. Even after the implementation of this reform, Wisconsin spends far more than many other states on social welfare programs. The governor of Wisconsin who led this state-level reform, Tommy Thompson, was appointed secretary of health and human services in the Bush administration.

In addition to state governments, citizens pay taxes to and receive services from an array of local governments that include such entities as counties, cities, districts for special services such as water and fire protection, and townships. These local entities have a different relationship to the states, however, than do states to the federal government. The local entities are statutory creations of the state and can be altered or eliminated by the state. In 2002, for example, Los Angeles voters considered (and rejected) a ballot measure that could have divided Los Angeles into as many as four separate cities. Thus, local governments have no independent constitutional standing (and are not a form of federalism).

Local governments are nevertheless very important in the system of American governance. They provide many of the direct services that the citizenry gets from the government. Most important among these is public education, which has traditionally been the responsibility of local governments. Because states and localities have different resources (often based on local property taxes) and different visions of the responsibilities of government, people in the United States can receive vastly different versions of the same government service depending simply on where they live. Again, education provides an example. Property tax–poor areas can spend just a few thousand dollars per year educating students while property tax–rich areas can spend $15,000 to $20,000 per student. Some states try to equalize education spending within the state, while others see disparities this great within the state, but there is no national effort, or constitutional authority, to equalize spending across states.

The Policy-Making Process

Separation of powers and constitutional limits on each branch of government create a federal policy-making process with no clear starting or ending point. Instead, citizens and organized interests have multiple points of entry and can contest outcomes through multiple venues. There is little centralization of policy-making except in a few areas where there is consensus among national leaders. Without centralization, policies often conflict with each other (for example, the United States currently subsidizes tobacco cultivation but seeks to hamper tobacco companies from selling cigarettes through high taxes, health warnings, and limits on advertising). Federalism further complicates policy-making. Each of the states sets policy in many areas, and states often have contradictory policies. State policy-making institutions are often used strategically to shape the debate around an issue or to influence other states or the federal government. In sum, policy advocates have many venues in which to propose new policies or change existing policies: congressional committees, individual members of Congress, executive branch regulatory agencies, state governments, and, in some states, direct ballot initiatives.

With so many entrance points, there are equally many points at which policies can be blocked. Once Congress passes a law, executive branch agencies must issue regulations to explain specifically how the law will be implemented. Subtle changes can be inserted as part of this process. On controversial issues, cabinet secretaries and other senior appointees set policy for the writing of regulations. Laws that must be imple-

mented by several agencies raise a possible role for the cabinet to craft government-wide solutions to policy needs, but recent presidents have not used the cabinet as a whole to structure policy-making in this way.

Furthermore, people or interest groups that feel disadvantaged by the regulations can contest regulations in the courts. They also can contest the law itself, if the assertion can be made that the law is unconstitutional or conflicts with another law or with state government responsibilities. Once a policy is in place, it can be opposed or undermined by creating a competing policy in another agency or at the state level.

The Constitution gives no guidance about the origins and outcomes of policy initiatives. The president is directed to present an annual report to Congress on the state of the nation. Over time, this has evolved into an organized set of policy proposals. In the absence of presidential leadership in policy-making, Congress partially filled the void. Enumerated powers in the Constitution direct Congress to take action in specific policy areas, such as setting tax policy, establishing a post office, and building public roads. Once Congress established committees to increase its efficiency (see Section 4), these committees offered forums for discussion of narrow policy areas of importance to society. These committees, however, are not mandated in the Constitution and are changed to reflect the policy needs of each era. Thus, while presidents can propose policies (and implement them), only Congress has the ability to deliberate about policy and pass it into law.

The courts have long provided a forum for debating the outcome of policy decisions but have rarely initiated policies on their own. Beginning in the 1970s, however, some federal courts experimented with initiating policy as a way of maintaining jurisdiction in cases brought before them. These efforts, such as court-mandated busing of public school students to achieve racial integration and control of state prison or mental health care systems, spurred much national controversy and caused the judiciary to decline in public opinion. Today, the courts are much more likely to block or reshape policies than to initiate them.

Because there is no clear starting point for initiating policies, individual citizens have great difficulty when they seek to advocate a new policy. Into this void have come extragovernmental institutions, some with narrow interests and some promoting collective interests. Prominent or wealthy individuals or groups can get Congress's or the president's attention through campaign contributions and other types of influence in support for their candidacies and the causes they support.

Mediating institutions have also emerged to represent mass interests. Political parties, organized on a mass basis in the 1830s, organize citizen demands and channel them to political leaders. The parties balance the needs of various interests in society and come as close as any other group in society to presenting comprehensive policy proposals (often summarized in the parties' platforms). Group-based interests also organize to make narrow demands. Veterans are an early example of a group in society that made a group-specific demand on federal policy-making. In the twentieth century, as both federal and state governments began to implement more widespread distributive and redistributive policies, more organized interest groups appeared. These interest groups have become the dominant form of mediating institution in U.S. politics (see Section 4). Unlike political parties, however, interest groups represent only a single issue or group or narrowly related issues. Thus, the complexity of policy-making in the United States has created an equally complex structure of making demands.

Section ❹ Representation and Participation

The Legislature

Of the three branches in the federal government, the founders envisioned that Congress would be at the center and would be the most powerful. They concentrated the most important powers in it and were most explicit about its responsibilities. For most of the nation's history, their expectations for the powers of Congress have been met.

One of the most important compromises of the Constitutional Convention involved the structure of Congress. States with large populations wanted seats in the national legislature to be allocated based on population. Small states feared they would be at a disadvantage under this system and wanted each state to have equal representation. The compromise was a **bicameral** system with two houses, one allocated by population—the House of Representatives—and the other with equal representation for each state—the Senate. This compromise has remained largely uncontested for the past two hundred years despite the growing gap in population between large and small states. Today, for example, the 494,000 residents of Wyoming elect two senators, the same number elected by the more than 35 million residents of California. The senatorial vote of each resident of Wyoming has seventy times the impact of each Californian.

These two legislative bodies are structured differently. The House has 435 members (a number that has been fixed since 1910) and is designed to be more responsive to the popular will. Terms are short (two years) and the districts are smaller than Senate seats except in the smallest states. After 2000, the average House seat had 646,952 constituents and will continue to grow. The Senate has only 100 members and is designed to be more deliberative, with six-year, staggered terms. Although unlikely, it is possible every two years to vote out an entire House of Representatives; the Senate could see only one-third of its members unseated any election year.

Membership in the U.S. Congress is slightly more diverse than the people who have held the presidency, though most members of Congress are white male Protestants. In the 1990s, approximately 12 percent of officeholders were women, 9 percent were African American, 4 percent were Latino, and 0.5 percent were Asian American. Most members of Congress, regardless of gender, race, or ethnicity, are highly educated professionals. Lawyer is the most common profession. The Senate is less diverse: one member is Native American, no Latinos or African Americans have been elected since the early 1990s, and only thirteen women served in the Senate between 2000 and 2002.

The two central powers of Congress are legislation and oversight. For a bill to become law, it must be passed in the same form by both the House and the Senate and signed by the president. Equally important, Congress has the ability to monitor the implementation of laws that it passes. Since it continues to control the appropriation of funds for programs each year (all government spending must begin with an appropriations bill in the House of Representatives), Congress can oversee programs being administered by the executive branch and shape their implementation through allocations of money or by rewriting the law.

Congress has organized itself to increase its efficiency. Discussion and debate take place primarily in committees and subcommittees. The committee system permits each member to specialize in specific areas of public policy, often areas that are of interest to their constituents or key supporters. Committees are organized topically, and members often seek to serve on committees that are of particular interest to their constituencies—for instance, a member of Congress from a rural area may seek to serve on the Agriculture Committee. All members seek to serve on committees that have broad oversight of a wide range of government activities, such as the Appropriations Committee through which all spending bills must pass. Specialization allows each member to have some influence while not requiring that she or he know the substance of all facets of government.

For a bill to become law, it must be reviewed by the committee and subcommittee that have responsibility for the substantive area that it covers. When a member proposes a bill, it is referred to committee based on the subject matter of the legislation and usually never gets any further. In each session, relatively few bills are given hearings before a subcommittee or committee. The House and Senate leadership (the Speaker of the House, the Senate majority leader, and committee chairs) are central to deciding which bills receive hearings. If the bill receives support from the committee, it must then be debated by the body as a whole. In the House, this may never occur because that institution has another roadblock: the Rules Committee, which determines what can be debated on the floor and under what terms. Only in the Senate can debate be unlimited (though even it can be limited by cloture, a vote of sixty senators to limit debate). These hierarchical structures strengthen the powers granted to the House and the Senate in the Constitution because they allow Congress to act efficiently and to use its powers to investigate federal programs, even though it does not administer these programs. As a result, Congress

places itself at the center of the policy-making process. When Woodrow Wilson, in his years as a political scientist before he ran for president, studied U.S. government, he saw Congress as the central branch of government and the committee system as its central organizational tool.[7] Although congressional power waned somewhat in the late twentieth century, it remains the foremost branch of American government.

This tension between the constitutional powers of Congress and the national focus on the president as the national leader became evident in the federal government's response to the September 11 attacks. Initially, President Bush shaped the public policy response, including a large emergency appropriation that included financial assistance for New York City, grants and loans to the airlines, and an increase in defense and intelligence spending and military action against Afghanistan. Congress quickly followed the presidential lead and appropriated funds, federalized airport security screening, and supported military action in Afghanistan that targeted the al Qaeda movement that took responsibility for the September 11 attacks and the Taliban government that provided a safe haven for al Qaeda.

As Bush administration policies evolved and the response came to focus on structural changes in the federal government, however, Congress began to reassert its constitutional prerogatives. It forced the president to seek and obtain congressional approval for any U.S. military action against Iraq. Congressional concern about the growth in executive power after September 11 was probably most evident in its reaction to Bush administration proposals to reorganize more than fifty federal agencies into the cabinet-level Department of Homeland Security. In addition to centralizing many (but not all) federal agencies with responsibilities for domestic intelligence collection and public safety, the Bush administration sought to fundamentally shift the protections federal workers in this new agency would have. The selection of federal agencies with responsibilities for security to exclude from the new department (most notably the Federal Bureau of Investigation) reflected White House sensitivities to agencies with strong support in Congress that would, though logically placed in the new agency, make it less likely to receive congressional approval. Democrats, and perhaps some Republicans, in Congress feared that granting the new Department of Homeland Security an exemption from worker civil service protections would make the new agency more subject to political pressures. When combined with its intelligence gathering and law enforcement responsibilities, this gave many in Congress concerns about the growth of executive power. With the election of a Republican senatorial majority in the 2002 elections, Congress did establish the Department of Homeland Security under the terms that President Bush proposed, but Congress is likely to continue to seek to limit the growth in executive branch powers. Congress has also manifested second thoughts about the federalization of airport security.

As congressional responses to presidential leadership on the U.S. response to September 11 should indicate, Congress did not sit idly by as the president gained power. It passed legislation to undermine presidential power and, equally important, applied its traditional authority to investigate federal programs to the president. Beginning with Watergate (the Nixon administration scandals in which Nixon and his aides used the institutions of the federal government to investigate and intimidate Nixon's political opponents), Congress directly investigated presidents. Congress also created a legal structure, the independent counsel, whereby the executive branch is forced to investigate itself. Although the statutory authority to appoint independent counsels expired in the late 1990s, in part in response to perceptions that independent counsels—and particularly Kenneth Starr, who investigated President Clinton—were overstepping their statutory authority, the precedent has been laid. Perceived criminal and ethical lapses by the executive branch will continue to be investigated, and presidents will pay a political price in declining popularity.

These investigations of presidents and their senior appointees weaken the connection between the presidency and the people (regardless of the specific charges being investigated or the outcome of the investigation). Investigations of Presidents Nixon and Clinton to determine charges for impeachment can be seen in terms of congressional efforts to weaken not just the presidents as individuals but the presidency as an office.

Political Parties and the Party System

Electoral politics in the United States is organized around two political parties. The roots of two-party politics can be found both in the nation's political culture and in the legal structures that govern elections. Today, the two major parties are the Democrats and the Republicans. The Democrats can trace their origins to the 1800 election, while the Republicans first appeared in 1856. Despite the fact that today's parties have consistently competed against each other in each of the past thirty-seven presidential elections, the coalitions that support them (and which they, in turn, serve) have changed continually.

Today, the Republicans depend on a coalition of upper-income voters, moral and religious conservatives, small-business owners, residents of rural areas, and evangelical Christians. They receive more support from men than from women and are strongest in the South and the Mountain West. The Republicans have tried to make inroads in minority communities but have been largely unsuccessful with the exception of Cuban Americans and some Asian American groups (see Table 1). President Bush has sought to bring a higher share of the Latino vote into the Republican fold. Although he was modestly successful when running for governor of Texas, his presidential campaign in 2000 succeeded only in returning the Republican share of the Latino vote to levels achieved by Ronald Reagan and George H. W. Bush in the 1980s and early 1990s. For Republicans to win Latino (or African American) votes on a wider scale, the party would have to be willing to alienate some core Republican constituencies.[8]

The contemporary Democratic coalition includes urban populations, the elderly, racial and ethnic minorities, owners of export-oriented businesses, unionized labor, and increasingly working women. Suburban voters have increasingly joined the Democratic coalition. Though diminished, this coalition formed in the 1930s in response to New Deal programs promoted by President Franklin D. Roosevelt, a Democrat. Today's Democrats are strongest in urban areas, in the Northeast, and on the West Coast. The Democrats have built a steady advantage among women voters. This is a double advantage for the Democrats: women have higher turnout rates than do men, and men split their votes more evenly.

The Democrats have maintained a steady dominance over the Republicans in terms of registration. Approximately 35 percent of registered voters are Democrats, 30 percent are Republicans, and 35 percent

Table 1

Candidate Vote in Presidential Elections, by Race and Ethnicity, 1976–2000 (in percentages)

	Whites	Blacks	Hispanics	Asian Americans
1976				
Carter (D)	47	83	76	n.a.
Ford (R)	52	16	24	n.a.
1980				
Reagan (R)	56	11	33	n.a.
Carter (D)	36	85	59	n.a.
Anderson (I)	7	3	6	n.a.
1984				
Reagan (R)	64	9	37	n.a.
Mondale (D)	35	90	62	n.a.
1988				
Bush (R)	59	12	30	n.a.
Dukakis (D)	40	86	69	n.a.
1992				
Clinton (D)	39	83	61	31
Bush (R)	40	10	25	55
Perot (I)	20	7	14	15
1996				
Clinton (D)	43	84	72	43
Dole (R)	46	12	21	48
Perot (I)	9	4	6	8
2000				
Bush (R)	54	8	31	41
Gore (D)	42	90	67	54
Nader (I)	3	1	2	4

Note: Data were not collected on Asian Americans until 1992. Data do not always add up to 100 because of votes for other candidates.

Source: Copyright © 2000 by the *New York Times*. Reprinted with permission.

are independent. Generally, Democrats, who are more likely to be poor, less educated, and younger than Republican voters, are less likely to turn out on Election Day. As a result, the Republicans have been the dominant party at the presidential level since 1968 and have had a slight advantage in governorships and state legislatures. After the 2002 election, the Republicans controlled governorships in twenty-six states, and the Democrats controlled twenty-four. The majority of members of the House of Representatives have been Republican since 1994. In 2003, the Republicans have a 229-to-205 majority (with one independent voting with the Democrats on organizational matters). The Republicans hold a two-vote majority in the Senate, but majority-control of that body has been somewhat fluid. The 2000 election left the Senate in a 50-50 tie (Republicans had made up the majority of the Senate since 1994). Since Republican Vice President Dick Cheney would be able to break ties in the Republicans' favor, the Republicans organized the majority (which gave Republican Senators key leadership roles). In May 2001, however, Republican Senator James Jeffords of Vermont switched his affiliation to independent and began to vote with the Democrats on organizational matters, giving Democrats leadership in the Senate.

The relative Republican advantage in holding federal offices in the last two decades of the twentieth century may be changing at this writing. Internal conflicts in the Democratic Party in the 1970s and 1980s limited its ability to present a cohesive message and reach out to new constituencies. As a result, it was not able to recruit new followers at rates comparable to the Republicans. These conflicts—particularly disputes over the size and scope of government, affirmative action (programs designed to redress past discrimination against racial and ethnic minorities and women) and other race-sensitive programs, and taxation and the deficit—subsided during the Clinton presidency and have remained quiet since he completed his term. Beginning in the 1990s, internal conflicts grew in the Republican Party. Moral conservatives and fiscal conservatives each wanted the party to focus on their interests and jettison the others' issues as a way of expanding the party's base of support. The future of each party's coalition is unclear at this writing, though it is worth noting that Democrats are more successful in the parts of the country seeing population growth (particularly suburbs of major cities) than are Republicans. The Republicans have begun to see growth in support in the so-called exurbs, or areas in transition from rural to suburban on the fringes or metropolitan areas.

These party divisions lead to speculation that new

parties might emerge. The political culture of the United States limits the likelihood that a faction of one of the parties (such as the religious right from the Republicans) will break off and form a party that competes in election after election. Instead, two coalitional parties are the norm.

Electoral law reinforces this situation. Most U.S. elections are conducted under a **single-member plurality (SMP) election system.** The candidate who wins the most votes wins the election, and only one person is elected from each district. One common variant is a single-member majoritarian system, in which a candidate must win a majority of votes cast (used primarily in the South as a tool to reduce the likelihood of African Americans' getting elected when the white vote divides). Single-member district-based elections (whether plurality or majoritarian) reward coalitional parties and diminish opportunities for single-issue parties or narrowly focused parties, such as the Green Party in today's politics (see "Citizen Action: The Green Party"). Broad coalitional parties can contest a seat election after election, while smaller parties are likely to dissolve after a number of defeats. Finally, since the existing parties have written the electoral laws in each of the states (the laws vary dramatically from state to state), they have made it difficult for new parties to get on the ballot.

Geography reinforces the difficulty faced by small and single-issue parties in an SMP system. There are more than 600,000 elected offices in the United States. To compete regularly in even a small percentage of these, a party must have a national presence and a national infrastructure. Most third parties fail long before they are able to compete in more than a few hundred of these 600,000 races. Despite rapid growth over the past fifteen years, for example, the Green Party fielded candidates in just one-tenth of one percent of offices nationwide in 2002 and held just 3 of every 10,000 elective offices.

Thus, it is unlikely that a new major party will emerge in the United States. Much more than in countries with proportional representation, the electoral law in the United States limits the ability of new parties to emerge and, if they do, to survive. Both the political culture and the geography of the United States, however, make this unlikely. The heterogeneity of the U.S. population and the range of regional needs and interests advantage a system that forces coalitions prior to elections, as does a system with just two political parties. The Constitution-driven inefficiency of U.S. government would become all the more dramatic if multiple parties (rather than two that must, by their nature, be coalitions) were competing in legislatures to shape outcomes.

Elections

The United States takes pride in its long practice of democracy. As an example of its commitment to democratic norms, it points to the frequency of elections and the range of offices filled through elections. As is not the case in parliamentary systems, these elections are conducted on a regular schedule: presidential elections every four years, Senate elections every six years, House of Representatives elections every two years. States and localities set the terms of state and local offices, but almost all have fixed terms. (Local judicial offices in some states are the rare exception.) General elections for federal offices are held the first Tuesday after the first Monday in November. States and localities establish dates for primary elections and for general elections for nonfederal offices. Thus, while elections are regularly scheduled, there are frequently multiple elections in the same year.

Fundamental to understanding U.S. elections is federalism. States set the rules for conducting elections and for who can participate and how votes are counted. When the nation was founded, this authority was almost complete, since the Constitution said little about elections. At the nation's founding, most states limited electoral participation to white male landholders. By the 1830s, many states had reduced or eliminated the property-holding requirement, in part in response to the emergence of competitive political parties that sought to build their memberships.

Further expansion of the U.S. electorate required the intervention of the federal government and amendment of the Constitution. The first of the efforts to nationalize electoral rules was initially a failure. This was the effort to extend the franchise to African Americans after the Civil War through the Fourteenth and Fifteenth Amendments. More successful was the Nineteenth Amendment, ratified in 1920, which extended the vote to women.[9] The Civil War amendments finally

Citizen Action: *The Green Party*

In 2000, the Green Party recruited a prominent consumer advocate and social critic, Ralph Nader, to head its ticket. Nader's national reputation as an advocate for consumer safety, governmental efficiency, and the power of mass interests over corporate interests indicated that the Green Party had achieved a new level of prominence. Nader ran a serious national campaign that challenged the two dominant parties in each of the fifty states in a way that a less prominent candidate (particularly one with few campaign contributions) could have. Although the parties used their control over the mechanisms of national campaigns, such as the presidential debates, to exclude Nader, he presented the Green Party in a positive light.

Arguably, Nader's candidacy also determined the outcome of the election. Exit polling indicated that had the Green Party not been on the presidential ballot in Florida, Nader's 97,488 Florida voters would have given Vice President Gore at least a two-to-one margin. These 32,000 extra Gore votes would have shifted his narrow defeat to a solid victory and would have given him Florida's electoral college votes and the presidency.

Because the Green Party is small, it has not had to develop a comprehensive platform that links all its candidates and supporters. It has identified ten key values that guide its agenda: grassroots democracy, social justice, ecological wisdom, nonviolence, decentralization, community-based economics, feminism, diversity, responsibility, and a focus on the future. Individual candidates or state parties emphasize some of these objectives over others. To the extent that Green Party candidates tap these key values, they are likely to draw more support from traditional Democratic voters than from traditional Republican voters. Green Party leaders express the hope that this agenda will draw new voters into U.S. elections, though there has been little evidence that this hope is being realized.

The Green Party has seen a steady growth in the number of candidates it runs in elections, the levels of office these candidates compete for, and the number of Green candidates who win election. Beginning with just three candidates in two states (none of whom won election) in 1985, the Greens fielded 547 candidates in 2002. These candidates competed for election in forty states and included candidates for election to all levels of office, including U.S. senator, U.S. House of Representatives, and governor. Seventy of these candidates won, though the victors tended to be candidates for local-level offices. Approximately 200 Green Party members hold elective office in 2003. California is the state with the largest number of Green Party officeholders, making up approximately one-third of Green Party officeholders nationwide.

Despite the Green Party's steady increase in the number of candidates running for office, the levels of office for which they are running, and the number who are winning, the party faces the limits that all third parties face in U.S. elections. In 2002, they fielded candidates for less than one-tenth of 1 percent of elective offices in the United States and saw their candidates holding just 3 of every 10,000 elective offices. While some of these campaigns are able to speak to a large share of the American public (as Ralph Nader's presidential campaign did), the party is, for the most part, dependent on individual candidates running in seats with no competition for its successes. At this writing, it seems unlikely that the party will be able to grow to compete routinely for more than a handful of seats and, as a result, will maintain the spoiler role that it played in 2000. Should it begin to see greater success in the electorate, it would still probably not become a dominant party. Instead, one of the existing parties—most likely the Democrats in the case of the Greens—would be likely to absorb some of the Green Party's key issues into its agenda.

had an impact with the passage of the Voting Rights Act (VRA) in 1965, which secured African Americans access to the ballot box. In 1975, Congress extended the VRA to other ethnic and racial groups who had previously seen their right to vote abridged based on their origin or ancestry: Hispanics, Asian Americans, Native Americans, and Alaskan Natives. The Twenty-Sixth Amendment gave the vote to all citizens between the ages of eighteen and twenty in 1971.

States continue to be able to regulate individual participation in elections through their control of the registration process. This process prescreens potential voters to make sure that they meet the state's requirements for voting, usually residence in the state and the jurisdiction for a set amount of time and the absence of felony convictions. While this may appear minimal and necessary to prevent voter fraud such as an individual's voting multiple times in the same election, the requirement to register in advance of the election prevents many from being able to vote.[10] In 1993, Congress sought to expand opportunities for registration by requiring the distribution of voter registration materials at certain state agencies such as motor vehicle offices (hence, the designation "motor voter" legislation). While not as sweeping in impact as the VRA, motor voter was a continuing effort to nationalize the rules for voting.

There is a second consequence of federalism on U.S. elections: the responsibility for holding elections, deciding which nonfederal offices are filled through elections, and determining how long nonfederal office-holders will serve before again having to be elected is the responsibility of the states and, if the states delegate the power, to localities. Thus, a local office that is elected in one state could be an appointed office in another. Terms for state and local offices, such as governors, vary. Elections are held at different points throughout the year. In states that have primary elections to determine each party's candidates, the primary can be just a month before the general election or as many as ten months before.

Finally, federalism shapes elections by delegating to the states responsibilities for determining how votes are collected and how they are counted, even in elections to national office. This became evident to the nation as a result of the controversy after the 2000 elections. Florida allowed local jurisdictions to design ballots, select voting machines, and establish rules for counting the ballots. One of the most controversial design decisions was Palm Beach County's "butterfly ballot," which led many voters who thought they were casting their vote for Al Gore actually to vote for Pat Buchanan. The several legal challenges filed by the Gore and Bush campaigns in state and federal courts after the elections focused on questions of the legality and constitutionality of ballot designs, counting rules, and deadlines established by Florida counties and the state.

What are the consequences of this federalist system of elections? At a minimum, it leads to confusion and burnout among potential voters. Many voters are unaware of elections that are not held on the same schedule

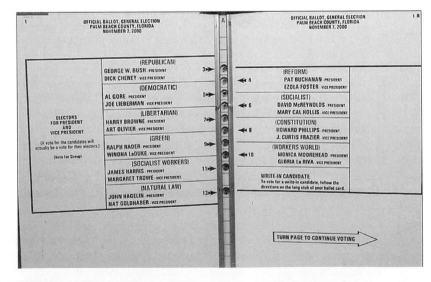

The confusing design of Palm Beach, Florida's, presidential ballot appears to have caused more than 3,000 Gore supporters to vote for Pat Buchanan. Had Gore won these votes, he would have won the presidency. *Source:* © Gary Rothstein/ Getty Images.

as national elections (with the general election in November). Others who are aware become overloaded with electoral responsibilities in jurisdictions that have frequent elections and so choose not to participate in local races.

One result of this decentralized system with a legacy of group-based exclusion is that increasing numbers of citizens do not vote. In the late 1800s, for example, turnout in national elections often exceeded 80 percent of those eligible to vote, and the poor participated at rates comparable to the rich. In 1996, turnout in the presidential election dropped below 50 percent (rising to 51 percent in 2000). In state and local races, turnouts in the range of 10 to 20 percent are the norm. Perhaps more important, turnout varies dramatically among different groups in society. The poor are less likely to vote than the rich, the young less likely than the old, and the less educated less likely than the more educated.[11] Because blacks and Hispanics are more likely to be poor and less likely to have high levels of formal education, they are less likely to vote than are whites. Hence, political institutions are less likely to hear their demands and respond to their needs.

These class- and age-driven differences in participation are not entirely the result of federalism and variation in the rules for individual participation and the conduct of elections. Declining party competitiveness also plays a role. Nevertheless, it is important to observe that the steady elimination of formal group-based exclusion has been replaced by the informal exclusion of the majority of some groups, such as African Americans and Hispanics. Thus, despite the expansion of the electorate to almost all adults, the nation has yet to live up to its democratic ideals. Many adults continue not to participate.

This declining participation should not obscure the dramatic changes in leadership and issues addressed that result from elections. The 1994 elections saw an unprecedented increase in Republican members of the House of Representatives that allowed Republicans to take control of the House for the first time in forty years. Republicans also took control of the Senate in that year and were able to pass legislation that dramatically changed the nation's welfare system and slowed the growth of the federal government. In 1998, Democrats unexpectedly gained seats in the sixth year of a presidential term by a member of their party. This gain in representation in the House of Representatives in the sixth year of a presidential term was the first such gain since 1822. This victory ensured the Senate's acquittal of President Clinton in his impeachment trial. In 2002, Republicans bucked a historical trend and gained seats at the midpoint of the presidential term of a member of their party. This was the first time since 1934 that the

Despite a steady liberalization of rules on who can vote, voting rates in the United States have declined for the past 100 years.
Source: By permission of Gary Varvel and Creators Syndicate, Inc.

party controlling the presidency won seats in the House of Representatives in the off-year election following its election to the presidency (see Figure 4). The long-term consequences of this victory cannot be gauged at this writing, but at a minimum, this Republican victory ensured the creation of the Department of Homeland Security and the confirmation of a large number of conservative judges to the federal courts who would not otherwise have been confirmed.

Political Culture, Citizenship, and Identity

The United States is a large nation with distinct regional cultures, ongoing immigration leading to distinct languages and cultures, class divisions, and a history of denying many Americans their civil rights. Despite these cleavages, the United States has maintained almost from its first days a set of core political values that have served to unify the majority of the citizenry. These values are liberty, equality, and democracy.

Liberty, as it is used in discussions of U.S. political culture, refers to liberty from restrictions imposed by

government. A tangible form of this notion of liberty appears in the Bill of Rights, the first ten amendments to the U.S. Constitution, which provide for the rights of free speech, free assembly, free practice of religion, and the absence of cruel and unusual punishment. Support for liberty takes a second form: support for economic liberty and free enterprise. Property rights and contract rights, for example, are protected at several places in the Constitution. Furthermore, Congress, not the states, which were perceived by the framers as to likely to serve mass interests, is empowered to regulate commerce.

Clearly, these liberties are not mutually exclusive. Protections of the Bill of Rights often conflict with each other: economic liberties reward some in the society at the cost of economic opportunities for others. Nevertheless, the idea that citizens should be free to pursue their beliefs and their economic objectives with only limited government interference has been a unifying element in U.S. political culture.

Equality is the second unifying American political value. In the Declaration of Independence, it is "self-evident" that "all men are created equal." Nevertheless, at various times in the nation's history, women, Native Americans, African Americans, Mexican Americans, Chinese Americans, Japanese Americans, and immigrants have been excluded from membership in the polity and, consequently, from access to this equality. But each of the excluded groups, such as African Americans during the civil rights movement, has used the widespread belief in equality to organize and demand that the nation live up to its ideals.

It is important to observe what this belief in equality is not. The equality that has long been sought is equality of opportunity, not equality of result, such as that sought in the communist states. There is support for the notion that people should have an equal opportunity to compete for economic rewards, not that they should end up at the same point.

The final unifying value is democracy. Throughout the nation's history, there has been a belief that government is legitimate only to the degree that it reflects the popular will. As with the notion of equality, the pool of citizens whose voices should be heard has changed over time, from white male property holders at the time of the founding to most citizen adults today (convicted felons are excluded from the franchise in many

Figure 4

Party Control of the U.S. House of Representatives, 1930–2003

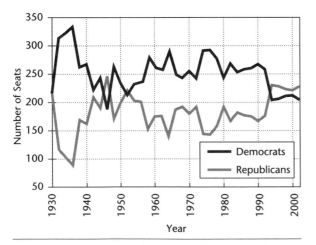

Source: Author's compilation based on U.S. House of Representatives, Office of the Clerk. http://clerk.house.gov/histHigh/Congressional_History/partyDiv.php (accessed November 27, 2002).

states). Nevertheless, excluded populations have continually sought to influence the polity.

These values are still at the heart of contemporary political debates. Leaders have marshaled these values throughout the nation's history to reduce potential cleavages in U.S. society. Since the United States cannot look to a common ethnicity of its people (as, for example, Germany can), to a sovereign with a historical tie to the citizenry (as in a monarchy), or to a purported common religion or ideology among its citizens (as does Iran or Cuba), the belief in these values has been used to unify the diverse peoples of the United States.[12] Voluntary membership based on belief in this creed serves to unify the disparate peoples of the United States.

Interests, Social Movements, and Protest

In the United States, political participation has long included activities other than elections and party politics. In the nation's story about its origins, protest proves central; the Revolution was spurred by acts of civil disobedience such as the Boston Tea Party. Similarly, protest and social movements repeatedly forced the nation to live up to its democratic ideals. From the woman's suffrage movement of the nineteenth century to the civil rights movement of the 1950s and 1960s, people defined as being outside the democratic community organized to demand that they be included. The success of these movements was enhanced by their ability to tap the political values discussed in the previous section.

These protest movements have also been able to tap the willingness of Americans to become involved in collective action. First chronicled by a visitor from France in the 1830s, Alexis de Tocqueville, this volunteerism and civic involvement have long been identified as stronger in the U.S. democracy than in other advanced democracies.

In recent years, however, observers of U.S. politics have noted a decline in this pattern of rich civic involvement. Although social movements remain, they have become much more driven by elites than their predecessors were. At the same time, voluntarism and civic involvement have declined, and the likelihood of participation has followed the patterns of voting, with the more educated, wealthier, and older generally more

likely to volunteer and be civically engaged.[13] This decline in civic involvement in U.S. politics has serious long-term implications for society. As civic involvement declines, Americans talk about politics less with their peers and have a lessened sense that they can shape political outcomes. Political scientist Robert Putnam has identified this as the "bowling alone" phenomenon.[14] Americans traditionally had many social venues, such as bowling leagues, where they had an outlet to talk about politics and, potentially, to organize when they were frustrated with political outcomes. There are fewer of these today (people are busier, have more job responsibilities, and spend more time watching television), and the decline in civic engagement has led to reduced political efficacy and greater frustration with the course of politics.

Protest, of course, remains an option for people who feel neglected by the political order. The decline in social movements and other ways to organize the politically marginalized (such as labor unions), however, has shifted the focus of protest from organized collective actions to more isolated and, often, violent protests (such as the 1995 bombing of the federal building in Oklahoma City) that fail to build more support for the demands of the people organizing the protest. Militia movements—organizations of individuals willing to take up arms to defend their own notion of U.S. political values and the Constitution, for example—represent the concerns of some in today's society, but few support their activities.

The twentieth century saw the rise of a new form of organized political activity: interest groups. Like political parties and candidates for office, these organizations try to influence the outcome of public policy by influencing policy-makers. They differ, however, in that they are usually organized to influence a single issue or a tightly related group of issues. Also unlike social movements, they rely on money and professional staff rather than on committed volunteers. Interest groups increased in prominence as the federal and state governments increasingly implemented distributive and redistributive policies. Beginning in the 1970s, a specialized form of interest group, the **political action committee (PAC),** appeared to evade restrictions on corporate and organized labor financial contributions to political candidates and political parties.

Interest groups are so numerous in contemporary U.S. politics that it is not possible to even venture a guess as to their number. To show their diversity, however, it is important to realize that they include national organizations, such as the National Rifle Association, as well as local groups, such as associations of library patrons who seek to influence city council appropriations. They include mass organizations, such as the American Association of Retired Persons, which claims to represent the interests of more than 30 million people over the age of fifty, and very narrow interests, such as oil producers seeking to defend tax protections for their industry.

Although interest groups and PACs are now much more common than social movements in U.S. politics, they do not replace one key function traditionally fulfilled by the social movements, which seek to establish accountability between citizens and government. Interest groups by definition are organized to protect the

needs of a cohesive group in the society and to make demands that government allocate resources in a way that benefits the interests of that group. Thus, they tend to include as members people who already receive rewards from government or are seeking new benefits. Their membership, then, tends to include more socially, financially, and educationally advantaged members of U.S. society. There is no place in the network of interest groups for individuals who are outside the democratic community or whose voices are ignored by the polity. The key role that social movements and protest have played in U.S. politics is being replaced by a more elite and more government-focused form of political organization. This is not to say that social movements and collective protest will not reappear in the future, but such a reappearance would require that the insider-focused strategy employed by interest groups could no longer ensure the outcomes that their members seek from government.

Section ❺ United States Politics in Transition

Political Challenges and Changing Agendas

The United States today faces some familiar and some new challenges that result from the nation's new place in the world of states. Primary among the continuing challenges is the need to live up to its own definition of the democratic idea and to balance this idea of representative government elected through mass participation with the divergent economic outcomes that result from its laissez-faire approach to governing the economy. As it has throughout its history, the United States must address these challenges with a system of government that was designed to impede the actions of government and a citizenry that expects much of government but frequently does not trust it to serve popular needs.

Although challenges to achieve the democratic idea are not new to U.S. political life, the circumstances in which they are debated are new for several reasons. Most important, the United States has assumed a relatively new role and set of responsibilities in the world of states, at least new as far as the past sixty years. U.S. governing institutions must now respond not just to their own people but more broadly to an international

political order that is increasingly interconnected and seeks rapid responses to international security, political, and economic crises. The institutional arrangements of U.S. government reduce the likelihood of quick responses. These institutional arrangements are reinforced by a citizenry that for the most part cares little about foreign policy (except when war threatens), expects quick and often unilateral solutions to international crises, and has little respect, and sometimes open animosity, for multinational political and economic institutions such as the UN and the IMF. Despite the citizenry's continued focus on domestic concerns, U.S. jobs and national economic well-being are increasingly connected to international markets. Over time, many in the United States may come to resent this economic integration (as is already evidenced in the political rhetoric of commentator and frequent presidential candidate Patrick Buchanan).

Economics is not the only role that the United States plays in the world of states, as has been brought home in the period since the September 11 attacks. Its military and its bilateral and multilateral defense arrangements guarantee that the U.S. military will have a global presence. Again, this represents a substantial change from the nation's historical role prior to World War II. Although the citizenry has demonstrated a willingness to pay the financial cost of a global military, it has been much less willing to sacrifice the lives of members of the military. As a result, U.S. leaders must continually balance their military objectives and responsibilities to allies and international organizations with an inability to commit U.S. forces to conflicts that might lead to substantial casualties.

This tension between U.S. reliance on a global economic order among developed nations and a willingness to pursue a unilateral military and defense policy appeared repeatedly after the September 11 attacks. The initial approach of national leaders as well as the citizenry was to pursue military actions against Afghanistan and Iraq alone if necessary. Although alliances formed for each military engagement, this threat of unilateral action made the building of long-term multilateral alliances all the more difficult.

In addition to its economic and military roles in the world of states, the United States exports its culture and language throughout the world. Certainly, this process contributes to economic development in the United States; equally important, it places the United States at the center of an increasingly homogenizing international culture. The process also can generate hostile reactions in defense of national and local cultures.

The substantial changes in the U.S. linkages to the world of states have not been matched by equally dramatic changes in the U.S. role in governing the economy. The laissez-faire governance that has characterized the nation from its earliest days continues. The United States tolerates income and wealth disparities greater than those of other advanced democracies. Equally important, business is less regulated and less taxed in the United States than in other democracies. Few in the polity contest this system of economic regulation.

Since the Great Depression, the United States has seen an expansion of redistributive programs to assist the poor. Beginning with Proposition 13 and coming to fruition with the 1996 welfare reform legislation, however, the nation has reduced its commitment to assisting the poor and established time limits for any individual to collect benefits. While some programs will undoubtedly survive, the current pattern indicates that the United States will not develop targeted programs to assist citizens in need that come anywhere close to those of other advanced democracies. Distributive programs targeted to the middle class, such as social security, Medicare, and college student loans, have also been implemented in the twentieth century. These have much more support among voters and will be harder to undermine or significantly change, even if they challenge traditional laissez-faire approaches to the U.S. role in governing the economy.

Regardless of whether the focus is domestic or international policy, the U.S. government faces a challenge to its sense of its own democratic idea that is more dramatic than that faced by other advanced democracies. Fewer Americans are choosing to participate in the electoral politics of the nation. Turnout in the 1996 presidential election was lower in percentage terms than in any other national election since the 1920s (just after women had been granted the right to vote, but before they voted in large numbers). Official turnout rates for 1996 indicated that fewer than half of eligible adults turned out to vote. In the 2000 election, the structure of the election should have produced increased turnout: there was no incumbent, and the two candidates were evenly balanced in the polls through much of the race. Yet turnout increased by only two percentage points, to 51 percent. Turnout in nonpresidential-year elections is even lower: approximately 39 percent of registered voters in 2002. As has been indicated, participation is not spread evenly across the population. Older, more affluent, and more educated citizens are much more likely to vote than are the young, the less educated, and the poor. As a result, non-Hispanic whites vote at considerably higher rates than blacks or Latinos. Thus, elected representatives are simultaneously receiving less guidance from a narrower subset of the people. Contributing to this process is the increasing cost of campaigns in the United States and the burdensome need to raise ever-increasing sums of money.

The breadth of nonelectoral politics is also narrowing. Previous study of the United States found rich networks of community-based organizations, voluntary organizations, and other forms of nonelectoral political activity. Community politics in the United States, however, began to decline in the 1950s (roughly when electoral turnout began to decline) and appears to be at record lows today. This is the "bowling alone" phenomenon discussed above.

This decline in electoral and nonelectoral politics magnifies a final dilemma that the United States faces as it looks to the future. The politics of collective identities has always been central to U.S. politics because the nation has been a recipient of large numbers of immigrants through much of its history. Each wave of immigrants has differed from its predecessors in terms of culture and religion. These differences forced the nation to redefine itself in order to live up to its democratic idea. The "old" group of each era also perceived the "new" group as a threat to the political values of the nation. Today, Asian and Hispanic immigrants are perceived as a challenge by the descendants of European immigrants who populated the nation before large-scale immigration of these groups began in 1965.[15] These political fears lead to periodic spasms of anti-immigrant rhetoric that disappear rapidly when it becomes evident that the new wave of immigrants has adopted the political values of the nation (in the long run, cultural differences are more tolerated).

The United States has experienced a long period of sustained high levels of immigration since 1965. Soon, the current period of high immigration (roughly from 1965 to the present) will exceed the previous period of sustained high immigration (beginning after the Civil War and extending to the 1920s). In this previous period, however, the final fifteen years were characterized by increasingly vitriolic national debates about limiting the volume of immigration and limiting immigration from parts of Europe (Southern and Eastern) that had only recently begun to send large numbers of immigrants to the United States. Immigration restriction, particularly of legal immigrants to permanent residence, is not a part of the current debate. It seems likely that sustained high levels of immigration, quite diverse in terms of its origins, will continue well into the future. (See "Current Challenges: Incorporating Immigrants.")

The absence of strong political parties, mediating institutions, and nonelectoral community politics may dampen the political integration of these immigrants and their children. The preliminary evidence is that naturalization rates are increasing, but that naturalized citizens vote and participate in other forms of politics at lower levels than comparably situated U.S.-born citizens. If these patterns continue, the nation faces a risk that has not come to pass in its long history of high levels of immigration: contemporary immigrants and their children may not be represented in the political order, even when these immigrants achieve formal political equality by naturalizing as U.S. citizens.

In the past, the weaknesses of the U.S. constitutional system could be overcome in part through institutional arrangements and mediating institutions. In terms of institutions, Congress dominated the executive until the New Deal era, after which the president dominated Congress until the Watergate scandal. This institutional dominance reflected the framers' intent through the Great Depression and after, at least in terms of the dominance of one branch. It is unclear that the framers envisioned a system where two, and occasionally all three, branches of government would compete for dominance and where the Congress and the presidency would be routinely controlled by different political parties.

Mediating institutions also played a role in the past that they are incapable of addressing today. Once they formed as mass institutions in the 1830s, the parties served a necessary role in unifying popular opinion and forcing elite compromise. Today, parties are in decline and have been replaced by a distinct type of mediating institution that does not seek compromise across issues and instead promotes narrow interests. Interest groups connect the citizenry to political institutions, as did parties, but the purpose of this connection is to advance a narrow agenda.

Thus, the United States faces the challenges that it has confronted throughout its history and continues to be limited by a governing system that seeks to inhibit government activity. In the past, it has been able to overcome these challenges through active citizen participation, often channeled through mediating institutions and the mobilization of new groups to active political participation. With citizen participation in decline (or becoming more selective) and mediating institutions less broadly based, the nation is more poorly situated to face challenges. As the United States is now centrally positioned in the international economic and political order, its ability to overcome challenges has implications not just for the people of the United States but for people throughout the world.

United States Politics in Comparative Perspective

From the perspective of the study of comparative politics, the United States may well remain something of an enigma. Its size, wealth, unique experiences with

Current Challenges: *Incorporating Immigrants*

That the United States is a nation of immigrants is a truism. What is often overlooked, however, is that the flow of immigrants to the United States is not even across its history. Instead, some periods, such as the current one, see high levels of immigration, and others see much more moderate levels. As each of these periods of high immigration reaches maturity, the nation has to relearn how to ensure that the new immigrants achieve the same levels of success as the children of previous periods of immigration.

Approximately 31 million residents of the United States were born abroad. These foreign-born residents make up more than 10 percent of the U.S. population. Although the number of foreign-born residents in the United States is at a historic high, they make up a lower share of the national population than in previous periods of high immigration because the national population is so much larger. Today's immigrants overwhelmingly trace their origins to Latin America and to Asia, two regions that sent few immigrants to the United States prior to the current immigrant wave (which began when U.S. immigration law was reformed in 1965).

Immigrants are generally more educated and better skilled than the average person from their countries of origin, but they have less education and fewer professional skills than the U.S. work force. While some immigrants are at the top of the U.S. work force and many can be found in positions in the technology industry, the average immigrant works in service, administrative, agriculture, or manufacturing. Immigrants are much more urban than the population as a whole. Immigrant households include more members than households headed by a U.S.-born resident and are more likely to have more than two generations in the household.

The experience of previous waves of immigrants offers a partial lesson for immigrant incorporation today. Immigrants bring with them a drive that facilitates economic advance. Immigrants, on average, work more hours and have more jobs than do the U.S.-born. Immigrant households have more workers than do households headed by the U.S.-born. This economic drive allows immigrant households in part to overcome the low salaries associated with the sectors of the economy in which they work. Even with this drive, however, immigrant households tend to earn less than those headed by the U.S.-born. This gap is particularly large for recent immigrants and those without legal status in the United States.

The U.S. economy is much changed from a century ago. Manufacturing and agriculture have declining labor needs, and the number of low-skill jobs that have absorbed immigrants over the past three decades is not growing. There are few job training resources to prepare low-skill immigrants for the needs of the U.S. economy. Thus, economic gains seen in immigrant populations over the past several decades may not continue in the future.

Immigrants are demonstrating a steady development of political ties to the United States, though they are slow to make these connections formal through naturalization. Survey data demonstrate that immigrants quickly develop ties to the political values of the United States (liberty, equality, and democracy), sometimes at levels greater than those of the U.S.-born. Immigrants show only moderate interest in the politics of their native lands. When disputes arise between the United States and the nation of origin, immigrants often agree with the U.S. government's position on the issue. Immigrants, however, are somewhat slow to naturalize. Approximately one-third of immigrants have naturalized. While this may reflect a failure among immigrants to choose to become citizens, a more likely explanation is that some immigrants are ineligible (those who are undocumented and those who immigrated legally within the past five years) and others are interested but find the application requirements too onerous or too expensive. With time, most immigrants naturalize, though few do as soon as they become eligible (after five years of legal residence) or for few years after.

A final measure supplements economic and political incorporation to assess whether immigrants are becoming full members of U.S. society, and, in this area, there is much less evidence. For the current wave of immigration to be successful, the children of today's immigrants must have opportunities comparable to those of other Americans. These children start with a structural disadvantage: they overwhelmingly reside in urban and suburban areas with poor tax bases and, hence, poor schools. It was schooling that allowed previous generations of immigrant children to improve their position in U.S. society. If equal educational opportunities are denied to today's children of immigrants, these past successes will likely not be repeated. Perhaps the greatest domestic challenge that the nation faces in the coming years is ensuring that its commitment to large-scale immigration is matched by a commitment to ensuring that those immigrants and their children become equal participants in the opportunities and political responsibilities of membership in the American polity.

immigration, history of political isolation from the world, and reliance on separation of powers and federalism do not have clear parallels among the other advanced democracies. This distinctness comes through perhaps most clearly in the way the nation engages its international political responsibilities. While the president has traditionally directed the scope of U.S. foreign policy, Congress, as it reasserts power relative to the president, will likely play an increasing role. Members of Congress, who represent narrow geographic districts and are more directly connected to mass interests, are less likely to take an internationalist perspective than is the president. When Congress speaks on international issues, it is often with multiple voices, including some that oppose U.S. involvement in multilateral organizations. This conflict over control and direction of foreign policy has become more evident since the end of the cold war. An example would be tensions over U.S. payments to support the United Nations. The objections of one, admittedly well-placed, senator, Jesse Helms, chair of the Senate Foreign Relations Committee, to his perceptions of excessive bureaucracy at the United Nations caused the United States to slow its support payments to the organization and risk its voice in the activities of UN agencies. Because Helms controlled the actions of the Foreign Relations Committee, which had to authorize the U.S. payments, he was able to alter U.S. policy and ultimately force the United Nations to change its policies. Most nations, let alone, individual legislators, do not have this sort of power. Only in the United States can a senator have more power than a president.

The impact of the constitutionally mandated structural and institutional weaknesses of U.S. government is not limited to the American people. The United States plays a dominant role in the world economy, as well as a central political role in international organizations. Thus, the inefficiencies and multiple entry points into U.S. policy-making shape the ability of the United States to respond to crises and develop coherent long-term policies in conjunction with its allies. In 1998, for example, as the world economy declined, the president, with the support of the chair of the Federal Reserve, proposed that the United States increase its contribution to the IMF by $18 billion so that the IMF could expand its ability to provide short-term loans to Asian and Latin American countries. Congress initially balked at this request for several reasons, none of which were apparent to the U.S. allies. Some opposed the new appropriations because of concerns about international organizations in general, reflecting the tradition of isolationism. Others sought to block presidential initiatives in general, because of the president's political weaknesses. Still others, likely the majority of those who opposed the initiative, thought that they could bargain with the president to earn his support for initiatives that they sought to pass. While the power of intransigence and horse trading makes a great deal of sense to analysts of U.S. politics, analysts abroad cannot so easily understand the seeming failure of the United States to act in a time of a crisis. Eventually Congress passed the added IMF appropriation.

In sum, despite its central role in the international economic system and in multilateral organizations, the United States often remains reluctant to embrace fully the international system that it helped shape. This hesitancy appears despite the active role of U.S. economic interests abroad and the importance of international trade to the U.S. economy. Although the United States has assumed many new international economic and security responsibilities since World War II and does not hesitate to impose its will abroad when it perceives its security threatened, it is sometimes unwilling to play by the rules that these international organizations create. Thus, despite its central role in the world of states, the United States is sometimes a hesitant leader.

Key Terms

Electoral College
Constitution
appropriations
Department of Homeland Security
North American Free Trade Agreement
manifest destiny
Declaration of Independence
Articles of Confederation
Bill of Rights
property taxes
interest group
federalism

separation of powers
free market
laissez-faire
police powers
Federal Reserve Board
regulations
distributive policies
redistributive policies
Marbury v. *Madison*
checks and balances
bicameral
single-member plurality electoral system
political action committee (PAC)

Suggested Readings

Amar, Akhil Reed. *The Bill of Rights: Creation and Reconstruction*. New Haven, Conn.: Yale University Press, 1998.

Burns, Nancy, Schlozman, Kay Lehman, and Verba, Sidney. *The Private Roots of Public Action: Gender, Equality, and Political Participation*. Cambridge, Mass.: Harvard University Press, 2001.

Dawson, Michael C. *Black Visions: The Roots of Contemporary African-American Political Ideologies*. Chicago: University of Chicago Press, 2002.

Deering, Christopher J., and Smith, Steven S. *Committees in Congress*. 3d ed. Washington, D.C.: Congressional Quarterly Books, 1997.

DeSipio, Louis. *Counting on the Latino Vote: Latinos as a New Electorate*. Charlottesville: University Press of Virginia, 1996.

Elkins, Stanley, and McKitrick, Eric. *The Age of Federalism*. New York: Oxford University Press, 1993.

The Federalist Papers. Edited by Clinton Rossiter. New York, Mentor, 1961.

Fenno, Jr., Richard F. *Home Style: House Members in Their Districts*. Glenview, Ill.: Scott, Foresman, 1978.

Hartz, Louis. *The Liberal Tradition in America*. New York: Harvest/HBJ, 1955.

Kupchan, Charles. *The End of the American Era: U.S. Foreign Policy and the Geopolitics of the Twenty-First Century*. New York: Knopf, 2002.

Judis, John B., and Teixeira, Ruy. *The Emerging Democratic Majority*. New York: Scribner, 2002.

Levinson, Sanford. *Constitutional Faith*. Princeton, N.J.: Princeton University Press, 1988.

Lowi, Theodore J. *The End of Liberalism: The Second Republic of the United States*. 2d ed. New York: Norton, 1979.

Nye, Joseph Jr. *The Paradox of American Power: Why the World's Only Superpower Can't Go It Alone*. New York: Oxford University Press, 2002.

Sniderman, Paul, and Piazza, Thomas. *The Scar of Race*. Cambridge, Mass.: Harvard University Press, 1993.

Tulis, Jeffrey A. *The Rhetorical Presidency*. Princeton, N.J.: Princeton University Press, 1988.

Verba, Sidney, Schlozman, Kay Lehman, and Brady, Henry. *Voice and Equality: Civic Voluntarism in American Politics*. Cambridge, Mass.: Harvard University Press, 1995.

Wilson, Woodrow. *Congressional Government: A Study in American Politics*. Baltimore: Johns Hopkins University Press, 1885.

Wolfinger, Raymond, and Rosenstone, Steven. *Who Votes?* New Haven, Conn.: Yale University Press, 1980.

Zaller, John. *The Nature and Origins of Mass Opinion*. New York: Cambridge University Press, 1992.

Suggested Websites

Find Law, Cases and Codes, U.S. Constitution
www.findlaw.com/casecode/constitution/
New York Times
www.nytimes.com/

Thomas, Legislative Information from the Library of Congress
thomas.loc.gov/
U.S. Census Bureau
www.census.gov/
White House
www.whitehouse.gov/

Notes

[1] U.S. Bureau of the Census, *Statistical Abstract of the United States 2001* (Washington, D.C.: U.S. Bureau of the Census, 2001), Table 1374.

[2] Rogers Smith, *Civic Ideals: Conflicting Visions of Citizenship in U.S. History* (New Haven, Conn.: Yale University Press, 1997).

[3] Louis Hartz, *The Liberal Tradition in America* (New York: Harvest/HBJ, 1955).

[4] Randall Robinson, *The Debt: What America Owes to Blacks* (New York: Plume, 2001).

[5] U.S. Immigration and Naturalization Service, *2000 Statistical Yearbook of the Immigration and Naturalization Services* (Springfield, Va.: National Technical Information Service, 2002).

[6] See *The Federalist Papers,* ed. Clinton Rossiter (New York: Mentor, 1961), particularly Federalist Nos. 10 and 51.

[7] Woodrow Wilson, *Congressional Government: A Study in American Politics* (Baltimore: Johns Hopkins University Press, 1885).

[8] Louis DeSipio, *Counting on the Latino Vote: Latinos as a New Electorate* (Charlottesville: University Press of Virginia, 1996).

[9] Kristi Anderson, *After Suffrage: Women in Partisan and Electoral Politics Before the New Deal* (Chicago: University of Chicago Press, 1996).

[10] Ruy A. Teixeira, *The Disappearing American Voter* (Washington, D.C.: Brookings Institution, 1992).

[11] Raymond Wolfinger and Steven Rosenstone, *Who Votes?* (New Haven, Conn.: Yale University Press).

[12] Sanford Levinson, *Constitutional Faith*. (Princeton, N.J.: Princeton University Press, 1988).

[13] Sidney Verba, Kay Lehman Schlozman, and Henry Brady, *Voice and Equality: Civic Voluntarism in American Politics* (Cambridge, Mass.: Harvard University Press, 1995).

[14] Robert D. Putnam, *Bowling Alone: The Collapse and Revival of American Community* (New York: Simon and Schuster, 2000).

[15] Louis DeSipio and Rodolfo O. de la Garza, *Making Americans/Remaking America: Immigration and Immigrant Policy* (Boulder, Colo.: Westview Press, 1998).

PART 3

Developing Democracies

CHAPTER 8

Russia

Joan DeBardeleben

Russian Federation

Land and People

Capital	Moscow
Total area (square miles)	6,520,800 (About 1.8 times larger than the U.S.)
Population	145.5

Annual population growth rate (%)	1975–2000	0.3
	2000–2015 (projected)	−0.6

Urban population (%)	72.9

Ethnic Composition (%)	Russian	81.5
	Tatar	3.8
	Ukrainian	3.0
	Chuvash	1.2
	Bashkir	0.9
	Belorussian	0.8
	Moldavian	0.7
	Other	8.1

Major language(s)	Russian

Religious affiliation (%)	Russian Orthodox	16.3
	Muslim	10.0
	Protestant	0.9
	Jewish	0.4
	Roman Catholic	0.3
	Other (mostly nonreligious)	72.1

Economy

Domestic currency	Ruble (RUB) US$1: 31.38 (2002 av.)
Total GDP (US$)	251.1 billion
GDP per capita (US$)	1,726
Total GDP at purchasing power parity (US$)	1.2 trillion
GDP per capita at purchasing power parity (US$)	8,377

GDP annual growth rate (%)	1997	0.9
	2000	9.0
	2001	5.0

GDP per capita average annual growth rate (%)	1975–2000	−1.2
	1990–2000	−4.6

Inequality in income or consumption (1998) (%)	Share of poorest 10%	1.7
	Share of poorest 20%	4.4
	Share of richest 20%	53.7
	Share of richest 10%	38.7
	Gini Index (1998)	40

Structure of production (% of GDP)	Agriculture	6.4
	Industry	39.0
	Services	54.6

Labor force distribution (% of total)	Agriculture	10.8
	Industry	27.8
	Services	61.4

Exports as % of GDP	46
Imports as % of GDP	25

Society

Life expectancy at birth	66.1
Infant mortality per 1,000 live births	18
Adult literacy (%)	99%

Access to information and communications (per 1,000 population)	Telephone lines	218
	Mobile phones	22
	Radios	418
	Televisions	421
	Personal computers	42.9

Women in Government and the Economy

Women in the national legislature		
Lower house or single house (%)		7.6
Upper house (%)		3.4
Women at ministerial level (%)		—
Female economic activity rate (age 15 and above) (%)		59.3
Female labor force (% of total)		49
Estimated Earned Income (PPP US$)	Female	6,611
	Male	10,383
2002 Human Development Index Ranking (out of 173 countries)		60

Political Organization

Political System   Federal state, semipresidential system.

Regime History   Re-formed as an independent state with the collapse of communist rule in December 1991; current constitution since December 1993.

Administrative Structure   Federal system with 89 subnational governments including 21 republics, 55 provinces (*oblast'*, *krai*), 11 autonomous districts or regions (*okrugs* or autonomous *oblast'*), 7 super districts, and 2 cities of federal status.

Executive   Dual executive (president and prime minister). Direct election of president; prime minister appointed by the president with the approval of the lower house of the parliament (State Duma).

Legislature   Bicameral. Upper house (Federation Council) made up of heads of regional executive and representative organs. Lower house (State Duma) chosen by direct election, with half of the 450 deputies chosen through a proportional representation system and half from single-member constituencies. Powers include proposal and approval of legislation, approval of presidential appointees.

Judiciary   Independent constitutional court with 19 justices, nominated by the president and approved by the Federation Council, holding 12-year terms with possible renewal.

Party System   Fragmented multiparty system with changing party names and coalitions.

Section **1** The Making of the Modern Russian State

Politics in Action

In May 2000, the offices of NTV, Russia's leading independent broadcaster, were raided and searched by Russian police, leading to a takeover by Gasprom, the giant natural gas monopoly whose majority shareholder was the Russian government. In early 2002, TV-6, which had taken over NTV's role in providing an independent media perspective, was temporarily taken off the air after a raid triggered by a court ruling enforcing bankruptcy charges. Majority owners of NTV and TV-6, before the raids, were industrial-financial conglomerates headed by business magnates Vladimir Gusinsky and Boris Berezovksy. Both had fallen out of favor with the Russian president. NTV was the nearly sole TV critic of the Kremlin's military action against the secessionist Republic of Chechnya; later, Berezovksy threatened to broadcast charges on TV-6 linking the government to 1999 apartment bombings that had been attributed to terrorists. In the face of these events, critics blamed the Russian government for the assault on the independent media. Suspicions that political motives were at work seemed plausible to many observers. President Vladimir Putin quickly asserted that the actions had nothing to do with press censorship; rather, they were part of the government's campaign to assure proper business practices by business **oligarchs,** a small group of powerful and wealthy individuals who had gained ownership and control of important sectors of Russia's economy. Gusinsky, who was charged with fraud and fled to Spain, also had close ties to President Vladimir Putin's political rival, Moscow mayor Luzhkov. Boris Berezovksy also was pushed into political exile.

These events spurred debates among political observers about the status of press freedom in Russia. Are they a sign that President Putin means business in his proclaimed attack on the oligarchs who had benefited from the privatization of state industry and now control the country's most lucrative firms? Although both Gusinsky and Berezovksy had posed as defenders of a free media in the NTV/TV6 conflict, their hands were not clean either; like other oligarchs, they had benefited from government largesse and political connections in the past.[1] Nevertheless, Putin's attacks on

the oligarchs seemed strangely focused on political opponents. Were the actions a dimly veiled assault on press freedom? With Russian citizens increasingly concerned about crime and corruption in high places, Putin's commitment to restoring legal order struck a chord with the Russian public, so the broader public outcry against the takeover of NTV and the short-lived assault on TV-6 quieted fairly quickly. Still, Putin's personal background in the Soviet secret service, the KGB, made some observers more skeptical of his motives; attacks on independent media outlets, particularly in the TV broadcasting sector, could give the Russian government and president control over the formation of public opinion, influencing electoral outcomes and creating an atmosphere of fear and intimidation.

Since 1991, Russia's faltering movement toward democratic political processes and a market economy have created numerous such contradictions. Behind the democratic facade, sometimes Russian politics looks like court intrigue with the role and interests of the public clearly in the background. Privatization of formerly state-owned industries has not decoupled economic from political power. Rather, a new, wealthy business class has found innovative methods, some legal and some not, of wielding political power. It is not surprising that the term *privatizatsiia* has come to mean "appropriation" in everyday Russian parlance. At the same time, new democratic institutions *have* made the government answerable to the public in a way unprecedented in Russian history.

Geographic Setting

In December 1991, the Soviet Union ceased to exist. Each of the fifteen newly independent states that emerged in early 1992 began the process of forming a new political entity. In this section, we focus on the Russian Federation, the most important of these fifteen successor states. With a population of just over 145 million, Russia is the largest European country in population and in size, and in terms of territory, it is the largest country in the world, spanning ten time zones.

Russia underwent a period of rapid industrialization and urbanization in the Soviet period; only 18 percent

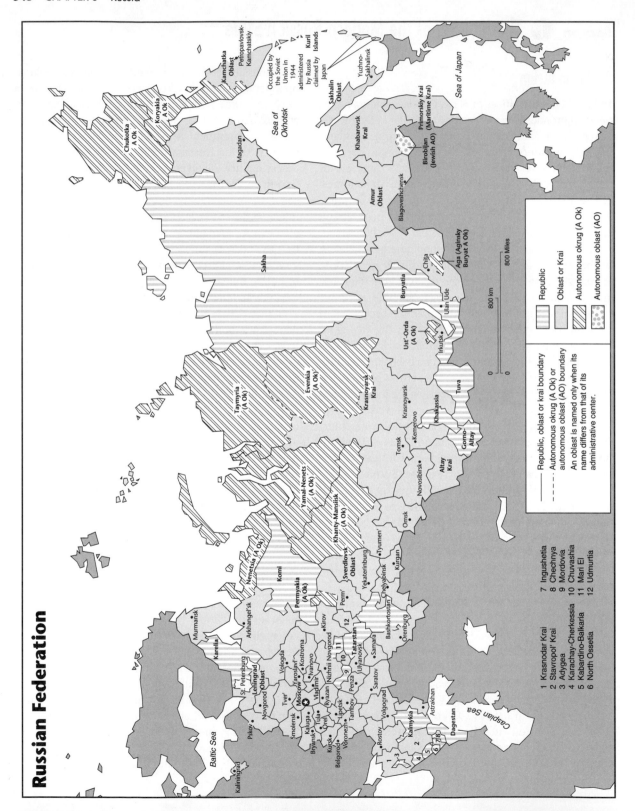

Russian Federation

Kamchatka Oblast
Petropavlovsk-Kamchatskiy

Koryakia A Ok

Chukotka A Ok

Magadan

Sea of Okhotsk

Occupied by the Soviet Union in 1944 administered by Russia claimed by Japan

Kuril Islands

Sakhalin Oblast

Yuzhno-Sakhalinsk

Sea of Japan

Sakha

Khabarovsk Krai

Amur Oblast

Blagoveshchensk

Primorsky Krai (Maritime Krai)

Birobijan (Jewish AO)

Buryatia

Chita

Aga (Aginsky Buryat A Ok)

Ulan-Ude

Taymyria (A Ok)

Evenkia (A Ok)

Krasnoyarsk Krai

Ust'-Orda (A Ok)

Irkutsk

Tuva

Krasnoyarsk

Khakassia

Kemerovo

Tomsk

Gorno-Altay

Altay Krai

Novosibirsk

Omsk

Yamal-Nemets (A Ok)

Khanty-Mansiisk (A Ok)

Nenetsia (A Ok)

Komi

Permyakia (A Ok)

Perm'

Sverdlovsk Oblast

Yekaterinburg

Tyumen'

Kurgan

Chelyabinsk

Bashkortostan

Orenburg

Murmansk

Arkhangel'sk

Karelia

Vologda

Tatarstan

Kirov

Nizhnii Novgorod

Ulyanovsk

Samara

Saratov

Penza

Tambov

Volgograd

Kalmykia

Astrakhan

Caspian Sea

Dagestan

Rostov

Voronezh

Lipetsk

Belgorod

Kursk

Bryansk

Orel

Tula

Kaluga

Smolensk

Moscow

Vladimir

Ivanovo

Kostroma

Yaroslavl

Tver'

Novgorod Oblast

Pskov

Leningrad Oblast

St. Petersburg

Baltic Sea

Kaliningrad

Ryazan

1 Krasnodar Krai
2 Stavropol' Krai
3 Adygea
4 Karachay-Cherkessia
5 Kabardino-Balkaria
6 North Ossetia
7 Ingushetia
8 Chechnya
9 Mordovia
10 Chuvashia
11 Mari El
12 Udmurtia

Republic

Oblast or Krai

Autonomous okrug (A Ok)

Autonomous oblast (AO)

—— Republic, oblast or krai boundary

- - - Autonomous okrug (A Ok) or autonomous oblast (AO) boundary

An oblast is named only when its name differs from that of its administrative center.

800 km

800 Miles

0

0

of the population lived in urban areas in 1917, rising to 73 percent in 1989. Despite its vast expanses, under 8 percent of Russia's land is arable, while 45 percent is forested.[2] Russia is rich in natural resources, which are generally concentrated in the vast regions of western Siberia and the Russian north, far from Moscow, the Russian capital. Russia's wealth includes deposits of oil, natural gas, mineral resources (including gold and diamonds), and extensive forest land.

Before the Communists took power in 1917, the Russian empire extended east to the Pacific, south to the Caucasus mountains and the Muslim areas of Central Asia, north to the Arctic Circle, and west into present-day Ukraine, eastern Poland, and the Baltic states. Unlike the empires of Western Europe with their far-flung colonial possessions, Russia's empire bordered its historic core. With its unprotected location between Europe and Asia, Russia had been repeatedly invaded and challenged for centuries. This exposure to outside intrusion encouraged an expansionist mentality among the leadership; some historians argue that this factor, combined with Russia's harsh climate, encouraged Russia's rulers to craft a centralizing and autocratic state.[3]

With the formation of the Soviet Union after World War I, the Russian Republic continued to form the core of the new multiethnic state. Russia's ethnic diversity and geographic scope have always made it a hard country to govern. In the contemporary period, although only one of Russia's **republics** (Chechnya, in the Caucasus region) has attempted outright secession from the Russian Federation, other regions have asserted their autonomy in a manner that has challenged the authority of the Russian state. Russia also faces pockets of instability and regional warfare on several of its borders, most notably in the Central Asian countries of Tadzhikistan and Afghanistan and in the countries of Georgia and Azerbaijan on Russia's southern border. On the west, Russia's neighbors include the newly independent states of Ukraine, Belarus, Estonia, Latvia, and Lithuania, as well as the formerly allied country of Poland. Several of these countries have unambiguously embraced a European identity, with policies directed toward joining Western institutions such as the European Union (EU) and the North Atlantic Treaty Organization (NATO). Poland, Hungary, and the Czech Republic were admitted to NATO in March 1999; in November 2002, seven additional post-communist countries (Latvia, Estonia, Lithuania, Slovakia, Slovenia, Bulgaria, and Romania) were invited to undertake accession talks to join NATO. Eight of these countries are expected to join the EU in 2004, with Bulgarian and Romanian membership to follow a few years later. The enlargement of the EU to include these countries will place Russia directly on the border of an increasingly integrated European continent.

Some have described Russia as Eurasian, reflecting the impact of both Asian and European cultural influences. Efforts to unite most of the former Soviet republics in the Commonwealth of Independent States, which was formed at the time of the Soviet collapse in December 1991, have produced few concrete results. A process set in place in December 1998 with the signing of a set of accords by Russia and Belarus pointing in the direction of a possible economic and political union of the two countries has been stillborn. Russia has turned its attention to other foreign policy concerns, above all, establishing a firmer and more cooperative form of relations with Western countries.

Critical Junctures

The Decline of the Russian Tsarist State

Until the revolution of 1917, Russia was ruled through an autocratic system headed by the tsar, the Russian monarch and emperor. The historian Richard Pipes explains that before 1917, Russia had a **patrimonial state,** that is, a state that not only ruled the country but owned the land as well.[4] Serfdom was an economic and agricultural system that tied the majority of the population (peasants) to the nobles whose land they worked. The serfs were emancipated by the tsar in 1861 as a part of his effort to modernize Russia, to make it militarily competitive with the West, and thus to retain its status as a world power. Emancipation freed the peasants from bondage to the nobility but did not destroy the traditional communal peasant organization in the countryside, the *mir.* Individual peasant farming did not develop in Russia on a significant scale.

A Russian bourgeoisie, or entrepreneurial class, also failed to emerge in Russia as it had in Western Europe. The key impetus for industrialization came from the state itself and from injections of foreign (especially French, English, German, and Belgian) capital in the form of joint-stock companies and foreign debt incurred by the tsarist government. The dominant role of state and foreign capital was accompanied by the emergence of large factories alongside small, private workshops. Trade unions were illegal until 1906, and even then their activities were carefully controlled. Under these conditions, worker discontent grew, culminating in the revolution of 1905, which involved widespread strikes in the cities and rural uprisings. Despite some transient reforms, the tsarist regime was able to retain control through increasing repression until its collapse in 1917.

The Bolshevik Revolution and the Establishment of Soviet Power (1917–1929)

In 1917, at the height of World War I, two revolutions occurred in Russia. The March revolution threw out the tsar (Nicholas II) and installed a moderate provisional government. In November, that government was overthrown by the Bolsheviks, a part of the Russian Social Democratic Labor Party led by Vladimir Lenin. This second revolution marked a major turning point in the history of Russia. Instead of trying to imitate Western European patterns, the Bolsheviks applied a dramatically different blueprint for economic, social, and political development.

The Bolsheviks were Marxists who believed their revolution reflected the political interests of a particular social class, the proletariat (working class). Most of the revolutionary leaders, however, were not themselves workers but were from the more educated and privileged strata, commonly referred to as the intelligentsia. But in 1917, the Bolsheviks' slogan, "Land, Peace, and Bread," appealed to both the working class and the discontented peasantry, which made up over 80 percent of Russia's population. With his keen political sense, Lenin was able to grasp the strategy and the proper moment for his party to seize state power.

The Bolsheviks formed a tightly organized political party based on their own understanding of democracy. Their strategy was founded on the notions of democratic centralism and vanguardism, concepts that differed significantly from the liberal democratic notions of Western countries. **Democratic centralism** mandated a hierarchical party structure in which leaders were elected from below with freedom of discussion

Critical Junctures in Soviet and Russian Political Development

1917	The Bolshevik seizure of power
1918–1921	Civil War and war communism
1921–1928	New Economic Policy
1929	Stalin consolidates power
1929–1953	Stalin in power
1929–1938	Collectivization and purges
1941–1945	Nazi Germany invades Soviet Union; "Great Patriotic War"
1953	Death of Stalin
1953–1955	Leadership change after Stalin's death
1956–1964	The Khrushchev era and de-Stalinization
1965–1982	The Brezhnev era and bureaucratic consolidation
1982–1985	Leadership change after Brezhnev's death
1985–1991	The Gorbachev era and *perestroika*
1991	Popular election of Boris Yeltsin as president of Russia (July); Collapse of the USSR and formation of fifteen independent states (December); establishment of the Russian Federation as an independent state
1992	Market reforms launched in Russia (January)
1993	Adoption of the new Russian constitution by referendum; first (multiparty) parliamentary elections in the Russian Federation (December)
1995	Second parliamentary elections in the Russian Federation; Communists win the most seats (December)
1996	The first presidential elections under the new Russian constitution; Yeltsin is re-elected
1998	Financial crisis and devaluation of the ruble
1999	Third parliamentary elections in the Russian Federation; Unity Party gains strong support, as does Communist party; resignation of Yeltsin as president (December)
2000	Election of Vladimir Putin as president of Russia

until a decision was taken, but strict discipline was required in implementing party policy. In time, the centralizing elements of democratic centralism took precedence over the democratic elements, as the party tried to insulate itself first from informers of the tsarist forces and later from both real and imagined threats to the new regime. The concept of a **vanguard party** governed the Bolsheviks' (and later the Communist Party's) relations with broader social forces: party leaders claimed that they understood the interests of the working people better than the people did themselves. In time, this philosophy was used to rationalize virtually all actions of the Communist Party and the state it dominated. Neither democratic centralism nor vanguardism emphasized democratic procedures or accountability of the leaders to the public. Rather, these concepts focused on achieving a "correct" political outcome that would reflect the "true" interests of the working class, as defined by the leaders of the Communist Party.

Once in power, the Bolsheviks formed a new government, which in 1922 brought the formation of the first Communist Party state, the Union of Soviet Socialist Republics (USSR), henceforth referred to as the Soviet Union. In the early years, the Bolsheviks felt compelled to take extraordinary measures to ensure the survival of the regime. The initial challenge was an extended civil war (1918–1921) for control of the countryside and outlying regions. The Bolsheviks introduced war communism to ensure the supply of materials necessary for the war effort. The state took control of key economic sectors and forcibly requisitioned grain from the peasants. Political controls also increased: the *Cheka*, the security arm of the regime, was strengthened, and restrictions were placed on other political groups, including other socialist parties. By 1921, the leadership recognized the political costs of war communism: the peasants resented the forced requisitioning of grain and the policy stymied initiative. In an effort to accommodate the peasantry, the New Economic Policy (NEP) was introduced in 1921 and lasted until 1928. State control over the economy was loosened. In agriculture, once in-kind taxes were paid, peasants were allowed to sell their product on the free market. In other sectors of the economy, private enterprise and trade were also revived. The state, however, retained control of large-scale industry and experimented with state control of the arts and culture.

Gradually throughout the 1920s the authoritarian elements of Bolshevik thinking eclipsed the democratic elements. Lacking a democratic tradition and bolstered by the vanguard ideology of the party, the Bolshevik leaders engaged in internecine struggles following Lenin's death in 1924. These conflicts culminated in the rise of Joseph Stalin and the arrest or exile of prominent party figures such as Leon Trotsky and Nikolai Bukharin. By 1929, all opposition, even within the party itself, had been eliminated. Sacrifices of democratic procedure were justified in the name of protecting class interests.

The Bolshevik revolution also initiated a period of international isolation for the new state. To fulfill their promise of peace, the new rulers had to cede important chunks of territory to Germany under the Brest-Litovsk Treaty (1918). Only the defeat of Germany by Russia's former allies (the United States, Britain, and France) reversed some of these concessions. However, these countries were hardly pleased with internal developments in Russia. Not only did the Bolshevik revolution bring expropriation of foreign holdings and Russia's withdrawal from the Allied powers' war effort, it also represented the first successful challenge to the capitalist order. As a result, the former allies sent material aid and troops to oppose the new Bolshevik government during the civil war.

Lenin had hoped that successful working-class revolutions in Germany and other Western countries would bolster the fledgling Soviet regime and bring it tangible aid. When this did not occur, the Soviet leaders had to rely on their country's own resources to build a viable economic structure. In 1923, Stalin announced the goal of building "socialism in one country." This policy defined Soviet state interests as synonymous with the promotion of socialism. It simultaneously set the Soviet Union on a course of economic isolation from the larger world of states. To survive in such isolation, the new Soviet leader, Stalin, pursued a policy of rapid industrialization and increased political control.

The Stalin Revolution (1929–1953)

From 1929 until Stalin's death in 1953, the Soviet Union faced another critical juncture. During this time, Stalin consolidated his power as Soviet leader by establishing the basic characteristics of the Soviet regime that substantially endured until the collapse of the Communist system in 1991. Russia's problems since 1991 reflect the difficulties of extracting Russia from the Stalinist system.

The Stalin revolution brought changes to virtually every aspect of Soviet life. The result was an interconnected system of economic, political, and ideological power. Under Stalin, the state became the engine for rapid economic development, with state ownership and control of virtually all economic assets (land, factories, housing, and stores). By 1935, over 90 percent of agricultural land had been taken from the peasants and made into state or collective farms. This **collectivization** campaign was justified as a means of preventing the emergence of a new capitalist class in the countryside, but it actually targeted the peasantry as a whole, leading to widespread famine and loss of life. Those who resisted were arrested or exiled to Siberia. In the industrial sector, a program of rapid industrialization favored heavy industries (steel mills, hydroelectric dams, machine building); production of consumer goods was neglected. Economic control was exercised through a complex but inefficient system of central economic planning, in which the state planning committee (Gosplan) set production targets for every enterprise in the country. The industrialization campaign was accompanied by social upheaval. People were uprooted from their traditional lives in the countryside and catapulted into the rhythm of urban industrial life. Media censorship and state control of the arts stymied creativity as well as political opposition. The party/state became the authoritative source of truth; anyone deviating from the authorized interpretation could be charged with treason.

In the early 1920s, the Communist Party was the only political party permitted to function, and by the early 1930s, opposition or dissent within the party itself had been eliminated. Gradually, the party became subject to the personal whims of Stalin and his secret police. Party bodies ceased to meet on a regular basis, and they no longer made important political decisions. Party ranks were periodically cleansed of potential opponents, and previous party leaders as well as citizens from many walks of life were violently purged (arrested, sentenced to labor camps, sometimes executed). Overall, an estimated 5 percent of the Soviet population

was arrested at one point or another under the Stalinist system, usually for no apparent cause. Social groups lost all autonomy. People could not form independent political organizations, and public discussion about controversial issues was prohibited. The arbitrary and unpredictable terror of the 1930s left a legacy of fear. Only among trusted friends and family members did people dare to express their true views. Forms of resistance, when they occurred, were evasive rather than active: peasants killed their livestock to avoid giving it over to collective farms; laborers worked inefficiently, and absenteeism was high; in some cases, citizens simply refused to vote for the single candidate offered in the elections.

Isolation of the Soviet citizen from interaction with the outside world was a key tool of Stalinist control. Foreign news broadcasts were jammed, travel abroad was highly restricted, and contacts with foreigners brought citizens under suspicion. The economy was also highly autarkic, that is, isolated from interaction with the international economic system. Although this policy shielded Soviet society from the effects of the Great Depression of the 1930s, which shook the capitalist world (indeed, the decade of the 1930s was a period of rapid economic growth in the Soviet Union), it also allowed an inefficient system of production to survive in the USSR. Protected from foreign competition, the economy failed to keep up with the rapid pace of economic and technological transformation in the West.

In 1941, Nazi Germany invaded the Soviet Union, and Stalin had little choice but to join the Allied powers. World War II had a profound impact on the outlook of an entire generation of Soviet citizens. Soviet propaganda dubbed it the Great Patriotic War, evoking images of Russian nationalism rather than of socialist internationalism; the sacrifices and heroism of the war period remained a powerful symbol of Soviet pride and unity until the collapse of Communist power. The period was marked by support for traditional family values and a greater tolerance for religious institutions, whose support Stalin sought for the war effort. Among the social corollaries of the war effort were a declining birthrate and a long-lasting gender imbalance as a result of high wartime casualties for men. The war also affected certain minority ethnic groups that were accused of collaborating with the enemy during the war effort and were deported to areas farther east in the

USSR. These included Germans, Crimean Tatars, and peoples of the northern Caucasus regions such as the Chechens, Ingush, and Karachai-Balkar. Their later rehabilitation and resettlement caused renewed disruption and conflict, contributing to the ethnic conflicts of the post-Soviet period. In sum, the war experience had a long-lasting influence on the development of postwar political elites, demographic patterns in the country, and ethnic relations.

The Soviet Union was a major force in the defeat of the Axis powers in Europe. After the war, the other Allied powers allowed the Soviet Union to absorb new territories into the USSR itself (these became the Soviet republics of Latvia, Lithuania, Estonia, Moldavia, and portions of western Ukraine), and they implicitly granted the USSR free rein to shape the postwar governments and economies in eastern Germany, Poland, Hungary, Czechoslovakia, Yugoslavia, Bulgaria, and Romania. Western offers to include parts of the region in the Marshall Plan were rejected under pressure from the USSR. With Soviet support, local communist parties gained control of all of these countries; only in Yugoslavia were indigenous communist forces sufficiently strong to gain power largely on their own and thus later to assert their independence from Moscow.

Following World War II, the features of Soviet communism were largely replicated in those areas newly integrated into the USSR and in the countries of Eastern Europe. The Soviet Union tried to isolate its satellites in Eastern Europe from the West and to tighten their economic and political integration with the USSR. The Council for Mutual Economic Assistance (CMEA) and the Warsaw Treaty Organization (a military alliance) were formed for this purpose. With its developed industrial economy, its military stature bolstered in World War II, and its growing sphere of regional control, the USSR emerged as a global superpower. But the enlarged Soviet bloc still remained insulated from the larger world of states. Some countries within the Soviet bloc, however, had strong historic links to Western Europe (especially Czechoslovakia, Poland, and Hungary), and in these areas, domestic resistance to Soviet dominance forced some alterations or deviations from the Soviet model. Over time, these countries served not only as geographic buffers to direct Western influence on the USSR but also as conduits for such influence. In the more Westernized Baltic republics of

the USSR itself, the population firmly resisted assimilation to Soviet rule and eventually spearheaded the disintegration of the Soviet Union in the late 1980s.

Attempts at De-Stalinization (1953–1985)

Stalin's death in 1953 triggered another critical juncture in Soviet politics. Even the Soviet elite realized that Stalin's system of terror could be sustained only at great cost to the development of the country. The terror stymied initiative and participation, and the unpredictability of Stalinist rule inhibited the rational formulation of policy. The period from Stalin's death until the mid-1980s saw a regularization and stabilization of Soviet politics. Terror abated, but political controls remained in place, and efforts to isolate Soviet citizens from foreign influences continued.

Nikita Khrushchev, who succeeded Stalin as the party leader from 1955 until his removal in 1964, embarked on a bold policy of de-Stalinization. Although his specific policies were only minimally successful, he initiated a thaw in political and cultural life, an approach that planted the seeds that ultimately undermined the Stalinist system. Khrushchev rejected terror as an instrument of political control. According to Khrushchev, the party still embodied the positive Leninist values that had inspired the 1917 revolution: the construction of an egalitarian and democratic socialist society that would protect the true interests of the working population. Khrushchev revived the Communist Party as a vital political institution able to exercise political, economic, and cultural authority. The secret police (KGB) was subordinated to party authority, and party meetings were resumed on a regular basis. However, internal party structures remained highly centralized, and elections were uncontested. In the cultural sphere, Khrushchev allowed sporadic liberalization, with the publication in the official media of some literature critical of the Stalinist system.

Leonid Brezhnev, Khrushchev's successor, who headed the party from October 1964 until his death in 1982, partially reversed the de-Stalinization efforts of the 1950s and early 1960s. Controls were tightened again in the cultural sphere. Individuals who expressed dissenting views (members of the so-called dissident movement) through underground publishing or publication abroad were harassed, arrested, or exiled.

However, unlike in the Stalinist period, the political repression was predictable: people knew when they were transgressing permitted limits of criticism. The Brezhnev regime could be described as primarily bureaucratic and conservative, seeking to maintain existing power structures rather than to introduce new ones.

During the Brezhnev era, a **tacit social contract** with the population governed state-society relations.[5] In exchange for political compliance, the population enjoyed job security; a lax work environment; low prices for basic goods, housing, and transport; free social services (medical care, recreational services); and minimal interference in personal life. Wages of the worst-off citizens, especially agricultural and industrial workers, were increased relative to those of the more educated and better-off portions of the population. For its part, the intelligentsia (historically Russia's social conscience and critic) was allowed more freedom to discuss publicly issues that were not of crucial importance to the regime.

Nonetheless, from the late 1970s, an aging political leadership was increasingly ineffective at addressing the mounting problems facing Soviet society. Economic growth rates declined, and improvements in the standard of living were minimal. Many consumer goods were still in short supply, and quality was often mediocre. As the economy stagnated, opportunities for upward career mobility declined. To maintain the Soviet Union's superpower status and competitive position in the arms race, resources were diverted to the military sector, gutting the capacity of the consumer and agricultural spheres to satisfy popular expectations. Russia's rich natural wealth was squandered, and the costs of exploiting new resource deposits (mostly in Siberia) soared. High pollution levels lowered the quality of life and health in terms of morbidity and declining life expectancy. At the same time, liberalization in some Eastern European states and the telecommunications revolution made it increasingly difficult to shield the population from exposure to Western lifestyles and ideas. Among a certain critical portion of the population, aspirations were rising just as the capacity of the system to fulfill them was declining. It was in this context that the next critical transition occurred.

Perestroika *and* Glasnost *(1985–1991)*

Mikhail Gorbachev took office as a Communist Party leader in March 1985 at the relatively young age of fifty-three. He hoped to reform the system in order to spur economic growth and political renewal, but without undermining Communist Party rule or its basic ideological precepts. Four important concepts formed the basis of Gorbachev's reform program: *perestroika, glasnost, demokratizatsiia,* and "New Thinking." *Perestroika* (restructuring) involved decentralization and rationalization of the economic structure to enable individual enterprises to increase efficiency and take initiative. The central planning system was to be reformed, not disbanded. To counteract the resistance of entrenched central bureaucracies, Gorbachev enlisted the support of the intelligentsia, who benefited from his policy of *glasnost. Glasnost* (openness) involved relaxing controls on public debate, the airing of diverse viewpoints, and the publication of previously prohibited literature. ***Demokratizatsiia*** (Gorbachev's conception of democratization) was an effort to increase the responsiveness of political organs to public sentiment, both within and outside the party. It did not endorse all components of Western liberal democracy, but it did place greater emphasis on procedural elements (competitive elections, a **law-based state,** freer political expression) than did the traditional Leninist approach. Finally, "New Thinking" in foreign policy involved a rethinking of international power in nonmilitary terms. Gorbachev advocated integration of the USSR into the world of states and the global economy, emphasizing the common challenges facing East and West, such as the cost and hazards of the arms race and environmental degradation.[6]

Gorbachev's policies triggered a fundamental change in the relationship between state and society in the USSR. Citizens pursued their interests and beliefs through a variety of newly created organizations at the national and local levels. These included ethnonationalist movements, environmental groups, groups for the rehabilitation of Stalinist victims, charitable groups, new or reformed professional organizations, political clubs, and many others. The existence of these groups implicitly challenged the Communist Party's monopoly of power. By March 1990, pressures from within and outside the party forced the Supreme Soviet (the Soviet parliament) to rescind Article 6 of the Soviet constitution, which provided the basis for single-party rule. Embryonic political parties challenged the Communist Party's monopoly of political control. In the spring of 1989, the first contested elections since the 1920s were held for positions in the Soviet parliament.

These were followed by elections at the republic and local levels in 1990, which, in some cases, put leaders in power who pushed for increased republic and regional autonomy.

The most divisive issues facing Gorbachev were economic policy and demands for republic autonomy. The Soviet Union was made up of fifteen **union republics,** each formed on the basis of an ethnic or national group, as only 50.8 percent of the Soviet population was ethnically Russian in 1989. In several of these union republics, popular front organizations formed, sometimes supported by a portion of the local Communist leadership. First in the three Baltic republics (Latvia, Lithuania, and Estonia) and then in other union republics (particularly Ukraine, Georgia, Armenia, Moldova [formerly Moldavia], and Russia itself) demands for national autonomy and, in some cases, for secession from the USSR were put forth. Gorbachev's efforts to bring consensus on a new federal system for the fifteen union republics failed, as popular support and elite self-interest took on an irreversible momentum, resulting in a "separatism mania."

Gorbachev's economic policies failed as well. They involved half-measures that sent contradictory messages to enterprise directors, producing a drop in output and national income and undermining established patterns that had kept the Soviet economy functioning, albeit inefficiently. The economic decline reinforced demands by union republics for economic autonomy even as central policy appeared to shackle any real improvement. To protect themselves, regions and union republics began to restrict exports to other regions, despite planning mandates. "Separatism mania" was accompanied by "the war of laws," as regional officials openly defied central directives. In response, Gorbachev issued numerous decrees; their number increased as their efficacy declined.

Gorbachev achieved his greatest success in the foreign policy sphere. Just as his domestic support was plummeting in late 1990 and early 1991, he was awarded the Nobel Peace Prize, reflecting his esteemed international stature. Under the guidance of his "New Thinking," the military buildup in the USSR was halted, important arms control agreements were ratified, and many controls on international contacts were lifted. In 1989, Gorbachev refused to prop up unpopular communist governments in the East European countries. First in Hungary and Poland, then in the German Dem-ocratic Republic (East Germany) and Czechoslovakia, pressure from below pushed the communist parties out of power, and a process of democratization and market reform ensued. More gradual transformations occurred in Bulgaria and Romania. Politicians in both East and West declared the cold war over. To Gorbachev's dismay, the liberation of Eastern Europe fed the process of disintegration in the Soviet Union itself.

Collapse of the USSR and the Emergence of the Russian Federation (1991 to the Present)

On August 19, 1991, a coalition of conservative figures attempted a coup d'état, temporarily removing Gorbachev from the leadership post to stop the reform initiative and prevent the collapse of the USSR. The failed coup proved to be the death knell of the Soviet system. While Gorbachev was held captive at his summer house (*dacha*), Boris Yeltsin, the popularly elected president of the Russian Republic, climbed atop a tank loyal to the reform leadership and rallied opposition to the attempted coup. Yeltsin declared himself the true champion of democratic values and Russian national interest. The Soviet Union collapsed at the end of 1991 when Yeltsin joined the leaders of Ukraine and Belorussia (later renamed Belarus) to declare the formation of a loosely structured entity, called the Commonwealth of Independent States, to replace the Soviet Union. In December 1991, the Russian Federation stepped out as an independent country in the world of states. Its independent status (along with that of the other fourteen former union republics of the USSR) was quickly recognized by the major world powers.

Yeltsin quickly proclaimed his commitment to Western-style democracy and market economic reform, marking a radical turn from the Soviet past. However, that program was controversial and proved hard to implement. The market reform produced severe and unpopular economic repercussions as traditional economic patterns were disrupted. The Russian parliament, elected in 1990, mirrored popular skepticism in its hesitancy to embrace the radical reform project. The president, in turn, relied heavily on the power of decree to try to implement his program, raising questions about the democratic nature of the new regime. The executive and legislative branches of the government failed to reach consensus on the nature of a new Russian constitution; the result was a bloody showdown in

The White House, seat of the Russian parliament, burns while under assault from troops loyal to President Yeltsin during the confrontation in October 1993.
Source: AP/Wide World Photos.

October 1993, after Yeltsin disbanded what he considered to be an obstructive parliament and laid siege to its premises, the Russian White House. The president mandated new elections and a constitutional referendum in December 1993. The constitution, adopted by a narrow margin of voters, put in place a set of institutions marked by a powerful president and a relatively weak parliament.

Yeltsin's economic reform program failed to produce an effective market economy; a major financial crisis in August and September 1998 was the culmination of this failed reform process. The financial crisis triggered a political one. In 1999, Yeltsin nominated a surprise candidate to the post of prime minister of Russia. Vladimir Putin, a little-known figure from St. Petersburg, was a former KGB operative in East Germany. His political advance was swift, and the rise in his popularity was equally meteoric. In December 1999, Yeltsin, apparently ill and unable to command the reins of power, resigned from his position as president of the Russian Federation. Elections were announced for March 2000; the result was a resounding victory for Putin, who carried a majority of the vote in the first round of the electoral process and won a plurality in al-

most every region of Russia. Putin's tenure as president benefited from auspicious conditions, as the devalued ruble helped to spur demand for domestically produced goods, and high international gas and oil prices fed tax dollars into the state's coffers. In 1999, the economy experienced its first real growth in over a decade, a trend that continued into the new millennium.

Following the terrorist attacks on the World Trade Center and the Pentagon on September 11, 2001, President Putin expressed his strong solidarity with the American people in their struggle against terrorism. A new warming trend in American-Russian relations ensued, and Russia was rewarded by being granted an enhanced status in relationship to organizations such as NATO and the Group of 7 (G-7, a group of leading industrial nations, which became the G-8 with Russia's addition). Here, again, however, skeptics questioned Putin's motives. Was he trying to mute Western criticism of Russian actions against the separatist rebels in the Russian republic of Chechnya by drawing analogies with the American struggle against terrorism? Or did the rapprochement represent a new, less conflictual era of Russian-American relations? To many, Russian policy seemed as enigmatic as ever.

Leaders: *Boris Nikolaevich Yeltsin*

On February 1, 1931, Boris Yeltsin was born to a working-class family in a village in the Russian province of Sverdlovsk located in the Ural Mountains. Like so many other men of his generation who later rose to top Communist Party posts, his education was technical, in the field of construction. His early jobs were as foreman, engineer, supervisor, and finally director of a large construction combine. Yeltsin joined the Communist Party of the Soviet Union in 1961, and in 1968 he took on full-time work in the regional party organization. Over the next ten years, he rose to higher positions in Sverdlovsk *oblast,* first as party secretary for industry and finally as head of the regional party in 1976. In 1981, Yeltsin became a member of the Central Committee of the CPSU and moved onto the national stage.

Because of Yeltsin's reputation as an energetic figure not tainted by corruption, Mikhail Gorbachev drafted him onto his leadership team in 1985. Yeltsin's first important post in Moscow was as head of the Moscow party organization. Gorbachev also selected Yeltsin to be a nonvoting member of the USSR's top party organ, the Politburo.

Yeltsin soon gained a reputation as an outspoken critic of party privilege. He became a popular figure in Moscow as he mingled with average Russians on city streets and public transport. In 1987, party conservatives launched an attack on Yeltsin for his outspoken positions; Gorbachev did not come to his defense. Yeltsin was removed from the Politburo and from his post as Moscow party leader in 1988; he was demoted to a position in the construction sector of the Soviet government. At the party conference in June 1988, Yeltsin defended his position in proceedings that were televised across the USSR. His popular support soared as the public saw him single-handedly taking on the party establishment.

Rivalry between Gorbachev and Yeltsin formed a backdrop for the dramatic events that led to the collapse of the Soviet Union in December 1991. Yeltsin represented a radical reform path, while Gorbachev supported gradualism.

Yeltsin established his political base within the Russian Republic; thus, Russia's self-assertion within the USSR was also a way for Yeltsin to secure his own position. Under his guidance, on June 8, 1990, the Russian Republic declared sovereignty (not a declaration of independence but an assertion of the right of the Russian Republic to set its own policy). One month later, Yeltsin resigned his party membership. On June 12, 1991, he was elected president of the Russian Republic by direct popular vote, establishing his legitimacy as a spokesman for democratization and Russian independence.

During the attempted coup d'état by party conservatives in August 1991, Yeltsin reinforced his popularity and democratic credentials by taking a firm stand against the plotters while Gorbachev remained captive at his *dacha* in the Crimea. Yeltsin's defiance gave him a decisive advantage in the competition with Gorbachev and laid the groundwork for the December 1991 dissolution of the USSR engineered by Yeltsin (representing Russia) and the leaders of Ukraine and Belorussia. In an unusual turn of events, the rivalry between Yeltsin and Gorbachev, as well as between their differing approaches to reform, was decided through the disbanding of the country Gorbachev headed.

In 1992, Yeltsin embarked on the difficult task of implementing his radical reform policy in the newly independent Russian Federation. Economic crisis, rising corruption and crime, and a decline of state authority ensued. Yeltsin's popularity plummeted. His reputation as a democratic reformer was marred by his use of force against the Russian parliament in 1993 and in the Chechnya war in 1994–1996. Although Yeltsin's campaign team managed to orchestrate an electoral victory in 1996, Yeltsin's day was past. Plagued by poor health and failed policies, Yeltsin could hope only to serve out his presidential term and groom a successor. He succeeded in the latter, designating Vladimir Putin as acting president on his own resignation in December 1999. How history will view Yeltsin is hard to say.

Russian President Vladimir Putin and American President George W. Bush brought a positive turn to United States–Russia relations at a summit in Slovenia in June 2001, reinforced by Russian support for American antiterrorist efforts after the September 11 attacks. New tensions emerged, however, in 2003 with the American attack on Iraq. *Source:* Getty Images.

Themes and Implications

Historical Junctures and Political Themes

For nearly a decade following the collapse of the Soviet system, the Russian Federation seemed mired in a downward spiral of economic collapse and political paralysis. By 1999, the Russian public was disillusioned and distrustful of its leaders, and international support for the new regime had faded. National humiliation intensified the bitter reality of economic decline. Resentment over the dismal results of the Western-inspired reform program reinforced Russian nationalism. The air attack carried out by the newly expanded NATO in early 1999 against Yugoslavia reinforced these sentiments, as many Russians viewed NATO's actions as an assertion of power against a historically close Slavic nation. These concerns, combined with the chaotic state of the economy and polity, raised questions about Russia's management of its nuclear arsenal. Although these concerns have not abated, the events of September 11 seemed to provide a new impetus for Russia's hope of taking its place in the alliance of leading nations.

By 2002, the Russian economy seemed to have weathered the worst of the economic downturn associated with the shift from a centralized to a quasi-market economy. Data from the Central Bank of Russia indicated that **capital flight** in 2000 had declined to nearly half its 1997 level,[7] and in the new millennium, Russian officials announced a budget surplus along with expectations of continued economic growth. The population showed a marked increase in economic confidence, even as wide disparities in wealth and income continued to plague the system. Questions, however, remained about the depth of the apparent economic recovery. Some experts estimated that a significant drop in oil prices or a global economic downturn could push Russia back into a renewed slump. Meanwhile, many problems had not been addressed, including control of quasi-monopolies in key sectors of the economy, rising rates of unemployment, the decline in the agricultural sector, and control by economic oligarchs and corruption. The public remained skeptical of many of the features of a market economic system, feeding suspicions that public optimism could easily turn sour in the face of a new economic jolt, such as occurred in 1998.

Concerns about the fate of Russian democracy are even more widespread. On the positive side, the constitution adopted in 1993 seems to have gained a surprising level of public acceptance, and Russia has passed what some consider a crucial test of democratic consolidation: the passing of power to a new president through a competitive electoral process. However, observers continue to express concern about the democratic credentials of the new Russian leader. Would his KGB past mark his style of leadership in the fledgling democratic state? While Russians clearly wanted order, couldn't this easily spill over into a revival of authoritarian tendencies?

Finally, Russians continue to seek new forms of collective identity. The loss of superpower status, the dominance of Western economic and political models, and the delegitimation of the previous ideology have all contributed to uncertainty about what it means to be Russian and where Russia fits into the world as a whole. Vladimir Putin's efforts to articulate a new definition of Russian identity are almost certainly a source of his popularity. Meanwhile, Russia itself suffers from internal divisions. Although overt separatism has been limited to the Republic of Chechnya, differing visions of collective identity have emerged in some of Russia's ethnic republics, particularly in Muslim areas. Other aspects of identity are also being reconsidered. Social class, a linchpin of Soviet ideology, may take on increasing importance in defining group solidarity as working people seek new organizational forms to assert their rights. Changing gender roles have challenged both men and women to reconsider not only their relationships to one another, but also the impact of these changes on children and community values.

Implications for Comparative Politics

Many countries in the world today are undergoing a process of transition from authoritarian rule to democratic political structures. The Russian experience is, however, unique in many respects. Indigenous political traditions and political culture influence the nature of political change in any country. In Russia's case, one of the most important factors is the tradition of the patrimonial state of tsarist times, which extended into the Soviet period. In addition, the intertwined character of politics, economics, and ideology in the Soviet Union has made democratization and economic reform difficult to realize. In effect, four transition processes were begun at once:

- The democratization of the political system, including the introduction of competitive elections and competing political parties
- Dismantling state dominance of the economy through privatization and the expansion of market relations, accompanied by rising inequality and inroads into traditional social guarantees
- A search for new forms of collective identity to replace those provided by the old Communist ideology
- A process of economic integration into the world of states and exposure to ideas and goods from the Western world

Whereas other democratizing countries may have undergone one or two of these transitions simultaneously, Russia has tackled all four at once. Thus, the stakes and the stress are high. As one analyst of Russia has suggested, Russia is building "democracy from scratch."[8] The search for methods to structure political conflict, build political legitimacy, and resolve policy problems is posed in a very stark form in the Russian case. In addition, the Russian case provides a striking example of the difficulty of extricating political from economic power. Because the former Communist elites had no private wealth to fall back on, corrupt or illegal methods were sometimes used to maintain former privileges, methods taken over by Russia's new capitalist class. Citizens, confronted with economic decline, have been less susceptible to nationalist appeals, demagogues, or antidemocratic movements than one might have expected, but no doubt economic uncertainty has made the Russian public willing to accept strong leadership and limits on political expression that would be resisted in many Western countries. Examining these strong linkages between political and economic forces in Russia may provide insights into understanding other political settings.

Section ② Political Economy and Development

In both tsarist and Soviet times, the state played a leading role in Russia's economic development. Following the collapse of the Soviet system in late 1991, the new Russian leadership brought in a sea change, involving a radically reduced economic role for the state and a reopening of the Russian economy to foreign influence. However, the difficulties of this transition have been marked by the legacies of the Soviet system, in which politics and economics were inextricably intertwined. The reform process also has created clear winners and losers, presenting policy-makers with political risks alongside the economic challenge. Going too quickly would tax the ability of institutions and individuals to adapt, but going too slowly would create confusion and contradictions.

Because political institutions have been changing as radically as the economy, the new Russian government has had to scramble to create adequate tools to guide economic reform. Pressures from the global economy have placed additional constraints on the choices that reformers could make. Following nearly a decade of decline and social upheaval, only since 1999 has Russia seemed finally to have regained a foothold to support a positive economic trajectory. In that year, economic growth revived, and other economic indicators began to move in a positive direction (see Table 1). One question that occupies experts is whether this upturn has much to do with state policies, or whether it is founded almost solely on short-term conditions, which could easily fade without more fundamental structural change.

State and Economy

Many observers have identified the weakness of state institutions as a main obstacle to the success of the economic reform agenda. These inadequacies have included weaknesses in areas such as tax collection, legal enforcement of contracts, protection of ownership rights, control of crime and corruption, and the creation of a reliable banking system. The tools used by the Soviet state to spur earlier economic development did not provide an adequate foundation for the new circumstances, so the new Russian state has undergone a difficult process of redefining its role and building new institutions appropriate to a market economy. But to understand the challenges they face, we need some background on the Soviet system.

The Soviet Economic System

Under the Soviet command economy, land, factories, and all other important economic assets belonged to the state. Immediate production goals as well as longer-term development were guided by one-year and five-year plans, which detailed targets for every branch of the economy. Although the plans had the force of law, they were frequently too ambitious to be fulfilled; productivity and efficiency were low in Soviet enterprises, and innovation was not rewarded. Prices were centrally controlled by the state and did not rise when demand was high and supplies were limited, as in a market economy. Only in the peasant markets and the illegal black market did prices fluctuate in response to conditions of shortage or surplus. Enterprises were to meet state-set production targets and were not motivated by the need to turn a profit. Therefore, producers had neither the incentive nor the resources to increase production of goods in short supply or to respond to consumer demands. Retail stores piled up stocks of unwanted goods, while goods in high demand were often unavailable. Shortages forced citizens to wait in line for basic items.

Environmental quality deteriorated under Soviet rule because ecological goals were subordinate to production quotas. Large nature-transforming projects (hydroelectric dams, huge factory complexes) were glorified as symbols of Soviet power. At the same time, many priority industries (metallurgy, machine building, chemicals, energy production) were highly polluting, resulting in a visibly higher incidence of respiratory and other ailments. High nitrate levels and other contaminants in food, resulting from excessive use of chemical fertilizers and pesticides, were present in many areas of the USSR. On paper, Soviet standards for industrial emissions were often impressive, but they were not enforced, partly because they were unrealistically ambitious. Inadequate technological safeguards and an insufficient regulatory structure led to the disastrous nuclear accident at Chernobyl (in Ukraine) in

Table 1

Economic Indicators for the Russian Federation (percent change from the previous year unless otherwise indicated)

	1991	1992	1993	1994	1995	1996	1997	1998	1999	2000	2001
Economic growth[a]	–5.0%	–14.5	–8.7	12.6	–4.0	–3.5	0.9	–4.9	5.4	9.0	5.0
Industrial gross output	–8.0%	18.0	–14.1	–20.9	–3.3	–4.0	1.9	–5.2	8.1	9.0	4.9
Agricultural gross output	–3.7%	–9.0	–4.4	–12.0	–7.6	–5.1	0.1	–12.3	2.4	4.0	6.8
Consumer price inflation[b]	93%	1526.0	875.0	307.0	197.0	48.0	15.0	28.0	86.0	21.0	22.0
Unemployment rate[c]	n.a.	4.8%	5.5	7.5	8.8	9.3	10.7	13.3	12.2	9.8	8.7
Rubles per U.S.$[d]	169.0	415.0	1247.0	3550.0	4640.0	5560.0	5960.0	9.7	24.6	28.1	29.1
Population (in millions, Jan. 1)	148.3	148.9	148.7	148.4	148.3	148.0	147.1	146.5	146.0	1145.2	144.5
Gini coefficient[e]		.26	.29	.40	.41	.38	.38	.38	.40	.40	.39	n.a.

[a]Growth in real domestic product (controlled for inflation).

[b]Average for the year.

[c]According to the definition of the International Labour Organization in the year indicated.

[d]At year end until 1997, average from 1998. Figures for 1998 and after are in new redenominated rubles, where one new ruble = 1,000 old rubles. The redenomination occurred in January 1998.

[e]A standard measure of income inequality, where a higher value is more unequal (ratio of income of top 20 percent of population to bottom 20 percent). Data for this line are from Millar (see below).

Sources: Data from 1991–1997 are reprinted from *Introduction to Comparative Politics* (Boston: Houghton Mifflin, 2000), 442; updates for 1997–2001 are from James Millar, "Normalization of the Russian Economy: Obstacles and Opportunities for Reform and Sustainable Growth," *NBR Analysis*, June 25, 2002, Table 1, from Ben Slay, "The Russian Economy: How Far from Sustainable Growth?" prepared for the Congressional Research Service, http://www.nbr.org/publications/analysis/vol13/no2/Table1.html (accessed August 1, 2002); Intelligence Economic Unit, Country Report: Russia (March 2002), p. 5,13; Transition Report 1999 (EBRD, 1999); Transition Report 2002 (EBRD,2002).

1986, which contaminated immense areas of agricultural land in Ukraine and Belorussia (now Belarus). By the l970s, easily accessible deposits of natural resources in the western part of the country approached depletion. To deal with this, Soviet leaders gave priority to the development of northern Siberia to permit exploitation of valuable deposits of oil, natural gas, and precious metals located there, resources that also served as valuable export commodities. However, Siberian development proved to be complicated and expensive. Costs were increased by permafrost conditions, transport distances, and the necessity of paying higher wages to attract workers. Technology was insufficient to deal with many problems, resulting in a massive waste of resources and serious environmental problems, such as oil pipeline leaks.

The Soviet authorities imposed controls on foreign economic contacts. Firms and individuals were not permitted to develop direct links to foreign partners; these were all channeled through the central economic bureaucracy. The insulation of the Soviet economy from outside forces had both negative and positive consequence. On the one hand, the USSR was shielded from business cycles that had an enormous impact on the capitalist world, including the Great Depression of the 1930s and periodic recessions thereafter. On the other hand, lacking foreign competition, the quality of many Russian consumer goods was low by Western standards, and both producers and consumers were denied access to many advances available in Western industrial society.

Despite these weaknesses, the Soviet economic model registered some remarkable achievements: rapid industrialization, provision of social welfare and mass education, relatively low levels of inequality, and advances in key economic sectors such as the military and space industries. Nonetheless, over time, the top-heavy nature of Soviet planning and the isolation of the Soviet economy could no longer deliver increased prosperity at home and competitive products for export. The inability of Russian industry to keep up with international standards was one factor that spurred Mikhail Gorbachev to initiate his program of restructuring (*perestroika*). However, Gorbachev's efforts to reform the economic system were halting and contradictory. The results were declining economic performance, increasing regionalism, and an uncertain economic environment. Only after the collapse of the USSR in 1991 did a concerted effort at fundamental economic change take place.

State and Economy in the Russian Federation

Following the collapse of the Soviet Union in December 1991, Boris Yeltsin immediately endorsed radical **market reform,** sometimes referred to as **shock therapy** because of the radical rupture it implies. The basic notions underlying the government's reform policy were to free prices from state control, take ownership of economic assets away from the state, and open the economy to international influences. Decision making about production and distribution of goods would be turned over to new private owners, who would be forced to respond to consumer demands and to increase efficiency and quality by exposure to a competitive economic environment. Foreign capital could be attracted to spur investment, which would be required because enterprises would no longer depend on state subsidies. For a time, at least, some key sectors of the economy (such as transport, defense, health care, education, culture, research, and certain portions of the energy sector) were to remain largely under state control, but some of these were privatized in later stages of the process. The changes were to be rapid and thorough, thus jolting the Russian economy into a new mode of operation.

Shock therapy would inevitably throw large parts of the economy into a downward spin; social benefits provided by the Soviet system, such as guaranteed employment and low prices on basic necessities, would be eliminated. It was hoped, however, that recovery would be relatively quick. To avoid hyperinflation, it was necessary to institute measures to stabilize the monetary system, especially strict controls on the emission of rubles by the state bank and on state budget expenditures. The final goal of the policy was to create a

Western-type market economy, integrated into the global economic system and capable of producing domestic prosperity.

Yeltsin's team quickly took first steps to implement the economic reform program but was repeatedly forced to make compromises to accommodate domestic political concerns. Three main pillars of reform were the lifting of price controls, encouragement of small private businesses, and the privatization of most state-owned enterprises. By January 1992, price controls on most goods were loosened or removed entirely. The result was a period of high inflation (reaching 1,354 percent in 1992), which was fueled by a soft monetary policy pursued by the Central Bank of Russia; money was printed with nothing tangible to back it up. At the same time, real wages (after controlling for the effects of inflation), on average, declined by an estimated 50 percent between late 1991 and January 1993. International lenders, most notably the International Monetary Fund (IMF), placed strict conditions on Russian loans in order to try to control inflationary tendencies, but the restrictions on the money supply that these policies implied produced their own problems. Debate still continues over whether such requirements were more helpful or detrimental to the reform project.[9]

Some private business activity was allowed even in the late Soviet period, but private entrepreneurs were more actively encouraged by the new Russian leadership. However, these new ventures faced a number of obstacles, including high and complicated taxes, lack of capital, and a poor infrastructure (transport, banking, communications) for doing business. With the breakdown of the Soviet distribution system, trade became a lucrative business, and this is the area in which many successful private enterprises started. These included not only thousands of small kiosks on city streets, but also restaurants and retail outlets. Less visible but equally important were the middlemen who operated behind the scenes, buying up stocks of goods and reselling them, often at inflated prices. Through the use of contacts, savvy, and bribes, some of these "businessmen" accumulated large profits and deposited them in banks abroad; other small entrepreneurs barely scraped by. Although the number of small businesses increased quickly in the early 1990s, growth tapered off after 1994.[10]

Another important component of the government's reform program was rapid privatization of the state sector. In the late 1980s and early 1990s, some enterprise managers and ministry bureaucrats transformed promising state enterprises into private entities without a clear legal framework for doing so. This **spontaneous privatization** permitted former elites to appropriate state property for private benefit. In 1992, a privatization law went into effect, providing a legal context for the process. By early 1994, an estimated 80 percent of medium-sized and large state enterprises in the designated sectors of the economy had been transformed into **joint-stock companies,** whose shareholders might include individuals, Russian and foreign businesses, societal organizations (e.g., trade unions or professional organizations), and the state itself.[11] As part of the government's privatization plan, each citizen of Russia (including children) in November 1992 was issued a **privatization voucher** with a nominal value of 10,000 rubles (at that time equivalent to about ten U.S. dollars). These vouchers could be used to buy shares in enterprises undergoing privatization, sold for cash, or invested through newly formed funds that handled investment choices for voucher holders. Some workers bought shares in their own enterprises, a practice encouraged by the law on privatization and by enterprise managers. Many people were confused about how to use the vouchers, and for most part the vouchers provided neither economic dividends nor tangible input to decision making.

A contentious issue involved the distribution of shares between workers and managers ("insiders"), on the one hand, and outside buyers, on the other. The privatization law established various options for the privatization of enterprises, in most cases to be chosen by the work collective; the most popular one gave managers and workers of the enterprise the right to acquire a controlling packet (51 percent) of enterprise shares at virtually symbolic prices, in part through the use of privatization vouchers. Remaining shares were temporarily held by a state agency or sold at voucher auctions. This path resulted in **insider privatization,** that is, placing the majority of enterprise shares (and thus effective control of the enterprise) in the hands of those who worked there. Many analysts consider insider privatization an obstacle to real reform of business operations. Because managers needed to maintain

worker support to gain the majority of shares for the work collective, they were reluctant to take radical measures that might alienate the work force and lead to labor conflict. Thus, excess labor was often retained, and work discipline remained lax in many cases. This might have been an acceptable cost if insider privatization had resulted in real workers' control. However, this was not the case. Protection of shareholder rights was weak, so that savvy managers found ways, over time, to buy out worker shares or prevent them from giving workers a real impact on decision making. Only in August 2001 was legislation protecting shareholder rights signed by the president. In addition, the most lucrative enterprises in the natural resource sector (oil, gas) were subject to a different privatization regime and came under the control of a small business elite.

Many managers did not have the necessary skills to restructure enterprise operations effectively, and some resisted badly needed outside investment that could threaten insider control. At the same time, some managers were able to extract personal profit from enterprise operations rather than investing available funds to improve production. Despite passage of a bankruptcy law in 1992, most unprofitable enterprises have not been forced to close. Over time, however, turnover of the managerial corps is bringing younger, more adaptable individuals to these positions.

At the second stage of privatization, firms could sell remaining shares for cash or investment guarantees. State-owned shares in already privatized companies could be sold through auctions, which has generated some revenue for the state. However, this phase of privatization proceeded much more slowly than expected. Many enterprises proved to be unattractive to potential Russian and foreign investors because they were pink elephants with backward technology, requiring massive infusions of capital for restructuring. Some of the more attractive enterprises (in sectors such as oil and gas production, telecommunications, mass communications, and minerals) were privatized through insider channels, with majority shares going into the hands of developing financial-industrial conglomerates. Government policies did not create a level playing field for potential buyers.

The loans-for-shares program of 1996 was a particularly controversial approach and is credited by some observers with helping to secure the position of Russia's wealthy and powerful business elite (the oligarchs). Under this program, favored businessmen were granted control of lucrative enterprises (through control of state shares) in exchange for loans to the cash-strapped Russian government. When the government could not repay the loans, the favored businesses gained ownership of the shares. In other cases, securities auctions gave advantages to large business interests. These business oligarchs became an increasingly powerful force on the Russian political scene in the late 1990s as politicians tried to win their favor, particularly before elections to secure sources of campaign financing.

Despite all of its problems, on balance the pace and scope of privatization in Russia were rapid and thorough compared to other postcommunist countries. However, the new joint-stock companies did not meet expectations. Productivity and efficiency did not increase significantly, unprofitable firms continued to operate, investment was weak, and the benefits of ownership were not widely or fairly distributed. The government continued to subsidize ineffective operations through various means, making most Russian firms uncompetitive and unattractive to potential investors.

Reform of agriculture produced even less satisfactory results than industrial privatization. Large joint-stock companies and associations of individual households were created on the basis of former state and collective farms. These privatized companies operated inefficiently, and agricultural output declined throughout the 1990s. Foreign food imports (including meat and a whole range of processed goods) also undercut domestic producers, contributing to a downward spiral in agricultural investment and production. The Russian government was unable to achieve consensus on private ownership of agricultural land, leaving this area to the jurisdiction of regional governments. Only in 2002 was a new Land Code passed (which took effect in January 2003) that allowed the sale of agricultural land for agricultural purposes, with some restrictions, including the exclusion of foreigner buyers.[12]

By 1999, it appeared that that the government's reform program had not achieved most of its underlying goals (see Figure 1). Russia was in the grip of a severe depression comparable to the Great Depression of the 1930s in the United States and Western Europe. Industrial production was less than half the 1990 level. Basic industrial sectors such as machine building, light

Figure 1

Downturn of the Russian Economy

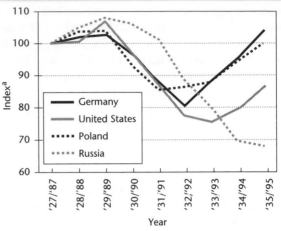

[a]100 equals 1927 GDP for the United States and Germany, and 1987 GDP for Poland and Russia.

Source: Copyright © 2002 by the National Bureau of Asian Research. Reprinted from Millar, James, R. "Normalization of the Russian Economy: Obstacles and Opportunities for Reform and Sustainable Growth," *NBR Analysis 13,* no. 2, April 2002, by permission of the National Bureau of Asian Research.

industry, construction materials, and wood products were the worst off. The depression fed on itself, as declining capacity in one sector deprived other sectors of buyers or suppliers. Deteriorating and expensive transport links also disrupted previous trading relationships. Consumer purchasing power dropped with the decline in real wages. Firms were unable to pay their suppliers, were in arrears to their employees, and owed taxes to the government. Even the state was behind in its wage payments and payments of social benefits such as pensions. Under these conditions, barter arrangements, often involving intertwined linkages of several enterprises or organizations, became common.

At the same time, other centers of power challenged the ability of the Russian government to pursue clear and effective policies. One set of concerns lay with the declining ability of the central state to exert its authority in relation to the eighty-nine regions of the Russian Federation (see Section 3). A second problem was the increasing power of the business oligarchs. Sergei Peregudov argues that in contrast to traditional Western elites, the Russian oligarchs were able to wield considerable political influence as they engaged in rent-seeking behavior, a term he defines as "extracting monopolistic rights or any sort of privilege from the state."[13] These new Russian capitalists were able to gain control of important economic assets but often did not reinvest their profits to spur business development; rather, wealth was siphoned off through capital flight, in which money was removed from the country and deposited in foreign accounts or assets. Diverse methods of laundering money to avoid taxes and extract a profit from the remaining state-owned entities also became widespread. Corruption involving government officials, the police, and operators abroad fed a rising crime rate, which spilled over into many Western countries. Rich foreigners, Russian bankers, and outspoken journalists became targets of the Russian **mafia.** Rather than controlling these abuses, policies of the Russian government itself had contributed to the creation of this new group of financial and business oligarchs.

A financial crisis in August 1998 brought the situation to a head. Within a two-week period, the ruble lost two-thirds of its value against the U.S. dollar, banks closed or allowed only limited withdrawals, store shelves were empty of foreign imports, and business accounts were frozen, forcing some firms to lay off employees and some to close their doors. Underlying the crisis was the Russian government's inability to pay its many creditors The government successively

took on new loans at progressively higher rates of interest in order to pay off existing debts, creating a structure of **pyramid debt.** Because the revenues the government acquired through these short-term loans were used, in large part, to pay interest on debt, they did not generate any usable income for the government. Following a sharp upturn in 1996–1997, the Russian stock market lost over 90 percent of its value by August 1998. In early September, the Ministry of Finance failed to meet its obligations to domestic and international lenders. Many Russian banks, holders of the Russian government's short-term bonds, were facing imminent bankruptcy, and with the Russian government itself in default, bailouts were unlikely. The government began to print more of the increasingly valueless rubles, threatening to undermine the ruble's value further and thus intensify the underlying financial crisis.

The government was finally forced to allow a radical devaluation of the overvalued ruble. In January 1999, the exchange rate was twenty-two rubles to one U.S. dollar compared to the precrisis level of about six to one. The crash of the ruble meant that prices of imported food items and durable goods soared, placing them out of the reach of most Russian consumers. Those who had benefited from the previous reform process—the new Russian middle class and affluent

"Welcome to the Russian Market." The market economy is not always a friendly place for the small firm. *Source*: Elkin, *Izvestiia*, August 29, 2002

strata in Moscow and St. Petersburg—were affected immediately by the crisis, but effects spread to the population as a whole.

In retrospect, it can be seen that despite the immediate disastrous effects the 1998 financial crisis, it ushered in positive changes in the Russian economy. First, the devalued ruble led to a sharp reduction in imports of Western commodities, bringing a revival to Russian producers, who were now again competitive. Firms were able to improve their products, put underused labor back to work, and thus increase productivity. The state budget benefited from improved tax revenues; barter declined, as did payment arrears.[14] Economic growth registered 5.4 percent in 1999, 9.0 percent in 2000, and 5.0 percent in 2001,[15] the first years of sustained economic recovery in the decade.

A second effect was less tangible. Before 1998, Russian policy-makers had tried to chart a precarious balance between popular discontent with shock therapy and conditions that Western and international agencies attached to the advice, assistance, and credits they offered the Russian reform project. At the same time, the reliance on outside aid instilled a mentality of both dependence and resentment; this psychology undermined development of policy instruments appropriate to Russia's unique conditions. Following the 1998 crisis, Russian policy-makers gained an appreciation of the fact that solution of the country's problems was ultimately in Russia's own hands. This sentiment was captured by Vladimir Putin, who harnessed this determination to fashion Russian solutions to Russian problems.

A third positive influence emerged in the late 1990s: international oil and gas prices rose sharply, generating new sources of revenue, which also spilled into government tax coffers, making up 20 percent of the budget.[16] The improvement in economic indicators, including gross domestic product (GDP) per capita and indicators of consumer purchasing power, continued into the new millennium with positive projections into the foreseeable future.

President Yeltsin nominated Vladimir Putin to the post of acting prime minister in August 1999; with Yeltsin's early resignation, Putin became acting president on December 31, 1999. In preparation for the presidential election of March 26, 2000, Putin failed to provide a clear economic program, and in the first year of his presidency, economic policy seemed sluggish.

However, he was laying the political groundwork for an active legislative program that emerged in 2001 and 2002. A new Ministry for Economic Development and Trade under the leadership of German Gref was charged with developing the underlying concept. One of the first steps was a simplification of the tax system, intended to increase tax compliance and facilitate enforcement. A 13 percent flat income tax was one very visible aspect of the package, but adjustments were also proposed for corporate taxes as well. Other government initiatives included amendments to the corporate governance law to protect shareholders' rights; legislation to control money laundering; provision for the sale of land to both domestic and foreign buyers (in the first instance, commercial and urban land only); a new labor code that tightened conditions for trade union organization; a new system governing the distribution of tax revenues between the center and the regions; and a new customs code. Other drafts were in the process of development or approval in 2002–2003, including pension reform, amendments to the bankruptcy law, simplification of licensing procedures for various types of business activity, municipal reform, civil service reform, and initiatives to reduce subsidization of housing and communal services. The active legislative program of the government and the latter's ability to secure the legislature's approval of key proposals suggested that the state might be successful in rebuilding its capacity to govern.

A second pillar of Putin's economy policy has been the attempt to rein in the power of the economic oligarchs. In the Yeltsin period, conflicts of interest had become endemic as state officials became involved in the bartering of concessions in exchange for economic benefits or political support. The result was that publicly espoused goals of the government succumbed to the politics of private economic interest. The "normalization" of the Russian economy would depend on the state's establishing a clear legal authority in relation to the oligarchs, but to do so would require the state to exercise autonomous authority. The Yeltsin team had failed to find an exit from this vicious circle. It remains unclear whether Putin will succeed in doing so. Observers have noted, however, that Putin's targeting of the oligarchs has been selective, focusing on critics or opponents such as Gusinsky and Berezovksy but leaving others untouched. Others feel that Putin's strategy is a corporatist one, involving patron-client relations,

Paying Taxes Helps You Sleep.
Father's words: "And then Snow White fell into a deep sleep."
Son's words: "Does that mean that she paid all her taxes?"
This young boy has taken to heart the Russian government's much touted slogan to improved tax compliance: "Pay your taxes and sleep well at night."
Source: Elkin, *Izvestiia*, Jan. 29, 2002

selective consultation, and use of designated groups to channel input, a form of soft authoritarianism involving control over dissent and opposition.[17]

Society and Economy

Soviet Social Policy

The Soviet system allowed the leadership to establish priorities with little input from society. One such priority was military production, but realization of social goals was also a policy focus, producing some of the most marked achievements of the Soviet system. Among benefits offered to the population were free health care, low-cost access to essential goods and services, maternity leave (partially paid), child benefits, and disability pensions. Mass education was another social priority of the Soviet regime, and this approach was bolstered by the belief that science and education are engines of progress. All segments of the population were provided free access to primary and secondary schooling. Private schools and universities were forbidden, and postsecondary education was free of charge,

with state stipends provided to university students. Following graduation, university graduates were assigned to particular jobs (sometimes in remote places) for a brief period as payment for the free education provided by the state.

Guaranteed employment and job security were other core elements of the tacit social contract; only in exceptional cases could an enterprise fire an employee. Participation in the labor market was high: almost all able-bodied adults, men and women, worked outside the home. As in China today, citizens received many of these benefits through their place of employment, thus making the Soviet workplace a social as well as an economic institution. The full-employment policy made unemployment compensation unnecessary. The retirement age was fifty-five for women and sixty for men, although in the early 1980s, about one-third of those beyond retirement age continued to work. Modest pensions were guaranteed by the state, ensuring a stable but minimal standard of living for retirement.

Although basic social needs were met in the Soviet Union, the system was plagued by shortages and low-quality service. For example, the availability of advanced medical equipment was limited, and sometimes under-the-table payments were required to prompt better quality service. Regional differences persisted as well. Many goods and services, although economically in the reach of every citizen, were in short supply, so queues were a pervasive part of everyday life. Housing shortages restricted mobility and forced young couples and their children to share a small apartment with parents. In the area of education and employment, the state found it difficult to match educational training to society's needs; therefore, many people were employed in jobs below their skill levels or in positions that did not match their formal training. In the employment sector, an irony of the system was that labor in many sectors was in constant short supply, reflecting the inefficient use of the work force. Labor productivity was low by international standards and work discipline weak: drunkenness and absenteeism were common. A Soviet saying of the time captured this element of the tacit social contract: "We pretend to work, they pretend to pay us." Whereas the lax work atmosphere reduced the likelihood and frequency of labor conflicts, it also kept production inefficient. Alcoholism and health problems due to environmental pollution were also significant problems in the Soviet period.

Another feature of the system was the relatively low level of inequality. As a matter of state policy, wage differentials between the best- and worst-paid were lower than in most Western economies. This approach seemed in harmony with overriding cultural values, but at the same it reduced the incentive for outstanding achievements and innovation. Because land and factories were state owned, individuals could not accumulate wealth in the form of real estate, stocks, or ownership of factories. Any privileges that did exist were modest by Western standards. Political elites did have access to scarce goods, higher-quality health care, travel, and vacation homes, but these privileges were hidden from public view. An underlying assumption of this approach seemed to be that a dismal equality was superior to the tensions and discontent that visible inequality might evoke.

Economic Reform and Russian Society

Social and economic patterns from the Soviet system have helped to define potential bases of collective identity, expectations about state policy, and grievances against authority in the new Russia. A market economy involves less direct state involvement in securing the types of social welfare that Russians had come to expect, and budget constraints necessitated cutbacks in state welfare programs at a time when there was a growing need for them. After 1991, pensions had decreased buying power, and state services to deal with increasing problems of homelessness and poverty proved inadequate. In line with the new market ideology, tuition fees for postsecondary education were introduced in many cases, and although a system of universal health care remained, higher-quality health care was made more obviously dependent on ability to pay. The cost of medicine rose beyond the reach of many citizens. Benefits provided through the workplace were cut back, as even viable businesses faced pressures to reduce costs and increase productivity.

Some groups have suffered more from the reform process than others, including children, pensioners, and the disabled. The number of homeless and beggars has skyrocketed, especially in large cities like Moscow, a magnet for displaced persons and refugees from war zones on Russia's perimeter. Alongside the "new poor" are the "new rich," probably less than 2 to 3 percent of the population, who enjoy a standard of living luxurious even by Western standards. These people, many of them multimillionaires with Western bank accounts, were able to take advantage of the privatization process to gain positions in lucrative sectors like banking, finance, oil, and gas. Between these two extremes, the mass of the Soviet population itself is affected by growing differentials in income. The percentage of the population with incomes below the subsistence level registered at 30 percent in 1999.[18] Dramatic declines in income have affected those without easily marketable skills, including unskilled laborers in low-priority sectors of the economy and people working in areas of public service such as education. Wage rates are highest for skilled workers in the natural resource sectors (e.g., oil and gas) and in new sectors such as banking and finance. Individuals who have marketable skills (e.g., accounting, knowledge of English or German) have also benefited. These growing income differentials are becoming more visible, but many Russians view them as illegitimate, seeing them as a sign of corruption rather than of hard work and initiative.

Public opinion surveys indicate that in 2001, the majority of Russians were increasingly optimistic about economic prospects and gradually adapting to the new economic circumstances. Since 2000, levels of personal consumption have grown following years of decline, but many individuals (particularly men) have two to three jobs just to make ends meet. Unemployment, an expected side effect of the shock therapy, has proven difficult to measure. Official measures showed an average rate of 9.8 percent in 2000 and 8.7 percent in 2001.[19] But these figures hide short-term layoffs, workers still employed but only sporadically paid, or people shifted to partial employment. On the other hand, some employment in the shadow economy goes unreported. Consumer price inflation remained at a high but tolerable rate of 20 to 21 percent in 2000–2001 after falling from 86 percent in 1999.

In some cases, economic strains have reinforced ethnic and national cleavages. Levels of unemployment are particularly high in some regions, including republics and regions with high ethnic minority populations.[20] Aboriginal groups in Russia's far north have suffered particularly adverse effects as a result of the economic decline. Northern regions depend on the maintenance of a fragile transport and communications system for deliveries of basic necessities such as fuel and food. Ethnic regions with rich natural resources, such as the Tatarstan, have sought greater economic autonomy to permit them to take advantage of potential profits from this natural wealth.

Women suffer many of the same hardships now that they did in the Soviet period. They continue to carry the bulk of domestic responsibilities, including shopping, cooking, housework, and child care. In addition, most women continue to feel compelled to work outside the home to help make ends meet. Many women take advantage of the permitted three-year maternity leave, which is only partially paid. Fathers play a relatively small role in child raising; many women must rely on grandparents to help out. Employers are sometimes reluctant to hire women of child-bearing age who have certain rights to maternity leave that employers may view as disruptive or expensive to fulfill. Some data suggest, however, that while women are more likely to register with unemployment offices and take longer to find new jobs, levels of actual unemployment are fairly equal for men and women.[21]

The birthrate in Russia fell from 16.6 births per 1,000 people in 1985 to a rate of 9.5 births in 2001, while the death rate was 13.85.[22] Life expectancy for Soviet men fell from 64 years in 1964–1965 to just over 60 by the end of the century (72.5 for women).[23] These demographic trends are a striking example of the social costs of the economic transformation. The decline in population has been tempered only by the immigration of ethnic Russians from other former Soviet republics (see Table 2). While declining birthrates are a common corollary of economic modernization, many couples in Russia are especially reluctant to have children because of daily hardships, future uncertainty, a declining standard of living, and continuing housing shortages—a line of thinking that reflects a dangerous demoralization of public life. Today, contraceptive devices and sanitary products are more widely available than in the past, but the former are expensive if they are of reliable quality.

Russian Political Culture and Economic Change

Alongside more objective factors, culture affects processes of economic change. Particular aspects of Russian political culture that may inhibit adaptation to a market economy include a weak tradition of individual entrepreneurship, a widespread commitment to egalitarian values, and a reliance on relations of personal trust rather than written contracts. Profit, as a measure of success, is less important to many Russians than is support for friends and coworkers; thus, firing redundant workers may be an unpalatable approach. Selection of business partners or recruitment of personnel may be strongly influenced by personal contacts and relationships rather than by merit. These and other features of the Soviet social contract have produced a work ethic that is not completely compatible with capitalist economic practices. Risk avoidance, low productivity, poor punctuality, absenteeism, lack of personal responsibility and initiative, and a preference for security over achievement are all work habits tolerated, perhaps even encouraged, by the Soviet system.[24] However, when offered appropriate incentives, employees of Western firms in Russia tend to operate at high levels of efficiency and, after a period of time, to adopt work habits rewarded by the employing organization.

Younger Russians are better able to adapt to the new economic conditions than their elders are. They are also more supportive of the market transition and are more oriented toward maximizing self-interest and demonstrating initiative. Thus, generational change is

Table 2

Migration Into and Out of Russia, 1995–2001

Year	Immigration from CIS and Baltic Countries	Emigration to CIS and Baltic Countries	Net Flow from CIS/Baltics	Immigration from Other Foreign Countries	Emigration to Other Foreign Countries	Net Flow from other Foreign Countries	Total Inflow from Immigration
1995	658,000	176,900	481,100	20,400	89,000	–68,600	412,500
1996	458,200	144,000	314,200	12,400	71,500	–59,100	255,100
1997	417,600	113,300	304,300	12,900	64,700	–51,800	252,500
1998	377,800	98,200	279,600	15,200	55,700	–40,500	239,100
1999	255,600	102,000	153,600	9,400	60,000	–50,600	103,000
2000	168,500	41,500	127,000	4,500	30,800	–26,300	100,700
2001	77,800	29,600	48,200	3,300	29,900	–26,600	21,600

This table is based on data from State Commission of the Russian Federation on Statistic, *Current Statistical Survey,* no. 4 (1996), no. 4 (1997), no. 4 (1998), no. 4 (1999), no. 3 (2001), p. 8, in each issue.

an important factor in understanding Russia's economic development. Nevertheless, a significant portion of Russians of all age groups still seem to question many of the values underlying the market reform process, preferring an economy that is less profit driven and places more emphasis on equality and the collective good but at the same time is somewhat less efficient and productive. Survey data suggest that although Russians support the idea of democracy and appreciate the freedom they have gained since the collapse of communism, they are much less enamored with the basic notions underlying the capitalist economic system.[25]

Russia and the International Political Economy

Right up to the end of the Soviet period, the economy remained relatively isolated from outside influences. Most of the USSR's trade (53 percent of imports, 51 percent of exports, in 1984) was carried out with the countries of Eastern Europe.[26] The ruble, the Soviet currency, was nonconvertible, meaning that its exchange rate was set by the state (at various levels for various types of exchange) and did not fluctuate freely in response to economic forces. Furthermore, the ruble could not legally be taken out of the country. All foreign trade was channeled through central state organs, so individual enterprises had neither the possibility nor the incentive to seek external markets. Accounts in Western currencies (so-called hard currency) were under state control. Russia's rich natural resource base,

particularly oil and gas, provided an important source of hard currency income and insulated the country from incurring a larger hard-currency debt.

Gorbachev sought to integrate the USSR more fully into the global economy by reducing international tensions, permitting some foreign investment through joint ventures, and reducing barriers to foreign contacts. The new Russia has pursued this policy even more aggressively. Over time, restrictions on foreign investment have been lifted, the value of the ruble has been allowed to respond to market conditions (although there are still restrictions on the export of the ruble), and firms are allowed to conclude agreements directly with foreign partners. In response, Western governments (with Germany at the top of the list) have made fairly generous commitments of technical and humanitarian assistance. Assistance programs have included training programs to help government officials, individual entrepreneurs, and social organizations adapt to the new challenges of market reform. The World Bank, the IMF, and the EU have also contributed substantial amounts of economic assistance, often in the form of repayable credits. In the past, release of money from a ruble stabilization fund established by the IMF was made contingent on Russia's pursuing a strict policy of fiscal and monetary control and lifting remaining price controls. The Russian government had difficulties in meeting these conditions, and thus the funds were released intermittently and often in limited amounts. In 2001, the Russian government owed international lenders $120.5 billion (of which $63 billion was inherited from the Soviet period); Russian banks and companies owed $36.4 billion.[27] After the August 1998 crisis, the Russian government defaulted first on the ruble-denominated short-term debt and then on the former Soviet debt. Since then, debt repayments have been made on time. In 2001, the Russian government decided to forgo additional IMF credits, possibly because of the government's more favorable budgetary balance, facilitated by improved collection of tax revenues and income from oil and gas sales abroad. However, debt repayment draws resources away from investment, which is needed to fuel the economic recovery. Current levels of investment, about 40 percent of 1990 levels, are inadequate to rebuild the structure of the economy.[28] Investment in public goods, such as education, has also declined.

Russia has had problems attracting foreign investment, even in its improved economic circumstances, since 1999. In 2002, an estimated 6 percent of total investment was of foreign origin.[29] Although a large number of foreign-Russian joint ventures are legally registered, many are not operational. Continued uncertainty and instability regarding government policy toward joint ventures as well as a few highly visible murders of prominent business figures have reduced investor confidence, particularly since August 1998. The focus of Russia's foreign trade activity has shifted significantly since the Soviet period. Whereas in 1994, Ukraine was Russia's most important trading partner, now Germany holds first place, receiving 9 percent of Russian exports, followed by the United States with 7.7 percent in 2000. Germany provided 11.5 percent of imports in 2000, followed by Belarus (11.1 percent), Ukraine (10.8 percent), and the United States (8.0 percent).[30] In the year 2000, over a third of Russia's exports were to countries of the EU, more than combined exports to Eastern European and the countries of the

Commonwealth of Independent States (CIS). An even larger proportion of imports came from the EU area (about 40 percent),[31] making efforts to work out special trade arrangements with the EU an important task. In November 2002, a point of tension between the EU and Russia was addressed when the EU agreed to accommodate Russian concerns to facilitate travel for Russian citizens through Lithuania (an EU candidate) between Kaliningrad *oblast* (a Russian province with no land connection to the rest of the country) and the rest of Russia.[32]

Russia's position in the international political economy remains undetermined. With a highly skilled work force and an advanced technological base in certain sectors (especially military sectors), Russia has many of the ingredients necessary to become a competitive and powerful force in the global economy. However, if the country's industrial capacity is not restored, Russia's reliance on natural resource exports will leave the country particularly vulnerable to global economic fluctuations in price and demand. At the same time, its wealth in natural resources has given Russia advantages compared to its neighbors, since these expensive materials do not need to be imported. In 2001, 54 percent of exports were fuels or energy resources, another 17 percent were metals, while only 8.9 percent were machinery and transport equipment. The latter made up nearly a third of imports, when 20.6 percent of Russia's imports were food and beverages, a striking figure for a country with Russia's land mass.[33] Ultimately, Russia's position in the global economy will depend on the ability of the country's leadership to fashion a politically viable approach to domestic economic problems. The clock cannot be turned back to the days of economic isolation that characterized the Soviet period. President Putin seems to recognize this and is moving Russia even further in the direction of global integration.

Section ❸ Governance and Policy-Making

Like everything else in Russia, the organization of the state has undergone dramatic change. Until December 1991, Russia was a union republic in a nominally federal Soviet Union; now Russia is an independent state with its own constitution and political institutions. Un-

der Soviet power, state organs had to answer to the Communist Party, the sole party permitted to function. After 1991, the executive state organs gained dominance, and political parties sprang up like mushrooms. Finally, in the Soviet period, the head of state was the leader of the Communist Party, whereas now he is a powerful popularly elected president. The basic edifice of democratic political institutions has been constructed in Russia. However, political analysts continue to debate whether democratic principles are actually being realized or whether the strong executive may lay the groundwork for a new "soft" authoritarian path.

Organization of the State

Since 1991, Russia has moved in the direction of adopting fundamental liberal democratic principles as the basis of its political institutions, similar to those underlying West European and North American polities. Ratification of a new constitution in 1993 was a contested political process, but the outcome was a document that provides for competitive elections within a multiparty context, separation of powers, an independent judiciary, federalism, and protection of individual civil liberties. While the institutional structures represent a mix of parliamentary and presidential features, a key characteristic is the strength of executive power. This feature of Russian political life is both a response to the demands for leadership required in a period of radical change and a reflection of Russia's political tradition, which has seen a strong role for central political authority. At the same time, Russia's multiparty system is fragmented and fluid, government bureaucratic organs have been repeatedly restructured, and the state has had only a limited capacity to implement policies and ensure compliance. While elections have been carried out on schedule and recognized by international observers as generally fair and genuinely competitive, a skewed distribution of economic power and media control has had a strong, sometimes even a decisive, impact on electoral and policy outcomes.

The Russian Federation inherited a complex structure of regional subunits from the Soviet period. Between 1991 and 1993, negotiations between the central government and the various regions led to the establishment of a complex federal structure with eighty-nine units. Although all of these eighty-nine federal units are given equal status by the constitution, in fact they are treated differently (and not always equally). Some of these subnational governments have resisted compliance with federal laws (and one, Chechnya, has demanded independence; see "Current Challenges: The Chechnya Crisis") generating a process of negotiation

and political conflict between the center and the regions that sometimes has involved regions' adopting policies that contradict the constitution or federal laws. The regularization of Russian federalism has been defined by the Putin administration as one of its most important goals.

The relationship between organs of the federal government has also been conflict ridden. The constitution makes the executive dominant, but still dependent on the agreement of the legislative branch to realize its programs. Tension between the two branches of government, which are selected in separate electoral processes, was a persistent obstacle to effective governance in the Yeltsin years and one that Putin also has tried, somewhat successfully, to address since his election in 2000. The executive itself has two heads (the president and the prime minister), introducing other possibilities for intrastate conflict. Relations between the executive and judicial branches were strained in the Yeltsin years, and the establishment of real judicial independence remains a significant political challenge. Finally, the poor salaries and the lack of professionalism of the civil service have opened the door to corruption and political influence.

Many of the difficulties facing the new Russian state are, at least in part, legacies of the Soviet period. While in many ways the new political leadership tried to wipe the slate clean and start anew after 1992, some political scientists have emphasized the importance of "path dependence," that is, the manner in which past experience shapes the choices and options available for change.[34] Many of the new Russian leaders, such as Yeltsin himself, were socialized in the Soviet system; new ways of conducting political life have not come naturally. The current Russian state represents a mix of old and new personnel and ways of conducting the affairs of state.

The Soviet State

Before Gorbachev's reforms, top organs of the Communist Party of the Soviet Union (CPSU) dominated the state. The CPSU was a hierarchical structure in which lower party bodies elected delegates to higher party organs, but these elections were uncontested, and top organs determined candidates for lower party posts. The Politburo, the top party organ, considered all important policy issues and was the real decision-making center. A larger body, the Central Committee, represented the broader political elite, including regional

Current Challenges: *The Chechnya Crisis*

Despite its small size and population (estimated at 600,000 in 1994), the breakaway republic of Chechnya holds an important position on Russia's southern border. The republic is widely perceived as a safe haven for criminal elements that operate in Russia. In the early 1990s, the Russian leadership feared that Chechnya's attempted secession from the Russian Federation might embolden other republics to pursue a similar course. These concerns motivated Russia to send troops into Chechnya on December 11, 1994, fueling a regional civil war.

The desire for independence has deep roots in Chechnya. Prior to its incorporation into the Russian Empire in 1859 and again after the Bolshevik revolution in 1917, local forces fought to maintain Chechnya's independence. In 1924, Chechnya was made part of the USSR, and in 1934 it was joined with an adjacent region, Ingushetia, to form a single autonomous republic within the Soviet Union. During World War II, following an anti-Soviet uprising, Stalin deported hundreds of Chechens to Soviet Central Asia.

Taking advantage of the ongoing political upheaval in the USSR, in October 1991 the newly elected president of the republic, Dzhokar Dudaev, declared Chechnya's independence from Russia. In 1992, Checheno-Ingushetia was officially recognized by the Russian government as two separate republics. Following the split, Chechen leaders continued to pursue independence, a claim rejected by the Russian government. Intervention by Russian military forces in December 1994 evoked criticism within the Russian Federation and its leadership circles. Some opposed the intervention completely, favoring a political solution; others were primarily critical of the ineffective manner in which the war effort was carried out. The campaign was poorly organized and internal dissension within the army and security forces demoralized the troops. Civilians in Chechnya and the surrounding regions suffered at the hands of both sides. On June 14, 1995, Chechen fighters took control of the city Budennovsk in the adjacent Russian province of Stavropol and held some 1,500 hostages in a local hospital. An attempt by Russian forces to storm the hospital led to the escape of only 150 hostages, while the others were killed. In January 1996, another hostage-taking in the adjacent republic of Dagestan again took the conflict beyond Chechnya's borders.

The unpopular war became an important issue in the 1996 presidential campaign and threatened to undermine Yeltsin's already fragile support. In late May 1996, a cease-fire agreement was signed, and in June, Yeltsin decreed the beginning of troop withdrawals. Apparently these steps were sufficient to prevent the issue from undermining Yeltsin's reelection prospects, but they were not sufficient to stop the war. Skirmishes continued. In September 1996 an agreement with the rebels was again signed. The joint declaration put off a decision on Chechnya's status for five years, leaving the issue unresolved.

On January 27, 1997, an election was held for the president of the Republic of Chechnya. Observers generally considered the vote to be fair, with 79 percent of the eligible population participating. In a race involving thirteen candidates, Aslan Mashkhadov received 59 percent of the vote. Relative to other leading candidates, Mashkhadov was considered to be a moderate. However, he publicly supported Chechnya's independence, and lawlessness continued to prevail in the Republic.

In 1999, terrorist bombings, attributed to Chechen rebels, occurred in apartment buildings in Moscow and two other Russian cities, causing about 300 deaths; Chechen insurgents again entered Dagestan. The second war against Chechnya was launched as Yeltsin sent nearly 100,000 Russian troops to regain control of the breakaway republic. The troops occupied the Chechen capital Grozny; refugees spilled into surrounding areas and beyond Chechnya's borders. Allegations of human rights violations were made both against Russian troops and Chechen rebels; Western governments and international organizations such as Human Rights Watch demanded that the Russian government comply with international human rights standards.

Russian authorities resist external involvement in the situation, maintaining that the Chechnya crisis is a domestic political issue. In September 2002, Russia threatened to send forces into the Pankisi Gorge in neighboring Georgia, alleging that the region was being used by Chechen rebels to launch cross-border attacks. President Putin has repeatedly emphasized the existence of links between Chechen rebels and international terrorist networks, including al Qaeda, in an effort to gain Western acceptance for Russia's military actions.

Since 1999, Russian authorities have periodically claimed imminent victory in the military struggle. However, Russian forces have proven unable to rout rebels from the mountainous regions of the republic. The Russian government has expressed its willingness to engage in negotiations on the condition that Chechen rebels release their hostages and that those charged with terrorist acts in Russia be extradited. Chechen rebels have refused to comply. On October 23, 2002, Chechen terrorists with explosives strapped to their persons took over a Moscow theater, holding 800 civilians hostage. In the face of the rebels' threat to blow up the building, Russian troops gassed and stormed the building; the gas led to the deaths of about 130 hostages and 41 hostage-takers.

Russia launched new offensives in Chechnya, and on December 27, 2002, Chechen rebels blew up the pro-Russian administrative building in Grozny, leading to approximately sixty deaths. Despite repeated Russian claims that the situation is under control, no end is in sight. Putin's failure to resolve the crisis has the potential to undermine Putin's popularity with the Russian public.

Adapted, with the help of Yevgen Shevchenko, from Joan DeBardeleben, *Russian Politics in Transition*, 2nd ed. Copyright 1997 by Houghton Mifflin Company. Reprinted with permission.

party leaders and representatives of various economic and social interests. Alongside the CPSU were Soviet state structures that formally resembled those of Western parliamentary systems but had little decision-making authority. The state bureaucracy, which was considerably larger than the party bureaucracy, had day-to-day responsibility in both the economic and political spheres but operated in subordination to the party's directives. People holding high state positions were appointed through the *nomenklatura* system, a mechanism that allowed the CPSU to fill key posts with politically reliable individuals. The Supreme Soviet, the parliament, was a rubber-stamp body; its members were directly elected by the population, but the single candidate who ran in each district was chosen by higher CPSU organs (but was not necessarily a party member).

In theory, the Soviet state was governed by a constitution, the last one adopted in 1977. In practice, however, the constitution was of symbolic rather than operational importance, since many of its principles were ignored. The constitution provided for legislative, executive, and judicial organs, but separation of powers was considered inapplicable to Soviet society because the CPSU claimed to represent the interests of society as a whole. With the power of appointment firmly under party control, it made little sense to speak of legislative or judicial independence. When the constitution was violated (as it frequently was), the courts had no independent authority to protect its provisions.

The Soviet Union was also designated a federal system; that is, according to the constitution, certain powers were granted to the fifteen union republics (which have since become independent states). However, this was "phony federalism," since all aspects of life were overseen by a highly centralized Communist Party. Nonetheless, the various subunits that existed within the Russian Republic (***autonomous republics, krais, oblasts,*** and ***okrugs***) were carried over into the Russian Federation in an altered form, an example of path dependence.

Gorbachev began a process of radical institutional change through the introduction of competitive elections, increased political pluralism, reduced Communist Party dominance, a revitalized legislative branch of government, and renegotiation of the terms of Soviet federalism. He also tried to bring the constitution into harmony with political reality, and many constitu-

tional amendments were adopted that altered existing political institutions. Together, these changes moved the political system slowly and unsurely in a direction resembling the liberal democratic systems of the West.

The New Russian State

Incremental changes in the political institutions of the Russian republic itself began before the Russian Federation achieved independence in December 1991. A new post of president was created for the Russian republic, and on June 12, 1991, Boris Yeltsin was elected by direct popular vote as its first incumbent. This election gave Yeltsin a base of popular legitimacy during his first years in the leadership post. Once Russia became an independent state, it quickly became clear that the existing institutional structures were not functioning well. A crucial turning point was the adoption by referendum of a new Russian constitution in December 1993. It is this constitution that governs current political institutions (see Figure 2). However, as in any other country, political practice goes far beyond constitutional provisions and sometimes alters their interpretation. In some ways, the evolution of governance and policy-making in the Russian Federation since 1991 can be seen as a laboratory for engineering democratic governance, somewhat analogous to the experience of Germany and Japan after World War II. The success and outcome of the Russian democratic experiment still hang in the balance.

The Executive

The constitution establishes a semipresidential system, formally resembling the French system but with stronger executive power. The president, who holds primary power, is the head of state, and the prime minister, appointed by the president but approved by the lower house of the parliament (the State *Duma*), is the head of government. The structure of the dual executive can introduce tensions within the executive branch, as well as between the president and the *Duma*. As a rule of thumb, the president has overseen foreign policy, relations with the regions, and the organs of state security, while the prime minister has focused his attention on the economy and related issues. However, with Yeltsin's continuing health problems in 1998 and 1999,

Figure 2

Political Institutions of the Russian Federation (R.F.), 2002

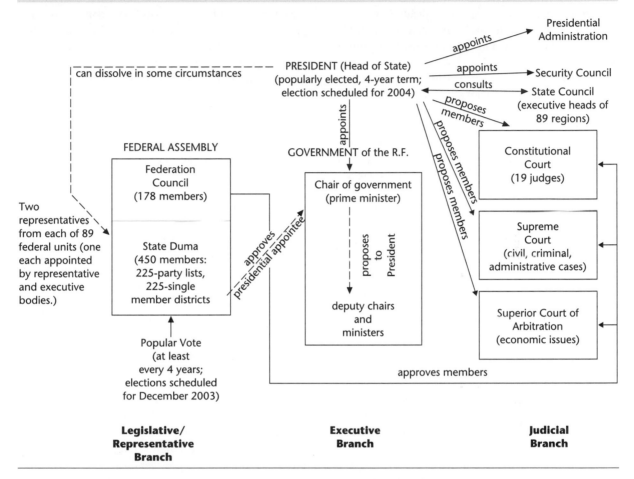

operative power shifted in the direction of the prime minister. Since the election of Vladimir Putin in March 2000, the primary locus of power has returned to the presidency; the prime minister, Mikhail Kasyanov, who rose through the Finance Ministry, has taken a major role in the economic sphere, but innuendoes of dissatisfaction with his performance by President Putin have raised persistent questions about his likely longevity in office.

The president is elected directly by the population every four years, and no individual may serve more than two terms. In 1996, the first presidential elections under Russia's new constitution were carried out. De-

spite Yeltsin's low popularity in early 1996, he waged a successful election campaign, but his declining health reduced his ability to deal with Russia's crisis conditions. In December 2000, Yeltsin resigned from office, making the prime minister, Vladimir Putin, acting president until the March 2000 elections, which he won handily.

One of the president's most important powers is the authority to issue decrees, which Yeltsin used frequently to address contentious issues such as privatization, salaries of state workers, the running of the economy, and anticrime measures. Presidential decrees have the force of law until formal legislation is passed, but because they can be annulled as quickly as they are approved, they do not command the same respect as actual laws. Although presidential decrees may not violate the constitution or specific legislation passed by the bicameral legislature (the Federal Assembly), policymaking by decree can allow the president to ignore an uncooperative or divided parliament. The president's decision in 1994 and again in 1999 to launch the offensive in Chechnya was not approved by either house of parliament, despite strong objections from a broad range of political groups. President Putin has also used his power of decree but less extensively than Yeltsin, in part because he has managed to forge a more cooperative relationship with the parliament and thus has been able to resolve many policy debates through the legislative process.

The president has other powers, including the right to call a state of emergency, impose martial law, grant pardons, call referenda, and temporarily suspend actions of other state organs if he deems them to contradict the constitution or federal laws. Some of these actions must be confirmed by other state organs (e.g., the upper house of the parliament, the Federation Council). The president is commander in chief of the armed forces and conducts affairs of state with other nations. Impeachment of the president is a complicated process involving the *Duma,* the Federation Council, the Supreme Court, and the Constitutional Court. If the president dies in office or becomes incapacitated, the post is filled by the prime minister until new presidential elections can be held.

The Russian government is headed by the prime minister and five deputy prime ministers. The president's choice of prime minister must be approved by the *Duma.* During the course of Yeltsin's presidency of the Russian Federation, six prime ministers held office, the longest being Viktor Chernomyrdin, from December 1992 until March 1998, and the final one being Vladimir Putin, appointed in August 1999. The prime minister can be removed by the *Duma* if it votes no confidence two times within three months; although the process has been attempted several times in the past decade, usually spearheaded by the Communist Party faction, it has never succeeded. If the *Duma* fails to approve a president's nominee, the *Duma* itself can be dissolved, so the legislative body has been reluctant to remove a sitting prime minister. The president has also, on occasion, had difficulty gaining approval of

his nominee for prime minister, most notably following the 1998 financial crisis when three prime ministers were in office over a seventeen-month period. Here too the *Duma* has ultimately been reluctant to defy the president because rejection of the candidate three times can lead to dissolution of the *Duma* itself. The prime minister has never been a member of the dominant party or coalition in the *Duma*; thus, principles of party accountability that apply in most Western parliamentary systems are not operative in Russia. Without disciplined parties and with no formal links between parties and the executive branch, the president and prime minister must work hard to gain parliamentary acceptance of their proposals.

The National Bureaucracy

The new Russian state inherited a large bureaucratic apparatus. Since market reform reduced the role of the state in economic management, a decrease in the size of the bureaucracy was widely expected. But despite proclaimed intentions, efforts to downsize the executive bureaucratic apparatus have been only partially successful. Alongside the state bureaucracy is the presidential administration, which serves the president directly. With some 2,000 employees, the presidential administration can duplicate or compete with the formal agencies of the state, while some government ministries (e.g., the Foreign Affairs Ministry, the Federal Security Service, and the Defense Ministry) report directly to the president.[35] The State Legal Office reviews all legislation before the president signs it. The president also uses consultants from outside formal government structures to advise his staff on particular issues. Other resources available to the presidential administration include the Academy of State Service in Moscow[36] and its regional affiliates, teaching and research institutions that served the Central Committee in Soviet times and now undertake commissioned research and host training programs and conferences at the behest of the presidential administration.

The president has created various advisory bodies that serve to solicit input from important political and economic actors, but also to co-opt them into support for government policies. These organs have no constitutional status, and thus could be abolished at will. The most important are the Security Council and the State Council. Formed in 1994, the Security Council advises the president in areas related to foreign policy and security (broadly conceived) and includes heads of appropriate government bodies (the so-called power ministries such as Defense and the Federal Security Service), the prime minister, and the heads of seven newly created federal districts. The State Council was formed in September 2000 as part of Putin's attempt to redefine the role of regional leaders in federal decision making (see below). The State Council, which includes all eighty-nine regional heads, has a consultative role, but without giving the regional executives any real power. A smaller presidium, made up of seven of the regional heads selected by the president, meets monthly, while the State Council itself meets at least every three months. While Putin appointed business leader, Aleksandr Abramov, as first secretary of the council, the president himself chairs the body and seems to keep a tight rein on its discussion agenda.

The bureaucratic agencies that make up the executive branch itself include ministries, state committees, and other agencies. Ministers other than the prime minister do not require parliamentary approval. The prime minister makes recommendations to the president, who appoints these officials. President Putin's May 2000 decree[37] outlining a reorganization of executive organs provided for twenty-four ministries, six state committees, two federal commissions, and twenty-five bodies of other types, such as the Federal Security Service and the Tax Inspectorate. Ministers and other agency heads are generally career bureaucrats who have risen through an appropriate ministry, although sometimes more clearly political appointments are made. Many agencies have been reorganized, often more than once. Reorganization of the state's bureaucracy results not only from restructuring of the economy and of state functions; top leaders also use restructuring to induce political loyalty and place their clients and allies in key positions in the new agencies. **Patron-client networks,** which were important in the Soviet period, continue to play a key role in both the presidential administration and other state organs. These linkages are similar to old-boy networks in the West (and they most often involve men in the Russian case); they underscore the importance of personal career ties between individuals as they rise in bureaucratic or political structures. For example, Putin has drawn heavily on colleagues with whom he worked earlier in St. Petersburg or in the security establishment in staffing a variety of posts in his administration. With the collapse of the *nomenklatura*

system and the absence of a functioning system of civil service appointments, politicians and government officials look to people they know and trust as they staffed their organizations.[38] Although this type of personal trust is very important in the Russian context, the operation of patron-client networks can undermine confidence in the competence and fairness of government agencies since merit may be less important than loyalty in determining who fulfills important positions. In an effort to increase the role of merit and the professional character of the civil service, the president himself issued a decree in August 2002; legislation to reform the civil service was presented to the Duma and passed on a first reading in January 2003.

In Putin's restructuring of government agencies, a new Ministry for Economic Development and Trade, headed by German Gref, took over functions of several previously existing ministries, as did a new Ministry of Industry, Science, and Technology. Observers question whether such reorganizations produce substantive benefits, and some are particularly controversial. For example, the State Committee for Environmental Protection was abolished by the May 2000 decree, with its responsibilities transferred to the Ministry of Natural Resources. The mixing of responsibility for overseeing both use and protection of natural resources in this single agency may be an indicator of the low priority of environmental protection (as compared to resource use). Functions of the State Committee on Northern Affairs were transferred to the Ministry for Economic Development and Trade, viewed by some as a downgrading of northern concerns on the government's agenda.

Other State Institutions

The Military and Security Organs

Because of Vladimir Putin's career background in the Soviet security agency (the KGB), he has drawn many of his staff from this arena. For example, five of the presidential representatives for the seven new federal districts (discussed below) have career backgrounds in the KGB, the military, or the Ministry of Internal Affairs. Thus, while the formal rank of the Federal Security Service has not changed, the actual impact of the security establishment has taken on increasing importance in the Putin era. This development preceded the events of September 11, 2001, and the important role placed on security concerns is reflective of the orientation of the current Russian state under Putin's leadership. Because many Russians are alarmed by the crime rate and terrorist bombings in the country, restrictions on civil liberties have not elicited the popular concern typical of many Western countries. At the same time, there is widespread public cynicism about the honesty of the ordinary police (*militsiia*); many believe that payoffs by the mafia and even by ordinary citizens can buy their cooperation in overlooking crimes or ordinary legal infractions such as traffic tickets, and they are likely correct.[39]

The Russian government believes that terrorist attacks carried out in Russia in the form of bombings of apartments and railway stations that have occurred since 1999 are linked to a terrorist network connected to the Chechen rebels but with international links involving the al Qaeda network. Attacks on civilians in the context of the Chechen war have elicited Western human rights protests, and earlier warnings issued by President Putin about the terrorist threat were apparently not taken seriously, perhaps because they were viewed as a ploy to mute Western criticism of Russia's Chechnya policy. Since the September 11 attacks, cooperation between Russian and Western security agencies has increased, as Russia has shared security information and accepted an American presence in neighboring Georgia and Tadzhikistan. In turn, Western governments have muted their public criticism of Russian actions in Chechnya.

The Soviet military ranked as one of the largest and most powerful forces in the world, second only to that of the United States and justifying the country's designation as a superpower. Since the military was given preferential treatment and was represented in the political structures (almost always having at least one representative on the Politburo), political loyalty to the civilian authorities represented a good bargain for the military establishment. The Communist Party controlled military appointments, and while the military did lobby for particular policies and sometimes played a role in Kremlin intrigues, it never usurped political power. During the August 1991 coup attempt, troops remained loyal to Yeltsin and Gorbachev even though the minister of defense was among the coup plotters; there were no orders to fire on Soviet citizens who took to the streets in defense of the government. In Oc-

tober 1993, despite some apparent hesitancy in military circles, military units defended the government's position, this time firing on civilian protesters and shocking the country. It is noteworthy that in not a single postcommunist country has the military intervened to take power, which suggests that communist rule helped to cement the principle of civilian political control, earlier exercised through the communist party and now through elected political figures.

In the postcommunist period, the political power and prestige of the military have declined radically. Both Gorbachev and Yeltsin oversaw a reduction in military expenditures, which undermined the privileged position of military interests, bringing a decline in facilities for military personnel and a reduction in conventional and nuclear forces. Plans to downsize the military have been a source of tension between the political leadership and the military establishment, and the Putin government has also proclaimed its commitment to continue the process. The military's failure to implement a successful strategy in the Chechnya war has led the government to increase the role of the Federal Security Service there instead of relying on the army alone.[40] Reports of deteriorating conditions in some Russian nuclear arsenals have raised international concerns about nuclear security. In addition, the situation of military personnel, from the highest officers to rank-and-file soldiers, has deteriorated dramatically, producing a potential source of political unrest.

As of 2002, the Russian Federation still maintained a system of universal male conscription, but noncompliance has been a persistent problem; a law to permit alternative military service was signed in 2002, to take effect in January 2004. While the concept is welcomed by critics of the military service law, criticism has focused on the restrictive conditions that are imposed on alternative service by the new law. Government proposals to replace the conscript army by a smaller professional military corps have been on the agenda for some time, with the apparent target date now set for 2004. Given opposition to the idea in certain military circles, the adoption of the proposal is by no means a forgone conclusion.

The Judiciary

Concepts such as judicial independence and the rule of law were poorly understood in both prerevolutionary

Russia and the Soviet era. Gorbachev, however, emphasized the importance of constructing a law-based state, judicial independence, and due process. These concepts have been embedded in the new Russian constitution and seem to be accepted by a broad spectrum of political forces as underlying concepts in the Russian Federation. However, their implementation has been difficult and not wholly successful.

In Russia, a Constitutional Court was formed in 1991. Its decisions were binding, and in several cases even the president had to bow to its authority. After several controversial decisions that challenged the president's authority, Yeltsin suspended the operations of the court in late 1993. However, the new Russian constitution again provided for a Constitutional Court with the power to adjudicate disputes on the constitutionality of federal and regional laws, as well as jurisdictional disputes between various political institutions. Justices are nominated by the president and approved by the Federation Council, a procedure that produced a stalemate after the new constitution was adopted, so that the court became functional only in 1995. Among the justices are political figures, lawyers, legal scholars, and judges. Since 1995, the court has established itself as a vehicle for resolving conflicts relating to the protection of individual rights and conformity of regional laws with constitutional requirements.[41] The court has been cautious in confronting the executive branch, on which it depends to enforce its decisions.

Alongside the Constitutional Court is an extensive system of lower and appellate courts, with the Supreme Court at the pinnacle. These courts hear ordinary civil and criminal cases. In 1995, a system of commercial courts was also formed to hear cases dealing with issues related to privatization, taxes, and other commercial activities. Supreme Court judges are approved by the Federation Council after nomination by the president, and the constitution also grants the president power to appoint judges at other levels. In practice, methods of judicial selection vary, since executive authorities in some regions appoint judges anyway.[42] Measures to shield judges from political pressures include criminal prosecution for attempting to influence a judge and protections from arbitrary dismissal and criminal prosecution. Low judicial salaries draw qualified personnel away, lowering the overall quality of judicial decision making. The Russian judicial system operates on a civil code system, similar to most of continental Europe. One innovation in the legal system has included introduction of jury trials for some types of criminal offenses.

Subnational Government

The collapse of the Soviet Union was precipitated by the demands of some union republics for more autonomy and then independence. After the Russian Federation became an independent state, the problem of constructing a viable federal structure resurfaced.

The Russian Federation inherited a complex structure of regional subunits from the Soviet period. Between 1991 and 1993, negotiations between the central government and the various regions led to the establishment of a federal structure that includes eighty-nine units, which have different historical origins designations (twenty-one republics, forty-nine *oblasts,* six *krais,* ten autonomous *okrugs,* one autonomous *oblast,* and two cities with federal status, namely, St. Petersburg and Moscow). One of the major challenges that has faced both the Yeltsin and Putin administrations has been finding a workable relationship with the regions that respects the principles of federalism and the desire of regional authorities and population for some autonomy, while still retaining a unified governing structure within a single legal space.

One of the first issues to arise in the development of Russia's federal system was whether all of the eighty-nine units should have equal status. The republics have viewed themselves as a special category because of their different status in the Soviet period due to the presence of significant minority groups within their borders. They have also been the most assertive in putting forth claims for autonomy or even sovereignty. The most extreme example is Chechnya, whose demand for independence led to a protracted civil war. The Russian government's determination to oppose Chechen secession is reflective of its fear that separatist sentiment could spread. This has not happened, although other republics have declared sovereignty, an ambiguous claim rejected by the Constitutional Court. The ethnic dimension complicates political relations with some of the republics. For example, in Tatarstan, one of the most populous and most assertive of the republics, the titular nationality (the Tatars) formed 48.5 percent of the population in 1989 (the last available census data).

Figure 3

Level of Trust in Various Institutions in Russia (September 2000)

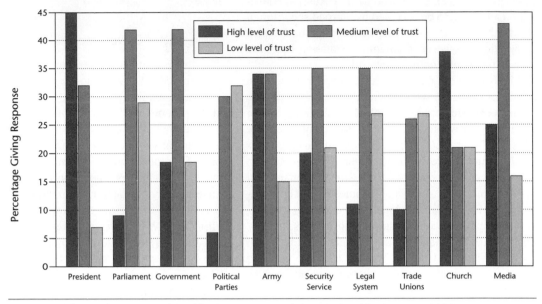

Source: Data from Russian Centre for Public Opinion Research (VTsIOM), *Public Opinion—2000,* www.wciom.ru (accessed October 2002).

In the Republic of Sakha (formerly Yakutia), which has valuable diamond reserves, Yakuts formed one-third of the population. The republics tend to be in peripheral areas of the Russian Federation (except for Tatarstan and Bashkortostan, which lie in the center of the country). Many are rich in natural resources, and an issue of dispute with the federal government has been control of these resources and the revenue they generate. While the constitution grants equal status to all eighty-nine units in the federation, republics have been given some special rights, such as declaring a second state language (in addition to Russian) and adopting their own constitutions. These documents may not contradict the federal constitution, but some provisions in fact do so. From 1994 to 1998, forty-six individual treaties were signed, first between the federal government and several of Russia's republics and then with other units of the federation. These treaties outlined the jurisdiction of each level of government and granted special privileges in some cases.

The de facto privileges granted to the republics drew protests from leaders of some of Russia's other regions—the *oblasts, krais,* and *okrugs;* some demanded their own agreements with the federal government, like those concluded with republics. This ad hoc approach produced a system of **asymmetrical federalism,** giving different regions varying privileges. The result was an escalation of regional demands and a drop in the perceived fairness of central policy. During the Yeltsin years, the central government's limited capacity to govern allowed subnational authorities to assume more power. In addition to control of natural resources, specific areas of conflict have involved ownership of property or factories, division of tax revenues, responsibility for social welfare programs (which the center wishes to transfer to the regions), provision of central subsidies for local enterprises or industrial restructuring, and issues of regional equalization.

It is no wonder that Putin identified the establishment of a uniform system of federal-regional relations, governed by uniform legal principles, as an important priority following the March 2000 election. He immediately took several steps to realize this objective, some of which were quite controversial because they appeared to involve a considerable recentralization of power, which might undermine the fragile federal arrangements outlined in the constitution. Putin continued Yeltsin's policy of appointing a special presidential representative to each region, but he also decreed the formation of seven new federal districts. Putin stated that these districts were not intended to replace the eighty-nine regional governments but were intended to oversee the work of federal offices operating in these regions and ensure compliance with federal laws and the constitution.

Most of the heads of these new federal districts had backgrounds in the security services, reinforcing concerns that the federal districts could become a powerful instrument of central control. In practice, the federal districts have been less intrusive than many feared. In some cases, there has been overt tension with assertive governors; in other cases, there has been apparently frictionless cooperation. No doubt some governors are hesitant to take a resistant stance that might alienate the powerful president and believe that cooperation will yield more benefits. The president set a deadline of 2002 for the rescinding of the special bilateral treaties that Yeltsin concluded first with the republics and then with other regions, but so far only a few regions have willingly given up the privileges that they afforded.

A second alteration to the federal-regional relationship introduced under Putin involves the role of the regional executives in national politics (referred to here as governors but called presidents in the republics). In the Yeltsin period, there was extensive political conflict over the method of selection of governors: initially, they were appointed by the president, but Yeltsin finally agreed to their popular election, which has given them a greater legitimacy and independence from Moscow. Since 1996, the governors, along with the heads of the each regional legislative body, sat as members of the upper house of the Russian parliament, the Federation Council. This arrangement gave the regional executives a direct voice in national legislative discussions and a presence in Moscow, but it divided their attention between their executive responsibilities in their home regions and their duties in Moscow. In 2001, Putin gained approval for a revision to the composition of the Federation Council; regional executives would, as of January 2002, no longer be members of the Federation Council. Rather, one regional representative would be appointed by the regional executive and the other by the regional legislature. Some governors re-

sisted this change, seeing it as an assault on their power (they would also lose the legal immunity that goes along with being a member of parliament). Putin made some concessions to make the change more palatable, for example, giving governors the right to recall their representatives. The State Council was formed to try to assure the regional executives that they would maintain some role in the federal policy-making arena, although losing their seats in the Federation Council. A final measure introduced by Putin, and upheld by the Constitutional Court, allows the president to remove a governor and disband a regional legislature if they engage in anticonstitutional activity, pending approval by a court. Although this measure has not been used, it communicated to regional executives that they should exhibit care in defying federal laws. The power was upheld by the Constitutional Court in 2002, but with many restrictions regarding its use.[43]

Fiscal federalism (the process of distribution of tax revenues between the various levels of government) has been another problematic area in center-regional relations. While the Soviet state pursued a considerable degree of regional equalization, regional differences have increased in the Russian Federation. The Putin government has accepted the legitimacy of some degree of regional equalization and has tried to create a more regularized system for determining the distribution of revenues, taking account of both the regional tax base and differences in the needs of various regions (e.g., northern regions have higher expenses to maintain basic services). An additional area requiring attention is the role and powers of local governments. Local governments have been saddled with responsibilities for social welfare but have not had adequate resources to fulfill them, a situation termed **unfunded mandates.** The Kozak Commission, formed in June 2001, was charged with developing a legislative foundation for the division of jurisdictions between the federal center, the regions, and local government, including the issue of unfunded mandates. Proposals presented in 2002 have evoked a lively political debate over the status of the various levels of government in the Russian Federation.

The Policy-Making Process

Policy-making occurs through both formal and informal mechanisms. The Russian constitution laid the ground rules for the adoption of legislation, one formal mechanism of policy-making. Although most legislation is proposed by the federal government, regional legislatures, the president, and his administration, individual deputies and some judicial bodies may also do so. Various organizations may be involved in the drafting of legislation, including the presidential administration, the parliamentary staff, and a special office within the federal government responsible for drafting economic legislation. Often, expert consultants are drawn into the process, involving organs such as the Security Council, special commissions (such as the Kozak Commission), and lobbyists representing regional, industrial, and sectoral interests. In August 2000, the president formed the Entrepreneurship Council to solicit input from the business elite; meetings were also held with the Russian Union of Industrialists and Entrepreneurs regarding issues relating to economic and social policy affecting the business sector.[44] Whereas in the Yeltsin years only 35 to 40 percent of legislation was based on initiatives issuing from the executive branch, the proportion rose to 60 percent in the first half of 2001.[45]

Sometimes the government, deputies, or parliamentary factions offer competing drafts of laws, leading to protracted and complicated bargaining. In order for a bill to become law, it must be approved by both houses of the parliament in three readings and signed by the president. If the president vetoes the bill, it must be passed again in the same wording by a two-thirds majority of both houses of parliament in order to override the veto. Budgetary proposals can be put forth only by the government, and they usually elicit sharp controversy in the parliament since proposed budget reductions affect key interests and groups, such as regional and local governments, other state agencies, the military, trade unions, enterprise directors, state employees, and pensioners. Many policy proclamations are made through presidential or governmental decrees, without formal consultation with the legislative branch. This decision-making process is much less visible and may involve closed-door bargaining rather than an open process of debate and consultation.

Informal groupings also have an important indirect impact on policy-making, very evident in the Yeltsin years. A prominent example is the industrialist lobby, which represents the managerial interests of some of Russia's large privatized industries. Business magnates were able to exert behind-the-scenes influence to gain benefits in the privatization of lucrative firms in sectors such as oil, media, and transport (see "Current Challenges: Russian Oligarchs: A New Ruling Class?"). A striking example was Boris Berezovsky, the founder of a company (LogoVAZ) that gained a powerful ownership interest in the media, banking, oil, and car dealership sectors. Berezovsky managed to gain control of the management of large enterprises in these sectors early in the privatization process and also to gain political influence through backroom dealing as well as campaign contributions. In late 1996 (after the 1996 presidential election), Yeltsin appointed Berezovsky deputy head of the Security Council, only to remove him in November 1997. Berezovsky was made executive secretary of the CIS in April 1998 (generally considered a position with lesser influence). Berezovksy has fallen out of favor, and it appears that Putin has been trying to formalize business input through bodies such as the Entrepreneurship Council. Some observers see this development as an example of corporatism, where the government identifies (or sometimes helps create) organizations that are consulted to represent designated societal interests (in this case business interests) in the policy-making process. The emerging Russian corporatism seems to be a state corporatist variant, a top-down variety where the government itself plays an active role in defining these vehicles of societal input.[46] One problem with this approach is that some interests, particularly those that are less powerful or well organized, may be excluded from the process. Another less formal linkage between the government and business is through continued government ownership of enterprise shares and thus the ability to influence leadership positions in key firms such as Gasprom. Through such personal links, the president can maintain some leverage in the economic sphere, even without a clear policy or legislative basis. These patron-client relations are not always transparent, masking patterns of mutual benefit and policy influence. In almost all cases, participation in policy-making does not extend to representatives of more broadly based citizens' groups.

A continuing problem is the inefficacy of policy implementation. Under Communist rule, the party's control over political appointments and promotions enforced at least some degree of conformity to central mandates. Under Yeltsin, the fragmented and decentralized nature of political power gave the executive branch few resources to ensure compliance. The government faced massive tax evasion, avoidance of military conscription, circumvention of a wide variety of regulations in spheres ranging from environmental protection to export of foreign currency, and regional policies violating federal laws. Pervasive corruption, including bribery and selective enforcement, hindered

enforcement of policy decisions. The mafia has demanded payoffs and protection money not only from private businesses but also from state organizations or public officials. While Putin has stated his commitment to restrict these types of irregularities, they no doubt continue. However, his commitment to reestablishing order and a rule of law has been an important foundation of his public support, which we explore in the next section.

Current Challenges: *Russian Oligarchs: A New Ruling Class?*

Privatization of Russia's previously state-owned enterprises in the early to mid-1990s brought opportunities for shrewd individuals to gain control of vast economic assets. Those who rose to the top of this pyramid of wealth and power are usually referred to as oligarchs, a small group of individuals who own or control a large share of Russian industrial enterprises, mass media companies, and banks, and who often have close ties with state authorities. Some individuals used their political positions as a springboard to win ownership rights in lucrative businesses, while others used their economic clout to exert political influence. In both cases a symbiotic relationship of mutual benefit between politicians and private economic interests emerged. What follows are brief profiles of three oligarchs who came from diverse backgrounds and pursued differing paths in establishing their positions of wealth and power.

Vladimir Potanin: Businessman with Political Influence

In 2002, the American business magazine *Forbes* ranked Vladimir Potanin at 234 in the list of 497 world billionaires, with total estimated wealth of US$1.8 billion.[1] Potanin's family held a relatively privileged position in the Soviet period; as an employee in the Soviet Foreign Trade Ministry, his father had postings in Turkey, Yemen, and New Zealand, giving the young Vladimir a perspective most Soviets did not enjoy. Potanin followed his father's footsteps, studying diplomacy and beginning his career in the Ministry of Foreign Trade, dealing with a Soviet state export company. In 1990 his entrepreneurial skills took flight. Using

some start-up capital he attracted from several small state-owned trade organizations, Potanin managed to found a small trading company of his own and a bank to serve the sector. As David F. Hoffman explains, things took off from there, when Potanin took advantage of a troubled Soviet state-owned bank: "Potanin appears to have effectively taken the deposits and assets away from the troubled state bank, while leaving behind the debts. Potanin inherited a $300 million windfall over a six-month period."[2] In 1993, Potanin founded Uneximbank, which, with help from government contacts, was to become one of Russia's largest financial-industrial groups.

In 1995 Potanin became a main mover in gaining government acceptance of the loan-for-shares program (see "State and Economy in the Russian Federation"). As a result, Potanin's Uneximbank obtained the controlling package of shares in Russia's largest nickel smelter, Norilsk Nikel, and in the oil company, Sidanko. In 1996, Potanin added some of Russia's largest print media to his empire, including widely read newspapers such as *Izvestiia* and *Komsomol'skaia pravda,* and the business magazine *Ekspert.* Throughout his business career, Vladimir Potanin has maintained close ties with the Russian political elite. A major contributor to President Yeltsin's 1996 presidential campaign, Potanin was shortly thereafter appointed deputy prime minister in charge of financial policy, a post he held until 1997. Although Potanin's role in politics has diminished since then, he continues to represent business interests in regular consultations between President Putin and the Russian Union of Industrialists and Entrepreneurs.

(continued)

Current Challenges: *Russian Oligarchs: A New Ruling Class? (cont.)*

Boris Berezovsky: From Oligarch to Exile

Born in 1946 in Moscow as the only child of a Jewish construction engineer and a pediatric nurse, Boris Berezovsky rose from his humble beginnings to become a mathematician at the prestigious Moscow Institute of Control Sciences during the Soviet period. Early in life he gained a reputation as an energetic and ambitious dealmaker with an entrepreneurial sense and a talent for cultivating connections. He put these talents to work in 1989 when he created the company, Logovaz, a move which provided an entrée to the giant Soviet automobile factory, Avtovaz. Avtovaz produced the Zhiguli, a car modelled after the Fiat. Berezovsky's Logovaz served as the intermediary for the Italian firm, Logosytem SpA, which carried out repairs on the line. Using his connections at the scientific research institute, Berezovksy was positioned to court the upper echelons of the faltering Avtovaz. Berezovsky then took advantage of high inflation and the inexperience of Avtovaz's economists with Russia's wild capitalism; he bought cars from Avtovaz's assembly line at bargain basement prices.[3] He later sold them for a large profit to Russian consumers who were eager for cars following Soviet-era shortages and the lure of the automobile culture. Berezovsky's Logovaz went on to become the centrepiece of his financial empire, selling 45,000 cars annually.

By 1994, Berezovsky had developed Logovaz into a media, banking, and oil empire with holdings and companies including Obedinionny Bank, Oil Finance Company, and Sibneft Oil, as well as large stakes in Russia's mass media. After falling out of favor with President Yeltsin, Berezovsky fled Russia in November 2000, in the face of auto theft charges and allegations that his banks bilked the Russian air carrier Aeroflot out of hundreds of millions of dollars. He is currently living in self-imposed exile in London, England.

Vagit Alekperov: Oil Magnate[4]

Vagit Alekperov is one of *Forbes* magazine's five richest Russians, whose net worth was estimated at US$1.4 billion in 2002. Of Azeri ethnicity, Alekperov was trained as an engineer and went to work in the nearby Caspian Sea oil fields, then in the oil fields of Western Siberia. In 1984, he was appointed general director of the state-owned gas and oil company, Kogalymneftgaz. In 1990 he left this post to go to Moscow, where he rose to the position of first deputy and then acting minister of fuel and energy (1992–1993). As acting minister, Alekperov was able to influence the breakup and privatization of the Soviet petroleum industry.

In 1993 Alekperov designed and then assumed the presidency of what has become the country's largest private oil company, Lukoil. Patterned after the vertically integrated oil companies of the West, Lukoil initially consisted of three production fields, the initials of which formed the company name. In August 1995, Prime Minister Viktor Chernomyrdin transferred four huge state-owned oil fields to Lukoil. Lukoil also acquired some other distribution and service companies. Alekperov expanded his business profile, buying refineries in Eastern Europe, building a fleet of tankers and snapping up the Getty gas station chain in the United States. Alekperov also moved into the banking and the media sector. In an apparent political vendetta, Lukoil used its position as minority shareholder in TV6 to bankrupt the network and push the rival and former oligarch Boris Berezovsky out of the television company.

Oil giants, such as Lukoil, enjoy a cooperative relationship with Russian state authorities. For example, Alekperov has looked to the Russian government to help ensure that in the wake of Saddam Hussein's fall, Lukoil will not lose its claim on assets in Iraq's West Kurna oil field, one of the world's largest, with estimated reserves of 20 billion barrels.

I am grateful to Stuart Chandler, Natalia Joukovskaia, and Yevgen Shevchenko for their assistance in assembling this material.

[1] http://www.forbes.com/2002/02/28/billionaires.html

[2] David Hoffman, *The Oligarchs: Wealth and Power in the New Russia* (New York: Public Affairs, 2002), 305.

[3] Hoffman, ch. 6.

[4] *Sources for this section: Forbes* website (http://www.forbes.com/2002/02/28/billionaires.html); Russian media sources (NTV Internet edition http://www.ntv.ru); Internet analytical portal Pravda.Ru (http://www.pracda.ru); and Hoffman, p. 299.

Section ④ Representation and Participation

Gorbachev's policies brought a dramatic change in the relationship between state and society. The communist political system was driven by an impetus to control society; out of this stifling environment, *glasnost* sparked new public and private initiatives. Most restrictions on the formation of social organizations were lifted, and a large number of independent groups appeared. Observers in the late 1980s began suggesting that **civil society** was emerging, that is, an autonomous sphere of social life that could act on but was not dependent on the state. Throughout the 1990s, however, concern grew that only a small stratum of Russian society was actually becoming actively engaged politically; the demands of everyday life as well as cynicism about politicians and state institutions led many people to withdraw into the private domain again. With the chaos and uncertainty of the early reform years, many citizens also wished for a strong leader who could impose order, control crime, and restore the predictability that was lost with the collapse of the Soviet system. Vladimir Putin drew on these sentiments in his bid for the presidency. Even after the honeymoon period following his election in 2000, Putin has maintained support levels of around 70 percent of the adult population, according to public opinion surveys. While higher levels of trust in the government are generally seen as a positive foundation for an active citizenry, it is not clear that the ability of public to affect government has increased.

The Legislature

The Russian legislature, the Federal Assembly, came into being after the parliamentary elections of December 12, 1993, when the referendum ratifying the new Russian constitution was also approved. The upper house, the Federation Council, represents Russia's constituent federal units. The lower house, the *Duma,* has 450 members and represents the people through direct popular vote for candidates and parties. This body was named after the short-lived assembly formed by the tsar following the revolution of 1905 and thus emphasizes continuity with the Russian (rather than the Soviet) tradition. The first Federal Assembly served only

a two-year term. Subsequent elections to the *Duma* occur at least every four years: the second set of parliamentary elections occurred in December 1995 and the third set in 1999. In some special circumstances, earlier elections can be called.

Within the *Duma,* factions unite deputies from the same or allied parties. The *Duma* also has a number of standing committees, made up of members from the various factions, to review legislation. The chairs and composition of membership of these committees have generally been distributed among the most important factions of the *Duma;* however, following a failed attempt by the Communist group to vote no confidence in the government in 2001, chairs were taken away from this important faction. The Speaker of the *Duma* is elected by the body and usually represents the strongest political faction, which was the Communist Party after the 1995 and 1999 elections. Gennady Seleznev, who became Speaker following the 1999 election, was expelled from the CPRF in May 2002 because the party considered that he did not represent its position after the removal of communist deputies from *Duma* committee chairs. However he appeared poised to take on a new role in the party in early 2003.

Compared to the Communist period, deputies in the representative bodies reflect less fully the demographic characteristics of the population at large. For example, in 1984, 33 percent of the members of the Supreme Soviet were women. In 1995, this declined to 10 percent and further to 7.6 percent following the 1999 elections.[47] In 2000, manual workers made up less than 1 percent of *Duma* deputies, in contrast to 35 percent in the 1985 Supreme Soviet.[48] It is important to remember that the implicit demographic quotas that the CPSU enforced in the Soviet period were primarily symbolic, since the Supreme Soviet was largely powerless. On the other hand, the underrepresentation of women and workers in the present *Duma* indicates the extent to which politics is the domain of male elites in the Russian Federation.

The upper house of the Federal Assembly, the Federation Council, represents Russia's eighty-nine regions and republics and serves a function analogous to the German *Bundesrat.* It includes two delegates from each federal unit. In 1993, they were directly elected by the population, but beginning in 1995, they were the head of the executive branch of the region (the governor) and the head of the legislative branch. As noted in Section 3, Putin proposed and received legislative approval in 2000 for a change that provided for appointment of the two representatives: one by the regional executive and one by the regional legislature. The new system was phased in over an eighteen-month period, to be completed by January 2002. Because of the prominence of businessmen among the new appointees, observers wonder whether the new system will ensure an adequate representation of most sectors of the population or whether this selection method will tighten the interdependence of regional governments with local business interests. The ability of the governor to control his appointee is reinforced by a power of recall given to him, and it may be that being freed from the post in the Council of the Federation will give governors more time to devote to matters in the region. Party factions do not play a significant role in the Federation Council as they do in the *Duma*. Deputies to the Federation Council, as well as to the *Duma*, are granted immunity from criminal prosecution.

The constitution grants parliament powers in the legislative and budgetary areas, but if conflict exists with the president or government, these powers can be exercised effectively only if parliament operates with a high degree of unity. In practice, parliamentary powers can often be overridden by the president through mechanisms such as the veto of legislation. To override the veto, two-thirds of the members of the Federal Assembly must support the original wording of the bill. Each house of parliament has the authority to confirm certain presidential appointees, in addition to the prime minister. For example, the *Duma* confirms the chair of the Central Bank of Russia, and the Federation Council confirms federal judges. In some cases, failure to approve the president's nominees has produced stalemate or prevented certain offices from functioning for a period of time.

Because presidential and parliamentary elections are entirely separate from one another in Russia, conflict between the president and the legislative branch has been frequent, since the president's supporters do not necessarily control the Federal Assembly. Following electoral rebuffs in the 1993 and 1995 parliamentary elections, Yeltsin confronted a parliament that obstructed many of his proposed policies, but the parliament did not have the power or unity to offer a constructive alternative. Following the 1999 elections, the situation was somewhat less conflictual, partly because the Unity Party, which Putin had supported, gained a significant portion of seats in the *Duma*. Thus, supporters of the government could form a coalition to usher through legislative proposals.

Society's ability to affect particular policy decisions through the legislative process is minimal. First, the blocs and parties in the parliament are isolated from the public at large and suffer low levels of popular respect. Many of the mechanisms that link parties and parliaments to citizens in Western democracies do not exist in Russia: interest associations to lobby the parliament are weak; party membership is low (except for the Communist Party); and the internal decision-making structures of parties are generally elite dominated. The fragmentation of the party system makes parties themselves weak institutions for influencing policy. Second, public hearings on controversial issues are rare. Nonetheless, through the parliament, Russian citizens have had the opportunity to select deputies in truly competitive elections, and politicians may take note of the election results to some degree.

Political Parties and the Party System

The most important political change that occurred with the collapse of communism was the shift from a single-party system to a multiparty system. In the Communist Party state, the CPSU not only dominated state organs but oversaw all social institutions, such as the mass media, trade unions, youth groups, educational institutions, and professional associations. It defined the official ideology for the country, set the parameters for state censorship, and, through the *nomenklatura* system, ensured that loyal supporters occupied all important offices. Approximately 10 percent of adults in the Soviet Union were party members, but there were no effective mechanisms to ensure accountability of the party leadership to its members. Because the CPSU did not have to compete for political office, it was a party of a special kind, whose authority could not be openly questioned.

National competitive elections were held for the

first time in the USSR in 1989, but new political parties were not formal participants in Russia until the 1993 elections. Since then, a confusing array of political organizations have run candidates in elections (see Table 3). These have included not only political parties but also political and socioeconomic movements, as well as coalitions of several parties or movements. In another Putin initiative, a new law on political parties went into effect in July 2001; the law tightened the conditions for party formation and registration, requiring that regional branches with at least 100 members exist in at least half of the regions of Russia. This legislation is likely to have a dampening effect on small parties and encourage the formation of coalitions between parties with similar positions. While critics have portrayed the new law as a muffling of democratic representation, one could view it as a necessary step to help bring order to a chaotic and fragmented party structure. Many electoral groupings had succeeded in registering under the new party law by late 2002, in preparation for the *Duma* elections scheduled for December 2003.[49] Under the new law, only organizations registered as political parties are permitted to nominate candidates independently in elections.

Russian political parties have some peculiarities when compared to their Western counterparts. First, they generally form around and are associated with a prominent individual. For example, one party, Yabloko, got its name from the first letters of the names of its founding leaders: Grigorii Yavlinsky, Yuri Boldeyev, and Vladimir Lukin. Even after Boldeyev and Lukin left the association, the name stuck. (The word *yabloko,* "apple," is easy for voters to remember.) In anticipation of the 1999 parliamentary elections, prominent political figures such as Moscow's mayor, Yuri Luzhkov, formed new parties or movements, which were distinguished primarily by who led them. The formation of the Unity Party in 1999 was a bit of an exception because its leader, Sergei Shoigu (head of the State Committee for Emergencies), was not a prominent political figure, but it appears that Prime Minister Putin's public statement that he intended to vote for the party had the same effect. The acronym for the full party name (Inter-regional Movement-Unity, *or* Me*zhregional'noe* D*vizhenie* Ed*instvo*) is the Russian word for "bear" (*medved*), a symbol of Russia's prowess and identity. The *Duma* ballots list not only the names of the blocs

and parties but also of their leaders.[50] The importance of individual leaders has increased political fragmentation, because groups with similar programs often split along lines of personal loyalties; political figures may also resist forming coalitions with potential allies because this could compromise personal political power. It remains to be seen whether the new party law will counteract this tendency.

Unlike most parties in the West, most Russian parties do not have a firm social base or stable constituency. Many Russians are hesitant to join a political party. Some recall their unhappy experience with the CPSU. Others simply distrust politics and politicians. Furthermore, other than the Communist Party of the Russian Federation (CPRF), Russian parties are young, so deeply rooted political identifications are absent. Finally, many citizens do not have a clear conception of their own interests or how parties might represent them. In this context, image making is as important as programmatic positions, so parties appeal to transient voter sentiments. As the situation in the country stabilizes, the interests of particular groups (for example, blue-collar workers, business entrepreneurs, or groups based on age, gender, or region) may take a more central role in the formation of parties.

Despite the personalistic nature of party politics, some key cleavages help explain the political spectrum. A major cleavage relates to economic policy. Nearly all parties and electoral groupings mouth support for the market transition, but those on the communist/socialist end of the spectrum are markedly muted in their enthusiasm. They support renationalization of some firms, continued state subsidies, more extensive social welfare policies, and limits on foreign economic investment. At the other end of the spectrum are liberal/reform groupings, which support rapid market reform, including privatization, free prices, limited government spending, and reduced emission of rubles by the Central Bank. Centrist formations, such as Unity/Fatherland (a 2001 merger of Unity with Luzhkov's party), take a middle position of commitment to market reform but in a less radical manner. Many of the centrist parties are closely associated with establishment political figures in the Russian government.

Parties and blocs are also divided on noneconomic issues, particularly those involving national identity and Westernization. The nationalist/patriotic parties

Table 3

Top Parties in the 1999 State Duma Elections[a]

Party or Bloc	Percent of 1993 Party List Vote[b]	Percent of 1995 Party List Vote[b]	Comments	Leader at Time of 1999 Election	Percent in 1999 Party List Vote[b]	Duma Seats from Party List Vote	Duma Seats from Single-Member Districts	Total Seats in Duma After Elections[c]
Centrist								
Unity (Inter-regional Movement, Unity)	—	—	New party	Sergei Shoigu, party favored by Vladimir Putin	23.3%	64	9	73
Fatherland, All Russia	—	—	New coalition	Yurii Lyzhkov, Evgenii Primakov	13.3	37	31	68
Women of Russia	8.1%	4.6%		Alevtina Fedulova	2.1	0	0	
Liberal/Reform								
Union of Rightist Forces	(15.4)	(3.9)	Russia's Choice (1993); Russia's Democratic Choice/United Russia (1995)	Sergei Kirienko	8.5	24	5	29
Yabloko	7.8	6.9		Grigorii Yavlinksy	5.9	16	4	20
Communist/ Socialist								
Communist Party of the Russian Federation	12.4	22.3		Gennady Zyuganov	24.3	67	46	113
Communist-Worker's Russia-For the Soviet Union	—	4.5	Radical communist	Viktor Anpilov	2.2	0	0	
Nationalist/Patriotic								
Bloc Zhirinovsky	22.8	11.2	In 1993, 1995 ran as Liberal Democratic Party of Russia	Vladimir Zhirinovsky	6.0	17	0	17

[a]Figures may not add up to 100 percent or to the total number of deputies in the State *Duma* because smaller parties and independents are excluded. Table includes only parties winning at least 4.5 percent of the national party list vote in one of the three elections (but not all such parties).

[b]Percentage of the total popular vote the party or bloc received on the proportional representation portion of the ballot in the year indicated. A dash indicates that the party or bloc was not included on that ballot or did not win a significant portion of the vote. Numbers in parentheses are votes for predecessor parties, similar to the one running in 1999.

[c]The sum of seats won in the proportional representation (party list) vote and the single-member district vote. Number of deputies in the faction changed over time following the elections.

Source: DeBardeleben, Joan, *Russian Politics in Transition,* 2nd ed. Copyright 1997 by Houghton Mifflin Company. Reprinted with permission. Centre for the Study of Public Policy, University of Strathclyde, and Russian Center for Public Opinion and Market Research, "Russia Votes" website, www.russiavotes.org (accessed March 12, 2003).

emphasize the defense of Russian interests over those of the West. They strongly criticize the expansion of NATO to include former Soviet bloc countries such as Poland, Hungary, and the Czech Republic. They also favor a strong military establishment, protection from foreign economic influence, and reconstitution of some former Soviet republics into a larger federation. Liberal/reform parties strongly support the integration of Russia into the global market and the adoption of Western economic and political principles, positions that go along with their general support for radical market reform.

It is intriguing that despite Russia's ethnic diversity, ethnic and regional parties have not had a significant impact on the national scene and only a minimal one in particular regions. Similarly, religion has not been an important political cleavage, probably because religious sentiments, although reviving among certain sectors of the population, have not developed a firm enough organizational or identity base, given their suppression in the communist period. Religion appears to have personal meaning rather than being a source of group identity, at least for Russians (who primarily adhere to the Russian Orthodox strain of Christianity). Ethnic and religious distinctions do overlap, particularly for the Islamic portion of the population, but even these groupings have not taken on a significant political character in the form of political parties.

Because of the primacy of both the economic and identity cleavages, one can conceive of the Russian party spectrum as being divided into three ideological groupings:

- The traditional left, represented by the CPRF, the Agrarian Party, and other smaller communist/socialist formations, which are hesitant about market reform and often mildly nationalistic
- The liberal/reform and centrist forces, which support Western-type market reform and political norms
- The nationalist/patriotic forces, which are not primarily concerned with economic issues but emphasize concerns of national identity

The most important parties in all three groupings, when not in power, have acted throughout as a loyal opposition; that is, they have not challenged the structure of the political system but have chosen to work within it.

The Russian Left: The Communist Party of the Russian Federation

By far the strongest parliamentary party after the 1995 elections was the CPRF, which won over one-third of the seats in the *Duma*. The CPRF maintained an equal showing in the 1999 elections, but its dominant position was undermined by the ability of the progovernment Unity Party to gain almost an equal number of votes and seats in the *Duma*.

The CPRF is the clearest successor of the old CPSU, although it is formally a new entity. Many former members and leaders of the CPSU have joined other parties or left politics, so that the leadership of the CPRF is new. Gennady Zyuganov has been the party leader since the first congress of the CPRF in March 1993. The party won about 12 percent of the popular party-list vote in 1993, 22 percent in 1995, and over 24 percent in 1999. The party won 157 of the 450 seats in the *Duma* in 1995 and 124 in 1999.

The party contains a variety of ideological tendencies, some more orthodox communist than others. Strong elements of Russian nationalism are evident in the party program. The CPRF supported the defense of the White House against the Yeltsin siege in 1993 and consistently criticized Yeltsin's economic reform program and often blocked legislation, such as the right to buy and sell agricultural land, which the reformers view as crucial. Nonetheless, the party accepts substantial elements of the market reform package, favoring a combination of state and private ownership. Primary among the party's concerns are the social costs of the reform process. Thus, it has supported state subsidies for industry to ensure timely payment of wages and prevent enterprise bankruptcies. Some critics have questioned the commitment of the party leadership to democratic governance, and there was speculation in 1996 about whether the party would have reverted to authoritarianism had Zyuganov won the presidential race. The party's detractors see its leaders as opportunistic rather than as true democrats, but others point out that communist governors in some of Russia's regions have become less ideological and more pragmatic once in power.

Support for the party is especially strong among older Russians, the economically disadvantaged, and rural residents. The party is no longer credible as a vanguard organization representing the working class. Instead, it appears to represent those who have adapted less successfully to the radical and uncertain changes that have occurred since the collapse of the Communist state, as well as some individuals who remain committed to socialist ideals. This feature raises questions about the future durability of the party's electoral base, although through 1999, no overall decline in electoral support was evident in parliamentary elections.

Centrist Parties: Unity and the Fatherland-All Russia

The amazing feature of Unity was its ability, within a few months after its formation in 1999, to come in as a close second runner to the CPRF in the 1999 *Duma* elections. In its first electoral foray, the party won 23.3 percent of the party list vote and seventy-three seats in the *Duma*. Previous centrist formations, despite their close association with the government and other political elites, had failed to develop a base of popular support. What explains Unity's success? It appears to be largely the appeal of Vladimir Putin, who gave his personal support to the party, as well as a successful effort on the part of party leaders to gain the support of regional leaders, who could use their resources to bolster support in their regions. A bandwagon effect and desire to be on the winning side also bolstered the party's fortunes. The party had a rather poorly defined program, which emphasized the uniqueness of Russia (as distinct from Western models), an appeal to values of order and law, and a continued commitment to moderate reform. Supporters of the Unity Party in the 1999 election represented a broad spectrum of the population. The party drew away voters from supporters of almost every other political grouping.

Previous, less successful centrist parties included Our Home Is Russia, Fatherland, All Russia, and Women of Russia. The strongest until late 1998 was Our Home Is Russia, led by Viktor Chernomyrdin, the Russian prime minister from late 1992 until early 1998. In the 1995 election, this bloc represented an important part of the political and economic establishment, including many government ministers and governors of some important Russian regions. But it won only 10 percent of the party-list vote, a dismal show-

ing to serve as a basis for governance. Part of the party's weakness was Chernomyrdin's lack of charisma and close association with the oil and gas industry.

Fatherland was formed by Moscow mayor Yuri Luzhkov and held its founding congress in December 1998. The party's platform was less important than the personal appeal of Luzhkov. Although he was associated with Moscow, a capital city whose privileges are both envied and resented in the regions, Luzhkov's success in modernizing the city gave him the image of an effective leader. The party joined with another centrist grouping, All-Russia, headed by Evgenii Primakov, in 1999. Fatherland–All Russia won a respectable 13.3 percent of the vote in the 1999 *Duma* party-list vote, bringing the total centrist vote (with Unity) up to 36.6 percent. It was widely expected that Primakov would run for president in March 2000, but presumably due to Putin's overwhelming popularity, he also got on the bandwagon.

Another centrist party, Women of Russia, had a surprisingly good showing in the 1993 elections, when it won 8 percent of the party-list vote. The party was formed in 1993 on the basis of an alliance of women's groups, most prominently the Union of Women of Russia, a renamed version of an official organization of women formed by the Soviet regime. Its program has emphasized social welfare issues. The party's success in the 1993 vote put twenty-three women in the *Duma,* otherwise dominated by men. But in 1995, Women of Russia won only 4.6 percent of the party-list vote, and in 1999 just over 2 percent, well below the 5 percent threshold needed to win seats from this part of the ballot in the parliament. Possible explanations for the decline include limited campaign funds, minimal media coverage of the party during the electoral campaign, and the failure of the party to make its positions adequately clear to the voters.[51]

Yabloko and Other Liberal/Reform Parties

More than any other grouping in the political spectrum, the liberal/reform parties have found it hard to build a stable and unified electoral base. Whether the division within this camp has been more a cause or an effect of this failure is hard to say. These groups espouse a commitment to traditional liberal values, such as limited interference of the state in economic affairs, support for free-market principles, and the protection of individual rights and liberties, and thus they were closest to the original agenda of the Yeltsin reform administration. Yeltsin's refusal to associate himself with any political party may have hindered the ability of these groupings to develop a unified political strategy in the early 1990s. Another possibility is that the unpopularity of Yeltsin's reform approach may have undermined support for its ideological soulmates, particularly because none of these parties had a sufficiently appealing leader to muster strong popular enthusiasm.

The liberal/reform parties, often referred to as the democrats, have been blamed for Russia's economic and national decline. A survey conducted in late 1995 found that 58 percent of respondents associated the use of the word *democracy* in Russia with negative developments, such as confusion, chaos, lawlessness, criminality, or poverty. Only 20 percent had positive associations with the word, such as freedom, freedom of speech, and free elections.[52] The tarnished image of Russian democracy both reflects and contributes to disillusionment with the liberal/reform parties.

Four parties or blocs running on a promarket reform plank won seats in the *Duma* in the 1993 elections, the most prominent being Russia's Democratic Choice, headed by Yegor Gaidar, and Yabloko, headed by Grigorii Yavlinsky. Support for liberal/reform parties generally is stronger among the young, the more highly educated, urban dwellers, and the well-off. Until 1999, Yabloko enjoyed the most success among the liberal/reform parties. An economist who became well known for his role in fashioning an economic program for the important region of Nizhnii Novgorod, Yavlinsky has been a consistent critic of the government, albeit a supporter of Western-style democratization and market reform. He charged the Yeltsin regime with being insufficiently democratic in its methods, citing the siege of the Russian White House in 1993, the attack on Chechnya, and the strong powers granted to the president in the new Russian constitution. On the economic front, Yavlinsky represents a softer version of market reform. He has sustained quite consistent support from a relatively narrow constituency, especially in educated circles.

An important obstacle that the liberal/reform forces face has been their inability to form a unified coalition. Several parties running on a liberal/reform platform split the vote in 1995, reducing their representation in the *Duma*. On November 21, 1998, the brutal murder by contract killers of the liberal/reform politician and *Duma* member Galina Starovoitova (one of Russia's most prominent female politicians) resulted in renewed efforts to form a united political bloc. The Union of Rightist Forces, which represented the coalition, got just over 8.5 percent of the party-list vote in 1999. Yabloko, with its more critical stance to the government, ran separately and won 5.9 percent of the vote.

Nationalist/Patriotic Parties

To the surprise of many observers, the Liberal Democratic Party of Russia (LDPR), headed by Vladimir Zhirinovsky, got the strongest support on the party ballot in 1993, winning almost 23 percent of the vote; this declined to 11 percent in 1995 and 6 percent in 1999. Neither liberal nor particularly democratic in its platform, the party might more properly be characterized as nationalist and populist. Its populism is based on Zhirinovsky's personal charismatic appeal. Some Russians believe he "speaks our language," while others radically oppose his provocative style and nationalist rhetoric. In his speeches, Zhirinovsky has openly appealed to the anti-Western sentiments that grew in the wake of Russia's decline from superpower status and the government's perceived groveling for Western economic aid. The party has supported revival of an expanded Russian state to include Ukraine, Belarus, and possibly other neighboring areas. Concern with the breakdown of law and order seems to rank high among the priorities of Zhirinovsky supporters. However, despite Zhirinovsky's radical demeanor, he has often supported the government on key issues, most notably the war in Chechnya. Zhirinovsky's support has been especially strong among working-class men and military personnel, but by the late 1990s, it had weakened, since Zhirnovsky's extreme political rhetoric and sometimes uncivilized public demeanor alienated many Russians. In addition, leaders of other parties took up patriotic themes. Zyuganov of the CPRF included nationalist elements in his appeals, and Putin's own emphasis on Russian's unique identity and path represents a more moderate version of these themes. An array of smaller extremist parties has also emerged, but they have failed to gain widespread support.

Elections

In the post-Communist period, elections seem to be a constant phenomenon in Russia. With its mixed presidential-parliamentary system, electoral contests for the two branches of government are completely separate from one another. There are also regular elections at the regional and local levels. The initial euphoria with the competitive electoral structure has been replaced by voter fatigue, although interest in federal elections remains quite high, with voter turnout at 60 percent for the 1999 *Duma* elections and around 69 percent for the second round of the 2000 presidential election. In regional and local contests, participation rates have at times fallen below the required minimum of 25 or 50 percent of eligible voters, necessitating repeat balloting. National elections receive extensive media coverage, and campaign activities begin as long as a year in advance of the contest. The widespread use of polling firms by candidates and parties to assess public opinion and devise campaign strategies has made political consulting a big business.

The electoral system for selecting the *Duma* resembles the one used for election of the German *Bundestag*, combining **proportional representation** with winner-take-all districts. Half of the 450 deputies are selected on the basis of nationwide party lists; any party gaining 5 percent of the national vote is entitled to a proportional share of these 225 deputies in the *Duma*. Particularly in 1995, a large percentage of voters chose small parties that did not win the 5 percent needed to cross the threshold, so these citizens, in effect, were not represented through that part of the balloting. Voters are also given the explicit option of voting against all candidates or parties. In the 1999 *Duma* election, 3.3 percent of those voters chose this option.[53] The remaining 225 deputies are elected in winner-take-all races in **single-member plurality districts;** these races usually involve local notables. Although a majority of candidates who win in single-member districts are associated with particular parties or blocs, many are not. Some of these independent candidates join party factions once in the parliament.

The impact of the electoral system on party fragmentation is ambiguous. Because Russian parties and electoral blocs are so fluid and politics is so personalized, proportional representation may both increase and decrease party fragmentation. Proportional representation gives parties a role in drawing up the candidate lists, and the 5 percent threshold for representation does, to some extent, encourage the formation of electoral coalitions. On the other hand, proportional representation allows fairly small parties to gain representation in the *Duma* and may discourage broader coalitions. The final balance of forces in the parliament is determined by the combined result of the party-list vote and the single-member district votes. The number of parties running on the party-list ballot has not shown a consistent decrease over time; in 1993, thirteen electoral groupings were on the ballot, in 1995 the number rose to forty-three, and in 1999 it declined to twenty-six. Of the twenty-six parties running in 1999, only six passed the 5 percent threshold, and they represented 81.4 percent of those voting. The winner-take-all races may not bolster the chances of large parties as much as they do in established democracies because well-known local figures may win in these races without being associated with a particular party or bloc.

In both the 1993 and 1995 parliamentary elections, forces opposing the government came out ahead, signaling broad public concern about the social consequences of the government's economic policy. Despite the electoral rebuff, Yeltsin kept Viktor Chernomyrdin as prime minister after both elections, leaving the impression that parliamentary elections had little impact on governance. Only in 1999 did parliamentary elections offer qualified support for the government, with the Unity Party winning almost as many votes as the Communists.

Results of presidential electors have not mirrored parliamentary election outcomes. While the CPRF topped the list in the 1995 *Duma* elections, the party leader, Zyuganov, was not able to defeat Yeltsin in the presidential election of 1996. Zyuganov did even more poorly against Putin in the 2000 vote; even in areas of traditional support (the so-called Red Belt in central European Russia), Putin often outscored him. Under the Russian constitution, presidential elections are held every four years. If no candidate receives a majority of the votes in the first round, a runoff election is held between the two top contenders. While the 1995 election went to a second round (Yeltsin won 35 percent in the first and 54 percent in the second round against Zyuganov), Putin won handily, with nearly 53 percent of the vote against ten other candidates in the first round in 2000. Although Putin was Yeltsin's designated successor, nonetheless, the peaceful democratic transfer of power may be a sign that the new political institutions are providing a viable framework for the peaceful transfer of power.

Political Culture, Citizenship, and Identity

Political culture can be a source of great continuity in the face of radical upheavals in the social and political spheres. Indeed, in many ways, attitudes toward government that prevailed in the tsarist period seem to have endured with remarkable tenacity. These include acceptance of a wide scope of state activity, a tradition of oligarchic or one-man leadership, support for economic egalitarianism, collectivist values, a tendency to utopian thinking, a simultaneous attraction to order and anarchy, and the desire for an authoritative source of truth. While depictions of political culture often oversimplify and therefore should be viewed with caution, they capture some of the distinctiveness of political orientations in particular countries. The Soviet regime embodied many traditional Russian values, but Soviet authorities also glorified science, technology, industrialization, and urbanization—values superimposed on the traditional way of life of the largely rural population. When communism collapsed, Soviet ideology was discredited, and the government embraced political and economic values from the West. Many citizens and intellectuals rejected this "imported" culture. A crisis of identity resulted for both elites and average citizens. What does it mean to be Russian, and on what basis should Russia's political society and structures be built? As Russians ponder these issues, those who study the country wonder whether traditional Russian political culture is compatible or in conflict with Western norms of liberal democracy and market economics. Can Russian political culture generate its own variant of democracy and economic prosperity, distinct from both the Soviet and the Western models?

One way to study political culture is to examine evidence from public opinion surveys. Such surveys suggest that there is considerable support for liberal democratic values such as competitive elections, an independent judiciary, a free press, and basic civil liberties. A survey carried out before the 1999 parliamentary elections indicated that 65 percent of respondents supported the idea of democracy, but at the same time, only 19 percent were willing to say that the system in Russia at the time was a democracy.[54] Colton and McFaul conclude from survey results that "a significant portion of the Russian population acquiesces in the abstract idea of democracy without necessarily looking to the West for guidance."[55] The authors find that Russians are divided on the proper balance between defense of individual rights and the maintenance of order; other experts conclude that Russians' desire for a strong state and strong leaders does not imply support for authoritarian government.[56] This may explain a large part of the current popular support for President Putin, whose emphasis on order, state capacity, and rule of law mirrors these concerns.

Another dimension of the search for identity relates to what it means to be Russian. The Russian language has two words for "Russian": *russkii,* which refers to an ethnicity, and *Rossiiskii,* a broader concept referring to people of various ethnic backgrounds included in Russia as a political entity. In the USSR, just over 50 percent of the population was ethnically Russian. Since most of the major ethnic minorities now reside in independent states, the Russian Federation is considerably more ethnically homogeneous than was the USSR, with Russians making up over 80 percent of the population. The largest minority group is the Tatars, a traditionally Muslim group residing primarily in Tatarstan, a republic of Russia. Other significant minorities are the Bashkirs, various indigenous peoples of the Russian north, the many Muslim groups in the northern Caucasus region, and ethnic groups (e.g., Ukrainians, Armenians) of other former Soviet republics. At the same time, some 25 million ethnic Russians reside outside the Russian Federation in other former Soviet republics.

Given this situation, it is significant whether one considers Russianness to be defined by ethnicity or by citizenship. In 1998, a Communist *Duma* deputy made public anti-Semitic statements, eliciting a heated discussion about political tolerance. Liberal/reform politicians wished to strip the deputy of immunity and bring legal action against him. Observers worried that crisis conditions might incite increasing racial and ethnic tension. Muslim groups from Russia's southern regions have also been the target of ethnic stereotyping. In addition, refugee flows from some of the war-torn regions of the Transcaucasus (Georgia, Azerbaijan, and neighboring regions of southern Russia such as Chechnya and Ingushetia) have heightened national tensions. Individuals from these regions play an important role in Russia's trade sector and are viewed by many Russians as speculators and crooks. Nonetheless, experts like Peter Reddaway and Dmitri Glinsky have argued that "Russia (perhaps not unlike the United States) is one of the few major countries of the world where nationalists pure and simple, whether democratic or not, simply have never had a broad-based popular appeal."[57] In explaining this, the authors note that the very word *natsionalizm* has a negative connotation in Russian and is associated with the extreme ethnic intolerance embodied in Nazism that Russians fought at great sacrifice in World War II.

Religion has long played a role in shaping Russian identity. Today, the Russian Orthodox Church appeals to many citizens who are looking for a replacement for the discredited values of the Communist system. Russia is experiencing a revival of religious practice as residents of many localities have focused on reconstructing or refurbishing churches, some of which were used for other purposes during the Soviet period. Religion has not, however, become a defining cleavage in the Russian political landscape. The government of President Yeltsin supported the revival of Russian Orthodoxy as a basis of national identity. A controversial law passed in 1997 made it harder for new religious groups to organize themselves; the law was directed primarily at Western proselytizers. Human rights advocates and foreign observers protested strongly, again raising questions about the depth of Russia's commitment to liberal democratic values.

In the Soviet period, the mass media, the educational system, and a variety of other social institutions played a key role in propagating the party's political values. Now, students are presented with a wider range of views, and the print media represent a broad spectrum of political opinion. Opposition newspapers publish sometimes scathing criticisms of the government. Nonetheless, restrictions on the ability of the press and other mass media to function freely still exist. First, financial constraints make their existence precarious. Many Russians cannot afford to buy newspapers regularly; therefore, readership has declined dramatically since Soviet times. A second factor affecting the ability of the press to give fair and complete coverage is the mafia. As already noted, courageous journalists have been a particular target of organized crime. Third, powerful financial interests exert influence over the media to sway public opinion, particularly during election campaigns. Politicians are concerned to receive favorable media coverage and therefore may be subject to pressures from the financial interests that control important media outlets. As noted in Section 1, the government itself has exerted pressure on the media to present issues favorably, although this pressure has rarely taken the form of overt censorship, as occurred after the October 1993 events. The electronic media are particularly susceptible to political pressure, given the costs and limited availability of the technology needed to run television stations. In the print media, both the national and regional governments still pressure editors to limit the publication of highly critical viewpoints, and in the extreme case, some editors have been forcibly removed from their posts. Because the major newspapers receive financial subsidies from the government, pressure can be exerted in this way, as well as through government taxation policy. The continued political interference in media affairs is but one example of the difficult process involved in transforming political culture.

Interests, Social Movements, and Protests

In the late 1980s, *glasnost* produced an outburst of public activity, involving the formation of a wide variety of political and social movements. In recent years, economic decline has dampened political activism. Citizens are preoccupied with personal economic survival, many times holding three or four jobs to make ends meet. This leaves little time for participation in political and societal organizations. Political and social organizations also face financial problems and are often unable to hire staff or support basic organizational functions. In this environment, the most successful interest associations have been those formed by better-off elements of society (such as new business entrepreneurs), officials, or groups receiving funding from international or foreign agencies. A main thrust of Western humanitarian assistance to Russia has been support for nongovernmental organizations. Most of this aid, however, comes with strings attached. For example, some Western organizations require particular attention to gender equality, an issue that is of less priority to many Russians.

Dozens and usually hundreds of political and social organizations exist in every region of Russia, alongside a large number of nationwide organizations representing the interests of children, veterans, women, environmental advocates, pensioners, the disabled, and cultural interests. Other groups are professional unions, sports clubs, trade unions, and organizations concerned with various aspects of social welfare. Most locally based interest associations have small staffs and rely for support on local government, grants from international organizations, contracts for work carried out, and commercial activities. Organizations generally must register with local authorities, and some develop such close relationships with the local administration as to possibly undermine their independence. Many groups are successors to Soviet-era associations, such as the trade union organizations and nature protection societies. Others are closely linked to international organizations, such as the YMCA and the Rotary Club, or receive assistance from international organizations such as the Soros Foundation, the Save the Children Federation, or TACIS (run by the EU). Many try to influence state policy, such as the Committee of Soldiers' Mothers of Russia, the Socio-Ecological Union, the "Chernobyl" Union, and the Society of Veterans. Others, such as hobby clubs or sports associations, bring together people with common interests or problems.

Environmental activism was particularly important in the late 1980s as *glasnost* increased public knowledge of pollution. The fate of the environmental movements in the 1990s is a paradigm for interest representation in general. Groups that in the late 1980s sometimes gained enough public support to force the temporary closure of polluting industries are less successful today because people fear the loss of jobs more than the effects of pollution. Nonetheless, numerous environmental organizations exist throughout the country, some operating under the national umbrella of the Socio-Ecological Union. Greenpeace, an international environmental organization, has a Russian affiliate, and

ecological parties have run, albeit unsuccessfully, in both parliamentary elections.

Labor issues have been another focus of public attention. The official trade unions established under Soviet rule have survived under the title Federation of Independent Trade Unions (FITU), although they are no longer an arm of the party or state as they were in the Soviet period. Still the largest union in Russia, FITU has lost the confidence of large parts of the work force. In some sectors, such as the coal industry, new independent trade unions have formed, mainly at the local level. Labor actions have become an important form of social protest through spontaneous strikes, transport blockages, and even hunger strikes. In the mid-to late 1990s, the main grievance was late payment of wages. In 1998, coal miners in Siberia and the Donetsk area of European Russia blocked railway arteries to protest late wage payment. Later that year, teachers from various regions of the country participated in protest actions against wage delays; in the city of Ulyanovsk, a hunger strike led to the death of one teacher. Immediate concessions are often offered in response to such protests, but the underlying problems are rarely addressed. These cases illustrate the helplessness felt by many citizens; the use of nontraditional forms of protest is a radical and desperate attempt to gain the attention of domestic and international authorities. In other cases, current economic insecurity inhibits workers from protesting too assertively for fear of losing their jobs. It may well be, however, that class conflict, along with pressures for regional autonomy, will generate the most pronounced collective identities in this century.

At this moment, one cannot say that civil society has really formed in Russia, except perhaps among elements of the intelligentsia. Whatever forms of collective identity have emerged, social forces do not easily find avenues to exert constructive and organized influence on state activity. As Russian citizens awaken to political awareness, they seem to sway between activism and apathy, and the political system wavers along a path between fledgling democratic innovations and renewed authoritarianism.

Section ⑤ Russian Politics in Transition

Political Challenges and Changing Agendas

On November 21–22, 2001, some five thousand Russian citizens descended on the Kremlin, the seat of Russian state power, to take part in the Civic Forum, an unprecedented all-Russian congress of nongovernmental organization activists. The event, sponsored by business interests and nonprofit organizations, was heralded as a significant stimulus to the development of civil society and was attended not only by ordinary citizens but also by many government ministers, *Duma* deputies, and representatives from the president's own staff. Prime Minister Mikhail Kasyanov addressed the delegates, assuring them that "the government is open to any contacts, including the most unconventional ideas, and the public, for its part, must 'spur on' the government in conducting effective reforms."[58] But some participants and observers were skeptical; while pleased that government participation signaled official recognition for the importance of civil society in the democratic reform process, some felt the event was mainly a public relations effort that would have no long-lasting impact. Proponents challenged the activists to take the opportunity and run with it, breathing life into the working groups established at the forum and using the congress as a spark to enliven public involvement in addressing important issues like human rights, environmental protection, and tax reform.[59] Did government support for the event signal a break with what Kasyanov called an age-old Russian malady—the "lack of connectedness and communication between the authorities and society"—or was it a reflection of the Kremlin's efforts to co-opt potential opposition and maintain firm control?[60]

When the first edition of this book was published in 1996, five possible scenarios for Russia's future were presented:

- A stable progression toward marketization and democratization
- The gradual introduction of "soft authoritarianism"
- A return to a more extreme authoritarianism of a quasi-fascist or communist variety
- The disintegration of Russia into regional fiefdoms or de facto individual states
- Economic decline, civil war, and military expansionism[61]

Just before Putin's appearance as a major political figure, it appeared that the more pessimistic scenarios were the more likely. Now, many observers maintain a tempered optimism, seeing soft authoritarianism as a possible vehicle for moving toward a more liberal, democratic outcome. The Civic Forum might be one faltering step in this direction.

Russia in the World of States

In the international sphere, Russia's flirtation with Westernization in the early 1990s produced ambiguous results, leading to a severe transitional recession and placing Russia in the position of a supplicant state requesting international credits and assistance. Russia's protests against unpalatable international developments such as NATO expansion, the Desert Fox operation against Iraq in December 1998, and NATO's bombing of Yugoslavia in 1999 revealed Moscow's underlying resentment against Western dominance, as well as the country's relative powerlessness in affecting global developments. With a weakened military structure and economy, Russia could do little more than issue verbal protests. The West's recognition that Russia's involvement was crucial to finding a diplomatic solution to the Kosovo crisis in 1999 marked the beginning of a turning point, heralding a new period of increased cooperation between Russia and the Western world. The events of September 11 reinforced these cooperative ventures, as Russia expressed solidarity with American losses and a commitment to join the battle against international terrorism. Evidence of warmer relations included the formation of a NATO-Russia Council in May 2002, marking an era of closer cooperation in areas such as control of international terrorism, arms control, nonproliferation, and crisis management.[62] The next month the G-8 announced that Russia would assume the presidency of the organization in 2006 and host the annual summit meeting.[63] The G-8 statement affirmed that "Russia has demonstrated its potential to play a full and meaningful role in addressing the global problems that we all face" and referred to "the remarkable economic and democratic transformation that has occurred in Russia in recent years and in particular under the leadership of President Putin."[64] As a further sign of the positive trend in U.S.-Russia relations, in May 2002 Presidents Bush and Putin agreed to a treaty involving further reductions in the nuclear arsenals of the two countries (see Figure 4).

Despite these positive indicators, disagreements remained, including Russia's criticism (although milder than expected) of American withdrawal from the Anti-Ballistic Missile Treaty and opposition to military action to depose Iraqi leader Saddam Hussein. While criticism of Russia's Chechnya policies by Western governments was tempered after the events of September 11, organizations such as Amnesty International and Human Rights Watch continued to charge Russia with acts of violence against the civilian population, as well as instances of arbitrary arrests and sexual attacks on women.[65]

Governing the Economy

The upturn in the Russian economy that began in 1999 may have been a watershed in the struggle to over-

come the transitional recession that plagued Russia from the late 1980s. At the same time, severe disparities in income and wealth remain, meaning that a restoration of economic growth may not bring an improved standard of living for large numbers of Russian citizens, particularly the elderly, children, the disabled, and those living in poorer northern regions. Questions also remain about whether income from oil and gas exports will feed the investment needs of other sectors of the economy, or whether they will be appropriated by a privileged elite. Making the economy attractive to foreign investors will require a continued development of the banking sector, legal institutions to ensure enforcement of contracts, and controls on crime and corruption. While the 1998 devaluation of the ruble brought decreased reliance on Western imports (as they become too expensive), the so-called Dutch disease, where heavy reliance on export income pushes the value of the currency up, now threatens to again undermine prospects for domestic producers. The Russian economy is no longer shielded from foreign and international influences; thus, reverberations in international markets and foreign economies can have a direct impact on the Russian economy as well. Perhaps the greatest economic challenge facing the Putin administration is the establishment of an appropriate vehicle for limiting the influence of powerful economic forces on policy-making. Control of the oligarchs would not only give the state the autonomy required to engage in sensible policy-making but also increase popular legitimacy of government.

The Democratic Idea

Russia's attempted democratization has been formally successful but marred by corruption, the power of big money, and the limited accountability of its leaders. The political structures put in place by the 1993 constitution have not produced the strong and effective government most Russians desire or permitted ordinary people to feel that their interests are being considered. A survey of public opinion carried out in four Russian regions in 1998 revealed that two-thirds of respondents assessed government performance as poor across areas such as economic policy, crime control, dealing with unemployment, social security, and health care; that figure dropped to 53 percent in mid-2000.[66]

Figure 4

Russian Attitudes Toward the West

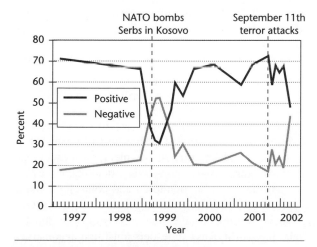

Source: Economist, May 25, 2002, p. 48.

Thus, although Putin's leadership has brought an increase in public confidence, it remains at very low levels. Russian citizens also continue to show higher levels of confidence in regional organs of power than in national ones. The disjuncture between high personal support for the president and a continuing lack of confidence in the ability of political central institutions to address the country's problems effectively suggests that the legitimacy of the system is still on thin ice. The more positive working relationship between the executive and legislative branches that has emerged under Putin's leadership, as well as efforts to regularize relations between the center and regions, provide prospects for improved institutional performance, but it may take many years of successful governance to counteract the cynicism many Russians feel about democracy in their country, the motives of politicians, and the trustworthiness of institutions.

At the same time, it is difficult to conceive that the freedoms that have been exercised since 1986 could be easily withdrawn. Russians value the personal freedom they have gained since the collapse of communism. Expanding contacts with the West have made increasingly broad circles aware of the benefits of civic participation, even if the Russian system does not yet realize these potentials. This new social context would make a return to full-blown authoritarianism difficult.

The Politics of Collective Identities

Despite changes in social consciousness, the formation of new political identities remains unfinished business. In the Soviet period, the state-imposed homogeneity of interests and political repression hindered the formation of diverse interest associations. Now other obstacles prevail. Most people are still preoccupied by the struggle to make ends meet; they have little time or energy to forge new forms of collective action to address underlying problems. Under such circumstances, the appeal to nationalism and other basic sentiments can be powerful, but if President Putin is able to channel these sentiments into support for the current constitutional order, then the danger of extreme populist appeals may be minimized. The weakness of Russian intermediary organizations (interest groups, political parties, or associations) means that

politicians can more easily appeal directly to emotions because people are not members of groups that help them evaluate the politicians' claims. These conditions are fertile ground for authoritarian outcomes, which the government itself might use to keep the public compliant. Still, the high level of education and increasing exposure to international media may work in the opposite direction. Exposure to alternative political systems and cultures may make people more critical of their own political system and seek opportunities to change it. A significant portion of the intelligentsia and some political elites provide potential leaders for this democratic subculture.

Russia remains in what seems to be an extended period of transition. Radical upheavals have been frequent over the past century, which provides some solace to Russians, as they see their current conditions in continuity rather than in contrast to the past. History has been hard on Russians, but the country has always muddled through. In the early 1990s, Russians frequently hoped for "normal conditions," that is, an escape from the shortages, insecurity, and political controls of the past. As the new situation becomes familiar, "normality" has been redefined in less glowing terms than conceived in the late 1980s. Russians seem to have a capability to adapt to change and uncertainty that North Americans find at once alluring, puzzling, and disturbing.

Russian Politics in Comparative Perspective

The way in which politics, economics, and ideology were intertwined in the Soviet period has profoundly affected the nature of political change in all of the former Soviet republics and generally has made the democratization process more difficult. Unlike developing countries currently experiencing democratization and economic transformation, Russia is a highly industrialized country with a skilled and educated work force. While this offers advantages, this high level of development is associated with a host of problems: a heavily damaged natural environment, obsolescent industries, entrenched bureaucratic structures, a nuclear arsenal that must be monitored and controlled, and a public that expects the state to provide a stable system of social welfare. Unlike modernizing elites in the developing world, Russian leaders must first deconstruct existing modern structures before constructing new ones. For example, inefficient or highly polluting factories may need to be closed, the military-industrial complex has been cut back or converted to other uses, and the state has reduced social benefits. These problems make it more difficult for the state to manage the domestic and international challenges it confronts.

How is Russia faring compared to some of the other post-communist systems that faced many of these same challenges? The nations of Eastern Europe and the former Soviet Union were all subjected to a similar system of economic, political, and ideological power during the period of communist rule. Some were under communist rule for a shorter period of time, but most parts of the Soviet Union shared with Russia more than seven decades of the Communist Party state. Despite the efforts of the Soviet leadership to establish conformity throughout the region, national differences did emerge. The countries of Eastern Europe had a history of closer ties and greater cultural exposure to Western Europe; ideas of liberalism, private property, and individualism were less foreign to citizens in countries such as Czechoslovakia, East Germany, and Hungary than in regions farther east, including Russia. The Roman Catholic Church in Poland provided a focal point for national identity, and Poland's historical antipathy to Russia produced a stronger resistance to the imposition of the Soviet model than in other Slavic countries of the region. Such cultural, geopolitical, and historical differences affected the shape that communist rule took in the various countries.

Within the Soviet Union, too, there was considerable variation among the union republics. The Baltic republics of Latvia, Lithuania, and Estonia took a more experimental approach in many spheres of activity and had a more Western European atmosphere; at the other extreme, the Central Asian republics retained aspects of traditional Muslim culture, preserved the extended family structure, and maintained within the construct of the Communist Party a greater prominence for links rooted in the clan system indigenous to the region. Only in Russia and Yugoslavia (as well as in China and Cuba) was communism largely an indigenous phenomenon rather than a pattern imposed by an outside force. In many ways, Russia's culture helped to define

the character of the communist system that it imposed throughout its sphere of influence.

All fifteen countries that gained independence after the collapse of the Soviet Union, as well as several countries of Central and Eastern Europe, have experienced the collapse of the communist system of power since 1989. Given the diversity of nations that were subject to the system, it is not surprising that paths of extrication from communist rule should also vary widely. How has Russia fared in the post-communist period compared to these other countries? We can say, "not the best, but not the worst either." All of the post-communist states have shared common problems, but the elites have responded in different ways, and differences in traditional cultures and the particular nature of the communist system in each country have affected its condition today.

Russia has almost certainly suffered more severe economic dislocations than most of the post-communist countries of Central Europe. Poland pursued the most radical variant of the shock therapy approach, and it appears that its strategy has been the most successful in terms of gross economic indicators. However, huge differentials in income and high unemployment rates have been costs of the approach. Russia's attempt to implement the radical reform strategy has been less successful than Poland's because state institutions have been weaker, internal political opposition has been more successful in moderating economic policy, and indigenous culture is probably less conducive to market structures.

Russia has not fared so badly compared to neighbors like Ukraine, Belarus, and most of the Central Asian states. In Belarus and the Central Asian states, democratization has not taken hold. In all of these countries, the leaders have embraced market reform with considerably less commitment than the Russian government. Because Russia possesses rich deposits of natural resources (including energy resources), it has been able to cope with the ruptured economic ties resulting from the collapse of the Soviet Union better than some of the less-well-endowed states. In addition, Ukraine and particularly Belarus are still suffering from the severe economic and health effects of the accident at the Chernobyl nuclear power plant, and the Central Asian states confront the disastrous effects of

Soviet-imposed emphasis on cotton production and associated environmental degradation (Aral Sea crisis). Russia (along with Ukraine) has been the focal point of international economic assistance because of its large nuclear arsenal, its size, and its geopolitical importance (see "Global Connection: Joining the West or Aid Recipient?"). Although this aid has been insufficient to make the government's overall reform program successful, other parts of the former Soviet Union (with the likely exception of the Baltic states) have received even less international assistance, despite their weaker economic position.

In the political sphere, virtually all of the post-communist states claim to be pursuing some form of democratization, but in some cases, this is more in name than in practice, particularly in Central Asia and parts of the Transcaucasian area. Belarus has a distinctively authoritarian government. In all of the post-communist states, the attempt to construct democratic political institutions has been characterized by repeated political crises, weak representation of popular interests, executive-legislative conflict, faltering efforts at constitutional revision, and corruption. These features are more marked in the more eastern countries. This may be the result of cultural differences between Russia and its more Europeanized western neighbors (particularly Poland, eastern Germany, the Czech Republic, and Hungary) as well as of the shorter period of Communist Party rule in Eastern Europe, the Baltics, and some of the western portions of the former USSR (where the Communist Party took power only after World War II). The cultural and geographical proximity of the post-communist countries of Central Europe to the West has also meant less ambivalence on the part of the population and elite toward Western notions of political democracy.

In Russia, there is considerable skepticism about adopting the Western model of political development, and the political elites who mouth Western values have to some degree not understood or internalized them. The question might be asked whether the patrimonial, collectivist, and egalitarian thrust of Russian culture, as well as some features of the cultures of Central Asia, Ukraine, and Belarus, are really compatible with Western economic and political ideas. Although the concept of democracy has a distinct appeal in the region (partly because it has been associated with Western

affluence), to much of the population in these countries, it means, above all, personal freedom rather than support for notions of political accountability, rule of law, or the civic role of the citizen.

Although Russian politics has been highly contentious and the government has operated at very low levels of efficacy and legitimacy for most of the past decade, with the exception of the Chechnya conflict, Russia has escaped major domestic violence and civil war, unlike Yugoslavia, Armenia, Azerbaijan, Georgia, Moldova, and the Central Asian state of Tadzhikistan. For all their problems, Russian politicians have conducted themselves in a relatively civil manner, and neither Yeltsin nor Putin has appealed to exclusivist definitions of Russian identity. Citizenship rights for all ethnic groups have been maintained, and state-sponsored racism is largely absent. Some opposition figures have not been so restrained in their political rhetoric, but the Russian government can be credited with avoiding marginalization of any major social groups.

Russia will undoubtedly continue to be a key regional force in Europe and Asia. Its vast geographic expanse, rich resource base, large and highly skilled population, and the legacy of Soviet rule will ensure this. Yet its former allies in Central Europe, as well as the Baltic states, are gradually drifting into the orbit of Western Europe economically and politically. They are seeking, and to a degree have already achieved, closer economic and political ties to the EU; those ties increasingly define their identity. Russian leaders seem to appreciate the isolation this could imply, unless they too embrace a positive form of integration into Western institutions and norms.

Thus, over the past few years, while Russia has resisted a monopolar world order dominated by the United States, its leaders have shown a desire and willingness to identify as a European country, still an outsider to some major institutions such as NATO and the EU but increasingly integrated into their norms in a relationship of active partnership.

On Russia's eastern side, the former Central Asian republics (Turkmenistan, Uzbekistan, Tadzhikistan, and Kyrgyzstan) are being courted by the Middle Eastern states with which they share linguistic, cultural, and religious ties, while also serving as a buffer against the unstable situation in Afghanistan and Pakistan. Here,

Global Connection: *Joining the West or Aid Recipient?*

With the collapse of the Iron Curtain, Western governments and international agencies were poised to help build market economies and democratic political structures in the former Communist countries of Central Europe and the former Soviet Union. To some extent the goals of this aid were self-interested: market economies would be more accessible to Western firms seeking external markets and profitable investment opportunities. Promotion of democratization was linked to a view that the West had won the cold war, and democratic countries were considered likely to be more cooperative and peaceful neighbors and partners.

International aid has many sources. Between 1991 and 1997 about 60 percent of assistance to Russia came from individual countries, most notably Germany, followed by the United States, and the United Kingdom. Other significant donors have included Norway, Canada, France, Japan, Italy, and Sweden. This particular kind of aid is bilateral (between two countries), and should not be confused with multilateral aid programs carried out by international institutions like the International Monetary Fund (IMF) and World Bank.

Much bilateral aid has taken the form of programs to provide training and knowledge in areas such as nuclear safety, legislative drafting, health care management, support for private entrepreneurs, encouragement of nongovernmental organizations, and development of the housing sector. Critics point out that a certain portion of such aid is expended in the donor country to pay consultants and training specialists' salaries that would be considered exorbitant in the recipient country. Also, it is often difficult to measure the direct impact of aid programs, although most assistance agencies try to do so. The most important effects may be immeasurable, in the form of long-term changes in attitudes or exposure to alternative models for social or economic undertakings. Some assistance programs have involved humanitarian or food aid, investment funds, and repayable credits. Bilateral aid programs may be administered by such national agencies as the U.S. Agency for International Development or the Canadian International Development Agency.

Alongside such bilateral aid programs, international organizations have also provided assistance, most often in the form of repayable credits. The most important of these agencies are discussed here.

International Organizations

The International Monetary Fund (IMF). The IMF was founded in 1944, and during most of the 1990s it was the most influential international agency in Russia. Its general mandate is to oversee the international monetary system and help maintain stability in exchanges between its 184 member countries, which can draw on the fund's resources. Funds were issued to Russia as short- and medium-term credits to help stabilize the ruble and Russia's internal and external monetary balance. The dispersal of these funds was made contingent on the fulfillment of certain conditions by the Russian government, particularly the maintenance of noninflationary fiscal and monetary policies. These policies, in turn, necessitated cutbacks in social services and subsidies to troubled economic sectors. Through conditions on its loans, the IMF was able to influence the direction of the Russian reform program. In 1999 a final loan was granted, and since then Russia has forgone further credits, choosing to manage its own macroeconomic fiscal policy. As of 2001, Russia managed to cut its outstanding IMF debt to US$7.5 billion, half of what it owed in 1999.[1] (www.imf.org)

The World Bank. Also founded in 1944, the World Bank has as its purpose to promote and finance economic development in the world's poorer countries. After World War II this involved assistance in financing reconstruction in war-torn Europe. The agency is an investment bank with 184 member countries. Through its International Bank for Reconstruction and Development (IBRD), the World Bank has provided loans to support development programs in Russia in sectors such as agriculture, environment, energy, and social welfare. From 1991 to 2002, Russia borrowed US$12.5 billion from the IBRD, and in 2002 its outstanding debt stood at just under $7 billion.[2] (www.worldbank.org)

(continued)

Global Connection: *Joining the West or Aid Recipient? (cont.)*

The European Bank for Reconstruction and Development (EBRD). The EBRD, formed in 1991, promotes the development of market economies in post-communist countries by supporting privatization and entrepreneurship as well as developing infrastructure for production. EBRD provides loans, guarantees, and supports equity investments. (www.ebrd.com)

The European Union initiated the Tacis program in 1991 as a vehicle for providing grants to finance the transfer of knowledge to Russia and other countries in the former Soviet Union. In 2001, Tacis provided 90 million euros to Russia alone and was projected to provide 96 million euros to Russia for the period 2002–2003.[3] (www.europa.eu.int/comm/dg1a/tacis)

Despite the broad scope of assistance programs, aid to Russia in 1994 represented only 0.6 percent of gross domestic product and was at a level of US$12 per capita. Compared to the Marshall Plan, which assisted the reconstruction of Europe after World War II, this is an extremely modest contribution. Many Russians feel that Western assistance efforts have not made a noticeable difference. Some Russian politicians criticize organizations like the IMF for forcing a development strategy on Russia that has produced only economic crisis and decline. Following the financial crisis of August 1998, many assistance agencies undertook a review of their approaches to development assistance for Russia. One positive effect of this has been to encourage Russia to seek solutions based on its own resources and capacities rather than on outside support.

Other International Connections

While being a recipient of international assistance and credits, the government of the Russian Federation has also sought to find its place as an equal partner in a variety of international economic organizations. Discussed here are two examples.

The G8 and Russia. In 1998 Russia was accepted as a full member into the G-8 (Group of Eight), an expanded G-7. The G-8 is an informal international body consisting of the leading industrial nations; G-8 countries hold regular summits dealing with such issues as the international economy, trade relations, and foreign exchange markets. While Russia is still too weak to exert much influence on G-8 issues, its membership in the organization is widely perceived to be valuable, allowing Russia to maintain a presence on the world stage. Russia is currently looking forward to hosting the G-8 for the 2006 summit. For an introduction to the G-8, go to www.g8.gc.ca/menu-en.asp.

The World Trade Organization (WTO) and Russia. The WTO is a powerful international organization, responsible for regulating international trade, settling trade disputes, and designing trade policy through meetings with its 144 member countries. Because of the increasingly global nature of trade, membership in the WTO is seen as an essential prerequisite for increasing economic prosperity and for avoiding international economic isolation. As such, Russia's anticipated entry into the WTO is seen as a milestone in its integration with the international economic community. While negotiations are extremely complex and far from over, current predictions are that Russia will gain entry into the WTO by 2005. (www.wto.org)

I am grateful to Stuart Chandler for assistance in updating this material.

[1]Michael Lelyveld, "Russia: Inflation Fears Forestall Increases for Gas, Electricity," Radio Liberty Radio Free Europe, *Weekday Magazine,* January 29, 2001, http://www.rferl.org/nca/features/indexes/2002/200201.asp (accessed March 4, 2003); http://www.worldbank.org.ru/eng/

[2]*World Bank Annual Report,* Vol II: Financial Statements and Appendices (Washington D.C., 2002), www.worldbank.org/annualreport/2002/Financials.htm, IBRD/IDA Appendices, Appendix 9, p. 135; and www.worldbank. org.ru/eng/group/strategy3/strategy12.htm (World Bank Group Website, accessed March 7, 2003.)

[3]European Union website, at http://europa.eu.int/comm/external_relations/russia/intro/ass.htm.

the pattern of economic and political transformation will be affected by traditions and cultures (including Islam) that play only a minimal role in the Christianized areas of the former Soviet bloc. And yet in many ways, these regions, along with Kazakhstan, retain strong links to Russia, rooted in decades of economic and political interdependence. The states in the middle (Russia, Ukraine, Belarus, Moldova, Bulgaria, Romania) still lie between East and West. Here, efforts to adapt a Western European model of economy and polity have at times seemed tortured and incongruous with indigenous traditions and aspirations. The tradition of a strong state and weak society has not been reversed; cultural tendencies to egalitarianism, state paternalism, clientelistic networks, and communalism conflict with efforts to adopt Western market structures and legal regimes. And yet exposure to Western lifestyles, affluence, and legal norms has instilled expectations and hopes, particularly in educated circles, for a more prosperous lifestyle, less encumbered by the bureaucratic control of the state. The global nature of politics and economics has made impossible the type of isolation that provided a bulwark for the legitimacy of the Soviet state for many decades. These states that lie between Western Europe and Asia will likely continue to be torn between conflicting values and international pressures, with Russia both a feared but influential model (either to emulate or reject) for the neighboring countries.

Will Russia be able to find a place for itself in the world of states that meets the expectations of its educated and sophisticated population? On the dawn of the new millennium, prospects look brighter than five years earlier. One thing is certain: Russia will continue to be an important factor by virtue of its size and its nuclear arsenal. If Russia's experiment of combining market reform and democratization gradually achieves success, then this may inspire movement in this direction in countries like China. If it fails, this may demoralize democratic movements elsewhere and lead to an increase in regional instability.

Key Terms

republics
oligarchs
patrimonial state
mir
democratic centralism
vanguard party

collectivization
tacit social contract
perestroika
glasnost
demokratizatsiia
law-based state
union republics
capital flight
market reform
shock therapy
spontaneous privatization
joint-stock companies
privatization voucher
insider privatization
mafia
pyramid debt
oblasts
autonomous republics
krai
okrugs
patron-client networks
asymmetrical federalism
unfunded mandates
civil society
proportional representation
single-member plurality district

Suggested Readings

Blasi, R. Joseph, Kroumova, Maya, and Kruse, Douglas. *Kremlin Capitalism: The Privatization of the Russian Economy.* Ithaca, N.Y.: Cornell University Press, 1997.

Bowker, Russell. *Russia After the Cold War.* Harlow, England: Longman, 1999.

Brown, Archie, ed. *Contemporary Russian Politics: A Reader.* New York: Oxford University Press, 2001.

Christensen, Paul T. *Russia's Workers in Transition: Labor, Management, and the State Under Gorbachev and Yeltsin.* DeKalb: Northern Illinois University Press, 1999.

Colton, Timothy J. *Transitional Citizens: Voters and What Influences Them in the New Russia.* Cambridge, Mass.: Harvard University Press, 2000.

Eckstein, Harry, Fleron, Frederic J. Jr., Hoffman, Erik P., and Reisinger, William M. *Can Democracy Take Root in Russia? Explorations in State-Society Relations.* Lanham, Md.: Rowman & Littlefield, 1998.

Fish, M. Steven, *Democracy from Scratch: Opposition and Regime in the New Russian Revolution.* Princeton, N.J.: Princeton University Press, 1995.

Freeland, Chrystia. *Sale of the Century: Russia's Wild Ride from Communism to Capitalism.* New York: Doubleday, 2000.

Getty, J. Arch. *Origins of the Great Purges: The Soviet Communist Party Reconsidered.* Cambridge: Cambridge University Press, 1985.

Hoffman, David E. *The Oligarchs: Wealth and Power in the New Russia.* New York: Public Affairs Press, 2002.

Hough, Jerry, and Fainsod, Merle. *How the Soviet Union Is Governed.* Cambridge, Mass.: Harvard University Press, 1979.

Lewin, Moshe. *The Gorbachev Phenomenon: A Historical Interpretation.* Berkeley: University of California Press, 1991.

Mickiewicz, Ellen. *Changing Channels: Television and the Struggle for Power in Russia* Durham, N.C.: Duke University Press, 1999.

Pipes, Richard. *Russia Under the Old Regime*. London: Widenfelt & Nicolson, 1974.

Reddaway, Peter, and Glinski, Dmitri. *The Tragedy of Russia's Reforms: Market Bolshevism Against Democracy*. Washington D.C.: U.S. Institute of Peace, 2001.

Remington, Thomas F. *Politics in Russia*. 2nd ed. New York: Longman, 2002.

Robinson, Neil, ed. *Institutions and Political Change in Russia*. Houndsmill, Basingstoke, Hampshire: Macmillan; New York: St. Martin's Press, 2000.

Silverman, Bertram, and Yanowitch, Murray. *New Rich, New Poor, New Russia: Winners and Losers on the Russian Road to Capitalism*. Armonk, N.Y.: M. E. Sharpe, 2000.

Solomon, Peter H., Jr., and Fogelson, Todd S. *Courts and Transition in Russia: The Challenge of Judicial Reform*. Boulder, Colo.: Westview Press, 2000.

Stavrakis, Peter J., DeBardeleben, Joan, and Black, J. L. *Beyond the Monolith: The Emergence of Regionalism in Post-Soviet Russia*. Washington, D.C.: Wilson Centre Press and Johns Hopkins University Press, 1997.

Tolz, Vera. *Russia*. London : Arnold; New York: Oxford University Press, 2001.

Suggested Websites

Center for Russian and East European Studies, University of Pittsburgh
www.ucis.pitt.edu/reesweb
"Friends and Partners," established by citizens of the United States and Russia
www.friends-partners.org/friends/index/html
Norwegian Institute of International Affairs
www.nupi.no/russland/russland.htm
Radio Free Europe/Radio Liberty
www.rferl.org/newsline/

Notes

[1]For background on Gusinsky and Berezovsky, see Chrystia Freeland, *Sale of the Century: Russia's Wild Ride from Communism to Capitalism* (New York: Doubleday, 2000), chap. 7.

[2]Gosudarstvennyi komitet Rossiiskoi Federatsii po Statistike (State Statistical Committee of the Russian Federation), *Regiony Rossii: informatsionno-statisticheskii sbornik* (Regions of Russia: information-statistical collection), vol. 1 (Moscow, 1997), 381, 615; and Central Intelligence Agency, *World Factbook 1997*.

[3]Richard Pipes, *Russia Under the Old Regime* (London: Widenfelt & Nicolson, 1974).

[4]Pipes, *Russia Under the Old Regime,* 22–24.

[5]Peter Hauslohner, "Politics Before Gorbachev: De-Stalinization and the Roots of Reform," in Alexander Dallin and Gail W. Lapidus (eds.), *The Soviet System in Crisis: A Reader of Western and Soviet Views* (Boulder, Colo.: Westview Press, 1991), 37–63.

[6]Mikhail Gorbachev, *Perestroika: New Thinking for Our Country and the World* (New York: Harper, 1987).

[7]Jacques Sapir, "Russia's Economic Rebound: Lessons and Future Directions," *Post-Soviet Affairs* 18, no. 1 (January–March 2002): 6.

[8]M. Steven Fish, *Democracy from Scratch: Opposition and Regime in the New Russian Revolution* (Princeton, N.J.: Princeton University Press, 1995).

[9]See, for example, Joseph Stiglitz, *Globalization and Its Discontents* (New York: WW Norton & Co., 2002).

[10]James R. Millar, "Normalization of the Russian Economy: Obstacles and Opportunities for Reform and Sustainable Growth," *NBR Analysis,* June 25, 2002, Table 5, http://www.nbr.orgn/publications/analysis/vol13no2/essay_millar.html) (accessed July 1, 2002).

[11]Radio Free Europe/Radio Liberty Daily Report (distributed by e-mail), April 8, 1994, May 17, 1994 (report by Keith Bush).

[12]Gregory Feifer, "Putin Tries Incrementation Rather than Radical Reform in the Countryside," *RFE/RL Russian Political Weekly*, Vol. 3, No. 8 (21 February 2003), http://www.rferl.org/rpw/archives.asp (accessed February 23, 2003).

[13]Sergei Peregudov, "The Oligarchic Model of Russian Corporatism," in Archie Brown (ed.), *Contemporary Russian Politics: A Reader* (New York: Oxford University Press, 2001), 259.

[14]Sapir, "Russia's Economic Rebound," 5–7.

[15]Economist Intelligence Unit (EIU), *Country Report: Russia* (London: EIU, March 2002), 5.

[16]EIU, *Country Report: Russia* (London: EIU, December 2001), 11.

[17]Lilia Shevtsova, "The Political Dimensions of Economic Reform Under Vladimir Putin: Obstacles, Pitfalls, and Opportunities," *NBR Analysis* 13, no. 2 (April 2002), http://www.nbr.org/publications/analysis/vol13no2/essay_Shevtsova.html (accessed July 25, 2002).

[18]Cited in Millar, "Normalization of the Russian Economy," Table 1.

[19]EIU, *Country Report: Russia* (March 2002), 13; Sapir, "Russia's Economic Rebound," 1.

[20]Gosudarstvennyi komitet Rossiiskoi Federatsii po Statistike (State Statistical Committee of the Russian Federation), *Regiony Rossii,* 440–442.

[21]Sarah Ashwin and Elaine Bowers, "Do Russian Women Want to Work?" in Mary Buckley (ed.), *Post-Soviet Women: From the Baltics to Central Asia* (Cambridge: Cambridge University Press, 1997), 23.

[22]Central Intelligence Agency, *The World Factbook 2001*, Russian Federation, http://www.cia.gov/cia/publications/factbook/index.html (accessed August 2, 2002)

[23]UN Human Development Report, Human Development Indicators, "Russian Federation," http://www.undp.org/statistics

(accessed April 15, 2003). The CIA *World Factbook 2001* gives a figure of 62.12 for men and 72.83 for women based on a 2001 estimate.

24Victor Zaslavsky, "From Redistribution to Marketization: Social and Attitudinal Change in Post-Soviet Russia," in Gail W. Lapidus (ed.), *The New Russia: Troubled Transformation* (Boulder, Colo.: Westview Press, 1994), 125.

25Joan DeBardeleben, "Attitudes Toward Privatization in Russia," *Europe-Asia Studies* 51, no. 3 (1999): 447–465.

26Figures adapted from Economist Intelligence Unit, *EIU Quarterly Economic Review of the USSR,* Annual Supplement (London: EIU, 1985), 20.

27Sapir, "Russia's Economic Rebound," 17.

28Sapir, "Russia's Economic Rebound," 18–19.

29Sapir, "Russia's Economic Rebound," 20.

30Millar, "Normalization of the Russian Economy," Table 9; EIU, *Country Report: Russia* (March 2002), 5.

31Sapir, "Russia's Economic Rebound," 24.

32Internationale Politik: Transatlantic Edition, April 15, 2003, 4/2002, vol. 3, www.dgap.org/english/tip/tip0204/Kaliningrad_111102.htm (accessed April 15, 2003).

33EIU, *Country Report: Russia* (March 2002), 5.

34For an example of path-dependent analysis, see David Stark and Laszlo Bruszt, *Postsocialist Pathways: Transforming Politics and Property in East Central Europe* (Cambridge, New York: Cambridge University Press, 1998).

35Thomas Remington, *Politics in Russia*, 2nd ed. (New York: Longman, 2001), 53–54.

36In Russian, this is the Akademiia Gosluzhby pri administratsii presidenta Rossiskoi Federatsiia. See at http://www.rags.ru

37A copy of the decree may be found at http://document.kremlin.ru/index.asp, Decree No. 86 (accessed August 20, 2002). I am grateful to Natalia Joukovskaia for research assistance on this point.

38The beginning of regularized competitive system for civil service appointments was provided in a July 1995 law, but its provisions have not been widely implemented. See Natalia Joukovskaia, "The Development State in Russia" (master's research essay, Carleton University, September 2002), 59–61.

39See Remington, *Politics in Russia,* 261–262.

40Fred Weir, "Putin's Endgame for Chechen Beartrap," *Christian Science Monitor,* January 25, 2001.

41Remington, *Politics in Russia,* 242–248. See the remainder of the chapter for a discussion of other aspects of legal reform.

42Eugene Huskey, "Russian Judicial Reform After Communism," in Peter H. Solomon, Jr. (ed.), *Reforming Justice in Russia, 1864–1996: Power, Culture, and the Limits of Legal Order* (Armonk, N.Y.: M. E. Sharpe, 1997), 336–337.

43Svetlana Mikhailova, "Constitutional Court Confirms Federal Authorities' Ability to Fire Governors, Disband Legislatures,"

Russian Regional Report, April 10, 2002, http://www.iews.org/rrrabout.nsf / (accessed Sept. 6, 2002).

44I am grateful to Natalia Joukovskaia for her assistance relating to these issues. See Aleksei Zudin, "Biznes i gosudarstvo pri Putina: stanovlenie novoi sistemy vzaimootnoshenii" (Business and the state under Putin: The creation of a new system of interrelations), *Russian Journal,* Dec.18, 2000, http://www.russ.ru/today/archive (accessed April 18, 2003).

45EIU, *Country Report: Russia* (September 2001), 13.

46On corporatism, see Philippe C. Schmitter and Gerhard Lehmbruch, *Trends Towards Corporatist Intermediation* (Thousand Oaks, Calif.: Sage, 1979).

47Fond razvitiia parlimentarizma v Rossii, *Federal'noe sobranie: Sovet Federatsii, Gosudarstvennaia Duma, Spravochnik* (The Federal Assembly, Council of the Federation, State Duma, handbook) (Moscow, 1996), 125; data from the Soviet period are from David Lane, *State and Politics in the USSR* (Oxford: Blackwell, 1985), 184–185; for 1999, the figures are from Thomas Remington, *Politics in Russia* (New York: Longman, 2001), 102, and Svetlana Aivazov and Gigory Kertman, "Parliamentary Elections of 1999," *Men and Women at the Elections: Gender Analysis of the Electoral Campaigns of 1999 and 2000 in Russia* (Moscow: Open Women Line, 2000), http://www.owl.ru/eng/books/election/chapter1.htm.

48*Politics in Russia,* 102.

49For a listing of parties, see the site of the Central Electoral Commission of the Russian Federation, http://www.cikrf.ru/_5/doc_1_1.htm.

50For a copy of the 1999 ballot, see Remington, *Politics in Russia,* 182–183.

51Mary Buckley, "Adaptation of the Soviet Women's Committee: Deputies' Voices from "Women of Russia," in Mary Buckley (ed.), *Post-Soviet Women: From the Baltics to Central Asia* (Cambridge: Cambridge University Press, 1997), 158, 163, 180.

52Timothy J. Colton and Michael McFaul, "Are Russians Undemocratic," *Post-Soviet Affairs* 18 (April-June 2002): 91–121; and Jon Pammett, "Elections and Democracy in Russia," *Communist and Post-Communist Studies* 32, no. 1 (1999).

53University of Essex, www2.essex.ac.uk/elect/er.index.htm (accessed April 15, 2003).

54Colton and McFaul, "Are Russians Undemocratic?" 96, 101.

55Colton and McFaul, "Are Russians Undemocratic?" 102.

56William M. Reisinger, Arthur H. Miller, Vicki L. Hesli, and Kristen Hill Maher, "Political Values in Russia, Ukraine, and Lithuania: Sources and Implications," *British Journal of Political Science* 24 (1994): 183–223.

57Peter Reddaway and Dmitri Glinski, *The Tragedy of Russia's Reforms: Market Bolshevism Against Democracy* (Washington, D.C.: United States Institute of Peace, 2001), 76.

58Quoted by Oksana Alekseyeva, "Premier Performance," *Kommersant*, Nov. 23, 2001, excerpted and translated in *The Current Digest of the Post-Soviet Press*, Dec. 19, 2001.

[59]For this viewpoint, see Olga Alexeeva, "Civic Forum or Civic Chorus? Russian NGOs Must Decide," *Alliance* 7, no. 2 (March 2000). http://www.globalpolicy.org/ngos/role/globalact/state/2002/ 0302russia.htm (accessed Sept. 12, 2002).

[60]Paraphrased by Alekseyev, "Premier Performance."

[61]Joan DeBardeleben, "Russia," in Mark Kesselman, Joel Krieger, and William A. Joseph (eds.), *Comparative Politics at the Crossroads* (Lexington, Mass.: Heath, 1996), 355–357.

[62]For the official statement, see the NATO website, "NATO-Russia Relations: A New Quality Declaration by Heads of State and Government of NATO Member States and the Russian Federation," http://www.nato.int/docu/basictxt/b020528e.htm (accessed Sept. 12, 2002).

[63]For background on the G-8, see the Canadian government site, "About the G8," http://www.g8.gc.ca/about-e.asp. (accessed Sept. 12, 2002)

[64]See the official summit statement at the Government of Canada web site, "Russia's Role in the G8," http://www.g8.gc.ca/sumdocs2002-en.asp (accessed April 12, 2002).

[65]For example, see the website of Human Rights Watch, http://www.hrw.org/campaigns/russia/chechnya/docs.htm (accessed September 12, 2002).

[66]Based on a survey carried by the author in conjunction with Russian partners headed by Vladimir Popov and the Academy of National Academy in Moscow and funded by the Consortium on Economic Policy Research and Advice (CEPRA). The research was conducted by regional partners in Stavropol *krai,* Nizhnegorodskaia *oblast,* Khanty-Mansiisk autonomous *okrug,* and Orlov *oblast.*

CHAPTER 9

Brazil

Alfred P. Montero

Federative Republic of Brazil

Land and People

Capital	Brasilia
Total area (square miles)	3,286,500 (Slightly smaller than the United States)
Population	170.4 million
Annual population growth rate (%)	1975–2000 1.8 2000–2015 (projected) 1.1
Urban population (% of total)	81.2
Ethnic composition (% of total)	White 55 (includes Portuguese, German, Italian, Spanish, Polish) Mixed white and black 38 Black 6 Other (includes Japanese, Arab, Amerindian) 1
Major language(s)	Portuguese
Religious affiliation (%)	Roman Catholic (nominal) 80

Economy

Domestic currency	Cruzeiro real
Total GDP (US$)	595.5 billion
GDP per capita (US$)	3484
Total GDP at purchasing power parity (US$)	1299.4 billion
GDP per capita at purchasing power parity (US$)	7625
GDP annual growth rate (%)	1997 3.3 2000 4.5 2001 1.0
GDP per capita average annual growth rate (%)	1975–2000 0.8 1990–2000 1.5
Inequality in income or consumption (1998)	Share of poorest 10% 0.7 Share of poorest 20% 2.2 Share of richest 20% 64.4 Share of richest 10% 48.1 Gini Index 60.7
Structure of production (% of GDP)	Agriculture 9.0 Industry 32.0 Services 59
Labor force distribution (% of total)	Agriculture 23 Industry 24 Services 53
Exports as % of GDP	12
Imports as % of GDP	11

Society

Life expectancy	67.7
Infant mortality per 1000 live births	32
Adult literacy (%)	Female 85.4 Male 85.1
Access to information and communications (per 1000 population)	Telephone lines 182 Mobile phones 136 Radios 433 Televisions 343 Personal computers 44.1

Women in Government and the Economy

Women in the National Legislature	
Lower house or single house (%)	6.8
Upper house (%)	6.3
Women at ministerial level	0
Female economic activity rate (age 15 and above)	43.8
Female labor force (% of total)	36
Estimated earned income (PPP US$)	Female 4557 Male 10,769
2002 Human Development Index Ranking (out of 173)	73

Political Organization

Political System   Federal republic, presidential with separation of powers.

Regime History   Democratic since 1946 with periods of military autoritarianism, especially 1964–1985.

Administrative Structure   Federal, with 26 states plus the Federal District, which also functions as a state. Subnational legislatures are unicameral. State governments have multiple secretariats, the major ones commonly being economy, planning, and infrastructure. The states are divided into municipalities (over 5,500), with mayors and councillors directly elected.

Executive   President, vice president, and cabinet. The president and vice president are directly elected by universal suffrage in a two-round runoff election for four-year terms.

Legislature   Bicameral: The Senate is made up of three senators from each state and from the Federal District, elected by plurality vote for an eight-year term; the Chamber of Deputies consists of representatives from each state and from the Federal District, elected by proprotional vote for a four-year term.

Judiciary   Supreme Court, High Tribunal of Justice, regional courts, labor courts, electoral courts, military courts, and state courts. Judiciary has financial and administrative autonomy. Most judges are elected for life.

Party System   Multiparty system including several parties of the right, center-left, and left. Elections are by open-list proportional representation. There is no restriction on the creation and merging of political parties.

Section ❶ The Making of the Modern Brazilian State

Politics in Action

In May 1997, thousands of Brazilians gathered outside the stock exchange in Rio de Janeiro while hundreds more collected inside the building. All were waiting for the beginning of an auction of *Companhia Vale do Rio Doce* (CVRD), a mining conglomerate that was Brazil's largest public firm. The sale of Vale, as the company is known, was the latest in a series of **privatization** moves that began in the early 1990s with the sale of Brazil's steel mills, fertilizer firms, and utility companies. Fifty-two state enterprises had already been sold, and now it was Vale's turn. For the Brazilians gathered outside the stock exchange, this event meant much more than a sale: a cherished piece of Brazil's past was being lost to the faceless market. Vale represented memories of the Brazilian economy that blossomed in the post–World War II era with ambitious industrialization projects led by large public firms. Now, all of that was under attack by "greedy capitalists" intent on exploiting the patrimony of the Brazilian people for personal gain. For the students, workers, and professionals who joined to protest the sale of the mining giant, it was too much to take. Minutes before the auction gavel fell, tempers flared. The angry crowd pushed against police barricades. Some threw punches; others were hurled to the floor and trampled; many would leave with bloodied faces. Everyone felt the painful defeat. The old Brazil was dead.

For those inside the stock exchange, the sale of Vale meant the birth of a new Brazil. By agreeing to privatize one of the most recognizable symbols of Brazilian industry, the country's leaders were embracing the importance of the market in modernizing Brazil. Despite its past successes, the state could no longer guarantee Vale or any other industrial firm the resources needed to become competitive in global markets. By putting Vale up for sale, Brazil's political leadership was guaranteeing that the firm would have a future. The new owners of Vale were young Brazilian industrialists and bankers as well as international investors, including U.S. firms such as NationsBank and the financier George Soros. Unlike most other Brazilian firms, which are family owned, the new Vale would be owned by share-

holders and operated by professional administrators, much as major U.S. and European multinational firms are. Nothing less would befit the world's largest exporter of iron ore. The new Vale was emblematic of the new Brazil: modern, competitive, and linked to global markets.

Although opponents were thwarted in their attempts to stop the sale, the opposition to the auctioning of Vale revealed aspects of the new Brazil. Only a week before the sale, opponents had filed 135 separate lawsuits in state courts to halt the privatization. In response, squads of lawyers for the National Development Bank, the federal agency responsible for organizing the sale of Vale, had traveled to the far corners of Brazil to defeat each and every lawsuit. Yet the absence of a centralized and hierarchical system for adjudicating the dispute highlighted both the weakness of democratic institutions in Brazil and the difficulty of ruling over such a large, decentralized political order. The new Brazil is a relatively young democracy, and like Russia and India, it is big and complicated.

Geographic Setting

Brazil's size is only the most obvious characteristic of this country of 170 million people. In land surface, Brazil is larger than the continental United States and occupies two-thirds of South America. It borders all the other countries of South America except Ecuador and Chile. Because of the expansion of the coffee economy in São Paulo state during the nineteenth century and the growth of an industrial economy during the twentieth century, Brazil's largest cities are concentrated in the southern and southeastern regions. More than 15 million inhabitants live in Greater São Paulo alone. This density contrasts with the northern, sparsely populated rain forest regions of the Amazon. Generally, however, Brazil's 18.2 inhabitants per square kilometer means that the country is more underpopulated than the United States.

The physical geography of Brazil is impressively diverse, including thick rain forest in the Amazon valley, large lowland swamps known as the *pantanal* in the central western states, and vast expanses of badlands

Brazil

known as the *sertão* in the north and northeast. The country is rich in natural resources and arable land. The Amazon has an abundance of tropical fruit and minerals; the central and southern regions provide most of the country's iron ore and coal; offshore and onshore sources of petroleum in Rio de Janeiro and the northeast coastline are also significant. Brazil's farmlands are particularly fertile, including large soy-producing areas in the central savannas called the *cerrados,* coffee areas of the Paraíba Valley near Rio de Janeiro and in São Paulo, and sugar and other agriculture along the narrow stretch off the northeast coast called the *litoral*. The Amazon's climate is wet, the *sertão* is dry, and the agricultural areas of the central, southeastern, and southern regions are temperate.

Centuries of voluntary and involuntary immigration of Europeans and Africans have contributed to the emergence of an ethnically mixed society. Combinations of Europeans, Africans, and Indians produced hundreds of distinct colors of people. Although this complexity makes any classification scheme precarious, the National Brazilian Institute of Geography and Statistics (IBGE) claims that 57 percent of the population is white, 37 percent is *pardo* (brown or mulatto), 6 percent is black, and 0.6 percent is Asian.[1] These numbers probably ignore people of mixed race, from indigenous and white parents, who are known as *mestizos* but are sometimes classified erroneously as being white or *pardo*. The indigenous people, who live in the vast Amazon basin and once numbered in the millions, were largely decimated by colonization and modernization; their number is usually estimated at 250,000. They occupy over 8.5 million square kilometers, 11 percent of the total area of Brazil.[2] The Asian population is dominated by people of Japanese descent who immigrated to the southeastern states and particularly São Paulo after 1925. Numbering over 2 million, São Paulo's community of Japanese descendants is the largest such grouping outside Japan.

Like other ethnically plural societies such as India, Mexico, Nigeria, Russia, Iran, and the United States, Brazil is a unique blend of distinct cultural influences. Unlike the people of India, Iran, and Nigeria, however, Brazilians are not greatly divided over religious differences. Roman Catholicism was imposed by Portuguese colonial rule, then reinforced by immigration from Catholic Italy, Spain, and Portugal at the end of the nineteenth century. In recent years, evangelical Protestants have made inroads and now compose about 11 percent of the population. Afro-Brazilian religions represent an older, and far more difficult to measure, tendency with religious practices that often mix Catholic and African traditions but are sometimes practiced independently. Indigenous religions and traditions are also part of the cultural landscape. More than religion, the dominance of Portuguese as the language of the land has served to keep this large country united.

Because of its size, large population, large internal market for foreign and domestic industry, and dominance over a majority of the rain forests in the Amazon (the so-called green lung of our planet), Brazil possesses resources that could make it a global superpower. Yet Brazil is a poor country that struggles to provide for its own people out of its impressive abundance of natural resources. Addressing the immense social problems of this big country requires administering its considerable resources with foresight. Unfortunately, Brazil's potential has often fallen victim to the political baggage from its past.

Critical Junctures

The Brazilian Empire (1822–1889)

Europeans first arrived in Brazil in 1500 with an expedition led by the Portuguese explorer Pedro Alvares Cabral. Unlike the other countries of Latin America, Brazil was a Portuguese colony, not a Spanish one. As a result, Brazil was spared the devastatingly violent wars of independence that afflicted other Latin American states, including Mexico. Violence, however, played

Critical Junctures in Brazil's Political Development

1822 Dom Pedro I declares himself emperor of Brazil, peacefully ending three hundred years of Portuguese colonial rule.

1824 Constitution drafted.

1888 Abolition of slavery.

1889 Dom Pedro II, who assumed throne in 1840, is forced into exile; landowning elites establish an oligarchical republic.

1891 A new constitution establishes a directly elected president.

1930 Getúlio Vargas gains power after a coup led by military and political leaders. His period of dictatorship (1937–1945) is known as the New State.

1945 Vargas calls for general elections. General Eurico Dutra of the Social Democratic Party wins.

1950 Vargas is elected president. Scandals precipitate his suicide in 1954.

1956 Juscelino Kubitschek becomes president.

1960 Jânio Quadros becomes president.

1961 Quadros resigns. João Goulart gains presidency despite an attempted military coup.

1964 A military coup places power in the hands of successive authoritarian regimes.

1985 *Diretas Já!* a mass mobilization campaign, calls for direct elections.

1985 Vice-presidential candidate José Sarney becomes president on the sudden death of elected president Tancredo Neves.

1988 A new constitution grants new social and political rights.

1989 Fernando Collor is elected president.

1992 Collor is impeached; Vice President Itamar Franco assumes presidency.

1994 Fernando Henrique Cardoso is elected president after his Real Plan controls inflation.

1998 Cardoso is reelected.

1999 The Real Plan weathers a financial crisis.

2002 Lula da Silva is elected president.

a prominent role in Brazil's conquest and development as indigenous peoples, and African slaves were mistreated and killed or died of disease.

In 1808, when Napoleon Bonaparte invaded Spain and Portugal, the Portuguese king, João VI, and his court escaped to Brazil. After the defeat of Napoleon, Dom João returned to Portugal to reclaim his throne, but he left his son, Dom Pedro, behind in Rio de Janeiro as prince regent. In September 1822, Dom Pedro declared Brazil independent and took the new title of emperor of Brazil. In 1824, a constitution was drafted, making Brazil the only constitutional monarchy in the Americas. In 1840, Dom Pedro I's son, Dom Pedro II, assumed the throne.

The Brazilian empire's chief concern was keeping control of the country's large, mostly unexplored territory. Complicating this task was the divisive issue of slavery, on which Brazil's plantation economy depended. The solution was to centralize authority in the emperor, who acted as a **moderating power** (*poder moderador*), mediating conflicts among the executive, legislative, and judicial branches of government and powerful landowning elites, known as the landed **oligarchy.** This centralization of authority provided a contrast with the other postcolonial Latin American states, which suffered numerous conflicts among territorially dispersed strongmen called *caudillos.* Brazil avoided the rise of figures such as Mexico's arch-strongman, Porfirio Díaz.

The constitutional empire marked the birth of Brazilian liberal institutions. In contrast with its neighbors, the country enjoyed several features of a functioning representative democracy: regularity of elections, the alternation of parties in power, and scrupulous observation of the constitution. In substance, however, liberal institutions only regulated political competition among the rural, oligarchical elites, reflecting the interests of a privileged minority and not the larger Brazilian population.

The Old Republic (1889–1930)

The next critical juncture in Brazilian history occurred in 1889 with the peaceful demise of the empire, the exile of Dom Pedro II, and the emergence of a republic ruled by the landowning oligarchy (the Old Republic). Many causes led to the end of the empire. The institu-

tions of slavery and the monarchy were topics of heated debate among landowners, politicians, and commercial elites. The international pressures of abolitionists to end slavery resulted in the freeing of slaves over sixty years of age and unborn children of slaves. Socioeconomic changes also paved the way for abolition. The dynamic coffee economy, concentrated in the state of São Paulo, had grown impressively since the 1830s. Unlike the plantation sugar economy of the northeast, coffee did not require the use of slave labor, which was prohibitively expensive. Under sustained pressure by the coffee elite, all slaves were freed in 1888. By this time, too, liberal political values in opposition to the centralization of political authority had taken root among the coffee oligarchy.

The Old Republic (1889–1930) consolidated the political rise of the coffee oligarchy and a small urban industrial class and commercial elite linked to the coffee trade. By the end of the nineteenth century, coffee had become the main economic commodity, with Brazil supplying most of the world's demand. The economic importance of coffee only added to the rapidly growing political influence of the southern coffee oligarchy.

The constitution of 1891, which was inspired by the U.S. model, established a directly elected president as the head of government, guaranteed the separation of church and state, and expanded the franchise to include all literate males (about 3.5 percent of the population before 1930). The **legitimacy** of the republican political system was established on governing principles that were limited to a privileged few, but no longer determined by the hereditary rights of the emperor. Power was decentralized to the states, which gained greater authority to formulate policy, spend money, levy taxes, and maintain their own militias.

Although the republican elite went further than the empire's elite in expressing liberal ideas in the constitution, republican liberalism was a sham to the majority of Brazilians. Most Brazilians continued to reside in rural areas where the landed oligarchy vigorously suppressed dissent. As in the southern United States and in Mexico, landed elites manipulated local political activity. The colonels, as these elites were called in Brazil, assumed extensive extralegal authority to gather their poor workers and "vote them" (use their votes to guarantee the election of officials favored by the local colonels). This process became widely known as *coronelismo.*

The ties that developed between the patron (the landowner) and the client (the peasant) during the Old Republic became the basis of modern Brazilian politics. In return for protection and occasional favors, the client did the bidding of the patron. As urbanization and the growth of the state's administrative and bureaucratic agencies proceeded, the process of trading favors and demanding action was transformed and became known as **clientelism.** *Coronelismo* in rural areas and clientelism in urban areas were extended to the politics of the national state. In this way, the state was dominated by **patrimonialism**—the injection of private interests into public policy-making. Pervasive corruption, graft, and outright bribery developed as means of reinforcing patrimonialism.

In contrast to the centralization of power during the empire, the Old Republic consecrated the power of local elites. Perhaps at no other time in Brazilian political history was the **politics of the governors** as blatant as it was during the years of the Old Republic. Regional elites, mainly from the coffee and cattle regions, dominated national politics. Three states in particular emerged as key players: São Paulo (coffee), Minas Gerais (coffee and ranching), and Rio Grande do Sul (ranching). These states profoundly influenced economic policy-making and the choice of presidential candidates. The presidency alternated almost on a regular basis between São Paulo and Minas Gerais. The pattern was so obvious that this period of Brazilian political history is popularly referred to as the rule of *café com leite* ("coffee with milk"), reflecting the dominance of the São Paulo coffee and Minas Gerais cattle elites.

The 1930 Revolution

The Great Depression of the 1930s upset the economic and political base of the Old Republic. As world demand for coffee plummeted, the coffee and ranch elites faced their worst crisis. Worker demonstrations and a resurgent Brazilian Communist Party challenged the legitimacy of the Old Republic. Among the ranks of discontented political elites, a figure emerged who would change the shape of Brazilian politics for the rest of the century: Getúlio Vargas (see "Leaders: Getúlio Dornelles Vargas").

After a disputed presidential campaign in 1930, Vargas came to power as the head of what he called a new "revolutionary government." He moved swiftly to crush middle-class and popular dissent and built a political coalition around a new economic project of industrialization led by the central government and based on central state resources. In contrast to the Old Republic, Vargas insisted on controlling the regional governments by replacing all governors (except in Minas Gerais) with hand-picked allies (*interventores*). Once again, the center of gravity of Brazilian politics swung back to the national state.

Under the Old Republic, calls for rights by workers and middle-class professionals had been treated as issues for the police to resolve with force. By contrast, Vargas believed he could win the support of these groups by answering their demands in a controlled way. They would be allowed to participate in the new political order, but only if they mobilized within state-created and state-regulated unions and associations.

This model of government was **state corporatism.** State corporatism refers to a method of organizing societal actors in state-sponsored associations. It rejects the idea of competition among social groups by having the state arbitrate all conflicts. For instance, when workers requested increases in their wages, state agencies would determine to what extent such demands were answered and how business would pay for them.[3]

By 1937, Vargas had achieved a position of virtually uncontested power. From such a vantage point, he implemented a series of reforms whose influence is still felt. During the next eight years, Vargas consolidated his state corporatist paradigm with labor codes, the establishment of public firms to produce strategic commodities such as steel and oil, and paternalistic social policies. Packaged with nationalist fervor, these policies were collectively called the **New State** (*Estado Novo*).

The New State was decidedly authoritarian. Vargas, who was called *pai do povo* (father of the people), could not be upstaged by competing political images and organizations. Parties and congressional politicians became mere onlookers. Brazilian society would be linked directly to the state and to Vargas as the state's primary agent. Although the New State's constitution had fascist overtones, Vargas's policies were as much inspired by the New Deal of U.S. President Franklin D. Roosevelt as by fascist Italy or Nazi Germany.[4] The new regime expanded the existing rudimentary social

Leaders: *Getúlio Dornelles Vargas*

Getúlio Dornelles Vargas (1883–1954) came from a wealthy family in the cattle-rich southernmost state of Rio Grande do Sul. Vargas's youth was marked by political divisions within his family between federalists and republicans, conflicts that separated Brazilians during the Old Republic and particularly in Rio Grande do Sul, which had a strong regional identity. Political violence, which was common in the state's history, also affected Vargas's upbringing. His two brothers were each accused of killing rivals, one at the military school in Minas Gerais that Getúlio attended with one of his older siblings. After a brief stint in the military, Vargas attended law school in Porto Alegre, where he excelled as an orator. Like many others in his generation, his university education was incomplete. He supplemented his studies by reading many books published in other countries.

After graduating in 1907, he began his political career as a district attorney. Later, he served as majority leader in the state senate. In 1923, Vargas was elected federal deputy for Rio Grande do Sul, and in 1924 he became leader of his state's delegation in the Chamber of Deputies. In 1926, he made another political career change when he was named finance minister for the Washington Luis administration (1926–1930). He served for a year before winning the governorship of his home state. Never an ideologue, Vargas embraced a highly pragmatic style of governing that made him one of Brazil's most popular politicians by the end of the 1920s.

Vargas's powerful political position as governor of Rio Grande do Sul catapulted him into national prominence in 1929. The international economic crisis compelled several regional economic oligarchies to unite in opposition to the coffee and financial policies of the government. The states, including the state of São Paulo, divided their support between two candidates for the presidency: Julio Prestes, who was supported by President Luis, and Vargas, head of the opposition. The two states of Minas Gerais and Rio Grande do Sul voted as a bloc in favor of Vargas, but he lost the 1930 election. Immediately after this loss, a conspiracy among discontented military and political leaders led to the coup of October 1930, which installed Vargas in power.

No other figure in Brazilian political history has ever affected the country as much as Getúlio Vargas. His New State launched a series of reforms that established the terms on which Brazilian society would be linked to the state for decades. Even today, his political legacy continues in the form of state agencies and laws protecting workers.

Getúlio Vargas as president in 1952. *Source:* Hulton/Getty Archive by Getty Images.

Source: For more on Vargas's life, see Robert M. Levine, *Father of the Poor? Vargas and His Era* (New York: Cambridge University Press, 1998).

insurance and pension programs into a broad welfare and health care system for urban workers. Although unemployment insurance was not envisaged by the new laws, workers were provided with insurance against occupational accidents, illness, and death. Vargas created a Ministry of Labor and labor courts to regulate and solve conflicts between employers and labor.

In the New State, the military became an ever more important institution in politics. The armed forces experienced marked improvements in armament production and recruitment. Professional standards of promotion, conduct, and the use of force were codified in the establishment of the Superior War College (*Escola Superior de Guerra*). The military even developed new doctrines to justify the use of public funds to own and operate industries seen as essential to the nation's security. The ideology of the military regimes that dominated Brazil from 1964 to 1985 emerged directly from these earlier experiences.[5]

The Populist Republic (1945–1964)

The ever-growing mobilization of segments of the working and middle classes as well as U.S. diplomatic pressure forced Vargas, in 1943, to call for full democratic elections to be held in December 1945. Three political parties emerged to contest the election: the Social Democratic Party (PSD), the Brazilian Labor Party (PTB), and the National Democratic Union (UDN). The PSD was a collection of *Estado Novo* supporters and members of clientelist political machines across the country. The PTB was created by Vargas to mobilize members of the official labor unions. The PSD and the PTB, which operated in alliance, were both dependent on the state. The UDN brought together the various regional, anti-Vargas forces, which advocated a return to the liberal constitutionalism of the Old Republic. The UDN continued to support the role of the state in promoting economic development, however. By October 1945, the bitterness of the campaign led the military to force Vargas's resignation, two months before the general election.

The turn to democracy in 1945 fell far short of breaking with the past. The new president, Eurico Dutra of the PSD, was one of the architects of the New State. Although the new 1946 constitution provided for periodic elections, state corporatism continued in full force.

The most important economic and social policies of the country were still decided by Brazil's far-flung state bureaucracy, not by the national legislature.

Populism, not democracy, became the defining characteristic of the new political order. In Brazil, the terms *populist* and *populism* refer to politicians, programs, or movements that seek to expand citizenship to previously disenfranchised sectors of society in return for political support. Populist governments tend to grant benefits to guarantee support, but they discourage lower-class groups from creating autonomous organizations. Populist leaders, around whom personality cults often form, were successful in Brazil and other Latin American countries in generating mass support among urban working and middle classes (and sometimes rural groups) through the provision of social insurance, health care, and higher wages. Yet in no way were these leaders directly representative of or accountable to their constituencies.

Populism was Vargas's most important tool after his elected return to the presidency in 1950 with PSD and PTB support. Brazilian workers supported his return because he promised to increase the minimum wage, improve the social insurance system, and provide subsidies for public transportation and basic foodstuffs. However, many of these promises were threatened by economic problems in the early 1950s as inflation increased and wages eroded. Opposition politicians charged that Vargas was no longer able to ensure Brazil's development and that if he were given a chance, he would impose another dictatorship on the country.[6] Already politically vulnerable, Vargas was soon swept up in a bizarre scandal involving the attempted assassination of a popular journalist. The crisis drove Vargas to take his own life on August 24, 1954.

Under Vargas's democratic successor, Juscelino Kubitschek (in office from 1956 to 1960), the economic picture improved. Brazilian industry expanded tremendously in the 1950s. Kubitschek was a master of political symbolism and **nationalism.** His administration promoted images of a new and bigger Brazil, capable of generating "fifty years of development in five." Chief among these symbols of the new Brazil was Kubitschek's decision to move the country's capital from Rio de Janeiro to a planned city called Brasília. The building of this utopian city served to divert attention from the country's economic and social problems. It also

Brazil's capital, Brasília. The planned city was designed by the world-famous Brazilian architect Oscar Niemeyer.
Source: Georges Holton/Photo Researchers.

acted as a political symbol to rally support among Brazil's business class for Kubitschek's developmentalist policies.

The weak point in Brazil's political economic order was the country's incoherent party system. After Kubitschek's term ended, a populist antiparty maverick, Jânio Quadros, won the presidency in 1960 because of fragmented party identities and unstable partisan alliances.[7] Economic bad times returned as inflation soared and growth slowed. Then, without much explanation, Quadros resigned, elevating João Goulart, Vargas's former minister of labor and Quadros's acting vice president, to the presidency.

Goulart embarked on an ill-fated campaign for structural reforms, mainly of the educational system and the federal administration, and a progressive agrarian policy. Meanwhile, Brazilian politics were becoming more polarized into right and left. New political actors burst onto the scene: peasant league movements, students, and professional organizations. Protests, strikes, and illegal seizures of land by poor Brazilians heightened ideological tensions. Goulart was severely hindered in responding to these problems by a congress that was almost perpetually stalemated in partisan bickering. Finally, industrial and landowning elites came down firmly against Goulart's reforms. Right-wing organizations flooded the streets of the main capital with anti-Goulart demonstrators. Convinced that the situation was out of control and that Goulart would soon resort to extraconstitutional measures, the military intervened in 1964, putting an end to Brazil's experiment with democratic populism.

The Rise of Bureaucratic Authoritarianism (1964–1985)

The military government that came to power in 1964 installed what the Argentine sociologist Guillermo O'Donnell has termed **bureaucratic authoritarianism** (BA).[8] These authoritarian regimes emerge in response to severe economic crises and are led by the armed forces and key civilian allies, most notably professional economists, engineers, and administrators. Repression in Brazilian BA varied from combinations of mild forms that constricted civil rights and other political freedoms and harsher forms that included wholesale censorship of the press through institutional acts, torture of civilians, and imprisonment without trial. The first and the last two military rulers, Castelo Branco (1964–1967), Ernesto Geisel (1974–1979), and João Figueiredo (1979–1985) presented less violent forms of authoritarianism, whereas the rule of Artur Costa e Silva (1967–1969) and of Emilio Médici (1969–1974) encompassed the worst forms of physical repression.

Initially, the military government envisioned a quick return to civilian rule and even allowed the continuation of democratic institutions, though in a limited form. Although purged in 1964 of perceived enemies of the military, the national congress continued to function afterward, and direct elections for federal legislators and most mayors (but not the president or state governors) were held at regular intervals. In November 1965, the military abolished all existing political parties and replaced them with only two: the National Renovation Alliance, or ARENA, and the Brazilian Democratic Movement, or MDB. ARENA was the military government's party, and MDB was the "official" party of the opposition. Although previous party labels were discarded, former members of the three major parties joined one of the two new parties. The most important party affiliations in ARENA belonged to former UDN and PSD members, while many PTB members flocked to MDB. Although the two parties did not operate until Castelo Branco left office in March 1967, the military hoped that the reform would give the BA regime a level of democratic legitimacy.[9]

Although these democratic institutions were more than pro forma, their powers were severely limited. The military government used institutional decrees to legislate the most important matters, thereby stopping the

congress from having an important voice. Few civilian politicians could speak out directly against the military for fear of being removed from office.

In economic policy, the military reinforced the previous pattern of state interventionism. The government actively promoted **state-led development** by creating hundreds of state corporations and investing millions in established public firms such as Vale. Under military leadership, Brazil implemented one of the most successful economic development programs in the Third World. Often called the Brazilian miracle, these programs demonstrated that, like France, Germany, and Japan in earlier periods, a developing country could create its own economic miracle.

The Transition to Democracy and the First Civilian Governments (1974–2002)

After the oil crisis of 1973 set off a wave of inflation around the world, the economy began to falter. Increasing criticism from Brazilian business led Geisel and Figueiredo to embrace a gradual process of democratization.[10] Initially, these leaders envisioned only a liberalizing, or opening (*abertura*), of the regime that would allow civilian politicians to contest for political office. As was the case with Gorbachev's *glasnost* in the Soviet Union, however, control over the process of liberalization gradually slipped from their hands and was captured by organizations within civil society. In 1974 the opposition party, the MDB, stunned the military government by increasing its representation in the Senate from 18 to 30 percent and in the Chamber of Deputies from 22 to 44 percent. These numbers did not give it a majority, but the party did capture a majority in both chambers of the state legislatures in the most important industrialized southern and southeastern states.[11]

Abertura accelerated in the following years. The opposition made successive electoral gains and used them to get concessions from the government. The most important of these concessions was the reestablishment of direct elections for governors in 1982, political amnesty for dissidents, the elimination of the government's power to oust legislators from political office, and the restoration of political rights to those who had previously lost them. The gubernatorial elections of November 1982 sealed the fate of promilitary candidates. Opposition gubernatorial candidates won landslide victories, capturing the most developed states: Minas Gerais, São Paulo, and Rio de Janeiro. The process of liberalizing the authoritarian regime was now irreversible.

The military, which wanted to maintain as much control over the succession process as possible, preferred to have the next president selected within a restricted electoral college. In 1983, mass mobilization campaigns seeking the right to elect the next president directly got off the ground. The *Diretas Já!* ("Direct Elections Now!") movement, comprising an array of social movements, opposition politicians, and labor unions, expanded in size and influence in 1984.[12] Their rallies exerted tremendous pressure on the military at a moment when the question of who would succeed General Figueiredo was not clear. The military's fight to keep the 1984 elections indirect alienated civilian supporters of the generals, many of whom broke with the regime and backed an alliance (the Liberal Front) with Tancredo Neves, the candidate of the opposition PMDB, or Party of the MDB. Neves's victory in 1984, however, was short-lived. His sudden death on the eve of his inauguration meant that Vice President José Sarney became the first civilian president of Brazil since 1964.

The sequence of events that led to Sarney's presidency was a keen disappointment to those who had hoped for a clean break with the authoritarian past. Most of the politicians who gained positions of power in the new democracy hailed from the former ARENA or its misleadingly named successor, the Democratic Social Party (PDS). Most of these soon joined Sarney's own PMDB or its alliance partner, the Party of the Liberal Front (PFL).[13] Labor unions in particular distrusted Sarney as a former political hack of the military. His administration failed to reform the old authoritarian modes of policy-making, including corporatist institutions and military prerogatives over civilian government.

A chance for fundamental change appeared in 1987 when the national Constituent Assembly met to draft a new constitution. Given the earlier success of the opposition governors in 1982, state political machines became important players in the game of constitution writing. The state governments petitioned for the devolution of new authority to tax and spend. Labor groups also exerted influence through their lobbying organization. Workers demanded constitutional protection of their right to strike and called for an extension of the right to public employees, who were heretofore prohibited from engaging in such activism. The constitution also granted workers the right to create their own unions without authorization from the Ministry of Labor.[14] As a whole, the constitution guaranteed a rich array of social and political rights, yet it also left vestiges from the corporatist past, including protection of public firms in petroleum and telecommunications from foreign investment and privatization.

The other primary issue of the day was inflation. Soon after Sarney's rise to power, annual rates of inflation began to skyrocket. The government invoked several stabilization plans to stop the explosion of prices, but to no avail. By the presidential elections of 1989, the first since the 1960s to be held as direct elections for that post, Brazilian society was calling for a political leader who would remedy runaway inflation and remove corrupt and authoritarian politicians from positions of power.

Rising from political obscurity, an ex-governor from Alagoas, a small state in the poor northeast, Fernando Collor de Mello, became president. Collor and his small party, the Party of National Reconstruction (PRN), had fought a grueling campaign against the popular left-wing labor leader and head of the Workers' Party (*Partido dos Trabalhadores,* or PT), Luiz Inácio "Lula" da Silva (see "Citizen Action: The Workers' Party" in the "Political Parties and the Party System" section later in this chapter). To counteract Lula's appeal among the Brazilian people, Collor's campaign rhetoric appealed to the poor, known as the *descamisados* ("shirtless ones"), who were attracted by his attacks against politicians and the social problems caused by bureaucratic inefficiency. A skillful campaigner on television, Collor convinced Brazilians that he could "kill inflation with one shot" and get rid of the "maharajahs"— corrupt public servants who collected massive salaries but did little work.

The Collor presidency was a critical juncture as the government's economic team began the privatization of state enterprises, deregulation of the economy, and the reversal of decades of policies that had kept Brazil's markets closed to the rest of the world. Yet Collor failed to solve the nagging problem of inflation and, ironically, was soon accused of bribery and influence peddling and was impeached in September 1992, an ignominious end for the first directly elected president since the 1960s.

Collor's impeachment brought to the presidency

Itamar Franco, a well-known politician in Minas Gerais who was less well known at the national level as Collor's vice president. Despite a high level of uncertainty during Franco's first year, including rumors of a military coup that was allegedly in the works in 1993, his government provided an important stabilizing role. Perhaps his most important decision was to support his minister of finance, Fernando Henrique Cardoso, a sociologist and senator from São Paulo, in a plan to conquer inflation. In July 1994, Cardoso implemented a plan to fight inflation, the Real Plan, which succeeded. By creating a new currency, the real, the government hoped to wipe away the populace's memories of its weak and unstable predecessors, cruzeiros and cruzados. The result was that monthly inflation fell from 26 percent to 2.82 percent in October 1994 (see Section 2).

Cardoso rode the success of the Real Plan to the Brazilian presidency, beating out Lula of the PT in 1994 and again in 1998 to become the first Brazilian president since the Vargas dictatorship to be reelected. After his inauguration in January 1995, Cardoso proved adept at keeping inflation low and consolidating some of the structural reforms of the economy. As the tale of Vale suggests, privatization moved forward. Other reforms, however, remained stuck in congress, including crucial reforms of the tax system. Brazil's budget and trade deficits increased, requiring the government to finance the shortfall with short- and medium-term debt. As in Mexico in 1994, these conditions caused foreign investors to abandon the Brazilian market, leading to billions of dollars in capital flight. Financial crisis in Asia and Russia worsened the crisis in 1998 and early 1999. Even Cardoso's reelection in October 1998 could not stop Brazil from becoming the latest casualty in a widening global financial crisis as the real crashed in January 1999. Yet the months following the crisis showed how resilient Brazilian democracy and the economic reform process could be. The real soon stabilized, hyperinflation did not return, and the country weathered the financial calamity of the Argentine economy's meltdown after December 2001 without turning back on any of the structural reforms implemented during the 1990s.

Following the October 2002 elections, the country experienced the first regular transfer of the presidential sash from one directly elected chief executive to his successor, Lula da Silva. Despite international financial uncertainty in response to Lula's rise to power, this fourth presidential election in twelve years reflected the maturity and stability of Brazilian democracy.

Themes and Implications

Historical Junctures and Political Themes

The state has played a central role in the story of modern Brazilian politics. In the world of states, both international and domestic factors have influenced the Brazilian state's structure, capacity, and relations with society. During the days of the empire, international opposition to slavery forced powerful oligarchs to turn to the state for protection. The coffee and ranch economies that provided the material base for the power of the Old Republic were intricately tied to Brazil's economic role in the world. Even the *Estado Novo,* with its drive to organize society, was affected by events outside Brazil. The defeat of fascism in Europe helped turn the New State's authoritarian project into a populist-democratic one. The return to democracy during the 1980s was also part of a larger global experience, as authoritarian regimes gave way all over Latin America, eastern Europe, southern Europe, and the Soviet Union.

Within Brazil, the state adjusted to changes in the distribution of power, the rise of new, politically active social classes, and the requirements of development. In the federal state, power shifted regularly between the central and subnational governments. From the centralizing, moderating power of the Brazilian emperor Dom Pedro II and the state corporatist *Estado Novo* of Getúlio Vargas, to the decentralized, power-sharing exchange of *café com leite,* the swings of the pendulum between center and local punctuated many of the critical junctures of Brazilian politics. In recent decades, the pendulum has swung between the centralization of political power required by bureaucratic authoritarianism and the liberalization (and decentralization) of power involved in the transition to democracy.

The inclusion of new political actors such as the working and middle classes reshaped the Brazilian state during the twentieth century. The state corporatism of Vargas's New State provided mechanisms for mobilizing and organizing workers and professionals. Populist democracy later provided these social segments protection from unsafe working environments, the effects of eroding wages, and the prohibitive expense of health care. Public firms such as Vale employed hundreds of thousands of Brazilians and dramatically altered the development possibilities of the country. These policies have now come under attack by reformists both within the government and in the international financial institutions who believe their reform requires another round of state restructuring, this time with a generous dose of market-oriented criteria. Privatization, deregulation, economic liberalization, and the reform of public employment and pension programs are dramatically altering the role of the Brazilian state and its relations with society.

As for Brazil's distinctive approach to governing the economy, no one should discount the legacies of state-led development in the country's history. During the twentieth century, Brazil was transformed from a predominantly agrarian economy into an industrialized economy. To some extent, markets and foreign investment played key roles in this process, but the state also provided crucial financial, technical, and political support that made this great transformation possible. As a result, Brazil's position in the global system of production and exchange was fundamentally guided by politics.

Nonetheless, the growth produced by state-led development was poorly distributed. Social problems that emerged from this unequal model of development are at the heart of the country's ongoing struggles with democracy. For many Brazilians living in poverty, it was not clear what benefits the return to democracy had produced.

Regarding the democratic idea, Brazil certainly has the institutions of a democracy, but in many ways, the decades of patrimonialism, populism, and corporatism undermine these institutions. Brazilian politicians typically cultivate personal votes (they are known as *personalist politicians*) and avoid following the rule of parties or alliances. Many switch parties several times in a political career. As a result, Brazilian political parties are extremely weak. Personalism in Brazilian politics persists because it is well rewarded. Once elected, politicians can remain in power through frequent use of clientelist relations, favoritism, nepotism, and outright bribery.

Yet even with these enduring shortcomings in democracy, Brazilians continue to prefer this form of government. The appeal of democracy is based in part on their negative memories of the repression they suffered under the authoritarian regime and the military's poor management of the economy. More important, Brazilians impute positive values to the improved access to decision-making processes that democracy gives them. Thousands of new political groups, social movements, civic networks, and economic associations have emerged in recent years. The Brazilian state is highly decentralized into twenty-six states, a federal district, and over 5,500 municipalities. Each of these centers of power has become a locus of demand-making by citizens and policy-making by elites. Under these circumstances, centralized rule following the model of the New State or the bureaucratic authoritarian period is impossible today and, in any case, seems undesirable to most Brazilians.

Collective identities remain uncertain in Brazil, although Brazilians are now more commonly linked through their place in the democratic order. Who are the Brazilians? has always been a vexing question, no less so now that Brazil's borders are becoming obsolete in a world of heavy flows of international commerce, finance, and ideas. One common response to the question is that the symbols of the Brazilian nation continue to tie Brazilians together: carnival, soccer, samba, and bossa nova. Yet even as these symbols have become more prevalent, they have also lost some of their meaning because of commercialization and export as part of a tourist-attracting image of Brazil. Catholicism is a less unifying force today as Pentecostalism and evangelism have eaten into the Church's membership. Women have improved both their social position and their political awareness as gender-based organizations have become a more important resource of civil society. Yet even here, Brazil remains an extremely patriarchal society: women are expected to balance motherhood and other traditional roles in the household while they are pressured by economic need to produce income.

Perhaps race, more than any other form of identity, remains the most difficult issue to understand in Brazilian politics and society. Racial identity continues to divide Brazilians, but not in the clear-cut manner it does blacks and whites in the United States. These categories are more fluid in Brazil. Racial mixing has been the basis for easier integration. But it has also undercut the political mobilization of blacks by weakening the kind of stark, black–white segregation that helped blacks in the United States coalesce around the civil rights movement.

Like race, class continues to separate Brazilians. Economic reforms and the erosion of populist redistribution have caused social gaps to widen further, making Brazil a highly fragmented society. Although it is one of the world's ten wealthiest economies, with a gross domestic product over US$588 billion, that wealth is poorly distributed. Like India, Brazil's social indicators such as income distribution, infant mortality, and nutrition consistently rank near the bottom in the world of states. Income disparities mirror racial differences, as the poor are represented by mostly blacks and mulattos, and the rich are almost invariably white. The poverty of the north and northeast also contrasts with the more industrialized and prosperous southeastern and southern states.

Implications for Comparative Politics

As a large, politically decentralized, and socially fragmented polity, Brazil presents several extraordinary challenges to the study of comparative politics. First, the Brazilian state is an anomaly. It has been both highly centralized and decentralized during different periods of its history. In each of these periods, the state produced lasting political legacies that have both strengthened and weakened its capacity for promoting development, democracy, and social distribution. Although political centralization has been an important factor in making the French state strong, decentralized states such as the U.S. and German federations have also proven to be successful formulas for government. The Brazilian case is a laboratory for evaluating which approach is likely to be more successful in other large, highly decentralized states in the developing world, such as Russia, China, and India.

While the complexity of the Brazilian state represents one problem area, the weakness of the country's democratic institutions suggests another, and perhaps more troubling, concern. Along with Russia, Brazil demonstrates how the lack of coherent party systems and electoral institutions can endanger democracy. In contrast to the highly organized polity of Germany and the strength of parties in parliamentary democracies like the United Kingdom and Japan, Brazil's experience highlights how anemic representative institutions can weaken democracy.

Paradoxically, as Brazil developed economically and made its way back to democracy in the 1980s, it also became a more socially unequal country. Established democracies like India and transitional democracies like Mexico and Russia have also experienced the reality that democratization does not improve the distribution of wealth. Yet the longest established democracies in our study—the United States, Britain, France, Germany, and Japan—are also the richest and, by and large, the countries where wealth is most equally distributed. Brazil and India therefore are a bit of a puzzle: If democracy and social development are intricately linked, shouldn't the distribution of wealth be getting better, not worse, in these two countries?

Finally, the complex divisions afflicting Brazilians' collective identities challenge all attempts to address the country's problems. Yet even today, Brazilians and outside observers continue to treat the country as a singular unit. In this regard, Brazil presents a puzzle for theories about collective identities: How has such a socially fragmented society remained a coherent whole for so long?

Section ❷ Political Economy and Development

Like most other countries in the developing world, Brazilian politics has always been shaped by the country's quest for economic and social development. Two processes in particular have left enduring legacies: the pattern of state intervention in the domestic market and the effects of external economic change. Historically these two factors have influenced each other. External economic crises—world depressions, fluctuations in the price of exported goods such as coffee, upsurges in the prices of imported goods—have compelled the Brazilian state to intervene in the domestic economy through protection, subsidies, and even the production of goods that it previously imported. In turn, policies aimed at promoting the industrial growth of the country have made Brazil one of the newly industrialized countries of the world, alongside states such as Mexico, Taiwan, South Korea, and Malaysia.

In order to clarify how political and economic development have been intertwined in Brazil, this section explores the state-led model of development, considers how the domestic effects of the state-led model and its reform generated enormous social costs, and discusses the international capitalist forces that shaped domestic economic policy and society.

State and Economy

Like its Latin American neighbors, Brazil's early economic development was based on **export-led growth,** that is, on the export of agricultural products such as sugar, cotton, coffee, and, for a short time in the early 1900s, rubber. In the nineteenth century, coffee emerged as the engine of growth in the Brazilian economy. By the time of the Old Republic, a strong demand for Brazilian coffee in Europe and North America gave the country a virtual monopoly in the global market. Cotton, sugar, and cereals continued to be important export products too, but they were secondary to coffee. By 1919, coffee composed 56 percent of Brazil's total exports. Only five years later, that figure had jumped to 75 percent.[15]

The dominance of coffee ensured that the Old Republic would keep Brazil active in the world market. That meant that the state had only a minimal role in promoting the export-led economy, which functioned so well that money generated by coffee provided a reservoir of capital to build railroads, power stations, and other infrastructure. These investments, in turn, spurred the growth of some light industries, mostly in textiles, footwear, and clothing.

The Brazilian state's role in the economy became far more **interventionist** during the 1930s when the Great Depression caused international demand for coffee to decline. As exports fell, imports of manufactured goods also declined. The coffee export sector had created demand for these goods among the urban population in the decades before the Great Depression. Therefore, as the coffee economy declined, incentives to boost domestic industrial production to substitute for previously imported manufactures increased.

During the 1930s, Brazil's economy pursued **import substitution industrialization** (ISI), a model of development that promoted domestic industrial production of previously imported manufactured goods. By 1937, this policy, which relied heavily on state intervention, became a major pillar of Vargas's New State. At first, large doses of state intervention were not necessary. The initial phase of ISI—the so-called light, or easy, phase—focused on manufactured products that required little capital or sophisticated technology. Most of these industries, such as textiles and food processing, were labor intensive and therefore created jobs. Although these conditions did not require large infusions of state capital, the New State provided limited subsidies and tariff protection to nascent ISI sectors.

At the end of World War II, new ideas about Third World development came to be adopted by various international agencies. The new goal was to "deepen" the ISI model by promoting heavy industry and capital-intensive production. In Brazil, as in Argentina, Mexico, and India, a new generation of **state technocrats**—experts in economic development—took an active role in designing new policies. Inspired by the texts of the United Nations Economic Commission for Latin America (ECLA), these technocrats targeted particular industrial sectors as strategic.[16] Then, through the use of industrial policies including planning, subsidies, and financial support, state agencies promoted the quick growth of these sectors.

Brazil was the epitome of ECLA-style **developmentalism,** the ideology and practice of state-sponsored growth, during the 1950s in Latin America. More than any other Latin American state, the Brazilian state was organizationally capable of implementing industrial policies to deepen ISI. New bureaucratic structures, such as a national development bank and national public firms, were created during the first and second Vargas governments. Petrobrás, the state oil firm, quickly became a model of what the Brazilian state wanted to become: a state that could produce as well as regulate. The producer state promoted private investment by extracting and distributing raw materials for domestic industries at prices well below the international market level. These lower prices were in effect subsidies to domestic industry. In this way, subsidized steel and subsidized credit from the national development bank fueled domestic industrialization. Other firms linked to sectors of the economy receiving these supports would benefit in a chain reaction.

Although growth rates achieved impressive levels during the 1950s and early 1960s and even higher levels in the 1970s (see Table 1), it was during this period that the first serious contradictions of ISI emerged.[17] Protection fostered noncompetitive, inefficient production because it removed incentives for competition. Although industries grew, they did so by depending too heavily on public subsidies. ISI also became import intensive. Businesses used subsidized finance to import technology and machinery. The government helped these firms by overvaluing the currency to make import prices cheaper. This overvaluation of the currency hurt export earnings, which were necessary to pay for imports. As a result, the export sector could not supply the state with much-needed revenues to sustain growth, prompting the government to print money, which in turn led to inflation. Under the Goulart government (1961–1964), the economy's capacity to import and export dwindled, and stagnation set in. The economic crisis that soon followed contributed to the coup of 1964 and Goulart's fall.

The failures of ISI during the 1960s inspired new thinking, at least in Brazilian and Latin American academe, on development. The so-called dependency school, whose adherents were known as *dependencistas*,

emerged in the social sciences around the idea that underdeveloped or "peripheral" countries faced tremendous obstacles to achieving sustained levels of industrialization and growth in a world dominated by "core" economies in North America and western Europe. ISI's failures, the *dependencistas* argued, were due to the ill-fated attempt to adjust marginally the inherently exploitative structure of world markets. Core economies had created a global capitalist structure that would always favor their interests and lead to the extraction of wealth from poor countries. This early attack on what we today call globalization inspired a new generation of progressive thinkers, among them the sociologist and future president Fernando Henrique Cardoso, who became one of the preeminent proponents of a variant of the dependency argument. The fall of Brazilian democracy, however, would provide little opportunity for these groups to take their ideas out of the universities and implement them as policy.

The rise of the military governments in 1964 led to reform but eventually to an attempt to deepen ISI through state-led development methods. From 1964 to 1985, the state continued to promote industrialization, especially the production of consumer durable goods such as automobiles, televisions, refrigerators, and machinery for the domestic market. Domestic entrepreneurs relied on the transfer of technology from foreign investors, particularly after 1970, when they collaborated with multinational firms to produce pharmaceuticals and later computers. Table 2 highlights the important contribution of industry to the Brazilian gross domestic product.

Para-statals, also known as public or state firms, played an important role in the military's development model. Large-scale projects in shipbuilding, mining, steel, oil, bauxite, and aluminum were financed and managed by bureaucratic agencies and state firms. These projects often operated in conjunction with larger development plans designed to attract domestic and foreign entrepreneurs. Peter Evans, an American political economist, insightfully characterized these complex relations among the state, foreign investors, and domestic capitalists as a "triple alliance."[18] The state, however, remained the dominant partner.

In the 1970s, Brazil's military leaders realized that the deepening of ISI could not rely on domestic capital

Table 1

Governing the Economy: GDP Growth Rates, 1940–2000	
Year	*GDP Growth Rate*
1940–1949	5.6%
1950–1959	6.1
1960–1969	5.4
1970–1979	12.4
1980–1989	1.5
1990–1996	2.1
1997–2000	0.8

Source: Brazilian Institute of Geography and Statistics (IBGE), *Anuario Estatístico Brasileiro* (Rio de Janeiro: IBGE, various years).

Table 2

Governing the Economy:
Sector Composition of the GDP, 1970–2000

Year	Agriculture	Industry	Services
1970	11.55%	35.87%	52.59%
1980	10.16	40.99	48.84
1990	9.26	34.20	56.54
2000	9.00	29.00	62.00

Source: IBGE and Werner Baer, *The Brazilian Economy:*
Growth and Development, 4th ed. (New York: Praeger,
1994), 382–383. Copyright © 1995 by Werner Baer.
Reprinted by permission of Greenwood Publishing Group,
Inc. All rights reserved.

alone. In order to finance the huge public expenditures of national industrial policy, the military turned to international financial markets, particularly private investment markets in North America and Europe. The military also began to emphasize primary exports such as coffee, iron ore, cereals, and other agricultural products. Policies designed to increase agricultural productivity and technological modernization that had already been implemented in the first years of military rule were expanded. Agriculture began to be integrated with industrial production.

The export of agricultural surplus and the sale of food products in the internal market were facilitated by a growing agribusiness sector. Spurred on by state subsidies, agribusiness supplied new resources and management for previously inefficient agricultural subsectors. Agricultural production in the agribusiness sector employed heavy machinery and advanced technologies that increased the size of the average yield. One of the most unusual agribusiness ventures occurred in the 1970s, when the military government introduced a plan to use sugarcane alcohol as a fuel source. Northeast agribusiness boomed during these years as the sugar economy became tied to the dynamic industrial economy of the southern and southeastern regions.

The Environmental Costs of State-Led Growth

The impressive growth of industry and agriculture was concentrated in the central and southern regions of Brazil. Centers of growth in the states of São Paulo,

Minas Gerais, Rio de Janeiro, and Rio Grande do Sul became the locomotives of the country's development and sites of environmental degradation. As capital-intensive industries became more common in Brazil, ecologically destructive technologies were used without much regulation. Before the mid-1970s, Brazilian policy-makers were unconcerned with the emission of toxic waste into the ground at major industrial zones, air pollution in overgrown urban areas, or pesticide and chemical fertilizer use in agricultural regions. Industrial growth was simply more important than these environmental factors.

The environmental costs of these attitudes became clear in the 1970s. Guanabara Bay and the Paraiba do Sul River basin, both in Rio de Janeiro state, were brought to the brink of biological death. Urban pollution in São Paulo devastated the Tietê River, which runs through the city, making it no better than a toxic waste dump in some areas and threatening the health of millions. By far the worst tragedy was in Cubatão, an industrial city 60 kilometers east of metropolitan São Paulo. There, petrochemical industries and steel mills wreaked havoc on the environment, pumping 1 million kilograms of pollutants into the surrounding ecological system each day. The conditions in the residential area of Cubatão became so bad that by 1981, one city council member reported that he had not seen a star in twenty years.[19] Thousands reported becoming afflicted with tuberculosis, pneumonia, bronchitis, emphysema, asthma, and cancer. Forty of every one thousand babies in Cubatão were stillborn.

Big development projects reached the forests of the Amazon River basin in the 1970s with Vale do Rio Doce's Carajás mining work in the eastern Amazon. This and other industrial projects threatened the tropical forests, as did cattle ranching, timber extraction, and slash-and-burn agriculture by poor farmers, a practice that allowed frequent rains to leech nutrients from the soil and prevent the return of tropical habitats. By the 1980s, it was clear that the primary result of these practices was the deforestation of the Amazon.

Brazil's worsening environmental problems received official attention after 1972, when the United Nations held its Conference on the Human Environment. Soon afterward, Brazil created an environmental secretariat, and in 1981 the government established the National Environmental Council (CONAMA), which included officials from national and state government and representatives from business, professional, and environmental groups. State governments also established their own environmental agencies and passed important legislation.[20] In 1975, São Paulo passed a comprehensive antipollution law. The cleanup of Cubatão began in 1983.

Partly as a result of the return to democracy in 1984, new environmental movements within and outside Brazil began to influence official and public opinion on the costs of resource degradation. Much attention was brought to these problems when the Brazilian government successfully persuaded the United Nations to hold its Conference on the Environment, a follow-up to the 1972 conference, in Rio de Janeiro in 1992. Thousands of delegates and hundreds of **nongovernmental organizations** gathered in Rio to discuss global environmental problems that were virtually all present in Brazil. By that time, numerous environmental organizations were already active in Brazilian politics.[21]

Despite the attention the Rio conference brought to the issue, rates of deforestation, pollution, and resource degradation fell only briefly after 1992 and have since returned to historically high levels. Brazilian business has shown only passing interest in the use of clean technologies because of their expense. In the third international UN conference on the environment, held in Kyoto, Japan, in 1997, Brazil was joined by the rest of the developing world in deflecting the finger of blame for ecological problems. However, it did play an important diplomatic role toward the end of the conference by supporting a U.S.-backed clean development fund. Nevertheless, Brazil lags behind its neighbor Argentina, which in November 1998 became the first developing country to adopt binding targets for controlling emissions of industrial waste gases.

The Fiscal System

In developed countries such as the United States, Germany, France, and Britain, governments can use tax policy to punish polluters. In Brazil, however, tax collection has been notoriously weak, making this a less useful instrument to regulate business or individuals. Tax evasion has been a chronic problem. The military governments attempted to change that through a constitutional reform in 1967 that created new taxes, made the federal government better able to collect taxes, and centralized fiscal policy and the control of revenues. However, because one of the military's primary objectives was to stimulate private savings and to increase capital formation, the new tax systems allowed for numerous costly exemptions and transfers of budgetary resources to private firms and to the upper and middle classes. As a result, the Brazilian tax system became more regressive by shifting the tax burden onto the middle and working classes.

As the Brazilian economy became more complex, new opportunities for evading taxes emerged. An **informal economy** of small firms, domestic enterprises, street vendors, and unregistered employees proliferated, virtually outside the domain of the taxable economy. In some cases, these enterprises acquired substantial size, accounting for the distribution of everything from artisans' goods to professional services. Legally registered companies began to subcontract unregistered professionals to render services beyond the reach of the tax system. Although reliable information is lacking, economists estimate that the informal economy represents close to half of Brazil's gross domestic product, or GDP (about US$300 billion) and employs about 30 million to 45 million people. More reliable figures on tax evasion in both the formal and informal sectors estimate that federal coffers lose over $95 billion a year.

Other problems developed for the tax system after the transition to democracy. The new constitution of 1988 decentralized the fiscal structure by allowing the states and municipalities to expand their collection of taxes and receive larger transfers of funds from Brasília. Significant gaps emerged in tax collection responsibilities and public spending as a result of these changes. Although the central state spent less than it collected in taxes between 1960 and 1994, Brazil's 5,500 municipal governments spent several times more than they collected. Subnational governments also gained more discretion over spending. More than 90 percent of funds transferred from the federal government to the states went unearmarked, so state governments could use these monies for their own purposes.

New reforms during the Collor administration began to reverse some of the adverse effects of fiscal decentralization and the weak tax system. In the 1980s, the state governments, which held almost half of Brazil's total debt, continued to roll over their debt with federal outlays and failed to cut expenditures. In the early 1990s, federal threats to cut off debt servicing and close down profligate regional banks owned by the state governments put an end to this unsustainable practice. Other reforms shifted some of the tax burden onto business, which helped to increase tax receipts to 25 percent of GDP.[22]

The Cardoso administration had some success in recovering federal tax revenues and reducing the fiscal distortions produced by Brazil's federal structure. Tax evasion was slowed as the federal tax collection agency was expanded and its surveillance powers enhanced. Legislation in 1994 and 1998 allowed the federal government to employ more discretion over transfers of funds constitutionally earmarked for the state and municipal governments and to cap the states' ability to acquire debt. That allowed the federal government to exert some leverage on state governments to control their spending. Brasília also shifted more spending responsibilities in health care, housing, and social policy to subnational governments. That has allowed the federal government to reduce its own spending and control how the states spend their resources. The most important reform in this area, the Fiscal Responsibility Law, which was passed in 2000, set strict limits on federal, state, and municipal expenditures, but its enforcement is still in doubt. Given still large civil service payrolls (often these constitute more than 70 percent of state and municipal revenues), governments are hard-pressed to implement the law. The National Confederation of Municipalities estimates that 80 percent of Brazil's mayors and sixteen of twenty-seven states are not in compliance with the law's strict requirements. These problems are at the center of Brazil's mounting public debt, which now hovers over 60 percent of GDP, and they have played a role in the country's recent financial crises.

The Problem of Inflation

Inflation deserves special mention in Brazil, for in no other country, with the possible exception of Germany, has this phenomenon had such a lasting impact on a country's politics. In Brazil, inflation accompanied state-led development, especially after 1974. Through various types of controls, the Brazilian state, business, and unions all attempted to govern prices, interest rates, and wages. Such manipulation distorted the value of goods and services, and facilitated inflation. With the return to democracy after 1985, successive governments attempted to control inflation. All of these "stabilization" packages failed as "hyperinflation" (four-digit inflation) returned repeatedly. Figure 1 illustrates this terrible track record.

The Sarney, Collor, and Franco governments sought to control the growth in prices by setting the price of some basic products and freezing wages while the government reduced spending. The plans failed for a mixture of reasons, but usually because one of these conditions could not be sustained. Once fixed prices could not be maintained or government spending could not be restrained or wages were increased in accordance with monthly inflation rates, the inflationary spiral would heat up.

Only Cardoso's Real Plan proved successful in reining in inflation. The Real Plan attempted to anchor the real, the new currency, in a unit of real value, which was itself indexed to the U.S. dollar. Unlike a similar plan in Argentina, the Real Plan did not fix the real to the dollar strictly but allowed it to float within bands, thus achieving more flexibility in the exchange rate.

Figure 1

*Governing the Economy:
Annual Rates of Inflation, 1989–1996*

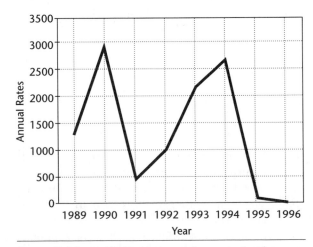

Source: Fundação Getúlio Vargas, *A Economia Brasileira em Gráficos* (Rio de Janeiro: FGV, 1996), 24.

This is one of the main reasons that the real was able to weather the kind of financial turmoil that led the Argentine economy to ruin in 2001–2002.

Paradoxically, the Real Plan's formula for success proved to be a source of weakness. Soon after the Mexican peso crisis of December 1994, Central Bank managers in Brasília became convinced that the real was overvalued, just as the peso had been before its crash. Overvaluation made exports more expensive abroad, raised the costs of production, and made imports cheaper. Brazil's trade deficit rose by more than 140 percent after 1995, threatening to scare away foreign investors. Despite dire predictions, though, Brazil's large foreign reserves (US$75 billion in mid-1998) kept investors confident in the economy, although turmoil in Asian financial markets led to the bleeding of these foreign reserves at $1 billion a day during October 1998. Improvements in tax collection, an influx of foreign investment, modest growth, and repeated attempts by the Cardoso administration to close the trade deficit by limiting imports and removing taxes on exports helped to keep the real's value stable. Yet high interest rates, escalating public debt, the inability to rein in spending, and monetary instability in Asia and Russia continued to threaten the real's stability. Signs of hope emerged in November 1998 when the International Monetary Fund (IMF) negotiated a US$42 billion bailout agreement with Brazil in order to keep the economy from sinking further into financial upheaval. These efforts proved unsuccessful. In January 1999, Itamar Franco, the ex-president and the newly elected governor of Minas Gerais, threatened his former minister of finance with a moratorium on the state government's debt to Brasília. The threat led to an upsurge in capital flight (US$6 billion in the first fourteen days of 1999) as investors lost confidence in Cardoso's government. Central Bank president Gustavo Franco, one of the Real Plan's chief defenders, resigned abruptly. The new president, Francisco Lopes, announced a "controlled" devaluation of 8 percent. Within just two days, pressures on the real forced the government to abandon the Real Plan's exchange rate regime altogether. The currency was forced to float, causing it to decline in value by more than 50 percent against the dollar. The devaluation generated renewed fears of inflation and refocused attention on the need to contain public sector spending. But hyperinflation did not return, and the government was successful in moderating the growth in public spending through reforms such as the Law of Fiscal Responsibility. Nevertheless, the massive public debt continued to grow to $245 billion by 2002, continuing to threaten the stability of the currency (see Figure 2).

Society and Economy

Brazil's astounding levels of industrialization during the 1950s, 1960s, and 1970s had lasting effects on the urban population. In 1950, 35 percent of the population lived in urban areas. By 1980, that number had increased to 68 percent. During the same period, employment in industry jumped from 14 percent to 24 percent, while employment in agriculture declined from 60 percent to 30 percent. Import substitution had created these jobs by expanding the domestic market. ISI led to a jump in the size of both the working and the middle classes. Service sector professionals like lawyers, doctors, and private teachers soon found clients as the domestic consumer market grew along with the working class.

Nevertheless, the number of jobs created in the industrial sector did not begin to absorb the huge number of unemployed Brazilians. Many of the new jobs required skilled and semiskilled specialized labor. Metallurgy, automobile production, and mining did not

Figure 2

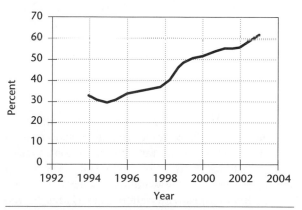

Consolidated Brazilian Public Sector Net Dezbt as a Percentage of GDP

Source: Based on numbers produced by the Central Bank of Brazil.

provide many opportunities for the large numbers of unskilled workers in the Brazilian labor market. In the late 1980s and 1990s, even skilled workers faced losing their jobs because of intense industrial restructuring. From 1990 to 1996, manufacturing jobs fell by 38.1 percent, and unemployment in metropolitan areas rose above 18 percent. Service sector employment increased, but not enough to make up for industrial job losses. These jobs also paid less and offered fewer protections from arbitrary dismissal.

Industrialization also failed to eradicate the racial inequalities inherited from slavery. Despite the impressive industrial development of Brazil, Afro-Brazilians continued to make less than their white colleagues and had fewer opportunities for upward mobility. According to one study, nonwhite men and women in Brazil have made real gains in their income because of improvements in education and occupation, but the gap separating nonwhite income from white income remains significant.[23] On average, blacks make 41 percent and mulattos make 47 percent of what whites make.

Women constitute 28 percent of the economically active population in Brazil and continue to enter the labor market in record numbers. Working women typically have more years of schooling than men and are better prepared to meet the demands of an increasingly technological economy. Despite such developments, women receive lower salaries than men employed at the same job. Women make 57 percent of what men make. Afro-Brazilian women, who are doubly disadvantaged by race and gender, are in a particularly precarious situation. Many are employed in underpaid and menial jobs, particularly as domestic servants, 90 percent of whom are black women. Mulatto women receive 46 percent of what white men make, and black women take in only 40 percent of what white men make.

The Welfare System

In a country of startling social inequalities, welfare policy plays a remarkably minor role in the lives of most Brazilians. Although welfare and education expenditures constitute about 11 percent of the GDP, among the highest levels in the world, the money has not improved Brazil's mediocre welfare state. Unlike the systems in Britain, France, Germany, and Japan, Brazil's welfare system has not reduced the high level of poverty or helped the majority of the poor. Vast sectors of the population, deprived of access to bank finance, higher education, and jobs, remain totally outside the reach of welfare services.

Brazil supports a public school system as well as a health, retirement, and social assistance system that includes funds for unemployment relief. Salaried workers are entitled to benefits such as health care, worker's compensation, retirement pensions, paid vacations, and overtime pay, yet only an estimated 15 percent of the Brazilian population qualify for these benefits. Workers in the informal sector, who are normally undocumented, cannot collect welfare since technically the federal government does not consider them employed. Corruption, clientelism, and outright waste make the welfare system incapable of delivering benefits to the people who need them the most.[24]

Part of the problem is that more people need welfare than actually contribute to the welfare state. Today, only half of the 70 million people who are economically active contribute to the welfare system. Between 1990 and 2000, while the population doubled, the number of retired people multiplied elevenfold, adding to the roster of those depending on public welfare spending. In 1995, the welfare system received US$3.5 billion less than was needed to pay the retirement pensions of the 15.2 million inactive workers and 3 million new beneficiaries. The shortfall was covered by public debt, thus adding to Brazil's fiscal problems. During the military period, changes to the welfare system produced additional distortions. Since the days of the New State, workers employed by a firm for ten years or more were guaranteed generous severance benefits. The military replaced these guarantees with a social insurance fund that prorated inferior benefits to the years of employment. The military expanded protection to several sectors of employment that previously had been outside the welfare system: rural workers, domestic workers, and professionals. But the chief beneficiaries of the new system continued to be public employees (including politicians and members of the military). Compared to total benefit payments of US$35.2 billion to 15 million inactive workers in the private sector, inactive public sector workers, who number 404,000, received $10.5 billion during the 1990s. That means that the average retired or unemployed civil servant received $2,188 monthly as compared to an average of $194 for private workers.

As in Margaret Thatcher's Britain, fundamental welfare reform in Brazil came with the rise of a new political figure. Fernando Collor began to dismantle the welfare system soon after his election to the presidency. The funding and quality of welfare services deteriorated to levels never seen in contemporary Brazilian history. Federal funds for health care fell 50 percent. In 1988, the federal welfare system devoted 25 percent of its revenues to health care; in 1990, that number was only 15 percent. In 1993, no funds were allocated. At present, the subnational governments have been left to take up the slack, with differing results throughout Brazil.

The combination of distortions in the distribution of welfare benefits and unavoidable social pressure to expand outlays to the poor caused the Cardoso administration to step up efforts to reduce tax evasion and reform the public pension system. Private employers and state companies (among the worst offenders) were increasingly obligated by federal authorities to pay their share of social welfare contributions. As in the United States, France, and all other countries in South America, the debate over welfare has begun to revolve around the issue of completely or partly privatizing the system. The experiences these other countries have with such ideas may influence Brazil's choices, but the final response will depend on whether state agencies and political parties can refrain from employing welfare as a means of clientelism.

Agrarian Reform

The restructuring of the rural economy in the 1960s and 1970s altered the rural social structure. The growing role of agribusiness created jobs for some segments of the rural working class while it crowded out small landowners. After 1964, various state welfare programs were launched in the agricultural sector: retirement policies for low-income producers, pension plans for rural workers, and financial support to community rural associations. These policies played a prominent role in breaking landowners' political and economic control of the rural population. During the 1970s and 1980s, rural workers were organized into rural unions that received welfare transfers from the state—medical plans, job security, and protection of wages against inflation.

Landownership in Brazil remains concentrated in the hands of only 1 percent of the landowning class. The arable land held by this small group of owners (about 58,000) is equal to the size of Venezuela and Colombia combined. Over 3 million other farmers survive on only 2 percent of the country's land. An additional 4.5 million Brazilians are farm laborers or squatters who own no land. In the 1980s and 1990s, several landless peasant movements grabbed headlines by sanctioning illegal land invasions and coming to blows with rural landowners and police. Among the most important of these groups, the Landless Workers' Movement (*Movimento dos Sem-Terra,* or MST) attracted the most attention by seizing some 1.38 million acres of land.

The Cardoso administration responded to these problems by expropriating some unproductive estates and settling 186,000 families on them. Substantial sums were set aside to provide financial support and the placement of additional rural families. However, these efforts fell far short of providing a lasting solution to rural poverty. Brazil continues to lack true agrarian reform.

Any serious effort to address rural poverty will affect urban poverty. Through rural-to-urban migration, the landless poor have swelled the rings of poverty that surround Brazil's major cities. During the 1950s and 1960s, the growth of industry in the south and southeast enticed millions to migrate to the states of São Paulo, Minas Gerais, and Rio de Janeiro in the hopes of finding new economic opportunities. The rapidity of rural-to-urban migration was striking. In the 1960s, over 13.8 million people (about 36 percent of the rural population in 1960) migrated to the cities of the south and southeast. In 1970, 17 million (approximately 42.2 percent of the rural population in 1970) moved from the countryside to the city. It took migrations in the United States eight decades to reach the same level of migrants as went from rural to urban areas in Brazil during the 1960s and 1970s. By the early 1980s, 68 percent of Brazil's population was living in urban areas. Between 1960 and 1980, rural-to-urban migration accounted for 58 percent of urban population growth.

The flood of migrants to urban areas and the growth of urban populations created terrible social problems. The pressures on Brazilian cities for basic services such as sanitation, education, and transportation soon overwhelmed the budgets of municipalities and state governments. Poor people were left to their own devices. Squatters soon took government land, settling on the outskirts of the major cities. Millions of these *descamisados* ("shirtless ones") built shelter out of cardboard, wood from dumps, and blocks of mortar and brick. Huge shantytowns called *favelas* sprang up around cities like Rio and São Paulo.

Regional disparities in income worsened during this period. The military governments addressed this problem by transferring revenues from the industrialized south and southeast to the poor north and northeast, where many of their supporters were based. The federal government subsidized communication and transportation in the poorer regions and created new state agencies to implement regional developmental projects. These policies had mixed results. The contribution of poor regions to GDP increased. The growth rate of the central and western regions was spurred on by agribusiness activities, mineral exploration, and financial services. The economic gap between regions narrowed, but social and income disparities within the underdeveloped regions increased.[25] Industrialization in the poorer regions was capital intensive and therefore labor saving but did not create jobs. Only the most skilled workers in these regions benefited from these changes. Poor agricultural management, ecological destruction, the murder of native Brazilians due to the need to expropriate land for mining and agriculture, and corruption all weakened the distributive effect of these policies.

Today, the northern and northeastern regions remain much poorer than those in the south and southeast. Whereas 15 percent of the population in the southeast subsist under the poverty line, more than 50 percent of the inhabitants of the northeast are below that marker. The life expectancy of a northeasterner—fifty-eight years—is nine years below that of a resident of São Paulo state (sixty-seven years) and fifteen years below that of a resident of Rio Grande do Sul (seventy-three years).[26]

The shrinking labor market for unskilled workers, the rapidity of rural-to-urban migration, and the regional disparities that add to poverty have all worked against the equalization of income distribution in Brazil. Compared with other developing countries, including Mexico and India, Brazil has the worst structure of income distribution in the world (see Table 3).

Brazil and the International Political Economy

As the financing needs of state-led industrialization outstripped the resources of the national development bank and domestic bankers, the deepening of ISI required Brazil to pursue international sources of credit. During the late 1960s and the 1970s, private lenders were eager to provide loans to Brazil and other fast-growing countries. As a result, Brazil became the largest single debtor country in the developing world.

External events had a hand in creating and then managing Brazil's external debt. By the end of the 1970s, the world economy had been hit with two oil

Favelas **in Rio de Janeiro.** *Source:* © Marc Valdecantos.

Table 3

Governing the Economy: Brazilian Income Distribution in Comparative Perspective				
		Percentage of Total Income Received		
Country	Year	10% Richest	20% Richest	40% Poorest	20% Poorest
Peru	1994	34.3%	50.4%	14.1%	4.9%
China	1995	30.9	47.5	15.3	5.5
United States	1994	28.5	45.2	15.3	4.8
India	1994	25.0	39.3	22.2	4.1
France	1989	24.9	40.1	19.9	7.2
Britain	1986	24.7	39.8	19.9	7.1
Brazil	1995	47.9	64.2	8.2	2.5
Chile	1994	46.1	61.0	10.1	3.5
Mexico	1992	39.2	55.3	11.9	4.1
Germany	1989	22.6	37.1	22.5	9.0
Poland	1992	22.1	36.6	23.1	9.3

Source: World Bank, *World Development Report 1998/99* (Washington, D.C.: World Bank, 1998), 198–199.

price shocks that sent inflation rates soaring in the United States and other industrialized countries. Many of these countries also held Brazilian debt. As the central banks in Europe and the Federal Reserve in the United States ratcheted interest rates upward to force prices back down, Brazil's interest payments soared.[27]

After Mexico declared a moratorium on interest payments in 1982, private investors began to shun Brazil and other Latin American debtors. During the 1980s, the so-called Lost Decade of slow growth and debt crisis, the IMF and the World Bank became important suppliers of badly needed credit. But only debtors who promised to take concrete steps to reduce inflation, open their domestic markets to foreign competition, promote exports, and privatize state industries were eligible for help.

Brazil, along with Argentina and Peru, rejected these conditions. The Sarney government refused to implement the free-market policies demanded by the international financial institutions. In 1987, his government took the ultimate gamble in resisting creditors by declaring a moratorium on debt repayment, a move that sent a signal to investors that Brazil would control its own reform agenda on its own terms. The moratorium, however, did not last. It was lifted a few months later under intense pressure from the international

financial community. Opposition to the moratorium within the country was also great among the business community, which feared that such aggressive action would scare off foreign investors and ruin the country's already tattered credit rating.

Collor reversed course. Partly in response to pressure from international creditors and partly in recognition that Sarney's alternative policies had failed, he agreed to put Brazil on the path of free-market policies. The Collor administration invoked both macroeconomic reforms to bring down inflation and reduce balance-of-payments deficits and structural adjustment policies to liberalize the domestic market, privatize state enterprises, and deregulate the economy. Although Collor's anti-inflation plans failed, his structural reforms provided a crucial catalyst for freeing up the economy from layers of bureaucratic red tape and inefficiency. These domestic changes were reflected externally as Collor began to normalize relations between Brazil and the multilateral agencies, especially the IMF.

The liberalization of markets opened Brazilian industry to higher degrees of foreign competition. As a result, the competitiveness of domestic firms has emerged as a core problem. Brazilian industrial productivity reached its lowest levels in 1992, when, on a list of fifty countries, Brazil was ranked forty-ninth, just ahead of Pakistan. One 1997 study showed that the overall productivity of Brazilian industry runs at only 27 percent of the U.S. level.[28] Although productivity levels improved by 7 percent after 1992, inherent inefficiencies caused by poor infrastructure, untrained labor, and lack of access to technology and capital continue to create obstacles to higher growth. The average Brazilian worker has only six years of schooling, half as much as the average worker in Japan or the United States. These problems undermine the rationale of IMF-style free-market policies, since they suggest that free markets alone cannot guarantee the country's growth.

How Brazil will fare in an increasingly interconnected and competitive global marketplace will also depend on its external political relations. During the 1980s, Brazil engaged in numerous conflicts with the United States over steel exports (one of Brazil's most export-competitive industries), computer hardware, and patent protection for multinational companies operating in Brazil. Washington threatened to slap protective tariffs on Brazilian products in retaliation. The political climate changed during the administrations of George H. W. Bush and Bill Clinton, when international free-trade accords, such as the North American Free Trade Agreement (NAFTA), received the support of both Washington and most Latin American governments. During the Summit of the Americas in Miami in December 1994, the leaders of the United States, Central America, the Caribbean (except Cuba), and South America agreed to form a Free Trade Area of the Americas (FTAA) by the year 2005. Several years later, Cardoso's skepticism about the schedule for FTAA's implementation and the nature of the agreement became apparent. At the Quebec summit of FTAA signatories in 2001, Brazil criticized growing U.S. protectionism, a view that was confirmed in 2002 when President George W. Bush imposed sweeping tariffs on steel, a major Brazilian export to the United States. Brazil is also more committed to its own subhemispheric group, the Market of the South (MERCOSUL), although enthusiasm for this common market was tempered by the collapse in 2001–2002 of the Argentine economy, Brazil's key trade partner in MERCOSUL. (See "Global Connection: Governing the Economy in a World of States: MERCOSUL.")

Brazil's degree of commitment to the international free-trade system will depend on the endurance of the country's domestic reform agenda. If inflation threatens to return, Brazil's leaders have already shown that they would be willing to sacrifice MERCOSUL and other commitments to free trade. For example, an attempt to stave off growing trade deficits that threatened the Real Plan in 1995 forced Brazilian policy-makers to increase tariffs on imported automobiles from 32 percent to 70 percent, an act that immediately angered Argentina. Although such disagreements are regularly resolved through MERCOSUL's dispute resolution mechanisms, a larger crisis could push Brazil to sacrifice these commitments on the altar of inflation control.

Domestic and international opposition to globalization are also factors to consider. When delegates from the advanced capitalist countries and largest global firms convened the World Economic Forum in Davos, Switzerland, in 2000, globalization opponents, led by Lula da Silva and including famous activists such as the French farm leader Jose Bové, gathered in Porto Alegre, Rio Grande do Sul, for the World Social Forum. The instability of developing country economies and Brazil's own persistent problems of growing external debt and the need to periodically negotiate bailouts with the IMF fueled the attacks on "unbridled globalization" at Porto Alegre. Cardoso and other leaders were burned in effigy as delegates accused them of betraying progressive ideas, abandoning social redistribution, and embracing neoliberalism, a label commonly used to refer to reforms meant to reduce the intervention of the state in the market. Moreover, Cardoso seemed to symbolize all of these attributes as a former intellectual in the "dependency school" now turned neoliberal reformer. It is still an open question whether Cardoso's successor in the presidency will embrace the ideas of Davos or Porto Alegre.

Global Connection: *Governing the Economy in a World of States: MERCOSUL*

After several years of negotiating the Treaty of Asunción, Brazil, Argentina, Paraguay, and Uruguay inaugurated MERCOSUL, a regional common market group, in January 1995. Under MERCOSUL (Mercosur in Spanish), Brazil and its trade partners agreed to reduce tariffs on imports from signatories gradually until 2006, when the 10,000 items that make up the tariff listings of all four countries must conform to a common external tariff (CET) regime.

During the negotiations over the Treaty of Asunción between March 26, 1991, and MERCOSUL's inauguration, trade among the partners increased from 8 to 20 percent, making the case for a subhemispheric common market stronger. After a rough start due to the Mexican peso crisis, the signatories reaffirmed their commitment to forge the common market. Efforts to remove gradually tariff protections and nontariff protections such as regulations that slow the flow of trade, proceeded with few disruptions.

At the center of MERCOSUL's evolution is the long list of products that the CET targets. However, the signatories are allowed to exclude up to 300 items (399 in Paraguay) as exceptions to the CET. The partners also agreed to numerous dispute-resolution mechanisms to avoid conflicts that might threaten the free-trade group.

MERCOSUL is only the latest in a list of common market schemes in Latin America. In 1960, the Latin American Association of Free Trade (ALALC) initiated a process for forming a common market in twelve years. Although this goal was unfulfilled because of persistent differences among the group's members, intraregional trade increased from 7.7 percent in 1960 to 13.8 percent in 1980. Subhemispheric common market groups unconnected to ALALC also emerged as the Andean Group in 1969 (Bolivia, Colombia, Ecuador, and Venezuela) and the Central American Common Market in 1960 (Costa Rica, Guatemala, El Salvador, Honduras, and Nicaragua). ALALC was replaced in 1980 with the Latin American Integration Association (ALADI). Unlike ALALC's mission of forming a common market, ALADI's goal was to foster the formation of preferential trade agreements among subhemispheric groups. These efforts received their most important boost soon after the administration of George H. W. Bush delivered its Enterprise for the Americas Initiative (EAI) in 1990, a plan of lofty goals for hemispheric economic integration, which are being implemented now through the Free Trade Area of the Americas (FTAA). Soon after the EAI was announced, the existing regional groups and a new wave of other groups formed preferential organizations. Besides MERCOSUL, the most important of these was the North American Free Trade Agreement (NAFTA), initiated on January 1, 1994.

MERCOSUL differs from NAFTA in several ways. First, it is designed to be a common market among developing countries and not, as NAFTA is, a tripartite free-trade area organized to reduce tariffs primarily across the U.S.-Mexico border. Second, MERCOSUL can evolve in ways unimagined in NAFTA, such as the creation of a common currency. Finally, MERCOSUL can and has negotiated free-trade agreements with other global blocks such as the European Union (EU). This gives these four developing countries more leverage on the international level. Mexico's interests as a developing country are arguably not given the same priority by its trade partners in NAFTA.

MERCOSUL also differs markedly from the EU. Because the EU is a supranational organization, its members shift important sovereign areas of policy such as commercial, competition, increasingly justice and home affairs, and for the members of the euro zone, monetary policy to Brussels. The signatories of MERCOSUL do not envision more than a commercial and perhaps monetary agreement, and all this is negotiated multilaterally. MERCOSUL does not have an executive body such as the EU Commission that regulates the behavior of members. It has dispute resolution mechanisms, but nothing like the European Court of Justice whose decisions are binding on EU members.

Like its predecessors, MERCOSUL was a product and a cause of increased commercial integration among its signatories. Since its creation, MERCOSUL has contributed to a threefold increase in trade among its members. The common market, however, is in dire straits now in the wake of the Argentine financial crisis and continued economic instability in Brazil, Uruguay, and Paraguay. MERCOSUL is also at a crossroads regarding the role it will play in the continuing FTAA process. President Lula da Silva will likely attempt to use Brazil's leadership within MERCOSUL to extract concessions from Washington on the type and pacing of trade liberalization in the hemisphere.

Source: Lia Valls Pereira, "Tratado de Assunção: Resultados e Perspectivas," in Antônio Salazar P. Brandão and Lia Valls Pereira, eds., *Mercosul: Perspectivas da Integração* (Rio de Janeiro: Fundação Getúlio Vargas, 1996), 11.

Section ③ Governance and Policy-Making

Organization of the State

The institutions of the Brazilian state have changed significantly since independence. Even so, a number of institutional legacies have endured and continue to shape Brazilian politics. The most important is the centralization of state authority in the executive. Paradoxically, a second legacy is the decentralized federal structure of the Brazilian state. The constitution of 1988 attempted to construct a new democratic order but left these contradictory tendencies in place. The president retained the authority to legislate on social and economic matters, but new powers governing the implementation of these policies were devolved to the state and municipal governments.

As a result, the 1988 constitution was simultaneously the focus of much hope and intense attack. It was to be the governing document for the new democracy, but it became an instrument used to confound political and economic reform. As a product of political horse-trading, it failed to provide a coherent vision of how institutions should be structured and what functions they should have. The separation of powers remains ill-defined in Brazil. Instead, ad hoc and stopgap arrangements continue to determine the boundaries of official authority, while informal relations and understandings play a major role in the interpretation of law.

Some generalizations about the organization of the Brazilian state can be made. First, the church and state are officially separated. The Catholic Church never controlled any portion of the state apparatus or directly influenced national politics as it did in other Catholic countries, including Spain. This does not mean, however, that the Catholic Church plays no role in Brazilian politics (see Section 4).

Second, Brazil has a presidential system of government. The directly elected president is the head of state, head of government, and commander in chief of the armed forces. The Brazilian state has traditionally placed vast power in the hands of the executive. Although the executive is one of three branches of government (the legislature and the judiciary being the other two), Brazilian presidents have traditionally been less bound by judicial and legislative constraints than their European or North American counterparts. Brazilian constitutions have granted the executive more discretion than the other branches in enforcing laws or in making policy. The legislature and the judiciary historically have played secondary roles.

The Brazilian state does not have the checks and balances of the U.S. government system. It differs also from the semipresidentialism of France, in which the president, although dominant over the legislature and judiciary, faces broader constraints in the possibility of having to work with a hostile parliamentary majority. Although the French prime minister is appointed by the executive and is not elected by the legislature as in other parliamentary systems, he or she is chosen from the party with the majority of elected representatives in parliament, which is not necessarily the president's party. Moreover, the French party system is more organized and less fragmented than its counterpart in Brazil, making the legislature more efficient and capable of checking executive actions.

Brazil's executive and the bureaucracy manage most of the policy-making and implementation functions of government. Both the federal legislature and the state governments look to the president and, in economic matters, to the minister of the economy for leadership on policy. The heads of the key agencies of the economic bureaucracy—the ministers of the economy and of planning, the president of the Central Bank, and the head of the national development bank—have more discretion over the details of policy than the president does. Although some Brazilian presidents have delegated less to bureaucratic agencies, recent presidents have had little choice but to delegate, given the growing complexity of economic and social policy. Ultimate authority nevertheless remains in the hands of the president, who may replace his ministers.

Although the Brazilian president is the dominant player among the three branches of government, the powers of the legislature and the judiciary are becoming stronger. Since the transition to democratic rule in 1985, these institutions have become critical to democracy. The 1988 constitution gave many oversight functions to the legislature and judiciary, so that much presidential discretion in economic and social policy is now subject to approval by either the legislature or the judiciary, or both. This gives these branches of government some independence and leverage over the presidency, although this power is not often employed effectively. Centralizing traditions are still strong in Brazil, making the obstacles to the deconcentration of executive power enormous.

A third generalization that may be offered on the Brazilian state is that it is decentralized. Like Germany, India, and the United States, the Brazilian state has a federal structure. The country's twenty-six states are divided into 5,500 municipal governments. Most of the country's presidents have relied on subnational bases of power to stay in office. The presidents of the Old Republic and even Getúlio Vargas counted on the support of local clientelist political machines led by self-interested governors and mayors.

With the transition to democracy, these "barons of the federation," as one study calls them, became a crucial source of political support for legislators as well as presidents.[29] By controlling indispensable reservoirs of patronage through their powers of appointment and spending, governors and even some mayors can wield extraordinary influence. In recent years, some of the harsher elements of reform legislation have been jettisoned to mollify this subnational constituency.

Seen as a whole, political decentralization, which was accelerated with the constitution of 1988, has further fragmented the Brazilian polity. At the same time, some subnational governments have become an important source of innovative policy-making.[30] Average Brazilian citizens have more access to their municipal and state governments than they do to their federal representatives, which suggests that decentralization may eventually strengthen democracy by making political elites more accountable to their local constituencies.

The Executive

A majority of delegates to the 1987 National Constituent Assembly that drafted the new democratic constitution favored the creation of a parliamentary system. President Sarney, who did not want to see his powers reduced, used his support among the governors to lobby against the parliamentary option. The best he could do was force the members of the assembly to defer the issue to a plebiscite in 1993. Yet the plebiscite, envisioned

by the constitution's framers as the climactic event that would determine Brazil's political structure, ended by giving a stamp of approval to the existing presidential system. With virtually no experience in parliamentary politics, Brazilians opted for presidentialism.

Why is there no parliamentarism in Brazil? For many Brazilians, governmental effectiveness has historically been identified with presidential supremacy. For the poor and for organized sectors such as workers and professionals, the presidency has always been the focus of their demands for improvements in living conditions and wages. As for the armed forces, few generals could imagine being led by a prime minister and a legislature. Although not a constitutional requirement, all Brazilian presidents, and most elected officials, have been men.

In 1993, widespread suspicion of legislative politics was fanned by the argument of the campaign to retain presidentialism that the parliamentary option was little more than a trick to "take the right to vote away from the people." The concept of a parliamentary system that would allow a prime minister to be elected by legislative elites and not directly by the citizenry seemed contrary to what Brazilians had fought for during the long struggle for democracy. Brazilians did not want to lose the ultimate check on the presidency: direct elections by voters every four years. This principle has become even more important as the Cardoso presidency gained the constitutional right to allow the president to run for a second term. Popular elections will now present a crucial test for presidents wishing to pursue their agendas for another four years.

If parliamentary government seemed a far-off goal, rules designed to rein in the power of the federal executive still found their way into the 1988 constitution. In part as a reaction to the extreme centralization of executive authority during military rule, the delegates restored some of the congressional prerogatives that had existed prior to 1964 and granted new ones. The congress gained oversight over economic policy and the right of consultation on executive appointments. Executive decrees, which allowed the president to legislate directly, were abolished. In their place "provisional measures" (also known as "emergency measures") were established, which preserved the president's power to legislate for thirty days, at the end of which congress can pass, reject, or allow the provisional law to expire.

President Sarney and his successors got around this restriction by reissuing their "provisional measures" indefinitely, yet to become law, they would need to survive a two-thirds vote of both houses of the congress. Finally, the 1988 constitution limited the president to a single term, a provision common to Latin American constitutions. In 1997, however, Cardoso succeeded in passing a constitutional amendment through congress that removed the no-reelect rule, allowing him and twenty-two governors to run again in 1998. This expansion of presidential power was later met with a restriction on the power to reissue provisional measures, which both houses of congress passed in 2001.

Despite these new constraints, Brazilian presidents were still able to use emergency measures with considerable success because of the sorry state of the economy. Given such crisis conditions, how could congress deny the president the right to railroad through much-needed reform legislation? Some presidents articulated such arguments with great frequency. Collor, for example, severely abused these powers. In his first year in office, Collor handed down 150 emergency measures. Technically, this meant that the country experienced a crisis situation every forty-eight hours.[31] Worse still, the Supreme Tribunal, the highest court in Brazil, did little to curb this obvious abuse of constitutional authority by the president. The use of presidential discretionary power has only reinforced the powers of the executive to legislate.[32] Even with the restrictions passed in 2001, over 80 percent of all legislation originates in the executive branch.

The president also retains extremely valuable powers of appointment over the huge Brazilian bureaucracy, particularly at the ministerial level. Among them are broad powers to select and dismiss close associates and select ministers for the armed forces according to the merit system prevailing in their respective branches. For most other positions, the president usually appoints ministers from groups of his long-time cronies and collaborators or from any of the existing parties. Although these appointees are not as cohesive a group as the presidential *camarillas* in Mexico, the close-knit and often personal networks binding the Mexican president and his chief ministers and advisors, this comparison serves to illustrate the importance of personal ties to the president in Brazil. Under the 1988 constitution, the president must negotiate with congress and some powerful groups (e.g., business associations, labor unions, bar associations) over certain positions in the cabinet, mainly those responsible for economic policy-making. Even so, the power of appointments in Brazil continues to be a source of great influence.

Among the chief cabinet posts, the ministries of Economy (also called Finance during certain administrations) and Planning have had extraordinary influence. Since the beginning of the military governments, the Ministry of Economy has had more authority than any other executive agency of the state. These powers were heightened as a result of the economic problems of the 1980s and the reform agenda of the 1990s. As a result of their control of the federal budget and the details of economic policy, recent ministers of the economy have had levels of authority typical of a prime minister in a parliamentary system. The success of Cardoso in the 1994 presidential campaign was due in large part to his effective performance as Itamar Franco's minister of economy.

The Bureaucracy: State and Semipublic Firms

Bureaucratic agencies and public firms have played key roles in Brazilian economic and political development during the twentieth century. After 1940, the state created a large number of new agencies and public enterprises. Many of these entities were allowed to accumulate their own debt and plan development projects without undue influence from the central ministries or politicians. Public firms became a key part of the triple alliance of state, foreign, and domestic capital that governed the state-led model of development. Yet it was the state that dominated this alliance. By 1981, ten of the top twenty-five enterprises in Brazil were owned by the federal government, and eight others were owned by state governments. Public expenditures as a share of GDP increased from 16 percent in 1947 to more than 32 percent in 1969, far higher than in any other Latin American country except socialist Cuba.[33]

Much of this spending (and the huge debt that financed it) was concentrated on development projects, many of gigantic proportions. Key examples include the world's largest hydroelectric plant, Itaipú; Petrobrás's petroleum processing centers; and steel mills such as the gargantuan National Steel Company in Volta Redonda, Rio de Janeiro; and Vale do Rio Doce, a public firm with interests in sectors as diverse as mining, transport, paper, and textiles. Under the past three military governments (Médici, Geisel, and Figueiredo), dozens of other projects were completed, including the trans-Amazonian highway, the Tucuruí hydroelectric plants, the Açominas metallurgy park, and the National Nuclear Reactor Program. These and hundreds of more modest projects accounted for much of the country's industrial production. On the eve of the debt crisis in 1982, the top thirty-three projects, including those just listed, absorbed US$88 billion in external debt, employed 1.5 million people, and added $47 billion to the GDP.

Managing the planning and finance of these projects required enormous skill. Several public agencies were responsible, but the National Bank for Economic and Social Development (*Banco Nacional de Desenvolvimento Economico e Social,* or BNDES) stands out as an important coordinator. Founded by Vargas in the early 1950s, the BNDES played a key role in channeling public funds to industrial projects. Among the bank's greatest achievements was the creation of an automobile sector based on subsidized public steel; foreign assemblers such as Ford, General Motors, and Volkswagen; and domestic suppliers of parts and labor. Under President Juscelino Kubitschek, the BNDES implemented an industrial policy in automobiles called the Plan of Goals (*Plano de Metas*), which coordinated domestic and international resources to create the largest automobile industry in Latin America.[34]

The experience of the BNDES demonstrated that despite Brazil's clientelist legacies, the Brazilian bureaucracy could function effectively. Meritocratic advancement and professional recruitment granted these agencies some autonomy from political manipulation. Such agencies were considered islands of efficiency in a state apparatus characterized by patronage and corruption.[35]

Other state and semipublic firms, however, were rife with clientelism. Civilian and military leaders often appointed their supporters as the heads of these enterprises, positions with quite generous salary and retirement packages. Many public firm managers took advantage of their positions to dole out government contracts to associates and even to their own companies in the private sector.

The fiscal crisis of the 1980s had put severe strains on the entire economic bureaucracy, but some things failed to change. The 1988 constitution did not alter significantly the concentration of power in the economic bureaucracy that made developmentalism with clientelism possible. In fact, the new constitution reinforced certain bureaucratic monopolies by codifying them as rights. For example, the state's control over petroleum, natural gas, the exploration of minerals, nuclear energy, and telecommunications was protected constitutionally. These sectors could not be privatized, much less sold to foreign governments or multinational companies.

What the writers of the new constitution did do in response to the fiscal crisis was place new restraints on the activity of state-directed industries. The fiscal independence of state firms was curtailed with restrictions on the amount of debt they could incur. The constitution imposed additional obstacles to the creation of public firms, including the requirement that congress approve any new state enterprises proposed by the executive branch.

Some of the constitutional protections of the public firms lasted only a few years. After his election in 1989, Fernando Collor began a sweeping reform of Brazil's public bureaucracy, beginning with the privatization of large public firms in steel, chemicals, and mining. In 1990, his government launched the National Destatization Program (*Programa Nacional de Destatização,* PND). Under the PND, more than US$20 billion in public firms were sold ($8.5 billion in the steel sector alone). Although the program slowed under the Franco administration, the selloffs of the steel firms were completed. The Cardoso administration went even further. The government convinced the congress to amend the constitution to remove the public monopoly on petroleum refining, telecommunications, and infrastructure, making these sectors available for auction. Electricity distribution, cellular phone bands, and the octopus-like structure of Vale were put up for privatization. In 1998, much of the public telecommunication sector was privatized, bringing in about $25 billion.

Paradoxically, the agency at the center of the privatization process in Brazil is the BNDES, which is also the agency most responsible for developmentalism. Faced with the fiscal crisis of the 1980s, BNDES managers adopted a new perspective on the state's role in the economy. Instead of targeting industries and spending large sums to promote them, its new mission was to provide financing to productivity-enhancing investments such as new technology and labor retraining, outlays that promise to make firms soon to be privatized and already privatized more competitive in international markets.[36] As a result, the economic bureaucracy in Brazil continues to play a crucial role in the country's development.

The Military and the Police

The military is another significant arm of the state. Like many other South American militaries, the Brazilian armed forces retain substantial independence from civilian presidents and legislators. Brazil has suffered numerous coups; those in 1930 and 1964 were critical junctures, while others brought in caretaker governments that eventually ceded to civilian rule. Although the military's grip on power was never as tight as in Nigeria during the Abacha regime (1993–1998), the generals have maintained influence in Brazilian politics, blocking policies they do not like and lobbying on behalf of those they favor.

The military's participation in Brazilian politics became more defined following the transition to democracy. Several laws governing areas of policy-making affecting the armed forces gave the military broad prerogatives to "guarantee internal order" and to play a "tutelary role" in civilian government. During the Sarney administration, members of the armed forces retained cabinet-level rank in areas of importance to the military, such as the ministries of the armed forces and the nuclear program. Military officers also kept middle- and lower-level positions in public firms and bureaucratic agencies. Most important, the armed forces were successful in obtaining amnesty for human rights abuses committed during the preceding authoritarian regime.

In an effort to professionalize the armed forces and keep them in the barracks, the Collor government slashed the military budget and replaced the top generals with officers who had few or no connections to the authoritarian regime and were committed to civilian leadership. Collor's reforms were helped by the decline of the country's arms industry, which lost key markets for ordnance, tanks, and guns in the Middle East during the 1980s. These industries had previously supplied capital and armaments to the Brazilian armed forces, keeping them autonomous from civilian control. The collapse and, in some cases, privatization of these military industries gave civilians more control over the generals.[37] One recent test of civilian authority was the successful removal of the commandant of the Brazilian Air Force, Brigadier Walter Werner Braüer, for alleged involvement in drug trafficking, money laundering, and organized crime activities. Despite public demonstrations by air force officers supporting Braüer, congressional investigations continued, and the general was dismissed at the end of 1999.

Police enforcement primarily falls into the domain of the state governments. The state police consists of two forces: the civil police force, which acts as an investigative unit and is not completely uniformed, and the uniformed military police force, which maintains order. The military police are not formally under the command of the military; the constitution stipulates that in the event of a national emergency, they can be called to perform active military service. Like the military, the military police are governed by a separate judicial system.

During the 1990s, urban crime became one of the most important political issues facing the country. Perhaps the most telling indicator of the rising level of violence is the fact that over fifty mayors were assassinated in Brazil between 1990 and 2000. Murders, kidnappings, rapes, and violent robberies are the talk of nightly news programs, and these subjects often dominate citizens' lists of chief concerns.

The specter of criminal violence has shocked Brazilians into voting for politicians who promise them better police security. Yet as more attention has focused on the use of police resources, Brazilians have learned that these forces themselves are often part of the problem. Despite official oversight of police authorities, in practice the military and civil police forces in many cities of the northeast, in São Paulo, and in Rio de Janeiro often act extrajudicially. Cases of arbitrary detention, torture, corruption, and systematic killings by Brazilian police have received much international attention. Human rights investigations have found that off-duty police officers are regularly hired by merchants and assorted thugs to kill street urchins whom they accuse of thievery. One study in Rio de Janeiro between 1993 and 1996 showed that police officers preferred the use of deadly force, shooting to kill rather than to disable.[38] The majority of victims were shot in the shoulders or the head; in 40 of the 697 cases, the victims were shot in the back of the head in gangland execution style. The victims were mostly young black men and boys and had no criminal records whatsoever. Other studies have shown that at least 10 percent of the homicides in Rio de Janeiro are committed by the police. In São Paulo, police violence is just as bad. In 1992 alone, the São Paulo police killed 1,470 people, accounting for one-third of all homicides in the state.[39]

The federal police force is a small unit of approximately 3,000 people. It operates as a combined U.S. Federal Bureau of Investigation, Secret Service, Drug Enforcement Agency, and Immigration and Naturalization Service. Under the authority of the executive, the federal police are responsible for providing security to public officials, cracking down on drug rings, administering customs regulations, and investigating federal crimes. The demands placed on this single agency have caused some Brazilian politicians to propose that the federal police be split up into more specialized units, as in the U.S. system.

Other State Institutions

The Judiciary

The Brazilian judiciary is composed of a network of state courts, which has jurisdiction over state matters, and a federal court system, not unlike the one in the United States, which maintains jurisdiction over federal crimes. A supreme court (the Supreme Federal Tribunal), similar in jurisdiction to the U.S. Supreme Court but lacking authority over the other branches of government, acts as the final arbiter of court cases. The eleven justices are appointed by the president and confirmed by an absolute majority of the Senate. The Superior Court of Justice, with thirty-three sitting justices, operates under the Supreme Federal Tribunal as an appeals court. Matters requiring interpretation of the constitution go to the Supreme Federal Tribunal. The military maintains its own court system. Most judges in the Brazilian judicial system serve for life.

The judiciary is designed to adjudicate political conflicts as well as civil and social conflicts. The Electoral Supreme Tribunal (*Tribunal Supremo Electoral,* TSE)

has exclusive responsibility for the organization and oversight of all issues related to voting. The seven-member TSE is composed of three justices elected from the members of the Supreme Federal Tribunal, two from the Superior Court of Justice, and two nominated by the president from a group of six attorneys of notable quality that are selected by the Supreme Federal Tribunal. The seven justices on the TSE serve for two years and they have the power to investigate charges of political bias by public employees, file criminal charges against persons violating electoral laws, and scrutinize and validate electoral results. In addition to these constitutional provisions, under electoral law and its own regulations, the TSE monitors the legal compliance of electoral campaigns and executive neutrality in campaigns. The integrity of the tribunal in the conduct of elections has remained very high, making fraud relatively rare in national elections. The TSE is assisted in this process by a system of regional electoral courts that oversee local elections.

As in the rest of Latin America, penal codes established by legislation govern the powers of judges. This makes the judiciary less flexible than its North American counterparts, which operate on case law, but it provides a more effective barrier against judicial activism—the tendency of the courts to render broad interpretations of the law.

Since the 1940s the judicial branch of government in Brazil in theory has been highly independent from the executive. In practice, especially under authoritarian rule, the judiciary has been dictated to by the executive branch. President Collor exercised sweeping executive powers without much judicial review. The Supreme Federal Tribunal was viewed as ceding significant extraconstitutional authority by not challenging Collor's rule by fiat. A year after Collor's anti-inflation asset freeze, some of the country's most renowned jurists decided to oppose further blockage of financial assets on the grounds that it was unconstitutional. Although their opposition came late, it began a national debate that continues to this day about the president's "emergency measures."

In recent years, the judiciary has been severely criticized for its perceived unresponsiveness to Brazil's social problems and the persistent corruption in the lower courts. These problems are particularly apparent in rural areas, where impoverished defendants are often denied the right to a fair trial by powerful landowners, who have undue influence over judges and procedures. Children are especially victimized; courts have refused to hear cases prosecuting those who profit from child prostitution, pornography, and murder of street urchins.

Official corruption in the judiciary became an important and high-profile issue in 2000 when a federal judge, Nicolau dos Santos, who was accused of embezzling US$90 million from official coffers, remained a fugitive for 227 days until he turned himself in. The ongoing investigation revealed a network of official corruption leading up to the ministerial level in some cases.

A more everyday indicator of systemic corruption is the difficulty citizens face in prosecuting the police. In the state of Rio de Janeiro, between January 1996 and July 1997, 68 percent of cases in military court involving the police were retired without a hearing because of insufficient evidence (which is often destroyed by the police) or because of the police's favorite excuse: that the defendant was injured or killed "while resisting arrest." Although federal legislation in 1996 granted civil courts jurisdiction over such matters, paradoxically the power to investigate these crimes was left in the hands of the police.

The Supreme Tribunal's reluctance to act on these matters leaves little hope for change in the short term. Judicial reform has thus far focused on speeding up the Supreme Tribunal's judicial review functions, avoiding the more difficult question of restructuring the judiciary to eliminate corruption.

Restructuring of the judiciary will continue to get attention as the 1988 constitution is revised. Proposals for reform include subjecting judges to external control through periodic elections. Members of the judiciary deeply resent and fear such a prospect. They argue that it would push the institution into the kind of partisanship that has marred policy debates on key social and political issues. Others view the structure of the judiciary and its approach to interpreting and implementing laws as the central obstacles to accomplishing policy goals. Like the Brazilian bureaucracy, the judiciary has a complex structure, with multiple jurisdictions at different levels of government. The problems inherent in this complex network of adjudication were made clear during the privatization of Vale, when opposition groups in different states and jurisdictions

were able to use the local courts to create numerous obstacles to the sale.

Subnational Government

The structure of subnational politics in Brazil is not unlike that of other federal systems throughout the world. Each state government consists of a governor; his chief advisers, who also usually lead key secretariats such as economy and planning; and a unicameral legislature, which is often dominated by the supporters of the governor. Governors are elected to four-year terms and, under the 1997 amendment of the 1988 constitution, may run for another term.

State and municipal governments wield tremendous influence in Brazilian politics. Since the days of the Old Republic, governors and mayors have been essential sources of support for presidents and federal legislators. This "politics of the governors" expanded with the transition to democracy. The fact that the 1982 elections created the first opportunity since the inauguration of the military regime for Brazilians to elect their governors directly made these subnational politicians crucial standard-bearers of the transition. It lent legitimacy to the governors' campaign to decentralize fiscal resources in the form of taxes and federal transfers.

The 1988 constitution provided much of what the governors and mayors wanted. First, the states and municipalities were promised a larger share of tax revenues. At the same time, however, the governors and mayors were successful in deflecting Brasília's attempts to devolve additional spending responsibilities to subnational government, particularly in the areas of education, health, and infrastructure. The governors also proved successful in protecting state banks from a major overhaul, which was greatly needed given that these financial institutions continued to fund irresponsible subnational spending by accumulating huge debts that the federal government agreed to roll over.

During the Collor administration, the federal government began to regain much of the fiscal authority it had lost to the states and municipalities. The Central Bank made good on its threats to intervene in bankrupt state banks and privatize them. The federal government also refused to roll over state debt without a promise of reform, including the privatization of money-losing utility companies. The Cardoso administration required states and municipalities to finance a larger share of social spending, including education and health care. At the same time, new legislation empowered Brasília to claim more discretionary authority over fiscal transfers and tax revenues that had previously devolved to subnational governments.

Despite these efforts, Brazilian presidents must continue to negotiate the terms of reform with governors as much as with the congress. Because they can now run for reelection, the governors and their political machines will represent an even more consistent element in national politics. The October 1998 elections proved the staying power of incumbent governors: fifteen of the twenty-two incumbents who ran were reelected, a turnover rate well below the high levels in the legislature (see Section 4).

Although most subnational politics are still preoccupied with the distribution of political favors in return for fiscal rewards, certain governors and mayors have devised innovative solutions to Brazil's social and economic problems. One recent study of the state of Ceará in the poor northern region has demonstrated that even the most underdeveloped subnational governments can produce important policies to promote industrial investment, employment, and social services.[40] Such an example is a useful reminder that not all states and municipalities are the same in a federal system. Much depends on the interests and quality of political and bureaucratic leadership.

The Policy-Making Process

Although policy-making continues to be fluid and ambiguous in Brazil, certain domains of policy are clearly demarcated. Foreign policy, for example, is exclusively within the purview of the executive branch. Political parties and the congress in general still have only inconsistent power over investment policies. Because most legislation originates in the executive branch, bureaucratic agencies have retained command over the details of social and economic policies.

The process of making policy in Brazil can be characterized by one common quality: the tendency of clientelism to inject itself at every stage, from formulation and decision making to implementation. Even when policies are formulated without the undue influence of societal and political actors, implementation is often obstructed or distorted by clientelism. Again, as noted, exceptions exist, but they are only that: exceptions.[41]

Complex formal and informal networks linking the political executive, key agencies of the bureaucracy, and private interests tend to be the chief players in clientelist circles. One of Cardoso's contributions to sociology before he became involved in Brazilian politics was his characterization of these clientelistic networks as **bureaucratic rings.** For Cardoso, the Brazilian state is highly permeable, fragmented, and therefore easily colonized by private interests that make alliances with midlevel bureaucratic officers. By shaping public policy to benefit these interests, bureaucrats gain the promise of future employment in the private sector. While in positions of responsibility, bureaucratic rings are ardent defenders of their own interests. Because they are entrenched and well connected throughout the Brazilian bureaucracy, few policies can be implemented without the resources and support of the most powerful bureaucratic rings.

One example of the role of bureaucratic rings is the creation of large development projects. The politics surrounding these decisions were often intense. Governors and mayors wanted lucrative public projects to be placed in their jurisdiction; private contractors yearned for the state's business; and politicians positioned themselves for all the attendant kickbacks, political and pecuniary.[42] Although the days of huge development projects are over, the public sector still formulates policy and allocates resources under the influence of bureaucratic rings.

Among the key sources of influence external to the state is organized business. Unlike business associations in some Asian and West European countries, Brazilian business groups have remained independent of corporatist ties to the state. There is no Brazilian version of the French agricultural association *Fédération Nationale des Syndicats d'Exploitants Agricoles* (FNSEA) or the para-public institutions of the Federal Republic of Germany. Business associations have also remained aloof from political parties. Brazil has nothing akin to Mexico's National Action Party (*Partido Acción Nacional,* or PAN), a party that claims to represent a large portion of the business class. That does not mean, however, that Brazilian business interests are not organized. Lobbying by Brazilian entrepreneurs is common, and their participation in bureaucratic rings is legendary. Few major economic policies are passed without the input of the Federation of São Paulo Industries (*Federação das Industrias do Estado de São Paulo,* or FIESP). Other business groups, some that have broken off from FIESP, continue to defend their interests energetically as Brazil reforms its economy.

The country's labor confederations and unions have had less consistent access to policy-making. Although unions were once directly organized and manipulated by the corporatist state, they gained autonomy in the late 1970s and the 1980s. From then on, they sought leverage over policy-making through outside channels, such as the link between the *Central Única dos Trabalhadores* (CUT, Workers' Singular Peak Association) and Lula da Silva's Workers' Party. Attempts to bring labor formally into direct negotiations with business and the state have failed. Shortly after assuming power, Sarney initiated talks among business, government, and representatives of the major labor federations. These talks quickly broke down. Widening cleavages within the Brazilian union movement tended to split sectors of organized labor, causing some segments to refuse to be bound by any

agreement. Later, during the Collor administration, a second attempt at tripartite negotiation, called the "sectoral chambers," took place in the São Paulo automotive sector. These talks produced some noteworthy accords, but the chambers did not last because of opposition from the Ministry of Economy and other agencies. These experiences contrast sharply with the legacy of codetermination in Germany and other formulas for maintaining collective bargaining with state mediation in West European countries.

Policy implementation is also highly politicized. Debate and lobbying do not stop in Brazil once laws are enacted. Policy implementation is a subject of perpetual bargaining. One popular phrase, *o jeito brasileiro* ("the Brazilian way"), captures this aspect of Brazilian politics.[43] The Brazilian way is to scoff at the law and find a way around it. If one wants to get something without really paying for it, one asks for a *jeito*. Paradoxically, *jeito* can be the source of great efficiency in Brazilian society, but it carries a heavy price in that the rule of law is not respected. Therefore, reform of the policy-making process will require more than restrictions on clientelism and legislative and judicial oversight of suspected bureaucratic rings. It will require a shift in thinking about the role of law in Brazilian society.

Section ❹ Representation and Participation

Because of urbanization and economic modernization, the Brazilian electorate grew impressively after 1945. Improved literacy and efforts by political parties to expand voter registration helped to increase the number of citizens eligible to vote. Voting rights were granted in 1981 to anyone eighteen or older (but not illiterates) and in 1988 to anyone over age sixteen. As a result of these changes, the percentage of the total population eligible to vote increased from 16.2 percent in 1945 to 60 percent in 1994. The Brazilian electorate stands at 106 million and regularly votes (for example, turnout in the October 2002 presidential vote was 82.2 percent in the first round and 79.5 percent in the second round).

The expansion of the Brazilian electorate coincided with the proliferation of political organizations

and movements dedicated to marshaling popular support. Mass appeal became an important element in campaigns and political alliances. With the return to democracy in the 1980s, newly independent labor unions and special-interest organizations emerged, making new alliances in civil society possible.

Nevertheless, the richness of political organization was restrained by the legacies of state-centered structures of social control. Despite the transition to democracy, state corporatism continued to govern important segments of the Brazilian polity. Some political parties and many of the new social movements and political organizations that helped end the military government lacked staying power. Clientelism continued to fragment the legislature and weaken other democratic institutions.

The Legislature

The 594-member national legislature is bicameral, consisting of an upper house, the Senate with 81 members, and a lower house, the Chamber of Deputies with 513 members. Each state and the federal district elects 3 senators, for a total of 81. Senators are elected by simple majority. Senators serve for eight-year terms and may be reelected without limits. Two-thirds of the Senate is elected at one time, and the remaining one-third is elected four years later. For example, in the elections of 1994, two-thirds of the Senate was renewed. In 1998, the remaining one-third was renewed. Senatorial elections are held concurrently with those for the Chamber of Deputies, which places all of its seats up for election after each four-year cycle. Federal deputies may be reelected without limits. The number of members in the Chamber of Deputies is, in theory, proportional to the population of each state and the federal district. Each state is allowed a minimum of 8 and a maximum of 70 deputies, regardless of population.

Both houses of the legislature have equal authority to make laws. In all cases, one chamber acts as a reviser of legislation passed by the other. Bills go back and forth between houses without going through a conference committee of the two chambers, as is the case in the United States. Once the bill is passed by both houses, the president may sign it into law, reject it as a whole, or reject it in part. The legislature can override a presidential veto with a majority of the vote in both houses during a joint session. Constitutional amendments must survive two three-fifths votes in each house of congress. Amendments may also be passed with an absolute majority in a special unicameral constituent assembly proposed by the president and created by both houses of congress. The Senate retains authority to try the president and other top officials, including the vice president and key ministers and justices, for impeachable offenses. It also has the power to approve appointments to high offices, including justices of the high courts, heads of diplomatic missions, and the directors of the Central Bank.

The formula for determining the proportionality of population to representatives is distorted by complex constitutional rules that favor the most sparsely populated states. Because these states are the most numerous in the federal system, they tend to be overrepresented

in the legislature. For example, between 1990 and 1994, the northern region had 4.85 percent of the voters but elected 11.33 percent of the deputies, while the southeastern region had 46 percent of the electorate but only 33.59 percent of the seats. Only 40 percent of the population elects a majority of the Chamber of Deputies. The least populated states are also the poorest and most rural in Brazil. Typically, they have been political bases for conservative landowning interests and, more recently, agribusiness. After 1964 the military cultivated support among conservative rural groups by granting statehood to sparsely populated territories in the north and northeast, reinforcing their overrepresentation in the Chamber. These precedents continued into the democratic period and largely explain why conservative landowners and agribusiness elites maintain positions of great influence in the Brazilian congress.

In contrast to the presidency, the Brazilian legislature has rarely played a dominant role in the country's politics. In part, that is due to the ability of the president to impose policy through corporatism and populism. However, the congress must accept some of the blame. Many senators and deputies are more interested in cultivating and dispensing patronage than in representing and being accountable to the voters. As a result, representatives have never organized their parties or large segments of the population in support of national policy. Only the rarest of exceptions exist to this rule of Brazilian congressional politics.

Legislators view their service primarily as a means to enhance their own income with generous public pensions and through kickbacks earned in the dispensing of political favors. Election to the federal legislature is often used as a steppingstone to even more lucrative, especially executive, posts.[44] After the presidency, the governorships of the industrialized states are the most coveted positions. Appointment to head any of the premier ministries and state firms also ranks high, since these are choice positions from which to distribute and receive favors. Although many members of congress are independently wealthy, most come from the middle or upper middle classes and therefore have much to gain in the economics of public administration.

The congress has largely failed to use the expanded powers granted by the 1988 constitution. Lack of a quorum to vote is a frequent problem, and recently acquired powers have provided greater opportunities for some legislators to practice corruption and backroom dealing, conditions that have helped to break down party loyalties and reinforce the self-serving nature of congressional politics. The many deficiencies of the Brazilian legislature were magnified in recent years by several corruption scandals. In the most serious case, a handful of senators and deputies were accused of embezzling from regional development projects or directly from the national treasury.

One response to legislative corruption has been the use of parliamentary commissions of inquiry to review cases of malfeasance by elected officials. Although these temporary committees have demonstrated some influence, most notably the parliamentary commission of inquiry that investigated Collor and recommended his impeachment, they have not always produced results. The temporary committees work alongside sixteen permanent legislative committees that treat issues as diverse as taxation and human rights. These committees, however, are not nearly as strong as the major committees in the U.S. Congress. Due to the self-interested focus of Brazilian politicians and the related weakness of political parties, legislative committees, both temporary and permanent, often fail to get to the end of an investigation or find solutions to persistent dilemmas in policy.

Political Parties and the Party System

The Brazilian political party system is one of the most mercurial in the world. Party names, party affiliations, and the structure of party alliances are constantly in flux. This is nothing new in Brazilian political history. Like many of the country's current problems, party instability stretches back to the New State of Getúlio Vargas and the centralization of politics in the Brazilian state. State corporatism and populism were hostile to the development of independent party organizations. Political parties, when they did emerge, were created by state managers. Populist redistribution reinforced these tendencies, as workers and the middle class became accustomed to asking what they would receive from a politician in return for support. Except for members of the Communist Party and other extreme organizations, Brazilian voters did not develop a strong sense of political identity linked to established parties.

Personalist loyalties and the distribution of goods and services were more important.

Many of the traditional weaknesses of the party system were reinforced after the transition to democracy, making parties even more anemic. The rules governing the party system made it easier for politicians to switch parties, virtually at will. One of the most important observers of Brazilian democracy, Scott Mainwaring, found that the 559 representatives of the 1987–1991 legislature had belonged to an average of over three parties per politician.[45] Politicians switched parties to increase their access to patronage. Other rules of the electoral system created incentives for politicians to ignore the importance of party labels. Brazil's experience with **proportional representation** (PR), which is used to elect federal and state deputies, is particularly important in this regard. (See "Institutional Intricacies: Proportional Representation.")

Brazil's mix of presidentialism and multiparty democracy creates other problems for the country's system of representation. Given the political fragmentation of the legislature and the weakness of the party system, presidents are unable to maintain majority alliances in congress, a requirement for stability in a multiparty system. In parliamentary systems, the party in power has an absolute majority or stands at the head of an alliance of parties that compose a majority. As a result, the ruling party or alliance can implement a programmatic approach to legislation. By contrast, in Brazil, the president has never been able to maintain a supraparty alliance in congress. More often, Brazilian presidents have attempted to govern above parties, dispensing favors to key congressional politicians to get legislation approved. Alternatively, presidents have not been shy about railroading reform through congress by using their discretionary authorities. As Timothy Power, a scholar of presidential authority in Brazil, has noted, "The [presidential] pen is mightier than the congress."[46]

In the midst of Brazil's confusing party system, a number of political organizations have emerged over the last few years. These parties can be defined ideologically, although discrete categories are often not possible (see Table 4). Brazilian political parties are internally eclectic.

Political parties on the right currently defend neoliberal economic policies designed to shrink the size of the public sector. They support the reduction and

Institutional Intricacies: *Proportional Representati█████*

Proportional representation was introduced in Brazil in 1932 and was later reaffirmed by the military governments. Unlike Mexico, Britain, and the United States, but like many of the European parliamentary democracies, Brazil is divided into electoral districts that choose more than one representative. The ability to choose more than one representative means that a broader range of voices may be heard in elected offices.

Minority parties can make alliances to pass the threshold of votes needed to achieve representation. Proportional representation may be based on either a closed-list or an open-list system. In a closed-list PR, the party selects the order of politicians, and voters cannot cross party lines. Because voters are effectively choosing the party that best represents them, this system encourages party loyalty among both the electorate and individual politicians. In an open-list PR system, the voters have more discretion and can cross party lines. Brazil's PR system is open-list. Voters cast single ballots for either a party label, which adds to the party's total for determining representation, or for individuals. No names appear on Brazilian ballots, so voters must write in their choices.

Electoral districts for the election of state and federal deputies are entire states in Brazil. In any given election, there may be between six and seventy federal deputies and from twelve to eighty-four state deputies running for office. With few limits on how many individuals and parties may run in the same electoral district, crowded fields discourage party loyalty and emphasize the personal qualities of candidates, who must stand out in the minds of voters. Party affiliations do little to reduce the confusion of the average Brazilian voter as he or she is confronted with dozens of names for each position. Worse still, the open-list PR system creates ██████ for politicians to ignore party la██████se voters can cross party lines with ease. That even leads to politicians from the same party running against each other for the same position within a district.

Open-list proportional representation explains why there are so many parties in Brazil. With so much emphasis on the personal qualities of politicians, ambitious individuals can ignore the established party hierarchies while achieving elected office. They need only create their own parties or form alliances to get on the ballot and gain enough votes to qualify for representation. As a result, Brazil has the most fragmented party system in Latin America and one of the most fragmented in the world.

As if the open-list PR system were not distorting enough, Brazilian electoral law also allows incumbents to keep their party affiliation and remain on the ballot for the next election. This provision strips political parties of any control over their members: an incumbent may ignore the party's interests while in office but still must be kept on the ballot during the next contest.

Brazil's electoral system differs from other open-list proportional representation systems in that state, not national, parties select legislative candidates. In most cases, Brazilian governors exert tremendous influence over who can be elected. This further weakens national party leaders, who remain beholden to governors who can reward them with supportive nominees or rivals.

Source: Scott Mainwaring, "Brazil: Weak Parties, Reckless Democracy," in Scott Mainwaring and Timothy R. Scully, eds., *Building Democratic Institutions: Party Systems in Latin America* (Stanford, Calif., Stanford University Press, 1995), 375.

partial privatization of the welfare state. A majority advocate a liberal trade policy and MERCOSUL, but a substantial minority press for protectionism and the continuation of subsidies, particularly in agriculture. No party of the right has yet emerged as a solid defender of neoliberal restructuring of the economy, although scholars have detected a significant trend in favor of these policies among the parties on the right. On constitutional reform, right-wing parties are fairly united in favor of curtailing the number and range of

Table 4

The Democratic Idea: The Major Parties in Brazil

Conservative/Right-Wing Parties

PFL: *Partido da Frente Liberal* (Party of the Liberal Front)

PL: *Partido Liberal* (Liberal Party)

PPB: *Partido Progressista Brasileiro* (Brazilian Progressive Party)

Centrist Parties

PMDB: *Partido do Movimento Democrático Brasileiro* (Party of the Brazilian Democratic Movement)

PSDB: *Partido da Social Democracia Brasileira* (Party of Brazilian Social Democracy)

PTB: Partido Trabalhista Brasileiro (Brazilian Labor Party)

Populist/Leftist Parties

PT: Partido dos Trabalhadores (Workers' Party)

PSB: *Partido Socialista Brasileiro* (Brazilian Socialist Party)

PCdoB: *Partido Comunista do Brasil* (Communist Party of Brazil)

PDT: Partido Democrático Trabalhista (Democratic Labor Party)

PPS: Partido Popular Socialista (ex-Partido Comunista Brasileiro) (Popular Socialist Party)

social rights protecting welfare entitlements and workers; they also advocate electoral reform—specifically, the establishment of a majority or mixed, rather than purely proportional, district voting system, although this is contentious within the rightist cohort.

A loose set of conservative parties currently struggles for the mantle of the right. In front of the pack is the PFL (Party of the Liberal Front), one of the largest parties in the Senate and the Chamber. Many wild card parties, with low to moderate levels of representation in congress, ally themselves with right-wing and center-right parties or advocate right-wing issues; the Brazilian Labor Party (PTB), the Brazilian Progressive Party (PPB), and the evangelistic Liberal Party (PL) are examples.

The two other large parties in congress are the PMDB (Party of the Brazilian Democratic Movement, a descendant of the old MDB) and the PSDB (the Party of Brazilian Social Democracy, originally an offshoot of the PMDB; Cardoso's party). These parties, while having disparate leftist and rightist elements, tend to dominate the center and center-left segment of the ideological spectrum. Along with the PFL, these have been the key governing parties during the democratic era. Some scholars argue that these parties have formed a disciplined pro-reform bulwark in congress for Cardoso especially; hence, they are "government parties."[47] Other scholars argue that although these parties seem to vote coherently in favor of reform, these votes are infrequent and, more important, they are the product of the president's dispensing large amounts of patronage to particular politicians to manufacture a coherent vote.[48] Yet there is agreement that these parties have become ideologically more coherent in favor of neoliberal reform, and hence they can be characterized as being on the right or center-right.[49]

Political parties on the left advocate reducing deficits and inflation, but also maintaining the public sector in public hands and improving the welfare state. Left-oriented parties want to expand the state's role in promoting and protecting domestic industry. On constitutional reform, they support the social rights guaranteed by the 1988 constitution.

On the left, the most important party continues to be the Workers' Party (PT). (See "Citizen Action: The Workers' Party.") Since 1985 the PT has occupied much of the left's political space, marginalizing already peripheral parties such as the Brazilian Socialist Party (PSB), the Brazilian Communist Party (PCB—renamed the Popular Socialist Party, or PPS, in 1992), and the Communist Party of Brazil (PC do B). The Democratic Labor Party (PDT), a populist organization led by Leonel Brizola, the ex-governor of Rio de Janeiro, advocates Vargas-era nationalism and state-led development. In the elections of October 1998, this party formed an alliance with the PT at the national level. The PPS is led by Ciro Gomes, a former finance minister under the Itamar Franco presidency and a former governor of Ceará. Gomes ran for president in 1998 and 2002 but did not make it to the second round in either contest.

As might be expected, the proliferation of political parties has only added to the incoherence of legislative politics. Currently, no party has more than 24 percent of the seats in either house of congress (see Figures 3 and 4). Cardoso's multiparty alliance of the PSDB-PFL-PTB-PPB controlled 57 percent of the vote in the lower house and 48 percent in the upper house. Lula's alliance of his PT, the PL, and some of the leftist and

Citizen Action: *The Workers' Party*

The creation of the Workers' Party (PT) in the early 1980s was a remarkable development in Brazilian history. The PT was founded by workers who had defied the military government and engaged in strikes in São Paulo's metalworking and automobile industries in 1978 and 1979. Although the PT began with a working-class message and leftist platform, its identity broadened during the 1980s and early 1990s. The party and its leader, Luiz Inácio "Lula" da Silva, increasingly campaigned for the support of the middle class, the rural and urban poor, and even segments of business and the upper classes. Unlike previous populist parties in Brazil, the PT aimed both to bring previously excluded groups into the political arena and to change the status quo substantively.

Lula da Silva ran for the presidency four times: in 1989, 1994, 1998, and 2002. In 1989, he qualified for, but lost, the runoff to Collor. In 1994 and 1998, he was beaten during the first round by Cardoso. In 1998, the PT forged an electoral alliance with Leonel Brizola's left-populist PDT, as well as with other leftist parties, including the PSB, PC do B, and the PCB. Despite a unified leftist ticket, da Silva captured 31.7 percent of the vote to Fernando Henrique Cardoso's 53.1 percent. Lula did much better in 2002, beating Cardoso's designated successor, José Serra, in the second round with 61.3 percent, the largest share for any presidential winner in the democratic period. The party's electoral success is a product of its demonstrated capacity for clean and effective government at all levels in Brazil's federal system.

As Margaret Keck, an American scholar of the PT, argues, the party was a novel development because it sought to represent the interests of workers and the poor. This had never before been attempted by a political organization that operated independently from the state. The PT also tries to be an internally democratic party. Its leaders

Luiz Inácio "Lula" da Silva, founder of the Workers' Party and Brazilian President (2002–2006). *Source:* © Jornal do Brasil, August 19, 1998, Alexandre Sassaki.

respect the views of grassroots organizers and ensure that their voices are heard in the party's decision making.

Source: Margaret Keck, *The Workers' Party and Democratization in Brazil* (New Haven, Conn.: Yale University Press, 1992), 219–220.

center-left parties might provide a "governing coalition" similar in size to Cardoso's. But because of party switching, merging, and clientelism, the loyalty of these "progovernment" parties to the administration remains remarkably soft. Consistency of support is difficult to maintain as turnover in the Chamber is high, with 50 to 60 percent of the members being replaced with each election. This reality has reinforced the common claim of the executive to be the only source of political order in the Brazilian democratic system.

Figure 3

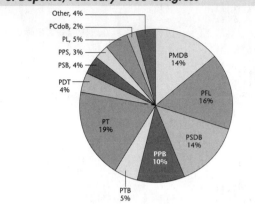

Share of Seats of the Major Parties in the Chamber of Deputies, February 2003 Congress

Source: Data from final TSE numbers.

The results of the October 1998 elections produced mounting recriminations among the leftist parties that a divided opposition was ineffectual. Conservative parties remained suspicious of Cardoso's social reform agenda, while center-left forces considered alternatives to right-wing support. Discussions have focused on the possibility of consolidating Brazil's political parties into a three- or four-party left-center-right structure. Yet the 2002 campaign produced no such major alliances. The right offered several candidates, including

Figure 4

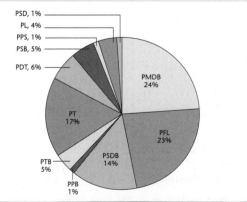

Share of Seats of the Major Parties in the Senate, February 2003 Congress

Source: Data from final TSE numbers.

the surprising Roseana Sarney, the PFL governor of Maranhão state and former president José Sarney's daughter, who dropped out of the race after being implicated in a widening embezzlement scandal. José Serra, Cardoso's PSDB health minister, quickly became the center-right's candidate to beat Lula, but opposition to Cardoso's government within the center and by populists such as Itamar Franco (PMDB) undercut his electoral standing prior to the second round of the presidential vote in October 2002. Lula, not needing any alliances with Brizola's PDT or Gomes's PPS (but forging a somewhat opportunistic tie to the Liberal Party, a probusiness, strongly evangelical party), proved that the PT could be successful at the presidential level. Yet without the support of the large conservative parties in congress and lacking a viable alliance of leftist parties, Lula's presidency will have great difficulty passing meaningful social and economic reform.

Elections

Contests for public office in Brazil are dominated by the rules of proportional representation (PR). Everything, from federal legislative to municipal council positions, is distributed on the basis of several mathematical calculations to ensure proportionality among political parties. Generally, the number of seats each party obtains is determined by multiplying the ratio between party and total votes by the total number of seats.

In addition to its effects on the party system, open-list PR (see "Institutional Intricacies: Proportional Representation") rules distort democratic representation in other ways. Given the multiplicity of parties, the unbalanced apportionment of seats among the states, and the sheer size of some electoral districts, candidates often have few incentives to be accountable to their constituency. In states with hundreds of candidates running in oversized electoral districts, the votes obtained by successful candidates are often scattered, limiting the accountability of those elected. In less populated states, there are more seats and parties per voter; the electoral and party quotients are lower. As a result, candidates often alter their legal place of residence immediately before an election in order to run for a safer seat, compounding the lack of accountability. Electoral laws are highly permissive regarding the candidate's change of residence. For example, ex-president Sarney, realizing that he would not be eligible to run for a Senate seat in his home state, successfully changed his residence only a few months before the 1990 elections.

As in all other modern nations, the media play a key role in Brazilian political campaigns. With the *abertura,* political parties gained the right to air electoral propaganda on radio and television. All radio stations and TV channels are required to broadcast, at no charge, two hours of party programming each day during a campaign season. The parties are entitled to an amount of time on the air proportional to their number of votes in the previous election. Some candidates have no more than a few seconds to present themselves and their platform to the public.

In recent years, elections, particularly presidential contests, have become touchstones of the country's progress in building democracy. Although the president was elected indirectly in 1984 and the eventual president, José Sarney (PMDB and PFL), had not been selected to be president in the first place, this first election set Brazil on the path to democracy. More important was the 1989 contest, which gave Brazilians their first opportunity to elect the president directly. Collor's (PRN) selection became an important precedent that further strengthened Brazilian democracy. Ironically, his impeachment two years later also promoted democracy, because it reinforced the rule of law and enhanced the oversight functions of the congress. Fernando Henrique Cardoso's election in 1994 and reelection in 1998 repeated and reinforced the 1989 precedent of direct elections for the presidency. Although elections cannot guarantee democracy, recent contests have shown how far Brazilian democracy has come in little over a decade.

Seen from the perspective of average Brazilians, however, the situation is a bit more complex. Although most Brazilians are suspicious of authoritarianism and wary of the return of the military or any other form of dictatorship, they seem to be disappointed with the results of democracy. The weakness of political parties, coupled with the persistence of clientelism, has discouraged average Brazilians with their country's politics. According to opinion polls, support for democracy as a viable system of government is under 50 percent nationwide. Brazilians vote, but they disparage politics and politicians regularly. For example, in the October 2002 presidential elections, 9.7 million voters turned in blank or spoiled ballots, a common indicator of voter discontent in Brazil. Electronic voting machines have reduced voter error in recent years making blank and null voting statistics even stronger indicators of the discontent of the electorate.

Political Culture, Citizenship, and Identity

The notion of national identity describes a sense of national community that goes beyond mere allegiance to a state, a set of economic interests, regional loyalties, or kinship affiliations. The cultivation of a national identity occurs through a process of nation building during which a set of national symbols, cultural terms and images, and shared myths consolidates around historical experiences that define the loyalties of a group of people.

Several developments made Brazilian nation building possible. Unlike nation formation in culturally, linguistically, and geographically diverse western Europe, Africa, and Asia, Brazil enjoyed a homogeneous linguistic and colonial experience. As a result, Brazilian history largely avoided the ethnic conflicts that have become obstacles to nation building in eastern Europe, Nigeria, and India. Immigrants added their ideas and value systems at the turn of the century, but they brought no compelling identities that could substitute for an overarching national consciousness. Regional secessionist movements were uncommon in Brazilian history and were short-lived experiences when they did emerge in the twentieth century.

Despite Brazil's rich ethnic makeup, racial identities in Brazil have seldom been the basis for political action. In part, this was the result of the historical myth that the country was racially mixed. Therefore, a singular racial consciousness emerged around the spurious idea that Brazil was a racial democracy. Even in the face of severe economic and political oppression of native peoples, Afro-Brazilians, and Asians, the myth of racial democracy has endured in the national consciousness. As a result, the unique contributions of different ethnic groups were not appreciated.

Brazilian literature, political discourse, and history textbooks reinforced the myth of racial democracy. For example, the famous Brazilian historian Gilberto Freyre, in his book *The Masters and the Slaves,* described the evolution of social relations among blacks and whites since colonial times, but he treated the underlying reality of racial conflict as an issue of secondary importance.[50] For such intellectuals, miscegenation had diminished racial differences and made conflict unlikely.

Carnival in Brazil, the world's largest floor show, is also an insightful exhibition of allegories and popular myths about the country, its people, and their culture.
Source: Bettmann/ Corbis.

This thinking buttressed the false belief that prejudice and discrimination were lacking among whites, blacks, indigenous peoples, and mulattos.

Like the myth of racial democracy, the major collective political identities in Brazilian history have sought to hide or negate the real conflicts in society. For example, the symbols and images of political nationalism tended to boost the quasi-utopian visions of the country's future development. Developmentalists under democratic leaders such as Kubitschek and the military governments espoused optimism that "Brazil is the country of the future." In the face of severe fiscal, social, and political problems, Brazilians continue to have faith in their country, even when their confidence in their politicians and democratic institutions has been shaken.

Both the persistence of optimistic myths about the country and an almost angry disengagement from politics are reflections of a weak system of political socialization. Given the dominance of corporatism and populism in twentieth-century Brazilian politics and the current crisis in these forms of mobilizing popular support, Brazilians lack avenues for becoming more involved in politics. The weakness of political parties is one problem. But an underfunded primary and secondary educational system and a largely uncritical media leave most Brazilians without the resources to become more politically aware. Brazil's illiteracy rate of 16.7 percent remains one of the highest in Latin America and is a key obstacle to mobilizing the electorate. The frenetic nature of political change in Brazil has confused the citizenry, further breaking down whatever continuous political identities might emerge. Perhaps the ultimate reflection of these distressing tendencies is the cynical joke among Brazilians that "Brazil is the country of the future and *will always be.*"

The political sentiments of Brazilian society are actually quite static because most Brazilians feel powerless to change their fates. Brazilians have always considered liberal democratic institutions, particularly individual rights, as artificial or irrelevant. Although this view may appear cynical, it is a deeply ingrained notion in Brazilian political culture. Since the end of the nineteenth century, Brazilians have made a distinction between the "legal" Brazil—that is, the formal laws of the country—and the "real" Brazil—what actually occurs. A prime example was the turn-of-the-twentieth-century liberal democracy, which concealed the patronage-ridden interior of Brazilian politics. Brazilian intellectuals developed the phrase *para ingles ver* ("for the English to see") to describe the notion that liberal democracy had been implanted to impress foreign observers, hiding the fact that real politics would be conducted behind the scenes. As Brazil struggles to balance the interests of foreign investors with those of its own people, many Brazilians continue to believe that much of the politics they observe is really "for the English to see."

One of the key outcomes of the sense of powerlessness among the majority of Brazilians was the belief that the state should organize society. This idea helped to justify both the Vargas dictatorship in 1937 and the military rule that followed the coup of 1964. The primacy of the state manifested itself in Brazilian political culture. The notion that the state had a duty to provide for its citizens' welfare placed the state at the center of the Brazilian polity and the president at the center of the state. It should be clear, based on this analysis, that both society and the state in Brazil developed a set of core ideas that favored the establishment of a strong central government with an overbearing presidentialism. These ideas were not just imposed on Brazilians by savvy politicians; they were the product of many decades of social and political conflict.

During the redemocratization process, new trends in Brazilian political culture emerged. Most segments of Brazilian society came to embrace "modernization with democracy," even if they would later raise doubts about its benefits. The Catholic Church played an important role in promoting democracy. During the transition, a number of Catholic political organizations and movements aided by the Church organized popular opposition to the military governments. After the transition, archbishops of the Catholic Church helped assemble testimonials of torture victims. The publication of these depositions in the book *Nunca Mais* (*Never Again*) fueled condemnation of the authoritarian past. In this way, an establishment that previously had been associated with social conservatism and political oppression became a mobilizer of popular opposition to authoritarianism.

Another trend that developed during and after the transition to democracy was the growth of a profound distrust of the state. Brazilians began to doubt the ability of the state to find solutions to the country's economic and social problems. Business groups assailed the failures of state-led development, while labor unions claimed that corporatist management of industrial relations could not satisfy the interests of workers. As a result, Brazilians became increasingly receptive to fringe voices that promised to eradicate the previous economic-political order. By 1989, most Brazilians were willing to trust a little-known politician, Fernando Collor, who told the electorate what they wanted to hear. Collor swore to go to war against indolent state employees, corrupt politicians, and inefficient state enterprises. The results were, at least in part, disastrous. By ceding their authority to an untested figure like Collor, Brazilians failed one of the most important tests of democracy: ensuring that elected officials will be accountable to the electorate. In the end, antistatism proved hostile to democracy.

A third trend in Brazilian political culture can be seen among the most elite segments of society. Soon after the transition to democracy, many journalists, economists, politicians, intellectuals, and entrepreneurs began to embrace the notion that national institutions could be adjusted incrementally to strengthen democracy and promote economic growth. Constitutional, administrative, and economic reform became priorities of politicians such as Fernando Henrique Cardoso.

For average Brazilians, the dynamics of institutional tinkering are virtually unintelligible. The electorate must feel substantial change, primarily in their pocketbooks. Cardoso was able to deliver in 1994 when his Real Plan reduced inflation and increased the buying power of most Brazilians. That success gave him the popular support he needed to become president and launch an array of institutional reforms. In 1998, facing another presidential contest, Cardoso struggled to convince voters that his government of technocrats had the answers to the country's problems. With his reforms stuck in congress, Cardoso had difficulty backing up his claim to deserve a second term. Economic growth began to stall, raising fears that Cardoso's reforms had run their course and were beginning to erode. Despite these problems, he was reelected, but he continued to struggle with congress on the reform agenda, as his successor surely will.

The task of selling even the most complex sets of

policies to a population with weak political socialization and poor general education has become central to gaining and maintaining political power in Brazil. That has placed a premium on the adept management of the media, particularly radio and television. The Brazilian media are free to criticize the government, and most of the broadcast businesses are privately owned. Although there is significant government influence over the resources necessary for media production and the advertising revenue from government campaigns, there is no overt government censorship, and freedom of the press is widely and constitutionally proclaimed. Government officials must engage in a complex dance of symbols and words to attract the attention of the private media and cast the most appealing image to a distrustful electorate.

The largest media organizations are owned by a small group of conglomerates. The Globo network is Brazil's preeminent media empire and one of the five largest television networks in the world. It has been formidable in shaping public opinion; some believe it played a prominent role in Collor's election in 1989. Conglomerates like Globo have played favorites in the past and no doubt will continue to do so. In return, the media giants expect licensing concessions from their political friends.

Media independence from government interference varies. The print media are generally less restrained than the broadcast media in criticizing politicians and governments. Though television newscasts, which attract millions of viewers, continuously cover events embarrassing to the government or criticize government policies, the majority of viewers hear woefully little information on how and why political decisions are made, why one policy is favored over another, and the ultimate results. Domestic broadcast news coverage in Brazil is often merely the broadcasting of official government versions.

Interests, Social Movements, and Protest

Despite the growing disengagement of most Brazilians from politics and the country's legacy of state corporatism, autonomous collective interests have been able to take positions of importance in the political landscape. The role of business lobbies, rural protest movements, and labor unions, particularly those linked to the Workers' Party, are all examples of how Brazilian civil society has been able to break through the vise of state corporatism and social control.

As noted, the Catholic Church was actively engaged in organizing grass-roots movements during and after the transition to democracy. After the profound changes in Catholic doctrine brought about by the Second Vatican Council in the early 1960s, the Church in Brazil became more active in advocating social and political reform. The Brazilian church, through the National Conference of Brazilian Bishops (CNBB), produced an array of projects to improve literacy, stimulate political awareness, and improve the working and living conditions of the poor. Although some conservative segments of the Brazilian church reacted violently against the Church's "messing in politics," the CNBB pressed on.

One well-known outcome of these changes was the development of liberation theology, a doctrine that argued that religion had to free people from both their sins and social injustice at the same time. In Brazil this thinking was associated with the Franciscan theologian Leonardo Boff. During the *abertura,* this doctrinal shift sought to relate theology to Brazilian reality by having priests become directly involved in improving the lot of poor Brazilians by defending their social and political needs.[51] By organizing community-based movements to press for improved sanitation, clean water, basic education, and, most important, freedom from oppression, Catholic groups mobilized millions of citizens. Among the Brazilian church's most notable accomplishments was the development of an agrarian reform council in the 1970s, the Pastoral Land Commission. The commission called for the extension of land tenure to poor peasants. The Brazilian Church also created ecclesiastical community movements to improve conditions in the *favelas.*

In the mid-1970s, Brazil witnessed a historic awakening of social and political organization: grass-roots popular movements; new forms of trade unionism; neighborhood movements; professional associations of doctors, lawyers, and journalists; entrepreneurial associations; and middle-class organizations. At the same time, a host of nongovernmental organizations (NGOs) became more active in Brazil; among them were Amnesty International, Greenpeace, and native Brazilian rights groups. Domestic groups active in these areas increasingly turned to the NGOs for resources and information, adding an international dimension to what was previously an issue of domestic politics.

Women's organizations played a significant role in popular urban social movements during the 1970s. By the 1980s, women were participating in and leading popular initiatives on a wide variety of issues related to employment and the provision of basic services. Many of these organizations enlisted the support of political parties and trade unions in battles over women's wages, birth control, rape, and violence in the home. Although practically absent in employers' organizations, women are highly active in urban unions. Out of the country's 5,324 urban unions, 14.8 percent have elected women directors. Fewer women are leaders of rural unions (6.6 percent), but they compose 78 percent of active membership. In recent years, Brazilian women have created over 3,000 organizations to address their issues. Included in this total are special police stations (*delegacias de defesa da mulher,* DDMs) dedicated to addressing crimes against women. The DDMs have emerged in major Brazilian cities, and particularly in São Paulo, where their performance has been highly rated.

Women's groups have seen their power increase as more women have joined the work force: 39 percent of women now work outside the home. That figure is higher than in Mexico (22 percent) and Argentina (33 percent). More than 20 percent of Brazilian families are supported exclusively by women. The share of domestic servants in the female work force has declined from 32 percent to 20 percent over the past ten years, suggesting that traditional roles for women have not absorbed the increase in the female work force.

Women have also made great strides in representative politics and key administrative appointments. In March 2000, Teresa Grossi was confirmed as the first woman to occupy the directorship of the Central Bank. Judge Ellen Gracie Northfleet became the first woman to occupy a seat on the STF, Brazil's Supreme Court, and Marta Suplicy became mayor of São Paulo. Roseanna Sarney's startling, yet ill-fated, performance during the presidential campaign of 2002 suggests that Brazilians are prepared to consider a women for president. The number of women with seats in congress nearly doubled following the election of October 2002.

Despite women's improved economic, social, and political importance, progress on women's issues is slow. On average, women earn only 57 percent of what men make. Only 7 percent of women with university degrees earn more than twenty times the minimum wage (about $75 per month), as compared to 28 percent of men. Thirty-four percent of illiterate women earn the minimum wage or less versus 5 percent of illiterate males.

In contrast to the progress of women's movements, a politically significant organization to address racial discrimination has not emerged. This fact is especially surprising because Brazil is one of the world's most racially mixed countries. Only during the 1940s did some public officials and academics acknowledge that prejudice existed against blacks. At that time, the problems of race were equated with the problems of class. Given the absence of legally sanctioned discrimination since the abolition of slavery in 1888, prejudice came to be viewed as class based, not race based. Attacking class inequality was thus considered a way to address prejudice against blacks. This belief seemed plausible because most poor Brazilians are either *pardo* (mulatto) or black. But it might be just as logical to suggest that they are poor because they are black. In any case, the relationship between race and class in Brazil is just as ambiguous as it is in the United States and other multiethnic societies.

Some analysts believe that a gradual and peaceful evolution of race relations is possible. Others argue that as a consequence of white domination, blacks lack the collective identity and political organization necessary to put race relations on the political agenda. Both sides seem to agree, however, that although poverty and color are significantly correlated, overt confrontation among races is uncommon. Ironically, this may explain why no serious national discussion of race relations has ever emerged in Brazil.

The rights of Brazil's indigenous peoples, the Indians of the Amazon, remain at the center of the debate on the country's most pressing social problems. Over the past half-century, the development of the Amazon has threatened the cultures and lives of Indians. For example, members of the Ianomami, a tribe with one of the largest reserves in Brazil, are frequently murdered by miners so they can gain access to mines in Indian territory. Many such massacres have occurred in territories legally provided by the central state to the Ianomami. During the military government, the national

Indian agency, FUNAI, turned a blind eye to such abuses with its claim that indigenous cultures represented "ethnic cysts to be excised from the body politic."[52] With the *abertura,* many environmental NGOs defended the human rights of indigenous people as part of their campaign to defend the Amazon and its people. The end of military rule and the economic crisis of the 1980s slowed exploitation of the Amazon.

The 1988 constitution recognized the rights of indigenous peoples for the first time, creating large reserves for tribes like the Ianomami. Yet these protections were eroded when President Cardoso, under pressure by landowning conservative allies from the northeast, implemented a policy to allow private interests to make claims on over half of all indigenous lands. Miners, loggers, and land developers invade native lands, often with destructive consequences for the ecology and indigenous people. Allied against these interests are members of the Workers' Party, a coalition of indigenous groups known as COIAB, and church-based missionary organizations. The Kayapó and their resistance

to large-scale development projects in the Amazon are a key example of how environmental, labor, and indigenous issues are melding together to form a powerful grass-roots campaign. Members of the Kayapó tribe have been successful in politically disrupting damming and mining projects through mass media campaigns.[53] Their struggle continues, but without more federal protection Amazonian Indians will continue to be threatened.

The sprouting of movements, associations, and interest groups may seem impressive, but they represent specific constituencies. Most Brazilians do not bother to participate in parties, movements, and unions because the basic functions of government such as security, justice, education, and health care simply do not reach them. When confronted with immediate deprivations, many Brazilians avoid organized and peaceful political action, often taking to the streets in sporadic riots. Such events demonstrate that many Brazilians feel they have only two choices in the face of unresponsive political and state organizations: violent protest or passivity.

Section ⑤ Brazilian Politics in Transition

Political Challenges and Changing Agendas

As the financial and monetary crisis that began in Asia in late 1997 continued to scare foreign investors throughout the developing world, Fernando Henrique Cardoso appeared on a Cable News Network (CNN) business show in December. The Brazilian president proclaimed his country a safe place for foreign money, a stable and growth-oriented economy sure to remain immune from the economic difficulties afflicting Asia. To scholars of Brazil, Cardoso's CNN appearance seemed paradoxical. Here was an avowed social democrat, an old theorist of leftist sociology, a former *dependencista,* pitching his country to international investors. They noted that Cardoso made no mention of his country's worsening social problems, its disparities in income, land tenure, and access to basic social and educational services. For many Brazilians on the left, Cardoso's comments were a ruthless betrayal of shared principles.

From a comparative perspective, we might interpret Cardoso's CNN interview in very different terms. Cardoso's remarks become more understandable when we consider the dilemmas connected to our theme of governing the economy. Much like other leaders of developing countries, Cardoso needs to preserve a stable domestic economy attractive to foreign investors, who are likely to turn to other countries at the first signs of instability. Not surprisingly, then, on CNN the president talked up his economic policy and downplayed the political and social negatives of investing money in Brazil. Rather than a betrayal of his social democratic principles, Cardoso's pitch could be seen as a pragmatic attempt to turn a necessity into a virtue. Five years later, the same paradox faces Brazil's new president, Lula da Silva. During the presidential campaign, Lula repeatedly stated his commitment to preserve the real and to avoid an Argentine-style default on Brazil's ever-expanding public debt. By his efforts to court business interests inside and outside Brazil, the suit-and-tie Lula (not the blue-collar labor party leader) opted for the same strategy as his predecessor.

At the same time, there are serious costs to the presidential strategy of reforming the Brazilian political and economic structure in order to become more competitive in global markets. The Brazilian president has had to embrace the very mechanisms of clientelism to curry center-right support that are at the heart of many of the inefficiencies that create a deadlock on the country's democratic institutions. Given a weak party system and constitutional requirements that all amendments survive two majority votes of 60 percent in both houses of congress, clientelism has become the presidency's most powerful mechanism for cultivating support. Only with the support of conservative and probusiness groups, which maintain a majority of votes in both houses of congress, will any Brazilian president have the support to implement the constitutional, administrative, and social security reforms needed to restructure the economy.

This strategy has created serious paradoxes for the Brazilian president. Rather than strengthen Brazil's weak political parties and fragmented legislature, these tactics have reinforced the factors that make the country's democratic institutions anemic. By kowtowing to clientelistic interests, Cardoso's administration put on hold reforms to the electoral and party system. In the process, members of his own party, the Brazilian Social Democratic Party (PSDB), rebuked the president for cultivating support from other parties, particularly the conservative Party of the Liberal Front (PFL), and sometimes hurting his own social democrats in congressional and gubernatorial contests. By wooing many conservative interests, mostly in the north and northeast regions, Cardoso strengthened groups that oppose significant agrarian reform, income distribution, and improvements in social services. Most important, his strategy depended on increased spending, financed with public debt at high interest. The result has been a soaring deficit and public debt. Despite Lula's strong leftist credentials, his presidency will face similar strategic choices and structural constraints. Systemic reforms will require legislative coalitions with centrist and even right-wing parties, especially in the Senate, and Lula will be under even greater pressure from a leftist partisan base if he strays too far from his promises to address social inequalities.

Despite the heady rhetoric of Cardoso's 1994 presidential campaign and the rising expectations of long-frustrated social democrats inside and outside Brazil, his administration offered little in the way of changing Brazilian politics for the long haul. Cardoso made only token progress on the country's persisting social inequalities. The Real Plan reduced the eroding effect of mega-inflation on the incomes of the poor, boosting consumption for millions of Brazilians. But other policies were less effective. Economic liberalization caused thousands of Brazilian firms to shave their labor costs, putting hundreds of thousands out of work. Privatization, for example, put an estimated 546,000 out of work as sold-off firms downsized to become viable market actors. As urban unemployment has increased, so have urban violence and crime. The government distributed more land to poor people in rural areas, but these efforts failed to make a dent in Brazil's concentrated system of land tenure. Some innovation in health reform and education emerged regarding improving the availability of anti-HIV drugs and state-level experiments, respectively, but wider reforms received only lip-service from the administration. Lula's presidency will certainly try to do more for the poor, but against the backdrop of Brazil's mounting debt and the nervousness of international investors, he might not be able to produce the kind of systemic change many of his voters would like to see.

Both the fiscal and the environmental limits to Brazil's economic development have been stretched almost to their breaking points. Even without a significant downturn in the global economy, the fate of the Brazilian economy is being threatened by the state's burgeoning indebtedness, the inability to cut public spending, and the social and ecological costs of the maldistribution of income and the abuse of natural resources. The tendency to see solutions to Brazil's economic problems in terms of promoting exports and enlarging the economy deepens these problems. Considering that many of Brazil's exports are still extractive (e.g., iron ore, lumber), these recommendations place ever more pressure on the country's ecology. The quality of life of most Brazilians can only suffer as a result.

The challenges facing Brazil and the way that the country's political leaders have chosen to deal with them are similar to experiences elsewhere. The Brazilian state lacks the resources to promote development as it did during the days of Vargas, Kubitschek, and military rule. As the needs of the Brazilian citizenry grow, the state appears less capable, and political leaders less willing, to respond. With the advent of the Real Plan, the priorities have been to attract foreign capital, boost export earnings, and favor the highest bidders in the privatization of public firms. The developmentalist state lives on only in some BNDES policies. Like former state-led industrializers India, Mexico, and France, Brazil has turned in the neoliberal direction, limiting the state's role in the economy. This shift in the state's organization reminds us of the importance of our theme of highlighting critical junctures in state formation.

In contrast to the corporatist and populist role of the state, the moderating power in Brazilian history, the central state has become a far more passive agent in society. Brazilian workers no longer negotiate labor issues with state mediation, as they still do in Germany. Instead, labor unions, when they are capable, negotiate directly with business. In most cases, given high urban unemployment, the interests of business usually prevail. Urban workers receive little or no compensation from the state when they suffer layoffs or reductions in their salaries and workplace benefits. Most rural workers, the millions in the informal sector, and minorities are in an even more precarious position, as they lack the few benefits and protections enjoyed by salaried urban workers. The weakness of the judiciary, the abusive use of police authority, and the tendency to vigilantism and class conflict in poor, rural areas reinforce the anemia of a civil society that increasingly discounts its role in politics.

In this context, Brazilian democracy has suffered greatly, the importance of which we highlighted in our theme of the democratic challenge. The poor feel doubly divorced from politics, both socially and politically disenfranchised from a process they view as unresponsive to their needs. Over time, this sense of disengagement has turned into open doubt about the utility of democracy itself. Stories of official corruption and the popular assumption that a politician's priority is his or her own pocketbook reinforce the idea that representatives are unaccountable to their constituencies. The weakness of political party loyalties and the fragmentation of interests compound the problem of

accountability. By contrast, much stronger democracies such as Germany, the United States, France, and Britain rely on well-defined rules that force political leaders to be accountable to other branches of government and to their own constituencies. Brazil's example has shown how difficult it is to embrace the democratic idea without these structures.

While some of Brazil's problems are unique, many take the same form they do elsewhere. Like all other major economies in the world, Brazil's is well integrated into the global economy. Despite the country's current problems with monetary stability and debt, Brazil is one of the world's key platforms for agricultural production and manufacturing. Brazil's share of the world market in iron ore, textiles, footwear, steel, machine parts, and autos makes it an important hub in the multinational production of several industrial products. It is a crucial supplier of raw materials as well as a large market for multinational producers. As such, it has advantages few other developing countries enjoy. That also means, however, that Brazilian firms and workers (not to mention the public sector itself) must be able to adapt to greater competition from abroad and the needs of foreign capital. Given the speed with which technology outpaces itself, the pressure to train workers, boost productivity, and enhance research and development has grown tremendously. Brazil is struggling just to keep pace with globalization.

As globalization and democratization have made Brazilian politics less predictable, older questions about what it means to be Brazilian have reemerged. Brazil highlights the point made in the discussion of our theme on political identities in the Introduction that political identities are often reshaped in changed circumstances. What it means to be Brazilian has become a more complex question given the way that Brazil, like the rest of the world, has been bombarded by foreign consumer images. Democracy has given ordinary Brazilians more of a voice, and they have used it to forge their own understandings, but mostly on local issues, not at the national level. Women, nongovernmental organizations, Catholics, Pentecostals, blacks, landless peasants, and residents of *favelas* have all organized in recent years around social and cultural issues. On the one hand, these movements have placed additional pressure on an already weakened state to deliver goods and services. On the other hand, these groups have supplied alternatives to the state by providing their own systems of social and cultural support. As the domain of the state in other countries is constrained by the need to compete in the global economy, space is created for nonstate actors to provide goods and services that were previously produced by the state. What is missing in all of this is a sense of the "national question." How are all these disparate groups linked? Do they have a common, national interest? If they are increasingly disconnected, then the proliferation of social movements and organizations is only a symptom of the wider disengagement from the state and political society already being practiced by most Brazilians.

Brazilian Politics in Comparative Perspective

The most important lesson that Brazil offers for the broader study of comparative politics is that fragmented polities threaten democracy, social development, and nation building. The Brazilian political order is fragmented on several levels. The central state is fragmented by conflicts between the executive and the legislature, divided alliances and self-interested politicians in the congress, decentralized government, and an indecisive judiciary with a complicated structure and an uncertain mission. Political parties are fragmented by clientelism and electoral rules that create incentives for politicians and voters to ignore party labels. Finally, civil society itself is fragmented into numerous, often conflictual, organizations, interest groups, professional associations, social movements, churches, and, most important, social classes and ethnic identities.

In some societies that are similarly fragmented, such as the United States and India, institutions have been successful in bridging the gaps between individualistic pursuits and the demand of the people for good government. Rich systems of social organization and reciprocity that are linked to the state through political parties, parliaments, and even informal associations help to strengthen democracy in these countries. Where these systems are faulty, as they are in Brazil, fragmentation reinforces the weakness of the state and the society.

Recent Brazilian politics shows that a weak state deepens the citizenry's sense that all politics is corrupt. Although corruption is present in all polities to some degree, it does not by itself produce the angry disengagement from politics that has emerged in Brazil. Much more is wrong with the Brazilian political order. Police brutality, judicial incompetence, and the inability of bureaucratic agencies to respond to social demands have just as powerful an effect in legitimizing civil disengagement.

This only reinforces the importance of creating systems of accountability to reduce the corruption, police abuse, and bureaucratic incompetence that have given rise to these doubts. Unfortunately, the English word *accountability* has no counterpart in either Portuguese or Spanish. Given Brazil's (and Latin America's) long history of oligarchical rule and social exclusion, the notion of making elites accountable to the people is so alien that the languages of the region lack the required vocabulary. Systems of accountability must be built from the ground up; they must be nurtured in local government and in community organizations and then in the governments of states and the central state. The judiciary, political parties, the media, and civil societal organizations must be able to play enforcement and watchdog roles. These are the building blocks of accountability, and the accountability of political elites is the fulcrum of democracy.

Without a system of elite accountability, representation of the citizenry is impossible. The 60 percent of the Brazilian population that is classified as poor or close to that status has few autonomous organizations to pressure government. More than business, labor, or professional groups, the poor depend on their elected officials to find solutions to their problems. Brazilian politicians have shown that through demagoguery and personalism, they can be elected. But being elected is not the same as guaranteeing a constituency its right to be represented. For this to occur, institutions must make political elites accountable to the people who elected them. When that condition is met, genuine representation of citizens' interests becomes possible.

Political fragmentation can also have a virulent effect on a country's sense of national purpose. Collective identities, by definition, require mechanisms that forge mutual understandings among groups of people. Fractured societies turn to age-old ethnic identities that, as the India-Pakistan and Nigerian experiences demonstrate, can produce destructive, internecine conflict. In Brazil, such extreme conflict has been avoided, but the divisive effects of a fragmented polity on collective identities are serious nonetheless. Divided by class, poor Brazilians continue to feel that politics holds no solutions for them, so they fail to mobilize for their rights. Blacks, women, and Indians share some of the same interests because they are paid less than white men are for the same kind of work. Yet few national organizations have been able to unite a coalition of interest groups to change business practices in this regard. Finally, all Brazilians should be concerned with the clearing of rain forests, the pollution of rivers and lakes, and the destruction of species, yet the major political parties and the congress seem incapable of addressing these issues on behalf of future generations. Such national concerns continuously take a back seat to the self-interests of politicians in Brazil.

Perhaps the most serious effect of political fragmentation on Brazil has involved the struggle to achieve the country's interests in an increasingly competitive, global marketplace. While globalization forces all countries, and particularly developing countries, to adapt to new technology, ideas, and economic interests, it also lets states take advantage of the opportunity to attract investment. Given the weakness of the Brazilian state, the social dislocation produced by industrial restructuring (e.g., unemployment), and the currently unstable nature of the international investment climate, Brazil maintains only an ambiguous vision of its role in the global capitalist order. Although Brazilian business, some unions, and key political leaders speak of the need to defend Brazil's interests in the international political economy, the country has few coherent strategies. Such questions are inherently complex and politically difficult, perhaps no less so in Brazil than in France. But dealing with these issues requires a somewhat consistent policy created by a political leadership with clear ideas about the interests of the country. In Brazil's fragmented polity, developing such unambiguous strategies is difficult.

Acting now on behalf of Brazil's interests in the world of states must be a priority of Cardoso's successor. In the post–September 11 world, issues of security are quickly outpacing matters of equity and development, a concern that Cardoso himself voiced in various summits with world leaders in 2002. Brazil is solidly in the antiterrorist camp, yet Brazilians care more about their security against crime, malnutrition, and ecological disaster than they do about fanatical political violence.

Finally, Brazil's experience with economic restructuring and democratization will continue to influence countries undergoing similar transformations in Latin America and the rest of the developing world. As a large and resource-rich country, Brazil presents a useful example for other big developing countries such as Mexico, Russia, India, and China. Its evolving federal structure as well as its efforts to manage its resources while dealing with environmental costs can inform similar processes in these countries.

As a transitional democracy, Brazil can provide insights into which governance systems work better than others. As a negative example, Brazil's ongoing experiment with presidentialism, multiparty democracy, and open-list PR might well confirm the superiority of alternative parliamentary systems in India and Germany or presidentialism in France and the United States. As a positive example, Brazil's experiences with keeping a diverse country united through trying economic times will have much to teach Russia and Nigeria, as these countries are weighed down by the dual challenges of economic reform and nation building.

Within Latin America, Brazil continues to consolidate its position as the preeminent economy of the region. Through MERCOSUL, Brazil exerts authority on commercial questions, and with its continued dominance of the Amazon basin, the country's political elite retains the world's attention when they speak on environmental issues in the developing world. Brazil's experiences with balancing the exigencies of neoliberal economic adjustment with the sociopolitical realities of poverty will keep it on center stage as the World Bank and the IMF and the region's political, economic, and academic leaders discuss the possibilities for a new model of development.

Brazil may not be "the country of the future," but it is a country with a future. None of the maladies of Brazilian politics and social development is immune to improvement. If political reform is consolidated in the next few years, the groundwork will have been laid for transforming Brazil into a country that deserves the respect of the world.

Key Terms

privatization

moderating power

oligarchy

legitimacy

clientelism

patrimonialism

politics of the governors

interventores

state corporatism

New State

populism

nationalism

bureaucratic
authoritarianism

state-led development

abertura

personalist politicians

export-led growth

interventionist

import substitution
industrialization

state technocrats

developmentalism

para-statals

nongovernmental
organizations

informal economy

favelas

bureaucratic rings

proportional repre-
sentation

Suggested Readings

Alvarez, Sonia. *Engendering Democracy in Brazil.* Princeton, N.J.: Princeton University Press, 1990.

Ames, Barry. *The Deadlock of Democracy in Brazil: Interests, Identities, and Institutions in Comparative Politics.* Ann Arbor: University of Michigan Press, 2001.

Baer, Werner, ed. *The Brazilian Economy: Growth and Development.* 4th ed. New York: Praeger, 1995.

Dean, Warren. *With Broadax and Firebrand: The Destruction of the Brazilian Atlantic Forest.* Berkeley: University of California Press, 1995.

Evans, Peter B. *Dependent Development: The Alliance of Multinational, State, and Local Capital in Brazil.* Princeton, N.J.: Princeton University Press, 1979.

Furtado, Celso. *The Economic Growth of Brazil: A Survey from Colonial to Modern Times.* Berkeley: University of California Press, 1963.

Keck, Margaret. *The Workers' Party and Democratization in Brazil.* New Haven, Conn.: Yale University Press, 1992.

Kingstone, Peter R., and Power, Timothy J., eds. *Democratic Brazil: Actors, Institutions, and Processes.* Pittsburgh: University of Pittsburgh Press, 2000.

Lamounier, Bolivar. "Brazil Towards Parliamentarism?" In Juan Linz and Valenzuela Arturo, eds., *The Failure of Presidential Democracy.* Baltimore: Johns Hopkins University Press, 1994.

Mainwaring, Scott. *Rethinking Party Systems in the Third Wave of Democratization: The Case of Brazil.* Stanford: Stanford University Press, 1999.

Matta, Roberto da. *Carnivals, Rogues, and Heroes: An Interpretation of the Brazilian Dilemma.* Notre Dame, Ind.: University of Notre Dame Press, 1991.

Roett, Riordan. *Brazil: Politics in a Patrimonial Society.* 4th ed. New York: Praeger, 1992.

Scheper-Hughes, Nancy. *Death Without Weeping: The Violence of Everyday Life in Brazil.* Berkeley: University of California Press, 1992.

Schneider, Ben Ross. *Politics Within the State: Elite Bureaucrats and Industrial Policy in Authoritarian Brazil.* Pittsburgh: University of Pittsburgh Press, 1991.

Skidmore, Thomas E. *Black into White: Race and Nationality in Brazilian Thought.* Durham, N.C.: Duke University Press, 1993.

———. *The Politics of Military Rule in Brazil, 1964—85.* New York: Oxford University Press, 1988.

Stepan, Alfred. *Rethinking Military Politics: Brazil and the Southern Cone.* Princeton, N.J.: Princeton University Press, 1988.

———, ed. *Democratizing Brazil: Problems of Transition and Consolidation.* New York: Oxford University Press, 1989.

Tendler, Judith. *Good Government in the Tropics.* Baltimore: Johns Hopkins University Press, 1997.

Weyland, Kurt. *Democracy Without Equity: Failures of Reform in Brazil.* Pittsburgh: University of Pittsburgh Press, 1996.

Suggested Websites

LANIC database, University of Texas-Austin, Brazil Resource page
lanic.utexas.edu/la/brazil/
U.S. Library of Congress Country Study Page for Brazil
lcweb2.loc.gov/frd/cs/brtoc.html
Political Resources for Brazil, Political Database of the Americas, Georgetown University
cfdev.georgetown.edu/pdba/Countries/countries.cfm?ID=43
SciELO Brazil, Searchable Database of Full-Text Articles on Brazil
www.scielo.br/
National Development Bank of Brazil, Searchable Database of Documents on Brazilian Economy and Development (many in English)
www.bndes.gov.br

Notes

[1]IBGE (Instituto Brasileiro de Geografia e Estatística), *PNAD–Síntese do Indicadores da Pesquisa Básica da PNAD de 1981 a 1989* (Rio de Janeiro: IBGE, 1990). For more on Brazil's multiclassification system, see George Reid Andrews, *Blacks and Whites in São Paulo, Brazil, 1888–1988* (Madison: University of Wisconsin Press, 1991).

[2]See Bertha K. Becker and Claudio A. G. Egler, *Brazil: A New Regional Power in the World Economy: A Regional Geography* (New York: Cambridge University Press, 1992), 5, and Terence Turner, "Brazil: Indigenous Rights vs. Neoliberalism," *Dissent* (Summer 1996): 67.

[3]For a complete treatment of state corporatism in Brazil during this period, see Ruth Berins Collier and David Collier, *Shaping*

the Political Arena: Critical Junctures, the Labor Movement, and Regime Dynamics in Latin America (Princeton, N.J.: Princeton University Press, 1991), 169–195.

[4]Robert M. Levine, *Father of the Poor? Vargas and His Era* (New York: Cambridge University Press, 1998), 8–9.

[5]For an analysis of this "new professionalism," see Alfred Stepan, *The Military in Politics: Changing Patterns in Brazil* (Princeton, N.J.: Princeton University Press, 1971).

[6]Thomas E. Skidmore, *Politics in Brazil, 1930–1964: An Experiment in Democracy* (New York: Oxford University Press, 1967), 101.

[7]Maria do Carmo Campello de Souza, *Estado e Partidos Políticos no Brasil (1930 a 1964)* (São Paulo: Editora Alfa-Omega, 1975).

[8]Guillermo O'Donnell, *Modernization and Bureaucratic-Authoritarianism: Studies in South American Politics* (Berkeley: Institute of International Studies, University of California, 1973).

[9]Thomas E. Skidmore, *The Politics of Military Rule in Brazil, 1964–85* (New York: Oxford University Press, 1988), 49.

[10]Leigh A. Payne, *Brazilian Industrialists and Democratic Change* (Baltimore: Johns Hopkins University Press, 1994), chap. 4.

[11]For an analysis of these critical elections, see Bolivar Lamounier, "Authoritarian Brazil Revisited: The Impact of Elections on the Abertura," in Alfred Stepan, ed., *Democratizing Brazil: Problems of Transition and Consolidation* (New York: Oxford University Press, 1989).

[12]Margaret Keck, *The Workers' Party and Democratization in Brazil* (New Haven, Conn.: Yale University Press, 1992), 219–220.

[13]Timothy J. Power, *The Political Right in Postauthoritarian Brazil: Elites, Institutions, and Democratization* (University Park: Pennsylvania State University Press, 2000).

[14]Margaret Keck, "The New Unionism in the Brazilian Transition," in Stepan, *Democratizing Brazil,* 284.

[15]See Celso Furtado, *The Economic Growth of Brazil: A Survey from Colonial to Modern Times* (Berkeley: University of California Press, 1963).

[16]For a more complete treatment of how developmentalist ideas cultivated in ECLA affected policy choices in Brazil, see Kathryn Sikkink, *Ideas and Institutions: Developmentalism in Brazil and Argentina* (Ithaca, N.Y.: Cornell University Press, 1991).

[17]More complete treatment of the ISI experience can be found in Albert O. Hirschman, *A Bias for Hope: Essays on Development and Latin America* (New Haven, Conn.: Yale University Press, 1971).

[18]Peter B. Evans, *Dependent Development: The Alliance of Multinational, State, and Local Capital in Brazil* (Princeton, N.J.: Princeton University Press, 1979).

[19]These and other examples of ecological destruction are analyzed in Werner Baer and Charles C. Mueller, "Environmental Aspects of Brazil's Development," in Werner Baer, ed., *The Brazilian Economy: Growth and Development*, 4th ed. (New York: Praeger, 1995).

[20]For more on state environmental efforts, see Barry Ames and Margaret E. Keck, "The Politics of Sustainable Development: Environmental Policy Making in Four Brazilian States," *Journal of Interamerican Studies and World Affairs* 39, no. 4 (Winter 1998), 1–40.

[21]Kathryn Hochstetler, "The Evolution of the Brazilian Environmental Movement and Its Political Roles," in Douglas Chalmers, Carlos M. Vilas, Katherine R. Hite, Scott B. Martin, Kerianne Piester, and Monique Segarra, eds., *The New Politics of Inequality in Latin America: Rethinking Participation and Representation* (New York: Oxford University Press, 1997).

[22]Alfred P. Montero, "Devolving Democracy? Political Decentralization and the New Brazilian Federalism," in Peter R. Kingstone and Timothy J. Power, eds., *Democratic Brazil: Actors, Institutions, and Processes* (Pittsburgh: University of Pittsburgh Press, 2000).

[23]Peggy A. Lovell, "Race, Gender, and Development in Brazil," *Latin American Research Review* 29, no. 3 (1994), 7–35.

[24]Kurt Weyland, *Democracy Without Equity: Failures of Reform in Brazil* (Pittsburgh: University of Pittsburgh Press, 1996).

[25]Wilson Cano, "Concentración, desconcentración y descentralización en Brasil," in José Luis Curbelo, Francisco Alburquerque, Carlos A. de Mattos, and Juan Ramón Cuadrado, eds., *Territorios en Transformación: Análisis y Propuestas* (Madrid: Fondo Europeo de Desarrollo Regional, 1994).

[26]Leonardo Guimarães Neto, "Desigualdades Regionais e Federalismo," in Rui de Britto Álvares Affonso and Pedro Luiz Barros Silva, eds., *Desigualdades Regionais e Desenvolvimento* (São Paulo: FUNDAP, 1995).

[27]Jeffry A. Frieden, *Debt, Development, and Democracy: Modern Political Economy and Latin America, 1965–1985* (Princeton, N.J.: Princeton University Press, 1991), 54–65.

[28]Diana Jean Schemo, "The ABC's of Business in Brazil," *New York Times*, July 16, 1998, B1, 7.

[29]Fernando Luiz Abrúcio, *Os Barões da Federação: O Poder dos Governadores no Brasil Pós-Autoritário* (São Paulo: Editora HUCITECU, 1998).

[30]Alfred P. Montero, *Shifting States in Global Markets: Subnational Industrial Policy in Contemporary Brazil and Spain* (University Park: Pennsylvania State University Press, 2002).

[31]Timothy J. Power, "Politicized Democracy: Competition, Institutions, and 'Civic Fatigue' in Brazil," *Journal of Interamerican Studies and World Affairs* 33, no. 3 (Fall 1991), 75–112.

[32]Argelina Figueiredo and Fernando Limongi, "O Congresso e as Medidas Provisórias: Abdicação ou Delegação?" *Novos Estudos CEBRAP* 47 (1997): 127–154.

[33]Thomas J. Trebat, *Brazil's State-Owned Enterprises: A Case Study of the State as Entrepreneur* (New York: Cambridge University Press, 1983).

[34]Helen Shapiro, *Engines of Growth: The State and Transnational Auto Companies in Brazil* (New York: Cambridge University Press, 1994).

[35]Peter B. Evans, "Predatory, Developmental, and Other Apparatuses: A Comparative Political Economy Perspective on the Third World State," *Sociological Forum* 4, no. 4 (1989), 561–587.

[36]Alfred P. Montero, "State Interests and the New Industrial Policy in Brazil: The Case of the Privatization of Steel, 1990–1994," *Journal of Interamerican Studies and World Affairs* 40, no. 3 (Fall 1998), 27–62.

[37]Wendy Hunter, *Eroding Military Influence in Brazil: Politicians Against Soldiers* (Chapel Hill: University of North Carolina Press, 1997).

[38]Paulo Sérgio Pinheiro, "Popular Responses to State-Sponsored Violence in Brazil," in Chalmers et al., eds., *The New Politics of Inequality in Latin America*.

[39]Human Rights Watch, *Police Brutality in Urban Brazil* (New York: Human Rights Watch, 1997), 13.

[40]Judith Tendler, *Good Government in the Tropics* (Baltimore: Johns Hopkins University Press, 1997).

[41]For a study of how these exceptions have emerged in Brazil, see Barbara Geddes, *Politician's Dilemma: Building State Capacity in Latin America* (Berkeley: University of California Press, 1994).

[42]Ben Ross Schneider, *Politics Within the State: Elite Bureaucrats and Industrial Policy in Authoritarian Brazil* (Pittsburgh: University of Pittsburgh Press, 1991).

[43]Lívia Neves de H. Barbosa, "The Brazilian Jeitinho: An Exercise in National Identity," in David J. Hess and Roberto A. DaMatta, eds., *The Brazilian Puzzle: Culture on the Borderlands of the Western World* (New York: Columbia University Press, 1995).

[44]Barry Ames, *The Deadlock of Democracy in Brazil: Interests, Identities, and Institutions in Comparative Politics* (Ann Arbor: University of Michigan Press, 2001).

[45]Scott Mainwaring, "Brazilian Party Underdevelopment in Comparative Perspective," *Political Science Quarterly* 107 (1993).

[46]Timothy J. Power, "The Pen Is Mightier Than the Congress: Presidential Decree Power in Brazil," in John M. Carey and Mathew S. Shugart, eds., *Executive Decree Authority: Calling Out the Tanks or Just Filling Out the Forms* (New York: Cambridge University Press, 1998).

[47]See Argelina C. Figueiredo and Fernando Limongi, "Presidential Power, Legislative Organization, and Party Behavior in Brazil," *Comparative Politics* 32 (January 2000): 151–170.

[48]See Ames, *Deadlock of Democracy*.

[49]See Power, *The Political Right in Postauthoritarian Brazil*.

[50]See especially Gilberto Freyre, *The Mansions and the Shanties: The Making of Modern Brazil* (New York: Knopf, 1963), chap. 12.

[51]Ralph Della Cava, "The 'People's Church,' the Vatican, and Abertura," in Stepan, *Democratizing Brazil*.

[52]Turner, "Brazil: Indigenous Rights vs. Neoliberalism," 67.

[53]William H. Fisher, "Megadevelopment, Environmentalism, and Resistance: The Institutional Context of Kayapó Indigenous Politics in Central Brazil," *Human Organization* 53, no. 3 (1994), 220–232.

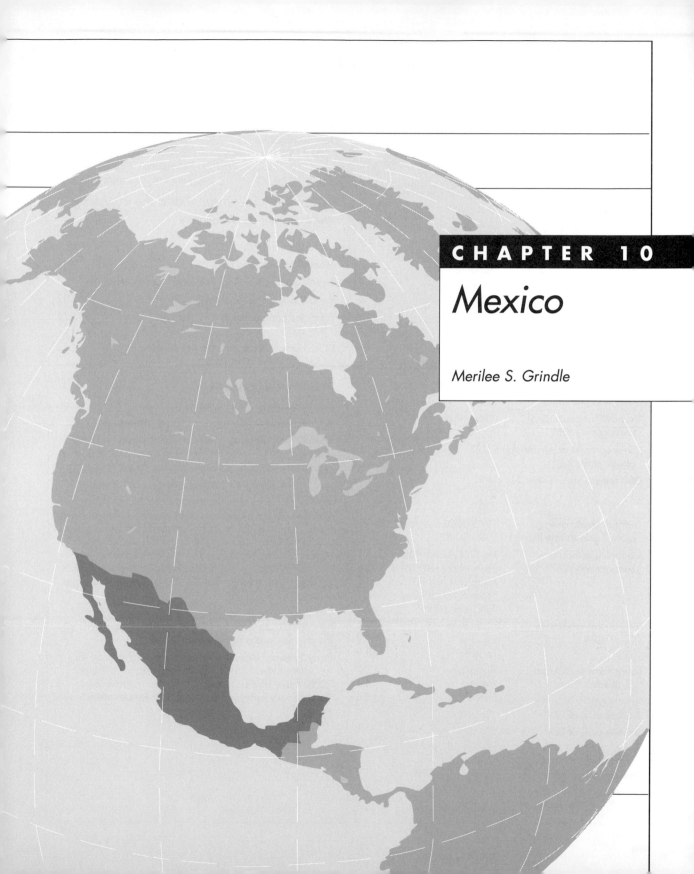

CHAPTER 10

Mexico

Merilee S. Grindle

United Mexican States

Land and People

Capital	Mexico City
Total area (square miles)	756,066 (about 3 times the size of Texas)
Population	98.6 million

Annual population growth rate (%)	1975–2000	2.1
	2000–2015 (projected)	1.2

Urban population (%)	74.4

Major language(s) (%)	Spanish	94.1
	Mayan, Nahuatl, and other indigenous languages	5.9

Religious affiliation (%)	Roman Catholic	89
	Protestant	6
	Other	5

Economy

Domestic currency	Peso (MXN) US$1: 9.66 MXN (2002 av.)
Total GDP (US$)	574.5 billion
GDP per capita (US$)	5,805
Total GDP at purchasing) power parity (US$	884.0 billion
GDP per capita at purchasing power parity (US$)	9,023

GDP annual growth rate (%)	1997	6.8
	2000	6.6
	2001	–0.3

GDP per capita average annual growth rate (%)	1975–2000	0.9
	1990–2000	1.4

Inequality in income or consumption (1995) (%)	Share of poorest 10%	1.4
	Share of poorest 20%	3.6
	Share of richest 20%	58.2
	Share of richest 10%	42.8
	Gini Index (1995)	53.7

Structure of production (% of GDP)	Agriculture	4.1
	Industry	27.9
	Services	68.0

Labor force distribution (% of total)	Agriculture	20
	Industry	24
	Services	56

Exports as % of GDP	31
Imports as % of GDP	33

Society

Life expectancy at birth	72.6
Infant mortality per 1,000 live births	25

Adult literacy (%)	Male	93.4
	Female	89.5

Access to information and communications (per 1,000 population)	Telephone lines	125
	Mobile phones	142
	Radios	320
	Televisions	283
	Personal computers	50.6

Women in Government and the Economy

Women in the national legislature		
Lower house or single house (%)		16.0
Upper house (%)		15.6

Women at ministerial level (%)		10.1
Female economic activity rate (age 15 and above) (%)		50
Female labor force (% of total)		32

Estimated earned income (PPP US$)	Female	4,978
	Male	13,152

2002 Human Development Index Ranking (out of 173 countries)	54

Political Organization

Political System   Federal republic.

Regime History   Current form of government since 1917.

Administrative Structure   Federal with 31 states and a federal district.

Executive   President, elected by direct election with a six-year term of office; reelection not permitted.

Legislature   Bicameral Congress. Senate (upper house) and Chamber of Deputies (lower house) elections held every three years. There are 128 senators, 3 from each of the 31 states, 3 from the federal (capital) district, and 32 elected nationally by proportional representation. The 500 members of the Chamber of Deputies are elected from 300 electoral districts, 300 by simple majority vote and 200 by proportional representation.

Judiciary   Independent federal and state court system headed by a Supreme Court with 11 justices appointed by the president and approved by the Senate.

Party System   Multiparty system. One-party dominant (Institutional Revolutionary Party) system from 1929 until 2000. Major parties: National Action Party, Institutional Revolutionary Party, and the Democratic Revolutionary Party.

Section ❶ The Making of the Modern Mexican State

Politics in Action

On December 1, 2000, Vicente Fox Quesada became president of Mexico. Although most of the inauguration ceremony followed long-established tradition for the transfer of power from one administration to the next, the event was historic. For the first time in seventy-one years, the president of Mexico did not represent the Institutional Revolutionary Party (PRI, pronounced "pree"), which had governed the country without interruption since 1929. Fox assumed the presidency under the banner of the National Action Party (PAN, pronounced "pahn"), a center-right party that had long opposed the PRI. He won the election largely because the old civil-authoritarian system could no longer ensure political stability, economic progress, and responsiveness to the demands of a society that was increasingly characterized by inequality.

The inauguration of Fox signaled a new stage in Mexico's quest for democracy. Under the PRI, political conflict had been largely limited to internal struggles within the party, and those who questioned its monopoly of power were usually co-opted into quiescence with promises and benefits or quietly but effectively repressed. The regime was sometimes called "the perfect dictatorship." For several decades, this system produced political stability and economic growth. Yet, increasingly during the 1980s and 1990s, Mexicans began to question the right of the PRI to monopolize political power. They organized to press for fairer elections and more responsive public officials. They demanded the right of opposition parties to compete for power on an equal basis with the PRI. They argued that the president had too much power and that the PRI was riddled with corruption. By 2000, a significant number of the country's 100 million citizens wanted political change.

Mexicans from every walk of life watched Fox's inauguration with trepidation. Just six years before, in 1994, despite widespread disillusionment with the political system, PRI candidate Ernesto Zedillo had easily won the presidency. At that time, many voters feared that political change might bring violence and instability more than they feared politics as usual under the continuation of a PRI government. And having spent all their lives under the PRI, some citizens remembered the party's triumphs of decades past and supported it. By 2000, however, a majority of the voters had had enough. Yet it was natural that they should be concerned about what government under the PAN would bring. Along with trepidations about change, many were expecting a great deal from the new government—more open political debate, more open government, more capacity to influence public policies, more economic growth, improved public services. President Fox had his job cut out for him.

In the two decades leading up to this historic change of administrations, the government had introduced major policy changes that affected virtually every aspect of the country's economy. Reformers of the 1980s and 1990s wanted Mexico to have a market-oriented economic system to replace one in which the state played a major role in guiding the process of development. They wanted to see the country's industry and agriculture thrive in a competitive global market. However, the new policies, together with a series of economic crises, affected many people adversely. Incomes fell, businesses went bankrupt, jobs were lost, and government services were cut back. Inequalities grew, and many blamed free-market policies and globalization for the plight of the country's poor and dispossessed. Despite growing disillusion with the reforms, the Fox government was committed to maintaining them and to seeking greater integration into the global marketplace.

Today, Mexicans are proud that their country has demonstrated its ability to move toward more democratic politics. Yet political and economic dissatisfaction continues to characterize the country. Regime change did not bring much evidence of improved capacity to respond to the needs of many. For elites, the opportunities of globalization have provided unprecedented wealth and cosmopolitan lifestyles. Yet indicators of increased poverty are everywhere. At least four of every ten Mexicans live on less than two dollars a day. The public education and health systems struggle with minimal resources to meet overwhelming demand. In the countryside, the peasant population faces destitution. Indigenous groups challenge government to end historical injustices and show respect for their cultures. In urban areas, the poor are forced to find meager sources of income however they can.

Thus, the advent of the Fox administration drew attention to ongoing and interrelated challenges of Mexico's development:

- Would a country with a long tradition of authoritarian government be able to sustain a democratic political system in the face of increasing demands and high expectations?
- Would a country that had long sought economic development through government activism and the domestic market be able to compete effectively in a competitive and market-driven global economy?
- Would a country long noted for severe inequalities between the rich and the poor be capable of providing better living standards for its growing population?

Geographic Setting

Mexico is one of the most geographically diverse countries in the world, encompassing snow-capped volcanoes, coastal plains, high plateaus, fertile valleys, rain forests, and deserts within an area slightly less than three times the size of Texas. To the north, it shares a 2,000-mile-long border with the United States, to the south, a 600-mile-long border with Guatemala and a 160-mile-long border with Belize. Two imposing mountain ranges run the length of Mexico: the Sierra Madre Occidental to the west and the Sierra Madre Oriental to the east. As a result, the country is noted for peaks, plateaus, and valleys that produce an astonishing number of microclimates and a rich diversity of plants and animals. Mexico's varied geography has historically made communication and transportation between regions difficult and infrastructure expensive. The mountainous areas tend to limit large-scale commercial agriculture to irrigated fields in the northern part of the country, while the central and southern regions produce a wide variety of crops on small farms. Soil erosion and desertification are major problems because of the steep terrain and unpredictable rainfall in many areas. The country is rich in oil, silver, and other natural resources but has long struggled to manage those resources wisely.

The human landscape is equally dramatic. With some 100 million inhabitants, Mexico is among the world's ten most populated countries—the second-largest nation in Latin America after Portuguese-speaking Brazil and the largest Spanish-speaking nation in the world. Sixty percent of the population is *mestizo,* or people of mixed **Amerindian** and Spanish descent. About 30 percent of the population claims indigenous (Amerindian) descent, although only about 6 percent of population speaks an indigenous language rather than Spanish. The rest of the population is Caucasian or people with other backgrounds. The largest **indigenous groups** are the Maya in the south and the Náhuatl in the central regions, with well over 1 million speakers each. Other important groups like the Zapotec, Mixtec, Otomí, Purépecha, and the Tarahumara number in the tens of thousands. There are also dozens and perhaps hundreds of smaller linguistic and social groups throughout the country. Although Mexicans pride themselves on their Amerindian heritage, problems of racism and classism run deep, and there is a great deal of ambivalence about issues of "Indianness."

Mexico was transformed from a largely rural to a largely urban country in the second half of the twentieth century, with over 74 percent of the population now living in urban areas. Mexico City has become one of the world's largest cities, with about 20 million inhabitants.[1] Population growth has slowed to about 1.5 percent, but society continues to adjust to the baby boom of the 1970s and early 1980s as these fifteen to thirty year olds seek jobs and form families. Migration both within and beyond Mexico's borders has become a major issue. Greater economic opportunities in the industrial cities of the north lead many men and women to seek work there in the *maquiladoras,* or assembly industries. Border cities like Tijuana and Ciudad Juárez have experienced tremendous growth in the past twenty years. Many job seekers continue on to the United States, lured by a larger job market and higher wages. The problem repeats itself in reverse on Mexico's southern border, with many thousands of Central Americans looking for better prospects in Mexico and beyond.

Critical Junctures

Mexicans are deeply affected by the legacies of their collective past, including centuries of colonialism and decades of political instability that followed Spanish rule. The legacies of the distant past are still felt, but the most formative event in the country's modern history was the Revolution of 1910. Mexico experienced

Mexico

the first great social revolution of the twentieth century, a conflict that lasted for more than a decade and claimed the lives of as many as 2 million people. Some died in violent confrontations, but the majority lost their lives through the massive destruction, dislocation, and famine caused by the shifting and sporadic nature of the conflict. The revolution was fought by a variety of forces for a variety of reasons, which made the consolidation of power that followed as significant as the revolution itself. The institutions and symbols of the current political regime emerged from these complex conflicts.

Independence and Instability (1810–1876)

Spain ruled Mexico for three centuries, administering a vast economic, political, and religious empire in the interests of the imperial country, its kings, and its representatives in North America (see "Global Connec-

tion: Conquest or Encounter?"). Colonial policy was designed to extract wealth from New Spain and to limit the possibilities for Spaniards in the New World to benefit from agriculture, commerce, or industry without at the same time benefiting Spain. It was also designed to ensure commitment to the Roman Catholic religion and the subordination of the Amerindian population.

In 1810, a parish priest in central Mexico named Miguel Hidalgo issued a rallying cry to a group assembled in a church in the town of Dolores. He called for an end to Spanish misrule. At the head of a motley band of rebels, he began the first of a series of wars of independence that pitted rebels against the Spanish Crown for eleven years. Although independence was gained in 1821, Mexico struggled to create a stable and legitimate government for decades after. Liberals and conservatives, federalists and centralists, those who sought to expand the power of the church and those

---

Critical Junctures in Mexico's Political Development

1810–1821 War of independence from Spain.

1876–1911 Dictatorship of Porfirio Díaz.

1910–1921 Mexican Revolution.

　　1917 Mexican Constitution.

　　1929 Plutarco Elías Calles founds PRI.

1934–1940 Presidency of Lázaro Cárdenas; entrenchment of corporatist state.

　　1968 Massacre of Tlaltelolco; 200 students killed.

1978–1982 State-led development reaches peak with petroleum boom and bust.

　　1982 Market reformers come to power in PRI.

　　1988 Carlos Salinas elected amid charges of fraud.

　　1989 First governorship won by an opposition party.

　　1994 NAFTA goes into effect; uprising in Chiapas; Colosio assassinated.

　　1996 Four largest political parties agree on electoral reform.

　　1997 Opposition parties advance nationwide; PRI loses absolute majority in congress for first time in its history.

　　2000 PRI loses presidency; Vicente Fox of PAN becomes president, but without majority support in congress.

---

who sought to curtail it, and those who wanted a republic and those who wanted a monarchy were all engaged in the battle for Mexico's soul during the nineteenth century. Between 1833 and 1855, thirty-six presidential administrations came to power.

Adding insult to injury during this disorganized period, Mexico lost half its territory to the United States. Its northern territory of Texas proclaimed and then won independence in a war ending in 1836. Then the Lone Star Republic was annexed to the United States by the U.S. Congress in 1845, and claims on Mexican territory north of the Rio Grande were increasingly heard from Washington. On the basis of a dubious claim that Mexico had invaded U.S. territory, the United States

declared war on its southern neighbor. The war was first fought along what was later to become the border between the two countries, and then, in 1847, the U.S. army invaded the port city of Veracruz. With considerable loss of civilian lives, U.S. forces marched toward Mexico City, where they engaged in the final battle of the war at Chapultepec Castle. An 1848 treaty gave the United States title to what later became the states of Texas, New Mexico, Utah, Nevada, Arizona, California, and part of Colorado for about $18 million, leaving a legacy of deep resentment toward the United States, the "Colossus of the North."

The loss of this war did not make it any easier to govern Mexico. Liberals and conservatives continued their struggle to resolve issues of political and economic order and, in particular, the power of the Catholic Church. The constitution of 1857 incorporated many of the goals of the liberals, such as republican government, a bill of rights, abolition of slavery, and limitations on the economic and political power of the church. The constitution did not guarantee stability, however. In 1861, Spain, Great Britain, and France occupied Veracruz to collect customs claims from the government, and the French army marched on Mexico City, subdued the weak government, and established the rule of Emperor Maximilian and Empress Carlota (1864–1867). Conservatives and Catholic loyalists welcomed this respite from the liberals. Benito Juárez, who occupied the presidency on three separate occasions, was back in office in 1867, spearheading reforms in economic, social, and political arenas, as well as building up the institutions of a new national government. He continues to be revered in Mexico as an early proponent of open and republican government.

The Porfiriato (1876–1911)

Over the next few years, a popular retired general named Porfirio Díaz became increasingly dissatisfied with what he thought was a "lot of politics" and "little action." After several failed attempts to win and then take the presidency, he finally succeeded in 1876. His dictatorship lasted thirty-four years and was at first welcomed by many because it brought sustained stability to the country.

Díaz imposed a highly centralized authoritarian

Global Connection: *Conquest or Encounter?*

The year 1519, when the Spanish conqueror Hernán Cortés arrived on the shores of the Yucatán Peninsula, is often considered the starting point of Mexican political history. But the Spanish explorers did not come to an uninhabited land waiting to be excavated for gold and silver. Instead, the land that was to become New Spain and then Mexico was home to extensive and complex indigenous civilizations that were advanced in agriculture, architecture, and political and economic organization—civilizations that were already over a thousand years old. The Mayans of the Yucatán and the Toltecs of the central highlands had reached high levels of development long before the arrival of the Europeans. By 1519, diverse groups had fallen under the power of the militaristic Aztec Empire, which extended throughout what is today central and southern Mexico.

The encounter between the Europeans and these indigenous civilizations was marked by bloodshed and violence. The great Aztec city of Tenochtitlán—the site of Mexico City today—was captured and largely destroyed by the Spanish conquerors in 1521. Cortés and the colonial masters who came after him subjected indigenous groups to forced labor, robbed them of gold, silver, and land, and introduced flora and fauna from Europe that destroyed long-existing aqueducts and irrigation systems. They also brought alien forms of property rights and authority relationships, a religion that viewed indigenous practices as the devil's work, and an economy based on mining and cattle—all of which soon overwhelmed existing structures of social and economic organization. Within a century, wars, savage exploitation at the hands of the Spaniards, and the introduction of European diseases reduced the indigenous population from an estimated 25 million to 1 million or fewer. The Indian population took three hundred years just to stop decreasing after the disaster of the conquest.

Even so, the Spanish never constituted more than a small percentage of the total population, and massive racial mixing between the Indians, Europeans, and to a lesser extent Africans produced a new *raza*, or *mestizo* race. This unique process remains at once a source of pride and conflict for Mexicans today. What does it mean to be Mexican? Is one the conquered or the conqueror? While celebrating Amerindian achievements in food, culture, the arts, and ancient civilization, middle-class Mexico has the contradictory sense that to be "Indian" nowadays is to be backward. Many Amerindians are stigmatized by mainstream society if they speak a native dialect. But perhaps the situation is changing, with the upsurge of indigenous movements from both the grass roots and the international level striving to promote ethnic pride, defend rights, and foster the teaching of Indian languages.

The collision of two worlds resonates in current national philosophical and political debates. Is Mexico a Western society? Is it colonial or modern? Third or First World? South or North? Is the United States an ally or a conqueror? Perhaps most important, many Mexicans at once welcome and fear full integration into the global economy, asking themselves: Is globalization the new conquest?

---

system to create political order and economic progress. In time, he relied increasingly on a small clique of advisers, known as *científicos* (scientists), who wanted to adopt European technologies and values to modernize the country, forcefully if necessary. Deeply disdainful of the vast majority of the country's population, Díaz and the *científicos* encouraged foreign investment and amassed huge fortunes, which they used to support lavish lifestyles and copy the latest European styles. During this period, known as the Porfiriato, this small elite group monopolized political power and reserved lucrative economic investments for itself and its allies. Economic and political opportunities were closed off for new generations of middle- and upper-class Mexicans, who became increasingly sensitive to the greed of the Porfirians and their own lack of opportunities.

The Revolution of 1910 and the Sonoran Dynasty (1910–1934)

In 1910, conflict broke out as reformers sought to end the dictatorship. Díaz had pledged himself to an open election for president, and in 1910, Francisco I. Madero, a landowner from the northern state of Coahuila, presented himself as a candidate. The slogan "Effective Suffrage, No Reelection" summed up the reformers' goals in creating opportunities for a new class of politically ambitious citizens to move into positions of power. When this opposition swelled, Díaz cancelled the election and tried to repress growing dissent. But it was too late. The clamor for change forced Díaz into exile. Madero was elected in 1911, but he was soon using the military to put down revolts from reformers and reactionaries alike. When Madero was assassinated, political order in the country virtually collapsed.

At the same time that middle-class reformers struggled to displace Díaz, a peasant revolt that focused on land claims erupted in the central and southern states of the country. This revolt had roots in legislation that made it easy for wealthy landowners and ranchers to claim the lands of peasant villagers. Encouraged by the weakening of the old regime and driven to desperation by increasing landlessness, villagers armed themselves and joined forces under a variety of local leaders. The most famous of these was Emiliano Zapata, who amassed a peasant army from Morelos, a state in southern Mexico. Peasant battalions swept through the countryside and grew in numbers; women as well as men flocked to fight under Zapata and other revolutionary leaders. Zapata's Plan de Ayala, first announced in 1911 and agreed to at a national meeting of revolutionary leaders in 1915, became the cornerstone of the radical agrarian reform that would be incorporated into the Constitution of 1917.

In the northern part of the country, Francisco (Pancho) Villa rallied his own army of workers, small farmers, and ranch hands. He presented a major challenge to the national army, now under the leadership of Venustiano Carranza, who had inherited Madero's middle-class reformist movement and eventually became president. Villa's forces recognized no law but that of their chief and combined military maneuvers with banditry, looting, and warlordism in the territories under their control. In 1916, troops from the United States entered Mexico to punish Villa for an attack on U.S. territory. Although this military operation was badly planned and poorly executed and Villa was never located by the U.S. forces, Mexican hostility toward the United States, already running high because of an invasion of Veracruz in 1914, increased.

The Constitution of 1917 was forged out of this diverse and often conflicting set of interests. It established a formal set of political institutions and guaranteed a range of progressive social and economic rights to citizens: agrarian reform, social security, the right to organize in unions, a minimum wage, an eight-hour workday, profit sharing for workers, universal secular education, and adult male suffrage. Despite these socially advanced provisions, the constitution did not provide suffrage for women, who had to wait until 1953 to vote in local elections and 1958 to vote in national elections. In an effort to limit the power of foreign investors, the constitution declared that only Mexican citizens or the government could own land or rights to water and other natural resources. It also contained numerous articles that severely limited the power of the Roman Catholic Church, long a target of liberals who wanted Mexico to be a secular state. The signing of the docu-

In 1914, Pancho Villa (right) met with Emiliano Zapata in Mexico City to discuss the revolution and their separate goals for its outcome. *Source:* Robert Freck/Odyssey/Chicago.

ment signaled the formal end of the revolution and the intent of the contending parties to form a new political regime. Despite such noble sentiments, violence continued as competing leaders sought to assert power and displace their rivals. By 1920 a modicum of stability had emerged, but not before many of the revolutionary leaders—Zapata, Villa, and Presidents Carranza and Obregon—had been assassinated in struggles over power and policy. There were, however, occasional outbreaks of violence among local warlords during this decade.

Despite this violence, power was gradually consolidated in the hands of a group of revolutionary leaders from the north of the country. Known as the Sonoran Dynasty, after their home state of Sonora, these leaders were committed to a capitalist model of economic development. During the 1920s, they skillfully outmaneuvered those who wished to see a socialist economy rise from the ashes of civil war. Eventually, one of the Sonorans, Plutarco Elías Calles, emerged as the *jefe máximo*, or supreme leader. Elected president in 1924, Calles managed to select and dominate his presidential successors from 1929 to 1934. The consolidation of power under his control was accompanied by extreme **anticlericalism,** which eventually resulted in warfare between conservative leaders of the Catholic Church and their followers, and the government.

In 1929, Calles brought together many of the most powerful contenders for leadership, including many regional warlords, to create a political party. The bargain he offered was simple: contenders for power would accommodate each others' interests in the expectation that without political violence, the country would prosper and they would be able to reap the benefits of even greater power and economic spoils. They created a political party, whose name was changed in 1939 and again in 1946, to consolidate their power, and for the next seven decades, Calles's bargain was effective in ensuring nonviolent conflict resolution among elites and the uninterrupted rule of the PRI in national politics.

Although the revolution was complex and the interests contending for power in its aftermath were numerous, there were five clear results of this protracted conflict. First, the power of traditional rural landowners was undercut. In the years after the revolution, wealthy elites would again emerge in rural areas, but they would never again be so powerful in national politics or their power so unchecked in local areas. Second, the power of the Catholic Church was strongly curtailed. Although the church remained important in many parts of the country, it no longer participated openly in national political debates. Third, the power of foreign investors was severely limited; prior to the revolution, foreign investors owned much of the country's land as well as many of its railroads, mines, and factories. Henceforth, Mexican nationalism would shape economic policy-making. Fourth, a new political elite consolidated power and agreed to resolve conflicts through accommodation and bargaining rather than through violence. And fifth, the new constitution and the new party laid the basis for a strong central government that could assert its power over the agricultural, industrial, and social development of the country.

Lázaro Cárdenas, Agrarian Reform, and the Workers (1934–1940)

In 1934, Plutarco Calles handpicked Lázaro Cárdenas, a revolutionary general and state governor, as his successor to the presidency. He fully anticipated that Cárdenas would go along with Calles's behind-the-scenes management of the country and continue the economic policies of the postrevolutionary coalition. To his great surprise, Cárdenas executed a virtual coup that established his own supremacy and sent Calles packing to the United States for an "extended vacation."[2] Even more unexpectedly, Cárdenas mobilized peasants and workers in pursuit of the more radical goals of the 1910 revolution. He encouraged peasant syndicates to petition for land and claim rights promised in the Constitution of 1917. During his administration, more than 17 million hectares of land were distributed (1 hectare is 2.471 acres). Most of these lands were distributed in the form of *ejidos* (collective land grants) to peasant groups. *Ejidatarios* (those who acquired *ejido* lands) became one of the most enduring bases of support for the government. Cárdenas also encouraged workers to form unions and demand higher wages and better working conditions. He established his nationalist credentials in 1938 when he wrested the petroleum industry from U.S. and British investors and placed it under government control.

During the Cárdenas years (1934–1940), the bulk of the Mexican population was incorporated into the political system. Organizations of peasants, workers, middle-class groups, and the military were added to the party, and the voices of the poor majority were heard within the councils of government, reducing the risk that they would become radicalized outside them. In addition, the Cárdenas years witnessed a great expansion of the role of the state as the government encouraged investment in industrialization, provided credit to agriculture, and created infrastructure.

Lázaro Cárdenas continues to be a national hero to Mexicans, who look back on his presidency as a period when government was clearly committed to improving the welfare of the country's poor. His other legacy was to institutionalize patterns of political succession and presidential behavior that continue to set standards for Mexico's leaders. He campaigned extensively, and his campaign travel took him to remote villages and regions, where he listened to the demands and complaints of humble people. Cárdenas served a single six-year term, called a *sexenio,* and relinquished full political power to the new president, Manuel Avila Camacho. Cárdenas's conduct in office created hallowed traditions of presidential style and succession that all subsequent national leaders have observed.

The Politics of Rapid Development (1940–1982)

Although Cárdenas had directed a radical reshuffling of political power in the country, his successors were

able to use the institutions he created to counteract his reforms. Ambitious local and regional party leaders and leaders of peasants' and workers' groups began to use their organizations as pawns in exchange for political favors. Gradually, the PRI developed a huge patronage machine, providing union and *ejido* leaders with jobs, opportunities for corruption, land, and other benefits in return for delivering their followers' political support. Extensive chains of personal relationships based on the exchange of favors allowed the party to amass far-reaching political control and limit opportunities for organizing independent of the PRI. These exchange relationships, known as **clientelism,** became the cement that built loyalty to the PRI and the political system.

This kind of political control translated into the capacity of post-Cárdenas presidents to reorient the country's development away from the egalitarian social goals of the 1930s toward a development strategy in which the state actively encouraged industrialization and the accumulation of wealth. Initially, industrialization created jobs and made available a wide range of basic consumer goods to Mexico's burgeoning population. Growth rates were high during the 1940s, 1950s, and 1960s, and Mexicans flocked to the cities to take advantage of the jobs created in the manufacturing and construction industries. By the 1970s, however,

Mexican presidential candidates are expected to campaign hard, traveling to remote locations, making rousing campaign speeches, and meeting with citizens of humble origins. Here, presidential candidate Vicente Fox Quesada is on the campaign trail. *Source:* R. Kwiotek/Zeitenspiegel/Corbis/ Sygma.

industrial development policies were no longer generating rapid growth and could not keep pace with the rapidly rising demand for jobs.

The country's economy was in deep crisis by the mid-1970s. Just as policy-makers began to take actions to correct the problems, vast new amounts of oil were discovered in the Gulf of Mexico. Soon, rapid economic growth was refueled by extensive public investment programs in virtually every sector of the economy. Based on the promise of petroleum wealth, the government and private businesses borrowed huge amounts of capital from foreign lenders, who were eager to do business with a country that had so much oil. Unfortunately for Mexico, international petroleum prices plunged sharply in the early 1980s. Almost overnight, there was no more credit to be had and much less money from petroleum to pay for economic expansion or the interest on the debts incurred in preceding years. Mexico plunged into a deep economic crisis that affected many other countries around the world.

Crisis and Reform (1982 to the Present)

This economic crisis helped two presidents, Miguel de la Madrid (1982–1988) and Carlos Salinas (1988–1994), introduce the first major reversal of the country's development strategy since the 1940s. New policies were put in place to limit the government's role in the economy and to make it easier for Mexican producers to export their goods. This period clearly marked the beginning of a new effort to become more important in international economic affairs. In 1993, by signing the **North American Free Trade Agreement** (NAFTA), which committed Mexico, the United States, and Canada to eliminating trade barriers among them, Mexico's policy-makers signaled the extent to which they envisioned the future prosperity of their country to be tied to that of its two neighbors to the north. Efforts to increase trade and investment to Latin American, European, and Asian countries also emphasized Mexico's new commitment to competitiveness in a global economy.

The economic reforms of the 1980s and 1990s were a turning point for the country's development and meant that Mexico's future development would be closely tied to conditions in the international economy. A major economic crisis at the end of 1994, in which billions of dollars of foreign investment fled the country, was indicative of this new international vulnerability. The peso lost half of its value against the dollar within a few days, and the government lacked the funds to pay its obligations. Suddenly, Mexico's status among nations seemed dubious once more, and the country felt betrayed by outgoing President Salinas, convinced that he had patched together a shaky house of cards only long enough to get himself out of office. The economy shrank by 6.2 percent in 1995, inflation soared, taxes rose while wages were frozen, and the bank system collapsed. The United States orchestrated a $50 billion bailout, $20 billion of which came directly from the U.S. Treasury. Faced with limited options, the administration of Ernesto Zedillo (1994–2000) implemented a severe and unpopular economic austerity program, which restored financial stability over the next two years. The actions taken to meet that crisis helped shield Mexico from the impact of the Asian financial crisis of 1997 and 1998. It was also helped by its increasing interconnection with the United States, whose economy was growing during this period.

Economic crisis was exacerbated by political concerns. On January 1, 1994, a guerrilla movement, the Ejército Zapatista National Liberation Front (EZLN), seized four towns in the southern state of Chiapas. The group demanded land, democracy, indigenous rights, and an immediate repeal of NAFTA. Many citizens throughout the country openly supported the aims of the rebels, pointing out that the movement brought to light the reality of two different Mexicos: those who enjoyed the fruits of wealth and influence and those who were getting left behind because of poverty and repression. The government and the military were criticized for inaction and human rights abuses in the state (See "Citizen Action: Rebellion in Chiapas"). A second guerrilla movement, the Popular Revolutionary Army (EPR), also challenged the government. This movement was far more mysterious, less ideological, and more committed to violence than the Zapatistas. Considered terrorist by the government, it claimed to have operatives throughout the country and took responsibility for several destructive actions.

Following close on the heels of rebellion came the assassination of the PRI's presidential candidate, Luis Donaldo Colosio, on March 23, 1994, in the northern border city of Tijuana. The assassination shocked all

Citizen Action: *Rebellion in Chiapas*

In the months after January 1994, indigenous women set out daily for the tourist zones of central Mexico City to sell handmade dolls. These dolls, dressed in brightly colored costumes, also sported black ski masks. They represented a symbolic connection to the rebels of the Ejército Zapatista National Liberation Front (EZLN) in the southern state of Chiapas, who wore ski masks to avoid identification by the government. Images of the ideological leader and public spokesman of the Zapatista movement, Subcomandante Marcos, also appeared throughout the country, and people of diverse ethnic, class, and political backgrounds began expressing support for the goals of the rebels.

The rebellion by some 2,000 members of the EZLN broke out on January 1, 1994, the day that NAFTA went into effect. The Zapatista army captured four towns in the state of Chiapas, including the city of San Cristobal de las Casas, a popular tourist destination. The EZLN demanded "jobs, land, housing, food, health, education, independence, freedom, democracy, justice and peace."[1] The peasant army also called on the government to repeal NAFTA. These demands and the progress of the rebellion were immediately transmitted throughout Mexico and around the globe by domestic and international media as camera crews and reporters flocked to this remote, poverty-stricken state.

The EZLN's call for an end to exploitation at the hands of voracious landowners and corrupt bosses of the PRI, as well as for social services and citizenship rights, resonated deeply throughout the country. Soon, a broad spectrum of local, regional, professional, and human rights groups took up the banner of the Chiapas rebels and called on the government to open the political system to more just and democratic elections, decision-making processes, and policies. By calling in the army to suppress armed peasants, most of whom were Mayan Indians, and to retake the four towns by force, the government only increased sympathy for the marginalized, impoverished indigenous groups. The Chiapas rebellion symbolized for many the reality of Mexico's political, economic, and social inequalities.

The Zapatistas were not seeking to overthrow the Mexican political system. They believed, however, that the system created and maintained by the PRI had become very much like the dictatorship of Porfirio Díaz, toppled in the Revolution of 1910. They were united in their demand that indigenous groups throughout Mexico be granted fair treatment and the means to escape their poverty and powerlessness.

They resorted to violence because they believed the government would not otherwise pay attention to their demands.

The Zapatista rebellion presented a major challenge to Mexico's image of political stability. It had a profound effect on the election of 1994, as competing political parties and candidates sought to identify with rebel demands for indigenous rights, economic justice, and honest elections. The rebels rejected a peace treaty that would have promoted the electoral fortunes of the PRI, arguing instead for increased space for political debate and dialogue. The government spent over $200 million on social programs and infrastructure projects in the state in the months leading up to the election, a 44 percent increase over what had been budgeted. Just weeks before the elections, however, the EZLN hosted a National Democratic Convention of a large number of groups committed to pressuring the government for fundamental political reform. The rebels insisted that economic assistance alone would not solve the problems in the southern part of the country. They pointed to the deeper causes of injustice: concentration of wealth in the hands of a brutal local elite and monopolization of power by a government that valued stability and compromise with local elites above all else.

In the aftermath of the rebellion, Mexican officials sought to erase the impression that the insurgency was an Indian uprising. They pointed out that many indigenous groups rejected the EZLN. Yet major indigenous organizations across Mexico and elsewhere in Latin America expressed solidarity with the Chiapas rebels and the decision to take up arms. While some argued that the Chiapas rebellion was a local phenomenon and an isolated set of incidents, others predicted the spread of the Mexican example of armed uprisings by indigenous groups. The roots of such insurrections are in economic and social exploitation, they argued, not in specific ethnic identities. A stalemate continued: talks broke down, foreign observers were expelled, and accusations of human rights violations by the government were on the rise. President Fox attempted to resolve the impasse by granting greater autonomy to indigenous communities, but congress altered his proposal and the EZLN rejected it.

---

[1]As cited in Neil Harvey, *Rebellion in Chiapas: Rural Reforms, Campesino Radicalism, and the Limits to Salinismo* (San Diego: Center for U.S.-Mexican Studies, University of California, 1994), 1.

citizens and shook the political elite deeply. Not since 1923, when a military revolt threatened presidential elections, had there been such uncertainty about who would lead the government for the next six years. Not since 1928, when president-elect Alvaro Obregón was assassinated, had a politician bound for the highest office met with violent death. Not since 1929, when the PRI was founded, had there been such fear that the political elite was so divided that overt violence, not accommodation and compromise, might be used to resolve disputes. The murder opened wide rifts within the PRI and unleashed a flood of speculation and distrust among the citizenry. Many Mexicans were convinced that the assassination was part of a conspiracy of party "dinosaurs," political hard-liners who opposed any kind of democratic transformation.[3] Fear of violence helped provide the PRI with strong support in the August 1994 elections, although the secretary-general of the PRI, José Francisco Ruiz Massieu, was assassinated the following month. In 1996, Raúl Salinas, brother of the former president, was indicted on charges of masterminding the murder of Ruiz Massieu as well as illicit enrichment and money laundering.

These shocks provoked widespread disillusionment and frustration with the political system. Many citizens, especially in urban areas, decided that there was no longer any reason to support the PRI. Buoyed by a 1996 electoral reform, important gains were made by the opposition in the legislative elections. For the first time in modern Mexican history, the PRI lost its absolute majority in the Chamber of Deputies. Since then, the congress has shown increasing dynamism as a counterbalance to the presidency, blocking executive decisions, demanding unrestricted information, and initiating new legislation. In addition, opposition parties have won important governorships and mayorships. The election of Vicente Fox was the culmination of this electoral revolution.

Themes and Implications

Historical Junctures and Political Themes

The modern Mexican state emerged out of a popular revolution that proclaimed goals of democratic government, social justice, and nationalism. In the chaotic years after the revolution, the state created conditions for political and social peace. By incorporating peasants and workers into party and government institutions and providing benefits to low-income groups during the 1930s, it became widely accepted as legitimate. In encouraging considerable economic growth in the years after 1940, it also created belief in its ability to provide material improvements in the quality of life for large portions of the population. These factors worked together to create a strong state capable of guiding economic and political life in the country. Only in the 1980s did this system begin to crumble.

In its external relations, Mexico has always prided itself on ideological independence from the world's great powers. For many decades, its large population, cultural richness, political stability, and front-line position regarding the United States prompted Mexico to consider itself a natural leader of Latin America and the developing world in general. After the early 1980s, however, the government rejected this position in favor of rapid integration into a global economy. The country aspired to the status of newly industrialized countries of the world, such as South Korea, Malaysia, and Taiwan. While the reforms of the 1980s and 1990s, and especially NAFTA, have advanced this goal, many citizens are concerned that the government has accepted a position of political, cultural, and economic subordination to the United States.

Mexico enjoyed considerable economic advancement after the 1940s, but economic and political crises after 1980 shook confidence in its ability to achieve its economic goals and highlighted conflict between a market-oriented development strategy and the country's philosophical tradition of a strong and protective state. The larger questions of whether a new development strategy can generate growth, whether Mexican products can find profitable markets overseas, whether investors can create extensive job opportunities for millions of unemployed and part-time workers, and whether the country can maintain the confidence of those investors over the longer term continue to challenge the country.

Politically, after the Revolution of 1910, the country opted not for true democracy but for representation through government-mediated organizations within a **corporatist state,** in which interest groups became an institutionalized part of state structure. This increased state power in relation to civil society. The state took the lead in defining goals for the country's development and, through the school system, the party, and the media, inculcated a broad sense of its legitimate right to set such goals. In addition, the state had extensive resources at its disposal to control or co-opt dissent and purchase political loyalty. The PRI was an essential channel through which material goods, jobs, the distribution of land, and the allocation of development projects flowed to increase popular support for the system or to buy off opposition to it.

This does not mean that Mexican society was unorganized or passive. Indeed, many Mexicans were actively involved in local community organizations, religious activities, unions, and public interest groups. But traditionally, the scope for challenging the government, insisting on basic civil rights, or demanding an open and responsive government was very limited. At the same time, Mexico's strong state did not become openly repressive except when directly challenged. On the contrary, officials in the government and the party generally worked hard to find ways to resolve conflicts peacefully and to use behind-the-scenes accommodation to bring conflicting interests into accord. In this conflict resolution system, the power of the PRI could not be successfully challenged, and the emergence of an effective democracy was curtailed for decades.

By the 1980s, cracks began to appear in the traditional ways in which Mexican citizens interacted with the government. As the PRI began to lose its capacity to control political activities and civic groups increasingly insisted on their right to remain independent from the PRI and the government, the terms of the state-society relationship were clearly in need of redefinition. Ethnic groups, religious organizations, community movements, private business, and regionalism all emerged to pressure government to be more responsive, fair, democratic, and effective. The administration of President Zedillo signaled its willingness to cede political power to successful opposition parties in fair elections, and electoral reform in 1996 and elections in 1997 were significant steps that led to the defeat of the PRI in 2000. Mexico's future stability depends on how well a more democratic government can accommodate conflicting interests while at the

same time providing economic opportunities to a largely poor population.

Implications for Comparative Politics

The Mexican political system is unique among developing countries in the extent to which it managed to institutionalize and maintain civilian political authority for a very long time. In a world of developing nations wracked by political turmoil, military coups, and regime changes, the PRI regime established enduring institutions of governance and conditions for political stability. Other countries have sought to emulate the Mexican model of stability based on an alliance between a dominant party and a strong development-oriented state, but no other government has been able to create a system that had widespread legitimacy for so long. The regime's revolutionary heritage, as well as its ability to maintain a sense of national identity, were important factors in accounting for its political continuity.

Currently, Mexico represents a nation undergoing significant political change without widespread violence, transforming itself from a corporatist state to a democratic one for the first time in its long history. At the same time, it struggles to resolve the conflicts of development through integration with its North American neighbors. Mexico has been categorized as a middle-income developing country, and its per capita income is comparable to countries such as Estonia, Malaysia, Poland, South Africa, and Uruguay.[4] It has made significant strides in industrialization, which accounts for about 28.4 percent of the country's gross domestic product (GDP). Agriculture contributes about 4.4 percent to GDP, and services contribute some 67.3 percent.[5] This structure is very similar to the economic profiles of Argentina, Brazil, Poland, and Hungary. But unlike those countries, Mexico is oil rich. The government-owned petroleum industry is a ready source of revenue and foreign exchange, but this commodity also makes the economy extremely vulnerable to changes in international oil prices.

Mexico's industrial and petroleum-based economy means a higher per capita income than in most other developing countries. If income were spread evenly among all Mexicans, each would receive $4,400 annually—far more than the per capita incomes of India ($450),

China ($780), and Nigeria ($310) but considerably less than those of Britain ($22,640), France ($23,480), and Germany ($25,350).[6] Of course, income is not spread evenly. Mexico suffers from great inequalities in how wealth is distributed, and poverty continues to be a grim reality for millions of Mexicans. The way the country promoted economic growth and industrialization is important in explaining why widespread poverty has persisted and why political power is not more equitably distributed.

Section ❷ Political Economy and Development

State and Economy

During the years of the Porfiriato (1876–1911), Mexico began to produce some textiles, footwear, glassware, paper, beer, tiles, furniture, and other simple products. At that time, however, policy-makers were convinced that Mexico could grow rich by exporting its raw materials to more economically advanced countries. Their efforts to attract domestic and international investment encouraged a major boom in the production and export of products such as henequin (for making rope), coffee, cacao (cocoa beans), cattle, silver, and gold. Soon, the country had become so attractive to foreign investors that large amounts of land, the country's petroleum, its railroad network, and its mining wealth were largely controlled by foreigners. Nationalist reaction against the power of these foreign interests played a significant role in the tensions that produced the Revolution of 1910.

In the postrevolutionary Mexican state, this nationalism combined with a sense of social justice inspired by popular revolutionary leaders such as Zapata. Mexicans widely shared the idea that the state had the responsibility to generate wealth for all its citizens. In addition, it was thought that only the state was powerful enough to mobilize the resources and stimulate the development necessary to overcome the destruction of the revolution. As a result, the country adopted a strategy in which the government guided the process of industrial and agricultural development and set the political conditions for its success.

Often referred to as **state capitalism,** this development strategy relied heavily on government actions to encourage private investment and lower risks for private entrepreneurs. In the twenty years following the revolution, many of those concerned about the country's development became convinced that economic growth would not occur unless Mexico could industrialize more fully. They argued that reliance on exports of agricultural products, minerals, and petroleum—called the agro-export model of development—forced the country to import manufactured goods, which, over the long term, would always cost more than what was earned from exports. Critics of the agro-export model also argued that prices of primary products shifted greatly from one year to the next. Countries that produced them were doomed to repeat boom-and-bust cycles as their domestic economies reflected sharp fluctuations in international prices for the goods they exported. Mexico, they believed, should begin to manufacture the goods that it was currently importing.

Import Substitution and Its Consequences

Between 1940 and 1982, Mexico pursued a form of state capitalism and a model of industrialization known as import substitution, or **import substituting industrialization** (ISI). Like Brazil and other Latin American countries during the same period, the government promoted the development of industries to supply the domestic market by encouraging domestic and international investment, providing credit and tax incentives to industrialists, maintaining low rates of inflation, and keeping wage demands low through subsidized food, transportation, housing, and health care for workers. It also fostered industrialization by establishing state-owned steel mills, electric power generators, ports, and petroleum production and by using tariffs and import licenses to protect Mexican industries from foreign competition. Between 1940 and 1970, over 40 percent of all fixed capital investment came from the government. These policies had considerable success. Initially, the country produced mainly simple products like shoes, clothing, and processed foods. But by the 1960s and 1970s, it was also producing consumer durables (refrigerators, automobiles, trucks), intermediate goods (steel, petrochemicals, and other products used in the manufacturing process), and capital goods (heavy machinery to produce manufactures).

Mexican agriculture was also affected by this drive to industrialize. With the massive agrarian reform of the 1930s (see Section 1), the *ejido* had become an important structure in the rural economy, accounting for half the cultivated area of the country and 51 percent of the value of agricultural production by 1940. After President Cárdenas left office, however, government policy-makers moved rapidly away from the economic development of the *ejidos*. They became committed instead to developing a strong, entrepreneurial private sector in agriculture. For them, "the development of private agriculture would be the 'foundation of industrial greatness.'"[7] They wanted this sector to provide foodstuffs for the growing cities, raw materials for industry, and foreign exchange from exports. To encourage these goals, the government invested in transportation networks, irrigation projects, and agricultural storage facilities. It provided extension services and invested in research. It encouraged imports of technology to improve output and mechanize production. Since policy-makers believed that modern commercial farmers would respond more to these investments and services than would peasants on small plots of land, the government provided most of its assistance to large landowners.

The government's encouragement of industry and agriculture set the country on a three-decade path of sustained growth. Between 1940 and 1950, GDP grew at an annual average of 6.7 percent, while manufacturing increased at an average of 8.1 percent. In the following two decades, GDP growth rates remained impressive, and manufacturing growth continued to outpace overall growth in the economy. In the 1950s, manufacturing achieved an average of 7.3 percent growth annually and in the 1960s, 10.1 percent annually. Agricultural production grew rapidly as new areas were brought under cultivation and green revolution technology (scientifically improved seeds, fertilizers, and pesticides) was extensively adopted on large farms. These were years of great optimism as foreign investment increased,

the middle class grew larger, and indicators for health and welfare steadily improved. Between 1940 and 1970, Mexico City grew from a modest-sized city of 1.5 million people to a major metropolis of over 8 million inhabitants. Even the poorest Mexicans believed that their lives were improving. Table 1 presents data that summarize a number of advancements during this period. So impressive was Mexico's economic performance that it was referred to internationally as the Mexican Miracle.

U.S. private investment was an important source of capital for the country's effort to industrialize. In the twenty years after 1950, it grew at an average of over 11 percent a year. In 1962, the United States accounted for 85 percent of all foreign investment in Mexico. Moreover, two-thirds of Mexico's imports typically came from the United States, while it regularly sent two-thirds of its exports there. Mexican policy-makers increasingly saw the closeness and size of the U.S. economy as a significant threat, and many policy initiatives—restricting foreign investment in industries considered important to national development and seeking to diversify trade relationships with other countries, for example—were undertaken to lessen the country's dependence on the United States.

While the government took the lead in encouraging industrialization, it was not long before a group of domestic entrepreneurs developed a special relationship with the state. Government policies protected their products through high tariffs or special licensing requirements, limiting imports of competing goods. Business elites in Mexico received subsidized credit to invest in equipment and plants; they benefited from cheap, subsidized energy; and they rarely had to pay taxes. Additionally, inflation was kept in check, and the government helped ensure a supply of cheap labor by providing workers' housing, transportation, and medical coverage and ensuring that low cost staple foods were available in urban areas.

Through the impact of such policies, an elite of protected businesses emerged as powerful players in national politics. In the 1940s and 1950s, they strengthened a set of industry-related interest groups that worked to promote and sustain favorable policies. With this organizational base, groups like the chambers of industry, commerce, and banking began to play increasingly important roles in government policy-making. They

Table 1

Mexican Development, 1940–2000

	1940	1950	1960	1970	1980	1990	2000[a]
Population (thousands)	19,815	26,282	38,020	52,771	70,416	88,598	96,585
Life expectancy (years)[b]	—	51.6	58.6	62.6	67.4	68.9	71.35
Infant mortality (per 1,000 live births)[b]	—	—	86.3	70.9	49.9	42.6	32.6
Illiteracy (% of population age 15 and over)	—	42.5	34.5	25.0	16.0	12.7	8.9
Urban population (% of total)	—	—	50.7	59.0	66.4	72.6	74.2
Economically active population in agriculture (% of total)	—	58.3	55.1	44.0	36.6	22.0	21.0

	1940–1950	1950–1960	1960–1970	1970–1980	1980–1990	1990–2000	
GDP growth rate (average annual percent)	6.7	5.8	7.6	6.7	1.6	3.3	
Per capita GDP growth rate	—	—	3.7	3.7	–0.7	1.0[c]	

[a]Except where noted, 2000 indicators are from *World Development Indicators 2002*.

[b]Five-year average.

[c]*Human Development Report 2001*. New York: Oxford University Press, 2001.

Sources: Statistical Abstract for Latin America (New York: United Nations, Economic Commission for Latin America, various years; Roger Hansen, *The Politics of Mexican Development* (Baltimore, Md.: Johns Hopkins University Press, 1971); *Statistical Bulletin of the OAS*. For 2000: *World Development Indicators 2002*, CD-ROM, and *Human Development Report 2001*, www.undp.org/hdr2001/.

were able to veto efforts by the government to cut back on their benefits and lobby for even more advantages. The government remained the source of most policy initiatives, but generally it was not able to move far in the face of opposition from those who benefited most from its policies. Perhaps just as important, business elites became adept at sidestepping government regulations; paying bribes to acquire licenses, credit, permits, and exemptions; and working out individual deals with officials.

Workers also became more important players in national politics. As mentioned in Section 1, widespread unionization occurred under President Cárdenas, and workers won many rights that had been promised in the Constitution of 1917. Cárdenas organized the unions into the National Confederation of Workers (CTM), which became the most powerful official voice of organized labor within the PRI. The policy changes

initiated in the 1940s, however, made the unions more dependent on the government for benefits and protection; the government also limited the right to strike. Wage standards were set through active annual negotiation between the CTM and the government, with employer groups largely sitting on the sidelines. Despite the fact that unions were closely controlled, organized workers continued to be an elite within the country's working classes. Union membership meant job security and important benefits such as housing subsidies and health care. These factors helped compensate for the lack of democracy within the labor movement. Moreover, labor leaders had privileged access to the country's political leadership and benefited personally from their control over jobs, contracts, and working conditions. In return, they guaranteed labor peace.[8]

In agriculture, those who benefited from government policies and services were primarily farmers who had enough land and economic resources to irrigate and mechanize and the capacity to make technological improvements in their farming methods and crops. By the 1950s, a group of large, commercially oriented farmers had emerged to dominate the agricultural economy.[9] They, like their urban counterparts in business, became rich and powerful. Industrialization also created a powerful class of government officials. Many abused their power to dispense jobs, licenses, and permits for a variety of activities, public works projects, and government investments by selling such favors in return for *mordidas* (bites, or bribes) or political support. They also became firm supporters of the continuation of government policies that provided them with special advantages.

There were significant costs to this pattern of economic and political development. Most important, government policies eventually limited the potential for further growth.[10] Industrialists who received extensive subsidies and benefits from government had few incentives to produce efficiently. High tariffs kept out foreign competition, further reducing reasons for efficiency or quality in production. Importing technology to support industrialization eventually became a drain on the country's foreign exchange. In addition, the costs of providing benefits to workers increased beyond the capacity of the government to generate revenue, especially because tax rates were kept low as a further incentive to investors. Mexico's tax rates, in fact, were among the lowest in the world, and opportunities to avoid payment were extensive. Eventually, the ISI strategy became less effective in generating new jobs as industrialists moved from investing in labor-intensive industries such as processed foods and textiles to capital-intensive industries such as automobiles, refrigerators, and heavy equipment.

But as the economy grew, and with it the power of industrial, agricultural, and urban interests, many were left behind. The ranks of the urban poor grew steadily, particularly from the 1960s on. Mexico developed a sizable **informal sector**—workers who produced and sold goods and services at the margin of the economic system and faced extreme insecurity. By 1970, a large proportion of Mexico City's population was living in inner-city tenements or squatter settlements surrounding the city.[11]

Also left behind in the country's development after 1940 were peasant farmers. Their lands were often the least fertile, plot sizes were minuscule, and access to markets was impeded by poor transportation and exploitive middlemen who trucked products to markets for exorbitant fees. The 1940s and 1950s were important years for increasing the gap between commercial agriculture, largely centered in the north and northwestern regions of the country, where much of Mexico's political elite originated, and subsistence agriculture, largely made up of small private farmers and *ejidatarios* who lived in central and southern parts of the country. Farming in the *ejido* communities, where land was held communally, was particularly difficult. Because *ejido* land could not be sold or (until the early 1980s) rented, *ejidatarios* could not borrow money from private banks because they had nothing to pledge as collateral if they defaulted on their payments. Government banks provided credit, but usually only to those who had political connections. The government invested little in small infrastructure projects throughout the 1960s, and agricultural research and extension focused on the large-farm sector. Moreover, because prices for basic foodstuffs were controlled, the *ejidatarios* saw little advantage to investing in farming. Not surprisingly, the *ejido* sector consistently reported low productivity.

Increasing disparities in rural and urban incomes, coupled with high population growth rates, contributed to the emergence of rural guerrilla movements and student protests in the mid- and late 1960s. The government was particularly alarmed in 1968, when a student movement openly challenged the government on the eve of the Olympic Games being hosted in Mexico City. Moreover, by the early 1970s, it was becoming evident that the size of the population, growing at a rate of some 3.5 percent a year, and the structure of income distribution were impeding further industrial development. The domestic market was limited by poverty; many Mexicans could not afford the sophisticated manufactured products the country would need to produce in order to keep growing under the import substitution model.

The Mexican government had hoped that industrialization would free the economy from excessive dependence on the industrialized world, and particularly on the United States, making the country less subject to abrupt swings in prices for primary commodities.

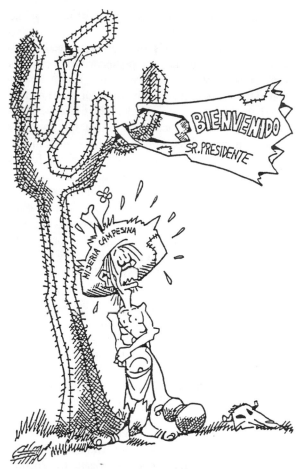

A farmer with a hat labeled "rural misery" hangs his shirt on a cactus: "Welcome, Mr. President." Among those who have benefited least from the government's development policies are the rural poor. *Source: Ausencias y Presencias Gente de Ayer y Hoy en su Tinta: Problematica Politica, Social, Vista por un Cartoonista Potosino by Luis Chessal, Unversidad Autonoma de San Luis Potosi, Mexico, 1984.*

Industrialization, however, highlighted new vulnerabilities. Advanced manufacturing processes required ever more foreign investment and imported technology. Concern grew about powerful multinational companies, which had invested heavily in the country in the 1960s and about purchasing foreign technology with scarce foreign exchange. By the late 1960s, the country was no longer able to meet domestic demand for basic foodstuffs and was forced to import increas-ingly large quantities of food, costing the government foreign exchange that it could have used for better purposes. By the 1970s, some policy-makers had become convinced that industrialization had actually increased the country's dependence on advanced industrial countries and particularly on the United States.

Sowing the Oil and Reaping a Crisis

In the early 1970s, Mexico faced the threat of social crisis brought on by rural poverty, chaotic urbanization, high population growth, and the questioning of political legitimacy. The government responded by increasing investment in infrastructure and public industries, regulating the flow of foreign capital, and increasing social spending. It was spending much more than it generated, causing the public internal debt to grow rapidly and requiring heavy borrowing abroad. Between 1971 and 1976, inflation rose from an annual average of 5.3 percent to almost 16 percent, and the foreign debt more than tripled. In response to mounting evidence that current policies could not be sustained, the government devalued the peso in 1976 and signed a stabilization agreement with the International Monetary Fund (IMF) to reduce government spending, increase tax collection, and control inflation. Little progress was made in changing existing policies, however, because just as the seriousness of the economic situation was being recognized, vast new finds of oil came to the rescue.

Between 1978 and 1982, Mexico was transformed into a major oil exporter. As international oil prices rose rapidly, from $13.30 per barrel in 1978 to $33.20 per barrel in 1981, so did the country's fortunes, along with those of other oil-rich countries such as Nigeria, Iran, Indonesia, and Venezuela. The administration of President José López Portillo (1976–1982) embarked on a policy to "sow the oil" in the economy and "administer the abundance" with vast investment projects in virtually all sectors and major new initiatives to reduce poverty and deal with declining agricultural productivity. Oil revenues paid for much of this expansion, but the foreign debt also mounted as both public and private sectors borrowed heavily to finance investments and lavish consumer spending.

By 1982, Mexico's foreign debt was $86 billion, and the exchange rate was seriously overvalued, making the peso and Mexican products more expensive on the world market. Oil accounted for 77.2 percent of the country's exports, causing the economy to be extremely vulnerable to changes in oil prices. And change they did. Global overproduction brought the international price for Mexican petroleum down to $26.30 a barrel. Revenues from exports declined dramatically. At the same time, the United States tightened its monetary policy, and access to foreign credit dried up. Wealthy Mexicans responded by sending vast amounts of capital out of the country just as the country's international creditors were demanding repayment on their loans. In August 1982, the government announced that the country could not pay the interest on its foreign debt, triggering a crisis that reverberated around the world.

The impact of these conditions on the Mexican economy was devastating. GDP growth in 1982 was −0.6 percent and fell to −4.2 percent the following year. New policy measures were put in place by the administration of Miguel de la Madrid (1982–1988) to deal with the economic crisis, but policy-makers were repeatedly overtaken by escalating inflation, financial sector panic, depleted foreign reserves, severe trade imbalances, and debt renegotiations. In 1986, petroleum prices dropped to $12 a barrel, exacerbating an already desperate situation.

The economic crisis had several important implications for structures of power and privilege in Mexico. First, faith in the import substitution policy was destroyed. The crisis convinced even the most diehard believers that import substitution created inefficiencies in production, failed to generate sufficient employment, cost the government far too much in subsidies, and increased dependency on industrialized countries. In addition, the power of interest groups and their ability to influence government policy declined. Prolonged economic crisis hit the business sector particularly hard. When the economy stagnated, declined, and failed to recover rapidly, private debts could not be repaid, inflation and unemployment reduced demand, government subsidies were repeatedly cut back, and most public investment plans were put on hold. The inevitable result was the failure of many Mexican companies. Bankruptcy and recession exacted their toll on the fortunes of even large entrepreneurs. As economic hardship affected their members, traditional business organizations lost their ability to put strong pressure on the government.

Similarly, the country's relatively privileged unions lost much of their bargaining power with government over issues of wages and protection. Union leaders loyal to the PRI emphasized the need for peace and order to help the nation get through tough times, while inflation and job loss focused many of the country's workers on putting food on the table. A shift in employment from the formal to the informal sector further fragmented what had once been the most powerful sector of the party. Cuts in government subsidies for public transportation, food, electricity, and gasoline created new hardships for workers. The combination of these factors weakened the capacity of labor to resist policy changes that affected the benefits they received.

In addition, new voices emerged to demand that the government respond to the crisis. During the recession years of the 1980s, wages lost between 40 and 50 percent of their value, increasingly large numbers of people became unemployed, inflation cut deeply into middle-class incomes, and budgets for health and education services were severely cut back. A wide variety of interests began to organize outside the PRI to demand that government do something about the situation. Massive earthquakes in Mexico City in September 1985 proved to be a watershed for Mexican society. Severely disappointed by the government's failure to respond to the problems created by death, destruction, disorientation, and homelessness, hundreds of communities organized rescue efforts, soup kitchens, shelters, and rehabilitation initiatives. A surging sense of political empowerment developed, as groups long accustomed to dependence on government learned that they could solve their problems better without government than with it.[12]

In addition, the PRI was challenged by the increased popularity of opposition political parties, one of them headed by Cuauhtémoc Cárdenas, the son of the country's most revered president, Lázaro Cárdenas. The elections of 1988 became a focus for protest against the economic dislocation caused by the crisis and the political powerlessness that most citizens felt. Carlos Salinas, the PRI candidate, received a bare majority of 50.7 percent, and opposition parties claimed widespread electoral fraud.

New Strategies and Democratic Institutions

Demands on the Salinas administration to deal with the economic and political crisis were extensive. At the same time, the weakening of the old centers of political power provided the government with a major opportunity to reorient the country's strategy for economic development. Between 1988 and 1994, the dependent relationship between industry and government was weakened when new free-market policies were put in place. Decreasing regulation was an important part of this restructuring of state-economy relationships. Deregulation gave the private sector more freedom to pursue economic activities and less reason to seek special favors from government. A number of large government industries, such as the telephone company, the banking sector, the national airlines, and steel and sugar mills, were reorganized and sold to private investors. A constitutional revision made it possible for *ejidatarios* to become owners of individual plots of land; this made them less dependent on government but more vulnerable to losing their land. In addition, financial sector reform that changed laws about banking and established a stock exchange encouraged the emergence of new banks and brokerage and insurance firms.

Salinas pursued, and Zedillo continued, an overhaul of the federal system and the way government agencies worked together. Called the New Federalism, it was an attempt to give power and budgetary responsibilities to state and local governments, which had been historically very weak in Mexico. Beginning with education and health, the presidents hoped decentralization would make government more efficient and effective. In addition, federal agencies began to be broken down into regional bureaus to work more closely with lower levels of government. This was a major change from the highly centralized government of the past. Additionally, the central bank became independent from the government in 1994, though exchange rates are still determined by the finance ministry.

Among the most far-reaching initiatives was NAFTA. This agreement with Canada and the United States created the basis for gradual introduction of free trade among the three countries. These changes were a major reversal of import substitution and economic intervention that had marked government policies in the past. However, the liberalization of the Mexican economy and opening up its markets to foreign competition increased the vulnerability of the country to changes in international economic conditions. These factors, as well as mismanaged economic policies, led to a major economic crisis for the country at the end of 1994 and profound recession in 1995. NAFTA has meant that the fate of the Mexican economy is increasingly linked to the health of the U.S. economy, sheltering it from the contagion of the 1997–1998 financial crisis in Asia and putting it at risk in the cool-down of the U.S. system in the early 2000s.

New economic institutions were followed by the emergence of more democratic structures. In 1996, an independent election board composed of private citizens helped ensure fairer and more competitive elections. Constitutional amendments helped ensure more fairness for political parties during campaigns. Now, election funds are mostly public, with private expenditures limited. Changes also introduced procedures for auditing the political parties. By 1997, it became much more possible for opposition parties to win elections from the PRI. In that year, the party of the old regime lost its majority in congress. Numerous governors and mayors were elected from the opposition. In 2000, the PRI lost the presidency.

Society and Economy

Mexico's economic development has had a significant impact on social conditions in the country. Overall, the standard of living improved markedly after the 1940s. Rates of infant mortality, literacy, and life expectancy have steadily improved. Provision of health and education services expanded until government cutbacks on social expenditures in the early 1980s. Among the most important consequences of economic growth was the development of a large middle class, most of whom live in Mexico's numerous large cities. By the 1980s, a third or more of Mexican households could claim a middle-class lifestyle: a steady income, secure food and shelter, access to decent education and health services, a car, some disposable income and savings, and some security that their children would be able to experience happy and healthy lives.

These achievements reflect well on the ability of the economy to increase social well-being in the country. However, the impressive economic growth through the early 1970s and between 1978 and 1982 could have produced greater social progress. In terms of standard indicators of social development—infant mortality, literacy, and life expectancy—Mexico fell behind a number of Latin American countries that grew less rapidly but provided more effectively for their populations. Costa Rica, Colombia, Argentina, Chile, and Uruguay had lower overall growth but greater social development in the period after 1940. These countries paid more attention to the distribution of the benefits of growth than did Mexico. Moreover, in its pursuit of rapid industrialization, Mexico City has become one of the most congested and polluted cities in the world. In some rural areas, oil exploitation left devastating environmental damage, destroying the lifestyles and opportunities of *ejidatarios* and small farmers.

Mexico's economic development also resulted in a widening gap between the wealthy and the poor and among different regions in the country. Although the poor are better off than they were in the early days of the country's drive toward industrialization, they are worse off when compared to middle- and upper-income groups. In 1950, the bottom 40 percent of the country's households accounted for about 14 percent of total personal income, while the top 30 percent had 60 percent of total income.[13] In 1995, it is estimated, the bottom 40 percent accounted for about 11 percent of income, while the top 40 percent shared 77.4 percent.[14] As in the United States, as the rich grew richer, the gap between the rich and the poor increased.

Among the poorest are those in rural areas who have little or no access to productive land and those in urban areas who do not have steady jobs. Harsh conditions in the countryside have fueled a half-century of migration to the cities. Nevertheless, some 25 million Mexicans continue to live in rural areas, many of them in deep poverty. Many of them work for substandard wages and migrate seasonally to search for jobs in order to sustain their families. Traditionally, those who, legally and illegally, crossed the border to the United States in search of jobs came from depressed rural areas. Increasingly, however, they come from urban areas.

Among rural inhabitants with access to land, almost half have five hectares or less. This land is usually not irrigated and depends on erratic rainfall. It is often leached of nutrients as a result of centuries of cultivation, population pressure, and erosion. The crops grown on such farms, primarily corn and beans, do not bring high prices in the markets. To improve production, peasant farmers would have to buy fertilizer, improved seeds, and insecticides, and they would have to find ways to irrigate their plots. But they generally have no money to purchase these supplies or invest in irrigation. In many areas, farm production provides as few as twenty to one hundred days of employment each year. Not surprisingly, underemployment is high in rural Mexico, as are rates of seasonal migration. The incidence of disease, malnutrition, and illiteracy is much higher in Mexico's rural areas than in urban areas. When the rebels in Chiapas called for jobs, land, education, and health facilities, they were clearly reflecting the realities of life in much of the country.

Poverty has a regional dimension in Mexico. The northern areas of the country are significantly better off than the southern and central areas. In the north, large commercial farms using modern technologies grow fruits, vegetables, and grains for export. The U.S. border, the principal destination of agricultural products, is close at hand, and transportation networks are extensive and generally in good condition. Moreover, industrial cities such as Monterrey and Tijuana provide steady jobs for skilled and unskilled labor. Along the border, a band of manufacturing and assembly plants, called *maquiladoras*, provides many jobs, particularly for young women who are seeking some escape from the burdens of rural life or the constraints of traditional family life.

In the southern and central regions of the country, the population is denser, the land poorer, and the number of *ejidatarios* eking out subsistence greater. Transportation is often difficult, and during parts of the year, some areas may be inaccessible because of heavy rains and flooding. Most of Mexico's remaining indigenous groups live in the southern regions, often in remote areas where they have been forgotten by government programs and exploited by regional bosses for generations. The conditions that spurred the Chiapas rebellion are found throughout the southern states.

The economic crisis of the 1980s had an impact on social conditions in the country as well. Wages declined by about half, and unemployment soared as businesses collapsed and the government laid off workers in public offices and privatized industries. The informal sector expanded rapidly. Here, people eked out a living by hawking chewing gum, umbrellas, sponges, candy, shoelaces, mirrors, and a variety of other items in the street; jumping in front of cars at stoplights to wash windshields and sell newspapers; producing and repairing cheap consumer goods such as shoes and clothing; and selling services on a daily or hourly basis. While the informal sector provides important goods and services, conditions of work are often dangerous, and insecurity about where the next peso will come from is endemic.

The economic crisis of the 1980s also reduced the quality and availability of social services. Expenditures on education and health declined after 1982 as the government imposed austerity measures. Salaries of primary school teachers declined by 34 percent between 1983 and 1988, and many teachers worked second and even third jobs in order to make ends meet. Per capita health expenditures declined from a high of about $19 in 1980 to about $11 in 1990. Hospitals, clinics, and schools were left in disrepair, and obtaining equipment and supplies became almost impossible. Although indicators of mortality did not rise during this troubled decade, the incidence of diseases associated with poverty—malnutrition, cholera, anemia, and dysentery—increased. The diet of most Mexicans became less rich in protein as they ate less meat and drank less milk. The crisis began to ease in the early 1990s, however, and many came to believe that conditions would improve for the poor. The government began investing in social services. When a new economic crisis occurred, however, unemployment surged, and austerity measures severely limited investments. Despite considerable recovery in the late 1990s, wages remain low for the majority of workers while taxes have increased. Subsidies on basic goods like tortillas, water, and gas have been lowered or eliminated, making the cost of living rise steeply for the poor and the working class.

Mexico and the International Political Economy

The crisis that began in 1982 altered Mexico's international policies. In response to that crisis, the government relaxed restrictions on the ability of foreigners to own property, reduced and eliminated tariffs, and did away with most import licenses. Foreign investment was courted in the hope of increasing the manufacture of goods for export. The government also introduced a series of incentives to encourage the private sector to produce goods for export. In 1986, Mexico joined the General Agreement on Tariffs and Trade (GATT), a multilateral agreement that seeks to promote freer trade among countries.

The government's effort to pursue a more outward-oriented development strategy culminated in the ratification of NAFTA in 1993, with gradual implementation beginning on January 1, 1994. This agreement is important to Mexico. In 2000, 89 percent of the country's exports were sent to the United States, and 74 percent of its imports came from that country. The next most active trading country with Mexico was Canada, which received only 2 percent of its exports and accounted for only 2.3 percent of its imports.[15] Access to the U.S. market is thus essential to Mexico and to domestic and foreign investors. NAFTA signaled a new period in U.S.-Mexican relations by making closer integration of the two economies a certainty. To date, trade among Mexico, Canada, and the United States has increased along with foreign direct investment. Additionally, NAFTA contains two parallel agreements regarding the environment and labor that were negotiated in order to pass the treaty in the U.S. Congress. These documents created trinational institutions to cooperate and mediate on these issues to prevent potentially damaging side effects from free trade. The new institutions have not been very active, however, and it is unknown what positive effect, if any, they are having. (See "Global Connection: NAFTA and Beyond.")

NAFTA also entails risks for Mexico. Domestic producers worry about competition from U.S. firms. Farmers worry that Mexican crops cannot compete effectively with those grown in the United States; for example, peasant producers of corn and beans have been hard hit by lower-priced U.S.-grown grains. In addition, many believe that embracing free trade with Canada and the United States indicates a loss of sovereignty. Certainly Mexico's economic situation is now more vulnerable to the ebb and flow of economic conditions in the U.S. economy. Some are also concerned with increasing evidence of "cultural imperialism" as

Global Connection: **NAFTA and Beyond**

On January 1, 1994, the North America Free Trade Agreement (NAFTA) between Mexico, Canada, and the United States went into effect. The day chosen for the EZLN's action was no coincidence: besides demanding social justice for indigenous groups, the rebels called on Carlos Salinas de Gortari's administration to revoke NAFTA. Since that time, Mexico has been both a subject of deep criticism for its evident failure to integrate those who have been gradually excluded by its development strategy, and respect for being able to negotiate—on a fairly equal basis—a major trade pact with the world's strongest economy. The coincidence of the Chiapas rebellion and the beginning of NAFTA was symbolic of the difficulty of at least one of the many "Mexicos" to catch up with the high-speed train of the country's aspirations to become a key player in the new international economy.

Almost a decade later, the debate surrounding free trade and its tangible benefits to the vast majority of Mexicans remains. While Mexico has achieved some successes in advancing economic development in the context of NAFTA and other trade agreements, economic growth has not only not contributed to poverty reduction but also has steadily increased income disparities, benefiting the better off at the expense of the poorest sectors. Mexico is the twelfth biggest economy in the world, but 42.5 percent of its more than 100 million inhabitants live on less than $2 a day and 17.9 percent on less than $1 a day. The Gini index for Mexico, a measure of inequality, was 53.7 in 2000. The United States and Canada had indexes of 40.8 and 31.5, respectively (the higher the number, the greater the inequality).

NAFTA was conceived as a mechanism through which Mexico's historical economic and political ties to the United States could become institutionalized on both sides of the border. NAFTA was perceived as the "seal of gold" to technocrats' efforts to pursue an outward-oriented development strategy. Since the mid-1980s and in a clear response to the negative traits associated with the protectionist model that culminated in the 1982 crisis, Mexico began a series of dramatic changes in its economic, fiscal, and monetary policies and legal and institutional frameworks, emphasizing the need to develop export platforms and liberalize trade. Beginning with President Miguel de la Madrid and followed by Presidents Carlos Salinas de Gortari, Ernesto Zedillo, and Vicente Fox, the idea of integrating Mexico into the global marketplace was formalized through the adoption of free-trade agreements, with NAFTA as the most important.

Today, Mexico is considered one of the most prolific signers of free-trade agreements in the world. Besides the United States and Canada, Mexico has signed trade accords with Argentina, Bolivia, Brazil, Chile, Colombia, Costa Rica, El Salvador, the European Union (Austria, Belgium, Denmark, Finland, France, Germany, Greece, Ireland, Italy, Luxembourg, the Netherlands, Portugal, Spain, Sweden, and the United Kingdom), the European Free-Trade Association (Norway, Switzerland, and Liechtenstein), Guatemala, Honduras, Israel, Nicaragua, and Venezuela. Formal negotiations continue with Ecuador, Japan, MERCOSUR (a free-trade area in southern Latin America), Panama, Peru, Singapore, Trinidad and Tobago, and the Free-Trade Area of the Americas. And while this list might seem comprehensive in proving Mexico's attempts to diversify its economic relationships with the rest of the world, Mexican-U.S. trade and political ties are stronger than ever before: currently the United States accounts for about 80 percent of Mexico's foreign trade.

Without any doubt, NAFTA signaled a new period in Mexican-U.S. relations. Mexico's foreign policy shift from historical commitment to nonintervention to one that is more proactive and assertive in international affairs, for example, has been considered a direct consequence of the strategic position gained through the new relationship with the United States. Also, further economic and political transformation has been undertaken to fulfill NAFTA requirements. Alas, NAFTA has also added more issues to an already complex and difficult relationship. In the years since it went into effect, the two countries have locked horns in various trade disputes, such as antidumping regulations to cross-border trucking provisions, and social and political sectors in the United States and Mexico continue to hold each other responsible for their respective misfortunes, particularly as electoral opportunities arise. In addition, antinarcotics efforts and undocumented immigration continue to fuel intense debate on both sides over the costs and benefits of managing economic integration.

Written by Bertha Angulo Curiel, Harvard University. Reprinted with permission.

U.S. movies, music, fashions, and lifestyles increasingly influence consumers.

In addition, the incorporation of Mexico into NAFTA has political ramifications. During negotiations for this agreement, new international political alliances developed. Environmental groups from the United States sought support in Mexico and Canada for fighting the agreement, and labor groups also looked across both borders for allies in opposing new trade relations. Environmental and labor groups united around concerns that Mexico would not enforce environmental protection and fair labor legislation. Some business interests allied across countries in supporting the agreement, anticipating opportunities for larger markets, cheaper labor, or richer sources of raw materials. For Mexico, which has traditionally feared the power of the United States in its domestic affairs, internationalization of political and economic relationships poses particularly difficult problems of adjustment.

On the other hand, the United States, newly aware of the importance of the Mexican economy to its own economic growth and concerned about instability on its southern border, hammered together a $50 billion economic assistance program composed of U.S., European, and IMF commitments to support its neighbor when crisis struck in 1994. The Mexican government imposed a new stabilization package that contained austerity measures, higher interest rates, and limits on wages. Remarkably, by 1998, Mexico had paid off all of its obligations to the United States.

Globalization is also stripping Mexico of some of the secrecy that traditionally surrounded government decision making, electoral processes, and efforts to deal with political dissent. International attention increasingly focuses on the country. Investors want clear and up-to-date information on what is occurring in the economy. The Internet and email, along with lower international telephone rates, are increasing information flow across borders. The government can no longer respond to events such as the peasant rebellion in Chiapas, alleged electoral fraud, or the management of exchange rates without considering how such actions will be perceived in Tokyo, Frankfurt, Ottawa, London, or Washington.

Section ❸ Governance and Policy-Making

Mexico is a federal republic, although until the 1990s, state and local governments had few resources and a limited sphere of action when compared with the national level. Under the PRI, the executive branch concentrated almost all power, while the legislative and judiciary branches followed the executive's lead and were considered rubber-stamp bodies. During the seventy-one years of PRI hegemony, the government was civilian, authoritarian, and corporatist. Currently, it has multiparty competitive elections, and power is less concentrated in the executive branch and the national government. Since the mid-1980s, great efforts have been made to reinvigorate the nation's laws and institutions and make the country more democratic.

Organization of the State

According to the supreme law of the land, the Constitution of 1917, Mexico's political institutions resemble those of the United States. There are three branches of government, and a set of checks and balances limits the power of each. The congress is composed of the Senate and the Chamber of Deputies. One hundred twenty-eight senators are elected, three from each of the country's thirty-one states and an additional three from the federal district (capital), Mexico City, and another thirty-two elected nationally by proportional representation. Five hundred deputies are elected from 300 electoral districts—300 by simple majority vote and 200 by proportional representation. States and local governments are also elected. The president, governors, and senators are elected for six years, and deputies (representatives in the lower house) and municipal officials are elected for three.

In practice, the Mexican system is very different from that of the United States. The constitution is a very long document that is easily amended, especially when compared to that of the United States. It lays out the structure of government and guarantees a wide range of human rights, including familiar ones such as freedom of speech and protection of the law, but also economic and social rights such as the right to a job and the right to health care. Economic and social rights are acknowledged but in practice do not reach all of the population. Although there has been some decentralization of power, the political system is still much more centralized than that of the United States. Congress is now more active as a decision-making arena and as a check on presidential power, but the executive remains central to initiating policy and managing political conflict.

The Executive

The President and the Cabinet

The Mexican presidency is the central institution of governance and policy-making. Until the 1990s, the incumbent PRI president always selected who would run as the party's next presidential candidate, appointed officials to all positions of power in the government and the PRI, and often named the candidates, who almost automatically won elections as governors, senators, deputies, and local officials. Even with a non-PRI incumbent, the president continues to set the broad outlines of policy for the administration and has numerous resources to ensure that those policy preferences are adopted. Until the mid-1970s, Mexican presidents were considered above criticism in national politics and revered as symbols of national progress and well-being. While economic and political events of the 1980s and 1990s diminished presidential prestige, the extent of presidential power remains a legacy of the long period of PRI ascendance.

Mexican presidents have a set of formal powers that allows them to initiate legislation, lead in foreign policy, create government agencies, make policy by decree or through administrative regulations and procedures, and appoint a wide range of public officials. More important, informal powers provide them with the capacity to exert considerable control. The president manages a vast patronage machine for filling positions in government and initiates legislation and policies that were, until recently, routinely approved by the congress. When Vicente Fox became president in 2000, he promised many fewer personnel changes in government than under previous incumbents. He promised more open government and greater diversity

among his cabinet and other appointees. His powers have been curtailed to some degree by a more forceful congress and his administration's lack of experience in governing.

Under the PRI, presidents were always male and almost always members of the outgoing president's cabinet. Several had served as ministers of the interior, the person responsible for maintaining law and order in the country. This was true of Miguel Alemán (1946–1952), Adolfo Ruiz Cortines (1952–1958), Gustavo Díaz Ordaz (1964–1970), and Luis Echeverría (1970–1976). With the expansion of the government's role in economic development, candidates in the 1970s and 1980s were selected from the ministries that managed the economy. José López Portillo (1976–1982) had been minister of finance, and Miguel de la Madrid (1982–1988) and Carlos Salinas (1988–1994) had served as ministers of planning and budgeting. The selection of Luis Donaldo Colosio, who had been minister of social development and welfare, was thought by political observers to signal renewed concern with problems of social development. When Colosio was assassinated in 1994, the selection of Ernesto Zedillo, who had first been minister of planning and budgeting and then minister of education, was interpreted as an ongoing concern with national social problems and as an effort to maintain the policies of economic liberalization that Salinas had introduced. With the victory of the PAN in 2000, this long tradition came to an end. Prior to running for president, Vicente Fox had been in business and had served as the governor of the state of Guanajuato (see "Leaders: Vicente Fox Quesada").

Candidates since the mid-1970s have had impressive educational credentials and have tended to be trained in economics and management rather than in the traditional field of law. Presidents since López Portillo have had postgraduate training at elite institutions in the United States. Miguel de la Madrid held a master's degree in public administration from Harvard; Carlos Salinas received a Ph.D. degree in political economy and government from Harvard; Luis Colosio studied for a Ph.D. degree in economics from the University of Pennsylvania; Ernesto Zedillo had a Ph.D. degree in economics from Yale; and Vicente Fox holds a certificate from the prestigious Advanced Management Program at the Harvard Business School. By the 1980s, a topic of great debate in political circles was

Leaders: *Vicente Fox Quesada*

When Vicente Fox Quesada was governor of the small but prosperous state of Guanajuato, he embarked on a major political gamble. In 1998, he declared himself a candidate for the presidency, even before gaining the backing of his political party, the National Action Party (PAN). He was not only gambling on the nomination of the party, by no means assured because he was not considered an insider by party leaders, but also on being able to campaign effectively for the presidency. For seven decades, the dominant party, the PRI, had controlled Mexico's presidency. In the fall of 1999, the conservative, probusiness PAN reluctantly gave the nomination to Fox, and he began active campaigning. His first major national test came in a presidential debate in April 2000, and most analysts declared him the winner. By May, he was leading in public opinion polls. On July 2, 2000, he won the election, and on December 1, he assumed the presidency. He had won his gamble. Mexicans were intrigued by their new president, the one who had upset the PRI after seventy-one years. Who was he? What were his plans for the country?

Vicente Fox was born on July 2, 1942, one of nine children. When he was a child, the family moved to a small town in Guanajuato, where he became familiar with rural life and the challenges of agriculture in a country that was rapidly industrializing. He also saw firsthand the poverty that afflicted many of those who lived in rural areas. He is reported to have said, "I grew up in an *ejido* with the children of peasants and the only difference between me and my childhood friends were the opportunities I had."[1] He attended the Iberoamerican University in Mexico City, where he majored in business administration. He also earned a certificate in advanced management from Harvard Business School. He became the father of four children, although his marriage dissolved in divorce some years later. In 1964, he became a route director for Coca-Cola in Mexico and gradually rose to become the president of Coca-Cola for Mexico and Latin America. He returned to Guanajuato to pursue interests in business and politics, becoming president of the Fox Group of farming, livestock, agro-industrial, shoe, and boot companies.

In the 1980s, Fox became a member of the PAN, which had long been tied to business interests in the north of the country and had long opposed the central government in Mexico City. He was elected to congress as a deputy in 1988, ran for governor and lost in 1991, and then won the gubernatorial election of 1995. His administration was recognized for its promotion of "good government," including greater efficiency and effectiveness in carrying out public policies and programs.

His path to the presidency was not smooth, however. PAN leaders, among them those who wanted to run for this important position, considered Fox to be a newcomer to the party, one who had not fully demonstrated his commitment to it. They recognized his growing reputation and popularity and tried to use party rules to keep him from gaining greater power. Fox, recognizing the uphill battle he would encounter with the PAN, organized his own electoral machine, the "Friends of Fox," to finance and lead his campaign. Eventually, the party was forced to recognize his candidacy, but the main vehicle for the election continued to be the Friends of Fox. When he became president, the tension between the candidate and the party continued, and Fox could not count on the support of the PAN when he sent legislation to congress.

As president, Fox committed himself to greater transparency in government decision making and continued efforts to liberalize the economy and encourage its global integration. He promised that citizens would have more information and that there would be greater responsiveness in public services. He had a difficult time delivering on these promises, however, as the PAN did not have a majority in congress and he did not have many experienced people to plan policy and manage government activities. Moreover, he made a number of widely broadcast political mistakes—spending lavishly on refurbishing the presidential residence, for example, and pursuing what was viewed as an improper relationship with his spokesperson, Martha Sahagun (they were married in 2001)—and at times seemed uncertain about the direction of his presidency. In a system that had always depended on the president to generate and promote a vision of government every six years, many Mexicans came to the conclusion that he lacked decisiveness. Nevertheless, the first president from an opposition party since 1929 earned high marks for bringing democratic change to Mexico and supporting a more open political system.

---

[1]www.presidencia.gob.mx.

the extent to which a divide between *políticos* (politicians) and *técnicos* (**technocrats**) had emerged within the national political elite. Among the old guard of the PRI, there was open skepticism about the ability of young technocrats like Carlos Salinas and Ernesto Zedillo to manage political conditions in the country. During the presidential campaign of 1994, considerable efforts were made to stress the more humble beginnings of Colosio and Zedillo and the fact that they had had to work hard to get an education. Under Fox, the ties of the president to business elites raised similar fears that the government would not respond to the concerns of everyday citizens.

Once elected, the president moves quickly to name a cabinet. Under the PRI, he usually selected those with whom he had worked over the years as he rose to political prominence. He also used cabinet posts to ensure a broad coalition of support; he might, for example, appoint people with close ties to the labor movement, business interests, or some of the regional strongholds of the party. Only in rare exceptions were cabinet officials not active members of the PRI. When the PAN assumed the presidency, the selection of a cabinet and close advisers was more difficult. Until then, the party had elected officials only to state and local governments and to congress. As a consequence, the range of people with executive experience whom Fox could turn to was limited. He appointed U.S.-trained economists for his economic team and business executives for many other important posts. Few of these appointees had close ties to the PAN, and few had prior experience in government. Over the years, few women have been selected for ministry-level posts—there are a handful of examples in recent administrations—and thus far only in those agencies that have limited influence over decision making, like Tourism, Ecology, and Foreign Relations.

The president has the authority to fill numerous other high-level positions, which allows him to provide policy direction and keep tabs on what is occurring throughout the government. Such appointments provide the president with the capacity to build a team of like-minded officials in government and ensure their loyalty to him. In turn, high-level appointees fill many jobs in their organizations. Like the president, they use this patronage power to put together loyal teams of officials whose career advancement is tied to their own

political fate. These officials, in turn, build their own teams, and so on down through middle levels in the bureaucracy. This system traditionally served the interests of presidents and the PRI well; under the PAN, given the limited number of its partisans who have experience at national levels, the system has not guaranteed the president as much power over the workings of the executive branch. In addition, when he assumed power, President Fox committed himself to retaining qualified people in their positions and making many fewer changes than customary.

Given the range of appointments that a president can make, the beginning of each administration is characterized by extensive turnover of positions, although under the PRI, many of the newly appointed officials served in other positions in prior administrations. While the PRI held power, little happened in government in the year prior to an election as officials bided their time or jockeyed for positions in the next administration. Even under alternative parties, little is likely to happen in the year following an election as newly appointed officials learn the ropes and assemble their teams. Nevertheless, when a president has set clear goals and expects high performance from his personally chosen officials, these people in turn must expect good performance from their staffs if they are to produce for the president. In many situations, then, the patronage system results in the potential for increased presidential leadership and effective performance, at least at high levels in government. Under the PRI, delivering for "the boss" might even result in a position in the next administration, if one's boss happened to be chosen as the presidential candidate or one of his ministers. Just as frequently, however, appointments to government service can mean opportunities to amass personal wealth, take bribes, and use insider information for personal benefit. Under more democratic conditions today, there is mounting pressure for a less politicized and more professional civil service.

Mexican presidents, though powerful, are not omnipotent. They, must, for example, abide by a deeply held constitutional norm, fully adhered to since 1940, to step down at the end of their term, and they must honor the political norm to step out of the political limelight to allow the successor to assume full presidential leadership. All presidents, regardless of party, must demonstrate their loyalty to the myths and symbols of Mexican nationalism, such as the indigenous roots of much of its culture, the agrarian origins of the revolution, and rhetorical commitment to social justice and sovereignty in international affairs. In addition, several factors tend to limit the extent of presidential discretion. PRI presidents were always creatures of the system, selected because they proved themselves adept at understanding and playing by the existing rules. Through their careers in politics or government, they became familiar with the range of interest groups in the country and demonstrated a willingness to compromise on policy and political issues so that these interests would not unduly challenge the government. They also proved themselves to be skillful in the fierce bureaucratic politics that surround career advancement and in guessing about whom the next PRI candidate for president was likely to be. Under more democratic conditions since 2000, presidential backgrounds and career trajectories can no longer be predicted. Indeed, Vicente Fox, although the standard-bearer of the PAN, was not close to the party apparatus and did not ascend through its ranks. This meant that he could not necessarily count on party support in the congress or its unconditional loyalty as launched new initiatives or sought to mobilize public support for his actions.

In the 1990s, President Zedillo relinquished a number of the traditional powers of the presidency. He announced, for example, that he would not select his PRI successor but would leave it up to the party to determine its candidate. In doing so, however, he created considerable conflict and tension as the PRI had to take on unaccustomed roles and as politicians sought to fill the void left by the "abandonment" of presidential power. President Fox inherited a system in which he was expected to set the policies and determine the priorities for a very wide range of government activity. Without a strong party in congress or many experienced people in government, he was often unable to deliver. In the absence of strong presidential leadership, government often seemed to flounder.

The Bureaucracy

Mexico's executive branch is large and powerful. Almost 1.5 million people work in the federal bureaucracy, most of them in Mexico City. An additional 1 million work for the large number of state-owned industries and semiautonomous agencies of the government. State and local governments employ over 1.5 million people. Pay scales are usually low, and in the past, the number of people filling lower-level positions such as drivers, messengers, secretaries, and maintenance people far exceeded the demand for them. In the 1980s, austerity measures cut down on some of this overstaffing.

Officials at lower levels in the bureaucracy are unionized and protected by legislation that gives them job security and a range of benefits. At middle and upper levels, most officials are called "confidence employees"; they serve as long as their bosses have confidence in them. These are the officials who are personally appointed by their superiors at the outset of an administration. Their modest salaries are compensated for by the significant power that they can have over public events. For aspiring young professionals, a career in government is often attractive because of the challenge of dealing with important problems on a daily basis and being part of the process of finding solutions to them. Some employees also benefit from opportunities to take bribes or use other means to promote their personal interests.

The Para-Statal Sector

The **para-statal** sector—composed of semiautonomous or autonomous government agencies, many of which produce goods and services—was extremely large and powerful in Mexico. Because the government provided significant support for the development of the economy as part of its post-1940 development strategy, it engaged in numerous activities that in other countries are carried out by the private sector. Thus, until the Salinas administration, the country's largest steel mill was state owned, as were the largest fertilizer producer, sugar mills, and airlines. In addition, the national electricity board still produces energy and supplies it at subsidized prices to industries. The petroleum company, PEMEX, grew to enormous proportions in the 1970s and 1980s under the impact of the oil boom. NAFIN, a state investment corporation, provides a considerable amount of investment capital for the country. At one point, a state marketing board called CONASUPO was responsible for the importation and purchase of the country's basic food supplies, and in the

1970s, it played a major role in distributing food, credit, and farm implements in rural areas.

This large para-statal sector was significantly trimmed by the economic policy reforms of the 1980s and 1990s. In 1970, there were 391 para-statal organizations in Mexico. By 1982, their number had grown to 1,155, in part because of the expansion of government activities under presidents Echeverría and López Portillo and in part because of the nationalization of private banks in 1982. In the 1980s and 1990s, concerted efforts were made to privatize many of these industries, including the telephone company, the national airline, and the nationalized banks. By 1994, only 215 state-owned industries remained, and efforts continued to sell or liquidate many of them. The Fox government, a partisan of the private sector, raised the possibility of privatizing PEMEX and the electricity board, but quickly retreated to very partial measures in the face of extensive opposition to private ownership of the "national patrimony."

Other State Institutions

The Military

Mexico is one of only a few countries in the developing world to have successfully marginalized the military from centers of political power. Much of the credit for this process belongs to Plutarco Calles, Lázaro Cárdenas, and subsequent presidents who introduced the rotation of regional commands so that generals could not build up regional bases of power. In addition, postrevolutionary leaders made an implicit bargain with the military leaders by providing them with opportunities to engage in business so that they did not look to political power as a way of gaining economic power. After 1946, the military no longer had institutional representation within the PRI and became clearly subordinate to civilian control.

This does not mean that the military has existed outside politics. It has been called in from time to time to deal with domestic unrest: in rural areas in the 1960s, in Mexico City and other cities to repress student protest movements in 1968, in 1988 in the arrest of a powerful labor leader, in 1989 to break a labor strike, in 1990 to deal with protest over electoral fraud, in Chiapas beginning in late 1994, and to manage the

Mexico City police in 1997. The military was also called in to deal with the aftermath of the earthquake in Mexico City in 1985, but its inadequate response to the emergency did little to enhance its reputation in the eyes of the public. In recent years, the military has been heavily involved in efforts to combat drug trafficking, and rumors abound about deals struck between military officials and drug barons. Such fears were confirmed when General Jesús Gutierrez Rebollo, the head of the antidrug task force, was arrested in February 1997 on accusations of protecting a drug lord. When the PAN government made it possible for citizens to gain greater access to government information, it was discovered that the military had been involved in political repression, torture, and killing in the 1970s and 1980s. The scandal created by such revelations further lowered its reputation.

Whenever the military is called in to resolve domestic conflicts, some Mexicans become concerned that the institution is becoming politicized and may come to play a larger role in political decision making. From time to time, rumors of preparations for a coup are heard, as during financial panics in the 1980s and in the aftermath of Colosio's assassination. Thus far, such fears have not been realized, and many believe that as long as civilian administrations are able to maintain the country's tradition of stability, the military will not intervene directly in politics. The fact that the country successfully observed the transfer of power from the PRI to the PAN also has increased a sense that the military will remain subordinate to civilian control.

The Judiciary

Unlike Anglo-American legal systems, Mexico's law derives from the Roman and Napoleonic tradition and is highly formalized and explicit. The Constitution of 1917 is a lengthy document that has been amended many times and contains references to a wide range of civil rights, including items as broad as the right to a healthy environment. As in other countries, regulatory agencies can also create rules and regulations, known as administrative law, regarding material under their jurisdiction. Because Mexican law tends to be very explicit and because there are no punitive damages, there are fewer lawsuits than in the United States. One important exception to this is the *amparo*, whereby citizens may ask for a writ of protection claiming that their constitutional rights have been violated by specific government actions or laws. Each citizen who wants an *amparo* must present a separate case.

There are federal and state courts in Mexico. The federal system is composed of the Supreme Court, which decides the most important cases in the country; circuit courts, which take cases on appeal; and district courts, where all cases enter the system. As in the United States, Supreme Court justices are nominated by the president and approved by the Senate. Since most of the important laws in Mexico are federal, state courts have played a subordinate role. However, this is changing. As Mexican states become more independent from the federal government, state law has been experiencing tremendous growth. In addition, there are many important specialized federal courts, such as labor courts, military courts, and electoral courts.

Like other political institutions in Mexico, the judiciary was for many decades politically, though not constitutionally, subordinate to the executive. The courts occasionally slowed the actions of government by issuing *amparos*; however, in almost every case in which the power of government or the president was at stake, the courts ruled on the side of the government. The administration of Ernesto Zedillo tried to change this by emphasizing the rule of law over that of powerful individuals. Increasing interest in human rights issues by citizens' groups and the media has added pressure to the courts to play a stronger role in protecting basic freedoms. Citizens and the government are increasingly resorting to the courts as a primary weapon against sticky problems like corruption and police abuse. President Zedillo's refusal to interfere with the courts' judgments also strengthened the judiciary. This trajectory continued under President Fox. Nevertheless, the judicial system remains the weakest branch of government.

Subnational Government

As with many other aspects of the Mexican political system, regional and local government in Mexico is quite different from what is described in the constitution. Mexico has a federal system, and each state has its own constitution, executive, unicameral legislature, and judiciary. Municipalities (equivalent to U.S. counties) are governed by popularly elected mayors and councils. But most state and municipal governments are poor. Most of the funds they command are transferred to them from the central government, and they have little legal or administrative capacity to raise their own revenue. States and localities also suffer greatly from the lack of well-trained and well-paid public officials. As at the national level, many jobs are distributed as political patronage, but even officials who are motivated to be responsive to local needs are generally ill equipped to do so. Since the early 1990s, the government has made several serious efforts to decentralize and devolve more power on state and local governments. At times, governors and mayors have resisted such initiatives because they meant that regional and local governments would have to manage much more complex activities and be the focus of demands from public sector workers and their unions. They were also worried that they would be unable to acquire the budgetary resources necessary to carry out their new responsibilities.

There are exceptions to this picture of regional and local government impoverishment and lack of capacity. State governments in the north of the country, such as Nuevo León, have been more responsive to local needs and better able to administer public services. In such states, local municipalities have become famous for the extent to which they differ from the norm in most of Mexico. Monterrey, in Nuevo León, for example, has a reputation for efficient and forward-looking city government. Much of this local capacity can be credited to a regional political tradition that has stressed independence from—and even hostility to—Mexico City and the PRI. In addition, states and localities that have stronger governments and a tradition of better service tend to be areas of greater wealth, largely in the north of the country. In these cases, entrepreneurial groups and private citizens have often invested time and resources in state and local government.

Until 1988, all governors were from the PRI, although many believe that only electoral fraud kept two governorships out of the hands of an opposition party in 1986. Finally, in 1989, a non-PRI governor assumed power in Baja California Norte, an important first. After the 2000 election, twelve states and the Federal District of Mexico City were governed by parties other than the PRI. By 2002, the number had grown to fourteen states and the Federal District. Also, municipalities have increasingly been the focus of authentic party competition. As opposition parties came to control these levels of government, they were challenged to improve services such as police protection, garbage collection, sanitation, and education. PRI-dominated governments have also tried to improve their performance because they are now more threatened by the possibility of losing elections.

The Policy-Making Process

The Mexican system is very dependent on the quality of its leadership and presidential understanding of how economic and social policies can affect the development of the country. As indicated throughout this chapter, the six-year term of office, the *sexenio*, is an extremely important fact of political life in Mexico. New presidents can introduce extensive change in positions within the government. They are able to bring in "their" people, who build teams of "their" people within ministries, agencies, and party networks. This generally provides the president with a group of high- and middle-level officials who share a general orientation toward public policy and are motivated to carry out his goals. When the PRI was the dominant party, these officials believed that in following presidential leadership, they enhanced their chances for upward political mobility. In such a context, even under a single party, it was likely that changes in public policies could be introduced every six years, creating innovation or discontinuity, or both. As indicated, the limited experience of the PAN in executive office and the increasing role of congress in policy-making meant that the influence of the president on government was less strong. Nevertheless, Mexicans continue to look to the president and the executive for policy leadership.

Together with the bureaucracy, the president is the focal point of policy formulation and political management. Until 1997, the legislature always had a PRI majority and acted as a rubber stamp for presidentially sponsored legislation. Since then, the congress has proven to be a more active policy-maker, blocking and forcing the negotiation of legislation, and even introducing its own bills. The president's skills in negotiating, managing the opposition, using the media to acquire public support, and maneuvering within the bureaucracy can be important for ensuring that his program is fully endorsed.

Significant limits on presidential power occur when policy is being implemented. In fact, in areas as diverse as the regulation of working conditions, antipollution laws, tax collection, election monitoring, and health care in remote rural areas, Mexico has extremely advanced legislation on the books. Yet the persistence of unsafe factory conditions, pollution in Mexico City, tax evasion, election fraud, and poor health care suggests that legislation is not always translated into practice. At times, policies are not implemented because public officials at the lower levels disagree with them or make deals with affected interests in order to benefit personally. This is the case, for example, with taxes that remain uncollected because individuals or corporations bribe officials to overlook them. In other cases, lower-level officials may lack the capacity or skills to implement some policies, such as those directed toward improving education or rural development services. For whatever reasons, Mexican presidents cannot always deliver on their intentions. Traditionally, they have been above criticism when this has occurred because of the willingness of Mexican citizens to blame lower-level officials for such slippage. However, exempting the president from responsibility for what does or does not occur during his watch became much less common after the 1970s.

Section ❹ Representation and Participation

How do citizen interests get represented in Mexican politics, given the high degree of centralization, presidentialism, and, until recently, PRI domination? Is it possible for ordinary citizens to make demands on government and influence public policy? In fact, Mexico

has had a relatively peaceful history since the revolution in part because the political system offers some channels for representation and participation. Through this long history, the political system emphasized compromise among contending elites, behind-the-scenes conflict resolution, and distribution of political rewards to those willing to play by the formal and informal rules of the game. It also responded, if reluctantly and defensively, to demands for change.

Often, citizens are best able to interact with the government through a variety of informal means rather than through the formal processes of elections, campaigns, and interest group lobbying. Interacting with government through the personal and informal mechanisms of clientelism usually means that the government retains the upper hand in deciding which interests to respond to and which to ignore. For many interests, this has meant "incorporation without power."[16] Increasingly, however, Mexican citizens are organizing to alter this situation, and the advent of truly competitive elections has increased the possibility that citizens who organize can gain some response from government.

The Legislature

Students in the United States are frequently asked to study complex charts explaining how a bill becomes a law, because the formal process of lawmaking affects the content of legislation. Under the old reign of the PRI in Mexico, while there were formal rules that prescribed such a process, studying them would not have been useful for understanding how the legislature worked. Because of the overwhelming presence of this political party, opposition to presidential initiatives by Mexico's two-chamber legislature, the Senate and the Chamber of Deputies, was rarely heard. To the extent that representatives did not agree with policies they were asked to approve, they counted on the fact that policy implementation was flexible and allowed for after-the-fact bending of the rules or disregard of measures that were harmful to important interests.

Members of congress are elected through a dual system of "first past the post" and proportional representation. Each state elects three senators. Two of them are determined by majority vote, and the third is determined by whichever party receives the second highest number of votes. In addition, thirty-two senators are determined nationally through a system of proportional representation that awards seats based on the number of votes cast for each party. The same system works in the Chamber of Deputies, with 300 selected on the basis of majority vote and 200 additional representatives

chosen by proportional representation. Representation in congress has become somewhat more diverse since the end of the 1980s. In 2001, women held 15.6 percent of seats in the Senate and 16 percent in the Chamber of Deputies. Some representatives also emerged from the ranks of community activists who had participated in activities such as urban popular movements.

The PRI's grip on the legislature was broken in 1988. The growing strength of opposition parties, combined with legislation that provided for greater representation of minority parties in the congress, led to the election of 240 opposition deputies (out of 500) that year, giving the PRI less than the two-thirds majority it needed for major pieces of legislation or constitutional amendments. After that, when presidential legislation was sent to the chamber, the opposition challenged the tradition of legislative passivity and insisted on real debate about issues. The two-thirds PRI majority was returned in 1991—amid allegations of voter fraud—and presidentialism was reasserted. Nevertheless, the strong presence of opposition parties continued to encourage debate as PRI delegates were challenged to defend proposed legislation. The 1994 elections returned a clear PRI majority of 300 deputies and 64 senators, but in 1997, the PRI lost this majority when 261 deputies and 51 senators (of 128) were elected from opposition parties. For the first time in its history, the PRI did not have an absolute majority in the Chamber of Deputies. The party composition of the Chamber of Deputies and the Senate after the elections of 2000 is shown in Figure 1.

Since that time, the role of congress in the policy process has been strengthened considerably.[17] The cost of greater sharing of powers between the executive and the legislature, however, has been to stall the policy process. Several important pieces of legislation, including efforts to manage private debts and approve the budget, were stalled under President Zedillo. Even PRI legislators became more willing to slow or alter presidential initiatives. Under the Fox administration, relations with congress have been even more confrontational. The president lacks a party majority and had a difficult time promoting his investment plan, labor code reform, and the liberalization of the energy sector. In a first-ever use of congressional power, the senate denied President Fox permission to go to the United States and Canada, greatly embarrassing him. As a

Figure 1

Congressional Representation by Party, 2000

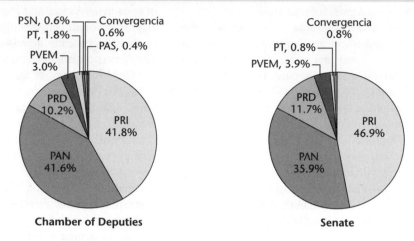

Chamber of Deputies

Senate

PRI = Partido Revolucionario Institucional
PAN = Partido Acción Nacional
PRD = Partido de la Revolución Democrática
PVEM = Partido Verde Ecologista de México
PT = Partido del Trabajo
Convergencia = Convergencia por la Democracia

Source: Instituto Federal Electoral, www.ife.org.mx.

consequence of this kind of muscle flexing, congressional committees that once were important only for their control over patronage have acquired new relevance, and committee members and chairs are becoming somewhat more like their U.S. counterparts in terms of the power they can wield. Party caucuses have also emerged as centers of power in the legislature. In addition, interest groups, which before 1997 had scant interest in lobbying for legislative action because this body did not make important decisions, have increased their lobbying activities in congress. Thus, as a genuine multiparty system emerged, the Mexican congress became a more important forum for a variety of political voices and points of view. PRI candidates now have to participate in competitive elections in many locales, and the number of safe seats for party stalwarts is declining.

Political Parties and the Party System

Mexico has a multiparty system. Even under the long reign of the PRI, a number of political parties existed. By the mid-1980s, some of them were attracting more political support, a trend that continued into the 1990s and 2000s. Electoral reforms introduced by the López Portillo, de la Madrid, Salinas, and Zedillo administrations made it easier for opposition parties to contest elections and win seats in the legislature. In 1990, an electoral commission was created to regulate campaigns and elections, and in 1996 it became fully independent of the government. Now all parties receive funding from the government and have access to the media. In addition to the PRI, two other political parties have demonstrated the capacity to acquire substantial support in elections.

The PRI

Mexico's Institutional Revolutionary Party—Partido Revolucionario Institucional—(PRI) was founded by a coalition of political elites who agreed that it was preferable to work out their conflicts within an over-arching structure of compromise than to continue to resort to violence. In the 1930s, the PRI incorporated a wide array of interests, becoming a mass-based party that drew support from all classes in the population. Over seven decades, its principal activities were to generate support for the government, organize the electorate to vote for its candidates, and distribute jobs and development resources in return for loyalty to the system.

Until the 1990s, party organization was based largely on the corporate representation of class interests. Labor was represented within party councils by the National Confederation of Labor (CTM), which includes industry-based unions at local, regional, and national levels. Peasants were represented by the National Confederation of Peasants (CNC), an organization of *ejido* and peasant unions and regional syndicates. The so-called popular sector, comprising small businesses, community-based groups, and public employees, had less internal cohesion but was represented by the National Confederation of Popular Organizations (CNOP). Of the three, the CTM was consistently the best organized and most powerful. Traditionally, the PRI's strongest support came from the countryside, where *ejidatarios* and independent small farmers were grateful for and dependent on rewards of land or jobs. As the country became more urbanized, the support base provided by rural communities remained important to the PRI, but produced many fewer votes than were necessary to keep the party in power.

Within its corporate structures, the PRI functioned through extended networks that distributed public resources—particularly jobs, land, development projects, and access to public services—to lower-level activists who controlled votes at the local level. This informal clientelist organization formed multiple chains of patron-client interaction that culminated at the highest level of political decision making within the PRI and the office of the president. In this system, those with ambitions to public office or to positions within the PRI put together networks of supporters from above (patrons), to whom they delivered votes, and supporters from below (clients), who traded allegiance for access to public resources. For well over half a century, this system worked extremely well. PRI candidates won by overwhelming majorities until the 1980s (see Figure 2). Of course, electoral fraud and the ability to distribute government largesse are central explanations for these numbers, but they also attest to an extremely well-organized party. Although the PRI became much weaker in the 1980s and 1990s, it was still the only political party that could boast a network of constituency organizations in virtually every village and urban community in the country. Its vast political machinery also allowed it to monitor events, even in remote areas.

Within the PRI, power was centralized, and the sector organizations (the CTM, the CNC, and the CNOP) responded primarily to elites at the top of the political pyramid rather than to member interests. Over time, the corporate interest group organizations, particularly the CTM and the CNC, became widely identified with corruption, bossism, centralized control, and lack of effective participation. By the 1980s, new generations of voters were less beholden to patronage-style politics and much more willing to question the party's dominance. When the administrations of de la Madrid, Salinas, and Zedillo imposed harsh austerity measures, the PRI was held responsible for the resulting losses in incomes and benefits. Simultaneously, as the government cut back sharply on public sector jobs and services, the PRI had far fewer resources to distribute to maintain its traditional bases of support. Moreover, it began to suffer from increasing internal dissension between the old guard—the so-called dinosaurs—and the "modernizers" who wanted to reform the party.

Until the elections of 1988, there was no question that the PRI candidate would be elected president. Victories recording 85 to 95 percent of the total vote for the PRI were the norm (see Table 2). After 1988, however, PRI candidates were challenged by parties to the right and left, and outcomes were hotly contested by the opposition, which claimed fraudulent electoral practices. In 1994, Zedillo won primarily because the opposition was not well organized and failed to present a program other than its opposition to the PRI. Presidents Salinas and Zedillo also distanced themselves from the party during their administrations, giving the first clear signals in PRI history that there was a distinction between the party and the government.

Figure 2

PRI Support in Congressional Elections, 1946–2000

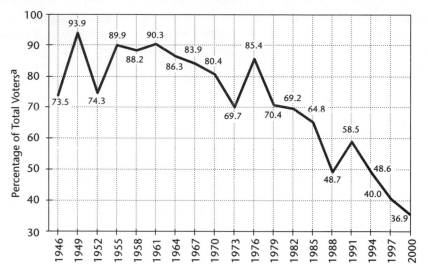

Sources: For 1946–1988: Juan Molinar Horcasitas, *El Tiempo de la legitimidad: Elecciones, autoritarismo y democracia en México* (México, D.F.: Cal y Arena, 1991). For 1991: Secretaría Nacional de Estudios, Partido Acción Nacional, *Análisis del Proceso Federal Electoral 1994, 1995.* For 1994: Instituto Federal Electoral, *Estadística de las Elecciones Federales de 1994, Compendio de Resultados* (Mexico, D.F., 1995). For 1997: www.ife.org.mx/wwworge/tablas/mrent.htm. For 2000: Instituto Federal Electoral, www.ife.org.mx.

As the PRI faced greater competition from other parties and continued to suffer from declining popularity, efforts were made to restructure and reform it. The CNOP was replaced by an organization that sought to incorporate a wide array of non-class-based citizen and neighborhood movements. In 1990, membership rules were altered to allow individuals and groups not identified with its corporate sector organizations to join. In addition, regional party organizations gained representation at the national level. Party conventions were introduced in an effort to democratize the internal workings of the party, and some states and localities began to hold primaries to select PRI candidates, a significant departure from the old system of selection by party bosses.

The PRI continues to face a difficult future. The Mexican electorate is now predominantly urban. Voters are younger, better educated, and more middle class than in the days of the PRI's greatest success—the 1940s, 1950s, and 1960s. The 1988 elections demon-strated the relevance of changing demographic conditions when only 27.3 percent of the population of Mexico City voted for the PRI candidate and only 34.3 percent of the population in other urban areas supported him. In 2000, Mexico City gave only 22.7 percent of its vote to the PRI. Most important, the election of 2000 demonstrated to everyone that the PRI could lose the pinnacle of power in the country, the presidency. Many analysts believe that opposition party campaigns tapped into a deep well of resentment against evidence of corruption and mismanagement in the PRI.

The PAN

The National Action Party—Partido Acción Nacional—(PAN) was founded in 1939 to represent interests opposed to the centralization and anticlericalism of the PRI. It was founded by those who believed that the country needed more than one strong political party and

Table 2

Voting in Presidential Elections, 1934–2000				
Year	Votes for PRI Candidate[a]	Votes for PAN Candidate	Votes for All Others[b]	Turnout (% Voters Among Eligible Adults)[c]
1934	98.2%	—	1.8%	53.6%
1940	93.9	—	6.1	57.5
1946	77.9	—	22.1	42.6
1952	74.3	7.8%	17.9	57.9
1958	90.4	9.4	0.2	49.4
1964	88.8	11.1	0.1	54.1
1970	83.3	13.9	1.4	63.9
1976[d]	93.6	—	1.2	29.6
1982	71.0	15.7	9.4	66.1
1988	50.7	16.8	32.5[e]	49.4[f]
1994	50.1	26.7	23.2	77.16
2000	36.1	42.5[g]	19.2[h]	64.0

[a]From 1958 through 1982, includes votes cast for the Partido Popular Socialista (PPS) and the Partido Auténtico de la Revolución Mexicana (PARM), both of which regularly endorsed the PRI's presidential candidate. In 1988, they supported opposition candidate Cuauhtémoc Cárdenas.

[b]Excludes annulled votes; includes votes for candidates of nonregistered parties.

[c]Eligible population base for 1934 through 1952 includes all males ages 20 and over (legal voting age: 21 years). Both men and women ages 20 and over are included in the base for 1958 and 1964 (women received the franchise in 1958). The base for 1970–1988 includes all males and females ages 18 and over (the legal voting age was lowered to 18, effective 1970).

[d]The PRI candidate, José Lopez Portillo, ran virtually unopposed because the PAN failed to nominate a candidate. The only other significant candidate was Valentín Campa, representing the Communist Party, which was not legally registered to participate in the 1976 election. More than 5 percent of the votes were annulled.

[e]Includes 31.1 percent officially tabulated for Cuauhtémoc Cárdenas.

[f]Estimated using data from the Federal Electoral Commission. However, the commission itself has released two different figures for the number of eligible voters in 1988. Using the commission's larger estimate of eligible population, the turnout would be 44.9 percent.

[g]Votes cast for Alianza por el Cambio, formed by the Partido Acción Nacional (PAN) and the Partido Verde Ecologista de Mexico (PVEM).

[h]Includes votes cast for Alianza por México, formed by the Partido de la Revolución Democrática (PRD), the Partido del Trabajo (PT), Convergencia por la Democracia, the Partido Alianza Social (PAS), and the Partido de la Sociedad Nacionalista (PSN).

Sources: From *Comparative Politics Today: A World View*, 4th ed. by Gabriel Almond and G. Bingham Powell, Jr. Copyright ©1988. Reprinted by permission of Addison-Wesley Educational Publishers, Inc. For 1994: Instituto Federal Electoral, *Estadística de las Elecciones Federales de 1994, Compendio de Resultados* (Mexico, D.F., 1995). For 2000: Instituto Federal Electoral, www.ife.org.mx.

that opposition parties should oppose the PRI through legal and constitutional actions. Historically, this party has been strongest in northern states, where the tradition of resistance to Mexico City is also strongest. It has also been primarily an urban party of the middle class and is closely identified with the private sector. The PAN has traditionally campaigned on a platform endorsing greater regional autonomy, less government intervention in the economy, reduced regulation of business, clean and fair elections, rapprochement with the Catholic Church, and support for private and religious education. When PRI governments of the 1980s and 1990s moved toward market-friendly and export-oriented policies, the policy differences between the two parties were significantly reduced. Nevertheless, a major difference of perspectives about religion continued to characterize the two parties. The PAN has always favored a closer relationship with the Catholic Church, and President Fox's public protestations of faith, including kissing the pope's ring when the pontiff visited Mexico in 2002, raised many an eyebrow in a system long noted for its commitment to secularism.

For many years, the PAN was able to elect 9 to 10 percent of all deputies to the national congress and capture control of a few municipal governments. Then, in the early 1980s, and especially after President López Portillo nationalized the banks, opposition to centralism and statism grew more popular. The PAN began to develop greater capacity to contest elections at higher levels of government. In particular, the party gained popularity among urban middle-class voters, won elections in several provincial cities, and came close to winning governorships in two states. In 1988, it captured 16.8 percent of the vote for president, 101 Chamber of Deputies seats, and one Senate seat. The following year, it won the governorship of the state of Baja California Norte. In the 1994 elections, PAN's candidate, Diego Fernández de Cevallos, garnered 26 percent of the presidential vote, and the party won 25 seats in the senate and 119 in the Chamber of Deputies. This number increased to 33 senate seats and 121 chamber seats in 1997. In 2000, the party elected 53 senators and 224 deputies and by 2002 controlled the governorships in ten states. And, of course, it won the presidency with 42.7 percent of the total vote. In these elections, the party ran in an electoral alliance, called the Alliance for Change, with the small Green Ecologist Party of Mexico (PVEM). The Fox campaign attracted many younger and well-educated voters.

The PAN has traditionally set relatively high standards for activism among its party members; as a consequence, the membership of the party has remained small, even as its capacity to attract votes has grown. In their efforts to control the development of the party, its leaders have had a difficult relationship with the PAN standard bearer, Vicente Fox. As Fox's political profile expanded while serving as the governor of the

state of Guanajuato, leaders of the party became concerned that he would emerge as a favorite for the presidency. They worked to limit his opportunities to run for office, forcing him to look for other sources of financing his campaign. In 1997, the Friends of Fox organization began to raise funds and promote his candidacy for president, and at the same time, the traditional leaders of the party were weakened significantly in electoral contests when the PAN made a poor showing. Fox gained in popularity throughout the country, and in 1999, the party had little option but to nominate him as its candidate. The Friends of Fox continued to provide the most important source of campaign support, however, and when Fox won the presidential election, the PAN organization was weak and not at all united in backing him. Further, although it made a very good showing in elections for the Chamber of Deputies and the Senate, it did not have a majority in either chamber.

The PRD

Another significant challenge to the PRI has come from the Democratic Revolutionary Party—Partido de la Revolucion Democrática—(PRD), a populist and nationalist alternative to the PRI, whose policies are left of center. Its candidate in the 1988 and 1994 elections was Cuauhtémoc Cárdenas, the son of Mexico's most famous and revered president. He was a PRI insider until party leaders virtually ejected him for demanding internal reform of the party and a platform emphasizing social justice. In the 1988 elections, Cárdenas was officially credited with winning 31.1 percent of the vote, and the party captured 139 seats in the Chamber of Deputies. He benefited from massive political defection from the PRI and garnered support from workers disaffected with the boss-dominated unions as well as peasants who remembered his father's concern for agrarian reform and investment in the poor. Mexico City gave him 50.4 percent of the vote, which also represented some middle-class support.

Even while the votes were being counted, the party began to denounce widespread electoral fraud and claim that Cárdenas would have won if the election had been honest. The PRD challenged a number of vote counts in the courts and walked out of Salinas's inaugural speech. Considerable public opinion supported the party's challenge. In the aftermath of the 1988 elections, then, it seemed that the PRD was a strong contender to become Mexico's second most powerful party. It was expected to have a real chance in future years to challenge the PRI's "right" to the presidency.

However, in the aftermath of these elections, the party was plagued by internal divisions over its platform, leadership, organizational structure, and election strategy. By 1994, it still lagged far behind the PRI and the PAN in establishing and maintaining the local constituency organizations needed to mobilize votes and monitor the election process. In addition, the PRD found it difficult to define an appropriate left-of-center alternative to the market-oriented policies carried out by the government. While the claims that such policies ignored the need for social justice were popular, policies to respond to poverty that did not imply a return to unpopular government intervention were difficult to devise. In the aftermath of the Colosio assassination, citizens also became more alarmed about violence, and some were concerned that the level of political rivalry represented by the PRD threatened the country's long-term political stability. In the 1994 elections, Cárdenas won only 17 percent of the votes, although the PRD elected seventy-one deputies and eight senators.

Thanks to the government's continued unpopular economic policies and the leadership of a successful grassroots mobilizer named Andrés Manuel López Obrador, who was elected to head the party in 1996, the PRD began to stage a remarkable turnaround. Factional bickering was controlled, and organizational discipline increased. In addition, the PRD proved successful in moving beyond its regional stronghold and established itself as a truly national party. In 1997, the party increased its share of seats to 125 in the Chamber of Deputies and 16 in the Senate. Most important, Cárdenas became the first popularly elected mayor of Mexico City. This provided him and the party with a critically important opportunity to demonstrate their ability to govern, not to mention a potential platform for the presidential elections of 2000. By this time, the PRD had managed to shed some of its reputation as a "one-horse show" and had won two governorships, with the PRI under question for fraud in a third. In 2000, López Obrador was elected mayor of Mexico City with 39.5 percent of the vote, signaling again the political importance of the capital city. In the presidential race,

Cárdenas ran again, but even in alliance with several small parties, the Alliance for Mexico, he was able to garner only 16.5 percent of the vote. Its performance in the legislative race was equally disappointing. The PRD alliance retained 16 seats in the senate, but lost 58 in the Chamber of Deputies, retaining only 67 seats. In 2000, three state governors represented the party, and by 2002, four were governed by the PRD, in addition to the Federal District of Mexico City.

Other Parties

There are a number of smaller parties that contest elections in Mexico. Some of them have always allied themselves with the PRI, supporting its candidates for president and other positions. Newer parties have also emerged to contest more democratic elections. In 2000, the Social Democracy Party—Partido Democrácia Social—(PDS) won 1.6 percent of the votes for president, and the Democratic Center Party—Partido de Centro Democrático—(PCD) won 0.6 percent. The PDS won 1.8 percent of votes for the Senate and 1.9 percent for the Chamber of Deputies, and the PCD won 1.1 percent each of votes for Senate and the Chamber of Deputies. This very poor performance raises questions about whether either party would survive. National law requires that parties must receive 2.5 percent of the vote in order to remain registered as political parties.

Elections

Each of the three main political parties draws voters from a wide and overlapping spectrum of the electorate. Nevertheless, a typical voter for the PRI is likely to be from a rural area or small town, to have less education, and to be older and poorer than voters for the other parties. A typical voter for the PAN is likely to be from a northern state, to live in an urban area, to be a middle-class professional, to have a comfortable lifestyle, and to have a high school or even a university education. A typical voter for the PRD is likely to be young, to be a political activist, to have an elementary or high school education, to live in one of the central states, and to live in a small town or an urban area. As we have seen, the support base for the PRI is the most vulnerable to economic and demographic changes in the country. Voting for opposition parties is an urban phenomenon, and Mexico continues to urbanize at the rate of 3 percent per year. This means that in order to stay competitive, the PRI will have to garner more support from urban areas. It must also be able to appeal to younger voters, especially the large numbers who are attracted to the PRD and the PAN.

Elections are becoming more competitive and fairer in Mexico. Electoral reforms introduced by the López Portillo, de la Madrid, Salinas, and Zedillo administrations made it easier for opposition parties to contest elections and win seats in the legislature. In 1990, an electoral commission was created to regulate campaigns and elections, and in 1996 it became fully independent from the government. Now all parties receive government funding and have ensured access to the media. These and other laws that limit campaign spending and campaign contributions were a response to demands that the government level the playing field between the PRI and the other parties. Voter registration was reformed to ensure that fraud would be more detectable. Election monitoring was also strengthened, and another reform increased the chances for opposition parties to win representation in the Senate. Beginning in 1994, elections have been much fairer, and subsequent congressional, state, and municipal elections reinforced the impression that electoral fraud is on the wane in many areas. PAN's victory in 2000 substantially increased this impression. Some state and local elections continue to be questioned, especially in rural areas in the south, where local PRI bosses remain powerful. For example, many citizens did not believe that the PRI had fairly swept the 1997 congressional elections in the state of Chiapas, where opposition to the government was strong.

Political Culture, Citizenship, and Identity

Most citizens in Mexico demonstrate overall commitment to the political system while expressing considerable criticism—and often cynicism—about how it works and how equitable it is. A survey of almost any *ejido*, for example, will uncover lengthy local histories of how *ejidatarios* have been mistreated, given the runaround by bureaucratic organizations, and cheated by local, regional, and national leaders of the CNC, the PRI, and government agencies. The survey will reveal deep commitment to the country's heroes and the institutions of government along with anger, distrust, frustration, and biting jokes told at the expense of the rich and powerful. Currently, many citizens criticize corruption in government and the PRI, but remain proud that their country has become more democratic.

Most Mexicans have a deep familiarity with how the political system works and the ways in which they might be able to extract benefits from it. They understand the informal rules of the game in Mexican politics that have helped maintain political stability despite extensive inequalities in economic and political power. Clientelism has long been a form of participation in the sense that through their connections, many people, even the poorest, are able to interact with public officials and get something out of the political system. This kind of participation emphasizes how limited resources, such as access to health care, can be distributed in a way that provides maximum political payoff. This informal system is a fundamental reason that many Mexicans continued to vote for the PRI for so long.

However, new ways of interacting with government are emerging, and they coexist along with the clientelistic style of the past. An increasing number of citizens are seeking to negotiate with the government on the basis of citizenship rights, not personal relationships. The movements that emerged in the 1980s sought to form broad but loose coalitions with other organizations and attempted to identify and work with reform-oriented public officials. Their suspicion of traditional political organizations such as the PRI or the CNC and the CTM also carried over to suspicion of close alliances with the PAN and the PRD.

As politics and elections became more open and competitive, the roles of public opinion and the mass media have become more important. In the past, public opinion polling was often contaminated by the dominance of the PRI, and some polling organizations were even subsidized by the party or the government. Increasingly, however, even the PRI and the government are interested in objective information and analysis of public opinion. These data have influenced the content and timing of government decisions and the development of strategies in election campaigns. In 1994 and 2000, politicians, citizens, and political activists closely followed the popularity polls of the three major candidates for president, and party officials monitored how the image of their contender could be molded to capture higher voter approval ratings. Because extensive public opinion polling is comparatively new in Mexico, it is difficult to assess how attitudes toward government have changed over time. Surveys taken in the 1980s and 1990s indicate that confidence fell extensively during the 1980s but rebounded somewhat in the 1990s. Fewer Mexicans claim a party preference today than in the past, and the percentage of citizens who identify with the PRI has fallen sharply.

Today, the media play an important role in public opinion formation. In the past, it was not easy for newspapers, magazines, or radio and television stations to be openly opposed to the government. For many years, the government used access to newsprint, which it controlled, to reward sympathetic news coverage and penalize coverage it considered hostile. In addition, the government subsidized the salaries of some reporters, and politically ambitious public and PRI officials paid stipends to those who covered their activities sympathetically. A considerable amount of the revenue of newspapers and other media organizations came from advertising placed by the government. Each of these mechanisms was used to encourage positive reporting of government activities, strong endorsement of presidential initiatives, and quashing of stories that reflected ill on the party or the government, all without resorting to outright government control of the media.

As with other aspects of Mexican politics, the media began to become more independent in the 1980s, enjoying a "spring" of greater independence and diversity of opinion.[18] There are currently several major television networks in the country, and many citizens have access to CNN and other global networks. The number of newspapers is expanding, as is their circulation, and several news magazines play the same role in Mexico that *Time* and *Newsweek* do in the United States. Citizens in Mexico today clearly hear a much wider range of opinion and much greater reporting of debates about public policy and criticism of government than at any time previously.

Interests, Social Movements, and Protests

The Mexican system has long responded to groups of citizens through pragmatic **accommodation** to their interests. This is one important reason that political tensions among major interests have rarely escalated into the kind of serious conflict that can threaten stability. Where open conflict has occurred, it has generally been met with efforts to find some kind of compromise solution. Accommodation has been particularly apparent in response to the interests of business. Mexico's development strategy encouraged the growth of wealthy elites in commerce, finance, industry, and agriculture (see Section 2). Although these elites were the primary beneficiaries of the country's development, they were never incorporated into the PRI. Instead, they represent themselves through a set of business-focused interest groups and personal relationships with influential officials. Through these networks, business organizations and individuals seek policies favorable to their interests.

Labor has been similarly accommodated within the system. Wage levels for unionized workers grew fairly consistently between 1940 and 1982, when the economic crisis caused a significant drop in wages. At the same time, labor interests were attended to in terms of concrete benefits and limitations on the rights of employers to discipline or dismiss workers. Labor union leaders controlled their rank and file in the interest of their own power to negotiate with government, but at the same time, they sought benefits for workers who continued to provide support for the PRI. The power of the union bosses has declined, in part because the unions are weaker than in the past, in part because union members are demanding greater democratization, and in part because the PRI no longer monopolizes political power.

Under the PRI, accommodation was often coupled with **co-optation** as a means of incorporating dissidents into the system so that they did not threaten its continuity. In 1968, for example, students protesting against authoritarianism, poverty, and inequity challenged the government just prior to the opening of the Olympic Games. The government responded with force—in one instance killing several hundred students in Mexico City—sparking even greater animosity. When Luis Echeverría became president in 1970, he recruited large numbers of the student activists into his administration. He also dramatically increased spending on social services, putting many of the young people to work in expanding antipoverty programs in the countryside and in urban slums. Through these actions, a generation of political and social activists was incorporated into the system, and there was some accommodation to their concerns. We also know now that his government allowed the military to kidnap, arrest, torture, and kill some political dissidents.

Despite the strong and controlling role of the PRI in Mexico's political history, the country also has a tradition of civic organizations that operate at community and local levels with considerable independence from politics. Local village improvement societies, religious organizations, and sports clubs are widespread. Many of their activities are not explicitly political, although they may have political implications in that they encourage individuals to work together to find solutions to problems or organize around common interests. Other organizational experiences are more explicitly political. The student movement of 1968 provided evidence that civil society in Mexico had the potential to contest the power of the state. The emergence of independent unionism in the 1970s was another indication of renewed willingness to question the right of the state to stifle the voices of dissent and the emergence of demands for greater equity and participation. The elections of 2000 were an announcement that the old system of accommodation, co-optation, and repression was no longer working.

The economic crisis of 1982 combined with this civic tradition to heighten demands for assistance from the government. In October 1983, as many as 2 million people participated in a civic strike to call attention to the crisis and demand a forceful government response. A less successful strike in June 1984 made the same point to the government. In urban areas, citizen groups demanded land rights in squatter settlements, as well as housing, infrastructure, and urban services, as rights of citizenship rather than as a reward for loyalty to the PRI.[19] In the aftermath of the 1985 earthquake, citizen groups became especially dynamic in demanding that government respond to the needs of citizens without reference to their history of party loyalty. Residents of Mexico City demanded that the government let them decide how to rebuild and relocate their neighborhoods and choose who would serve as mayor and represent them.[20] Many also became active in groups that share concerns about quality-of-life issues such as clean air

and safe neighborhoods. See "Citizen Action: Urban Popular Movements."

In rural areas, peasant organizations also demanded greater independence from government and the leaders of the PRI and the CNC in the 1980s.[21] In addition to greater access to land, they demanded better prices for the crops they produced, access to markets and credit, development of better infrastructure, and the provision of better education and health services. They began to form alliances with other groups. For example, in the Yucatán peninsula, PEMEX's exploration and production of oil caused massive ecological damage and was carried out with complete disregard for the rights of local *ejidatarios*. By the late 1970s, environmental groups had joined peasant organizations and student activists in protesting against PEMEX. Since 1994, the rebels in Chiapas have become a focal point for broad alliances of those concerned about the rights of indigenous groups (ethnic minorities) and rural poverty. Indigenous groups have also emerged to demand that government be responsive to their needs and respectful of their traditions.

A variety of groups have also organized around middle-class and urban issues. In Mexico City, community groups and broader citizen alliances have been active in calling attention to the disastrous levels of air,

Mexicans demonstrate for better housing in Mexico City's central plaza. *Source:* Robert Freck/Odyssey/Chicago.

Citizen Action: **Urban Popular Movements**

In October 1968, hundreds of students and working-class people took to the streets of Mexico City to protest high unemployment and the authoritarianism of the government. What began as a peaceful rally in Tlaltelolco Plaza ended in a tragedy when government troops opened fire on the crowd and killed more than two hundred people. The political activism of the students heralded the birth of urban popular movements in Mexico. The massacre in Tlaltelolco became a symbol of a government that was unwilling or unable to respond to citizen demands for economic and political equity. The protest movements sparked by the events of 1968 sought to transcend class boundaries and unite voices around a range of urban issues, from housing shortages to inadequate urban services to lack of land to centralized decision making. Such social movements forged new channels for poor and middle-class urban residents to express their needs. They also generated forums for demanding democratic government that the traditional political system was not providing. In May 1980, the first national congress of urban movements was held in Monterrey in northern Mexico.

Urban popular movements, referring to activities of low- and modest-income (popular) groups, gained renewed vitality in the 1980s. When the economic crisis resulted in drastic reductions of social welfare spending and city services, working- and middle-class neighborhoods forged new coalitions and greatly expanded the national discussion of urban problems. The Mexico City earthquake of 1985 encouraged the formation of unprecedented numbers of grass-roots movements in response to the slow and poorly managed relief efforts of the government. Turning to each other, earthquake victims organized to provide shelter, food, and relocation. The elections of 1988 and 1994 provided these groups with significant opportunities to press parties and candidates to respond to their needs. They insisted on their rights to organize and protest without fear of repression or co-optation by the government or the PRI. As the opposition parties expanded rapidly, some leaders of urban movements enrolled as candidates for public office.

Urban popular movements bring citizens together around needs and ideals that cut across class boundaries. Neighborhood improvement, the environment, local self-government, economic development, feminism, and professional identity have been among the factors that have forged links among these groups. As such identities have been strengthened, the need of the political system to negotiate and bargain with a more independent citizenry has increased. Urban popular movements have helped to transform political culture on the most local level, one reason the PAN was able to garner so many votes in the 2000 election.

water, and noise pollution in the capital. Women, with a strong cultural role as caretakers of the home, have begun to mobilize in urban areas around demands for community services, equal pay, legal equality, and opportunities in business traditionally denied them.[22] Religious groups, both Catholic and Protestant, have begun to demand greater government attention to problems of poverty and inequity, as well as more government tolerance of religious education and religious practices. In the early 1990s, the government's social development program, which many critics claim was a ploy by President Salinas to win back respect for his government after the flawed elections of 1988, helped organize thousands of grassroots organizations and possibly contributed to a trend in broader mobilization independent of PRI clientelist networks.[23] In 1997 and 2000, unprecedented numbers of citizens volunteered their time to civic associations that observed the vote to ensure, ballot box by ballot box, that the votes were counted accurately. Where this occurred, mostly in urban areas, there were few accusations of fraud. Overall, then, civil society in Mexico is becoming more pluralist and less easily controlled and there is broader scope for legitimate protest, opposition, and dissent.

Section 5 Mexican Politics in Transition

Political Challenges and Changing Agendas

Mexico confronts a world of increasing interdependence among countries. For all countries, economic integration raises issues of national sovereignty and identity. Mexicans define themselves in part through a set of historical events, symbols, and myths that focus on the country's troubled relationship with the United States. Among numerous national heroes and martyrs are those who distinguished themselves in confrontations with the United States. The myths of the Revolution of 1910 emphasize the uniqueness of the country in terms of its opposition to the capitalists and militarists of the northern country. In the 1970s, Mexicans were encouraged to see themselves as leading Third World countries arguing for increased bargaining positions in relation to the industrialized countries of the north. This view stands in strong contrast to more recent perspectives touting the benefits of an internationally oriented economy and the undeniable reality of information, culture, money, and people flowing back and forth across borders. Mexicans see NAFTA as the beginning of closer integration with trading partners in Latin America, Asia, and Europe.

The country's sense of national identity is affected by international migration. Of particular importance in the Mexican case is labor migration. Every year, large numbers of Mexicans enter the United States as workers. Many return to their towns and villages with new values and new views of the world. Many stay in the United States, where Hispanics have become the largest ethnic population in the country. Most continue to believe that Mexican culture is preferable to American culture, which they see as excessively materialistic and violent. Although they believe that Mexico is a better place to nurture strong family life and values, they are nevertheless strongly influenced by U.S. mass culture, including popular music, movies, television programs, fast food, and consumer goods.

The inability of the Mexican economy to create enough jobs pushes additional Mexicans to seek work in the United States. Extensive migration to the United States has been occurring since the 1880s, when Mexican workers were recruited to help build railroads. In the 1920s and between 1942 and 1964, Mexico and the United States concluded a number of bilateral agreements to provide workers to help the United States meet labor shortages. When such programs ended, a greater proportion of the labor migrants crossed the border into the United States illegally. Differences in wage levels and the jobs lost during the Mexican economic crisis added to the number of workers seeking employment in the United States. The U.S. Congress passed stiff legislation to contain illegal immigration in 1986, but it has been largely ineffective. The difference in wages between the two countries will persist for a long time, which implies that migration will also persist. In fact, the militarization of the border and the increasing danger of crossing lead more illegal immigrants to settle permanently in the United States rather than risk continued trips back and forth across the border. Remittances sent back to Mexico from those working abroad contribute over $6 billion to Mexico's economy each year.

There is disagreement about how to respond to the economic challenges the country faces. Much of the debate surrounds the question of what integration into a competitive international economy really means. For some, it represents the final abandonment of Mexico's sovereignty. For others, it is the basis on which future prosperity must be built. Those who are critical of the market-based, outward-oriented development strategy are concerned about its impact on workers, peasants, and national identities. They argue that the state has abandoned its responsibilities to protect the poor from shortcomings of the market and to provide for their basic needs. They believe that U.S. and Canadian investors have come to Mexico only to find low-wage labor for industrial empires located elsewhere. They see little benefit in further industrial development based on importation of foreign-made parts, their assembly in Mexico, and their export to other markets. This kind of development, they argue, has been prevalent in the *maquiladoras*, or assembly industries, many of which are located along the U.S.-Mexico border. Those who favor closer integration with Canada and the United States acknowledge that some foreign investment does not promote technological advances or move the work force into higher-paying and more skilled jobs. They emphasize, however, that most investment will occur because the country has a relatively well-educated population, the capacity to absorb modern technology, and a large internal market for industrial goods.

In addition to the economic challenges it faces, Mexico provides a testing ground for the democratic idea in a state with a long history of authoritarian institutions. The democratic ideas of citizen rights to free speech and assembly, free and fair elections, and responsive government are major reasons that the power of the PRI came under so much attack. Currently, Mexico is struggling with opening up its political institutions to become more democratic. Vicente Fox, for example, promised to make information about government activities much more widely available to the population, and extensive files about violent military and police repression of political dissent in the past have been made available to citizens. The government also created the independent National Human Rights Commission, which has been active in protecting citizens' rights. (See "Current Challenges: Human Rights in Mexico.") Yet many citizens remain ill informed about government procedures and decision making and are trying to find ways to make their voices heard more effectively in politics. Meanwhile, when Fox demonstrated little capacity to set priorities and communicate a vision for his government, many government agencies found it difficult to act, given a long history of dependence on presidential leadership. This has left many citizens with questions about the effectiveness of more democratic institutions.

Centralization of power and decision making is another legacy that Mexico is trying to revise. Countries around the globe increasingly recognize that the solutions to many policy problems lie at regional and local levels. Issues such as how to ensure that children are receiving a high-quality education, how to relieve chronic and massive traffic congestion, how to dispose of garbage in ways that do not threaten public health, and how to reduce air and water pollution require state and municipal governments that have money, authority, and capable public officials—precisely the conditions that only a very few regional and local governments in Mexico have had. While the government has introduced the decentralization of a number of activities and services, state and municipal governments are struggling to meet the demands of citizens who want competence, responsiveness, and accountability from their local and regional public officials.

The complexity of contemporary problems and the inability of national governments to deal with them all at once make the politics of collective identities more important. The pressure for change in Mexico and many other countries is accelerating as modern technology increases the extent to which people in one country are aware of what is occurring in others and the degree to which citizens are able to communicate their concerns and interests among themselves and to government. The formation of a strong civil society capable of articulating its interests and ensuring that government is responsive to its needs is the other side of political reform.

Human and social development in a country make such a functioning civil society more possible. Improving social conditions is an important challenge for Mexico. While elites enjoy the benefits of sumptuous lifestyles, education at the best U.S. universities for their children, and luxury travel throughout the world, large numbers of Mexicans remain ill educated, poorly served with health care, and distant from the security of knowing that their basic needs for food, shelter, and employment can be met. The Chiapas rebellion of 1994 made the social agenda a topic of everyday conversation by reminding Mexicans that some people lived in appalling conditions with little hope for the future.

What to do about these conditions is debated. As in the United States, some argue that economic growth and expanded employment will resolve the major problems of poverty in the country. They believe that prosperity, tied to Mexico's economic future internationally, will benefit everyone in the long run. For this to occur, however, they insist that education will have to be improved and made more appropriate for developing a well-educated work force. They also believe that improved education will come about when local communities have more control over schools and curriculum and when parents have more choice between public and private education for their children. From their perspective, the solution to poverty and injustice is fairly clear: more and better jobs and improved education.

For those critical of the development path on which Mexico embarked in the 1980s and 1990s, the problems of poverty and inequity are more complex. Solutions involve understanding the diverse causes of

Current Challenges: *Human Rights in Mexico*

The government of Vicente Fox (2000–2006) committed itself to opening up government and improving the state of human rights in Mexico. In the past, the government had been able to limit knowledge of its repressive actions, use the court system to maintain the political peace, and intimidate those who objected to its actions. The president appointed human rights activists to his cabinet and ordered that secret police and military files be opened to public scrutiny. He instructed government ministries to supply more information about their activities and the rights that citizens have to various kinds of services. He also invited the United Nations to open a human rights office in Mexico. He encouraged the ratification of the Inter-American Convention on Enforced Disappearance of Persons. The government also sought to protect the rights of Mexicans abroad, and the United States and Mexico have established a working group to improve human rights conditions for migrants.

The results of these actions have been dramatic. For the first time, Mexicans learned of cases of hundreds of people who had "disappeared" as a result of police and military actions. In addition, citizens have come forward to announce other disappearances, ones they were unwilling to report earlier because they feared reprisals. In 2002, former president Luis Echvererría was brought before prosecutors and questioned about government actions against political dissent in 1968 and 1971, a kind of accountability unheard of in the past. The National Human Rights Commission has been active in efforts to hold government officials accountable and to protect citizens nationally and abroad from repetitions of the abuses of the past.

Yet challenges to human rights accountability remain. Opening up files and setting up systems for prosecuting abusers need to be followed by actions to impose penalties on abusers. The judicial system is weak and has little experience in human rights cases. In addition, action on reports of disappearances, torture, and imprisonment has been slowed by contention about civil and military jurisdictions. In an embarrassing revelation to the government, Amnesty International reported several cases of disappearances that occurred after Fox assumed leadership of the country. There were also reports of arbitrary detentions and extrajudicial executions. In October 2001, Digna Ochoa, a prominent human rights lawyer, was shot. In the aftermath of this assassination, the government was accused of not doing enough to protect her, even when it was widely known that she had been targeted by those opposed to her work. Human rights activists claimed that police and military personnel, in particular, still had impunity to the laws. The strength of the Fox administration was tested in these events, and although human rights were much more likely to be protected than in the past, the government continued to have a long way to go in safeguarding the rights of indigenous people, political dissidents, migrants, gays and lesbians, and poor people whose ability to use the judicial system is limited by poverty and lack of information.

poverty, including not only lack of jobs and poor education but also exploitation, geographic isolation, discriminatory laws and practices, and families disrupted by migration, urbanization, and the tensions of modern life. In the past, Mexicans looked to government for social welfare benefits, but their provision was deeply flawed by inefficiency and political manipulation. The government consistently used access to social services as a means to increase its political control and limit the capacity of citizens to demand equitable treatment. Thus, although many continue to believe that it is the responsibility of government to ensure that citizens are well educated, healthy, and able to make the most of their potential, the populace is deeply suspicious of the government's capacity to provide such conditions fairly and efficiently.

Finally, Mexico is confronting major challenges of adapting newly democratic institutions to reflect ethnic and religious diversity and provide equity for women in economic and political affairs. The past decade has witnessed the emergence of more organized and politically independent ethnic groups demanding justice and equality from government. These groups claim that they suffered for 300 years under colonial rule, for almost 200 years under an independent government, and for 70 years under the PRI and that they are no longer willing to accept poverty and marginality as their lot. The Roman Catholic Church, still the largest organized religion in the country, is losing members to Protestant sects that appeal particularly to the everyday concerns of poor Mexicans. Women, who make up 27 percent of the formal labor force but 40 percent of professional and technical workers, are becoming more organized, but they still have a long way to go before their wages equal those of men or they have equal voice in political and economic decisions.

Mexican Politics in Comparative Perspective

Mexico faces many of the same challenges that beset other countries: creating equitable and effective democratic government, becoming integrated into a global economy, responding to complex social problems, and supporting increasing diversity without losing national identity. Indeed, these were precisely the challenges that the United States faced at the millennium, as did India, Nigeria, China, Japan, Germany, and others. Mexico confronts these challenges within the context of a unique historical and institutional evolution. The legacies of its past, the tensions of the present, and the innovations of the future will no doubt evolve in ways that continue to be uniquely Mexican.

What will the future bring? How much will the pressures for change and the potential loss of national identity affect the nature of the political system? In 1980, few people could have predicted the extensive economic policy reforms and pressures for democracy that Mexico faced in the next two decades. Few would have predicted the outcome of the elections of 2000. In considering the future of the country, it is important to remember that Mexico has a long tradition of relatively strong institutions. It is not a country that will easily slip into sustained political instability. A tradition of constitutional government, a strong presidency, a political system that has incorporated a wide range of interests, a weak tradition of military involvement in politics, and a strong sense of national identity: these

are among the factors that need to be considered in predicting the political consequences of democratization, economic integration, and greater social equality.

Mexico represents a pivotal case for the Northern Hemisphere. If it can successfully bridge the gap between its past and its future and move from centralization to effective local governance, from regional vulnerability to global interdependence, and from the control of the few to the participation of the many, it will set a model for other developing countries that face the same kind of challenges.

Key Terms

mestizo	corporatist state
Amerindian	state capitalism
indigenous groups	import substituting
maquiladoras	industrialization
anticlericalism	informal sector
ejidos	technocrats
ejidatarios	para-statal
sexenio	accommodation
clientelism	co-optation
North American Free Trade Agreement	

Suggested Readings

Babb, Sarah L. *Managing Mexico: Economists from Nationalism to Neoliberalism.* Princeton, N.J.: Princeton University Press, 2001.

Chand, Vikram K. *Mexico's Political Awakening.* Notre Dame, Ind.: University of Notre Dame Press, 2001.

Collier, Ruth Berins. *The Contradictory Alliance: State-Labor Relations and Regime Change in Mexico.* Berkeley: University of California Press, 1992.

Cook, Maria Lorena, Middlebrook, Kevin J., and Molinar, Juan (eds.). *The Politics of Economic Restructuring in Mexico.* San Diego: Center for U.S.-Mexican Studies, University of California, 1994.

Cornelius, Wayne A. "Nation-Building, Participation, and Distribution: The Politics of Social Reform Under Cárdenas." In Gabriel A. Almond, Scott Flanagan, and Robert J. Mundt (eds.), *Crisis, Choice, and Change: Historical Studies of Political Development.* Boston: Little, Brown, 1973.

Cornelius, Wayne A., Craig, Ann L., and Fox, Jonathan (eds.). *Transforming State-Society Relations in Mexico: The National Solidarity Strategy.* San Diego: Center for U.S.-Mexican Studies, University of California, 1994.

Cornelius, Wayne A., Eisenstadt, Todd A., and Hindley, Jane (eds.). *Subnational Politics and Democratization in Mexico.*

San Diego: Center for U.S.-Mexican Studies, University of California, 1999.

Domínguez, Jorge I., and McCann, James A. *Democratizing Mexico: Public Opinion and Electoral Choices*. Baltimore, Md.: Johns Hopkins University Press, 1996.

Eckstein, Susan (ed.). *Power and Popular Protest: Latin American Social Movements*. Berkeley: University of California Press, 1989.

Foweraker, Joe, and Craig, Ann L. (eds.). *Popular Movements and Political Change in Mexico*. Boulder, Colo.: Lynne Rienner, 1990.

Gonzales, Michael J. *The Mexican Revolution, 1910–1940*. Albuquerque: University of New Mexico Press, 2002.

Grindle, Merilee S. *Challenging the State: Crisis and Innovation in Latin America and Africa*. Cambridge: Cambridge University Press, 1995.

Hansen, Roger. *The Politics of Mexican Development*. Baltimore, Md.: Johns Hopkins University Press, 1971.

Harvey, Neil. *The Chiapas Rebellion: The Struggle for Land and Democracy*. Durham, N.C.: Duke University Press, 1998.

Lawson, Chappell H. *Building the Fourth Estate: Democratization and the Rise of a Free Press in Mexico*. Berkeley: University of California, 2002.

Levy, Daniel C., and Bruhn, Kathleen. *Mexico: The Struggle for Democratic Development*. Berkeley: University of California Press, 2001.

Lustig, Nora. *Mexico: The Remaking of an Economy*. 2nd ed. Washington, D.C.: Brookings Institution, 1998.

Meyer, Michael C., and Sherman, William L. *The Course of Mexican History*. 5th ed. New York: Oxford University Press, 1995.

Paz, Octavio. *The Labyrinth of Solitude: Life and Thought in Mexico*. New York: Grove Press, 1961.

Suárez-Orozco, Marcelo (ed.). *Crossings: Mexican Immigration in Interdisciplinary Perspective*. Cambridge, Mass.: Harvard University Press, 1998.

Ugalde, Luis Carlos. *The Mexican Congress: Old Player, New Power*. Washington, D.C.: Center for Strategic and International Studies, 2000.

Ward, Peter. *Mexico City*. New York: Wiley, 1998.

Womack, John, Jr. *Zapata and the Mexican Revolution*. New York: Vintage Books, 1968.

———, (ed.). *Rebellion in Chiapas: An Historical Reader*. New York: New Press, 1999.

Suggested Websites

Bank of Mexico (in English and Spanish)
www.banxico.org.mx
Economist Intelligence Unit (registration required)
www.eiu.com
Mexico (search engine for Mexican web sites)
www.Mexico.com (in English and Spanish)
New York Times
www.nytimes.com/pages/world/americas/index.html

Office of the President (in English and Spanish)
www.presidencia.gob.mx
Treasury ministry (in English and Spanish)
www.shop.gob.mex
Washington Post
www.washingtonpost.com/wp-dyn/world/americas/northamerica/mexico/
Public Broadcasting System
www.pbs.org/newshour/bb/latin_america/mexico_index.html
Government of Mexico
www.precisa.gob.mx (in Spanish only)

Notes

Bertha Angulo Curiel of Harvard University assisted in the preparation of this chapter.

[1] This figure represents an estimate of the metropolitan area of Mexico City, which extends beyond the official boundaries of the city.

[2] An excellent history of this event is presented in Wayne A. Cornelius, "Nation-Building, Participation, and Distribution: The Politics of Social Reform Under Cárdenas," in Gabriel A. Almond, Scott Flanagan, and Robert J. Mundt (eds.), *Crisis, Choice and Change: Historical Studies of Political Development* (Boston: Little, Brown, 1973).

[3] Although the self-confessed "lone gunman" was jailed, the ensuing investigation raised concerns about a possible conspiracy involving party and law enforcement officials as well as drug cartels. Rumors circulated about a cover-up scandal. Eventually, skepticism about the integrity of the inquiry was so great that President Salinas called for a new investigation. At this point, little remains known about what exactly happened in Tijuana and why.

[4] United Nations Development Programme, *Human Development Report* (2001), http//www.undp.org/hdr2001/back.pdf.

[5] World Bank, *World Development Indicators 2002*, CD-ROM.

[6] World Bank, *World Development Report, 2001* (New York: Oxford University Press, 2001).

[7] Merilee S. Grindle, *State and Countryside: Development Policy and Agrarian Politics in Latin America* (Baltimore, Md.: Johns Hopkins University Press, 1986), 63, quoting President Avila Camacho (1940–1946).

[8] Kevin J. Middlebrook (ed.), *Unions, Workers, and the State in Mexico* (San Diego: Center for U.S.-Mexican Studies, University of California, 1991).

[9] Grindle, *State and Countryside*, 79–111.

[10] For a description of this process, see Carlos Bazdresch and Santiago Levy, "Populism and Economic Policy in Mexico," in Rudiger Dornbusch and Sebastian Edwards (eds.), *The Macroeconomics of Populism in Latin America* (Chicago: University of Chicago Press, 1991), 72.

[11]For an assessment of the mounting problems of Mexico City and efforts to deal with them, see Diane E. Davis, *Urban Leviathan: Mexico City in the Twentieth Century* (Philadelphia: Temple University Press, 1994).

[12]Joe Foweraker and Ann L. Craig (eds.), *Popular Movements and Political Change in Mexico* (Boulder, Colo.: Lynne Rienner, 1989).

[13]Roger Hansen, *The Politics of Mexican Development* (Baltimore, Md.: Johns Hopkins University Press, 1971), 75.

[14]World Bank, *World Development Report, 2001*, 283.

[15]Economist Intelligence Unit, *Country Commerce, Mexico* (London: EIU, September 2001), 43.

[16]Daniel Levy and Gabriel Székely, *Mexico: Paradoxes of Stability and Change* (Boulder, Colo.: Westview Press, 1983), 100.

[17]See Luis Carlos Ugalde, *The Mexican Congress: Old Player, New Power* (Washington, D.C.: Center for International and Strategic Studies, 2000).

[18]See Chapell H. Lawson, *Building the Fourth Estate: Democratization and the Rise of a Free Press in Mexico* (Berkeley: University of California Press, 2002).

[19]Susan Eckstein (ed.), *Power and Popular Protest: Latin American Social Movements* (Berkeley: University of California Press, 1989).

[20]Wayne A. Cornelius and Ann L. Craig, "Politics in Mexico," in Gabriel Almond and G. Bingham Powell (eds.), *Comparative Politics Today*, 5th ed. (Boston: Scott Foresman, 1992), 502.

[21]Jonathan Fox and Gustavo Gordillo, "Between State and Market: The Campesinos' Quest for Autonomy," in Wayne A. Cornelius, Judith Gentleman, and Peter H. Smith (eds.), *Mexico's Alternative Political Futures* (San Diego: Center for U.S.-Mexican Studies, University of California, 1989).

[22]Foweraker and Craig, *Popular Movements and Political Change in Mexico*.

[23]Wayne A. Cornelius, Ann L. Craig, and Jonathan Fox (eds.), *Transforming State-Society Relations in Mexico: The National Solidarity Strategy* (San Diego: Center for U.S.-Mexican Studies, University of California, 1994).

CHAPTER 11

Nigeria

Darren Kew and Peter Lewis

Federal Republic of Nigeria

Land and People

Capital	Abuja
Total area (square miles)	356,669 (more than twice the size of California)
Population	130 million

Annual population growth rate (%)

1975–2000	2.9
2000–2015 (projected)	2.7

Urban population (%)	38

Ethnolinguistic composition (% of population)

Hausa-Fulani	32
Yoruba	21
Igbo	18
Ibibio	6
Various dialects	14
Other	8

Official Language	English

Religious affiliation (%)

Muslim	50
Christian	45
Indigenous	5

Economy

Domestic currency	Naira (NGN) US$1: 135 NGN (2003 av.)
Total GDP (US$)	44 billion (2002)
GDP per capita (US$)	363 (2002)
Total GDP at purchasing power parity (US$)	113.7 billion
GDP per capita at purchasing power parity (US$)	896

GDP annual growth rate (%)

1997	2.7
2000	3.8
2001	4.0
2002	3.4

GDP per capita average annual growth rate (%)

1975–2000	−0.7
1990–2000	−0.4

Inequality in income or consumption (1996–1997) (%)

Share of poorest 10%	1.6
Share of poorest 20%	4.4
Share of richest 20%	55.7
Share of richest 10%	40.8
Gini Index (1996–1997)	50.6

Structure of production (% of GDP)

Agriculture	41
Industry	32
Services	27

Labor force distribution (% of total)

Agriculture	60
Industry	8
Services	32

Exports as % of GDP	52
Imports as % of GDP	41

Society

Life expectancy at birth	52.7
Infant mortality per 1,000 live births	110

Adult literacy (%)

Male	72.4
Female	55.7

Access to information and communications (per 1,000 population)

Telephone lines	4
Mobile phones	1
Radios	200
Televisions	68
Personal computers	6.6

Women in Government and Economy

Women in the national legislature

Lower house or single house (%)	3.4
Upper house (%)	2.8

Women at ministerial level (%)	22.6
Female economic activity rate (age 15 and above) (%)	47.6
Female labor force (% of total)	36

Estimated earned income (PPP US$)

Female	532
Male	1,254

2002 Human Development Index Ranking (out of 173 countries)	148

Political Organization

Political System   Democracy.

Regime History   Democratic government took office in May 1999, after 16 years of military rule. The most recent elections were held in 2003.

Administrative Structure   Power is centralized largely under the presidency and the governors. Nigeria is a federation 36 states, plus the Federal Capital Territory (FCT) in Abuja.

Executive   U.S.-style presidential system, under Olusegun Obasanjo.

Legislature   A bicameral civilian legislature was elected in April 2003. The 109 senators are elected on the basis of equal representation: three from each state, and one from the FCT. The 360 members of the House of Representatives are elected from single-member districts.

Judiciary   The Nigerian judicial system resembles that of the United States with a network of local and district courts as well as state-level courts. The state-level judiciaries are subordinate to the Federal Court of Appeal and the Supreme Court of Nigeria, which consists of 15 appointed associate justices and the chief justice. Every state of the federation can also opt to establish a system of Islamic law (*shari'a*) courts for cases involving only Muslims in customary disputes (divorce, property, etc.); the secular courts, however, retain supreme jurisdiction at the federal level if any conflict arises over which system to use. Most Nigerian states feature such courts, which share a Federal *Shari'a* Court of Appeal in Abuja. Twelve Northern states since 1999 have also instituted the *shari'a* criminal code, which allows for cutting off hands for stealing, stoning to death for adultery, and other extreme sentences. This aspect of the *shari'a* remains contentious, however, and may soon be challenged at the Supreme Court, which is likely to dismantle it.

Party System   Three parties were registered by the Nigerian electoral commission in December 1998: the Alliance for Democracy (AD), All People's Party (APP—now the All Nigerian People's Party, ANPP), and People's Democratic Party (PDP). PDP won the presidency, majorities in both houses of the National Assembly, and control of many of the governorships, state assemblies, and local governments. 27 more parties were registered in 2002.

Section ❶ The Making of the Modern Nigerian State

Politics in Action

Olusegun Obasanjo took office as president in May 1999 amid tremendous domestic and international goodwill as Nigeria's first elected civilian leader in nearly twenty years. Flanked by Nelson Mandela and other global dignitaries, Obasanjo boldly stated his intentions to reform the corrupt Nigerian state, reverse its economic decline, and restore the nation to greatness. A succession of oppressive, thieving military leaders in the 1980s and 1990s had stolen billions from the national coffers, leaving this oil-rich nation in tremendous debt and making it an international pariah; 120 million Nigerians looked to Obasanjo to rectify the political sins of the past and pull them out of impoverishment. The president promised to do both, and in 1999 he set out with an ambitious political agenda.

Three years later, the National Assembly set out to impeach him. Members of Obasanjo's own party, including the Speaker of the House, sponsored the resolution to instigate impeachment proceedings. The legislators spoke in public of the president's unconstitutional behavior, but in private they were more outraged by his heavy-handed methods—and by the fact that he refused to disburse their personal allowances for the year.

President Obasanjo's struggles with the National Assembly are symptomatic of the larger obstacles his government faces in trying to revive the dysfunctional Nigerian state. His ambitious agenda has run aground on the many contradictions in governance left by years of military rule, such as a disproportionately powerful presidency married to an inexperienced legislature in search of power and relevance. In addition, the young democracy faces the challenge of managing the country's incredible diversity. Colonialism left Nigerians with a project as complex as the construction of the European Union, trying to build a single political structure out of many nations yet without the high levels of political and economic development that the Europeans enjoy. Furthermore, years of economic decline and political corruption have left most Nigerians with little patience to wait for Obasanjo's fragile, self-conflicted government to deliver significant progress.

The military left power in 1999 as a discredited institution, but it is slowly rebuilding, and the clock is ticking against the civilians: Will public frustrations with the slow pace of reform hold off long enough for democracy to consolidate sufficiently to meet minimal public expectations?

Although Nigeria has developed well beyond the point in the 1950s when its leaders saw it as a mere geographic expression, the development of national consciousness and character has progressed, often in spite of the nation's political direction. Many Nigerians intermarry across ethnic and religious lines, share common traditions like chewing kola nuts with friends, work (often their whole lives) and invest in cities outside their ethnic homelands, and unite in support of their national sports teams. Yet when talk turns to politics, southern Nigerians will complain of northern domination of the government, Igbos will claim that Yorubas cannot be trusted for their "betrayal" of Biafra during the civil war, Christians will complain that Muslims want an Islamic fundamentalist state, and so on.

Nigeria offers, within a single case, characteristics that identify Africa. These opposing forces are rooted in the constant struggle in Nigeria between **authoritarian** and democratic governance, the push for development and the persistence of underdevelopment, the burden of public corruption and the pressure for accountability. Nigeria, like all other African countries, has sought to create a viable nation-state out of the social incoherence created by its colonial borders. Over 250 competing nationalities—or ethnic groups, largely defined by language differences—in Nigeria have repeatedly clashed over economic and political resources. All of these factors combine to produce the political entity known as Nigeria with a low level of popular **legitimacy** and **accountability** and a persistent inability to meet the most basic needs of its citizens. The country therefore provides a crucible in which to examine questions of democracy and authoritarianism, the pressures and management of ethnic conflict, and economic underdevelopment brought about by both colonial oppression and independent Nigeria's mismanagement of its vast resources.

Much about Nigeria is contentious. Since gaining

independence from British colonial rule in 1960, Nigeria has undergone several political transitions, from democratic governments to autocratic regimes, both military and civilian, and from one military regime to another. After nearly four decades as an independent nation, Nigeria has yet to witness an orderly and constitutional transition from one democratic regime to another, although it will try once again to do so in 2003. It has experienced six successful coups (most recently in November 1993) and many unsuccessful attempted coups, and it was torn by three years of civil war that claimed over 100,000 military and over 1 million civilian casualties. Against this background, Nigeria today remains essentially an **unfinished state** characterized by instabilities and uncertainties.

Nigeria reached another critical turning point in 1999 when a military government transferred power to civilians for the second time since the British left in 1960. The civilians held their own elections in 2003 for the first time since 1983, which were so flawed then that the public welcomed a military coup. The 2003 elections also showed evidence of tampering. Will Nigeria return to the discredited path of authoritarianism and greater underdevelopment, or will the civilian leadership rise to achieve a consolidated democracy and sustainable growth?

Geographic Setting

Nigeria, with 130 million people inhabiting 356,669 square miles, ranks as the most populous nation in Africa and among the ten largest in the world. A center of West African regional trade, culture, and military strength, Nigeria is bordered by four countries—Benin, Niger, Chad, and Cameroon, all of them Francophone—and by the Gulf of Guinea in the Atlantic Ocean to the south. The modern country of Nigeria, however, like nearly all the other contemporary states in Africa, is not even a century old.

Nigeria was a British colony from 1914 until its independence on October 1, 1960, although foreign domination of much of the territory had begun in the mid-nineteenth century. Nigeria's boundaries had little to do with the borders of the precolonial African nations in the territory that the British conquered. Instead, these boundaries merely marked the point where British influence ended and France's began. Britain ruled northern and southern Nigeria as two separate colonies until 1914, when it amalgamated its Northern and Southern Protectorates. In short, Nigeria was essentially an arbitrary creation reflecting British colonial interests. The consequences of this forced union of a myriad of formerly independent African nations under one political roof remain a central feature of Nigerian political life today.

Nigeria's location in West Africa, its size, and its oil-producing status have made it a hub of regional activity. Demographically, it overwhelms the other fifteen countries in West Africa, with a population that is nearly 60 percent of the region's total. Moreover, Nigeria's gross domestic product (GDP) typically represents more than half of the total GDP for the entire subregion.

Nigeria's ethnic map can be divided into six inexact areas or "zones." The northwest (or "core North") is dominated by Nigeria's largest ethnic group, the Hausa-Fulani, two formerly separate groups that over the past century have largely merged. The northeast is a minority region, the largest of whom are the Kanuri. Both regions in the north are predominantly Muslim. A large swath of territory stretching across the center of the country, called the Middle Belt, is also home to a wide range of minority groups of both Muslim and Christian identification. The southwest (referred to as the Western Region in the First Republic) is dominated by the country's second largest ethnic group, the Yoruba, who are approximately 40 percent Muslim, 40 percent Christian (primarily Protestant), and 20 percent practitioners of Yoruba traditional beliefs. The southeast (which formed the hub of the First Republic's Eastern Region) is the Igbo homeland, Nigeria's third largest group, who are primarily Christian, and where Protestant evangelical movements have become popular. Between the Yoruba and Igbo regions of the south is the southern minority zone, which stretches across the Niger Delta areas and east along the coast as far as Cameroon.

Critical Junctures

A number of critical junctures helped shape the character of the Nigerian state and illustrate the difficult path that the country has taken during the past century. This path features influences from the precolonial period,

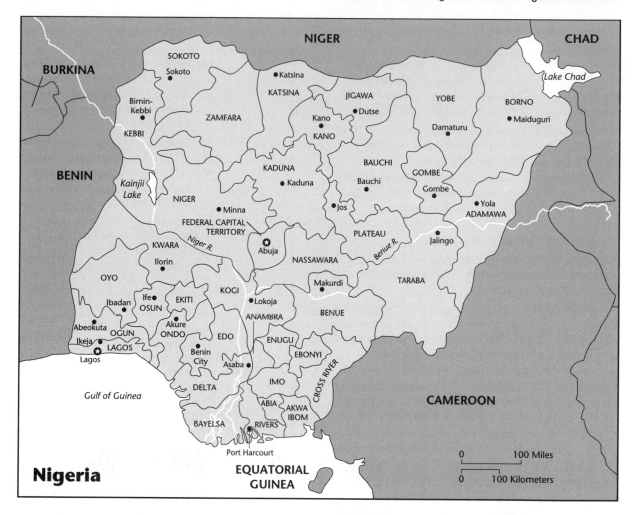

Nigeria

British colonialism, the alternation of military and civilian rule after independence, and the post-1980 economic collapse, precipitated by Nigeria's political corruption and overreliance on its petroleum industry.

The Precolonial Period (800–1900)

Much of Nigeria's precolonial history before 1000 has been reconstructed from oral histories because, with few exceptions, literate cultures evolved much later. In contrast to the peoples of the forest belt to the south, the more open terrain in the north, with its need for irrigation, encouraged the early growth of centralized states. Such states from the eighth century included Kanem-Bornu in the northeast and the Hausa states in

the northwest. Another attempt at state formation led to the emergence of a Jukun kingdom; however, by the end of the seventeenth century, the Jukun became a tributary state of the Bornu empire.

A major element that shaped the course of events in the savanna areas of the north was trade across the Sahara Desert with northern Africa. Trade brought material benefits as well as Arabic education and Islam, which gradually replaced traditional spiritual, political, and social practices. In 1808, the Fulani, who came from lands west of modern Nigeria through a holy war (*jihad*) led by Uthman dan Fodio, established an Islamic empire, the Sokoto Caliphate. Portions of the region to the south, the present day Middle Belt, were able to repel the *jihad* and preserve their independence

Critical Junctures in Modern Nigerian Political Development

1960   Independence. Nigeria consists of three regions under a Westminster parliamentary model. **Abubakar Tafawa Balewa,** a Northerner, is the first prime minister.

January 1966   Civilian government deposed in coup. **General Aguiyi Ironsi,** an Igbo, becomes head of state.

July 1966   Countercoup led by **General Yakubu Gowon** (an Anga, from the "Middle Belt") with aid from northern groups.

1967–1970   Biafran civil war.

July 1975   Military coup deposes Gowon; led by **General Murtala Muhammed,** a northerner.

February 1976   Murtala Muhammed assassinated in failed coup led by Middle Belt minorities. Muhammed's second-in-command, **General Olusegun Obasanjo,** a Yoruba, assumes power.

September 1978   New constitution completed, marking the adoption of the U.S. presidential model in a federation with 19 states.

October 1979   Elections held. A majority in both houses is won by NPN, led by Northern/Hausa-Fulani groups. **Alhaji Shehu Shagari** is elected Nigeria's first executive president.

December 1983   Military coup led by **General Muhammadu Buhari,** a northerner.

August 1985   Buhari is overthrown by **General Ibrahim B. Babangida**, a Middle Belt Muslim, in a palace coup. Babangida promises a return to democracy by 1990, a date he delays five times before being forced from office.

June 12, 1993   **Moshood Abiola** wins presidential elections, but Babangida annuls the election 11 days later.

August 1993   Babangida installs **Ernest Shonekan** as "interim civilian president" until new presidential elections could be held later that autumn.

November 1993   Defense Minister **General Sani Abacha** seizes power in a coup. Two years later he announces a three-year transition to civilian rule, which he manipulates to have himself nominated for president in 1998.

July–Sept. 1994   Pro-democracy strike by the major oil union, NUPENG, cuts Nigeria's oil production by an estimated 25 percent. Sympathy strikes ensue, followed by arrests of political and civic leaders.

June 1998   General Abacha dies; succeeded by General **Abdulsalami Abubakar**, a Middle Belt Muslim from Babangida's hometown. Abubakar releases nearly all political prisoners and installs a new transition program. Parties are allowed to form unhindered.

1999   Former head of state **Olusegun Obasanjo** and his party, the PDP, sweep the Presidential and National Assembly elections, adding to their majority control of state and local government seats. The federation now contains 36 states.

November 1999   Zamfara state in the North is the first of 12 to institute the *shari'a* criminal code. That same month, President Obasanjo sends the army to the Niger Delta town of Odi to root out local militias, leveling the town in the process.

2000   Communal conflicts erupt in Lagos, Benue, Kaduna, and Kano states at different times over localized issues.

Spring 2002   The Supreme Court passes several landmark judgments, overturning a PDP-biased 2001 electoral law, and ruling on the control of offshore oil and gas resources. In November the Court opens the legal door for more parties to be registered.

August 2002   The National Assembly begins impeachment proceedings against President Obasanjo over budgetary issues. The matter ends by November, with the president apologizing.

and religious diversity. The Sokoto Caliphate used Islam and a common language, Hausa, to forge unity out of the disparate groups in the north. The Fulani empire held sway until British colonial authority was imposed on northern Nigeria by 1900.

Toward the southern edge of the savanna lived such groups as the Tiv, whose political organizations seldom extended beyond the village level. Within such societies, politics was generally conducted along kinship lines, and the fundamental political unit was the extended family. Political authority was diffused rather than centralized, such that later Western contacts described them as "stateless," or **acephalous societies.** Because they lacked complex political hierarchies, these societies escaped much of the upheaval experienced under colonialism by the centralized states, and they retained much of their autonomy.

The development of collective identities in southern Nigeria was equally complex. Groups included the highly centralized Yoruba empires and kingdoms of Oyo and Ife; the Edo kingdom of Benin in the midwest; the fragmentary, acephalous societies of the Igbo to the east; and the trading city-states of the Niger Delta and its hinterland, peopled by a wide range of ethnicities.

Several precolonial societies had democratic elements that scholars speculate might have led to more open and participatory polities had they not been interrupted by colonialism. Governance in the Yoruba and Igbo communities involved principles of accountability: rulers could not disregard the views and interests of the governed or they would risk revocation of consent and loss of their positions. Another element was representation, defined less in terms of formal procedures for selecting leaders, and more in terms of assurances that rulers adhered to culturally mandated principles and obligations that forced them to seek out and protect the interests of their subjects.

Among the Islamic communities of the north, political society was highly structured, reflecting local interpretations of Qur'anic principles. Leadership structures

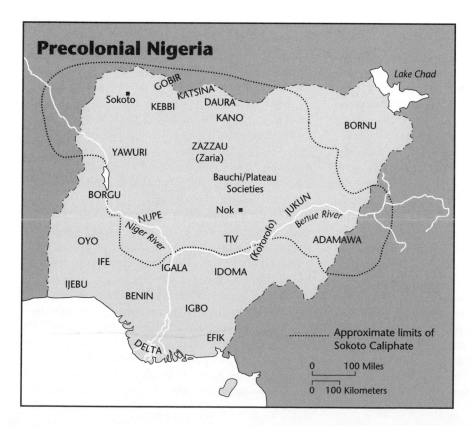

Precolonial Politics and Societies. *Source:* K. Michael Barbour, Julius Oguntoyinbo, J.O.C. Onyemelukwe, and James C. Nwafor, *Nigeria in Maps* (New York: Africana Publishing Company, 1982), 37.

were considerably more hierarchical than those of the south, dominated by a few educated elites in positions of authority. In addition (although some of the pre-Islamic indigenous beliefs showed deference to important women spirit leaders), women were consigned to a subordinate position in systems of governance. The Islamic Fulani empire was a confederation in which the rulers, **emirs,** owed allegiance to the sultan, who was the temporal and spiritual head of the empire. The sultan's powers, in turn, were circumscribed by the obligation to observe the principles of Islam in fulfilling his duties.

Colonial Rule and Its Impact (1860–1945)

Competition for trade and empire drove the European imperial powers into Africa after 1860. During the colonial period, Nigeria's resources were extracted and its people exploited as cheap labor to further the growth of British society and defray administrative costs of the British Empire. Colonialism left its imprint on all aspects of Nigeria's existence, bequeathing a political system that was inappropriate in many respects.

Where centralized monarchies existed, particularly in the north, the British ruled through a policy known as **indirect rule,** which allowed traditional structures to persist as subordinates to the British governor and a small administrative apparatus. Where more democratic and acephalous societies existed, particularly among the Igbo and other groups in the southeast, the colonizers either strengthened the authority of traditional chiefs and kings or appointed **warrant chiefs** (who ruled by warrant of the British Crown), weakening the previous practices of accountability and participation.

The British played off ethnic and social divisions to keep Nigerians from developing organized political resistance to colonial rule, and where resistance did develop, the colonizers were not afraid to employ repressive tactics, even as late as the 1940s. They instilled two sets of rules: one for political leaders and another for the citizenry. Yet the British also promoted the foundations of a democratic political system before they left in 1960. This dual standard left a conflicted democratic idea: formal democratic institutions yet an authoritarian political culture. Colonialism also strengthened the collective identities of Nigeria's mul-

tiple ethnic groups by fostering political competition among them, primarily among the three largest: the Hausa-Fulani, Yoruba, and Igbo.

Divisive Identities: Ethnic Politics Under Colonialism (1945–1960)

Based on the British example, leaders of the anticolonial movement came to regard the state as an exploitative instrument, and its control as an opportunity to pursue personal and group interests rather than broad national interests. Thus, once the British in the 1940s announced their intention to negotiate the terms of their gradual exit from Nigeria, whatever semblance of unity had existed among the anticolonial leaders soon evaporated, and political competition became increasingly fierce.

Nigerian leaders quickly turned to ethnicity as the preferred vehicle to pursue this competition and mobilize public support. The three largest ethnic groups—the Hausa-Fulani, Igbo, and Yoruba, which together comprise approximately 65 percent of Nigeria's population—have dominated the political process since the 1940s. By pitting ethnic groups against each other for purposes of "divide and rule" and by structuring the administrative units of Nigeria based on ethnic groups, the British ensured that ethnicity would be the primary element in political identification and mobilization.

Nigerian ethnic groups, championed by educated local elites, began to propound tales of origin and to create standardized languages and histories to foster a more exclusivist identity and heritage. They rallied followers based on common ethnic identity and challenged the colonial administration in competition with rivals from other ethnic groups.

The early ethnically based associations were initially concerned with nonpolitical issues: promoting mutual aid for housing and education, as well as sponsoring cultural events. With the encouragement of ambitious leaders, however, these groups took on a more political character. Nigeria's first political party, the National Council of Nigeria and the Cameroons (later the National Convention of Nigerian Citizens, NCNC), initially drew supporters from across Nigeria. As the prospects for independence increased, however, indigenous elites began to divide along ethnic lines to mobilize support for their differing political agendas.

Recognizing the multiethnic character of their colony, the British divided Nigeria into a federation of three regions with elected governments in 1954. Each of the federated units soon fell under the domination of one of the three largest ethnic groups and their respective parties. The Northern Region came under the control of the Northern Peoples Congress (NPC), associated with and dominated by Hausa-Fulani elites. In the southern half of the country, the Western Region was controlled by the Action Group (AG), which was controlled by the elites of the Yoruba group. The Igbo, the numerically dominant group in the Eastern Region, were closely associated with the NCNC, which became the ruling party there. Thus, the distinctive and often divisive ethnic and regional characteristics of modern Nigeria were reinforced during the transition to independence.[1]

Chief Obafemi Awolowo, leader of the AG, caught the sentiment of the times when he wrote in 1947 that "Nigeria is not a nation. It is a mere geographical expression. There are no 'Nigerians' in the same sense as there are 'English,' 'Welsh,' or 'French.' The word 'Nigerian' is merely a distinctive appellation to distinguish those who live within the boundaries of Nigeria from those who do not."[2]

The First Republic (1960–1966)

The British granted Nigeria independence in 1960 to a civilian parliamentary government. Nigerians adopted the British Westminster model at the federal and regional levels, in which the chief executive, the prime minister, was chosen by the majority party. Northerners came to dominate the federal government by virtue of their greater population, based on the 1952–1953 census. The ruling coalition for the first two years quickly turned into a northern-only coalition when the NPC achieved an outright majority in the legislature. Having benefited less from the economic, educational, and infrastructural benefits of colonialism, the northerners who dominated the First Republic set out to redistribute resources in their own direction. This NPC policy of northernization brought them into direct conflict with their southern counterparts, particularly the Yoruba-based AG and later the Igbo-dominated NCNC.

When an AG internal conflict led to a political crisis in the Western regional assembly in 1962, the NPC-led national government seized the opportunity to subdivide the Western (largely Yoruba) Region in two, diluting Yoruba political power. Violence escalated among the Yoruba factions in the West as the

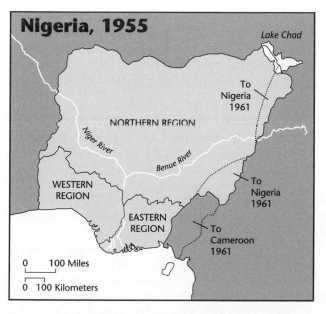

Nigeria, 1955

Lake Chad

To Nigeria 1961

NORTHERN REGION

Niger River

Benue River

WESTERN REGION

To Nigeria 1961

EASTERN REGION

To Cameroon 1961

0   100 Miles

0   100 Kilometers

Nigeria in 1955: Divided into Three Federated Regions. The administrative division of Nigeria into three regions later became the basis for ethnoregional conflicts. (Note: At the time of independence, the southeastern part of the country, which had been governed as a trust territory, opted to become part of independent Cameroon; two northern trust territories opted to become part of independent Nigeria.) Source: K. Michael Barbour, Julius Oguntoyinbo, J.O.C. Onyemelukwe, and James C. Nwafor, *Nigeria in Maps* (New York: Africana Publishing Company, 1982), 39.

NPC-dominated government engaged in extensive political corruption. A fraudulent census, falsified ballots, widespread violence, and intimidation of supporters and candidates alike ensured the NPC a tarnished victory in 1965.

Rivalries intensified as the NPC sat atop an absolute majority in the federal parliament with no need for its former coalition partner, the NCNC. NCNC leader Nnamdi Azikiwe, who was also president in the First Republic (then a largely symbolic position), and Tafawa Balewa, the NPC prime minister, separately approached the military to ensure that if it came to conflict, they could count on its loyalty. Thus, "in the struggle for personal survival both men, perhaps inadvertently, made the armed forces aware that they had a political role to play."[3]

Civil War and Military Rule (1966–1979)

With significant encouragement from contending civilian leaders, a group of largely Igbo officers seized power in January 1966. Aguiyi Ironsi, also an Igbo, became head of state by dint of being the highest-ranking officer rather than a coup plotter. His announced aim was to end violence in the Western Region and to stop political corruption and abuses by the northern-dominated government by centralizing the state apparatus, thereby replacing the federation with a unitary state. Although Ironsi claimed to be ethnically plural in his outlook, other Nigerians, particularly northerners, were deeply suspicious of his revocation of federalism. A second coup in July 1966 killed General Ironsi and brought Yakubu Gowon, a Middle Belt Christian, to power as a consensus head of state among the non-Igbo coup plotters.[4]

Because many northern officials had been killed in the initial coup, a tremendous backlash against Igbos flared in several parts of the country during 1966, especially after the second coup. Igbo migrant laborers were persecuted in the north, and many fled to their home region in the east. By 1967, the predominantly Igbo population of eastern Nigeria attempted to secede and form its own independent nation, called Biafra. The secessionists wanted to break free from Nigeria, believing that the north, by virtue of its greater numbers, would permanently lock the other regions out of power. General Gowon built a military-led government of national unity in what remained of Nigeria (the North and West) and, after a bloody three-year war of attrition and starvation tactics, defeated Biafra by January 1970. The conflict exacted a heavy toll on Nigeria's populace, including at least a million deaths.

After the war, Gowon presided over a policy of national reconciliation, which proceeded fairly smoothly with the aid of growing oil revenues. In order to dilute the power of the "big three" ethnic groups, he broke the four-state federation into twelve states, later increased to nineteen by his successor. He also oversaw an increase in the armed forces from about 10,000 men in 1966 to nearly 250,000 by 1970. Senior officers reaped the benefits of the global oil boom in 1973–1974, and corruption was widespread. Influenced by the unwillingness of the military elite to relinquish power and the spoils of office, Gowon opted to postpone a return to civilian rule, which he had pledged originally to complete by 1976. He was overthrown in 1975 by Murtala Muhammed, who promptly reactivated the transition program.

Muhammed was committed to the restoration of democracy, but he was assassinated in 1976. General Olusegun Obasanjo, Muhammed's second-in-command who took power after the assassination, peacefully ceded power to an elected civilian government in 1979, which became known as the Second Republic. Obasanjo retired but would later reemerge as a civilian president in 1999.

The Second and Third Republics, and Predatory Military Rule (1979–1999)

The president of the 1979–1983 Second Republic, Shehu Shagari, and his ruling National Party of Nigeria (NPN, the successor party to the First Republic's northern-dominated NPC), did little to assuage the mistrust between the various parts of the federation, or to stem rampant corruption. After the NPN "won" its 1983 reelection through massive fraud, the military, led by Major General Muhammadu Buhari, seized power within months.

When General Buhari refused to pledge a rapid return to democratic rule and failed to revive a plummeting economy, his popular support wavered, and in August 1985 General Ibrahim Babangida seized power. Although Babangida announced a program of transition

General Olusegun Obasanjo was the Nigerian head of state who supervised the transition to civilian rule from 1976 to 1979. In 1995 he was arrested and convicted in a secret trial in connection with an alleged attempt to overthrow the regime of General Abacha. After his release, he won the presidency in 1999 as a candidate for the PDP. *Source:* Bettmann/Corbis.

to democratic rule as one of his first acts as the new head of state, he and his cohort engaged in an elaborate set of stalling tactics in order to extend their tenure in office. What promised to be the dawn of a Third Republic ended in betrayal when Babangida annulled the presidential election of June 12, 1993, which should have preceded a full withdrawal of the military from the political scene. In stark contrast to all prior elections since independence, the 1993 election was widely acclaimed as fair (despite military restrictions on the scope of competition), and was evidently won by Yoruba

businessman Chief Moshood Abiola. The annulment provoked an angry reaction from a population weary of postponed transitions, military rule, and deception. Babangida could not resist the pressure to resign, but he did manage to handpick his successor, Ernest Shonekan, and a civilian caretaker government.

Following the pattern set by his predecessors, General Sani Abacha seized power in November 1993 from Shonekan. Shonekan's government, never regarded as legitimate after Babangida installed it in August 1993, was vulnerable to increasing agitation from both civilian and military ranks, providing an opportunity for Abacha to remove it. As head of state, General Abacha prolonged the now established tradition of military dominance and combined increased repression with frequent public commitments to restore constitutional democracy. Like Babangida, Abacha announced a new program of transition to civilian rule and regularly delayed the steps in its implementation. Only Abacha's sudden death in June 1998 saved the country from certain crisis, as his scheme to orchestrate the outcome of the transition to produce his own "election" as president became clearer. General Abdulsalami Abubakar, Abacha's successor, announced in his first broadcast to the nation his intention to return power to civilians. Within two months, Abubakar had established a new transition program and promptly handed over to an elected civilian government led by President Olusegun Obasanjo and the People's Democratic Party (PDP) in May 1999.

The Fourth Republic (1999 to the Present)

Obasanjo was called out of retirement by the leaders of the PDP to run for president for several reasons. First, many Yoruba people, particularly leaders, felt that their group had long been cheated out of the presidency by northern elites, especially when Moshood Abiola's election victory was annulled in 1993. Yet most northern leaders did not trust the prominent Yoruba politicians. Obasanjo, although he is Yoruba, as military head of state in 1979 had handed power to the northerner Shehu Shagari at the dawn of the Second Republic. The northern political establishment that dominated the PDP, when faced with the real prospect that the Yoruba might rebel if they did not win the presidency in 1999, concluded that the "detribalized"

General Sani Abacha, a prominent member of Nigerian military regimes since December 1983, took over the government in November 1993, disbanded all elective institutions, and suppressed opposition forces. His death in June 1998 was celebrated in the streets; he and his close supporters looted billions of U.S. dollars from the nation's coffers. *Source:* AP/Wide World Photos.

Obasanjo was the only Yoruba candidate they could trust. In addition, it was thought that, as an ex-military leader, Obasanjo could better manage the thorny task of keeping the military in the barracks once they left power.

Yet precisely because Obasanjo had handed power to Shagari in 1979, he was widely unpopular among his own Yoruba people, and he assumed the presidency in 1999 with few Yoruba votes, in an election marred by irregularities at the polls. Nonetheless, Obasanjo claimed a broad mandate from the Nigerian people to arrest the nation's decline by reforming the state and economy. Within weeks, he electrified the nation by retiring all the military officers who had held positions of political power under the previous military governments, seeing them as the most likely plotters of future coups.

Obasanjo then turned to the economy. The critical oil sector was targeted for new management, while the president lobbied foreign governments to forgive Nigeria's massive debts. The minimum wage was raised dramatically, a "truth and reconciliation" commission and an anticorruption commission were set up to ad-dress past and future offenses, and a special commission was created to channel an increased portion of oil revenues back to the impoverished and environmentally degraded Niger Delta region, where the oil is extracted. Civil society groups thrived on renewed political freedoms, and the media grew bold in exposing corrupt practices in government, forcing a Speaker of the House of Representatives and two Senate presidents to resign.

Despite his ambitions for reform, Obasanjo felt obliged to appoint the powerful leaders of his PDP party to ministerial positions in government. Consequently, his first cabinet included some of the same corrupt politicians who had brought down the nation's previous republics and had colluded with Generals Babangida and Abacha in the 1980s and 1990s. They and similarly corrupt politicians in the legislature, state governments, and local governments grew increasingly bold in lining their own pockets with public funds. With President Obasanjo's decision to run for reelection in 2003, however, he needed many of these same politicians to deliver their home states' support, rendering the president's anticorruption machinery largely dormant in his first term.

Having surrounded himself with politicians whom he did not particularly trust, Obasanjo largely kept his own counsel on matters of state. When it came to the National Assembly, members of which he referred to as "small boys," Obasanjo was openly disdainful. In the light of rampant corruption in the legislature, his views were not altogether without merit. When Obasanjo refused to pay half of funds allocated by the Assembly in the 2002 budget on account of a sharp drop in oil revenues, members of his own party in the legislature joined in motions to impeach him. After weeks of tense negotiations, including some legislative concessions and an apology by the president (and persistent rumors of money changing hands), the impeachment drive relented, marking an important victory for the National Assembly.

Themes and Implications

Historical Junctures and Political Themes

Nigeria's adoption of a federal democracy has been a strategy to ensure "unity in diversity" (the national motto) by building a coherent nation-state out of over 250 different ethnic groups and blending traditional democratic values with modern, accountable government. In reality, as a consequence of many years of colonial and military rule, a unitary system emerged in a federal guise: a system with an all-powerful central government surrounded by weak and economically insolvent states.

Another consequence of military rule is the relative overdevelopment of the executive arm at all levels of government—federal, state, and local—at the expense of weak legislative and judicial institutions. Executive superiority was a key feature of the colonial era and has been strengthened by each period of military rule in the postcolonial era. The current civilian government works under a military-authored constitution, which again placed tremendous powers in the presidency. Unchecked executive power under the military, and a dominant executive under the civilians, has encouraged the arbitrary exercise of authority, accompanied by patronage politics, which sap the economy of its vitality, prevent accountability, and undermine the rule of law.

Since the return of democratic rule in 1999, the state governments, the National Assembly, and the judiciary have been whittling away at the powers of the national executive. The president, however, remains the dominant figure in Nigerian politics.

Nigeria in the World of States: Oil Dependence and Decline.   Although Nigeria enjoys economic and military power within the West African region, on a global level, it has become increasingly marginalized and vulnerable. Nigeria, with its natural riches, has long been regarded as a potential political and economic giant of Africa. Yet the World Bank lists it among the poorest 20 percent of the countries of the world, with a GDP per capita of just $300. Instead of independent growth, today Nigeria depends on unpredictable oil revenues, sparse external loans, and aid, a victim of its leaders' bad policies and poor management. Owing to underinvestment in and neglect of agriculture, Nigeria moved from self-sufficiency in the production of basic foodstuffs in the mid-1960s to heavy dependence on imports of those goods less than twenty years later. Manufacturing activities, after a surge of investment by government and foreign firms in the 1970s, suffered from inefficiency and disinvestment in subsequent decades, sagging to levels not seen since independence.

Nigeria's economy remains dependent on oil, and its heavy indebtedness gives foreign creditors and the International Monetary Fund (IMF) tremendous influence over its macroeconomic policies. Years of predatory military rule made Nigeria a political and economic pariah in the 1990s, and its declining political institutions have made the country a way station for international drug trafficking to the United States and international commercial fraud.

The installation of a democratic government in 1999 ended the nation's political isolation, but its economy remains subject to the vicissitudes of the international oil market. For most of its independent history, Nigeria has aligned itself with the United States, and President Obasanjo has given strong public support to the U.S. war on terrorism in the wake of the September 11, 2001, attacks. Partly in response to this support, the Bush administration is seeking to rely more on Nigerian oil and less on that from the Middle East.

Governing Nigeria's Economy.   Nigeria's oil dependency is a symptom of deeper structural problems.

The very concept of the state was introduced into the colony in large part to restructure and subordinate the local economy to European capitalism. The Nigerian colonial state was conceived and fashioned as **interventionist,** with broad license to intrude into major sectors of the economy and society. The principal goals of the British colonial enterprise were to control the Nigerian economy and to marshal the flow of resources from the colonies to the metropole. A secondary concern was the creation of an economy hospitable to free markets and private enterprise. Nigeria's interventionist state extended its management of the economy, including broad administrative controls and significant ownership positions in areas as diverse as agriculture, banking, commerce, manufacturing, transportation, mining, education, health, employment, and, eventually, oil and natural gas.

After independence in 1960, Nigeria's civilian and military rulers alike expanded the interventionist state, which came to dominate all facets of the nation's economic life. Successive governments began in the late 1980s to reverse this trend, but privatization and economic reform have been piecemeal at best. By 2000, President Obasanjo promised to sell off government interests in the telephone, power, and oil sectors, though the state remains by far the largest source of economic activity.

Democratic Ideas Amid Colonialism and Military Rule. Colonialism introduced a cultural dualism— a clash of customs, values, and political systems— between the traditions of social accountability in precolonial society, and emerging Western ideas of individualism. These pressures weakened indigenous bases for the accountability of rulers and responsibility to the governed, along with age-old checks on abuses of office. Although the colonial rulers left Nigeria with the machinery of parliamentary democracy, they largely socialized the local population to be passive subjects rather than responsive participants. Even as colonial rule sought to implant democracy in principle, in practice it bequeathed an authoritarian legacy to independent Nigeria. Military rule continued this pattern from 1966 to 1979 and again from 1983 to 1999, as juntas promised democratization yet governed with increasing severity.

This dualism promoted two public realms to which individuals belonged: the communal realm, in which people identified by ethnic or subethnic groups (Igbo, Tiv, Yoruba, and others), and the civic realm under the colonial administration and its successors in which citizenship was universal.[5] Both realms fed on each other, though the communal realm was often stronger in certain respects than the civic realm. Thus, Nigerians faced a regular dilemma of loyalty and citizenship. Does one govern or serve the interests of one's ethnic group or those of a greater Nigeria? Viewing the colonial state and its "civic" realm as an alien, exploitative force, Nigerians came to view the state as the realm from which rights must be extracted, duties and taxes withheld, and resources plundered (see Section 4). This view was encouraged by the style of rule under military regimes in the post-colonial era.

The British policy of indirect rule had profoundly different effects on the northern and southern regions. The south experienced both the benefits and burdens of colonial occupation. The proximity of Lagos, Calabar, and their regions to the Atlantic Ocean made them important hubs for trade and shipping activity, around which the British built the necessary infrastructure— schools (promoting Christianity and Western education), roads, ports, and the like—and a large African civil service to facilitate colonialism. In northern Nigeria, where more developed hierarchical political structures were already present, the British used indigenous structures and left intact the emirate authorities and Islamic institutions of the region. The north consequently received few infrastructural benefits and little Christian missionary activity, and its traditional administration was largely preserved.

A pattern of uneven development resulted, with the south enjoying the basis for a modern economy and exposure to democratic institutions and the north remaining largely agricultural and monarchical. These disparities between northern and southern Nigeria propelled northern leaders in the First and Second Republics to secure control of the federal government in order to redistribute resources to the north, while military rulers pursued their own goals by selectively colluding with and manipulating northern fears and southern resentments.

Nigeria's Fragile Collective Identity. This division between north and south is overlaid with hundreds of ethnic divisions across the nation, which military governments and civilians alike have been prone to manipulate for selfish ends. Over three decades after the Biafran civil war, Nigeria often seems as divided as it was in the prelude to that conflict. Fears of another civil war rose during the mid-1990s.

These many cultural divisions have been continually exacerbated by the triple threats of **clientelism,** corruption, and unstable authoritarian governing structures, which together foster ethnic group competition and hinder economic potential.[6] Clientelism is the practice by which a particular group receives disproportionate policy benefits or political favors from a political patron, usually at the expense of the larger society. In Nigeria, patrons are often linked to clients by ethnic, religious, or other cultural ties, and these ties have generally benefited only a small elite. By fostering political competition along cultural lines, clientelism tends to undermine social trust and political stability, which are necessary conditions for economic growth. Clientelism thus reduces the state to an arena of struggle over distribution of the "national cake" among primarily ethnic clients rather than serving as a framework of governance.

Despite the prevalence of ethnicity as the primary form of political identity and the accompanying scourge of ethnic-based clientelism, the idea of Nigeria has taken root among the country's ethnic groups over forty years of independence. Most public discourse does not question the idea of a single cohesive country, but instead revolves around finding an equitable balance among different ethnic groups within the context of a united Nigeria. This can be seen in recent calls from some organizations for a national conference to restructure the federation. Most Nigerians enjoy many personal connections across ethnic and religious lines, and elites in both the north and the south hold significant business investments throughout the country. Nevertheless, ethnicity remains a critical flashpoint that has led to localized ethnic violence on many occasions, and politicians continue to use ethnic identification to forward their political objectives, often divisively.

Implications for Comparative Politics

The saying that "as Nigeria goes, so goes the rest of sub-Saharan Africa" may again be relevant. With a population of 130 million, Nigeria is by far the largest country in Africa and among the ten most populous countries in the world. One out of every five black Africans are Nigerians. Unlike most other countries on the continent, Nigeria has the human and material resources to overcome the vicious cycle of poverty and **autocracy.** Hopes for this breakthrough, however, have been regularly frustrated over four decades of independent rule. If Nigeria, with its vast resources, cannot succeed in breaking this cycle, what does that mean for the rest of sub-Saharan Africa?

Nigeria remains the oldest surviving federation in Africa. At a time when other federations are dissolving, whether peacefully, as in the former Czechoslovakia, or violently, as in the former Yugoslavia, Nigeria manages to maintain its fragile unity. That unity has come under increasing stress, and a major challenge is to ensure that Nigeria does not go the way of Yugoslavia. One fact is certain: Nigeria's multiethnic, multireligious, multiclass, and multiregional nature makes it an especially valuable case for the study of social cleavages in conflict and cooperation. Even the United States, which is nearing a demographic transition from a white majority, can learn from Nigeria's efforts to find unity amid cultural diversity.

Nigeria's past failures to sustain democracy and economic development also render it an important case for the study of resource competition and the perils of corruption, and its experience demonstrates the interrelationship between democracy and development. Democracy and development depend on other factors, including leadership, political culture, institutional autonomy, and the external economic climate. Nigeria has much to teach us on all these topics.

At this stage, it is uncertain whether Nigeria will return to the path of autocracy, underdevelopment, and fragmentation or shift to a course of democratic renewal and national construction. In the following sections, we will explore these issues and evaluate how they may shape Nigerian politics in the years ahead.

Section ❷ Political Economy and Development

We have seen how colonialism bequeathed Nigeria an interventionist state and how governments in the post-independence period continued this pattern. The state became the central fixture in the Nigerian economy, stunting the private sector and encumbering industry and commerce. As the state began to unravel in the late 1980s and 1990s, leaders grew more predatory, plundering the one major revenue-generating sector remaining, oil, and keeping the nation's vast economic potential largely unrealized.

State and Economy

Through direct ownership of industry and services or through regulation and administrative control, the Nigerian state plays the central role in making decisions about the extraction, deployment, and allocation of scarce economic resources. Any major economic activity involves the state in some way, whether through licenses, taxes, contracts, legal provisions, trade and investment policy, or direct involvement of government agencies. The state's premier role in the economy arises from control of the most productive sectors, particularly the oil industry. Most of the nation's revenues, and nearly all of its hard currency, are channeled through the government. The discretion of leaders in spending those earnings, known as **rents,** forms the main path for channeling money through the economy. Consequently, winning government contracts—for supplies, construction, services, and myriad functions connected to the state—becomes a central economic activity, and control of the state makes its occupants the gatekeepers of contracting, licenses, and other areas of economic attainment.[7]

As individuals, groups, and communities jostled for state control or access, economic and social life became thoroughly politicized and consumed by **rent-seeking** behavior. The state has evolved beyond the role of regulator and manager, as seen in a less interventionist environment like Hong Kong. In most societies, access to the state and its leadership confers some economic advantages, but it can literally be a matter of life and death in impoverished countries like Nigeria.

Perhaps 70 percent of Nigerians struggle along without such access, surviving on petty trade and subsistence agriculture—the so-called informal sector of the economy—where taxes and regulation rarely reach. A number of analysts estimate that the Nigerian informal sector can be valued at approximately 20 percent of the entire Nigerian GDP, much of it earned through cross-border trade.

Origins of Economic Decline

In the colonial and immediate postcolonial periods, Nigeria's economy was centered on agricultural production for domestic consumption as well as for export. Peasant producers were induced by the colonial state to produce primary export commodities—cocoa in the west, palm oil in the east, and groundnuts and cotton in the north—through direct taxation, forced cultivation, and the presence of European agricultural firms. Despite the emphasis on exports, Nigeria was self-sufficient in food production at the time of independence. Vital to this effort was small-scale local production of sorghum and maize in the north and cassava and yams in the south. Some rice and wheat were also produced. It was not until later in the 1960s that emphasis shifted to the development of nonfood export crops through large-scale enterprises.

The nearly exclusive state attention to large-scale, nonfood production meant that small farmers were left out and received scant government support. Predictably, food production suffered, and food imports were stepped up to meet the needs of a burgeoning population. Despite government neglect, agriculture was the central component of the national economy in the First Republic. Michael Watts points to a combination of three factors that effectively undermined the Nigerian agricultural sector. The first was the Biafran War (1967–1970), which drastically reduced palm oil production in the east, where the war was concentrated. Second, severe drought in 1969 produced a famine from 1972 through 1974. Finally, the development of the petroleum industry caused a total shift in economic focus from agriculture (in terms of both labor and capital investment) to petroleum production. Agricultural export production plummeted from 80 percent of exports in 1960 to just 2 percent by 1980. To compensate for widening food shortfalls, food imports surged by 700 percent between 1970 and 1978.[8]

With the 1970s boom in revenues from oil, Nigeria greatly increased its expenditures on education, defense, and infrastructure. The university system was expanded, roads and ports were built, and industrial and office buildings were constructed. Imports of capital goods and raw materials required to support this expansion rose more than seven-fold between 1971 and 1979. Similarly, imports of consumer goods rose dramatically (600 percent) in the same period as an increasingly wealthy Nigerian elite developed a taste for expensive imported goods.[9] By 1978, the Nigerian government had outspent its revenues and could no longer finance many of its ambitious projects; consequently, the government was forced to borrow money to make up the deficit, causing external debt to skyrocket.

The acceleration in oil wealth was mirrored by a corresponding increase in corruption. Many public officials became very wealthy by setting up joint ventures with foreign oil companies. Other officials simply stole public funds for their own benefit. The economic downturn of the 1980s created even greater incentives for government corruption, and the Babangida and Abacha administrations became infamous for avarice. A Nigerian government commission reported that some $12.2 billion had been diverted to special off-budget accounts between 1988 and 1993. These funds were supposedly earmarked for national security and infrastructure, but they were never audited and their expenditure remains entirely unaccounted.[10] Within three years of seizing power, General Abacha allowed all of Nigeria's oil refineries to collapse, forcing this giant oil-exporting country into the absurd situation of having to import refined petroleum. Shamelessly, Abacha's family members and friends, who essentially served as fronts for him, monopolized the contracts to import this fuel in 1997. Small-time scam artists meanwhile proliferated, such that by 2002, Internet scams had become one of Nigeria's top five industries, earning over $100 million annually.

In sum, the oil boom was a double-edged sword for Nigeria. On one hand, it has generated tremendous income; on the other, it has become a source of external dependence and has badly skewed the Nigerian econ-

omy. Since the early 1970s, Nigeria has relied on oil for over 90 percent of its export earnings and about three-quarters of government revenues, as shown in Table 1. Hasty, ill-managed industrial and infrastructural expansion under both military and civilian regimes, combined with the neglect of the agricultural sector, further weakened the Nigerian economy. As a result, the economy was unable to offset the sharp fall in world oil prices after 1981 and descended into crisis.

From 1985 to the Present: Deepening Economic Crisis and the Search for Solutions

Structural Adjustment.   The year 1985 marked a turning point for the Nigerian state and economy. It ushered in Ibrahim Babangida's eight-year rule and revealed the economy's precarious condition. Within a year of wresting power from General Buhari in August 1985, the Babangida regime developed an economic **structural adjustment program (SAP)** with the active support of the World Bank and the IMF (also referred to as the **international financial institutions,** or **IFIs**). The decision to embark on the SAP was made against a background of increasing economic constraints arising from a combination of factors: the continued dependence of the economy on waning oil revenues, a growing debt burden, **balance of payments** difficulties, and lack of fiscal discipline.[11] (See "Global Connection: Structural Adjustment Programs.")

The large revenues arising from the oil windfall enabled the state to increase its involvement in direct production. Beginning in the 1970s, the government created a number of para-statals (state-owned enterprises; see Section 3) including large shares in major banks and other financial institutions, manufacturing, construction, agriculture, public utilities, and various services. This practice has ensured that the state remains the biggest employer as well as the most important source of revenue, even for the private sector. By the 1980s, the public bureaucracy in Nigeria had swollen to over 3 million employees (most employed by the federal and state governments), representing more than 60 percent of employment in the modern, formal sector of the economy.

Conversely, the share of the private sector in the economy fell from 45 percent in the 1960s to as little as 15 percent in the 1980s The stated goal of Nigerian

Table 1

Oil Sector Statistics, 1970–2003

	Annual Output (million barrels)	Average Price Index	Oil Exports as Percent of Total Exports	Government Oil Revenue (Naira millions)	Percent of Total Revenue
1970	396	37	58	166	26
1971	559	43	74	510	44
1972	643	40	82	767	54
1973	750	39	83	1,016	60
1974	823	162	93	3,726	82
1975	651	109	93	4,271	77
1976	756	115	94	5,365	79
1977	761	115	93	6,081	76
1978	692	100	89	4,556	62
1979	840	237	93	8,881	81
1980	753	220	96	12,353	81
1981	525	225	97	8,563	70
1982	470	212	99	7,814	66
1983	451	200	96	7,253	69
1984	508	190	97	8,268	74
1985	544	180	97	10,915	75
1986	534	75	94	8,107	66
1987	464	90	93	19,027	76
1988	507	60	91	20,934	77
1989	614	87	95	41,334	82
1990	–	125	–	–	–
1991	–	80	–	–	–
1992	714	79	98	164,078	86
1993	720	62	91	162,102	84
1994	733	70	85	160,192	79
1995	705	65	95	244,902	53
1996	783	95	95	266,000	51
1997	803	85	95	250,000	80
1998	700	62	90	248,500	70
1999	1950	–	–	–	76
2000	2040	–	–	–	65
2001	2083	–	98	1,668,000	79
2002	2068	–	94	1,884,000	80
2003*	2291	–	91	2,194,000	78

*Projected.

Sources: Output is from *Petroleum Economist* (1970–1989); price index and exports are from IMF, *International Financial Statistics* (1970–1984) and from Central Bank of Nigeria, *Annual Reports* (1985–1989); revenues are from Central Bank of Nigeria, *Annual Reports* (various years). From Tom Forrest, *Politics and Economic Development in Nigeria.* (Boulder: Westview Press, 1993), 134. 1990s statistics are from the Nigerian Federal Office of Statistics, *Annual Abstract of Statistics: 1997 Edition*, from the 1998 IMF *Annual Report*, and from Vision 2010, *Report of the Vision 2010 Committee: Main Report* (Abuja: Federal Government of Nigeria, September 1997). Nigerian Economic Summit Group, *Economic Indicators* (Vol. 8, no. 2, April–June 2002). Compilation and some calculations by Darren Kew.

Global Connection: *Structural Adjustment Programs*

The solutions to Nigeria's economic woes depend, in the first instance, on its own people and government, but assistance must also come from outside its borders. In addition to bilateral (country-to-country) assistance, multilateral economic institutions are a key source of loans, grants, and other forms of development aid. Two multilateral institutions that have become familiar players on the African economic scene are the International Monetary Fund (IMF) and the World Bank. These international financial institutions (IFIs) were established following World War II to provide short-term credit facilities to encourage growth and expansion of trade and longer-term financing packages, respectively, to rebuild the countries of war-torn Europe. Today, the functions of the IFIs have adapted and expanded to meet contemporary needs, including efforts to stabilize and restructure faltering economies. One area of emphasis by the IFIs, particularly among African countries, is the structural adjustment program (SAP).

Assistance from the World Bank and the IMF comes with many strings attached. These rigorous programs, which are intended to reduce government intervention and develop free markets, call for immediate austerity measures by recipient governments. SAPs generally begin with currency devaluation and tariff reductions. These actions are followed by measures aimed at reducing budget deficits, restructuring of the public sector (particularly employment practices), privatizing state-owned enterprises, agricultural reform (especially raising producer prices), and the reduction of consumer subsidies on staple foods. The social and economic hardships of these programs, particularly in the short term, can be severe. SAPs result in considerable economic, and frequently social, dislocation; dramatic price increases in foodstuffs and fuel, plus rising unemployment, are seldom popular with the general population.

At Babangida's insistence, Nigeria's SAP was developed and deployed in 1986 independent of the IMF and the World Bank. The program was, however, endorsed by the IFIs, making Nigeria eligible to receive disbursements of funds from the IMF and the World Bank and to reschedule $33 billion of external debt with the Paris and London clubs of lenders. Ironically, Nigeria's SAP was in many regards more rigorous than an initial program designed by the IMF. Like SAPs elsewhere, the Nigerian program was designed to encourage economic liberalization and promote private enterprise in place of a reliance on state-owned enterprises and public intervention. The logic was that competition leads to more efficient products and markets. Recovery among Africa's struggling economies has, however, been limited. Africa's economic problems are deeply entrenched; although an economy may be stabilized relatively quickly, comprehensive structural adjustment takes considerably longer. Thus far, Nigeria's SAP—in part because of the popular reaction to austerity measures, continued corruption in its implementation, and the complicating factor of unstable military rule—has failed to revitalize the economy. The final years of the Babangida administration (1985–1993) saw a marked slippage in the reform program, and the Abacha regime continued that trend. Abacha did enact a number of economic policies in 1995 and 1996 that lowered inflation, stabilized the exchange rate, and fostered mild GDP growth, but by 1997, these achievements had been squandered. President Obasanjo has sought to uphold the overall policies of SAP without calling it such, including attempts to end subsidies on fuel and to finish the privatization of the major government para-statals.

governments since the mid-1980s has been to reduce unproductive investments in the public sector, improve the sector's efficiency, and promote the growth of the private sector. **Privatization,** which is central to Nigeria's adjustment program, means that state-owned businesses would be sold to private (nonstate) investors, domestic or foreign. Privatization is intended to generate revenue, reduce state expenditures for loss-making operations, and improve efficiency. However, privatization also typically results in the loss of jobs. President Obasanjo entered office with a renewed commitment to privatization, beginning most prominently with the telecommunications network. There is also discussion of selling the jewel in the economic crown, the government's share of oil industry, sometime after the elections of 2003.

Expectations that privatization would encourage Nigerian and foreign investment in manufacturing have been largely disappointed. On a domestic level, Nigerian entrepreneurs have found that trading, government contracting, and currency speculation offer more reliable yields than manufacturing. Potential foreign investors remain hesitant to risk significant capital in an environment characterized by political and social instability, unpredictable economic policies, and endemic corruption. Only a few attractive areas such as telecommunications, utilities, and oil and gas are likely to draw significant foreign capital.

Economic Planning. Beginning in 1946, when the colonial administration announced the ten-year Plan for Development and Welfare, national plans have been prepared by ministries of finance, economic development, and planning. Five-year plans were the norm from 1962 through 1985, when their scope was extended to fifteen years. The national plan, however, has not been an effective management tool. The reasons are the absence of an effective database for planning and a great lack of discipline in plan implementation. The state strives to dictate the pace and direction of economic development, but lacks the tools and political will to deliver on its obligations.

Nigerian and foreign business leaders revived dialogue with government on economic direction with the 1994 establishment of the annual Nigerian Economic Summit (NES). This differed from previous planning efforts in that it was based on the coequal participation of government and private sector representatives. Two years later, General Abacha initiated the Vision 2010 process (see "Current Challenges: Vision 2010"). Participants in Vision 2010 advocated reductions in government's excessive role in the economy with the goals of increasing market efficiency and reducing competition for control of the state. The Obasanjo administration accepted much of the Vision 2010 agenda, although it did not say so publicly because of the plan's association with General Abacha's predatory regime. Many of the private sector participants in Vision 2010 continue to meet regularly through the Economic Sum-

mit. Advice from the NES continues to influence the economic policies of both the Obasanjo administration and the National Assembly.

Although the Economic Summit and Vision 2010 provide a basis for reform, many problems must still be overcome in the economy: low investment, low capacity utilization, unreliable distribution, stifling corruption, and overregulation. Average annual GDP growth rates were negative from 1981 through 1987 and have risen only mildly above the rate of population growth since Obasanjo took office in 1999. Consumption and investment have also recorded negative growth (see Table 2).

Nigeria's heavy foreign debt exacerbates the nation's economic stagnation (see Table 3). President Obasanjo made debt relief one of his highest priorities on taking office in 1999 and promptly undertook numerous visits to the capitals of Europe, Asia, and the United States to urge the governments of those countries to forgive most of Nigeria's obligations. His pleas fell largely on deaf ears, however, as Nigeria's National Assembly showed little inclination to spend within the nation's means. Obasanjo's government also showed a weak commitment to fiscal discipline, wastefully spending on such expensive prestige projects as a new football stadium in Abuja. Nigeria, once considered a country likely to achieve self-sustaining growth, now ranks among the more debt-distressed countries in the developing world. It cannot earn enough from the export of goods to service its foreign debt and also meet the basic needs of the population.

Social Welfare. Given the continued decline in its economic performance since the early 1980s, it is not surprising that Nigeria's social welfare has suffered greatly as well. Since 1986, there has been a marked deterioration in the quantity and quality of social services, complicated by a marked decline in household incomes (see Table 4). The SAP program and subsequent austerity measures emphasizing the reduction of state expenditures, have forced cutbacks in spending on social welfare.

Budgetary austerity and economic stagnation have hurt vulnerable groups such as the urban and rural poor, women, the young, and the elderly. Indeed, Nigeria performs poorly in meeting basic needs: life expectancy is barely above fifty years, and infant mortality is estimated at more than 80 deaths per 1,000 live births.

Current Challenges: *Vision 2010*

In the early 1990s, concerned with the nation's economic decline, a number of the larger Nigerian businesses and key multinational corporations decided to pursue new initiatives. With the August 1993 appointment of Ernest Shonekan, the former chairman of West Africa's largest local corporation, UAC, as head of state, these businesses sensed an opportunity to alter the course of Nigeria's economic policies. With Shonekan's involvement, they arranged the first Economic Summit, a high-profile conference that advocated numerous policies to move Nigeria toward becoming an "emerging market" that could attract foreign investment along the lines of the high-performing states in Asia.

Shortly after the first Economic Summit, however, General Abacha took control and continued the ruinous economic approach of Babangida's later years. The Economic Summit meanwhile continued to meet annually. After his flawed 1994 budget sent the Nigerian economy into a tailspin, Abacha was ready to listen to the summit participants. He accepted several of their recommendations, and by 1996 the economy began to make modest gains. Therefore, when key members of the summit proposed Vision 2010, General Abacha seized the opportunity presented and endorsed it in September 1996. Chief Shonekan was named the chair.

Vision 2010 relies on a model of strategic planning that begins with a visioning process to identify key corporate goals and the paths of action to realize these goals. The process brings together key stakeholders and implementers, who are expected to bring goals to fruition. Malaysia and other developing countries successfully employed this model in the 1980s to devise blueprints for development. As part of the visioning process, the government adopts a package of business-promoting economic reforms, while business pledges to work toward certain growth targets consistent with governmental priorities in employment, taxation, community investment, and the like. General Abacha's estimation of the potential of Vision 2010 was so great that he quickly increased its scope beyond its initial economic intentions. Committees were set up to develop plans for Nigeria's sports teams, interethnic relations, media development, and even for civil-military relations under the expected democratic rule. Along with government and business leaders, key figures were invited to participate from nearly all sectors of society, including the press, nongovernmental organizations, youth groups, market women's associations, and others. Government-owned media followed Vision 2010's pronouncements with great fanfare, while the private media reviewed them with a healthy dose of skepticism regarding Abacha's intentions and the elitist nature of the exercise.

In September 1997, on schedule, the Vision 2010 executive committee presented its final report. Its four volumes painted a surprisingly candid picture of where Nigeria stood and recommended how the country could transform itself into a strong emerging-market democracy by 2010. The recommendations called for, in part, restoring democratic rule, restructuring and professionalizing the military, lowering the population growth rate, rebuilding education, meaningful privatization, diversifying the export base beyond oil, supporting intellectual property rights, and central bank autonomy.

Whatever its merits, Vision 2010 was imperiled because of its association with Abacha. When the new Obasanjo administration took office in 1999 lacking a comprehensive economic plan of its own, however, it quietly approached Shonekan for the detailed recommendations and data produced by Vision 2010. Consequently, the general economic strategy and objectives of Vision 2010 are largely echoed in those of the current government. The Economic Summit, meanwhile, continues to provide annual assessments of the Nigerian economy and critical economic advice to policy-makers.

Source: Vision 2010 Final Report, *September 1997.*

Table 2

Selected Economic Indicators, 1980–1998

	Real GDP (Naira billions) (1993 = 100)	GDP (% Growth)	Manufacturing Capacity Utilization (%)*	Inflation Rate (%)
1980	96.2	5.5	70.1	9.9
1985	68.9	9.4	37.1	5.5
1990	90.3	8.1	40.3	7.4
1991	94.6	4.8	42.0	13.0
1992	97.4	3.0	41.8	44.6
1993	100.0	2.7	37.2	57.2
1994	101.0	1.3	30.4	57.0
1995	103.5	2.2	29.3	72.8
1996	106.9	3.3	32.5	29.3
1997	111.1	3.9	–	8.5
1998	113.3	2.0	–	9.0
1999	114.4	1.0	–	6.7
2000	118.8	3.8	–	6.9
2001	123.5	4.0	–	18.9
2002	127.7	3.4	–	16.9
2003	133.1	4.2	–	13.5

GDP % Growth

1976–1986	–1.3
1987–1997	1.6

*Manufacturing capacity utilization is the average (across the economy) percentage of full production capabilities at which manufacturers are producing.

Sources: Vision 2010. *Report of the Vision 2010 Committee: Main Report.* Abuja: Federal Government of Nigeria, September 1997; World Bank, "Nigeria at a Glance," 1998 (www.worldbank.org) the 1998 IMF *Annual Report.* Nigerian Economic Summit Group, *Economic Indicators* (Vol. 8, no. 2, April–June 2002).

Table 3

Nigeria's Total External Debt (millions of US$; current prices and exchange rates)

1975–1979	1980	1981	1982	1983
3,304	8,934	12,136	12,954	18,540
1984	**1985**	**1986**	**1987**	**1988**
18,537	19,551	24,043	31,193	31,947
1989	**1994**	**1995**	**1996**	**1997**
32,832	34,000	35,010	33,442	32,906
1999	**2000**	**2001**	**2002**	**2003**
29,358	34,134	33,766	33,723	33,740

Nigeria's Debt Compared to its Earnings:

	1976	1986	1996	1997	1999
Total Debt/GDP	3.7	109.9	72.0	63.1	83.8
Total Debt Service/ Exports	3.7	28.4	15.2	15.9	204

	2000	2001	2002	2003
Total Debt/GDP	97.3	86.9	76.5	72.6
Total Debt Service/ Exports	147.6	147	177.5	159.5

Sources: UNDP, World Bank, *African Development Indicators* (Washington, D.C.: World Bank, 1992), 159; UNDP *1998 Human Development Report;* World Bank, "Nigeria at a Glance," 1998 (www.worldbank.org). Nigerian Economic Summit Group, *Economic Indicators* (Vol. 8, no. 2, April–June 2002).

Nigeria's provision of basic education is also inadequate. Moreover, Nigeria has failed to develop a national social security system, with much of the gap filled by family-based networks of mutual aid. President Obasanjo took an important step in meeting basic needs when he raised the minimum wage nearly tenfold in 1999. Since wage levels had hardly been raised in years despite the inflation of the previous decade, the gains for workers with formal sector jobs were more meager than the increase suggests.

The provision of health care and other social serv-ices—water, education, food, and shelter—remains woefully inadequate in both urban and rural areas. Beyond the needless loss of countless lives to preventable and curable maladies, Nigeria's neglect of the health and social net will likely bear more bitter fruit. The nation stands on the verge of an AIDS epidemic of catastrophic proportions. The United Nations estimates—conservatively—that HIV infection rates are at approximately 6 percent of the population and are likely to spread to 10 percent by the end of the decade, dooming perhaps 15 million Nigerians to the slow death of that disease without access to the medications or treatment that can delay HIV's effects. The government has made AIDS a secondary priority, leaving much of the initiative to a small group of courageous but underfunded nongovernmental organizations.

Table 4

Index of Real Household Incomes of Key Groups 1980/81–1986/87, 1996, 2001
(Rural self-employed in 1980/81 = 100)

	1980/81	1981/82	1982/83	1983/84	1984/85	1985/86	1986/87	1996*	2001*
Rural self-employed	100	103	95	86	73	74	65	27	32
Rural wage earners	178	160	147	135	92	95	84	48	57
All rural households	105	107	99	89	74	84	74	28	33
Urban self-employed	150	124	106	94	69	69	61	41	48
Urban wage earners	203	177	164	140	101	101	90	55	65
All urban households	166	142	129	109	80	80	71	45	53

*Estimated, based on 1980/81 figures adjusted for a 73 percent drop in per capita GDP from 1980 to 1996, and an 18 percent increase in per capita GDP from 1996 to 2001. The FOS lists annual household incomes for 1996 as $75 (N 6,349) for urban households and $57 (N 4,820) for rural households, suggesting that the gap between urban and rural households is actually 19 percent closer than our estimate.

Sources: National Integrated Survey of Households (NISH), Federal Office of Statistics (FOS) consumer price data, and World Bank estimates. As found in Paul Collier, *An Analysis of the Nigerian Labour Market,* Development Economics Department Discussion Paper (Washington, D.C.: World Bank, 1986). From Tom Forrest, *Politics and Economic Development in Nigeria* (Boulder: Westview Press, 1993), 214. 1996 data from FOS *Annual Abstract of Statistics: 1997 Edition,* p. 80.

Society and Economy

Because the central government in Nigeria controls access to most resources and economic opportunities, the state has become the major focus for competition among ethnic, regional, religious, and class groups. In such an environment, elite members of these groups become conflict generators rather than conflict managers.[12] A partial explanation for the failure of economic strategies can be found within Nigerian society itself—a complex mix of contending ethnic, religious, and regional constituencies.

Ethnic and Religious Cleavages

Nigeria's ethnic relations have generated tensions that sap the country's economy of much needed vitality.[13] Competition among the largest groups is centered on access to national economic and political resources. The dominance of the Hausa-Fulani, Igbo, and Yoruba in the country's national life and the conflicts among political elites from these groups bias economic affairs. Religious cleavages have also affected economic and social stability. Some of the federation's states in the far north are populated mainly by Muslims, whereas others, particularly in the middle and eastern parts of the south, are predominantly Christian.

A combination of government ineptitude—or outright manipulation—and growing Islamic and Christian assertion, have heightened conflicts between adherents.[14] Christians have perceived past northern-dominated governments as being pro-Muslim in their management and distribution of scarce resources as well as in their policy decisions, some of which jeopardized the secular nature of the state. These fears have increased since 1999, when several northern states instituted expanded versions of the Islamic legal code, the *shari'a.* For their part, Muslims now fear that President Obasanjo, a born-again Christian, is tilting the balance of power and thus the distribution of economic benefits against the north.

The decline in the Nigerian economy also contributed to the rise of Christian and Muslim fundamentalism, which have spread among unemployed youths and others in a society suffering under economic collapse. In northern Nigeria, disputes over economic and political issues have sometimes escalated into physical attacks on Christians and members of southern ethnic groups residing in the north. A demonstration led by Islamist groups in Kano against U.S. intervention in Afghanistan after the September 11, 2001, terrorist attacks, for instance, degenerated into a Muslim-Christian conflict when gangs of youths used the occasion to loot some Christian neighborhoods. Occasionally, religious revivalism among the various Christian sects has provoked violent protests by Muslims.

Evangelical Christian churches swept across the south and Middle Belt in the 1990s, growing with the general rise in poverty and social dislocation. Offering music, dancing, community, and even instant miracles (especially in regard to fertility, relationships, and finances), these churches have sprouted in nearly every neighborhood where Christians are to be found. The evangelical churches augment the more established denominations, including Anglicans, Catholics, and Methodists.

Northern-led governments after independence, fearing a "southern tyranny of skills,"[15] sought to use the political clout of their numerical majority to keep the south in check and to redistribute resources to the north. Early military governments (1966–1979) tried to maintain some measure of ethnic and religious balance, but the Babangida regime in the 1980s became increasingly northern dominated and more willing than any of its predecessors to manipulate Nigeria's ethnic divisions. General Abacha's Provisional Ruling Council (PRC) tilted overwhelmingly in favor of northerners, specifically Hausa-Fulani, in its membership. Numerous attacks were perpetrated against prominent southern civilians, particularly Yoruba, often using Abacha's secret hit squads. His regime also closed universities and detained a number of activists, particularly in the south.

Yoruba groups were not the only ones adversely affected by Abacha's rule. The Ogoni, Ijaw, and other southern minorities of the oil-producing regions were brutalized by military and police forces when they protested the scant oil revenues remitted to the region, as well as the environmental degradation from the irresponsible oil industry. The Ogoni in particular were organized through the Movement for the Survival of the Ogoni People (MOSOP), under the leadership of internationally renowned writer and environmentalist Ken Saro-Wiwa. The military's abrupt hanging of Saro-Wiwa and eight Ogoni compatriots in 1995 following a kangaroo trial was widely criticized as "judicial murder" by human rights groups, and led to Nigeria's suspension from the Commonwealth (an international organization composed of Britain and its former colonies). A subsequent UN mission of inquiry declared the executions illegal under both Nigerian and international law.

MOSOP under Saro-Wiwa effectively blended claims for **self-determination,** which in this case meant increased local political autonomy and national political representation, with concerns over oil industry pollution in the Niger Delta, primarily on the part of global oil giant Royal Dutch/Shell, as a platform to forge alliances with international environmental and human rights organizations. Many other Niger Delta minority groups have subsequently followed MOSOP's lead in pushing a combination of self-determination, political rights, environmental concerns, and demands for greater control over the oil pumped from their lands.

Since the return of democracy in 1999, many ethnic-based and religious movements have taken advantage of restored political freedoms to mobilize and press the federal government to address their grievances. Some mobilization has been peaceful, but many armed groups have also formed, at times with the encouragement or complicity of the mainstream political movements.

Youths from the Niger Delta minorities, primarily the Ijaw, have occupied Shell and Chevron facilities on several occasions to protest their economic marginalization. One spectacular incident on an offshore oil platform in 2002 saw a group of local women stage a peaceful takeover using a traditional form of protest: disrobing in order to shame the oil companies and local authorities. Most of the protests have ended peacefully, although a large-scale upheaval in the Warri region in 2003 caused the deaths of several policemen, soldiers, and oil workers. The Obasanjo government has periodically responded to these incidents and other disturbances with excessive force. After Ijaw militias killed several policemen in the village of Odi in late 1999, the army was ordered to track down the perpetrators. The military subsequently flattened the village, raping and killing many innocent people in the process. Army units committed similar retaliatory atrocities in 2001 among villages in the Middle Belt state of Benue, when ethnic militias apparently killed several soldiers engaged in a peacekeeping mission during an interethnic dispute. In the Niger Delta, the struggle of the minority communities with the federal government and multinational oil corporations has been complicated by clashes among the minority groups themselves over control of land and access to government rents. Fighting among the Ijaws and the Itsekiris near Warri in 2003 claimed more than 100 lives. Ethnic-based mobilization has increased across Nigeria in general since 1999, including ethnic vigilantes. Political leaders unfortunately have built alliances with these groups and are increasingly using them to harass and even kill political opponents. Nigerian political and business elites have also demonstrated a propensity toward accentuating sectional cleavages. Culture or ethnicity is used to fragment rather than to integrate the country, with grave consequences for the economy and society.

These divisive practices overshadow certain positive aspects of sectional identities. For example, associations based on ethnic and religious affinities often serve as vehicles for mobilizing savings, investment, and production, such as informal credit associations. In addition, professional associations—comprising lawyers, doctors, journalists, business and trade groups, academics, trade unions, or students' organizations—played a prominent role in the anticolonial struggle. These groups, which form the core of civil society, have continued to provide a vehicle for political expression while also reflecting the divisive pressures of Nigeria's cultural pluralism.

Gender Differences

Although the Land Use Act of 1978 stated that all land in Nigeria is ultimately owned by the government, land tenure in Nigeria is still governed by traditional practice, which is largely patriarchal. Despite the fact that women, especially from the south and Middle Belt areas, have traditionally dominated agricultural production and form the bulk of agricultural producers, they are generally prevented from owning land, which remains the major means of production. Trading, in which women feature prominently, is also controlled in many areas by traditional chiefs and local government councilors, who are overwhelmingly male.

Women have not succeeded in transforming their economic importance into political clout, but important strides are being made in this direction. Their past inability and current struggle to achieve direct access to state power is a reflection of several factors. Women's associations in the past tended to be elitist, urban based, and mainly concerned with issues of trade, children, welfare, and religion. The few that did have a more political orientation have been largely token appendages of the male-dominated political parties or instruments of the government. An example of the latter was the Better Life Program, directed by the wife of Babangida, and its successor, the Family Support Program, directed by Abacha's wife. Women are grossly underrepresented at all levels of the governmental system; only eight (of 469) national legislators are women.[16]

Reflecting the historical economic and educational advantages of the south, women's interest organizations sprouted in southern Nigeria earlier than in the north. Although these groups initially focused generally on nonpolitical issues surrounding women's health and children, organizations like Women in Nigeria began to form in the 1980s with explicit political goals, such as getting more women into government and increasing funds available for education.

By the 1990s, northern women had become nearly as active as southerners in founding nongovernmental organizations (NGOs). As in the south, northern women's NGOs at first focused on less politicized issues, but by the end of the decade, explicitly political organizations such as the 100 Women Groups, which sought to elect 100 women to every level of government, emerged. Northern groups also showed tremendous creativity in using Islam to support their activities, which was very important considering that tenets of the religion have been regularly used by Nigerian men to justify women's subordinate status. Women's groups in general have been much more dynamic than male-dominated NGOs, nearly all of which are entirely dependent on foreign or government funding, in developing income-generating projects to make their organizations and the women they assist increasingly self-reliant.

Nigeria and the International Political Economy

At the international level, the state has remained weak and dependent on Western industrial and financial interests four decades after Nigeria became a full-fledged member of the world community. The country suffers from an acute debt burden. In addition, Nigeria is reliant on the developed industrial economies for finance capital, production and information technologies, basic consumer items, and raw materials. Nigeria strives to provide leadership at the continental (African) and subregional (West African) levels. Most of its policy and intellectual elites support this self-image.

In recent years, Nigeria has played a major role in reorienting the focus of the Nonaligned Movement toward issues of economic development and cooperation. In bodies such as the Organization of African Unity (OAU) and the UN, Nigeria generally took firm positions to promote decolonization and the development of the Third World and against the apartheid regime in South Africa. Unfortunately, much of this international goodwill was largely squandered by the Babangida and Abacha regimes. Since taking office in 1999, President Obasanjo has made over 100 foreign visits, seeking to restore Nigerian credibility and status. Debt relief, or outright cancellation, has been an important goal of these trips. This has been such a central focus, in fact, that some of his critics charge that he is more interested in traveling abroad than addressing the problems at home.

Nigeria and the Regional Political Economy

Nigeria has aspired to be a regional leader in Africa. These aspirations have not been dampened by its declining position in the global political economy. Nigeria was a major actor in the formation in 1975 of the **Economic Community of West African States (ECOWAS)** and has carried a disproportionately high financial and administrative burden for keeping the organization afloat. Under President Obasanjo's initiative, ECOWAS voted to create a parliament and a single currency for the region as the next step toward a European Union–style integration. These lofty goals will take several years of concerted efforts from the region's troubled governments to become a reality, and the lackluster results of past integration efforts do not bode well for success.

Nigeria has also been the largest contributor of troops to the West African peacekeeping force, the ECOWAS Monitoring Group (known as ECOMOG). Under Nigerian direction, the ECOWAS countries dispatched ECOMOG troops to Liberia from 1990 to 1997 to restore order and prevent the Liberian civil war from destabilizing the subregion. Ironically, despite military dictatorship at home, Nigerian ECOMOG forces invaded Sierra Leone in May 1997 to restore its

democratically elected government, a move generally endorsed by the international community. The United Nations assumed leadership of the operation in 1999, but Nigeria continues to contribute troops. Nigeria under President Obasanjo has also sought to mediate crises in Guinea-Bissau and Ivory Coast, and in Congo and Zimbabwe outside the ECOWAS region.

Because it is the largest economy in the West African subregion, Nigeria has at times been a magnet for immigration. At the height of the 1970s oil boom, many West African laborers, most of them Ghanaians, migrated to Nigeria in search of employment. When the oil-based expansion ceased and jobs became scarce, Nigeria sought to protect its own workers by expelling hundreds of thousands of West Africans in 1983 and 1985. Many Nigerians now flock to the high-flying Ghanaian economy for work and to countries across the continent, including far-off South Africa.

Nigeria and the Political Economy of the West

Nigeria's global influence peaked in the 1970s at the height of the oil boom. Shortly after the 1973–1974 global oil crisis, Nigeria's oil wealth was perceived by the Nigerian elite largely as a source of strength. In 1975, for example, Nigeria was selling about 30 percent of its oil to the United States and was able to apply pressure to the administration of President Gerald Ford in a dispute over Angola.[17] By the 1980s, however, the global oil market had become a buyers' market. Thereafter, it became clear that Nigeria's dependence on oil was a source of weakness, not strength. The depth of Nigeria's international weakness became more evident with the adoption of structural adjustment in the mid-1980s. Given the enormity of the economic crisis, Nigeria was compelled to seek IMF/World Bank support to improve its balance of payments and facilitate economic restructuring and debt rescheduling, and it has had to accept direction from foreign agencies ever since.

In addition to its dependence on oil revenues, Nigeria remains dependent on Western technology and Western industrial expertise for exploration and extraction of its oil reserves. Nevertheless, oil can be an important political resource. For example, after General Babangida cancelled presidential elections in 1993, pressure on their home governments by U.S. and

European oil companies, along with a few well-paid Abacha lobbyists, ensured that severe economic sanctions on Nigeria were never imposed. The United States is now turning toward Nigerian oil to diversify its supply base beyond the Middle East, which should improve Nigerian government revenues but may not significantly alter the overall dependency of the economy.

In the end, although oil creates dependencies, it also provides advantages: Nigeria's global leverage stems directly from oil. Nigeria remains a highly visible and influential member of the Organization of Petroleum Exporting Countries (OPEC), selling on the average 2 million barrels of petroleum daily and contributing approximately 8 percent of U.S. oil imports. Britain, France, and Germany each has over $1 billion in investments. Nigeria's oil wealth and its great economic potential have tempered the resolve of Western nations in combating human rights and other

abuses, notably during the Abacha period from 1993 to 1998.

With the end of the ruinous Abacha years, President Obasanjo enjoyed much goodwill among Western governments when he assumed office in 1999. They were, however, hesitant to forgive much of Nigeria's enormous debt without some evidence of fiscal responsibility. By the end of his first term in 2003, Obasanjo had little to show for his international persuasion efforts, because neither his administration nor the National Assembly succeeded in reining in Nigeria's budget or checking rampant public sector corruption.

The West has nevertheless been strongly supportive of the return of Nigeria's leadership across Africa at large under the president. Together with President Thabo Mbeki of South Africa, Obasanjo was instrumental in 2002 in convincing the continent's leaders to transform the OAU into the African Union (AU),

Despite being sub-Saharan Africa's largest crude oil exporter, Nigeria faces chronic fuel shortages. General Abacha allowed the nation's four refineries to collapse, forcing the country into the absurd situation of importing fuel—through middlemen who gave enormous kickbacks to Abacha and his family. Shortages have resurfaced periodically since 1999.
Source: Jay Oguntuwase-Asope, *The Guardian* (Lagos), August 12, 1998.

modeled on European-style processes to promote greater political integration across the continent. The AU's first item of business, largely promoted by Mbeki and Obasanjo, was to endorse the New Partnership for Africa's Development (NEPAD), through which African governments committed to specific political and economic reforms in return for access to Western markets and financial assistance. Western leaders endorsed NEPAD in principle at a summit of the world's largest economies in 2002, but were short on what specific actions they would take if African governments met their target reforms.

Despite its considerable geopolitical resources, Nigeria's economic development profile is bleak. Nigeria is listed very close to the bottom of the UNDP's Human Development Index (HDI), 142 out of 174, behind India and Haiti. Gross national product (GNP) per capita in 2001 was $300, less than 2 percent of which was recorded as public expenditures on education and health, respectively. These figures compare unfavorably with the $860 per capita GNP for China and $390 per capita for India. On the basis of its per capita GDP, the Nigerian economy is the nineteenth poorest in the world in a 1997 World Bank ranking. For comparative purposes, the same study ranks Ghana as thirty-first poorest and India twenty-seventh.

Section ❸ Governance and Policy-Making

The rough edges of what has been called the "unfinished Nigerian state" can be seen in its institutions of governance and policy-making. What seemed like an endless political transition under the Babangida and Abacha regimes was rushed through in less than a year by their successor, Abdulsalami Abubakar, by 1999. President Obasanjo thus inherited a government that was close to collapse, riddled with corruption, unable to coherently perform basic tasks of governance, yet facing high public expectations to deliver considerable progress.

Organization of the State

The National Question and Constitutional Governance

After four decades as an independent nation, Nigerians are still debating the basic political structures of the country, who will rule and how, and indeed, even if the country should remain united. They call this fundamental governance issue the "national question." How is the country to be governed given its great diversity? What should be the institutional form of the government? How can all sections of the country work in harmony and none feel excluded or dominated by the others? Nigerian leaders have attempted to answer these questions in various ways. Since the creation of Nigeria by the British, one path has been reliance on the Anglo-American tradition of rule by law rather than by individuals. Another path has been military guidance. Nigeria has stumbled along under hybrids of these two tendencies. As a consequence, the country has produced many constitutions but has yet to entrench constitutionalism.

Since the amalgamation of northern and southern Nigeria in 1914, the country has introduced, or nearly inaugurated, nine constitutions—five under colonial rule (in 1922, 1946, 1951, 1954, and 1960) and four after colonial rule: the 1963 Republican Constitution, the 1979 Constitution of the Second Republic, the 1989 Constitution intended for the Third Republic, and the current 1999 Constitution, which essentially amended the 1979 version. Despite the expenditure of huge sums on constitution making by the Babangida and Abacha regimes, Nigeria experienced the anomaly of conducting national elections in 1998–1999 without a settled constitutional document. Civil society groups, meanwhile, continue to advocate rewriting the 1999 Constitution.

In the United States, the U.S. Constitution is perceived as a living document and subject to interpretation, yet the document itself has endured for over 200 years with just twenty-seven amendments. In contrast, Nigerian constitutions have earned no such respect from military or civilian leaders, who have been unwilling to observe legal and constitutional constraints. Governance and policy-making in this context are conducted within fragile institutions that are often swamped by personal and partisan considerations. Military rule bolstered these tendencies and personalized governance and policy-making. With this in mind, we will discuss key elements of recent periods of military rule, their continued influence in the present, and the young institutions of the Fourth Republic.

Federalism and State Structure

Nigeria's First Republic experimented with the parliamentary model, in which the executive is chosen directly from the legislative ranks in a manner inspired by the British system. The First Republic was relatively decentralized, with the locus of political power in the three federal units: the Northern, Eastern, and Western Regions. The Second Republic constitution, which went into effect in 1979, adopted a U.S.-style presidential model. The Fourth Republic continues with the presidential model: a system with a strong executive who is constrained by a system of checks and balances on authority, a bicameral legislature, and an independent judicial branch charged with matters of law and constitutional interpretation.[18]

Like the United States, Nigeria also features a federal structure comprising 36 states and 774 local government units empowered to enact their own laws within their individual jurisdictions, but limited in scope by the constitution and federal laws. Together, these units constitute a single national entity with three levels of government. The judicial system also resembles that of the United States with a network of local and district courts, as well as state-level courts.

Under a true federal system, the formal powers of the different levels of government would be clearly delineated and the relationships among and between them defined. In Nigeria, by contrast, these institutions have been radically altered by military rule, and the military-authored 1999 Constitution reflects the contradictions of that period. The military perceived their role as preservers of the federation, and they brooked little dissent. Consequently, they left a constitution that retains enormous powers in the federal government, and the executive in particular. In addition, so many years of military rule left a pattern of governance—a political culture—that retains many authoritarian strains despite the formal democratization of state structures.

The control of oil wealth by this centralized command structure has further cemented economic and political control in the center, resulting in a skewed federalism in which states enjoy nominal powers, but in reality are totally dependent on the central government. The powers of the state and local governments are delineated by the federal constitution, and most of them receive their entire budget from what the federal government decides is their share of the oil revenues.

Another aspect of federalism in Nigeria has been the effort to arrive at some form of elite accommodation to moderate some of the more divisive dimensions of cultural pluralism. For example, recruitment of local elements into the army shortly after independence followed a quota system. Through such a system, it was hoped the army would reflect the country's complex ethnic makeup more closely. A similar practice, reflecting what Nigerians now refer to as "federal character," was introduced into the public service and formally codified the 1979 Constitution. (See "Current Challenges: Nigeria's Federal Character.")

Because federal character is also perceived as a tool of ethnic management, disputes about its application have tended to focus on ethnic representation rather than on representation of state interests. Although this principle was originally regarded as a positive Nigerian contribution to governance in a plural society, its application has tended to intensify rather than reduce intergroup rivalries and conflicts. In recent years, there have been calls for the use of merit over federal character in awarding public sector jobs. (See "Current Challenges: Federalism in Nigeria.")

The Executive

Evolution of the Executive Function

In the Second Republic, the earlier parliamentary system was replaced by a presidential system based on the American model. The president was chosen directly by the electorate rather than indirectly by the legislature. The rationale for the change was based on the experience of the First Republic; the instability and ultimate failure of that government, which was less a result of the parliamentary model than of underlying societal cleavages, left a bitter legacy. In addition, there was a widespread belief that a popularly elected president, a truly national figure, could serve as a symbol of unity. Finally, the framers of the Second Republic's constitution believed that placing the election of

Current Challenges: **Nigeria's Federal Character**

What is Nigeria's "federal character"? Federal character, in principle, is an "affirmative action" program to ensure representation of all ethnic and regional groups, particularly in the civil service. Although *federal character* is regarded as a euphemism for *ethnic balancing*, in practice it has provoked ethnic instability, rivalry, and conflict. Federal character goes beyond federalism in the traditional Western and territorial sense, although it definitely contains a territorial element. Federalism as a principle of government has a positive connotation (especially with regard to mitigating ethnic conflict); however, federal character elicits the unevenness and inequality in Nigerian politics, especially when it comes to the controversial use of ethnic-based quotas in hiring, the awarding of government contracts, and the disbursement of political offices.

The pursuit of ethnic balancing has had numerous ill effects, several of which are identified by Nigerian scholar Peter Ekeh.* First, federal charac-

ter has created benefit-seeking and autonomy-seeking groups in areas where they did not previously exist. Second, federal character and federalism have overloaded the political system in terms of personnel and other costs. Federal character has also "invaded the integrity of the public bureaucracy" by ignoring merit. Finally, the thirty-six states that currently exist in Nigeria are vying for control of the center in order to extract the greatest benefits, using ethnic quotas as a lever. None of these conditions is likely to change in the near future. Federal character, and everything that goes with it, appears to be a permanent part of Nigeria's political and social landscape.

---

*See Peter Ekeh, "The Structure and Meaning of Federal Character in the Nigerian Political System," in Peter Ekeh and Eghosa E. Osaghae (eds.), *Federalism and the Federal Character in Nigeria* (Ibadan: Heinemann, 1989).

---

the president in the hands of the electorate, rather than parliament, would mitigate the effects of a lack of party discipline in the selection of the executive.

The Second Republic's experiment with presidentialism lasted for only four years before it was ended by the 1983 coup. Although some Nigerian intellectuals call for a return to parliamentarism, the presidential model has become entrenched in the nation's political arena. The return of military rule in 1983 further concentrated power in the hands of the chief executive, first with head of state Major-General Muhammadu Buhari, until his removal in a 1985 palace coup. His successor, General Babangida, although obviously unelected, assumed the title of president, the first Nigerian military ruler to do so. After ousting Chief Shonekan in November 1993, Sani Abacha also assumed the title of president. Thus, when President Obasanjo took office in 1999, the first elected Nigerian president since Shehu Shagari in 1983, he inherited an executive structure that towered above all other arms of the federal government, far beyond the careful balance envisioned when the model was adopted in 1979.

The Executive Under Military Rule

The styles and leadership approaches among Nigeria's seven military heads of state varied widely. The military regime of General Gowon (1966–1975) was initially consensual, but as he clung to power for five years after the war, his authority declined, and he increasingly relied on a small group of advisers. Although all military leaders talked of "transitions to democracy," only Generals Obasanjo (1976–1979) and Abubakar (1998–1999) fulfilled the pledge of yielding power to an elected government.

After a few years of relatively consensual governance, the Babangida regime (1985–1993) drifted into a more personalized and repressive mode of governance. Abacha (1993–1998) outdid them all, however, and his harsh autocratic rule included the 1994 suspension of habeas corpus and the hounding of outspoken Nigerians into exile. General Abubakar, in contrast, moved quickly to release political prisoners, institute a rapid democratization program, and curb the abuses of the security services.

Current Challenges: *Federalism in Nigeria*

Despite the high-handed methods of its institution and reform, ironically, the federal system has enjoyed wide support within Nigeria historically. With the "national question" unanswered, however, the federal structure endures increasing strain. At the conclusion of the civil war in 1970, many had assumed that the question of national unity had been finally settled. Thus, attempts to include clauses on the right to secede in the constitutions of 1979 and 1989 were roundly rejected by the drafting committees. Yet the Abubakar transition period featured a number of public debates about secession, particularly among the Yoruba, and other groups have complained since 1999 about their continuing marginalization. Other widely held beliefs are now questioned by some elements in society. For example, will Nigeria continue to be a secular state, as outlined in the 1999 Constitution, and persist as a federation to accommodate the country's ethnic, cultural, and religious heterogeneity?

Some northerners have advocated turning Nigeria into an Islamic state, prompting fear among many Christians.

To resolve these issues, some Nigerians have called for a national conference to review the basis of national unity and even to consider the restructuring of Nigeria into a loose confederation of autonomous states, perhaps along the lines of the First Republic. Such calls were ignored by the military, which refused to permit any debate on the viability of a united Nigeria, thus maintaining the geographic status quo. President Obasanjo has so far resisted calls for a national conference. Instead, he created an expert commission to make recommendations for constitutional amendments, and the National Assembly has also stated its intention to debate constitutional reforms. A number of critical civil society groups continue to push for a national conference, however, and the issue is likely to regain attention after the 2003 elections.

Under military administrations, the president, or head of state, made appointments to most senior government positions.[19] Since the legislature was disbanded, major executive decisions (such as decrees) were subject to the approval of a ruling council of high-level military officers. By the time of Abacha's Provisional Ruling Council (PRC), however, this council had become largely unwilling to disagree with the head of state. Given this highly personalistic character of military politics, patron-client relationships flourished during this period. Not surprisingly, ethnic, religious, and regional constituencies have paid close attention to the pattern of appointments to the executive branch.

The military emerged structurally weakened from their long years in power, having been politicized and divided by these patron-client relationships. Within days of his taking office in 1999, President Obasanjo promptly retired over ninety military officers who had held political offices (such as military governorships) under the previous military juntas, seeing them as the most likely plotters of future coups. This lightning act,

unthinkable just a year before, caught the nation, including the military, by surprise, and the officers left quietly. Since 1999, the print media have reported rumors of several possible coup plots that were thwarted, but for the most part, the military has remained loyal and outside of politics.

Under Babangida and Abacha, the military was transformed from an instrument that guarantees national defense and security into another predatory apparatus, one more powerful than political parties. Three decades after the first military coup of January 1966, most Nigerians now believe that the country's political and economic development has been profoundly hampered by military domination and misrule.

In addition, President Obasanjo has paid close attention to keeping the military professionally oriented—and in the barracks. Because he is an ex-military head of state himself, this should not be surprising. U.S. military advisers and technical assistance have been invited to redirect the Nigerian military toward regional peacekeeping expertise—and to keep them busy outside of politics. So far, this strategy seems effective, but the military remains a threat should the civilians fail to gain popular approval.

The Obasanjo Administration

After the abrupt retirement of the political military officers, President Obasanjo raised the minimum wage dramatically, to regain some of the value lost from years of inflation. He also pushed international donors, though without success, to forgive much of Nigeria's debt (see Section 2).

Obasanjo then turned to the conflict-ridden Niger Delta. The initial goodwill he won by visiting the region and meeting local leaders, including youths, soon turned to hostility when he refused to negotiate claims by delta communities for greater control of the revenues from oil drilled on their lands. Instead, he proposed a Niger Delta Development Commission (NDDC) to disburse the 13 percent of oil revenues constitutionally mandated to return to the delta states. Community groups rejected the plan, governors of the Niger Delta states took Obasanjo to court, and youth militias returned to harassing the police and kidnapping oil workers for ransom. One such attack killed several policemen in November 1999, prompting Obasanjo to send the military after the perpetrators. Military units then destroyed the village of Odi and massacred many of its innocent inhabitants.[20] Obasanjo's NDDC, meanwhile, took two years for approval by the National Assembly, and little of its funds have so far reached the impoverished communities of the Niger Delta.

Obasanjo also sought to root out public sector corruption. His initial appointments to manage the oil industry drew early praise for their clean management and contracting policies, and the persistent fuel scarcities of the Abacha years largely disappeared. By 2001, however, familiar patterns of clientelism and financial kickbacks for oil licenses began to resurface. Obasanjo also proposed an Anti-Corruption Commission with sweeping statutory powers to investigate and prosecute public officials, but this commission also took over two years to be enacted, and until 2003, indicted only one minor official. Several months before the 2003 elections, however, the commission shockingly announced that several governors and prominent members of the National Assembly were under investigation, almost all of whom were Obasanjo opponents. Legis-lators said that the announcements were politically motivated, and promptly revoked the commission's authority. Its future remains unresolved.

In response to calls by civil society groups for some accounting for the injustices committed during years of military rule, Obasanjo set up the Peace and Reconciliation Commission in 1999. Unlike the famous Truth and Reconciliation Commission set up by South Africa at the end of the apartheid years, the Nigerian Commission did not have the power to grant amnesty in exchange for admissions of guilt, which would have better ensured that testimony would be accurate. Consequently, the stories and mutual recriminations given by former Abacha henchmen that riveted the nation in nightly television broadcasts created high political drama. The commission conducted some of its most sensitive inquiries in secret, and when it submitted its report in 2002 to the president, he refused to make its findings public. The report purportedly contains evidence that former military leader General Babangida arranged for the death of a prominent journalist in 1986. The billionaire Babangida, a major financial backer of the president's People's Democratic Party (PDP) and other parties, managed to get a court order blocking its publication, and the Obasanjo administration has so far refrained from pursuing the matter.

To some extent, President Obasanjo's own PDP members hampered his reform efforts. The PDP was a collection of powerful politicians from Nigeria's First and Second Republics, many of whom had grown rich from their complicity with the Babangida and Abacha juntas. These "big men" approached Obasanjo in 1998, and their political machines delivered him the election victory in 1999, an election in which former U.S. President Jimmy Carter and his observation team recorded numerous procedural violations. As apparent reward for this support, Obasanjo filled his cabinet with many of these dubious political kingpins and did not scrutinize their handling of ministry budgets. With a difficult reelection bid in 2003, Obasanjo again turned to these "fixers" to deliver a victory for him and the PDP. Not surprisingly, allegations of corruption at the highest levels of the Obasanjo administration have increased—and gone largely uninvestigated. Personal differences between President Obasanjo and PDP leaders in the National Assembly, particularly the Speaker of the

House, meanwhile, led them to instigate impeachment proceedings against the president in mid-2002, as will be discussed in Section 4.

The Bureaucracy

The bureaucracy touches upon all aspects of Nigerian government. The colonial system relied on an expanding bureaucracy to govern Nigeria. As government was increasingly "Africanized," the bureaucracy became a way to reward individuals in the patrimonial, prebendal system (see "Current Challenges: Prebendalism"). Bureaucratic growth was no longer determined by function and need; increasingly, individuals were appointed on the basis of patronage, ethnic group, and regional origin rather than merit.

It is conservatively estimated that federal and state government personnel increased from a modest 72,000 at independence to well over 1 million by the mid-1980s and beyond. The salaries of these bureaucrats presently consume an estimated 80 to 90 percent of government expenditures, leaving a paltry 10 percent or so for the other responsibilities of government, from education and health care to building the roads.

Para-statals

The largest component of the national bureaucracy in Nigeria is the state-owned enterprises, or **para-statals.** Para-statals in Nigeria are corporate enterprises owned by the state and established to provide specific commercial and social welfare services. They are a hybrid, somewhere between institutions that engage in traditional government operations, such as customs or the

---

Current Challenges: **Prebendalism**

Prebendalism, the peculiarly Nigerian version of corruption, is the disbursing of public offices and state rents to one's ethnic-based clients.* It is an extreme form of clientelism that refers to the practice of mobilizing cultural and other sectional identities by political aspirants and officeholders for the purpose of corruptly appropriating state resources. Prebendalism is an institutionalized pattern of political behavior that justifies the pursuit of and the use of public office for the personal benefit of the officeholder and his clients. The official public purpose of the office becomes a secondary concern. As with clientelism, the officeholder's "clients" comprise a specific set of elites to which he is linked, typically by ethnic or religious ties, and this linkage is key to understanding the concept. There are thus two sides involved in prebendalism, the officeholder and the client, and expectations of benefits by the clients (or supporters) perpetuate the prebendalist system.

As practiced in the Babangida and Abacha eras, when official corruption occurred on an unprecedented scale, prebendalism deepened sectional cleavages and eroded the resources of the state. It also discouraged genuinely productive activity in civil society and expanded the class of individuals who live off state patronage.

As long as prebendalism remains the norm of Nigerian politics, a stable democracy will be elusive. These practices are now deeply embedded in Nigerian society and therefore are more difficult to uproot. The corruption resulting from prebendal practices is blamed in popular discourse for the enormous flight of internally generated capital into secret accounts in overseas banking institutions. The lion's share of the $12.2 billion Gulf War windfall is believed to have been pocketed by Babangida and senior members of his regime and the Central Bank, an example of the magnitude of the systematic pilfering of public resources. General Abacha continued this pattern and is accused of diverting $5 billion from the Nigerian central bank. There are so many current officeholders in Nigeria who indulge in these practices, albeit at less gargantuan levels, that Transparency International regularly lists Nigeria among the most corrupt countries.

---

*Richard Joseph, *Democracy and Prebendal Politics in Nigeria: The Rise and Fall of the Second Republic* (Cambridge: Cambridge University Press, 1987) 55–68.

postal service, and those in the private sector that operate primarily for profit. In organizational terms, such para-statals are similar to private enterprises in having their own boards of directors. In principle, they are autonomous of the government that established them. In reality, however, such autonomy is limited since their boards are appointed by, and ultimately answerable to, the government through the supervising government ministry.

In general, para-statals are established for several reasons. First, they furnish public facilities, including water, power, telecommunications, ports, and other transportation. A second rationale for the establishment of para-statals is the need to accelerate economic development by controlling the commanding heights of the economy, including steel production, petroleum and natural gas production, refining, petrochemicals, fertilizer, and certain areas of agriculture. Third, para-statals are intended to provide basic utilities and services to citizens at low costs, held below the levels that would be needed by private firms to generate profit. Finally, there is a nationalist dimension that relates to issues of sovereignty over sectors perceived sensitive for national security.

Para-statals such as agricultural commodity boards and the Nigerian National Petroleum Corporation (NNPC) have served as major instruments of the interventionist state. They have been used to co-opt and organize business and societal interests for the purpose of politically controlling the economy and dispensing state largesse. These enterprises are major instruments of patronage and rent-seeking. In Nigeria, as in the rest of Africa, most para-statal enterprises are a tremendous drain on the economy. It is not surprising, therefore, that one of the major requirements of the economic structural adjustment program discussed in Section 2 is the privatization of most of these enterprises. Privatizing the para-statals remains a central part of reform strategy under the Obasanjo administration. The telecommunications and power industries are already up for sale, and parts of the oil industry are slated for auction in 2003.

Other State Institutions

Other institutions of governance and policy-making, including the federal judiciary and subnational governments (incorporating state and local courts), operate within the context of a strong central government dominated by a powerful chief executive.

The Judiciary

At one time, the Nigerian judiciary enjoyed relative autonomy from the executive arm of government. Aggrieved individuals and organizations could take the government to court and expect a judgment based on the merits of their case. This situation changed as each successive military government demonstrated a profound disdain for judicial practices, and eventually it undermined not only the autonomy but also the very integrity of the judiciary as a third branch of government.

The principal instrument that the Babangida and Abacha regimes used to achieve this outcome was a spate of repressive decrees that contained clauses disallowing judicial review. Such clauses were regularly inserted in government decrees barring any consideration of their legality by the courts, as well as any actions taken by government officials under them. Other methods included intimidation by the security services, the creation of parallel special military tribunals that could dispense with various legal procedures and due process, and disrespect for courts of record.

Through the executive's power of appointment of judicial officers to the high bench, as well as the executive's control of funds required for the running of the judiciary, the government can dominate the courts at all levels. In addition, what was once regarded as a highly competent judiciary has been undermined severely by declining standards of legal training as well as bribery.

The decline of court independence reached a new low in 1993 when, in what some analysts labeled "judicial terrorism," the Supreme Court endorsed a government position that literally placed all actions of the military executive beyond the pale of judicial review. The detention and hanging of Ken Saro-Wiwa and eight other Ogoni activists in 1995 (see Section 2) underscored the politicization and compromised state of the judicial system. With the return of civilian rule in 1999, however, the courts have slowly begun to restore some independence and credibility. The Supreme Court in particular has suddenly returned as a critical player in national political development after years of docility and self-imposed irrelevance. In early 2002, it passed two landmark judgments. The first struck down a 2001 election law that Obasanjo and the PDP-dominated legislature passed that would have prevented new parties from contesting the national elections in 2003. Second, the Court decided against the governors of Nigeria's coastal states over control of the vast offshore gas reserves, declaring that these were under the jurisdiction of the federal government.

State and Local Judiciaries.   The judiciaries at the state level are subordinate to the Federal Court of Appeal and the Supreme Court. Some of the states in the northern part of the country with large Muslim populations maintain a parallel court system based on the Islamic *shari'a* (divine law). Similarly, some states in the Middle Belt and southern part of the country have subsidiary courts based on customary law. Each of these maintains an appellate division. Otherwise, all courts of record in the country are based on the English common law tradition, and all courts are ultimately bound by decisions handed down by the Supreme Court.

How to apply the *shari'a* has been a source of continuing debate in Nigerian politics. For several years, some northern groups have participated in a movement to apply *shari'a* to all of Nigeria, and some even have advocated that it be made the supreme law of the land. The military government of Obasanjo blocked the expansion of *shari'a* in 1979. Demands for a broader application of Islamic law were made during the drafting of the 1989 Constitution, but these were again thwarted.

Prior to 1999, *shari'a* courts had jurisdiction only among Muslims in civil proceedings and in questions of Islamic personal law. In November 1999, however, the northern state of Zamfara instituted a version of the *shari'a* criminal code, which included cutting off hands for stealing, and stoning to death for those (especially women) who committed adultery. Eleven other northern states adopted the criminal code by 2001, prompting fears among Christian minorities in these states that the code might be applied to them and creating a divisive national issue. Although the *shari'a* criminal code appears to contradict Nigeria's officially secular constitution, President Obasanjo has so far been unwilling to take these states to court and appears to be pushing for a political solution.

State and Local Government

Because the creation of new states and local governments opens new channels to the oil wealth accumulated at the federal level, localities and groups are constantly clamoring for more. Sensing opportunities to buy support for their regimes, Babangida and Abacha nearly doubled the number of states and tripled that of local governments (see Table 5). Although they touted these moves as answering the "national question" by increasing opportunities for local self-determination, the limited fiscal and political autonomy of these units has in fact bolstered central government control. Several states have added local governments since 2000, but it is uncertain whether they have the constitutional authority to do so.

In response to this proliferation of states, the political parties have turned to the notion of six zones in Nigeria, correlated roughly with the major ethnic regions in the country: Hausa-Fulani, Igbo, Yoruba, and three minority-dominated areas. Political appointments are roughly balanced among the six zones and rotate over time.[21] For instance, the presidency is currently held by the southwest (Yoruba) zone; the next president, by informal agreement, will likely be from one of the Middle Belt minorities, the Northeast, or from the South-South zone—the Niger Delta. Virtually the entire process of constituting and reconstituting this federal arrangement, including the addition of a third level of local government, has occurred under the nondemocratic auspices of colonial and military rule.

The Nigerian experience has promoted a distributive approach to federalism. The lofty claims for federalism as a way of promoting unity through diversity are lost amid the intense competition among "local communities and elites for access to national patronage in the form of oil revenues that are collected, and then appropriated or redistributed, by the federal administration" through the states. (See Table 6.)

State governments are generally weak and dependent on federally controlled revenues. Most of them would be insolvent and unable to sustain themselves without substantial support from the central government, because of the states' weak resource and tax base. About 90 percent of state incomes are received directly from the federal government, which includes a lump sum based on oil revenues, plus a percentage of

Table 5

Political Divisions, 1963–1996					
1963	**1967**	**1976**	**1987**	**1991**	**1996**
					(Northwest zone)
Northern Region	North Central	Kaduna	Kaduna	Kaduna	Kaduna
			Katsina	Katsina	Katsina
	Kano	Kano	Kano	Kano	Kano
				Jigawa	Jigawa
	North Western	Sokoto	Sokoto	Sokoto	Sokoto
					Zamfara
				Kebbi	Kebbi
					(North-Central zone)
		Niger	Niger	Niger	Niger
	Benue-Plateau	Benue-Plateau	Benue-Plateau	Benue	Benue
				Plateau	Plateau
					Nassarawa
		Abuja	Abuja	FCT (Abuja)[c]	FCT (Abuja)
	West Central	Kwara	Kwara	Kwara	Kwara
				Kogi[a]	Kogi
					(Northeast zone)
	North Eastern	Bauchi	Bauchi	Bauchi	Bauchi
					Gombe
		Borno	Borno	Borno	Borno
				Yobe	Yobe
		Gongola	Gongola	Adamawa	Adamawa
				Taraba	Taraba
					(Southeast zone)
Eastern Region	East Central	Anambra	Anambra	Anambra	Anambra
				Enugu	Enugu
					Ebonyi
		Imo	Imo	Imo	Imo
				Abia	Abia
					(South-south zone)
	South Eastern	Cross River	Cross River	Cross River	Cross River
			Akwa Ibom	Akwa Ibom	Akwa Ibom
	Rivers	Rivers	Rivers	Rivers	Rivers
					Bayelsa
Mid-West Region	Mid-Western	Bendel	Bendel	Edo	Edo
				Delta	Delta
					(Southwest zone)
Western Region	Western	Ogun	Ogun	Ogun	Ogun
		Ondo	Ondo	Ondo	Ondo
					Ekiti
		Oyo	Oyo	Oyo	Oyo
				Osun	Osun
Lagos[b]	Lagos	Lagos	Lagos	Lagos	Lagos

[a]Kogi state was created by combining parts of Benue and Kwara states.

[b]Lagos was excised from the Western Region in 1954 and became the federal capital. In 1967, it also became capital of the new Lagos State, which included Badagry, Ikeja, and Epe districts from the Western Region.

[c]Abuja replaced Lagos as the federal capital in December 1991, although its boundaries were first delineated in the 1970s.

Source: Tom Forrest, *Politics and Economic Development in Nigeria* (Boulder, Colo.: Westview Press, 1993), 214; Darren Kew.

oil income based on population. The states and local governments must, however, generate more resources of their own to increase the efficiency of both their administrations and private economic sectors. In all likelihood, only Lagos and Kano states could survive without federal subsidies.

In the same way that states depend on federal handouts, local governments have remained dependent on both state and federal governments. This practice has continued despite reforms of the local government system initiated by the Babangida regime in 1988, supposedly to strengthen that level of government. The state and local governments have the constitutional and legal powers to raise funds through taxes. However, Nige-

rians share a pronounced unwillingness, especially those in self-employment, trade, and other informal sector activities, to pay taxes and fees to a government with such a poor record of delivering basic services. The result is a vicious cycle: government is sapped of resources and legitimacy and cannot adequately serve the people. Communities, in turn, are compelled to resort to self-help measures to protect these operations and thus withdraw further from the reach of the state. Because very few individuals and organizations pay taxes, even the most basic government functions cannot be performed (see Table 7).

The return of democratic rule has meant the return of conflict between the state and national governments,

Table 6

Percentage Contribution of Different Sources of Government Revenue to Allocated Revenue, 1980–2002

	Oil Revenue Petroleum Profits Tax	Mining Rents and Royalties	Nonoil Revenue Customs and Excise Duties	Others	Total
1980	58.1	25.7	12.3	3.9	100.0
1981	55.5	19.6	20.4	4.5	100.0
1982	44.5	27.3	21.5	6.7	100.0
1983	35.7	33.4	18.9	12.0	100.0
1984	44.8	32.4	15.2	7.6	100.0
1985	47.8	30.0	14.7	7.5	100.0
1986	40.5	25.3	14.6	19.6	100.0
1987	50.6	25.4	14.3	9.7	100.0
1988	46.7	31.5	15.9	5.9	100.0
	Oil Revenues (Combined)		Nonoil Revenue	Other	Total
1992	86.2		8.4	5.4	100.0
1993	84.0		8.0	8.0	100.0
1994	79.3		9.1	11.6	100.0
1995	53.2		8.1	38.7*	100.0
1996	51.1		10.6	38.3*	100.0
2001	79.7		17.6	2.7	100.0
2002	78.6		19.4	2.0	100.0
2003	78.1		19.9	2.0	100.0

*Beginning in 1995, the Nigerian government began including surplus foreign exchange as federally collected revenue in its accounting.

Sources: Federal Ministry of Finance and Economic Development, Lagos. From Adedotun Phillips, "Managing Fiscal Federalism: Revenue Allocation Issues," *Publius: The Journal of Federalism,* 21, no. 4 (Fall 1991), p. 109. Nigerian Federal Office of Statistics, *Annual Abstract of Statistics: 1997 Edition.* Nigerian Economic Summit Group, *Economic Indicators* (Vol. 8, no. 2, April–June 2002).

much like during the Second Republic (1979–1983). The primary vehicle for conflict since 1999 has been a series of "governors' forums," one for the seventeen southern governors, one for the nineteen northern governors, and one for all thirty-six governors. Ad hoc committees on specific issues have also arisen. The governors' forums have not only taken the federal government to court on a number of occasions, they have also made policy pronouncements and have sought to mediate between the president and National Assembly. Much as at the national level, the state-level executives have far more power than their legislatures. These state assemblies, however, have not been docile, and on several occasions they have moved to impeach their state governors.

A number of governors, particularly in the Igbo-dominated southeast, have increasingly turned to armed militias and vigilante groups to provide security in their states and to intimidate political opponents. Many of these groups were initially local responses to the corrupt and ineffective police force, but several of the governors have sensed the larger political usefulness of these groups. Consequently, and disturbingly, political assassinations and violence increased as the 2003 elections approached.

The Policy-Making Process

Nigeria's prolonged experience with military rule has resulted in a policy process based more on top-down directives than on consultation, political debate, and legislation. Yet four years of democratic government have seen some important changes, as the legislatures, courts, and state governments have begun to force the presidency to negotiate its policies and work within a constitutional framework.

First, we must explore how military rule shaped policy-making in Nigeria. Because of their influence in recruitment and promotions, as well as through their own charisma or political connections, senior officers often develop a network of supporters of the same or lower rank, creating what is referred to as a "loyalty pyramid."[22] Once in power, the men at the top of these pyramids in Nigeria have access to tremendous oil wealth, which is passed on through the lower echelons of the pyramid to reward support. Often these pyramids feature ethnic or religious affiliations (see the discussions of corruption in Section 2 and **prebendalism** in Section 3) such as the "Kaduna Mafia" of northern elites, but pyramids like the "Babangida" or "Abacha Boys" included a patchwork of officers beyond their

Table 7

Share of Total Government Expenditure (%)

	1961	1965	1970	1975	1980	1987	1992	1996	2001	2002
Federal Government	49	53	73	72	66	75	72	74	57	52.3
State Government	51	47	27	28	34	25	28*	26*	24	26
Local Government**	–	–	–	–	–	–	–	–	20	21.7
Total Expenditure (millions Naira)	336	445	1,149	10,916	21,349	29,365	128,476	327,707	1,008,780	1,111,950

* Note that 67% of state spending in 1992 and 49% of it in 1996 came from federal government oil earnings, part of which are allocated annually to all the states roughly in proportion to their population size.

**Local government expenditures are included in state government figures in 1961 and 1965, and federal figures from 1970 through 1996.

Sources: Central Bank of Nigeria, Annual Report and Statement of Accounts; Federal Office of Statistics, Abstract of Annual Statistics (Lagos: Federal Government Printer, 1961, 1965, 1970, 1975, 1980, 1987, and 1997). From Izeubuwa Osayimwese and Sunday Iyare, "The Economics of Nigerian Federalism: Selected Issues in Economic Management," Publius: The Journal of Federalism, 21, no. 4 (Fall 1991), p. 91. Nigerian Economic Summit Group, Economic Indicators (Vol. 8, no. 2, April–June 2002). 1990s percentage calculations by Darren Kew.

ethnic circle. In addition, the well-developed pyramids have allies or personal connections in the bureaucracy, business, and the private sector.

The personal ambitions of leaders commonly eclipse the corporate mission of the military to "save" the nation. Personal goals and interests often become the defining characteristic of the regime and its policies, with the only check on personal power being another coup. In many African countries, a coup signifies the ascension of one particular loyalty pyramid into power, often at the expense of others. Nigeria's first coup in 1966 appeared to signal the rise of a group of Igbo officers under General Ironsi, although he tried to maintain a more nationalist image. General Gowon helped to establish a collegial (or consensus) model of military governance in which important decisions were made by an ethnically balanced body consisting of the leaders of the major loyalty pyramids. The Muhammed and Obasanjo regimes also employed this model, as did Buhari and, at first, Babangida.

General Babangida, however, signified the turning point within the military when national concerns became increasingly subsumed by personal ambitions.[23] He was a master at playing the different loyalty pyramids off against each other, lavishing the nation's oil wealth on friends and buying the support of opponents he could not crush. Once in power, General Abacha made little pretense of accommodating other factions, instead ruthlessly centralizing nearly all government decision making and spreading little of the largesse for which Babangida was famous.

Abacha's personal plunder of the nation's revenues dispelled the notion that the military was a cohesive, nationalist institution capable of governing Nigeria any more efficiently than the civilians. A parallel structure of junior officers loyal to Abacha acted as his gatekeepers, circumventing and humiliating the military's normal chain of command. General Abubakar thus took the reins of a military in June 1998 that was divided and demoralized. Abubakar was more of a professional than his predecessors, purging the government of "Abacha boys" and swiftly returning the country to civilian rule. Despite having returned to the barracks, others in the military clearly yearn for their turn at the top. The civilian politicians appear well aware of this danger. It remains to be seen whether the civilians can forge a new role for the mil-

itary and develop for themselves a sustainable coalition of support among civil society groups and public constituencies.

Because the military dominated Nigeria for three-quarters of its existence, civilian politics bears strong a resemblance to the politics of loyalty pyramids among the military.[24] Many of the current civilian politicians belonged to the loyalty pyramids of different military men—as bureaucrats, members of military cabinets, business partners to exploit Nigeria's oil wealth, and so on. Now that these civilians are in power, some of whom are former military themselves, they are taking up the reins of the civilian portions of these pyramids, although they do retain some influence with military figures as well.

Nigerians often refer to the politicians who sit atop these civilian loyalty pyramids as "big men." Unlike the military leaders, however, the civilian big men do not typically have access to formal coercive instruments, so to maintain their pyramids they must rely on financial kickbacks and promises of rents from the state: government jobs, contracts, and so on. (Section 4 discusses these clientelistic and prebendal patterns of the loyalty pyramids in greater detail.)

Thus, in patterns reminiscent of the struggles among military loyalty pyramids, the policy-making process today in Nigeria under democratic rule is a function of the clash of interests among the big men and their clients. The vice president, party leaders of the PDP, many of the ministers, and leaders in the National Assembly are all big men vying for larger rents from the state and increased influence and status. Ironically, President Obasanjo was not a big man when he was elected; he rode to power on the backs of these big men and their supporters now in intense competition with each other.

Consequently, policy-making during the Obasanjo administration, after the early honeymoon period when the president was able to get much of what he wanted, has developed a pattern. Obasanjo and his closest advisers formulate a policy and announce it. If legislation is required, the big men in the National Assembly struggle to have their interests appeased in the process. Once the legislation is passed or if no legislation is required, the powerful ministers who must implement the policy alter it to reflect their interests, and then the policy moves on down through the bureaucracy. Not surprisingly, if the policy involves financial disbursements, little of the funds actually reach their intended targets.

In short, civilian policy-making in present day Nigeria is a story of the president introducing reform policies, which are then filtered through the interests of the big men. Invariably, their interests conflict with those of the president and each other, which leads the policy to be blocked or significantly altered to the point that at times, the reformist agenda is lost or ineffectual. The president has grown increasingly adept at navigating these interests, but soon enough his reformist agenda took a backseat to his own overarching interest: reelection in 2003. On this point, however, his ministers were agreed, and policy-making by the administration was undertaken with the goal of getting the president reelected by any possible means.

Section ④ Representation and Participation

Representation and participation are two vital components in modern democracies; however, Nigeria is at best a nascent democracy. Nigerian legislatures, when they have been allowed to function, have been sidelined or reduced to subservience by the powerful executive, and fraud, elite manipulation, and regular military interference have marred the party system and elections. Consequently, Nigerian society has found modes of participation outside the official structures. An important focus of this section will therefore be unofficial (that is, nongovernmental) methods of representation and participation through the institutions of civil society. Whereas the institutions of political society include such entities as parties, constitutions, and legislatures, those of **civil society** include professional associations, trade unions, religious organizations, and various interest groups.

The Nigerian experience described in this section emphasizes the complex nature of the relationship between representation and participation. It shows that formal representation does not necessarily enhance participation. In fact, there are situations in which the most important modes of political participation are found outside of and in opposition to the institutional modes such as elections and legislatures.

The Legislature

Not surprisingly, Nigeria's legislature has been a victim of the country's political instability. Legislative structures and processes prior to 1999 suffered abuse, neglect, or peremptory suspension by the executive arm. As a consequence, the politicians who took office at the state and federal levels in 1999 had little understanding of and less practice with legislative functions and responsibilities. In addition, they stood in the shadow of the overly powerful executive that had dominated Nigerian politics under the military.

Until the first coup in 1966, Nigeria operated its legislature along the lines of the British Westminster model, with an elected lower house and a smaller upper house composed of individuals selected by the executive. For the next thirteen years of military rule, a Supreme Military Council performed legislative functions by initiating and passing decrees at will. During the second period of civilian rule, 1979–1983, the legislature was structured similar to the U.S. system. As in the United States, Nigeria employed a bicameral structure, with both houses (Senate and House of Representatives) consisting of elected members. The Fourth Republic maintains the U.S.-inspired legislative system, called the National Assembly.

As part of the Babangida regime's transition program, the civilian members of the National Assembly, elected in July 1992, held meetings until mid-1993. Once seated, however, they were barred by military decree from deliberating on issues other than those dealing with uncontroversial topics. When Abacha took over in late 1993, he dismissed both houses, as well as all other elected officials at the state and local levels.

Only one woman sat among the 91 senators and two among the 593 representatives in the Third Republic, and only eight women were elected in 1999 to sit in the Fourth Republic's National Assembly. This reflects the limited political participation of Nigerian women in formal institutions, as discussed in Section 2. Election to the Senate is on the basis of equal state representation, with three senators from each of the thirty-six states, plus one senator from the federal capital territory, Abuja. The practice of equal representation in the Senate is identical to that of the United States, except that each Nigerian state elects three senators instead of two. Election to the Nigerian House of Representatives was also based on state representation but weighted to reflect the relative size of each state's population, again after the U.S. example.

An innovation added during the failed transition to the Third Republic is that local government structures now enjoy greater autonomy from control by the state governments. The federal executive has, however, dominated other branches of government, partly as a consequence of the frequency of military coups. It is standard practice among coup leaders to replace all elected representatives with ruling councils, handpicked by the military executive. Indeed, General Abacha's first act as head of state in November 1993 was to abolish all political institutions, including the duly elected national and state legislatures.

Thus, Nigerian legislatures under military government were either powerless or nonexistent. Even under elected civil administrations prior to 1999, however, Nigerian legislatures were subjected to great pressure by the executive and never assumed their full constitutional role. Because the executive and majority interests in the National Assembly belonged to the same party, this influence has been easily exercised through the actions of party machines and by outright bribery. This situation has been exacerbated by legislative dependence on the executive for their allowances and the resources to meet the relentless demands from their constituents for jobs, contracts, and other favors. This is the critical difference between the Nigerian and U.S. systems: in Nigeria, the president gathers and disburses public revenues, which the Assembly only influences by its right to pass the budget, whereas the U.S. Congress controls the public purse.

The National Assembly that took office in 1999 therefore began its work with great uncertainty over its role in Nigerian politics. Both the House and the Senate were overwhelmingly controlled by the People's Democratic Party (PDP), as was the presidency. Thus, many observers expected the familiar pattern of executive dominance of the legislature through the party structures to continue as it had under the Second and Third Republics.

Initially, these expectations were largely fulfilled. Legislators spent most of their time clamoring for their personal spending funds to be disbursed by the executive. Some of their first acts were to vote themselves pay raises and exorbitant furniture expenditures (the latter move provoking a protest strike by trade unions). Other legislators tested the legislative waters for the first time with a variety of radical bills that never emerged from committee, including one that would have asked the United States to invade Nigeria if the military staged another coup. The first Speaker of the House was forced to resign when a newspaper discovered that he had lied about his age and was too young to run for office. Dramatically, two Senate presidents were also forced to resign within the first year when the media unearthed their corrupt practices. The president, meanwhile, referred to legislators as "small boys" and rarely accorded them the respect of an equal branch of government.

Gradually, however, the National Assembly began to fight back and gain some relevance. The one constitutional power of the Assembly that President Obasanjo could not circumvent was the authority to approve the national budget. In 2001, negotiations between the president and Assembly leaders over the budget became deadlocked, and it was eventually passed several months after it was due. The 2002 budget negotiations were even more bruising, and the president was ultimately forced to sign a budget that was much higher than the revenues expected for that year. When oil revenues dipped even lower than expected, Obasanjo unilaterally chose to disburse only a portion of the budgeted funds to programs of his choosing. Among the funds withheld were those for the National Assembly. Unpaid and feeling disrespected, legislators gradually escalated their demands that Obasanjo negotiate. In August 2002, both the House and the Senate began impeachment proceedings against the president, despite being controlled by Obasanjo's own party. Alarmed at the deadlock, PDP party leaders sought desperately to mediate between the two arms of government. A face-saving compromise, and an apology from the president, was reached through a combination of negotiation and reported side-payments to key legislators.

The impeachment move was not so much a serious attempt to remove the president as it was a statement to Obasanjo that he had to deal with the legislature with respect and as an equal partner in governance. The motives of legislators were hardly pure, since most were primarily concerned with getting their personal slices of the budget, but the president had clearly overstepped his constitutional role by arbitrarily choosing which portions of the budget he would or would not respect. Some of the big men in the Assembly, particularly the Speaker of the House, have personal grudges against Obasanjo that were also at play in the impeachment move. Overall, however, the legislature emerged strengthened from the encounter.

Legislatures at the state level face a similar imbalance of power with the governors, who control large local bureaucracies and disburse the funds received from the federally shared revenues. The politics of these state assemblies have been chaotic and often vicious, with behavior ranging from throwing chairs to storming the assembly hall with supporters, and increasingly, the use of political violence.

The Party System and Elections

The unfortunate legacy of the party and electoral systems after independence in 1960 was that political parties were associated with certain regions and ethnic groups.[25] This extreme factionalization was encouraged by the tendency of most Nigerians to perceive politics as a zero-sum struggle (or winner-take-all) for access to scarce state resources. Unlike Mexico and, to some extent, India, Nigeria did not develop an authoritarian dominant-party system after independence that might have transcended some of these social cleavages. Instead, the multiparty system reinforced and deepened existing social divisions.

Nigeria's use of a first-past-the-post plurality electoral system produced legislative majorities for parties with strong ethnic and regional identities. All of the parties of the First and Second Republics were more attentive to the welfare of the regions from which they drew the most support than to the development of Nigeria as a whole. Control of the center, or at least access to it, ensured access to substantial financial resources. In a polity as potentially volatile as Nigeria, however, these tendencies intensified political fragmentation and resentment among the losers. Nigerian parties during the First Republic were dominated by

the largest ethnic groups and interests in each of the three regions. During subsequent democratic experiments, many of the more recent parties could trace their roots to their predecessors in the First Republic.

In the Second Republic, the leading parties shared the same ethnic and sectional support, and often the same leadership, as the parties prominent in the first civilian regime. The Unity Party of Nigeria, UPN (mainly Yoruba), was headed by former Action Group leader Chief Obafemi Awolowo, the Nigerian Peoples Party, NPP (mainly Igbo), was led by Nnamdi Azikiwe (formerly of the NCNC), the Peoples Redemption Party, PRP (organized and located around Kano city in northern Nigeria), was led by Mallam Aminu Kano, while the Great Nigeria Peoples Party, GNPP (organized around the Kanuri northeast), was a somewhat new tendency under Waziri Ibrahim. The dominant party in the Second Republic, the National Party of Nigeria (NPN), brought together a diverse cross-ethnic coalition, under a predominantly northern leadership that had been associated with the Northern People's Congress (NPC) under the previous civilian regime.

In its wavering steps toward the civilian Third Republic, General Babangida's administration in October 1989 announced a landmark decision to establish, by decree, only two political parties.[26] The state provided initial start-up funds, wrote the constitutions and manifestos of these parties, and designed them to be "a little to the right and a little to the left," respectively, on the political-ideological spectrum.

Interestingly, the elections that took place between 1990 and 1992 at local, state, and federal levels indicate that despite their inauspicious beginnings, the two parties cut across the cleavages of ethnicity, regionalism, and religion in their membership and electoral performance and demonstrated the potential within Nigeria to move beyond ethnicity.[27] Presidential victor Moshood Abiola, a southern Muslim, won a number of key states in the north, including the hometown of his opponent. Once the election was annulled, however, the more familiar north-south divisions reemerged, fostered by both the regime and, ironically, Abiola's most determined advocates.

As shown in Table 8, northern-based parties dominated the first and second experiments with civilian rule. Given this historical trend, it is significant that a southerner was able to win the presidency in 1993, the first time in Nigeria's history that a southerner defeated a northerner in elections to lead the nation. Southerners therefore perceived the decision by the northern-dominated Babangida regime to annul the June 12 elections as a deliberate attempt by the military and northern interests to maintain their decades-long domination of the highest levels of government.

Yet Abiola's victorious Social Democratic Party (SDP) was an impressive coalition of Second Republic party structures, including elements of the former UPN, NPP, PRP, and GNPP. The opposing National Republican Convention (NRC) was seen as having its roots in northern groups that were the core of the National Party of Nigeria (NPN).

New Alignments: Abacha's Ambition and Abubakar's Promise

Nigerians in general greeted General Abacha's 1993 coup and subsequent banning of the SDP and NRC with expressions of anger, while the response of party members, with a few exceptions, was muted. Southern-based human rights and prodemocracy groups, in alliance with student unions and other organizations, launched street demonstrations, and trade union strikes brought the economy to a halt by mid-1994. With the unions crushed and Abiola in jail by the end of 1994, Abacha started his own transition program in October 1995. It featured a series of elections from the local to the federal levels over the following three years in a manner reminiscent of the Babangida program.

Once the ban on political associations was lifted, some of the Second Republic party structures resurfaced and applied for accreditation with the election commission. To general surprise, a party favored by northern oligarchs was not registered, and most of the other parties led by powerful figures were also barred. In late 1996, the Abacha government registered only five parties, most of whose members had no public constituency and little political experience. By the time local government elections were held in January 1997, the few people who did vote had little idea for whom they were voting; some of the candidates confessed publicly that they had never even seen their party's manifesto.

During 1997, the five parties, which Chief Bola Ige, a prominent Yoruba political figure and victim of political assassination in 2002, branded "five fingers of a leprous hand," began to clamor for General Abacha to run for president. Public participation in delayed state assembly elections in December 1997 was abysmal, as each of the parties proclaimed, one after another, that Abacha was their candidate. Despite strong resistance from some of its leaders, the fifth party finally succumbed to the pressure and nominated Abacha in April 1998, making the presidential elections scheduled for August 1998 a mere referendum, endorsed by the chief justice of the Supreme Court as being legally permissible. The "transition" process had become a travesty.[28] Throughout the Abacha transition, the military influenced or became actively involved in the parties. Key generals in the regime would orchestrate party policies and provide supplementary funding for the groups already funded by the government. The government actively disqualified party candidates just days before the casting of ballots and peremptorily reversed some election results.

In 1996–1997, condemnation of the Abacha government came primarily from Lagos-based human rights and pro-democracy groups, exiles abroad, international nongovernmental organizations, and foreign governments. By April 1998, once Abacha's plan to be certified as president became a certainty, domestic opposition increased. A group of former governors and political leaders from the north (many former NPN and PRP members) publicly petitioned Abacha not to run for president. They were later joined by colleagues from the south, forming what they called the Group of 34 (G-34). Human rights and pro-democracy organizations began again to form alliances to organize protests, and critical press coverage recovered some of its former boldness. Even General Babangida voiced his opposition to Abacha's continuing as president. Although public disenchantment and apathy were pervasive after years of economic struggle and broken political promises, the only real obstacle to Abacha's plan for "self-succession" was whether the military would allow it.

Rumors of Abacha's ill health had circulated for a year, but his sudden death on June 8, 1998, was still a great surprise. The following day, General Abubakar, chief of Defense Staff, was sworn in as head of state. Shortly after, he promised a speedy transition to democracy and began releasing political prisoners. There were

Table 8

Federal Election Results in Nigeria, 1959–2003

Presidential Election Results, 1979–2003

	Victor (% of the vote)	Leading Contender (% of vote)
1979	Shehu Shagari, NPN (33.8)	Obafemi Awolowo, UPN (29.2)
1983	Shehu Shagari, NPN (47.3)	Obafemi Awolowo, UPN (31.1)
1993	M.K.O. Abiola, SDP (58.0)	Bashir Tofa, NRC (42.0)
1999	Olusegun Obasanjo, PDP (62.8)	Olu Falae, AD/APP alliance (37.2)
2003	Olusegun Obasanjo, PDP (61.9)	Mohammadu Buhari, ANPP (32.1)

Parties Controlling the Parliament/National Assembly by Ethno-Regional Zone, First to Fourth Republics

		Northwest	North-Central	Northeast	Southwest	South-South	Southeast
First	1959	**NPC**	**NPC** (NEPU)	**NPC**	*AG*	*AG*	*NCNC**
	1964–65	**NPC**	**NPC**	**NPC**	*NNDP** (AG)**	*NNDP** (AG)**	*NCNC*
Second	1979	**NPN**	PRP **(NPN, UPN)**	GNPP **(NPN)**	*UPN* **(NPN)**	**NPN** *(UPN)*	NPP*
	1983	**NPN**	**NPN** (PRP)	**NPN**	*UPN* **(NPN)**	**NPN**	NPP**
Third	1992	**NRC**	*SDP* **(NRC)**	*SDP* **(NRC)**	*SDP*	**NRC** *(SDP)*	**NRC**
Fourth	1999	**PDP** *(APP)*	**PDP**	**PDP** *(APP)*	AD **(PDP)**	**PDP** *(APP)*	**PDP**
	2003	*ANPP*	**PDP** *(ANPP)*	*ANPP* **(PDP)**	**PDP** *(AD)*	**PDP**	**PDP**

Boldfaced: Ruling party

Italicized: Leading opposition

*: Coalition with ruling party

**: Coalition with opposition

1998 Local Government Elections*

	Total Council Chairs	Total States with majority (out of 36, plus FCT)
PDP	459	28 (including FCT)
APP	188	2 (one tied with PDP)
AD	100	6
Others	8	—

*Preliminary results December 9, 1998, in *The Guardian* (Lagos, Nigeria).

1999 State Gubernatorial and House of Assembly Elections (out of 36)

	Total Seats	House of Assembly majorities
PDP	21	23
APP	9	8
AD	6	5

Table 8 *(continued)*

Federal Election Results in Nigeria, 1959–2003

1999 National Assembly Elections

	Senate (out of 109)	House (out of 360)
PDP	63	214
APP	26	77
AD	20	69

Table 9

List of Acronyms used in Table 8

AG	Action Group
AD	Alliance for Democracy
APP	All People's Party
GNPP	Great Nigerian Peoples' Party
NAP	Nigerian Advance Party
NCNC	National Convention of Nigerian Citizens (formerly, National Council of Nigeria and the Cameroons)
NEPU	Northern Elements Progressive Union
NNDP	Nigerian National Democratic Party
NPC	Northern People's Congress
NPF	Northern Progressive Front
NPN	National Party of Nigeria
NPP	Nigerian People's Party
NRC	National Republican Convention
PRP	People's Redemption Party
PDP	People's Democratic Party
SDP	Social Democratic Party
UPN	Unity Party of Nigeria

immediate calls for Abiola's release and his appointment to head an interim government of national unity. Abiola's fatal heart attack on July 7, 1998, removed the last obstacle to the holding of entirely new elections, the preferred option of the Abubakar administration. New parties quickly formed, and even Yoruba political leaders agreed by August to participate, although they insisted that the next president should be a Yoruba to compensate their people for having been robbed of their first elected presidency.

Once again, political associations centered on well-known personalities—the big men—emerged around the country, and intense bargaining and mergers among the smaller groups took place. The G-34, the prominent group of civilian leaders who had condemned

Abacha's continuation plans, tried to transform itself into a political party. They created the People's Democratic Party (PDP) in late August, minus most of the key Yoruba members of G-34, who joined a primarily Yoruba-based Alliance for Democracy (AD). At least twenty more parties applied for certification to the electoral commission, INEC, many of which were truly grass-roots movements, including a transformed human rights organization and a trade union party. The Abubakar administration evidently played no role in party formation, nor did it provide government funds for their functioning (unlike its two predecessors, the Babangida and Abacha regimes).

To escape the ethnic-based parties of the First and Second Republics, INEC required that parties earn at least 5 percent of the votes in twenty-four of the thirty-six states in the December 1998 local government elections in order to proceed to the state and federal levels. This turned out to be an ingenious way of reducing the number of parties for the most important elections and also to oblige them to seek to broaden their appeal. The only parties to meet INEC's requirements were the PDP, AD, and the All Peoples Party (APP); the APP included a mixture of groups from the Middle Belt, the southeast, and the far north. With the big men of the PDP wielding tremendous resources across the country, the AD and APP formed an alliance in the elections for the presidency in February 1999.

In comparison to the failed experiments of Babangida and Abacha, the transition process under Abubakar moved ahead peacefully, if problematically. One important challenge was the continuing unrest in the southern Niger Delta region. A number of minority groups there, in some areas engaged in low-level conflict since 1997, complained of being excluded from the process. In September 1998, they seized several production sites from multinational oil corporations and

demanded more local government access, development projects, and a greater share of the oil wealth.
Bayelsa state elections were disrupted and had to be
rescheduled, as were some local government contests
in the region. Voter turnout in the Niger Delta region
for the presidential and National Assembly elections
was abysmal; the political parties fraudulently inflated
the returns.

The three registered parties rely on elite-centered
structures established during previous civilian governments and transition programs. The PDP includes core
members of the northern establishment NPN and the
northern progressive PRP of the Second Republic.
From the Second Republic, the AD drew key individuals from the Yoruba-dominated UPN and the APP
(now ANPP) from the GNPP, a party dominated by the
Kanuri-Middle Belt. The ANPP also featured southern
politicians who had prominent roles in the five Abacha
parties. Demonstrating the cross-ethnic alliances that
have forged and reworked despite the political disruptions of a quarter-century, only the AD reflected a specific ethnic configuration. General Obasanjo and other
Yoruba leaders joined PDP. In a fiercely contested
nomination battle, Obasanjo was chosen as the PDP's
presidential nominee, defeating Second Republic Vice
President Alex Ekwueme, who is Igbo. Interestingly,
Obasanjo again defeated Ekwueme for the PDP nomination in 2003. Obasanjo then went on to defeat the
AD/APP alliance candidate, Chief Olu Falae, also
Yoruba, in the presidential contest in February 1999.

ANPP is truly a multiethnic collection, drawing
northern politicians of royal lineage, northeastern and
Middle Belt minorities, Igbo business moguls, and
southern minority leaders. AD appears to be as Yoruba-
centric as its Second Republic UPN and First Republic
AG predecessors. Yet like these earlier parties, it has
attracted dynamic politicians from other areas such as
Arthur Nwankwo, an Igbo. It is important to note the
political pragmatism of the Abubakar administration
(and the INEC) in registering the AD, despite its
ethno-regional base, and allowing it to compete for the
presidency in alliance with the then-APP. It made
sense to accommodate rather than alienate the Yoruba
people on account of the deep sense of grievance toward
the federal government provoked by the 1993 annulment of Abiola's victory and the subsequent five years
of bitter conflict.

The rapidity of the Abubakar-supervised electoral
process benefited civilian politicians and recently retired military officers with access to substantial financial resources. The civil society groups that led much
of the struggle against the Abacha dictatorship found
themselves at a disadvantage in trying to influence,
and participate in, this process.

Thus, the leaders of the Fourth Republic political
parties essentially represent alliances of convenience
among powerful individuals, the big men, who retain
their own resource and client bases and lack a common
ideology or clear policy agenda. In contrast to the parties of the First and Second Republics, the current parties (with the exception of the AD, which showed
signs of partial disintegration by the end of the first
electoral cycle) are not associated with a single predominant ethnic group. Ethnicity is still a critical factor in party politics, but the locus of competition is
within the parties themselves rather than among the
parties using the levers of government against each
other, as in the interethnic competition of the earlier
failed republics.

Because the current parties are mere alliances of
convenience among the big men, however, they suffer
an instability that their predecessors did not. They
stand for little beyond the interests of their masters, so
the loyalties among their members are weak, as are
their connections to the wider populace. Squabbles
among the leaders of the AD caused the party to im-
plode not long after the election, and the APP faced a
crisis of relevance. Thus, the Fourth Republic has enjoyed no real opposition movement at the national
level. Without a viable opposition to challenge it, the
ruling PDP was also prey to internal division. Bonds
among the PDP leaders had grown so frayed by 2002
that the PDP Speaker of the House could spearhead
impeachment moves against the PDP president. The
approach of the 2003 elections to some extent reinvigorated all three parties, but they may well continue to
unravel thereafter.

The Independent National Electoral Commission
(INEC) complicated matters in 2002 when it registered three new political parties, each of them pragmatic alliances among disgruntled politicians from the
existing parties, primarily the PDP, as well as a few
new faces. One of the new parties merged with the
APP to form the ANPP, the All Nigerian Peoples Party.

Late in 2002, however, the Supreme Court overruled the INEC's restrictive policies on registering parties, and dozens of new parties were permitted to contest the 2003 elections. In all, some thirty associations participated at the polls. Revealing its pro-Abacha roots, the ANPP nominated as its 2003 presidential candidate former head of state, General (retired) Muhammadu Buhari, a well-known supporter of the *shari'a* movement. The AD declined to nominate a 2003 presidential candidate in exchange for the PDP not mounting serious challenges against other AD candidates in the Yoruba region. However, the PDP reneged on the backroom deal and stunningly defeated the AD at all levels in five of the six southwestern states in 2003.

Political Culture, Citizenship, and Identity

Traditionally, institutions that represent and mobilize society in the political sphere include legislatures, political parties, trade unions, and other major elements of civil society. In the process, they help to shape, organize, and express political culture and identities, thus nurturing qualities of citizenship. During military rule, which held sway for about thirty years of the post-independence period, these institutions were proscribed and disbanded (in the case of legislatures and political parties) or muzzled (in the case of labor unions). Their roles have been largely assumed by other groups and institutions, including ethnic and religious organizations, the mass media, and professional and trade groups. In many of these circles, the state (federal government) is regarded as a distant entity of questionable legitimacy. The state's unwillingness or inability to deliver appropriate services to the populace, its rampant corruption, and the frequency of military coups have fostered a political culture of apathy and alienation among many Nigerians and militant opposition among particular communities and groups.

Thus, military rule left Nigeria with strong authoritarian influences in its political culture. Most of the younger politicians of the Fourth Republic came of age during military rule, so naturally they learned the business of politics from Abacha, Babangida, and their military governors. Nigeria's deep democratic traditions discussed in Section 1 remain vibrant among the larger polity, but they are in constant tension with the values imbibed during years of governance when po-litical problems were often solved by military dictate, power, and violence rather than by negotiation and respect for law. This tension was manifest in the irony that the leading presidential contenders in 2003 were all former military men, one of whom—Buhari—was the ringleader of the 1983 coup that overthrew the Second Republic.

Modernity Versus Traditionalism

The terrain of political culture, citizenship, and identity is a contested arena within Nigeria. The interaction of modern (colonial, Western) elements with traditional (precolonial, African) practices has created the tensions of a modern sociopolitical system that rests uneasily on traditional foundations. Nigerians straddle two worlds, each undergoing constant evolution. On one hand, the strong elements in communal societies that promoted accountability have been weakened by the intrusion of Western culture oriented toward individuality. On the other hand, the modern state has been unable to free itself fully from rival ethnic claims organized around narrow, exclusivist constituencies.

As a result, exclusivist identities continue to dominate Nigerian political culture and define the nature of citizenship.[29] Individuals tend to identify with their immediate ethnic, regional, and religious (or subethnic, subregional, and subreligious) groups rather than with state institutions, especially during moments of crisis. Nigerians usually seek to extract as many benefits as possible from the state but hesitate when it comes to performing basic civic duties such as paying taxes or taking care of public property. Entirely missing from the relationship between state and citizen in Nigeria is a fundamental reciprocity—a working social contract based on the belief that there is a common interest that binds them.

Religion

Religion has been a persistent basis of conflict in Nigerian history. Islam began to filter into northeast Nigeria in the eleventh and twelfth centuries, spread to Hausaland by the fifteenth century, and greatly expanded in the early nineteenth century. In the north, Islam first coexisted with, then gradually supplanted, indigenous religions. Christianity arrived later, but it expanded rapidly through missionary activity in the south dating from the early nineteenth century. The amalgamation of northern and southern Nigeria in 1914 brought together the two regions and their belief systems.

These religious cultures have consistently clashed over political issues such as the application of the *shari'a* criminal code in the northern states. For most Muslims, the *shari'a* represents a way of life and supreme (personal) law that transcends secular and state law; for many Christians, the expansion of *shari'a* law threatens the secular nature of the Nigerian state and their position within it. The pull of religious versus national identity becomes even stronger in times of economic hardship. The Babangida period corresponded to a rise in both Islamic fundamentalist movements and evangelical Christian fundamentalism. Where significant numbers of southern Christians are living in predominantly Muslim states (for example, Kaduna state), many clashes have erupted, with great loss of life and the extensive destruction of churches, mosques, and small businesses.

The Press

The plural nature of Nigerian society, with the potential to engender a shared political culture, can be seen in virtually all aspects of public life. The Nigerian press, for instance, has long been one of the liveliest and most irreverent in Africa. The Abacha regime moved to stifle its independence, banning several publications and threatening the suspension of others. Significantly, most of the Nigerian press has been based in a Lagos-Ibadan axis in the western part of Nigeria and has frequently been labeled "southern." In 1994, Abacha closed several of the most influential and respected southern Nigerian newspapers and magazines, including the *Guardian, Concord* (owned by Abiola), and the *Punch,* leaving less critical and more biased publishers intact. In this regard, he was following the nefarious example of his predecessor, Babangida, especially during the final and increasingly conflicted years of his rule. A northern paper, the *New Nigerian,* published in Kaduna, succumbed at times to overt sectionalism. The fact that the media are sometimes regarded as a captive of ethnic and regional constituencies has weakened its capacity to resist attacks on its rights and privileges.

Recently, however, independent television and radio stations have proliferated, and forests of satellite towers now span across Nigerian cities to support the boom in Internet cafés and telecommunications. The freer environment of democracy has also allowed investigative journalism to flourish. One Speaker of the House and two Senate presidents have been brought down by timely media exposés of their misconduct, and other public figures are being scrutinized in the press.

Interests, Social Movements, and Protests

Issues relating to political attitudes, political culture, and identities are still dominated and defined largely by elite, male, urban-based interests. These interests include ethnic as well as professional and associational groups. The few nonelite groups, such as urban-based market women's associations, often serve as channels for disseminating the decisions and agendas of male-dominated groups. In essence, nonelite and rural elements continue to be marginalized and manipulated by elites and urban groups. Lacking competence in the language of public discourse, namely English, and access to financial networks, nonelites have difficulty confronting, on their own, the decision-making centers of the state and society.

Elite and nonelite Nigerians alike come together in civic organizations and interest groups such as labor unions and student and business associations. Because the political machinery was in the hands of the military, Nigerian citizens sought alternative means of representation and protest in an effort to have an impact on political life. Historically, labor has played a significant role in Nigerian politics, as have student groups, some women's organizations, and various radical and populist organizations. Business groups have frequently supported and colluded with corrupt civilian and military regimes. In the last year of the Abacha regime, however, even the business class, through mechanisms like Vision 2010, began to suggest an end to such arbitrary rule. The termination of military rule has seen civil society groups flourish across Nigeria.

Labor

Organized labor once played an important role in challenging governments during both the colonial and postcolonial eras in several African countries, including Nigeria. Continuous military pressure throughout the 1980s and 1990s forced a decline in the once independent and powerful role of organized labor in Nigerian politics. The Babangida regime implemented strategies of **state corporatism** designed to control and co-opt various social forces such as labor. When the leadership of the Nigerian Labour Congress (NLC), to which all unions compulsorily belong, however, took a vigorous stand against the government, the government sacked the leaders and appointed conservative replacements. When prodemocracy strikes during the summer of 1994 by the National Petroleum Employees Union (NUPENG) and other sympathetic labor groups significantly reduced oil production and nearly brought the country to a halt, the Abacha regime arrested and disbanded its leadership.

The Nigerian labor movement has been vulnerable to reprisals by the state and private employers. First, the state has always been the biggest single employer of labor in Nigeria, as well as the recognized regulator of industrial relations between employers and employees. Second, ethnic, regional, and religious divisions have often hampered labor solidarity while being deliberately manipulated by the state.

Military policy to centralize and co-opt the unions caused their militancy and impact to wane, until General Abubakar removed the government-appointed union administrators in 1998 and allowed the unions to elect their own leaders again. Within a year, labor had regained its footing. National strikes in 2000 forced the Obasanjo government to forgo plans to raise the price of fuel, and strikes in 2001 and 2002 had similar positive impacts on wage increases.

Labor still claims an estimated 2 million members across Nigeria and remains one of the most potent forces in civil society. It therefore has a great stake in the consolidation of constitutional rule in the Fourth Republic and the protections that allow it to organize and act freely on behalf of its members and, more broadly, the masses of disadvantaged people in Nigeria.

The Business Community

Nigeria has a long history of entrepreneurialism and business development. This spirit, however, is compromised by the tendencies toward rent-seeking and the appropriation of state resources. Members of the Nigerian business class are often characterized as "pirate capitalists" because of the high level of cor-

rupt practices and collusion with state officials.[30] Many wealthy individuals have served in the military or civilian governments, or indirectly protect their access to state resources by sponsoring elected officials. Nevertheless, as economic and political conditions in Nigeria deteriorated, the state offered fewer avenues for businesspeople and can no longer provide even the necessary infrastructure for business development.

Private interests have proved surprisingly resilient, as organized groups have emerged to represent the interests of the business class and promote economic development generally. These associations have proliferated throughout Nigeria and in many areas represent diverse groups, from butchers, to manufacturers, to car-hire firms. In a number of cases, they have demonstrated social responsibility by building roads, schools, market stalls, and similar infrastructure, rather than relying on uncertain government provisions.

Many local or regional groups arc also members of national organizations. National business associations, such as the Nigerian Association of Chambers of Commerce, Industry, Mines, and Agriculture (NACCIMA), the largest in the country, have taken an increasingly political stance pressing the military leadership to resolve the June 12 crisis and advocating better governance. In their bid to reduce uncertainty, halt economic decline, and protect their economic interests, large business associations increasingly perform what are clearly political roles. The continuing influence of the Economic Summit and other business associations in shaping government economic policies underscores this trend.

Other Social Groups

Student activism continues to be an important feature of Nigerian political life. University and other higher-level student groups play an important political role. Along with their teachers, they have suffered government harassment, banning, and attempts to engineer divisions in their unions and associations, including countless closings of the universities during the Babangida and Abacha regimes. Many professional associations of doctors and lawyers have also become champions of human rights. They often support campaigns conducted by human rights organizations, which have proliferated since the founding of the Civil Liberties Organization (CLO) in 1987.

The activities of these organizations increased

significantly with the introduction of the structural adjustment program (SAP). Marginal groups, including women and the young, the urban poor, and people in rural areas, perceived an imbalance in the distribution of the benefits and burdens generated by the SAP program. Not surprisingly, the flagrant display of wealth by senior members of the military alienated these groups and encouraged a "culture of rage" among youths, artisans, the urban poor, and the unemployed.

This rage over economic hardship and military oppression led to a sharp increase in the number of human rights groups and other nongovernmental organizations (NGOs) in the 1990s.[31] Greater funding for NGOs from governments and private foundations in Europe and the United States assisted the growth of this sector, most notably in the south but gradually in the north as well. They generally focus on such issues as civil protection, gender law, health care, media access, and public housing. Most are urban based, although efforts to develop rural networks are underway.

Personality conflicts, ethnic divisions, and intense competition for funding hampered the challenge posed by these civil society organizations to military dictatorship.[32] Prodemocracy efforts by NGOs peaked in the 1993–1994 struggle over June 12, when they managed to stage numerous successful stay-home strikes in Lagos and several other southern cities. The Campaign for Democracy in 1993 and then the National Democratic Coalition (NADECO) in 1994 built an antimilitary front among the NGOs that also included students, academics, some labor unions, and other groups. As Abacha moved forward with his "self-succession" campaign in 1997–1998, this sector once again was able to mount numerous street demonstrations and other protests to counter the regime's orchestration, even under very restrictive political conditions.

The return of political freedoms under the Fourth Republic in 1999 has allowed these groups, battle hardened from the Abacha years, to proliferate and become influential. Yet the end of military government has also left many of the prodemocracy and human rights groups without the strong central focus they had in the 1990s. Specialized groups are gradually supplanting the older, broader organizations, while many of the leaders of the prodemocracy struggles in the 1990s ran for office in the 2003 elections, although most were unable to dislodge the ruling politicians.

Civil society groups are, in short, making a substantial contribution to consolidating democracy in Nigeria. Their relationships with the political parties, however, remain largely distant. Nigeria's prospects for building a sustainable democracy during the Fourth Republic will depend, in part, on the willingness of many of these advocacy groups to increase their collaboration with the political parties, while maintaining a high level of vigilance and activism.

Section ⑤ Nigerian Politics in Transition

Despite the slow progress of the Fourth Republic, Nigerians remain overwhelmingly in favor of democratic government over military rule. About 80 percent of respondents in a recent survey said that they still prefer democracy to any other alternative, but their frustration is growing with the slow pace of reform and continued corruption in politics.[33] Will democracy in Nigeria consolidate sufficiently to meet even minimal levels of public satisfaction before Nigerians are again willing to accept authoritarian rule? So long as the civilian politicians treat government offices more as personal feeding frenzies rather than as positions of public service, the clock is ticking closer to the hour of the next military coup.

Several patterns in Nigerian politics must change if the entrepreneurs in the military are to be kept in the barracks and democracy is to become more stable in Nigeria. First and foremost, the nation must turn from a system of politics dominated by big men—what is, for all intents and purposes, a semicompetitive oligarchy—to a more popular mode of politics that engages and addresses the fundamental interests of the public. Second, but ultimately determined by the first, Nigerians must conclusively settle the national question and commit to a political arrangement that reflects and respects the nation's great diversity but allows its government to move beyond limited ethnic struggles so that it may address the larger national interests of economic development and good governance.

The popular vote on June 12, 1993, in which

Moshood Abiola won many of the states outside his own ethnic region, provided a radical departure from the sectionalism of the past and offered a refreshing opportunity to develop a more national political agenda. June 12 was a historic breakthrough, the day the ordinary people of Nigeria rose against the ethnic, religious, and regional prejudices and the divisive politics with which colonialism and the political class had oppressed them for a half a century. Babangida's annulment of the June 12 election followed by Abacha's predatory rule, however, placed ethnicity, religion, and regionalism back firmly on the agenda. Nonetheless, and despite the flaws of the May 1999 elections, President Obasanjo was elected *despite* having lost the popular vote in his own ethnic region. Northerners, Igbos, and minority groups across Nigeria, rather than Obasanjo's own Yoruba ethnicity, voted for him overwhelmingly and put him into office. Nigeria's Fourth Republic must find ways of moving beyond patrimonial politics and develop a truly national political process in which mobilization and conflicts along ethnic, regional, and religious lines gradually diminish.

Political Challenges and Changing Agendas

Nigeria's fitful transition to democratic rule from 1985 to 1999 was halting in part because it was planned and directed from above. This approach contrasts sharply with the popular-based movements that unseated autocracies in Central and Eastern Europe beginning in the spring of 1989. Promises of democratic transition were made periodically during Nigeria's political history as a ploy by the military to stabilize and legitimize their governments. General Abubakar dutifully handed power to the civilians in 1999, but only after ensuring that the military's interests would be protected under civilian rule, and creating an overly powerful executive that reinforces **patrimonialism,** a system of power in which authority is maintained through patronage. His rapid transition program produced a tenuous, conflicted democratic government facing daunting tasks of restoring key institutions, securing social stability, and reforming the economy. The continuing strength and influence of collective identities, defined on the basis of religion or ethnicity, are often more binding than "national" (that is, all-Nigerian) ones and remain problematic. The parasitic nature of the Nigerian economy is a further source of instability. Rent seeking and other unproductive, often corrupt, business activities remain accepted norms of wealth accumulation.

Nonetheless, Nigerians are sowing seeds of change in all of these areas. Attitudes toward the military in government have shifted dramatically. The decline in the appeal of military rule can be attributed to the abysmal performances of the Babangida and Abacha regimes in economic policies and governance. Many now recognize that the military, apart from its contributions to national security, is incapable of promoting economic and social progress in Nigeria. With the military discredited for the moment, the nature and outcome of the struggles among the big men will decide the direction of political and economic change. Thus, the current struggles among Nigeria's patrimonial big men may actually support democratic development in the long run if stable coalitions appear among them over time and if these political kingpins are generally willing to respect the democratic rules.

So far, they have generally confined their struggles within the constraints of the democratic system: taking each other to court, attacking each other in the media, introducing competing bills in the Assembly, and even threatening to impeach the president. All of these efforts actually strengthen the system not just by using it, but by forcing the personal struggles of powerful individuals into the public realm. These opposing coalitions of powerful individuals, who gather under the umbrellas of political parties, have used the system to police each other and keep each other's ambitions in check.

The next critical step down the long road of democratic development for Nigeria is the development of a viable, multiethnic opposition party that is also "loyal," meaning that it plays by the rules of the system. Opposition parties help to reduce corruption in the system because they have an interest in exposing the corruption of the ruling party, which in turn forces them to reduce their own corrupt practices. Furthermore, in order to unseat the ruling party and win elections, opposition parties need to engage the public to win their votes. In this manner, issues of interest to the public become of interest to the powerful individuals leading the parties.

The introduction of so many new parties in 2002 may facilitate the development of a viable, loyal opposition, especially if the PDP continues to be riven with internal division. On the other hand, these new parties may further dilute the opposition and allow the PDP to govern largely unchecked, except by its own factions. Even worse, if these parties manage to win only narrow ethnic constituencies, and if the electoral commission does not rigorously apply the multiethnic rules of contest, Nigeria might return to the ruinous ethnic politics of the past.

In addition to loyal multiethnic opposition, democratic development also requires that parties compete within the confines of the law and, more so, that elections stay generally free of rigging or other corrupt practices. The parties of the First and Second Republics, particularly the NPC and NPN, were willing to rig the system with reckless abandon, and they were able to do so primarily because they held unchallenged control over their own states, and thus the electoral systems within their states.

Although the elections of 1999 saw serious violations of the rules, the public and the international observers present were largely willing to accept them in order to get the military out of power. Nonetheless, Obasanjo, a former military ruler, and the PDP received extensive financial support from other retired military officers, including the same individual who annulled the 1993 elections, Ibrahim Babangida. In the 2003 election, the PDP and its tarnished backers showed that it was willing to circumvent the system as it did four years prior. Local election commissions were packed with PDP loyalists, while the national commission, appointed by the president, showed a willingness to alter the process to accommodate PDP interests. Also disturbing was the reliance by a number of governors and other leaders on local ethnic militias to harass and intimidate their competitors.

Ironically, however, because the PDP has such national dominance, the critical event may not have been the elections but the PDP party convention held late in 2002. To the degree that the party's list of candidates were acceptable to its powerful patrimonial leaders this reduced the temptation to rig, except in areas where PDP candidates faced significant competition. Yet the elections were still contentious: the ANPP's nomination of the pro-*shari'a* Buhari and 2003 election victories across northwest and north-central Nigeria promise to aggravate the Muslim-Christian, North-South divide, and in part explains why the Yoruba-dominated AD shifted its support to Obasanjo. If the opposition

parties emerging from the 2003 elections are able to organize a viable coalition to challenge the PDP, they will have an interest in cleaning up the electoral system.

Democratic development also requires further decentralization of power structures in Nigeria. The struggle on the part of the National Assembly and the state governors to wrest power away from the presidency has already begun this process. The administration's efforts to privatize government para-statals will also reduce the power of the presidency over time, since it will no longer control all the productive sectors of the economy. A more decentralized system allows local problems to be solved locally rather than engaging national institutions and the consequent interethnic competition. Decentralization also lowers the stakes for holding national offices, so that they are less likely to be viewed as life-or-death contests. Moving businesses out of government control and into the private sector will also attract individuals interested in making their fortunes from government into the private sector, where market forces will then regulate them.

Decentralization and a viable opposition movement of themselves, however, will not necessarily change the elite, and hence unaccountable, character of Nigerian politics. Civil society groups are the final link in democratic consolidation in Nigeria. These groups are critical players in connecting the Nigerian state to the Nigerian people. They aggregate and articulate the interests of the sector they represent into the policy realm, and they advocate on behalf of their members. If the political parties are to reflect anything more than the elite interests of the big men and their clients, the parties must reach out and build alliances with civil society groups. So far, however, the parties continue to be an elite business, and civil society groups must strike or find other ways to gain more than the cursory attention of party leaders. For opposition parties to become a viable opposition movement capable of checking the power of the PDP, they will have to build alliances with civil society groups in order to mobilize large portions of the population.

Foreign pressure also plays an important role in maintaining the quest for democracy and sustainable development. In recent years, major external forces have been more forthright in supporting civil society and democratization in Nigeria. The United States, Britain, and some member states of the European Union were quite visible in exerting pressure on Babangida to leave and in applying modest sanctions in support of democracy. This has been made possible, in part, by a changing international environment, especially the willingness of the major industrial countries and the international financial institutions to support democracy in the Third World. Nigeria's increasingly weak economy and enormous debt, now estimated at $33 billion, have made it susceptible to this kind of pressure.

Western commitment to development and democracy in Africa is not guaranteed. Much of the initiative for Africa's growth therefore needs to emerge from within. In Nigeria, such initiatives will depend on substantial changes in the way Nigerians do business. It will be necessary to develop a more sophisticated and far less corrupt form of capitalist enterprise and the development of entrepreneurial interests within Nigeria who will see their interests tied to the standard principles of democratic politics and private economic initiative. The middle class is beginning to grow under democratic rule, but it remains small and vulnerable to economic and political instability.

In addition, the project of building a coherent nation-state out of competing nationalities remains largely unfinished and under constant siege by resurgent ethno-nationalism and religious fundamentalism. The challenge here is to achieve a proper balance between ethnic-based symbols and institutions and those of a "transethnic" nature. Ironically, because the parties of the Fourth Republic generally do not represent any particular ethnic interest—indeed, they do not represent anyone's interests except those of the leaders and their clients—ethnic associations and militias have risen to articulate ethnic-based grievances. Ethnic consciousness cannot be eliminated from society, but ethnicity should not become the main basis for political competition. If the current ethnic mobilization can be contained within ethnic associations arguing over the agenda of the parties, then it can be managed. If any of the ethnic associations captures one of the political parties or joins with the militias to foment separatism, instability will result.

Nigerian politics has been characterized by turmoil and periodic crises since the British relinquished colonial power in 1960. Over forty years later, the country is still trying to piece together a fragile democracy, and per capita incomes are scarcely higher than they were at independence. Despite a number of positive trends, the nation continues to wrestle with stagnation and decline of major productive sectors, collapsed infrastructure and institutions, heightened sociopolitical tension, an irresponsible elite, and an expanding mass culture of despondency and rage. Only a responsible government combined with sustained civil society action can reverse this decline and restore the nation to what President Obasanjo has called "the path to greatness."

Nigerian Politics in Comparative Perspective

The study of Nigeria has important implications for the study of African politics and, more broadly, of comparative politics. The Nigerian case embodies a number of key themes and issues that can be generalized to increase social science knowledge, and these themes deserve careful consideration. We can learn much about how democratic regimes are established and achieve stability by understanding the pitfalls Nigeria has encountered. By analyzing the historical dynamics of Nigeria's ethnic conflict, for example, we can identify institutional mechanisms that may be effective in reducing ethnic conflict in other states. We can also learn much about how viable and sustainable economies are developed by contrasting their evolution with Nigeria's. Each of these issues offers comparative lessons for the major themes explored in this book: the world of states, governing the economy, the democratic idea, and the politics of collective identities.

A World of States

Nigeria exists in two "worlds" of states: one in the global political economy and the other within Africa. We have addressed at length Nigeria's position in the world. Economically, Nigeria was thrust into the world economy in a position of weakness, first as a British colony and later as an independent nation. Despite its resources and the potential of oil to provide the investment capital needed to build a modern economy, Nigeria has grown weaker. It has lost much of its international clout, and, in place of the respect it once enjoyed in diplomatic circles, it was regularly criticized for persistent human rights abuses throughout the 1990s. The return of democracy in 1999 has restored some of Nigeria's former stature, but its economic vulnerability and persistent corruption keep it a secondary player in the world of states.

This chapter has quoted the statement, "As Nigeria goes, so goes the rest of sub-Saharan Africa." The future of democracy, political stability, and economic renewal in other parts of Africa, and certainly in West Africa, will be greatly influenced, for good or ill, by unfolding events in Nigeria. Beyond the obvious demonstration effect, the economy of the West African subregion can be revitalized by resumed growth of the Nigerian economy. International political, scholarly, and business attention has shifted steadily to the south of the continent, focusing chiefly on South Africa and its stable neighboring states of Botswana and Namibia. That shift portends a greater danger of marginalization, as Africa becomes divided into a zone of growth that attracts investment and a zone of decay.

Governing the Economy

Nigeria provides important insights into the political economy of underdevelopment. At independence in 1960, Nigeria was stronger economically than its Southeast Asian counterparts, Indonesia and Malaysia. Independent Nigeria appeared poised for growth, with a wealth of natural resources, a large population, and the presence of highly entrepreneurial groups in all regions of the country. Today, Nigeria is among the poorest countries in the world in terms of per capita income, while many of its Asian counterparts have joined the ranks of the newly industrializing countries (NICs). One critical lesson Nigeria teaches is that a rich endowment of resources is not enough to ensure economic development. In fact, it may encourage rent-seeking behavior that undermines more productive activities.[34] Sound political development must come first.

Other variables are critically important, notably, political stability from democracy and a capable developmental state. A developmentalist ethic, and an institutional structure to enforce it, can set limits to corrupt behavior and constrain the pursuit of short-term personal gain at the expense of national economic growth. Institutions vital for the pursuit of these objectives include a professional civil service, an independent judiciary, and a free press. Nigeria has had each of these, yet they were gradually undermined and corrupted under military rule. The public "ethic" that has

come to dominate Nigerian political economy has been prebendalism. Where corruption is unchecked, as in Nigeria, the Philippines under Ferdinand Marcos, and Latin American countries such as Mexico and Venezuela, economic development suffers accordingly.

Nigeria also demonstrates that sustainable economic development requires sound economic policy. Without export diversification, commodity-exporting countries are buffeted by the price fluctuations of one or two main products. This situation can be traced back to overreliance on primary commodity export-oriented policies bequeathed by the British colonial regime. Yet other former colonies, such as Malaysia and Indonesia, have managed to diversify their initial export base. Nigeria, by contrast, has substituted one form of commodity dependence for another; and it has allowed its petroleum industry to overwhelm all other sectors of the economy. Nigeria even became a net importer of products (for example, of palm oil and palm nuts) for which it was once a leading world producer. In comparative perspective, we can see that natural resource endowments can be tremendously beneficial. The United States, for example, has parlayed its endowments of agricultural, mineral, and energy resources into one of the world's most diversified modern economies. Meanwhile Japan, which is by comparison poorly endowed with natural resources, has one of the strongest economies in the world, achieved in large part through its unique developmental strategies. Each of these examples illustrates the primacy of sound economic policies implemented through consolidated political systems.

The Democratic Idea

Many African countries have experienced transitions from authoritarian rule.[35] With the end of superpower competition in Africa and the withdrawal of support from the former Soviet Union and the United States for Africa's despots, many African societies experienced a resurgence of popular pressures for greater participation in political life and more open forms of governance. Decades of authoritarian, single-party, and military rule in Africa have left a dismal record: arbitrary imprisonment and silenced political opposition; harassment of civic, professional, and religious institutions; stifled public discourse and free speech; and bankrupted treasuries and mismanaged economies. At the same time, a handful of elites have acquired large fortunes through wanton corruption. The examples, sadly, are plentiful. Consider Nigeria's "missing" $2.3 billion windfall in oil revenues after the Gulf War in 1991 or the fact that former Zairian president Mobutu Sese Seko's personal wealth was estimated to be several billion dollars—perhaps as much as half the external debt of the entire country. Or that Kenya's former president Daniel Arap Moi is considered among the richest men in Africa, a group to which Ibrahim Babangida and the late Sani Abacha of Nigeria have belonged. The devious ways in which these fortunes were acquired and dispensed make it difficult to give concrete figures. They do, however, suggest that the exercise of postcolonial authoritarian rule in Africa has contributed to economic stagnation and decline. The difficulty that such countries as Cameroon, Togo, and Zimbabwe have experienced in moving to democratic systems is a reflection, among other factors, of the ruling elites' unwillingness to cede control of the political instruments that made possible their self-enrichment.

Nigeria exemplifies the harsh reality of authoritarian and unaccountable governance. Corruption, fraud, mismanagement, and the restriction of political liberties were tolerated in the past by populations numbed into complacency by political repression and the daily struggles for economic survival. Nigeria has endured six military regimes, countless attempted coups, and a bloody civil war that claimed over 1 million lives. They have also seen a once-prospering economy reduced to a near shambles. Today, democracy has become a greater imperative because only such a system provides the mechanisms to limit abuses of power and render governments accountable.

Collective Identities

Nigeria presents an important case in which to study the dangers of ethnically based competition in a society with deep cultural divisions. How can multiethnic countries manage their diversity? What institutional mechanisms can be employed to avert tragedies such as the 1967–1970 civil war or the continuing conflicts that have brought great suffering to the former Yugoslavia and Rwanda? This chapter has suggested institutional reforms such as constitutionally encouraged multiethnic political parties, decentralization, and a strengthened federal system that can contribute to reducing tensions and minimizing conflict.

Insights from the Nigerian experience may explain why some federations persist and identify the factors that can undermine them. Nigeria's complex social situation, and its varied attempts to create a nation out of its highly diverse population, enhances our understanding of the politics of cultural pluralism and the difficulty of accommodating sectional interests under conditions of political and economic insecurity. Federal character in Nigeria has been distorted into a form of ethnic and regional favoritism and a tool for dispensing patronage. Yet the country has benefited in some ways from the attention devoted to creating state and local governments and from giving people in different regions a sense of being stakeholders in the entity called "Nigeria."

The challenges that Nigeria faces concern not only its people's frustrated hopes for a better life, stable government, and a democratic political order, but also the potential contributions that this country and its peoples could make to the entire continent and to the world at large. The nation's leaders in partnership with civil society must deliver responsive and prosperous democratic governance before public frustration reaches the point where military entrepreneurs, or ethnic and religious extremists, seize the opportunity to return Nigeria to the cycles of coups, decline, and possibly collapse.

Key Terms

authoritarian
legitimacy
accountability
unfinished state
jihad
acephalous societies
emirs
indirect rule
warrant chiefs
interventionist
clientelism
autocracy
rents
rent-seeking
structural adjustment
   program (SAP)

international financial
   institutions
balance of payments
privatization
self-determination
Economic Community of
   West African States
   (ECOWAS)
para-statals
shari'a
prebendalism
civil society
state corporatism
patrimonialism

Suggested Readings

Aborisade, Oladimeji, and Robert J. Mundt. *Politics in Nigeria,* 2nd Edition. New York: Longman, 2002.

Achike, Okay. *Public Administration: A Nigerian and Comparative Perspective.* London: Longman, 1978.

Adamolekun, L. *Politics and Administration in Nigeria.* London: Hutchinson, 1986.

Agbaje, Adigun. *The Nigerian Press: Hegemony and the Social Construction of Legitimacy, 1960–1983.* Lewiston, N.Y.: Edwin Mellen Press, 1992.

———. "Twilight of Democracy in Nigeria." *Africa Demos* 3, no. 3:5. Atlanta: The Carter Center of Emory University, 1994.

Beckett, Paul A., and Crawford Young, eds. *Dilemmas of Democracy in Nigeria.* Rochester, NY: University of Rochester Press, 1997.

Bienen, Henry. *Political Conflict and Economic Change in Nigeria.* London: Frank Cass, 1988.

Diamond, Larry. *Class, Ethnicity and Democracy in Nigeria: The Failure of the First Republic.* London: Macmillan, 1988.

Diamond, Larry, "Nigeria: The Uncivic Society and the Descent into Praetorianism," in Larry Diamond, J. Linz, and S. M. Lipset, eds. *Politics in Developing Countries: Comparing Experiences With Democracy,* 2nd Edition. Boulder, Colo.: Lynne Rienner Publishers, 1995, 417–491.

Decalo, Samuel. *Coups and Army Rule in Africa,* 2nd edition. New Haven: Yale University Press, 1990.

Dudley, Billy. *An Introduction to Nigerian Government and Politics.* Bloomington: Indiana University Press, 1982.

Ekeh, Peter P., and Eghosa E. Osaghae, eds. *Federal Character and Federalism in Nigeria.* Ibadan: Heinemann, 1989.

Falola, Toyin. *Violence in Nigeria: The Crisis of Religious Politics and Secular Ideologies.* Rochester, NY: University of Rochester Press, 1999.

Forrest, Tom. *Politics and Economic Development in Nigeria.* Boulder, Colo.: Westview Press, 1993.

Horowitz, Donald L. *Ethnic Groups in Conflict.* Berkeley: University of California Press, 1985.

Joseph, Richard A. *Democracy and Prebendal Politics in Nigeria: The Rise and Fall of the Second Republic.* Cambridge: Cambridge University Press, 1987.

Kew, Darren. "Political Islam in Nigeria's Transition Crisis," *Muslim Politics Report* (Council on Foreign Relations: New York), May–June, 1996.

Kirk-Greene, Anthony, and Douglas Rimmer. *Nigeria Since 1970: A Political and Economic Outline.* London: Hodder and Stoughton, 1981.

Lewis, Peter M. "Endgame in Nigeria? The Politics of a Failed Democratic Transition." *African Affairs* 93 (1994): 323–340.

Lewis, Peter M., Barnett R. Rubin, and Pearl T. Robinson. *Stabilizing Nigeria: Pressures, Incentives, and Support for Civil Society.* New York: Century Foundation, for the Council on Foreign Relations, 1998.

Lubeck, Paul. *Islam and Urban Labor in Northern Nigeria.* Cambridge: Cambridge University Press, 1987.

Luckham, Robin. *The Nigerian Military: A Sociological Analysis of Authority and Revolt, 1960–67* Cambridge: Cambridge University Press, 1971.

Melson, Robert, and Howard Wolpe, eds. *Nigeria: Modernization and the Politics of Communalism,* East Lansing: Michigan State University Press, 1971.

Nyang'oro, Julius, and Tim Shaw, eds. *Corporatism in Africa: Comparative Analysis and Practice.* Boulder, Colo.: Westview Press, 1989.

Olukoshi, Adebayo, ed. *The Politics of Structural Adjustment in Nigeria.* London: James Currey Publishers, 1993.

Osaghae, Eghosa. *Crippled Giant: Nigeria Since Independence.* Bloomington: Indiana University Press, 1998.

Oyediran, Oyeleye, ed. *Nigerian Government and Politics Under Military Rule.* London: Macmillan, 1979.

Reno, William. *Warlord Politics and African States.* Boulder, Colo.: Lynne Rienner Publishers, 1998.

Sklar, Richard L. *Nigerian Political Parties: Power in an Emergent African Nation.* New York: NOK Publishers, 1983.

Soyinka, Wole. *Open Sore of a Continent.* Oxford: Oxford University Press, 1996.

Suberu, Rotimi. *Federalism and Ethnic Conflict in Nigeria.* Washington, D.C.: U.S. Institute of Peace, 2001.

Watts, Michael, ed. *State, Oil, and Agriculture in Nigeria.* Berkeley: University of California Press, 1987.

Wunsch, James S., and Dele Olowu, eds. *The Failure of the Centralized State: Institutions and Self-Governance in Africa.* Boulder, Colo.: Westview Press, 1990.

Young, Crawford. *The Rising Tide of Cultural Pluralism: The Nation-State at Bay?* Madison: University of Wisconsin Press, 1993.

Suggested Websites

British Broadcasting Corporation: A 2002 interview with President Obasanjo.
news.bbc.co.uk/2/hi/talking_point/1800826.stm
Gamji: A collection of news stories from Nigerian newspapers, as well as opinion pieces and other news links.
www.gamji.com/
The Guardian, Nigeria's leading daily newspaper
www.ngrguardiannews.com/
Human Rights Watch reports
www.hrw.org/africa/nigeria.php
International Institute for Democracy and Electoral Assistance
www.idea.int/frontpage_nigeria.htm
Stanford University's Center for African Studies
www.stanford.edu/dept/AFR/

Notes

[1]Much of this context is recounted in James S. Coleman, *Nigeria: Background to Nationalism* (Berkeley: University of California Press, 1958).

[2]Obafemi Awolowo, *Path to Nigerian Freedom* (London: Faber and Faber, 1947), 47–48.

[3]Billy Dudley, *An Introduction to Nigerian Government and Politics* (Bloomington: Indiana University Press, 1982), 71.

[4]Robin Luckham, *The Nigerian Military: A Sociological Analysis of Authority and Revolt 1960–67* (Cambridge: Cambridge University Press, 1971).

[5]Peter Ekeh, "Colonialism and the Two Publics in Africa: A Theoretical Statement," *Comparative Studies in Society and History* 17, no. 1 (January 1975).

[6]Richard A. Joseph, *Democracy and Prebendal Politics in Nigeria: The Rise and Fall of the Second Republic* (Cambridge: Cambridge University Press), 55–58.

[7]Gavin Williams and Terisa Turner, "Nigeria," in John Dunn, ed., *West African States: Failure and Promise* (Cambridge: Cambridge University Press,1978), 156–157 .

[8]Michael J. Watts, *State, Oil and Agriculture in Nigeria* (Berkeley: University of California Press, 1987), 71.

[9]Watts, *State Oil and Agriculture in Nigeria,* 67.

[10]See Peter M. Lewis, "From Prebendalism to Predation: The Political Economy of Decline in Nigeria," *Journal of Modern African Studies* 34, no. 1 (1996), 79–103.

[11]Tom Forrest, *Politics and Economic Development in Nigeria,* 2nd Edition (Boulder, Colo.: Westview Press, 1995), 207–212.

[12]Dele Olowu, "Centralization, Self-Governance, and Development in Nigeria," in *The Failure of the Centralized State: Institutions and Self-Governance in Africa,* ed. James S. Wunsch and Dele Olowu (Boulder, Colo.: Westview Press, 1991), 211.

[13]Robert Melson and Howard Wolpe, *Nigeria: Modernization and the Politics of Communalism* (East Lansing: Michigan State University Press, 1971).

[14]Toyin Falola, *Violence in Nigeria: The Crisis of Religious Politics and Secular Ideologies* (Rochester, NY: University of Rochester Press, 1998).

[15]Billy J. Dudley, *Instability and Political Order: Politics and Crisis in Nigeria* (Ibadan: Ibadan University Press, 1973), 35.

[16]Pat A. Williams, "Women and the Dilemma of Politics in Nigeria," in Crawford Young and Paul Beckett, eds., *Dilemmas of Democracy in Nigeria* (Rochester, NY: University of Rochester Press, 1997), 219–241.

[17]Anthony Kirk-Greene and Douglas Rimmer, *Nigeria Since 1970: A Political and Economic Outline* (London: Hodder and Stoughton 1981), 49.

[18]Rotimi Suberu, *Federalism and Ethnic Conflict in Nigeria* (Washington, D.C.: U.S. Institute of Peace, 2001).

[19]Henry Bienen, *Armies and Parties in Africa* (New York: Africana Publishing, 1978), 193–211.

[20]Human Rights Watch, *The Destruction of Odi and Rape in Choba* (New York: Human Rights Watch, December 22, 1999).

[21]Suberu, *Federalism and Ethnic Conflict in Nigeria,* 119–120.

[22]Samuel DeCalo, *Coups and Army Rule in Africa* (New Haven: Yale University Press, 1976), 18.

[23]Larry Diamond, "Nigeria: The Uncivic Society and the Descent into Praetorianism," in Larry Diamond, J. Linz, and S.M. Lipset, eds., *Politics in Developing Countries: Comparing Experiences With Democracy,* 2nd Edition (Boulder, Colo.: Lynne Rienner Publishers, 1995).

[24]Joseph, *Democracy and Prebendal Politics in Nigeria,* 52–53.

[25]Richard Sklar, *Nigerian Political Parties* (Princeton: Princeton University Press, 1963).

[26]Babafemi Badejo, "Party Formation and Party Competitition" in Larry Diamond, Anthony Kirk-Greene, and Oyeleye Oyediran, eds., *Transition Without End: Nigerian Politics and Civil Society Under Babangida* (Boulder, Colo.: Lynne Rienner Publishers, 1997), 179.

[27]Eghosa Osaghae, *Crippled Giant: Nigeria Since Independence* (Bloomington: Indiana University Press 1999), 233–239.

[28]Peter M. Lewis, Barnett Rubin, and Pearl Robinson, *Stabilizing Nigeria: Pressures, Incentives and Support for Civil Society* (New York: Council on Foreign Relations, 1998), 87.

[29]Rotimi Suberu, *Public Policies and National Unity in Nigeria,* Research Report No. 19 (Ibadan: Development Policy Centre, 199), 9–10.

[30]Sayre Schatz, " 'Pirate Capitalism' and the Inert Economy of Nigeria," *Journal of Modern African Studies* 22, no. 1 (March 1984), 45–57.

[31]Adebayo Olukoshi, "Associational Life" in Diamond, Kirk-Greene, and Oyediran, *Transition Without End*, 385–86.

[32]Osaghae, *Crippled Giant*, 301.

[33]Peter Lewis, Etannibi Alemika, and Michael Bratton, *Down to Earth: Changes in Attitudes to Democracy and Markets in Nigeria*, Afrobarometer Working Paper No. 20, Michigan State University, August 2002.

[34]See Terry Lynn Karl, *The Paradox of Plenty* (Berkeley: University of California Press, 1997). And Michael Ross, "The Political Economy of the Resource Curse," *World Politics* 51 (January 1999), 297–322.

[35]Michael Bratton and Nicolas van de Walle, *Democratic Experiments in Africa* (Cambridge: Cambridge University Press, 1997).

PART 4

Non-Democracies

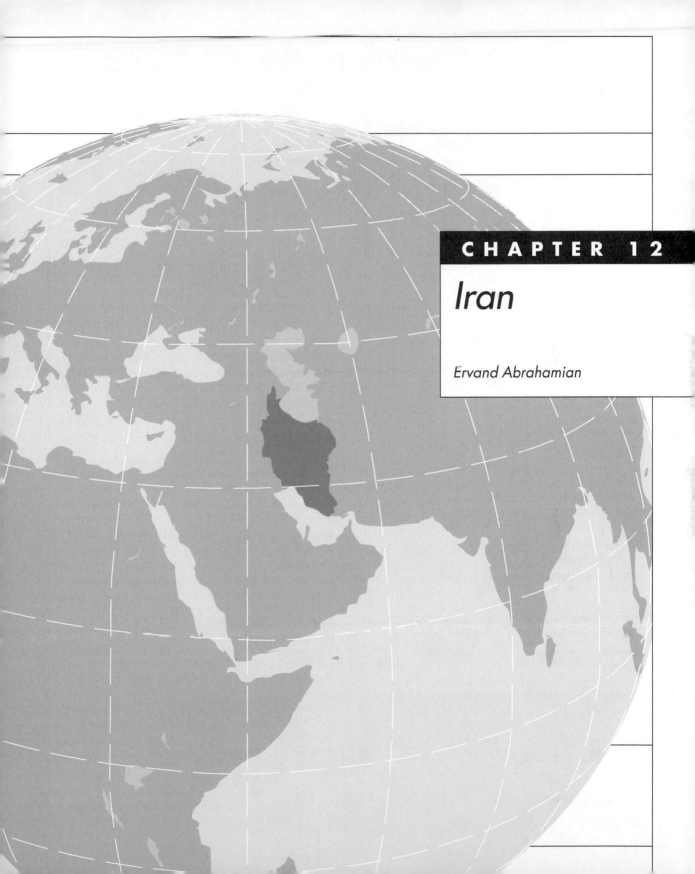

CHAPTER 12

Iran

Ervand Abrahamian

Islamic Republic of Iran

Land and People

Capital	Tehran
Total area (square miles)	634,562 (slightly larger than Alaska)
Population	64.6 million

Annual population growth rate (%)	1975–2000	3.0
	2000–2015 (projected)	1.2

Urban population (%)	64.0

Ethnic composition (% of total population)	Persian	51
	Azeri	24
	Gilaki and Mazandarani	8
	Kurd	7
	Arab	3
	Other	7

Major language(s) (%)	Persian (Farsi)	58
	Turkic	26
	Kurdish	9
	Other	7

Religious affiliation (%)	Shi'a Muslim	89
	Sunni Muslim	10
	Zoroastrian, Jewish, Christian, and Baha'i	1

Economy

Domestic currency	Rial (IRR)
	US$1: 1743.9 IRR (2002 av.)
Total GDP (US$)	104.9 billion
GDP per capita (US$)	4690
Total GDP at purchasing power parity (US$)	374.6 billion
GDP per capita at purchasing power parity (US$)	5,884

GDP annual growth rate (%)	1997	3.4
	2000	5.9
	2001	4.6

GDP per capita average annual growth rate (%)	1975–2000	–0.7
	1990–2000	1.9

Inequality in income or consumption (1996–1997) (%)	Data Not Available for Iran

Structure of production (% of GDP)	Agriculture	18.9
	Industry	22.3
	Services	58.8

Labor force distribution (% of total)	Agriculture	30
	Industry	25
	Services	45

Exports as % of GDP	35
Imports as % of GDP	21

Society

Life expectancy at birth	69
Infant mortality per 1,000 live births	41

Adult literacy (%)	Male	83.2
	Female	69.3

Access to information and communications (per 1,000 population)	Telephone lines	149
	Mobile phones	15
	Radios	281
	Televisions	163
	Personal computers	62.8

Women in Government and the Economy

Women in the national legislature

Lower house or single house (%)	4.1
Women at ministerial level (%)	9.4

Female economic activity rate (age 15 and above) (%)	29
Female labor force (% of total)	27

Estimated earned income (PPP US$)	Female	2,524
	Male	9,088

2002 Human Development Index Ranking (out of 173 countries)	98

Political Organization

Political System Theocracy (rule of the clergy) headed by a cleric with the title of Supreme Leader. The clergy rule by divine right.

Regime History Islamic Republic since the 1979 Islamic Revolution.

Administrative Structure Centralized administration with 28 provinces. The Interior Minister appoints the provincial governor-generals.

Executive President and his cabinet. The president is elected by the general electorate every four years. The president chooses his cabinet ministers, but they need to obtain the approval of the *Majles* (parliament).

Legislature Unicameral. The *Majles,* formed of 270 seats, is elected every four years. It has multiple member districts with the top runners in the elections taking the seats. Bills passed by the *Majles* do not become law unless they have the approval of the clerically dominated Council of Guardians.

Judiciary A Chief Judge and a Supreme Court independent of the exective and legislature but appointed by the Supreme Leader.

Party System The ruling clergy restrict all party and organizational activities.

Section ❶ The Making of the Modern Iranian State

Politics in Action

Iran shook the world, not to mention its own establishment, first in 1997 by electing Muhammad Khatami, a relatively unknown liberal cleric, as president of the Islamic Republic in a landslide victory, and then again in 2001 by reelecting him with even a larger majority. Khatami, a former director of the National Library, was a mild-mannered middle-ranking cleric, a hojjat al-Islam ("Proof of Islam"), not a high-ranking **ayatollah** or grand ayatollah ("Sign of God"). In the elections, he vigorously campaigned on the theme of creating "civil society" and improving the "sick economy." He stressed the importance of an open society that would protect individual liberties, freedom of expression, women's rights, political pluralism, and, most essential, the rule of law. He even authored books applauding Western thinkers such as Locke, Voltaire, and Rousseau. It was as if he were transferring principles found in political science textbooks into practical politics. His electoral campaigns also stressed the need for a "dialogue between civilizations." This was a far cry from the early days of the 1979 Iranian Revolution, when its leader, Grand Ayatollah Ruhollah Khomeini, had denounced the United States as the "Great Satan" and incited students to seize the U.S. embassy. This takeover and "hostage crisis" lasted 444 days and prompted a break in U.S.-Iranian diplomatic relations that lasts to this day.

Khatami's initial electoral success was especially surprising since much of the religious establishment had openly endorsed his conservative rival. Most commentators, both inside and outside the country, had considered the election a shoo-in for the conservative candidate. After all, he had been endorsed by an impressive array of establishment newspapers, radio stations, television programs, state institutions, quasi-state foundations, clerical organizations, and local mosques (Muslim houses of worship). They had warned that any opening up of the system could endanger the whole regime and that Khatami could become another Mikhail Gorbachev, the reformist leader who had inadvertently presided over the demise of the Soviet Union. Even the Supreme Leader of the Islamic Republic, Ayatollah Ali Khamenei, had implicitly endorsed the conservative

candidate. In the upset election, Khatami took 70 percent of the vote in a campaign that attracted 80 percent of the electorate. Much of Khatami's vote came from women, university students, and young adults throughout the country—even from those serving in the armed forces. He followed up his victory by trying to liberalize the press, establishing political parties, and initiating a "dialogue" with the United States. He even bolstered the case for liberalization by citing *Democracy in America,* the famous book by nineteenth-century French writer Alexis de Tocqueville. Khatami also assured the West that Iran had no intention of implementing the *fatwa* (religious decree) that Ayatollah Khomeini had placed on Salman Rushdie, the Muslim-born British writer. Khomeini had condemned Rushdie to death on the grounds that his book, *Satanic Verses,* blasphemed Islam and thus proved that its author was an apostate from Islam, which is a capital offense according to a narrow interpretation of Islamic law. The 2001 presidential elections further strengthened Khatami's mandate: he took 77 percent of the vote and increased his overall support by over 1 million.

These two presidential elections vividly illustrated the main dilemmas confronting the Islamic Republic that had been established by Ayatollah Khomeini in the aftermath of the 1979 revolution. The Islamic Republic of Iran today is a mixture of **theocracy** and democracy: it is a political system based on clerical authority as well as popular sovereignty, on the divine right of the clergy as well as the rights of the people, on concepts derived from early Islam as well as from modern democratic principles such as the separation of powers. The country has regular elections for the presidency and the *Majles* (Parliament), but a clerically dominated **Guardian Council** determines who can and cannot run in these elections. The president is the formal head of the executive branch of government, but he can be overruled, even dismissed, by the chief cleric known as the **Supreme Leader.** The president appoints the minister of justice, but the whole judiciary is under the supervision of the chief judge, who is appointed directly by the Supreme Leader. The *Majles* is the legislative branch of government, but its bills do not become law unless the Guardian Council deems them compatible with Islam and the Islamic constitution. In short, contemporary Iranian politics resonates with both *vox dei* (the voice of God) and *vox populi* (the voice of the people).

Geographic Setting

Iran—three times the size of France, slightly larger than Alaska, and much larger than its immediate neighbors—is notable for two geographic features. The first is that much of its territory is inhospitable to agriculture. A vast arid zone known as the Great Salt Desert covers much of the central plateau from the capital city, Tehran, to the borders with Afghanistan and Pakistan. A mountain range known as the Zagros takes up the western third of the country. Another range, the Elborz, stretches across the north. Rain-fed agriculture is confined mostly to the northwest and the provinces along the Caspian Sea. In the rest of the country, population settlements are located mostly on oases, on the few rare rivers, and on constructed irrigation networks. Only pastoral nomads can survive in the semiarid zones and in the high mountain valleys. Thus, 67 percent of the total population of 65 million is concentrated on 27 percent of the land—mostly in the Caspian provinces, in the northwest, and in the cities of Tehran, Qom, Isfahan, Shiraz, and Ahwaz. In the past, the inhospitable environment was a major obstacle to economic development. In recent decades, this obstacle has been partly alleviated by oil revenues. Iran is the second largest oil

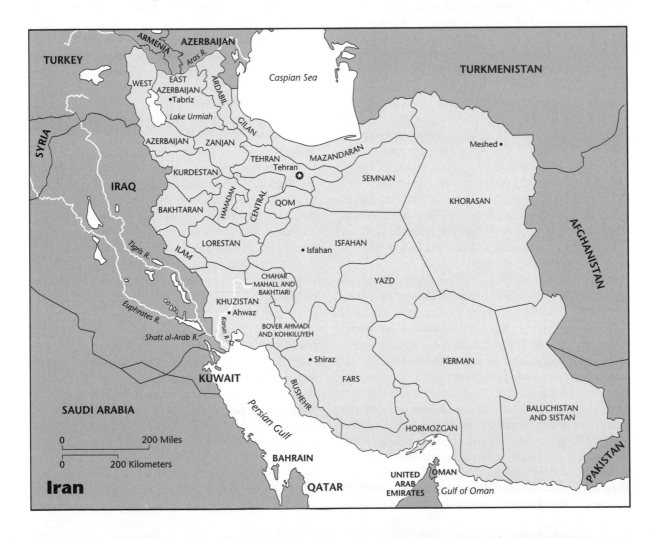

producer in the Middle East and the fourth largest in the world. Its oil wells help fuel many industrial economies. These oil revenues account for the fact that Iran is now urbanized and partly industrialized and can be described as a developing rather than a stagnant society. Nearly 63 percent of the population lives in urban centers; 68 percent of the labor force is employed in industry and services; 67 percent of adults are literate; life expectancy has reached sixty-nine years; and the majority of Iranians enjoy a standard of living well above that found in most of Asia and Africa.

Iran's second notable geographic feature is that it lies on the crossroads between Central Asia and Asia Minor, between the Indian subcontinent and the Middle East, between the Arabian Peninsula and the Caucasus Mountains. This has made the region vulnerable to invaders: Indo-Europeans in the distant past (they gave the country the name of Iran, Land of the Aryans), Islamic Arab tribes in the seventh century, and a series of Turkic incursions in the Middle Ages. The population today reflects these historic invasions. Some 51 percent of the country speaks Persian **(Farsi),** an Indo-European language, as their first language; 26 percent speak various dialects of Turkic, mainly Azeri and Turkmen; 8 percent speak Gilaki or Mazandarani, distant Persian dialects; 7 percent speak Kurdish, another Indo-European language; and 3 percent speak Arabic. Although since the Middle Ages, Europeans have referred to the country as Persia, Iranians have traditionally called their country Iran and their main language Farsi, after the central province (Fars) where the language originated. In 1935, Iran formally asked the international community to cease calling the country Persia.

Critical Junctures

Although modern Iran traces its roots to the ancient Iranian empire of sixth century B.C. and its Islamic religion to the Arab invasions of the seventh century, its current national identity, geographic boundaries, particular interpretation of Islam—**Shi'ism**—and political system were formed by four more recent critical junctures: the Safavid (1501–1722), Qajar (1794–1925), and Pahlavi (1925–1979) dynasties and the Islamic Revolution of 1979, which led to establishment of the current Islamic Republic.

Critical Junctions in Modern Iran's Political Development

1921	Colonel Reza Khan's military coup
1925	Establishment of the Pahlavi dynasty
1941–1945	Allied occupation of Iran
1951	Nationalization of the oil industry
1953	Coup against Mosaddeq
1963	White Revolution
1975	Establishment of the Resurgence Party
1979	Islamic Revolution
1979–1981	U.S. hostage crisis
December 1979	Referendum on the constitution
January 1980	Bani-Sadr elected president
March 1980	Elections for the First Islamic *Majles*
1980–1988	War with Iraq
June 1981	President Bani-Sadr ousted
October 1981	Khamenei elected president
1984	Elections for the Second Islamic *Majles*
1988	Elections for the Third Islamic *Majles*
1989	Khomeini dies; Khamenei appointed Supreme Leader; Rafsanjani elected president
1992	Elections for the Fourth Islamic *Majles*
1996	Elections for the Fifth Islamic *Majles*
1997	Khatami elected president on reform platform
2000	Reformers win elections for the Sixth Islamic *Majles*
2000	Khatami reelected president with a huge majority

The Safavids (1501–1722)

Modern Iran, with its Shi'i Islamic identity and its present-day boundaries, can be traced to the sixteenth century, when the Safavid family conquered the territory with the help of fellow Turkic-speaking tribes and established their dynasty. They revived the ancient Iranian titles of shah-in-shah (King of Kings) and Shadow of God on Earth, and proceeded to convert their subjects to Shi'ism forcibly. Although small Shi'i communities had existed in this area since the beginning of Islam, the vast majority had adhered to the majority Sunni branch (see "Background: Islam and Shi'ism"). The Safavid motivation for this drastic conversion was to give their state and population a distinct identity separate from the surrounding Sunni powers: the Ottomans in the west, the Uzbeks in the north, and the Afghans in the east.

By the mid-seventeenth century, the Safavids had succeeded in converting nearly 90 percent of their subjects to Shi'ism. Sunnism survived among the peripheral tribal groups: Kurds in the northwest, Turkmens in the northeast, Baluchis in the southeast, and Arabs in the southwest. It should be noted that the Safavids, despite their conquests, failed to capture from the Ottomans the two most holy Shi'i places located in modern Iraq: Karbala, the site of the martyrdom in 680 B.C.

of Imam Husayn, one of the most important figures in the history of Shi'ism, and Najaf, the main theological center.

In addition to the Sunni minority, Safavid Iran contained small communities of Jews, Zoroastrians, and Christians (Armenians and Assyrians). These small minorities lived mostly in Isfahan, Shiraz, Kerman, Yazd, and Azerbaijan. Jews had lived in Iran since ancient times, predating the great diaspora prompted by the Roman destruction of Jerusalem. Zoroastrians were descendants of those who retained their old religion after the Arab invasions. The Christians had lived in the northwest long before the advent of Islam. To strengthen their foothold in central Iran, the Safavids transported there some 100,000 Armenians, encouraging them to

Background: Islam and Shi'ism

Islam, with some 1 billion adherents, is the second largest religion in the world. Islam means literally "submission to God," and a Muslim is someone who has submitted to God—the same God that Jews and Christians worship. Islam has one central tenet: "There is only one God, and Muhammad is His Prophet." Muslims, in order to consider themselves faithful, need to perform the following four duties to the best of their ability: give to charity; pray every day facing Mecca, where Abraham is believed to have built the first place of worship; make a pilgrimage at least once in a lifetime to Mecca, which is located in modern Saudi Arabia; and fast during the daytime hours in the month of Ramadan to commemorate God's revelation of the Qur'an (Koran, or Holy Book) to the Prophet Muhammad. These four, together with the central tenet, are known in the West as the Five Pillars of Islam.

From its earliest days, Islam has been divided into two major branches: the Sunnis and the Shi'is. The Sunnis, meaning literally "followers of tradition," are by far in the majority worldwide. The Shi'is, literally "partisans of Ali," constitute less than 10 percent of Muslims worldwide and are concentrated in Iran, southern Iraq, Azerbaijan, and southern Lebanon. Although both branches accept the Five Pillars, they differ mostly over who should have succeeded the Prophet Muhammad (d. 632). The Sunnis recognized the early dynasties that ruled the Islamic empire with the exalted title of caliph ("Prophet's Deputy"). The Shi'is, however, argued that as soon as the Prophet died, his authority should have been passed on to Imam Ali, the Prophet's close companion, disciple, and son-in-law. They further argue that Imam Ali passed his authority to his direct male heirs, the third of whom, Imam Husayn, had been martyred fighting the Sunnis in 680, and the twelfth of whom had supposedly gone into hiding in 941. The Shi'is are also know as Twelvers since they follow the Twelve Imams. They refer to the Twelfth Imam as the *Mahdi*, the Hidden Imam, and believe him to be the Messiah who will herald the end of the world. Furthermore, they argue that in his absence, the authority to interpret the *shari'a* (religious law) should be in the hands of the senior clerical scholars—the ayatollahs. Thus, from the beginning, the Shi'is harbored ambivalent attitudes toward the state, especially if the rulers were Sunnis or lacked genealogical links to the Twelve Imams. For Sunnis, the *shari'a* is based mostly on the Qur'an and the teachings of the Prophet. For Shi'is, it is also based on the teachings of the Twelve Imams.

become craftsmen and merchants, especially in the lucrative silk trade. The Safavids, like most other Muslim rulers but unlike medieval Christian kings, tolerated religious minorities as long as they paid special taxes and accepted royal authority. According to Islam, Christians, Jews, and Zoroastrians were to be tolerated as legitimate **People of the Book.** They were respected both because they were mentioned in the Holy **Qur'an** and because they had their own sacred texts: the Bible, the Torah, and the Avesta.

The Safavids established their capital in Isfahan, a Persian-speaking city, and recruited Persian scribes into their court administration. Such families had helped administer the ancient Iranian empires. They proceeded to govern not only through these Persian scribes and Shi'i clerics but also through local magnates: tribal chiefs, large landowners, religious notables, city merchants, guild elders, and urban ward leaders.

The Safavid army was formed mostly of tribal cavalry led by local chieftains. Financial constraints prevented the Safavids from creating a large bureaucracy or an extended standing army. Their revenues came mostly from land taxes levied on the peasantry. In theory, the Safavids claimed absolute power; Europeans labeled them Oriental despots. In reality, their power was limited, since they lacked a central state and had no choice but to seek the cooperation of many semi-independent local leaders. The central government was linked to the general population not so much through coercive institutions as through provincial and hereditary notables. It survived for the most part because the society below was sharply fragmented by geographic barriers (especially mountains) and by regional, tribal, communal, and ethnic differences. Moreover, some of the senior clerics resided in Najaf, safely out of royal reach. The monarch did not control society. Rather, he hovered over it, systematically orchestrating its many existing rivalries.

The Qajars (1794–1925)

The Safavid dynasty collapsed in 1722 when Afghan tribesmen invaded the capital. The invasion was followed by a half-century of civil war until the Qajars, another Turkic tribe, reconquered much of Iran. The Qajars moved the capital to Tehran and recreated the Safavid system of central manipulation and court administration, including the Persian scribes. They also declared Shi'ism to be the state religion even though they, unlike the Safavids, did not boast of genealogical links to the Twelve Imams. This was to have far-reaching repercussions. Since these new shahs did not pretend to wear the imam's mantle, the Shi'i clerical leaders could claim to be the main interpreters of Islam. In addition, many of them safeguarded their independence from the state by continuing to reside in Iraq and collecting religious contributions directly from the faithful in Iran. These contributions came mainly from wealthy merchants.

Qajar rule coincided with the peak of European imperialism. The Russians seized parts of Central Asia and the Caucasus from Iran and extracted a series of major economic concessions, including a monopoly to fish for sturgeon in the Caspian Sea and exemption from import duties, internal tariffs, and the jurisdiction of local courts. The British Imperial Bank won the monopoly to issue paper money. The Indo-European Telegraph Company got a contract to extend communication lines through the country. Exclusive rights to drill for oil in the southwest were sold to a British citizen. The later Qajars also borrowed heavily from European banks to meet lavish court expenses. By the end of the century, these loans had become so heavy that the Qajars were obliged to guarantee repayments by placing the country's entire customs service under European supervision. Iranians felt that their whole country had been auctioned off and that the shah had given away far too many concessions, or capitulations, as they called them.

These resentments culminated in the constitutional revolution of 1905–1909. The revolution began with shopkeepers and moneylenders demonstrating against the handing over of customs collections to Europeans. They suspected that the shah would renege on local debts in favor of repaying his foreign loans. They also protested that the government was not doing enough to protect native merchants and local industries. The protests intensified when the government, faced with soaring sugar prices due to political turmoil in Russia, publicly whipped two major sugar merchants.

The revolutionary movement peaked in 1906, when some 14,000 protesters took sanctuary inside the gardens of the British legation in Tehran and demanded a written constitution. After weeks of haggling, the shah conceded because the British diplomats advised compromise and because the unpaid Cossack Brigade, the regime's sole standing army, threatened to join the protesters. Led by Russians and named after the tsar's praetorian guards, the Cossack Brigade was the only force in Iran resembling a disciplined army. A British diplomat commented, "The shah with his unarmed, unpaid, ragged, starving soldiers, what can he do in face of the menace of a general strike and riots?"[1]

The 1906 constitution, modeled after the Belgian one, introduced essential features of modern government into Iran: elections, separation of powers, laws made by a legislative assembly, and the concepts of popular sovereignty and the nation (*mellat*). It also generated a heated debate, with some arguing that democracy was inherently incompatible with Islam and others countering that true Islam could not be practiced unless the government was based on popular support. Some even argued in favor of secularism—complete separation of religion from politics, church from state, clergy from government authority, the affairs of the next world from those of this world.

While retaining the monarchy, the new constitution centered political power in a national assembly called the *Majles*. It hailed this assembly as "the representative of the whole people" and guaranteed seats to the recognized religious minorities: Jews, Zoroastrians, and Christians. Significantly, no seats were given to the Baha'is, a nineteenth-century offshoot of Shi'ism. The clerical leaders deemed the Baha'is to be apostates from Islam and Baha'i to be a "sinister heresy linked to the imperial powers."

The constitution endowed the *Majles* with extensive authority over all laws, budgets, treaties, loans, concessions, and the composition of the cabinet. The ministers were accountable to the *Majles,* not to the shah. "Sovereignty," declared the constitution, "is a trust confided (as a divine gift) by the people to the person of the shah." The constitution also included a bill of rights guaranteeing citizens equality before the law, protection of life and property, safeguards from arbitrary arrest, and freedom of expression and association.

Although the constitution was modeled on the European liberal secular system of government, it made some concessions to Shi'ism. Shi'ism was declared Iran's official religion. Only Shi'is could hold cabinet posts. Clerical courts retained the right to implement the *shari'a* (religious law), especially in family matters. A Guardian Council formed of senior clerics elected by the *Majles* was given veto power over parliamentary bills deemed not to be Islamic. In short, popular sovereignty was to be restricted by a clerical veto power. In actual fact, this Guardian Council was not convened until the 1979 Islamic Revolution. Divisions within the clerical establishment as well as opposition from parliament forestalled implementation of the Guardian Council.

The initial euphoria that greeted the constitutional revolution gave way to deep disillusionment in the subsequent decade. Pressures from the European powers continued, and a devastating famine after World War I took some 1 million lives, almost 10 percent of the total population. Internal conflicts polarized the *Majles* into warring liberal and conservative factions. The former, mostly members of the intelligentsia, championed social reforms, especially the replacement of the *shari'a* with a modern law code. The latter, led by landlords, tribal chiefs, and senior clerics, vehemently opposed such reforms, particularly land reform, women's rights, and the granting of full equality to religious minorities.

Meanwhile, the central government, lacking any real army, bureaucracy, or tax-collecting machinery, was unable to administer the provinces, especially the regions inhabited by the Kurds, Turkmens, and Baluchis. Some tribes, equipped with modern breech-loading European rifles, had more firepower than the central government. Moreover, during World War I, Russia and Britain formally carved up Iran into three zones. Russia occupied the north and Britain the south. Iran was left with a small "neutral zone" in the middle.

By 1921, Iran was in complete disarray. The shah was gathering his crown jewels to flee south. The British, in their own words, were hoping to "salvage" some "healthy limbs" in their southern zone. Left-wing rebels, helped by the new communist regime in Russia, had taken over Gilan province and were threatening nearby Azerbaijan, Mazandaran, and Khorasan. According to a British diplomat, the propertied classes, fearful of communism, were anxiously seeking "a savior on horseback."[2]

The Pahlavis (1925–1979)

That savior appeared in February 1921 in the person of Colonel Reza Khan, the recently appointed commander of the 3,000-man Cossack Brigade. Carrying out a typical military coup d'état, he replaced the cabinet and, while paying lip service to the monarch, consolidated power in his own hands, especially the post of commander in chief of the armed forces. Four years later, he emerged from behind the throne, deposed the Qajars, crowned himself shah-in-shah in the style of his hero, the French emperor Napoleon, and established his own Pahlavi dynasty, adopting a name associated with the glories of ancient Iran. This was the first nontribal dynasty to rule the whole of Iran. To forestall opposition from Britain and the Soviet Union, he assured both countries that Iran would remain strictly nonaligned. A compliant *Majles* endorsed this transfer of power from the Qajars to the Pahlavis.

Reza Shah ruled with an iron fist until 1941, when the British and the Soviets invaded Iran to forestall Nazi Germany from establishing a foothold there. Reza Shah promptly abdicated in favor of his son, Muhammad Reza Shah, and went into exile, where he soon died. In the first twelve years of his reign, the young shah retained control over the armed forces but had to live with a free press, an independent judiciary, competitive elections, assertive cabinet ministers, and boisterous parliaments. He also had to confront two vigorous political movements: the communist Tudeh (Masses) Party and the National Front, led by the charismatic Dr. Muhammad Mosaddeq (1882–1967).

The Tudeh drew its support mostly from working-class trade unions. The National Front drew its support mainly from the salaried middle classes and campaigned to nationalize the British-owned company that had a monopoly over the drilling, refining, and sale of all petroleum in Iran. Mosaddeq also wanted to sever the shah's links with the armed forces. He argued that according to the constitution, the monarch should reign, not rule, and that the armed forces should be supervised by cabinet ministers responsible to parliament. In 1951, Mosaddeq was elected prime minister and promptly nationalized the oil industry. The period of relative freedom, however, ended abruptly in 1953, when royalist officers overthrew Mosaddeq and in-

stalled the shah with absolute power. Since this 1953 coup was financed by the U.S. Central Intelligence Agency (CIA) and the British, it intensified anti-British sentiment and created a deep distrust of the United States. It also made the shah appear to be a puppet of the foreign powers. Muhammad Reza Shah ruled much in the style of his autocratic father until he was overthrown by the 1979 Islamic Revolution.

During their fifty-four-year rule, the Pahlavis built a highly centralized state, the first in Iran's history. This state rested on three pillars: the armed forces, the bureaucracy, and the royal patronage system. The armed forces grew from fewer than 40,000 men in 1925 to 124,000 in 1941 and to over 410,000 in 1979. In 1925, the armed forces had been formed of a motley crew of cossacks, city policeman, and gendarmes (rural policemen). By the mid-1930s, they had the power to disarm the tribes and impose the will of the state on the provinces. By 1979, they constituted the fifth largest army in the world, the largest navy in the Persian Gulf, the largest air force in western Asia, and one of the best-equipped tank brigades in the Third World. They were supplemented with a pervasive secret police known as SAVAK—the Persian acronym for the Organization to Protect and Gather Information for the State.

The bureaucracy expanded from a haphazard collection of hereditary scribes, some without fixed offices, to twenty-one ministries employing over 300,000 civil servants in 1979. The powerful Interior Ministry appointed the provincial governors, town mayors, district superintendents, and village headmen. Since it also appointed electoral supervisors, it could rig *Majles* elections and provide the shah with rubber-stamp parliaments. Thus, the 1905–1909 constitutional laws survived only on paper. The Education Ministry grew twentyfold, administering 26,000 primary schools with some 4 million children and 1,850 secondary schools with 740,000 pupils. Meanwhile, the Ministry of Higher Education supervised 750 vocational schools with 227,000 students and thirteen universities with 154,000 students.

The Justice Ministry supplanted the *shari'a* with a European-style civil code and the clerical courts with a modern judicial system. This included district courts, provincial courts, and a Supreme Court. To practice in these courts, lawyers and judges had to pass government-administered exams based on European jurisprudence. The system was further secularized in the 1960s, when the shah decreed a controversial Family Protection Law. This contradicted the traditional interpretation of the *shar'ia* on a number of points. It raised the marriage age to twenty for men and eighteen for women. It allowed women to override spousal objections and work outside the home if they got court permission. It restricted polygamy by stipulating that husbands could marry more than one wife only if they first obtained permission from previous wives and the courts. For some, the state had extended its arm to reach into the most intimate area of existence: family life.

Other ministries experienced similar expansion. For example, the Transport Ministry built an impressive array of bridges, ports, highways, and railroads known as the Trans-Iranian Railway. The Ministry of Industries financed the construction of numerous factories specializing in consumer goods. The Agricultural Ministry attained prominence in 1962 when the shah made land reform the centerpiece of his much-heralded "White Revolution," which was designed partly to forestall the possibility of a communist-led "red revolution." The government bought land from large absentee owners and sold it to small farmers through low-interest, long-term mortgages. It also undertook the task of transforming small farmers into modern commercial entrepreneurs by providing them with fertilizers, cooperatives, distribution centers, irrigation canals, dams, and tractor repair shops. The White Revolution included the extension of the vote to women, the Family Protection Law, and a Literacy Corps to eradicate illiteracy in the countryside. Thus, by 1979, the state had set up a modern system of communications, initiated a minor industrial revolution, and extended its reach into even the most outlying villages.

The state also controlled a number of major institutions: the National and the Central Banks; the Industrial and Mining Development Bank, which channeled money to private entrepreneurs; the Plan Organization in charge of economic policy; the national radio-television network, which monopolized the airwaves (by the 1960s, most villages had access to transistor radios); and most important, the National Iranian Oil Company, which grew from a leasing firm in the 1950s to become a large exploring, drilling, refining, and exporting corporation.

The Pahlavi state was further bolstered by court patronage. Reza Shah, the son of a small landowner, used coercion, confiscations, and diversion of irrigation water to make himself one of the largest landowners in the Middle East. In the words of a British diplomat, Reza Shah had an "unholy interest in property," especially other people's property.[3] This wealth transformed the shah's court into a large military-landed complex, providing work for thousands employed in its numerous palaces, hotels, casinos, charities, companies, and beach resorts. This patronage system grew under Muhammad Reza Shah, particularly after he established his tax-exempt Pahlavi Foundation. By the 1970s, the Pahlavi Foundation controlled 207 large companies active in tourism, insurance, banking, agribusiness, mining, construction, and manufacturing.

Although the Pahlavi state looked impressive, it lacked solid foundations. The drive for secularization, centralization, industrialization, and social development won some favor from the urban propertied classes. But arbitrary rule, the 1953 coup, the disregard for constitutional liberties, and the stifling of independent newspapers, political parties, and professional associations produced widespread resentment, particularly among the clergy, the intelligentsia, and the urban masses. In short, this state was strong in the sense that it controlled the modern instruments of coercion and administration. But its roots were very shallow because of its failure to link the new state institutions to the country's social structure. The Pahlavi state, like the Safavids and the Qajars, hovered over, rather than embedded itself into, the society. Furthermore, much of the civil society that had existed in traditional Iran had now been suffocated by the modern state.

As if the Pahlavi state did not have enough social control, the shah in 1975 announced the formation of the Resurgence Party. He declared Iran to be a one-party state and threatened imprisonment and exile to those refusing to join the party. In heralding the new order, the shah replaced the traditional Islamic calendar with a new royalist one, jumping from the Muslim year 1355 to the royalist year 2535; 2,500 years were allocated to the monarchy in general and 35 years for the shah's own reign. The King of Kings and the Shadow of God also accrued two new titles: Guide to the New Great Civilization and Light of the Aryans (Aryamehr).

The Resurgence Party was designed to create yet another organizational link with the population, especially with the **bazaars** (traditional marketplaces), which, unlike the rest of society, had managed to retain their guilds and thus escape direct government control. The Resurgence Party promptly established bazaar guilds as well as newspapers, women's organizations, professional associations, and labor unions. It also prepared to create a Religious Corps, modeled on the Literacy Corps, to go into the countryside to teach the peasants "true Islam." The state was venturing into areas where previous rulers had feared to tread.

The Resurgence Party promised to establish an "organic relationship between rulers and ruled," "synthesize the best of capitalism and socialism," and chart the way toward the New Great Civilization. It also praised the shah for curbing the "medieval clergy," eradicating "class warfare," and becoming a "spiritual guide" as well as a world-renowned statesman. For his part, the shah told an English-language newspaper that the party's philosophy was "based on the dialectical principles of the White Revolution" and that nowhere else in the world was there such a close relationship between a ruler and his people. "No other nation has given its commander such a carte-blanche [blank check]."[4] The terminology, as well as the boast, revealed much about the shah at the height of his power—or, as some suspected, his megalomania.

The Islamic Revolution (1979)

On the eve of the 1979 Islamic Revolution that overthrew the shah, an exiled Iranian newspaper denounced the Pahlavis in an issue entitled "Fifty Indictments of Treason During Fifty Years of Treason."[5] It charged the shah and his family with establishing a military dictatorship; collaborating with the CIA; trampling on the constitution; creating SAVAK; rigging parliamentary elections; organizing a fascistic one-party state; taking over the religious establishment; and undermining national identity by disseminating Western culture. It also accused the regime of inducing millions of landless peasants to migrate into urban shantytowns; widening the gap between rich and poor; funneling money away from the small bourgeoisie into the pockets

of the wealthy comprador bourgeoisie (the entrepreneurs linked to foreign companies and multinational corporations); wasting resources on bloated military budgets; and granting new capitulations to the West—the most controversial being the extension of diplomatic immunity to U.S. military advisers in Iran.

These grievances were given greater articulation when a leading anti-shah cleric, Ayatollah Ruhollah Khomeini—from his exile in Iraq—began to formulate a new version of Shi'ism (see "Leaders: Ayatollah Ruhollah Khomeini"). His version has often been labeled Islamic **fundamentalism;** it would better be described as Shi'i populism or political Islam. The term *fundamentalism,* derived from American Protestantism, implies religious dogmatism, intellectual inflexibility and purity, political traditionalism, social conservatism, rejection of the modern world, and the literal interpretation of scriptural texts. Khomeini, however, was less concerned about literal interpretations of the Qur'an than about articulating resentments against the elite and the United States. He was more of a political revolutionary than a social conservative.

Khomeini denounced monarchies in general and the Pahlavis in particular as part and parcel of the corrupt elite exploiting the oppressed masses. For him, the oppressors consisted of courtiers, large landowners, high-ranking military officers, wealthy foreign-connected capitalists, and millionaire palace dwellers. The oppressed consisted of the masses, especially landless peasants, wage earners, bazaar shopkeepers, and shantytown dwellers. His proclamations often cited the Qur'anic term *mostazafin* (dispossessed) and the biblical promise that "the poor (meek) shall inherit the earth."

In calling for the overthrow of the Pahlavi monarchy, Khomeini injected a radically new meaning into the old Shi'i term *velayat-e faqih* (**jurist's guardianship**). He argued that jurist's guardianship gave the senior clergy—namely, the grand ayatollahs such as himself—all-encompassing authority over the whole community, not just over widows, minors, and the mentally disabled, as had been the interpretation previously. He insisted that only the senior clerics had the sole competence to understand the *shari'a;* that the divine authority given to the Prophet and the imams had been passed on to their spiritual heirs, the clergy; and that throughout history, the clergy had championed the rights of the people against bad government and

Leaders: *Ayatollah Ruhollah Khomeini*

Ruhollah Khomeini was born in 1902 into a landed clerical family well known in central Iran. During the 1920s, he studied in the famous Fayzieh Seminary in Qom with the leading theologians of the day, most of whom were scrupulously apolitical. He taught at the seminary from the 1930s through the 1950s, avoiding politics even during the mass campaign to nationalize the British-owned oil company. His entry into politics did not come until 1962, when he, along with most other clerical leaders, denounced Muhammad Reza Shah's White Revolution. Forced into exile, Khomeini taught at the Shi'i center of Najaf in Iraq from 1964 until 1978. During these years, he developed his own version of Shi'i populism by incorporating socioeconomic grievances into his sermons and denouncing not just the shah but the whole ruling class. Returning home triumphant in the midst of the Iranian Revolution, he was declared the Supreme Leader, the Founder of the Islamic Republic, the Guide for the Oppressed Masses, and imam of the Muslim community. In the past, Iranian Shi'is, unlike the Arab Sunnis, had reserved the special term *imam* only for Imam Ali and his twelve direct heirs, whom they deemed to be semidivine and thereby infallible. For many Iranians in 1979, Khomeini was charismatic in the true sense of the word: a man with a special gift from God. Khomeini ruled as Imam and Supreme Leader of the Islamic Republic until his death in 1989.

foreign powers. He further insisted that the clergy were the people's true representatives, since they lived among them, listened to their problems, and shared their everyday joys and pains. He claimed that the shah secretly planned to confiscate all religious endowments and replace Islamic values with "cultural imperialism." These pronouncements added fuel to an already explosive situation.

By 1977, Iran needed a few sparks to ignite the revolution. These sparks came in the form of minor economic difficulties and international pressures to curb human rights violations. In 1977–1978, the shah tried to deal with a 20 percent rise in consumer prices and a 10 percent decline in oil revenues by cutting construction projects and declaring war against "profiteers," "hoarders," and "price gougers." Not surprisingly, shopkeepers felt that the shah was diverting attention from court corruption and planning to replace them with government-run department stores and that he was intending to destroy the bazaar, which some felt was the "the real pillar of Iranian society."

The pressure for human rights came from Amnesty International, the United Nations, and the Western press, as well as from the recently elected Carter administration in the United States. In 1977, after meeting with the International Commission of Jurists, the shah permitted Red Cross officials to visit prisons and allowed defense attorneys to attend political trials. In the words of Khomeini's first postrevolution prime minister, Mehdi Bazargan, this international pressure had allowed the opposition to breathe again after decades of suffocation.[6]

This slight loosening of the reins, coming in the midst of the economic recession, sealed the fate of the shah. Political parties, labor organizations, and professional associations—especially lawyers, writers, and university professors—regrouped after years of being banned. Bazaar guilds regained their independence from the government party. College, high school, and seminary students, especially in the religious center of Qom, took to the streets to protest the quarter-century of repression. On September 8, 1978, known as Bloody Friday, troops in Tehran fired into a crowded square, killing hundreds of unarmed demonstrators. By late 1978, a general strike brought the whole economy to a halt, paralyzing not only the oil industry, the factories, the banks, and the transport system but also the civil service, the media, the bazaars, and the whole educational establishment. The oil workers vowed that they would not export any petroleum until they had exported the "shah and his forty thieves."[7]

Meanwhile, in the urban centers, local committees attached to the **mosques** and financed by the bazaars were distributing food to the needy, supplanting the police with militias known as *pasdaran* (Revolutionary Guards), and replacing the judicial system with ad hoc courts applying the *shari'a*. Equally significant, antiregime rallies were now attracting as many as 2 million protesters. The largest rally was held in Tehran in December 1978 on the day commemorating the martyrdom of Imam Husayn in the seventh century. Protesters demanded the abolition of the monarchy, the return of Khomeini, and the establishment of a republic to preserve national independence and provide the masses with social justice in the form of decent wages, land, and a proper standard of living.

Although these rallies were led by pro-Khomeini clerics, they drew support from a broad variety of organizations: the National Front; the Lawyer's, Doctor's, and Women's associations; the communist Tudeh Party; the Fedayin, a Marxist guerrilla group; and the Mojahedin, a Muslim guerrilla group formed of nonclerical intellectuals. The rallies also attracted students, from both high schools and colleges, as well as shopkeepers and craftsmen from the bazaars. A secret Revolutionary Committee in Tehran coordinated protests throughout the country, kept in telephone contact with Khomeini in exile in Paris, and circulated his tapes within Iran. This was a revolution made in the streets and propelled forward by audiotapes. It was also one of the first revolutions to be televised worldwide.

After a series of such mass rallies in late 1978, the *Washington Post* concluded that "disciplined and well-organized marches lent considerable weight to the opposition's claim of being an alternative government."[8] Similarly, the *Christian Science Monitor* stated that the "giant wave of humanity sweeping through the capital declared louder than any bullet or bomb could the clear message, 'The shah must go.'"[9] Confronted by this opposition and aware that increasing numbers of soldiers were deserting to the opposition, the shah decided to leave Iran. A year later, when he was in exile and dying of cancer, there was much speculation, especially in the United States, that he might have mastered the upheavals if he had been healthier, possessed a stronger personality, and received full support from the United States. But even a healthy man with an iron will and full foreign backing would not have been able to deal with 2 million demonstrators, massive general strikes, and debilitating defections from his own army rank and file.

On February 11, 1979—three weeks after the shah's departure from Iran and ten days after Khomeini's return—armed groups, especially Fedayin and Mojahedin guerrillas, supported by air force cadets, broke into the main army barracks in Tehran, distributed arms, and then assaulted the main police stations, the jails, and eventually the national radio-television station. That same evening, the radio station made the historic announcement: "This is the voice of Iran, the voice of true Iran, the voice of the Islamic Revolution." A few hours of street fighting had completed the destruction of the fifty-four-year-old dynasty that claimed a 2,500-year-old heritage.

The Islamic Republic (1979 to the Present)

Seven weeks after the February revolution, a nationwide referendum replaced the monarchy with an Islamic Republic. Of the 21 million eligible voters, over 20 million—97 percent—endorsed the change. Liberal and lay supporters of Khomeini, including Mehdi Bazargan, his first prime minister, had hoped to offer the electorate a third choice: that of a democratic Islamic Republic. But Khomeini overruled them on the grounds that the term *democratic* was redundant because Islam itself was democratic. The structure of this new republic was to be determined later. Khomeini was now hailed as the Leader of the Revolution, Founder of the Islamic Republic, Guide of the Oppressed Masses, Commander of the Armed Forces, and most potent of all, Imam of the Muslim World, since in Shi'ism, the term **imam** implies "infallible authority."

The constitution itself was drawn up in late 1979 by a constituent body named the Assembly of Religious Experts (*Majles-e Khebregan*). Although this seventy-three-man assembly was elected by the general public, almost all secular organizations as well as clerics opposed to Khomeini boycotted the elections on the grounds that the state media were controlled, independent papers had been banned, and voters were being intimidated by club-wielding vigilantes known as the **Hezbollahis** ("Partisans of God"). The vast majority of those elected, including forty **hojjat al-Islams** and fifteen ayatollahs, were pro-Khomeini clerics. They proceeded to draft a highly theocratic constitution vesting much authority in the hands of Khomeini in particular and the clergy in general—all this over the

The Shah's statue on the ground, February 1979.
Source: © Abbas/ Magnum Photos.

strong objections of Prime Minister Bazargan, who wanted a French-style presidential republic that would be Islamic in name but democratic in structure.

Khomeini submitted this clerical constitution to a national referendum in December 1979, at the height of the American hostage crisis. In fact, some suspect that the hostage crisis was engineered to undercut Bazargan. As soon as Bazargan threatened to submit his own secular constitution to the public, the state television network, controlled by the clerics, showed him shaking hands with U.S. policy-makers. Meanwhile, Khomeini declared that the U.S embassy had been a "den of spies" plotting a repeat performance of the 1953 coup. A month after the embassy break-in and Bazargan's resignation, Khomeini submitted the theocratic constitution to the public and declared that all citizens had a divine duty to vote. Although 99 percent of the electorate endorsed it, voter participation was down to 75 percent—this, despite full mobilizations by the mass media, the mosques, and the Revolutionary Guards. Some 5 million voters abstained. The clerics had won their constitution but at the cost of eroding their broad support.

In the first decade after the revolution, a number of factors helped the clerics consolidate power. First, few could afford to challenge Khomeini's overwhelming charisma. Second, the Iraqi invasion of Iran in 1980—prompted by Saddam Hussein's ambition to gain control over vital borders—rallied the Iranian population; after all, their homeland was in danger. Third, world petroleum prices shot up, sustaining oil revenues. The price of a barrel of oil, which had hovered around $30 in 1979, jumped to over $50 by 1981. Thus, despite war and revolution, the new regime was able to continue to finance social programs launched by the previous one. In fact, in the 1980s, modern amenities, especially electricity, indoor plumbing, televisions, telephones, refrigerators, motorcycles, and medical clinics, made their first significant appearance in the countryside.

The second decade after the revolution brought the clerics serious problems. Khomeini's death in June 1989 removed his decisive presence. His successor, Ali Khamenei, lacked not only his charisma but also his scholastic credentials and seminary disciples. Khamenei had been considered a mere hojjat al-Islam until the government-controlled press elevated him to the rank of ayatollah and Supreme Leader. Few grand ayatollahs deemed him their equal. The 1988 UN-brokered cease-fire in the Iran-Iraq War ended the foreign danger. The drastic fall in world oil prices after 1984 placed a sharp brake on economic development. By 1998, the price of a barrel of oil dipped down to less than $10. Even more serious, by the late 1990s, the regime was facing a major ideological crisis, with many of Khomeini's followers, including some of his closest disciples, now stressing the importance of public participation over clerical hegemony, of political pluralism over theological conformity, of populism over fundamentalism, and of civil society over state authority—in other words, of democracy over theocracy.

Themes and Implications

Historical Junctures and Political Themes

These historical junctures have shaped contemporary Iran, especially the way it deals with the democratic idea, its role in the world of states, its attempts to govern the economy and meet the rising expectations of its citizens, and its need to overcome internal ethnic divisions.

In internal affairs, by far the most important challenge facing the republic is the task of reconciling Islam with democracy. Iran has been Muslim since the seventh century and Shi'i Muslim since the sixteenth century. It has also aspired to attain democracy, mass participation, and popular sovereignty since the 1905 constitutional revolution. The dual aspirations for Islam and for democracy culminated in the 1979 Islamic Revolution and appeared to be reconcilable as long as the vast majority supported Khomeini and accepted his notion of the jurist's guardianship. Human rights did not seem to contradict the divine right of the clergy. As Khomeini liked to argue, Islam and democracy were compatible since the vast majority supported the clerics, had faith in them, respected them as the true interpreters of the *shari'a,* and wanted them to oversee the activities of state officials. Islam and democracy, however, appear less reconcilable now that the public has lost its enthusiasm for the clergy. Consequently, some Khomeini followers have continued to give priority to his concept of theocracy, but others have begun to emphasize the need for democracy. In other words, Khomeinism has divided into two

divergent branches: political liberalism and clerical conservatism.

The fate of democracy in Iran is bounded by the very nature of the *shari'a.* Democracy is based partly on the two principles that all individuals are equal, especially before the law, and that all people have inalienable natural rights, including the right to choose their own religion. The *shari'a,* at least in its traditional and conventional interpretations, rejects both of these democratic principles. Formulated in the seventh century, the *shari'a* is based on the principle of inequality, especially between men and women, between Muslims and non-Muslims, between legitimate minorities, known as the People of the Book, and illegitimate ones, known as unbelievers. In addition, the *shari'a,* like all other religious law, not only considers rights to emanate from God rather than nature, but also deems the individual to be subordinate to the larger religious community. This is of special concern for Muslims who lose their faith or join another religion, since the *shari'a* can condemn them to death as apostates. This is no mere technicality; over 250 Baha'is and over 400 leftist prisoners have been executed on just such grounds. The latter were hanged after admitting that they did not believe in God, the Resurrection, and the divinity of the Qur'an. But there are many moderate clerics in Iran who want to reform the *shari'a* to make it compatible with the modern concepts of individual freedom and human rights. They also favor treating those who do not believe in religion in the traditional manner of "don't ask, don't tell."

In international affairs, the Islamic Republic is determined to remain the dominant power in the Persian Gulf, even though it attained this position under the shah thanks mainly to the United States. In his last years, the shah had become known as the American policeman in the Gulf region. By denouncing the United States as an "arrogant imperialist," canceling military agreements with the West, and condoning the taking of U.S. diplomats as hostages, Khomeini certainly asserted Iranian autonomy and authority in the region, but he also inadvertently prompted Saddam Hussein to launch the Iraq-Iran War. When his government ministers suggested renaming the Persian Gulf the Muslim Gulf to improve relations with Arab countries, all of which call it the Arab Gulf, Khomeini responded that it should remain what it had always been: the Persian

Gulf. Khomeini was as much an Iranian nationalist as a Muslim revolutionary.

Before he died, Khomeini initiated policies that have made it difficult for his successors to improve relations with the West, especially the United States. He called for revolutions throughout the Muslim world, denouncing Arab rulers in the region, particularly in Saudi Arabia, as the "corrupt puppets of American imperialism." He strengthened Iran's navy, and bought nuclear submarines from Russia. He launched a research program to build medium-range missiles and nuclear weapons. He denounced the proposals for Arab-Israeli negotiations over Palestine. He sent money as well as arms to Muslim dissidents abroad, particularly Shi'i groups in Lebanon, Iraq, and Afghanistan. He permitted the intelligence services to assassinate some one hundred exiled opposition leaders living in Western Europe, and he issued the *fatwa* death decree against the British writer Salman Rushdie. These policies helped isolate Iran not only from the United States but also from the European Community, human rights organizations, and the United Nations. Khomeini's successors have had to grapple with this heritage, especially since these acts have direct bearing on economic development and the prospects for obtaining foreign investment.

The Islamic Republic began with the conviction that it could rapidly develop the economy if it relied less on oil exports and more on agriculture and manufacturing. It blamed the shah for the one-export economy, the migration of peasants into the towns, the increasing gap in incomes, the continued high illiteracy rate, the lack of medical and educational facilities, and, in general, the low standard of living. It also blamed the former regime for failing to make Iran self-sufficient and instead making it vulnerable to the vagaries of the world economy by building assembly plants rather than factories that would produce industrial goods.

The new regime soon discovered that the country's underlying economic problems were formidable. Peasants continue to migrate to the cities because of the lack of both agricultural land and irrigated water. Industry remains limited because of the lack of capital. Real per capita income has fallen due to forces outside the control of the state, particularly the price fluctua-

tions of the international petroleum market. The real price of oil has plummeted; by 1999, it was less than it had been before the dramatic quadrupling of prices in 1974. Meanwhile, the population has grown to almost 64 million. In other words, the population has steadily increased, whereas the oil revenues have fluctuated widely. Not surprisingly, Iran continues to struggle with financial problems such as inflation, high unemployment, and capital shortages. To deal with this economic crisis, some have favored conventional state-interventionist strategies: price controls, five-year plans, and further redistribution of wealth through high taxation and social investment. Others have advocated equally conventional laissez-faire strategies: open markets, removal of state controls, more business incentives, and the wooing of foreign capital. Some clerics now openly admit that religion does not have answers to such problems as inflation, unemployment, and the volatility of world oil prices. This is a sharp contrast to the early days of the revolution, when Khomeini had confidently declared that Islam had all the solutions and that economics was a subject best left to "donkeys."

Finally, the Islamic Republic began with a broad collective identity, since 99 percent of Iran's population is Muslim. But this major asset has been squandered in the two decades after the revolution. The stress on Shi'ism naturally alienated the Sunnis, who constitute some 10 percent of the population. The triumph in neighboring Afghanistan of the Taliban, an ultraconservative Sunni organization supported initially by Pakistan and indirectly by the United States, complicated the situation. The Taliban armed Sunni dissidents in Iran; Iran, in turn, armed Shi'i dissidents inside Afghanistan. In addition, the regime's insistence on building the constitution on Khomeini's controversial concept of theocracy antagonized other top clerics as well as lay secular Muslims, who lead most of the political parties. Similarly, the inadvertent association of Shi'ism with the central Persian-speaking regions of Iran carries with it the potential danger of eventually alienating the important Turkic minority in Azerbaijan province. Thus, the Iranian regime, like most other developing states, has to solve the problem of how to allocate scarce resources without exacerbating ethnic, regional, and sectarian differences.

Implications for Comparative Politics

The Iranian Revolution, the emergence of religion in Middle Eastern politics, and the collapse of the Soviet Union convinced many Americans that a new specter was haunting the West: that of Islamic fundamentalism. Some experts on international relations predicted that "clash of civilizations" would replace the cold war; that the fault lines in world politics would no longer be over economics and ideology but over religion and culture; and that the main confrontation would be between the West and the Islamic world, headed by the Islamic Republic of Iran.[10] Islam was seen as a major threat not only because of its size but also because it was deemed "inherently bellicose," "militant," and antagonistic to the West.

These dire predictions have turned out to be gross exaggerations. It is true that the Islamic Republic began denouncing the United States, arming militants in other parts of the Middle East, and calling for a struggle, sometimes termed a *jihad* (crusade), against the West. But these rhetorical denunciations became muted as time passed, as reflected in the election of the reformist Muhammad Khatami as president. The call for Muslim unity has fallen on deaf ears, especially in Sunni countries, such as Saudi Arabia. External assistance to Shi'i Muslims was limited to Iraq, Lebanon, and Afghanistan, where, as part of the Northern Alliance, they helped the United States overthrow the Taliban in 2002. Islam has proved not to be a monolith. What is more, Iranians themselves, including the clerics, have divided sharply into ultra-conservatives, conservatives, liberals, and radicals. They even use the Western terms *left, right,* and *center* to describe themselves. Iran shows that the notion of Muslim politics has as little meaning as that of Christian politics. In the same way that one does not study the Bible to understand modern Europe, one does not need the Qur'an to analyze Middle Eastern politics.

It is true that Iran is a major power in the Middle East. It has one of the region's biggest armies, a large land mass, considerable human resources, a respectable gross national product (GNP), and vast oil production. It has the largest navy in the Persian Gulf. In the days of the shah, this navy safeguarded the flow of oil to the West, but it now poses a threat to that same flow of oil. Iran also has plans, predating the Islamic Revolution, to build nuclear weapons.

But it is also true that Iran is in many ways a much weakened power. Its GNP is only about that of New Jersey, and its armed forces are a mere shadow of their former selves. The brutal eight-year conflict with Iraq made the military war-weary. The officer ranks have been decimated by constant purges. The country's military hardware has been depleted by war, obsolescence, and lack of spare parts. In the last years of the shah, military purchases accounted for 17 percent of the GNP. They now take less than 2 percent. Plans to build nuclear weapons are bogged down in financial, technical, and logistical problems. Iran is unlikely to obtain nuclear weapons, not to mention nuclear delivery capabilities, in the foreseeable future. Moreover, a U.S. fleet cruises the Persian Gulf, counterbalancing the Iranian navy, to say nothing of the increased American military presence in the region since the terrorist attacks of September 11, 2001.

It is true that Iran has viewed itself as the vanguard of the Islamic world. But that world turns out to be as illusory for its champions as for its detractors. The Muslim world is formed not of one unitary bloc but of many rival states, each with its own national self-interest. In theory, their rulers stress the importance of Islamic solidarity. In reality, they pursue conventional national interests, even if it necessitates allying with non-Muslims against Muslims. For example, at the height of the American hostage crisis, Iran obtained military equipment from Israel and the United States to pursue the war against Iraq. Similarly, in recent years, Iran has sided with Hindu India against Muslim Pakistan, with Christian Armenia against Muslim Azerbaijan, and with Russia against Muslim Chechnya. Those who see the future as a clash of civilizations and a replay of the medieval Christian-Muslim wars forget that the crusaders themselves, both Muslim and Christian, were often divided, with some siding against their own coreligionists. The Muslim world is no more united now than it was in the days of the medieval crusaders. Iran, like its neighbors, formulates state policies based on national interests, not on cultural and so-called civilizational sentiments.

Section ❷ Political Economy and Development

State and Economy

In 2002, Iran drafted a dramatically new investment law permitting foreigners to own as much as 100 percent of any firm in the country, to repatriate profits, to be free of state meddling, and to have assurances against both arbitrary confiscations and high taxation. Its intention was to attract foreign investments, especially from the European Union, and pave the way for joining the World Trade Organization (WTO). Iran's application to join the WTO in 1996 had failed in part because of its legal impediments against foreign investments and in part because of U.S. opposition. The new investment law was a far cry from the early days of the revolution when Khomeinists had vociferously denounced foreign investors as imperialist exploiters, waxed eloquent about economic self-sufficiency, and criticized the 1965 investment law, which limited foreign capital to less than 49 percent of any firm, as another example of the shah's selling out to the country to Western corporations. Although some leaders continued to warn against Western consumerism and cultural imperialism, the regime as a whole was now eager to attract foreign investment and to rejoin the world economy.

The Economy in the Nineteenth Century

The integration of Iran into the world system began in a modest way in the latter half of the nineteenth century. Before then, commercial contact with the outside world had been limited to a few luxury goods and the famous medieval silk route to China. A number of factors account for this nineteenth-century integration: the economic concessions granted to the European powers; the opening up of the Suez Canal and the building of the Trans-Caspian and the Batum-Baku railways; the laying of telegraph lines across Iran to link India with Britain; the outflow of capital from Europe after 1870; and, most important, the Industrial Revolution in Europe and the subsequent export of manufactured goods to the rest of the world.

In the course of the nineteenth century, Iran's foreign trade increased tenfold. Over 83 percent of this trade was with Russia and Britain; 10 percent with Germany, France, Italy, and Belgium; and less than 7 percent with countries in the Middle East. Exports were confined to carpets and agricultural products, including silk, raw cotton, opium, dried fruits, rice, and tobacco. Imports were mostly tea, sugar, kerosene, and such industrial products as textiles, glassware, guns, and other metal goods. Also in this period, modest foreign investment flowed into banking, fishing, carpet weaving, transport, and telegraph communications.

Contact with the West had far-reaching repercussions. It produced economic dependency, a situation common to much of the Third World, in which less developed countries become too reliant on developed countries; poorer nations are vulnerable to sudden fluctuations in richer economies and dependent on the export of raw materials, the prices of which often stagnate or decline, while the prices of the manufactured products they import invariably increase. Some scholars argue that this type of dependency lies at the root of the present-day economic problems in much of Africa, Latin America, and Asia, including the Middle East.

The nineteenth-century influx of mass-manufactured goods devastated some traditional handicrafts, especially cotton textiles. According to a tax collector in Isfahan, the import of cheap, colorful cotton goods undercut not only the local weavers, dyers, and carders but also the thousands of women who in the past had supplemented their family incomes with cottage industries and home spindles.[11] They naturally blamed foreign imports for their plight. Carpet manufacturers, however, benefited, since they found a ready market in Europe and North America.

The introduction of cash crops to be sold on the market, especially cotton, tobacco, and opium, reduced the acreage available for wheat and other edible grains. Many landowners ceased growing food and turned to commercial export crops. This paved the way for a series of disastrous famines in 1860, 1869–1872, 1880, and 1918–1920. Opium cultivation in Iran was particularly encouraged by British merchants eager to meet the rising demands of the Chinese market brought about by the notorious Opium Wars of the mid-nineteenth century.

Furthermore, the competition from foreign

merchants, together with the introduction of the telegraph and the postal systems, brought the many local merchants, shopkeepers, and workshop owners together into a national middle class aware for the first time of their common statewide interests against both the central government and the foreign powers. In short, the bazaars were transformed into a propertied middle class conscious of its shared grievances against the state. This awareness played an important role in Iran's constitutional revolution of 1905.

The Oil Economy

The real integration of Iran into the world system came in the twentieth century. Its main engine was oil. British prospectors struck oil in Khuzistan in 1908, and the British government in 1912 decided to fuel its navy with petroleum rather than coal. It also decided to buy most of its fuel from the Anglo-Iranian Oil Company, in which it was a major shareholder. Iran's oil revenues increased modestly in the next four decades, reaching $16 million in 1951. After the nationalization of the oil industry in 1951 and the agreement with a consortium of U.S. and British companies in 1955, oil revenues rose steadily, from $34 million in 1955 to $5 billion in 1973 and, after the quadrupling of oil prices in 1974, to over $20 billion in 1975 and $23 billion in 1976. Between 1953 and 1978, the cumulative oil income came to over $100 billion.

Oil became known as Iran's black gold. It financed over 90 percent of imports and 80 percent of the annual budget and far surpassed total tax revenues. Oil also enabled Iran not to worry about feeding its population, a problem that confronts many developing countries. Instead, it could undertake ambitious development programs that other states implemented only if they could squeeze scarce resources from their populations. In fact, oil revenues created what is known as a **rentier state,** a country that obtains a lucrative income by exporting raw materials or leasing out natural resources to foreign companies. Iran as well as Iraq, Algeria, and the Gulf states received enough money from their wells to be able to disregard their internal tax bases. The Iranian state became relatively independent of society. Society, in turn, had few inputs into the state. Little taxation meant little representation. It also meant that the state was totally reliant on one commodity, oil, whose worth was dependent on the vagaries of the world market.

Muhammad Reza Shah tried to reduce Iran's dependency on oil by encouraging other exports and attracting foreign investment into nonoil ventures. Neither policy succeeded. Despite some increase in carpet and pistachio exports, oil continued to dominate: on the eve of the 1979 revolution, it still provided 97 percent of the country's foreign exchange. The new nonoil industries faced difficulties finding export markets. Furthermore, Iran failed to draw external capital despite concerted efforts. Even after the oil boom, foreign firms, mostly U.S., European, and Japanese, invested no more than $1 billion. Much of this was not in industry but in banking, trade, and insurance. In Iran, as in the rest of the Middle East, foreign investors were put off by government corruption, labor costs, small internal markets, potential instability, and fear of confiscations. Apparently foreign companies did not share their government's confidence that Iran was an island of stability in the Middle East.

Society and Economy

Oil revenues financed Muhammad Reza Shah's development projects. It is true, as the opposition liked to publicize, that some revenue was squandered on palaces, bureaucratic waste, outright corruption, ambitious nuclear projects, and ultrasophisticated weapons too expensive even for many NATO countries. But it is also true that significant sums were channeled into socioeconomic development. GNP grew at the average rate of 9.6 percent every year from 1960 to 1977, making Iran one of the fastest-developing countries in the Third World at that time. The land reform project, the linchpin of the White Revolution, created over 644,000 moderately prosperous farms (see Table 1). The number of modern factories tripled from fewer than 320 to over 980 (see Table 2). Enrollment in primary schools grew from fewer than 750,000 to over 4 million; in secondary schools from 121,000 to nearly 740,000; in vocational schools from 2,500 to nearly 230,000; and in universities from under 14,000 to more than 154,000. The Trans-Iranian Railway was completed, linking Tehran with Tabriz, Meshed, Isfahan, and the Gulf. Roads were built connecting most villages with the provincial cities.

The expansion in health services was equally impressive. Between 1963 and 1977, the number of hospital beds increased from 24,126 to 48,000; medical clinics from 700 to 2,800; nurses from 1,969 to 4,105; and doctors from 4,500 to 12,750. These improvements, together with the elimination of epidemics and famines, mainly due to food imports, lowered infant mortality and led to a population explosion. In the two decades prior to the 1979 revolution, the overall population doubled from 18 million to nearly 36 million. This explosion gave the country a predominantly youthful age structure. By the mid-1970s, half the population was under sixteen years of age. This was to have far reaching repercussions in the street politics of 1977–1979 when young people were one of the driving forces leading up to the Islamic Revolution.

Socioeconomic development did not necessarily make the shah popular. On the contrary, his approach to development tended to increase his unpopularity with many sectors of Iranian society. The Industrial and Mining Development Bank channeled over $50 billion of low-interest loans to court-connected entrepreneurs, industrialists, and agribusinessmen. The shah believed that if economic growth benefited those who were already better off, some of the wealth that was produced would gradually trickle down to the lower levels of society. But in Iran, as elsewhere, the benefits of this development strategy got stuck at the top of society and never trickled down. By the mid-1970s, Iran had one of most unequal countries in the world in terms of income distribution.[12] Similarly, land reform, despite high expectations, created a small stratum of prosperous farmers but left the vast majority of peasants landless or nearly landless; over 1.2 million received less than 10 hectares (approximately 24.7 acres), not enough to survive as independent farmers (see Table 1). Not surprisingly, many of the rural poor flocked to the urban shantytowns in search of work.

The factories spawned by the shah's modernization program drew criticism on the grounds that they were mere assembly plants and poor substitutes for real industrial development (see Table 3). His medical programs left Iran with one of the worst doctor-patient ratios and child mortality rates in the Middle East. Educational expansion created only one place for every five university applicants, failed to provide primary

Table 1

Land Ownership in 1977

Size (hectares)	Number of Owners
200+	1,300
51–200	44,000
11–50	600,000
3–10	1,200,000
Landless	700,000

Note: One hectare is equal to approximately 2.47 acres.
Source: E. Abrahamian, "Structural Causes of the Iranian Revolution," *Middle East Research and Information Project,* no. 87 (May 1980).

Table 2

Number of Factories

Size	1953	1977
Small (10–49 workers)	Fewer than 1,000	More than 7,000
Medium (50–500 workers)	300	830
Large (over 500 workers)	19	159

Source: E. Abrahamian, "Structural Causes of the Iranian Revolution," *Middle East Research and Information Project,* no. 87 (May 1980).

Table 3

Industrial Production

Product	1953	1977
Coal (tons)	200,000	900,000
Iron ore (tons)	5,000	930,000
Steel (tons)	—	275,000
Cement (tons)	53,000	4,300,000
Sugar (tons)	70,000	527,000
Tractors (no.)	—	7,700
Motor vehicles (no.)	—	109,000

Source: E. Abrahamian, "Structural Causes of the Iranian Revolution," *Middle East Research and Information Project,* no. 87 (May 1980), 22.

schools for 60 percent of children, and had no impact on 68 percent of the country's illiterates. In fact, the population explosion increased the absolute number of illiterates in Iran. The priority given to the development of Tehran increased disparities between the capital and the provinces. By the mid-1970s, Tehran contained half the country's doctors and manufacturing plants. According to one study, the per capita income in the richest provinces was ten times more than in the poorest ones. By the end of the shah's rule, Iran had the second highest (after Brazil) regional income disparity in the developing world.[13] According to another study, the ratio of urban to rural incomes was 5 to 1, making it one of the worst in the world.[14]

These inequalities created a **dual society** in Iran.

On one side was the modern sector, headed by the elites with close ties to the oil state. On the other side was the traditional sector comprising the clergy, the bazaar middle class, and the rural masses. Each sector, in turn, was sharply stratified into unequal classes. Thus, Iranian society was divided vertically into the modern and the traditional and horizontally into a number of urban as well as rural classes (see Figure 1).

The upper class—the Pahlavi family, the court-connected entrepreneurs, the military officers, and the senior civil servants—constituted less than 0.01 percent of the population. In the modern sector, the middle class—professionals, civil servants, salaried personnel, and college students—formed about 10 percent of the population. The bottom of the modern sector—the

---

Iranian society was divided sharply not only into horizontal classes, but also into vertical sectors—the modern and the transitional, the urban and the rural. This is known as a dual society.

Figure 1

Iran's Class Structure in the Mid-1970s

Upper Class

Pahlavi Family; Court-Connected Entrepreneurs; Senior Civil Servants and Military Officers	0.1%

Middle Class

Traditional (Propertied)	13%		Modern (Salaried)	10%
Clerics Bazaaris Small Factory Owners Commercial Farmers			Professionals Civil Servants Office Employees College Students	

Lower Classes

Rural	45%		Urban	32%
Landed Peasants Near Landless Peasants Landless Peasants Unemployed			Industrial Workers Wage-Earners in Small Factories Domestic Servants Construction Workers Peddlers Unemployed	

urban working class, which included factory workers, construction laborers, peddlers, and unemployed—constituted over 32 percent. In the traditional sector, the middle class—bazaar merchants, small retailers, shopkeepers, workshop owners, and well-to-do family farmers—made up 13 percent. The rural masses—landless and near-landless peasants, nomads, and village construction workers—made up about 45 percent of the population.

The government's own statistics reveal the widening inequality. In 1972, the richest 20 percent of urban households accounted for 47.1 percent of total urban family expenditures; by 1977, it accounted for 55.5 percent. In 1972, the poorest 40 percent accounted for 16.7 percent of urban family expenditures; by 1977, it accounted for 11.7 percent (see Table 4).

These inequalities fueled resentments against the ruling elite, which were expressed more in cultural and religious terms than in economic and class terms. Articulating these resentments was a gadfly writer named Jalal Al-e-Ahmad (1923–1969). A former communist who had rediscovered his Shi'i roots in the 1960s, Al-e-Ahmad shook his contemporaries by publishing a polemical pamphlet entitled *Gharbzadegi* (*The Plague from the West*). He argued that the ruling class was destroying Iran by blindly imitating the West; neglecting the peasantry; showing contempt for popular religion; worshipping mechanization, regimentation, and industrialization; and flooding the country with foreign ideas, tastes, luxury items, and mass-consumption goods. He stressed that developing countries such as Iran could survive this "plague" of

Western imperialism only by returning to their cultural roots and developing a self-reliant society, especially a fully independent economy. Al-e-Ahmad inspired the long search for cultural authenticity and economic self-sufficiency.

These themes were developed further by another young intellectual, Ali Shariati (1933–1977). Studying in Paris during the turbulent 1960s, Shariati was influenced by Marxist sociology, Catholic liberation theology, the Algerian revolution, and, most important, Frantz Fanon's theory of violent Third World revolutions against colonial oppression as laid out in his famous book, *Wretched of the Earth*. Shariati returned home with what can be called a fresh and revolutionary interpretation of Shi'ism, echoes of which would later appear in Khomeini's writings.

Shariati argued that history was a continuous struggle between oppressors and oppressed. Each class had its own interests, its own interpretations of religion, and its own sense of right and wrong, justice and injustice, morality and immorality. To help the oppressed, Shariati believed, God periodically sent down prophets, such as Abraham, Moses, Jesus, and Muhammad. In fact, Muhammad had come to launch a dynamic community in "permanent revolution" toward the ultimate utopia: a perfectly classless society in this world.

Although Muhammad's goal had been betrayed by his illegitimate successors, the caliphs, his radical message had been preserved for posterity by the Shi'i imams, especially by Imam Husayn, who had been martyred in the seventh century to show future generations that human beings had the moral duty to fight oppression in all places at all times. Shariati equated Imam Husayn with Che Guevara, the famous Latin American guerrilla leader killed in Bolivia in 1967. According to Shariati, the contemporary oppressors were the imperialists, the feudalists, the corrupt capitalists, and their hangers-on, especially the "tie-wearers" and "the palace dwellers," the carriers of the "Western plague." He criticized the conservative clerics who had tried to transform revolutionary religion into an apolitical public opiate. Shariati died on the eve of the 1979 revolution, but his prolific works were so widely read and so influential that many felt that he, rather than Khomeini, was the true theorist of the 1979 Islamic Revolution.

Table 4

Measures of Inequality of Urban Household Consumption Expenditures

Year	Percentage Share in Total Expenditures		
	Poorest 40%	Middle 40%	Richest 20%
1972	16.7	36.2	47.1
1977	11.7	32.8	55.5

Source: V. Nowshirvani and P. Clawson, "The State and Social Equity in Postrevolutionary Iran," in M. Weiner and A. Banuazizi (eds.), *The Politics of Social Transformation in Afghanistan, Iran, and Pakistan* (Syracuse, N.Y.: Syracuse University Press, 1994), 248.

Iran and the International Political Economy

Under the Shah

The oil boom in the 1970s gave the shah the opportunity to play a significant role in international politics. As the second most important member of the **Organization of Petroleum Exporting Countries (OPEC),** Iran could cast decisive votes for raising or moderating oil prices. At times, the shah curried Western favor by moderating prices. At other times, he pushed for higher prices to finance his ambitious projects and military purchases. These purchases rapidly escalated once President Richard Nixon began to encourage U.S. allies, such as the shah, to take a greater role in policing their regions. Moreover, Nixon's secretary of state, Henry Kissinger, openly argued that the United States should finance its ever-increasing oil imports, most of them from the Persian Gulf, by exporting more military hardware to the region. The shah was now able to buy from the United States almost any ultrasophisticated weapon he desired. Arms dealers began to jest that the shah read their technical manuals in the same way that some men read *Playboy.* The shah's arms buying from the United States jumped from $135 million in 1970 to a peak of $5.7 billion in 1977. Between 1955 and 1978, Iran spent more than $20.7 billion on U.S. arms alone.

This military might gave the shah a reach well beyond his immediate boundaries. He occupied three small but strategically located Arab islands in the Strait of Hormuz, thus controlling the oil lifeline through the Persian Gulf but also creating distrust among his Arab neighbors. He talked of establishing a presence well beyond the Gulf on the grounds that Iran's national interests reached into the Indian Ocean. "Iran's military expenditures," according to a 1979 U.S. congressional report, "surpassed those of the most powerful Indian Ocean states, including Australia, Indonesia, Pakistan, South Africa, and India."[15]

In the mid-1970s, the shah dispatched troops to Oman to help the local sultan fight rebels. He offered Afghanistan $2 billion to break its ties with the Soviet Union, a move that probably prompted the Soviets to intervene militarily in that country. The shah, after supporting Kurdish rebels in Iraq, forced Baghdad to concede to Iran vital territory on the Shatt al Arab estuary. This had been a bone of contention between the two countries ever since Iraq had come into existence after World War I. A U.S. congressional report summed up Iran's overall strategic position: "Iran in the 1970s was widely regarded as a significant regional, if not global, power. The United States relied on it, implicitly if not explicitly, to ensure the security and stability of the Persian Gulf sector and the flow of oil from the region to the industrialized Western world of Japan, Europe, and the United States, as well as to lesser powers elsewhere."[16]

These vast military expenditures, as well as the oil exports, tied Iran closely to the industrial countries of the West and to Japan. Iran was now importing millions of dollars' worth of rice, industrial tools, construction equipment, pharmaceuticals, tractors, pumps, and spare parts. The bulk of the rice and wheat, and a substantial portion of the tractors, medicines, and construction equipment, came from the United States. Trade with neighboring and other developing countries was insignificant. In the words of the Department of Commerce in Washington, "Iran's rapid economic growth [provided America with] excellent business opportunities."[17]

The oil revenues thus had major consequences for Iran's political economy, all of which paved the way for the Islamic Revolution. They allowed the shah to pursue ambitious programs that inadvertently widened class and regional divisions within the dual society. They drastically raised public expectations without necessarily meeting them. They made the rentier state independent of society. They also made the state highly dependent on oil prices and imported products. Iran was no longer a simple rentier state but an oil-addicted one, vulnerable to the world market. Economic slowdowns in the industrial countries could lead to a decline in their oil demands, which could diminish Iran's ability to buy such essential goods as food, medicine, and industrial spare parts. One of the major promises made by the Islamic Revolution was to end this economic dependency on oil and the West.

The Islamic Republic

The Islamic Republic began with high hopes of rapidly developing the economy and becoming fully independent of oil and the West. The results have been mixed, illustrating the constraints that political economy can place on society. The Pahlavi monarchy and the Islamic Republic may have differed in many respects, but they governed the same economy and therefore faced similar financial problems.

The main problem plaguing the Islamic Republic has been instability in the world oil market. This instability has occurred despite the efforts of OPEC to preserve prices by limiting production and setting quotas for its members. The price of a barrel of oil, which had quadrupled from $5 to $20 in 1974, peaked at $52 in late 1980 but plunged sharply thereafter, reaching $18 in 1985, hovering around $12 to $14 in the late 1980s and 1990s, and descending to a new low of $10 in 1999. This meant that Iran's oil revenues, which continued to provide the state with 80 percent of its hard currency and 75 percent of its total revenues, fell from $20 billion in 1978 to less than $10 billion in 1998. They did not improve until 2000, when they rose to $27 per barrel. Iran, still a rentier state, remains vulnerable to the vagaries of the international petroleum market.

The decline in the world price of oil was due to a number of factors outside Iran's control: the slackening of the demand in the industrialized countries (especially with the recession in the late 1990s); the glutting of the international market by the entry of non-OPEC producers, such as Britain and Mexico; and the tendency of some OPEC members to preserve their revenues by cheating on their production quotas. Iran's oil revenues were also affected by the war with Iraq and its own failure to raise production. In some years, Iran was not able to meet even its OPEC quotas. To raise production, Iran needs an influx of capital and new deep-drilling technology, both of which can be found only in the West. This explains the recent about-turn on foreign investments by the Islamic Republic.

This oil crisis has been compounded by the population explosion, the Iran-Iraqi war, and the emigration of some 3 million Iranians. The annual population growth rate, which had hit 2.5 percent in the late 1970s, jumped to nearly 4 percent by the late 1980s, mainly because the new regime encouraged large families. This was the highest rate in the world, causing a major strain on government resources, especially social services and food imports. The Iraqi war not only

hurt the oil industry but also wrought as much as $600 billion in property damage—whole border cities were flattened. It also led to half a million Iranian casualties. The Islamic Revolution itself frightened many professionals and highly skilled technicians, as well as wealthy entrepreneurs, and industrialists into fleeing to the West. Of course, they carried their portable assets with them.

The overall result was a twenty-year economic crisis that lasted into the late 1990s. GNP fell 50 percent, per capita income declined 45 percent, and inflation hovered around 20 to 30 percent every year. The value of real incomes, including salaries and pensions, dropped by as much as 60 percent. Unemployment hit 20 percent; over two-thirds of entrants into the labor force could not find jobs. The absolute number of illiterates increased. Peasants continued to flock to urban shantytowns. Tehran grew from 4.5 million to 12 million people. The total number of families living below the poverty level increased. By the late 1990s, over 9 million urban dwellers lived below the official poverty line.[18] Shortages in foreign exchange curtailed vital imports, even of essential manufactured goods. The value of the currency plummeted. Before the revolution, the U.S. dollar had been worth 70 Iranian rials; by 1998, it was worth as much as 1,750 rials on the official exchange rate, and more than 9,000 rials on the black market. What is more, the regime that came to power advocating self-sufficiency now owed foreign banks and governments over $30 billion, forcing it to renegotiate foreign loans constantly.

Despite this ongoing economic crisis, the Islamic Republic scored some notable successes, especially after the war with Iraq ended. The Reconstruction Ministry, established mainly for the rural population, built 30,000 miles of paved roads, 40,000 schools, and 7,000 libraries. It brought electricity and running water to more than half of the country's 50,000 villages. The number of registered vehicles on the roads increased from 27,000 in 1990 to over 2.9 million in 1996. More dams and irrigation canals were built, and the Agricultural Ministry distributed some 630,000 hectares of confiscated arable land to peasants and gave farmers more favorable prices, especially for wheat. By the late 1990s, most independent farmers had such consumer goods as radios, televisions, refrigerators, and pickup trucks. The extension of social services narrowed the gap between town and country and between the urban poor and the middle classes. The overall literacy rate grew from 50 percent to nearly 76 percent, and by 2000 the literacy rate among those in the age range from six to twenty-nine years was 97 percent. The infant mortality rate fell from 104 per 1,000 in the mid-1970s to 25 per 1,000 in the late 1990s. Life expectancy climbed from fifty-five years in 1979 to sixty-eight in 1993 and further to sixty-nine in 2002, which is one of the highest in the Middle East. The UN estimates that by 2000, 94 percent of the population had access to health services and 95 percent to safe water. On the whole, the poor in Iran are better off now than their parents had been before the Islamic Revolution. Moreover, the country, despite initial setbacks, was able to become more self-sufficient in food production. By the mid-1990s, it was importing no more than 5 percent of its wheat, rice, sugar, and meat requirements. Furthermore, the regime was able to diversify foreign trade and become less dependent on the West. By 2000, Iran's main trade partners were Japan, South Korea, and Russia.

The Islamic Republic regime also made major strides toward population control. At first, it closed down birth control clinics, claiming that Islam approved of large families and that Iran needed workers. But it reversed direction once the ministries responsible for social services felt the full impact of this growth. The regime also realized that only food imports could meet the rising demands. In 1989, the government declared that Islam favored healthy rather than large families and that one literate citizen was better than ten illiterate ones. It reopened birth control clinics, cut subsidies to large families, and announced that the ideal family should consist of no more than two children. It even took away social benefits from those having more than two children. By 2003, the regime boasted that it had reduced the annual rate of population growth to 1.2 percent. It is an impressive accomplishment. It is also a sign that the regime is highly pragmatic when it comes to economic issues.

The 2000–2002 rise in petroleum prices further helped the situation. Oil revenues jumped from less than $10 billion in 1998 to over $28 billion in 2001. Foreign reserves increased to $4.8 billion, wiping out the external debt, stabilizing the currency, and improving the country's creditworthiness. Iran became one of the few developing countries to be free of foreign debt and was even able set aside some oil revenues as a hedge against leaner times. The GDP grew 6 percent in 2000 and 5 percent in 2001. The official unemployment rate fell from 16 to 12.5 percent, and inflation was reduced to 13 percent. The rial stabilized at 1,750 per U.S. dollar on the official rate and 8,000 in the unofficial rate. The government floated its first international bond and succeeded in attracting European investors despite American opposition. The World Bank lent Iran $232 million for medical services and sewage lines, again despite American opposition. Meanwhile, foreign investments—to the tune of $12 billion—have been contracted to flow into oil and gas ventures, petrochemicals, minerals, and car factories. What is more, the government could now afford to channel additional revenues into the infrastructure, especially into power stations, hydroelectric dams, and education. In the 1980 and 1990s, Iran had been considered one of the world's most inhospitable places for foreign investors. In the early 2000s, it was rated by European and Japanese investors as safe. The earlier oil bust had brought Iran economic stagnation; the new boom brought it some hope.

Section ③ Governance and Policy-Making

The political system of Iran is unique in the contemporary world. It is neither presidential, parliamentary, military, monarchical, nor totalitarian. Instead, it is a theocracy with some concessions to democracy. It is a theocracy for the simple reason that the clergy—in other words, the theocrats or the theologians—control most of the important positions. The system nevertheless contains an element of democracy, with some high officials, including the president, elected directly by the general public. Although this combination is unprecedented, similar ones could emerge in other parts of the Middle East if more Islamic countries have similar revolutions.

Organization of the State

The Iranian state rests on the Islamic constitution designed by the Assembly of Religious Experts immediately after the 1979 revolution. It was amended between April and June 1989 during the last months of Khomeini's life by the Council for the Revision of the Constitution, handpicked by Khomeini himself. These amendments were ratified by a nationwide referendum in July 1989, immediately after Khomeini's death. The final document, with 175 clauses and some 40 amendments, is a highly complex mixture of theocracy and democracy.

The constitution's preamble affirms faith in God, Divine Justice, the Qur'an, the Resurrection, the Prophet Muhammad, the Twelve Imams, the eventual return of the Hidden Imam (the Mahdi), and, of course, Khomeini's doctrine of jurist's guardianship. All laws, institutions, and state organizations have to conform to these "divine principles."

The Supreme Leader

The constitution named Khomeini to be the Supreme Leader for life on the grounds that the public overwhelmingly recognized him as the "most just, pious, informed, brave, and enterprising" of the senior clerics—the grand ayatollahs. It further described him as the Leader of the Revolution, the Founder of the Islamic Republic, and, most important, the imam of the whole community. It stipulated that if no single Supreme Leader emerged after his death, then all his authority would be passed on to a leadership council of two or three senior clerics. After Khomeini's death, however, his followers so distrusted the other senior clerics that they did not set up such a council. Instead, they elected one of their own, Ali Khamenei, a middle-ranking cleric, to be the new Supreme Leader. Most of Khomeini's titles, with the exception of imam, were bestowed on Khamenei. The Islamic Republic has often been described as a regime of the ayatollahs (high-ranking clerics). It could be more aptly called a regime of the hojjat al-Islams (middle-ranking clerics), since

few senior clerics want to be associated with it. None of the grand ayatollahs and few of the ordinary ayatollahs subscribed to Khomeini's novel notion of jurist's guardianship. On the contrary, most disliked his radical populism and political activism.

The constitution gives wide-ranging powers to the Supreme Leader. Enshrined as the vital link between

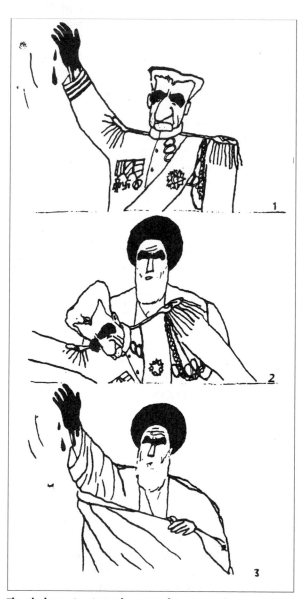

The shah turning into Khomeini, from an émigré newspaper. *Source:* Courtesy Nashriyeh.

the three branches of government, he can mediate between the legislature, the executive, and the judiciary. He can "determine the interests of Islam," "supervise the implementation of general policy," and "set political guidelines for the Islamic Republic." He can eliminate presidential candidates as well as dismiss the duly elected president. He can grant amnesty. As commander in chief, he can mobilize the armed forces, declare war and peace, and convene the Supreme Military Council. He can appoint and dismiss the commanders of Revolutionary Guards as well as those of the regular army, navy, and air force.

The Supreme Leader can nominate and remove the chief judge, the chief prosecutor, and the revolutionary tribunals. He can remove lower court judges. Even more important, he nominates six clerics to the powerful twelve-man Guardian Council. This council can veto parliamentary bills. It has also obtained (through separate legislation) the right to review all candidates for elected office, including the presidency and the *Majles.* The other six on the Guardian Council are jurists nominated by the chief judge and approved by the *Majles.*

The Supreme Leader is also authorized to fill a number of important nongovernment posts: the preachers **(Imam Jum'ehs)** at the main city mosques, the director of the national radio-television network, and the heads of the main religious endowments, especially the **Foundation of the Oppressed,** the successor to the privileged Pahlavi Foundation (see below). By 2001, the Office of the Supreme Leader employed over six hundred in Tehran and had representatives placed in most sensitive institutions throughout the country. The Supreme Leader has obtained more constitutional powers than dreamed of by the shah.

The later constitutional amendments expanded and transformed the Assembly of Religious Experts into an eighty-six-man house elected every four years. Packed with clerics, the assembly not only elected Khamenei as Khomeini's successor but also reserved the right to dismiss him if it found him "mentally incapable of fulfilling his arduous duties." In effect, the Assembly of Religious Experts has become an upper chamber to the regular *Majles.* Its members are required to have a seminary degree equivalent to a master's degree. Figure 2 illustrates the hierarchy established by the constitution.

The general public elects the *Majles,* the president, and the Assembly of Religious Experts. But the Supreme Leader and the Guardian Council decide who can compete in these elections.

Because the constitution is based on Khomeini's theory of jurist's guardianship, it gives wide-ranging judicial powers to the Supreme Leader in particular and to the clerical strata in general. Laws are supposed to conform to the religious law, and the clergy are regarded as the ultimate interpreters of the *shari'a.* In fact, the constitution makes the judicial system the central pillar of the state, overshadowing the executive and the legislature. Bills passed by the Islamic *Majles* are reviewed by the Guardian Council to ensure that they conform to the *shari'a.* All twelve members of this Guardian Council are either clerics or lay jurists knowledgeable in the *shari'a.* The minister of justice is chosen by the president but needs the approval of both the *Majles* and the chief judge. The judicial system itself has been Islamized all the way down to the district courts, with seminary-trained jurists replacing university-educated judges. The Pahlavis purged the clergy from the judicial system; the Islamic Republic purged the university-educated from the same judiciary.

The Executive

The President and the Cabinet

The constitution, particularly after the amendments, reserves some power for the president. He is described as the chief executive and the highest state official after the Supreme Leader. He is chosen every four years through a national election. He must be a pious Shi'i faithful to the principles of the Islamic Republic. He cannot be elected to more than two terms. He draws up the annual budget, supervises economic matters, and chairs the plan and budget organization. He can propose legislation to the *Majles.* He conducts the country's internal and external policies. He signs all international treaties, laws, and agreements. He chairs the National Security Council responsible for defense matters. He can select his own vice presidents and cabinet ministers. The minister of intelligence, however, has to be a cleric according to a separate parliamentary law.

The president appoints most senior officials, including provincial governors, town mayors, and

The general public elects the *Majles*, the president, and the Assembly of Religious Experts. But the Supreme Leader and the cleric-dominated Guardian Council decide who can compete in these elections.

Figure 2

The Islamic Constitution

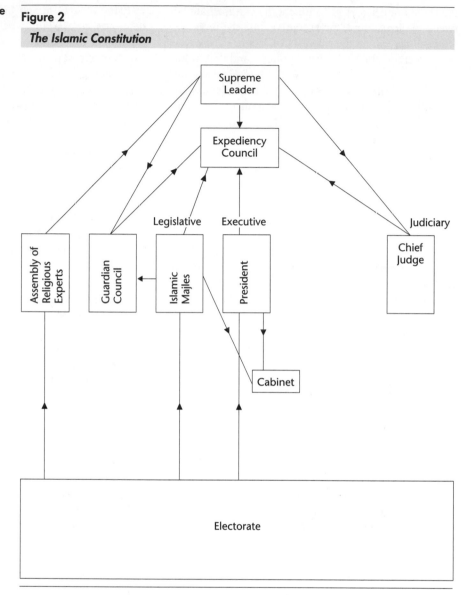

ambassadors. Furthermore, as head of the executive, he names the directors of some of the large public organizations, such as the National Iranian Oil Company, the National Electricity Board, and the National Bank.

Although during the revolution Khomeini often promised that trained officials would run the executive, clerics in fact have dominated the presidency. Of the four presidents since the revolution, three have been clerics: Khamenei, Rafsanjani, and Khatami (see "Leaders: Ayatollah Ali Khamenei," "Leaders: Hojjat al-Islam Ali-Akbar Hashemi Rafsanjani," and "Leaders: Sayyid Muhammad Khatami"). The exception, Abol-Hasan Bani-Sadr, was ousted in 1981 precisely because he denounced the regime as "a dictatorship of the mullahtariat," comparing it to a communist-led "dictatorship of the proletariat."

Leaders: *Ayatollah Ali Khamenei*

Ali Khamenei succeeded Khomeini as Supreme Leader in 1989. He was born in 1939 in Meshed into a minor clerical family originally from Azerbaijan. He studied theology with Khomeini in Qom and was briefly imprisoned in 1962. Active in the opposition movement in 1978, he was given a series of influential positions immediately after the revolution, even though he held only the middle-level clerical rank of hojjat al-Islam. He became Friday prayer leader of Tehran, head of the Revolutionary Guards, and, in the last years of Khomeini's life, president of the republic. After Khomeini's death, he was elevated to the rank of Supreme Leader even though he was neither a grand ayatollah nor a recognized senior expert on Islamic law. He had not even published a theological treatise. The government-controlled media, however, began to refer to him as an ayatollah. Some ardent followers even referred to him as a grand ayatollah qualified to guide the world's whole Shi'i community. After his elevation, he built a constituency among the regime's more diehard elements: traditionalist judges, conservative war veterans, and antiliberal ideologues. Before 1989, he often smoked a pipe in public, a mark of an intellectual, but put away the habit when he became Supreme Leader.

The Bureaucracy

The president, as the chief of the executive branch, heads a huge bureaucracy. In fact, this bureaucracy continued to proliferate after the revolution even though Khomeini had often taken the shah to task for having a bloated government. It expanded, for the most part, to provide jobs for the many college and high school graduates. On the eve of the revolution, the ministries had 300,000 civil servants and 1 million employees. By the early 1990s, they had over 600,000 civil servants and 1.5 million employees. The Iranian Revolution, like many others, ended up creating a bigger bureaucracy.

Of the new ministries, Culture and Islamic Guidance censored the media and enforced "proper conduct" in public life; Intelligence has replaced SAVAK as the main security organization; Heavy Industries manages the recently nationalized factories; and Reconstruction has the dual task of expanding social services and taking "true Islam" into the countryside. Its mission is to build bridges, roads, schools, libraries, and mosques in the villages so that the peasantry will learn the basic principles of Islam. "The peasants," declared one cleric, "are so ignorant of true Islam that they even sleep next to their unclean sheep."[19]

The clergy dominate the bureaucracy as they do the presidency. They have monopolized the most sensitive ministries—Intelligence, Interior, Justice, and Culture and Islamic Guidance—and have given posts in other ministries to their relatives and protégés. These ministers appear to be highly trained technocrats, sometimes with higher degrees from the West, but in fact are powerless individuals chosen by, trusted by, and related to the ruling clergy.

Semipublic Institutions

The Islamic Republic has set up a number of semipublic institutions. They include the Foundation of the Oppressed, the Alavi Foundation (named after Imam Ali), the Martyrs Foundation, the Pilgrimage Foundation, the Housing Foundation, the Foundation for the Publication of Imam Khomeini's Works, and the Fifteenth of Khordad Foundation, which commemorates the date (according to the Islamic calendar) of Khomeini's 1963 denunciation of the shah's White Revolution. Although supposedly autonomous, these foundations are directed by clerics appointed personally by the Supreme Leader. According to some estimates, their annual income may be as much as half that of the government.[20] They are exempt from paying state taxes and are allocated foreign currencies, especially U.S. dollars, at highly favorable exchange rates subsidized by the oil revenues. Most of their assets are property confiscated from the old elite.

The largest of these institutions, the Foundation for the Oppressed, administers over 140 factories,

Leaders: *Sayyid Muhammad Khatami*

Muhammad Khatami was elected president of the Islamic Republic in 1997 and reelected in 2000. He was born in 1944 into a prominent clerical family in central Iran. His father, an ayatollah, was a close friend of Khomeini. His mother came from a prosperous landed family. He studied theology in Qom and philosophy at Isfahan University. At the outbreak of the revolution, he was in charge of a Shi'i mosque in Germany. After the revolution, he first headed a state publishing house, then sat in the *Majles*, and then served as minister of culture and Islamic guidance. Arousing the wrath of the conservatives, he resigned from the last post in 1992 and took up the teaching of philosophy at Tehran University. He uses the title *sayyid* and wears a black turban to indicate that he is a male descendant of the Prophet. Although a cleric by appearance and training, he seems to many more like a university professor interested in political philosophy.

120 mines, 470 agribusinesses, and 100 construction companies. It also owns the country's two leading newspapers, *Ettela'at* and *Kayhan*. The Martyrs Foundation, in charge of helping war veterans, controls property of the old elite that was confiscated in 1979 but not handed over to the Foundation for the Oppressed. It also receives an annual subsidy from the government. These foundations together control $12 billion in assets and employ over 400,000 people. They can be described as states within a state—or rather, as clerical fiefdoms favored by the Supreme Leader.

Other State Institutions

The Military

The clergy have taken special measures to control the armed forces—both the regular military of 388,000, including 220,000 conscripts, and the irregular forces formed of 100,000 Revolutionary Guards established immediately after 1979 and 200,000 volunteers of the Mobilization of the Oppressed (*Basej-e Mostazafin*) created during the war against Iraq. The Supreme Leader, as commander in chief, appoints the chiefs of staff as well as the top commanders. He also fills the post of defense minister with his own confidants, who report directly to him, bypassing the president and the cabinet. Moreover, he places chaplains, who function like political commissars in communist party-states, in regular military units to watch over officers.

To further safeguard the republic against the regular army built by the Pahlavis, the new regime purged the top ranks, placed officers promoted from the ranks of the Revolutionary Guards in command positions over the regular divisions, and built up the Revolutionary Guards as a parallel force with its own uniforms, budgets, munitions factories, recruitment centers, and even small air force and navy. According to the constitution, the regular army defends the borders, while the Revolutionary Guards protect the republic. Despite these measures, political sentiments about the Islamic Republic remain unknown, if not ambivalent, in the regular military, especially among the 18,000 professionals in the navy, 45,000 in the air force, and 125,000 in the conventional army.

The Judiciary

The Islamic Republic regime Islamized the judiciary by enacting a penal code, the Retribution Law, based on a reading of the *shari'a* that was so narrow that it prompted many modern-educated lawyers to resign in disgust, charging that it contradicted the United Nations Charter on Human Rights. It permitted injured families to demand blood money on the biblical and Qur'anic principle of "an eye for an eye, a tooth for a tooth, a life for a life." It mandated the death penalty for a long list of "moral transgressions," including adultery, homosexuality, apostasy, drug trafficking, and habitual drinking. It sanctioned stoning, live burials, and finger amputations. It divided the population into male and female and Muslims and non-Muslims, and treated

Leaders: *Hojjat al-Islam Ali-Akbar Hashemi Rafsanjani Ali-Akbar*

Rafsanjani was born in 1934 into a fairly prosperous business and farming family in the heartland of the Shi'i and Persian-speaking provinces. He studied in Qom with Khomeini, found himself in prison four times during the 1960s, set up a number of commercial companies, including one that exported pistachios, and wrote a book praising a nineteenth-century prime minister who had made an abortive attempt to industrialize the country. Nevertheless, Rafsanjani remained active enough in clerical circles to be considered a hojjat al-Islam. After the revolution, he became a close confidant of Khomeini and attained a number of cabinet posts, culminating with the presidency in 1989. After serving two four-year terms, the maximum allowed by the constitution, he was given the chairmanship of the powerful Expediency Council. In some ways, his institutional power rivals that of President Khatami, but not, of course, that of Supreme Leader Khamenei.

them unequally. For example, in court, the evidence of one male Muslim is equal to that of two female Muslims. The regime also passed a "law on banking without usury" to implement the *shari'a* ban on all forms of interest taking and interest giving.

Although the law was Islamized, the modern centralized judicial system was not dismantled. For years, Khomeini argued that in a truly Islamic society, the local *shari'a* judges would pronounce final verdicts without the intervention of the central authorities. Their verdicts would be swift and decisive. This, he insisted, was the true spirit of the *shari'a*. After the revolution, however, he discovered that the central state needed to retain ultimate control over the justice system, especially over life and death. Thus, the new regime retained the appeals system, the hierarchy of state courts, and the power to appoint and dismiss all judges. State interests took priority over the spirit of the *shari'a*.

Practical experience led the regime to broaden the narrow interpretation of the *shari'a* gradually. To permit the giving and taking of interest, without which modern economies would not function, the regime allowed banks to offer attractive rates as long as they avoided the taboo term *usury*. To meet public sensitivities as well as international objections, the courts rarely implemented the harsh corporal punishments stipulated by the *shari'a*. They adopted the modern method of punishment, imprisonment, rather than the traditional one of corporal public punishment. By the early 1990s, those found guilty of breaking the law were treated much as they would be in the West: fined or imprisoned rather than flogged in the public square.

Subnational Government

Although Iran is a highly centralized state, it is divided administratively into provinces, districts, subdistricts, townships, and villages. Provinces are headed by governors-general, districts by governors, subdistricts by lieutenant governors, towns by mayors, and villages by headmen.

The Islamic constitution promises elected councils on each level of administration. The constitution declares that the management of local affairs in every village, town, subdistrict, district, and province will be under the supervision of councils whose members would be elected directly by the local population. It also declares that governors-general, governors, mayors, and other regional officials appointed by the central government's Interior Ministry have to consult local councils. These clauses creating local councils had been incorporated into the constitution mainly because of mass demonstrations organized in 1980 by the left—notably the Mojahedin and the Fedayin. The **Assembly of Experts** would have preferred to remained silent on the issue.

Despite these clauses, no steps were taken to hold council elections until 1999 when Khatami, the new president, insisted on holding the country's very first nationwide local elections. Over 300,000 candidates, including 5,000 women, competed for 11,000 council seats—3,900 in towns and 34,000 in villages. Khatami's supporters won a landslide victory taking 75 percent of the seats, including twelve of the fifteen in Tehran. The top vote getter in Tehran was Khatami's former interior minister, who had been impeached by the conservative *Majles* for issuing too many publishing licenses to reform-minded journals and newspapers. These local elections showed that the conservative clergy, despite their mosque pulpits, could not stem the reformist tide. They also showed that participatory democracy had come to the grass-roots level in Iran.

The Policy-Making Process

Iran's policy-making system is highly complex in part because of the cumbersome constitution and in part because factional conflicts within the ruling clergy have resulted in more amendments, which have made the original constitution even more complicated. Laws can originate in diverse places, and they can be modified by pressures coming from diverse directions. They can also be blocked by a wide variety of state institutions. In short, the decision-making process is highly fluid and diffuse, often reflecting the regime's factional divisions.

The clerics who destroyed Iran's old order remained united while building the new one. They were convinced that they alone had the divine mandate to govern. They formed a distinct social stratum as well as a cohesive political group. They followed the same leader, admired the same texts, cited the same potent symbols, remembered the same real and imaginary indignations under the shah, and, most important, shared the same vested interest in preserving the Islamic Republic. Moreover, most had studied at the same seminaries and came from the same lower-middle-class backgrounds. Some were even related to each other through marriage and blood ties.

But once the constitution was in place, the same clerics drifted into two loose but identifiable blocs: the Society (*Majmu'eh*) of the Militant Clergy, and the Association (*Jam'eh*) of the Militant Clergy. The former can be described as statists, populists, or radical reformers and the latter as laissez-faire (free-market) conservatives. The populists hoped to consolidate lower-class support by redistributing wealth, eradicating unemployment, nationalizing enterprises, confiscating large

The clerical regime and its two stilts: the sword and the oil wells. *Source: Courtesy Mojahed* (in exile).

estates, financing social programs, rationing and subsidizing essential goods, and placing price ceilings on essential consumer goods. In short, they espoused the creation of a comprehensive welfare state. The conservatives hoped to retain middle-class support, especially in the bazaars, by removing price controls, lowering business taxes, cutting red tape, encouraging private entrepreneurs, and balancing the budget, even at the cost of sacrificing subsidies and social programs. In recent years, the statist reformers have begun to emphasize the democratic over the theocratic features of the constitution, stressing the importance of individual rights, the rule of law, and government accountability to the electorate. In many ways, they have become like social democrats the world over.

The conservatives were originally labeled middle-roaders and traditionalists. The statists were labeled progressives, seekers of new ideas, and followers of the imam's line. The former often denounced the latter as extremists, leftists, and pro-Soviet Muslims. The latter countered by denouncing the free-marketers as medievalists, rightists, capitalists, mafia bazaaris, and pro-American Muslims. Both could bolster their arguments with apt quotes from Khomeini.

This polarization created a major constitutional gridlock, since the early Islamic *Majles* was dominated by the radicals, whereas the Guardian Council was controlled by the conservatives. Khomeini had appointed conservatives to the Guardian Council to preserve his links with the bazaars and to build bridges to the grand ayatollahs, who distrusted his whole revolutionary movement. Between 1981 and 1987, over one hundred bills passed by the *Majles* were vetoed by the Guardian Council on the grounds that they violated the *shari'a,* especially the sanctity of private property. The vetoed legislation included a labor law, land reform, nationalization of foreign trade, a progressive income tax, control over urban real estate transactions, and confiscation of the property of émigrés whom the courts had not yet found guilty of counterrevolutionary activities. Introduced by individual deputies or cabinet ministers, these bills had received quick passage because the radical statists controlled the crucial *Majles* committees and held a comfortable majority on the *Majles* floor. Some ultraconservatives had countered by encouraging the faithful not to pay taxes and instead to contribute to the grand ayatollahs of their choice. After all, they argued, one could find no mention of income tax anywhere in the *shari'a.*

Both sides cited the Islamic constitution to support their positions. The free-marketers referred to the long list of clauses protecting private property, promising balanced budgets, and placing agriculture, small industry, and retail trade in the private sector. The statists referred to an even longer list promising education, medicine, jobs, low-income housing, unemployment benefits, disability pay, interest-free loans, and the predominance of the public sector in the economy.

To break the constitutional gridlock, Khomeini boldly introduced into Shi'ism the Sunni Islamic concept of *maslahat*—that is, "public interest" and "rea-

sons of state." Over the centuries, Shi'i clerics had denounced this as a Sunni notion designed to bolster the illegitimate caliphs. Khomeini now claimed that a truly Islamic state could safeguard the public interest by suspending important religious rulings, even over prayer, fasting, and the pilgrimage to Mecca. He declared public interest to be a primary ruling and the others mere secondary rulings. In other words, the state could overrule the views of the highest-ranking clerics. In the name of public interest, it could destroy mosques, confiscate private property, and cancel religious obligations. Khomeini added that the Islamic state had absolute authority, since the Prophet Muhammad had exercised absolute (*motalaq*) power, which he had passed on to the imams and thus eventually to the Islamic Republic. Never before had a Shi'i religious leader claimed such powers for the state, especially at the expense of fellow clerics.

As a follow-up, Khomeini set up a new institution named the Expediency Council for Determining the Public Interest of the Islamic Order, known now as the **Expediency Council.** He gave this Expediency Council the task of resolving the conflicts between the Islamic *Majles* and the Guardian Council. He packed the council with thirteen clerics, including the president, the chief judge, the Speaker of the *Majles,* and six jurists from the Guardian Council. The Expediency Council eventually passed some of the more moderate bills favored by the statists. These included a new income tax, banking legislation, and a much-disputed labor law providing workers in large factories with a minimum wage and some semblance of job security.

The constitutional amendments introduced after Khomeini's death institutionalized the Expediency Council. The new Supreme Leader could now not only name its members but also determine its tenure and jurisdiction. Not surprisingly, Khamenei packed it with his supporters—none of them prominent grand ayatollahs. Even more important, he made its meetings secret and allowed it to initiate entirely new laws rather than restrict itself to resolving legislative differences between the Guardian Council and the *Majles.* In effect, the Expediency Council is now a secretive supra-constitutional body accountable only to the Supreme Leader. In this sense, it has become a powerful body rivaling the Islamic *Majles* even though it did not exist in the original constitution. By 2002, the Expediency

Council contained thirty-two members. These included the president; chief judge; Speaker of the *Majles;* ministers of intelligence, oil, culture, and foreign affairs; chief of the General Staff; commander of the Revolutionary Guards; jurists from the Guardian Council; directors of radio and television as well as of the Central Bank, Atomic Energy Organization, and National Oil Company; heads of the main religious foundations; chairman of the Chamber of Commerce; and editors of the main conservative newspapers. Seventeen were clerics. These thirty-two can be considered the most powerful men in the Islamic Republic.

Section ④ Representation and Participation

Although the Islamic Republic is a theocracy, some supporters of the regime claim that it is still compatible with democracy. According to the constitution, the government represents the general electorate. The president is directly elected by the people, and the Supreme Leader is chosen by the Assembly of Religious Experts, which in turn is elected by the general population. What is more, the elected legislature, the Islamic *Majles,* retains considerable power, and according to one of the founders of the regime, it is the centerpiece of the Islamic constitution.[21] Another architect of the constitution has argued that the Iranian people, by carrying out an Islamic Revolution in 1979, implicitly favored a type of democracy that would be confined within the boundaries of Islam and within the rubric of jurist's guardianship.[22] But another declared that if he had to choose between the democracy and jurist's guardianship, he would not hesitate to choose the latter, since it came directly from God.[23] On the eve of the initial referendum on the constitution, Khomeini himself had declared: "This constitution, which the people will ratify, in no way contradicts democracy. Since the people love the clergy, have faith in the clergy, want to be guided by the clergy, it is only right that the supreme religious authority oversee the work of the ministers to ensure that they don't make mistakes or go against the law of the Qur'an."[24]

The Legislature

According to Iran's constitution, the *Majles* "represents the nation" and is granted many powers, including enacting or changing ordinary laws (with the approval of the Guardian Council), investigating and supervising all affairs of state, and approving or ousting the cabinet ministers. In describing this branch of government, the constitution uses the term *qanun* (statutes) rather than *shari'a* (divine law) so as to gloss over the fundamental question of whether legislation passed by the *Majles* is derived from God or the people. The rationale is that the divine law (*shari'a*) comes from God, but statutes (*qanuns*) are made by the people's elected representatives.

The *Majles* originally contained 270 seats and was elected every four years through secret direct balloting by all citizens over the age of fifteen. It now contains 290 seats and is elected by citizens over the age of sixteen. The *Majles* has considerable authority. It can pass *qanun* as long as the Guardian Council deems it compatible with the *shari'a* and the Islamic constitution. It can interpret legislation as long as these interpretations do not contradict the judicial authorities. It can choose, from a list drawn up by the chief judge, six of the twelve-man Guardian Council. It can investigate at will cabinet ministers, affairs of state, and public complaints against the executive and the judiciary. It can remove cabinet members—with the exception of the president—through a parliamentary vote of no confidence. It can withhold approval for government budgets, foreign loans, international treaties, and cabinet appointments. It can hold closed debates, provide its members with immunity from arrest, and regulate its own internal workings, especially the committee system.

Although the 1989 constitutional amendments weakened the *Majles* in relation to the presidency and the Expediency Council, the *Majles* nevertheless remains a highly important political institution in Iran. On occasion, it has changed government budgets, criticized cabinet policies, modified development plans, and forced the president to replace his ministers as well as the director of national radio-television. In 1992, 217 deputies circulated an open letter that explicitly emphasized the prerogatives of the *Majles* and thereby implicitly downplayed those of the Supreme Leader. Likewise, the Speaker of the House in 2002 threatened to close down the whole *Majles* if the judiciary violated parliamentary immunity and arrest one of his liberal deputies.

Political Parties and the Party System

The constitution guarantees citizens the right to organize, and a law passed in 1980 permits the Interior Ministry to issue licenses to political parties. But political parties were not encouraged until Khatami's 1997 election as president. Since then, three parties have been active, especially in the heated parliamentary elections of 2000: the Islamic Iran Participation Front and the Islamic Labor Party, both formed by Khatami supporters, and the Servants of Reconstruction created by Hojjat al-Islam Ali-Akbar Hashemi Rafsanjani, the former president and now chairman of the Expediency Council. According to the Interior Ministry, licenses have been granted to some seven hundred political, social, and cultural organizations, but all are led by people deemed politically acceptable by the regime. This limited form of political participation might be called "guided democracy." The real political opposition has been forced into exile, mostly in Europe:

- **The Liberation Movement.** Established in 1961 by Mehdi Bazargan, who became Khomeini's first premier in 1979, the Liberation Movement is a moderate Islamic party similar in ideology to Germany's Christian Democrats. Beginning in the early 1980s, the government gradually tightened control over its activities, especially after it criticized the Islamic Republic for prolonging the war with Iraq, giving too much influence to the clergy, and mismanaging the economy. In 2002, the judiciary banned the Liberation Movement as a subversive organization. Despite its religious orientation, the party advocates secularism and the strict separation of mosque from state.
- **The National Front.** Originating in the campaign to nationalize the country's oil resources in the early 1950s, the National Front remains committed to Mossadeq's twin political ideals of nationalism and

secularism. Because the conservative clergy feel threatened by the National Front's potential appeal, they have banned the organization and forced it into exile.
- **The Mojahedin.** Formed in 1971 as a guerrilla organization to fight the shah's regime, the Mojahedin tried to synthesize Marxism and Islam. It interpreted Shi'i Islam to be a radical religion favoring equality, social justice, martyrdom, and redistribution of wealth. Immediately after the revolution, the Mojahedin attracted a large following among college and high school students, especially when it began to denounce the clergy for establishing a new dictatorship. The regime retaliated with mass executions and forced the Mojahedin to move their base of operations into Iraq. Not unexpectedly, the Mojahedin became associated with the national enemy and thereby lost much of its appeal within Iran.
- **The Fedayin.** Also formed in 1971, the Fedayin modeled itself after the Marxist guerrilla movements of the 1960s in Latin America, especially those inspired by Che Guevara and the Cuban revolution. Losing more fighters than any other organization in the guerrilla war against the shah, the Fedayin came out of the revolution with much revolutionary mystique and popular urban support. But it soon lost much of its strength because of massive government repression and a series of internal splits.
- **The Tudeh (Party of the Masses).** Established in 1941, the Tudeh is a mainstream, formerly pro-Soviet communist party. Although the Tudeh initially supported the Islamic Republic as a "popular anti-imperialist state," it was banned, and most of its organizers were executed during the period 1983 through 1989. It survives mostly in Europe.

Elections

Iran's constitution promises free elections. In practice, however, *Majles* elections have varied from relatively free but disorderly in the early days of the republic, to controlled and highly unfair in the middle years, and back again to free—and now orderly—in recent years. The main obstacle to fair elections has been the Guardian Council with its power to vet candidates. For example, in 1996, the Guardian Council excluded over 44 percent of some 5,000 parliamentary candidates by questioning their loyalty to the concept of jurist's guardianship. Other factors help restrict electoral freedom. The government-controlled radio-television network, the main source of information for the vast majority, favors some candidates, ignores others, and denounces yet others. The Interior Ministry can ban dissident organizations, especially their newspapers and meetings, with the claim that they are anti-Islamic and antirevolutionary. Ballot boxes are placed in mosques, and at the time the Revolutionary Guards supervise voting. Neighborhood clerics are on hand to help illiterates complete their ballots. Club-wielding gangs, the Hezbollahis, have been known to assault their opponents. Some elections are timed to coincide with high religious holidays. The Supreme Leader inevitably denounces those tempted to abstain as "secret agents of the devil." The electoral law, based on a winner-take-all majority system rather than on proportional representation, was designed to minimize the voice of the opposition. The Islamic Republic has had six *Majles* elections so far: 1980, 1984, 1988, 1992, 1996, and 2000.

The First Majles (1980)

In the election for the First *Majles* in 1980, shortly after the founding of the Islamic Republic, there were over 4,400 candidates, over 40 parties, over 200 dailies and weeklies, and thousands of workplace organizations in the bazaars, campuses, high schools, factories, and offices. The parties represented the whole range of the political spectrum from the far right, through the center, to the extreme left. By shattering the old state structures, the revolution had released a wide variety of political, social, and ethnic groups. It was as if, after years of silence, every professional and occupational association, every political party and ideological viewpoint, and every interest and pressure group rushed into the open to air its views, print its newspapers and broadsheets, and field its parliamentary candidates.

On the right was the Islamic Republican Party (IRP), which was established immediately after the revolution by Khomeini's closest disciples. It had the support of two highly conservative religious groups that had survived the old regime: the Fedayan-e Islam and the Hojjatieh Society. It also had the support of the Islamic Association of Bazaar Guilds, Islamic Association of Teachers, Islamic Association of University Students, the Association of Seminary Teachers of Qom, and, most important, the Association of the Militant Clergy in Tehran. Not surprisingly, it championed Khomeini's notion of jurist's guardianship.

At the center of the political spectrum was Bazargan's Liberation Movement. Bazargan had been appointed premier in February 1979 by Khomeini himself, but had resigned in disgust ten months later when the Revolutionary Guards had permitted students to take over the U.S. embassy. The Liberation Movement favored free markets, limited government, cordial relations with the United States, and a pluralistic political system in which all parties, religious and nonreligious, would compete in fair elections. The Liberation Movement also favored a regime built on its own liberal interpretation of Islam, one in which the clergy would guide and advise rather than rule. Bazargan was a former member of Mosaddeq's National Front, the organization instrumental in nationalizing the oil industry in 1951. But Bazargan, unlike Mosaddeq, liked to sprinkle his speeches with religious quotations.

Closely allied with the Liberation Movement was the National Front, a mere shadow of its former self, and its offshoots, the National Party and the Democratic National Front. These parties, like the Liberation Movement, were led by Western-educated, middle-aged professionals and technocrats. But unlike the Liberation Movement, they avoided making political use of Islam. Like their deceased mentor, Mosaddeq, they preferred to separate politics from religion and to treat the latter as primarily a private matter. The Liberation Movement can be defined as a liberal Muslim party; the National Front and its offshoots as liberal secular parties.

The left was fragmented even more into religious and nonreligious groups. The religious groups included such Muslim yet anticlerical ones as the People's Mojahedin, the Movement of Militant Muslims, and the Movement for the Liberation of the Iranian People. The nonreligious groups included a number of Marxist and ethnic parties: the Tudeh, the Majority and Minority Fedayin, the Kurdish Democratic Party, and at least a dozen small Marxist-Leninist parties. To complicate matters further, Abul-Hassan Bani-Sadr, a French-educated intellectual supporter of Khomeini who had been elected president of Iran in January 1980, was distancing himself from the Islamic Republican Party by fielding a number of his own candidates. Many of these political parties had their own student, labor, professional, and women's organizations. For example, in the early years of the revolution, there were over a dozen women's organizations in Tehran alone.

Not surprisingly, the elections for this First *Majles* were extremely lively, even though the IRP manipulated the state machinery, especially the Interior Ministry and the national radio-television network, to favor its candidates. On the eve of the voting, the minister of the interior declared that all were free to run, but only "true Muslims" would be permitted to sit in the forthcoming parliament.[25] Some 80 percent of the electorate participated in the first round.

The competition in the 1980 election was so intense in some constituencies, particularly Kurdistan, Kermanshah, West Azerbaijan, and the Caspian provinces, that the Interior Ministry stepped in, impounded the ballot boxes, harassed candidates, and postponed the second round indefinitely. The second round was not held until late 1981. By then, the regime had cracked down on the opposition, forcing Bani-Sadr into exile, banning many leftist parties, and executing hundreds of Mojahedin organizers.

Of the 216 deputies elected in 1980, 120 were supporters of the IRP, 33 of Bani-Sadr, and 20 of the Liberation Movement; 33 described themselves as independent. The independents included two Kurdish Democrats and five National Front leaders. The latter had their parliamentary credentials promptly rejected on the grounds that documents found in the recently occupied U.S. embassy "proved" them to be U.S. spies. The IRP had won only 35 percent of the popular vote but had collected over 60 percent of the filled seats. The Mojahedin, on the other hand, had won 25 percent of the popular vote but had not obtained a single seat. The electoral law based on majority rather than proportional representation had paid off for Khomeini.

Once the IRP carried out the second round and replaced the purged members, including Bani-Sadr's supporters, it gained a solid majority. This included 105 clerics—more than 38 percent of the *Majles*—making it by far the highest clerical representation in Iran's parliamentary history. Most were medium-ranking clerics serving as court judges and town preachers (Imam Jum'ehs). The others were white-collar employees and high school teachers, some of whom were seminary graduates. Over 90 percent came from the propertied middle class. Their fathers had been clerics, bazaar merchants, guild elders, or small farmers.

The Second Majles (1984)

The elections for the Second *Majles* in 1984 were carried out under very different circumstances. The "spring of the Iranian Revolution" was over. The opposition was now either banned outright or else highly restricted in its activities. The IRP monopolized the political scene, manipulating state institutions and controlling a vast array of organizations, including large foundations, local mosques, Revolutionary Guards, and thousands of town preachers. Not surprisingly, it won a landslide victory, leaving a few seats to independent-minded clerics with their own local followings. Also not surprisingly, voter participation fell sharply, to less than 60 percent, even though Khomeini declared that abstaining was tantamount to betraying Islam.

Over 54 percent of the 270 deputies were clerics, almost all middle ranking. Most of the nonclerics had doctoral, master's, bachelor's, or associate's degrees or high school diplomas. Only eleven had not completed high school. Twenty-seven of the lay members had at one time or another attended seminary. As before, most were in their late thirties or early forties.

In 1987, Khomeini dissolved the IRP in preparation for the Third *Majles*. No reason was given, but the decision was prompted by the conflict between the radical statists demanding economic reforms and the conservative free marketers favoring the bazaars. One radical deputy claimed that "the party had been infiltrated by opportunistic time-servers pretending to be devout followers of the Imam's Line."[26] In the *Majles*, the radicals could muster 120 votes and the conservatives some 90; the remainder moved back and forth between these poles.

In dissolving the IRP, Khomeini declared that the clergy were free to establish two competing organizations as long as both opposed imperialism, communism, and capitalism and supported Islam, the Islamic Republic, and the jurist's guardianship. "Political differences," he commented, "are natural. Throughout history our religious authorities have differed among themselves. . . . Besides Iranians should be free to express themselves."[27] He could have added, "within reason and within the context of Islam as defined by myself."

In preparation for the next elections, the radicals left the Association of the Militant Clergy and formed their Society of the Militant Clergy. From then on, there were two rival clerical organizations: on one side, the statist reformers with their society and at least five major newspapers; on the other side, the conservative free marketers with their association and a major newspaper called *Resalat* (*Message*). The conservatives became known as the Resalat group. Both had adherents in the seminaries and among the local preachers (Imam Jum'ehs). This was political pluralism, but one restricted to those subscribing to Khomeini's interpretation of Shi'ism.

The Third (1988), Fourth (1992), and Fifth (1996) Majleses

The radicals won the lackluster 1988 elections for the Third *Majles*. In the new parliament, there were eighty-six clerics, a 23 percent decline from the previous assembly. This, however, did not signify the demise of clerical power. Some clerics had gone on to higher positions, especially to the Assembly of Religious Experts. Moreover, many of the new lay deputies were young protégés of the clerics recruited into their fold from the students who had taken over the U.S. embassy.

Although the radical clerics began the Third *Majles* with a clear majority, their influence soon ebbed because of Khomeini's death in June 1989 and because the new Supreme Leader Khamenei and President Rafsanjani began to adopt free-market policies as soon as the war with Iraq ended. During the war, both men had been vocal advocates of price controls, rationing, high taxes, nationalization, and large government budgets. Now, with the cease-fire, they argued that the only way to jump-start the economy was to encourage private enterprise and cut government expenditures.

Rafsanjani launched this new economic course for Iran in giving his eulogy for Khomeini. He downplayed Khomeini as the revolutionary leader of the downtrodden and oppressed and instead praised him as a world-famous statesman who had restored Iran's national sovereignty. He also praised him as a highly reputable scholar-theologian who had intellectually

"awakened the moribund seminaries" from their "medieval graves."

In the following months, Rafsanjani, and to a lesser extent Khamenei, acknowledged that the revolution had been "guilty of excesses." They asked their followers to put away "childish slogans." They talked increasingly of realism, stability, efficiency, managerial skills, work discipline, expertise, individual self-reliance, modern technology, entrepreneurship, and business incentives. They warned that the worst mistake a state could make was to spend more than its revenue. Rafsanjani declared, "Some people claim that God will provide. They forget that God provides only for those willing to work." Khamenei sermonized on how Imam Ali, the founder of Shi'i Islam, had taken great pride in his plantations. Khomeini had often depicted Imam Ali as a humble water carrier; Khamenei now depicted him as an entrepreneurial plantation owner.

To ensure that the change of economic course would go smoothly, Khamenei handed over the two main newspapers, *Kayhan* and *Ettela'at,* to the conservative free marketers and authorized the Guardian Council to monitor the 1992 *Majles* elections. The Guardian Council announced that all candidates had to prove their "practical commitment to the Supreme Leader and the Islamic Republic." The Guardian Council further restricted the campaign to one week, permitting candidates to speak in mosques and run newspaper advertisements but not to debate each other in open forums. The head of the Guardian Council announced that he would use pesticides to cleanse parliament of anyone with "difficult attitudes." Seventy-five radical candidates withdrew. Forty were disqualified by the Guardian Council. Only a handful of radicals were allowed to be elected. Voter participation dropped to a new low. In Tehran, less than 55 percent of the eligible voters bothered to cast ballots despite Khamenei's pronouncement that it was the "religious obligation of everyone to participate."

Ayatollah Khalkhali, a vocal radical, was barred from running on the grounds that he did not have appropriate theological training. Yet the same Khalkhali had been considered qualified enough from 1978 to 1987 to sit as a high court judge dispatching hundreds of political prisoners to their deaths as enemies of the Islamic Republic. Khalkhali retorted that his candidacy had been rejected by conservatives who had sat out the revolution but were now weaseling their way into the Guardian Council. He warned that "true servants of the revolution," like himself, had been subjected to a political purge as a prelude to a future physical purge. Another disqualified candidate, who had earlier dismissed any talk of human rights as a "foreign conspiracy," now complained that the Guardian Council had grossly violated the UN Charter on Human Rights. It had failed to inform him of the charges brought against him, given him insufficient time to respond, and denied him the right to defend himself in a proper court of law.

The Guardian Council said, in turn, that its decisions had been kept out of the mass media in order to protect state secrets and the public reputations of those it had decided were unqualified to serve in the *Majles*. Those who had been purged were expected to be grateful for this sensitivity. It also argued that it had followed precedent, reminding the radicals that they themselves had used similar procedures to keep out "undesirables" from the previous three parliaments— undesirables such as the Mojahedin, the Fedayin, the Tudeh, the National Front, the Liberation Movement, and the "pseudo-clerics," who did not believe in jurist's guardianship.

The purge of the *Majles* was relatively easy to carry out. For one thing, the extensive constitutional powers entrusted to the Supreme Leader left the radicals vulnerable. As Hojjat al-Islam Mohtashami, a leading radical, complained, the institution of jurist's guardianship was now being used to clobber revolutionary heads. When radicals complained that they were being slandered as traitors for merely questioning the turn to free-market economic policies, their opponents countered that disobedience to the Supreme Leader was tantamount to disobedience to God. They argued that only proponents of "American Islam" would dare question the decisions of the Supreme Leader. They also reminded them that the new oath of office required parliamentary deputies to obey the Supreme Leader as "the Vice Regent of the Hidden Twelfth Imam." Khamenei may not have inherited Khomeini's title of imam, but he had obtained the new exalted position of the Hidden Imam's Spokesman.

The conservatives also effectively used populist rhetoric against the radicals. They described them as the "newly moneyed class" and as "Mercedes-Benz clerics." They accused them of misusing official positions to line their own pockets, open slush funds and secret foreign accounts, give lucrative contracts to their friends, sell contraband, and deceive the masses with unrealistic promises. "They," exclaimed one conservative, "act like a giant octopus, giving with one tentacle but taking away with the others." They also placed the responsibility for the country's economic malaise squarely on the shoulders of the radicals. They argued that a decade of statist policies had further increased poverty, illiteracy, inflation, unemployment, and slum housing. Before the revolution, these problems were blamed on the shah and his family. Now they were blamed on the "extremist pseudo-clerical radicals."

The purge was so decisive that the radicals suspended the activities of their Society of the Militant Clergy soon after the 1992 elections for the Fourth *Majles*. Some radicals went to head foundations and libraries. Some took up seminary positions. Others began to write for newspapers, occasionally arguing that the public should choose the Supreme Leader and that the Guardian Council should stay out of the whole electoral process. Yet others remained politically active, mildly criticizing the regime and quietly awaiting a better day.

This expectation was not far-fetched. The conservative majority in the Fourth *Majles* began to divide as soon as President Rafsanjani implemented a series of probusiness reforms. He relaxed price controls, liberalized imports, trimmed the ration list, disbanded courts that penalized price gougers, returned some confiscated property, and ended all talk of further nationalization, land reform, and income distribution. He also set up a stock exchange in Tehran and free-trade zones in the Persian Gulf. One bloc of deputies, associated with Supreme Leader Khamenei and the newspaper *Resalat,* supported these measures but also favored highly conservative cultural policies. They advocated strict control over the media, the silencing of liberal intellectuals, and the rigid implementation of the dress code for women. They were also reluctant to challenge the financial privileges of the large foundations or open up the economy to international and émigré capital; foreign competition was seen as a threat to the bazaar economy. These conservatives could muster some 170 votes in the *Majles*. Meanwhile, another bloc, also advocating laissez-faire policies but associated more with President Rafsanjani, favored foreign capital and greater cultural liberalization. They also favored balancing the budget by downsizing the large clerical foundations and cutting state subsidies. This bloc could muster some forty votes. The remaining sixty deputies were independent, voting sometimes with the majority and other times with the minority.

To get a working majority in the *Majles,* Rafsanjani had to water down his programs. He had to remove his own brother from the directorship of the national radio-television network. He could take only limited measures to privatize large enterprises, trim the foreign exchange privileges of the huge clerical foundations, and cut subsidies that absorbed much of the oil revenue. Moreover, he was unable to increase business taxes: all the taxes raised by the bazaar guilds together still constituted less than 9 percent of the government's annual tax income. Moreover, he had to shelve his daring bill designed to attract foreign investment. This bill would have raised the share that foreign interests could own in Iranian enterprises from 49 percent to 100 percent. It would have been a total policy reversal, since the Islamic revolutionaries had relished accusing the shah of selling the country to foreign capitalists. Rafsanjani now argued that he could not revive the ailing economy without an injection of massive foreign capital. The bill, however, met stiff resistance and failed to pass into law during Rafsanjani's terms as president.

Frustrated by these setbacks, Rafsanjani created a new political organization, the Servants of Reconstruction, to win control of the Fifth *Majles* that was to be elected in 1996. Although supported by many cabinet ministers and the popular mayor of Tehran who had made the capital more livable by building highways, libraries, and parks, this party won only 80 seats. Over 140 seats went to the conservatives endorsed by the Chamber of Commerce, the Association of the Militant Clergy, and the Teachers of Qum Seminaries. Some radical reformers even voted for the Servants of Reconstruction; most stayed away from the polls. The Fifth *Majles* turned out to be a continuation of the gridlocked Fourth *Majles.* The conservatives prevented liberalization—in either the economy or the media. Meanwhile, the Judiciary imprisoned the mayor of Tehran on trumped-up "embezzlement" charges and closed down the newspaper, *Zanan (Women),* which

was edited by Rafsanjani's daughter, on the grounds that it had offended religious susceptibilities. Rafsanjani's position was further weakened by term limits since the constitution stipulated that presidents could serve no more than two terms. This, together with Khatami's upset victory in the 1997 presidential election, opened the way for the Sixth *Majles* elections in 2000, the first to be both orderly and competitive since the founding of the Islamic Republic in 1979.

The Sixth Majles (2000)

The reformers—labeling themselves the Khordad Front after the month (in the Islamic calendar) when Khatami had won his first presidential election in 1997—ran a highly successful campaign in 2000. The Khordad Front brought together the Islamic Iran Participation Front (headed by Khatami's brother; the Society of Militant Clergy; the Islamic Labor Party and the Workers House, a quasi-union; the Servants of Reconstruction, at least, initially; and the Mojahedin Organization of the Islamic Revolution); a twenty-year-old group of radical technocrats and intellectuals not to be confused with the antiregime guerrilla Mojahedin; a new university campus organization called the Office for Strengthening Solidarity; and a host of Islamic associations, including the Islamic Association of Women. These associations had previously supported the regime but had recently spoken out in favor of a free press, government accountability, and fewer privileges for the clergy. Their views were articulated by a number of prominent intellectuals and journalists who had started their careers as staunch regime supporters—even as student occupants of the U.S. embassy in 1979–1980—but who had come to the conclusion that the democratic features of the constitution should take priority over the theocratic ones.

The best known of these reformist intellectuals was Abdol-Karim Soroush. Soroush had begun his political career as a militant supporter of Ali Shariati, the radical intellectual who had developed a revolutionary interpretation of Shi'ism that had greatly influenced Khomeini. But he now argued that Islam had become an overbloated ideology and should be limited to private ethics and individual morality. He and his fellow reformers often denounced intolerant conservatives as "religious fascists." If the works of Shariati and

Khomeini had been replete with such terms as *revolution, imperialism, cultural roots, martyrdom, the dispossessed,* and the *Western plague,* those of Soroush and the new reformers were full of concepts such as civil society, pluralism, democracy, freedom, equality, modernity, citizenship, dialogue, human rights, rule of law, and political participation. These new reformers not only championed liberal concepts but also tried to make them compatible with Islam.

These reformers took the Sixth *Majles* elections in 2000 in a landslide, winning 80 percent of the vote in a campaign that drew over 70 percent of the electorate. In elections held for the Assembly of Experts a few months earlier, the reformers had abstained, and consequently voter participation had dropped to 46 percent. Over 6,800 candidates competed for the 290 seats in the Sixth *Majles*. Although the Guardian Council axed some prominent reformers from the list of those allowed to run in the election, it permitted most of them to participate, probably because of pressure from the Supreme Leader Khamenei. The reformers won over 195 seats. Former president Rafsanjani, who in the last days had openly courted the conservatives, was humiliated in his bid to be elected to the *Majles*. He came in thirtieth in the first round of the Tehran election and quietly withdrew instead of continuing in the runoffs. Many supporters of secular parties, all banned from the campaign, voted for the reformers as a better alternative to the die-hard conservatives. Conservative candidates endorsed by the Association of Militant Clergy, Teachers of Qum Seminaries, and the bazaar Coalition of Islamic Societies won fewer than forty seats. The total number of "turbaned deputies" (clerics) fell to a new low of thirty-seven. Khatami's brother, who had created the Islamic Iran Participation Party, topped the winners in Tehran. Many prominent conservatives with long experience in high positions failed to get elected even in provincial constituencies. Even Qom, the country's religious capital, voted overwhelmingly for the reformers. After the elections, the London *Economist* magazine commented: "Iran, although an Islamic state, imbued with religion and religious symbolism, is an increasingly anti-clerical country. In a sense, Iran resembles some Roman Catholic countries where religion is taken for granted, without public display, and with ambiguous feeling towards the clergy. Iranians tend to mock their mullahs, making mild little

jokes about them; they certainly want them out of their bedrooms. In particular, they dislike their political clergy."[28]

Political Culture, Citizenship, and Identity

In theory, the Islamic Republic should be a highly viable state. After all, Shi'ism is the religion of both the state and the vast majority of the population. It can also be described as the central component of popular culture. Moreover, the constitution guarantees basic rights to religious minorities as well as to individual citizens. All citizens, regardless of race, color, language, or religion, are promised the rights of free expression, worship, and organization. They are guaranteed freedom from arbitrary arrest, torture, and police surveillance. In short, the constitution incorporates the modern concepts of individual rights and civil society.

The constitution gives further guarantees to the recognized religious minorities: the Christian, Jews, and Zoroastrians. Although Christians (Armenians and Assyrians), Jews, and Zoroastrians form just 1 percent of the total population, they are allocated five *Majles* seats. They are permitted their own places of worship, their own community organizations, including schools, and their own marriage, divorce, and inheritance laws. The constitution, however, is ominously silent concerning Baha'is and Sunnis. The former are deemed defectors from Islam; the latter are treated as equal in theory to the Shi'is, but their status is not spelled out.

The constitution also gives guarantees to non-Persian speakers. Although 83 percent of the population understands Persian, thanks to the educational system, over 50 percent continue to speak non-Persian languages at home—languages such as Azeri, Kurdish, Turkic, Gilaki, Mazandarani, Arabic, and Baluchi. The constitution promises them rights unprecedented in Iranian history. It states that "local and native languages can be used in the press, media, and schools." It also states that local populations have the right to elect provincial, town, and village councils. These councils can watch over the governors-general and the town mayors, as well as their educational, cultural, and social programs.

These generous promises have often been honored more in theory than in fact. The local councils— the chief institutional safeguard for the provincial minorities—were not convened until twenty years after the revolution. Subsidies to non-Persian publications and radio stations remain meager. Jews have been so harassed as "pro-Israeli Zionists" that more than half—40,000 out of 80,000—have left the country. Armenian Christians had to accept Muslim principals in their schools. They also had to end coeducational classes, adopt the government curriculum, abide by Muslim dress codes, including the veil, and close their community clubs to Muslims. The Christian population has declined from over 300,000 to fewer than 200,000.

The Baha'is, however, have borne the brunt of religious persecution. Their leaders have been executed as "apostates" and "imperialist spies." Adherents have been fired from their jobs, had their property confiscated, and been imprisoned and tortured to pressure them to convert to Islam. Their schools have been closed, their community property expropriated, and their shrines and cemeteries bulldozed. It is estimated that since the revolution, one-third of the 300,000 Baha'is have left Iran. The Baha'is, like the Jews and Armenians, have migrated mostly to Canada and the United States, especially New York and California. This persecution did not ease until the election of President Khatami.

The much larger Sunni Muslim population, which forms as much as 10 percent of the total, has its own reasons for being alienated from the regime. The state religion is Shi'ism. High officials have to be Shi'i. Citizens have to subscribe to Khomeini's concept of government, a notion derived from Shi'ism. Few institutions cater to Sunni needs. There is not a single Sunni mosque in the whole of Tehran. The regime also tends to overlook the existence of Sunnis among Iran's Kurds, Turkmens, Arabs, and Baluchis. It is no accident that in the period 1979 through 1981, the newborn regime faced its most serious challenges in precisely the areas of the country where these people live. It succeeded in crushing the revolts by rushing in tens of thousands of Revolutionary Guards from the Persian Shi'i heartland of Isfahan, Shiraz, and Qom to the Sunni regions.

Thus, the Islamic Republic has its strongest cultural roots in the Persian Shi'i heartland. Its weakest roots are among the non-Shi'is: the Sunnis, Baha'is, Jews, Christians, and Zoroastrians. Its base among the Azeris, who are Shi'i but not Persian speakers, remains to be tested. In the past, the Azeris, who form 24 percent of the population and dwarf the other minorities, have not posed an ethnic problem. They are part and parcel of the Shi'i community. They have prominent figures, such as President Khamenei, in the Shi'i hierarchy. Many Azeri merchants, professionals, and workers live throughout the regions of Iran.

In short, Azeris can be considered well integrated into Iran. But the 1991 creation of the Republic of Azerbaijan on Iran's northeastern border following the disintegration of the Soviet Union has raised new concerns, since some Azeris on both sides of the border have begun to talk of establishing a larger unified Azerbaijan. It is no accident that in the war between Azerbaijan and Armenia in the early 1990s, Iran favored the latter. So far, the concept of a unified Azerbaijan has little appeal among Iranian Azeris. The recent elections show that the Sunni and Azeri populations remain politically integrated into Iran and that they place much of their hopes in Khatami and his reform movement.

Interests, Social Movements, and Protests

In the first two decades after its founding, the Islamic Republic often violated its own constitution. It closed down newspapers, professional associations, labor unions, and political parties. It banned demonstrations and public meetings. It incarcerated tens of thousands without due process. It systematically tortured prisoners to extract false confessions and public recantations. And it executed some 25,000 political prisoners, most of them without due process of law. The United Nations, Amnesty International, and Human Rights Watch all took Iran to task for violating the UN Human Rights Charter as well its own Islamic constitution. Most victims were Kurds, military officers from the old regime, and leftists, especially members of the Mojahedin and Fedayin. Iran's Islamic Revolution, like many other revolutions in history, devoured its own children.

Although the violation of individual liberties affected the whole population, it aroused special resentment among three social groups: the modern middle class, educated women, and organized labor. The modern middle class, especially the intelligentsia, has been secular and even anticlerical ever since the 1905 revolution. Little love is lost between it and the Islamic Republic. Not surprisingly, the vast majority of those executed in the 1980s were teachers, engineers, professionals, and college students. In 1999, eighteen different campuses throughout the country, including Tehran University, erupted into mass demonstrations against the chief judge, who had closed down a reformist newspaper. Revolutionary Guards promptly occupied the campuses, killing and seriously injuring an unknown number of students. And again in late 2002, thousands of students protested the death sentence handed down by the courts to a reformist academic who was accused of insulting Islam.

Every year university students show their strength by commemorating December 7, the day in 1953 when three student demonstrators were shot dead by the shah's army. Youth and college students are now political forces to be reckoned with in Iran: over half the population was born after the 1979 revolution; and in 1997 there were more than 1.15 million students in higher education.

Educated women in Iran also harbor numerous grievances against the conservative clerics in the regime, especially in the judiciary. Although the Western press often dwells on the veil, Iranian women consider the veil one of their less important problems. Given a choice, most would probably continue to wear it out of personal habit and national tradition. More important are work-related grievances: job security, pay scales, promotions, maternity leave, and access to prestigious professions. Furthermore, judges often interpret the *shari'a* in a narrow fashion, treating women as second-class citizens, especially in marriage disputes, child custody disputes, and even criminal cases. They consider women to be wards of male relatives. Adult women are not allowed to travel without written permission from their male relatives. The conservatives also favor social policies to encourage women to stay home raising children rather than enter the university and the professions. Despite these patriarchal attitudes, educated women have become a major factor in Iranian society. They now form 54 percent of college students, 45 percent of doctors, 25 percent of government employees, and 13 percent of the general labor force, up from 8 percent in the 1980s. They have established their own organizations and journals reinterpreting Islam to conform with modern notions of equality. One grand ayatollah has even argued that women should be able to hold any job, including president, Supreme Leader, and court judge, a position from which they have been barred since 1979. He also said they should have the right to abort fetuses in the first trimester; that compensation to a family for the loss of life of a relative, known as blood money, should be the same for men and women; and that wives should have the same rights as husbands in divorce cases.

Factory workers in Iran are another significant social group with serious grievances. Their concerns deal mostly with high unemployment, low wages, declining incomes, lack of decent housing, and an unsatisfactory labor law, which, while giving them mandatory holidays and some semblance of job security, denies them the right to call strikes and organize independent unions. Since 1979, wage earners have had a Workers' House—a government-influenced organization—and its affiliated newspaper, *Kar va Kargar* (*Work and Worker*), and, since 1999, the Islamic Labor Party to represent their interests. In most years, the Workers' House flexes political muscle by holding a May Day rally. In 1999, the rally began peacefully with a greeting from a woman reform deputy who had received the second-most votes in the 1996 Tehran municipal elections. But the rally turned into a protest when workers began to march to parliament denouncing conservatives who had spoken in favor of further watering down of the Labor Law. Bus drivers spontaneously joined the protest, shutting down most of central Tehran.

President Khatami's reform movement draws much of its core support precisely from these three social groups: college youth, women, and workers. In the 1997 and 2001, presidential campaigns, as well as in the elections for municipal councils and the Sixth *Majles,* crucial roles were played by the Islamic Student Associations, the Office of Student Solidarity, the Islamic Women's Association, and the Workers' House. The reformers were also supported by a number of newspapers, which have quickly gained a mass circulation even though they initially catered mainly to the intelligentsia. For example, the reformist *Hayat-e No,* launched in late 2000, had a circulation of over 235,000 by April 2001, almost double that of the long-established conservative newspaper *Ettela'at.*

Section ⑤ Iranian Politics in Transition

Political Challenges and Changing Agendas

As of 2002, President Khatami and his reform movement dominate both the executive and the legislative branches of Iran's government and continue to enjoy overwhelming support among the general electorate. But the conservative opposition still controls the judiciary and receives substantial support from the powerful religious foundations, Revolutionary Guards, and intelligence services. In political terms, this amounts to ongoing clash between reformers and conservatives. In institutional terms, it is a clash between the executive and the legislature against the judiciary. In ideological terms, it is a clash between democracy and theocracy. At times, the conflict is open, vociferous, and even violent. At other times, it is hidden, managed, and kept behind the scene. But it is ever present and underscores nearly everything that happens in Iran's politics. Khatami hopes to keep the conflict out of the streets and convince Supreme Leader Khamenei that alienating the general public would be fatal for the Islamic Republic, and he has tried to persuade Khamenei to nudge the die-hard conservatives to accept needed reforms.

Khatami has managed to score some successes. He placed reformers in charge of most cabinet posts. The Interior Ministry first went to Hojjat al-Islam Abdullah Nouri, an innovative interpreter of Islam. The Labor Ministry portfolio was given to the head of the Workers' House. Khatami also removed the previous intelligence minister and chief judge, and although he was unable to replace them with his own supporters, he managed to give these vital positions to less conservative clerics. He eased out military officers who had initiated the campus bloodshed, a general who had talked of cutting out the tongues of liberals, and a prison warden notorious for his cruelty. The new Intelligence minister brought to account officials responsible for a series of high-profile political assassinations, claiming that they had been out-of-control rogues; their leader conveniently "committed suicide" in prison. The culture minister issued some 200 newspaper licenses, relaxed censorship, which boosted both publishing and the film industry, and, in an act of great symbolic significance, made Mossadeq's home into a national heritage monument. The Justice minister named women judges to family courts for the first time since 1979. The Revolutionary Guards lost their autonomy and were merged into the Ministry of Defense. Moreover, the Revolutionary Guards and the Hezbollahi vigilantes

President Khatemi of Iran. *Source:* Angel Franco, *The New York Times,* November 10, 2001.

were instructed not to harass the public over dress codes, hair styles, videos, music cassettes, Internet cafés, and satellite dishes.

Meanwhile, reform deputies in the *Majles* have drafted a number of controversial bills. They proposed raising the legal marriage age for girls from nine to fifteen; giving women equal rights in divorce, and even the right to separate from husbands; and allowing girls to study in foreign universities. They tried to combat AIDS with safer-sex education, condom distribution, and even legalized prostitution. They favored ratifying the UN Declaration on All Forms of Discrimination Against Women. They drafted an investment law to attract foreign capital, a judicial law stipulating courts to have juries, and another one reiterating the constitutional ban on torture. They tried to get the Guardian Council to render its decisions in writing and to pass on its authority to vet parliamentary candidates to the Interior Ministry. Khatami warned of the dangers of "religious fascism" in Iran and openly argued that the long-term survival of the Islamic Republic would remain in doubt unless needed reforms were accepted. He even hinted that he would appeal directly to the public to obtain new constitutional powers. "We cannot speak of democracy if we are not ready to play by its rules," he declared. "The main feature of democracy is the right of people to change a government if they do not like it."[29]

The conservatives have fought back. The Guardian Council initially vetoed the new bills, but the Expediency Council, probably pushed by the Supreme Leader, eventually accepted some of them in watered-down versions. For example, the investment law was accepted. The marriage age was raised to thirteen, and divorced women were guaranteed a portion of their ex-husband's income. The Revolutionary Courts and the Special Court for the Clergy also waged a concerted campaign to silence the reformers. Over sixty newspapers, including the most popular ones, were banned for publishing supposedly antiregime materials in what became known as the "newspaper massacre." And a long array of prominent reformers and Khatami advisers, headed by Nouri, were accused by the courts of questioning the concept of jurist's guardianship and thus undermining not only the Islamic Republic but also Islam. In other words, they were accused of apostasy, blasphemy, and heresy. These measures,

however, were less dramatic than they sound. New newspapers replaced those that were closed down. The show trials boomeranged against the conservatives since the accused reformers were able to turn them into arenas for propagating their popular views. The reformers even equated the courts that were trying them to the Spanish Inquisition in medieval Europe. What is more, most of the defendants, after being charged with capital offenses, were given prison sentences and then, after relatively short intervals, were released through amnesties and appeals to the Supreme Leader.

The conflict between the reformers and conservatives has complicated Iran's foreign policy. Difference in foreign policy, which had existed from the early days of Khatami's administration, became stark in the aftermath of the September 11, 2001, terrorist attacks on the United States. Khatami promptly extended condolences to the American people, and his supporters held well-publicized candlelight vigils in Tehran. His foreign minister received his British counterpart in Tehran, promised help in the "war on terrorism," offered military assistance to American soldiers in Afghanistan, stepped up supplies to the Northern Alliance fighting the Taliban, and, once that regime was overthrown, extended financial and diplomatic aid to the pro-American administration in Kabul.

Supreme Leader Khamenei, however, continued to denounce Washington, implied that America had brought September 11 upon itself, and forbade any public debate about improving relations with the United States. His intransigence was ironically helped when U.S. President George W. Bush, in his January 2002 State of the Union address, lumped Iran together with Iraq and North Korea in an alleged "axis of evil" that supported terrorism and threatened world peace. President Khatami, however, while keeping his distance from the United States, has continued to improve relations with the rest of the world, especially with European and Arab countries. He paid state visits to Moscow, Rome, Tokyo, and Paris, where he laid wreaths at the Pantheon for French cultural icons Jean-Jacques Rousseau, Emile Zola, and Victor Hugo. He also signed contracts with European oil companies, attracted considerable foreign investment to Iran, and required foreign companies to pay for oil in euros rather than U.S. dollars.

Iranian Politics in Comparative Perspective

Iran is both like and unlike other developing countries. It is unlike most Third World countries in that it is an old state with institutions that go back to ancient times. It is also not a country that only relatively recently achieved independence since it was never formally colonized by the European imperial powers. Unlike many other developing nations that have a weak connection between state and society, Iran has a religion that links the elite with the masses, the cities with the villages, the government with the citizenry. Shi'ism, as well as Iranian national identity, serves as a social cement, giving the population a strong collective identity. Iran possesses rich oil resources that give it the potential for rapid economic growth that would be the envy of most developing countries. Finally, Iran produced two popular upheavals in the twentieth century: the constitutional (1905) and the Islamic (1979) revolutions in which the citizenry actively intervened in politics, overthrew the old regime, and shaped the new. Both of these revolutions were the result of authentic home-grown political movements, not foreign imports.

Yet Iran shares some problems with other Third World countries. It has failed to establish a full-fledged democracy. Its economy remains underdeveloped, highly dependent on one commodity, and unable to meet the rising expectations of its population. Iran's collective identity is strained by internal fault lines, especially those of class, ethnicity, and interclerical conflicts. And its ambition to enter the world of states as an important player has been thwarted by international as well as domestic and regional realities that have combined to keep the country pretty much on the global sidelines. This thwarted ambition has helped to undermine democracy and economic development in Iran.

Democracy has been constricted by theocracy. Some argue that Islam made this inevitable. But Islam, like Christianity and the other major religions, can be interpreted in ways that either support or oppose democracy. Islam, as interpreted by some Muslims, stresses the importance of justice, equality, and consultation. It has a tradition of tolerating other religions. Its *shari'a* explicitly protects life, property,

and honor. In practice, it has often separated politics from religion, statutes from holy laws, spiritual affairs from worldly matters, and the state from the clerical establishment.

Moreover, the theocracy in Iran originates not in Islam but in jurist's guardianship, a concept developed by Khomeini. On the whole, Sunni Islam considers clerics to be theological scholars, not a special political stratum. This helps explain why the Iranian regime has found it difficult to export the revolution to the rest of the Muslim world. The failure of democracy in Iran should be attributed less to Islam than to the confluence of crises between 1979 and 1981 that allowed a group of clerics to seize power. Whether they remain in power into the twenty-first century depends not so much on Islam but on how they handle the opposition, their own differences, and, most important, the country's economic problems.

The Islamic Republic of Iran is sharply divided over how to manage an economy beset by rising demands, wildly fluctuating petroleum revenues, and the nightmarish prospect that in the next two generations, the oil wells will run dry. Most clerics favor a rather conventional capitalist road to development, hoping to liberalize the market, privatize industry, attract foreign capital, and encourage the propertied classes to invest. Others envisage an equally conventional statist road to development, favoring central planning, government industries, price controls, high taxes, state subsidies, national self-reliance, and ambitious programs to eliminate poverty, illiteracy, slums, and unemployment. Khatami has charted a third road, combining elements of state intervention with free enterprise. This is strikingly similar to the social democracy favored in other parts of the world.

As the clock of history ticks, Iran's population grows, oil revenues fluctuate, and the per capita national income threatens to fall. Economic problems like those that undermined the monarchy could well undermine the Islamic Republic. The country's collective identity has also come under great strain in recent years. The emphasis on Shi'ism has antagonized Iran's Sunnis as well as its non-Muslim citizens. The emphasis on clerical Shi'ism has further alienated all secularists, including lay liberals, radical leftists, and moderate nationalists. Furthermore, the emphasis on Khomeini's brand of Shi'ism has alienated Shi'is who reject the whole notion of jurist's guardianship. The elevation of Khamenei as the Supreme Leader has also antagonized many early proponents of jurist's guardianship.

In sum, the regime has gradually reduced its social base of support to a bare minimum. Only time will tell whether the growing discontent in Iran will be expressed through apolitical channels, such as drug addiction, emigration, and quietist religion, or whether those seeking change will look to reformist movements such as that led by President Khatami and the reformist clerics remaining within the regime, or turn to more radical insurrectionary organizations or ethnic-based movements.

Finally, the Islamic Republic's initial attempt to enter the international arena as a militant force proved to be counterproductive. It has diverted scarce resources to the military, especially the Revolutionary Guards. It frightened Saudi Arabia and the Gulf sheikdoms into the arms of the United States. It has prompted the United States to isolate Iran, discouraging investment and preventing international organizations from extending economic assistance. It also alarmed neighboring secular Islamic states such as Turkey, Tadzhikistan, and Azerbaijan. In recent years, President Khatami has managed to overcome many of these problems. He has won over Iran's Arab neighbors and has established cordial relations with Turkey and Afghanistan. Most important, he has managed to repair bridges between Iran and the European Community. Whether he can do the same with the United States is an open question that will be answered by decision makers in Tehran and Washington.

Key Terms

ayatollah	*shari'a*
fatwa	bazaars
theocracy	fundamentalism
Majles	jurist's guardianship
Guardian Council	mosques
Supreme Leader	*pasdaran*
Farsi	imam
Shi'ism	Hezbollahis
People of the Book	hojjat al-Islam
Qur'an	*jihad*

rentier state	Foundation of the
dual society	Oppressed
Organization of Petro-	Assembly of Experts
leum Exporting	*maslahat*
Countries	Expediency Council
Imam Jum'ehs	

Suggested Readings

Abrahamian, E. *Iran Between Two Revolutions.* Princeton, N.J.: Princeton University Press, 1982.

———. *Khomeinism.* Berkeley: University of California Press, 1993.

Akhavi, S. *Religion and Politics in Contemporary Iran.* Albany: State University of New York Press, 1980.

Bakhash, S. *Reign of the Ayatollahs.* New York: Basic Books, 1984.

Baktiari, B. *Parliamentary Politics in Revolutionary Iran.* Gainesville: University Press of Florida, 1966.

Bill, J. *The Eagle and the Lion.* New Haven, Conn.: Yale University Press, 1988.

Buchta, W. *Who Rules Iran?* Washington, D.C.: Washington Institute for Near East Policy, 2000.

Chehabi, H. *Iranian Politics and Religious Modernism.* Ithaca, N.Y.: Cornell University Press, 1990.

Dabashi, H. *Theology of Discontent: The Ideological Foundation of the Islamic Revolution in Iran.* New York: New York University Press, 1993.

Fischer, M. *Iran: From Religious Dispute to Revolution.* Cambridge, Mass.: Harvard University Press, 1980.

Halliday, F. *Iran: Dictatorship and Development.* London: Penguin, 1979.

Hooglund, E. *Twenty Years of Islamic Revolution.* Syracuse: Syracuse University Press, 2002.

Huntington, Samuel P. *The Clash of Civilizations and the Remaking of the World Order.* New York: Simon & Schuster, 1996.

Kazemi, F. "Civil Society and Iranian Politics." In A. Norton (ed.), *Civil Society in the Middle East.* Leiden: Brill, 1996.

Keddie, N. *Roots of Revolution.* New Haven, Conn.: Yale University Press, 1981.

Mackey, S. *The Iranians: Persia, Islam, and the Soul of a Nation.* New York: Penguin, 1996.

Milani, M. *The Making of Iran's Islamic Revolution.* Boulder, Colo.: Westview Press, 1994.

Mir-Hosseini, Z. *Islam and Gender.* Princeton, N.J.: Princeton University Press, 1999.

Moin, B. *Khomeini: Life of the Ayatollah.* London: Tauris, 1999.

Mottahedeh, R. *The Mantle of the Prophet.* New York: Simon & Schuster, 1985.

Schirazi, A. *The Constitution of Iran.* London: Tauris, 1997.

Suggested Websites

British Broadcasting Corporation
www.bbc.co.uk/persian/revolution

Guide to Iranian media, including English-language sources
www.gooya.org
Iranian Mission to the United Nations
www.un.int/iran.org
Radio Free Europe
www.iranreport@list.rferl.org
Weekly Digest of News
www.times@iranian.com

Notes

[1]Quoted in E. Browne, *The Persian Revolution* (New York: Barnes and Noble, 1966), 137.

[2]British Financial Adviser to the Foreign Office in Tehran, *Documents on British Foreign Policy, 1919–39* (London: Her Majesty's Stationery Office, 1963), First Series, XIII, 720, 735.

[3]British Minister to the Foreign Office, *Report on the Seizure of Lands,* Foreign Office 371/Persia 1932/File 34-16007.

[4]*Kayhan International,* November 10, 1976.

[5]"Fifty Indictments of Treason During Fifty Years of Treason," *Khabarnameh,* no. 46 (April 1976).

[6]M. Bazargan, "Letter to the Editor," *Ettela'at,* February 7, 1980.

[7]*Iran Times,* January 12, 1979.

[8]*Washington Post,* December 12, 1978.

[9]*Christian Science Monitor,* December 12, 1978.

[10]Samuel P. Huntington, *The Clash of Civilizations and the Remaking of World Order* (New York: Simon & Schuster, 1996).

[11]Mirza Hosayn Khan Tahvildar-e Isfahan, *Jukhrafiha-ye Isfahan* (The Geography of Isfahan) (Tehran: Tehran University Press, 1963), 100–101.

[12]International Labor Organization, "Employment and Income Policies for Iran" (Unpublished report, Geneva, 1972), Appendix C, 6.

[13]A. Sharbatoghilie, *Urbanization and Regional Disparity in Post-Revolutionary Iran* (Boulder, Colo.: Westview Press, 1991), 4.

[14]*Wall Street Journal,* November 4, 1977.

[15]U.S. Congress, *Economic Consequences of the Revolution in Iran* (Washington, D.C.: U.S. Government Printing Office, 1979), 184.

[16]U.S. Congress, *Economic Consequences of the Revolution in Iran,* 5.

[17]U.S. Department of Commerce, *Iran: A Survey of U.S. Business Opportunities* (Washington, D.C.: U.S. Government Printing Office, 1977), 1–2.

[18]Cited in H. Amirahmadi, *Revolution and Economic Transition* (Albany: State University of New York Press, 1960), p. 201.

[19]Cited in *Iran Times,* July 9, 1993.

[20]J. Amuzegar, *Iran's Economy Under the Islamic Republic* (London: Taurus Press, 1994), 100.

[21]A. Rafsanjani, "The Islamic Consultative Assembly," *Kayhan,* May 23, 1987.

[22]S. Saffari, "The Legitimation of the Clergy's Right to Rule in the Iranian Constitution of 1979," *British Journal of Middle Eastern Studies* 20, no. 1 (1993): 64–81.

[23]Ayatollah Montazeri, *Ettela'at,* October 8, 1979.

[24]O. Fallaci, "Interview with Khomeini," *New York Times Magazine,* October 7, 1979.

[25]*Kayhan,* March 6, 1980.

[26]*Kayhan,* April 21, 1987.

[27]*Kayhan-e Hava'i,* November 16, 1988.

[28]*Economist,* February 9, 2000.

[29]*New York Times,* August 27, 2002.

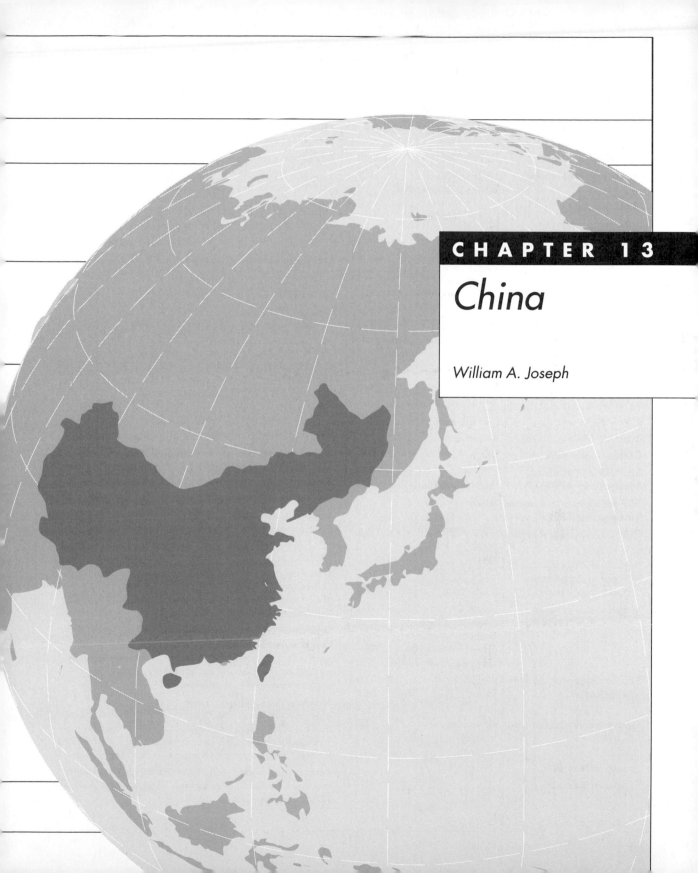

CHAPTER 13

China

William A. Joseph

People's Republic of China

Land and People

Capital	Bejing
Total area (square miles)	3,696,100 (slightly larger than the U.S.)
Population	1.275 billion
Annual population growth rate (%)	1975–2000 1.3 2000–2015 (projected) 0.7
Urban population (%)	36
Ethnic composition (% of total population)	Chinese (Han) 92 Others 8
Major language(s)	Chinese (various dialects, including Mandarin and Cantonese)
Religious affiliation (%)	Atheist* 94–96 Christian 3–4 Muslim 1–2

*Although officially atheist, many people practice Buddhism and traditional folk and other religions, e.g., Daoism (Taoism).

Economy

Domestic currency	Renminbi ("People's Currency") CNY US$1: 8.28 CNY (2002 av.)
Total GDP (US$)	1.08 trillion
GDP per capita (US$)	866
Total GDP at purchasing power parity (US$)	5.02 trillion
GDP per capita at purchasing power parity (US$)	3,976
GDP annual growth rate (%)	1997 8.8 2000 7.9 2001 7.3
GDP per capita average annual growth rate (%)	1975–2000 8.1 1990–2000 9.2
Inequality in income or consumption (1998) (%)	Share of poorest 10% 2.4 Share of poorest 20% 5.9 Share of richest 20% 46.6 Share of richest 10% 30.4 Gini Index (1995) 40.3
Structure of production (% of GDP)	Agriculture 50.9 Industry 15.9 Services 33.2
Labor force distribution (% of total)	Agriculture 50 Industry 23 Services 27
Exports as % of GDP	26
Imports as % of GDP	23

Society

Life expectancy at birth	70.5	
Infant mortality per 1,000 live births	32	
Adult literacy (%)	Male	91.7
	Female	76.3
Access to information and communications (per 1,000 population)	Telephone lines	112
	Mobile phones	66
	Radios	339
	Televisions	293
	Personal computers	15.9

Women in Government and the Economy

Women in the national legislature Lower house or single house (%)		21.8
Women at ministerial level (%)		5.1
Female economic activity rate (age 15 and above) (%)		72.7
Female labor force (% of total)		42
Estimated earned income (PPP US$)	Female	3,132
	Male	4,773
2002 Human Development Index Ranking (out of 173 countries)		96

Political Organization

Political System Communist party-state; officially, a socialist state under the people's democratic dictatorship.

Regime History Established in 1949 after the victory of the Chinese Communist Party (CCP) in the Chinese civil war.

Administrative Structure Unitary system with 22 provinces, 5 autonomous regions, 4 centrally administered municipalities, and 2 Special Administrative Regions (Hong Kong and Macao).

Executive Premier (head of government) and president (head of state) formally elected by legislature, but only with approval of CCP leadership; the head of the CCP, the general secretary, is in effect the country's chief executive.

Legislature Unicameral National People's Congress; 2985 delegates elected indirectly from lower-level people's congresses for five-year terms. Largely a "rubber-stamp" body for Communist Party policies, although in recent years has become somewhat more assertive.

Judiciary A nationwide system of people's courts, which is constitutionally independent but, in fact, largely under the control of the CCP; a Supreme People's Court supervises the country's judicial system and is formally responsible to the National People's Congress, which also elects the court's presidents.

Party System A one-party system, although in addition to the ruling Chinese Communist Party, there are eight politically insignificant "democratic" parties.

Section ❶ The Making of the Modern Chinese State

Politics in Action

When it was announced in July 2001 that Beijing had been chosen as the site of 2008 Summer Olympics, an estimated 200,000 Chinese citizens poured into Tiananmen ("Gate of Heavenly Peace") Square in the heart of China's capital to celebrate the honor that had been bestowed on their country. They saw the awarding of the games to Beijing by the International Olympics Committee (IOC) as overdue recognition of the remarkable modernization of the Chinese economy, the stunning successes of Chinese athletes in international sports competitions, and the emergence of the People's Republic of China (PRC) as major global power.

But there were also many voices that were extremely critical of the IOC's decision. Human rights organizations such as Amnesty International argued that the decision rewarded one of the world's most oppressive governments. Some compared the Beijing Games to those held in Berlin, Germany, in 1936, shortly after Hitler had come to power and which the Nazis used to gain international legitimacy. The Dalai Lama, the exiled spiritual leader of Tibet, which has been occupied by China since 1950, strongly objected to awarding the games to Beijing. As his spokesman noted, "This will put the stamp of international approval on Beijing's human rights abuses and will encourage China to escalate its repression."[1] Critics of the Beijing games also pointed out the irony that the Olympics celebrations in Tiananmen Square were held very near the place where, in 1989, China's Communist leaders ordered troops to crush a prodemocracy movement, which led to the killing of hundreds of civilians, many of them college students.

Others argued that hosting the Olympics could be a force for positive change in China. PRC leaders would not want to risk an international boycott of the Beijing Games by engaging in highly visible repression. This, in turn, could embolden China's democracy activists, who have been largely silent since the Tiananmen massacre. In this way, the 2008 Beijing Olympics might spur much-needed political reform, as did the 1988 Olympics in Seoul, an important impetus to South Korea's transition from a military dictatorship to a democracy.

The controversy over the Beijing Olympics reflects the fundamental contradictions that define contemporary Chinese politics. The People's Republic of China is one of only a few countries in the world that is still a **communist-party state** in which the ruling party claims an exclusive monopoly on political power and proclaims allegiance (at least officially) to the ideology of **Marxism-Leninism.** At the same time, the country has experienced dramatic economic and social liberalization—and even some political relaxation since the bloodshed in Tiananmen—and is more fully integrated into the world than at any other time in its history. But the Chinese Communist Party (CCP) rejects any meaningful movement toward democracy, and the rift between an oppressive political system and an increasingly modern and globalized society remains deep and ominous.

Geographic Setting

The PRC is located in the eastern part of mainland Asia at the heart of one of the world's most strategically important and volatile regions. It shares land borders with more than a dozen countries, including Russia, India, Pakistan, Vietnam, and the Democratic People's Republic of Korea (North Korea) and is a relatively short distance by sea from Japan, the Philippines, and Indonesia. China, which had largely assumed its present geographic identity by the eighteenth century, is slightly bigger than the United States in land area, making it the third largest country in the world, after Russia and Canada.

The PRC is bounded on all sides by imposing physical barriers: the sea to the east; mountains to the north, south, and west (including the world's largest, Mount Everest); deserts, vast grasslands, and dense forests in various parts of the north; and tropical rain forests to the south. In traditional times, these barriers isolated China from extensive contact with other peoples and contributed to the country's sense of itself as the "Middle Kingdom" (which is how the Chinese word

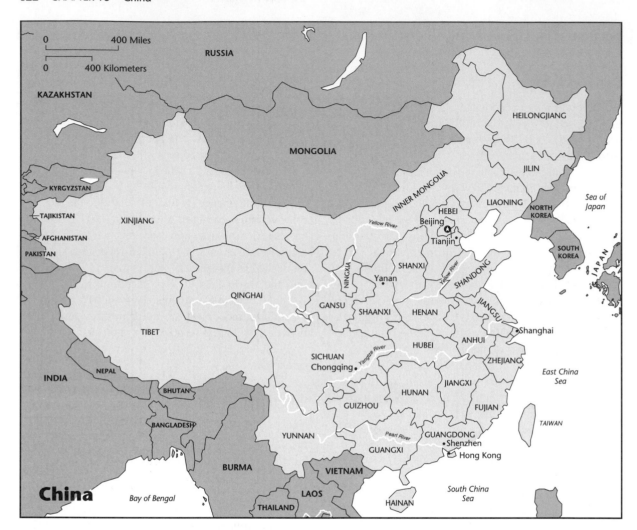

China

for China, *Zhongguo*, is translated) that lay not only at the physical but also at the political and moral center of its known world.

Administratively, the PRC is made up of twenty-two provinces, five **autonomous regions,** and four centrally administered cities (including the capital, Beijing), and two Special Administrative Regions (Hong Kong and Macao). The sparsely populated but territorially vast western part of the country is mostly mountains, deserts, and high plateaus. The northeast, which is much like the U.S. plains states in terms of weather and topography, is both a wheat-growing area and China's industrial heartland. Southern China has a much warmer, and in places even semitropical, climate, which allows year-round agriculture and inten-

sive rice cultivation. The country is very rich in natural resources, particularly coal and petroleum (including significant, but untapped onshore and offshore reserves), and is considered to have the world's greatest potential for hydroelectric power.

Although China and the United States are roughly equal in geographic size, China's population of about 1.3 billion—by far the world's largest—is five times greater. But only a relatively small part of China's land is usable for agriculture. China has a little over 20 percent of the world's population but only 10 percent of the world's arable land. The precarious balance between people and the land needed to feed them has been a dilemma for China for centuries and remains one of the government's major concerns.

Industrialization and urbanization have expanded significantly in recent years. The PRC now has more than thirty cities of 1 million or more, the three largest being Shanghai (16.7 million), Beijing (13.8 million), and Tianjin (10.0 million). In 1997, the former British colony of Hong Kong, one of the world's great commercial centers (population 6.8 million), became part of the PRC. Nevertheless, about 65 percent of China's people still live and work in rural areas. The countryside has played—and continues to play—a very important role in China's political development.

China's population is highly concentrated along the eastern seaboard and in the most agriculturally fertile areas around the country's three great rivers: the Yellow River, the Yangtze (Yangzi), and the Pearl River. The vast majority (92 percent) of China's citizens are ethnically Chinese (referred to as the Han people, after one of China's earliest dynasties). The remaining 8 percent is made up of more than fifty ethnic minorities, who differ from the Han in several major ways, including race, language, culture, and religion. Most of these minority peoples live in the country's geopolitically vital border regions, including Tibet. This makes the often uneasy and sometimes hostile relationship between China's minority peoples and the central government in Beijing a crucial and sensitive issue in Chinese politics today.

Critical Junctures

The PRC was founded in 1949. But understanding the critical junctures in the making of the modern Chinese state requires that we go back much further into China's political history. Broadly considered, that history can be divided into three periods: the imperial period (221 B.C.–1911 A.D), during which China was ruled by a series of dynasties and emperors; the relatively brief and unstable republican period (1912–1949), when a weak central government was plagued by civil war and foreign invasion; and the Communist period, from the founding of the People's Republic of China in 1949 to the present.

From Empire to Republic (221 B.C.–1911 A.D)

Modern China is heir to one of the world's oldest cultural and political traditions. The roots of Chinese culture date back more than 4,000 years, and the Chinese empire first took political shape in 221 B.C., when a number of small kingdoms were unified under the Emperor Qin, who laid the foundation of an imperial system that lasted for more than twenty centuries until its overthrow in 1911. During those many centuries, China was ruled by more than a dozen different dynasties and experienced extensive geographic expansion and far-reaching political, economic, social, and cultural changes. Nevertheless, many of the core features of the imperial system remained remarkably consistent over time.

There are several reasons that the Chinese empire survived for such a long time. First, imperial China developed a sophisticated and effective system of national government long before the strong monarchical states of Europe took form in the seventeenth century. Second, the traditional Chinese economy was a source of great strength to the empire. Urbanization expanded in China much sooner than it did in Europe, and Westerners, like Marco Polo, who journeyed to China as early as the thirteenth century were amazed by the grandeur of the Middle Kingdom's cities.

Third, the structure of traditional Chinese society, especially in the million or more small villages that were its foundation, gave imperial China great staying power. The vast majority of the village population was made up of poor and relatively poor peasants. But life was dominated by landlords and other local elites who worked with the national government to maintain and sustain the system.

Fourth, the traditional order was supported by the enduring influence in Chinese society of Confucianism. This philosophy, based on the teachings of Confucius (c. 551–479 B.C.), stresses the importance of the group over the individual, deference to one's elders and superiors, and the need to maintain social harmony. Confucianism did contain a teaching, the "Mandate of Heaven," that the people could overthrow an unjust ruler. Nevertheless, Confucianism was basically a conservative philosophy that justified and preserved an autocratic state, a patriarchal culture, and a highly stratified society. Finally, the Chinese imperial system endured because, throughout most of its history, China was by far the dominant political, military, and cultural force in its known world.

In the late eighteenth and early nineteenth centuries, imperial China experienced a population explosion and economic stagnation, along with a significant rise in official corruption and exploitation of the peasants by both landlords and the government. Social unrest culminated in the Taiping Rebellion (1850–1864), a massive revolt that took 20 million lives and nearly toppled the ruling Qing dynasty.

In the meantime, the West, which had surged far ahead of China in industrial development and military technology, was pressing the country to open its markets to foreign trade. China showed little interest in such overtures and tried to limit the activities of Westerners in China. But Europe, most notably Britain, in the midst of its era of mercantile and colonial expansion, used its military supremacy to compel China to engage in "free" trade with the West. China's efforts to stop Britain from selling opium in China led to military conflict between the two countries. After suffering a humiliating defeat in the Opium War (1839–1842), China was literally forced to open its borders to foreign merchants, missionaries, and diplomats on terms dictated by Britain and other Western powers. China lost control of significant pieces of its territory to foreigners (including Hong Kong), and important sectors of the Chinese economy fell into foreign hands.

There were many efforts to revive or reform the dynasty in the late nineteenth and early twentieth centuries, but political power in China remained largely in the hands of staunch conservatives who resisted change. As a result, when change came, it was in the form of a revolution in 1911 that toppled the Qing dynasty and brought an end to the 2,000-year-old imperial system.

Warlords, Nationalists, and Communists (1912–1949)

The Republic of China was established on January 1, 1912, with Dr. Sun Yat-sen,* then China's best-known revolutionary, as president. However, the Western-educated Sun was not able to hold onto power, and China soon fell into a lengthy period of conflict and disintegration, with parts of the country run by rival warlords. Sun set about organizing another revolution to

---

*In China, the family name, or surname (e.g., *Sun*) comes before the personal, or given, name (e.g., *Yat-sen*). Therefore, Sun Yat-sen would be referred to as President Sun.

Critical Junctures in Modern China's Political Development
1911 Revolution led by Sun Yat-sen overthrows 2,000-year-old imperial system and establishes the Republic of China.
1912 Sun Yat-sen founds the Nationalist (*Guomindang*) Party to oppose warlords who have seized power in the new republic.
1921 Chinese Communist Party (CCP) founded.
1927 Civil war between Nationalists (now led by Chiang Kai-shek) and Communists begins.
1934 Mao Zedong becomes leader of the CCP.
1937 Japan invades China, marking the start of World War II in Asia.
1949 Chinese Communists win the civil war and establish the People's Republic of China.
1958–1960 Great Leap Forward.
1966–1976 Great Proletarian Cultural Revolution.
1976 Mao Zedong dies.
1978 Deng Xiaoping becomes China's paramount leader.
1989 Tiananmen massacre.
1997 Deng Xiaoping dies; Jiang Zemin becomes China's most powerful leader.
2002–2003 Hu Jintao succeeds Jiang as head of the CCP and president of the People's Republic of China.

defeat the warlords and reunify the country under his Nationalist Party (the *Guomindang*).

In 1921, the Chinese Communist Party (CCP) was established by a few intellectuals who had been inspired by the Communist revolution in Russia in 1917 and by the anti-imperialism of the newly founded Soviet Union to look for more radical solutions to China's problems. In 1924, the small Communist Party, acting on Soviet advice, joined with Sun Yat-sen's Nationalists to fight the warlords. After some initial successes, this alliance came to a tragic end in 1927 when Chiang Kai-shek, a military leader who had become the head of the Nationalist Party after Sun's death in 1925, turned against his coalition partners and ordered a bloody suppression that nearly wiped out the Communists. Chiang then proceeded to unify the Republic of China under his personal rule, largely by striking an accommodation with some of the country's most powerful remaining warlords who supported him in the civil war against the communists

Ironically, the defeat of the CCP created the conditions for the eventual triumph of the man who would lead the party to nationwide victory. Mao Zedong, who had been one of the junior founders of the Communist Party, strongly advocated paying more attention to China's suffering peasants as a potential source of support. "In a very short time," he wrote in 1927, "several hundred million peasants will rise like a mighty storm, like a hurricane, a force so swift and violent that no power, however great, will be able to hold it back."[2]

In 1934–1935, the party undertook its fabled Long March, an epic journey of 6,000 miles through some of China's roughest terrain, to escape attack by Chiang's forces. At the end of the Long March, the CCP established a base in Yanan, a remote rural area in northwestern China. In Yanan, Mao consolidated his political and ideological leadership of the CCP, sometimes through coercive means, and was elected party chairman in 1943, a position he held until his death in 1976.

Japan's invasion of China in 1937 pushed the Nationalist government deep into the country's southwest and effectively eliminated it as an active combatant against Japanese aggression. In contrast, the CCP base in Yanan was on the front line against Japan's troops in northern China, and Mao and the Communists successfully mobilized the peasants to use **guerrilla warfare** to fight the invaders. By the end of World War II in 1945, the CCP had vastly expanded its membership and controlled much of the countryside in north China. The Nationalists, on the other hand, were isolated and unpopular with many Chinese because of the corruption, political repression, and economic mismanagement of Chiang Kai-shek's regime.

After the Japanese surrender, Communist forces won decisively against the U.S.-backed Nationalists, who were forced to retreat to the island of Taiwan, 90 miles off the Chinese coast. (See "Global Connection: The Republic of China on Taiwan.") On October 1, 1949, Mao Zedong stood on a rostrum in Tiananmen near the entrance to the former imperial palace in Bei-

jing and declared the founding of the People's Republic of China.

Mao in Power (1949–1976)

The CCP came to power on the crest of an enormous wave of popular support because of its reputation as being a party of social reformers and patriotic fighters. Chairman Mao and the CCP quickly turned their attention to some of the country's most glaring problems. For instance, a massive land reform campaign redistributed property from the rich to the poor and increased productivity in the countryside. Highly successful drives eliminated opium addiction and prostitution from the cities, and a national law greatly enhanced the legal status of women in the family and allowed many women to free themselves from unhappy arranged marriages. Although the CCP did not hesitate to use violence to achieve its objectives and silence opponents, the party gained considerable legitimacy because of its successful policies during these years.

Between 1953 and 1957, the PRC implemented a Soviet-style five-year economic plan. The complete nationalization of industry and **collectivization** of agriculture carried out as part of this plan were decisive steps away from the mixed state-private economy of the early 1950s and toward **socialism.** Although the plan achieved good economic results, Mao was troubled by the persistence of inequalities in China, especially those caused by the emphasis on industrial and urban development and relative neglect of the countryside. In response, he launched the **Great Leap Forward** (1958–1960), a utopian effort to accelerate the country's economic development by relying on the labor and willpower of the masses while also propelling China into a radically egalitarian era of true **communism.**

The Great Leap was a great flop and turned into "one of the most extreme, bizarre, and eventually catastrophic episodes in twentieth-century political history."[3] In the rural areas, irrational policies, wasted resources, poor management, and the lack of labor incentives combined with bad weather to produce a famine that claimed between 20 and 30 million lives. An industrial depression soon followed the collapse of agriculture, causing a terrible setback to China's economic development.

Global Connection: *The Republic of China on Taiwan*

Despite the victory of the Chinese Communist Party in the civil war and the founding of the People's Republic of China on the Chinese mainland in October 1949, the Republic of China (ROC) under Chiang Kai-shek and the Nationalist Party continued to function on Taiwan. The Chinese Communists would likely have taken over Taiwan at the end of the civil war if the United States had not intervened to protect the island. The U.S. government, alarmed by the outbreak of the Korean War in 1950, saw the defense of the Nationalist government on Taiwan as part of the effort to stop the further expansion of communism in Asia.

When Chiang Kai-shek and his supporters fled to Taiwan in 1949, the island was already firmly under the control of Nationalists, who had killed or arrested many of their opponents on Taiwan in the aftermath of a popular uprising in February 1947. The harsh dictatorship imposed by Chiang's Nationalists deepened the sharp divide between the "mainlanders," who had come over to escape the Communists, and the native Taiwanese majority, whose ancestors had settled on the island centuries before and who spoke a distinctive Chinese dialect.

Economically, Taiwan prospered under Chiang Kai-shek's rule. With large amounts of U.S. aid and advice, the Nationalist government sponsored a successful and peaceful program of land reform and rural development, attracted extensive foreign investment, and encouraged an export-led strategy of economic growth that made Taiwan a model newly industrializing country (NIC) by the 1970s. The government also invested heavily in the modernization of Taiwan's roads and ports, and it promoted policies that have given the island health and education levels that are among the best in the world and a standard of living that is one of the highest in Asia.

Political change, however, came more slowly to Taiwan. After his death in 1975, Chiang Kai-shek was succeeded as president by his son, Chiang Ching-kuo, whom most people expected to continue the authoritarian rule of his father. Instead, the younger Chiang permitted some opposition and dissent, and he gave important government and party positions previously dominated by mainlanders to Taiwanese. When he died in 1988, the presidency of the republic passed to the Taiwanese vice president, Lee Teng-hui, who also became head of the Nationalist Party.

Under President Lee, Taiwan made big strides toward democratization. Laws used to imprison dissidents were revoked, the media were freed of all censorship, and open multiparty elections were held for all local and island-wide positions. In presidential elections in 1996, Lee Teng-hui won 54 percent of the vote in a hotly contested four-way race, reflecting both the new openness of the political system and the credit that Taiwan's voters gave the Nationalist Party for the island's progress.

But in 2000, an opposition party candidate, Chen Shui-bian of the Democratic Progressive Party (DPP), won the presidency, which many observers saw as reflecting a further maturing of Taiwan's democracy. Chen's victory was due in part to a combination of the desire for change, especially in the light of a serious downturn in the island's economic growth and a split within the National Party.

The most contentious political issue in Taiwan, which is still formally called the Republic of China, is whether the island should continue to work, however slowly, toward reunification with the mainland, as was the Nationalists' policy under Lee Teng-hui, or declare formal independence. A big factor in Chen's election was the growing popularity of the DPP's position that Taiwan should seriously consider the independence option. Beijing still regards Taiwan as a renegade province and has threatened to use force if the island moves toward formal separation.

Taiwan and the PRC have developed extensive, if indirect, economic relations with each other, and millions of people from Taiwan have gone to the mainland to do business, visit relatives, or just sightsee. The PRC and ROC have engaged in some negotiations about possible reunification, but the two sides remain far apart because of their vastly differing political, economic, and social systems.

Taiwan

Land area (sq. miles)	13,895 (about one-third the size of Virginia)
Population	22.5 million
Ethnic composition	Taiwanese 84%, mainland Chinese 14%, aborigine 2%
GDP (purchasing power parity)	$386 billion
GDP per capita (purchasing power parity)	$17,200
GDP growth rate:	–2.2% (2001)
Life expectancy	Male, 74; Female, 80
Infant mortality (per 1,000 live births)	6
Literacy	94%

In the early 1960s, Mao took a less active role in day-to-day decision making. Two of China's other top leaders at the time, Liu Shaoqi and Deng Xiaoping, were put in charge of efforts to revive the economy and used a combination of careful planning and some market-oriented policies to stimulate production, particularly in agriculture.

This strategy did help the Chinese economy, but once again Mao found himself profoundly unhappy with the consequences of China's development. By the mid-1960s, the chairman had concluded that the policies of Liu and Deng had led to a resurgence of elitism and inequality that were threatening his revolutionary goals for China by setting the country on the road to capitalism.

The result of Mao's disquiet was the **Great Proletarian Cultural Revolution** (1966–1976), an ideological crusade designed to jolt China back toward his vision of socialism. Like the Great Leap Forward, the Cultural Revolution was a campaign of mass mobilization and utopian idealism, but its methods were much more violent, and its main objective was the political purification of the party and the nation through struggle against so-called class enemies, not accelerated economic development. Using his unmatched political clout and charisma, Mao put together a potent coalition of radical party leaders, loyal military officers, and student rebels (called Red Guards) to purge anyone thought to be guilty of **revisionism,** that is, betrayal of his version of Marxism-Leninism known as Mao Zedong Thought.

In the Cultural Revolution's first phase (1966–1969), 20 million or so Red Guards went on a rampage across the country, harassing, torturing, and killing people accused of being class enemies, particularly intellectuals and discredited party leaders. During the next phase (1969–1971), Mao used the People's Liberation Army (PLA) to restore political order, while the final phase (1972–1976) involved intense factional conflict over who would succeed the aging Mao as party chairman. Mao died in September 1976 at age eighty-two. A month later, the power struggle was settled when a coalition of the moderate leaders masterminded the arrest of their radical rivals, the so-called Gang of Four, who were led by Mao's wife, Jiang Qing. The arrest of the Gang (who were sentenced to long prison terms) marked the end of the Cultural Revolution, which had claimed at least a million lives and brought the nation to the brink of civil war.

Deng Xiaoping and the Transformation of Chinese Communism (1977–1997)

In order to help them repair the damage caused by the Cultural Revolution, China's new leaders restored to office many of the veteran officials who had been purged by Mao and the radicals, including Deng Xiaoping. By 1978, Deng had clearly become the most powerful member of the CCP leadership—though he preferred to install a loyal lieutenant in the formal position of party leader rather than take it for himself. He lost little time in putting China on a path of reform that dramatically transformed the nation.

Deng's policies were a profound break with the Maoist past. State control of the economy was significantly reduced, and market forces were allowed to play an increasingly important role in all aspects of production. Private enterprise was encouraged, and the economy was opened to unprecedented levels of foreign investment. On the cultural front, Chinese artists and writers saw the shackles of party dogma that had bound them for decades greatly loosened. Deng took major steps to revitalize China's government by bringing in younger, better-educated officials. The results of Deng's initiatives were, by any measure, astounding. After decades of stagnation, the Chinese economy experienced spectacular growth throughout the 1980s and beyond (see Figure 1).

Then came June 1989 and the massacre near Tiananmen Square. Discontent over inflation and official corruption, as well as a desire, especially among students and intellectuals, for more democracy, inspired large-scale demonstrations in Beijing and several other Chinese cities that spring. The demonstrations in Beijing grew through April and May, and at one point more than 1 million people from all walks of life gathered in and around Tiananmen. For several months, the CCP, constrained by internal divisions about how to handle the protests and intensive international media coverage, did little other than engage in some threatening rhetoric to dissuade the demonstrators. But China's leaders ran out of patience, and the army was ordered to clear the square during the very early morning hours of June 4. By the time dawn broke in Beijing,

Figure 1

The Economic Transformation of Post-Mao China

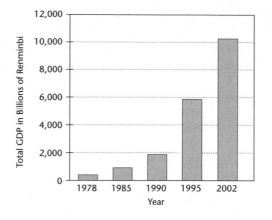

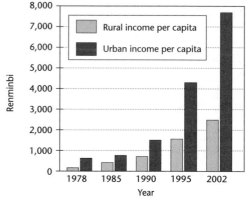

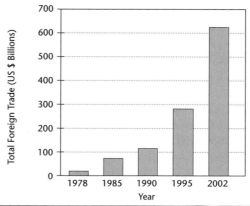

These charts show how dramatically the Chinese economy has been transformed since the market reforms were introduced by Deng Xiaoping in 1978. *Sources: China Statistical Yearbook 1997 and 2001; Statistical Communique of the People's Republic of China on the 2002 National Economic and Social Development.*

Tiananmen Square had indeed been cleared, but with a death toll that still has not been revealed.

Following the Tiananmen massacre, China went through a few years of intensified political repression and economic retrenchment. Then in early 1992, Deng Xiaoping took some bold steps to accelerate reform of the economy. He did so in large part because he hoped it would help the PRC avoid a collapse of the Communist system such as had occurred just the year before in the Soviet Union.

From Revolutionary Leaders to Technocrats (1997 to the Present)

Another important consequence of the 1989 Tiananmen crisis was the replacement as formal head of the CCP of one Deng protégé, Zhao Ziyang, by another, Jiang Zemin. Zhao was ousted by Deng because he was considered too sympathetic to the student demonstrators, and Jiang was promoted from his previous posts as mayor and CCP chief of Shanghai because of his firm but relatively bloodless handling of similar protests in that city. Although Deng remained the power behind the throne for several years, he gradually turned over greater authority to Jiang, who, in addition to his positions as head (general secretary) of the CCP and chair of the powerful Central Military Commission, became president of the PRC in 1993. When Deng Xiaoping died in February 1997, Jiang was secure in his position as China's top leader.

Jiang Zemin retired at age seventy-six as head of the Communist Party in late 2002 and as president of the PRC in early 2003. Under his leadership, China continued the process of economic reform and its record of remarkable economic growth. China became even more fully integrated into the global economy, as exemplified by its admission to the World Trade Organization (WTO) in 2001, and enhanced both its regional and international stature as a rising power. Overall, the country was politically stable during the Jiang era. But the CCP still ruthlessly repressed any individual or group perceived as challenging its authority and faced serious problems, including mounting unemployment, pervasive corruption, and widening gaps between the rich and the poor that threatened to disrupt the calm.

Jiang was succeeded as CCP general secretary in November 2002 and PRC president in March 2003 by

This cartoon captures the contradiction between economic reform and political repression that characterized China under the leadership of Deng Xiaoping. *Source:* © 1992, *The Boston Globe.* Distributed by Los Angeles Times Syndicate. Reprinted with permission.

Hu Jintao, who had previously served as China's vice president. At age sixty when he took these offices, Hu Jintao was considerably younger than most of China's recent leaders. But both Jiang and Hu represented a new kind of leader for the PRC. Mao Zedong and Deng Xiaoping were professional revolutionaries who had participated in the CCP's long struggle for power and were among the founders of the Communist regime when it was established in 1949. In contrast, Jiang and Hu were "technocrats," party officials with academic training (in their cases, as engineers) who worked their way up the political ladder by a combination of competence and loyalty.

The most significant aspect of the transfer of power from Jiang to Hu was how predictable and orderly it was. In fact, some observed that it was the first relatively tranquil top-level political succession in China in more than 200 years. Jiang had retired after two terms in office, as required by both party rules and the state constitution, and Hu had, for several years, been expected to succeed Jiang.

This smooth leadership transition, however, masked much that echoed the secretive and highly personalistic politics that has long characterized Chinese politics. First, Hu Jintao had been designated years before by Deng Xiaoping to be Jiang's successor. So Hu's "election" to the posts of CCP general secretary and PRC president was less the result of an institutionalized process than of personal and factional machinations.

Second, despite retiring from all party and government positions, Jiang Zemin retained considerable political power and influence. He was, in various ways, able to orchestrate his enshrinement as the successor to Mao and Deng as one of the great luminaries in party history. He also kept at least an ear in the inner sanctum of decision making through the placement of numerous close associates in the party's most powerful organizations. Most significant, Jiang did not relinquish his position as chair of the Military Commission, which meant that he was following in Deng's footsteps by keeping control of the country's armed forces even though he did not hold any of the country's top executive offices. Nevertheless, the coming to power of Jiang Zemin and then Hu Jintao did mark a critical juncture in that it reflected the passing of power from the revolutionary to the technocratic generation of Chinese Communist leaders.

Themes and Implications
Historical Junctures and Political Themes

The World of States.   When the People's Republic was founded, China was in a weak position in the international system. For more than a century, its destiny had been shaped by incursions and influences from abroad that it could do little to control. Mao made many tragic and terrible blunders, but one of his great

Student demonstrators erected a statue called the "Goddess of Democracy" in Beijing's Tiannmen Square in late May 1989 to symbolize their demands for greater political freedom in China. In the background is an official portrait of former Chinese Communist Party leader, Mao Zedong. Chinese troops toppled and destroyed the statue after they occupied the square on June 4, 1989, a process that also resulted in the death of many protestors. *Source:* AP/ Wide World Photos.

achievements was to build a strong state able to affirm and defend its sovereignty. China's international stature has increased as its economic and military strength have grown in recent decades. Although still a relatively poor country by many per capita measures, the sheer size of its economy makes the PRC an economic powerhouse whose import and export policies have an important impact on many other countries. China is a nuclear power with the world's largest conventional military force, and it is an active and influential member of nearly all international organizations, including the United Nations, where it sits as one of the five permanent members of the Security Council. Clearly, China has become one of the major players in the world of states

The making of the modern Chinese state has also been profoundly influenced at several critical points by China's encounters with other countries. The end of the Middle Kingdom's relative isolation from the non-Asian world and the conflict with the militarily superior West in the nineteenth century was a major factor in the collapse of the imperial system in 1911. Anger over European and U.S. treatment of China, admiration for the Russian Revolution, and the invasion of China by Japan in the 1930s all played a role in propelling the CCP to power in 1949.

American hostility to the new Communist regime in Beijing helped push the PRC into an alliance with the Soviet Union and follow the Soviet model of development in the early 1950s. But Mao's disapproval of the direction in which Soviet Communist leaders were taking their country greatly influenced his decisions to launch both the Great Leap Forward in 1958 and the Cultural Revolution in 1966. In the early 1970s, Mao supported the beginnings of détente with the United States in response to what he saw as a growing and more immediate threat to China from the Soviet Union. The relationship between China and the United States deepened throughout the 1970s and paved the way for the marketization and globalization of the Chinese economy under Deng Xiaoping.

Sino-American interaction (*sino* means "China," as derived from the Latin) is, arguably, the most important bilateral diplomatic relationship in the post–cold war world. There have been numerous ups and downs in that relationship since the two countries resumed ties in the 1970s. A particularly low point came after the 1989 Tiananmen massacre, when the United States cut back contacts with the Beijing regime. But shared economic and geopolitical interests have brought the United States and China closer since then, although issues such as human rights, arms control, and trade policies have sometimes caused serious friction. American presidential administrations have differed about whether the PRC should be seen as a rising power best dealt with by cooperation or containment.

The terrorist attacks of September 11, 2001, had a significant impact on Sino-American relations. The PRC became a key ally in the U.S.-led war on terrorism, which led to a downgrading of any and all outstanding disagreements between Beijing and Washington. When Presidents Bush and Jiang met in Texas in October 2002, their mutual interest in dealing with the terrorist threat was practically the only matter for discussion. This was after a period in which Sino-American ties had been strained by the accidental bombing of the PRC embassy in Belgrade, Yugoslavia, by U.S. aircraft during the Kosovo war in July 1999 and the collision of an American spy plane with a Chinese jet fighter off the coast of China in April 2001. Common ground in the war on terrorism has led to a distinct warming of U.S.-China relations as issues that had become contentious between the two nations, including human rights, the trade imbalance, and Chinese arms exports, were put on the diplomatic back burner. China's leaders were quite happy to have tensions with the United States off their already overly burdened agenda. Indeed, one observer concluded that "the country that has benefited most from 9-11 is China."[4]

Governing the Economy.   Economic issues were central to the revolutionary process that resulted in the founding of the People's Republic. The Western powers were primarily motivated by the lure of the China market in their aggressive policies toward the Chinese empire in the nineteenth century. Chiang Kai-shek's Nationalist government lost popular support partly because of its mismanagement of the economy and inability to control corruption. Mass poverty and terrible inequality fueled the Chinese revolution and led millions of peasants and workers to back the Communist Party in the civil war.

The history of the PRC is largely the story of experimentation with a series of very different economic systems: a Soviet-style planning system in the early 1950s, the radical egalitarianism of the Maoist model, and Deng Xiaoping's market-oriented policies. Ideological disputes within the CCP over which of these development strategies China should follow were the main cause of the ferocious political struggles, such as the Cultural Revolution, that have so often wracked the country. Deng's bold reforms were, in large measure, motivated by his hope that improved living standards would restore the legitimacy of the CCP, which had been badly tarnished by the economic failings of the Maoist era. The remarkable successes of those reforms under Deng and his successors have helped sustain the CCP in power at a time when most other Communist regimes have disappeared. Continuing China's economic progress will be one of the most important challenges facing Hu Jintao and China's other leaders.

The Democratic Idea.   The CCP also faces major political challenges, especially the challenge of the democratic idea, which has had a troubled history in modern China. The revolution of 1911, which overthrew the imperial system and established the Republic of China under Sun Yat-sen, was the culmination of the first effort to establish a Chinese government in which citizens would have a greater voice. But the combination of warlordism, civil war, world war, and Chiang Kai-shek's sharp turn toward dictatorship undermined any real progress toward democracy. Any hope that the democratic idea might take root in the early years of Communist rule in China was violently dispelled by the building of a one-party Communist state and Mao's unrelenting campaigns against alleged enemies of his revolution. The Deng Xiaoping era brought much greater economic, social, and cultural freedom for the Chinese people, but time and again the CCP acted to strangle the stirrings of the democratic idea, most brutally near Tiananmen Square in 1989. Jiang Zemin has been a faithful disciple of Deng; he not only has vigorously championed economic reform in China, but also has also made sure that the CCP retains its firm grip on power. Although it is unlikely that Hu Jintao will act any differently, he could face increasing pressure for political change as Chinese society becomes more modernized, complex, and globalized. In fact, in his first months in power, Hu struck a number of populist themes in his speeches and travels that could portend an effort to establish a "close to the people" leadership style distinct from that of the more aloof Jiang.

The Politics of Collective Identity.   Because of its long history and high degree of cultural homogeneity, China has a very strong sense of national identity.

Memories of past humiliations and suffering at the hands of foreigners still influence the international relations of the PRC. For example, Beijing's insistence that Britain return Hong Kong to Chinese control in 1997 largely on its terms was shaped by the desire to redress what it saw as one of the most blatant injustices of China's defeat in the Opium War of the mid-nineteenth century. China also believes that Japan should apologize more fully for atrocities committed by the Japanese army during World War II before the two Asian powers can have completely cordial diplomatic relations. And as faith in communist ideology has weakened, party leaders have increasingly turned to nationalism as a means to rally the Chinese people behind their government, as reflected in the large-scale public celebrations that greeted Beijing's selection as the site for the 2008 Summer Olympics

China's cultural homogeneity has also spared it the kind of ethnic or religious violence that has plagued so many other countries in the modern world. The exception has been in the border regions of the country, where there is a large concentration of minority peoples, particularly in Tibet and the Muslim areas of China's northwest (see Section 4).

But China did experience a particularly vicious and destructive kind of identity politics during the Maoist era. Although landlords and capitalists had lost their private property and economic power by the mid-1950s, Mao continued to promote class struggle that pitted workers, peasants, and loyal party activists against "capitalist roaders" and other alleged counterrevolutionaries. When he took over in the late 1970s, Deng Xiaoping called for an end to such divisive class struggles and proclaimed an era of social harmony in which the whole nation could concentrate its energies on the overarching goal of economic development, a trend that was continued and deepened by his successor, Jiang Zemin. But economic reform has led to new (or renewed) cleavages in Chinese society, including glaring inequalities between those who have profited handsomely from the marketization of the economy and those who have done less well or even been disadvantaged by the changes. These inequalities could become the basis of class, regional, or other kinds of identity-based conflicts that severely test the economic and political management skills of China's leaders.

Implications for Comparative Politics

China is a particularly important and interesting case for the study of comparative politics. First, the PRC can be compared with other communist party-states with which it shares or has shared many political and ideological features. From this perspective, China raises intriguing questions: Why has China's communist party-state so far proved more durable than that of the Soviet Union and nearly all other similar regimes? By what combination of reform and repression has the CCP held onto power? What signs are there that it is likely to continue to be able to do so for the foreseeable future? What signs suggest that Communist rule in China may be weakening? Studying Chinese politics is important for understanding the past, present, and future of a type of political system, the communist party-state, that has had a major impact on the modern world.

China can also be fruitfully compared with other developing nations that face similar economic and political challenges. Although the PRC is part of the Third World as measured by the average standard of living of its population, its record of growth in the past several decades has been far better than almost all other developing countries. Furthermore, the educational and health levels of the Chinese people are quite good when compared with many other countries at a similar level of development, for example, India and Nigeria. How has China achieved such relative success in its quest for economic and social development? On the other hand, while much of the Third World has gone through a wave of democratization in recent decades, China remains a one-party dictatorship. How and why has China resisted this wave of democracy? What does the experience of other developing countries say about how economic modernization might influence the prospects for democracy in China?

Napoleon Bonaparte, emperor of France in the early nineteenth century, is said to have remarked, "Let China sleep. For when China wakes, it will shake the world."[5] No doubt China has awakened, and given the country's geographic size, vast resources, huge population, surging economy, and formidable military might, it will certainly be among the world's great powers in the near future. China should command the attention of all students of comparative politics.

Section ❷ Political Economy and Development

The growth of China's economy since reform began in the late 1970s has been called "one of the century's greatest economic miracles," which has led to "one of the biggest improvements in human welfare anywhere at any time."[6] Such superlatives seem justified in describing overall economic growth rates that averaged about 10 percent per year for nearly two decades while most of the world's other economies were growing much more slowly. China's gross domestic product (GDP), in dollar terms, is now the sixth largest in the world (about the same as that of France). In terms of purchasing power parity (which adjusts for price differences between countries), China has the second largest economy in the world after the United States and accounts for nearly 12 percent of global GDP. Between 1980 and 2000, the average income of the Chinese people increased more than fifteen-fold. Although there are still many very poor people in China, more than 200 million have been lifted from living in absolute poverty to a level where they have a minimally adequate supply of food, clothing, and shelter. China's economic miracle has involved much more than growth in GDP and personal income. There has also been a profound transformation of the basic nature of economic life in the PRC from what it had been during the Maoist era.

State and Economy

The Maoist Economy

When the CCP came to power in 1949, the Chinese economy was suffering from the devastating effects of more than a hundred years of rebellion, invasion, civil war, and bad government. The first urgent task of China's new Communist rulers was the stabilization and revival of the economy. Although a lot of property was seized from wealthy landowners, rich industrialists, and foreign companies, much private ownership and many aspects of capitalism were allowed to continue in order to gain support for the government and get the economy going again.

Once production had been restored, the party turned its attention to economic development by following the Soviet model of state socialism. The essence of this model was a **command economy,** in which the state owns or controls most economic resources, and economic activity is driven by government planning and commands rather than by market forces.

The command economy in China was at its height during the First Five-Year Plan of 1953–1957, when the government took control of the production and distribution of nearly all goods and services. The First Five-Year Plan yielded some impressive economic results, but it also created huge bureaucracies and new inequalities, especially between the heavily favored industrial cities and the investment-starved rural areas. Both the Great Leap Forward and the Cultural Revolution embodied a Maoist approach to economic development that was intended to be less bureaucratic and more egalitarian than the Soviet model.

For example, in the Great Leap, more than 1 million backyard furnaces were set up throughout the country to prove that steel could be produced by peasants in every village, not just in a few huge modern factories in the cities. In the Cultural Revolution, revolutionary committees, controlled by workers and party activists, replaced the Soviet-style system of letting managers run industrial enterprises. Both of these Maoist experiments were less than successful. The backyard furnaces yielded great quantities of useless steel and squandered precious resources, while the revolutionary committees led many factories to pay more attention to politics than production.

The economic legacy of Maoism is mixed. Under Mao, the PRC "did accomplish, in however flawed a fashion, the initial phase of industrialization of the Chinese economy, creating a substantial industrial and technological base that simply had not existed before."[7] In addition, by the end of the Maoist era, the people of China were much healthier and more literate than they had been in the early 1950s. But for all of its radical rhetoric, the Maoist strategy of development never broke decisively with the basic precepts of the command system. Political interference, poor management, and ill-conceived projects led to wasted resources of truly staggering proportions. Overall, China's economic growth rates, especially in agriculture, barely kept pace with population increases, and the standard of living changed little between the 1950s and Mao's death in 1976.

China Goes to Market

After he consolidated power in 1978, Deng Xiaoping took China in an economic direction far different from Mao's or from that which had ever been followed by a communist party-state anywhere. His pragmatic views on how to promote development were captured in his famous 1962 statement, "It doesn't matter whether a cat is white or black, as long as it catches mice."[8] Deng meant that China should not be overly concerned about whether a particular policy was socialist or capitalist if it in fact helped the economy. It was just such sentiment that got him in trouble with Mao and made Deng one of the principal victims of the Cultural Revolution.

Once he was in charge, Deng spearheaded a program of far-reaching reforms that remade the Chinese economy, touched nearly every aspect of life in the PRC, and redefined socialism in China. These reforms greatly reduced the role of government control while allowing market mechanisms, such as the profit motive, to operate in increasingly large areas of the economy. They also involved a significant degree of decentralization in the economy. Authority for making economic decisions passed from bureaucrats to individual families, factory managers, and private entrepreneurs, all of them presumably motivated by the desire to make more money.

Almost all prices are now set according to supply and demand, as in a capitalist economy, rather than by administrative decree, and in most sectors of the economy decisions about what to produce and how to produce it are no longer dictated by the state. The Chinese government also encourages private ownership of factories and businesses. According to some estimates, private and semiprivate enterprises, including those in industry, services, commerce, and agribusiness, now account for between 50 and 60 percent of China's GDP and employ nearly 200 million people.

In many areas of the economy, government monopolies have given way to fierce competition between state-owned and non-state-owned firms. For example, the government-run national airline, which was the country's only airline until 1985, now competes with dozens of foreign and domestic carriers. Several government-approved stock markets, which sell shares in enterprises to private individuals, have been established, and many more unauthorized ones have sprung up around the country.

A decade ago there were over 100,000 state-owned enterprises (SOEs) in China; now there are fewer than half that number. But these so-called economic dinosaurs still employ nearly 80 million workers, produce a significant share of China's total industrial output, and continue to dominate critical sectors of the economy, such as the production of steel and petroleum. Nevertheless, the role of the state sector is rapidly shrinking as private industries and so-called collective enterprises (which are usually run by combinations of local governments and private entrepreneurs) are expanding at a much faster rate (see Figure 2). Moreover, even SOEs must now be responsive to market forces. Those that are unable to turn a profit are forced to restructure or even threatened with bankruptcy. It is estimated that between 45 and 60 million SOE employees have been laid off in recent years. Many are too old or too unskilled to find good jobs in the modernized and marketized economy, and China has very little in the way of unemployment insurance or social security for its displaced workers.

Some SOEs have been privatized, but most of those that remain are vastly overstaffed and have outdated facilities and machinery, which make them very unattractive to potential foreign or domestic buyers. They remain a huge drain on the country's banking system and hinder modernization of key sectors of the Chinese economy. But the country's leaders are understandably concerned about the political and social consequences that would result from an even more massive layoff of industrial workers.

The economic results of China's move to the market have been phenomenal. The PRC has been the fastest-growing major economy in the world for more than two decades and even weathered, relatively unscathed, the severe financial crisis that struck the rest of East Asia in the late 1990s. China's GDP per capita (that is, the total output of the economy divided by the total population) grew at an average rate of 9.2 percent per year from 1990 to 2000. By way of comparison, the per capita GDP of the United States grew at 2.2 percent

Figure 2

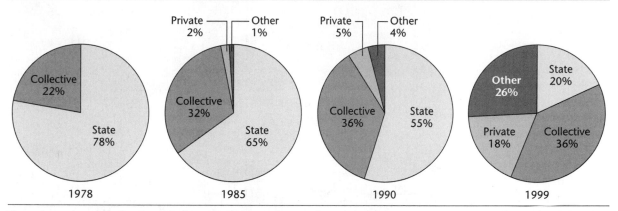

China's Industrial Output by Ownership Type

1978 1985 1990 1999

These charts show how the share of China's total industrial output that comes from state-owned enterprises has declined sharply since economic reforms began in 1978. The category "Collective" consists mostly of rural township and village enterprises (TVEs), which are owned by local governments, but operate according to the market rather than by state planning. "Private" refers to industries owned by individuals, and "Other" includes foreign-owned enterprises and various kinds of mixed ownership. *Source: China Statistical Yearbook 1998 and 2000.*

per year during the same period, India's at 4.1 percent, and Brazil's at 1.5 percent.

A booming economy and rapidly rising incomes have unleashed a consumer revolution in the PRC. To cite just one example, in the late 1970s, hardly anyone owned a television of any kind; now nearly every urban household has a color TV, and a large proportion of rural families have at least a black-and-white set.

The PRC says that it currently has a **socialist market economy.** Although this terminology may seem to be mere ideological window dressing to allow the introduction of capitalism into a country still ruled by a communist party, the phrase conveys the fact that China's economy now combines elements of both socialism and capitalism. In theory, the market remains subordinate to government planning and CCP leadership, which is supposed to prevent too much capitalist-like exploitation and inequality.

Despite these far-reaching changes, the Chinese economy is not fully marketized. Central planning, though greatly refined and reduced, has not been eliminated altogether, and national and local bureaucrats still exercise a great deal of control over the production and distribution of goods, resources, and services. The extent of private property is still restricted, and

unproductive state enterprises continue to exert a considerable drag on key economic sectors. Although the market reforms have gained substantial momentum that would be nearly impossible to reverse, the CCP still wields the power to decide the future direction of China's economy.

Remaking the Chinese Countryside

The economic transformation of China has been particularly striking in the countryside, where over 700 million people live and work.

One of the first major efforts launched by the CCP after it came to power in 1949 was a land reform campaign that confiscated the property of landlords and redistributed it as private holdings to the poorer peasants. But in the mid-1950s, as part of the transition to socialism, China's peasants were reorganized into collective farms made up of about 250 families each. The land then belonged to the collective, and production and labor were directed by local officials working in coordination with the state plan. Individuals were paid according to how much they worked on the collective land, while most crops and other farm products had to be sold to the state at low fixed prices. During

This picture, taken in Shanghai in the 1990s, graphically captures how the modern and the traditional exist side-by-side in China. It also shows how the market-style reforms introduced by Deng Xiaoping greatly increased disparities in wealth, a problem that could lead to growing social and political tensions in the future. *Source:* Dan Habib.

the Great Leap Forward, the collective farms were merged into gigantic **people's communes** with several thousand families. Although the size of the communes was scaled back following failure of the Leap, the commune system remained the foundation of the rural economy throughout the rest of the Maoist period. The system of collectivized agriculture proved to be one of the weakest links in China's command economy. Per capita agricultural production and rural living standards were essentially stagnant from 1957 to 1977.

The first changes in the organization of agriculture in post-Mao China came from the spontaneous actions of local leaders who were looking for ways to boost production. They moved to curtail the powers of the commune and allow peasants more leeway in planting and selling their crops. In the early 1980s, Deng Xiaoping used his newly won political power to support this trend and moved to "bury the Maoist model once and for all" in the countryside.[9] The communes were replaced by a **household responsibility system,** which remains in effect today. Under this system, farmland is contracted out to individual families, who take full charge of the production and marketing of crops. Families can sign contracts for thirty years or more, but there has been no move to privatize agriculture fully by selling the land to individuals. The freeing of the rural economy from the constraints of the communal system led to a sharp increase in agricultural productivity and income for farm families.

But nothing contributed more to the remaking of the Chinese countryside than the spread of a rural industrial and commercial revolution that, in speed and scope, was unprecedented in the history of the modern world. Although the foundations of rural industrialization were laid during the Maoist period, **township and village enterprises** (TVEs) expanded enormously under Deng Xiaoping's economic reforms. These rural factories and businesses, which vary greatly in size, are generally owned and run by local government and private entrepreneurs. Although they are called collective enterprises, TVEs operate outside the state plan, make their own decisions about all aspects of the business process, and are responsible for their profits and losses.

For much of the 1980s and 1990s, TVEs were the

fastest-growing sector of the Chinese economy, producing 80 percent of the nation's clothes and, by 1998, accounting for nearly 30 percent of China's total economic output. But the economic Darwinism of the market caught up with the rapid expansion of TVEs by the turn of the century, and many were forced out of business. Nevertheless, they can still be found in nearly every part of the country, except the poorest areas of the interior, and they employ tens of millions of people.

The transformation of the Chinese countryside has not been without serious problems, however. Local officials who run TVEs "often behave more like business tycoons than public servants" and pay more attention to making money for themselves than to their civic duties.[10] Peasant protests, which sometimes turn violent, against high taxes, corrupt local officials, and delays in payments for agricultural products purchased by the government have increased significantly in recent years.

There have also been concerns about China's ability to produce enough food to feed its big population. Now that the state no longer commands farmers to give priority to the production of grain (which dropped 9 percent in 2001) and other essential foods, they often choose to raise more lucrative cash crops, such as flowers and vegetables. In fact, China has recently had to import fairly large quantities of grain. And overall, the growth of agriculture has slowed considerably since the first burst of reform: it averaged a little over 4 percent per year in the 1990s and dropped to 2.4 percent in 2000 and 2.8 percent in 2001. It is likely that there needs to be more investment, particularly in technology, and deeper structural changes in the rural economy if agriculture is going to resume rapid growth.

The social services safety net provided for China's rural dwellers by the communes has all but disappeared with the return to household-based farming. Many rural clinics and schools closed once government financial support was eliminated. The availability of health care, educational opportunities, disability pay, and retirement funds now depends on the relative wealth of families and villages, which has led to very large gaps between the prosperous and the poor areas of the country. Economic factors, such as the need for larger families in situations where income is dependent on household labor, have also contributed to peasant efforts to circumvent China's controversial one-child popula-

tion control policy (see "Current Challenges: China's One-Child Policy").

The Political Impact of Economic Reform

Efforts to transform the economy through market-style policies have had an important impact on China's domestic politics. First, both Deng Xiaoping and then Jiang Zemin faced opposition from other party leaders who believe that China has moved too fast and too far toward a market economy. The critics of reform are worried about the spread of capitalist influences, including calls for more democracy, at home and from abroad. Deng was able to accommodate such challenges, and the emergence of Jiang and, more recently, Hu Jintao as Deng's successors has kept power in the hands of leaders strongly committed to continuing economic reform. But a major economic setback or widespread political turmoil could still lead to a resurgence of antireform elements in the party.

Second, the **decentralization** of economic decision making, which has been an important factor in the success of the market reforms, has also greatly increased the autonomy of subnational governments. Local governments often defy or ignore the central government by, for example, evading taxes or undertaking massive construction projects without consulting Beijing. Such seepage of economic and political power from the central to the local levels poses serious questions about the ability of the national government to maintain control in the country.

Finally, China's economic transformation has brought far-reaching social change to the country, creating new pressures on the political system and new challenges to the CCP. The party wants the Chinese people to believe that economic growth depends on the political stability that only its firm leadership can provide. CCP leaders hope that growing prosperity will leave most people satisfied with the party and reduce demands for political change. But economic reform has created many groups—entrepreneurs, professionals, middle-class consumers, the hundreds of thousands of Chinese students who have studied abroad—who cannot be repressed if the party wants to sustain the country's economic progress. In time, these and other emerging groups are likely to press their claims for a more independent political voice and confront the

Current Challenges: **China's One-Child Policy**

While he was in power, Mao Zedong did not see a reduction of China's population growth rate as an important national priority. On the contrary, he viewed vast amounts of human labor and the revolutionary enthusiasm of the masses as precious national resources. As a result, little was done to promote family planning in China during most of the Maoist era.

By the early 1970s, China's population had reached over 800 million, and because of greatly improved health conditions, it was growing at about 2.8 percent per year. This meant that the number of people in China would double in just twenty-five years, which would put a great strain on the country's resources. Cutting the birthrate came to be seen as major prerequisite to economic development. Since the 1980s, the Chinese government implemented a stringent population control policy that has used various means to encourage or even force couples to have only a single child. Intensive media campaigns have lauded the patriotic virtues and material benefits of small families. Positive incentives such as more land or preferred housing have been offered to couples with only one child, and fines or demotions have been meted out to those who violate the policy. In some places, contraceptive use and women's fertility cycles are monitored by workplace medics or local doctors, and a couple must have official permission to have a child. Defiance has sometimes led to forced abortion or sterilization.

The one-child campaign, the modernizing economy, and a comparatively strong record in improving educational and employment opportunities for women have all played a role in bringing China's population growth rate to under 0.9 percent per year. This figure is *very* low for a country at China's level of economic development. India, for example, has also had some success in promoting family planning, but its annual population growth rate is 1.5 percent, while Nigeria's is 2.5 percent. These might not seem like big differences, but consider this: at these respective growth rates, it will take seventy-seven years for China's population to double, whereas India's population will double in forty-seven years and Nigeria's in just twenty-eight years!

There have been some very serious problems with China's population policy. The compulsory, intrusive nature of the family planning program and the extensive use of abortion as one of the major means of birth control has led to some international criticism, which Beijing has rejected as interference in its domestic affairs.

Many farmers have evaded the one-child policy—for example, by not registering births—because the return to household-based agriculture has made the quantity of labor an important ingredient in family income. The still widespread belief that male children will contribute more economically to the family and that a male heir is necessary to carry on the family line causes some rural families to take drastic steps to make sure that they have a son. Female infanticide and the abandonment of female babies have increased dramatically, and the spread of ultrasound technology has led to large number of sex-selective abortions of female fetuses. As a result, China has an unusual gender balance among its young population: normally, 105 to 107 boys are born for every 100 girls, but China's last census, completed in 2000, showed a gender ratio of 116.9 boys for every 100 girls and as high as 135 to 100 in some regions. As a result, there are hundreds of thousands (perhaps millions) of "missing girls" in China's population under the age of thirty. One estimate suggests that there are 70 million more males in China than females, and some worry this has already led to "bride stealing" and other kinds of trafficking in women.

Partly in response to rural resistance and international pressure, the Chinese government has relaxed its population policies somewhat; forced abortion is now infrequent, though sex-selective abortion is not. Rural couples are now often allowed to have two children. In the cities, where there has been more voluntary compliance with the policy because of higher incomes and limited living space, the one-child policy is still basically in effect.

regime with some fundamental questions about the nature of Communist power in China.

Society and Economy

Market reform and globalization of the Chinese economy have created a much more diverse and open society. People are vastly freer to choose careers, travel about the country and internationally, practice their religious beliefs, buy private homes, join nonpolitical associations, and engage in a wide range of other activities that were prohibited or severely restricted during the Maoist era. But economic change has also caused grave social problems. There has been a sharp increase in crime, prostitution, and drug use; although such problems are still far less prevalent in China than in many other countries, they are serious enough to be a growing concern for national and local authorities.

Economic reform has also brought significant changes in China's basic system of social welfare. The Maoist economy was characterized by what was called the **iron rice bowl.** As in other state socialist economies such as the Soviet Union, this meant that employment, a certain standard of living (albeit, a low one), and basic cradle-to-grave benefits were guaranteed to most of the urban and rural labor force. In the cities, the workplace was more than just a place to work and earn a salary; it also provided its employees with housing, health care, day care, and other services.

China's economic reformers believe that such guarantees led to poor work motivation and excessive costs for the government and enterprises, and they have implemented policies designed to break the iron rice bowl. Income and employment are no longer guaranteed but are more directly tied to individual effort. Workers in the remaining state-owned enterprises still have rather generous health and pension plans, but employees in the rapidly expanding semiprivate and private sectors usually have few benefits.

The breaking of the iron rice bowl has increased productivity and motivated people to work harder in order to earn more money. But it has also led to a sharp increase in unemployment, which is estimated to be as high as 20 percent of the total urban labor force (the official number is about 4 percent). Labor unrest, including strikes, slowdowns, demonstrations, and sit-ins, has been rising, particularly in China's rust belt,

where state-owned industries have been particularly hard-hit. In early 2002, 50,000 laid-off workers demonstrated in Daqing, a one-time model Maoist oil field in northeastern China, demanding unpaid benefits, and 30,000 workers in another northeastern city staged protests against official corruption and nonpayment of wages.

In the past, the CCP has not dealt gently with protesting workers: the army was ordered to crush the 1989 Tiananmen demonstrations partly because party leaders were alarmed by the large number of workers who had joined the protests under the banner of an unauthorized union. If inefficient state-owned firms are shut down or downsized as the current leadership has promised, another 30 million workers might lose their jobs. Unemployment and labor unrest could be a political time bomb for China's communist party-state.

Market reforms have also opened China's cities to a flood of rural migrants. After the agricultural communes were disbanded in the early 1980s, many of the peasants who were not needed in the fields found work in the rapidly expanding township and village enterprises. But many others, no longer constrained by the strict limits on internal population movement enforced in the Mao era, headed to the urban areas to look for jobs. The 80 to 120 million people who make up this so-called floating population are mostly employed in low-paying temporary jobs such as unskilled construction work—when they can find any work at all. These migrants are putting increased pressure on urban housing and social services, and their presence in Chinese cities could become politically destabilizing if they find their aspirations thwarted by a stalled economy or if they are treated too roughly or unfairly by local governments, which often see them as intruders.

China's economic boom has also created enormous opportunities for corruption. In a country in transition from a command to a market economy, officials still control many resources and retain power over many economic transactions from which large profits can be made. Bribes are common in this heavily bureaucratized and highly personalized system. Because the rule of law is often weaker than personal connections (called **guanxi** in Chinese), nepotism and cronyism are rampant. Recognizing the threat that corruption poses to its legitimacy, the government has repeatedly launched well-publicized campaigns against official graft, with severe punishment, including execution, for some serious offenders, but with little effect in curbing such nefarious practices.

The benefits of economic growth have spread throughout most of China. But there has also been a growth in inequality—a contradiction for a country led by a party that still claims to believe in socialist ideals. China's market reforms and economic boom have created sharp class differences, generally benefiting people who live in the cities much more than those in the countryside (see Figure 1), particularly since agricultural growth rates started to fall in the 1990s. There is also widening gap between the more developed coastal regions and the inland areas, though recent poverty alleviation programs, including a "Develop the West" campaign, have brought some economic progress to some of poorest parts of the country. Hu Jintao, China's new president and party leader, has also taken steps to portray himself as the champion of the poor, promising to place their plight at the top of his administration's agenda.

Gender inequalities also appear to have increased in some ways since the introduction of the market reforms. There is no doubt that the overall situation of women in China has improved enormously since 1949 in terms of social status, legal rights, employment, and education. Women have also benefited from rising living standards and expanded economic opportunities that the reforms have brought. But the trend toward marketization has not benefited men and women equally. In the countryside, it is almost always the case that only male heads of households may sign contracts for land, and therefore men dominate rural economic life. This is true despite the fact that farm labor has become increasingly feminized as many men move to jobs in rural industry or migrate to the cities. Economic and cultural pressures have also led to an alarming suicide rate (the world's highest) among rural women. Over 70 percent (about 120 million) of illiterate adults in China are female. Although China has one of the world's highest rates of female urban labor participation, the market reforms have "strengthened and in some cases reconstructed the sexual division of labor, keeping urban women in a transient, lower-paid, and subordinate position in the workforce."[11] Women

workers are the first to be laid off or are forced to retire early when a state-owned enterprise downsizes.

Finally, the momentous economic changes in China have had serious environmental consequences. As in the former Soviet Union and East-Central Europe, China's environment suffered greatly under the old state socialist system, but in some ways, ecological damage has gotten even worse in the profit-at-any-cost atmosphere of the market reforms. Industrial expansion is fueled primarily by the use of highly polluting coal, which has made the air in China's cities and even many rural areas among the dirtiest in the world. Soil erosion, the loss of arable land, and deforestation are serious problems for the countryside. The dumping of garbage and toxic wastes goes virtually unregulated, and it is estimated that 80 percent of China's rivers are badly polluted. One of the most serious problems is a critical water shortage in north China due to urbanization and industrialization. To meet this need, a $60 billion megaproject was begun in December 2002 to build a system of channels and pump stations to divert water from the central part of the country to the north. The government has also enacted some policies to protect the environment and increased environmental spending. However, "as is the case in most developing countries, the quest for economic development has superseded concern over environmental pollution."[12]

Dealing with some of the negative social consequences of China's market reforms and economic growth is one of the main challenges facing the government. The ability of labor, women's, or environmental movements to get these social issues on the political agenda remains limited by the party's tight control of political life and restrictions on the formation of autonomous interest groups in China (see Section 4).

China and the International Political Economy

Deng Xiaoping's program for transforming the Chinese economy rested on two pillars: the market-oriented reform of the domestic economy and the policy of opening China to the outside world. The extensive internationalization of the Chinese economy that has taken place in recent decades contrasts sharply with the semi-isolationist policy of economic self-reliance pursued by Mao Zedong.

China was not a major trading nation when Deng took power in 1978. Total foreign trade was about $20 billion (about 10 percent of GDP), and foreign investment in China was minuscule, as the stagnant economy, political instability, and heavy-handed bureaucracy were not attractive to potential investors from abroad.

In the early 1980s, China embarked on a strategy of using trade as a central component of its drive for economic development, following in some ways the model of export-led growth pioneered by Japan and **newly industrializing countries** (NICs) such as the Republic of Korea (South Korea). The essence of this model is to take advantage of low-wage domestic labor to produce goods that are in demand internationally and then to use the earnings from the sale of those goods to finance the modernization of the economy.

China's foreign trade totaled more than $620 billion in 2002 (about 50 percent of GDP), making the PRC the sixth largest trading nation in the world. Seventy percent of China's exports are garments, shoes, furniture, small electronic goods, and toys; the country manufactures 60 percent of the world's bicycles and 86 percent of those sold in the United States. The PRC imports mostly machinery, technology, and raw materials needed to support modernization. Despite having large domestic sources of petroleum and significant untapped reserves, China became a net importer of oil for the first time in 1993 because of the huge energy demands of its economic boom. And in 2002, in order to meet the voracious appetite for steel generated by a construction boom and surge in automobile production, China surpassed the United States as the world's largest importer of that commodity, even though it already produces more steel than the United States and Japan combined.

Much of China's trade is in East Asia, particularly with Japan, South Korea, Taiwan, and Hong Kong (which is now administratively part of the PRC but is a highly developed, capitalist economy; see "Global Connection: Hong Kong—From China to Britain and Back Again"). The financial crisis that hit that part of the world in the late 1990s caused a sharp drop in the rate of growth of Chinese exports (from 27 percent in 1997 to 0.5 percent in 1998). But China's export growth rate rebounded to about 6 percent in 2001 and to 22 percent in 2002. Nevertheless, there are still serious doubts about the long-run viability of an economic development strategy that is so heavily dependent on foreign trade.

The United States has also become one of the PRC's major trading partners and is now the biggest market for Chinese exports (over 20 percent of the total in 2001). In 2000, China surpassed Japan as the country with which the United States had the largest trade deficit by a small margin, but as Japan continued to be mired in a deep recession, the U.S. deficit with China in 2002 ($103 billion) far exceeded that with Japan ($70 billion). The growing trade imbalance was a source of some tension in U.S.-China relations, especially over the issue of restricted access to China's domestic market for American goods and the violation of U.S. copyrights by Chinese firms that produce compact discs, video recordings, and computer software. The United States and a number of China's other big trading partners hope that the PRC's accession to the WTO will help remedy some of these problems and open the Chinese market to more imported goods.

Foreign investment in China has also skyrocketed. From close to zero in 1978, by 2001, more than $700 billion in investments had been pledged (and over $400 billion actually used) in nearly 400,000 different enterprises, ranging from small factories producing toys and clothing for export to huge firms producing goods and services for the Chinese market, like Coca-Cola, Motorola, and General Motors. China is now the world's largest absorber of foreign direct investment, and more than 400 of the world's 500 top corporations have operations in the PRC. The low cost of labor in China is a major attraction to foreign firms: manufacturing wages average about 60 cents per hour.

Many of these foreign ventures are located in Special Economic Zones (SEZs) set aside by the government to attract overseas investors through incentives such as tax breaks, modern infrastructure, and the promise of less bureaucratic red tape. The SEZs are even more free-wheeling and faster growing than the Chinese economy as a whole and have also become hotbeds of speculation, corruption, and crime. The largest SEZ, Shenzhen (near Hong Kong), has been transformed in less than twenty years from a nondescript border town of 70,000 people into China's most modern city, with a population of about 7 million.

Global Connection: *Hong Kong: From China to Britain—and Back Again*

Hong Kong became a British colony in three stages during the nineteenth century as a result of what China calls the "unequal treaties" imposed under military and diplomatic pressure from the West. Two parts of Hong Kong were ceded permanently to Britain in 1842 and 1860, respectively, but the largest part of the tiny territory was given to Britain in 1898 with a ninety-nine-year lease. It was the anticipated expiration of that lease that set in motion negotiations between London and Beijing in the 1980s over the future status of Hong Kong. In December 1984, a joint declaration was signed by the two countries in which Britain agreed to return all of Hong Kong to Chinese sovereignty on July 1, 1997. On that date, Hong Kong became a Special Administrative Region (SAR) of the People's Republic of China.

Britain ruled Hong Kong in a traditional, if generally benevolent, colonial fashion. A governor sent from London presided over an administration in which foreigners rather than the local people exercised most of the power. There was a free press, a fair and effective legal system, and other important features of a democratic system. In the last years of British rule, there were efforts to appoint more Hong Kong Chinese to higher administrative positions and expand the scope of elections in choosing some members of the colony's executive and representative bodies. The British, who controlled Hong Kong for over a century, were criticized for taking steps toward democratization only on the eve of their departure from the colony. They allowed only a small number of Hong Kong residents to emigrate to the United Kingdom before the start of Chinese rule.

Hong Kong flourished economically under the free-market policies of the British and became one of the world's great centers of international trade and finance. Hong Kong has the highest standard of living in Asia outside of Japan and Singapore. At the same time, Hong Kong was and is characterized by extremes of wealth and poverty. When it took over Hong Kong in 1997, China pledged to preserve capitalism in the SAR for at least fifty years under the principle of "one country, two systems." Because of the extensive integration of the economies of Hong Kong and southern China, the PRC has a strong motivation not to do anything that might destroy the area's economic dynamism.

Although the PRC took over full control of Hong Kong's foreign policy and has stationed troops of the People's Liberation Army in Hong Kong, Beijing has generally fulfilled its promise that the SAR will have a high degree of political as well as economic autonomy. Civil liberties, the independence of the judiciary, and freedom of the press have largely been maintained.

The PRC nevertheless has made sure that it keeps a grip on political power in Hong Kong. The SAR is headed by a chief executive, Tung Chee-hwa, a wealthy businessman appointed by the PRC, and PRC-approved civil servants wield enormous authority in the government. Although democratic parties critical or at least skeptical of the Chinese Communist Party have a strong presence among the elected members of the SAR's legislature, a majority of seats are chosen by an indirect process that strongly favors pro-China candidates. Beginning in 2001, the Hong Kong government started to tighten rules on holding public demonstrations and banned visits by some prominent Chinese dissidents. And in late 2002, it took steps to implement a law that prohibited "any act of treason, secession, sedition, subversion against the Central People's Government, or theft of state secrets." Some residents and politicians who favor democracy in Hong Kong fear this antisedition law will pave the way for a clampdown on free speech and reinforces their worry that British colonialism has only been replaced by Chinese authoritarianism.

Hong Kong

Land area (sq. miles)	401.5 (about six times the size of Washington, D.C.)
Population	6.9 million
Ethnic composition	Chinese, 95%; other, 5%
GDP (US$)	$163 billion
GDP per capita (US$)	$25,153
GDP growth rate	0% (2001)
Human Development Index	23 (out of 173)
Life expectancy	Male, 77; female, 82
Infant mortality (per 1,000 live births)	5.73
Literacy	94%

The admission of the PRC to the WTO in December 2001 was a significant step in the country's integration into the global economy. The WTO is the major international organization that oversees and regulates commerce between nations, and membership in it is a great benefit to any country that engages in foreign trade. The United States and other highly developed countries agreed to let China in only once they felt that its economy was more "market" than "state" dominated and that China would play by the rules of free trade. The United States also was inclined to speed up approval of WTO membership for the PRC in late 2001 in order to encourage China's support for and participation in the post–September 11 war on terrorism.

In agreeing to the terms of joining the WTO, China had to promise to make some fundamental changes in its trade practices and domestic economic policies. Most important is the further opening of the Chinese economy to foreign investment and competition. Tariffs (i.e., taxes) on imported goods must be drastically cut, and sectors of the economy that have been largely closed to foreign companies, such as banking, insurance, and agriculture, will have to be unbarred. China's state-owned enterprises, government monopolies, and lagging rural economy will likely find this step toward deeper globalization particularly challenging, but the advantages to the PRC are an expected large increase in foreign trade and investment.

China has a major, but somewhat contradictory, position in the international economy. On the one hand, its relatively low level of economic and technological development compared to the industrialized countries makes it very much a part of the Third World. On the other hand, the total output and rapid growth of its economy, expanding trade, and vast resource base (including its population) make it a potential economic superpower among nations. In the years ahead, China is certain to become an even more active participant in the global economy. At the same time, international influences are likely to play an increasingly important role in China's economic and political development.

Section ❸ Governance and Policy-Making

The PRC is by far the most important of the world's few remaining communist party-states in terms of size and power. The basic political organization of the PRC, like that of the Soviet Union before its collapse in 1991, includes Communist Party domination of all government and social institutions, the existence of an official state ideology based on Marxism-Leninism, and the repression of any political opposition. The CCP, which had about 66 million members as of late 2002, claims that only it can govern in the best interests of the entire nation and therefore it has a right to exercise the leading role throughout Chinese society. Although China has moved sharply toward a market economy in recent decades, the CCP still asserts that it is building socialism with the ultimate objective of creating an egalitarian and classless communist society.

Organization of the State

"The force at the core leading our cause forward is the Chinese Communist Party," observed Mao Zedong in a speech given in 1954 at the opening session of China's legislature, the National People's Congress, which according to the constitution adopted at that meeting, was the "highest organ of state power" in the People's Republic.[13] Mao's statement was a blunt reminder that the party was in charge of the national legislature and all other government organizations. This same line was the very first entry in *The Little Red Book,* the bible of Mao quotes used by the Red Guards who ransacked the country in the name of ideological purity during the Cultural Revolution. Although many party members became targets of the Cultural Revolution, the prominence of this quotation reflected the fact that even at the height of the movement's near anarchy, Mao and his supporters did not intend to call into question the primacy of Communist rule in China. Even Deng Xiaoping, the architect of China's economic reforms, was unwavering in his view that the country should "never dispense with leadership by the party."[14] Despite the many fundamental changes that have taken place in recent decades, party leadership remains an unchallengeable principle of political life in China, and the nation's rulers still claim allegiance to communist ideology. Any analysis of governance and policy-making in China therefore must begin with a discussion of the ideology and power of the Communist Party.

Mao Zedong Thought is said to have made a fundamental contribution to communist ideology by adapting Marxism-Leninism to China's special circumstances, particularly its emphasis on the peasant-based revolution that brought the party to power. In 1997, the CCP added Deng Xiaoping Theory to its official ideology to reflect the late leader's role in justifying a self-proclaimed socialist country's use of market forces to promote the growth of the economy. And in 2002, even Jiang Zemin's ideas (the Three Represents) about expanding the CCP to incorporate all sectors of Chinese society, including private entrepreneurs, in the drive for modernization was enshrined in the party constitution when he retired as general secretary (see Section 4).

Although the focus of Chinese communism has shifted from an emphasis on revolutionary change to economic development, most people in China have lost faith in the ideology because of the CCP's erratic and repressive leadership over the past several decades, or they consider ideology largely irrelevant to their daily lives. Many of those who join the party now do so mainly for career advancement. There are numerous other sources of beliefs and values in society, such as the family and religion, that are more important to most people than the official ideology. But the latest Chinese communist variant of Marxism-Leninism still provides the framework for governance and policy-making and sets the boundaries for what, in the party's view, is permissible in politics.

The underlying organizing principles of China's political system are clearly laid out in the PRC constitution, which is a totally different document from the party (CCP) constitution.[15] The preamble makes repeated reference to the fact that the country is under "the leadership of the Communist Party of China." Article 1 defines the PRC as "a socialist state under the people's democratic dictatorship" and declares that "disruption of the socialist system by any organization or individual is prohibited." Such provisions imply that the Chinese "people"—implicitly defined as those who support socialism and the leadership of the party— enjoy democratic rights and privileges; but the Chinese

constitution also gives the CCP the authority to exercise dictatorship over any person or organization that it believes is opposed to socialism and the party.

Constitutional change (from amendments to total replacement) has reflected the shifting political winds in China. The character and content of the document in force at any given time bear the ideological stamp of the prevailing party leadership. For example, in 1993, the current PRC constitution (adopted in 1982) was amended to replace references to the superiority of central planning and state ownership with phrases more consistent with economic reform, including the statement (Article 15) that China "practices a socialist market economy."

The constitution of the People's Republic specifies the structures and powers of subnational levels of government, including the country's provinces, autonomous regions, and centrally administered cities. But China is not a federal system (like Brazil, Germany, India, Nigeria, and the United States), in which subnational governments have considerable policy-making autonomy. Provincial and local authorities operate "under the unified leadership of the central authorities" (Article 3), which makes China a unitary state (like France and Japan), in which the national government exercises a high degree of control over other levels of government.

The Executive

The PRC government is organizationally and functionally distinct from the Chinese Communist Party. For example, the PRC executive consists of both a premier (prime minister) and a president, whereas the CCP is headed by a general secretary. But there is no alternation of parties in power in China, and the Communist Party exercises direct or indirect control over all government organizations and personnel. Therefore, real executive power in the Chinese political system lies with the top leaders and organizations of the CCP (see Table 1). The government essentially acts as the administrative agency for carrying out and enforcing policies made by the party. Nevertheless, to fully understand governance and policy-making in China, it is necessary to look at both the Chinese Communist Party and the government of the People's Republic of China (the "state") and the relationship between the two.

Table 1

Who's Who In Beijing: China's Most Important Party and State Leaders Since 1949		
Leader	*Highest Positions Held*	*Comment*
Mao Zedong (1893–1976)	CCP Chairman (1943–1976) PRC President (1949–1959) Military Commission Chair (1949–1976)	Became effective leader of the CCP in 1934–1935 during the Long March, although not elected Chairman until 1943.
Liu Shaoqi (1898–1969)	PRC President (1959–1966) CCP Vice Chairman (1949–1966)	Purged as a "capitalist roader" during the Cultural Revolution. Died in detention.
Zhou Enlai (1898–1976)	PRC Premier (1949–1976) PRC Foreign Minister (1949–1958) CCP Vice Chairman (1949–1969; 1973–1976)	Long-time Mao ally, but a moderating influence during the Cultural Revolution. Architect of détente with U.S. in early 1970s.
Lin Biao (1907–1971)	CCP Vice Chairman (1958–1971) PRC Vice Premier (1954–1971) PRC Defense Minister (1959–1971)	One of Mao's strongest supporters in the Cultural Revolution. Allegedly killed in plane crash after a failed coup attempt against Mao.
Jiang Qing (1914–1991)	Deputy Director, Cultural Revolution Group (1966–1969) Member, CCP Politburo (1969–1976)	Former movie actress who married Mao in 1939. One of the leaders of the Cultural Revolution. Arrested after Mao's death in 1976 and sentenced to life in prison, where she died.
Hua Guofeng (1920–)	CCP Chairman (1976–1981) PRC Premier (1976–1980) Military Commission Chair (1976–1981)	Became CCP chairman after Mao's death and purge of Jiang Qing and her radical followers. Removed from power by Deng Xiaoping, who saw him as too weak and a neo-Maoist.
Deng Xiaoping (1904–1997)	PRC Vice-Premier (1952–1966; 1973–1976; 1977–1980) CCP Vice-Chairman (1975–1976; 1977–1987) Military Commission Chair (1981–1989)	Purged twice during Cultural Revolution. Became China's most powerful leader in 1978 and remained so until shortly before his death.
Jiang Zemin (1926–)	CCP General Secretary[a] (1989–2002) PRC President (1993–2003) Military Commission Chair (1989–)	Former Shanghai mayor promoted by Deng as a safe choice to carry out his policies after Tiananmen crisis. Consolidated his own power after Deng's death in 1997.
Hu Jintao (1942–)	CCP General Secretary (2002–) PRC President (2003–)	Chosen by Deng Xiaoping before his death to succeed Jiang Zemin as head of the CCP. A relatively young technocrat.

[a]The position of CCP chairman was abolished in 1982 and replaced by the general secretary as the party's top position.

The Chinese Communist Party

The constitution of the CCP specifies local and national party structures and functions, the distribution of authority among party organizations, the requirements for joining, the behavior expected of members, and procedures for dealing with infractions of party rules. But such details do not negate the fact that individual power, factional maneuvering, and personal connections are ultimately more important than formal constitutional arrangements for understanding how the party works.

For example, Deng Xiaoping, who was indisputably the most powerful individual in China from 1978 until he became physically incapacitated a year or so before his death in 1997, never occupied any of the top executive offices in the party or the government. Even when he no longer played an active role in day-to-day governance, no major decision was made without his approval, and he was regularly referred to as China's "paramount leader." The sources of Deng's immense power came from informal factors, such as his seniority as one of the founding leaders of the regime and his long advocacy of now widely supported ideas about how China should develop into a strong and modern nation.

But by the late 1990s, most of the elderly men (including Deng) who had wielded great informal authority in post-Mao China were dead. Despite the persisting strong influence of personal ties in Chinese politics, the formal structures of power have assumed greater importance for understanding who has the power and how decisions are made.

According to the CCP constitution, the "highest leading bodies" of the party are the National Party Congress and the Central Committee (see Figure 3). But its infrequent, short meetings (for one week every five years) and large size (more than 2,100 delegates) mean that the role of the Congress in the party is more symbolic than substantive. The essential function of the National Party Congress is to approve decisions already made by the top leaders and provide a showcase for the party's current policies. For example, the party congress that convened in November 2002 was a highly orchestrated celebration of Jiang Zemin's leadership and installation of Hu Jintao as the new general secretary. There was little debate about policy and no contested voting of any consequence.

The Central Committee, which currently has 198 full and 158 alternate members, is the next level up in the pyramid of party power and consists of party leaders from around the country. It meets annually for about a week. It is elected by the National Party Congress by secret ballot, and there is limited choice of candidates. Contending party factions may jockey to win seats, but the overall composition of the Central Committee is closely controlled by the top leaders to ensure compliance with their policies. The Central Committee elected in late 2002 continued the trend toward promoting younger and better-educated party members who are strong supporters of economic reform.

The Central Committee directs party affairs when the National Party Congress is not in session, but its size and relatively short and infrequent meetings (called plenums) also greatly limit its effectiveness. However, Central Committee plenums and occasional informal work conferences do represent significant gatherings of the party elite, which can be a very important arena of political maneuvering and decision making.

The most powerful political organizations in the communist party-state are the two small executive bodies at the very top of the CCP's structure: the Politburo (or Political Bureau) and its even more exclusive Standing Committee. These bodies are elected by the Central Committee from among its own members under carefully controlled conditions. The Politburo elected in 2002 had twenty-four members (plus one alternate) and the Standing Committee, the formal apex of power in the CCP, had nine. People who study Chinese politics scrutinize the membership of the Politburo and Standing Committee for clues about leadership priorities, the balance of power among party factions, and the relative influence of different groups in policy-making.

The Politburo and Standing Committee are not responsible to the Central Committee or any other institution in any meaningful sense. The workings of these organizations are shrouded in secrecy. Most of their work goes on, and many of the top leaders live, in a high-security compound called Zhongnanhai ("Central and Southern Seas"), which is adjacent to the former imperial palace near Tiananmen Square.

Power in the CCP is highly concentrated in the hands of those who control the highest party organizations. Prior to 1982, the top position in the party was the

Figure 3

Organization of the Chinese Communist Party

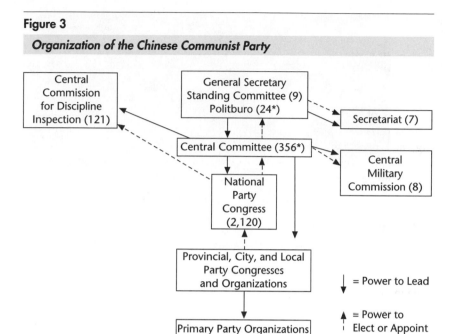

*Indicates full and alternate members

Numbers in parentheses refer to the number of members as of 2003.

chairman of the Politburo's Standing Committee, which was occupied by Mao Zedong (hence *Chairman* Mao) for more than three decades until his death in 1976. The title of chairman was abolished in 1982 to symbolize a break with Mao's highly personalistic and often arbitrary style of leadership. Since then, the party's leader has been the general secretary, who presides over the Politburo and the Standing Committee, a position held from 1989 to 2002 by Jiang Zemin. Although Jiang clearly emerged as China's most powerful individual in the late 1990s, he did not have the personal clout or charisma of either Deng or Mao and therefore governed as part of a collective leadership that included his fellow members on the Standing Committee and Politburo. It will certainly be the same with Hu Jintao, who succeeded Jiang as general secretary.

Hu Jintao is said to be the core of the "fourth generation" of CCP leadership, while Jiang was the core of the "third generation." (Mao Zedong and Deng Xiaoping were, respectively, the core leaders of the first and second "generations.") The transition in power from the Mao-Deng generations to the Jiang-Hu generations represents a shift from revolutionary to technocratic leadership. Indeed, both Jiang and Hu, as well as all nine members of the Politburo Standing Committee elected in 2002, were trained and worked as engineers before embarking on political careers.

Two other party organizations deserve brief mention. The Secretariat manages the day-to-day work of the Politburo and Standing Committee and coordinates the party's complex and far-flung structure with considerable authority in organizational and personnel matters. The Central Commission for Discipline Inspection is responsible for monitoring the compliance of party members with the CCP constitution and other rules. The commission has been used as a vehicle against thousands of party members accused of corruption. In a recent three-year period, more than 861,900 cases were filed by discipline organs at different levels across the country, resulting in 137,711 people being expelled from the party; 37,790 of them were also prosecuted in the courts. Many of those punished were

Former Chinese president and communist party leader, Jiang Zemin, confers with his successor, Hu Jintao, during a meeting of the National People's Congress in March 2003. *Source:* © Reuters NewMedia, Inc. / Corbis.

leading officials at the county provincial and ministry levels.

Below the national level, the CCP has a hierarchy of local party organizations in provinces, cities, and counties, each headed by a party committee. There are also more than 3 million primary party organizations, called branches and cells, which are found in workplaces, schools, urban neighborhoods, rural towns, villages, and army units. Local and primary organizations extend the party's reach throughout Chinese society and are designed to ensure the subordination of each level of party organization to the next-higher level and ultimately to the central party authorities in Beijing.

The Government of the PRC

Government (or state) authority in China is formally vested in a system of people's congresses that begins with the National People's Congress at the top and continues in hierarchically arranged levels down through provincial people's congresses, municipal people's congresses, rural township people's congresses, and so on (see Figure 4). In theory, these congresses (the legislative branch) are empowered to supervise the work of the "people's governments" (the executive branch) at the various levels of the system, but in reality, government executives (such as cabinet ministers, provincial governors, and mayors) are ultimately subject to party authority rather than to the people's congresses. Unlike the parallel system of party congresses, the people's

congresses are supposed to represent all of the citizens at the relevant level, not just the minority who are members of the CCP. Like the party congresses, the people's congresses play a politically limited, but symbolically important, role in policy-making.

The National People's Congress elects the president and vice president of China. But there is only one candidate, chosen by the Communist Party, for each office. The president's term is concurrent with that of the congress (five years), and there is a two-term limit. The position is largely ceremonial, although a senior party leader has always held it. As China's head of state, the president meets and negotiates with other world leaders. Jiang Zemin revived the practice that the leader of the CCP serve concurrently as PRC president, as Mao had done from 1949 to 1959. Hu Jintao followed Jiang's example and was elected president of China at the National People's Congress in March 2003.

The premier (prime minister) is the head of the government and has authority over the bureaucracy and policy implementation. The premier is formally appointed by the president with the approval of the National People's Congress. But in reality, the Communist Party decides who will serve as premier, and that post has always been held by a very high-ranking member of the CCP Standing Committee. Like the president, the premier may serve only two five-year terms. Wen Jiabao, a geologist and a former vice premier in charge of agriculture, the financial system,

Figure 4

Organization of the Government of the People's Republic of China

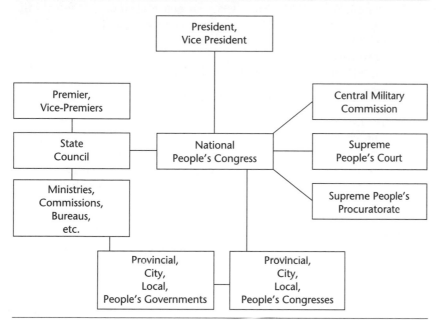

flood control, and poverty alleviation, was chosen as premier in March 2003.

The Bureaucracy

The premier directs the State Council, which is constitutionally "the highest organ of state administration" (Article 85) in the PRC. The State Council is formally appointed by the National People's Congress, though its membership is determined by the party leadership. It functions much like the cabinet in a parliamentary system and includes the premier, a few vice premiers, the heads of government ministries and commissions, and several other senior officials.

The size of the State Council varies as ministries and commissions are created, merged, or disbanded to meet changing policy needs. At the height of the state socialist planned economy, there were more than one hundred ministerial-level officials. In the 1990s, there were forty ministries and commissions, and in 2003 the number was cut to twenty-eight, reflecting the decreased role of central planning and the administrative

streamlining undertaken to make the government more efficient. The ministers run either functionally specific departments, such as the Ministry of Public Health, or organizations with more comprehensive responsibilities, such as the Science, Technology, and Industry Commission. Beneath the State Council is an array of support staffs, research offices, and other bureaucratic agencies charged with policy implementation.

The so-called central leading groups are important and flexible instruments of coordinated decision making in the PRC. These bodies are formed by the CCP and are made up of government officials who are also high-ranking party members. Current leading groups include those on national security, finance and economics, and information technology.

Government administration in the PRC is based on the principle of **dual rule,** which was adapted from the Soviet political system. Dual rule means that government organizations below the national level are under both the vertical supervision of the next higher level of government and the horizontal supervision of the Communist Party at their own level. For example, the organization in charge of education in one of China's provinces would be subject to both administrative supervision by the Ministry of Education in Beijing and political control by the province's CCP committee. Such a system leads to complex and sometimes conflicting lines of authority within the Chinese bureaucracy. It also reinforces two key aspects of governance and policy-making in the PRC: centralization and party domination. Nevertheless, since the 1980s, government administration in China has become increasingly decentralized as the role of central planning has been reduced and more power has been given to provincial and local authorities, particularly in economic matters. Efforts have also been made to reduce party interference in administrative work.

China's bureaucracy is immense in size and expansive in the scope of its reach throughout the country. The total number of **cadres**—people in positions of authority who are paid by the government or party—in the PRC is in the range of 40 million. A minority of these work directly for the government or the CCP. The remainder occupy key posts in economic enterprises (e.g., factory directors); schools (e.g., principals); and scientific, cultural, and other state-run institutions. Not all party members are cadres; in fact, most party members are ordinary workers, farmers, teachers, and so on. And most cadres (25 million) are not party members, though party cadres ultimately have power over nonparty cadres. In 2001, the government announced a plan to reduce the size of the bureaucracy by 10 percent, particularly at the city, county, and township levels, over the next five to ten years. There have also been substantive moves toward professionalizing the bureaucracy, particularly at the city level of government, by making more official positions subject to competition through civil service exams rather than the still-prevalent method of appointment from above.

One of the most significant administrative reforms of the post-Mao era—and one that is quite unprecedented in a communist party-state—has been the implementation of measures to limit how long officials can stay in their jobs. Depending on their position, both government and party cadres must now retire between the ages of sixty and seventy. A two-term limit has been set for all top cadres. In 1998, Premier Li Peng became the first central leader of the People's Republic to leave office at the end of a constitutionally

specified term limit. But exceptions are still sometimes made for core leaders such as Jiang Zemin (born in 1926), who stayed on as CCP general secretary until he was seventy-six and as chair of the Central Military Commission even beyond that.

Other State Institutions

The Military and the Police

China's People's Liberation Army (PLA), which encompasses all of the country's ground, air, and naval armed services, is the world's largest military force, with about 2.5 million active personnel (down from nearly 4 million in 1989). The PLA also has a formal reserve of another 1 million or so and a backup people's militia of 12 to 15 million, which could be mobilized in the event of war, although the level of training and weaponry available to the militia are generally minimal. There is a draft in China, but serving in the PLA is considered a prestigious option for many young people, particularly for rural youth who might not have many other opportunities for upward mobility.

In recent years, China has increased its defense spending quite substantially (over 17 percent in both 2001 and 2002) in order to modernize its armed forces and raise the pay of its military personnel. But the Chinese military is quite small in relation to China's total population. In the late 1990s, the PRC had 1.9 military personnel per 1,000 population, considerably fewer than the U.S. ratio of 3.2 per 1,000. China said that it would spend $20 billion on defense in 2002, compared with $379 billion by the United States. Many analysts think that the PRC vastly understates its defense budget and estimate that it is really closer to three times the official figures; still, China devotes a much smaller part of its annual government spending to defense than does the United States.

The military has never held formal political power in the PRC, but it has been a very important influence on politics and policy. Ever since the days of the revolution and the civil war, there have been close ties between the political and military leaders of the CCP, with many top leaders (such as Mao and Deng) serving in both political and military capacities. One of the most famous quotes from Chairman Mao's writings, "Political power grows out of the barrel of a gun," conveyed his belief that the party needed strong military backing in order to win and keep power. However, the often overlooked second half of the quote, "Our principle is that the party commands the gun, and the gun must never be allowed to command the party," made the equally important point that the military had to be kept under civilian (that is, CCP) control.[16] Although there have been a few periods when the role of the military in Chinese politics appeared to be particularly strong (such as during the Cultural Revolution), the party has always been able to keep the "gun" under its firm command.

Nevertheless, the PLA continues to play an important, if muted, role in Chinese politics. Military support remains a crucial factor in the factional struggles that still figure prominently in inner-party politics. Deng Xiaoping's long-standing personal ties to many very senior PLA officers were critical to his success in defeating the efforts of conservative party leaders to slow economic reform. Jiang Zemin, who had no such ties and lacks any military experience, paid close attention to building political bridges to the PLA by supporting increased defense spending and promoting generals who are loyal to him. There are no military officers on the party's most elite body, the Standing Committee, but two of the twenty-four full members of the Politburo are generals, and PLA representatives make up about 20 percent of the full members of the Central Committee.

Chinese Communist leaders have long been divided over the issue of what kind of armed forces the PRC needed. Mao was a strong advocate of equality between rank-and-file soldiers and officers and the use of guerrilla tactics ("people's war") even in modern warfare. He also stressed the importance of ideological education within the military and the extensive use of the PLA in nonmilitary tasks such as the construction of public works projects and the training of citizen paramedics ("barefoot doctors"). Some of China's foremost military leaders believed just as strongly that the PLA ought to emphasize the discipline, professionalism, and modernization needed to defend the nation. In the post-Mao era, the military leadership has been able to keep politics and ideology in the armed forces to a minimum and focus on making the PLA an effective, modern fighting force. But the PLA is also an instrument for keeping the CCP in power. The party

extends its control of the PLA through a system of party committees and political officers who are attached to all military units.

The key organizations in charge of the Chinese armed forces are the CCP and PRC Central Military Commissions (CMC). On paper, these are two distinct organizations, but, in fact, they overlap entirely in membership and function. The chair of the state Military Commission is "elected" by the National People's Congress, but is always the same person as the chair of the party CMC. The CMC chair is, in effect, the commander in chief of China's armed forces. This position has almost always been held by the most powerful party leader, for example, by Deng Xiaoping from 1981 to 1989, or his protégé, as was the case when Jiang Zemin took over the chairmanship in 1989 under Deng's auspices. The fact that Jiang held onto the CMC chairmanship after retiring as CCP general secretary in November 2002 and as PRC president in March 2003 was seen as a reflection that he was retaining a lot of formal power as well as informal influence in Chinese politics.

Beginning in the 1980s, the PLA climbed on the economic reform bandwagon in order to supplement its official budget by converting a number of its military factories to the production of consumer goods such as refrigerators and motorcycles, running hotels and even discos, and opening up some of its formerly secret facilities to foreign tourists. At one point, it was estimated that the PLA was running more than 15,000 nonmilitary enterprises at home and abroad with over $10 billion in revenues. In 1998, the government, concerned about both corruption and the need for the military to concentrate on its defense responsibilities, ordered the PLA to sell off many of its commercial ventures.

China's internal security apparatus consists of several different organizations. The Ministry of State Security is responsible for combating espionage and gathering intelligence at home and abroad. A 1 million strong People's Armed Police (under the PLA) guards public officials and buildings, carries out some border patrol and protection, and is used to quell serious public disturbances, including worker or peasant unrest. The Ministry of Public Security is responsible for the maintenance of law and order, the investigation of crimes, and the surveillance of Chinese citizens and foreigners in China suspected of being a threat to the state. Local Public Security Bureaus are under the command of central ministry authorities in Beijing. In effect, then, China has a national police force stationed throughout the country. There are also local police forces, but they do little more than supervise traffic.

Public Security Bureaus have the authority to detain indefinitely people suspected of committing a crime without making a formal charge and can use administrative sanctions, that is, penalties imposed outside the court system, to levy fines or sentence detainees to up to three years. For people convicted of serious crimes, including political ones, the Ministry of Public Security maintains an extensive system of labor reform camps. These camps, noted for their harsh conditions and remote locations, are estimated to have millions of prisoners. They have, at times, become a contentious issue in U.S.-China relations because of claims that they use political prisoners as slave labor to produce millions of dollars worth of products (such as toys) that are then exported to U.S. and other foreign markets. China has agreed to curtail the export of prison-produced goods, but it maintains that productive work by prison inmates (common in many countries, including the United States) helps to rehabilitate prisoners and is a legitimate part of the penal system.

The Judiciary

China has a four-tiered "people's court" system reaching from a Supreme People's Court down through higher, intermediate, and basic people's courts. The Supreme People's Court supervises the work of lower courts and the application of the country's laws, but it hears few cases and does not exercise judicial review over government policies. A nationwide organization called the "people's procuratorate" serves in the courts as both public prosecutor and public defender and also has investigatory functions in criminal cases. Citizen mediation committees based in urban neighborhoods and rural villages play an important role in the judicial process by settling a large majority of civil cases out of court.

China's judicial system came under attack as a bastion of elitism and revisionism during the Cultural Revolution. The formal legal system pretty much ceased to operate during that period, and many of its functions were taken over by political or police organizations, which often acted arbitrarily in making arrests or administering punishments.

In recent decades, the legal system of the PRC has been revitalized. There are now more than 100,000 lawyers in China (by way of comparison, there are about 1 million lawyers in the United States), and legal advisory offices have been established throughout the country to provide citizens and organizations with legal assistance. Many laws and regulations have been enacted, including new criminal and civil codes, in the effort to regularize the legal system. In 1997, the government revoked a vaguely worded law against "counterrevolutionary crimes," which had given the authorities broad powers to detain political dissidents, but the government has found other ways to accomplish the same ends.

In recent years, there has been an enormous surge in the number of lawsuits filed (and often won) by people against businesses, local officials, and government agencies. Chinese courts can provide a real avenue of redress to the public for a wide range of nonpolitical grievances, including loss of property, consumer fraud, and even unjust detention by the police.

China's criminal justice system works swiftly and harshly. Great faith is placed in the ability of an official investigation to find the facts of a case, and the outcome of cases that actually do come to trial is pretty much predetermined: there is a conviction rate of 98 to 99 percent for all criminal cases. Prison terms are long and subject only to cursory appeal. A variety of offenses in addition to murder—including, in some cases, rape and particularly serious cases of embezzlement and other "economic crimes"—are subject to capital punishment, which is carried out within days of sentencing by a single bullet in the back of the convicted person's head. Particularly large numbers of people have been executed during the periodic government-sponsored anticrime "Strike Hard" campaigns. Between April and July 2001, an estimated 1,781 people were executed in China—more than the total number of people executed in the rest of the world in the previous three years. China has been harshly criticized by human rights organizations such as Amnesty International for its extensive use of the death penalty.

Although the Chinese constitution speaks of judicial independence, China's courts and other legal bodies remain under rigorous party control. The appointment of judicial personnel is subject to party approval, and the CCP can and does bend the law to serve its interests. Recent legal reforms in China have been undertaken because China's leaders are well aware that economic development requires detailed laws, professional lawyers and judicial personnel, predictable legal processes, and binding documents such as contracts. China has, by and large, become a country where there is rule by law, in which the CCP uses the law to carry out its policies and enforce its rule. But it is still far from having established the rule of law, in which everyone and every organization, including the CCP, is accountable and subject to the law.

Subnational Government

There are four main layers of state structure beneath the central government in China: provinces, cities, counties, and rural towns. There are also four so-called very large centrally administered cities (Beijing, Shanghai, Tianjin, and Chongqing) and five autonomous regions, which are areas of the country with large minority populations (such as Tibet and Mongolia). Each of these levels has a representative people's congress that meets infrequently and briefly and plays a limited role in managing affairs in the area under its jurisdiction.

Day-to-day administration at each subnational level is carried out by a people's government, which consists of an executive (for instance, a provincial governor or city mayor), various functional bureaus, and judicial organs. According to China's constitution, the work of a local government is to be supervised by the local people's congress. But, in fact, the principle of dual rule makes local officials accountable more to higher levels of state administration and party organizations than to the local congresses.

Economic reform has led to considerable decentralization of decision making. As a result, local governments are becoming more vigorous in pursuing their own interests, but they are also experiencing enormously increased financial pressures. The latter has led many local governments, particularly in rural towns, to impose largely arbitrary fees for all sorts of services; this in turn has fed popular resentment that has sometimes exploded in violent protest.

Despite decentralization, the central government still retains the power to intervene in local affairs when and where it wants. This power of the central authorities derives not only from their ability to set binding national priorities but also from their control over the military and the police, critical energy sources, resource allocation, and the construction of major infrastructure projects. A number of political scientists in China and abroad have suggested that the PRC, given its continental size and great regional diversity, would be better served by a federal system with a more balanced distribution of power between the national, provincial, and local levels of government, but such a move would be inconsistent with the highly centralized structure of a communist party-state.

Beneath the formal layers of state administration are China's 700,000 or so rural villages, which are home to the majority of the country's population. These villages are technically self-governing and are not formally responsible to a higher level of state authority. In recent years, village leaders and representative assemblies have been directly and competitively elected by local residents (see Section 4), which has brought an important degree of grass-roots democracy to village government. Nevertheless, the most powerful person in Chinese villages is still the local Communist Party leader (the party secretary).

The Policy-Making Process

At the height of Mao's power, many scholars described the policy process in China as a "Mao-in-command" system. Then the Cultural Revolution led many analysts to conclude that policy-making in China was best understood as a result of factional and ideological struggles within the Chinese political elite. More recently, emphasis has shifted to analyzing the importance of bureaucratic actors and institutions in the policy process. Rather than portraying policy-making as simply a matter of the top party leaders' issuing orders, a model of fragmented authoritarianism sees policy outcomes as the result of conflict, competition, and bargaining among party and government organizations at various levels of the system.[17] The national focus on economic development has also led to the growing influence of nonparty experts in the policy loop.

Nevertheless, policy-making at all levels is still ultimately under the control of the CCP. Public debate, media scrutiny, and the influence of truly independent interest groups play little, if any, role in the policy process in the communist party-state. The CCP uses a weblike system of organizational controls to make sure that the government bureaucracy complies with the party's will in policy implementation. Almost all key government officials are also party members and therefore subject to party discipline. The CCP also exercises control over the policy process through party organizations that parallel government agencies at all levels of the system. For example, each provincial government works under the watchful eye of a provincial party committee. In addition, through its committees, branches, cells, and "leading members groups," the CCP maintains an effective presence inside every government organization.

Another means by which the CCP exercises control over the policy process is through the use of a cadre list, or as it was known in the Soviet Union, the **nomenklatura** system. The cadre list covers millions of positions in the government and elsewhere (including newspapers, hospitals, banks, and trade unions). Any personnel decision involving appointment, promotion, transfer, or dismissal that affects a position on this list must be approved by the party organization department, whether or not the official involved is a party member. In recent years, the growth of nonstate sectors of the economy and administrative streamlining have led to a reduction in the number of positions directly subject to party approval. Nevertheless, the *nomenklatura* system remains one of the major instruments by which the CCP tries to "ensure that leading institutions throughout the country will exercise only the autonomy granted to them by the party."[18]

No account of the policy process in China is complete without noting the importance of *guanxi* ("connections"), the personal relationships and mutual obligations based on family, friendship, school, military, professional, or other ties. The notion of *guanxi* has its roots in Confucian culture and has long been an important part of political, social, and economic life in China. These connections are still a basic fact of life within the Chinese bureaucracy, where personal ties are often the key to getting things done. Depending on how they are used, *guanxi* can either help cut red tape and increase efficiency or bolster organizational rigidity and feed corruption.

Guanxi also count mightily in the highly personalized world of elite politics within the CCP, where key policy decisions are made. Much of the informal power that Jiang Zemin appeared to wield even after his term as head of the party ended in late 2002—and which led some observers to dub him China's "de-facto Number One leader"—derived from his close personal ties (often based on common roots in Shanghai) to fifteen of the twenty-four full members of the CCP Politburo and five of the nine members of its Standing Committee.

In sum, the power of the Communist Party, particularly the nearly unchecked power of the two dozen or so top leaders, is at the heart of governance and policymaking in China. Party domination, however, does not mean that the system "operates in a monolithic way"; in fact, the system "wriggles with politics" of many kinds, formal and informal.[19] In order to get a complete picture of the policy process in China, it is important to look at how various influences, including ideology, factional struggles, bureaucratic interests, and *guanxi* shape the decisions made by the Communist Party leadership.

Section ❹ Representation and Participation

The Chinese Communist Party describes the political system of the People's Republic as a **socialist democracy,** which it claims is superior to democracy in a capitalist country. Unlike the *social* democracy of Western European's center-left political parties, however, which is rooted in a commitment to competitive politics, China's *socialist* democracy is based on the unchallengeable leadership of the Chinese Communist Party.

Nevertheless, representation and participation do play important roles in the PRC political system. There are legislative bodies, elections, and organizations like labor unions and women's associations, all of which are meant to provide citizens with ways of influencing public policy-making and the selection of government leaders. But such mechanisms of popular input are strictly controlled and bounded by the party's continuing insistence that all politics and policies in the country be guided by the CCP.

The Legislature

The Chinese constitution grants the National People's Congress (NPC) the power to enact and amend the country's laws, approve and monitor the state budget, and declare and end war. The NPC is also empowered to elect (and recall) the president and vice president of the PRC, the chair of the state Central Military Commission, the head of China's Supreme Court, and the procurator-general (something like the U.S. attorney general). It also has final approval over the selection of the premier and members of the State Council. At least on paper, these powers make China's legislature the most powerful branch of the government, but in fact these powers are exercised only in the manner allowed by the Communist Party.

The NPC is a unicameral legislature. It is elected for a five-year term and meets annually for only about two weeks in March. Deputies to the NPC are not full-time legislators but remain in their regular jobs and home areas except for the brief time when the congress is in session. The precise size of the NPC is set by law prior to each five-year electoral cycle. The NPC that was elected in 2003 consisted of nearly 3,000 deputies. All the delegates, except those who represent the People's Liberation Army, are chosen on a geographic basis from China's provinces, autonomous regions, and major municipalities. About 73 percent of the deputies elected in 2003 were members of the CCP, while the others either belonged to one of China's few non-Communist (and powerless) political parties or had no party affiliation.

Workers and farmers made up about 18 percent of the deputies elected in 2003, intellectuals and professionals made up another 21 percent, government and party cadres accounted for a little under a third, 9 percent were from the military, and the remainder consisted of representatives of other occupational categories, such as entrepreneurs. Women made up 20 percent and ethnic minorities 14 percent of the deputies.

The annual sessions of the NPC are hailed with great fanfare in the Chinese press as an example of socialist democracy at work, but generally legislation is passed and state leaders are elected by an overwhelming majority. For instance, Hu Jintao was elected president of China in March 2003 by a vote of 2,937 for him, 4 against, and 3 abstentions. Nevertheless, some debate and dissent do occur. For example, in 1992, about a third of NPC deputies either voted against or abstained from voting on the construction of the hugely expensive ($70 billion) and ecologically controversial Three Gorges dam project now being built on the Yangtze River. And in 2003, nearly 10 percent of deputies opposed relecting the outgoing party leader and president Jiang Zemin as chair of the Central Military Commission. On very rare occasions, government legislative initiatives have even been defeated. But all NPC proceedings are subject to party scrutiny, and the congress never debates politically sensitive issues. The CCP also monitors the election process to make sure that no outright dissidents are elected as deputies.

Still, as economics has replaced ideology as the main priority of China's leaders, the NPC has become a much more important and lively part of the Chinese political system than it was during the Mao era. Many NPC deputies are now chosen because of their ability to contribute to China's modernization rather than simply on the basis of political loyalty, and some have become a bit more assertive in expressing their opinions on various issues.

Political Parties and the Party System

China is usually called a one-party system because the country's politics are so thoroughly dominated by the Chinese Communist Party. In fact, China has eight political parties in addition to the CCP, but these parties neither challenge the basic policies of the CCP nor play a significant part in running the government, although they do sometimes provide important advice in the policy-making process.

The Chinese Communist Party

At the time of the National Party Congress that met in November 2002, the Chinese Communist Party had about 66 million members. The party has grown steadily since it came to power in 1949, when it had just under 4.5 million members. Only during the Cultural Revolution was there a sharp drop in membership due to the purge of "capitalist roaders" from party ranks, and many of those purged were welcomed back into the CCP after the death of Mao.

The CCP is the largest political party in the world in terms of total formal membership. But as with all other former and current ruling communist parties, its members make up a small minority of the country's population. CCP members are now about 5 percent of China's population, or about 8 percent of those over eighteen, the minimum age for joining the party.

The social composition of the CCP's membership has changed considerably in recent decades. In the mid-1950s, peasants made up nearly 70 percent of party membership. In 2002, a generic category that included "industrial workers, laborers in township enterprises, farmers, herdsman, and fishermen" accounted for only 45 percent of the CCP even though the party constitution still claims that "Members of the Communist Party of China are vanguard fighters of the Chinese working class imbued with communist consciousness" (Article 2). The majority of CCP members are not manual laborers of any sort, but are government officials, enterprise managers, military personnel, professionals, and retirees. In mid-2001, in a major speech commemorating the eightieth anniversary of the CCP, Jiang Zemin proclaimed that in order to serve the cause of national economic development, the party must include "worthy people from all sectors of society," by which he specifically meant that private entrepreneurs (capitalists) would be welcomed as members.[20] This important policy change was certainly a recognition of the rapidly changing nature of economic life in China, including the growth of the private sector in industry, commerce, and services. But it will also likely change the social composition of the CCP and perhaps even lead to a gradual redefinition of the party's political role in China.

Women make up less than 20 percent of the CCP as a whole and only 2.5 percent of full members of Central Committee (and 14 percent of alternates) elected in 2002. There is one female member of the Politburo, Wu Yi, who is also a senior government official and former minister of foreign trade. There are no women on the party's most powerful organization, the Politburo Standing Committee.

Despite the party's tarnished image since Tiananmen and what many Chinese feel is the increasing irrelevance of communist ideology to their lives and the nation's future, the CCP still recruits about 1 million new members each year. Party membership provides unparalleled access to influence and resources, especially given the current quasi-market nature of China's economy, and being a party member is still a prerequisite for advancement in many careers in China, particularly in government.

China's Noncommunist Parties

The eight noncommunist political parties in the PRC are referred to as the "democratic parties," a designation meant to signify the role they play in representing different interests in the political process and to lend some credibility to China's claim that it is a socialist democracy. Each noncommunist party draws its membership from a particular group in Chinese society. For example, the China Democratic League consists mostly of intellectuals, whereas the Chinese Party for the Public Interest draws on returned overseas Chinese and experts with overseas connections.

The democratic parties, all of which were founded before the CCP came to power, have a total membership of fewer than 500,000. These parties do not contest for power or challenge CCP policy. Their function is to provide advice to the CCP and generate support within their particular constituencies for CCP policies. Individual members of the parties may assume important government positions. But organizationally these parties are relatively insignificant and function as little more than "a loyal non-opposition."[21]

Elections

Elections in the PRC are basically mechanisms to give the party-state greater legitimacy by allowing large numbers of citizens to participate in the political process under very controlled circumstances.

China has both direct and indirect elections. In direct elections, all eligible citizens vote for candidates for offices in a particular government body. For example, all the voters in a rural county would vote for the deputies to serve in the county-level people's congress. In indirect elections, higher-level bodies are elected by lower-level government bodies rather than by the voters at large. For example, deputies to the National People's Congress are elected by the provincial-level people's congresses, which have been elected by lower-level people's congresses. Most elections in China are indirect, and there are no direct elections at the provincial or national levels. Turnout for direct elections is heavy—usually over 90 percent of eligible voters.

For several decades after the founding of the PRC, only one candidate stood for each office, so the only choice facing voters was to approve or abstain. Since the early 1980s, many direct and indirect elections have had multiple candidates for each slot, with the winner chosen by secret ballot. The nomination process has also become more open. Any group of more than ten voters can nominate candidates for an election. Most candidates in direct elections are now nominated by the voters, and there have been a significant number of cases where independent candidates have defeated official nominees, though even independent candidates are basically approved by the CCP.

The most significant progress toward real democratic representation and participation in China has occurred in the rural villages. Laws implemented since the late 1980s have provided for directly elected village representative assemblies and the election, rather than the appointment from above, of village officials. These are, for the most part, multicandidate, secret-ballot elections, though still carried out under the watchful eye of the CCP. Outside observers have been split on whether such direct grass-roots elections in China represent the seeds of real democracy or are merely a facade designed by the Communist Party to appease international critics and give the rural population a way to express discontent with some officials without challenging the country's fundamental political organization.

Recent electoral reform has certainly increased popular representation and participation in China's government. But elections in the PRC still do not give citizens a means by which they can exercise effective control over the party officials and organizations that have the real power in China's political system. In a major speech in December 1998 marking twenty years of economic reform, President Jiang Zemin stated bluntly, "The model of the West's political system should not be copied." He vowed that China would adhere to a system of socialist democracy in which "the Communist Party, being the ruling party . . . leads and supports the people in controlling and exercising the power to manage the country." And in his political report to the Sixteenth Party Congress in November

2002, Jiang, the retiring general secretary of the CCP, repeatedly reminded the delegates that, while pursuing economic development and socialist democracy, China had to preserve the leadership of the Communist Party, which was, in his words, "the very foundation on which we build our country."[22] There is little reason to think that this bottom-line framework for political representation and participation in China will change much in the foreseeable future.

Political Culture, Citizenship, and Identity

From Communism to Consumerism

Since the PRC's founding in 1949, its official political culture has been based on communist ideology, and the party-state has made extensive efforts to get people's political attitudes and behavior to conform to the currently prevailing version of Marxism-Leninism. But this ideology has gone through such severe crises and profound changes during the turbulent decades of Communist rule that its future in China is seriously in doubt.

At the height of the Maoist era, Mao Zedong Thought was hailed as "an inexhaustible source of strength and a spiritual atom bomb of infinite power" that held the answer to all of China's problems in domestic and foreign policy.[23] By the mid-1970s, however, the debacles of the Mao years had greatly tarnished the appeal of communism in China.

After Deng Xiaoping came to power in 1978, he set about trying not only to restore the legitimacy of the Communist Party through economic reforms but also to revive communist ideology by linking it directly to China's development aspirations. Toward the end of 1997, the CCP amended the party constitution to add Deng Xiaoping Theory to its official ideology. One key part of Deng's theory, often referred to under the rubric of "Building Socialism with Chinese Characteristics," was a major departure from Maoism and emphasizes that China is a relatively poor country in the "primary stage of socialism" and therefore must use any means possible, even capitalist ones, to develop the economy. The other central component of Deng's ideology, and one fully consistent with Maoist theory and practice, is his so-called **Four Cardinal Principles:** upholding the socialist road, the people's democratic dictatorship, the leadership of the Communist Party, and Marxism-Leninism. In essence, then, Deng Xiaoping Theory is an ideological rationale for the combination of economic liberalization and party dictatorship that characterizes contemporary China.

In an effort to have himself placed on a historical pedestal equal to that of Deng and Mao as he neared semiretirement, Jiang Zemin offered his own variation on Chinese communism, the Three Represents, which was said to sum up his contribution to the party's ideology. According to the amended party constitution, the Three Represents depict the CCP as the faithful representative of the "development trend of China's advanced productive forces, the orientation of China's advanced culture, and the fundamental interests of the overwhelming majority of the Chinese people." In other words, the Communist Party (and Jiang) take the credit for the country's vastly improved economic fortunes.

The CCP tries to keep communist ideology—now officially called "Marxism-Leninism, Mao Zedong Thought, Deng Xiaoping Theory, and the Important Thought of the Three Represents"—viable and visible by continued efforts to influence public opinion and socialization—for instance, by controlling the media and overseeing the educational system. Although China's media are much livelier and more open than during the Maoist period, there is no true freedom of the press. Reduced political control of the media has, to a large extent, meant only the freedom to publish more entertainment news, human interest stories, local coverage, and some nonpolitical investigative journalism. The Chinese film industry has emerged as one of the best in the world, with many of its directors, stars, and, productions winning international acclaim, including a Best Film award at Cannes and an Oscar nomination in 1993 for *Farewell My Concubine.* But movie making in the PRC is subject to political controls, and some films made in China are not distributed in the country.

Internet access is growing extremely fast in the PRC, with more than 58 million users as of 2002 and wired cafés found in even some quite remote towns. The government, worried about the potential influence of email and electronic information it cannot control, has at times blocked access to certain foreign websites, shut down unlicensed cybercafés, which it likened to the opium dens of the past, and even arrested people it

has accused of disseminating subversive material over the Internet, including, in December 2002, the publisher of an online prodemocracy journal. Nevertheless, the party-state has found it very difficult to control these new technologies as tightly as it would like; indeed, in mid-2002, an outlawed spiritual group, the Falun Gong (see below), hacked into the state-run television network to briefly broadcast its own message. But in another sign of the times, both the government of the PRC and the CCP have set up numerous Internet sites of their own.

Schools are one of the main institutions through which all states instill political values in their citizens. Educational opportunities have expanded enormously in China since 1949. Although enrollment rates drop sharply at the secondary school level, primary school enrollment is close to 100 percent of the age-eligible population (ages six to eleven). In Maoist China, students at all levels spent a considerable amount of time studying politics and working in fields or factories, and teaching materials were often overlaid with a heavy dose of political propaganda. Today, political study (recently with an emphasis on learning the Three Represents) is a required but relatively minor part of the curriculum at all levels of education. Much greater attention is paid to urging students to gain the skills and knowledge they need to further their own careers and help China modernize.

Yet schools in China are by no means centers of critical or independent thinking, and teachers and students are still closely monitored for political reliability. More than 80 percent of China's youth between the ages of seven and fourteen belong to the Young Pioneers, an organization designed to promote good social behavior, patriotism, and loyalty to the party among school children.

The party's efforts to keep socialist values alive in China do not appear to be meeting with much success, and public confidence in the party and in communist ideology is very low. Alternative sources of socialization are growing in importance, although these do not often take expressly political forms because of the threat of repression. In the countryside, peasants have replaced portraits of Mao and other Communist heroes with statues of folk gods and ancestor worship tablets, and the influence of extended kinship groups such as clans often outweighs the formal authority of the party in the villages. In the cities, popular culture, including gigantic rock concerts, shapes youth attitudes much more profoundly than do party messages about the Three Represents. Throughout China, consumerism and the desire for economic gain rather than communist ideals of self-sacrifice and the common good provide the principal motivation for much personal and social behavior.

Religion, which was ferociously repressed during the Mao era, is attracting an increasing number of Chinese adherents. Buddhist temples, Christian churches, and other places of worship operate more freely than they have in decades. However, religious life is still strictly controlled and limited to officially approved organizations and venues. The Chinese Catholic Church is prohibited from recognizing the authority of the Vatican, and clergy of any religion who defy the authority of the party-state are still imprisoned. Clandestine Christian communities, called house churches, have sprung up in many areas of China among people who reject the government's control of religious life and are unable to worship in public. The regime has reacted with particular harshness toward this underground movement, arresting leaders and lay people alike and bulldozing the private homes where the services have been held.

Citizenship and National Identity

China in the early twenty-first century is going through a profound and uncertain transformation in its national identity. Party leaders realize that most citizens view communist ideology as irrelevant to their lives. Therefore, the CCP has turned increasingly to patriotic themes to rally the country by portraying itself as the best guardian of China's national interests. The official media put considerable emphasis on the greatness and antiquity of Chinese culture, with the not-so-subtle message that it is time for the Chinese nation to reclaim its rightful place in the world order—under the leadership of the CCP.

The party-state also does all it can to get political capital by touting its leading role in China's impressive economic achievements, winning the 2008 Summer Olympics for Beijing, and securing the return to China of territories like Hong Kong and Macao (a former Portuguese colony) that were lost long ago to Western imperialist powers. Some observers have expressed

concern that such officially promoted nationalist sentiments could lead to a more aggressive foreign and military policy, particularly toward areas such as the potentially oil-rich South China Sea, where the PRC's historical territorial claims conflict with those of other countries like Vietnam and the Philippines.

China's Non-Chinese Citizens

The PRC calls itself a multinational state with fifty-six officially recognized ethnic groups, one of which is the majority Han people. The defining elements of a minority group in China involve some combination of language, culture (including religion), and race that distinguish them from the Han. The fifty-five minorities number a little more than 100 million, or about 8.5 percent of the total population of the PRC. These groups range in size from 16 million (the Zhuang of southwest China) to about 2,000 (the Lhoba in the far west of the country). Most of these minorities have come under Chinese rule over many centuries through territorial expansion rather than through migration into China.

China's minority peoples are highly concentrated in the five autonomous regions of Guangxi, Inner Mongolia, Ningxia, Tibet, and Xinjiang, although only in the last two do minority groups outnumber Han Chinese. These five regions are sparsely populated, yet they occupy about 60 percent of the total land area of the PRC. Some of these areas are resource rich, and all are located on strategically important borders of the country, including those with Vietnam, India, and Russia.

The Chinese constitution grants autonomous areas the right of self-government in certain matters, such as cultural affairs, but their autonomy is in fact very limited, and the minority regions are kept firmly under the control of the national party-state. Minority peoples are given some latitude to develop their local economies as they see fit, religious freedom is generally respected, and the use of minority languages in the media and literature is encouraged, as is bilingual education. In order to keep the already small minority populations from dwindling further, China's stringent family planning policy is applied much more loosely among minorities, who are often allowed to have two or more children per couple rather than the one-child prescribed limit for most Chinese.

There has also been a concerted effort to recruit and promote minority cadres to run local governments in autonomous areas. But the most powerful individual in minority areas, the head of the regional or local Communist Party, is likely to be Han Chinese: in 2002, the party secretary in all five autonomous regions was Han. Also despite significant progress in modernizing the economies of the minority regions, these areas remain among the poorest in China.

The most extensive ethnic conflict in China has occurred in Tibet, which has been under Chinese military occupation since the early 1950s. Hu Jintao, the newly elected general secretary of the CCP, served as the party chief in Tibet from 1988 to 1992. This gives him vastly more personal experience in this troubled part of the country than any previous national leader. Some see this experience as a cause for optimism, while others are critical of Hu's record of enforcing repressive Chinese control of the region (see "Current Challenges: Tibet and China").

According to official PRC statistics, there are about 20 million Muslims in China (though some outside observers put the number at several times that). China's Muslims live in many parts of the country and are spread among several different ethnic minorities, the largest of which are the Hui (9 million) and Uighur (7 million). The highest concentration of Muslims is in the far west of China in the Ningxia Hui and Xinjiang Uighur autonomous regions, the latter of which borders the Islamic nations of Afghanistan and Pakistan and the Central Asian states of the former Soviet Union.

In recent years, there has been growing unrest among Uighurs in Xinjiang (the more secular Hui are better integrated into Han Chinese society). The government has clashed with Uighur militants who want to create a separate Islamic state of "East Turkestan" and have sometimes used violence, including bombings and assassinations, to press their cause. One of the reasons that the PRC became an eager ally of the United States in the post–September 11 war on terrorism was that it allowed China to justify its crackdown on the Xinjiang-based East Turkestan Islamic Movement (ETIM), which Washington has included on its list of organizations connected to Osama bin Laden and al Qaeda.

China's minority population is relatively small and geographically isolated, and where ethnic unrest has occurred, it has been limited, sporadic, and easily quelled. Therefore, the PRC has not had the kind of intense identity-based conflict experienced by countries with more pervasive religious and ethnic cleavages, such as India and Nigeria. But it is very likely that in the future, both domestic and global forces will cause identity issues to become more visible and volatile on China's national political agenda.

Interests, Social Movements, and Protests

The formal structures of the Chinese political system are designed more to extend party-state control of political life than to facilitate citizen participation in politics. Therefore, people make extensive use of their personal connections (*guanxi*) based on kinship, friendship, and other ties to help ease their contacts with the bureaucrats and party officials who wield such enormous power over so many aspects of their lives. Patron-client politics is also pervasive at the local level in China, as it is in many other developing countries where ordinary people have little access to the official channels of power. For example, a village leader (the patron) may help farmers (the clients) avoid paying some taxes by reporting false production statistics in exchange for their support to keep him in office. Such clientelism can be an important way for local communities to resist state policies that they see as harmful to their interests.

Organized interest groups and social movements that are truly independent of party-state authority are not permitted to influence the political process in any significant way. Rather, the party-state tries to preempt the formation of autonomous groups and movements through the use of official "mass organizations." These organizations provide a means for interest groups to express their views on policy matters within strict limits.

China has numerous mass organizations formed around social or occupational categories, with a total membership in the hundreds of millions. Two of the most important mass organizations are the All-China Federation of Trade Unions, to which most Chinese factory workers belong, and the All-China Women's Federation, the only national organization representing the interests of women in general. Both federations are top-down, party-controlled organizations, and neither constitutes an independent political voice for the

Current Challenges: *Tibet and China*

Tibet is located in the far west of China on the border with India, Burma, Nepal, and Bhutan. It is a large area (about 470,000 square miles, which is nearly 13 percent of China's total area) and is ringed by some of the world's highest mountains, including the Himalayas and Mt. Everest. Ninety-four percent of Tibet's 2.6 million people are Tibetans, who are ethnically, linguistically, and culturally distinct from the Chinese. Another 2.5 million ethnic Tibetans live elsewhere in China, mostly in provinces adjacent to Tibet.

In the thirteenth century, Tibet became a theocracy in which absolute power was held by a Buddhist priest, called the Dalai Lama, who ruled the country with the help of other clergy and the aristocracy. Traditional Tibetan society was sharply divided between the tiny ruling class and the common people, most of whom were serfs living and working under difficult and often brutal conditions.

Tibet became subordinate to China in the early eighteenth century, although the Dalai Lama and other Tibetan officials continued to govern the country. After the collapse of China's imperial system in 1911, Tibet achieved de facto independence. However, Britain, which saw Tibet in the context of its extensive colonial rule in South Asia, exercised considerable influence in Tibetan affairs.

Shortly after coming to power, the Chinese Communists made known their intention to end foreign intervention in Tibet, which they, like previous Chinese governments, considered to be part of China. In 1951 the Dalai Lama agreed to the peaceful incorporation of Tibet into the People's Republic of China rather than face a full-scale military assault. Although some Chinese troops and officials were sent to Tibet, the Dalai Lama remained in a position of symbolic authority for much of the 1950s. In 1959 a widespread revolt against Chinese rule led to the invasion of Tibet by the People's Liberation Army. The Dalai Lama and over 50,000 of his supporters fled to exile in India, and Chinese rule was even more firmly established. In 1965 the Tibetan Autonomous Region was officially formed, but Chinese political and military officials have kept a firm grip on power in Tibet.

During the Maoist era, traditional Tibetan culture was suppressed by the Chinese authorities. Since the late 1970s, Buddhist temples and monasteries have been allowed to reopen, and Tibetans have gained a significant degree of cultural freedom; the Chinese government has also significantly increased investment in Tibet's economic development. However, China still considers talk of Tibetan political independence to be treason, and Chinese troops have violently crushed several anti-China demonstrations in Lhasa, the capital of Tibet.

The Dalai Lama is very active internationally in promoting the cause of independence for Tibet. In 1989, he was awarded the Nobel Peace Prize. He has met with several U.S. presidents, addressed Congress, and spoken widely to universities and other audiences in the United States. In 1999, the U.S. State Department appointed a special coordinator for Tibetan issues. The Chinese government considers these events as proof of tacit American support for Tibetan independence.

There have been some tentative talks between the Dalai Lama's representatives and Chinese officials about the conditions under which the Dalai Lama might return to Tibet. In September 2002, a high-level delegation from the Dalai Lama's government-in-exile visited Beijing and Lhasa to further explore better relations. But the PRC insists that the Dalai Lama renounce independence as a goal for Tibet, and the two sides appear far from any agreement. Tensions between Tibetans and Chinese in Tibet also remain high and potentially explosive.

groups they are supposed to represent. But they do sometimes act as an effective lobby in promoting the nonpolitical interests of their constituencies. For example, the Trade Union Federation has pushed for legislation to reduce the standard work week from six to five days, and the Women's Federation has become a strong advocate for women on issues ranging from domestic violence to economic rights.

Since the late 1990s, there has been huge increase in the number of nongovernmental organizations (NGOs) less directly subordinate to the CCP than the traditional mass organizations. There is an enormous variety of national and local NGOs, including those that deal with the environment (e.g., the China Green Foundation), health (e.g., the China Foundation for the Prevention of STDs and AIDS), charitable work (e.g., the China Children and Teenagers Fund), and legal issues (e.g., the Beijing Center for Women's Law Services). These NGOs have considerable latitude to operate within their functional areas without direct party interference *if* they steer clear of politics and do not challenge official policies.

Although they remain subordinate to the CCP, the various government bodies and other organizations discussed in this section should not be dismissed. They do "provide important access points between the Party and the organized masses, which allow the voicing of special interests in ways that do not threaten Party hegemony and yet pressure the shaping of policy."[24]

Mechanisms of Social Control

While China has certainly loosened up politically since the days of Mao Zedong, the party-state's control mechanisms still penetrate to the basic levels of society and serve the CCP's aim of preventing the formation of groups or movements that could challenge its authority. In the rural areas, the small-scale, closely knit nature of the village facilitates control by the local party and security organizations. The major means of control used by the party-state in urban China, called the unit (or *danwei*) system, is more complex. In the cities, almost everyone belongs to a unit, usually their place of work, and the *danwei* is the center of economic, social, and political life for most urban residents.

The unit holds meetings to discuss the official line on important policies or events. The personnel departments of units also keep a political dossier on every employee. The dossier contains a detailed record of the political activities and attitudes of the employee and his or her immediate family members. If a person changes jobs, which often can be done only with the *danwei*'s approval, the dossier moves too. In these and other ways, the unit has acted as a check on political dissidents. Residents' committees are another instrument of control in urban China. These neighborhood-based citizen organizations, which are often staffed by retired persons, housewives, or others not attached to a work unit, combine service and surveillance and effectively extend the unofficial reach of the party-state down to the most basic level of urban society.

As Chinese society continues to change because of the impact of economic reform, these control mechanisms are weakening. The growth of private and semi-private enterprises, increasing labor and residential mobility, and new forms of association (such as discos and coffeehouses) and communication (for example, cell phones, email, fax machines, and TV satellite dishes) are just some of the factors that are making it much harder for the party-state to monitor citizens as closely as it has in the past.

Protest and the Party-State

The Tiananmen massacre of 1989 showed the limits of protest in China. The leadership was particularly alarmed at signs that a number of grass-roots organizations, such as the Beijing Federation of Autonomous Student Unions and the Beijing Workers' Autonomous Union, were emerging from the demonstrations. The success of Solidarity, the independent Polish workers' movement, in challenging the power of the Communist Party in Poland in the 1980s was much in the minds of China's leaders as they watched the Tiananmen protests unfold. Massive repression was their way of letting it be known that the "Polish disease" would not be allowed to spread to China and that neither open political protest nor the formation of autonomous interest groups would be tolerated.

There have been no large-scale political demonstrations in China since 1989, and prodemocracy groups have been driven deep underground or abroad. Known dissidents are continuously watched, harassed, imprisoned, and, recently and more benevolently, expelled from the country, sometimes as a conciliatory diplomatic gesture. In late December 2002, one of China's leading democratic activists, Xu Wenli, was released and sent to the United States for medical care after spending sixteen of the previous twenty-one years in prison: he was most recently sentenced to a thirteen-year jail term in 1998 for his efforts to organize an independent political party.

But repression has by no means put an end to all forms of citizen protest in the PRC. Ethnic protests occur sporadically on China's periphery. The biggest and most continuous demonstrations against the party-state in recent years have been carried out by the Falun Gong (literally, Dharma Wheel Practice). Falun Gong (FLG) is a spiritual movement that combines philosophical and religious elements drawn from Buddhism and Taoism with traditional Chinese physical and meditative exercises (similar to *tai chi*). It was founded in the early 1990s by Li Hongzhi, a one-time low-level PRC government employee now living in the United States. The movement claims 70 million members in China and 30 million in more than forty other countries: these numbers may be exaggerated, but there is no doubt that the FLG has an enormous following. Its promise of inner tranquility and good health has proven very appealing to a wide cross-section of people in China as a reaction to some of the side effects of rapid modernization, including crass commercialism, economic insecurity, and the rising crime rate.

The Chinese authorities, reacting to the movement's growing popularity, began a crackdown on Falun Gong in 1999. Ten thousand FLG followers responded that April by holding a peaceful protest outside the gates of Zhongnanhai, the walled compound in the center of Beijing where China's top leaders live and work. The government then outlawed Falun Gong and deemed it an "evil cult" that spread lies, fooled people to the point that they rejected urgently needed medical care, encouraged suicides, and generally threatened social stability. It is not only the movement's size that alarms the Chinese party-state but also its ability to communicate with and mobilize its members and spread its message through both electronic means and by word of mouth.

The intense suppression of Falun Gong has included destruction of related books and tapes, jamming of websites, and the arrest of thousands of practitioners, many of whom, the movement claims, have been not only jailed but also beaten (sometimes to death) and

sent to psychiatric hospitals or labor camps. But the movement is far from being crushed. Although there have been no more protests as large as that of April 1999, FLG followers have staged numerous public demonstrations, including several in Tiananmen Square, most of which are stopped by quick arrests, and one in January 2001 that involved self-immolation by five believers.

Labor unrest has been growing in China, with reports of thousands of strikes and other actions in recent years. There have been big demonstrations at state-owned factories by workers angry about the ending of the iron rice bowl system, layoffs, the nonpayment of pensions or severance packages, and the arrest of grass-roots labor leaders. Workers at some foreign-owned enterprises have gone on strike to protest unsafe working conditions or low wages. Most of these actions have remained limited in scope and duration, so the government has usually not cracked down on the protesters and has, on occasion, actually pressured the employers to meet the workers' demands.

The countryside has also seen a rising tide of protest, especially in the poorer areas of central China. Farmers have attacked local officials and rioted over exorbitant taxes and extralegal fees, corruption, and the government's failure to pay on time for agricultural products it has purchased. These protests have not spread beyond the locales where they started and have focused on farmers' immediate material concerns, not on grand-scale issues like democracy. They have usually been contained by the authorities through a combination of coercion and concessions to some of the farmers' demands. But if the countryside is left too far behind in the process of economic development, rural discontent could spread and translate into more generalized anger against the regime.

The political situation in China early in the twenty-first century presents a rather contradictory picture. Although people are freer in many ways than they have been in decades, repression can still be intense, and open political dissent is almost nonexistent. But there are many signs that the Chinese Communist Party is losing some of its ability to control the movements and associations of its citizens and can no longer easily limit access to information and ideas from abroad. Some forms of protest also appear to be increasing and in places may come to pose a serious challenge to the authority of the party-state.

Section ⑤ Chinese Politics in Transition

Political Challenges and Changing Agendas

Scenes from the Chinese Countryside

The economic and political circumstances of China's vast rural population differ dramatically depending on where in the countryside you look.[25]

Guanqiao, Hubei Province.   In many ways, this rural village looks like an American suburb: spacious roads lined with two-story townhouses, potted plants on doorsteps, green lawns, and luscious shade trees. Some homes have leather living room furniture, studies with computers, and exercise rooms. And the village is spotless: garbage is picked up house by house every morning. But the pigsties and chicken coops are a good clue that this is farm country, not suburbia.

Things were not always so prosperous in Guanqiao. In 1978, the average annual income was only about $80, and the state had to provide the village with grain relief most every year. Now a typical young couple might earn $6,000 annually—about ten times the income of the average rural household in China.

This transformation came about in stages beginning in the early 1980s when the Maoist communes were replaced with household-based farming and agricultural production was diversified by the planting of profitable tea trees. Then came the establishment of a few small-scale village enterprises, such as ice cream making and brick factories. Under the leadership of the savvy farmer-turned-entrepreneur who was the village leader, enough capital was accumulated to allow for expansion into more sophisticated industries in the 1990s, the most recent of which is the production of steel cables used in bridge construction. Guanqiao is doing so well that much of the cost of the modern townhouses was paid for out of village funds.

Meishu, Yunnan Province.   This rural village is located in one of the areas known as China's Third World, where persistent poverty rather than growing prosperity is still the common lot in life. There are no townhouses here; most families have a total income of less than $50 a year and live in one-room, mud-brick houses with no running water that they often share with pigs or other farm animals. There are no paved roads.

The children, dressed in grimy clothes and ragged cloth shoes, are not starving, but they do not seem to be flourishing either. Education, professional health care, and other social services are minimal or nonexistent. There is no industry, and the land barely supports those who work it. Tens of millions of Chinese peasants in villages like Meishu remain mired in poverty and have benefited little from the country's economic boom.

Daolin, Hunan Province.   A few years ago, thousands of angry farmers marched on the township government headquarters to protest excessive taxes and the gross corruption of local officials. One farmer was killed and dozens injured when the police used clubs and tear gas to disperse the crowd. Shortly afterward, nine people suspected of being ringleaders of the protests were arrested. The demonstrations had been spurred by a grass-roots organization called Volunteers for Publicity of Policies and Regulations, formed to bring attention to local violations of a national law that limits taxes on farmers to 5 percent of their income. In many parts of rural China, villagers are subject to a wide range of arbitrary fees: charges for slaughtering pigs, for sending children to school, for permits to get married or to have a baby, for registering land, and for outhouse renovations—to name just a few. As a result of such local fees, Daolin's farmers were paying double the legal tax rate, which for people with an annual per capita income of only $170 was quite a burden. People were even more furious because the extra fees often went to support the wining and dining of township bureaucrats rather than for worthy local projects.

Beiwang, Hebei Province.   This was one of the first villages in China to hold democratic elections for a representative assembly to supervise the work of local government officials. Among the first decisions made by the representatives was to reassign the contracts for tending the village's 3,000 pear trees. After the rural communes were disbanded in the 1980s, each of the five hundred or so families in the village was given six trees to look after under the new household responsibility system. The assembly, however, decided that it would be better to reassign the trees to a very small number of families who would care for them in a more efficient and productive manner. The local Communist Party branch objected on the grounds that the village might lose much of the revenue that it earned from signing contracts with many households, which was used to pay for various public works projects such as road maintenance. The party was probably also concerned about the ideological implications of a less egalitarian distribution of the village's trees and the income derived from them. Nevertheless, assembly representatives were able to generate strong support from their constituents for their proposal, and the party branch allowed the trees to be recontracted to just eleven households. In a short time, pear production zoomed. The new system proved to be economically beneficial not only to the few families who looked after the trees but also to the village as a whole because of the local government's share of the increased profits.

The scenes just described make several important points about Chinese politics today. First, they remind us of the central role that China's rural areas will play in the nation's future. Most Chinese still live in the countryside, and China's political and economic fate will be greatly influenced by what goes on there. These scenes also reflect the enormous diversity of the Chinese countryside: prosperity and poverty, mass protests and peaceful politics. It is very hard to generalize about such a vast and varied nation by looking at what is going on in only one small part of the country.

The scene from Beiwang reminds us that in China, as in other countries, not all politics involves matters of national or international significance. For many, perhaps most, Chinese, who looks after the village pear trees matters more than what goes on in the inner sanctums of the Communist Party or the outcomes of U.S.-China presidential summits. The victory of the Beiwang representative assembly on the pear tree issue shows that even in a one-party state, the people sometimes prevail against the those with power, and democracy works on the local level—as long as the basic principle of party leadership is not challenged.

The Guanqiao scene is just one example of the astonishing improvement in living standards in much of rural China brought about by decollectivization and industrialization. But huge pockets of severe poverty, like that in Meishu, still persist, especially in inland regions that are far removed from the more prosperous coastal regions. Most of rural China falls somewhere

between the affluence of Guanqiao and the extreme poverty of Meishu. And it is in these in-between areas, such as Daolin, where the combination of new hopes brought about by economic progress and the anger caused by blatant corruption, growing inequalities, stagnating incomes, and other frustrations may prove to be politically explosive.

Economic reform has yielded a better life and higher hopes for most of China's farmers. The CCP must now deal with the challenge of having to satisfy those hopes or risk the wrath of a social group that for decades has been the bedrock of the party's support.

Economic Management, Social Tension, and Political Legitimacy

The problems of China's rural areas are part of a larger challenge facing the country's leadership: how to sustain and effectively manage the economic growth on which the CCP's legitimacy as China's ruling party is now largely based. The party is gambling that continuing solid economic performance will literally buy it legitimacy in the eyes of the Chinese people and that most citizens will care little about democracy if their material lives continue to get better.

Despite the overall success of the reforms, the Chinese Communist Party faces a number of very serious challenges in governing the economy that will affect the party's political fortunes. Failure to keep inequality under control, especially between city and countryside, or to continue providing opportunities for advancement for the less well off could become a source of social instability and a liability for a political party that still espouses a commitment to socialist goals. One of the government's most formidable tasks will be to create enough new jobs for the millions of workers who are expected to be laid off by the closure or restructuring of state-owned enterprises. This situation will very likely be compounded by those displaced from industries that are no longer competitive in China's increasingly globalized economy.

The considerable autonomy gained by provinces and localities as a result of the decentralization of economic decision making has fostered a growing regionalism that poses a potentially serious threat to the political control of the central government. Corruption, which affects the lives of most people more directly than does political repression, has become so blatant and widespread that it is probably the single most corrosive force eating away at the legitimacy of the Chinese Communist Party.

An increasingly serious issue on China's national agenda, and one with the potential to turn into a major crisis, is the spread of AIDS. Recent surveys estimate the number of infected citizens to be between 850,000 and 1 million. Unless the current infection rate is slowed, predictions are that there could be 10 million AIDS victims in China by 2010.

AIDS first spread in China in the early 1990s among needle-sharing heroin users, mostly in the border regions of the west and southwest. It has since spread to all areas of the country through drug use and sexual activity. There was also an extensive outbreak of AIDS in several provinces among blood donors and their families. In these cases, poor farmers had sold their blood for cash at unscrupulous and unsafe collection stations run by local "entrepreneurs," doctors, and officials. Some villages in Henan Province have an HIV infection rate of over 60 percent of the population.

The government has recently taken active steps to deal with the situation, including increased funding for AIDS prevention, support for AIDS awareness campaigns, improved access to cheaper drugs, and punishment of some blood dealers, as well as new laws regulating the blood supply. But responding effectively to the problem will require concerted action on the local level and the involvement of nongovernmental organizations and experts best equipped to address the root causes of the looming epidemic.

It was not an encouraging sign that China's leading AIDS activist, Dr. Wan Yanhai, was detained by the authorities in mid-2002 for "revealing state secrets," a reference to his role in exposing the Henan blood scandal. Wan was released a month later, after he admitted his "mistake" in distributing a classified government report on AIDS through foreign journalists and websites. As one authoritative article observed, "There are few countries in the world with a comparable level of governmental infrastructure and control, or that have experienced such steady and dynamic economic growth. China must muster the political will and resources to prevent this progress from quickly unraveling as a result of AIDS."[26]

Clearly, the leaders of the PRC will have to make some difficult policy choices in deciding how to manage China's rapidly modernizing economy and respond to its radically changing society.

China and the Democratic Idea

China has evolved in recent decades toward a system of what has been called "market Leninism," a combination of increasing economic openness and continuing political rigidity under the leadership of a ruling party that adheres to a remodeled version of communist ideology.[27] The major political challenges now facing the CCP and the country emerge from the sharpening contradictions and tensions of this hybrid system.

In the short run, the CCP's gamble that the country's economic boom would divert the attention of most Chinese from politics to profits has paid off. However, as the people of China become more secure economically, better educated, and more aware of the outside world, they are likely to become politically less quiescent. The steadily expanding class of private entrepreneurs may want political clout to match their economic wealth. Scholars, scientists, and technology specialists may become more outspoken about the limits on intellectual freedom. And the many Chinese citizens who travel or study abroad may find the political gap between their party-state and the world's growing number of democracies to be increasingly intolerable.

There are reasons to be both optimistic and pessimistic about the future of the democratic idea in China.[28] On the negative side, China's long history of bureaucratic and authoritarian rule and the hierarchical values of still-influential Confucian culture seem to be mighty counterweights to democracy. And although its political legitimacy may be weak and some aspects of its social control have broken down, the coercive power of China's communist party-state remains formidable. The PRC's relatively low per capita standard of living, a largely rural population and vast areas of extreme poverty, and state-dominated media and means of communications also impose some impediments to democratization. Finally, many in China are rather apathetic about national politics (preferring to focus on their immediate economic concerns) or fearful of the violence and chaos that radical political change might unleash.

On the positive side, the impressive successes of democratization in Taiwan in the past decade, including free and fair multiparty elections from the local level up to the presidency, strongly suggest that the values, institutions, and process of democracy are not incompatible with Confucian culture. And though it is still a developing country, China has a higher literacy rate, more extensive industrialization and urbanization, a faster rate of economic growth, and less inequality (though there are some worrisome trends here) than most other countries at its level of economic development—conditions widely seen by social scientists as favorable to democracy.

Despite the CCP's continuing tight hold on power, there have been a number of significant political changes in China that could be planting the seeds of democracy: the decentralization of political and economic power to local governments; the setting of a mandatory retirement age and term limits for all officials; the coming to power of younger, better educated, and more worldly leaders; the increasingly important role of the National People's Congress in the policy-making process; the introduction of competitive elections in rural villages; the strengthening and partial depoliticization of the legal system; tolerance of a much wider range of artistic, cultural, and religious expression; and the important freedom (unheard of in the Mao era) for individuals to be apolitical.

Furthermore, the astounding spread of democracy around the globe has created a trend that will be increasingly difficult for China's leaders to resist. The PRC has become a major player in the world of states, and its government must be more responsive to international opinion in order to continue the country's deepening integration with the international economy and growing stature as a responsible and mature global power.

One of the most important political trends in China has been the resurgence of civil society, a sphere of independent public life and citizen association, which, if allowed to thrive and expand, could provide fertile soil for future democratization. The development of civil society among workers in Poland and intellectuals in Czechoslovakia, for example, played an important role in the collapse of communism in East-Central Europe in the late 1980s by weakening the critical underpinnings of party-state control.

The Tiananmen demonstrations of 1989 reflected the stirrings of civil society in post-Mao China. The brutal crushing of that movement showed the CCP's determination to thwart the growth of civil society before it could seriously challenge Communist authority. But as economic modernization and social liberalization have deepened in the PRC, civil society has begun to stir again. Some stirrings, like the Falun Gong movement, have met with vicious repression by the party-state. But others, such as the proliferation of semiautonomous nongovernmental organizations, have been encouraged by the authorities. Academic journals and conferences have recently had surprisingly open, if tentative discussions about future political options for China, including multiparty democracy.

At some point, the leaders of the CCP will face the fundamental dilemma of whether to accommodate or, as they have done so often in the past, repress organizations, individuals, and ideas that question the principle of party leadership. On the one hand, accommodation will require less party-state control and more meaningful citizen representation and participation. On the other hand, repression would likely derail the country's economic dynamism and could have terrible costs for China.

Chinese Politics in Comparative Perspective

As mentioned at the end of Section 1, students of comparative politics should find it particularly interesting to compare China with other nations from two perspectives. First, the People's Republic of China can be compared with other communist party-states with which it shares or has shared many political characteristics. Second, China can be compared with other developing nations that face similar economic and political challenges.

China as a Communist Party-State

Why has the Chinese communist party-state been more durable than other regimes of its type? The PRC's successful economic restructuring and the rapidly rising living standard of most of the people have saved the CCP from the kinds of economic crises that greatly weakened other Communist systems, including the Soviet Union. China's leaders believe that one of the biggest mistakes made by the last Soviet party chief, Mikhail Gorbachev, was that he went too far with political reform and not far enough with economic change, and they are convinced that their reverse formula is a key reason that they have not suffered the same fate.

The fact that the Chinese Communists won power through an indigenous revolution with widespread popular backing and did not depend on foreign military support for their victory also sets China apart from the situation of most of the now-deposed East-Central European communist parties. Therefore, although repression and corruption may be harming the popularity of the CCP, the party still has a deep reservoir of historical legitimacy among large segments of the population.

But China also has many things in common with other communist party-states, including the basic features of what has been often called its totalitarian political system. **Totalitarianism** (a term also applied to fascist regimes such as Nazi Germany) describes a system in which the ruling party prohibits all forms of meaningful political opposition and dissent, insists on obedience to a single state-determined ideology, and enforces its rule through coercion and terror. Such regimes also seek to bring all spheres of public activity (including the economy and culture) and even many parts of its citizens' private lives (including reproduction) under the total control of the party-state in the effort to modernize the country and, indeed, to transform human nature.

China offers an interesting comparative perspective on the nature of change in totalitarian systems. Partly because of their inflexibility, totalitarian regimes in Russia and East-Central Europe collapsed quickly and thoroughly, to be replaced by democracies in the 1990s. The CCP appears to be trying to save Communist rule in China by abandoning or at least moderating many, if not all, of its totalitarian features. In order to promote economic development, the CCP has relaxed its grip on many areas of life, and citizens are now free to pursue their interests without state interference as long as they steer clear of sensitive political issues.

In this sense, the PRC has evolved from Maoist totalitarianism toward a less intrusive, but still dictatorial, "consultative authoritarian regime" that "increasingly recognizes the need to obtain information, advice, and support from key sectors of the population, but insists on suppressing dissent . . . and maintaining ultimate political power in the hands of the Party."[29] Thus, China seems, at least for the moment, to be going through a type of post-totalitarian transition characterized by bold economic and social reform, but which also leads to another type of dictatorship rather than to democracy.

China as a Third World State

The record of Communist rule in China raises many issues about the role of the state in economic development. It also provides an interesting comparative perspective on the complex relationship between economic and political change in the Third World.

When the Chinese Communist Party came to power in 1949, China was a desperately poor country, with an economy devastated by a century of civil strife and world war. It was also in a weak and subordinate position in the post–World War II international order. Measured against this starting point, the PRC has made remarkable progress in improving the well-being of its citizens, building a strong state, and enhancing the country's global role.

Why has China been more successful than so many other nations in meeting some of major challenges of development? Third World governments have often served narrow class or foreign interests more than the national interest. Many political leaders in Africa, Asia, and Latin America have been a drain on development rather than a stimulus. The result is that Third World states have many times become defenders of a status quo built on extensive inequality and poverty rather than agents of needed change. In contrast, the PRC's recent rulers have been quite successful in creating what social scientists call a **developmental state** in which government power and public policy are used effectively to promote national economic growth.

Whereas much of the Third World seems to be heading toward democracy without development—or at best very slow development—China seems to be following the reverse course of very fast development without democracy. There is a sharp and disturbing contrast between the harsh political rule of the Chinese communist party-state and its remarkable accomplishments in improving the material lives of the Chinese people. This contrast is at the heart of what one journalist has called the "riddle of China" today, where the government "fights leprosy as aggressively as it attacks dissent. It inoculates infants with the same fervor with which it arrests its critics. Partly as a result, a baby born in Shanghai now has a longer life expectancy than a baby born in New York City."[30] This "riddle" makes it difficult to settle on a clear evaluation of the overall record of Communist rule in China, particularly in the post-Mao era. It also makes it hard to predict the future of the Chinese Communist Party, since the regime's economic achievements could provide it with the support, or at least compliance, it needs to stay in power despite its serious political shortcomings.

The CCP's tough stance on political reform is in part based on its desire for self-preservation. But in keeping firm control on political life while allowing the country to open up in other important ways, the Chinese Communist Party also believes it is wisely following the model of development pioneered by the newly industrializing countries (NICs) of East Asia such as South Korea, Taiwan, and Singapore.

The lesson that the CCP draws from the NIC experiences is that only a strong "neoauthoritarian" government can provide the political stability and social peace required for rapid economic growth. According to this view, democracy—with its open debates about national priorities, political parties contesting for power, and interest groups squabbling over how to divide the economic pie—is a recipe for chaos, particularly in a huge and relatively poor country. Chinese leaders point out that democracy has not often been conducive to successful economic development in the Third World. In India, for example, a democratic but weak government has been unable to respond effectively to internal ethnic strife and has been stymied by entrenched interests in its efforts to alleviate poverty.

But another of the lessons from the East Asian NICs—one that most Chinese leaders have been reluctant to acknowledge so far—is that economic development, social modernization, and global integration also create powerful pressures for political change from below and abroad. In both Taiwan and South Korea, authoritarian governments that had presided over economic miracles in the 1960s and 1970s gave way in the 1980s and 1990s to the democratic idea, largely in response to domestic pressures.

The dynamic expansion and transformation of the Chinese economy indicate that the PRC is in the early stages of a period of growth and modernization that will lead it to NIC status. However, in terms of the extent of industrialization, per capita income, and the strength of the middle and professional classes, China's economic development is still far below the level at which democracy succeeded in Taiwan and South Korea. It is important to remember that "authoritarian governments in East Asia pursued market-driven economic growth for decades without relaxing their hold on political power."[31]

Nevertheless, economic reform in China has already created groups and processes, interests and ideas that are likely to become sources of pressure for more and faster political change. And the experience of the NICs and other developing countries suggests that such pressures are likely to intensify as the economy and society continue to modernize. Therefore, at some point in the not-too-distant future, the Chinese Communist Party may again face the challenge of the democratic idea. How China's new generation of leaders responds to this challenge is perhaps the most important and uncertain question about Chinese politics in the early twenty-first century.

Key Terms

communist party-state	township and village
Marxism-Leninism	enterprises
autonomous regions	decentralization
guerrilla warfare	iron rice bowl
collectivization	*guanxi*
socialism	newly industrializing
Great Leap Forward	countries
communism	dual rule
Great Proletarian	cadres
Cultural Revolution	*nomenklatura*
revisionism	socialist democracy
command economy	Four Cardinal Principles
socialist market	*danwei*
economy	totalitarianism
people's communes	developmental state
household responsibility	
system	

Suggested Readings

Bernstein, Thomas P., and Xiaobo Lü. *Taxation Without Representation in Contemporary Rural China*. Cambridge: Cambridge University Press, 2003.

Blecher, Marc J. *China Against the Tides: Restructuring Through Revolution, Radicalism, and Reform*. London: Pinter, 1997.

Chang, Jung. *Wild Swans: Three Daughters of China*. New York: Simon & Schuster, 1991.

Fairbank, John King, and Goldman, Merle. *China: A New History*. Cambridge, Mass.: Harvard University Press, 1998.

Gao Yuan. *Born Red: A Chronicle of the Cultural Revolution*. Stanford, Calif.: Stanford University Press, 1987.

Hutchings, Graham. *Modern China: A Guide to a Century of Change*. Cambridge, Mass.: Harvard University Press, 2001.

Judd, Ellen R. *The Chinese Women's Movement Between State and Market*. Stanford, Calif.: Stanford University Press, 2002.

Lampton, David M. *Same Bed, Different Dreams: Managing U.S.-China Relations, 1989–2000*. Berkeley: University of California Press, 2001.

Lardy, Nicholas R. *Integrating China into the Global Economy*. Washington, D.C.: Brookings Institution Press, 2002.

Li, Cheng. *China's Leaders: The New Generation*. Lanham, Md.: Rowman & Littlefield, 2001.

MacFarquhar, Roderick (ed.). *The Politics of China: The Eras of Mao and Deng*. 2nd ed. Cambridge: Cambridge University Press, 1998.

Ogden, Suzanne. *Inklings of Democracy in China*. Cambridge, Mass.: Harvard University Press, 2002.

Perry, Elizabeth J., and Selden, Mark (eds.). *Chinese Society: Change, Conflict and Resistance*. New York : Routledge, 2000.

Saich, Tony. *Governance and Politics of China*. New York: Palgrave Macmillan, 2001.

Solinger, Dorothy J. *Contesting Citizenship in Urban China: Peasant Migrants, the State, and the Logic of the Market*. Berkeley: University of California Press, 1999.

Spence, Jonathan. *Mao Zedong*. New York: Viking, 1999.

Spence, Jonathan D., and Annping Chin. *The Chinese Century: A Photographic History of the Last Hundred Years*. New York: Random House, 1996.

Starr, John Bryan. *Understanding China: A Guide to China's Economy, History, and Political Culture*. 2nd ed. New York: Hill and Wang, 2001.

Unger, Jonathan. *The Transformation of Rural China*. Armonk, N.Y.: M. E. Sharpe, 2002.

Zweig, David. *Internationalizing China: Domestic Interests and Global Linkages*. Ithaca, N.Y.: 2002.

Suggested Websites

China Links, Professor William A. Joseph, Wellesley College
www.wellesley.edu/Polisci/wj/China/chinalinks.html
Embassy of the People's Republic of China in the United States
www.china-embassy.org
Finding News About China
chinanews.bfn.org/
PRC China Internet Information Center

www.china.org.cn/english/index.htm
Washington Post.com: China
www.washingtonpost.com/wp-dyn/world/asia/eastasia/china

Notes

[1]"Beijing Win Divides World Opinion," CNN.com, http://www.cnn.com/2001/WORLD/asiapcf/east/07/13/beijing.win/.

[2]Mao Zedong, "Report on an Investigation of the Peasant Movement in Hunan," March 1927, in *Selected Readings from the Works of Mao Tsetung* (Beijing: Foreign Languages Press, 1971), 24.

[3]David Bachman, *Bureaucracy, Economy, and Leadership in China: The Institutional Origins of the Great Leap Forward* (Cambridge: Cambridge University Press, 1991), 2.

[4]Fareed Zakaria, "The Big Story Everyone Missed," *Newsweek*, December 30, 2002, 52.

[5]See, for example, "When China Wakes," *Economist*, November 28, 1992; and Nicholas D. Kristof and Sheryl WuDunn, *China Wakes: The Struggle for the Soul of a Rising Power* (New York: Time Books, 1994).

[6]"When China Wakes," 3, 15.

[7]Barry Naughton, "The Pattern and Legacy of Economic Growth in the Mao Era," in Kenneth Lieberthal et al. (eds.), *Perspectives on Modern China: Four Anniversaries* (Armonk, N.Y.: M. E. Sharpe, 1991), 250.

[8]Deng Xiaoping first expressed his "cat theory" in 1962 in a speech, "Restore Agricultural Production," in the aftermath of the failure and famine of the Great Leap Forward. In the original speech, he actually quoted an old peasant proverb that refers to a "yellow cat or a black cat," but it is most often rendered "white cat or black cat." See *Selected Works of Deng Xiaoping (1938–1965)* (Beijing: Foreign Languages Press, 1992), 293.

[9]Kathleen Hartford, "Socialist Agriculture Is Dead; Long Live Socialist Agriculture! Organizational Transformation in Rural China," in Elizabeth J. Perry and Christine P. W. Wong (eds.), *The Political Economy of Reform in Post-Mao China* (Cambridge, Mass.: Council on East Asian Studies, Harvard University, 1985), 55.

[10]Christine P. W. Wong, "China's Economy: The Limits of Gradualist Reform," in William A. Joseph (ed.), *China Briefing, 1994* (Boulder, Colo.: Westview Press, 1994), 50.

[11]Emily Honig and Gail Herschatter, *Personal Voices: Chinese Women in the 1980s* (Stanford, Calif.: Stanford University Press, 1988), 337.

[12]Baruch Boxer, "China's Environment: Issues and Economic Implications," in Joint Economic Committee of Congress, *China's Economic Dilemmas in the 1990s: The Problems of Reform, Modernization, and Interdependence*, vol. 1 (Washington, D.C.: Government Printing Office, 1991), 306–307.

[13]Mao Zedong, "Strive to Build a Great Socialist Country," September 15, 1954, in *Selected Works of Mao Tsetung*, vol. 5 (Beijing: Foreign Languages Press, 1977), 149.

[14]Deng Xiaoping, "Uphold the Four Cardinal Principles," March 30, 1979, in *Selected Works of Deng Xiaoping (1977–1982)*, (Beijing: Foreign Languages Press, 1984), 178.

[15]The constitution of the People's Republic of China can be found on line at the website of China's People's Daily, http://english.peopledaily.com.cn/constitution/constitution.html. The full text of the most recently amended version of the constitution of the Chinese Communist Party can be found at the website of the party's Sixteenth National Congress held in November 2002, http://www.16congress.org.cn/english/features/49109.htm.

[16]Mao Zedong, "Problems of War and Strategy," November 6, 1938, in *Selected Works of Mao Tsetung,* vol. 2 (Beijing: Foreign Languages Press, 1972), 224.

[17]Kenneth Lieberthal and David Michael Lampton (eds.), *Bureaucracy, Politics, and Decision-Making in Post-Mao China* (Berkeley: University of California Press, 1992).

[18]John P. Burns, *The Chinese Communist Party's Nomenklatura System: A Documentary Study of Party Control of Leadership Selection, 1979–1984* (Armonk, N.Y.: M. E. Sharpe, 1989), ix–x.

[19]Gordon White, *Riding the Tiger: The Politics of Economic Reform in Post-Mao China* (Palo Alto, Calif.: Stanford University Press, 1993), 20.

[20]Jiang Zemin, "Speech at the Meeting Celebrating the 80th Anniversary of the Founding of the Communist Party of China," July 1, 2001, http://www.china-un.ch/eng/14905.html.

[21]James D. Seymour, *China's Satellite Parties* (Armonk, N.Y.: M. E. Sharpe, 1987), 87.

[22]For Jiang's 1999 speech, see the People's Daily website, http://www.peopledaily.com.cn/english/50years/news/19991001A117.html). For the 2002 speech, see the official website of the Sixteenth Party Congress, http://www.16congress.org.cn/english/features/49007.htm.

[23]Lin Biao, "Foreword to the Second Edition," *Quotations from Chairman Mao Tse-tung* (Beijing: Foreign Languages Press, 1967), iii.

[24]James R. Townsend and Brantly Womack, *Politics in China,* 3d ed. (Boston: Little, Brown, 1986), 271.

[25]The following scenes are extrapolated from Wang Zhe, "Behind the Dream of a Village," *Beijing Review,* June 14, 2001, 13–16; Lu Xueyi, "The Peasants Are Suffering, the Villages Are Very Poor," *Dushu* (Readings), January 2001, in U.S. Embassy (Beijing, China), PRC Press Clippings, http://www.usembassy-china.org.cn/sandt/peasantsuffering.html); Erik Eckholm, "Heated Protests by Its Farmers Trouble Beijing," *New York Times,* February 1, 1999, A; Susan V. Lawrence, "Democracy, Chinese-Style: Village Representative Assemblies," *Australian Journal of Chinese Affairs,* no. 32 (July 1994): 61–68.

[26]Joan Kaufman and Jun Jing, "China and AIDS—The Time to Act Is Now," *Science,* June 28, 2002, 2340.

[27]Nicholas D. Kristof, "China Sees 'Market-Leninism' as Way to Future," *New York Times,* September 6, 1993, 1, 5.

[28]Many of the points in this section are based on Martin King Whyte, "Prospects for Democratization in China," *Problems of Communism* (May–June 1992): 58–69; Michel Oksenberg, "Will China Democratize? Confronting a Classic Dilemma," *Journal of Democracy* 9, no. 1 (January 1998): 27–34; and Minxin Pei, "Is China Democratizing?" *Foreign Affairs* 77, no. 1 (January–February 1998), 68–82.

[29]Harry Harding, *China's Second Revolution: Reform After Mao* (Washington, D.C.: Brookings Institution, 1987), 200.

[30]Nicholas D. Kristof, "Riddle of China: Repression as Standard of Living Soars," *New York Times,* September 7, 1993, A1, A10.

[31]Nicholas Lardy, "Is China Different? The Fate of Its Economic Reform," in Daniel Chirot (ed.), *The Crisis of Leninism and the Decline of the Left* (Seattle: University of Washington Press, 1991), 147.

Glossary

abertura (Portugese for "opening"; *apertura* in Spanish) in Brazil, refers to the period of authoritarian liberalization begun in 1974 when the military allowed civilian politicians to contest for political office in the context of a more open political society. See also **glasnost.**

accommodation an informal agreement or settlement between the government and important interest groups that is responsive to the interest groups' concerns for policy or program benefits.

accountability a government's responsibility to its population, usually by periodic popular elections and by parliament's having the power to dismiss the government by passing a motion of no confidence. In a political system characterized by accountability, the major actions taken by government must be known and understood by the citizenry.

acephalous societies literally "headless" societies. A number of traditional Nigerian societies, such as the Igbo in the precolonial period, lacked executive rulership as we have come to conceive of it. Instead, the villages and clans were governed by committee or consensus.

administrative court court that hears cases from private citizens and organizations involving allegations of bureaucratic violations of rules and laws. In Germany, the third branch of the court system, consisting of the Labor Court, the Social Security Court, and the Finance Court. In France, the highest administrative court is the Council of State.

administrative guidance in Japan, informal guidance, usually not based on a statute or formal regulation, that is given by a government agency, such as a ministry and its subdivisions, to a private organization, such as a firm, or a lower-level government. The lack of transparency of the practice makes it subject to criticisms as a disguised form of collusion between a government agency and a firm.

Aegis a term derived from the mythological armor of the Greek god Zeus; refers to the most advanced naval combat system that exists today. It combines high-powered radar, command and decision, and weapons-control elements, which enable an Aegis-equipped ship with a capability to engage simultaneously in antiair, antisurface, and antisubmarine warfare. Originally developed for the U.S. Navy, it is currently installed on a dozen U.S. cruisers and destroyers, four Japanese destroyers, and a few Spanish frigates.

amakudari a Japanese practice, known as "descent from heaven," in which government officials retiring from their administrative positions take jobs in public corporations or private firms under their own ministry's jurisdiction.

Amerindian original peoples of North and South America; indigenous people.

ancien régime the monarchical regime that ruled France until the Revolution of 1789, when it was toppled by a popular uprising. The term is used to describe long-established regimes in other countries ruled by undemocratic elites.

anticlericalism opposition to the power of churches or clergy in politics. In some countries, for example, France and Mexico, this opposition has focused on the role of the Catholic Church in politics.

appropriations government spending that must be approved by the U.S. Congress each year. All government spending must begin with a bill proposed in the House of Representatives.

Articles of Confederation the first governing document of the United States, agreed to in 1777 and ratified in 1781. The Articles concentrated most powers in the states and made the national government largely dependent on voluntary contributions of the states.

Asia-Pacific Economic Cooperation a regional organization of Asian and Pacific rim nations established in 1989 to promote cooperation among member states, especially in foreign investment and the standardization and compilation of statistical data. Currently composed of eighteen members (including the United States and Canada), it advocates "open regionalism," cooperation among nations within the region that neither precludes nor impedes cooperation between them and nations outside the region.

Asian Development Bank (ADB) a regional bank established in 1966 to promote economic development in and cooperation among nations in Asia. The bank mediates pub-

---

*Note: Boldface terms *within* a definition can be found as separate entries in the Glossary.

lic and private investments in, and loans for, selected developmental projects. The current members include fifty-six nations and areas in Asia and sixteen others, including the United States.

Assembly of Experts   nominates the **Supreme Leader** and can replace him. The assembly is elected by the general electorate but almost all its members are clerics.

Association of Southeast Asian Nations (ASEAN)   an organization formed in 1967 to promote regional economic and political cooperation. As of 2003, ASEAN consisted of ten member states: Brunei, Cambodia, Indonesia, Laos, Malaysia, Myanmar, the Philippines, Singapore, Thailand, and Vietnam.

asymmetrical federalism   a system of governance in which political authority is shared between a central government and regional or state governments, but where some subnational units in the federal system have greater or lesser powers than others.

authoritarian   See **authoritarianism.**

authoritarianism   a system of rule in which power depends not on popular legitimacy but on the coercive force of the political authorities. Hence, there are few personal and group freedoms. It is also characterized by near absolute power in the executive branch and few, if any, legislative and judicial controls. See also **autocracy; patrimonialism.**

autocracy   a government in which one or a few rulers has absolute power, thus, a **dictatorship.** Similar to authoritarianism.

autonomous region   in the People's Republic of China, a territorial unit equivalent to a province that contains a large concentration of ethnic minorities. These regions have some autonomy in the cultural sphere but in most policy matters are strictly subordinate to the central government.

autonomous republic   a territorial unit in the Soviet Union that was a constituent unit of the **union republic** within which it was located. Autonomous republics were populated by a large national (ethnic) group, after which the autonomous republic was generally named. They enjoyed little actual autonomy in the Soviet period. Once Russia adopted its new constitution in 1993, those autonomous republics within Russian territory became constituent units (now called republics) of the Russian Federation.

ayatollah   literally, "sign of God." High-ranking clerics in Iran. The most senior ones—often no more than half a dozen—are known as grand ayatollahs.

balance of payments   an indicator of international flow of funds that shows the excess or deficit in total payments of all kinds between or among countries. Included in the calculation are exports and imports, grants, and international debt payments.

basej   Persian word for "mobilization"; used to describe the volunteer army of young and old men formed in Iran to help the regular army and Revolutionary Guards in the war against Iraq.

Basic Law (*Grundgesetz*)   German document establishing the founding of the Federal Republic of Germany (West Germany) in 1949. Similar to a written constitution.

bazaar   an urban marketplace where shops, workshops, small businesses, and export-importers are located.

bicameral   a legislative body with two houses, such as the U.S. Senate and the U.S. House of Representatives. Just as the U.S. Constitution divides responsibilities between the branches of the federal government and between the federal and the states, it divides legislative responsibilities between the Senate and the House.

Bill of Rights   the first ten amendments to the U.S. Constitution (ratified in 1791), which established limits on the actions of government. Initially, the Bill of Rights limited only the federal government. The Fourteenth Amendment and subsequent judicial rulings extended the provisions of the Bill of Rights to the states.

Brahmin   highest caste in the Hindu caste system.

bureaucracy   an organization structured hierarchically, in which lower-level officials are charged with administering regulations codified in rules that specify impersonal, objective guidelines for making decisions. In the modern world, many large organizations, especially business firms and the executives of developed states, are organized along bureaucratic lines.

bureaucratic-authoritarianism   a term developed by Argentine sociologist Guillermo O'Donnell to interpret the common characteristics of military-led authoritarian regimes in Brazil, Argentina, Chile, and Uruguay in the 1960s and 1970s. According to O'Donnell, bureaucratic authoritarian regimes led by the armed forces and key civilian allies emerged in these countries in response to severe economic crises.

bureaucratic rings   a term developed by the Brazilian sociologist and president Fernando Henrique Cardoso that refers to the highly permeable and fragmented structure of the state bureaucracy that allows private interests to make alliances with midlevel bureaucratic officers. By shaping public policy to benefit these interests, bureaucrats gain the promise of future employment in the private sector. While in positions of responsibility, bureaucratic rings are ardent defenders of their own interests.

bushi the warrior class in medieval Japan, known also as samurai. The class emerged around the tenth century A.D., and a dominant band established Japan's first warrior government in the twelfth century. The last warrior government was overthrown in the Meiji Restoration of the mid-nineteenth century.

cabinet the ministers who direct executive departments. In parliamentary systems, the cabinet and high-ranking subcabinet ministers (also known as the government) are considered collectively responsible to parliament.

cadre a person who occupies a position of authority in a **communist party-state;** cadres may or may not be Communist Party members.

capital flight the transfer of funds from the national currency of a country into a foreign currency (e.g., Russian rubles into U.S. dollars) and the short-term investment of these funds either inside (e.g., dollar deposits in Russian banks) or outside of the country.

caste system India's Hindu society is divided into castes. According to the Hindu religion, membership in a caste is determined at birth. Castes form a rough social and economic hierarchy. See also **Brahmin; untouchables.**

central planning See **command economy.**

chancellor the German head of government. Functional equivalent of prime minister in other parliamentary systems.

charisma the ability of a leader to attract an intensely devoted following because of personal characteristics that supporters believe endow the charismatic leader with extraordinary and heroic qualities.

checks and balances a governmental system of divided authority in which coequal branches can restrain each other's actions. For example, the U.S. president must sign legislation passed by Congress for it to become law. If the president vetoes a bill, Congress can override that veto by a two-thirds vote of the Senate and the House of Representatives.

Citizen Action Groups formed in Germany in the 1970s, forerunner of the Greens Party.

civil servants state employees who make up the bureaucracy.

civil society refers to the space occupied by voluntary associations outside the state, for example, professional associations (lawyers, doctors, teachers), trade unions, student and women's groups, religious bodies, and other voluntary association groups. The term is similar to *society,* although

civil society implies a degree of organization absent from the more inclusive term *society.*

clientelism (or **patron-client networks**) an informal aspect of policy-making in which a powerful patron (for example, a traditional local boss, government agency, or dominant party) offers resources such as land, contracts, protection, or jobs in return for the support and services (such as labor or votes) of lower-status and less powerful clients; corruption, preferential treatment, and inequality are characteristic of clientelist politics. See also **patrimonialism; prebendalism.**

co-determination German legal mechanism that authorizes trade union members in firms with 2,000 or more employees to have nearly 50 percent of the seats on the firm's board of directors.

cohabitation the term used by the French to describe the situation in the Fifth Republic when a president and prime minister belong to opposing political coalitions.

cold war the hostile relations that prevailed between the United States and the USSR from the late 1940s until the demise of the Soviet Union in 1991. Although an actual (hot) war never directly occurred between the two superpowers, they clashed indirectly by supporting rival forces in many wars occurring in the Third World.

collectivization a process undertaken in the Soviet Union under Stalin in the late 1920s and early 1930s and in China under Mao in the 1950s, by which agricultural land was removed from private ownership and organized into large state and collective farms.

command economy a form of **socialism** in which government decisions ("commands") rather than market mechanisms (such as supply and demand) are the major influences in determining the nation's economic direction; also called central planning.

communism a system of social organization based on the common ownership and coordination of production. According to Marxism (the theory of German philosopher Karl Marx, 1818–1883), communism is a culminating stage of history, following capitalism and **socialism.** In historical practice, leaders of China, the Soviet Union, and other states that have proclaimed themselves seeking to achieve communism have ruled through a single party, the Communist Party, which has controlled the state and society in an authoritarian manner, and have applied **Marxism-Leninism** to justify their rule.

communist See **communism.**

communist party-state a type of nation-state in which the Communist Party attempts to exercise a complete monopoly on political power and controls all important state institutions. See also **communism.**

comparative politics the study of the domestic politics, political institutions, and conflicts of countries. Often involves comparisons among countries and through time within single countries, emphasizing key patterns of similarity and difference.

comparativists political scientists who study the similarities and differences in the domestic politics of various countries. See also **comparative politics.**

Confucianism a social philosophy based on the teachings of the Chinese sage Confucius (c. 551–479 B.C.) that emphasizes social harmony, righteous behavior toward others, and deference to one's superiors. Confucianism remains a major source of cultural values in the countries of East Asia, including China and Japan.

conservative the belief that existing political, social, and economic arrangements should be preserved. Historically, this has involved a defense of the inequalities (of class, race, gender, and so on) that are part of the existing order; often used to identify the economic and social policies favored by right-of-center parties.

Constitution the governing document of the United States. The Constitution was drafted in 1787 and ratified in 1788. It has been amended twenty-seven times since ratification.

constitutional monarchy system of government in which the head of state ascends by heredity, but is limited in powers and constrained by the provisions of a constitution.

constructive vote of no confidence provision in the German political system of requiring any opposition party or group of parties to have an alternative majority government that would replace the current one. This provision was placed into the Basic Law in 1949 to avoid the Weimar practice of voting governments out of office and producing numerous political crises.

co-optation incorporating activists into the system while accommodating some of their concerns.

corporatism a pattern of organizing interests and influencing public policy in which the state gives favored status to certain **interest groups**; typically involves tripartite (three-way) consultations among representatives of business, labor, and government over economic policy. Corporatism can occur in democratic and **authoritarian** settings. However, it is usually criticized because it limits open debate and representative processes. See also **corporatist state, democratic corporatism, state corporatism.**

corporatist state a state in which **interest groups** become an institutionalized part of the structure. See also **corporatism; democratic corporatism; state corporatism.**

country a territorial unit controlled by a single state. Countries vary in the degree to which groups within them have a common culture and ethnic affiliation. See also **nation-state; state.**

danwei a Chinese term that means "unit" and is the basic level of social organization and a major means of political control in China's **communist party-state.** A person's *danwei* is most often his or her workplace, such as a factory or an office.

decentralization policies that aim to transfer some decision-making power from higher to lower levels of government, typically from the central government to subnational governments.

Declaration of Independence the document asserting the independence of the British colonies in what is now the United States from Great Britain. The Declaration of Independence was signed in Philadelphia on July 4, 1776.

democratic centralism a system of political organization developed by V. I. Lenin and practiced, with modifications, by all communist party-states. Its principles include a hierarchical party structure in which (1) party leaders are elected on a delegate basis from lower to higher party bodies; (2) party leaders can be recalled by those who elected them; and (3) freedom of discussion is permitted until a decision is taken, but strict discipline and unity should prevail in implementing a decision once it is made. In practice, in all Communist parties in China, the Soviet Union, and elsewhere, centralizing elements tended to predominate over the democratic ones.

democratic corporatism a set of institutions or forums that bring representatives from employers, trade unions, and government together to negotiate issues affecting workplaces, industry structure, and national economic policy.

demokratizatsiia the policy of democratization identified by former Soviet leader Mikhail Gorbachev in 1987 as an essential component of *perestroika.* The policy was part of a gradual shift away from a **vanguard party** approach toward an acceptance of **liberal** democratic norms. Initially, the policy embraced multicandidate elections and a broadening of political competition within the Communist Party itself; after 1989, it involved acceptance of a multiparty system.

Department of Homeland Security the cabinet-level department established by the Bush administration in 2002 to centralize many, but not all, U.S. government agencies responsible for domestic security. The department was established in response to perceived security lapses that led to the September 11, 2001, attacks on the World Trade Center and the Pentagon.

deregulation the process of dismantling state regulations that govern social and economic life. Deregulation increases the power of private actors, especially business firms.

détente a relaxation of tensions between formerly hostile nations that moves them toward more normal diplomatic relations. Often used to describe a thaw in the **cold war** beginning in the 1960s.

developmental state a **nation-state** in which the government carries out policies that effectively promote national economic growth.

developmentalism an ideology and practice in Latin America during the 1950s in which the state played a leading role in seeking to foster economic development through sponsoring vigorous **industrial policy.** See also **import substituting industrialization.**

dictatorship See **authoritarianism; autocracy; totalitarianism.**

dirigisme a French term denoting that the state plays a leading role in supervising the economy. In contrast to **socialism** or communism, firms remained privately owned under a system of *dirigisme.* At the other extreme, *dirigisme* differs from the situation where the state has a relatively small role in economic governance.

dirigiste (See *dirigisme.*)

distributional politics the use of power, particularly by the state, to allocate some kind of valued resource among competing groups.

distributive policies policies that allocate state resources into an area that lawmakers perceive needs to be promoted. For example, leaders today believe that students should have access to the Internet. In order to accomplish this goal, telephone users are being taxed to provide money for schools to establish connections to the Internet (which, in large part, uses telephone lines to transfer data).

Domei the Japanese Confederation of Labor founded in 1964 through the merger of several federations of right-wing labor unions opposed to the leftist labor organization *Sohyo.* Dominated by private sector unions and closely allied with the Democratic Socialist Party, *Domei* advocated harmonious management-labor relations and a corporatist relationship with the government. *Domei* was disbanded in 1987 when all its affiliated unions joined *Rengo* at its founding.

dual rule a system of administration used in China (adapted from the Soviet Union) that places a government body under the authority of both a higher-level government organization and a Communist Party organization.

dual society a society and economy that are sharply divided into a traditional, usually poorer, and a modern, usually richer, sectors.

dual-structure system a structure of an industrial economy characterized by a sharp division between a modern corporate sector composed of large and powerful enterprises, on the one hand, and a traditional small-business sector, on the other. The latter tend to be dependent on and often controlled by the former. The pre–World War II Japanese economy was characterized by such a structure.

Economic Community of West African States (ECOWAS) the organization established in 1975 among the sixteen governments in West Africa. Its goals are to strengthen and broaden the economies in the region through the removal of trade barriers among its members (such as import quotas and domestic content laws), freedom of movement for citizens, and monetary cooperation.

economic liberalization the dismantling of government controls on the economy.

ejidatario recipient of *ejido* land grant in Mexico.

ejido land granted by Mexican government to an organized group of peasants.

Electoral College the body that formally elects the president of the United States. Voters in U.S. presidential elections actually elect electors (most of whom are unknown to them) who meet approximately a month after the election in each state capital to cast their votes for president. Most states award Electoral College votes on a winner-take-all system.

Emergency (1975–1977) the period when Indian Prime Minister Indira Gandhi suspended many formal democratic rights and ruled in an **authoritarian** manner.

emir traditional Islamic ruler. The emir presides over an "emirate," or kingdom, in northern Nigeria.

European Union (EU) An organization of European countries created in 1958 to promote economic integration and political cooperation among European states. At first, the EU's mandate was primarily to reduce tariff barriers among West European states. Since then, more countries throughout Europe have joined the EU, and its powers have vastly expanded to include promoting common policies on immigration, technical standards, and economic and monetary regulation.

executive the agencies of government that implement or execute policy. The highest levels of the executive in most countries is a president or prime minister and cabinet. The top executive officeholders supervise the work of administrative departments and bureaus.

Expediency Council a committee set up in Iran to resolve differences between the *Majles* and the Guardian Council.

export-led growth economic growth generated by the export of a country's commodities. Export-led growth can occur at an early stage of economic development, in which case it involves primary products, such as the country's mineral resources, timber, and agricultural products; or at a later stage, when industrial goods and services are exported.

Farsi Persian word for the Persian language. Fars is a province in central Iran.

fatwa a pronouncement issued by a high-ranking Islamic cleric.

favelas in Brazil, huge shantytowns of homes made out of cardboard, wood from dumps, and blocks of mortar and brick. These shantytowns create rings of extreme poverty around cities like Rio de Janeiro and São Paulo. Similar shantytowns can be found in other Latin American cities, although terms to describe them vary by country. In Peru, for example, these shantytowns are called *barriadas*.

Federal Reserve Board the U.S. central bank established by Congress in 1913 to regulate the banking industry and the money supply. Although the president appoints the chair of the board of governors (with Senate approval), the board operates largely independently. Many criticize its policies as reflecting the needs of banks and international capital over the needs of citizens, particularly workers.

federal system (state) nation-state with subnational units (states or provinces) that have significant independent political powers. A federal system differs from a unitary state that has few autonomous regional political institutions. See also **federalism.**

federalism a system of governance in which political authority is shared between the national government and regional or state governments. The powers of each level of government are usually specified in a federal constitution.

5 percent rule provision of the German electoral law requiring all parties to win at least 5 percent of the vote to obtain seats for representation.

foreign direct investment ownership of or investment in cross-border enterprises in which the investor plays a direct managerial role.

Foundation of the Oppressed a clerically controlled foundation in Iran set up after the revolution there.

Four Cardinal Principles ideas first enunciated by Chinese leader Deng Xiaoping in 1979 asserting that all policies should be judged by whether they uphold the socialist road, the dictatorship of the proletariat, the leadership of the Communist Party, and Marxism-Leninism-Mao Zedong Thought. The main purpose of the Four Cardinal Principles was to proscribe any challenge to the ultimate authority of the Chinese Communist Party, even during a time of far-reaching economic reform. The Principles have been reaffirmed by Deng's successors and continue to define the boundaries of what is politically permissible in China.

framework regulation German style of regulation in which the general patterns of public policy are outlined, but specific details of policy are left to policy-makers' discretion as long as they remain within the general framework.

franchise the right to vote.

free market A system in which government regulation of the economy is absent or limited. Relative to other advanced democracies, the United States has traditionally had a freer market economically. See **laissez-faire.**

free trade international commerce that is relatively unregulated or constrained by tariffs (special payments imposed by governments on exports or imports).

fundamentalism a term recently popularized to describe radical religious movements throughout the world.

fusion of powers a constitutional principle that merges the authority of branches of government, in contrast to the principle of **separation of powers.** In Britain, for example, Parliament is the supreme legislative, executive, and judicial authority. The fusion of legislature and executive is also expressed in the function and personnel of the cabinet.

Gastarbeiter (guest workers) A program instituted by the German government in the early 1960s that brought workers from Southern Europe into Germany to address a labor shortage.

gender social division based on the cultural and political significance ascribed to sexual difference.

gender gap politically significant differences in social attitudes and voting behavior between men and women.

glasnost Gorbachev's policy of "openness" or "publicity," which involved an easing of controls on the media, arts, and public discussion, leading to an outburst of public debate and criticism covering most aspects of Soviet history, culture, and policy.

globalization the intensification of worldwide interconnectedness associated with the increased speed and magnitude of cross-border flows of trade, investment and finance, and processes of migration, cultural diffusion, and communication.

grandes écoles prestigious and highly selective schools of higher education in France that train top civil servants, engineers, and business executives.

grands corps elite networks of graduates of selective training schools in France.

grass-roots democracy term used to describe activist, local political action, and community control. Used frequently by the Green Party in Germany and many social movements elsewhere.

Great Leap Forward a movement launched by Mao Zedong in 1958 to industrialize China very rapidly and thereby propel it toward communism. The Leap ended in economic disaster in 1960, causing one of the worst famines in human history.

Great Proletarian Cultural Revolution the political campaign launched in 1966 by Chairman Mao Zedong to stop what he saw as China's drift away from socialism and toward capitalism. The campaign led to massive purges in the Chinese Communist Party, the widespread persecution of China's intellectuals, and the destruction of invaluable cultural objects. The Cultural Revolution officially ended in 1976 after Mao's death and the arrest of some of his most radical followers.

green revolution a strategy for increasing agricultural (especially food) production, involving improved seeds, irrigation, and abundant use of fertilizers.

guanxi a Chinese term that means "connections" or "relationships," and describes personal ties between individuals based on such things as common birthplace or mutual acquaintances. *Guanxi* are an important factor in China's political and economic life.

Guardian Council a committee created in the Iranian constitution to oversee the *Majles* (the parliament).

guerrilla warfare a military strategy based on small bands of soldiers (the guerrillas) who use hit-and-run tactics to attack a numerically superior and better-armed enemy.

health insurance funds a semipublic system in Germany that brings all major health interests together to allocate costs and benefits by way of consultation and group participation.

hegemonic power a state that can control the pattern of alliances and terms of the international order, and often shapes domestic political developments in countries throughout the world.

Hezbollahis literally "partisans of God." In Iran, the term is used to describe religious vigilantes. In Lebanon, it is used to describe the Shi'i militia.

Hindus India's main religion is Hinduism, and its adherents are called Hindus.

hojjat al-Islam literally, "the proof of Islam." In Iran, it means a medium-ranking cleric.

household responsibility system the system put into practice in China beginning in the early 1980s in which the major decisions about agricultural production are made by individual farm families based on the profit motive rather than by a **people's commune** or the government.

imam leader. Iranians traditionally reserved this title for the twelve early Infallible Leaders of **Shi'ism.** During the Islamic Revolution, this title was bestowed on Khomeini to elevate him above the other grand ayatollahs.

Imam Jum'ehs prayer leaders in Iran's main urban mosques. Appointed by the **Supreme Leader,** they have considerable authority in the provinces.

import substituting industrialization (ISI) strategy for industrialization based on domestic manufacture of previously imported goods to satisfy domestic market demands. See also **developmentalism.**

Indian Administrative Service (IAS) India's civil service, a highly professional and talented group of administrators who run the Indian government on a day-to-day basis.

indicative planning a term used to describe the development of a national economic plan that indicates what the plan specifies as desirable priorities for economic development. Indicative planning can be distinguished from plans developed under **command economies.**

indigenous groups population of **Amerindian** heritage in Mexico.

indirect rule a term used to describe the British style of colonialism in Nigeria and India in which local traditional rulers and political structures were used to help support the colonial governing structure.

industrial policy a generic term to refer to a variety of policies designed to shape leading sectors of the economy and enhance competitiveness, especially for industries that are considered strategic to national interests. Countries differ substantially regarding the degree to which their states consciously pursue industrial policies.

informal sector (economy) an underground economy.

insider privatization a term used in relation to Russia to refer to the transformation of formerly state-owned enterprises into **joint-stock companies** or private enterprises in which majority control of the enterprise is in the hands of employees and/or managers of that enterprise.

interest group organizations that seek to represent the interests—usually economic—of their members in dealings with the government. Important examples are associations representing people with specific occupations, business interests, racial and ethnic groups, or age groups in society.

International Financial Institutions (IFIs) generally refers to the International Bank for Reconstruction and Development (the World Bank) and the International Monetary Fund (IMF), but can also include other international lending institutions. See also **structural adjustment program (SAP).**

interventionist an interventionist state acts vigorously to shape the performance of major sectors of the economy.

interventores in Brazil, allies of Getúlio Vargas (1930–1945, 1950–1952) picked by the dictator during his first period of rulership to replace opposition governors in all the Brazilian states except Minas Gerais. The *interventores* represented a shift of power from subnational government to the central state. See also **politics of the governors.**

iron rice bowl a feature of China's socialist economy that provided guarantees of lifetime employment, income, and basic cradle-to-grave benefits to most urban and rural workers. Economic reforms beginning in the 1980s that aimed at improving efficiency and work motivation sought to smash the iron rice bowl and link employment and income more directly to individual effort.

iron triangles a term coined by students of American politics to refer to the relationships of mutual support formed by particular government agencies, members of congressional committees or subcommittees, and interest groups in various policy areas. Synonymous with "cozy triangles," the term has been borrowed by some students of Japanese politics to refer to similar relationships found among Japanese ministry or agency officials, *Diet* (parliament) members, and special interest groups.

jihad literally "struggle" Although often used to mean armed struggle against unbelievers, it can also mean spiritual struggle for more self-improvement.

joint-stock company a business firm whose capital is divided into shares that can be held by individuals, groups of individuals, or governmental units. In Russia, formation of joint-stock companies has been the primary method for privatizing large state enterprises.

judicial review the prerogative of a high court (such as the U.S. Supreme Court) to nullify actions by the executive and legislative branches of government that in its judgment violate the constitution.

Junkers reactionary land-owning elite in nineteenth-century Prussia. Major supporters of Bismarck's attempts to unify Germany in 1871.

jurist's guardianship Khomeini's concept that the Iranian clergy should rule on the grounds that they are the divinely appointed guardians of both the law and the people. He developed this concept in the 1970s.

keiretsu a group of closely allied Japanese firms that have preferential trading relationships and often interlocked directorates and stock-sharing arrangements. The relationships among *keiretsu* member firms have been regarded as collusive and harmful to free trade by some of Japan's principal trading partners.

Keynesianism named after the British economist John Maynard Keynes, an approach to economic policy in which state economic policies are used to regulate the economy in an attempt to achieve stable economic growth. During recession, state budget deficits are used to expand demand in an effort to boost both consumption and investment and create employment. During periods of high growth when inflation threatens, cuts in government spending and a tightening of credit are used to reduce demand.

koenkai usually translated as "support association," *koenkai* is a Japanese campaign organization for a particular candidate, consisting mainly of the candidate's relatives, friends, alumni, coworkers, and their acquaintances. Networks of *koenkai* organizations are far more important and effective than political parties in assisting politicians' election campaigns. Since it costs politicians a great deal to maintain these networks, *koenkai*-centered elections encourage corruption.

krai one of the six territorial units in the Russian Federation that are defined by the constitution of 1993 to be among the eighty-nine members of the federation, with a status equal to that of the republics and *oblast.* Like the *oblasts* during the Soviet period, the *krai* were defined purely as territorial-administrative units within a particular **union republic** of the Soviet Union. A *krai* differed from an *oblast* in that part of its border was on an external boundary of the USSR or it included a mixture of diverse ethnic territories (or both). Generally a *krai* is a geographically large unit, but relatively sparsely populated.

Kulturkampf "cultural struggle" between Protestant and Catholic forces in late-nineteenth-century Germany.

laissez-faire the doctrine that government should not interfere with commerce. Relative to other advanced democracies, the United States has traditionally taken a more laissez-faire attitude toward economic regulation, though regulation increased in the twentieth century. See also **free market.**

land reform the process of reducing gross inequalities in the ownership of farm land by either confiscating or buying it from large owners and redistributing it to those who have little or no land.

law-based state a state where the rule of law prevails, so that actions of the government as well as of nongovernmental actors are subject to the requirements of the law. The creation of a law-based state in the Soviet Union was one of the explicit goals of Gorbachev's reform process, thus limiting the ability of state agencies or the Communist Party of the Soviet Union arbitrarily to circumvent laws or legal provisions.

legitimacy a belief by powerful groups and the broad citizenry that a state exercises rightful authority. In the contemporary world, a state is said to possess legitimacy when it enjoys consent of the governed, which usually involves democratic procedures and the attempt to achieve a satisfactory level of development and equitable distribution of resources.

liberal classically liberal in the 19th-century European sense, favoring free-market solutions to economic problems and extensive personal freedoms for individuals.

lifetime employment the practice common among Japanese government agencies and large business firms to keep newly hired high school and university graduates on payroll until they reach mandatory retirement age. As a rule, the practice applies only to male employees and, moreover, is on the decline in contemporary Japan, where both the general population and work force are rapidly "graying" and the ratios of temporary, part-time, and female employees are rising.

Lok Sabha the lower house of parliament in India where all major legislation must pass before becoming law.

macroeconomic policy government policy intended to shape the overall economic system at the national level by concentrating on policy targets such as inflation or growth.

mafia a term borrowed from Italy and widely used in Russia to describe networks of organized criminal activity that pervade both economic and governmental structures in that country and activities such as the demanding of protection money, bribe taking by government officials, contract killing, and extortion.

Maharajas India's traditional rulers—monarchs—who retained their positions during the colonial period but were removed from power when the Indian republic was established.

Majles Arabic term for "assembly"; used in Iran to describe the parliament.

manifest destiny The public philosophy in the nineteenth century that the United States was not only entitled but also destined to occupy territory from the Atlantic to the Pacific.

maquiladora factories that produce goods for export, often located along the U.S.-Mexican border.

Marbury* v. *Madison the 1803 U.S. Supreme Court ruling that the federal courts inherently had the authority to review the constitutionality of laws passed by Congress and signed by the president. The ruling, initially used sparingly, placed the courts centrally in the system of checks and balances.

market reform a strategy of economic transformation embraced by the Yeltsin government in Russia and the Deng Xiaoping government in China that involves reducing the role of the state in managing the economy and increasing the role of market forces. In Russia, market reform is part of the transition to postcommunism and includes the extensive transfer of the ownership of economic assets from the state to private hands. In China, market reform has been carried out under the leadership of the Chinese Communist Party and involves less extensive privatization.

Marxism-Leninism the theoretical foundation of communism based on the ideas of the German philosopher, Karl Marx (1818–1883), and the leader of the Russian Revolution, V. I. Lenin (1870–1924). Marxism is, in essence, a theory of historical development that emphasizes the struggle between exploiting and exploited classes, particularly the struggle between the bourgeoisie (capitalists) and the proletariat (the industrial working class). Leninism emphasizes the strategy and organization to be used by the communist party to overthrow capitalism and seize power as a first step on the road to communism.

maslahat Arabic term for "expediency," "prudence," or "advisability." It is now used in Iran to refer to reasons of state or what is best for the Islamic Republic.

mestizo a person of mixed white, indigenous (Amerindian), and sometimes African descent.

middle-level theory seeks to explain phenomena in a limited range of cases, in particular, a specific set of countries with particular characteristics, such as parliamentary regimes, or a particular type of political institution (such as political parties) or activity (such as protest).

Minamata disease   organic mercury poisoning caused by eating contaminated river fish and clams, which produces paralysis of limbs and speech impairment. Occurred in Japan in the 1950s and 1960s as a result of industrial firms' discharge of toxic wastes. The disease is regarded as one of the most tragic examples of the widespread industrial pollution that characterized postwar Japanese society at the height of its dramatic economic growth.

mir   a traditional form of communal peasant organization in Russia that survived until the collectivization campaign of the late 1920s and involved a periodic redistribution of strips of land among families of the commune.

moderating power (*poder moderador***)**   a term used in Brazilian politics to refer to the situation following the 1824 constitution in which the monarchy was supposed to act as a moderating power, among the executive, legislative, and judicial branches of government, arbitrating party conflicts, and fulfilling governmental responsibilities when nonroyal agents failed.

monetarism   an approach to economic policy that assumes a natural rate of unemployment determined by the labor market, and rejects the instrument of government spending to run up budgetary deficits for stimulating the economy.

mosque   Muslim place of worship, equivalent to a church, temple, or synagogue.

most different case analysis   the logic of most different case analysis is that, by comparing cases that differ widely, one seeks to isolate a factor or factors (termed the independent variable or variables) that both cases share—despite their differences in other respects—that might explain an outcome (or dependent variable).

Muslims   followers of Islam.

nationalism   an ideology seeking to create a **nation-state** for a particular community; a group identity associated with membership is such a political community. Nationalists often proclaim that their state and nation are superior to others.

nationalization   the take-over by the government of privately owned business firms.

nation-state   distinct, politically defined territory with its own state, relatively coherent culture, economy, and ethnic and other social identities. See also **country.**

Nazi   acronym for Adolf Hitler's National Socialist German Worker's Party.

neoliberalism   a term used to describe government policies aiming to promote free competition among business firms within the market, notably, liberalization and **monetarism.**

new social movements   grass-roots associations that may be differentiated from more established social movements and from interest groups by their greater tendency to raise basic questions about social values, social goals, and political styles; examples include environmentalism, women's rights, peace, and gay rights.

New State (*Estado Novo***)**   in Brazil, an authoritarian government led by Getúlio Vargas in 1937 that legitimized its rule through state corporatism, massive public sector investment through para-statals, and paternalistic social policies.

newly industrializing countries (NICs)   a term used to describe a group of countries that achieved rapid **economic development** beginning in the 1960s largely stimulated by robust international trade (particularly exports) and guided by government policies. The core NICs are usually considered to be Taiwan, South Korea, Hong Kong, and Singapore, but other countries, including Argentina, Brazil, Malaysia, Mexico, and Thailand, are often included in this category.

nomenklatura   a system of personnel selection under which the Communist Party maintained control over the appointment of important officials in all spheres of social, economic, and political life. The term is also used to describe individuals chosen through this system and thus refers more broadly to the privileged circles in the Soviet Union and China.

nonaligned bloc   countries that refused to ally with either the United States or the USSR during the **cold war** years.

nongovernmental organization (NGO)   a private group that seeks to influence public policy and deal with certain problems that it believes are not being adequately addressed by governments, such as Amnesty International (human rights), Oxfam (famine relief), and Greenpeace (the environment).

nontariff barriers (NTBs)   policies designed to prevent foreign imports in order to protect domestic industries, such as quotas, health and safety standards, packaging and labeling rules, and unique or unusual business practices. A form of protectionism that does not use formal tariffs.

North American Free Trade Agreement (NAFTA)   a treaty among the United States, Mexico, and Canada implemented on January 1, 1994, that largely eliminates trade barriers among the three nations and establishes procedures to resolve trade disputes. NAFTA serves as a model for an eventual Free Trade Area of the Americas zone that could include most Western Hemisphere nations.

oblast   one of forty-nine territorial units in the Russian Federation defined by the constitution of 1993 to be among the eighty-nine members of the federation, with a status equal to that of the republics and *krai.* An *oblast* generally lacks a non-Russian national/ethnic basis. During the Soviet period, the *oblasts* were defined purely as territorial-administrative units located within a particular **union republic** of the Soviet Union. See also *okrug;* **autonomous republic.**

okrug   one of ten territorial units in the Russian Federation that are defined by the constitution of 1993 to be among the eighty-nine members of the federation with a status equal to that of the republics, *oblasts*, and *krai.* An *okrug* generally was originally formed due to the presence of a non-Russian national/ethnic group residing in the territory. Alongside their status as equal units of the Russian Federation, most of the *okrugs* are physically located within and constituent parts of an *oblast* or *krai*. This situation has created ambiguity regarding the relationship between the *okrug* and the *oblast* or *krai* they are located in.

oligarchs   a small group of powerful and wealthy individuals who gained ownership and control of important sectors of Russia's economy in the context of the privatization of state assets in the 1990s.

oligarchy   narrowly based, undemocratic government, often by traditional elites. See also **autocracy; authoritarianism.**

OPEC   Organization of Petroleum Exporting Countries. Founded in 1960 by Iran, Venezuela, and Saudi Arabia, it now includes most oil-exporting states with the notable exceptions of Mexico and former members of the Soviet Union. It tries to regulate prices by regulating production.

Other Backward Classes   the middle or intermediary castes in India that have been accorded reserved seats in public education and employment since the early 1990s.

overlapping responsibilities (policy)   refers to the unique pattern of German federalism in which federal and state governments share administrative responsibility for implementation of public policies.

panchayats   In India, elected bodies at the village, district, and state levels that have development and administrative responsibilities.

para-statals   state-owned, or at least state-controlled, corporations, created to undertake a broad range of activities, from control and marketing of agricultural production to provision of banking services, operating airlines, and other transportation facilities and public utilities. See also **interventionist.**

parliamentary democracy   system of government in which the chief executive is answerable to the legislature and may be dismissed by it. Parliamentary democracy stands in contrast to a presidential system, in which the chief executive is elected in a national ballot and is independent of the legislative branch.

parliamentary sovereignty   a constitutional principle of government (principally in Britain) by which the legislature reserves the power to make or overturn any law without recourse by the executive, the judiciary, or the monarchy. Only parliament can nullify or overturn legislation approved by Parliament; and Parliament can force the cabinet or the government to resign by voting a motion of no confidence.

party democracy   a term used to describe the strong role that German political parties are allowed to play in the Federal Republic. Unlike the U.S. Constitution where parties are not mentioned, the Basic Law explicitly enables political parties to play a crucial linking role between citizen and state.

pasdaran   Persian term for guards, used to refer to the army of Revolutionary Guards formed during Iran's Islamic Revolution.

patrimonial state   see **patrimonialism.**

patrimonialism (or neopatrimonialism)   a system of governance in which a single ruler treats the state as personal property (patrimony). Appointments to public office are made on the basis of unswerving loyalty to the ruler. In turn, state officials exercise wide authority in other domains, such as the economy, often for their personal benefit and that of the ruler, to the detriment of the general population. See also **authoritarianism; autocracy; prebendalism.**

patron-client networks (or patron-client politics)   see **clientelism.**

People of the Book   the Muslim term for recognized religious minorities, such as Christians, Jews, and Zoroastrians.

people's communes   large-scale rural communities that were in charge of nearly all aspects of political, social, and economic life in the Chinese countryside from the late 1950s until the early 1980s, when they were disbanded and replaced by a system of household and village-based agricultural production.

perestroika   the policy of restructuring embarked on by Gorbachev when he became head of the Communist Party of the Soviet Union in 1985. Initially, the policy emphasized decentralization of economic decision making, increased enterprise autonomy, expanded public discussion of policy issues, and a reduction in the international isolation of the Soviet economy. Over time, restructuring took on a more political tone, including a commitment to *glasnost* and *demokratizatsiia.*

personalist politicians demagogic political leaders who use their personal charisma to mobilize their constituency.

personalized proportional representation German voters cast two votes on each ballot: the first for an individual candidate and the second for a list of national and regional candidates grouped by party affiliation. This system has the effect of personalizing list voting because voters have their own representative but also can choose among several parties.

police powers powers that are traditionally held by the states to regulate public safety and welfare. Police powers are the form of interaction with government that citizens most often experience. Even with the growth in federal government powers in the twentieth century, police powers remain the primary responsibility of the states and localities.

political action committee (PAC) a narrow form of interest group that seeks to influence policy by making contributions to candidates and parties in U.S. politics.

political culture the attitudes, beliefs, and symbols that influence political behavior; often defined in terms of specific national political-cultural orientations.

political development the stages of change producing more modern and effective political institutions.

political economy the study of the interaction between the state and the economy, that is, how the state and political processes affect the organization of production and exchange (the economy) and how the organization of the economy affects political processes.

political institutions the formal rules, structured relationships, and organizations within the state and, more broadly, within the political sphere. Some key examples are the executive, legislature, judiciary, military, and political parties.

politics of the governors in Brazil, refers to periods of history in which state governors acquire extraordinary powers over domains of policy that were previously claimed by the federal government. The term refers most commonly to the Old Republic and the current state of Brazilian federalism. See also **federalism.**

populism gaining the support of popular sectors. When used in Latin American politics, this support is often achieved by manipulation and demagogic appeals.

power sharing compulsory coalition government in South Africa in which all parties that obtained 5 percent or more of the ballot in the 1994 election would be entitled to seats in the cabinet. A transitional measure included in the 1993 constitution to reassure white South Africans that their political leaders would remain in government for an interim period. Power sharing is also used to describe **cohabitation** in France.

prebendalism patterns of political behavior that rest on the justification that official state offices should be competed for and then utilized for the personal benefit of officeholders as well as of their support group or clients. Thus, prebendal politics is sustained by the existence of **patron-client networks.** See also **patrimonialism; clientelism.**

predominant-party system a multiparty political system in which one party maintains a predominant position in parliament and control of government for a long period of time.

prefects French administrators appointed by the minister of the interior to coordinate state agencies and programs within the one hundred French departments or localities. Prefects had enormous power until decentralization reforms in the 1980s transferred some of their responsibilities to elected local governments.

privatization the sale of state-owned enterprises to private companies or investors. Those who support the policy claim that private ownership is superior to government ownership because for-profit entities promote greater efficiency. Privatization is a common central component of **structural adjustment programs** to curtail the losses associated with these enterprises and generate state revenue when they are sold. For Russia, see **spontaneous privatization.**

privatization voucher a certificate worth 10,000 rubles issued by the government to each Russian citizen in 1992 to be used to purchase shares in state enterprises undergoing the process of privatization. Vouchers could also be sold for cash or disposed of through newly created investment funds.

proletarian see **proletariat.**

proletariat the industrial working class, which, according to **Marxism-Leninism,** is destined to seize power and replace capitalism with socialism.

property taxes taxes levied by local governments on the assessed value of property. Property taxes are the primary way in which local jurisdictions in the United States pay for the costs of primary and secondary education. Because the value of property varies dramatically from neighborhood to neighborhood, the funding available for schools—and the quality of education—also varies from place to place.

proportional representation (PR) a system of political representation in which seats are allocated to parties within multimember constituencies, roughly in proportion to the votes each party receives. PR usually encourages the election to parliament of more political parties than single-member-district winner-take-all systems.

protectionism government policies that aim to prevent imported goods from competing with a country's domestic industries. The most common example is tariffs, a tax on imported, but not domestic, products.

pyramid debt a situation when a government or organization takes on debt obligations at progressively higher rates of interest in order to pay off existing debt. In some cases, a structure of pyramid debt can result in a default on the entire debt obligation if interest owed becomes unmanageable.

quangos acronym for quasi-nongovernmental organizations, the term used in Britain for nonelected bodies that are outside traditional governmental departments or local authorities. They have considerable influence over public policy in areas such as education, health care, and housing.

Qur'an the Muslim Bible.

Rayja Sabha India's upper house of parliament; considerably less significant politically than the **Lok Sabha.**

redistributive policies policies that take resources from one person or group in society and allocate them to a different, usually more disadvantaged, group. The United States has traditionally opposed redistributive policies to the disadvantaged.

referendum an election in which citizens are asked to approve (or reject) a policy proposal.

regulations the rules that explain the implementation of laws. When Congress passes a law, it sets broad principles for implementation, but how the law is actually implemented is determined by regulations written by executive branch agencies. The regulation-writing process allows interested parties to influence the eventual shape of the law in practice.

Rengo the General Confederation of Japanese Labor founded in 1987 under the leadership of private sector unions. The largest labor organization in Japanese history, *Rengo* consists today of 336 unions with the combined membership of about 7.2 million.

rentier state a country that obtains much of its revenue from the export of oil or other natural resources.

rents above-market returns to a factor of production. Pursuit of economic rents (or "rent-seeking") is profit seeking that takes the form of nonproductive economic activity.

republic in contemporary usage, a political regime in which leaders are not chosen on the basis of their inherited background (as in a monarchy). A republic may, but need not be, democratic. For Russia, a republic is one of twenty territorial units in the Russian Federation that are defined by the constitution of 1993 to be among the eighty-nine members of the federation with a status equal to that of other federal units such as the *oblasts* and *krai.* A republic generally was originally formed in recognition of the presence of a non-Russian national or ethnic group residing in the territory. In the Soviet period, most of these units were called **autonomous republics.**

reservations jobs or admissions to colleges reserved by the government of India for specific social groups, particularly underprivileged groups.

revisionism a label used by the Chinese Communist Party during the late Maoist era (1965–1976) to refer to the ideology of those political parties (including the Communist Party of the Soviet Union) or individuals judged to have betrayed what they believed to be the true meaning of the theory and practice of **Marxism-Leninism.**

revolution the process by which an established political regime is replaced (usually by force and with broad popular participation) and a new regime established that introduces radical changes throughout society. Revolutions are different from coups d'état in that there is widespread popular participation in revolutions, whereas coups d'état are led by small groups of elites.

scheduled castes the lowest caste groups in India; also known as the untouchables. See also **untouchables.**

Self-Defense Forces (SDF) inaugurated in Japan as a police reserve force with 75,000 recruits in August 1950, following the outbreak of the Korean War. Known as SDF since 1954, it today consists of approximately 250,000 troops equipped with sophisticated modern weapons and weapons systems. The constitutional status and operational mandates of these forces are controversial.

self-determination the right of a sovereign state or an ethnic or other group that shares cultural and historical ties to live together in a given territory and in a manner they desire. It is often the basis of the claim by a state or group for political independence and cultural autonomy.

semipresidential system a form of government in which presidents are more than just figureheads but are ultimately subordinate to parliament.

separation of powers an organization of political institutions within the state in which the executive, legislature, and judiciary have autonomous powers and no one branch dominates the others. This is the common pattern in presidential systems, as opposed to parliamentary systems, in which there is a **fusion of powers.**

sexenio   the six-year administration of Mexican presidents.

shari'a   Islamic law derived mostly from the **Qur'an** and the examples set by the Prophet Muhammad.

Shi'ism   a branch of Islam. It literally means the followers or partisans of Ali. The other branch is known as Sunni, or the followers of tradition.

shock therapy   a variant of **market reform** that involves the state simultaneously imposing a wide range of radical economic changes, with the purpose of "shocking" the economy into a new mode of operation. Shock therapy can be contrasted with a more gradual approach to market reform.

Sikhs   an important religious minority in India.

single-member plurality (SMP) electoral system   an electoral system in which candidates run for a single seat from a specific geographic district. The winner is the person who receives the most votes, whether or not that is a majority. SMP systems, unlike systems of proportional representation, increase the likelihood that two national coalition parties will form.

social class   common membership in a group whose boundaries are based on a common economic location, notably, occupation and income. Members of the same social class often share similar political attitudes.

social market economy   term describing the German economy that combines an efficient competitive economy with generous welfare state benefits for large segments of the population.

social movements   grass-roots associations that demand reforms of existing social practices and government policies. Social movements are less formally organized than **interest groups.** See also **new social movements.**

social security   national systems of contributory and non-contributory benefits to provide assistance for the elderly, sick, disabled, unemployed, and others similarly in need of assistance. The specific coverage of social security, a key component of the welfare state, varies by country.

socialism   in a socialist regime, the state plays a leading role in organizing the economy, and most business firms are publicly owned. A socialist regime, unlike a **communist party-state,** may allow the private sector to play an important role in the economy and be committed to political pluralism. In **Marxism-Leninism,** socialism refers to an early

stage in development of communism. Socialist regimes can be organized in a democratic manner, in that those who control the state may be chosen according to democratic procedures. They may also be governed in an undemocratic manner when a single party, not chosen in free competitive elections, controls the state and society.

socialist democracy   the term used by the Chinese Communist Party to describe the political system of the People's Republic of China. Also called the *people's democratic dictatorship.* The official view is that this type of system, under the leadership of the Communist Party, provides democracy for the overwhelming majority of people and suppresses (or exercises dictatorship over) only the enemies of the people. Socialist democracy is contrasted to bourgeois (or capitalist) democracy, which puts power in the hands of the rich and oppresses the poor.

socialist market economy   the term used by the government of China to refer to the country's current economic system. It is meant to convey the mix of state control (socialism) and market forces (capitalism) that China is now following in its quest for economic development. The implication is that socialism will promote equality, while the market (especially the profit motive) will encourage people to work hard and foreign companies to invest.

Sohyo   the General Council of Trade Unions of Japan founded in 1950 by seventeen left-wing industrial unions drawn mainly from the public sector. Throughout the 1950s and 1960s, *Sohyo* was closely allied with the Japan Socialist Party and played a prominent role in a series of campaigns on controversial issues, such as Japanese rearmament and the United States–Japan Mutual Security Treaty. *Sohyo*'s influence began to decline in the mid-1970s, and it was absorbed by *Rengo* in 1989.

spontaneous privatization   a process that occurred in the late 1980s and early 1990s in Russia in which existing managers or ministry bureaucrats transformed promising state-owned enterprises into privatized entities in their own hands, without the existence of a clear legal framework for doing so. See also **privatization.**

spring labor offensive   an annual event in Japan since 1955, the spring labor offensive refers to a series of negotiations between labor unions in major industries and management that take place each spring. The wage increases and changes in working hours and working conditions negotiated in this manner set the standards for management-union negotiations in other industries in the given year.

state   a unified political entity. The state comprises a country's key political institutions that are responsible for making, implementing, enforcing, and adjudicating important policies in that country. States have also been defined as those institutions within a country that claim the right to control force within the territory comprising the country and to make binding rules (laws), which citizens of that country must obey. See also **civil society.**

state capitalism strategy in which government guides industrial and agricultural development and sets political conditions for its success.

state corporatism a political system in which the state requires all members of a particular economic sector to join an officially designated **interest group**. Such interest groups thus attain public status, and they participate in national policy-making. The result is that the state has great control over the groups, and groups have great control over their members. See also **corporatism; corporatist state.**

state formation the historical development of a state, often marked by major stages, key events, or turning points (critical junctures) that influence the contemporary character of the state.

state-led economic development the process of promoting economic development using governmental machinery.

statist a situation in which the state intervenes extensively to direct economic and social activity within a country.

structural adjustment program (SAP) medium-term (generally three to five years) programs (which include both action plans and disbursement of funds) established by the World Bank intended to alter and reform the economic structures of highly indebted Third World countries as a condition for receiving international loans. SAPs often involve the necessity for **privatization,** trade liberalization, and fiscal restraint. See also **international financial institutions (IFIs).**

Supreme Commander for the Allied Powers (SCAP) the official title of General Douglas MacArthur between 1945 and 1951 when he led the Allied Occupation of Japan.

Supreme Leader the head of the Islamic Republic of Iran.

suspensive veto if the German *Bundesrat* votes against a bill, the *Bundestag* can override the *Bundesrat* by passing the measure again by a simple majority. If, however, a two-thirds majority of the *Bundesrat* votes against a bill, the *Bundestag* must pass it again by a two-thirds margin.

tacit social contract an idea put forth by some Western analysts that an unwritten informal understanding existed between the population and the party/state in the post-Stalinist Soviet Union, which helped form the basis of social and political stability; the implicit agreement involved citizens granting political compliance with Soviet rule in exchange for benefits such as guaranteed employment, free social services, a lax work environment, and limited interference in personal life.

Taisho Democracy a reference to Japanese politics in the period roughly coinciding with Emperor Taisho's reign, 1919–1925. The period was characterized by the rise of a popular movement for democratization of government by the introduction of universal manhood suffrage and the reduction of the power and influence of authoritarian institutions of the state.

technocrats career-minded bureaucrats who administer public policy according to a technical rather than a political rationale. In Mexico and Brazil, these are known as the *técnicos.* For contrasting concepts, see **clientelism; patrimonial state; prebendalism.**

theocracy a state dominated by the clergy, who rule on the grounds that they are the only interpreters of God's will and law.

Tokai Village a seaside community lying about ninety miles northeast of Tokyo that is Japan's major nuclear research center that hosts reprocessing and enrichment plants. It is also known as the site of the two worst nuclear accidents the nation has experienced. In the first that occurred, in March 1997, thirty-seven workers were exposed to radiation in fires and an explosion at a reprocessing plant, although none was injured. In the second, an accident at a uranium processing plant, more than 600 people who lived near the facility were exposed to radiation and two employees died. Despite these accidents, Japan continues to rely on nuclear energy for about 14 percent of its energy needs.

totalitarianism a political system in which the state attempts to exercise total control over all aspects of public and private life, including the economy, culture, education, and social organizations, through an integrated system of ideological, economic, and political control. The term has been applied to both **communist party-states** and fascist regimes such as Nazi Germany.

township and village enterprises (TVEs) nonagricultural businesses and factories owned and run by local governments and private entrepreneurs in China's rural areas. TVEs operate largely according to market forces and outside the state plan.

typology a method of classifying by using criteria that divide a group of cases into smaller numbers. For example, in this book, we use a typology of countries that distinguishes among established democracies, transitional democracies, and nondemocracies.

unfinished state a state characterized by instabilities and uncertainties that may render it susceptible to collapse as a coherent entity.

unfunded mandates obligations (e.g., on local governments) without provision of adequate funds for their fulfillment.

union republic one of fifteen territorial units that constituted the federal system of the Soviet Union and subsequently became independent states with the breakup of the Soviet Union in December 1991.

unitary state by contrast to the federal systems of Germany, India, Canada, or the United States, where power is shared between the central government and state or regional governments, in a unitary state (such as Britain) no powers are reserved constitutionally for subnational units of government.

untouchables the lowest caste in India's **caste system,** whose members are among the poorest and most disadvantaged Indians.

vanguard party a political party that claims to operate in the "true" interests of the group or class it purports to represent, even if this understanding doesn't correspond to the expressed interests of the group itself. The Communist parties of the Soviet Union and China are good examples of vanguard parties.

vertically divided administration also known as "sectionalism," the term refers to the extreme autonomy of each Japanese government agency or its subdivision, a situation that seriously interferes with "horizontal" coordination between two or more agencies or their subdivisions.

warrant chiefs employed by the British colonial regime in Nigeria. A system in which "chiefs" were selected by the British to oversee certain legal matters and assist the colonial enterprise in governance and law enforcement in local areas.

welfare state not a form of **state,** but rather a set of public policies designed to provide for citizens' needs through direct or indirect provision of pensions, health care, unemployment insurance, and assistance to the poor.

Westminster model a form of democracy based on the supreme authority of Parliament and the **accountability** of its elected representatives; named after the Parliament building in London.

works councils legally mandated workplace organizations that provide collective representation for workers with their employers. Separate organization from the trade unions.

zaibatsu giant holding companies in pre–World War II Japan, each owned by and under the control of members of a particular family. The largest were divided into a number of independent firms under the democratization program during the postwar occupation but were later revived as *keiretsu,* although no longer under the control of any of the original founding families.

zamindars landlords who served as tax collectors under the British colonial government. The *zamindari* system was abolished after independence.

zoku members of the Japanese *Diet* (parliament) with recognized experience and expertise in particular policy areas such as agriculture, construction, and transportation, and close personal connections with special interests in those areas.

Zollverein 1834 Customs Union among various preunification German states. Fostered economic cooperation that led to nineteenth-century German unification (1871).

About the Editors and Contributors

Ervand Abrahamian is Distinguished Professor of History at Baruch College and the Graduate Center of the City University of New York. His recent publications include *Khomeinism: Essays on the Islamic Republic* (University of California Press, 1993) and *Tortured Confessions: Prisons and Public Recantations in Modern Iran* (University of California Press, 1999).

Christopher S. Allen is an Associate Professor of International Affairs at the University of Georgia, where he teaches courses in comparative politics and political economy. He is the editor of *The Transformation of the German Political Party System* (Berghahn, 1999 and 2001), coauthor of *European Politics in Transition* (Houghton Mifflin, 2002), and is doing research on democratic representation in parliamentary and presidential systems.

Amrita Basu is Professor of Political Science and Women's and Gender Studies at Amherst College. Her main areas of interest are social movements, religious nationalism, and gender politics in South Asia. She is the author of *Two Faces of Protest: Contrasting Modes of Women's Activism in India* (University of California Press, 1992) and several edited books, including *Localizing Knowledge in a Globalizing World, Community Conflicts and the State in India* (with Atul Kohli) (Syracuse University Press, 2002), and *Appropriating Gender: Women's Activism and Politicized Religion in South Asia* (Routledge, 1998).

Joan DeBardeleben is Professor of Political Science and of European and Russian Studies at Carleton University in Ottawa, Ontario. She has published widely on Russian politics, with a focus on Russian federalism, public opinion, and elections. Recent articles have been published in *Europe-Asia Studies*, *Sotsiologicheskie issledovaniia* (Sociological Research), and *Party Politics*. She is a contributing author to *Microeconomic Change in Central and East Europe* (Carol S. Leonard, ed., 2002, Palgrave Macmillan, 2002) and *The Struggle for Russian Environmental Policy* (Ilmo Masso and Veli-Pekka Tynkkynen, eds., Kikimora, 2001). Dr. DeBardeleben is also Director of Carleton University's Centre for European Studies.

Louis Desipio is an Associate Professor in the Department of Political Science and the Chicano/Latino Studies Program at the University of California, Irvine. He is the author of *Counting on the Latino Vote: Latinos as a New Electorate* (University Press of Virginia, 1996) and the coauthor, with Rodolfo O. de la Garza, of *Making Americans/Remaking America: Immigration and Immigrant Policy* (Westview Press, 1998). He is also the author and editor of a six-volume series on Latino political values, attitudes, and behaviors. The seventh volume in this series, on Latino politics in the 2000 election, will be published in 2004.

Shigeko N. Fukai is Professor of Political Science in the Faculty of Law at Okayama University (Japan). She has written on Japan's land problems and policy-making, Japan's role in the emerging regional economic order in East Asia, and Japan's electoral and party politics.

Haruhiro Fukui is Professor Emeritus at the University of California, Santa Barbara, and currently serves as the director of the Hiroshima Peace Institute. His recent publications include *Informal Politics in East Asia* (co-edited with Lowell Dittmer and Peter Nan-shong Lee; Cambridge University Press, 2000), "Foreign Policy by Coalition: Deadlock, Compromise, and Anarchy" (co-authored with Joe D. Hagan, Philip P. Everts, and John D. Stempel), *International Studies Review* 3:2 (Summer 2001), and "East Asian Studies, Politics," in Neil J. Smelser and Paul B. Baltes, eds., *International Encyclopedia of the Social and Behavioral Sciences*, Vol. 6 (Elsevier Science, 2001).

Merilee S. Grindle is Edward S. Mason Professor of International Development at the John F. Kennedy School of Government, Harvard University. She is a specialist on the comparative analysis of policy-making, implementation, and public management in developing countries and has written extensively on Mexico. Her most recent book is *Audacious Reforms: Institutional Innovation and Democracy in Latin America* (The Johns Hopkins University Press, 2000).

William A. Joseph is Professor of Political Science at Wellesley College and an Associate of the Fairbank Center for East Asian Research at Harvard University. His research focuses on contemporary Chinese politics and ideology. He is the editor of *China Briefing: The Contradictions of Change* (M.E. Sharpe, 1997), co-editor of *New Perspectives on the Cultural Revolution* (Harvard University Press,

1991), and contributing editor of *The Oxford Companion to Politics of the World* (Oxford University Press, 2nd ed., 2001).

Mark Kesselman is Professor of Political Science at Columbia University. A specialist on the French and European political economy, his recent publications include contributions to *The Mitterrand Era: Policy Alternatives and Political Mobilization in France* (Macmillan, 1995), *Mitterrand's Legacy, Chirac's Challenge* (St. Martin's Press, 1996), and *Diminishing Welfare: A Cross-National Study of Social Provision* (Greenwood, 2002). He is the coauthor of *A Century of Organized Labor in France* (St. Martin's Press, 1997).

Darren Kew is Assistant Professor in the Graduate Program in Dispute Resolution at the University of Massachusetts, Boston. He studies the role of civil society in democratic development and conflict prevention in Africa. Professor Kew has written on elections, civil society, and conflict prevention in Nigeria. He has worked with the Council on Foreign Relations' Center for Preventive Action to provide analysis and blueprints for preventing conflicts in numerous areas around the world, including Nigeria, Central Africa, and Kosovo, and he has also observed elections in Nigeria.

Atul Kohli is Professor of Politics and International Affairs at Princeton University. His principal research interest is the comparative political economy of developing countries, especially India. He is the author of *Democracy and Discontent: India's Growing Crisis of Governability* (Cambridge University Press, 1990). His current research involves a comparative analysis of industrialization in South Korea, Brazil, India, and Nigeria.

Joel Krieger is Norma Wilentz Hess Professor of Political Science at Wellesley College. His publications include *British Politics in the Global Age: Can Social Democracy Survive?* (Polity Press, 1999) and *Reagan, Thatcher, and the Politics of Decline* (Oxford University Press, 1986). He was also editor-in-chief of *The Oxford Companion to Politics of the World* (Oxford University Press, 1993; 2nd ed., 2001).

Peter Lewis is Associate Professor at the School of International Service, American University. He has written extensively on Nigerian political economy, as well as on broader regional issues of participation, democratic transition, and economic adjustment in Africa. He is currently working on a study of the comparative political economies of Indonesia and Nigeria.

Alfred P. Montero is Assistant Professor of Political Science at Carleton College. His research focuses on the political economy of decentralization and comparative federalism in Latin American and European countries. He is the author of *Shifting States in Global Markets: Subnational Industrial Policy in Contemporary Brazil and Spain* (Penn State University Press, 2002) and co-editor of *Decentralization and Democracy in Latin America* (University of Notre Dame Press, 2003). He has also published his work in several edited volumes and journals such as *Latin American Politics and Society, Comparative Politics, Studies in Comparative International Development, Publius: The Journal of Federalism,* and the *Journal of Interamerican Studies and World Affairs.*

Index

---

*Numbers in boldface indicate the page where a key term is defined.